THE

Judicial Dictionary

OF

WORDS AND PHRASES JUDICIALLY INTERPRETED.

BY

F. STROUD,

OF LINCOLN'S INN, BARRISTER-AT-LAW.

THE LAWBOOK EXCHANGE, LTD.
Clark, New Jersey

ISBN 978-1-58477-263-7

Lawbook Exchange edition 2003, 2022

The quality of this reprint is equivalent to the quality of the original work.

THE LAWBOOK EXCHANGE, LTD.
33 Terminal Avenue
Clark, New Jersey 07066-1321

Please see our website for a selection of our other publications and fine facsimile reprints of classic works of legal history:
www.lawbookexchange.com

Library of Congress Cataloging-in-Publication Data

Stroud, Frederick, 1835-1912
The judicial dictionary of words and phrases judicially interpreted / by F. Stroud.
p. cm.
Originally published: London: Sweet and Maxwell, 1890.
Includes index.
ISBN 1-58477-263-8 (cloth: alk. paper)
1. Law—Great Britain—Dictionaries. 2. Law———Dictionaries. I. Title: Judicial dictionary. II. Title.

KD313 .S77 2002
340'.03—dc2 1 2002024331

Printed in the United States of America on acid-free paper

THE

Judicial Dictionary

OF

WORDS AND PHRASES JUDICIALLY INTERPRETED.

BY

F. STROUD,

OF LINCOLN'S INN, BARRISTER-AT-LAW.

LONDON:
SWEET AND MAXWELL, LIMITED,
3, CHANCERY LANE.
Law Publishers.
MEREDITH, RAY, & LITTLER, MANCHESTER;
HODGES, FIGGIS, & CO., AND E. PONSONBY, DUBLIN;
THACKER, SPINK, & CO., CALCUTTA;
C. F. MAXWELL, MELBOURNE.
1890.

LONDON:
BRADBURY, AGNEW, & CO. LIMD., PRINTERS, WHITEFRIARS.

To the Cherished Memory of

H. S.,

Friend and Wife,

Ever, and in all things, full of wise counsel and steadfast courage,

Who took an affectionate interest in this enterprise,

But whose too early death has taken away its charm,

This Book

is reverently and lovingly

Dedicated.

Easter, 1890.

PREFACE.

THIS work in no sense competes with, nor does it cover the same ground as, the Law Lexicons of Jacob, Tomlins, Wharton or Sweet. As its name imports, it is a Dictionary of the English Language (in its phrases as well as single words), so far as that language has received interpretation by the Judges.

Its chief aim is that it may be a practical companion to the English-speaking lawyer, not only in the Mother Country, but also in the Colonies and Dependencies of the Queen. The hope is also indulged that it may be not without utility to the man of business, nor without interest to the student of word-lore.

Its few archaisms will, possibly, be excused; for "Of all these you shall read in ancient bookes, charters, deeds and records: and to the end that our student should not be discouraged for want of knowledge when he meeteth with them, we have armed him with the signification of them, to the end he may proceed in his reading with alacrity, and set upon and know how to worke into with delight these rough mines of hidden treasure" (Co. Litt. 5 b, 6 a).

Interpretation Clauses in Acts of Parliament are not, as a rule, within its scope, unless when themselves judicially interpreted. But in some few instances of general importance this rule has been departed from, whilst the important Interpretation Act of 1889 is given *in extenso* in the Appendix.

In many instances where a word, or phrase, has been determined in a special sense, or brevity seemed preferable to a lengthy definition, only a reference to the authorities has been given.

Whenever available, the very words of a judicial exposition have been given. And so, when a convenient definition has been found in a work of repute,—*e.g.*, Jarman on Wills; Elphinstone, Norton and Clarke on the Interpretation of Deeds; Mr. Justice Stephen's Digest of the Criminal Law,—such definition has been adopted.

Where a statute is cited as having been interpreted, it must not be assumed that the statute is unrepealed. A judicial interpretation once delivered is a permanent possession; and though its immediate utility will be diminished by the repeal of the statute on which it was founded, it none the less should find a place here, as an authority on the same word when used *in pari materia*, or as furnishing a guide to interpreting similar expressions.

The printing of a word or phrase in SMALL CAPITALS is an indication to refer to such word or phrase in its alphabetical place in the Dictionary.

The references to each case have, since the sheets were in type, been verified by Mr. R. Riches, the Librarian of the Inns of Court Bar Library, Royal Courts of Justice, whose well-known ability and experience will be accepted as a guarantee of accuracy.

For the Tables of Cases and Statutes I am indebted to my son, Mr. Lewis Stroud.

Projected more than twenty years ago, and prosecuted at such intervals as could be obtained from an active professional life, this book will, I fear, offend by omissions, inequalities, and, possibly, worse faults. Yet merely to lay the foundations, search for the materials, and bit by bit build up the Vocabulary, has been, of itself, a task the difficulty and labour of which may well soften criticism and excuse imperfections.

It is, however, impossible to rise from these labours without a deepened admiration for the Judges of our land. It is extraordinary that so many minds, working through so many centuries, and upon such various matters, should have been able so harmoniously to lay down the law for such an expansive and ever-widening civilisation as that of the British Empire. And probably in no sphere of their duties has the work of the Judges been more distinguished than in their dealing with the composite subtleties of English Diction. To study that work, though involving labour, has brought delight; and this attempt to systematize its results will, it is hoped, be useful.

A companion volume based on American decisions is in a forward state of preparation.

2, NEW COURT, LINCOLN'S INN.
7th April, 1890.

CONTENTS.

TABLE OF CASES.

B.

C.

F.

H.

K.

L.

M.

N.

Q.

PAGE

R.

S.

T.

TABLE OF STATUTES.

TABLE OF ABBREVIATIONS.

Where Dates are given in the last column of this Table, that indicates that the item against which it appears is a Series, or Volume, of Reports of Cases, and these Dates also indicate the period covered by such Reports.

A.

ABBREVIATIONS.	EXPLANATIONS	PERIOD.
Add. C.	Addison on Contracts, 8th Ed.	
Add. T.	Addison on Torts, 5th Ed.	
Ads., or Admors.	Administrators.	
A. & E.	Adolphus and Ellis	1834—1841
Amb.	Ambler	1737—1783
And.	Anderson	1558—1603
Ann. Pr.	Annual Practice; the reference is usually to the Order and Rule of Court, and is applicable to any Edition; where a page is given the Edition for 1887-8 is meant.	
Anstr.	Anstruther	1792—1796
App. Ca.	Law Reports, Appeal Cases	1875, and in progress.
Arch. Bank.	Archbold on Bankruptcy, 11th Ed.	
Arch. Cr.	Archbold's Pleading and Evidence in Criminal Cases, 20th Ed.	
Arch. P. L.	Archbold's Poor Law, 14th Ed.	
Arnold	Arnold	1838—1839
Arn.	Arnould on Marine Insurance, 5th Ed.	
Assn.	Association,—chiefly in names of cases.	
Asp.	Aspinall	1871, & i.p.
Atk.	Atkyns	1736—1755
A.-G.	Attorney-General,—in names of cases.	

B.

ABBREVIATIONS.	EXPLANATIONS	PERIOD.
Baldwin	Baldwin on Bankruptcy, 5th Ed.	
Ball & Beatty	Ball and Beatty	1807—1814
Bankry.	Bankruptcy.	
Bankry. Act, 1869	Bankruptcy Act, 1869, 32 & 33 V. c. 71.	
Bankry. Act, 1883	Bankruptcy Act, 1883, 46 & 47 V. c. 52.	
B. & Ad.	Barnewall and Adolphus	1830—1834
B. & Ald.	Barnewall and Alderson	1817—1822
B. & C.	Barnewall and Cresswell	1822—1830
Beatty	Beatty	1814—1830

Abbreviations.	Explanations.	Period.
Bea.	Beavan	1838—1866
Bell, C. C.	Bell, Crown Cases	1858—1860
Benj.	Benjamin on Sales of Personal Property, 3rd Ed.	
B. & S.	Best and Smith	1861—1870
Bills of Ex. Act, 1882	Bills of Exchange Act, 1882, 45 & 46 V. c. 61.	
Bills of S. Act, 1854	Bills of Sale Act, 1854, 17 & 18 V. c. 36.	
Bills of S. Act, 1878	Bills of Sale Act, 1878, 41 & 42 V. c. 31.	
Bills of S. Act, 1882	Bills of Sale Act, 1882, 45 & 46 V. c. 43.	
Bing.	Bingham	1822—1834
Bing. N. C.	Bingham, New Cases	1834—1840
Blackb.	Blackburn on Sales, 2nd Ed.	
Bl. H.	Blackstone, Henry	1788—1796
Bl. W.	Blackstone, William	1746—1780
Bligh	Bligh	1819—1821
Bligh, N. S.	Bligh, New Series	1827—1837
B. & P.	Bosanquet and Puller	1796—1804
B. & P. N. R.	Bosanquet and Puller, New Reports	1804—1807
Bott	Bott	1768—1827
Brod. & B.	Broderip and Bingham	1819—1822
B. & F.	Broderick and Fremantle.	
Bro. C. C.	Brown's Chancery Cases	1778—1794
Brown P. C.	Brown's Parliamentary Cases	1702—1800
Brownl. & Gold.	Brownlow and Goldesborough	1558—1625
Brown. & Lush.	Browning and Lushington	1863—1866
B. & Macn.	Browne and Macnamara	1881, & i. p.
Buckl.	Buckley on the Companies Acts, 5th Ed.	
Bulst.	Bulstrode	1603—1649
Burr.	Burrow	1756—1772
Burr. S. C.	Burrow's Settlement Cases	1732—1776
Byles	Byles on Bills of Exchange and Promissory Notes, 14th Ed.	

C.

Abbreviations.	Explanations.	Period.
Cab. & El.	Cababé and Ellis	1882—1885
Camp.	Campbell	1807—1816
C. & K.	Carrington and Kirwan	1843—1853
C. & M.	Carrington and Marshman	1841—1842
C. & P.	Carrington and Payne	1823—1841
Carth.	Carthew	1688—1701
Ca. t. Hard.	Cases, temp. Hardwicke	1733—1737
Ca. t. Talb.	Cases in Equity, temp. Talbot	1733—1737
Ch. Ca.	Cases in Chancery	1660—1693
Ch. D.	Law Reports, Chancery Division	1875, & i. p.
Ch. Rep.	Reports in Chancery	1625—1710
Ch.	Law Reports, Chancery Appeals	1865—1875
Ch.	Chapter.	
Chitty	Chitty	vol. i., 1819, vol. ii., 1770—1822

ABBREVIATIONS.	EXPLANATIONS.	PERIOD.
Chitty, Eq. Ind.	Chitty's Equity Index, 4th Ed.	
Cl. & F.	Clark and Finelly	1831—1846
Co. Litt.	Coke upon Littleton.	
Coll.	Collyer	1844—1846
Colt. Reg. Ca.	Coltman, Registration Cases	1879—1885
Commrs.	Commissioners,—chiefly in names of cases.	
C. B.	Common Bench Reports	1845—1856
C. B. N. S.	Common Bench Reports, New Series	1856—1865
Com. L. Pro. Act, 1852	Common Law Procedure Act, 1852, 15 & 16 V. c. 76.	
Com. L. Pro. Act, 1854	Common Law Procedure Act, 1854, 17 & 18 V. c. 125.	
Com. L. Pro. Act, 1860	Common Law Procedure Act, 1860, 23 & 24 V. c. 126.	
C. P. D.	Law Reports, Common Pleas Division	1875—1880
Co.	Company.	
Comp. C. C. Act, 1845	Companies Clauses Consolidation Act, 1845, 8 V. c. 16.	
Cp.	Compare.	
Com.	Comyn	1696—1740
Com. Dig.	Comyn's Digest.	
Con. & L.	Connor and Lawson	1841—1843
Conv. & L. P. Act, 1881	Conveyancing and Law of Property Act, 1881, 44 & 45 V. c. 41.	
Conv. Act, 1882	Conveyancing Act, 1882, 45 & 46 V. c. 39.	
Coote	Coote on Mortgages, 5th Ed.	
Co. Co.	County Court.	
Cowp.	Cowper	1774—1778
Cox, Ch.	Cox's Chancery Cases	1745—1797
Cox, C. C.	Cox's Criminal Cases	1843, & i.p.
Cr. & Ph.	Craig and Phillip	1840—1841
Cro. Eliz. Cro. Jac. Cro. Car.	Croke, temp. Elizabeth, James I. and Charles I.	1581—1641
Cr. & J.	Crompton and Jervis	1830—1832
Cr. & M.	Crompton and Meeson	1832—1834
Cr. M. & R.	Crompton, Meeson and Roscoe	1834—1835
Cru. Dig.	Cruise's Digest.	
Curt.	Curteis	1834—1844

D.

Dan. Ch. Pr.	Daniell's Chancery Practice, 6th Ed.	
Dart	Dart on Vendors and Purchasers, 6th Ed.	
D. & M.	Davison and Merivale	1843—1844
Deacon	Deacon	1835—1840
Dea & C.	Deacon and Chitty	1832—1835
Dears.	Dearsley, Crown Cases	1852—1856
Dears. & B.	Dearsley and Bell	1856—1858
Debtors Act, 1869	Debtors Act, 1869, 32 & 33 V. c. 62.	

Abbreviations.	Explanations.	Period.
D. G.	De Gex	1844—1848
D. G. F. & J.	De Gex, Fisher and Jones	1859—1862
D. G. & J.	De Gex and Jones	1856—1859
D. G. J. & S.	De Gex, Jones and Smith	1862—1865
D. G. M. & G.	De Gex, Macnaghten and Gordon	1851—1857
D. G. & S.	De Gex and Smale	1846—1852
Den.	Denison	1844—1852
Dick.	Dickens	1559—1792
Doug.	Douglas	1778—1785
Dow	Dow	1812—1818
Dow & Cl.	Dow and Clark	1827—1831
Dowl.	Dowling, Practice Cases	1830—1841
Dowl. N. S.	Dowling, Practice Cases, New Series	1841—1843
Dowl. & L.	Dowling and Lowndes	1843—1849
D. & R.	Dowling & Ryland	1822—1827
Drew.	Drewry	1852—1859
Dr. & Sm.	Drewry and Smale	1859—1865
Dru.	Drury, temp. Sugden	1843—1844
Dr. & Wal.	Drury and Walsh	1837—1841
Dr. & War.	Drury and Warren	1841—1843
Dwar.	Dwarris on Statutes, 2nd Ed.	
Dyer, or Dy.	Dyer	1513—1582

E.

Abbreviations.	Explanations.	Period.
East	East	1800—1812
East, P. C.	East's Pleas of the Crown.	
Eden	Eden	1757—1766
E. & B.	Ellis and Blackburn	1852—1858
E. B. & E.	Ellis, Blackburn and Ellis	1858
E. & E.	Ellis & Ellis	1858—1861
Elph.	Elphinstone, Norton and Clark on the Interpretation of Deeds.	
Eq. Ca. Ab.	Equity Cases Abridged, 5th Ed.	
Esp.	Espinasse	1793—1810
Ex.	Exchequer Reports	1847—1856
Ex. D.	Law Reports, Exchequer Division	1875—1880
Exs., or Exors.	Executors.	

F.

Abbreviations.	Explanations.	Period.
Finch	Finch, Heneage	1673—1680
Fisher	Fisher on Mortgages, 4th Ed.	
F. N. B.	Fitz-Herbert, Natura Brevium.	
Fon. B. C.	Fonblanque, Bankruptcy Cases	1849—1852
Fort.	Fortescue	1695—1738
F. & F.	Foster and Finlason	1856—1867

G.

Abbreviations.	Explanations.	Period.
G. & D.	Gale and Davison	1841—1843
Giff.	Giffard	1857—1865
Gilb. Eq. Rep.	Gilbert's Equity Reports	1706—1727
Gould.	Gouldsborough	1586—1602
Gow	Gow	1818—1820
G. N. Ry.	Great Northern Railway.	
G. W. Ry.	Great Western Railway.	

H.

Hagg. Adm.	Haggard, Admiralty Cases	1822—1838
Hagg. Con.	Haggard, Consistorial Cases	1789—1802
Hagg. Ecc.	Haggard, Ecclesiastical Cases	1827—1833
H. & Tw.	Hall and Twells	1849—1850
Hard.	Hardres	1655—1660
Hare	Hare	1841—1853
H. & R.	Harrison and Rutherford	1865—1866
Hawk.	Hawkins, on the Construction of Wills.	
Hawk. P. C.	Hawkins' Pleas of the Crown.	
Hayes	Hayes	1830 –1832
H. & M.	Hemming and Miller	1862—1865
H. Bl.	Henry Blackstone	1788—1796
Heredits.	Hereditaments.	
Hob.	Hobart	1603—1625
Hodges	Hodges	1835—1837
Hogan	Hogan	1816—1834
Holt	Holt	1688—1710
Holt, N. P.	Holt, Nisi Prius Cases	1815—1817
Hop. & Colt.	Hopwood and Coltman	1868—1878
H. & P.	Hopwood and Philbrick	1863—1867
H. L.	House of Lords.	
H. L. Ca.	House of Lords Cases	1847—1866
Hud. & Bro.	Hudson and Brooke	1827—1831
H. & C.	Hurlstone and Coltman	1862—1866
H. & N.	Hurlstone and Norman	1856—1862

I.

Inl. Rev.	Inland Revenue,—chiefly in names of Cases.	
Insrce.	Insurance,—chiefly in names of Cases.	
Interp. Act, 1889	Interpretation Act, 1889, 52 & 53 V. c. 63, given *in extenso* in the Appendix.	
Ir. Ch. Rep.	Irish Chancery Reports	1850—1866
Ir. Com. Law Rep.	Irish Common Law Reports	1850—1866
Ir. Eq. Rep.	Irish Equity Reports	1838—1851
Ir. L. R.	Irish Law Reports	1838—1852
Ir. Rep. C. L.	Irish Reports, Common Law	1866—1877
Ir. Rep. Eq.	Irish Reports, Equity	1866—1877

J.

Abbreviations.	Explanations.	Period.
Jac.	Jacob	1821—1822
Jac. & W.	Jacob and Walker	1819—1821
Jarm.	Jarman on Wills, 4th Ed.	
Jebb & Sy.	Jebb and Symes	1838—1841
Johns.	Johnson	1858—1860
J. & H.	Johnson and Hemming	1859—1862
Jo. T.	T. Jones	1667—1684
J. & La T.	Jones and La Touche	1844—1846
Jdgmt.	Judgment.	
Jud. Act, 1873	Judicature Act, 1873, 36 & 37 V. c. 66.	
Jud. Act, 1875	Judicature Act, 1875, 38 & 39 V. c. 77.	
Jur.	Jurist	1837—1854
Jur. N. S.	Jurist, New Series	1854—1866

K.

Abbreviations.	Explanations.	Period.
Kay	Kay	1853—1854
K. & J.	Kay and Johnson	1854—1858
Keble	Keble	1661—1679
Keen	Keen	1836—1838
Keilwey	Keilwey, Ed. of 1688	1496—1578

L.

Abbreviations.	Explanations.	Period.
Lands C. C. Act, 1845	Lands Clauses Consolidation Act, 1845, 8 V. c. 18.	
L. J. O. S. Ch.	Law Journal, Old Series, Chancery	1822—1831
L. J. O. S. K. B.	,, ,, King's Bench	1822—1831
L. J. O. S. C. P.	,, ,, Common Pleas	1822—1831
L. J. O. S. Ex.	,, ,, Exchequer	1830—1831
L. J. O. S. M. C.	,, ,, Magistrates' Cases	1826—1831
L. J. Bank.	,, New Series, Bankruptcy	1832, & i. p.
L. J. Ch.	,, ,, Chancery	1831, & i. p.
L. J. K. B., or Q. B.	,, ,, King's, or Queen's, Bench (in and from 1876, Queen's Bench Division)	1831, & i. p.
L. J. C. P.	,, ,, Common Pleas (in and from 1876 to 1880, Common Pleas Division)	1831—1880
L. J. Ex.	,, ,, Exchequer (in and from 1876 to 1880, Exchequer Division)	1831—1880
L. J. M. C.	,, ,, Magistrates' Cases	1831, & i. p.
L. J. P. C.	,, ,, Privy Council	1865, & i. p.

ABBREVIATIONS.	EXPLANATIONS.	PERIOD.
L. J. P. & M.	Law Journal, New Series, Probate and Matrimonial.	1858—1859 1865—1875
L. J. P. M. & A.	,, ,, Probate, Matrimonial and Admiralty	1860—1865
L. J. Adm.	,, ,, Admiralty	1865—1875
L. J. Ecc.	,, ,, Ecclesiastical	1865—1875
L. J. P. D. & A.	,, ,, Probate, Divorce and Admiralty	1875, & i. p.
L. R. Ir.	Law Reports, Ireland	1878, & i. p.
L. T. O. S.	Law Times, Old Series	1843—1859
L. T.	,, New Series	1859, & i. p.
Lee, Ecc.	Lee	1752—1758
L. & C.	Leigh and Cave	1861—1865
Leon.	Leonard	1540—1615
Lev.	Levinz	1660—1697
Lewin	Lewin on Trusts, 8th Ed.	
Lewin, C. C.	Lewin, Crown Cases	1822—1833
Lindl.	Lindley on Partnership, 5th Ed.	
Litt. Rep.	Littleton	1626—1632
L. & G. t. Plunk.	Lloyd and Goold, temp. Plunkett	1833—1839
L. & G. t. Sug.	Lloyd and Goold, temp. Sugden.	1835
L. B. & S. Ry.	London, Brighton & South Coast Railway.	
Lond. & N. W. Ry.	London & North Western Railway.	
Lond. & S. W. Ry.	London & South Western Railway.	
Lowndes	Lowndes on Insurance.	
L. M. & P.	Lowndes, Maxwell and Pollock	1850—1851
Lush.	Lushington	1859—1862
Lutw.	Lutwyche, Registration Cases	1843—1853
Lutw. E.	Lutwyche, Edward	1683—1704

M.

ABBREVIATIONS.	EXPLANATIONS.	PERIOD.
Mac. & G.	Macnaghten and Gordon	1849—1852
Macq. H. L.	Macqueen, Scotch Appeals	1851—1865
MacS.	MacSwinney on Mines, Quarries and Minerals.	
Mad.	Maddock	1815—1822
Manchester S. & L. Ry.	Manchester, Sheffield & Lincolnshire Railway.	
M. & G.	Manning and Granger	1840—1844
M. & R.	Manning and Ryland	1827—1830
Manwood	Manwood's Forest Laws.	
M. W. P. Act, 1882	Married Women's Property Act, 1882, 45 & 46 V. c. 75.	
Marsh.	Marshall	1813—1816
Maude & P.	Maude and Pollock on Merchant Shipping, 4th Ed.	
M. & S.	Maule and Selwyn	1813—1817
Maxwell	Maxwell on the Interpretation of Statutes, 2nd Ed.	
M'Cle.	M'Cleland	1824
M'Cle. & Y.	M'Cleland and Younge	1824—1825
M. & W.	Meeson and Welsby	1836—1847
Mer.	Merivale	1815—1817

ABBREVIATIONS.	EXPLANATIONS.	PERIOD.
Metrop. Man. Act, 1855	Metropolis Management Act, 1855, 18 & 19 V. c. 120	
,, ,, 1862	Metropolis Management Amendment Act, 1862, 25 & 26 V. c. 102.	
,, ,, 1878	Metropolis Management and Building Acts Amendment Act, 1878, 41 & 42 V. c. 32.	
Mod.	Modern	1669—1732
Moll.	Molloy	1827—1828
Mont.	Montague	1829—1832
Mont. & Ayr.	Montague and Ayrton	1833—1838
Mont. & B.	Montague and Bligh	1832—1833
Mont. & Chitt.	Montague and Chitty	1838—1840
Mont. D. & D.	Montague, Deacon and De Gex	1840—1844
Mont. & M'A.	Montague and McArthur	1826—1830
Moody	Moody	1824—1844
Moo. & M.	Moody and Malkin	1826—1830
Moo. & R.	Moody and Robinson	1830—1844
Moore	Moore, Francis	1512—1621
Moore, C. P.	Moore, J. B.	1817—1827
Moore, P. C.	Moore, Privy Council Appeals	1836—1862
Moore, P. C. N. S.	Moore, Privy Council Appeals, New Series	1862—1873
Moore & P.	Moore and Payne	1827—1831
Moore & S.	Moore and Scott	1831—1834
Morr.	Morrell	1884, & i. p.
My. & C.	Mylne and Craig	1835—1841
My. & K.	Mylne and Keen	1832—1835

N.

N. & M.	Neville and Manning	1832—1836
N. & P.	Neville and Perry	1836—1838
N. R.	New Reports	1862—1865
Notes of Ca.	Notes of Cases	1841—1850
Noy	Noy	1559—1649

O.

O'M. & H.	O'Malley and Hardcastle	1869, & i. p.
Owen	Owen	1556—1615

P.

Palm.	Palmer	1619—1629
Park.	Parker	1743—1767
Peake	Peake	1790—1812
P. Wms.	Peere Williams	1695—1735
P. & D.	Perry and Davison	1838—1841

Abbreviations.	Explanations.	Period.
Phil. Ecc.	Phillimore	1809—1821
Phill.	Phillips	1841—1849
Platt	Platt, on Leases.	
Plowd.	Plowden	1550—1580
Pop.	Popham	1592—1627
Pr. Ch.	Precedents in Chancery, Finch	1689—1722
Price	Price	1814—1824
P. H. Act, 1848	Public Health Act, 1848, 11 & 12 V. c. 63.	
P. H. Act, 1875	,, 1875, 38 & 39 V. c. 55.	

Q.

Q. B.	Queen's Bench Reports	1841—1852
Q. B. D.	Law Reports, Queen's Bench Division	1875, & i. p.

R.

Ry.	Railway,—chiefly in names of Cases, and then signifying Railway Company.	
Rail. Ca., or Ry. Ca.	Railway and Canal Cases	1835—1854
Ry. C. C. Act, 1845	Railway Clauses Consolidation Act, 1845, 8 V. c. 20.	
Raym. T.	T. Raymond	1660—1684
Raym. Ld.	Lord Raymond	1694—1732
Rep.	Coke	1572—1617
Rob. Ecc.	Robertson, Ecclesiastical Cases	1844—1853
Rob. C.	Robinson, Christopher	1798—1808
Robson	Robson on Bankruptcy, 5th Ed.	
Rogers	Rogers on Elections, 14th Ed.	
Rolle	Rolle	1614—1625
Rol. Ab.	Rolle's Abridgement.	
Rosc. Cr.	Roscoe's Digest of the Law of Evidence in Criminal Cases, 15th Ed.	
Rosc. N. P.	Roscoe's Digest of the Law of Evidence at Nisi Prius, 15th Ed.	
Rose	Rose	1810—1816
R. S. C.	Rules of the Supreme Court, 1883.	
Russ.	Russell	1823—1829
Russ. & My.	Russell and Mylne	1829—1833
Russ. & Ry.	Russell and Ryan	1800—1823
Ry. & Moo.	Ryan and Moody	1823—1826
Rop.	Roper on Legacies, 4th Ed.	

S.

Salk.	Salkeld	1689—1712
Saund.	Saunders	1666—1672
Sayer	Sayer	1751—1756

Abbreviations.	Explanations.	Period.
Sch. & Lef.	Schoales and Lefroy	1802—1807
Sc.	Scott	1834—1840
Sc. N. R.	Scott, New Reports	1840—1845
Sess. Ca.	Sessions Cases, Scotch	1874, & i. p.
Seton	Seton on Decrees, 4th Ed.	
Show.	Shower	1678—1694
Sid.	Siderfin	1657—1670
Sim.	Simons	1826—1852
Sim. N. S.	Simons, New Series	1850—1852
Sim. & St.	Simons and Stuart	1822—1826
Skinner	Skinner	1681—1697
Sm. & G.	Smale and Giffard	1852—1858
Sm. L. C.	Smith's Leading Cases, 9th Ed.	
Socy.	Society,—chiefly in names of Cases.	
S. J.	Solicitors' Journal.	
S. E. Ry.	South Eastern Railway.	
Spelm.	Spelman's Glossarium Archaiologicum.	
Spinks	Spinks, Ecclesiastical & Admiralty	1853—1855
Sto.	Story, on Equitable Jurisprudence.	
Starkie	Starkie	1815—1823
Steph. Cr.	Stephen's Digest of the Criminal Law, 3rd Ed.	
Stone	Stone's Justices' Manual, 24th Ed.	
Stra.	Strange	1715—1748
Sty., or Style	Style	1646—1655
Sucn. Dy. Act, 1853	Succession Duty Act, 1853, 16 & 17 V. c. 51.	
Sug. Pow.	Sugden on Powers, 8th Ed.	
Sug. V. & P.	Sugden on Vendors and Purchasers, 14th Ed.	
Swabey	Swabey	1855—1859
Sw. & Tr.	Swabey & Tristram	1858—1865
Swanst.	Swanston	1818—1819
Sch.	Schedule.	
Sq.	But, this is questioned.	
Sv.	But see, or See however.	
Svh.	But see hereon.	
Svth.	But see thereon.	

T.

Abbreviations.	Explanations.	Period.
Taunt.	Taunton	1807—1819
T. R.	Term Reports, same as Durnford and East	1785—1800
Termes de la Ley.	Termes de la Ley,—the Edition used being that published in London and "printed by Jo. Beale & Ric. Hearne for the benefit of all that are studious in the Common Lawes of this Realme, 1641."	
Theobald	Theobald, on Wills, 3rd Ed.	
Touch.	The Touch-Stone, commonly cited as Shep. Touch.	

ABBREVIATIONS.	EXPLANATIONS.	PERIOD.
Tudor, Char. Trusts.	Tudor, on Charitable Trusts, 3rd Ed.	
Tudor's L. C. R. P.	Tudor's Leading Cases in Real Property.	
T. & R.	Turner and Russell	1822—1825
Tyr.	Tyrwhitt	1830—1835
Tyr. & G.	Tyrwhitt and Granger	1835—1836

V.

Vaugh.	Vaughan	1665—1674
Ventr.	Ventris	1668—1684
Vern.	Vernon	1681—1719
Vern. & S.	Vernon and Scriven	1786—1788
Ves.	Vesey, junior,—when the Volume cited has a higher number than 2	1795—1817
Ves. jun.	Vesey, junior	1754—1795
Ves. sen.	Vesey, senior	1746—1755
V. & B.	Vesey and Beames	1812—1814
Vin. Ab.	Viner's Abridgment.	
V.	See,—except between the names of cases.	
Va.	See also.	
Vf.	See further.	
Vh.	See hereon.	
Vth.	See thereon.	

W.

Watson, Eq.	Watson's Practical Compendium of Equity. 2nd Ed.	
Webster	Webster, Patent Cases	1601—1855
W. R.	Weekly Reporter	1852, & i. p.
Wight.	Wightwick	1810—1811
Wilberforce	Wilberforce, on Statute Law.	
Willes	Willes	1737—1758
W. Bl.	William Blackstone	1746—1780
Wms. Bank.	Williams, on Bankruptcy, 4th Ed.	
Wms. Exs.	Williams, on Executors and Administrators, 8th Ed.	
Wms. on Commons	Williams, on Commons.	
Wms. P. P.	Williams, on Personal Property, 3rd Ed.	
Wms. R. P.	Williams, on Real Property, 4th Ed.	
Wms. Saund.	Williams' Saunders.	
Wils.	Wilson	1818—1819
Wood	Wood, on Mercantile Agreements.	
Wood	Wood, Tithe Cases	1650—1798
Woodf.	Woodfall, on Landlord and Tenant, 13th Ed.	
Wh.	Which.	

Y.

Abbreviations.	Explanations.	Period.
Yate Lee	Yate Lee, on Bankruptcy, 2nd Ed.	
Yelv.	Yelverton	1602—1613
Younge	Younge	1830—1832
Y. & C., Ch.	Younge and Collier, Chancery Cases	1841—1843
Y. & C., Ex.	Younge and Collier, Exchequer Cases	1834—1842
Y. & J.	Younge and Jervis	1826—1830

INTRODUCTORY CHAPTER

ON THE

CONSTRUCTION OF DOCUMENTS.

THE documents whereby conclusions or directions are recorded are various in kind, and the rules for their interpretation must somewhat vary.

But underlying the special rules for construing the different classes of documents, there are two fundamental rules.

I. Every Document must be read in its true light.

Bearing that Rule in mind we get the full and proper meaning of the doctrine enunciated by Lord Wensleydale in *Grey* v. *Pearson* (a), that;—

II. "In construing Wills, and, indeed, Statutes and all Written Instruments, the grammatical and ordinary sense of the words is to be adhered to, unless that would lead to absurdity, or some repugnance or inconsistency with the rest of the instrument; in which case the grammatical and ordinary sense of the words may be modified so as to avoid that absurdity, repugnancy, or inconsistency, but no further."

In repeating this latter canon in *Abbott* v. *Middleton* (b), Lord Wensleydale said,—" This rule was in substance laid down by Mr. Justice Burton in *Warburton* v. *Loveland* (c). It had previously been

(a) 26 L. J. Ch. 481 ; 6 H. L. Ca. 106.
(b) 28 L. J. Ch. 114 ; 7 H. L. Ca. 114, 115.
(c) 1 Hud. & Bro. 648.

described by Lord Ellenborough in *Doe* v. *Jessep* (*d*), as 'a rule of common sense as strong as can be.' It had been stated (by Lord Cranworth when Chancellor) as 'a Cardinal Rule,' from which, if we departed, we should launch into a sea of difficulties not easy to fathom (*e*); and as the **Golden Rule** when applied to Acts of Parliament, by Chief Justice Jervis, in *Mattison* v. *Hart* (*f*), and by Mr. Justice Maule as 'the most general of rules, a general rule of great utility,' in *Gether* v. *Capper* (*g*)."

But a little reflection will show that this Golden Rule cannot be properly applied until the document under discussion has been put in its true light. How otherwise can the "Ordinary Sense" of the words employed be rightly determined? A word ordinarily employed in one sense in the time of Queen Elizabeth, may have quite another ordinary sense now. So that in construing statutes some regard must be had to the time of their enactment (*h*). So of a Will, the circumstances which the testator would, or ought to, consider when making it, must be borne in mind (*i*). So in construing a Mercantile Document before you can begin to read it in its ordinary sense, you have to know somewhat of the trade to which it relates, and it is often required to know the sense in which the phrases employed are used in that trade. That is to say, you must put the document in its true mercantile light. So again a word sometimes has a legal meaning, different from its popular meaning; and then the circumstances at the inception of the document, have to be attended to in order that it may be seen whether the word in question is a phrase of art, and so to receive its ordinary legal meaning, or whether it has been used as the language of common life, and, therefore, to receive its ordinary popular meaning. In such a case either meaning would be the ordinary meaning; and what would have, in the first instance, to be determined would be,—which ordinary meaning ought to be adopted? That could only be done by, first of all, putting the document in its true

(*d*) 12 East, 293.

(*e*) *Gundry* v. *Pinniger*, 1 D. G. M. & G. 502; 21 L. J. Ch. 405.

(*f*) 23 L. J. C. P. 108; 14 C. B. 385.

(*g*) 24 L. J. C. P. 71; 15 C. B. 706: *Va. Rhodes* v. *Rhodes*, 51 L. J. P. C. 53; 7 App. Ca. 192: and per Halsbury, L. C., *Leader* v. *Duffy*, 58 L. J. P. C. 16; 13 App. Ca. 301.

(*h*) *Vth. Ward* v. *Folkestone W. Works Co.*, 24 Q. B. D. 334.

(*i*) Per Ld. Blackburn, *Bowen* v. *Lewis*, 54 L. J. Q. B. 67; 9 App. Ca. 913.

light,—by considering the circumstances out of which the document arose.

Written documents cannot dispense with extrinsic illumination. Indeed many documents need the aid of parol evidence (*j*). And though the general rule of law prevents the admissibility of extrinsic evidence to vary a written document; yet it is conceived that that rule (to which there are many exceptions) only shuts out evidence of extrinsic facts directly and specially relating to the document in question, and never prohibits the consideration of the circumstances that are general to the class of documents of which that in question is one. In other words, there is no rule of law which prevents any document being read, as it ought to be read, in its true light.

The law indeed interposes to determine what extrinsic circumstances may be employed by the light of which particular classes of documents may be read. Hereon the reader is referred to the works which will be found enumerated at the close of this chapter.

It is, however, safe to say that it is better (where possible) to gather the circumstances out of which the document under consideration arose from the document itself. This can mostly be done by considering its recitals and general structure; whilst the meaning of individual phrases is frequently, even if not generally, shown by the context, on the principle that words, like men, are known by the company they keep (*Noscitur a sociis*),—in truth "every possible expression a man can use may be explained away by the context" (*k*).

It may possibly be objected that the first canon here proposed is only a part of that so firmly laid down by Lord Wensleydale. But though the two canons are intimately associated, yet the first is quite distinct from the second. The first is the intimate preface of the second. By applying the first a knowledge is obtained about a document; the second then guides to its true interpretation. As to this second canon of construction, those who say a document is not to be read literally must show some reason why (*l*). Not so very long ago one used to hear something about the Equity of a Statute, and about construing private documents on their broad principle. But though narrow technicalities are not now

(*j*) *V.* Obs. of Jessel, M. R., *Shardlow* v. *Cotterill*, 51 L. J. Ch. 356; 20 Ch. D. 93.
(*k*) Per Wood, V.-C., *Holmes* v. *Prescott*, 33 L. J. Ch. 271.
(*l*) Per Jessel, M. R., *Sutton* v. *Sutton*, 52 L. J. Ch. 336; 22 Ch. D. 516.

favoured by the Courts, yet it is perhaps not too much to say that the principle laid down in *Grey* v. *Pearson* is now universally applied so as to hold all documents to mean what they say,—*the* question now being, What *does* the document say? If it speaks plainly, that plain meaning is to be followed: if it speaks ambiguously, or doubtfully, the meaning of what it says must be ascertained in a natural and grammatical manner, and by such aids as the law allows: if it speaks so as to lead to absurdity, repugnancy or inconsistency, that absurd, repugnant or inconsistent conclusion is rejected because it could not have been meant (*m*). In every case, therefore, what has to be sought is, What does the document say?—*e.g.*, a case must be within the words of a statute; it is not enough to say that it is within the mischief intended to be prevented (*n*).

Sweeping general words often present a difficulty. Their wide terms induce the doubt as to whether they were employed in their absolutely literal sense, and whether so to construe them would not conduct to absurdity. In such cases it has been said:—"One of the safest guides to the construction of sweeping general words, which it is difficult to apply in their full literal sense, is to examine other words of like import in the same instrument, and to see what limitations must be imposed on them. If it is found that a number of such expressions have to be subjected to limitations or qualifications, and that such limitations or qualifications are of the same nature, that forms a strong argument for subjecting the expression in dispute to a like limitation or qualification" (*o*).

But, probably, it is not possible to formulate any rule that would guide safely to the conclusion that the literal meaning of any given phrase is to be set aside on the ground of its leading to absurdity, repugnancy or inconsistency; and still less as to what should be the reading in lieu of that so set aside. Each case of that kind, unless covered by authority, would have to take care for itself, subject to this one general principle, which would probably be of universal acceptation, that the argument of convenience ought not to prevail except as a last resource (*p*).

(*m*) Per Parke, B., *Miller* v. *Salomons*, 21 L. J. Ex. 191; 7 Ex. 546.

(*n*) *Scott* v. *Legg*, 2 Ex. D. 39; 46 L. J. M. C. 267.

(*o*) *Blackwood* v. *The Queen*, 52 L. J. P. C. 14; 8 App. Ca. 94.

(*p*) Per Jessel, M. R., *Spencer* v. *Metrop. Bd. of Works*, 52 L. J. Ch. 255; 22 Ch. D. 167.

To say, as even eminent judges have said, that documents are to be construed by the light of Common Sense does not seem to render verbal problems more easy of solution. Common Sense, as here applied, is a term of the pumpkin order. It is round, smooth and fair to view —but hollow. It was Common Sense which proved to the wise men of antiquity that there could be no antipodes: for how could people walk with their heads downwards like flies from a ceiling?

It is, perhaps, more to the purpose to say that "Popular language should be expounded popularly" (*q*). But before that rule can be brought into operation it must be ascertained whether the words in question are popular ones or not. To this end the first canon here stated may, possibly, be useful. Thus, Acts of Parliament, as proceeding from a popular assembly, frequently, and Mercantile Contracts, as employing the language of the market, generally, will be interpreted in a popular sense (*r*); whilst Deeds, Wills professionally prepared, and such-like solemn and formal documents are usually couched in the language of conveyancers, and the "Ordinary Sense" of such language would be its technical meaning.

But irrespective of the distinction between technical and popular meanings, a word may have different meanings, and then we get this Rule,—"Where we find a term which is used in more than one sense, which has a primary, secondary and tertiary meaning, the rule of construction is this—The law has settled which of its several meanings is the primary one, and then you require a context to give it one of its other meanings" (*s*). To say that the law "*has*" settled the primary meaning of words is only true in a very limited measure indeed. The primary legal meaning of a word can never be absolutely predicated until the authorities on that word are duly considered; and then not always. When, however, such primary meaning is known (and it is hoped that this Dictionary may to some degree help in that knowledge), then the rule as stated in *Pigg* v. *Clarke* guides to the "Ordinary Sense" of a word having more than one meaning. But when the primary legal meaning has not been settled by decision, then it is necessary to remember that

(*q*) Per Pollock, C. B., *Aggs* v. *Nicholson*, 25 L. J. Ex. 350; 1 H. & N. 165.
(*r*) *V.* per Esher, M. R., on Charter-Parties, *Nottebohm* v. *Richter*, 56 L.J. Q. B. 34.
(*s*) Per Jessel, M. R., *Pigg* v. *Clarke*, 45 L. J. Ch. 850; 3 Ch. D. 674.

the legal primary meaning would not necessarily be the primary etymological meaning, but would be collected from the ordinary import of the word as used in ordinary conversation (*t*).

In the uncertainty arising from the different meanings of words there is some help frequently to be derived from the rule that,—When it can be seen that a word is clearly used in a particular sense in one part of a document, that will be its meaning throughout the document (*u*). But even this rule is not of universal application; for the same word may be used in different senses in different parts of the same document (*v*).

One other general rule may be added, viz.,—Such a construction of doubtful words and phrases should be adopted as will give a reasonable meaning to every word and phrase in the document.

The time in relation to which a document is to be construed is the time when it comes into life. That is to say :—

An *Act of Parliament*, when it comes into operation (s. 36, Interp. Act, 1889):
A *Contract*, its date :
A *Deed*, its delivery (*w*) :
A *Will* "shall be construed, with reference to the Real Estate and Personal Estate comprised in it, to speak and take effect as if it had been executed immediately before the death of the testator, unless a contrary intention shall appear by the Will" (*x*).

There remains to bear in mind, in concluding these remarks on the fundamental canons of construction, and also in the use of the Dictionary, that cases on construction help the Court in determining the true meaning of words and phrases ; but they lay down no absolute rule which prevents the Court of construction arriving at its

(*t*) *Re Terry*, 19 Bea. 580 : Elph. 48.

(*u*) *Courtauld* v. *Legh*, 38 L. J. Ex. 49 ; L. R. 4 Ex. 130 : *Fermoy's Case*, 5 H. L. Ca. 745 : *Blackwood* v. *The Queen*, *ante* : 2 Jarm. 842.

(*v*) *Courtauld* v. *Legh*, sup. : *Doe* d. *Angell* v. *Angell*, 15 L. J. Q. B. 193 ; 9 Q. B. 328 (cited *post*, p. 671) : *Gill* v. *Barrett*, 29 Bea. 372 : *R.* v. *Allen*, L. R. 1 C. C. R. 371, 373, 374 ; 41 L. J. M. C. 99, 100 : per Bowen, L. J., *Cooke* v. *New River Co.*, 57 L. J. Ch. 389 ; 38 Ch. D. 56 ; 58 L. T. 830 ; affd. 14 App. Ca. 698.

(*w*) Co. Litt. 35 b : *Clayton's Case*, 5 Rep. 1 : Touch. 72 : Elph. 119.

(*x*) s. 24, 1 V. c. 26.

own conclusion in the absence of decision upon the same instrument, or on the same word or phrase (*y*).

The Rules of Construction of the several classes of documents will be found fully treated and illustrated in the following works: —

Acts of Parliament.	Dwarris on Statutes. Maxwell on the Interpretation of Statutes. Wilberforce on Statute Law. Broom's Maxims, Ch. 1, sect. 2. Bacon's Maxims, Reg. 10, 16, 19. Barrington on Statutes.
Contracts.	Addison on Contracts, Book I., Ch. 2. Chitty on Contracts, Ch. 5. Leake on Contracts, Ch. 4, sects. 2 and 3. Anson on Contracts, Part 4. Pollock on Contracts, Ch. 8, Part 3. 2 Smith's Leading Cases, *Roe* v. *Tranmarr*. Broom's Maxims, Ch. 8. Lindley on Partnership, 5th Ed., Book 3, Ch. 9. 1 Maude & Pollock on Shipping, Ch. 6. Abbott on Shipping, Part 4. MacLachlan on Shipping. Scrutton on Bills of Lading and Charter-Parties. Wood on Mercantile Agreements.
Deeds.	Elphinstone, Norton and Clark on the Rules for the Interpretation of Deeds; with a Glossary. Platt on Covenants. Platt on Leases, Part 5. Hamilton on Covenants. Broom's Maxims, Ch. 8. Co. Litt. 36 a. Bacon's Maxims, Reg. 21. The Touchstone, Ch. 5.

(*y*) Per Jessel, M. R., *Athill* v. *Athill*, 50 L. J. Ch. 126; 16 Ch. D. 223, 224.

Wills.	Hawkins on the Construction of Wills. Jarman on Wills, *passim*, but especially Ch. 51. Williams on Executors, Part 3, Book 3, Ch. 2. Theobald on Wills. Wigram on Extrinsic Evidence. Tudor's Leading Cases on Real Property. Tudor on Charitable Trusts, Ch. 5. Gilbert on Wills.
Miscellaneous Writings.	Broom's Maxims, Ch. 8. Bacon's Maxims, Reg. 3, 4, 8, 10, 13, 16, 19, 20, 23.

ADDENDA.

These Additions and Corrections are nearly all necessitated by cases which have been reported whilst this Book was going through the Press. It is suggested that they should be written-up in their respective places in the Dictionary.

Add to page

12 **ACRE.**—After Elph. 558, add, *Portman* v. *Mill*, 2 Russ. 570.

15 **ACTUAL VALUE.**—*V.* VALUE, towards end.

20 **ADVERSE.**—To cases on "Adverse Litigation," add, *Re Catling*, 34 S. J. 364.

21 **AFFAIRS.**—"Conduct and Affairs" of a Bankrupt, s. 28 (2), Bankry. Act, 1883; *V. Re Jones*, 34 S. J. 349. CONDUCT.

23 **AGENCY TERMS.**—*V.* USUAL AGENCY TERMS.

33 **AMOUNT SECURED.**—To reference to *Re Neath Bg. Socy.*, add, 59 L. J. Ch. 3.

34 **ANIMAL.**—*Semble*, a Duck, or other Domestic Fowl, is not an "Animal" within s. 61, 24 & 25 V. c. 100 (*Vh. R.* v. *Brown*, 24 Q. B. D. 357).

39 **ANTICIPATE.**—Where there is a gift for life to a married woman, subject to a restraint on alienation, and on her "anticipating" the same, then over, the gift over will not take effect on her mortgaging her life estate, because she has no power to mortgage; "anticipating" will not be construed "attempting to anticipate" (*Re Wormald, Frank* v. *Moozeen*, 34 S. J. 252).

41 **APOTHECARY.**—"An Apothecary is a person who professes to judge of internal disease by its symptoms, and applies himself to cure that disease by medicines" (per Cresswell, J., *Apothecaries Co.* v. *Lotinga*, 2 Moo. & R. 499); "a Chemist may prepare and vend, but not prescribe or administer medicine" (per Best, C. J., *Allison* v. *Haydon*, 4 Bing. 621: *Vf.* on this distinction *Apothecaries Co.* v. *Greenough*, 1 Q. B. 799). These decisions were on 55 G. 3, c. 194, ss. 20, 21; and a person acts as an Apothecary within s. 20, if he selects and supplies medicines for the purpose of individual cure, even though he may also be an Herbalist, and as such protected by 34 & 35 H. 8, c. 8 (*Apothecaries Co.* v. *Welch*, Times, 21st March, 1890).

Add to page

James 1 incorporated the Apothecaries of London (6 & 7 W. 3, c. 4, s. 1); and it has been contended that this statute was the first recognition of the right of apothecaries to attend patients, as well as make up and sell medicines, though *Rose* v. *Coll. of Physicians* (5 Brown, P. C. 553) is sometimes cited as having first established such right (1 Q. B. Rep. 805, n.).

49 **ARRANGEMENT.**—To reference to *Re Jones*, add, 59 L. J. Ch. 31.

56 **ASSIGNMENT.**—"Assignment," s. 10, 23 & 24 V. c. 154, does not include transmission of a tenant's interest by operation of law (*Kennelly* v. *Enright*, 8 L. R. Ir. 33).

57 **ASSIGNS.**—After HEIRS AND ASSIGNS, add, SPIRITUOUS LIQUORS.

58 **ASSURED.**—If in executing a Power of Appointment the appointor adds that the appointee "will, I am assured," do something outside the limits of the Power, that does not, necessarily, mean that there has been a bargain for that outside thing between appointor and appointee so as to void the appointment; the phrase may only mean, "I feel certain he will do it" (*Re Crawshay*, 34 S. J. 218).

81 **BILL OF SALE.**—As to what is a specific description of Goods in a Bill of Sale; *V.* SPECIFIC.

86 **BOONS.**—A Power to Lease, conditional on "reserving ancient, usual, and accustomed rents, *boons*, heriots and services;" *V. Cardigan* v *Montagu*, Sug. Pow. 918, 832.

87 **BOXES.**—"Boxes," held not to include Rollers in a Patent Specification (*Barber* v. *Grace*, 1 Ex. 339; 17 L. J. Ex. 122).

96 **BUSINESS.**—After CARRY ON, add, TRANSACT BUSINESS: then add,

"Business," the conducting of which is punishable under 16 & 17 V. c. 119, ss. 1, 3, does not mean the general, or any part of the, business of a place in which betting may be carried on, but means, "the Business of a Betting-house Keeper" in that place (per Hawkins, J., *R.* v. *Cook*, 13 Q. B. D. 384; 51 L. T. 21; 32 W. R. 796; 48 J. P. 694). *Vf. Davis* v. *Stephenson*, 34 S. J. 334; 6 Times Rep. 242.

After *Re Henton*, add,

So a bequest, by a Corn and Wool Factor, of "my said Business, and the Goodwill thereof, with the premises in which the same shall be carried on," was held not to pass the testator's capital in his business, nor his book-debts (which were regarded as part of capital), nor his stock-in-trade; but that sacks, horses and drays, "forming, as it were, part of the implements of trade," did pass (*Delany* v. *Delany*, 15 L. R. Ir. 55).

99 **BY RETAIL.**—*V.* RETAIL.

100 **BY WEIGHT.**—*Smith* v. *Wood*, affd. on appeal, 59 L. J. Q. B. 5.

Add to page

105 **CAPITAL.**—Book-debts are part of a tradesman's Capital (*Delany* v. *Delany*, 15 L. R. Ir. 55).

106 **CARE OR MANAGEMENT.**—"Care or Management" of a Place for Betting, ss. 1, 3, 16 & 17 V. c. 119; *V. R.* v. *Cook*, 13 Q. B. D. 377; 51 L. T. 21; 32 W. R. 796; 48 J. P. 694: *Davis* v. *Stephenson*, 34 S. J. 334; 6 Times Rep. 242.

118 **CERTAIN PRINCIPAL SUM.**—"Certain Principal Sum," "Certain Amount of Stock;" *V.* Settlement.

119 **CHARACTER.**—To reference to *Re Dale and Plant*, add, 43 Ch. D. 255; 59 L. J. Ch. 180.

120 **CHARGE.**—Following *Sunderland* v. *Alcock*, add, *Hornsey* v. *Monarch Bg. Socy.*, 59 L. J. Q. B. 105; and to reference to *R.* v. *Holt*, add, 59 L. J. Q. B. 113; nom. *R.* v. *Land Registry*, 24 Q. B. D. 178.

124 **CHEMIST.**—As distinguished from Apothecary, "a Chemist is one who sells medicines which are asked for;" he does not select the medicines (per Cresswell, J., *Apothecaries Co.* v. *Lotinga*, 2 Moo. & R. 500): "a Chemist may prepare and vend, but not prescribe or administer medicine" (per Best, C. J., *Allison* v. *Haydon*, 4 Bing. 621). *V.* Apothecary.

127 **CHILD.**—To reference to *Reigate* v. *Croydon*, add, 59 L. J. M. C. 29; to *West Derby* v. *Atcham*, add, 59 L. J. M. C. 17.

137 **COLLUSION.**—*Butler* v. *Butler*, affd. 38 W. R. 390.

137 **COMBINATION.**—"'Combination of Machinery,' which has become a favourite form of words with Patentees, is nothing but an extended expression of the word 'Machine.' It is 'machine' writ large" (per Westbury, L. C., *Foxwell* v. *Bostock*, 4 D. G. J. & S. 311).

145 **CONCLUSIVE PROOF.**—*V.* Proof.

147 **CONDUCT.**—A judgment in a breach of promise of marriage action, which is the only debt proved in a Bankruptcy, may be considered on the question of the "Conduct and Affairs" of the Bankrupt, under s. 28 (2), Bankry. Act, 1883 (*Re Jones*, 34 S. J. 349; 6 Times Rep. 254, wherein the dicta in *Re Betts* were considered and explained).

149 **CONSENT.**—What amounts to "Consent" to a Marriage by Trustees of a Will or Settlement; *V. Re Smith, Keeling* v. *Smith*, 6 Times Rep. 183.

Vh. Parent.

50 To reference to *Stuart* v. *Diplock*, add, 43 Ch. D. 343.

Add to page

150 **CONSEQUENCE.**—*Vh. The City of Lincoln*, 59 L. J. P. D. & A. 1. "Consequent" means, traceable to, directly or indirectly: "Damage Consequent upon Collision," in a Marine Policy, means damage immediately consequent upon collision, or leakage caused by collision (per Mathew, J., *Pink* v. *Fleming*, 6 Times Rep. 213; 59 L. J. Q. B. 151).

154 **CONTRACT.**—"All contracts" by Infants for Money Lent, Goods (other than Necessaries), or on Account Stated are void (Infants Relief Act, 1874, 37 & 38 V. c. 62); *Vth. Duncan* v. *Dixon*, 6 Times Rep. 222.

164 **COSTS ONLY.**—Add to reference to Ann. Pr., *Bazett* v. *Morgan*, 59 L. J. Q. B. 44.

169 **CREDITOR.**—Debenture-holders are Creditors within s. 2, Joint Stock Companies Arrangement Act, 1870, 33 & 34 V. c. 104 (*Re Empire Mining Co.*, 25 L. J. Notes of Cases, 38).

170 **CRIMINAL CAUSE.**—A Contempt of Court is a "Criminal Cause" (*O'Shea* v. *O'Shea*, 34 S. J. 298; 6 Times Rep. 221).

179 **DAMAGE.**—At end add, *V.* WILFUL AND MALICIOUS.

183 **DEBENTURE.**—After quotation from jdgmt. of Chitty, J., add, "Debenters" were, on the 24th Decr., 1647, ordered to be given to the "Souldiery" of the Parliament for the arrears of their pay (cap. 113, Ordinances of the Long Parliament, printed in Scobell's Collection, p. 148, where, in the *Title* to the Ordinance, the word is spelt "Debentures"). "Debenture" is also used in s. 7, 41 G. 3, c. 75.

195 **DEFECT.**—Or danger arising from the non-fencing of machinery (*Morgan* v. *Hutchings*, 6 Times Rep. 219). To follow *Weblin* v. *Ballard*, cited DEFECT.

196 **DEFINITE.**—"Definite and Certain Principal Sum," "Definite and Certain Amount of Stock;" *V.* SETTLEMENT.

198 **DEMESNE.**—An exception, in a Power to Lease, of the Demesnes of a Manor, includes its copyholds (*Winter* v. *Loveday*, Carth. 428: *Vth.* Sug. Pow. 736).

202 **DESCEND.**—A devise of fee-simple estates to testator's sons A. and B. equally, "*to descend* to the heirs of A. and B. for ever, but in the event of both dying without issue, then to be equally divided between my daughters;" held, that "descend" aptly controlled the devolution to the *lineal* heirs or descendants of A. and B.; therefore that A. and B. took estates tail with cross remainders between them, and not estates in fee with executory devises over (*Fay* v. *Fay*, 5 L. R. Ir. 274).

Add to page

205 **DESIROUS OF WORKING.**—To reference to *Mid. Ry.* v. *Robinson*, add, 15 App. Ca. 19.

207 **DETERMINATION.**—After *R.* v. *Maconochie*, add, nom. *Re Paul, Ex p. Portarlington*, 59 L. J. Q. B. 30; 24 Q. B. D. 247.

212 **DIFFERENCE.**—So "Difference," Arbitration Act, 1889, includes a question of construction (*Van Eeghen* v. *Jones*, Times, 22nd Feb., 1890).

Add to 2nd par., DIFFERENCE.

213 **DIRECTLY AFFECTED.**—To reference to *Re Webber*, add, 24 Q. B. D. 313.

223 **DISTRESS.**—To reference to *Phillips* v. *Rees*, add, 59 L. J. Q. B. 1.

226 **DOMICIL.**—As employed in Art. 63, Civil Code of Lower Canada, "Domicil" means Residence, and does not refer to international domicil (*McMullen* v. *Wadsworth*, 59 L. J. P. C. 7).

229 **DRY.**—"Dry," *e.g.* "Dry Arsenic Acid," in a Patent Specification; *V. Simpson* v. *Holliday*, 5 N. R. 340; L. R. 1 H. L. 315; 35 L. J. Ch. 811.

230 **DUE DILIGENCE.**—There is no general time rule as to what is "Due Diligence" in "commencing" litigation, after a Threat respecting a Patent within proviso to s. 32, 46 & 47 V. c. 57; each case will depend on its own circumstances (*Barrett* v. *Day*, 43 Ch. D. 435; 38 W. R. 362: *Colley* v. *Hart*, 34 S. J. 282; W. N. (90) 46).

"Due Diligence" in "prosecuting" such litigation, within the same proviso, does not necessarily require that it should be carried on to trial (*Colley* v. *Hart*, sup.).

239 **EDUCATIONAL ENDOWMENT.**—After *Re Holgate's School*, add, *Christ's Hospital* v. *Charity Commrs.*, 62 L. T. 10.

245 **ENDORSE.**—In *R.* v. *Fitzroy Cowper* (59 L. J. Q. B. 26), "indorse" was held to be equivalent to "sign."

250 **ENTITLED.**—To reference to *Fisher* v. *Shirley*, add, 43 Ch. D. 290; 59 L. J. Ch. 29.

252 **EQUITABLE.**—"Equitable Execution;" to reference to *Re Shepard*, add, 59 L. J. Ch. 83.

263 **EXISTING.**—On death of A. "without issue, his part of the property to fall to whatever Existing Member of my Family he may be disposed to will it to;"—"existing" means, living at the date of A.'s Will (*Sinnott* v. *Walsh*, 5 L. R. Ir. 27).

Add to page

266 **EXPRESSLY REFER.**—*Phillips* v. *Cayley*, affd. 59 L. J. Ch. 177; 43 Ch. D. 222.

At end of title add, *V.* POWER.

274 **FAMILY.**—The primary meaning of "Family" is "Children," per Deasy, L. J.: the word has no primary meaning, per FitzGibbon, L. J. (*Sinnott* v. *Walsh*, 5 L. R. Ir. 27; *Vth.* per FitzGibbon, L. J., 21 L. R. Ir. 119). In *Re Mulqueen* (7 L. R. Ir. 127), "Family" was construed "Children."

284 **FINAL ORDER.**—To reference to *Re Giles*, add, 59 L. J. Ch. 226; 43 Ch. D. 391.

304 **FOUNDATION.**—"Foundation" requiring instruction "according to the Doctrines or Formularies of any particular Church," s. 19 (2), Endowed Schools Act, 1869, 32 & 33 V. c. 56, does not comprise Christ's Hospital, London, as being specially attached to the Church of England (*Christ's Hospital* v. *Charity Commrs.*, 62 L. T. 10).

311 **FROM.**—"As from the 31st March next after the passing of this Act," s. 24 (1), (2), Local Government Act, 1888: *V. Ex p. West Riding of Yorkshire*, 6 Times Rep. 265.

311 **FROM AND AFTER.**—To reference to *Re Jobson*, add, 59 L. J. Ch. 245.

313 **FRONT MAIN WALL.**—As used in s. 3, 51 & 52 V. c. 52; *V. Ravensthorpe* v. *Hinchcliffe*, 59 L. J. M. C. 19.

333 **GOODWILL.**—After *Vernon* v. *Hallam*, add, *Bristol Aerated Bread Co.* v. *Maggs*, 38 W. R. 393; W. N. (90) 60; 6 Times Rep. 227.

After EFFECTS, add, STOCK-IN-TRADE: BUSINESS.

343 **HEAR: HEARING.**—After 24 & 25 V. c. 100, add, *Vh. Reed* v. *Nutt*, 6 Times Rep. 266.

361 **HUNTING.**—*Vh. Devonshire* v. *O'Connor*, 24 Q. B. D. 468.

380 **INCOME.**—To reference to *Re West Riding Socy.*, add, 43 Ch. D. 407.

385 **INFAMOUS CONDUCT.**—To reference to *Leeson* v. *Gen. Medical Council*, add, 59 L. J. Ch. 233; 43 Ch. D. 366.

388 **INHERIT.**—Bequest to A., but if he die "without leaving any children legally to inherit," then lapse; A. died in testator's lifetime, leaving children; held, that his children took the bequest by implication (*M'Clean* v. *Simpson*, 19 L. R. Ir. 528).

Add to page

390 **INJURIOUSLY AFFECTED.**—Diverting a Highway which is the proximate access to land, is to "injuriously affect" the land (*Metrop. Bd. of Works* v. *Howard*, 5 Times Rep. 732).

To references to *Gower's Walk Schools and Lond. Tilbury and Southend Ry.*, add, 59 L. J. Q. B. 162.

391 **INJURY TO PROPERTY.**—For "per Field, J.," read, "per Fry, J.;" at end add, *V.* WILFUL AND MALICIOUS.

392 **INQUIRY.**—To reference to *Leeson* v. *Gen. Medical Council*, add, 59 L. J. Ch. 233; 43 Ch. D. 366.

395 **INSURANCE COMPANY.**—To reference to *Colquhoun* v. *Heddon*, add, 24 Q. B. D. 491; 59 L. J. Q. B. 142.

402 **INVENTED WORD.**—"Satinine," for starch, blue, and other preparations for laundry purposes, is a descriptive word, and not an "Invented Word" within s. 10, ss. 1 (*d*) Trade Marks Act, 1888 (*Le Mayerstein*, 38 W. R. 440).

410 **JUDGE.**—To reference to *Leeson* v. *Gen. Medical Council*, add, 59 L. J. Ch. 233; 43 Ch. D. 366.

419 **LADIES' OUTFITTER.**—To reference to *Stuart* v. *Diplock*, add, 43 Ch. D. 343.

428 **LEAVING.**—In *Armstrong* v. *Armstrong* (21 L. R. Ir. 119), Fitz-Gibbon, L. J., speaks of "the great infirmities of V.-C. Bacon's reasoning and decision in *White* v. *Hight*."

434 **LIABILITY.**—To reference to *Re West Riding Bg. Socy.*, add, 43 Ch. D. 407.

457 **MANSION.**—"Principal Mansion House," s. 15, Settled Land Act, 1882; *V. Re Thompson*, 21 L. R. Ir. 109.

470 **MEMBER.**—A Depositing Member of a Building Society who has given Notice of Withdrawal, is still a "Member" for the purpose of signing an Instrument of Dissolution of the Society under s. 32 (3), Building Societies Act, 1874, 37 & 38 V. c. 42; and must be taken into consideration in estimating the two-thirds consents thereunder (*Sibun* v. *Pearce*, 34 S. J. 378; W. N. (90) 73).

481 **MOIETY.**—When a person goes into an auction room, where a "Moiety" of a piece of ground is being sold, and bids for the same at so much per yard, that means that his bids are for the interest in the property (*i.e.*, the half part thereof) which is being sold, at so much per yard, not

Add to page

that he is bidding for the entirety of the property at so much per yard; his purchase money will, accordingly, be the amount of his successful bid multiplied by the number of yards, not half that amount (per Cottenham, L. C., *Chamberlain* v. *Lee*, 8 L. J. Ch. 266).

507 **NEW STREET.**—After *Evans* v. *Newport*, add, *Roberts* v. *Richards*, Times, 28th March, 1890.

509 **NEXT HEIR.**—*V.* WORLD.

THE

JUDICIAL DICTIONARY.

A—ABA

A.—"A" is sometimes read as "the;" *e.g.* an act done "with *a* view" of giving a creditor a fraudulent preference (Bankry. Act, 1869, s. 92; and now Bankry. Act, 1883, 46 & 47 V. c. 52, s. 48), means with *the* view,—the real, effectual, substantial, dominant view of giving a preference (*Ex p. Hill, Re Bird,* 52 L. J. Ch. 903; 23 Ch. D. 695: *Ex p. Taylor,* 18 Q. B. D. 295: *Vh. Re Mills,* 58 L. T. 871; 4 Times Rep. 284).

But more frequently "a" is the equivalent of "any:" and therefore where by s. 52, Agricultural Holdings Act, 1883 (46 & 47 V. c. 61), bailiffs for levying a distress on an agricultural holding are to be appointed in writing "by the judge of *a* County Court," that does not mean "of *the* County Court in the district of which the holding is," but means "of *any* County Court"; so that a bailiff appointed by any County Court judge may levy an agricultural distress anywhere (*Re Sanders, Ex p. Sergeant,* 54 L. J. Q. B. 331).

A grant of "a" right of sporting on land, gives only a concurrent right; but "the" right would give it exclusively (*Graham* v. *Ewart,* 25 L. J. Ex. 47).

So a clergyman may be "a" minister of a church, without being "the" minister. *V.* MINISTER.

By a covenant not to erect any building "except *a* private dwelling-house," not merely the class of building is defined in the exception but only one of that class is permitted thereby (per Denman, J., *Smith* v. *Standing,* 32 S. J. 734).

V. ONE: THE.

ABANDON.—"Abandon or expose" a child under two years of age, s. 27, 24 & 25 V. c. 100. These words "include a wilful omission to take charge of the child on the part of a person legally bound to do so, and any mode of dealing with it calculated to leave it exposed to risk without protection" (Steph. Cr. 196, citing *R.* v. *White,* L. R. 2 C. C. R. 311; 40 L. J. M. C. 134: *R.* v. *Falkingham,* L. R. 2 C. C. R. 222; 39 L. J. M. C. 47). *Vf.* Arch. Cr. 788, 789; Rosc. Cr. 398.

ABANDONMENT.—In a policy of *Marine Insurance* Abandonment is of the essence of a claim for constructive total loss.

"The word 'abandon' is one in ordinary and common use, and in its natural sense well understood; but there is not a word in the English language used in a more highly artificial and technical sense than the word 'abandon'; in reference to constructive total loss, it is defined to be a cession or transfer of the ship from the owner to the under-writer, and of all his property and interest in it, with all the claims that may arise from its ownership, and all the profits that may arise from it, including the freight then being earned" (per Martin, B., *Rankin* v. *Potter*, 42 L. J. C. P. 200; L. R. 6 H. L. 139).

To constitute Abandonment of a *Trade-Mark* an intention to abandon must be shewn: mere evidence of non-user is insufficient (*Mouson* v. *Boehm*, 53 L. J. Ch. 932; 26 Ch. D. 398). *V.* COMMENCEMENT.

ABATE.—"'Abate' is both an English and French word, and signifieth, in his proper sense, to diminish or take away, as here (s. 475, Litt.) by his entrie he diminisheth and taketh away the freehold in law descended to the heire: and so it is said, to abate an account, signifying subtraction or withdrawing, &c., and to abate the courage of a man. In another sense it signifieth to prostrate, beat downe, or overthrow, as to abate castles, houses and the like, and to abate a writ; and hereof commeth a word of art, *abatamentum*, which is an entrie by interposition" (Co. Litt. 277 a; *Vf. Ib.* 134 b).

ABATEMENT.—*V.* DEDUCTIONS.

ABDUCTION.—*V.* Steph. Cr. 191–194, stating 24 & 25 V. c. 100, ss. 53, 54, as explained by the authorities there cited. *Vf.* Arch. Cr. 795–803; Rosc. Cr. 267–272.

ABET.—*V.* AID OR ABET.

ABEYANCE.—"'In abeiance': That is, in expectation, of the French word *bayer*, to expect. For when a parson dieth, wee say that the freehold is in abeyance, because a successor is in expectation to take it" (Co. Litt. 342 b).

ABIDE THE EVENT.—*V.* EVENT.

ABILITY.—In the sense of being able to pay, as used in 9 G. 4, c. 14, s. 6; *V. Lyde* v. *Barnard*, 1 M. & W. 101; 5 L. J. Ex. 117; 1 Sm. L. C. 195–197.

ABLE.—A gift of residue to an infant "if he shall be *able* to discharge the executors" is good, because, by action in Ch. D., he is "able" to discharge the executors (*Ledward* v. *Hassells*, 25 L. J. Ch. 311; 2 K. & J. 370).

An acknowledgment to pay "*when* able" or "as soon as I can," throws the onus of proving the debtor's ability to pay on the creditor (*Davies* v.

Smith, 4 Esp. 36 : *Besford* v. *Saunders*, 2 H. Bl. 116 : *Tanner* v. *Smart*, 6 B. & C. 603 : *Philips* v. *Philips*, 3 Hare, 281, 299 : *Smith* v. *Thorne*, 18 Q. B. 139 ; 21 L. J. Q. B. 199 : *Meyerhoff* v. *Froehlich*, 4 C. P. D. 63 ; 48 L. J. C. P. 43) ; and the Statute of Limitations, on such an acknowledgment, runs from the time when, in fact, the debtor is able, whether that state of things be known to the creditor or not (*Waters* v. *Thanet*, 2 Q. B. 757 ; *Hammond* v. *Smith*, 33 Bea. 452).

ABODE.—"Abode," "Place of Abode." *V.* PLACE : *Va.* USUAL PLACE OF ABODE : LAST.

ABOUT.—*V. Bourne* v. *Seymour*, 24 L. J. C. P. 202 ; 16 C. B. 337 : *Alcock* v. *Leeuw*, 1 Cab. & El. 98. *Va.* MORE OR LESS : SAY : THEREABOUTS : IN OR ABOUT.

ABSENTS.—S. 4 (*d*) Bankry. Act, 1883 :—"The result of the cases is that a man's intentionally keeping away from any place, where he would in the ordinary course of things be, is absenting himself, though it is not an act of Bankry. unless it be with intent to defeat or delay his creditors" (Yate Lee, citing *Ex p. Meyer, Re Stephany*, L. R. 7 Ch. 188). *Vf.* Yate Lee, 47–50 ; Wms. Bankry. 19 ; Robson, 141 ; Baldwin, 58. *V.* DEPART.

To "absent himself" from his service within s. 3, 4 G. 4, c. 34 (repealed), meant absent himself without lawful excuse (*Re Turner*, 9 Q. B. 80 ; 15 L. J. M. C. 140 : *Re Geswood*, 23 L. J. M. C. 35 ; 2 E. & B. 952), and knowing he had no such excuse (*Rider* v. *Wood*, 29 L. J. M. C. 1). *Vf. Willett* v. *Boote*, 30 L. J. M. C. 6 ; 6 H. & N. 26 ; *Ashmore* v. *Horton*, 29 L. J. M. C. 13.

ABSOLUTE.—*V.* ABSOLUTE ASSIGNMENT : ABSOLUTE DAMAGE : DISCRETION : DISPOSAL.

ABSOLUTE ASSIGNMENT.—An "Absolute Assignment" entitling an assignee to sue in his own name for a chose in action under sub-s. 6, s. 25, Jud. Act, 1873, need not, necessarily, be an assignment equivalent to a sale out-and-out.

An assignment by way of mortgage is "absolute" if in terms it is so ; and though such an assignment is for the purpose of securing payment of a debt, yet it is not "by way of charge only," for a "charge" is a mere appropriation of a particular fund to a particular debt (*Burlinson* v. *Hall*, 53 L. J. Q. B. 222 ; 12 Q. B. D. 347). But it has been said, that if a mortgage assignment contains a proviso for reconveyance, it is not "absolute" within the section (*Nat. Prov. Bank* v. *Harle*, 50 L. J. Q. B. 437 ; 6 Q. B. D. 626). But can this latter distinction be maintained ? *Semble*, not (*Tancred* v. *Delagoa Bay Ry.*, 23 Q. B. D. 239 ; 58 L. J. Q. B. 459 ; 5 Times Rep. 587).

An authority from A. to B., to pay C. so much periodically "until further order," is an "Absolute Assignment" (*Knill* v. *Prowse*, 33 W. R. 163); but a cheque is not (*Schroeder* v. *Central Bank*, 24 W. R. 710; 34 L. T. 735; *V.* CHARGE).

ABSOLUTE DAMAGE.—As to the phrase, in a Marine Insurance, "Absolute Damage caused by the Perils insured against;" *V. Forwood* v. *North Wales Mut. Mar. Insrce. Co.*, 9 Q. B. D. 732; 49 L. J. Q. B. 243, 593.

ABSOLUTELY ENTITLED.—Trustees for sale, having now power to give a complete discharge for the purchase money, are persons "absolutely entitled" within s. 69, Lands C. C. Act, 1845 (*Re Hobson*, 47 L. J. Ch. 310; 7 Ch. D. 708: *Re Thomas*, W. N. (82) 7; 30 W. R. 244. But *Re Hobson* was doubted in *Re Smith*, 40 Ch. D. 386; 58 L. J. Ch. 108), even though the power of sale has not become exerciseable (*Re Evans*, 14 Ch. D. 511: *Re St. Luke's, Middlesex*, W. N. (80) 58); and so (when acting jointly with a Tenant for Life) are Trustees who hold upon trust for sale on request of the Tenant for Life (*Re Ward*, 54 L. J. Ch. 231; 28 Ch. D. 719). *Vh. Ex p. Haberdashers' Co.*, 31 S. J. 126; 55 L. T. 758: *Re Curwen*, W. N. (80) 83.

A Tenant for Life is not a person "absolutely entitled" within s. 23, Trustee Act, 1850 (13 & 14 V. c. 60), except for the purpose of an application limited to the income only; nor is one of two or more trustees (*Mackenzie* v. *Mackenzie*, 21 L. J. Ch. 385; 5 D. G. & S. 338; 16 Jur. 723). But persons duly appointed new trustees are so "absolutely entitled" (*Re Russell*, 20 L. J. Ch. 196; 1 Sim. N. S. 404: *Re Baxter*, 2 Sm. & G. App. v.: *Re Ellis*, 24 Bea. 426; Lewin, 1022).

ABSOLUTELY SELL.—A conveyance, made by a Railway Co. selling Superfluous Land, provided that the purchase-money should not be payable until two years after the statutory period for such a sale: Held, that whether the company did "absolutely sell and dispose of" the land, within s. 127, Lands C. C. Act, 1845, was too doubtful for the title to be forced on a subsequent purchaser (*Re Thackwray & Young*, 58 L. J. Ch. 72; 40 Ch. D. 34, on consideration of judicial dicta in *Lond. & S. W. Ry.* v. *Gomm*, 51 L. J. Ch. 530; 20 Ch. D. 562).

ABSTRACT.—An "Abstract of Title," within the meaning of a Condition of Sale restrictive of requirements, means a *perfect* abstract,—*i.e.*, perfect so far as the vendor *ought* to make it, and that condition will (in the absence of patent and substantial errors or omissions) be generally fulfilled if the vendor honestly makes the abstract as perfect as he can, having regard to the materials within his control (Dart, 321). Copies of plans on abstracted deeds,—at any rate when the plans are of the essence of the description,—should be delivered with the Abstract to make it "perfect" (Dart, 345; *V. n.* 30 S. J. 796). *Sv. Blackburn* v. *Smith* (18 L. J. Ex. 187; 2 Ex. 783), in which Parke, B., in delivering the judgment of the court said,—"We are not aware that a map or plan is ever deemed to be necessary as a part of an Abstract." *Vf.* DELIVERY.

"Abstract," as used in s. 3 (6), Conv. & L. P. Act, 1881, is to be distinguished from "Abstract of Title" (*Re Johnson*, 54 L. J. Ch. 889; 30 Ch. D. 42).

ABUSE.—*V.* CRUELTY *to Animals.*

ABUTTING.—*V.* ADJOIN: BOUNDING: FRONTING.

&c.—*V.* ET CETERA.

ACCELERATION.—*V.* EXTINCTION.

ACCEPTANCE.—For definition and requisites of, and liabilities on, "Acceptance" of a *Bill of Exchange*, *V.* ss. 17, 18, 19, and 54, Bills of Exchange Act, 1882; "Acceptance for Honour, supra protest," ss. 65, 66, 67, *Ib.*

As to the difference between "Acceptance" and "Receipt" *of Goods* under the Statute of Frauds, *V.* Blackb. 30, citing *Boulter* v. *Arnott*, 1 Cr. & M. 333: *Vf.*, as to "Acceptance," *Castle* v. *Sworder*, 6 H. & N. 833; 29 L. J. Ex. 235; 30 *Ib.* 310: *Marvin* v. *Wallace*, 25 L. J. Q. B. 369: *Gardiner* v. *Grout*, 29 L. T. O. S. 110: *Nicholson* v. *Bower*, 28 L. J. Q. B. 97: *Holmes* v. *Hoskins*, 9 Ex. 753: *Currie* v. *Anderson*, 29 L. J. Q. B. 87: *Cusack* v. *Robinson*, 30 L. J. Q. B. 261; 1 B. & S. 299: *Smith* v. *Hudson*, 34 L. J. Q. B. 145: *Farrer* v. *Kirkby*, 4 Times Rep. 543.

Acceptance *of Shares* in a Co.; *V. Bog Lead Mining Co.* v. *Montague*, 30 L. J. C. P. 380; 10 C. B. N. S. 481.

ACCEPTED.—Goods sold are "accepted" by the buyer, within s. 17, Stat. of Frauds, when they, or a part of them, have been, actually or constructively, received by him under such circumstances as import a recognition of the contract. Acceptance of goods sold in order to examine their quality, is none the less an acceptance within the section (*Page* v. *Morgan*, 54 L. J. Q. B. 434; 15 Q. B. D. 228; 33 W. R. 793). As to constructive acceptance, *V.* Add. C. 921.

Guarantee of all Bills of Ex. "accepted" by A, construed by Pollock, C.B. and Martin, B. (diss. Bramwell, B.), as referring to future Bills (*Broom* v. *Batchelor*, 25 L. J. Ex. 299; 1 H. & N. 255). *V.* GIVEN.

"Accepted Office"—*e.g.* of Town Councillor—has a colloquial, as well as a technical meaning; and whether a person has "accepted" is a conclusion to be collected from all the circumstances (*R.* v. *Slatter*, 9 L. J. Q. B. 115; 11 A. & E. 507; 3 P. & D. 263).

ACCESS.—"In my judgment, the word 'Access' as used in s. 3, 2 & 3 W. 4, c. 71—('access and use of Light')—does not refer to the access through the orifice, through the aperture, through the window, but to the freedom of passage over the servient tenement, and I think some confusion has arisen from supposing that the access referred to there, is the access through the window of the dominant tenement. Undoubtedly the two are closely connected together, because the right acquired under this section of the statute by the dominant tenement is governed and measured by the access to the dominant tenement, and therefore the aperture which lets the light into the dominant tenement defines in a manner familiar to us all the area which must be kept free over the servient tenement. The two things are closely connected together; the one is the measure of the other; but they are not the same thing" (Per Fry, L. J., *Scott* v. *Pape*, 55 L. J. Ch. 432; 31 Ch. D. 554; 54 L. T. 389; 34 W. R. 465. *Vf. Greenwood* v. *Hornsey*, 55 L. J. Ch. 917; 33 Ch. D. 471; 55 L. T. 135; 35 W. R. 163: *Cooper* v. *Straker*, 58 L. J. Ch. 29; 40 Ch. D. 20).

V. Actually Enjoyed.

ACCESSORY.—"An Accessory *Before the Fact* is one who directly or indirectly counsels, procures, or commands any person to commit any felony or piracy which is committed in consequence of such counselling, procuring, or commandment. Knowledge that a person intends to commit a crime, and conduct connected with and influenced by such knowledge, is not enough to make the person who possesses such knowledge, or so conducts himself, an accessory before the fact to any such crime, unless he does something to encourage its commission actively" (Steph. Cr. 32: *Vf. Ib.* Art. 40–44). *Vh.* Arch. Cr. 1096.

"Every one is an Accessory *After the Fact* to felony who, knowing a felony to have been committed by another, receives, comforts, or assists him, in order to enable him to escape from punishment; or rescues him from an arrest for the felony; or having him in custody for the felony, intentionally and voluntarily suffers him to escape; or opposes his apprehension:—Provided that a married woman who receives, comforts, or relieves her husband knowing him to have committed a felony, does not thereby become an accessory after the fact" (Steph. Cr. 35). *Vf.* Arch. Cr. 1107; Rosc. Cr. 181–189.

"Accessory to or Conniving at" Adultery, s. 30, 20 & 21 V. c. 85. *V.* Connivance.

ACCIDENT.—"An effect is said to be accidental when the act by which it is caused is not done with the intention of causing it, and when its occurrence as a consequence of such act is not so probable that a person of ordinary prudence ought, under the circumstances in which it is done, to take reasonable precautions against it" (Steph. Cr. 143).

An exception in a Charter-Party against "Riots, Strikes, or any other *Accident*," does not include a snow-storm. "An accident is not an ordinary occurrence, but something which happens out of the ordinary course of things. A snow-storm, however, is one of the ordinary operations of nature, and may be described rather as an incident than an accident" (per Willes, J., *Fenwick* v. *Schalmz*, 37 L. J. C. P. 80; L. R. 3 C. P. 313: *Vf.*

1 Maude & P. 357; *Laurie* v. *Douglas*, 15 M. & W. 746). *V.* Dangers: Perils of the Sea.

Death by drowning (*Trew* v. *Ry. Insrce. Co.*, 30 L. J. Ex. 317; 6 H. & N. 839), even if the insured were drowned in shallow water whilst in a state of insensibility (*Reynolds* v. *Accidental Insrce. Co.*, 22 L. T. 820), is an "Accident" within a Policy against accidents. But sun-stroke is not (*Sinclair* v. *Maritime Assrce.*, 30 L. J. Q. B. 77; 3 E. & E. 478). *V.* Secondary: Caused by.

"Accident," s. 22, Factories Act, 7 V. c. 15: *V. Lakeman* v. *Stephenson*, 37 L. J. M. C. 57; L. R. 3 Q. B. 192; 9 B. & S. 54. "Accident," s. 15, Peak Forest Canal Act, 34 G. 3, c. 26: *V. Evans* v. *Manchester, S. & L. Ry.*, 3 Times Rep. 691.

V. Poison.

ACCIDENTALLY.—By s. 86, 14 G. 3, c. 78, a person in whose premises a fire "*accidentally* begins" is exonerated from liability to his neighbour for damage occasioned by such fire. "Accidentally" there is not used in contradistinction to "wilfully," but means "a fire produced by mere chance, or incapable of being traced to any cause;" and does not mean a fire arising from negligence (*Filliter* v. *Phippard*, 17 L. J. Q. B. 89; 11 Q. B. 347; *Vh.* Add. T. 341, and cases there cited). As to the common law responsibility for damage caused by fires, see Add. T. 339, and obs. at commencement of Lord Lyndhurst's judgment in *Canterbury* v. *The Queen*, 12 L. J. Eq. 281; 1 Phil. Ch. c. 318.

ACCOMMODATION.—"An Accommodation Party to a Bill is a person who has signed a Bill, as Drawer, Acceptor, or Indorser, without receiving Value therefor, and for the purpose of lending his name to some other person.

"(2) An Accommodation Party is liable on the Bill to a Holder for Value, and it is immaterial whether, when such Holder took the bill, he knew such party to be an Accommodation Party or not" (s. 28, Bills of Ex. Act, 1882): and so of an Accommodation Party to a Note (s. 89, *Ib.*).

"Works for the Accommodation of Lands adjoining the Ry.," s. 68, Ry. C. C. Act, 1845, do not, *semble*, comprise matters beneath the surface of the land, *e.g.*, Drains (*R.* v. *Fisher*, 32 L. J. M. C. 12; 3 B. & S. 191; 7 L. T. 325). *V.* Works.

ACCORDANCE.—*V.* In accordance with the form.

ACCORDING TO THE STOCKS.—*V.* Per Stirpes.

ACCORDING TO THE TERMS.—*V.* Terms.

ACCORDINGLY.—Agreeably; conformably; or in that capacity (*Lindley* v. *Girdler*, 13 L. J. Q. B. 53).

ACCOUNT.—"Wholly or in part matters of Mere Account," s. 3,

Com. L. Pro. Act, 1854 ;—The meaning of the power of ordering a Compulsory Arbitration under these words is, "that where the matter in dispute consists, either wholly or in part, of matters of Mere Account, the compulsory reference may be either of the whole, or of part only, of the matter in dispute, as the Court or Judge may think fit" (per Jervis, C. J. delivering judgment of the Court in *Browne* v. *Emerson*, 25 L. J. C. P. 105, 106 ; 17 C. B. 361). But in *Clow* v. *Harper* (47 L. J. Ex. 393 ; 3 Ex. D. 198), Cockburn, C. J., said that "when the matter in dispute involves mere matter of account, then it is competent to the Court to send the whole matter for the decision of the arbitrator. But when it is only *in part* a matter of account, and quoad the rest a matter of fact or law, the latter part is not a proper subject of the Order, but the Order must be limited to the questions of account." Brett, L. J., concurred in that opinion ; Bramwell, L. J., doubted. But it was not necessary to the decision, as the whole liability of the defendant was denied. Still, having regard to the weight of such an opinion, it seems difficult to see how *Imhof* v. *Sutton* (36 L. J. C. P. 130 ; L. R. 2 C. P. 406), or *Birmingham Gas Co.* v. *Ratcliffe* (40 L. J. Ex. 136 ; L. R. 6 Ex. 224), can now be regarded as authorities for the proposition in *Browne* v. *Emerson* (sup.), especially as Kelly, C. B., dissented from the decision in the *Birmingham Gas Co.* case.

An action for Dilapidations, or for breach of covenant to Repair "is one of Mere Account" where only the quantum is in dispute (*Cummins* v. *Birkett*, 27 L. J. Ex. 216 ; 3 H. & N. 156 : *Angell* v. *Felgate*, 31 L. J. Ex. 41 ; 7 H. & N. 396) ; *secus* if the liability is disputed (*Clow* v. *Harper*, sup.).

Vh., as to reluctance to limit the Judge's discretion in making the Order, *Sheard* v. *Learoyd*, 2 Times Rep. 632.

V. Accounts : Books of Account : On the Account : Merchant's Accounts.

ACCOUNTABLE.—*V.* Not liable.

ACCOUNTABLE RECEIPT.—*V.* Receipt.

ACCOUNTANT.—A person who carried on business as Agent to an Accountant, and was employed as accountant by other persons, was held to be properly described as "Accountant," for the purposes of the Bills of Sale Acts (*Briggs* v. *Boss*, 37 L. J. Q. B. 101 ; L. R. 3 Q. B. 268) ; but a clerk in the Accountant's Office of a Railway, who occasionally works for other people after office hours, is not properly described as "Accountant" (*Larchin* v. *North Western Deposit Bank*, 44 L. J. Ex. 71 ; L. R. 10 Ex. 64). In the latter case, Mellor, J., said, "I think in *Briggs* v. *Boss* we went to the extreme limit."

ACCOUNTS.—As used in the power of reference given by s. 57, Jud. Act, 1873, "Accounts" is widely interpreted, so as to include questions requiring scientific investigation (*Rowcliffe* v. *Leigh*, 3 Ch. D. 292).

V. Account.

ACCRUE.—A Title "accrues" when the instrument creating it, or the fact constituting it, first becomes operative; therefore s. 5, M. W. P. Act, 1882, applies only to property of a married woman her original title to which accrued after the commencement of the Act, and it does not embrace property in remainder at the time of, but which comes into possession after, the commencement of the Act (*Reid* v. *Reid*, 55 L. J. Ch. 294; 31 Ch. D. 402; 34 W. R. 332). *Cp.* ACQUIRE; *V.* TITLE.

A cause of action for a Tort "accrues" when it becomes effective, *i.e.*, when the resulting damage manifests itself. *V.* CAUSE OF ACTION.

"Accruing Debt;" *V.* DEBT.

"Arising or Accruing;" *V.* ARISING.

"Accruing *Share and Interest;*" *V. Greenwood* v. *Sutcliffe*, 23 L. J. C. P. 98; 14 C. B. 226.

V. FIRST ACCRUED.

ACCUMULATION.—"It cannot, perhaps, be considered as quite settled whether an accumulation which arises, not by the *direction* of the settlor, but by *operation of law*, is within the Thellusson Act," 39 & 40 G. 3, c. 98 (Watson, Eq. 5, *wh. V.* for consideration of cases thereon). The word "accumulate" is not necessary; a direction to "invest," or the like, for a period prohibited is within the Act (*Matthews* v. *Keble*, 37 L. J. Ch. 8, 657; L. R. 4 Eq. 467; 3 Ch. 691). *Vf.* hereon generally, Watson, Eq. 4, Tit. "Accumulations."

ACCUSTOMABLY.—*V.* USUALLY.

ACCUSTOMED RENT.—"Old and Accustomed Rent;" *V. Mountjoy's case*, 5 Rep. 3 b.

"Accustomed Rent;" *V. Doe* d. *Douglas* v. *Lock*, 4 L. J. Q. B. 113; 2 A. & E. 705; 4 N. & M. 807.

"Ancient and Accustomed Rent;" *V. Doe* d. *Biddulph* v. *Hole*, 20 L. J. Q. B. 57; 15 Q. B. 848.

"Yearly Firm or Rent . . . . accustomably yielden or paid;" s. 2, 32 H. 8, c. 28, 13 Eliz. c. 10; *V. Doe* d. *Tennyson* v. *Yarborough*, 7 Moo. 258; 1 Bing. 24.

V. ANCIENT RENT.

ACKNOWLEDGE.—"I acknowledge A. B. to be my heir-at-law;" held to pass the testator's lands in fee (*Parker* v. *Nickson*, 32 L. J. Ch. 397; 1 D. G. J. & S. 177). In giving judgment in that case Westbury, L. C., said,—"Nothing is better settled in our law than that the words 'I *make* A. B. my heir,' or 'I *declare* A. B. to be my heir,' or even the words 'A. B. *is* my heir,' amount to a devise to A. B. in fee of all the inheritable lands of the testator:" for as "Jerman, J., said (*Tayler* v. *Web*, Styles, 301, 319), 'the word *Heir* implies two things: first, that he shall have the lands; secondly, that he shall have them in fee simple.'" So of a nomination of an heir by such expressions as "I *appoint*" or "I *nominate*" (*Spark* v.

Purnell, Hob. 75). So where a testator constituted his dearly-beloved wife sole executrix and "Heiress of all his lands and real and personal estate," to sell same at pleasure and to pay debts and legacies, she was held entitled to retain the surplus proceeds after payment of debts and legacies, and that there was no resulting trust in favour of the heir as regards such surplus (*Rogers* v. *Rogers*, 3 P. W. 193, stated 1 Jarm. 570). *V.* Sole Heir.

V. Acknowledgment.

ACKNOWLEDGMENT.—At p. 108, 1 Jarm., the following rules are deduced from the cases, there cited, as to what is an Acknowledgment by a testator of the signature to his Will:—

"(a) The signature to be acknowledged may be made by the testator, or by another for him.

"(b) A testator, whether speechless or not, may acknowledge his signature by gestures.

"(c) There is no sufficient acknowledgment unless the witnesses either saw, or might have seen, the signature, not even though the testator should expressly declare that the paper to be attested by them is his Will."

(Note: This proposition cited and approved by Jessel, M. R., *Blake* v. *Blake*, 51 L. J. P. D. & A. 36; 7 P. D. 102; which case upholds Dr. Lushington's ruling hereon in *Hudson* v. *Parker*, 1 Robert. 14; but overrules that of Sir Cresswell Cresswell in *Gwillim* v. *Gwillim*, 3 Sw. & Tr. 200, and of Ld. Penzance in *Beckett* v. *Howe*, L. R. 2 P. & D. 1; 39 L. J. P. & M. 1.)

"(d) When the witnesses either saw or might have seen the signature, an express acknowledgment of the signature itself is not necessary, a mere statement that the paper is his Will, or a direction to them to put their names under his, or even a request by the testator, or by some person in his presence, to sign the paper is sufficient." *Vh. Daintree* v. *Fasulo*, 57 L. J. P. D. & A. 76; 13 P. D. 102; 58 L. T. 661.

"(e) When the signature is seen or expressly acknowledged, it is not material that the witnesses are not told that the instrument is a Will, or are deceived into thinking that it is a deed.

"(f) It is of course sufficient, on a re-execution, merely to acknowledge the signature made on a former execution."

ACQUIESCENCE.—This word does not mean simply an active intelligent consent, but will be implied if a person is content not to oppose irregular acts which he knows are being done (per Cairns, L. C., *Evans* v. *Smallcombe*, 37 L. J. Ch. 793; L. R. 3 H. L. 249).

"If a person having a right, and seeing another person about to commit, or in the course of committing an act infringing upon that right, stands by in such a manner as really to induce the person committing the act, and who might otherwise have abstained from it, to believe that he assents to its being committed, he cannot afterwards be heard to complain of the act.

This, as Lord Cottenham said in *Duke of Leeds* v. *Earl Amherst* (2 Ph. 117; 16 L. J. Ch. 5; 10 Jur. 956), is the proper sense of the term "Acquiescence," and in that sense may be defined as quiescence under such circumstances as that assent may be reasonably inferred from it, and is no more than an instance of the law of estoppel by words or conduct" (per Thesiger, L.J., *De Bussche* v. *Alt*, 8 Ch. D. 314; 47 L. J. Ch. 389; 38 L. T. 370). But "'Acquiescence' imports full knowledge" (per Turner, L. J., *Life Assn. of Scotland* v. *Siddal*, 3 D. G. F. & J. 58, 74). *Vf. Redgrave* v. *Hurd*, 20 Ch. D. 1; 51 L. J. Ch. 113; 45 L. T. 485; 30 W. R. 251; Buckl. 441–445.

It is not necessary to bring an action in order to show that a person has not "submitted to or acquiesced in" an interruption of an Easement within s. 4, Prescription Act, 2 & 3 W. 4, c. 71; "Acquiescence" under that section is a question of fact (*Bennison* v. *Cartwright*, 33 L. J. Q. B. 137; 5 B. & S. 1).

ACQUIRE.—Moneys of a deserted wife, not reduced into possession by her husband before desertion, and payable after desertion, are "acquired" by the wife after the desertion within s. 21, 20 & 21 V. c. 85 (*Nicholson* v. *Drury Building Co.*, 47 L. J. Ch. 192; 7 Ch. D. 48; *Vf. Cooke* v. *Fuller*, 26 Bea. 99); but rents of the wife's leaseholds received after her desertion by an agent appointed by her before the marriage, are not within the word (*Kingsman* v. *Kingsman*, 50 L. J. Q. B. 81; 6 Q. B. D. 122; 29 W. R. 207; 44 L. T. 124; 45 J. P. 357).

Property which a wife, after a judicial separation, "may *acquire*, or which may *come to* or *devolve* upon her," s. 25, 20 & 21 V. c. 85; *V. Re Insole*, 35 L. J. Ch. 177; 35 Bea. 92; L. R. 1 Eq. 470: *Re Coward & Adams*, L. R. 20 Eq. 179; 44 L. J. Ch. 384; *Waite* v. *Worland*, 38 Ch. D. 135; 59 L. T. 185; 57 L. J. Ch. 655; 36 W. R. 484.

V. Come to: Conquest. *Cp.* Accrue.

ACQUISITION OF GAIN.—*V.* Gain.

ACQUITTAL.—"'*To acquite him*': *acquite* is compounded of *ad*, and the old verbe *quietare*, and signifieth in law to discharge, or keepe in quiet, and to see that the tenant be safely kept from any entries, or other molestation for any manner of service issuing out of the land to any lord that is above the mesne. And hereof commeth Acquitall, and *quietus est*, (that is) that he is discharged; and he that is discharged of a felony, &c., by judgment, is said to be acquitted of the felony, *acquietatus de feloniâ*; and if he be drawne in question againe, he may plead *auterfoits acquite*" (Co. Litt. 100 a).

"The word 'Acquittal' is *verbum equivocum*, and may in ordinary language be used to express either the verdict of a jury, or the formal judgment of the Court, that the prisoner go thereof without day" (per Tindal, C. J., *Burgess* v. *Boetefeur*, 13 L. J. M. C. 126; 7 M. & G. 481).

ACQUITTANCE.—A "Clearance" Certificate, from one branch of a Friendly Society to another, is not an "Acquittance" within s. 23, 24 & 25 V. c. 98 (*R.* v. *French*, 39 L. J. M. C. 58; L. R. 1 C. C. R. 217).

ACRE.—"By the grant of an Acre of land, doth pass so much as is an acre by measure in that country, by the ordinary account and measure of the country (*V.* Co. Litt. 5 b: *O'Donnell* v. *O'Donnell*, 13 L. R. Ir. 227). By the grant of a Rood of land, doth pass ten perches, the fourth part of an acre" (Touch. 95, 96: whence is this statement that 10 perches are the fourth part of an acre ?).—*Vf.* Elph. 558.

ACROSS.—*V.* THROUGH.

ACROSS COUNTRY.—*V.* *Evans* v. *Pratt*, 11 L. J. C. P. 87; 3 M. & G. 759.

ACT.—Continuing a thing in its former condition, is not an act done (*Wordsworth* v. *Harley*, 1 B. & Ad. 391). *Sv.* DONE.

V. PURPOSES.

ACT JUSTLY.—*V.* PRECATORY TRUST.

ACT OF GOD.—"Act of God" means not a mere misfortune, but something overwhelming (per Martin, B., *Oakley* v. *Portsmouth Steam Packet Co.*, 25 L. J. Ex. 101; 11 Ex. 623), such as storms, lightning, and tempests, which could not happen by the intervention of man (*Forward* v. *Pittard*, 1 T. R. 33), and loss from which could not have been prevented, or avoided, by any reasonable amount of foresight, pains, or care (*Nugent* v. *Smith*, 45 L. J. C. P. 697, 708; 1 C. P. D. 441, 444).

"In the older, simpler days, I have myself never had any doubt but that this phrase does not mean Act of God in the Biblical sense of the term, under which everything almost is said to be the act of God; but that, in a mercantile sense, it means an extraordinary circumstance which could not be foreseen, and which could not be guarded against" (per Esher, M. R., *Pandorf* v. *Hamilton*, 55 L. J. Q. B. 548; 17 Q. B. D. 675).—*Vf.* *Nichols* v. *Marsland*, 46 L. J. Ex. 174; L. R. 10 Ex. 255; 2 Ex. D. 1: *Nitro-phosphate Co.* v. *L. & S. Katherine's Dock Co.*, 9 Ch. D. 503; 1 Maude & P. 350; Benj. 551: *R.* v. *Essex Commrs. of Sewers*, 14 Q. B. D. 561; 11 App. Ca. 449.

ACT OF PARLIAMENT.—*V.* LOCAL ACT OF PARLIAMENT.

ACT OR DEFAULT.—"Wrongful Act or Default;" *V.* DEFAULT.

ACT OR PRACTICE.—*V.* PRACTICE.

ACTING TRUSTEE.—An "acting" Trustee is one who has taken upon himself to perform some of the trusts; the phrase does not include one who, *in limine*, has refused to act (*Sharp* v. *Sharp*, 2 B. & Ald. 405; stated Lewin, 655: *Vf.* Lewin, 665). *Cp.* CONTINUING TRUSTEE.

ACTION.—This is a generic term, and means a litigation in a civil court for the recovery of individual right or redress of individual wrong, inclusive, in its proper legal sense, of suits by the Crown (*Bradlaugh* v. *Clarke*, 52 L. J. Q. B. 505; 8 App. Ca. 354; 48 L. T. 681: *Va.* jdgmt. of Brett, M.R., in *A.-G.* v. *Bradlaugh*, 54 L. J. Q. B. 214; 14 Q. B. D. 667; 52 L. T. 589; 33 W. R. 673). "*Action, n'est auter chose que loyall demande de son droit*" (Co. Litt. 285 a).

For the purpose of the Jud. Acts, "Action" means "a *Civil Proceeding* commenced by Writ or in such other manner as may be prescribed by Rules of Court; and shall not include a Criminal Proceeding by the Crown" (s. 100, Jud. Act, 1873). An Originating Summons is within this definition (*Re Fawsitt, Galland* v. *Burton*, 54 L. J. Ch. 1131; 30 Ch. D. 231; 34 W. R. 26, 158: *Re Vardon*, 55 L. J. Ch. 259; 31 Ch. D. 275; 53 L. T. 895; 34 W. R. 185); but an Interpleader Issue is not (*Hamlyn* v. *Betteley*, 6 Q. B. D. 63; 50 L. J. Q. B. 1; 29 W. R. 275; 43 L. T. 790), nor are Garnishee proceedings (*Mason* v. *Wirral*, 4 Q. B. D. 459), nor proceedings on a Petition (*Re Wallis*, 23 L. R. Ir. 7).

V. CAUSE: WRIT OF SUMMONS.

An action *in rem*, apart from statutory definition, is not generally included in the word "Action," *e.g.* in a provision requiring notice before action (*The Longford*, 58 L. J. P. D. & A. 33; 14 P. D. 34).

"Action founded on Contract or Tort;" *V.* FOUNDED ON: CONTRACT: TORT.

ACTIONS.—"Where one releases to another all 'Actions,' not only actions depending, but also causes of actions are released" (*Altham's Case*, 8 Rep. 153 a, 153 b); "but within a submission of all actions to arbitrement, causes of action are not contained" (Co. Litt. 285 a). *V.* SUIT.

ACTS.—"The covenant (*i.e.* for Quiet Enjoyment) is that the lessee should hold the premises without any lawful eviction, interruption, &c., by or from the lessor, or by or through her 'Acts, Means, right, title, forfeiture, privity or procurement.' Now the word 'Acts,' means something done by the person against whose acts the covenant is made; and the word 'Means' has a similar meaning, something proceeding from the person covenanting." (Per cur., *Spencer* v. *Marriott*, 1 B. & C. 459; 2 D. & Ry. 665. *Vf. Dennett* v. *Atherton*, L. R. 7 Q. B. 316; 41 L. J. Q. B. 165; 20 W. R. 442: *Stevenson* v. *Powell*, 1 Bulstr. 182: Dart, 884: Sug. V. & P. 602: Elph. 487, 488: 2 Platt, 310).

But "'Means and Procurement' have a large extent" (Palm. 340): and where a husband procured a conveyance to himself, remainder to his wife, the wife was held as claiming by "means" of her husband, "although she claims by title derived from another" (*Butler* v. *Swinnerton*, Palm. 339; 2 Rol. Rep. 286; Cro. Jac. 657).

All "*Reasonable* Acts," in a covenant for Further Assurance, mean such as the law requires; but do not include an unnecessary act (per Wood, B., *Warn* v. *Bickford*, 9 Pri. 51. *V. Pudsey* v. *Newsam*, Yelv. 44: Dart, 887: Sug. V. & P. 613), or one that is impracticable (Elph. 493).

ACTUAL.—The word "actual" does not, usually, advance the meaning. Speaking generally a thing is not more itself because it is spoken of as "actual," nor is an act more done or enjoined because it is said, or required, to be "actually" done. Thus the phrase "Actual *Seizure*" in s. 1, Mer. Law Amendt. Act, 1856 (19 & 20 V. c. 97), means no more than "Seizure" (*Gladstone* v. *Padwick*, 40 L. J., Ex. 154; L. R. 6 Ex. 203). *V.* SEIZURE.

But where a word has a constructive legal meaning not completely corresponding to the fact it indicates, then the addition of "actual" will intensify that word, so that it will not be fully satisfied by such legal meaning. Thus where, as in s. 26, Reform Act, 1832 (2 W. 4, c. 45), a freeholder, &c., must, in order to qualify for his vote, have been "in the actual *Possession*" or receipt of the rents and profits of his tenement for six months before the last day of July, that means a possession in fact as distinguished from a possession in law; and therefore the owner of a Rent-charge is not in such possession or receipt until he has had "the manual receipt of the rent itself, or some part of it, or something in lieu of it" (per Tindal, C. J., *Murray* v. *Thorniley*, 15 L. J. C. P. 155; 2 C. B. 217; the decision in which was followed in *Hayden* v. *Tiverton*, 16 L. J. C. P. 88; 4 C. B. 1: and *Webster* v. *Ashton-under-Lyne; Orme's case*, 42 L. J. C. P. 38; L. R. 8 C. P. 281). But where a conveyance of a Rent-charge is framed so as to operate under the Statute of Uses (27 H. 8, c. 10), then for the purposes of the Reform Act, the Rent-charge is in "actual possession" of the grantee from the date of the conveyance, because a long course of authority and practice has established that the "possession" into which Uses are converted by that Statute is equivalent to "actual possession" (*Heelis* v. *Blain*, 34 L. J. C. P. 88; 18 C. B. N. S. 90: *Webster* v. *Ashton-under-Lyne; Hadfield's case*, 42 L. J. C. P. 146; L. R. 8 C. P. 306).

But from the doubting way in which the Court (especially Bovill, C. J.) followed in *Hadfield's case*, the authority of *Heelis* v. *Blain*, it may be questioned whether a ruling similar to that in the two last-named cases would be adopted for the interpretation of any Act except the one then under consideration. *V.* POSSESSION: OCCUPATION.

Heirloom to the person for the time being "in the actual *Enjoyment and Possession*" of an estate; *V. Hogg* v. *Jones*, 32 L. J. Ch. 361; 32 Bea. 45.

ACTUAL ANNUAL INCOME.—A testator bequeathed all his real and personal estate to trustees upon trust for his wife with directions to sell and convert the same into money, and declared that his real estate, directed to be sold, should, in equity, be considered as converted into personalty as from the time of his decease, and that the "Actual Annual Income" for the time being of his unconverted real and personal estate should be considered income for the purposes of his Will, and be applied accordingly; Held, that the widow was entitled to the actual dividends becoming due after the testator's death in the case of all the securities, except such as in their nature bore interest *de die in diem* (*Unwin* v. *Eykyn*, W. N. (66) 268).

ACTUAL BODILY HARM.—*V.* INFLICT.

ACTUAL CAPTURE.—*V. Banda and Kirwee Booty*, 35 L. J. Adm. 17.

ACTUAL COSTS AND EXPENSES.—When an Order, for an account on the wrongful taking of Minerals, directs allowance to be made for "Actual Costs and Expenses" or "Disbursements," profit or trade allowances will not be included (*United Merthyr Co.*, L. R. 15 Eq. 46: *V.* MacS. 538).

ACTUAL MILITARY SERVICE.—The privilege of making Nuncupative Wills given to "any Soldier being *in actual military service*" (Stat. of Frauds, s. 22; Wills Act, 1 V. c. 26, s. 11) is limited, by the words italicised, "to those who are *on an expedition:* And consequently that the Will of a soldier made while he was quartered in barracks, either at home (*Drummond* v. *Parish*, 3 Curt. 522; 7 Jur. 538) or in the Colonies (*White* v. *Repton*, 3 Curt. 818: *Sv. Re Phipps*, 2 Curt. 368: *Re Johnson*, 2 Curt. 341: *Re Pery*, 2 L. T. (O. S.) 335), is not privileged. The same was held of the Will of a soldier made at Bangalore, whilst in command of the Mysore Division of the army there stationed, and who died whilst on a tour of inspection of the troops under his command (*Re Hill*, 1 Rob. 276):" Wms. Exs. 118. So of a sergeant, with his regiment at Malta, under orders for the West Indies (*Re Norris*, 3 Notes of Ecc. Cases, 197).

But a soldier passing from one regiment to another,—both regiments being in active service against the enemy (*Herbert* v. *Herbert*, D. & Sw. 10; 4 W. R. 182),—or joining a regiment with the view of marching against the enemy (*Re Thorne*, 34 L. J. P. M. & A. 131; 4 Sw. & Tr. 36; 11 Jur. N. S. 569), is within the privilege. So is one who has received a *mortal* wound on the battle-field (*Re Farquhar*, 4 Notes of Ecc. Cases, 651: *Re Churchill*, ib. 47: *Re Prendergast*, 5 ib. 92).

ACTUAL POSSESSION.—*V.* ACTUAL.

ACTUAL SEIZURE.—*V.* ACTUAL.

ACTUAL TOTAL LOSS.—*V.* TOTAL LOSS.

ACTUALLY CHARGEABLE.—*V.* CHARGEABLE.

ACTUALLY DELIVERED.—*V.* DELIVERED IN EXECUTION.

ACTUALLY ENJOYED.—The words "actually enjoyed," in s. 3, Prescription Act (2 & 3 W. 4, c. 71), are satisfied where a house exists with ordinary windows through which light and air have in fact passed, although there has been no occupation in the sense of personal occupation (*Courtauld* v. *Legh,* 38 L. J. Ex. 45 ; L. R. 4 Ex. 126). "Enjoying the use cannot mean shall have *continuously* used. If that had been the intention of the statute some such word as 'continuously' would be found in this section. I take 'enjoyed' to mean, 'having had the amenity or advantage of using' the access of light. That is nearly equivalent to 'having had the use,' the intention being that the owner of a house may acquire the right to have the access of light over adjoining land to an opening which he has used in such manner as suited his convenience for the passage of light during 20 years" (per Kay, J., *Cooper* v. *Straker,* 58 L. J. Ch. 29 ; 40 Ch. D. 21). *V.* ACCESS : INTERRUPTION.

ACTUALLY PAID.—As to the meaning of the phrase "Rent actually paid," in an Act authorising rating assessments ; *V. Bristol Waterworks Co.* v. *Uren,* 54 L. J. M. C. 97 ; 15 Q. B. D. 637.

ACTUALLY PENDING.—*V.* PENDING.

ACTUALLY RECEIVED.—Gift over on death "without having actually received" legacy ; *V. Martin* v. *Martin,* L. R. 2 Eq. 404 ; 35 L. J. Ch. 679 : *Johnson* v. *Crook,* 48 L. J. Ch. 777 ; 12 Ch. D. 639 : *Bubb* v. *Padwick,* 49 L. J. Ch. 178 ; 13 Ch. D. 519.

V. RECEIVABLE : RECEIVED.

ADDITION.—A legacy "in addition to," or "substitution for," or "instead of," another will *primâ facie* be taken on the same conditions, out of the same funds, and with the same privileges as that other (1 Jarm. 185),—a meaning, however, which may be varied by a context (*Ib.* n. ; 2 ib. 603). *Vf. Thomas* v. *Nurse,* W. N. (68) 181 : *Re Benyon,* 53 L. J. Ch. 1165 : *Lee* v. *Pain,* 4 Hare, 218.

V. LIEU.

ADHERING TO THE QUEEN'S ENEMIES.—"Every one commits High Treason who, either in the Realm or without it, actively assists a public enemy at war with the Queen. Rebels may be public enemies within the meaning of this definition" (Steph. Cr. 42). *Vf.* Arch. Cr. 837, 838.

ADJACENT.—"Adjacent Lands ;" *V. Birmingham* v. *Allen,* 46 L. J. Ch. 673 ; 6 Ch. D. 284.

ADJOIN : ADJOINING.—This word, in a penal statute, means "absolutely contiguous, without anything between" (per Parke, J., in *R.* v. *Hodges,* Moo. & M. 343), and it was there held that ground, separated from a house by a narrow walk and a paling with a gate in it, was not "adjoining" the house within s. 38, 7 & 8 G. 4, c. 29.

But, not so strict is the meaning of "adjoining" and "adjoin" in ss. 127, 128, Lands C. C. Act, 1845 (*Lond. & S. W. Ry.* v. *Blackmore*, 39 L. J. Ch. 713 ; L. R. 4 H. L. 610 ; and *V.* obs. of Manisty, J., *Hobbs* v. *Mid. Ry.*, 51 L. J. Ch. 324) ; nor in s. 150, P. H. Act, 1875 (*V.* FRONTING).

As to the meaning of a Devise of a house "with the piece of land *thereto adjoining;*" *V. Josh* v. *Josh*, 28 L. J. C. P. 100 ; 5 C. B. N. S. 454, stated, 1 Jarm. 784.

ADJOINING OWNER.—The owner of land, which land is separated from surplus lands of a Railway by only a private road over which such owner has a right of way, is an adjoining owner within s. 128, Lands C. C. Act, 1845 (*Coventry* v. *L. B. & S. Ry.*, 37 L. J. Ch. 90 ; L. R. 5 Eq. 104 ; 16 W. R. 267), and a person may be an "Adjoining Owner" within the section, although he purchased such adjoining lands from the Company itself against which he claims pre-emption (*L. & S. W. Ry.* v. *Blackmore*, 39 L. J. Ch. 713 ; L. R. 4 H. L. 610).

"'The Adjoining Owner' is *primâ facie* the person to whom the soil belongs : *e.g.* the lord of the manor as opposed to the persons entitled to a right of herbage (*Hooper* v. *Bourne*, 3 Q. B. D. 258 ; 5 App. Ca. 1 ; 47 L. J. Q. B. 437 ; 37 L. T. 594 ; 42 Ib. 97 ; 26 W. R. 295 ; 28 Ib. 493), and in connection with the expression 'Adjoining Owner' it must be clearly understood that there is a plain obvious distinction between the person in whom, under s. 127, the superfluous lands are, in default of sale, to vest, and the persons to whom the option of purchase is to be given under s. 128 (*Hobbs* v. *Mid. Ry.*, 20 Ch. D. 418 ; 51 L. J. Ch. 320 ; 46 L. T. 270 ; 30 W. R. 516) :" Dart, 861.

V. OCCUPIER.

ADJOINING PROPERTY.—As to this phrase in a covenant giving protection from annoyance ; *V. Harrison* v. *Good*, 40 L. J. Ch. 295 ; L. R. 11 Eq. 338 : ANNOYANCE : NEIGHBOURING.

ADJUDGED.—*V.* SUM ADJUDGED.

ADJUDICATION.—*V.* ORDER OF ADJUDICATION.

ADMEASUREMENT.—A Condition of Sale that provides that "the admeasurements are presumed to be correct," and negativing allowance for errors, does not imply that there has been an actual admeasurement prior to sale, and the Condition means,—if the quantity stated is incorrect neither party is to have any claim (*Cordingley* v. *Cheesebrough*, 31 L. J. Ch. 617 ; 3 Giff. 496). *V.* ERROR : *Cp.* ESTIMATED.

ADMINISTER.—A person who supplies a woman with a drug, for her to take and which she takes in his absence, "administers" it, within s. 58,

24 & 25 V. c. 100 (*R.* v. *Wilson*, 26 L. J. M. C. 18 ; D. & B. 127 : followed in *R.* v. *Farrow*, D. & B. 164). "If I call in a physician and he writes his prescription, and I take the medicines, is that not an administering by him?" (per Park, J., *R.* v. *Harley*, 4 C. & P. 369).—*Vf.* Arch. Cr. 819 ; Rosc. Cr. 274. *V.* CAUSE TO BE TAKEN.

ADMINISTRATION.—*V.* ORDER OF ADJUDICATION.

ADMINISTRATORS.—*V.* EXECUTORS.

ADMIRALTY.—*V.* s. 12 (4) Interp. Act, 1889.

ADMIRALTY CAUSE.—An action against a Pilot for Collision-damage caused by a vessel under his charge, is not an "Admiralty Cause" within ss. 3, 5, 31 & 32 V. c. 71, and 32 & 33 V. c. 51 (*Flower* v. *Bradley*, 44 L. J. Ex. 1, which *V.* for prior authorities : *Scovell* v. *Bevan*, 56 L. J. Q. B. 604 ; 19 Q. B. D. 428). *Vf. R.* v. *Essex Co. Co.*, 53 L. J. Q. B. 423 ; 13 Q. B. D. 142.

ADMISSION.—"'*Admission & institution.*' In proprietie of speech, admission is, when the bishop upon examination admitteth him (*i.e.* a Clerk) to be able and saith *Admitto te habilem.* Institution is, when the bishop saith, *Instituo te rectorem talis ecclesiæ cum curâ animarum, & accipe curam tuam & meam.* But sometimes in a more large sense, *admissus* doth include *institutus* also : *cujus præsentatus sit admissus,* (*i.e.*) *institutus.*" (Co. Litt. 344 a.)

"Upon Admission," 9 G. 4, c. 17, s. 2 ; *V. R.* v. *Humphrey*, cited, UPON.

ADMIT.—*V.* LIABILITY.

ADMITTED.—"Admitted" a Member of the Court of a City Company is equivalent to being "elected" (*R.* v. *Saddlers Co.*, 32 L. J. Q. B. 337 ; 10 H. L. Ca. 404).

"Admitted or Proved ;" *V.* PROVE.

ADMITTED SET-OFF.—*V.* OTHERWISE.

ADMIXTURE.—*V.* DECLARE.

ADULTERATION.—"'Adulteration,' means the infusion of some foreign substance" (per Cockburn, C. J., *Francis* v. *Maas*, 47 L. J. M. C. 84 ; 3 Q. B. D. 341). *V.* DYE.

An article of food is "adulterated" when any substance other than that which the article purports to be is mixed with, or added to, or placed upon it, either to increase the bulk or weight or apparent size of the article, or to give it a deceptive appearance (*Fitzpatrick* v. *Kelly*, 42 L. J. M. C. 132 ; L. R. 8 Q. B. 337 : *Roberts* v. *Egerton*, 43 L. J. M. C. 135 ; L. R. 9 Q. B. 494). But "milk from which the cream had been extracted would, probably, not fall within the designation of 'not pure'" (Maxwell, 400, 401).

V. As Unadulterated.

ADVANCE.—"In consideration of your being *in Advance* to A." (*Haigh* v. *Brooks*, 10 A. & E. 309), or "having this day advanced" to A. (*Goldshede* v. *Swan*, 1 Ex. 154), may be explained by parol not to refer to a past consideration.

V. Advancement.

ADVANCED.—In a devise containing a direction that "any moneys which might have been advanced to my children, or any of them, or to my sons-in-law in my life, and also any sums of money which might be owing from them, or any of them to me at my death," it was held that the word "advanced" was not used by the testator in a technical sense, and that money lent by the testator to one of his sons-in-law, though by reason of his bankruptcy it was not owing to the testator at his death, must be brought into hotchpot (*Astbury* v. *Beasley*, W. N. (69), 96). *V.* Unadvanced.

ADVANCEMENT.—A power to apply money for a person's "Advancement" in the world, means that when "an occasion really arises to advance such person in life, a proper provision may be made" (per Kay, J., *Abram* v. *Aldridge*, 20 April, 1886. *V.* as to this word, *Lowther* v. *Bentinck*, 44 L. J. Ch. 197 ; L. R. 19 Eq. 167).

Under the Statute of Distribution.—By the Statute of Distribution (22 & 23 Car. 2, c. 10, s. 5), a child "*advanced* by the intestate in his lifetime by portion," has to bring the amount of the advancement into hotchpot if claiming to participate in the distribution of the intestate's personal estate. This provision only applies to the estates of intestate *fathers* (*Holt* v. *Frederick*, 2 P. Wms. 357) ; and generally speaking it relates to gifts to children early in life (per Jessel, M. R., *Taylor* v. *Taylor*, 44 L. J. Ch. 720 ; L. R. 20 Eq. 155) ; and it means that "Wherever a sum is paid for a particular purpose, which is thought good and right by the father, and which the child desires, if it be money which is drawn out in considerable amount, *and not a small sum* (*V.* Wms. Exs. 1510), it must be treated as an advance. The payment of the money is the important thing, the Court does not look to the application" (per Wood, V.-C., *Boyd* v. *Boyd*, L. R. 4 Eq. 305 ; 36 L. J. Ch. 877). In that case it was accordingly held that a sum given by a father for the payment of his son's debts is an Advancement,—a decision followed by Pearson, J., in *Re Blockley* (54 L. J. Ch. 722 ; 29 Ch. D. 250), wherein he refused to follow the opposite view of Jessel, M.R., in *Taylor* v. *Taylor* (sup.).

Though it seems that apprenticing a child is not such an advancement (note to *Pusey* v. *Desbouvrie*, 3 P. Wms. 317) ; yet beyond doubt articling a young man to a solicitor is (*Boyd* v. *Boyd*, sup.). So the payment of a son's entrance fees to an Inn of Court is an advancement within the statute ; but not so the dues of the Inn, or the son's fee on entering the chambers of a Special Pleader (*Taylor* v. *Taylor*, sup.).

Voluntary periodical allowances which may or may not vary are not Advancements (*Taylor* v. *Taylor*, sup.) ; but a fixed and agreed annuity is, —*viz.*, its value at the date of the grant (Wms. Exs. 1509).

A Settlement, whether voluntary, or for a *good* consideration (as that of marriage), is an Advancement within the statute (*Edwards* v. *Freeman*, 2 P. Wms. 440 : *Phiney* v. *Phiney*, 2 Vern. 638). *Vf.* Wms. Exs. 1504–1511. *V.* BENEFIT.

ADVANTAGE.—*V.* UNDUE PREFERENCE.

ADVANTAGES.—" Commodities, Emoluments, Profits and Advantages . . . all of which four words are of one sense and nature, implying things gainful " (*London* v. *Southwell*, Hob. 304).

ADVENTURE.—" 'Adventure' (in questions relating to Marine Insurance) means, either one of the perils insured against, as in the clause in a policy commencing 'Touching the adventures and perils' ; or the liability or risk undertaken by the insurers, as in the clause in a policy commencing 'Beginning the adventure upon the said goods and merchandizes' ; or the speculation or undertaking to protect which the assured effected the insurance (*Fenwick* v. *Robinson*, 3 C. & P. 324 : *Jenkins* v. *Power*, 6 M. & S. 289) ; or a subject of insurance which has been exposed to the risks insured against (*Inglis* v. *Stock*, 10 App. Ca. 269 ; 54 L. J. Q. B. 582) :" Wood, 348.

" Trade, Adventure or Concern," Income Tax Act ; *V.* TRADE.

ADVERSE.—" Adverse *Litigation*," s. 80, Lands C. C. Act, 1845 ; *V.* *Haynes* v. *Barton*, L. R. 1 Eq. 422 ; 35 L. J. Ch. 233 ; 13 L. T. 787 ; 14 W. R. 257 : *Henniker* v. *Chafy*, 28 Bea. 621 : *Re Longworth*, 1 K. & J. 1 ; 23 L. J. Ch. 104 ; 22 L. T. O. S. 197 ; 2 W. R. 124 : *Askew* v. *Woodhead*, 14 Ch. D. 27, 36 ; 49 L. J. Ch. 320 ; 42 L. T. 567 ; 28 W. R. 874 ; 44 J. P. 570 : *Re Bareham*, 17 Ch. D. 329 ; 29 W. R. 525 : *Re Fenton, Armitage* v. *Askham*, 3 W. R. 331 ; 1 Jur. N. S. 227 : *London & S. W. Ry.* v. *Bridger*, 4 N. R. 261 ; 12 W. R. 948 ; 10 L. T. 689 ; 10 Jur. N. S. 650 : Dart, 809, 1263 : Dan. Ch. Pr. 2164.

As to what acts constitute "Adverse *Possession;*" *V.* MacS. 524–526, 532.

An " Adverse *Witness*," within s. 22, Com. L. Pro. Act, 1854, is one who, *in the opinion of the presiding judge*, is hostile (*Greenough* v. *Eccles*, 28 L. J. C. P. 160 ; 5 C. B. N. S. 786 ; 7 W. R. 341. *Va. Martin* v. *Travellers' Insrce. Co.* 1 F. & F. 505 : *Pound* v. *Wilson*, 4 F. & F. 301 : *Rice* v. *Howard*, 16 Q. B. D. 681 ; 55 L. J. Q. B. 311 ; 34 W. R. 532). *Vf. Price* v. *Manning*, 58 L. J. Ch. 649.

" *Adversely to any Charity;*" *V.* Tudor, Char. Trusts, 474, 482.

ADVISE.—*V.* PRECATORY TRUST.

ADVISEDLY.—"Advisedly," 13 Eliz., c. 12, s. 2, means not intentionally, or avowedly, but deliberately (*Heath* v. *Burder*, 1 B. & F. 212; 10 W. R. 673).

ADVOWSON : ADVOCATION.—"The right of presentation or collation to a church" (Elph. 558, citing Co. Litt. 119 *b*. *V.* Co. Litt. 17 *b* : Spelm. : 1 Burn's Eccles. Law, Tit. *Advowson*).

"Advowsons" and "Rectories," in s. 13, 1 & 2 V. c. 110, only embrace Advowsons in lay hands (*Hawkins* v. *Gathercole*, 24 L. J. Ch. 332; 6 D. G. M. & G. 1; 1 Sim N. S. 63; 1 Drew. 12).

AFFECT.—"Shall not affect" any estate, &c. (proviso to s. 2, 33 V. c. 14, Naturalization Act, 1870),—"*I.e.*,—Shall not validate or invalidate" (1 Jarm. 41, citing *Sharp* v. *St. Sauveur*, 41 L. J. Ch. 576; 7 Ch. 343. *Vf.* 2 Jarm. 651, where it is said "primâ facie 'Affect' is neutral.") *V.* INTERFERE.

A covenant in a lease of a Public-house that the lessee will do nothing that can or may "*affect, lessen or make void*" the License, is not broken by a Conviction which might have been, but was not, endorsed on the license (*Wooler* v. *Knott*, 1 Ex. D. 265; 45 L. J. Ex. 313; 34 L. T. 362; 24 W. R. 1004).

V. IMPEACHED.

AFFECTED.—*V.* DIRECTLY AFFECTED : INJURIOUSLY AFFECTED.

AFFECTING.—"Any act, &c., affecting *land* within the jurisdiction," Ord. 11, R. 1 (*b*), R. S. C.; *V.* Ann. Pr.: *Kaye* v. *Sutherland*, 57 L. J. Q. B. 68; 20 Q. B. D. 147; 58 L. T. 56; 36 W. R. 508.

V. INCUMBRANCES.

AFFIDAVIT.—*V.* OATH.

AFFIXED.—*V.* WINDOW : FIXED AND FASTENED : FIXTURES.

AFFRAY.—"An Affray is the fighting of two or more persons in a public place to the terror of Her Majesty's subjects" (Steph. Cr. 48). *Vf.* Arch. Cr. 961. "If the fighting be in private, it is not an Affray, but an Assault" (Rosc. Cr. 277).

AFLOAT.—*V.* ALWAYS AFLOAT.

AFORE.—"Afore Execution had." *V.* EXECUTION.

AFORESAID.—When this word is used as an adjective it can hardly create much difficulty. The man, or premises, "aforesaid," can mean nothing else than the man or premises which has been before indicated.

But when used,—*e.g.* in Wills,—adverbially, as in the expressions "as aforesaid," "in manner aforesaid,"—phrases of equal import with "as before," "in like manner," "on the same terms and conditions," and such like,—then difficulty may very easily arise. Generally speaking such referential expressions indicate the manner in, or conditions on which, not the persons by whom, benefits are to be taken. Thus where a Will, having contemplated the possibility of the death of testator's daughter under 21 without leaving a husband, gave certain directions "in case of the death of his daughter under age *as aforesaid*," that meant, under age and not leaving a husband (*Weddell* v. *Mundy*, 6 Ves. 341). So a successive gift "in manner aforesaid," following a prior gift for life, is also a gift for life (*Doe* d. *Woodall* v. *Woodall*, 16 L. J. C. P. 28; 3 C. B. 349). So if there were a gift to a class living at testator's death *as tenants in common*, and that was followed by a gift to another class "*in the same manner*," that would rather indicate that such other class would take as tenants in common, than that its members were to be ascertained by the fact of being alive at the testator's death (1 Jarm. 746, n.): *secus*, if the words were "at the same time and in the same manner" (*Swift* v. *Swift*, 32 L. J. Ch. 479). So in a "general survivorship clause, the words 'in manner aforesaid,' or similar terms, will have the effect of subjecting all the accrued shares to the same terms, restrictions and limitations over, as the original shares" (2 Jarm. 717, citing *Milsom* v. *Awdry*, 5 Ves. 465: *Giles* v. *Melsom*, L. R. 5 C. P. 614; L. R. 6 C. P. 532; L. R. 6 H. L. 24; 42 L. J. C. P. 122; *nom. Melsom* v. *Giles*, 40 L. J. C. P. 233; 39 Ib. 325). *Vf. Bessant* v. *Noble*, 26 L. J. Ch. 236: *Surtees* v. *Hopkinson*, 36 L. J. Ch. 305; L. R. 4 Eq. 98: LIKE.

Sometimes "as aforesaid" means "such" (*Walker* v. *Petchell*, 14 L. J. C. P. 211; 1 C. B. 652).

In a gift to testator's "aforesaid nephews and nieces" none having been mentioned, "aforesaid" was rejected, and all the nephews and nieces were held to be included (*Campbell* v. *Bouskell*, 27 Bea. 325, cited 1 Jarm. 370).

"Damage done by foresaid operations;" *V. Dixon* v. *White*, 8 App. Ca. 833.

To assist in baiting Animals "as aforesaid," s. 3, 12 & 13 V. c. 92, refers back to all the conditions mentioned in the preceding part of the section, and therefore only created the offence of assisting when the baiting is in a place kept for the purpose (*Clarke* v. *Hague*, 29 L. J. M. C. 105; 2 E. & E. 281). *V.* PLACE.

Vh. 10 Rep. 138, 107; 8 Ib. 47.

For distinction between "*in formâ prædictâ*" and "*in eâdem formâ;*" *V.* Co. Litt. 20 b.

AFTER.—Where an act has to be done within so many days "after" a given event, the day of such event is not to be reckoned, and the party to do the act has the whole of the last day of the prescribed time in which to do it (*Williams* v. *Burgess*, 10 L. J. Q. B. 10; 12 A. & E. 635: *Robinson* v. *Waddington*, 18 L. J. Q. B. 250); and if a time "after" an event has to expire before something else is done, that means clear time (*Blunt* v. *Heslop*, 7 L. J. Q. B. 216 ; 8 A. & E. 577).

V. At : From : Of : On : Passing : Thereafter.

A Devise "after," or "from and after," a previous interest is not, by such words, postponed in vesting (1 Jarm. 806, 816).

As to effect of testamentary gift "after" *death; V.* 2 Jarm. 517, 522 ; On : Before or After.

"After default ;" *V.* Default.

"After the fact committed ;" *V.* Fact.

AFTERWARDS.—*V. Chalmers* v. *North*, 28 Bea. 175 : but that case disapproved, *Drewitt* v. *Seaward*, 31 Ch. D. 234.

AGAINST.—In a devise on marrying *with* consent followed by a gift over on marrying "against" consent, the latter word was construed as "without," to effect the alternative (*Long* v. *Ricketts*, 2 S. & St. 179. *Vf. Creagh* v. *Wilson*, 2 Vern. 573).

AGED.—*V.* Sick.

AGENT.—Where the witness to a Claim for the Lodger Franchise described himself therein as "Agent," he being in fact a registration agent, and the Revising Barrister amended accordingly, although holding the original description sufficient ; held, that the description of "Agent" was sufficient (*Campbell* v. *Chambers*, 22 L. R. Ir. 460).

"Agent," in an Order for Inspection of Documents ; *V. Draper* v. *Manchester, S. & L. Ry.*, 30 L. J. Ch. 236 ; 3 D. G. F. & J. 23 : *Bonnardet* v. *Taylor*, 30 L. J. Ch. 523 ; 1 Jo. & H. 383.

AGENT INTRUSTED.—"Agent Intrusted" with goods or documents of title, within the Factors Act, 1877 (40 & 41 V. c. 39) ; *V. Baines* v. *Swainson*, 32 L. J. Q. B. 281 ; 4 B. & S. 270 : *Cole* v. *North Western Bank*, 44 L. J. C. P. 233 ; L. R. 10 C. P. 354 : Seton, 1097, 1098.—*Vf.* Intrusted.

AGER.—"An acre, a hide : Spelm. Seebohm says (Eng. Vill. Com. 167), that ager, agellus, or agellulus, was the word used by the ecclesiastical writers in the charters for the land belonging to a 'ham'" (Elph. 559).

AGGRAVATED ASSAULT.—*V. Holden* v. *King*, 46 L. J. Ex. 75.

AGGRAVATED MISCONDUCT. — As to what amounts to "Aggravated Misconduct" on the part of a husband, disentitling him to participate in a fund to which his wife has an Equity to a Settlement ; *V. Reid* v. *Reid*, 55 L. J. Ch. 756 ; 33 Ch. D. 220 ; 55 L. T. 153 ; 34 W. R. 715.

AGGRIEVED.—A person who has consented to a thing cannot be "aggrieved" by it (*Harrop* v. *Bayley*, 25 L. J. M. C. 107 ; 6 E. & B. 218 : but *Cp. Ex p. Poulton*, inf.).

As to meaning of "person aggrieved" within R. 33, *Trade Marks Rules*, Feb. 1883; *V. Re Ralph*, 53 L. J. Ch. 188; 25 Ch. D. 194: *Re Palmer*, 51 L. J. Ch. 673; 24 Ch. D. 504. It means there a person injured or damaged in a legal sense; but a person carrying on business out of England is not necessarily excluded (*Re Riviere*, 53 L. J. Ch. 455, 578; 26 Ch. D. 48). As to this phrase in s. 90, Patents, &c., Act, 1883; *V. Re Trade Mark, Normal*, 35 Ch. D. 231: *Re Gianaclis*, 58 L. J. Ch. 782.

As to a similar expression in s. 14, *Copyright Act* (5 & 6 V. c. 45); *V. Ex p. Hutchings & Romer*, 48 L. J. Q. B. 505; 4 Q. B. D. 483: *Chappell* v. *Purday*, 13 L. J. Ex. 7; 12 M. & W. 303: *Ex p. Walker*, 39 L. J. Q. B. 31; 10 B. & S. 680; W. N. (69) 168. In *Ex p. Poulton* (53 L. J. Q. B. 320) it was held that a person who himself has made a wrongful entry, is entitled under the section just cited to apply for its rectification as one "aggrieved" thereby.

For the purposes of an appeal under the *Intoxicating Liquor Laws*, a person "aggrieved" must be one who is "immediately aggrieved"; and a rival innkeeper is not such a person by reason of a new license being granted within a short distance of his premises (*R.* v. *Middlesex*, 3 B. & Ad. 938). A mortgagee is a person "aggrieved" by a refusal of a renewal license to his mortgagor, especially when he is the irrevocable attorney of the mortgagor to keep alive the license (*Garrett* v. *Marylebone*, 53 L. J. M. C. 81; 12 Q. B. D. 620); but an owner is not a person "aggrieved" by the indorsement of his tenant's license (*R.* v. *Andover*, 55 L. J. M. C. 143; 16 Q. B. D. 711; 55 L. T. 23; 34 W. R. 456; 50 J. P. 549).

For the purpose of an *Appeal in Bankruptcy* (s. 104 (2), Bankry. Act, 1883), a Trustee of a deed of Arrangement may be a "person aggrieved" by a Receiving Order (*Re Batten, Ex p. Milne*, 58 L. J. Q. B. 333). A Creditor is a "person aggrieved" by an Order of Discharge (*Re Payne*, 56 L. J. Q. B. 625; 18 Q. B. D. 154; 35 W. R. 89). So the Official Receiver, or the Board of Trade, may be a "person aggrieved" (*Re Reed & Co.*, 19 Q. B. D. 174; 56 L. J. Q. B. 447; 56 L. T. 876; 35 W. R. 660: *Re Stainton*, 19 Q. B. D. 182; 57 L. T. 202; 35 W. R. 667. *Va. Re Sidebotham*, 49 L. J. Bank. 41; 14 Ch. D. 458); so is a Bill of Sale holder when his document is the alleged act of bankry (*Re Ellis*, 45 L. J. Bank. 64, 159; 2 Ch. D. 229, 797), or a third person whose title to property is affected by the adjudication (*Ex p. Learoyd, Re Foulds*, 48 L. J. Bank. 17; 10 Ch. D. 3: *Qy.*, Is *Re Whelan*, 48 L. J. Bank. 43, an authority under the present Bankry. Act?) But a competing petitioning creditor cannot well be "aggrieved" by an adjudication, even though it be effected by collusion with the debtor (*Re White, Ex p. Mason*, 49 L. J. Bank. 56; 14 Ch. D. 71).

Persons "aggrieved" by a *Pauper Settlement Order*, s. 2, 13 & 14 Car. 2, c. 12, include the pauper as well as the parish (*R.* v. *Hartfield*, Carth. 222; 2 Bott. 940); but not mere ratepayers (*R.* v. *Colbeck*, 12 A. & E. 161; 9 L. J. M. C. 61: *R.* v. *Bishop Wearmouth*, 5 B. & Ad. 942), unless there be no officers of their parish (*R.* v. *Westmoreland*, 12 L. J. M. C. 113; 1 D. & L. 178).

A person "aggrieved" by diverting or stopping a *Highway*, s. 88, 5 & 6 W. 4, c. 50, does not include one who only uses the road as one of the general public; to bring a person within this phrase he must be living in the neighbourhood of the Highway, and in the habit of using it (*R.* v. *Taunton St. Mary*, 3 M. & S. 465: *R.* v. *Incledon*, 1 Ib. 268: *R.* v. *Williamson*, 7 T. R. 32: *R.* v. *Townsend*, 5 B. & Ald. 420: *Vf.* Glen on Highways, 390).

As to who is "a party aggrieved," within s. 253, *Public Health Act*, 1875, by fabricated voting papers; *V. Verdin* v. *Wray*, 46 L. J. M. C. 170; 2 Q. B. D. 608; 41 J. P. 484. The Clerk to a Local Board, who fearing dismissal resigns, is not, within that section, "a party aggrieved" by a disqualified person acting on the Board (*Rochfort* v. *Atherley*, 1 Ex. D. 511).

"Whether the near relations of a person whose body has been disinterred for dissection, are 'parties aggrieved' is doubtful" (Dwar. 689, 690, citing *R.* v. *Toole*, 1 M. & R. 728).

As regards a *Qui Tam* action; *V. Boyce* v. *Higgins*, 23 L. J. C. P. 5; 14 C. B. 1: *Hollis* v. *Marshall*, 27 L. J. Ex. 235; 2 H. & N. 755: *R.* v. *Blanshard*, 30 J. P. 280: *Robinson* v. *Curry*, 50 L. J. Q. B. 561; 7 Q. B. D. 465.

Vh. article discussing this word, 51 J. P. 705.

AGREED AND DECLARED.—"The rule is that where you have such words as 'It is hereby agreed and declared between and by the parties to these presents,' that some one will do an act or make a payment,—and that some one is a party to the deed,—it is a covenant by him with the others, not a covenant by all of them. Anything more absurd than to hold it a covenant by all of them could not be imagined. Suppose you had these words; 'Provided always it is hereby agreed and declared between and by the parties to these presents that the said A. B. shall pay £5000 to the said C. D. on the 6th of January next,' it would be absurd to say that this amounts to a covenant by C. D., the recipient of the money, that A. B. shall pay him, as well as a covenant by A. B. that he will pay him. If, therefore, we find that no act is to be done except by one of the parties, these words only amount to a covenant by that one party with the others" (per Jessel, M.R., *Dawes* v. *Tredwell*, 18 Ch. D. 359: cited and applied by Kay, J., in *Re De Ros*, 55 L. J. Ch. 73, and in which case it was held, on the construction of the deed, that the wife's after-acquired separate estate was bound, although the direct covenant to settle same was only entered into by the husband. *Vf.* Elph. 426, 502: *Ramsden* v. *Smith*, 23 L. J. Ch. 757; 2 Drew. 298: *Butcher* v. *Butcher*, 14 Bea. 222: *Re D'Estampes*, 53 L. J. Ch. 1117; 32 W. R. 978. The lastly named case was also decided by Kay, J., and in his judgment he reviews the previous authorities).

AGREEMENT.—"*Agreamentum* is a word compounded of two words,—viz., of *aggregatio* and *mentium*, so that aggreamentum est aggregatio mentium in re aliqua facta vel facienda. And so by the contraction of the two words, and by the short pronunciation of them, they are made one word, viz., *aggreamentum*, which is no other than an union, collection, copulation, and conjunction of two or more minds in anything done or to be done" (*Reniger* v. *Fogossa*, Plowd. 17*a*. *Va*. Com. Dig. "Agreement," and per Ellenborough, C. J., *Wain* v. *Warlters*, 5 East 16; 2 Sm. L. C. 266). In *Wain* v. *Warlters*, it was held that "Agreement," in the Statute of Frauds, meant the whole agreement, including the consideration for it: *Va*. obs. of Cockburn, C.J., *Williams* v. *Lake* (29 L. J. Q. B. 1). But "the Agreement or Contract" justifying a stoppage out of wages under the Truck Act (1 & 2 W. 4, c. 37, s. 23), need not specify the amounts to be deducted (*Cutts* v. *Ward*, 36 L. J. Q. B. 161; L. R. 2 Q. B. 357; 15 W. R. 445; 15 L. T. 614).

As to the distinction between "Agreement" in s. 4, Stat. of Frauds, and "Bargain" in s. 17 Ib.; *V*. Benj. 193, 194. *Va*. BARGAIN.

"Agreement" contrasted with "Conveyance;" *V*. *Inl. Rev*. v. *Angus*, 23 Q. B. D. 579.

V. COVENANT.

"Agreement in Writing;" *V*. IN WRITING.

AGRICULTURAL.—An "Agricultural" *Holding* (s. 54, Agricultural Holdings Act, 1883), "I take it refers only to land cultivated for profit in some way and not to natural grass land;" a "Pastoral" holding refers to grass land (per Judge Stephen, *Morley* v. *Jones*, 32 S. J. 630). But a holding may be "wholly agricultural," or "wholly pastoral," within the section, though it include a house, if such house be merely auxiliary to the land with which it is held; *secus*, where such house is independent of the land and, *à fortiori*, if the house be the chief part of the holding (Ib.). *Cp*. SERVANT IN HUSBANDRY.

A steam engine let and used for hauling straw and manure for farming operations, and no other purpose, is within s. 32, Highway Act, 1878, as being "a Locomotive used solely for Agricultural *Purposes*" (*Ellis* v. *Hulse*, 23 Q. B. D. 24).

AID.—*V*. IN AID.

AID OR ABET.—"To constitute an aider or abettor, some active steps must be taken, by word or action, with intent to instigate the principal or principals. Encouragement does not, *of necessity*, amount to aiding and abetting. It may be intentional or unintentional. A man may unwittingly encourage another in fact by his presence, by mis-interpreted words or gestures, or by his silence or non-interference;—or he may encourage intentionally by expressions, gestures, or actions, intended to signify approval. In the latter case he aids and abets; in the former he does not. It is no criminal offence to stand by a mere passive spectator of a crime, even of a murder. Non-interference to prevent a crime is not itself a crime. But the fact that a person was voluntarily and purposely present witnessing the commission of a crime, and offered no opposition to it, though he might reasonably be expected to prevent it, and had the power so to do or at least to express his dissent, might, under some circumstances, afford cogent evidence upon which a jury would be justified in finding that he wilfully encouraged, and so aided and abetted. But it would be purely a question for the jury whether he did so or not," (per Hawkins, J., *R.* v. *Coney*, 51 L. J. M. C. 78). In accordance with those principles the majority of the Court held, in the case cited, that the mere voluntary presence of persons at a prize-fight does not make them guilty of aiding or abetting an assault (51 L. J. M. C. 66; 8 Q. B. D. 534). *Vh. Ex p. Whiteley*, 39 J. P. 70: *R.* v. *Cheshire Jus.*, 40 J. P. 148.

AIT.—*V.* Hath.

ALE.—*V.* Spirituous Liquors.

ALEHOUSE.—An "Alehouse" is a place (licensed under the 9 G. 4, c. 61, and the Acts amending the same) where exciseable liquors are sold, by retail, to be consumed on the premises. The word is, probably, synonymous with "Public-house" and "Tavern," which latter words were employed in the covenants under discussion in *London and Suburban Land Co.* v. *Field* (50 L. J. Ch. 549; 16 Ch. D. 645; 44 L. T. 444) and *Holt* v. *Collyer* (50 L. J. Ch. 311; 16 Ch. D. 718; 44 L. T. 214; 29 W. R. 502).

A covenant in a Lease prohibiting the user of the premises "as a Public-house or Alehouse," will comprise a Beer-house (1 W. 4, c. 64, s. 31).

V. Public-house: Beer-house.

ALIEN.—"To Alien;" *V.* Alienation: Assign: Charge or Incumber.

An Alien is one who "is born out of the ligeance of our soveraigne lord the King" (Litt. s. 198; *Vth.* Co. Litt. 128 b, 129 a). *Vh. Calvin's Case*, 7 Rep. 1: *Isaacson* v. *Durant*, 55 L. J. Q. B. 331; 17 Q. B. D. 54; 54 L. T. 684; 34 W. R. 547.

ALIENATION.—A clause of Forfeiture on "Alienation" "will extend only to a disposition by the act of the party, and not to a transfer by operation of law; unless it can be collected from the context that the term was intended by the settlor to have so wide a signification" (Lewin 102, citing *Dommett* v. *Bedford*, 6 T. R. 684: *Cooper* v. *Wyatt*, 5 Mad. 482: *Ex p. Eyston*, 47 L. J. Bank. 62; 7 Ch. D. 145). Therefore bankruptcy *at the suit of creditors* is not such an alienation (*Lear* v. *Leggett*, 2 Sim. 479, and other cases cited, Lewin 102); *secus*, if the bankruptcy, or other cessio bonorum, be on the petition of the beneficiary (*Re Amherst*, 41 L. J. Ch. 222 ; L. R. 13 Eq. 464 : *Sv. Ex p. Dawes, Re Moon*, 17 Q. B. D. 275 : *Vf.* Lewin 103). A mere Declaration of Insolvency is not an alienation or attempt at alienation (*Graham* v. *Lee*, 26 L. J. Ch. 395 ; 23 Bea. 388). As to a Warrant of Attorney or Marriage being an alienation ; *V.* Lewin 102.

Vh. Co. Litt. 118 *b.* *V.* ASSIGN : RESTRAINT ON ALIENATION.

ALIKE.—A testamentary gift to two or more "alike," or "to be enjoyed alike" is synonymous with its being given EQUALLY, and creates a tenancy in common (per Lord Mansfield, *Loveacres* v. *Blight*, Cowp. 352. *Vf. Thorowgood* v. *Collins*, Cro. Car. 75 : *Page* v. *Page*, 2 P. Wms. 489, cited 2 Jarm. 258. In *Thorowgood* v. *Collins*, the words to be construed were "part and part-like"). *V.* SHARE AND SHARE ALIKE.

ALL.—"*Qui omne dicit, nihil excludit* ;" therefore, *omnes viduæ*, Stat. of Merton, c. 2, included all kinds of Dower, though there were five (2 Inst. 81).

"All," is equivalent to "each and every" (*V.* jdgmt. of Lord Fitzgerald, *Burnett* v. *G. N. of Scotland Ry.*, 54 L. J. Q. B. 539) ; but, by a context, it may mean "any" (1 Jarm. 504).

A testamentary gift of "All," without more, is indefinite and void (*Bowman* v. *Milbanke*, 1 Lev. 130 ; Sid. 191 ; T. Raym. 97 ; cited and commented on, 1 Jarm. 357, 358).

"The words 'All his Estate' will pass everything a man has" (per Lord Mansfield, *Hogan* v. *Jackson*, 1 Cowp. 306). So of the words "All I am *worth*" (*Huxtep* v. *Brooman*, 1 Bro. C. C. 437, cited and commented on, 1 Jarm. 738, 739), or "All I *have*" (per Bayley, J., *Doe* v. *Morgan*, 6 B. & Cr. 518 ; 9 D. & Ry. 633).

"But if the word 'All' is coupled with the word 'Personal,' or a local description, there, the gift will pass only personalty, or the specific estate particularly described" (per Lord Mansfield, *Hogan* v. *Jackson*, sup.). Thus "All my *Effects*" will not pass realty (*Henderson* v. *Farbridge*, 1 Russ. 479 ; cited 1 Jarm. 742). Qy. will such words as "All that I *possess*" or "all that I am or may die *possessed of*" pass *Realty ? Cp. Noel* v. *Hoy* (5 Mad. 38) : *Thomas* v. *Phelps* (4 Russ. 348) : *Wilce* v. *Wilce* (5 Moo. & P. 682 ; 7 Bing. 664 ; 9 L. J. O. S. C. P. 197) : *Evans* v. *Jones* (46 L. J. Ex. 280) : *Day* v. *Daveron* (12 Sim. 200 ; 10 L. J. Ch. 349) : and *Davenport* v. *Coltman* (11 L. J. Ch. 262 ; 12 Sim. 588 ; 9 M. & W. 481) : with *Monk* v. *Mawdsley* (1 Sim. 286): and *Cook* v. *Jaggard* (35 L. J. Ex. 76 ; L. R. 1 Ex. 125) ; and *V.* these cases stated 1 Jarm. 730, 731, 739–742.

Where a testator made a specific devise of part of his realty and by a subsequent part of the same Will made another devise of "*all* his real and personal estate ;"—Held, that "all" meant "all the Residue" (*Doe* d. *Snape* v. *Nevell*, 17 L. J. Q. B. 119 ; 11 Q. B. 466). So the generality of a devise of "all my Lands" may be restricted by the context (*Re Portal*, 54

L. J. Ch. 1012 ; 30 Ch. D. 50). But in *King* v. *George* (4 Ch. D. 435 ; 5 Ib. 627 ; 46 L. J. Ch. 670), a bequest of "*All that I have power over*, namely, plate, linen," &c., was an unlimited residuary gift, and not restricted to the classes of goods enumerated. *Va. Sidgreaves* v. *Brewer*, 49 L. J. Ch. 514 ; 15 Ch. D. 594.

"*All the Rest;*" *V.* REST.

As to the efficacy of "*All the Rest*" to pass lapsed legacies; *V. Re Pringle*, 17 Ch. D. 819 ; 50 L. J. Ch. 689.

When "all" is found in conjunction with specified property,—*e.g.* "all my property in the Funds,"—the bequest is specific (*Hayes* v. *Hayes*, 5 L. J. Ch. 243 ; 1 Keen 97 : *Vincent* v. *Newcombe*, You. 599).

"All my *Property*, Leasehold and Freehold;" *V. Re Roberts*, *Kiff* v. *Roberts*, 56 L. J. Ch. 628 ; 54 L. T. 386; 34 W. R. 626; W. N. (86) 165. "All my Property, Brewery, &c. ;" *V. Waite* v. *Morland*, W. N. (66) 139. *Vf.* PROPERTY.

"All my *Just Debts*." *V.* DEBTS.

As to effect of Revocation of "All Wills, &c.;" *V. Re Kingdon*, 55 L. J. Ch. 598.

As to invalidity on account of vagueness through the unqualified use of "All," especially in an Assignment of future things ; *V. Belding* v. *Read*, 34 L. J. Ex. 212 ; 3 H. & C. 955 ; 11 Jur. N. S. 547 : but that case is now overruled by *Tailby* v. *Official Receiver*, 58 L. J. Q. B. 75 ; 13 App. Ca. 523. *Va. Re Clarke*, 56 L. J. Ch. 981 : VAGUE : FUTURE.

"All *Proceedings*" in R. 1, Ord. 65, R. S. C., means all proceedings in respect of which there is an existing jurisdiction as to Costs (*Re Mills*, 56 L. J. Ch. 60).

"All *Rates* made for the relief of the Poor," which are to be paid to qualify for the parliamentary franchise, s. 3, sub-s. 3, 30 & 31 V. c. 102, mean only those made since the 5th January of the year preceding the qualifying year (*Cull* v. *Austin*, *Austin* v. *Cull*, 41 L. J. C. P. 153 ; L. R. 7 C. P. 227).

A stipulation to accept a cargo on receipt of "all the *Shipping Documents*," will be satisfied by production of three, of the five, parts of the Bill of Lading, if the sellers are unable to supply more (*Cederberg* v. *Borries*, 2 Times Rep. 201).

V. ENGAGEMENTS : INTEREST : MONEY : WAYS.

ALL AND EVERY.—For an illustration of effect of this phrase, *V. Re Sibley*, 46 L. J. Ch. 387 ; 5 Ch. D. 494 ; but see that decision, as based on this phrase, criticised by Kay, J., in *Re Webster*, 52 L. J. Ch. 768 ; 23 Ch. D. 737.

A bequest to A. and after her decease to "all and every her child and children, and his, her and their executors, administrators and assigns, for his, her, and their own absolute use and benefit ;" held, to create a joint tenancy in the children (*Morgan* v. *Britten*, L. R. 13 Eq. 28 ; 41 L. J. Ch. 70).

ALL FAULTS.—*V.* Faults.

ALL INTENTS AND PURPOSES.—An act disgavelling lands to "all intents and purposes," and declaring that they should be "descendible as lands at common law," was held only to disgavel quà descent (*Wiseman* v. *Cotton*, 1 Lev. 80).

V. Void.

ALL TIMES.—*V.* At all Times: At all Times of Tide.

ALLEGED.—*V.* As Alleged.

ALLOTMENT.—*V.* On Allotment.

ALLOWANCE.—A mere "Allowance," agreed to by a Lessor by a memorandum on the lease, does not operate as a reduction of the rent reserved, but only as an independent agreement (*Davies* v. *Stacey*, 9 L. J. Q. B. 393; 12 A. & E. 506; 4 P. & D. 157).

ALLOWANCES.—"Allowances," s. 189, P. H. Act, 1875; *V.* *Burgess* v. *Clark*, 14 Q. B. D. 735: *Edwards* v. *Salmon*, 58 L. J. Q. B. 571; 23 Q. B. D. 531: *Whiteley* v. *Barley*, 57 L. J. Q. B. 643; 21 Q. B. D. 154; 36 W. R. 823; 52 J. P. 595: *R.* v. *Ramsgate*, 58 L. J. Q. B. 352; 23 Q. B. D. 66.

V. Just Allowances.

ALLOWING.—*V.* Being.

ALLOWS.—*V.* So far as.

ALMS.—The disqualification to be enrolled as a Burgess of an Incorporated Borough arising from the receipt of "parochial relief or *other Alms*" (5 & 6 W. 4, c. 76, s. 9, and now by 32 & 33 V. c. 55, s. 1), applies only to such alms as are parochial (*R.* v. *Lichfield*, 11 L. J. Q. B. 122; 2 Q. B. 693; 2 G. & D. 10). But as regards the Parliamentary franchise, the disqualification arises from the receipt of "parochial relief or other alms *which by law of parliament now disqualify from voting*" (Reform Act, 2 W. 4, c. 45, s. 36); and that amplification differentiates the parliamentary from the municipal disqualification, and alms which will disqualify for the parliamentary franchise are not confined to those that are parochial: but any alms of a precarious tenure to persons so indigent that they are dependent on the charity will work the latter disqualification (*Smith* v. *Hall*, 33 L. J. C. P. 59; 15 C. B. N. S. 485; *Harrison* v. *Carter*, 46 L. J. C. P. 57; 2 C. P. D. 26: *Edwards* v. *Lloyd*, 57 L. J. Q. B. 121; 20 Q. B. D. 302; 58 L. T. 409; 52 J. P. 519). *Vf.* Rogers, 196–200: Parochial Relief.

ALMSHOUSE.—*V.* Hospital.

ALNETUM.—"A wood of elders" (Touch. 95; *Va.* Co. Litt. 4 b).

ALODIUM.—"In Domesday, *alodium* (in a large sense) signifieth a free mannor, and *alodiarii* or *alodarii*, lords of the same ; and *lannemanni* there signifie lords of a mannor, having *socam et sacam de tenentibus et hominibus suis* " (Co. Litt. 5 a).

ALONG.—*V.* THROUGH.

ALONG WITH.—" Along with any other Persons," Ord. 21, R. 11, R. S. C. ; *V. Dear* v. *Sworder*, 4 Ch. D. 482 ; 46 L. J. Ch. 100 : *Vf.* Ann. Pr. 342.

"Along with other Sums" construed "in addition to," not as "including" (*Pilkington* v. *Myers*, 8 L. T. 720).

ALONGSIDE.—Cargo " shall be Brought Alongside " for shipment, in a Charter-party, means that the charterer is to bring the cargo as near to the ship as practicable, and it is for the jury to say whether that has been done (*Holman* v. *Dasnieres*, 2 Times Rep. 480, 607). *Vf. Fletcher* v. *Gillespie*, 3 Bing. 635 : *Trindade* v. *Levy*, 2 F. & F. 441 : CARGO.

ALSO.—" Also," or " And Also," may be (1) the beginning of an entirely independent sentence, or (2) a copulative carrying on the sense of the immediately preceding words into those immediately succeeding. If the latter, the conditions of the preceding words would be read into those succeeding. Thus, "I give Blackacre to C. and his heirs, *and also* Whiteacre," gave C. the fee in Whiteacre (per Levinz, J., 1 Jarm. 497 n. : *Vf. Hopewell* v. *Ackland*, 1 Salk. 239 : *Willis* v. *Curtois*, 1 Bea. 189 ; 8 L. J. Ch. 105). Of course no such construction obtains when " Also " is the commencement of an independent sentence (*Doe* d. *Ellam* v. *Westley*, 4 B. & C. 667 ; 7 D. & Ry. 112 : on which *V.* Wms. Exs. 1087; 1 Jarm. 497).

Words importing a tenancy in common in one bequest will not be extended by implication to another bequest which is merely connected with the former by " also " (2 Jarm. 256, citing *Cookson* v. *Bingham*, 17 Bea. 262 ; 23 L. J. Ch. 127).

A general description of property introduced by " And also " or the like, and following a particular description, will usually receive an *ejusdem generis* interpretation (Elph. 173 *et seq.*).

V. LIKEWISE.

ALTARAGIUM.—" Properly, that which is offered on the altar, and the profit which arises to the priest by reason of the altar ; Spelm. It is sometimes said to include all vicarial or small tithes ; but this construction will not be adopted unless the word occurs in an old endowment, and is supported by usage ; *Franklin* v. *St. Cross*, Bunb. 79 " (Elph. 560).

ALTERED.—*V.* MATERIALLY ALTERED.

ALTOGETHER.—" Wound up altogether," s. 161, Companies Act, 1862 ; *V. Re Hafod Hotel Co.*, W. N. (68), 86.

ALWAYS AFLOAT.—" So near thereto as she may safely get at all times of tide, *and always afloat,*" in a Charter party; *V. Horsley* v. *Price,* 52 L. J. Q. B. 603; 11 Q. B. D. 244: *Caffarini* v. *Walker,* Ir. Rep. 9 C. L. 431: *Nielsen* v. *Wait,* 14 Q. B. D. 516.

AM.—In a devise "such an expression as, 'all the lands of which I *am* seized in A.,' must be read as if written just before the testator's death: *Doe* v. *Walker,* 13 L. J. Ex. 153; 12 M. & W. 591" (per Kay, J., *Re Portal to Lamb,* 53 L. J. Ch. 1163). The decision in that latter case was reversed (54 L. J. Ch. 1012; 30 Ch. D. 50), without, however, affecting the proposition above cited. *Vf.* 1 Jarm. 333, 334: Now.

AMERCIAMENT.—"Explained and distinguished from a Fine; *Beecher's Case,* 8 Rep. 58 a: *Godfrey's Case,* 11 Rep. 42 a; Co. Litt. 126 b. *et seq.,* where the Latin for Amerciament is said to be *misericordia:* Spelm. gives an explanation differing from that of Coke. The reason why an unsuccessful defendant was said in old time 'to be in mercy, &c.,' was that he was liable to be amerced for not having obeyed the King's writ immediately" (Elph. 560, which *V.* for further references).

"There is a manifest diversity between a ransome and an amerciament; for ransome is ever when the law inflicteth a corporal punishment by imprisonment (and so is also a fine); but otherwise it is of an amerciament" (Co. Litt. 127 a). *V.* Fine: Ransom.

AMIABLES COMPOSITEURS.—"What is the force and meaning of that expression, 'Amiables Compositeurs,' by Canadian law? We find it in the 1346th Article of the Code of Civil Procedure: 'Arbitrators must hear the parties, and their respective proofs, or establish default against them, and decide according to the rules of law, unless they are dispensed from so doing by the terms of the submission, or unless they have been appointed as Amiables Compositeurs.' That is to say, if they are Amiables Compositeurs, they are to be exempt at all events from the strictness of the obligations expressed in the previous words. Their lordships would, no doubt, hesitate much before they held that to entitle arbitrators named as Amiables Compositeurs to disregard all law, and to be arbitrary in their dealings with the parties; but the distinction must have some reasonable effect given to it, and the least effect which can reasonably be given to the words is, that they dispense with the strict observance of those rules of law the non-observance of which, as applied to awards, results in no more than irregularity" (per Selborne, E., *Rolland* v. *Cassidy,* 57 L. J. P. C. 100; 13 App. Ca. 770).

AMONG.—A testamentary gift to two or more "among," or "amongst," them creates a tenancy in common (2 Jarm. 257; Hawk. 112). *V.* Between.

AMOUNT SECURED.—"Amount secured," s. 15 (2) Building

Society Act, 1874, 37 & 38 V. c. 42, is not confined to principal money; but includes all moneys secured, whether for Principal, Interest, Fines or otherwise, and also all Instalments secured though not presently payable (per Chitty, J., *Re Neath Building Society*, 34 S. J. 11; 6 Times Rep. 13).

AMUSEMENT.—*V.* ENTERTAINMENT.

AN.—"An" is sometimes read in the most absolute sense as meaning "any,—whatsoever." "I am of opinion that the expression, '*an* Act of Bankruptcy' (in s. 5 Bankry. Act, 1883), includes everything which by legislative enactment is made to be an act of bankruptcy whether by this Act itself or by some other Act passed before it came into operation" (per Cotton, L. J., in *Ex p. Pratt*, 53 L. J. Ch. 614).

ANCESTOR.—"*Ancestor* is derived of the *Latine* word *antecessor*, and in law there is a difference between *antecessor* and *prædecessor*. For *antecessor* is applied to a natural person; but *prædecessor* is applied to a body politique or corporate" (Co. Litt. 78 b).

"The word 'Ancestor' does not mean, either etymologically or technically, a lineal ancestor only; in illustration of which proposition I may refer to a passage in Com. Dig., Vol. I., 5th Ed., 705, as to the English writ of 'Mort d'Ancestor;' which (it is said) 'does not lie upon the death of any Ancestor, except a father, mother, brother, sister, uncle, aunt, nephew or niece; for upon the death of another Ancestor, an *aiel*, *besaiel*, or *cosinage* lies'" (per Selborne, L. C., *Zetland* v. *Ld. Advocate*, 3 App. Ca. 520). And per Ld. Hatherley (Ib.) the word "Ancestor," as used in the Sucn. Dy. Act, 1853 (*V.* SUCCESSION), is properly assignable to the person who really preceded in the estate, although that person may not be the progenitor of the Successor.

ANCHORAGE TOLL.—An Anchorage Toll is a Toll for every anchor—(and sometimes in respect of a vessel having no anchor),—cast in a port, or on anchorage ground proved, or legally presumed, to have once formed part of a port (*Foreman* v. *Free Fishers of Whitstable*, 38 L. J. C. P. 345; L. R. 4 H. L. 266: explaining *Gann* v. *Free Fishers of Whitstable*, 35 L. J. C. P. 29; 11 H. L. Ca. 192).

V. TOLLS.

ANCHORITE.—*V.* RECLUSE.

ANCIENT DEMESNE.—*V.* Elph. 560.

ANCIENT INCLOSURES.—*V.* OLD INCLOSURES.

ANCIENT MEADOW.—Meadow not broken up for 20 years (*Murphy* v. *Daly*, 13 Ir. Ch. Rep. 239).

ANCIENT RENT.—Where a Power of Leasing "is in the form (which, however, is now uncommon), that the 'Ancient Rents' shall be reserved, this would seem to mean, the rent reserved under the latest lease (if any), granted before the creation of the power. But subsequent leases may be looked at; and the question, where the leases vary, is one of fact for the jury" (Watson, Eq. 869, 870, citing *Doe* d. *Douglas* v. *Lock*, 2 A. & E. 705; 4 L. J. K. B. 113; 4 N. & M. 807: *Doe* d. *Egremont* v. *Stephens*, 6 Q. B. 208: *Doe* d. *Biddulph* v. *Hole*, 15 Q. B. 848; 20 L. J. Q. B. 57). In the lastly cited case, however, it was held that if the ancient custom is uniform, and the single lease varying therefrom is granted just before the creation of the Power, such exceptional lease cannot be taken as evidence of the custom.

On the construction of "Ancient," "Accustomed," or "Usual" rent, *V.* Sug. Pow. 790; Farwell on Powers, 494; 1 Platt, 414—423.

The phrase generally employed now is BEST RENT, *wh. V.*

AND.—"And" has generally a cumulative sense, requiring the fulfilment of all the conditions that it joins together, and herein it is the antithesis of OR. Sometimes, however, even in such a connection it is, by force of a context, read as "Or": *V.* OR READ AS AND.

"And" may be relative as well as copulative (Dwar. 681).

Where there is a string of *adjectives* between the two last of which there is the conjunction "and," each adjective is, generally speaking, independent of its fellows. Thus a bequest for "Benevolent, Charitable and Religious" purposes, means that it may be applied in either of those ways, and, as some are too indefinite, the bequest is bad (*Williams* v. *Kershaw*, 5 Cl. & F. 111 *n*). But sometimes the first adjective (especially when there are only two) is the controlling word of the enumeration which is merely qualified by that which follows. Thus in *Re Sutton* (54 L. J. Ch. 613; 28 Ch. D. 464; 33 W. R. 519), Pearson, J., held that a bequest for "Charitable and Deserving" objects was good, because such a collocation only contemplated one class of objects,—"the word 'Charitable' governs the whole sentence." In that case the learned judge gave the following illustration,—"Instead of giving to young persons 'under 21' you might add the words 'and unmarried,' and those words would undoubtedly restrict the meaning of the former words."

As to the construction and apportionment where charitable and other *ascertained* objects are coupled in a bequest, *V.* 1 Jarm. 217, 218; *Crafton* v. *Frith*, 20 L. J. Ch. 198.

V. EXECUTORS.

AND READ AS BUT.—For an instance of this, *V.* jdgmt. Coleridge, C. J., *R.* v. *Barclay*, 51 L. J. M. C. 48; 8 Q. B. D. 486.

AND READ AS OR.—*V.* OR.

AND ALSO.—*V.* ALSO.

ANIMAL.—*V.* DOMESTIC ANIMAL.

ANNATS.—"'Annats or Annates;' the first fruits of an ecclesiastical benefice; *V.* 25 H. 8, c. 20; 26 H. 8, c. 3; 12 Rep. 45; Spelm." (Elph. 560).

ANNOYANCE.—A covenant against doing anything which may be a "Nuisance or Annoyance" to a neighbourhood, is broken by a Sanatorium for the reception of six boys affected with infectious disease (*Watson* v. *Leamington College*, 25 S. J. 30). In that case, Jessel, M. R., said it might perhaps be difficult to appreciate the difference between "Nuisance" and "Annoyance," but as both words were used, "annoyance," evidently, meant something less than "nuisance." And in *Tod-Heatley* v. *Benham* (58 L. J. Ch. 83; 40 Ch. D. 80), it was held that "Annoyance" has, in this connection, a wider meaning than "Nuisance," though it was there doubted whether it was not too much to say that no "Nuisance" would be within such a covenant, unless it amounts to an indictable nuisance. *V.* NUISANCE.

In *Bramwell* v. *Lacy* (48 L. J. Ch. 339; 10 Ch. D. 691), the words were "Annoyance, Damage, Injury, Prejudice or Inconvenience;" whilst in *Tod-Heatley* v. *Benham* (sup.) they were "Annoyance, Nuisance, Grievance or Damage:" and in the first of those cases an out-patient Branch of a Hospital for throat and chest diseases was held to be an "Annoyance, Inconvenience and Injury;" whilst in the latter, a Hospital for throat, nose, ear, skin and eye diseases, and diseases of the rectum, was held an "Annoyance or Grievance," those two words being, apparently, bracketed as synonymous.

"I think an act which is an interference with the pleasurable enjoyment, in reason, of a house is an 'Annoyance or Grievance.' It is not necessary, in order to bring the case within the words, that the plaintiff should show that any particular man may object to it; but we must be satisfied by argument and by evidence, that reasonable people, having regard to the ordinary use of a house for pleasurable enjoyment, would be annoyed or aggrieved by what is being done there. It is not necessary, in order to show that there has been reasonable ground for annoyance or grievance, to show that, in fact, there is danger or risk of infection. A reasonable apprehension of nuisance from acts done by the defendant will produce such interference with the pleasurable and reasonable enjoyment of the adjoining houses as to come within the words 'Annoyance and Grievance'" (per Cotton, L. J., *Tod-Heatley* v. *Benham*, sup.). "The expression 'Annoyance' is wider than 'Nuisance;' and a thing that reasonably troubles the mind and pleasure,—not of a fanciful person or of a skilled person who knows the truth, but,—of the ordinary sensible English inhabitant of a house, seems to me to be an 'Annoyance,' although it may not appear to amount to physical detriment to comfort" (per Bowen, L. J., Ib.).

An "Annoyance," &c. caused by a business, is none the less within such a covenant, because the business is such as would not be prohibited by accompanying words levelled against certain businesses (*Tod-Heatley* v. *Benham*, sup.).

Vf. hereon *Re Davis* v. *Cavey,* 58 L. J. Ch. 143 ; 40 Ch. D. 601.

ANNUAL EMOLUMENT.—Compensation for loss of office calculated on two-thirds "Annual Emolument," s. 8 (7), 31 & 32 V. c. 110 ; *V. R.* v. *Postmaster-Gen.*, 47 L. J. Q. B. 435 ; 3 Q. B. D. 428.

ANNUAL INCOME.—*V.* Actual Annual Income.

ANNUAL NET VALUE.—*V.* Annual Value : Net.

ANNUAL PROCEEDS.—" Rents, Dividends, and Annual Proceeds," held, on the context, equivalent to "Annual Rents, Dividends, and Proceeds" (*Re Green,* 40 Ch. D. 610).

ANNUAL PROFITS.—*V.* Profits.

ANNUAL RACK-RENT.—*V.* Rack-rent.

ANNUAL RENT.—*V. Smith* v. *Birmingham,* 52 L. J. M. C. 81; 11 Q. B. D. 195 : Annual Value.

ANNUAL VALUE.—" Value means *net* value" (per Ld. Bramwell, *Dobbs* v. *Grand Junc. Waterworks Co.*, 53 L. J. Q. B. 52). And on the authority of the same noble and learned lord in the same case, and on the authority of *Re Elwes* (28 L. J. Ex. 46 ; 3 H. & N. 719), it may be laid down that the general *primâ facie* meaning of "Annual Value" of property is that provided for " Net Annual Value" by s. 1 of the Parochial Assessment Act, 1836 (6 & 7 W. 4, c. 96) viz.—" The rent at which the same might reasonably be expected to let from year to year, free of all usual tenants' rates and taxes, and tithe commutation rent-charge (if any), and deducting therefrom the probable average annual cost of the repairs, insurance, and other expenses (if any) necessary (*V.* Necessary) to maintain them in a state to command such rent ;" and to that definition it may now be added that in estimating such lettable value regard is to be had to the worth of the premises as used for the purposes for which they are, for the time being, occupied (*West Middlesex W. W. Co.* v. *Coleman,* 54 L. J. M. C. 70 ; 14 Q. B. D. 529. As to what "expenses" may be deducted, *V. R.* v. *Gainsborough Union,* 41 L. J. M. C. 1; L. R. 7 Q. B. 64 : *R.* v. *Smith,* 55 L. J. M. C. 49 ; 54 L. T. 431 ; 50 J. P. 215 : *Stevens* v. *Bishop,* 19 Q. B. D. 442 ; 56 L. J. Q. B. 454 ; 57 L. T. 482 ; 35 W. R. 839).

That is the principle which the Metropolitan Waterworks Companies must adopt in making their charges on "Annual Value" (*Dobbs* v. *Grand Junc. Waterworks Co.*, 53 L. J. Q. B. 50 ; 9 App. Ca. 49). But such a phrase may be enlarged by a context, *e.g.* "gross" (*Bristol Waterworks Co.*

v. *Uren*, 54 L. J. M. C. 102; 15 Q. B. D. 637); or "rack-rent" (*Stevens* v. *Barnet Water Co.*, 57 L. J. M. C. 82; 36 W. R. 924).

So, too, where a Waterworks Co. are empowered to charge "on the annual value at which the premises are assessed to the poor-rate," that means the annual *rateable* value (*Warrington Waterworks Co.* v. *Longshaw*, 51 L. J. Q. B. 498; 9 Q. B. D. 145).

In cases of Small Tenements let at weekly rents,—the landlord doing the repairs and paying the rates and taxes,—the proper way of assessing the "annual value" or "annual rent" on which the Water-Rate is to be charged, is to multiply the weekly rent by 52, and deduct from the gross amount so ascertained a fair allowance for the average of empty houses and also the actual amount paid for poor and borough rates (*Smith* v. *Birmingham*, 52 L. J. M. C. 81; 11 Q. B. D. 195); and as to mode of assessing annual value of such tenements for the Poor-Rate; *V. Smith* v. *Birmingham*, 58 L. J. M. C. 33, 161; 22 Q. B. D. 211.

As to mode of calculating annual value of the buildings of a School Board; *V. R.* v. *West Bromwich School Bd.*, 53 L. J. M. C. 153; 13 Q. B. D. 929: *R.* v. *London School Bd.*, 55 L. J. M. C. 169; 17 Q. B. D. 738; 55 L. T. 384; 34 W. R. 583; 50 J. P. 419: and as to exemption where the owners and occupiers are prohibited from selling or leasing,—*e.g.* Owen's College, Manchester; *V. Owen's College* v. *Chorlton-upon-Medlock*, 56 L. J. M. C. 29; 18 Q. B. D. 403; 56 L. T. 373; 35 W. R. 236; 51 J. P. 356: *Sv. Burton-on-Trent Case*, 34 S. J. 94.

In a case under ss. 21 & 22 of the Sucn. Dy. Act, 1853, Watson, B., in delivering the judgment of the Court of Exchequer, said,—"The words 'annual value of the land' are not words of art; but mean, in common parlance, a rack-rent, *or* the value of the gross produce of the land, *minus* all payments, expenses, interest, labour, and charges on the land or on the tenant" (*Re Elwes*, 28 L. J. Ex. 47).

So also the "value" "By the Year" of lands, &c., for the purpose of giving County Courts jurisdiction in Ejectment (Co. Co. Act, 1888, s. 59), is the market value of the property,—the convenient mode for ascertaining which is prescribed by s. 1, Parochial Assessment Act, 1836 (*Elston* v. *Rose*, L. R. 4 Q. B. 4; 38 L. J. Q. B. 6: *V.* Rent Payable): but the premises to be valued are those actually in dispute,—*e.g.*, if there be a dispute over a party-wall, it is the wall, and not the premises of which it is part, that has to be valued (*Stolworthy* v. *Powell*, 55 L. J. Q. B. 228).

Rule 1 of s. 60, Income Tax Act (5 & 6 V. c. 35), provides that for the purposes of that Act the "annual value" of lands, &c., shall be the rack-rent; but the subsequent Rules of the Act would seem to bring this definition nearly identical with that in the Parochial Assessment Act: *Vf. Re Elwes*, sup.: *Coltness Co.* v. *Black*, 6 App. Ca. 315; 51 L. J. Q. B. 626; 29 W. R. 717; 45 L. T. 145.

The meaning of "Annual Value" of a resigned Benefice, as used in s. 8, Incumbents' Resignation Act, 1871 (34 & 35 V. c. 44: *Vh.* s. 11), is its

Net Annual Value at the time it is resigned; and the pension based on such value is not subject to diminution because the value of the Benefice afterwards declines (*Robinson* v. *Dand*, 55 L. J. Q. B. 585).

"Clear Yearly Value," Reform Act, 1832; *V.* CLEAR.

"Net Annual Value;" *V.* NET.

ANNUALLY.—"Profits and Gains received annually," 6th case, Sch. D., s. 100, Income Tax Act, 5 & 6 V. c. 35,—*i.e.* for the current year; *V. Ryhope Co.* v. *Foyer*, 7 Q. B. D. 485; 45 L. T. 404.

ANNUITY.—"An annuity is a yearly payment of a certaine summe of money granted to another in fee, for life or yeares, charging the person of the grantor onely" (Co. Litt. 144 b.; *Vf.* Wms. Exs. 816).

The gift of an "Annuity" generally means an annual sum during the life of the annuitant (*Re Taber*, 51 L. J. Ch. 721), "and nothing more" (per Fry, J., *Blight* v. *Hartnoll*, 51 L. J. Ch. 163; 19 Ch. D. 294: *Vf. Re Foster*, 23 L. R. Ir. 269); but where there is a direction to purchase an annuity, or a dedication of a fund out of which it is to be purchased, or where the annuity is dealt with as being in existence and operative beyond the life of the first annuitant and no other period can be fixed for such further duration short of making it perpetual, the annuity will be in perpetuity,—*i.e.*, it is a bequest of such a sum as will produce the income intended for the legatee, who may (notwithstanding a direction to the contrary) elect to take that sum or have the annuity; and in the event of his death before the annuity is purchased the sum which would have been needed for its purchase will go to his representatives (Wms. Exs. 1200, 1201, and cases there cited: *Stokes* v. *Heron*, 2 Dru. & W. 89; 12 Cl. & F. 161: *Ross* v. *Borer*, 31 L. J. Ch. 709; 2 Jo. & H. 469: *Bent* v. *Cullen*, 40 L. J. Ch. 250; 6 Ch. 235: *Stokes* v. *Cheek*, 29 L. J. Ch. 922; 28 Bea. 620: *Blight* v. *Hartnoll*, 51 L. J. Ch. 162; 19 Ch. D. 294).

"Annuity," s. 8, Legacy Dy. Act (36 G. 3, c. 52); *V. Crow* v. *Robinson*, 31 L. J. Ch. 516.

V. LEGACY: PECUNIARY LEGACY.

"Annuities or Periodical Sums;" *V.* PERIODICAL.

ANOTHER.—A promise "To answer for Another," s. 4, Stat. of Frauds, 29 Car. 2, c. 3, means that the promise is to be made to the original Creditor (*Eastwood* v. *Kenyon*, 9 L. J. Q. B. 409; 11 A. & E. 438; 3 P. & D. 276: *Reader* v. *Kingham*, 32 L. J. C. P. 108; 13 C. B. N. S. 344: *Cripps* v. *Hartnoll*, 32 L. J. Q. B. 381; 4 B. & S. 414). *Vh.* Add. C. 166; Rosc. N. P. 431.

ANSWER.—A certificate of indemnity to which a witness is entitled who shall "answer" questions, means that he shall "truly answer" (*R.* v. *Hulme*, 39 L. J. Q. B. 149; L. R. 5 Q. B. 377). In that case Lush, J., said, "Wherever the legislature speaks of 'answering' questions, it means that which is intended by the words 'true answer,'—'answer' in the sense in which the word is ordinarily and popularly used."

"'*Presently answer*,' held, in Plowden, only presently become debtor, not presently pay" (Dwar. 690).

ANSWERABLE.—*V.* INDEMNIFY.

"Answerable *in Damages*," s. 54, Mer. Shipping Act, 1862; *V. Sloomvart Maatschappy Nederland* v. *P. and O. Nav. Co.*, 7 App. Ca. 795: over-ruling *Chapman* v. *Royal Netherlands Co.*, 48 L. J. Ch. 449; 4 P. D. 157.

ANTICIPATION.—A restraint on "Anticipation" is equivalent to a restraint on "Alienation" (*Re Currey*, 55 L. J. Ch. 906; 32 Ch. D. 361: *Re Grey*, 56 L. J. Ch. 207).

ANTIQUITY.—*V.* LAW LIBRARY.

ANY.—"Any" is a word which excludes limitation or qualification (per Fry, L. J., *Duck* v. *Bates*, 53 L. J. Q. B. 344; 12 Q. B. D. 79): "as wide as possible" (per Chitty, J., *Beckett* v. *Sutton*, 51 L. J. Ch. 433). A remarkable instance of this wide generality is furnished in *Re Farquhar* (4 Notes of Ecc. Cases, 651, 652, cited Wms. Exs. 119, 120), wherein the words "any Soldier," &c., in s. 11, 1 V. c. 26, were construed as including minors, so that soldiers and seamen, within that section, can make Nuncupative Wills though under age.

But its generality may be restricted by the subject matter or the context. Thus under R. 295, Bankry. R. 1870, "any *Creditor*" might oppose registration of resolutions; but that meant "any creditor who had previously proved his debt" (*Ex p. Bagster*, 53 L. J. Ch. 124; 24 Ch. D. 477). So "any other *Person*," in R. 32, Ord. 42, R. S. C., means, by the context, any Officer of a judgment-debtor Corporation (*Irwell* v. *Eden*, 18 Q. B. D. 588; 56 L. J. Q. B. 446; 56 L. T. 620; 35 W. R. 511); and by a context "any Person" may mean any eligible person (*Tobacco Pipe Makers* v. *Woodroffe*, 7 B. & C. 838: *Vf. Metrop. Bd. Works* v. *L. & N. W. Ry.* 49 L. J. Ch. 355; 14 Ch. D. 521).

So "under a Devise to three persons as tenants in common in tail, and in default of such issue 'of *any of them*,' over, Cross Remainders were implied, and 'any,' in effect, read '*all*'" (Watson, Eq. 1410, citing *Powell* v. *Howell*, L. R. 3 Q. B. 654; 37 L. J. Q. B. 294; 9 B. & S. 704: *V. Holmes* v. *Meynell*, T. Raym. 452).

But the words "any *Person*," in s. 13 (3) Debtors Act, 1869, is not restricted to cases of bankruptcy, and applies to any person whether bankrupt or not (*R.* v. *Rowlands*, 51 L. J. M. C. 51; 8 Q. B. D. 530). *Va. Ex p. Harper, Re Tait*, 52 L. J. Ch. 117, and *Ex p. Norris, Re Sadler*, 56 L. J. Q. B. 93; 17 Q. B. D. 728; 35 W. R. 19, as to the phrase, "*at any Time*" in the Bankry. Act.

As to the phrase "any *Party*," R. S. C. 1883; *V. Shaw* v. *Smith*, 56

L. J. Q. B. 174 ; 18 Q. B. D. 193 ; 56 L. T. 40 ; 35 W. R. 188; explaining *Brown* v. *Watkins*, 55 L. J. Q. B. 126 ; 16 Q. B. D. 125.

The penalty for an unauthorized representation of "any *Part*" of a Dramatic Piece (3 & 4 W. 4, c. 15, s. 2), is not incurred unless a material and substantial part of it be given (*Planché* v. *Braham*, 7 L. J. C. P. 25 ; 4 Bing. N. C. 17 : *Chatterton* v. *Cave*, 47 L. J. C. P. 545 ; 3 App. Ca. 483).

A Power of Sale of "any Part" of an estate would, probably, authorize the sale of the whole of it (*Rendlesham* v. *Meux*, 14 Sim. 249 : *V. Cooke* v. *Farrand*, 7 Taunt. 122) : and a Power to appoint, or a Bequest of, "any part" of testator's estate enables the donee to take or appoint it all (1 Jarm. 361, 362, citing *Cooke* v. *Farrand*, sup. : *Arthur* v. *Mackinnon*, W. N. (79), 93). But the power to sell "any Part" of mortgaged property (s. 19 (1) Conv. & L. P. Act, 1881), means "a separable part of the mortgaged property in the state in which it was subjected to the mortgage" (per Bowen, L. J., 57 L. J. Ch. 705), and the power does not enable a mortgagee to break up or dismantle the property—*e.g.*, by selling fixtures separately from the building to which they are affixed (*Re Yates, Batcheldor* v. *Yates*, 57 L. J. Ch. 697 ; 38 Ch. D. 112 ; 59 L. T. 47 ; 36 W. R. 563).

As to effect of "any Part" in a stipulation against subletting ; *V.* ASSIGN : UNDERLEASE.

A local Harbour Act which imposed a penalty on "*any person*" who placed articles "on any quay, wharf or landing place, within 10 feet of the quay head, or on any space of ground immediately adjoining the said haven, within 10 feet from high-water mark," so as to obstruct the free passage, was held inapplicable to private property over which there was no public right of way (*Harrod* v. *Worship*, 30 L. J. M. C. 165 ; 1 B. & S. 381).

The usual clause in Conditions of Sale giving interest, if from "any *Cause* whatever" the purchase be delayed, may, *semble*, be modified by the Court (*Kershaw* v. *Kershaw*, L. R. 9 Eq. 56 ; 21 L. T. 651 ; 18 W. R. 477 : *Monckton to Gilzean*, 54 L. J. Ch. 257 ; 27 Ch. D. 555 ; 51 L. T. 320 ; 32 W. R. 973 : *Sv.* Dart, 143, 144, 719–723 : *Vf. Re Gold and Norton*, W. N. (85) 6 ; 52 L. T. 321 ; 33 W. R. 333 : but the last case not followed in *Re Riley to Streatfield*, 34 Ch. D. 386).

"Any *other Cause* whatever ;" *V. Sun Insrce.* v. *Hart*, 58 L. J. P. C. 69.

"Any Bird of Game ;" *V.* GAME, *Animals.*

"Any *Gaming*" (s. 17, sub-s. 1, 35 & 36 V. c. 94), prohibits a licensed person from allowing even lawful games on his premises, if played for money or money's worth (*Foot* v. *Baker*, 6 Sc. N. R. 306 ; 5 M. & G. 335 ; 11 J. P. 444 : *Danford* v. *Taylor*, 33 J. P. 277 : *Luff* v. *Leaper*, 36 J. P. 54 : *R.* v. *Ashton*, 22 L. J. M. C. 1 ; 1 E. & B. 286 : *Bew* v. *Harston*, 47 L. J. M. C. 121 ; 3 Q. B. D. 454 ; 26 W. R. 915 ; 42 J. P. 808 : *Dyson* v. *Mason*, 58 L. J. M. C. 55 ; 22 Q. B. D. 351).

"Any of the Inhabitants ;" *V.* INHABITANTS.

"Any *Land*," s. 8 Real Prop. Limitation Act, 1874, includes only land within the jurisdiction (*Sutton* v. *Sutton*, W. N. (83) 88 ; *V.* S. C. for "any *Sum* secured by mortgage").

"In any *Manner* vest ;" *V. Re De Ros*, 31 Ch. D. 81 ; 55 L. J. Ch. 73 ; 53 L. T. 524 ; 34 W. R. 36.

"Any Misdemeanour ;" *V.* MISDEMEANOUR.

"On any *Money received* ;" *V. Fisher* v. *Drewitt*, W. N. (78) 151.

"Any Officer ;" *V.* OFFICER.

"Profits accruing to "Any *Person* . . . from any kind of *Property* whatever," s. 2, Sch. D., 16 & 17 V. c. 34 ; *V. Colquhoun* v. *Brooks*, 57 L. J. Q. B. 439 ; 21 Q. B. D. 52 ; 59 L. T. 661 ; 36 W. R. 657 ; Affd. W. N. (89), 168.

"Any other *Purpose ;*" *V. Re Norris*, W. N. (83) 35, 65.

Vf. Harrison v. *Cornwall Minerals Ry.*, 51 L. J. Ch. 98 ; 18 Ch. D. 334 ; *Fletcher* v. *Hudson*, 49 L. J. Ex. 793 ; 5 Ex. D. 287 ; 45 J. P. 5.

V. ONE : PROCEEDING.

APOTHECARY.—An "Apothecary," within the late Bankruptcy definition of "Trader," included a man (*e.g.* Palmer, the Rugeley murderer) who carried on the business of Surgeon and Apothecary, and made up medicines for his patients, but did not make them up from other persons' prescriptions, or sell drugs to the public (*Ex p. Crabb, Re Palmer*, 25 L. J. Bank. 45 ; 8 D. G. M. & G. 277).

APPAREL.—*V.* TACKLE.

APPARENT.—By s. 64, Bills of Ex. Act, 1882, an alteration in a Bill which is not "apparent" will not affect a HOLDER IN DUE COURSE. "By the word 'apparent' I do not think it is meant that the holder only should not have had the means of detecting the alteration. If *the party sought to be bound* can at once discern by some incongruity on the face of the (Bill or) Note and point out to the holder that it is not what it was—that is to say, that it has been materially and fraudulently altered—I think the alteration is an 'apparent' one, even if it is not an obvious one to all mankind" (per Denman, J., *Leeds Bank* v. *Walker*, 52 L. J. Q. B. 594 ; 11 Q. B. D. 84).

V. OBVIOUS : POSSESSION.

"Apparent," s. 21, 1 V. c. 26, means apparent on the face of the instrument in the condition in which it is left by the testator (*Re Horsford*, 44 L. J. P. & M. 9 ; L. R. 3 P. & D. 211).

APPARENT EASEMENT.—Apparent Easements are "not only those which must necessarily be seen, but those which may be seen and known on a careful inspection by a person ordinarily conversant with the subject" (Gale on Easements, 2nd Ed. 100, adopted *Pyer* v. *Carter*, 26 L. J. Ex. 261 ; 1 H. & N. 922).

V. NECESSARY.

APPARENT POSSESSION.—*V.* POSSESSION.

APPEAL.—The right of "Appeal" is only by statute. It is not in itself a necessary part of the procedure in an action, but "is the right of entering a Superior Court and invoking its aid and interposition to redress the error of the Court below. It seems absurd to denominate this paramount right, part of the practice of the inferior tribunal" (per Westbury, L. C., *A.-G.* v. *Sillem,* 33 L. J. Ex. 209 ; 10 H. L. Ca. 704).

V. PRACTICE.

"Appeale of felonie" (Litt. s. 500) ;—"*Appellum* signifieth *accusatio,* an accusation, and therefore to appeale a man is as much as to accuse him ; and in ancient bookes he that doth appeale is called *accusator,* and is peculiarly in legall signification applyed to appeales of three sorts,"—*i.e.* (1) Wrong to Ancestor ; (2) Wrong to Husband ; (3) Wrong to self. "The word appellum is derived of *appeller,* to call, because *appellans vocat reum in judicium,* he calleth the defendant to judgement, and the plaintife is called the appellant" (Co. Litt. 287 b).

APPEAL COURT.—*V.* s. 13 (2), Interp. Act, 1889.

APPEAR.—A Condition of a Legacy, that legatee "personally appear before exors" and prove identity, is performed by delivering such proof to two of the exors and to the agent of the third (*Tanner* v. *Tebbutt,* 12 L. J. Ch. 216).

APPEARANCE.—The actual "Appearance" of the parent is not a condition precedent to making an order for Vaccination under s. 31, 30 & 31 V. c. 84 (*R.* v. *Cinque Ports Jus.,* 55 L. J. M. C. 157 ; 17 Q. B. D. 191 : *Dutton* v. *Atkins,* 40 L. J. M. C. 157 ; L. R. 6 Q. B. 373) ; and a similar rule was laid down as regards the power, under an old Act, to discharge an Indenture of Apprenticeship "on the master's appearance" (*Ditton's Case,* 2 Salk. 489).

APPENDAGES AND APPURTENANCES.—An assignment of "all the appendages and appurtenances" of a Ship, includes her chronometer (1 Maude & P. 53, citing *Langton* v. *Horton,* 11 L. J. Ch. 299).

"The case upon the ship *Dundee* (1 Hagg. 121), upon which we have a judgment by Lord Stowell and by Lord Tenterden, has only gone to the extent of establishing that, under 53 G. 3, c. 159, in the expression 'Ship and her appurtenances,' the word '*Appurtenances*' must be construed to extend to anything belonging to the owners which is on board a ship for the *accomplishment* of the object of the voyage and adventure on which she is engaged ; but the Cargo itself is the object and purpose of the adventure, and not something provided as a means for the attainment of the object" (per Langdale, M. R., *Langton* v. *Horton,* 11 L. J. Ch. 238 ; 5 Bea. 9) ; and it was accordingly there held that a cargo of oil, though acquired by a whaler during her adventure, was not included in an assignment of her "Appurtenances." *V.* APPURTENANCES, at end.

APPENDANT.—"Appendant is any inheritance belonging to another, that is superior or more worthy. In law it is called *pertinens, quasi invicem tenens*, holding one another; a word indifferent both to things appendant, and things appurtenant. The quality and nature of the things do make the difference. Appendants are ever by prescription; but appurtenants may be created in some cases at this day" (Co. Litt. 121 b.).

APPERTAINING.—The primary sense of "Appertaining" is much the same as APPURTENANCES, *wh. V.*

"There is, however, a difference between the devise of a house *and the appurts*, and of a house *with the lands appertaining thereto.* It is clear that by the latter expression *some* lands are intended, and therefore the primary sense of the word 'appertaining' is excluded" (1 Jarm. 782, and cases there cited).

Vf. Williams v. *Phillips*, 51 L. J. Q. B. 102; 8 Q. B. D. 437: *Townsend* v. *Champernowm*, 1 Y. & J. 538: BELONGING.

APPLICABLE.—British laws prescribed for a Colony "In so far as applicable;" *V. Jex* v. *McKinney*, 58 L. J. P. C. 67.

APPLICATION.—"Application," in Ord., 58 R. 15, R. S. C., includes the hearing of the action as well as an interlocutory proceeding (*International Financial Socy.* v. *Moscow Gas Co.*, 47 L. J. Ch. 258; 7 Ch. D. 241).

APPOINT.—A power "to appoint" to such persons as the donee may think fit enables him to appoint to himself or wife (Sug. Pow. 25).

So under a power "to appoint" an Executor to a Will, the donee may appoint himself (*Re Ryder*, 31 L. J. P. M. & A. 215; 2 Sw. & T. 127): but, *semble*, a person nominated to appoint a New Trustee cannot appoint himself (*Re Skeats*, 58 L. J. Ch. 656), but in that case the decision proceeded also on the ground that the power was given to appoint "any *other* person."

V. ACKNOWLEDGE.

APPOINTMENT.—A Power to appoint "by Will *or Appointment*," to be signed and sealed in the presence of one or more witnesses, may be exercised by Deed (Sug. Pow. 211).

APPORTION.—"Apportion signifieth a division or partition of a rent, common, &c., or a making of it into parts" (Co. Litt. 147 b).

"To apportion,"—*e.g.* expenses,—does not, *per se*, mean equally to divide; and therefore the apportionment of expenses of street-paving, under s. 77, Metrop. Man. Act, 1862, need not be made on any uniform principle, but is in the discretion of the vestry or board, and can only be challenged for *mala fides* (*Stotesbury* v. *St. Giles, Camberwell*, 57 L. J.

M. C. 114 ; 59 L. T. 473 ; 53 J. P. 5). So when it is said that County Court costs "shall be paid by or *apportioned* between the parties" as the judge shall think just (s. 113, Co. Co. Act, 1888), obviously no equal division is meant.

Apportionment Acts ; *V.* FIXED PERIOD : PERIODICAL : DIVIDEND.

APPRECIATE.—*V.* INAPPRECIABLE.

APPREHENSION.—"Apprehension," s. 8, Extradition Act, 1870 (33 & 34 V. c. 52), includes detention (*R.* v. *Weil,* 53 L. J. M. C. 74 ; 9 Q. B. D. 701 ; 47 L. T. 630 ; 31 W. R. 60 ; 15 Cox, C. C. 189).

APPROACH.—*V.* IMMEDIATE APPROACH.

APPROBATION.—*V.* CONSENT.

APPROPRIATE.—A power in a Will enabling a person to "Appropriate" or "Select," for his own use, such parts of testator's property as he may desire, intimates a confidence that a reasonable selection, and not the whole, will be taken ; and though the exact extent to which the donee may go in benefiting himself could not, in the nature of things, be laid down beforehand, yet it is submitted that the Court would find a mode of restraining any palpably unreasonable exercise of the power (*Kennedy* v. *Kennedy,* 10 Hare, 438 : *Vf. Davis* v. *Davis,* 1 H. & M. 255 : *Reid* v. *Reid,* 30 Bea. 388). But where the power extends over only a small class of property,—*e.g.* testator's plate,—and the donee be his widow, it would seem she might take the whole of it (*Arthur* v. *Mackinnon,* W. N. (79) 93). *Vh.* 1 Jarm. 362.

APPROPRIATED.—In a general testamentary gift of all property of whatever description that testator might die possessed of, to be "appropriated" as donee might think fit, Leach, V.-C., thought a criticism founded upon the words "possessed of" and "appropriated" too nice to exclude realty (*Noel* v. *Hoy,* 5 Mad. 38 ; stated 1 Jarm. 730).

APPROPRIATION.—"The word 'Appropriation' may be understood in different senses. It may mean a selection on the part of the vendor, where he has a right to choose the article which he has to supply in performance of the contract ; and the contract will show when the word is used in that sense. Or the word may mean that both parties have agreed that certain articles shall be delivered in pursuance of the contract, and yet the property may not pass in either case. 'Appropriation' may also be used in another sense, viz., where both parties agree upon the specific article in which the property is to pass, and nothing remains to be done in order to pass it" (per Parke, B., *Wait* v. *Baker,* 2 Ex. 8, 9 ; 17 L. J. Ex. 310, 311).

Appropriation of *Goods ; V.* Blackb. 128 *n.*, citing *Laidler* v. *Burlinson,*

2 M. & W. 602; 6 L. J. Ex. 160: *Atkinson* v. *Bell*, 8 B. & C. 277: *Anderson* v. *Morice*, L. R. 10 C. P. 58, 609; 1 App. Ca. 713; 44 L. J. C. P. 10, 341; 46 Ib. 11: *Calcutta* v. *De Mattos*, 32 L. J. Q. B. 322; 33 Ib. 214. *Vf. Colonial Insrce. Co. of New Zealand* v. *Adelaide Insrce. Co.*, 12 App. Ca. 128.

Appropriation of *Payments;* "Where the purchaser owes more than one debt to the vendor, and makes a payment, it is his right to apply (or in technical language 'appropriate') the payment to whichever debt he pleases" (Benj. 726).

"'Appropriation;' the annexing of an ecclesiastical benefice to the proper and perpetual use of a spiritual corporation or college" (Elph. 561; *wh. V.* for references).

APPROVAL.—*V.* SUBJECT TO.

APPROVED AGREEMENT.—A sale "subject to an Approved Agreement" is not a concluded transaction (per Butt, J., *Harman* v. *Homer*, 32 S. J. 752; cited at SUBJECT TO).

APPROVED BILL.—"I think the phrase 'Approved Bill' could only mean a Bill to which no reasonable objection could be made, and which ought to be approved" (per Ellenborough, C. J., *Hodgson* v. *Davies*, 2 Camp. 531; *V.* Benj. 721).

"Approved Bankers' Bill;" *V. Smith* v. *Mercer*, L. R. 3 Ex. 51.

APPROVED SECURITIES.—"A power to lend on 'Approved Securities,' though it will justify an investment on an ordinary Mortgage, might not be held to extend to Railway Securities (*Re Simson*, 1 J. & H. 89). And where trustees are empowered to lend 'on such securities *as they may approve*,' they are still bound to make enquiries, and exercise a sound discretion whether the securities are of sufficient value; and if in such a case the trustees lend on any irregular securities, the onus lies on the trustees to show the sufficiency of the security (*Stretton* v. *Ashmall*, 3 Drew. 9; 24 L. J. Ch. 277: *Va. Zambaco* v. *Cassavetti*, L. R. 11 Eq. 439: *New London and Brazilian Bank* v. *Brocklebank*, 51 L. J. Ch. 711; 21 Ch. D. 302)." (Lewin, 326.)

APPROVEMENT.—An enclosure by a lord of part of the waste of his manor, leaving sufficient common for the commoners. *Vh.* Wms. on Commons, 103 *et seq.;* Elph. 561: SUFFICIENT PASTURE.

APPURTENANCES.—"By the grant of a messuage, or a messuage *with the appurtenances*, doth pass no more than the dwellinghouse, barn, dovehouse, and buildings adjoining, orchard, garden, and curtilage, *i.e.* a little garden, yard, field, or piece of void ground, lying near *and belonging to* the messuage, and houses adjoining to the dwellinghouse, and the close upon which the dwellinghouse is built, at the most. And so much also may pass by the grant of a house. So that the quantity of an acre of ground, or thereabouts, in orchard, garden, and out-let, may pass by either of these names, but more than this will not pass by the grant that is made in either of these words, albeit more have been occupied with it, and albeit more be intended to be passed by the grant. And therefore if there be a messuage or dwellinghouse, and divers acres of land thereunto belonging, called altogether by the name of Hedges, and a grant is made by these words, of all that messuage with the appurtenances commonly called by the name Hedges ; by this grant nothing shall pass but the messuage, garden, and curtilage, and yet if a manor, or farm, be commonly called by the name of a messuage, there by the grant of a messuage the whole manor, or farm, may pass " (Touch. 94). In this latter case it is not the word " appurts " that has to be construed, but rather the extent and meaning of the *name* of the messuage (*V. Lister* v. *Pickford,* inf.).

The Touchstone, after the extract given above, goes on to say, " and by the grant of a messuage, or house, and all lands thereunto *appertaining,* will pass all the land usually *occupied therewith.*" This, however, is incorrect. A thing may be " used and enjoyed " or " occupied " with something else, without " belonging or appertaining " thereto : and if these latter words only were used they would only cover such things as are appurtenant to and form part of the property which is the principal subject of the instrument (*Barlow* v. *Rhodes,* 2 L. J. Ex. 91 ; 1 Cro. & M. 439 ; 3 Tyr. 280 : *Wardle* v. *Brocklehurst,* 29 L. J. Q. B. 145 : *Maitland* v. *Mackinnon,* 32 L. J. Ex. 49 : *Bolton* v. *Bolton,* 48 L. J. Ch. 467 ; 11 Ch. D. 968). *Secus,* where the words are " used," " enjoyed," or " occupied " (*James* v. *Plant,* 6 L. J. Ex. 260 ; 4 A. & E. 749 ; 6 N. & M. 282). But the word " appurtenant " may be used in a secondary sense as equivalent to such a phrase as " usually enjoyed with " (Elph. 188 ; *Bayley* v. *G. W. Ry.,* 26 Ch. D. 434 ; 51 L. T. 337 ; and *Vth,* and generally hereon, Dart, 609, 610). *V.* RIGHT.

In *Lister* v. *Pickford* (34 L. J. Ch. 582 ; 34 Bea. 576), Lord Romilly said,—" It is settled by the earliest authority, and acted upon and confirmed without contradiction down to the latest, that *Land cannot be appurtenant to Land:* and that the word ' Appurtenances ' includes incorporeal hereditaments, such as rights of way, of common, of piscary and the like ; but does not include land to be added to that which was granted." But though *Lister* v. *Pickford,* and *Evans* v. *Angell* (26 Bea. 202), were especially pressed on Kay, J., in *Cuthbert* v. *Robinson* (51 L. J. Ch. 238) he there, after briefly reviewing the authorities, said,—" The law seems to be clearly this : Neither in a Deed nor in a Will does the word ' Appurtenances ' include land, if the principal subject of gift is land or a messuage. But if, from the circumstances at the date of the Will and the whole context, it is clear that land is intended to pass as appurtenant, the word ' Appurtenant ' is flexible enough to carry it." (*Va.* Cary, 24, per Bromley, L. C.). So a gift of " my freehold messuage or Mansion-house, with the offices, garden, lawn and Appurtenances thereto, now in my occupation," was held, by force of the word "Appurtenances," to pass meadows without which the house would be no better than a suburban villa (*Leach* v. *Leach*, W. N. (78) 79). But it would seem that the burden of proof lies on those who contend for this enlarged meaning (1 Jarm. 781, 782).

It is sometimes said that the phrase "with the appurtenances," adds but little, if anything to the meaning, as the principal carries the accessory (Touch. 89 ; *Vth.* Elph. 186–189). Still some weight will frequently be attachable to the phrase ; and "it is construed more strictly in a Deed than in a Will" (Elph. 189, citing *Ongley* v. *Chambers*, 1 Bing. 483). In a Conveyance executed since the Conv. & L. P. Act, 1881, the phrase could scarcely add anything to the wide General Words which, by s. 6 of that Act, are implied. In a Lease it is flexible (*Dobbyn* v. *Somers*, 13 L. R. Ir. 592).

Vf. as to the meaning of "Appurtenances," Woodf. 141, 142 ; 2 Platt, 33 ; *Pheysey* v. *Vicary*, 16 M. & W. 484 : *Ackroyd* v. *Smith*, 19 L. J. C. P. 315 : *Thomas* v. *Owen*, 57 L. J. Q. B. 198 ; 20 Q. B. D. 225 ; 58 L. T. 162 ; 36 W. R. 440 ; 52 J. P. 516 : *Roe* v. *Siddons*, 22 Q. B. D. 224.

V. Appertaining : Appendages.

"Appurtenances" of a *Ship* must be such things as are appropriated to her exclusively ; and do not include such things as she uses indiscriminately with other ships (*Re Salmon & Woods, Ex p. Gould*, 2 Morr. 137).

APPURTENANT.—*V.* Appendant.

APT.—"Apt and Fit to execute" an Office ; *V.* Fit.

AQUA.—*V.* Waters.

ARBITRARILY.—*V.* Unreasonably.

ARBITRATION.—"An arbitration is a reference to the decision of one or more persons, either with or without an umpire, of a particular *matter in difference* between the parties" (per Romilly, M. R., *Collins* v. *Collins*, 28 L. J. Ch. 186). Accordingly if parties sell and buy, and leave the price on compensation for errors to be fixed by valuation, any question that may arise respecting such valuation is not such a difference as will make the case one of "arbitration" within ss. 11, 12, Com. L. Pro. Act, 1854 (*Collins* v. *Collins*, 28 L. J. Ch. 184 ; 26 Bea. 306 : *Bos* v. *Helsham*, 36 L. J. Ex. 20 ; L. R. 2 Ex. 72 : *Re Dawdy*, 54 L. J. Q. B. 574 ; 15 Q. B. D. 426 : but though in *Bos* v. *Helsham* the Court rejected the award of an arbitrator on a question of compensation under Conditions of Sale, Jessel, M. R., gave effect to such an award in *Re Turner & Skelton*, 49 L. J. Ch. 114 ; 13 Ch. D. 130). The object of the valuation in such a case is to *prevent* differences and is a mere appraisement valuation. "If," however, "two persons enter into an agreement for the sale of property, and try to settle the terms, but cannot agree, and after dispute and discussion respecting the price, say, we will refer the question of price to A. B., he shall settle it, and they agree that the matter shall be referred to his arbitration, that would appear to be 'Arbitration' in the proper sense of the term within the meaning of the Act" (per Romilly, M. R., *Collins* v. *Collins*, sup.). And so if there be a distinct agreement providing for the appointment of an umpire to determine differences between valuers, that would be an "Arbitration" (*Re Hopper*, 36 L. J. Q. B. 97 ; L. R. 2 Q. B. 367 : *Re Dawdy*, sup.). *V.* VALUATION.

A reference of possible disputes to a Foreign Court is an agreement for "Arbitration" within the sections cited (*Law* v. *Garrett*, 8 Ch. D. 26).

The sections cited repealed, and other provisions made, by the Arbitration Act, 1889.

ARE.—"Now are ;" *V.* NOW.

ARISING.—"Arising *from* ;" *V.* CAUSED BY.

Loss "Arising *off* their lines ;" *V. Kent* v. *Mid. Ry.*, L. R. 10 Q. B. 1.

"Arising *out of* the bankruptcy," s. 102, Bankry. Act, 1883 ; *V. Re Hawke, Ex p. Scott*, 55 L. J. Q. B. 302 ; 16 Q. B. D. 503 ; 54 L. T. 54 ; 34 W. R. 167.

Profits "arising or accruing" in the United Kingdom, s. 2, Sch. D., Income Tax Act, 1853, 16 & 17 V. c. 34, mean Profits coming to the person's hands or received by him in the United Kingdom (*Colquhoun* v. *Brooks*, 57 L. J. Q. B. 439 ; 21 Q. B. D. 52 ; 59 L. T. 661; 36 W. R. 657; 52 J. P. 645).

"Question arising ;" *V.* QUESTION.

Exception in an Accidental Insurance of Death from causes "arising *within the system* of the insured ;" *V. Smith* v. *Accident Insrce.*, L. R. 5 Ex. 302 ; 39 L. J. Ex. 211 : *Fitton* v. *Accidental Death Insrce.*, 34 L. J. C. P. 28 ; 17 C. B. N. S. 122.

ARMS.—*V.* FORCE.

ARRAIGN.—"No man is said to be arraigned, but merely at the suit of the king, upon an enditement found against him, or other record wherewith he is charged. And there the arraignment of the prisoner is to take order that he appeare, and for the certainty of the person to hold up his hand, and to plead a sufficient plea to the enditement or other record, whereupon they which follow for the king may orderly proceed" (Co. Litt. 263 a).

ARRANGEMENT.—"The term 'Arrangement' is a very wide and indefinite one" (per Parke, B., *Manning* v. *Eastern Counties Ry.*, 13 L. J. Ex. 265 ; 12 M. & W. 237) ; in which case it was held that a verdict of a jury, on a claim for compensation against a Railway Company and receipt of compensation under such verdict, was an "Arrangement with" the Company.

"Arrangement," identical with Agreement in writing (*Cave* v. *Hastings*, 50 L. J. Q. B. 575; 7 Q. B. D. 125). *V.* Balance.

A testamentary power enabling Trustees to wind-up testator's affairs "and in so doing to make any sales and Arrangements they shall judge expedient," authorises them to give a mortgage on the realty (*Re Jones, Dutton* v. *Brookfield*, 34 S. J. 11).

ARRAY.—"And herein you shall understand, that the jurors' names are ranked in the pannel one under another; which order or ranking the jurie is called the array, and the verbe, to array the jurie; and so we say in common speech, *battaile array* for the order of the battaile" (Co. Litt. 156 a).

ARREARS.—The bequest of "Arrears" of a Debt, will only pass the interest in arrear, and not the principal (Wms. Exs. 1203, citing *Hamilton* v. *Lloyd*, 2 Ves. 416).

"Arrears of Rent and Interest;" *V. Hele* v. *Gilbert*, 2 Ves. 430.

ARREST.—"Arrest of Goods," in a Marine Policy, "is a taking with the intention of restoring them at one time or another" (per Brett, J., *Rodocanachi* v. *Elliott*, L. R. 8 C. P. 659; 42 L. J. C. P. 254: *Vh.* 1 Maude & P. 488); and is equivalent to Seizure (*Johnston* v. *Hogg*, 52 L. J. Q. B. 343).

V. Restraints of Kings.

ARRIVE.—*Condition of Legacy*, that legatee "arrive" at a place; *V. Burgess* v. *Robinson*, cited Return.

"It appears on a review of the result of the decisions on *Contracts of Sales* 'to arrive':

1st. Where the language is that goods are sold 'on arrival' per ship A, or ex ship A, or *to arrive* per ship A, or ex ship A (for these two expressions mean precisely the same thing) it imports a *double condition precedent*, viz., that the ship named shall arrive, *and* that the goods sold shall be on board on her arrival.

2nd. Where the language asserts the goods to be on board of the vessel named, as '1170 bales now on passage, and expected to arrive per ship A,' or other terms of like import, there is a warranty that the goods are on board, and a *single condition precedent*, to wit the arrival of the vessel. *V.* Expected to arrive.

3rd. The condition precedent that the goods shall arrive by the vessel will not be fulfilled by the arrival of goods answering the description of those sold, but not consigned to the vendor, and with which he did not affect to deal; but, *semble*, the condition will be fulfilled if the goods which arrive are the same that the vendor intended to sell, in the expectation, which turns out to be unfounded, that they would be consigned to him." (Benj. 566, 567, citing *Neill* v. *Whitworth*, 18 C. B. N. S. 435; 34 L. J. C. P. 155.)

"When goods are to be sold on a condition to take effect at some future time, I agree in thinking that it is more rational to construe the words 'to arrive' in the light of a condition than as amounting to a warranty" (per Alderson, B., *Johnson* v. *Macdonald*, 9 M. & W. 606 ; 12 L. J. Ex. 99).

"On arrival" and "to arrive" mean the same thing (per Parke, B., *Johnson* v. *Macdonald*, 9 M. & W. 601 ; 12 L. J. Ex. 99).

"After Arrival;" *V. Lindsay* v. *Janson*, 28 L. J. Ex. 315 ; 4 H. & N. 699 : *Lidgett* v. *Secretan*, L. R. 5 C. P. 190; 39 L. J. C. P. 196 ; L. R. 6 C. P. 616 ; 40 L. J. C. P. 257.

Vf. Blackb. 230, 239 ; Benj. 560 : *Montgomery* v. *Middleton*, 13. Ir. C. L. Rep. 173.

V. Convoy.

ARSON.—For a statement of the statutory definition of Arson in 24 & 25 V. c. 97 ; *V.* Steph. Cr. 318 *et seq.* *Vf.* Arch. Cr. 575 ; Rosc. Cr. 284–289.

V. Set Fire.

ARTICLE.—A horse is an "Article" within s. 25, Llandaff and Canton District Markets Act, 1858 (21 & 22 V. c. cv.), (*Llandaff Market Co.* v. *Lyndon*, 30 L. J. M. C. 105 ; 8 C. B. N. S. 515).

Stock in the funds, held not included in a bequest of "every other Article belonging to me both in and out of my house and which may not be herein mentioned" (*Collier* v. *Squire*, 3 Russ. 467).

"Any other Article or Thing," in s. 37, Prisons Act, 1865, is not to be read *ejusdem generis* with the preceding enumeration, but means any other Article or Thing of any other kind, sort or description whatsoever, *e.g.*, a crowbar (*R.* v. *Payne*, 35 L. J. M. C. 170 ; L. R. 1 C. C. 27).

Semble, a ship is not an "Article" within the definition in s. 3 (7), 30 & 31 V. c. 103, by which "*Manufacturing Process*" is defined to mean any Manual Labour exercised by way of trade, or for purposes of gain, in or incidental to the *making of any Article*, or part of an article, or in or incidental to the altering, repairing, ornamenting, finishing or otherwise adapting for sale any Article (*Palmer Shipbuilding Co.* v. *Chaytor*, 38 L. J. M. C. 63 ; 10 B. & S. 177 ; L. R. 4 Q. B. 209).

"Articles;" *V.* Covenant.

ARTICLE DEMANDED.—"The 'Article demanded,'—s. 6, 38 & 39 V. c. 63,—must be held to be, the Article meant by an ordinary purchaser to be obtained,—not in any scientific definition" (per Ld. Justice Clerk, *Morton* v. *Green*, 4 Couper's Justiciary Rep. 469 ; *White* v. *Bywater*, 19 Q. B. D. 582 ; 51 J. P. 821 ; 3 Times Rep. 631). But the section is not limited in its application to adulterated articles (*Knight* v. *Bowers*, 14 Q. B. D. 845 ; 54 L. J. M. C. 108).

Vh. Coffee Case, *Higgins* v. *Hall*, 50 J. P. 788 : Milk Case, *Lane* v. *Collins*, 54 L. J. M. C. 76 ; 14 Q. B. D. 193 ; 33 W. R. 365 ; 49 J. P. 88 ; 52 L. T. 257 : Mustard Case, *Horder* v. *Grainger*, 44 J. P. 188 : Tincture of Opium Case, *White* v. *Bywater*, sup.

V. Nature : Prejudice of Purchaser.

ARTIFICER.—"An 'Artificer' is a skilled workman" (per Brett, L. J., *Morgan* v. *Lond. Gen. Omnibus Co.*, 53 L. J. Q. B. 352 ; 13 Q. B. D. 832). *V.* LABOURER : WORKMAN.

A designer of patterns for a calico-printer was held an "Artificer" within the repealed statute, 4 G. 4, c. 34, s. 3 (*Ex p. Ormerod*, 13 L. J. M. C. 73 ; 1 Dow. & L. 825). In that case Williams, J. (as reported in Dow. & L.) said,—"I cannot conceive that the word 'Artificer' only applies to persons engaged in such occupations as require *merely* manual labour. The party who makes this application to the court, himself states that he is a 'pattern designer,' a person in fact who makes the drawing of the pattern, which is then engraved on the printing rollers, and, subsequently, transferred in colours to the fabric itself. He is therefore the party who sets all in motion. He contributes in the most material degree to the printing of calico, and may therefore, I think, be properly included under the term 'Artificer.'" As reported in the *Law Journal*, Williams, J., commenced these observations thus :—"I cannot conceive that the term 'Artificer,' used in the statute, is confined to those instances only in which *great* manual labour is required." But whether "mere," or "great," were the word used by that learned judge, there can be little doubt that the personal exercise of some manual labour, and that of a skilled kind, is essential to the term "Artificer." And under the statute last cited, a Journeyman Tailor (*Ex p. Gordon*, 25 L. J. M. C. 12) was an "Artificer." Nor would an "Artificer" be less so, under that statute, because at liberty to employ other workmen under him (*Lawrence* v. *Todd*, 32 L. J. M. C. 238 ; 14 C. B. N. S. 554).

But though Erle, J. said (in *Lawrence* v. *Todd*, sup.), that the Truck Act (1 & 2 W. 4, c. 37), was *in pari materiâ* with 4 G. 4, c. 34, and though, of course, the kind of work which would make a man an "Artificer" would be the same for the purposes of each Act,—yet (notwithstanding such cases as that of the Butty colliers, *Bowers* v. *Lovekin*, 25 L. J. Q. B. 371 ; 6 E. & B. 584 ; 4 W. R. 600 ; 27 L. T. O. S. 168 : or of the Collier having liberty to employ others under him, *Weaver* v. *Floyd*, 21 L. J. Q. B. 151),—the principle of *Lawrence* v. *Todd* is not generally applicable to the Truck Act, and an "Artificer," labourer or other person within that Act must be one who contracts for his own labour exclusively, as distinguished from one who contracts to supply the *result* of the labour of others, or of himself and others (*Ingram* v. *Barnes*, 26 L. J. Q. B. 82, 319 ; 7 E. & B. 132 ; 5 W. R. 232, 726 ; 29 L. T. O. S. 297 ; 21 J. P. 822 : *Sleeman* v. *Barrett*, 33 L. J. Ex. 153 ; 2 H. & C. 934 ; 12 W. R. 411 ; 9 L. T. 834 ; 28 J. P. 232 : establishing *Riley* v. *Warden*, 18 L. J. Ex. 120 ; 2 Ex. 59 ; 10 L. T. O. S. 420 : and *Sharman* v. *Sanders*, 22 L. J. C. P. 86 ; 13 C. B. 166 ; 1 W. R. 152 ; 20 L. T. (O. S.) 247) ; but if the contract does not contemplate the sub-employment of others, but enables the employer whenever he chooses to require the employee to devote his own labour to the work, such an employee may be an "Artificer" within the Truck Act though he may have the opportunity (*e.g.* by taking the work home) of being assisted in his work by others (*Pillar* v. *Llynvi Co.*, 38 L. J. C. P. 294 ; L. R. 4 C. P. 752 ; 17 W. R. 1123 ; 20 L. T. 923).

ARUNDINETUM.—"Where reeds grow" (Co. Litt. 4 b).

AS.—*V.* WHEN.

This word is sometimes used as an *exempli gratia* (*V.* 1 Jarm. 753 n), or, as Ld. Coke phrases it, as "similitudinary" (Co. Litt. 43 b) ; but sometimes it is to be understood positively (Ib. 17 b).

AS A TRADER.—Notwithstanding what Bacon, V. C., is reported to have said in *The Colonial Bank* v. *Whinney* (51 L. T. 354) this phrase is not identical with "in the course of his trade or business" (*Re Jenkinson*, 54 L. J. Q. B. 602).

V. IN HIS TRADE OR BUSINESS.

AS AFORESAID.—*V.* AFORESAID.

AS ALLEGED.—A pleading denying terms of agreement "as alleged" is evasive (*Thorp* v. *Holdsworth*, 3 Ch. D. 637 ; 45 L. J. Ch. 406).

AS BEFORE.—*V.* AFORESAID.

AS COUNSEL SHALL ADVISE.—A covenant for Further Assurance "as Counsel shall advise," refers to the Counsel of the covenantee (*Higginbottom's Case*, 5 Rep. 19), but not the covenantee himself "although he be learned in the law" (*Rosewel's Case*, Ib.) ; *Vf.* Elph. 493, 494.

"A Direction to Settle 'as Counsel shall advise,' affords a strong indication that the trusts are executory" (Elph. 533, citing *White* v. *Carter*, 2 Amb. 670 ; 2 Ed. 366 ; *Vh.* Obs. by Sugden, C., *Rochfort* v. *Fitzmaurice*, 2 Dr. & War. 21, quoted Elph. 534).

AS DESCRIBED.—*V.* *Noseworthy* v. *Buckland*, 43 L. J. C. P. 27 ; L. R. 9 C. P. 233 : *Hinks* v. *Safety Lighting Co.*, 4 Ch. D. 607.

Invention "as *herein* described ;" *V.* *Thomas* v. *Welch*, L. R. 1 C. P. 192.

AS DEVISED.—*V.* *Cooch* v. *Walden*, 46 L. J. Ch. 639.

AS FAR AS.—*V.* SO FAR AS APPLICABLE : POSSIBLE.

AS IF.—"As if this Act had not been made ;" *V.* NOTWITHSTANDING.

"As if he was naturally dead ;" *V.* DEAD.

AS IN OTHER CASES.—Ord. 16, R. 31, R. S. C. ; *Vh.* Ann. Pr. 259.

AS IT STANDS.—A contract to take, *e.g.*, a Cargo, "as it stands" (though it specify a quantity), means that the cargo is "to be taken by the purchaser for better for worse, for less or for more" (per Campbell, C. J., *Covas* v. *Bingham*, 23 L. J. Q. B. 29 ; 2 E. & B. 836 ; *Vth.* Benj. 565).

AS NEAR AS.—*V.* So far as.

AS NEAR THERETO.—*V.* Near thereto as she may safely get.

AS OF.—"In, or as of" a Term ; *e.g.*,—in a Warrant of Attorney to sign judgment ; *V. Alcock* v. *Sutcliffe*, 16 L. J. Q. B. 129.
"As of Fee ;" *V.* Elph. 572, n.
"As of Right ;" *V.* Right.

AS OFTEN AS.—As to the value of this phrase in a covenant for renewal of a Lease, and as to its inefficiency to give the right to a perpetual renewal ; *V. Swinburne* v. *Milburn*, 54 L. J. Q. B. 6.

AS REQUIRED.—"It was held no defence to an action by the buyer for non-delivery 'as required,' that he had not requested delivery within a reasonable time" (Benj. 691, citing *Jones* v. *Gibbons*, 8 Ex. 920 ; 22 L. J. Ex. 347).

AS SOON AS.—*V.* Able : Possible : When.

AS SUCH.—Notice of a prejudicial instrument, etc., to counsel, solicitor or agent "as such" (s. 3, Conv. Act, 1882), means notice to counsel, etc., in and during the transaction sought to be affected (*Re Cousins*, 55 L. J. Ch. 662).

AS TENANT.—*V.* Tenant.

AS THE CROW FLIES.—*V.* Distance.

AS TO.—"As to" does not necessarily mark the commencement of an independent sentence (*Gordon* v. *Gordon*, L. R. 5 H. L. 254).

AS UNADULTERATED.—The offence of selling Food or Drink "*as* unadulterated," s. 2, 35 & 36 V. c. 74, does not need an express representation for its completion ; to supply on sale an article, *e.g.* Butter, which ought to be unadulterated, is to sell it "as unadulterated" (*Fitz-patrick* v. *Kelly*, 42 L. J. M. C. 132 ; L. R. 8 Q. B. 337).

ASCERTAINED.—This word has two meanings, (1) "known," (2) "made certain" (*Sidebottom* v. *Sidebottom*, L. R. 2 P. & D. 365 ; 41 L. J. P. & M. 23). In that case as used in a Residuary Clause it was construed "made certain."

Where money to be paid, or service to be rendered, has "to be ascertained" in a certain way, "the words 'to be ascertained' are very strong words, and they look very like a condition precedent" (per Crompton, J., *Braunstein* v. *Accidental Insrce. Co.*, 31 L. J. Q. B. 24).

ASSART.—"Grubbing woods in a man's own lands in a forest, so as to make the same arable" (Elph. 561, *wh. Vf.*).

ASSAULT.—"An Assault is (a) an attempt unlawfully to apply any the least actual force to the person of another directly or indirectly; (b) the act of using a gesture towards another, giving him reasonable gronnds to believe that the person using that gesture meant to apply such actual force to his person as aforesaid; (c) the act of depriving another of his liberty: in either case, without the consent of the person assaulted, or with such consent if it is obtained by fraud" (Steph. Cr. 177). But free consent will not always relieve a case of being a criminal assault, for the combatants at a prize fight, and all persons aiding or abetting therein, are guilty of an indictable Assault (*R.* v. *Coney*, 51 L. J. M. C. 66; 8 Q. B. D. 534; *wh.* case *V.* for a very full citation of authorities).

"A *Battery* is an assault whereby any the least actual force is actually applied to the person of another, or to the dress worn by him, directly or indirectly.

"Provided that such acts as are reasonably necessary for the common intercourse of life, are not Assaults or Batteries, if they are done for the purpose of such intercourse only and with no greater force than the occasion requires.

"No mere words can in any case amount to an Assault" (Steph. Cr. 177).

Vf. Arch. Cr. 750–790; Rosc. Cr. 300–310.

"Assault occasioning Actual Bodily Harm;" *V.* INFLICT.

ASSEMBLE.—The offence of knowingly suffering prostitutes or persons of bad character "to assemble and meet together," or "to assemble," or "to meet together," in an Inn or Beerhouse, means allowing them to be there as prostitutes or in their other evil character; but does not include a case of allowing them to be there merely to get refreshments and for no longer time than reasonably necessary for such refreshments to be consumed (*Greig* v. *Bendeno*, 27 L. J. M. C. 294; E. B. & E. 133; 22 J. P. 816: *Belasco* v. *Hannant*, 31 L. J. M. C. 225; 3 B. & S. 13; 6 L. T. 577: *Vf. Parker* v. *Green*, 6 L. T. 46: *Marshall* v. *Fox*, 24 L. T. 751). *Cp.* s. 14, 35 & 36 V. c. 94.

Cp. HARBOUR.

ASSEMBLY.—An "Assembly" of persons would seem to mean three or more; *V.* UNLAWFUL ASSEMBLY: *Cp.* MULTITUDE.

ASSESSED.—*V.* RATED OR ASSESSED.

ASSESSMENTS.—"Assessments," in the collocation in a lessee's covenant to pay "Taxes, Rates, and Assessments," means Assessments of a nature similar to that of Taxes and Rates, and does not comprise an exceptional burden imposed by a local authority and ordinarily to be borne by the landlord (*Tidswell* v. *Whitworth*, 36 L. J. C. P. 103 ; L. R. 2 C. P. 326 : *Hartley* v. *Hudson*, 48 L. J. Q. B. 751 ; 4 C. P. D. 367 : *Allum* v. *Dickinson*, 52 L. J. Q. B. 190 ; 9 Q. B. D. 632 : *Wilkinson* v. *Collyer*, 53 L. J. Q. B. 278 ; 13 Q. B. D. 1).

V. TAXES : OUTGOINGS : RATED OR ASSESSED.

ASSETS.—"*Assets* in the hands of the executor or administrator, that is,—'sufficient,' from the French *assez*, to make him chargeable to a creditor, and a legatee or party in distribution, so far as such property extends" (Wms. Exs. 1661 ; and as to Assets generally, *V.* Ib., Pt. 4, Bk. 1, ch. 1).

V. EFFECTS.

ASSIGN.—As to when this word is effectual to revive a merged term ; *V.* Elph. 45.

"A covenant not to assign or otherwise part with the premises, or any part thereof, for the whole *or any part of the term*, is broken by a sub-lease (*Doe* d. *Holland* v. *Worsley*, 1 Camp. 20 ; Cole, Ejec. 435) ; but a covenant 'not to assign, transfer, set over or otherwise do or put away the lease or premises' is not (*Crusoe* d. *Blencowe* v. *Bugby*, 2 W. Bl. 766 ; 3 Wils. 234 : *Kinnersley* v. *Orpe*, 1 Doug. 56 : *Church* v. *Brown*, 15 Ves. 258). A covenant against sub-letting will restrain an Assignment (*Greenaway* v. *Adams*, 12 Ves. 395) ;" Woodf. 659. *V.* UNDERLEASE : PUT AWAY.

"A covenant 'not to alien, sell, assign, transfer, set over or otherwise part with the lease or premises' was ruled, before the Jud. Act, not to be broken by a Deposit of the Lease as a security for a loan (*Doe* d. *Pitt* v. *Hogg*, 1 C. & P. 160 ; 4 D. & Ry. 226 ; cited and approved in *Greenslade* v. *Tapscott*, 3 L. J. Ex. 328 ; 1 Cr. M. & R. 59 ; 4 Tyr. 566) ; but the effect of s. 24 of that Act would seem to be to alter the law in this respect ;" (Woodf. 660). *Sq.*

A covenant not to assign is not broken by giving a Warrant of Attorney (*Doe* d. *Mitchinson* v. *Carter*, 8 T. R. 57), unless it be expressly given for the purpose of enabling the judgment creditor to take the term in execution (Ib. 8 T. R. 300).

Not "to grant away, assign, or let, charge or dispose of ;" *V. Croft* v. *Lumley*, 25 L. J. Q. B. 73, 223 ; 27 Ib. 321 ; 6 H. L. Ca. 672.

V. ALIENATION : ASSIGNS : NEGOTIATE.

ASSIGNEE.—"When a statute speaks of an 'Assignee,' it is to be intended of such complete Assignee as has all the ceremonies and incidents requisite by the law to such character ; not taking away any form or circumstance which the law requires. Therefore, Assignee by Fine shall not, under 32 H. 8, c. 34, take advantage of a Condition without attornment." (Dwar. 683, citing *Mallory's Case*, 5 Rep. 112.)

The word "Assignee," in the phrase "executor, administrator, or assignee" in s. 37, Solicitors Act, 1843 (6 & 7 V. c. 73), is not confined to a person resembling a personal representative of a deceased person; but is equivalent to an "Assign" (*Ingle* v. *McCutchan*, 53 L. J. Q. B. 311; 12 Q. B. D. 518: *Penley* v. *Anstruther*, 52 L. J. Ch. 367. *Vf. Re Ward*, 28 Ch. D. 719). *Cp.* "Assignee" as used in s. 25 (6), Jud. Act, 1873.

V. ASSIGNS.

ASSIGNING.—*V.* BEING.

ASSIGNMENT.—*V.* TRANSFER.

A written direction to trustees of a Will by a beneficiary thereunder to pay to a third person money due to the beneficiary, is an "Assignment' of the money within s. 25 (6), Jud. Act, 1873 (*Harding* v. *Harding*, 55 L. J. Q. B. 462; 17 Q. B. D. 442; 34 W. R. 775. *Va. Brice* v. *Bannister*, 47 L. J. Q. B. 722; 3 Q. B. D. 569).

ASSIGNS.—"Assignee cometh of the verb *assigno*. And note there be assignes in deed, and assignes in law: whereof see more in the Chapter of Warrantie, Sect. 733" (Co. Litt. 8 b). *V.* ASSIGNEE.

"Where a discretionary *legal power* is expressly limited to 'A. *and his assigns*,' the grantee or devisee of A., and even a claimant under him by operation of law (as an heir or executor), may exercise the power (*How* v. *Whitfield*, 1 Vent. 338, 339; 1 Freem. 476); but in a *trust*, if an estate be vested in a trustee upon trust that he, his heirs, exors, admors, *or assigns*, shall sell, &c., the introduction of the word 'assigns' will not authorize the trustee to assign the estate to a stranger, nor, if the assignment be made, will a stranger be capable of exercising the power" (Lewin, 603).

Where a trust for sale, or otherwise involving discretion, is limited to a person, his heirs *and assigns*, such trust may be executed by a devisee of the trustee (*Titley* v. *Wolstenholme*, 13 L. J. Ch. 410; 7 Bea. 425: *Hall* v. *May*, 26 L. J. Ch. 791; 3 K. & J. 585; 30 L. T. (O. S.) 64: *Vf.* 1 Jarm. 711; Lewin, 231–233). But now, since 31st Dec., 1881, *V.* s. 30, Conv. & L. P. Act, 1881.

As to value of "Assigns" in a mortgage power of sale; *V. Saloway* v. *Strawbridge*, 24 L. J. Ch. 393; 1 K. & J. 371.

Semble,—where in a Will "assigns" is subjoined to "exors and admors," the phrase is always one of limitation, and does not designate next of kin (2 Jarm. 115; LEGAL REPRESENTATIVES); and when the word "assigns" is used in association with "exors and admors," it will not make an interest assignable which otherwise is not transferable (*Gathercole* v. *Smith*, 50 L. J. Ch. 671; 17 Ch. D. 1; 29 W. R. 434).

Covenants relating to land of inheritance and made since 31st Dec., 1881, extend to heirs and assigns though not named (s. 58, Conv. & L. P. Act, 1881).

A covenant incurring liability for one's "Assigns" will not comprise a compulsory assign,—*e.g.* a Railway Company taking under compulsory powers (*Baily* v. *De Crespigny,* 38 L. J. Q. B. 98; 10 B. & S. 1; L. R. 4 Q. B. 180).

A limitation to A. "*and his assigns*" for life, "until he make or attempt to make assignment, or charge or incumber," is not sufficient to render nugatory the clause of forfeiture (*Craven* v. *Brady,* 4 Ch. 296; 38 L. J. Ch. 345; 17 W. R. 505: *Re Kelly, West* v. *Turner,* 33 S. J. 234).

"In preparing Covenants which are intended to *run with the land,* the 'Assigns' should always be mentioned, for though some covenants will bind them although not mentioned, and others will not bind them although mentioned, yet there is a middle class, in which assignees are bound if mentioned, but not otherwise; and it is prudent to provide for the possibility of a covenant being held to belong to this class" (Woodf. 162). *V.* Heirs and Assigns.

"Assigns" in a *Bill of Lading* refers to the Bill itself, not to the goods (*Glyn* v. *E. & W. India Dock Co.,* 50 L. J. Q. B. 62; 52 Ib. 156; 6 Q. B. D. 475; 7 App. Ca. 610).

Vf. Mitcalfe v. *Westaway,* 34 L. J. C. P. 113; 17 C. B. N. S. 658: *Saloway* v. *Strawbridge,* 25 L. J. Ch. 121; 7 D. G. M. & G. 594: *Greenaway* v. *Hart,* 23 L. J. C. P. 115; 14 C. B. 340.

ASSIST.—*V.* Unshipping.

ASSIZE.—"*Assisa* properly commeth of the Latin word *assideo,* which is to associate or set together; so as properly assise is an association or sitting together" (Co. Litt. 153 b).

"Court of Assize;" *V.* s. 13 (4), Interp. Act, 1889.

ASSIZES.—*V.* s. 13 (5), Interp. Act, 1889.

ASSOCIATION.—*V.* Company.

"Association," for purposes of Booty, must be military; political Association is not within the phrase (*Banda and Kirwee Booty,* 35 L. J. Adm. 17).

ASSURANCE.—Where, in any given set of circumstances, the only thing which validates a contract for the sale of goods is an entry in the auctioneer's book, such entry is an "Assurance" of the goods within s. 4, Bills of Sale Act, 1878 (*Re Roberts, Evans* v. *Roberts,* 36 Ch. D. 196; 56 L. J. Ch. 952; 57 L. T. 79; 35 W. R. 684; 51 J. P. 757; 3 Times Rep. 678); but a mere receipt, not intended to and not containing the contract between the parties, is not such an Assurance (*Newlove* v. *Shrewsbury,* 57

L. J. Q. B. 476 ; 21 Q. B. D. 41 ; 36 W. R. 835 : *Woodgate* v. *Godfrey*, L. R. 4 Ex. 59, 5 Ib. 24 : *Grace* v. *Gard*, Times, 30 Nov. 1889. *V.* Receipt.) A mortgage of Freeholds having Trade Fixtures thereto annexed which pass by such mortgage, is not an "Assurance" of the Fixtures within that section (*Re Yates, Batcheldor* v. *Yates*, 57 L. J. Ch. 697 ; 38 Ch. D. 112 ; 59 L. T. 47 ; 36 W. R. 563 : *Sv. Climpson* v. *Coles*, 23 Q. B. D. 465).

Vf. Coburn v. *Collins*, 35 Ch. D. 373 ; 56 L. J. Ch. 504 ; 56 L. T. 431 ; 35 W. R. 610, where an Agreement for sale of business effects by trustees, reserving a lien for the purchase money, was held an "Assurance" by the purchaser requiring registration.

ASSURANCE COMPANY.—A Friendly Society is not an "Assurance Co." (*Coppinger* v. *Gubbins*, 3 J. & La. T. 397).

ASSURED: HAVE FULL ASSURANCE.—*V.* Precatory Trust.

"Assured," in a Marine Policy ; *V. Gt. Britain Steamship Assn.* v. *Wyllie*, 58 L. J. Q. B. 614.

AT.—Where there is a bequest to several in common for life with a gift over "at," or "after," or "from," or "from and after" their decease to their children or other issue,—the gift over is to be read distributively and as a gift of the share of each to his children or other issue respectively (*Arrow* v. *Mellish*, 1 D. G. & S. 355 : *Willes* v. *Douglas*, 10 Bea. 47 : *Wills* v. *Wills*, 44 L. J. Ch. 582 ; L. R. 20 Eq. 342 : *Turner* v. *Whittaker*, 23 Bea. 196 : *Abrey* v. *Newman*, 22 L. J. Ch. 627 ; 16 Bea. 431 : *Alt* v. *Gregory*, 8 D. G. M. & G. 221 : *Waldron* v. *Boulter*, 22 Bea. 284 : *Re Hutchinson*, 51 L. J. Ch. 924). *Vf.* as to effect of testamentary gift "at" *death*, 2 Jarm. 517, 524 ; On.

A legacy given "at," "on," or "upon" a particular age or time, confers a contingent interest, such word, in such a context, being equivalent to "if" the event shall happen (*Parker* v. *Hodgson*, 30 L. J. Ch. 590 ; 1 Dr. & S. 568 ; Wms. Exs. 1237 ; Watson, Eq. 1218).

The 38 G. 3, c. 87, s. 1, as extended by 21 & 22 V. c. 95, s. 18, gives power to the Probate Court in cases where the exor or admor to whom probate or administration has been granted is out of the jurisdiction "*at* the expiration of twelve months" from testator's death, to grant special administration to a creditor, legatee or next of kin ; "At" there, means "at or after" (*Re Ruddy*, 41 L. J. P. & M. 63 ; L. R. 2 P. & M. 330 : *Re Colclough*, 19 L. R. Ir. 235) ; and a like interpretation applies to such a phrase as "at an interval" of a given period (*Re Railway Sleepers Co.*, 54 L. J. Ch. 720 ; 29 Ch. D. 204 : *Vh. Re Miller's Dale Co.*, 31 Ch. D. 211).

Where, under Rules of Court, an application to deprive a plaintiff of costs had to be made "at" the Trial, it was held in time when made an hour after the trial was over (*Kynaston* v. *Mackinder*, 47 L. J. Q. B. 76) ;

but an amendment which may be made "at" the Trial means (*semble*) before verdict (*Wickens* v. *Steel*, 26 L. J. C. P. 241 ; 2 C. B. N. S. 488).

So, under s. 3, 20 & 21 V. c. 43, recognizances are entered into "at the time of the application" for a Case, if entered into within the 3 days given for applying (*Chapman* v. *Robinson*, 28 L. J. M. C. 30 ; 1 E. & E. 25).

Under s. 25, Companies Act, 1867, a contract for paid-up shares simultaneously issued will be registered "at" the Issue of the shares if registered as soon as practically possible after the completion of the transaction (*Re Tunnel Mining Co.*, 56 L. J. Ch. 104 ; 3 Times Rep. 584).

As to a requirement that a deposit is to be paid "at *or before*" entering an Appeal ; *V. Ex p. Rosenthal, Re Dickinson*, 51 L. J. Ch. 736 ; 20 Ch. D. 315 : *Ex p. Luxon, Re Pidsley*, 51 L. J. Ch. 928 ; 20 Ch. D. 701.

A statement that the consideration of a Bill of Sale was paid "at or before" its execution (though such a phrase is somewhat elastic) is not true if not paid till 7 days afterwards (*Ex p. Rolph*, W.N. (81) 136).

In *Lloyd* v. *Gregory* (Cro. Car. 502) a reversionary lease to commence "at" a stated Feast Day, was construed as "*from*" such day.

When "at" is used as denoting a place, it refers to some fixed and definite place ; *e.g.*, therefore, a Marine Policy on pumps whilst engaged "*at* the wreck" of a vessel, will not cover the loss of the pumps when "on" the vessel after she has been got away from the scene of her wreck, and is moving about from place to place in an endeavour to get her into port (*Difiori* v. *Adams*, 53 L. J. Q. B. 437 : *Vf. Wingate* v. *Foster*, 47 L. J. Q. B. 525 ; 3 Q. B. D. 582). "At *as above*" in such a Policy ; *V. Joyce* v. *Realm Mar. Insrce*, 41 L. J. Q. B. 356 ; L. R. 7 Q. B. 580.

When "at" is used in a Will or Deed as descriptive of the situation or locality of property, its meaning is synonymous with IN. But in such a phrase as "*at or within*," the word "at" is rather used in the sense of "near to," or "adjacent to" (*Homer* v. *Homer*, 47 L. J. Ch. 635 ; 8 Ch. D. 758 ; cited 1 Jarm. 796 : *Sv. Doe* d. *Browne* v. *Greening*, 3 M. & S. 171 : *Evans* v. *Angell*, 26 Bea. 202).

An Advowson cannot properly be said to be "at" a place ; and, *primâ facie*, a devise of hereditaments "at" a place will not pass an Advowson (*Crompton* v. *Jarratt*, 54 L. J. Ch. 1109 ; 30 Ch. D. 298).

"*At, in or near* ;" *V.* 1 Jarm. 794.

AT A FAIR VALUATION.—*V.* FAIR VALUATION.

AT ALL TIMES.—A covenant in a Mining Lease to work the Mine "at all Times," is frequently incapable of literal performance (*Abinger* v. *Ashton*, L. R. 17 Eq. 358 : *Vth. Strelley* v. *Pearson*, 15 Ch. D. 113).

AT ALL TIMES OF TIDE.—Where a charter-party provides for delivery of the cargo at a port or as near thereto as the vessel may safely get "at all times of tide," even though it be added "always afloat," the phrase "at all times of tide" is in relief of the ship-owner, so that when the vessel is as near to the port as she can safely get, though from the state of the tide it is not near enough to unload, the Lay Days will begin to run, as the voyage will then be terminated (*Horsley* v. *Price*, 52 L. J. Q. B. 603 ; 11 Q. B. D. 244). The insertion of this phrase in a charter-party will accordingly materially qualify the usual phrase of as NEAR THERETO AS SHE MAY SAFELY GET.

AT AND FROM.—The risk on a Marine Policy begins at, and as soon as the ship is within, the port when the words are "At and From" (*Palmer* v. *Marshall*, 8 Bing. 79, 317 : *Haughton* v. *Empire Mar. Insrce.*, 35 L. J. Ex. 117 ; L. R. 1 Ex. 206 ; 4 H. & C. 44 : *Foley* v. *United Insrce.*, L. R. 5 C. P. 155) ; but at the commencement of the voyage when only "From" is used (*Small* v. *Gibson*, 20 L. J. Q. B. 152 ; 16 Q. B. 156). *Vh. New Zealand Col. Insrce.* v. *Adelaide Mar. Insrce.* (12 App. Ca. 128 ; 56 L. J. P. C. 19) in which a proposal "at and from," was accepted "from" a port ; and in which, on the construction of the letter of acceptance, it was held that parties were *ad idem* and the proposal accepted.

Vf. Wingate v. *Foster*, 3 Q. B. D. 582 ; 47 L. J. Q. B. 525.

AT ANY ONE TIME.—*V.* ONE TIME.

AT ANY TIME.—In a *Mining* Lease, a power to surrender "at any Time," on giving a specified notice, is literally construed as meaning "at any time of any year of the tenancy ;" and does not mean that the notice is to expire at the end of any year (*Bridges* v. *Potts*, 33 L. J. C. P. 338 ; 17 C. B. N. S. 314).

AT HIS DEATH.—"At his death" read "from and after his death" (*Thelwall* v. *Finney*, W. N. (68) 313).

AT HIS WILL OR PLEASURE.—*V.* CONVENIENCE.

AT HOME.—As to when property is said to be "at home," and the effect thereof ; *V.* Lewin, 949, 950 ; Watson, Eq. 112.

AT LEAST.—Where time is to be computed as so many days "at least," that means clear days (*R.* v. *Salop*, 7 L. J. M. C. 56 ; 8 A. & E. 173 : *Mitchell* v. *Forster*, 9 Dowl. P. C. 527 ; 12 A. & E. 472 ; 9 L. J. M. C. 95 : *Young* v. *Higgon*, 9 L. J. M. C. 29 ; 6 M. & W. 49 : *Robinson* v. *Robinson*, 30 L. J. P. M. & A. 189). But in *Re Ry. Sleepers Co.* (54 L. J. Ch. 722 ; 29 Ch. D. 204), Chitty, J., said, "I do not see any distinction between '14 days' and 'at least 14 days.'"

V. CLEAR.

AT MERCHANT'S RISK.—*V.* MERCHANT'S RISK.

AT ONE TIME.—*V.* ONE TIME.

AT OWNER'S RISK.—*V.* OWNER'S RISK.

AT SEA.—"In a policy of marine insurance where the vessel was described as 'At Sea' it was held by the Supreme Colony of Victoria that the condition was complied with, as she had then left port, although she was in a navigable river which had at its mouth a bar difficult to cross." (Wood, 241, citing *Fisher* v. *Adelaide Insrce. Co.*, 2 Victorian Rep. 90.)

"Mariner at Sea;" *V.* MARINER.

AT SIGHT.—"A Note payable at sight, by the terms of the contract, must be shown before action brought: that was the case of *Holmes* v. *Kerrison*, 2 Taunt. 323" (per Parke, B., *Norton* v. *Ellam*, 6 L. J. Ex. 121; 2 M. & W. 461). But *V.* s. 10, Bills of Ex. Act, 1882. *Va.* ON DEMAND.

As to what is a "Sight;" *V. Way* v. *Bassett*, 15 L. J. Ch. 1; 5 Hare, 55.

AT THE END.—*V.* END.

AT THE KING'S PLEASURE.—When a punishment is to be imposed "at the King's pleasure," this is to be done in his Courts and by his Justices (1 Hale, 375; Dwar. 675; Maxwell, 427).

AT THE KING'S WILL.—*V.* FELONY.

AT THE PLEASURE.—*V.* PLEASURE.

AT THE PRESENT TIME.—"The business at the Present Time returns a net profit of 17 % on the capital employed;" *V. Glasier* v. *Rolls*, 58 L. J. Ch. 331.

V. CAPITAL EMPLOYED.

AT THE TIME OF.—*V. Brown* v. *Wilkinson*, 16 L. J. Ex. 34; 15 M. & W. 391.

AT THEIR DEATH.—Bequest to two or more, and "at their death" to their children, read "at their respective deaths" (*Wills* v. *Wills*, L. R. 20 Eq. 342; 44 L. J. Ch. 582).

AT VARIANCE.—*V.* VARIANCE.

ATTACHED.—This word does not always mean physically fastened; it may also mean superincumbent upon. Thus in citing from the jdgmt. of Cockburn, C.J., *Laing* v. *Overseers of Bishopswearmouth* (47 L. J. M. C. 41; 3 Q. B. D. 299), that whatever is "attached" to premises has to be estimated for the purpose of ascertaining its rating value, Esher, M.R., said:—

"Now does the word 'attached' there, mean attached by some physical fastening such as screws or bolts? If it does, a thing weighing tons, which cannot be and never was intended to be lifted, would not be taken into account if not fastened to some part of the building; whereas if it were fastened it would. That, as it seems to my mind, would be a monstrous consequence. I do not think the word 'attached' does there mean 'physically fastened,' so as to determine whether the thing is to be taken into account or not" (*Tyne Boiler Works Co.* v. *Overseers of Longbenton*, 56 L. J. M. C. 12). It was held in that case that heavy machinery kept *in situ* by its own weight had to be taken into account in assessing the rateable value of the premises.

ATTACHES.—"When the liability of the underwriter commences under the contract, the technical mode of expressing this is by saying that 'the policy attaches,' or 'the risk begins to run' from that time" (Arn. 17).

ATTACHMENT FOR DEBT.—A committal under Debtors' Act, 1869, for non-payment of a Judgment debt, being punitive, though it may be got rid of by payment, is not an "Attachment *for* Debt" within s. 14, Sheriffs Act, 1887, 50 & 51 V. c. 55 (*Mitchell* v. *Simpson*, 58 L. J. Q. B. 425; 53 J. P. 694); the remarkable thing of that decision is, that the judges seem to have conceded that if the phrase "Attachment for Debt" did not cover such a committal it was, in the present state of the law, meaningless.

ATTACHMENT OF PLEAS OF THE CROWN.—*V. Jewison* v. *Dyson*, 9 M. & W. 540; 11 L. J. Ex. 401; 2 M. & R. 377.

ATTAIN.—A limitation to those "who attain," or "such as attain" a particular age, or marry, creates a condition precedent (*Duffield* v. *Duffield*, 3 Bli. N. S. 260); but, in some cases the estate would vest at once, subject to be divested on the event not happening (*Muskett* v. *Eaton*, 45 L. J. Ch. 22; 1 Ch. D. 435). *Vf.* the cases cited Watson, Eq. 1219.

Devise to T. for life, remainder to his second son "*on* his attaining 21, but in default of there being a second son" then over, does not give, to a second son dying under 21, an estate in fee with an executory devise over, but only a remainder contingent on his attaining 21 (*Alexander* v. *Alexander*, 24 L. J. C. P. 150; 16 C. B. 59).

ATTEMPT.—A mere offer to give security on property if it can be effectually done, is not an "attempt" to anticipate or incumber the property within a clause of forfeiture (*Graham* v. *Lee*, 26 L. J. Ch. 395; 23 Bea. 388; 29 L. T. O. S. 46); *V.* ALIENATION.

"An Attempt to commit a crime is an act done with intent to commit that crime, and forming part of a series of acts which would constitute its actual commission if it were not interrupted.

The point at which such a series of acts begins cannot be defined; but depends upon the circumstances of each particular case.

An act done with intent to commit a crime, the commission of which in the manner proposed was, in fact, impossible, is not an attempt to commit that crime.

The offence of attempting to commit a crime may be committed in cases in which the offender voluntarily desists from the actual commission of the crime itself" (Steph. Cr. 37, 38 : *Vf. R.* v. *Cheeseman*, L. & C. 140 ; 31 L. J. M. C. 89).

ATTENDANCE.—"Attendance" (41 V. c. 16, s. 23) means "attendance of a child at a morning or afternoon meeting of a school during not less than 2 hours of instruction in secular subjects" (Lond. Gaz. 31 Dec., 1878).

ATTENDING.—*V.* GOING TO.

ATTEST: ATTESTATION.—To "Attest" an instrument is not merely to subscribe one's name to it as having been present at its execution, but includes also, essentially, the being in fact present at its execution (*Roberts* v. *Phillips*, 24 L. J. Q. B. 171 ; 4 E. & B. 450 : *Bryan* v. *White*, 2 Robert. 315 : *Sharp* v. *Birch*, 51 L. J. Q. B. 64 ; 8 Q. B. D. 111 : *Va. Doe* d. *Spilsbury* v. *Burdett*, 4 A. & E. 1 ; 9 A. & E. 936 ; 1 P. & D. 670 ; 10 Cl. & F. 340 : *Freshfield* v. *Reed*, 11 L. J. Ex. 193 ; 9 M. & W. 404).

"'To Attest' is to bear witness to a fact. Take a common example: a notary public attests a Protest; he bears witness not to the statements in that protest, but to the fact of the making of those statements; so, I conceive, the witnesses in a Will bear witness to all that the statute requires attesting witnesses to attest, namely that the signature was made or acknowledged in their presence" (per Dr. Lushington, *Hudson* v. *Parker*, 1 Robert. 26 : *Vf.* 1 Jarm. 109).

"Attest and Subscribe" a Will; *V. Griffiths* v. *Griffiths*, L. R. 2 P. & M. 300 : *Re Maddock*, 3 Ib. 169 : *Roberts* v. *Phillips*, sup.

"The word 'attestation' is there,—*i.e.* in s. 10, Bills of Sale Act, 1878,—used for 'attestation clause'" (per Jessel, M. R., *Ex p. Bolland*, 52 L. J. Ch. 116 ; 21 Ch. D. 543).

V. SUBSCRIBE : *Cp.* SIGNED.

ATTORNEY.—"'*Attorney*' is an ancient English word, and signifieth one that is set in the turne, stead, or place of another; and of these some be private (whereof our author here speaketh, Litt. s. 66), and some be publike, as attorneys at law, whose warrant from his master is, *ponit loco suo talem attornatum suum*, which setteth in his turne or place such a man to be his attorney" (Co. Litt. 51 b).

Attorney "expressly named;" *V.* EXPRESSLY NAMED.

ATTORNMENT.—"'Attornment' is an agreement of the tenant to the grant of the seigniorie, or of a rent, or of the donee in tayle, or tenant for life or yeeres, to a grant of a reversion or remainder made to another" (Co. Litt. 309 a; Touch. 253; *Vh.* Woodf. 266).

An Attornment Clause in a Mortgage, is an "Attornment" within s. 6, Bills of Sale Act, 1878 (*Re Willis, Ex p. Kennedy,* 57 L. J. Q. B. 634; 21 Q. B. D. 384; 36 W. R. 793: over-ruling *Hall* v. *Comfort,* 18 Q. B. D. 11; 56 L. J. Q. B. 185).

AUCTION.—A covenant not to "permit any sale by Public Auction" to take place on the premises, is broken by the covenantor giving a Bill of Sale which enables the grantee, on default, to sell the goods on the premises "by private contract or public auction" (*Toleman* v. *Portbury,* 41 L. J. Q. B. 98; L. R. 7 Q. B. 344; 26 L. T. 292; 20 W. R. 441).

AUMONE.—"Tenure by divine service, as distinguished from frankalmoigne; Co. Litt. 96 b, 97 a; *V.* 2 Inst. 460; Britton, 164; Cowell, Law Dict." (Elph. 561).

AUTHOR.—A person who employs another to adapt a foreign drama for representation in England and who merely suggests the subject, is not the "Author" of the adaptation within s. 1, 3 & 4 W. 4, c. 15 (*Shepherd* v. *Conquest,* 25 L. J. C. P. 127; 17 C. B. 427); and to constitute a person a joint author he must co-operate in the production of the drama itself, and merely touching it up so as to make it more attractive on the stage does not constitute a joint authorship (*Levy* v. *Rutley,* 40 L. J. C. P. 244; L. R. 6 C. P. 523); *Vf. Hatton* v. *Kean,* 29 L. J. C. P. 20; 7 C. B. N. S. 268: *Wallerstein* v. *Herbert,* 16 L. T. 453.

"Author" in 5 & 6 V. c. 45, includes Alien authors (*Low* v. *Routledge,* 35 L. J. Ch. 114; 1 Ch. 42): under 8 Anne, c. 19, this was not so (*Jefferys* v. *Boosey,* 24 L. J. Ex. 81; 4 H. L. Ca. 815).

Not the proprietor of the business as such, but the actual operator who takes (or superintends the taking of) the negative is the "Author" of a Photograph within the Copyright Act, 1862 (25 & 26 V. c. 68) (*Nottage* v. *Jackson,* 52 L. J. Q. B. 760; 11 Q. B. D. 627). To use the language of Brett, M. R., in the last case, the superintending operator is "the person who effectively is as near as he can be the cause of the picture which is produced." Note: a photographic portrait cannot be published without the authority of the customer (*Pollard* v. *Photographic Co.,* 58 L. J. Ch. 251; 40 Ch. D. 345).

AUTHORITY OR LICENSE.—An Agreement authorizing a Brewer to distrain for goods supplied to a tied house, is an "Authority or License to take possession of personal chattels as security for any Debt" (s. 4, Bills of Sale Act, 1878), and requires registration (*Pulbrook* v. *Ashby,* 56 L. J. Q. B. 376; 35 W. R. 779).

AUTHORITY OR REQUEST.—"Warrant, Order, Authority, or Request," ss. 23 and 24, 24 & 25 V. c. 98;—a paper merely describing the goods;—*e.g.* "One quart kettle, James Haywod,"—amounts to a "Request" (*R.* v. *Pulbrook*, 9 C. & P. 37); a Deposit Receipt of a Building Society may be a "Warrant, Authority or Request" (*R.* v. *Kay*, 39 L. J. M. C. 118; L. R. 1 C. C. 257; 22 L. T. 557).

AUTHORIZE AND EMPOWER.—*V.* PRECATORY TRUST.

AUTHORISED.—*V.* REQUIRED.

AUXILIARY.—*V.* INCIDENTAL OR CONDUCIVE.

AVAILABLE.—An Act of Bankruptcy "available against him (the bankrupt) for *adjudication*" (s. 94 (3), Bankry. Act, 1869) was one which might have been acted upon by anybody at the date of the order for adjudication (*Hood* v. *Newby*, 52 L. J. Ch. 204; 21 Ch. D. 605: *Re Bedell*, 47 L. J. Bank. 19; 7 Ch. D. 123). "Available" is used in a similar connection in the present Bankry. Act, 1883, s. 49, subs. 2.

S. 198, Bankry. Act, 1861, 24 & 25 V. c. 134, prescribed that after registration of an Arrangement Deed, under s. 192, no process should be "available" against the debtor; held that "available" meant "put in force,"—*e.g.* that caption, not detention, was meant (per Holroyd, Commr., *Re Chaundy*, 5 L. T. 526). *Vf. Ewart* v. *Jones*, 15 L. J. Ex. 18; 14 M. & W. 774.

AVENUE.—"Avenue to a house," 5 & 6 W. 4, c. 5, s. 54; *V. Ramsden* v. *Yeates*, 50 L. J. M. C. 135; 6 Q. B. D. 583; 29 W. R. 628; 44 L. T. 612.

AVERAGE.—"The word 'Average' is from the Italian, 'Averia,' damage" (1 Maude & P. 491).

"The word 'Average,' far from being a term of art—(except in so far as, according to the evidence, usage may have limited its meaning to loss or damage to the goods themselves),—or a word with a rigid or unchanging signification, necessarily including expenses in the defence or safeguard of the subject-matter insured, is a word used in a great variety of phrases, as applicable to different subject-matters, and not with any fixed or settled application" (per Willes, J., *Kidston* v. *Empire Mar. Insrce.*, 35 L. J. C. P. 256; L. R. 1 C. P. 535).

As to the meaning of "Average" in the Contract of Affreightment; *V.* 1 Maude & P. 426.

As to the meaning of "Average" in a Marine Insurance; *V.* 1 Maude & P. 491; Arnould on M. Insrce; Maclachlan on Merchant Shipping: *Kidston* v. *Empire Insrce.*, sup.

"Average due on the Salvage"; *V. Broomfield* v. *Southern Insrce.*, L. R. 5 Ex. 192 : 39 L. J. Ex. 186.

An exception in a Marine Time Policy thus,—"'*free from average*' under (say) 3 per cent.," means that the losses are to be settled at the end of each voyage,—and not that the losses on all the voyages made by the ship during the time covered by the Policy are to be added together,—and only the damage exceeding the agreed percentage on each distinct voyage is recoverable under the policy (*Stewart* v. *Merchants' Mar. Insrce.*, 55 L. J. Q. B. 81; reversing Stephen, J., 54 L. J. Q. B. 387; 16 Q. B. D. 619; and commenting on *Blackett* v. *Royal Ex. Assrce.*, 1 L. J. Ex. 101; 2 Cr. & J. 244, and *Donnell* v. *Columbian Insrce.*, 2 Sumner, 366 : *Brooks* v. *Oriental Insrce.*, 7 Pickering, 258).

Vf. Marine Insrce. v. *China Transpacific Co.*, 56 L. J. Q. B. 100; 11 App. Ca. 573; 55 L. T. 491; 35 W. R. 169; 6 Asp. 68 : *Price* v. *A1. Ships Small Damage Insrce.*, 57 L. J. Q. B. 459; 58 Ib. 269 : Rosc. N. P. 403 : General Average.

"'Average,' *avera, averiæ, averii, affri*;—beasts of burden, oxen, farm horses : *Averagium*, the work done by them; particularly where it was done as a service due to the lord; Spelm. Gloss. *Avera*; 1 Ellis, Introd. Domesday, 263; Seebohm, Eng. Vill. Comm. 57, 297. *Averum* means revenue, effects, goods; Spelm.; Hale, Domesday of St. Paul's (Camd. Soc.), Introd. lxvi" (Elph. 561).

AVERAGE QUALITY.—*V.* Fair Average Quality.

AVERMENT: AVER.—*V.* Co. Litt. 362 b; Elph. 105 n.

AVOIDANCE.—*V.* Next Avoidance.

BACK FREIGHT.—*V. The Cargo ex Argos*, L. R. 5 P. C. 134; 42 L. J. Adm. 1. *Vth.* 1 Maude & P. 364, *n.* (*c*): *Gunnsstad* v. *Price*, L. R. 10 Ex. 65.

BACK STREET.—*V. Shiel* v. *Sunderland*, 30 L. J. M. C. 215; 6 H. & N. 796.

BAIL.—*V.* BAILIFF.

BAILEE.—"Bailee" is the receiver of a BAILMENT.

BAILIFF.—"'*To the bailife* (a le baily),' s. 79, Litt. This word bailie, as some say, commeth of the *French* word *baylife*, in-*Latin ballivus;* but in truth baily is an old *Saxon* word, and signifieth a safe keeper or protector, and *baile* or *ballium* is safe keeping or protection: and thereupon we say, when a man upon surety is delivered out of prison, *traditur in ballium*, he is delivered into bayle, that is, into their safe keeping or protection from prison: and the sherife that hath *custodiam comitatûs* is called *ballivus*, and the county *balliva sua*" (Co. Litt. 61 b).

BAILMENT.—"When one person delivers, or causes to be delivered, to another any moveable thing in order that it may be kept for the person making the delivery, or that it may be used, gratuitously or otherwise, by the person to whom the delivery is made, or that it may be kept as a pledge by the person to whom delivery is made, or that it may be carried, or that work may be done upon it by the person to whom delivery is made gratuitously or not, and when it is the intention of the parties that the specific thing so delivered, or the article into which it is to be made shall be delivered either to the person making the delivery or to some other person appointed by him to receive it, the person making the delivery is said to bail the thing delivered; the act of delivery is called a Bailment; the person making the delivery is called the bailor; the person to whom it is made is called the bailee" (Steph. Cr. 215).

The term "Bailment," according to its ordinary legal sense, "relates to something which is in the hands of a person who is to return it in specie" (per Cockburn, C. J., *R.* v. *Hassall*, 30 L. J. M. C. 175; L. & C. 58: *R.* v. *Ashwell*, 16 Q. B. D. 190; 55 L. J. M. C. 65; 53 L. T. 773; 34 W. R. 297; 50 J. P. 181. *Sv. R.* v. *Flowers*, 16 Q. B. D. 643; 55 L. J. M. C. 179; 54 L. T. 547; 34 W. R. 367; 50 J. P. 648: *R.* v. *De Banks*, 53 L. J. M. C. 132; 13 Q. B. D. 29).

As to the distinction between a Bailment and a Sale; *V. South Australian Insrce.* v. *Randell*, L. R. 3 P. C. 101.

Vf. Coggs v. *Bernard*, 1 Sm. L. C. 201; Add. C. 343–382; Arch. Cr. 390–393.

BAITING.—Coursing rabbits with dogs in an inclosure from which they cannot escape, is not "Baiting" within s. 3, 12 & 13 V. c. 92 (*Pitts* v. *Millar*, 43 L. J. M. C. 96; L. R. 9 Q. B. 380; 38 J. P. 615). In that case, Cockburn, C. J., said, "The word has usually been understood to apply to the case of an animal which is tied to a stake or peg, or so confined as not to be able to get away."

BALANCE.—"Balance," Ord. 21, R. 17, R. S. C.; *Vth.* cases Ann. Pr. 345.

"Balance," in a letter, held to couple with it a previous receipt, so that both documents constituted a sufficient mem. within the St. of Frauds (*Studds* v. *Watson*, 28 Ch. D. 305). For a similar purpose, "Purchase" was held to mean "Agreement to Purchase" (*Long* v. *Millar*, 4 C. P. D. 450). *Vf. Cave* v. *Hastings*, cited, ARRANGEMENT.

"Balance of Account;" *V. Pope* v. *Banyard*, 3 M. & W. 424; 7 L. J. Ex. 182: *Townson* v. *Jackson*, 13 M. & W. 374; 14 L. J. Ex. 57.

"Balance Order;" *V. Re Sanders*, 1 Morr. 185: *Re Tennant*, 3 Ib. 166.

Bequest of "Balance" (*Hill* v. *Mason*, 2 Jac. & W. 248); of "Small Balance" (*Page* v. *Young*, L. R. 19 Eq. 501; 23 W. R. 479).

BALE.—"Bale," "is an ambiguous word which may mean many things, and therefore it is for a jury to say what it means in a Mercantile Contract" (per Cresswell, J., *Gorrissen* v. *Perrin*, 27 L. J. C. P. 32); and in that case the jury were supported in finding that a Bale of Gambier meant a compressed package weighing about 2 cwt. (27 L. J. C. P. 29; 2 C. B. N. S. 681).

"In the Cotton Trade at Alexandria, Surat, and Calcutta,—a Bale means a compressed bale" (Wood, 369, citing *Taylor* v. *Briggs*, 2 C. & P. 525). "In the cotton trade at Charlestown a 'Round Bale' of cotton means an uncompressed bale; and a 'Square Bale' a compressed one" (Wood, 372, citing *Benson* v. *Schneider*, 7 Taunt. 271).

BALK.—"The unploughed strip between two *seliones;* Seebohm, Eng. Vill. Comm. 2, 20" (Elph. 562, *wh. Vf.*).

BALTIC.—In a Marine Insurance on a voyage "to any port in the *Baltic*," evidence is admissible to prove that the Gulf of Finland is within the Baltic, although the two seas are treated as separate and distinct by geographers (*Uhde* v. *Walters*, 3 Camp. 15).

"London Baltic printed Rates;" *V. Southampton Colly. Co.* v. *Clark*, L. R. 6 Ex. 53.

BANK.—"Bank" of a Canal, includes its towing-paths (*Mon. Ry. & Can. Co.* v. *Hill*, 28 L. J. Ex. 283; 4 H. & N. 421).

BANK OF ENGLAND.—*V.* s. 12 (18), Interp. Act, 1889.

BANK OF IRELAND.—*V.* s. 12 (19), Interp. Act, 1889.

BANK STOCK.—Bequest of ; *V. Bignall* v. *Rose,* 24 L. J. Ch. 27.

BANKER.—A "Banker," within the late Bankruptcy definition of "Trader," included a person acting as a Banker, though keeping no open banking-house nor usual bankers' books (*Ex p. Wilson,* 1 Atk. 218) ; also a member of a Joint Stock Banking Co. (*Ex p. Hall,* 3 Dea. 405 : *Ex p. Wyndham,* 1 M. D. & D. 146 : *Sv. Ex p. Brundrett,* 2 Dea. 219) : but not an Army or Navy Agent (*Ex p. Wilson,* sup. : *Richardson* v. *Bradshaw,* 1 Atk. 129). *Vf.* s. 9, 42 V. c. 11 : s. 11 (2), 45 & 46 V. c. 72.

BANKRUPTCY.—There is no "bankruptcy," within the meaning of a clause of forfeiture, if it be annulled before income is payable (*White* v. *Chitty,* 35 L. J. Ch. 343 ; L. R. 1 Eq. 372 : *Lloyd* v. *Lloyd,* L. R. 2 Eq. 722 : *Trappes* v. *Meredith,* 39 L. J. Ch. 366 ; L. R. 9 Eq. 229 : *Robins* v. *Rose,* 43 L. J. Ch. 334. *Sv. Samuel* v. *Samuel,* 12 Ch. D. 152, in which *White* v. *Chitty* was questioned : *Va. Smallcombe* v. *Olivier,* 13 L. J. Ex. 305 ; 13 M. & W. 77).

BAPTIZED.—*V.* Unbaptized.

BAR.—"'Barred' is a word common as well to the English as to the French, of which cometh the nowne, a Bar, *barra.* It signifieth legally a destruction for ever, or taking away for a time of the action of him that right hath" (Co. Litt. 372 a).

BARE TRUSTEE.—A "Bare Trustee" is a Trustee who has no duty to perform, and who, on request, would be compellable to convey or transfer to his cestui que trust (*Christie* v. *Ovington,* 1 Ch. D. 279).

After a judgment for sale in an action, a married woman trustee, beneficially interested, is a "Bare Trustee" within s. 6 Ven. & Pur. Act, 1874, and can convey real estate without acknowledgment (*Re Docwra,* 54 L. J. Ch. 1121 ; 29 Ch. D. 693). An unpaid Vendor, or any other person having only a beneficial interest, is not a "Bare Trustee" within s. 48 Land Transfer Act, 1875 (*Morgan* v. *Swansea,* 9 Ch. D. 582).

BARGAIN.—"A 'Bargain' is only another name for a 'Contract'" (per Hawkins, J., in delivering jdgmt. of the Court in *Crossman* v. *The Queen,* 56 L. J. Q. B. 245); and as used in s. 17 Stat. of Frauds "Bargain" means the terms on which the parties contract (*Kenworthy* v. *Schofield,* 2 B. & C. 947 ; *Archer* v. *Baynes,* 20 L. J. Ex. 54 ; 5 Ex. 625 : *Goodman* v. *Griffiths,* 26 L. J. Ex. 145). *V.* Agreement.

As to this word in Sch. 2, R. 64, P. H. Act, 1875 ; *V. Fletcher* v. *Hudson,* 51 L. J. Q. B. 48 ; 7 Q. B. D. 611 : The sale of a shilling's worth of stationery would be within the meaning of the word (per Bramwell, B., *Lewis* v. *Carr,* 46 L. J. Ex. 314 ; 1 Ex. D. 484).

BARGAIN AND SALE.—"A 'Bargain and Sale' was an expression of very definite meaning in use in the old forms of pleading ; it stands for what is sometimes called an 'Executed Contract,' that is one where the property has passed" (Blackb. 124 : *Va.* Benj. 1).

BARGAIN OR CONTRACT.—Letting Rooms to a Local Authority by one of its officers is a "Bargain or Contract" within s. 193, P. H. Act, 1875 (*Burgess* v. *Clark*, 14 Q. B. D. 735). *Vf. Melliss* v. *Shirley*, 16 Q. B. D. 446 : *Whiteley* v. *Barley*, cited, ALLOWANCES.

BARLEY.—In the Corn Trade 'fine' barley is different from, and superior to, 'good' barley (*Hutchinson* v. *Bowker*, 5 M. & W. 535 ; 9 L. J. Ex. 24).

"Seed Barley ;" "Chevalier Seed Barley ;" *V. Carter* v. *Crick*, 28 L. J. Ex. 238 ; 4 H. & N. 412.

BARONIA.—*V.* Elph. 562.

BARRATRY.—"The word 'Barratry' is derived from the Italian *barratrare*, to cheat. Any illegal, fraudulent, or knavish conduct of the master or mariners of a ship by which the freighters or owners are injured is, by our law, Barratry . . . . In order to constitute Barratry, the act must generally be done fraudulently and with a criminal intent ; and it is not sufficient that it is merely against the interest of the owner" (1 Maude & P. 145 ; *Vf. Taylor* v. *Liverpool & Gt. Wn. Steam Co.*, L. R. 9 Q. B. 546 ; 43 L. J. Q. B. 205). Negligence in steering, though in breach of a statutory rule, is not Barratry (*Grill* v. *General Iron Screw Collier Co.*, 35 L. J. C. P. 321 ; 37 Ib. 205 ; L. R. 1 C. P. 600 ; 3 Ib. 476 : *Cp.* WILFUL DEFAULT) : but wilful illegal trading involving condemnation of the ship is Barratry, though, if successful, the trading would have been profitable to the owner (*Earle* v. *Rowcroft*, 8 East, 126) ; and so is the carrying of prohibited persons if involving forfeiture of the ship (*Australasian Insrce.* v. *Jackson*, 33 L. T. 286). *Vf. Jones* v. *Nicholson*, 23 L. J. Ex. 330 ; 10 Ex. 28 ; 1 Maude & P. 146.

BARRETOR.—"'*Barrettors.*' A barretor is a common moover and exciter, or maintainer of suits, quarrels, or parts, either in courts, or elsewhere in the countrey" (Co. Litt. 368 a).

"'Barretor' is derived of this word (*barret*) which signifieth not only a wrangling suit, but also such brawles and quarrels in the countrey as are aforesaid" (Ib. 368 b).

BASTARD.—A "Bastard" is a person "that be borne out of lawfull marriage" (Co. Litt. 244 a). And the husband of a woman being "within the foure seas" (Ib.), is not now conclusive to legitimatize her offspring ; proof, positive or presumptive, of non-access may be given (*Pendrell* v. *Pendrell*, 2 Stra. 925 : *R.* v. *Luff*, 8 East, 204 : *Goodright* d. *Tompson* v. *Saul*, 4 T. R. 356 : *Morris* v. *Davies*, 5 Cl. & F. 163 : *Hawes* v. *Draeger*, 23 Ch. D. 173 ; 52 L. J. Ch. 449 : *Aylesford Peerage*, 11 App. Ca. 1), even though there has been opportunity of access (*Cope* v. *Cope*, 1 M.

& Rob. 269 : *R.* v. *Mansfield*, 1 Q. B. 450, 452 ; 10 L. J. M. C. 97 ; 1 G. & D. 7 : *Bosville* v. *A.-G.*, 12 P. D. 177 : *Burnaby* v. *Baillie*, 58 L. J. Ch. 842). But where husband and wife are living together, the presumption of the legitimacy of the wife's offspring is so strong, that it can only be rebutted by evidence absolutely irresistible (*Head* v. *Head*, 1 Sim. & St. 152 ; Turn. & R. 138 : *Banbury Peerage*, 1 Sim. & St. 153 : *Morris* v. *Davies*, sup. : *Legge* v. *Edmonds*, 25 L. J. Ch. 125).

If the husband was under the age of procreation (Co. Litt. 243 a), or if his habit of body was such as to make his begetting children an impossibility (*Lomax* v. *Holmden*, 2 Stra. 940), the children of the wife would be bastardized.

BATTERY.—*V.* ASSAULT.

BAWDY HOUSE.—*V.* COMMON BAWDY HOUSE.

BEADLE.—" Bedell is derived of the French word *Beadeau*, which signifies a messenger of the court, or under baylife, in *Latine Bedellus* " (Co. Litt. 234 b).

BEAR.—The use of " Bear " in collocation with " Pay,"—*e.g.* in a tenant's covenant to " bear and pay " taxes, rates, duties, &c.—has " the effect of more distinctly developing its very comprehensive character " (per Baggallay, L.J., *Budd* v. *Marshall*, 50 L. J. Q. B. 29).

Semble, there is a difference between a gift to descendants who " *bear* " a particular Name, and a gift to Descendants " *of* " such name (*Re Roberts*, 50 L. J. Ch. 265 ; s. c. on App. 19 Ch. D. 520).

BEARER.—The " Bearer," of a Bill or Note, " means the person in possession of a Bill or Note which is payable to Bearer " (s. 2, Bills of Ex. Act, 1882).

A Debenture payable " to Bearer " is, in effect, a Promissory Note, and passes from hand to hand free from any equities which might have attached to it as between the Company and the original holder (*Re Marseilles Imperial Land Co.*, 40 L. J. Ch. 93).

BEAST GATE.—*V.* CATTLE GATE.

BEASTS.—" The Beasts of *Parque* or *Chase*, properly extend to the Bucke, the Doe, the Foxe, the Marten, the Roe ; but, in a common and legall sense, to all the Beasts of the Forrest." (Co. Litt. 233 a.)

" Beasts of *Forrests* be properly Hart, Hinde, Bucke, Hare, Boar and Wolfe ; but legally all wild beasts of venery." (Ib.)

Beasts of the *Warren* are " Hares, Conies and Roes." (Ib.)

Beasts of the *Plough* ; *V.* Co. Litt. 47 a, b ; Woodf. 449.

" Beasts that gain his land " (51 H. 3, stat. 4), does not include cart Colts and young Steers, unbroken to harness or the plough (*Keen* v. *Priest*, 4 H. & N. 236 ; 28 L. J. Ex. 157).

BECOME.—"Become a Bankrupt," s. 7 (2) Bills of Sale Act, 1882; *V. Ex p. Allam,* 14 Q. B. D. 43.

V. ENTITLED: ELDEST.

BEER.—Summer's Botanic Beer, manufactured from fermented sugar and water, and flavoured with herbs, is "Beer" within the meaning of the Inl. Rev. Act, 1885; and to retail it necessitates the holding of an Excise license (*Howorth* v. *Minns,* 56 L. T. 316; 51 J. P. 181). The effect of such a ruling would seem to be that no kind of "Beer" containing over 2 per cent. of proof spirit can be sold without a license.

V. EXCISEABLE LIQUOR: SPIRITUOUS LIQUORS.

BEER-HOUSE.—"Beer-house" means a place where beer is sold to be consumed *on* the premises; but a "Beer-shop" means a place where Beer is sold by retail, and it is immaterial whether it is to be consumed on the premises or not (*London and Suburban Land Co.* v. *Field,* 50 L. J. Ch. 549; 16 Ch. D. 645; 44 L. T. 444: *Holt* v. *Collyer,* 50 L. J. Ch. 311; 16 Ch. D. 718; 44 L. T. 214; 29 W. R. 502: *St. Alban's* v. *Battersby,* 47 L. J. Q. B. 571; 3 Q. B. D. 359; 26 W. R. 679; 38 L. T. 685: *Nicoll* v. *Fenning,* 51 L. J. Ch. 166; 19 Ch. D. 258; 30 W. R. 95; 45 L. T. 738). Therefore a covenant against a "Beer-*Shop*" will prohibit a "Beer-*House*:" not so, *vice versâ* (*London & N. W. Ry.* v. *Garnett,* 39 L. J. Ch. 25; L. R. 9 Eq. 26; 21 L. T. 352; 18 W. R. 246: *Holt* v. *Collyer,* sup.).

V. ALE-HOUSE: PUBLIC-HOUSE.

BEER-SHOP.—*V.* BEER-HOUSE.

BEFORE.—"Before" in s. 40, subs. (b) Bankry. Act, 1883, means "next before" (*Re Smith,* 55 L. J. Q. B. 288; 17 Q. B. D. 4; 54 L. T. 307; 34 W. R. 535).

V. AFORESAID: AT: NOT BEFORE.

BEFORE OR AFTER.—"Dying before or after;" *V. Kendall* v. *Burt,* W. N. (73), 151.

BEFORE PAYABLE.—Gift over "before payable;" *V.* Chitty, Eq. Ind. 7412: "before becoming entitled;" *V.* Ib. 7415.

BEFORE THE PEOPLE.—"Their Lordships are of opinion that the words 'Before the People' (Rubric preceding Prayer of Consecration in Communion Office) coupled with the direction as to the manual acts, are meant to be equivalent to 'In the Sight of the People.' They have no doubt that the Rubric requires the manual acts to be so done that, in a reasonable and practical sense, the communicants, especially if they are conveniently placed for receiving the Holy Sacrament, as is pre-supposed in the Office, may be witnesses of, *i.e.*, may see them. What is ordered to be done 'Before the People,' when it is the subject of the sense, not of hearing, but of sight, cannot be done 'Before' them unless those of them who are properly placed for that purpose can see it. It was contended that 'Before the People,' meant nothing more than 'In the Church,' to guard against an anterior and secret consecration of the elements. But if the words 'Before the People' were absent, the manual acts, and the rest of the Service, could not be performed elsewhere than in the Church and in that sense *coram populo*, nor could the sacrament be distributed except in the place and at the time of its consecration; this argument would, therefore, reduce to silence the words 'Before the People,' which are an emphatic part of the declaration of the purpose for which the preparatory acts are to be done. That declaration applies not to the Service as a whole, nor to the consecration of the elements as a whole, but to the manual acts separately and specifically" (per Cairns, L. C., delivering jdgmt. of P. C. *Ridsdale* v. *Clifton*, 46 L. J. P. C. 61; 2 P. D. 276).

BEG.—*V.* Precatory Trust.

BEGIN.—"Begin to Demolish;" *V.* Demolish.
"Begin to form a New Street;" *V.* New Street.

BEGOTTEN.—*V.* 2 Co. Litt. 20 b: Born: To be Born.

BEHALF.—*V.* In that behalf: On behalf.

BEHIND.—As to the phrase "Leaving no Issue *behind him*;" *V.* 2 Jarm. 509.

BEING.—"Being," as used in a sense similar to that of the ablative absolute, has sometimes been translated as "having been;" but it properly denotes a state or condition existent at the time when the conclusion of law or fact has to be ascertained.

Thus the phrase, "*being a Trader*," in the Bankry. Act, 1869 (32 & 33 V. c. 71) meant "carrying on trade at the time when the act in question is committed" (per Jessel, M. R., *Ex p. McGeorge*, 51 L. J. Ch. 910; 20 Ch. D. 697). Therefore a trader who had absolutely ceased trading was not liable to the consequences of a trader-debtor's summons under sub-s. 6, s. 6 of that Act (*Ex p. Schomberg*, 10 Ch. 172; 23 W. R. 204); nor to be adjudicated bankrupt for departing from his dwelling under sub-s. 3, s. 6 (*Ex p. McGeorge*, sup.); but if he had the intention to resume trading he was still a trader (*Ex p. Salaman*, 21 Ch. D. 394; 47 L. T. 495; 31 W. R. 282).

"Being *in England*;" *V.* Living.

V. Entering or Being: Time Being.

Machinery, &c., "standing or being;" *V.* Erected.

"Being," may create a covenant,—*e.g.* in a lessee's covenant to repair premises, "the same *being* first put in repair by the lessor," these latter words create a covenant by the lessor (*Cannock* v. *Jones*, 3 Ex. 233 ; 5 Ib. 713 ; 18 L. J. Ex. 204); and so, probably, in such a covenant, do the words "being allowed sufficient rough timber" (*Martyn* v. *Clue*, 22 L. J. Q. B. 147 ; 18 Q. B. 661 ; *Va. Mucklestone* v. *Thomas*, Willes, 146), but in the way *Martyn* v. *Clue* was presented, it was only necessary to regard the phrase as creating a condition precedent, on which latter point *Vf. Neale* v. *Ratcliffe*, 20 L. J. Q. B. 130 ; 15 Q. B. 916 : *Coward* v. *Gregory*, 36 L. J. C. P. 1 ; L. R. 2 C. P. 153, 172. So, in such a covenant, lessor "*Finding, Allowing* and *Assigning* timber sufficient" was held to create a condition precedent (*Thomas* v. *Cadwallader*, Willes, 496); but "*Having or Taking*" bote, was held only to amount to a license to the lessee (*Bristol* v. *Jones*, 28 L. J. Q. B. 201 ; 1 E. & E. 484). *V.* FINDING.

BELIEF.—"In the full Belief;" *V.* PRECATORY TRUST.

BELONG.—An under-bailiff sending unwholesome meat to market, is not a "person to whom the same belongs" within s. 117, P. H. Act, 1875 (*Newton* v. *Monkcom*, 58 L. T. 231 ; 4 Times Rep. 205).

BELONGING.—Salvage for saving the lives of "persons belonging to" a *Ship*, s. 458 (2), Merchant Shipping Act, 1854, comprises passengers as well as the crew (*The Fusilier*, 34 L. J. P. M. & A. 25 ; 3 Moo. N. S. 51). In that case Dr. Lushington said, "I think that nothing is more common than to say of passengers by a ship, that they are passengers 'belonging' to the ship, and would be included under the expression 'persons.'"

By Sturges Bourne's Act (59 G. 3, c. 12), s. 17, churchwardens and overseers are to hold as a body corporate all buildings, &c., "belonging" to the *Parish*. Property, though applicable to general parochial purposes, is not within this phrase if the legal estate therein be vested in known existing Trustees (*St. Nicholas, Deptford*, v. *Sketchley*, 17 L. J. M. C. 17 ; 8 Q. B. 394 : over-ruling *Rumball* v. *Munt*, 15 L. J. Q. B. 180 ; 8 Q. B. 382). *Vf.* Tudor, Char. Trusts, 240–243.

As to the phrase "*Belonging or appertaining;*" *V. Williams* v. *Phillips*, 51 L. J. Q. B. 102 ; 8 Q. B. D. 437. These "are not words of art" (per Pollock, C.B., *Maitland* v. *Mackinnon*, 32 L. J. Ex. 49 ; 1 H. & C. 607). *Vf.* as to their interpretation, and as to the phrase "*Thereunto Belonging;*" 1 Jarm. 782 ; 2 Platt, 34 : *Kingsmill* v. *Millard*, 11 Ex. 313. "The words 'thereto belonging' may, perhaps, *primâ facie*, be considered to mean something held under the same title as and *occupied* with the subject-matter of the devise to which they are annexed" (Watson, Eq. 1322).

Bequest of "Effects belonging to the *Business*," includes the Fixtures (*Pinder* v. *Pinder*, 18 W. R. 309).

V. APPERTAINING : MILL.

BELOVED WIFE.—"A bequest by a husband to his '*beloved* wife,' not mentioning her by name, applies exclusively to the individual who answers the description at the date of the Will, and is not to be extended to an after-taken wife" (Wms. Exs. 1108, citing *Garratt* v. *Niblock*, 1 R. & M. 629). In the note, however, it is added, "this point cannot arise since the new Wills Act; for the second marriage would revoke the Will. But a similar question may occur in respect of a bequest by a testator to the wife of another person : *V. Boreham* v. *Bignall*, 8 Hare, 131 ; 19 L. J. Ch. 461 : *Re Lyne*, L. R. 8 Eq. 65 ; 38 L. J. Ch. 471." *Vf. Re Morrisson*, W. N. (88) 212.

V. WIFE.

BENEFICE.—This word occurs in cap. 14, Magna Carta. It is "a large word, and is taken for any ecclesiasticall promotion or spirituall living whatsoever" (2 Inst. 29 ; *Vf.* 3 Ib. 155 ; Elph. 562). As to what is a "Benefice with Cure" within 13 Eliz. c. 20 ; *V. M'Bean* v. *Deane*, 30 Ch. D. 520 ; 55 L. J. Ch. 19 ; 33 W. R. 924 ; 1 Times Rep. 624.

BENEFICIAL.—"Beneficial" and "Profitable" are not convertible terms (Dwar. 683).

A testamentary appointment of all property over which the testator has "any beneficial *Disposing Power*" is not confined to a Power exerciseable for the benefit of the testator or his estate (per Pearson, J., *Von Brockdorff* v. *Malcolm*, 55 L. J. Ch. 121 ; 30 Ch. D. 172 ; 53 L. T. 263 ; 33 W. R. 934) ; but the contrary was held by Fry, J., in *Ames* v. *Cadogan* (48 L. J. Ch. 762 ; 12 Ch. D. 868).

The "Beneficial *Enjoyment*" of property by a successor, as mentioned in s. 21, Sucn. Dy. Act, 1853, "means no more than in his own right, and for his own benefit, not as a trustee for another" (per Ld. Wensleydale, *A.-G.* v. *Sefton*, 34 L. J. Ex. 104. *V.* BENEFICIALLY ENTITLED.) So, also, "beneficial *Interest*" in s. 2 of the same Act means "a beneficial enjoyment in contradistinction to holding as trustee" (per Ld. Chelmsford, Ib. 106).

A direction in a Will that a Solicitor Trustee shall have his profit Costs, is a "beneficial *Gift* or Interest" within s. 15, 1 V. c. 26 (*Re Barber*, 55 L. J. Ch. 373 ; 31 Ch. D. 665 ; 54 L. T. 375 ; 34 W. R. 395 : *Re Pooley*, 40 Ch. D. 1).

"Beneficial *Interest*," Part 2, Merchant Shipping Act, 1854; *V.* s. 3, Mer. Shipping Act, 1862 ; and *Vth.* 1 Maude & P. 55, 56. "Beneficial *Interest*" in a Telegraph, s. 7, 31 & 32 V. c. 110 ; *V. R.* v. *Coleridge*, 45 L. J. Q. B. 649.

There must be a "Beneficial *Occupation*" of a tenement to make the occupier assessable to Poor Rate under the Statute of Elizabeth. The word "beneficial" in that connection is not the same as "profitable" to the person or corporation rated (*V.* the cases hereon collected, 3 Chitt. Stat. 3rd Ed., Tit. "Poor," 1019 *et seq.*). The border-line of these cases was set by *Gambier* v. *Lydford* (23 L. J. M. C. 69 ; 3 E. & B. 346 ; confirmed by

Martin v. *West Derby*, 11 Q. B. D. 145 ; 52 L. J. M. C. 66 : *Vf. Mersey Docks* v. *Llanelian*, 54 L. J. Q. B. 49 ; 14 Q. B. D. 770 : *Dewsbury W. Works Bd.* v. *Penistone*, 55 L. J. M. C. 121 ; 50 J. P. 644 ; 17 Q. B. D. 384 ; 54 L. T. 592 ; 34 W. R. 622, and cases there cited). As a general rule, where a tenement is *capable* of beneficial occupation it is rateable, unless occupied by the Crown or its servants for Crown purposes (*Jones* v. *Mersey Docks*, 11 H. L. Ca. 443 ; 35 L. J. M. C. 1 ; 13 W. R. 1069). A Reformatory School is rateable (*Tunnicliffe* v. *Birkdale*, 56 L. J. M. C. 109 ; 20 Q. B. D. 450 ; 36 W. R. 360 ; 52 J. P. 452 : overruling *Sheppard* v. *Bradford*, 33 L. J. M. C. 182 ; 16 C. B. N. S. 369 ; 12 W. R. 867), and so are School Board premises (*R.* v. *West Bromwich*, 53 L. J. M. C. 153 ; 13 Q. B. D. 929 : *R.* v. *London School Bd.*, 55 L. J. M. C. 169 ; 17 Q. B. D. 738 ; 55 L. T. 384 ; 34 W. R. 583 ; 50 J. P. 419) ; and so is a Sewage Farm worked by a Local Authority (obliged to sewer) and worked by them at an inevitable loss (*Burton-on-Trent Case*, 34 S. J. 94 : *Va. Metrop. Bd. of Works* v. *West Ham*, 40 L. J. M. C. 30 ; L. R. 6 Q. B. 193) ; but not Owen's College, Manchester, which cannot be sold or let (*Owen's College* v. *Chorlton-upon-Medlock*, 56 L. J. M. C. 29 ; 18 Q. B. D. 403 ; 56 L. T. 373 ; 35 W. R. 236 ; 51 J. P. 356).

"Beneficial *Owner* ;" *V. Re Roulston*, 21 L. R. Ir. 503.

"Beneficial *Winding-up*" of a Company, s. 131, Companies Act, 1862 ; *V. Hire Purchase Co.* v. *Richens*, 20 Q. B. D. 387 ; 58 L. T. 460 ; 36 W. R. 365 ; 4 Times Rep. 184.

BENEFICIALLY ENTITLED.—"Beneficially entitled to possession" (s. 2, subs. 5, Settled Land Act, 1882), "does not mean entitled and deriving a benefit from possession, but beneficially entitled in the sense of being entitled for one's own benefit, if there is any benefit to be derived from the estate, and not simply as trustee for others" (per Cotton, L.J., *Re Jones*, 53 L. J. Ch. 811 ; 26 Ch. D. 736). *Vf. Re Clitheroe*, 31 Ch. D. 135 : *Re Atkinson*, Ib. 577 : *Re Strangways*, 34 Ch. D. 423.

BENEFICIALLY INTERESTED.—"A person having a contingent interest in real estate (*Re Sheppard*, 4 D. G. F. & J. 423 ; 9 Jur. N. S. 59) is a person 'Beneficially Interested' within the meaning of s. 37, Trustee Act, 1850 ; and so is a creditor who has obtained a decree for the administration and sale of real estate (*Re Wragg*, 1 D. G. J. & S. 356) ; and also, it seems, a purchaser under a decree who has paid his purchase money into Court (*Ayles* v. *Cox*, 17 Bea. 584). The committee of lunatic *cestui que trusts* is not a person 'Beneficially Interested' within this section (*Re Bourke*, 2 D. G. J. & S. 426) :" Dan. Ch. Pr. 2120.

BENEFIT.—A Power to Trustees to make advances for a person's "Benefit," enables them to make advances to set up in business that person's husband (*Re Kershaw*, 37 L. J. Ch. 751 ; L. R. 6 Eq. 322) ; or to pay the person's debts (*Lowther* v. *Bentinck*, 44 L. J. Ch. 197 ; L. R.

19 Eq. 167 : *Sv. Re Price*, 34 Ch. D. 603). *Vf. Re Hargreaves*, W. N. (85) 174. *V.* ADVANCEMENT.

Assignment of Copyright with all "Property and Benefit;" *V. Ex p. Hutchins and Romer*, 4 Q. B. D. 90, 483.

"Benefit of Children;" *V. Re Pocock*, 6 Ch. 445 : *Scotney* v. *Lomer*, 29 Ch. D. 535 ; 31 Ib. 380 : *Urquhart* v. *Butterfield*, 36 Ch. D. 55 ; 37 Ib. 358.

BENEFIT OF SURVIVORSHIP.—"There is a difference between a gift over of the shares of any prior legatees to the survivors, and a gift to several 'with Benefit of Survivorship.' The latter expression is very general, and may without impropriety be held to pervade the whole fund, so as to carry accrued as well as original shares" (2 Jarm. 714, citing *Re Crawhall*, 8 D. G. M. & G. 480 : *Sv. Vorley* v. *Richardson*, Ib. 126 ; 25 L. J. Ch. 335).

As to this phrase giving a vested interest ; *V. Corneck* v. *Wadman*, L. R. 7 Eq. 80, wherein *Donald* v. *Bryce*, 16 Bea. 581, was doubted : *Va. Daniel* v. *Gosset*, 19 Bea. 478.

BENERTH.—"*Benerth* signifieth the service of the plough and cart" (Co. Litt. 86 a). "*Ben-erth* was precarious tillage service with horse and cart : *gavel-erth* was tillage service certain : *ben-rip* is a precarious service of reaping : *gavel-rip* was the same service only certain" (Elton, Ten. Kent, 34). *Va.* Spelm. ; Cowell, Law Dict. ; PRECARIÆ.

BENEVOLENCE: BENEVOLENT.—A bequest for objects of "Benevolence and Liberality" (*Morice* v. *Bp. of Durham*, 9 Ves. 399, 10 Ib. 522), or for "Benevolent Purposes" (*James* v. *Allen*, 3 Mer. 17 : *Re Jarman*, 47 L. J. Ch. 675 ; 8 Ch. D. 584) is not good.

V. CHARITY.

BENEWORK.—*V.* PRECARIÆ.

BEN-RIP.—*V.* BENERTH.

BEQUEATH.—*V.* DEVISE.

BEQUEATHED.—The word "Bequeathed" (though perhaps not in itself a technical word) is primarily applicable only to property passing under a testamentary disposition (*Re Armstrong*, 49 L. J. Ch. 53 ; 42 L. T. 823).

V. DEVISE.

BERCARIA.—"*Berquarium* or *bercaria*, commeth of *berc*, an old Saxon word, used at this day for barkes and rindes of trees, and signifieth a tan-house, or a heath-house, where barkes or rindes of trees are laid to tan withal : and *berquarii* are mentioned in Domesday. It signifieth also, and more legally, a sheep-cote, of the French word *bergerie*" (Co. Litt. 5 b). *Vf.* Cowell, Law Dict. ; Touch. 95.

BEREWICA.—"*Berewica*, or *berewit*, in Domesday signifieth a towne" (Co. Litt. 116 a). But it is also said to mean "a manor, or rather a detached member of a manor, a town, a hamlet, a sub-manor, a corn farm" (Elph. 563, citing Spelm.; Cowell, Law Dict.; 1 Ellis, Introd. Domesday, 240).

BESEECH.—*V.* PRECATORY TRUST.

BESET.—"Picketing" workmen is to "Beset" them within s. 7, sub-s. 4, Conspiracy and Protection of Property Act, 1875, 38 & 39 V. c. 86 (*R.* v. *Bauld*, Stone, 465). But s. 7 of the Act provides that "attending at or near the house or place where a person resides, or works, or carries on business, or happens to be, or the approach to such house or place, *in order merely to obtain or communicate information*, shall not be deemed a 'Watching or Besetting,' within the meaning of this section."

BESIDES.—When provisions are made for children "besides" an eldest son, no children take unless there be a son; *secus*, if the phrase is "OTHER THAN" (*Walcott* v. *Bloomfield*, 4 Dr. & War. 235; 6 Ir. Eq. 227: *Vth. Simpson* v. *Frew*, 5 Ir. Ch. 517).

BEST ENDEAVOURS.—*V.* UTMOST.

BEST RENT.—The "Best Rent" means the most rack-rent that can reasonably be gotten for the whole term of the lease to be granted, having regard to the solvency of the proposed tenants and what may fairly be considered for the permanent benefit of the property; and when a power to grant a lease at the "Best Rent" be exercised fairly and honestly, a reasonable latitude will be allowed to the donee of the power, so that when he has to choose between two or more responsible offers, not widely differing in amount, he is not bound to accept the highest offer (1 Platt, 483–489; Woodf. 388, 389).

The Settled Land Act, 1882, enabling Tenants for life to grant Leases, provides (s. 2, subs. 7), that "Every Lease shall reserve the *Best Rent* that can reasonably be obtained, regard being had to any Fine taken, and to any money laid out or to be laid out for the benefit of the settled land, and generally to the circumstances of the case." The value of a contemporaneously surrendered Lease may be taken into consideration in determining such "Best Rent" (*Re Rawlins*, L. R. 1 Eq. 286).

V. ANCIENT RENT.

BETTING HOUSE.—*V.* COMMON BETTING HOUSE.

BETWEEN.—A testamentary gift to two or more "between," or "between or amongst," them creates a tenancy in common (Wms. Exs. 1469: 2 Jarm. 257: *A.-G.* v. *Fletcher*, L. R. 13 Eq. 128; 41 L. J. Ch. 167); and so though the phrase be "jointly and between them" (*Perkins*

v. *Baynton*, 1 B. C. C. 118 : *Richardson* v. *Richardson*, 14 Sim. 526). *V.* AMONG.

As to an agreement and declaration "between and by the parties hereto ;" *V.* AGREED AND DECLARED.

BEYOND SEAS.—By the 19 & 20 V. c. 97, s. 12, no part of the United Kingdom of Great Britain and Ireland, nor the islands of Man, Guernsey, Jersey, Alderney, and Sark, or any islands adjacent to any of them are to be deemed to be "Beyond Seas" within the meaning of the Statute of Limitation, 4 & 5 Anne, c. 16. (Prior to 19 & 20 V. Ireland was "beyond seas" *quà* 4 & 5 Anne, *Lane* v. *Bennett*, 1 M. & W. 70).

The words "Beyond Seas" are not to be construed literally but are synonymous with "out of the realm or territories," and include, *e.g.* India (Add. T. 59, citing *Ruckmaboye* v. *Lulloobhoy Mottichund*, 8 Moo. P. C. 4). *V.* REALM.

"Offences committed on *Land beyond the Seas*, for which an indictment may legally be preferred in England or Wales," s. 2, 11 & 12 V. c. 42 ; *V. R.* v. *Eyre*, 37 L. J. M. C. 159 ; L. R. 3 Q. B. 487.

BIGAMY.—"Every one commits the felony called Bigamy, who, being married, marries any other person during the life of his or her wife or husband.

"The expression 'being married' means legally married. The word 'marries' means go through a form of marriage which the law of the place where such form is used recognizes as binding, whether the parties are by that law competent to contract marriage or not, and although by their fraud the form employed may, apart from the Bigamy, have been insufficient to constitute a binding marriage.

"Provided that this definition does not extend (a) to a second marriage contracted elsewhere than in England and Ireland by any other than a subject of Her Majesty ; nor (b) to any person marrying a second time, whose husband or wife has been continually absent from such person for seven years then last past, and has not been known by such person to be living within that time (or whose husband or wife is reasonably believed to be dead, *R.* v. *Tolson*, 58 L. J. M. C. 97 ; 23 Q. B. D. 168 ; 60 L. T. 899) ; (c) nor to any person who at the time of such second marriage was divorced from the bond of the first marriage, nor to any person whose first marriage has been declared void by the sentence of any Court of competent jurisdiction.

"A *Divorce* à vinculo matrimonii pronounced by a foreign Court between persons who have contracted marriage in England and who continue to be domiciled in England, on grounds which would not justify such a Divorce in England, is not a Divorce within the meaning of this clause" (Steph. Cr. 188, 189, citing 24 & 25 V. c. 100, s. 57, as explained by the authorities there also cited).

Vf. Arch. Cr. 1008–1015 : Rosc. Cr. 326–342.

BILL.—"Bill, Placard or Poster," s. 18, 46 & 47 V. c. 51, s. 14, 47 & 48 V. c. 70; *V. Barstow Case*, 5 Times Rep. 159: *Denbigh and Flint Case*, Ib. 160: *Shrewsbury Case*, Ib. 160.

BILL OF EXCHANGE.—"A Bill of Exchange is an Unconditional Order in Writing, addressed by one person to another, signed by the person giving it, requiring the person to whom it is addressed to pay, ON DEMAND, or at a fixed or DETERMINABLE FUTURE TIME, a SUM CERTAIN in money to or to the order of a specified person, or to bearer" (s. 3, Bills of Ex. Act, 1882). That section further provides that,

"An Order to pay out of a particular fund is not Unconditional within the meaning of this section; but an unqualified Order to pay, coupled with (a) an indication of a particular fund out of which the drawee is to reimburse himself or a particular account to be debited with the amount, or (b) a statement of the transaction which gives rise to the Bill, is unconditional." And further that

"A Bill is not invalid by reason—

(a) That it is not dated;

(b) That it does not specify the value given, or that any value has been given therefor;

(c) That it does not specify the place where it is drawn, or the place where it is payable."

V. APPROVED BILL: *Cp.* PROMISSORY NOTE.

A document otherwise in the form of a Bill of Exchange but having no drawer's name to it, is not a Bill of Exchange within s. 22, 24 & 25 V. c. 98 (*R.* v. *Harper*, 50 L. J. M. C. 90; 7 Q. B. D. 78).

BILL OF SALE.—An Agreement for sale of furniture on the ordinary Hire and Purchase System is not a Bill of Sale by the vendee (*Ex p. Crawcour*, 9 Ch. D. 419; nom. *Re Robertson*, 47 L. J. Bank. 94); nor is a Building Agreement, which provides that all materials brought by the builder on the land shall become the property of the freeholder (*Reeves* v. *Barlow*, 12 Q. B. D. 436; 53 L. J. Q. B. 192: *Vth. Re Hall, Ex p. Close*, 54 L. J. Q. B. 43; 14 Q. B. D. 386; 51 L. T. 795; 33 W. R. 228); nor is a "Letter of Hypothecation accompanying a deposit of goods by merchants or factors, or pawn-tickets given by pawnbrokers, or in fact any case where the object and effect of the transaction are immediately to transfer the possession from the grantor to the grantee" (per Cave, J., *Re Hall, Ex p. Close*, sup.: *Va. Hilton* v. *Tucker*, 57 L. J. Ch. 973; 39 Ch. D. 669; 59 L. T. 172; 36 W. R. 762: *Re Hardwick*, 55 L. J. Q. B. 490; 17 Q. B. D. 690; 35 W. R. 2). *Vf. Manchester, S. & L. Ry.* v. *North Central Wagon Co.*, 58 L. J. Ch. 219; 13 App. Ca. 554: *Redhead* v. *Westwood*, 59 L. T. 293: *Ex p. Collins, Re Yarrow*, 34 S. J. 23, 33.

The definition of a Bill of Sale, for the purposes of the B. of S. Acts, 1878 and 1882, is given in s. 4 of the Act of 1878. But whilst this definition has been adopted for the Act of 1882 by s. 3 of the latter, that same section provides that the peculiar provisions of the Act of 1882 shall not apply to a B. of S. not given "by way of security for the payment of money."

As to what is an ASSURANCE; AUTHORITY OR LICENSE; RECEIPT; TRANSFER; ORDINARY COURSE within that definition, or MARRIAGE SETTLEMENT; or VESSEL within its exception; *V.* those words respectively.

Va. Rosc. N. P. 1151, 1152; Reed on Bills of Sale, 6 Ed. 12–26.

As to "Bill of Sale" in s. 11, Trinidad Ordinance, No. 15, 1884; *V. Tennant* v. *Howatson,* 57 L. J. P. C. 110; 13 App. Ca. 489; 58 L. T. 646.

BILL WITH OPTION OF CASH.—*V.* CASH WITH OPTION OF BILL.

BIND.—By s. 62, Com. L. Pro. Act, 1854, a garnishee order *nisi* shall "bind" the debt in the garnishee's hands. That means, "that the debtor, or those claiming under him, shall not have power to convey or do any act as against the right of a party in whose favour the debt is bound; and we construe it as not giving any property in the debt in the nature of a mortgage or lien, but a mere right to have the security enforced" (per Campbell, C. J., in delivering the jdgmt. of the Q. B. in *Holmes* v. *Tutton,* 24 L. J. Q. B. 351: 5 E. & B. 67).

But in construing an obligation whereby a Joint Stock Co. did "Bind" themselves and their undertaking, James, L. J., said,—"It seems to me that the word 'Charge,' that the word 'Bind,' and the word 'Oblige,' (whatever may be the ordinary use by conveyancers of one or the other of them), in point of English language and of legal language mean the same. 'To Bind' means 'to Charge,' and 'to Charge' means 'to Bind,' and 'Oblige' means to charge or bind. All these words are in my opinion absolutely synonymous." (*Re Florence Land Co., Ex p. Moor,* 48 L. J. Ch. 145; 10 Ch. D. 530: *Sv.* jdgmt. of Jessel, M. R., in that case.) Yet it seems clear that "to Charge" property is to create a lien on it (*V.* CHARGE); whilst in *Holmes* v. *Tutton* (sup.) that was held to be a quality which did not inhere in the word "Bind," at least in the section there being construed.

BIND OVER.—Where power is given to Justices to "bind over," or to cause a person to do a certain thing, and such person being present, shall refuse to be bound or to do such thing, a power is implied to commit to prison until compliance (Dwar. 672). *Vf. R.* v. *Dunn,* 12 Q. B. 1026; 18 L. J. M. C. 41.

BINDING.—"Made Binding;" *V.* REQUIRED.

BIRD OF GAME.—*V.* GAME, *Animals.*

BLACK: BLACK-LEG, &c.—It was said by counsel, arg., in *Barnett* v. *Allen* (27 L. J. Ex. 412; 3 H. & N. 376; 31 L. T. O. S. 217), that the prefix "Black" has always a bad meaning in such terms as "Blackguard," "Black-leg," "Black-sheep." Either word would probably be Libel if written; but neither, probably, would, *per se,* be Slander.

"Black-*leg:*" "Black-*sheep:*"—In *Barnett* v. *Allen* (sup.) the Court was equally divided as to whether calling a man a "Black-*leg*," as meaning a disreputable gambler, was actionable Slander. But to write of a person that he is a "Black-leg," or "Black-sheep," with an innuendo that the phrase imputed that the person was of a bad character, would be Libel (*McGregor* v. *Gregory*, 12 L. J. Ex. 204 ; 11 M. & W. 289 ; 2 Dowl. P. C. 769 : *O'Brien* v. *Clement*, 16 L. J. Ex. 77 ; 16 M. & W. 159). In *Barnett* v. *Allen*, Pollock, C. B., said that the sense in which he had always understood "Black-leg" was "a professed gambler, a person who makes a business of betting—not necessarily dishonest, though disreputable." Watson, B., thought the word had no precise signification ; but Martin and Bramwell, BB., thought it imputed the indictable offence of cheating at cards, within s. 17, 8 & 9 V. c. 109.

V. Professed Gambler.

BLASPHEMY.—"Every publication is said to be blasphemous which contains matter relating to God, Jesus Christ, the Bible, or the Book of Common Prayer, intended to wound the feelings of mankind, or to excite contempt and hatred against the Church by law established, or to promote immorality.

"Publications intended in good faith to propagate opinions on religious subjects, which the person who publishes them regards as true, are not blasphemous (within the meaning of this definition) merely because their publication is likely to wound the feelings of those who believe such opinions to be false, or because their general adoption might tend by lawful means to alterations in the constitution of the Church by law established" (Steph. Cr. 108, 109 ; *wh: V.* for an alternative and stricter definition, which as there pointed out would probably not be now adopted).

Vf. Arch. Cr. 890, 891 ; Rosc. Cr. 695, 696.

BLOOD.—*V.* In Blood.

BOARD.—*V.* Fire on Board : On Board.

BOARD OF GUARDIANS.—*V.* s. 16 (1), (3) Interp. Act, 1889.

BOARD OF TRADE.—*V.* s. 12 (8), Interp. Act, 1889.

BOAT.—"Boat" includes a Steamboat (*Tisdell* v. *Combe*, 7 L. J. M. C. 48 ; 7 A. & E. 788).

BOCLAND.—*V.* Co. Litt. 6 a, 58 a ; Spelm. ; 1 Stubbs' Constit. Hist. ch. 5 ; 1 Ellis, Introd. Domesday, 230 n.

BODILY HARM.—*V.* Inflict.

BODY CORPORATE.—"Every Body Politic, or Corporate, and person and persons," s. 65, 4 G. 4, c. 95 ; held to include Parishes (*R.* v. *Barton*, 9 L. J. M. C. 23 ; 11 A. & E. 343 ; 3 P. & D. 190).

The entrance fees and subscriptions of a Social Club are not "funds voluntarily contributed to any Body Corporate or Unincorporate" within 48 & 49 V. c. 51, s. 11 (6); and the Club is, therefore, not exempt from the duty imposed by that Act (*Re New University Club*, 18 Q. B. D. 720; 56 L. J. Q. B. 462; 56 L. T. 909; 35 W. R. 774).

BOG.—*V.* Turf Moss.

BOILLOURIE.—*V.* Saliva.

BONÂ FIDE.—The equivalent of this phrase is, "honestly." The correct province of this phrase is, therefore, to qualify things or actions that have relation to the mind or motive of the individual; and it has no meaning when joined to things or actions common to all mankind, though sometimes it is thus used in a figurative, but inaccurate, sense. A fact completely within physical apprehension can neither be *bonâ*, nor *malâ fide*: a mental fact may be either.

Thus the phrase "bonâ fide *Traveller*" in s. 1, 17 & 18 V. c. 79, means just the same thing as "Traveller;" for, as Williams, J., very pertinently asked, "Can a man be said to be a *malâ fide* traveller? The question is,—Was he a traveller?" (*Atkinson* v. *Sellers*, 28 L. J. M. C. 13; and *Vh.* Traveller).

So "*bonâ fide*" in the phrase, "the actual and bonâ fide *Occupation*" of lands or tenements in s. 18, Reform Act, 1832, would seem surplusage,—for how could an "actual" occupation be *malâ fide*?

"I suppose anybody would have a difficulty in defining the difference between a '*Parishioner*' and a 'bonâ fide Parishioner.' I do not know what difference there is between them" (per Bramwell, B., *Etherington* v. *Wilson*, 45 L. J. Ch. 158; 1 Ch. D. 160).

But there may be a Bonâ fide Act, Belief, Intention, Claim, Objection, or Mistake; or a person's Conduct may be bonâ fide. Each of these is, so to speak, a mental fact having its origin in the individual.

As to a *Conveyance* being bonâ fide within 13 Eliz. c. 5; *V. Twyne's Case*, 3 Rep. 81; 1 Sm. L. C. 1; and for the cases on "Bonâ fide" as used in the old Bankry. Acts, and on "Good Faith" as used in the Act of 1869; *V.* Yate Lee, 436.

"Bonâ fide *Charitable Gift*;" *V. Fulham* v. *Thanet*, 7 Q. B. D. 539.

Bonâ fide *Lease*, s. 2, 12 & 13 V. c. 26; *V. Moffett* v. *Gough*, 1 L. R. Ir. 331.

As to the bonâ fide *Belief* that a first wife or husband is dead so as to excuse from Bigamy; *V. R.* v. *Tolson*, 58 L. J. M. C. 97; 23 Q. B. D. 168; 60 L. T. 899: Steph. Cr. 27, n. 4.—Bonâ fide belief by a Constable that an offence has been committed; *V. Ballinger* v. *Ferris*, 5 L. J. M. C. 133; 1 M. & W. 628.—Bonâ fide belief in statements made in Co. Prospectus; *Derry* v. *Peek*, 58 L. J. Ch. 864; 14 App. Ca. 337; 38 W. R. 33; 61 L. T. 265; 5 Times Rep. 625.

"Payments really and bonâ fide made," s. 82, 6 G. 4, c. 16, mean payments which the party does not intend to reclaim (*Gibson* v. *Muskett*, 11 L. J. C. P. 225 ; 3 Sc. N. S. 419).

A "bonâ fide *Purchaser*" as mentioned in s. 26, 3 & 4 W. 4, c. 27 (and as it should seem, as a general phrase) means one who is "really a purchaser, and not merely a donee taking a gift under the form of a purchase" (per James, L.J., *Vane* v. *Vane*, 42 L. J. Ch. 299 ; 8 Ch. 383). A Judgment Creditor is not a purchaser within 27 Eliz. c. 4 (*Beavan* v. *Oxford*, 6 D. G. M. & G. 507) ; nor though he has taken out a garnishee summons is he "a bonâ fide purchaser" within s. 28, 23 & 24 V. c. 127 (*Dallow* v. *Garrold*, 14 Q. B. D. 543 ; 54 L. J. Q. B. 76 ; 52 L. T. 240 ; 33 W. R. 219).

The phrase "*bonâ fide*" is employed in several sections of Lord St. Leonards' Act to Amend the Law of Property (22 & 23 V. c. 35).

As to what will constitute a bonâ fide *Claim of Right* so as to oust the jurisdiction of inferior tribunals ; *V. White* v. *Feast*, 41 L. J. M. C. 81 ; L. R. 7 Q. B. 353 : *Cole* v. *Miles*, 57 L. J. M. C. 133 ; 36 W. R. 784 : *Leicester* v. *Holland*, 57 L. J. M. C. 75 : *Thompson* v. *Ingham*, 19 L. J. Q. B. 189 ; 1 L. M. & P. 216 : *R.* v. *Cridland*, 27 L. J. M. C. 28 ; 7 E. & B. 853 : *Hudson* v. *McRae*, 33 L. J. M. C. 65 ; 12 W. R. 80 : *Williams* v. *Adams*, 31 L. J. M. C. 109 ; 2 B. & S. 312 ; *V.* Fair and Reasonable.

As to what is a bonâ fide *Objection to Church Rates*, within s. 7, 53 G. 3, c. 127, so as to oust justices' jurisdiction ; *V. Pease* v. *Chaytor*, 31 L. J. M. C. 1 ; 1 B. & S. 658 : *R.* v. *Blackburn*, 32 L. J. M. C. 41 : and as to Quakers under s. 4, 7 & 8 W. 3, c. 34, *Backhouse* v. *Bishopwearmouth*, 30 L. J. M. C. 118.

A "bonâ fide *Mistake*" under Ord. 16, R. 2, R. S. C., includes a mistake of law as well as of fact (*Duckett* v. *Gover*, 46 L. J. Ch. 407 ; 6 Ch. D. 82 ; 25 W. R. 455 : *Mason* v. *Harris*, 11 Ch. D. 106 : *Tryon* v. *National Provident Inst.*, 16 Q. B. D. 678) ; but it must be a genuine mistake, and not an erroneous view of the law which has been deliberately adopted (*Clowes* v. *Hilliard*, 46 L. J. Ch. 271 ; 4 Ch. D. 413 ; 25 W. R. 224).

Execution "bonâ fide executed and levied," 2 & 3 V. c. 29, s. 1, meant "bona fides of the creditor who caused execution to issue and of the sheriff who is his minister" (per Abinger, C. B., *Belcher* v. *Magnay*, 13 L. J. Ex. 52; 12 M. & W. 109 : *Vf. Hall* v. *Wallace*, 10 L. J. Ex. 133 ; 7 M. & W. 358).

The modern phrase for a bonâ fide holder for value of a *Bill or Note* without notice of any imperfection, is "Holder in due course" (s. 29, B. of Ex. Act, 1882) ; *V.* Holder for Value.

As to a bonâ fide holder for value of *Bonds*, &c. ; *V. London & County Bank* v. *London & River Plate Bank*, 32 S. J. 128.

V. Good Faith.

BONDS.—Gift of ; *V. Hudleston* v. *Gouldsbury*, 10 Bea. 547 : *Mercer* v. *Mercer*, 10 Ir. Ch. 505 : *Kent* v. *Tapley*, 11 Jur. 940 : *Roberts* v. *Kuffin*, 2 Atk. 112.

BOOK : BOOKS.—By the Copyright Act of 1842 (5 & 6 V. c. 45), s. 2, a " Book " is to be construed to mean " every volume, part or division of a volume, pamphlet, sheet of letter-press, sheet of music, map, chart or plan separately published." Does this include a newspaper ? (*V. Cox* v. *Land and Water Journal Co.*, L. R. 9 Eq. 324 ; 39 L. J. Ch. 152 : *Walter* v. *Howe*, 17 Ch. D. 708 : *Cate* v. *Devon & Exeter Newspaper Co.*, 40 Ch. D. 500) ; *Punch* is such a "book" (*Bradbury* v. *Hotten*, 42 L. J. Ex. 28 ; L. R. 8 Ex. 1). Prints of all kinds (qy. also photographs) published together in a volume, form a " book," whether there be letter-press or not ; or " there may be such things as picture-books for those who cannot read letter-press " (per Jessel, M.R., *Maple* v. *Junior Army and Navy Stores*, 52 L. J. Ch. 71 : but *cp. Schove* v. *Schmincke*, inf.) ; and prints bound in a volume are none the less a " book " entitled to copyright because they are bound up with letter-press or with other prints not so entitled ; and so also of bound letter-press, for a " book " includes every part of a book (*Bogue* v. *Houlston*, 5 D. G. & S. 267 ; 21 L. J. Ch. 470, which case see explained in *Maple* v. *Junior Army and Navy Stores*, sup.) ; nor is a " book," whether composed of letter-press or prints only, or of both combined, less within the protection of the Copyright Act because it is used as an advertisement distributed gratis,—*e.g.* a trade catalogue, whether illustrated or not (*Hotten* v. *Arthur*, 1 Hem. & M. 603 ; 32 L. J. Ch. 771 : *Grace* v. *Newman*, L. R. 19 Eq. 623 ; 44 L. J. Ch. 298 : *Maple* v. *Junior Army and Navy Stores*, sup., which latter case definitely overrules *Cobbett* v. *Woodward*, L. R. 14 Eq. 407 ; 41 L. J. Ch. 656). *Vf.* PERIODICAL.

But an envelope with the following words printed on the outside,— " Entered at Stationers' Hall. Key enclosed. The Christograph : The Christians' Puzzle. Suitable for all sects and denominations. Every family should have it. Price, with key, 6d.," and containing inside a piece of card-board which, when held up to the light, cast a shadow resembling the well-known picture " Ecce Homo," and a slip of paper on which was printed an extract from Longfellow, was held not to be a " Book " within the Copyright Act (*Cable* v. *Marks*, 52 L. J. Ch. 107) ; nor is the printed face of a Forecast Barometer such a " book " (*Davis* v. *Committi*, 54 L. J. Ch. 419 ; 52 L. T. 539 ; 1 Times Rep. 216) ; nor an illustrated Album (*Schove* v. *Schmincke*, 55 L. J. Ch. 892 ; 33 Ch. D. 546 ; 55 L. T. 212 ; 34 W. R. 700). *V.* FIRST PUBLICATION.

Bound Manuscript Notes will sometimes (generally ?) pass under a *Bequest* of " Books " (*Willis* v. *Curtois*, 8 L. J. Ch. 105 ; 1 Bea. 189 ; Wms. Exs. 1205).

BOOK DEBTS.—Include all such debts as, in the ordinary course of carrying on business, would be entered in books, although not actually entered (*Shipley* v. *Marshall*, 32 L. J. C. P. 258 ; 14 C. B. N. S. 566) : *Va.* per Esher, M.R., *Offl. Rec.* v. *Tailby*, 56 L. J. Q. B. 33 : *Re Stevens*, W. N. (88) 110, 116.

An Assignment of "all" Book Debts "due and owing or which, during the continuance of this security, may become due and owing" to the grantor, is not too vague to include future debts (*Tailby* v. *Official Rec.*, 58 L. J. Q. B. 75; 13 App. Ca. 523, overruling *Belding* v. *Read*, 3 H. & C. 955; 34 L. J. Ex. 212; 11 Jur. N. S. 547; and *Tadman* v. *D'Epineuil*, 20 Ch. D. 758).

A Bequest of "Book Debts," held to include the testator's share of trade debts of a Partnership (*Toplis* v. *Vanderheyde*, 9 L. J. Ex. Eq. 27; 4 Y. & C. 173). *Vf. Terry* v. *Terry*, 33 Bea. 232; 12 W. R. 66; 9 L. T. 469: *Chick* v. *Blackmore*, 23 L. J. Ch. 622; 2 Sm. & G. 274; 2 W. R. 488.

BOOK OF ACCOUNTS.—The "Books of Accounts" mentioned in R. 259, Bankry. Rules, 1883, mean such books of account as are usual in the bankrupt's business, and do not extend to "letters, cheques, and vouchers from which books of account can be made up" (per Cave, J., *Re Winslow*, 55 L. J. Q. B. 238; 16 Q. B. D. 696; 54 L. T. 306; 34 W. R. 534; 3 Morr. 60).

BOOK OF ANTIQUITY.—*V.* LAW LIBRARY.

BOOKING UP.—*V. Walsh* v. *Walley*, 43 L. J. Q. B. 102; L. R. 9 Q. B. 367.

BOOKLAND.—*V.* BOCLAND.

BOONWORK.—*V.* PRECARIÆ.

BORDARII.—"In Domesday there be often named *bordarii seu borduanni*, *cosces*, *coscet*, *cotucami*, *cotarii*, who are all in effect bores or husbandmen, or cottagers, saving that *bordarii*, which commeth of the French word *borde* for a cottage, signifieth there bores holding a little house, with some land of husbandry bigger than a cottage; and *coterelli* are meere cottagers, *qui cotagia et curtilagia tenent*" (Co. Litt. 5 b). *V.* VILLANI. *Cp.* COTTAGE.

BORDLANDS.—"Lands kept by a lord in his own hands for the maintenance of his table" (Elph. 563, citing Termes de la. Ley, 100; Spelm. *Bordarii*, &c.).

BORN.—The word "Born" or "Begotten," in gifts to children as a class, do not exclude after-born children (2 Jarm. 183: *Vf.* Elph. 236).

In such a connection, the word "Born," or "Living," is synonymous with *procreated*, so as to include a child *en ventre* (Ib. 185). But the fiction, or indulgence, of the law which treats a child *en ventre* as actually born, applies only for the purpose of enabling a child *to take a benefit* to which if actually born it would have been entitled; in all other cases the word "Born" must have its natural interpretation (*Blasson* v, *Blasson*, 34 L. J. Ch. 18; 2 D. G. J. & S. 665: *Pearce* v. *Carrington*, 42 L. J. Ch. 516, 900; 8 Ch. 969).

Vf. "Born," "To be born," Watson, Eq. 1381–3 ; To be Born.

"If A. shall not *have had* a child," embraces a child *en ventre* (*Pearce* v. *Carrington*, sup.).

BOROUGH.—*V.* s. 15 (4), Interp. Act, 1889.

BOROUGH OR PLACE.—This phrase in s. 31, 11 & 12 V. c. 43, means, a place having a Court of Quarter Sessions (*R.* v. *Dale*, 22 L. J. M. C. 44 ; 17 J. P. 68 : *Winn* v. *Mossman*, 38 L. J. Ex. 200 ; 33 J. P. 743 : *Reigate* v. *Hunt*, 37 L. J. M. C. 70 ; 32 J. P. 342 : *Vh.* Stone, 458).

BORROW.—*V.* Hereafter borrow.

BOSCUS.—*V.* Wood.

BOTE.—"*House-Bote*, is a sufficient allowance of wood to build or repair the house, or to burn in it, which latter is sometimes called *Fire-Bote. Plough-Bote* and *Cart-Bote*, are wood to be employed in making and repairing all instruments of husbandry, as ploughs, carts, harrows, rakes, forks, &c. *Hay-Bote* or *Hedge-Bote* is wood for repairing hedges or fences, as pales, stiles, and gates to secure enclosures" (Woodf. 694, 695). "*Common of Estovers*, is right to cut wood for these purposes in another man's land" (Elph. 564, citing Spelm. *Bota: Estovarium;* Wms. on Settlements, 230 ; Wms. on Commons, *pass.*). *V.* Estovers.

"*Bote* is an ancient Saxon word, and sometimes signifieth Amerciament or Compensation, as *Theftbote, Manbote;* or freedome from the same, as *Brigbote, Castlebote, Burghbote*" (Co. Litt. 127 a).

BOTH SIDES.—*V.* Nephew.

BOUND.—*V.* Bind.

BOUND TO RELINQUISH.—*V.* Relinquish.

BOUNDING.—"Bounding or abutting" on a new street within s. 77, 25 & 26 V. c. 102 ; *V. Williams* v. *Wandsworth*, 53 L. J. M. C. 187 ; 13 Q. B. D. 211 : *Hackney* v. *G. E. Ry.*, 51 L. J. M. C. 57 ; 52 Ib. 105 ; 8 App. Ca. 687 : *L. B. & S. Ry.* v. *St. Giles*, 48 L. J. M. C. 184 ; 4 Ex. D. 239.

V. Forming : Fronting.

BOVATA TERRÆ.—*V.* Oxgange.

BRANCHES.—*V.* Younger.

BRANDY.—"Brandy," sold simply as such, must not be reduced more than 25 degrees under proof (Sale of Food and Drugs Act Amendment Act, 1879, 42 & 43 V. c. 30, s. 6). *Sv.* Gin, and the case there cited.

BRAWLING.—*V.* s. 2, 23 & 24 V. c. 32, and *Vth. Asher* v. *Calcraft*,

56 L. J. M. C. 57 ; 18 Q. B. D. 607 ; 56 L. T. 490 ; 35 W. R. 651 ; 51 J. P. 598.

BREACH OF CONDITION.—*V.* FORFEITURE.

BREACH OF CONTRACT OR DUTY.—These words, in s. 6, Admiralty Ct. Act, 1861 (24 V. c. 10), " have been held to be limited to a breach of contract contained in a Bill of Lading (*The Pieve Superiore*, L. R. 5 P. C. 482 ; 43 L. J. Adm. 20), and they do not give jurisdiction in respect of a breach of Charter-Party committed before the goods were put on board (*The Dannebrog*, L. R. 4 A. & E. 386 ; 44 L. J. Adm. 21) :" 1 Maude & P. 400.

BREACH OF COVENANT.—*V. Goodhand* v. *Ayscough*, 52 L. J. Q. B. 97 ; 10 Q. B. D. 71.

BREACH OF TRUST.—Liability incurred by means of " Fraud or Breach of Trust," s. 49, Bankry. Act, 1869 ; *V. Emma Co.* v. *Grant*, 50 L. J. Ch. 449 ; 17 Ch. D. 122 : *Ramskill* v. *Edwards*, 55 L. J. Ch. 81 ; 31 Ch. D. 100 ; 53 L. T. 949 ; 34 W. R. 96. Note : The corresponding phrase in s. 30, Bankry. Act, 1883, is "*fraudulent* Breach of Trust :" qy. is the sense altered ? *Vh. Re Parker, Ex p. Sheppard*, 19 Q. B. D. 84.

BREAK.—A burglarious breaking is effected by breaking, or further breaking, any part of a dwelling-house, or unloosing or forcing any of its fastenings ; or by feloniously obtaining admission by a trick or threat, or by getting down the chimney (for the cases, *V.* Arch. Cr. 568 ; Rosc. Cr. 360 ; and for another definition, *V.* Steph. Cr. 248).

BREAK BULK.—To " break bulk" is not now necessary to constitute Larceny by a Bailee (s. 3, 24 & 25 V. c. 96, re-enacting s. 4, 20 & 21 V. c. 54). The cases were very numerous, and turned on nice distinctions, as to what amounted to " breaking bulk " (*V.* Russell on Crimes, 3 ed. 58–62).

BREAK OUT.—" The expression 'Breaks Out' (in the offence of Breaking Prison) means an actual breaking of the place in which the party is confined, whether intentional or not" (Steph. Cr. 102. *Vf.* Rosc. Cr. 359, 386).

BREAKAGE.—*V.* LEAKAGE AND BREAKAGE.

BRIBERY.—For the definition of Bribery at Parliamentary Elections ; *V.* Corrupt Practices Prevention Act, 1854 (17 & 18 V. c. 102), s. 2 ; Corrupt and Illegal Practices Prevention Act, 1883 (46 & 47 V. c. 51), s. 3, and Sch. 3, Part 3 ; and also adopted for Municipal Elections (47 & 48 V. c. 70, s. 2). *Vh.* Leigh & Le Marchant, 4 ed. 3–25 ; Mattinson & Macaskie, 2 ed. 4–39 ; Rogers, ch. 11.

Vf. Arch. Cr. 1076, 1077 ; Rosc. Cr. 343—348.

BRICK-BUILT.—" A house described as 'brick-built,' is understood to be brick-built in the ordinary sense of the words ; not composed externally partly of brick, and partly of timber, and lath and plaster" (Dart, 137, 155, citing *Powell* v. *Doubble*, Sug. 29 : *Arnold* v. *Arnold*, 14 Ch. D. 270 ; 42 L. T. 705 ; 28 W. R. 635 : *English* v. *Murray*, 49 L. T. 35 ; 32 W. R. 84).

BRIDGE.—As to what is a Bridge and whether an Arch, or a number of Arches, constructed over *stagnant* water may be considered a Bridge ; *V. R.* v. *Derbyshire*, 11 L. J. M. C. 51 ; 2 G. & D. 97.

As to the phrase, " Bridge broken in a Highway " (22 H. 8, c. 5); *V. R.* v. *Southampton*, No. 1, 55 L. J. M. C. 158 ; 17 Q. B. D. 424 ; 55 L. T. 322 ; 35 W. R. 10 ; 50 J. P. 773 : *Sv.* S. C., No. 2, 19 Q. B. D. 590 ; 56 L. J. M. C. 112 ; 57 L. T. 261.

"Bridge," in s. 46, Ry. C. C. Act, 1845, includes the roadway over a bridge as well as the structure of the bridge itself, and therefore the cost of metalling and paving such roadway is payable by the Railway Company (*Bury* v. *Lancashire and Yorkshire Ry.*, 14 App. Ca. 417 ; 57 L. J. Q. B. 280 ; 20 Q. B. D. 485 ; 59 L. T. 193 ; 36 W. R. 491 ; 52 J. P. 341).

The Mutiny Act exemption of soldiers from toll on crossing " Bridges," does not extend to a steam ferry boat, though it be called a floating bridge (*Ward* v. *Gray*, 34 L. J. M. C. 146 ; 6 B. & S. 345).

BRING FORWARD.—The prohibition against "Bringing Forward" a house or building beyond the front wall of the building on either side of it (s. 156, P. H. Act, 1875), does not apply to a new house or building on a new site (*Williams* v. *Wallasey*, 55 L. J. M. C. 133 ; 16 Q. B. D. 718 ; 34 W. R. 517).

BRITISH CUSTOM.—" Average, if any, to be adjusted according to British Custom ; " *V. Stewart* v. *W. India and Pacific Co.*, L. R. 8 Q. B. 88, 362.

BRITISH DOMINIONS.—For the purposes of the Copyright Act, 5 & 6 V. c. 45, "the words 'British Dominions' shall be construed to mean and include all parts of the United Kingdom of Great Britain and Ireland, the islands of Jersey and Guernsey, all parts of the East and West Indies, and all the Colonies, Settlements and Possessions of the Crown which now are or hereafter may be acquired " (s. 2). That extends to Canada (*Low* v. *Routledge*, 35 L. J. Ch. 114 ; 1 Ch. 42).

BRITISH INDIA.—In all Acts of Parliament passed after the 31st Dec. 1889, "'British India' shall mean all territories and places within Her Majesty's dominions which are for the time being governed by Her Majesty through the Governor-General of India, or through any Governor or other officer subordinate to the Governor-General of India" (s. 18 (4) Interp. Act, 1889) ; and,

"'India' shall mean British India together with any territories of any native prince or chief under the suzerainty of Her Majesty exercised through the Governor-General of India, or through any Governor or other officer subordinate to the Governor-General of India" (s. 18 (5) Ib.).

BRITISH ISLANDS.—In all Acts of Parliament passed after the 31st Dec. 1889, "'British Islands,' shall mean the United Kingdom, the Channel Islands, and the Isle of Man" (s. 18 (1) Interp. Act, 1889).

Cp. definition in Bills of Ex. Act, 1882, *quà* Inland Bills: *V.* INLAND.

BRITISH POSSESSION.—In all Acts of Parliament passed after the 31st Dec. 1889, "'British Possession,' shall mean any part of Her Majesty's dominions exclusive of the United Kingdom; and where parts of such dominions are under both a central and a local legislature, all parts under the central legislature shall, for the purposes of this definition, be deemed to be one British Possession" (s. 18 (2) Interp. Act. 1889).

BRITISH SHIP.—A ship built in England for a foreign owner and not registered, or intended to be registered, as a British Ship, is not a British Ship within the Merchant Shipping Act, 1854 (*Union Bank of London* v. *Lenanton*, 47 L. J. C. P. 409; 3 C. P. D. 243).

V. SHIP: RECOGNIZED BRITISH SHIP.

BROKER.—*V.* FACTOR.

As to meaning of "Broker" in 6 Anne, c. 16, and 6 G. 1, c. 18; *V.* *Clark* v. *Powell*, 2 L. J. K. B. 145; 4 B. & Ad. 846: *Smith* v. *Lindo*, 27 L. J. C. P. 196, 335; 4 C. B. N. S. 395: *Milford* v. *Hughes*, 16 L. J. Ex. 40; 16 M. & W. 174. In the last case Rolfe, B., said that a case of brokerage "must relate to goods and money, and not merely to personal contracts for work and labour."

"Broker," as used in the late Bankruptcy definition of "Trader," included not only barterers of merchandize, but also assurance-brokers (*Ex p. Stevens*, 4 Mad. 256); Bill-brokers (*Ex p. Phipps*, 2 Dea. 487); Pawn-brokers (*Rawlinson* v. *Pearson*, 5 B. & Ald. 124); Ship-brokers (*Pott* v. *Turner*, 4 M. & P. 551; 6 Bing. 702); and Stock-brokers (Cullen, 12, Note 2, 48).

"Broker" is a sufficient description of a Ship-broker, for the purposes of the Bills of Sale Acts (*Gugen* v. *Sampson*, 4 F. & F. 974).

BROTHER: SISTER.—A gift to "Brothers;" "Sisters,"—includes the half-blood; "and so with regard to every other degree of relationship" (2 Jarm. 154). "I think that, in general, when a man speaks of his brothers and sisters he speaks of them, not with reference to the definition of the word in the dictionary, but as a class standing in the same relation to *one or both* of his parents in which he himself stands. Though the half-blood are not descended from both the same parents, they are,—as it is said in *Les Termes de la Ley*, p. 123, tit. *Demy Sangue*,—'after a sort, brothers,' 'brothers by the father's side,' 'brothers by one mother;' and however others might describe them or they might designate themselves,

I think that, if required to give a precise description of the nature and degree of the relation subsisting between them, they, in ordinary parlance, would be called and would call themselves, Brothers and Sisters" (per Turner, V. C., *Grieves* v. *Rawley*, 22 L. J. Ch. 625 ; 10 Hare, 63). But this construction may be varied by a context (*Re Reed*, 57 L. J. Ch. 790 ; 36 W. R. 682).

The widower of a sister is not a "Brother," nor is the widow of a brother a "Sister," there being no blood relationship (*Hussey* v. *Berkeley*, 2 Eden, 194).

V. Nephew.

BROUGHT ALONGSIDE.—*V.* Alongside.

BROUGHT BEFORE.—A person is sufficiently "brought before" a magistrate, within s. 24, 2 & 3 V. c. 71, if he appear in answer to a summons; and it is not necessary that he should have been actually arrested and brought in custody (*Hadley* v. *Perks*, 35 L. J. M. C. 177; L. R. 1 Q. B. 444 ; 7 B. & S. 375). *Vf. R.* v. *Willcox*, 37 W. R. 686.

BROUGHT INTO QUESTION.—*V.* Jdgmt. of Willes, J., *Cooper* v. *Hubbuck*, 31 L. J. C. P. 326 ; 12 C. B. N. S. 456.

BRUERA.—"A man grants *omnes brueras suas;* the soile where heath doth growe passeth. It is derived from *bruyer*, a French word for heath; and it is called *ros* in the British tongue" (Co. Litt. 4 b, 5 a; *V.* Touch. 95).

BUILD.—*V.* Erect.

BUILDER.—A "Builder," within the late Bankry. definition of "Trader," was one who built houses for sale, whether on land purchased or leased by him for that purpose, or who built for other persons by hire or contract (*Ex p. Neirinckx*, 4 L. J. Bank. 73 ; 2 M. & A. 384). But the purchasing land with unfinished houses thereon, and employing persons to complete the houses was not trading as a "Builder" (*Ex p. Edwards*, 9 L. J. Bank. 11 ; 4 Jur. 153 ; 1 M. D. & D. 3). *Vf. Ex p. Stewart*, 18 L. J. Bank. 14 ; 13 Jur. 581 ; 3 Ex. 700 ; 3 D. G. & S. 557 : *Re Fowler*, Fon. 201.

BUILDING.—What is a "Building" must always be a question of degree.

"The masonry on the sides of a Canal is not sufficient to constitute it a 'building.' A London street, though paved and faced with stonework, would yet be 'land;' whilst the Holborn Viaduct would be a 'Building'" (per Blackburn, J., *R.* v. *Neath Canal Nav.*, 40 L. J. M. C. 197). A Bay Window is a "Building," and its addition to a house will be a breach of a covenant not to erect "any building" in advance of the house (*Manners* v. *Johnson*, 45 L. J. Ch. 404 ; L. R. 1 Ch. D. 673). So a wooden advertisement-hoarding is a contravention of a covenant not to erect a "Building or Erection" on the premises (per Matthew, J., *Pocock* v. *Gilham*, 1 Cab. & El. 104).

"Possibly a 'Silo' may be called a 'Building' within the meaning of Settled Land Act, 1882, s. 25 (xi.)" (per Cotton, L.J., *Re Broadwater*, 54 L. J. Ch. 1105).

A "Building, Structure or Erection" to be within s. 75, 25 & 26 V. c. 102, must be one on a space theretofore vacant; and a new building, &c., erected on the site of an old one recently pulled down, is not within the section (*Auckland* v. *Westminster*, 41 L. J. Ch. 723; 7 Ch. 597: *Vf. Barlow* v. *St. Mary Abbotts*, 55 L. J. Ch. 680; 11 App. Ca. 257; 55 L. T. 221; 34 W. R. 521; 50 J. P. 691). A small conservatory over a projecting shop-front is not within this section (*St. George, Hanover Sq.* v. *Sparrow*, 33 L. J. M. C. 118; 16 C. B. N. S. 209); nor is a conservatory which projects from a dwelling-house a "Building" within a By-Law under the P. H. Act, 1875 (*Hibbert* v. *Acton*, 5 Times Rep. 274).

"Building" within the Acts relating to the Metropolis; *V. Stevens* v. *Gourley*, 29 L. J. C. P. 1; 7 C. B. N. S. 99.

"House, Warehouse, Counting House, Shop, *or other Building*," to confer the franchise under s. 27, Reform Act, includes, in its last term, only buildings of a permanent character used for residentiary or commercial purposes (*Pownall* v. *Dawson*, 21 L. J. C. P. 14; 11 C. B. 9); and does not include a tool shed (*Powell* v. *Boraston*, 34 L. J. C. P. 73; 18 C. B. N. S. 175). *Sv. Morrish* v. *Harris*, L. R. 1 C. P. 155: Qy., Is a Pig-sty such a "Building"? (*Powell* v. *Farmer*, 34 L. J. C. P. 71; 18 C. B. N. S. 168). A Cow-house may be (*Whitmore* v. *Wenlock*, 13 L. J. C. P. 55).

"Dwelling-house, Workshop, *or other Building*," s. 3, 2 & 3 W. 4, c. 71, means *quà* "Building," one analogous to those mentioned (*Harris* v. *De Pinna*, 33 Ch. D. 238; 54 L. T. 38).

"Sewer, Drain, Privy, Cesspool, Ashpit, *Building*," in a local Act relating to public health, held to include in its last term a Dwelling-house (*Pearson* v. *Kingston*, 35 L. J. M. C. 36; 3 H. & C. 921).

An arch used as a store-house is a "Building" within s. 7, Gas Clauses Act, 1847 (*Thompson* v. *Sunderland Gas Co.*, 46 L. J. Ex. 710; 2 Ex. D. 429).

An unfinished house is a "Building" within s. 6, 24 & 25 V. c. 97 (*R.* v. *Manning*, L. R. 1 C. C. R. 338; 41 L. J. M. C. 11; 25 L. T. 573).

"Corporate Buildings," s. 92, 5 & 6 W. 4, c. 76; *Semble*, a Corporation Pew is within this phrase (*R.* v. *Warwick*, 15 L. J. Q. B. 306; 8 Q. B. 926).

V. New Building: House: Erection.

BUILDING LAND.—"'Building Land' is a term frequently used for land capable of being built on—land suitable for being built on in the judgment of those who come to that conclusion" (per Hatherley, L.J., *L. & S. W. Ry.* v. *Blackmore*, 39 L. J. Ch. 716; L. R. 4 H. L. 610).

BUILDING LEASE.—A Building Lease must contain a covenant by the lessee to build (*Jones* v. *Verney,* Willes, 169 : *Re Hallett,* 52 L. J Ch. 804 ; 24 Ch. D. 624).

For the purposes of the Conv. & L. P. Act, 1881, a Building Lease " is a Lease for building purposes, or purposes connected therewith," s. 2 (x.). A similar definition is provided for the Settled Land Act, 1882 ; *V.* s. 10 (iii.).

BUILDING LINE.—*V. Barlow* v. *St. Mary Abbotts,* 11 App. Ca. 257 ; 55 L. J. Ch. 680 ; 55 L. T. 221 ; 34 W. R. 521 ; 50 J. P. 691.

BUILDING PURPOSES.—The phrase, land " used for Building Purposes " in s. 128, Lands C. C. Act, 1845, does not mean what is ordinarily called " building land ; " but means " land actually used for building purposes, not land contemplated to be used for building purposes, or intended to be used for building purposes, or suitable for building purposes " (per Hatherley, L.C., *L. & S. W. Ry.* v. *Blackmore,* 39 L. J. Ch. 717 ; L. R. 4 H. L. 610 : *Va. Coventry* v. *L. B. & S. Ry.,* 37 L. J. Ch. 90 ; L. R. 5 Eq. 104 ; 16 W. R. 267).

BUILT UPON.—As to this phrase as used in s. 128, Lands C. C. Act, 1845 ; *V.* jdgmt. of Hatherley, L.C., *L. & S. W. Ry.* v. *Blackmore,* 39 L. J. Ch. 713 ; L. R. 4 H. L. 610.

BULK.—*V.* BREAK BULK ; LEFT.

BURDEN.—The exemption from tolls given by subs. 6, s. 19, 32 & 33 V. c. 14, for vehicles used for the conveyance " of any goods or *Burden,*" does not extend to such things as a travelling show. Neither does " Burden " include persons. " I cannot think that if a tradesman deals in an article, and sends his traveller out in a gig, the gig would be exempt on the ground that the traveller could be said to be a Burden " (*Speak* v. *Powell,* 43 L. J. M. C. 19 ; L. R. 9 Ex. 25).

Upon the construction of the Act for establishing a Ferry across the Tyne, " Burthen " held to mean capacity for carrying, not register admeasurement (*North Shields Ferry Co.* v. *Barker,* 2 Ex. 136).

BURGLARY.—" Burglary " is a term of art (*Holford* v. *Bailey,* 18 L. J. Q. B. 109 ; 13 Q. B. 426 : *R.* v. *Gray,* 33 L. J. M. C. 78 ; L. & C. 365), and means the breaking and entering by night of the dwelling-house of another with intent to commit a felony therein (3 Inst. 63 ; 4 Bl. Com. 224) ; " or, being in such dwelling-house, shall commit any felony therein, and shall in either case break out of the said dwelling-house in the night " (24 & 25 V. c. 96, s. 51). *Vf.* Arch. Cr. 558–573 ; Rosc. Cr. 359–388. *V.* BREAK.

BURN : BURNING.—The singeing of the cover is not a " burning " of a Will so as to revoke it ; nor is a fraudulent burning of something else, instead of the Will, which the testator has directed to be burnt, a revocation (*Doe* d. *Reed* v. *Harris*, 6 A. & E. 209 ; 6 L. J. K. B. 84 ; stated 1 Jarm. 131).

"A strong intention to burn is not a burning. There must be, at all events, a partial burning of the instrument itself; I do not say that a quantity of words must be burnt ; but there must be a burning of the paper on which the Will is" (per Patteson, J., Ib.). Coleridge, J., whilst agreeing that a total destruction was not necessary, added,—" but there should be such a burning as destroys the entirety of the Will, for in such a case the Will of the testator no longer exists as he framed it."

BURTHEN.—*V.* Burden.

BUSINESS.—Companies, for the acquisition of gain, of more than 20 persons for " carrying on any other business " (*i.e.* other than banking) must be registered (s. 4, The Companies Act, 1862, 25 & 26 V. c. 89).

"'Business,' has a more extensive meaning than the word 'Trade'" (per Willes, J., *Harris* v. *Amery*, 35 L. J. C. P. 92).

In *Smith* v. *Anderson* (50 L. J. Ch. 43 ; 15 Ch. D. 258), Jessel, M. R., after citing definitions of "Business" from several dictionaries, said, "anything which occupies the time and attention and labour of a man, *for the purpose of profit* (*Sv.* post), is business." Further on he remarks,—" There are many things which in common colloquial English would not be called a Business, when carried on by a single person, which would be so called when carried on by a number of persons. For instance, a man who is the owner of a house divided into several floors and used for commercial purposes, *e.g.* offices, would not be said to carry on a business because he let the offices as such. But suppose a Company was formed for the purpose of buying a building, or leasing a house, to be divided into offices and to be let out,—should not we say, if that was the object of the Company, that the Company was carrying on business for the purpose of letting offices ? The same observation may be made as regards a single individual buying or selling land, with this addition, that he may make it a business, and then it is a question of continuity. When you come to an Association or Company formed for a purpose, you would say at once that it is a business, because there you have that from which you would infer continuity. So in the ordinary case of investments, a man who has money to invest, the object being to obtain his income, invests his money, and he may occasionally sell the investments and buy others, but he is not carrying on a business." The decision of which the observations just quoted were the preface was reversed on appeal ; without, however, as it would seen, affecting the value of those observations in regard to its use in s. 4 of the Companies Act. Within that section a mutual Marine Insurance Association is a "Business" (*Re Padstow Assrce.*, 51 L. J. Ch. 344 ; 20 Ch. D. 137) ; so is Farming though it could not properly be called a trade (*Harris* v. *Amery*, sup.) ; and so is a Mutual Benefit Society the object of which is to lend money to its members only (*Shaw* v. *Benson*, 52 L. J. Q. B. 575 ; 11 Q. B. D. 563) ; or a Building Society one of whose objects is to win minerals (*Crowther* v. *Thorley*, 31 W. R. 564 ; 32 Ib. 330 ; 48 L. T. 644 ; 50 Ib. 43). Such transactions however, as were contemplated by the Government and Guaranteed Permanent Trust, or by the Submarine Cables Trust, are not a "Business ; " the Trustees being such in deed as well as in name, and not being agents with power to enter into contracts (*Smith* v. *Anderson*, sup.: over-ruling *Sykes* v. *Beadon*, 48 L. J. Ch. 522 ; 11 Ch. D. 170).

But though the contemplation of making profit was stated by Jessel, M. R., in *Smith* v. *Anderson*, to be an ingredient in determining whether a sequence of things done would form a "Business," and though that idea runs through the other cases just cited, yet that portion of the definition would seem to be confined to cases under the Companies Act, or those of a like kind. It is indeed clear law that there may be a "Business" offending against a prohibitory covenant, without pecuniary profit being at all contemplated. In such a connection especially "Business" is a very much larger word than "Trade :" and the word "Business" is employed in order to include occupations which would not strictly come within the meaning of the word "Trade,"—the larger word not being limited by association with the lesser (per Pearson, J., *Rolls* v. *Miller*, 53 L. J. Ch. 101). Therefore a covenant not to permit the carrying on of any "Trade or Business" is broken by allowing the premises to be used as an out-patient branch of a Hospital (*Bramwell* v. *Lacy*, 48 L. J. Ch. 339 ; 10 Ch. D. 691 ; 40 L. T. 361; 27 W. R. 463 : *Tod-Heatly* v. *Benham*, 40 Ch. D. 80 ; 58 L. J. Ch. 83 ; 37 W. R. 38) ; or as a Home for working girls (*Rolls* v. *Miller*, 53 L. J. Ch. 99, 510, 682 ; 25 Ch. D. 206 ; 27 Ib. 71). And the Council of Law Reporting carry on (probably) a Trade, and certainly a Business within the phrase "Trade or Business" in s. 11 (5), Customs & Inl. Rev. Act, 1885, 48 & 49 V. c. 51 (*Re Law Reporting Council*, 58 L. J. Q. B. 90).

On the other hand there may be a sequence of acts from which profit is anticipated without a "Business" being constituted. Thus where a Barrister occupying a house and 79 acres of land as a private residence, and which he had originally taken for pleasure, but some of which land he used for breeding cattle and horses and raising vegetables, fruits, and flowers, which he sold, and he also occasionally bought and sold cattle and horses ; it was held on the evidence that he did not carry on "Business" within the Bankry. Act, 1883, and therefore that his Trustee was not entitled to claim as against a Bill of Sale holder, by virtue of the reputed ownership clause (s. 44) (*Re Wallis, Ex p. Sully*, 14 Q. B. D. 950 ; 29 S. J. 323).

A Boys-School (*Doe* d. *Bish* v. *Keeling*, 1 M. & S. 95), or a Girls-School (*Kemp* v. *Sober*, 20 L. J. Ch. 602 ; 1 Sim. N. S. 517), is a "Business or Calling," or a "Public Trade or Business" (*Wickenden* v. *Webster*, 25 L. J. Q. B. 264 ; 6 E. & B. 387 ; 27 L. T. O. S. 122) within a restrictive covenant. So is a Pay-Hospital (*Portman* v. *Home Hospitals Assn.*, 27 Ch. D. 81, n.; 50 L. T. 599). It is questioned whether keeping a Lodging House is a "Business" within such a covenant (Woodf. 665); but surely it is a "Business," though not a "Trade."

V. TRADE: CARRY ON.

It seems that a patentee is engaged in a "Business" within R. 4, Trades Marks Rules, Feb., 1883, so long as he receives royalties under his patent, even though he does not himself manufacture (*Re Ralph,* 53 L. J. Ch. 188; 25 Ch. D. 194).

Filling up vacancies in a Local Board of Health, is "Business" within Sch. 1, Part 1, R. 2, P. H. Act, 1875 (*Newhaven Loc. Bd.* v. *Newhaven School Bd.,* 30 Ch. D. 350).

"Business *in any Action,*" &c., in R. 2, Solrs. Remuneration Ord., 1882, does not include conveyancing business (*Re Merchant Taylors' Co.,* 54 L. J. Ch. 867; 30 Ch. D. 28: *Vh. Re Atkinson,* 24 L. R. Ir. 182). "Business" in R. 6 of the Ord. means, any part of the business which would be covered by the Scale Fee (*Re Allen,* 56 L. J. Ch. 487; 34 Ch. D. 433; 56 L. T. 6; 35 W. R. 218: *Hester* v. *Hester,* 56 L. J. Ch. 247; 34 Ch. D. 607; 55 L. T. 862; 35 W. R. 233; 51 J. P. 438: *Re Metcalf,* 57 L. J. Ch. 82; 57 L. T. 925; 36 W. R. 137). *V.* BUSINESS CONNECTED WITH: UNDERTAKING.

"Business *of any Mine,*" s. 29, 24 & 25 V. c. 97; *V.* ERECTION.

V. OUT OF THE BUSINESS.

A Bequest of a "Business," does not include a freehold shop in which the Business is carried on (*Re Henton,* 30 W. R. 702).

BUSINESS CONNECTED WITH.—The negotiations (*Re Field,* 54 L. J. Ch. 661; 29 Ch. D. 608; 33 W. R. 553), and a preliminary agreement (*Re Emanuel & Simmonds,* 55 L. J. Ch. 710; 33 Ch. D. 40; 34 W. R. 613), are "Business connected with" a Lease, within Rule 2, Solicitors' Remuneration Order, 1882, and as such comprised within the work for which the *ad val.* remuneration is provided by the Order. But abortive negotiations with persons other than the actual lessee is not such Business (*Re Martin,* 41 Ch. D. 381; 5 Times Rep. 426).

V. BUSINESS.

BUSINESS DAYS.—"Non-business Days" for the purposes of the Bills of Ex. Act, 1882, mean—

"(a) Sunday, Good Friday, Christmas Day:

(b) A Bank Holiday, under the Bank Holidays Act, 1871, or Acts amending it:

(c) A day appointed by Royal proclamation as a Public Fast or Thanksgiving Day.

Any other day is a Business Day" (s. 92, Bills of Ex. Act, 1882).

BUSINESS PREMISES.—As to effect of a description in Particulars of Sale of property as "Business Premises;" *V. Re Davis & Cavey,* 58 L. J. Ch. 143; 40 Ch. D. 601.

BUSINESS TRANSACTIONS.—The "usual and proper" Books of Account sufficiently disclosing a person's "Business Transactions and *Financial Position*" the omission to keep which is a Bankry offence (46 & 47 V. c. 52, s. 28 (3, a)), need only disclose a Bankrupt's Transactions and Position "in the business carried on by him," and need not disclose matters outside such business,—*e.g.* a building speculation, the Bankrupt not being a builder (*Re Mutton*, 19 Q. B. D. 102; 56 L. J. Q. B. 395; 56 L. T. 802; 35 W. R. 561).

BUT.—"Where gifts are intended to be cut down, the words cutting them down are generally introduced by some stronger word than 'But;' and there must, therefore, be a distinction made between cases where gifts are properly cut down and those where such a result is only to be inferred from imperfect statements of the event on which the testator intended to found the gift over" (per Ld. St. Leonards, *Abbott* v. *Middleton*, 28 L. J. Ch. 113; 7 H. L. Ca. 68; *Sv.* jdgmt. of Ld. Wensleydale in that case).

The word "But" following a covenant "suggests a qualification," but is insufficient to create an independent covenant (per Hall, V.-C., *Sear* v. *House Property Co.*, 50 L. J. Ch. 77; 16 Ch. D. 387), in which case a lessee's covenant not to assign without lessor's consent, was held to be only qualified by the added phrase "but such consent not to be unreasonably withheld," and that such phrase did not amount to a covenant by the lessor on which a breach could be assigned; *Vf. Broughton* v. *Conway*, F. Moo. 58; Dy. 240 a: *Gervis* v. *Peade*, Cro. El. 615; Dy. 240 a; Elph. 469.

BUTCHER.—The business of a "Butcher" is carried on, within the meaning of a restrictive covenant, if raw meat be sold on the premises though the animals be slaughtered elsewhere (*Doe* d. *Gaskell* v. *Spry*, 1 B. & Ald. 617); and so the exposure of pork-meat for sale is carrying on the business of a "Pork-Butcher" (*Doe* d. *Davis* v. *Elsam*, Moo. & M. 189). But in *Cleaver* v. *Bacon* (4 Times Rep. 27), Kekewich, J., cited from the Imperial Dictionary the definition of "Butcher" as, "One who slaughters animals for market; or one whose occupation is to kill animals for the table;" and, the learned judge added, "One who simply sells meat does not seem to enter into that definition:" but that was an *obiter dictum*, yet still the case involved the construction of a restrictive covenant; *V.* Offensive.

BUTT.—"A piece of land; *e.g.*, Register of Worcester Priory, fol. 49 b (Cam. Soc.). Where a selio abruptly meets others, or abuts upon a boundary at right angles, it is sometimes called a Butt; Seebohm, 6" (Elph. 564).

BUTTY COLLIER.—"Butty Colliers are two or more working colliers who join together, and enter into an agreement with a mine owner to get coal or iron-stone from the mine at so much a yard or so much a ton, and sometimes at so much a day. They are not allowed to underlet the work or leave it; but they employ other workmen under them; and they are responsible for their wages. They usually work manually themselves; and they may bind themselves to the mine owner to do so; *V. Bowers* v. *Lovekin,* 6 E. & B. 584; 25 L. J. Q. B. 371; 4 W. R. 600; 27 L. T. O. S. 168: *Sleeman* v. *Barrett,* 2 H. & C. 934; 33 L. J. Ex. 153; 12 W. R. 411; 9 L. T. 834;" MacS. 520, n. 4. *Bowers* v. *Lovekin* laid down that a Butty Collier is an "Artificer" within the Truck Act; *Sv.* ARTIFICER.

BY.—The difference between "By" and "In" is exemplified in *Edmunds* v. *Waugh* (35 L. J. Ch. 234; L. R. 1 Eq. 418; 14 W. R. 257). There the question arose on the Statute of Limitations, 3 & 4 W. 4, c. 27, s. 42, which prohibits the recovery of more than six years' arrears of rent or interest "*by any Distress, Action or Suit.*" In giving judgment, Kindersley, V.-C., pointed out that the word was "by" not "in;" and accordingly it was held that though a mortgagee's estate is being administered "in" an action, yet the section does not prevent him or his representatives from retaining more than 6 years' arrears of interest out of the proceeds in their hands arising from the sale of the mortgaged property (*Vf. Re Marshfield,* 56 L. J. Ch. 599; 34 Ch. D. 721; 56 L. T. 694; 35 W. R. 491: distinguishing *Mason* v. *Broadbent,* 33 Bea. 296; *V.* RECOVER).

BY AND BETWEEN.—*V.* AGREED AND DECLARED.

BY BILL.—Payment to be made "By Bill" does not mean, and parol evidence cannot be received to shew it to mean, "By Approved Bill" (*Hodgson* v. *Davies,* 2 Camp. 530; *V.* Benj. 721); *V.* APPROVED BILL.

BY CONSENT.—*V.* CONSENT.

BY DEED OR WRITING.—*V.* IN WRITING.

BY DIRECTION OF THE EXECUTORS.—*V.* PROPRIETOR.

BY FORCE.—"By force of the statutes in that case made and provided," in an Indictment, is surplusage (*A.-G.* v. *Le Revert,* 9 L. J. Ex. 163; 6 M. & W. 405).

BY HIMSELF.—*V.* HIMSELF.

BY INHERITANCE—*V.* INHERITANCE.

BY LAW.—This phrase means, by implication of law as distinguished from stipulation by contract; and therefore on a contract providing a specified notice to quit, s. 33, Agricultural Holdings Act, 1883 (prescribing a year's in lieu of a half-year's notice), has no application (*Barlow* v. *Teal*, 54 L. J. Q. B. 564; 15 Q. B. D. 501; 1 Times Rep. 491). *V.* LEGAL NOTICE: SIX MONTHS.

So "Debts payable *by law* out of Personal Estate," s. 23, 5 & 6 V. c. 79, mean such debts as in themselves, and in their own nature and character are payable out of personal estate, and has no relation to any testamentary provision (*Percival* v. *The Queen*, 33 L. J. Ex. 289; 3 H. & C. 217).

"Devolution by Law;" *V.* DISPOSITION.

But it seems difficult to see how "By Law" can have the meaning just stated, as it is used in s. 210, Com. L. Pro. Act, 1852, which relates to proceedings for the forfeiture of a lease when a half-year's rent is in arrear and the landlord "hath right *by law* to re-enter for the non-payment thereof:" Can such a right be other than contractual?

"By operation of law;" *V.* DEVOLUTION.

BY PAYMENT.—*V.* REDUCED BY PAYMENT.

BY POISON.—*V.* POISON.

BY POST.—Where an Act passed after 31st Dec. 1889, "authorizes or requires any Document to be served 'By Post' (whether the expression 'Serve,' 'Give,' or 'Send,' or any other expression is used) then, unless the contrary intention appears, the service shall be deemed to be effected by properly addressing, pre-paying, and posting a letter containing the Document, and (unless the contrary is proved) to have been effected at the time at which the letter would be delivered in the ordinary course of post" (s. 26, Interp. Act, 1889). *Vh.* ORDINARY COURSE: SEND.

BY PURCHASE.—As to the effect of this phrase in a Limitation to prevent application of rule against Perpetuities; *V.* Watson, Eq. 245, 246. *V.* PURCHASE.

A covenant to settle such future property as may be acquired "by purchase," will include a subsequently effected Life Policy and the moneys payable thereunder (*Re Turcan*, 58 L. J. Ch. 101; 40 Ch. D. 5).

BY REASON.—"Costs sustained by the defendant by reason of" an Indictment or Information for Libel, s. 8, 6 & 7 V. c. 96, includes the costs of unsuccessfully showing cause against the Rule *nisi* for filing the Information (*R.* v. *Steel*, 45 L. J. Q. B. 391; 1 Q. B. D. 485; disapproving *R.* v. *Cavendish*, 12 Ir. L. R. 230).

V. CONTRACT.

BY THE YEAR.—*V.* VALUE.

BY VIRTUE.—"By virtue or in pursuance of;" *V.* PURSUANCE.

"By virtue of the Stat. of Distribution;" *V. Sturge and G. W. Ry.*, 19 Ch. D. 444.

BY WAY OF.—"By way of *Gaming;*" *V.* GAMING OR WAGERING CONTRACTS. "By way of *Jointure;*" *V. Jamieson* v. *Trevelyan,* 23 L. J. Ex. 281; 10 Ex. 269.

V. SUCCESSION.

BY WEIGHT.—To sell Bread "By Weight," s. 4, 6 & 7 W. 4, c. 37, the Bread, after it is baked, must be weighed; it is not enough to weigh the dough before baking and make an allowance for loss of weight in the oven (*Jones* v. *Huxtable,* 36 L. J. M. C. 122; L. R. 2 Q. B. 460; 15 W. R. 900; 31 J. P. 534; 8 B. & S. 433: *Hill* v. *Browning,* L. R. 5 Q. B. 453; 22 L. T. 584; 34 J. P. 774); but, *semble,* if a fair sample of a few loaves from each batch are weighed after the batch has been baked, and as a test of the weight of all the loaves in the batch, that would suffice (*Webb* v. *Manders,* 12 S. J. 1020). The point is, that in some fair way the baked Bread must be weighed shortly before sale. "I do not say that it is strictly the duty of the seller to weigh a loaf *at the time of sale;* but unless the loaf were weighed then, or shortly before, that would be evidence of a sale otherwise than 'By Weight'" (per Blackburn, J., *Jones* v. *Huxtable,* sup.).

In *Williams* v. *Deggan* (31 J. P. 807), Cockburn, C. J., is reported to have said that a baker ought to weigh his bread in the presence of his customer; and so he ought, and he runs risk if he do not; but there would seem no compulsion that he must (*Jones* v. *Huxtable,* sup.: *R.* v. *Kennet,* L. R. 4 Q. B. 565; 33 J. P. 824: *Mitton* v. *Troke,* 20 L. T. 563; 33 J. P. 821).

V. FRENCH BREAD.

Selling Coals, 1 & 2 W. 4, c. lxxvi, s. 57; *V. Smith* v. *Wood,* 58 L. J. Q. B. 611.

BY WHOSE ACT.—"Person by whose Act, Default, Permission or Sufferance the Nuisance arises," s. 12, 18 & 19 V. c. 121; *V. Brown* v. *Bussell,* 37 L. J. M. C. 65; 9 B. & S. 1; L. R. 3 Q. B. 251.

BY WILL.—*V.* WRITING.

BY WRITING.—*V.* WRITING.

BYE.—"*Bye* signifieth a dwelling, *bye,* an habitation, and *byan* to dwell" (Co. Litt. 5 b).

BYE LAW.—"Is not a Bye Law, a law governing the corporate body, and which they are authorized to make?" (per Alderson, B., *Hopkins* v. *Swansea,* 8 L. J. Ex. 125; 4 M. & W. 621). *Vh.* 5 Rep. 63: *James* v. *Tutney,* Cro. Car. 497, 498; Selwyn's Nisi Prius, 12 Ed. 1187–1191.

C—CAL

C. F. I.—Cost, Freight and Insurance; *wh. V.*

CABIN OR OTHER ALLOWANCES.—In *Best* v. *Saunders*, (Mo. & Mal. 268), Lord Tenterden was of opinion these words did not apply to an allowance in the nature of Primage. *Vh.* 1 Maude & P. 121, 122.

CABLISH.—"Brushwood, or, more properly, windfalls; Spelm.: browsewood; 4 Inst. 308" (Elph. 564).

CÆTERIS PARIBUS.—A statutory power to appoint to a Living was vested in trustees who were to appoint a fit and proper person duly qualified, provided that in such appointment such person should be preferred, "cæteris paribus," who should belong to a certain class;—held, that "cæteris paribus" referred to the being fit and proper and duly qualified, and not to the general qualifications of a clergyman (*A.-G.* v. *Powis*, 24 L. J. Ch. 218; Kay, 186).

CALCULATED TO BENEFIT.—Scheme of Arrangement "calculated to benefit the general body of Creditors," s. 18 (6), Bankry. Act, 1883;—*V. Re Aylmer*, 19 Q. B. D. 33; 56 L. J. Q. B. 460; 56 L. T. 801; 35 W. R. 532. *Vf.* S. C., 20 Q. B. D. 258; 57 L. J. Q. B. 168; 36 W. R. 231.

CALCULATED TO DECEIVE.—The prohibition in s. 6, Trade Marks Registration Act, 1875 (38 & 39 V. c. 91), against registering, in connection with a trade mark, words "calculated to deceive," refers to deceptiveness inherent in the words themselves, and not as arising from similarity to words comprised in other trade marks (*Re Horsburgh*, 53 L. J. Ch. 237).

As to the same phrase in Patents, Designs and Trade Marks Act, 1883, s. 72 (2); *V. Re Speer*, W. N. (87) 8; 55 L. T. 880: *Australian Wine Importers & Mason*, 58 L. J. Ch. 380; W. N. (89) 51.

CALCUTTA LINSEED.—*V. Wieler* v. *Schilizzi*, 25 L. J. C. P. 89; 17 C. B. 619.

CALENDAR MONTH.—"A 'Calendar Month' is a legal and technical term; and in computing time by calendar months, the time must be reckoned by looking at the calendar and not by counting days" (per Brett, L. J., *Migotti* v. *Colville,* 48 L. J. C. P. 695 ; 4 C. P. D. 233 ; 27 W. R. 744 ; 43 J. P. 620). Therefore, *e.g.,* "one calendar month's imprisonment is to be calculated from the day of imprisonment to the day numerically corresponding to that day in the following month, less one" (Ib.). When there is no such corresponding day in the last month of the imprisonment, the prisoner's term will be up on the last day of such last month. Thus a prisoner "sentenced to a calendar month's imprisonment will never be imprisoned for a greater number of days than there are in the month in which he was sentenced" (per Cotton, L. J., (*Migotti* v. *Colville,* sup.). So as regards the requirement of a calendar month's Notice of Action,—"In considering what is the length of a Calendar Month, it is sufficient, when the months are broken whatever be the length of either, to go from one day in one month to the corresponding day in the other" (per Cockburn, C. J., *Freeman* v. *Read,* 11 W. R. 802 ; 4 B. & S. 184).

V. Month.

CALL.—*V.* Liberty to Call.

CALLED.—"My estate *called* A." is a general description, not confined to a particular locality, and therefore extrinsic evidence may be given of what is included in such a devise ; *secus,* if there were a description of lands "at" or "in" a particular locality (*Ricketts* v. *Turquand,* 1 H. L. Ca. 472 ; cited 1 Jarm. 427, 428). *V.* Of.

CALLING.—Carrying on a School is a "Calling," within a restrictive covenant (*Doe* v. *Keeling,* 1 M. & S. 95 : *Kemp* v. *Sober,* 20 L. J. Ch. 602 ; 1 Sim. N. S. 517).

V. Ordinary Calling.

CALUMNIATOR.—*V.* Challenge.

CAN BE.—"Can be" means "can reasonably be" (per Knight-Bruce, L. J., *Whicker* v. *Hume,* 21 L. J. Ch. 406 ; 1 D. G. M. & G. 506 ; 14 Bea. 509 : adopted by P. C. in *Jex* v. *McKinney,* 58 L. J. P. C. 69 ; 14 App. Ca. 77).

CAN TRANSFER.—*V.* Left.

CANCELLED.—*V.* To be Cancelled.

CANDIDATE.—"The correct sense of the word 'Candidate' is, a person offering himself to the suffrages of the people" (per Lord Ellenborough, *Morris* v. *Burdett,* 2 M. & S. 217). But on this the question arises, when does a person so offer himself ? This question, according to the purpose for which it is asked, will vary in its answer.

A person who, with his consent, received a parliamentary nomination, but who declined to go to the poll, was not a "Candidate" liable to expenses of polling booths, &c., within s. 71, Reform Act, 2 W. 4, c. 45 (*Muntz* v. *Sturge*, 10 L. J. Ex. 234 ; 8 M. & W. 302). But a candidate cannot now withdraw from nomination, except "during the time appointed for the election" (35 & 36 V. c. 33, s. 1),—*i.e.* the hours for nomination,—or by neglecting, on request, to find security for the returning officer's expenses within one hour afterwards (38 & 39 V. c. 84, s. 3). How far then would *Muntz* v. *Sturge* be now operative in case no request for security be made within the time prescribed by the section last cited, and yet the candidate, before the expenses of the polling had been incurred, repudiated his candidature and consequent liability? Such a person would not be a "Candidate" within s. 71, Reform Act, and on the other hand the returning officer would not have availed himself of s. 3, 38 & 39 V. c. 84. How then could he claim for services repudiated before rendered? If it be said that the time for withdrawing the nomination being past, the nominee remains a "Candidate" in spite of himself, and all the machinery of an election must go on, and that that would be the nominee's fault; it may be replied, that the fault is equally the returning officer's for not having required the security, which request would have at once settled the matter. It would seem, therefore, that in the case supposed the returning officer would be without remedy (but see a contrary opinion, Cunningham on Elections, 66, 67).

A person who, with his consent, received a parliamentary nomination, but declined to go to the poll, was held to be a "Candidate" within 17 & 18 V. c. 102, and the 21 & 22 V. c. 87; and as such liable to the fee of £10 to the election auditor, an office abolished by 26 & 27 V. c. 29 (*Edwards* v. *Whitehurst*, 29 L. J. Ex. 329 ; 5 H. & N. 131).

But the most important aspect in which the question can be put, of when and how a person becomes a Parliamentary Candidate, is as it affects his return or the liability of himself or agents for corrupt practices. In this view the statutory definition is given in s. 63 of the Corrupt and Illegal Practices Prevention Act, 1883 (46 & 47 V. c. 51), and is as follows:—

"Candidate at an election," and "Candidate," "unless the context otherwise requires, shall include (1) any person elected to serve in parliament at such election, and (2) any person who is nominated as a candidate at such election, or is declared by himself or by others to be a candidate *on or after the day of the issue of the writ for such election, or after the dissolution or vacancy in consequence of which such writ has been issued.*

Provided that where a person has been nominated as a candidate or declared to be a candidate, by others, then,—

(*a*) If he was so nominated or declared without his consent, nothing in this Act shall be construed to impose any liability on such person, unless he has afterwards given his assent to such nomination or declaration, or has been elected; and (*b*) If he was so nominated or declared, either without his consent or in his absence, and he takes no part in the election, he may, if he thinks fit, make the Declaration respecting election expenses contained in the 2nd Part of the 2nd Sch. to this Act, and the election agent shall, so far as circumstances admit, comply with the provisions of this Act with respect to expenses incurred on account of or in respect of the conduct or management of the election in like manner as if the candidate had been nominated or declared with his consent."

This definition establishes two classes of candidates :

1. Successful :
2. Unsuccessful.

1. As regards successful candidates, a person "*elected*" is a candidate, and is responsible for all the acts of himself, or, his agents for the time being, that bear upon his election (*Youghal*, 21 L. T. 306 ; 1 O'M. & H. 291). There is no limitation of time. A successful candidate is a "candidate" as soon as he begins to operate with a view to his election ; and thenceforward all the liabilities, disqualifications, and penalties of a "candidate" attach to him (The *Boston* Case, 1874, was a memorable instance of this, 2 O'M. & H. 161 : *Malcolm* v. *Ingram*, L. R. 10 C. P. 168 ; 44 L. J. C. P. 121).

2. As regards unsuccessful candidates, the difference is indicated above by italics. An unsuccessful candidate would not be a "candidate" penally responsible, except for acts done on or after the day of the issuing of the writ or after the dissolution or vacancy.

CANISTER.—*V.* CASE OR CANISTER.

CANNOT.—"Cannot" includes a legal inability, as well as a physical impossibility (*The Newbattle*, 54 L. J. P. D. & A. 16 ; 10 P. D. 33).

CANONRY.—*V. Walrond* v. *Pollard*, 3 Dy. 294 a : *Ecc. Commrs.* v. *Kildare*, 8 Ir. Ch. Rep. 100.

CANTARIA.—*V.* CHAUNTRY.

CAPABLE.—"Capable of taking effect ;" *V.* SUBSISTING.
V. INCAPABLE.

CAPACITY.—A claim arising in respect of moneys improperly received and retained by a Director of a Building Society, is not a Dispute "in his Capacity of a member of the Society" within s. 2, Building Societies Act, 1884 (47 & 48 V. c. 41), so that it ought to be referred to arbitration (*Municipal Permanent Bg. Socy.* v. *Richards*, 39 Ch. D. 372 ; 58 L. J. Ch. 8 : *Cp.* CHARACTER).

CAPITA.—*V.* PER CAPITA.

CAPITAL.—"The word 'Capital' for the purposes of a Joint Stock Co., may have any one of at least three meanings, viz. :—

(1.) Nominal Capital :—the amount named in the Memorandum of Association, say, £100,000 in 10,000 shares of £10 each.

(2.) Issued Capital :—say 5,000 shares of £10 each, part of the above nominal capital.

(3.) Paid-up Capital :—say £25,000, being £5 per share on each of the above 5,000 shares.

In which one of these meanings it is used in the Acts, it is very difficult to say : probably it is used sometimes in one and sometimes in another. In the *Dronfield Co.* (17 Ch. D. 76, 86 ; 50 L. J. Ch. 387), Jessel, M.R., pointed out that in s. 12 of the Companies Act, 1862, and s. 9 of the Companies Act, 1867, it must mean not merely 'Nominal Capital' but 'Issued Capital' or 'Trading Capital.' By s. 3 of the Companies Act, 1877, the word as used in the Companies Act, 1867, is to 'include' paid-up capital ; and looking at s. 5 of the Companies Act, 1877, it must include unissued capital, for that section gives power to reduce capital by cancelling unissued shares. The result, therefore, would seem to be that the Acts of 1867 and 1877 in fact cover all three meanings." (Buckl. 511).

CAPITAL EMPLOYED.—On the sale of a business, a representation as to the "Capital employed" therein by the vendor, means "the amount in pounds, shillings, and pence which he has invested therein, and which, if not so invested, might be in his pocket, or otherwise expended on his account" (per Kekewich, J., *Glazier* v. *Rolls*, 58 L. J. Ch. 330 ; 37 W. R. 430 ; reversed on app. on a ground not affecting the above definition, 5 Times Rep. 691).

V. AT THE PRESENT TIME.

CAPITAL MONEY.—The definition of "Capital Money" in s. 2 (9), Settled Land Act, 1882, should be transposed thus,—"Capital Money arising under this Act and receivable for the trusts and purposes of the Settlement, is, in this Act referred to as Capital Money arising under this Act" (per Esher, M.R., *Marlborough* v. *Majoribanks*, 32 Ch. D. 5 ; 55 L. J. Ch. 339 ; 34 W. R. 377 ; 54 L. T. 914).

Proceeds from sale of Heir-looms (*Marlborough* v. *Majoribanks*, sup.), a Fine on granting a Lease (s. 4, 47 & 48 V. c. 18), Money required for Enfranchisement or for Equality of Exchange or Partition (s. 18, S. L. Act, 1882), Money in Court, or in the hands of trustees, liable to be laid out in purchase of lands (ss. 32, 33, Ib. : *Re Byron*, 23 Ch. D. 171 ; 53 L. J. Ch. 152 ; 48 L. T. 515 ; 31 W. R. 517 : *Re Mackenzie*, 23 Ch. D. 759 ; 52 L. J. Ch. 726 ; 48 L. T. 936 : *Clarke* v. *Thornton*, 35 Ch. D. 314 ; 56 L. J. Ch. 302 ; 35 W. R. 603 ; 56 L. T. 294 : *Sv.* as to the last case, *Burke* v. *Gore*, 13 L. R. Ir. 367) are "Capital Moneys" within the Settled

Land Act, 1882; but accumulations of surplus rents are not (*Re Newcastle*, 24 Ch. D. 129; 52 L. J. Ch. 645; 48 L. T. 779; 31 W. R. 782).

Vh. Tudor, Char. Trusts, 280, 281.

CAPITAL NOT CALLED UP.—Includes unissued Shares (*English Channel Steamship Co.* v. *Rolt*, 17 Ch. D. 715).

CAPTIVES.—*V.* Prisoner.

CAPTORS.—*V.* Joint Captors.

CAPTURE.—"Capture," in a Marine Insurance, and generally, means a hostile seizure with intent to keep or to deprive the owner of the thing seized (*Johnston* v. *Hogg*, 52 L. J. Q. B. 343; 10 Q. B. D. 432; and dicta there cited). In *Cory* v. *Burr* (52 L. J. Q. B. 659; 8 App. Ca. 393), which was also a case on a Marine Policy and contained the usual warranty against "Capture and Seizure," Selborne, L.C., said,—"I am disposed to agree that if the word 'Capture' had stood alone it might have appeared to point to a *belligerent* capture."

V. Seizure.

CARE: CUSTODY.—"Whether the custody be domestic or not, if a person,—no matter who he is or in what relation he stands,—has the care and custody of a Lunatic, and during the course of that care or custody abuses, ill-treats, or wilfully neglects a lunatic he is within" s. 9, 16 & 17 V. c. 96, and liable to its penalty (per Coleridge, C.J., *Buchannan* v. *Hardy*, 56 L. J. M. C. 45; 18 Q. B. D. 486; 35 W. R. 453; 51 J. P. 741). In that case it was accordingly held that a parent is within the section; and the decision in *R.* v. *Rundle* (24 L. J. M. C. 129; 1 Dears. 482), that a husband is not, was adversely criticised. A brother is within the section (*R.* v. *Porter*, 33 L. J. M. C. 126).

CARGO.—"The word 'Cargo,' as referred to a Ship, is very intelligible, and must mean the whole loading. It may as well be said that the word 'Ship' is uncertain, one being much bigger than another" (per Cur. *Sargent* v. *Reed*, 2 Stra. 1228).

"Generally speaking the term 'Cargo,' unless there is something in the context to give it a different signification, means the entire load of the ship which carries it" (per Mellish, L.J., *Borrowman* v. *Drayton*, 2 Ex. D. 19; 46 L. J. Q. B. 276). So when a contract shews that the buyer of a "Cargo" is to have complete control over the destination of the vessel, "Cargo" means the entire ship-load and not a shipment, and the buyer of *e.g.*, "a Cargo of from 2,500 to 3,000 Barrels (seller's option)," may reject a tender of 3,000 Barrels on the ground that other Barrels had been shipped by the same vessel and therefore that a "Cargo" was not tendered (*Borrowman* v. *Drayton*, sup.: *Va. Kreuger* v. *Blanck*, L. R. 5 Ex. 179; 39 L. J. Ex. 160: *Vf.* 1 Maude & P. 313). And, on the other hand, the buyer of a "Cargo," the quantity being mentioned, is bound to take the

Cargo, whatever its quantity, unless the contrary is very plainly shewn (*Levi* v. *Berk*, 2 Times Rep. 898).

Where, however, the question is on a Policy of Insurance, "Cargo" does not necessarily mean the whole loading (*Houghton* v. *Gilbart*, 7 C. & P. 701 : *V.* that case contrasted with *Sargent* v. *Reed*, sup. in jdgmt. of Cleasby, B., *Kreuger* v. *Blanck*, sup.).

As to the meaning of "*Full and Complete* Cargo;" *V. Southampton Steam Co.* v. *Clarke*, L. R. 4 Ex. 73; 6 Ib. 53 ; 38 L. J. Ex. 54 ; 40 Ib. 8 ; *Duckett* v. *Satterfield*, L. R. 3 C. P. 227 ; 37 L. J. C. P. 144 : *Morris* v. *Levison*, 1 C. P. D. 155 ; 45 L. J. C. P. 409. And as to the effect of custom on the mode of loading a "full and complete cargo" of sugar; *V. Cuthbert* v. *Cumming*, 10 Ex. 809 ; 11 Ib. 405 ; *Vth.* 1 Maude & P. 294.

"Cargo to be brought to and taken from *alongside* free of expense and risk to the ship;" *V.* 1 Maude & P. 291, citing *Wright* v. *New Zealand Shipping Co.*, 4 Ex. D. 165.

"Cargo is to be discharged with all despatch according to the custom of the port;" *V.* 1 Maude & P. 292, citing *Postlethwaite* v. *Freeland*, 4 Ex. D. 155 ; 5 App. Ca. 599 ; 48 L. J. Ex. 353 ; 49 Ib. 630.

Vh. Benj. 684, 688 ; Blackb. 217, 223.

CARNAL KNOWLEDGE.—"Carnal Knowledge means the penetration to any the slightest degree of the organ known, by the male organ of generation" (Steph. Cr. 186) ; *Vf.* Arch. Cr. 803 ; Rosc. Cr. 897.

CARPENTER.—A "Carpenter" within the late Bankry definition of "Trader" meant "a person who purchases timber and other materials which he works up as a Carpenter, and not a person who merely works at the trade" (Arch. Bankry. 11 Ed. 35, citing *Chapman* v. *Lamphire*, 3 Mod. 155; 1 Cooke, B. L. 49).

CARRIAGE.—Speaking generally a "Carriage" includes anything on which men or goods are carried: therefore a Bicycle is a "Carriage" within the Highway Act (5 & 6 W. 4, c. 50, s. 78), although bicycles were not in vogue when the Act passed (*Taylor* v. *Goodwin*, 4 Q. B. D. 228 ; 48 L. J. M. C. 104 ; 27 W. R. 489 ; 43 J. P. 653). "A carriage need not be necessarily on wheels ; for instance, it may be drawn as a sledge, so as to facilitate its use on a road" (Ib.). "Bicycles, Tricycles, Velocipedes, and other similar Machines," are now expressly declared to be "Carriages" within the Highway Acts (s. 85, Local Gov. Act, 1888).

But where a private Turnpike Act imposed a toll "for every *Carriage* of whatever description and for whatever purpose which shall be drawn or impelled or set or kept in motion by steam or any other power or agency than being drawn by any horse or beast ;" it was held that a Bicycle was *not* included, and that those words applied "only to carriages of a heavy description which both wear the road and are impelled by some mechanical power" (*Williams* v. *Ellis*, 5 Q. B. D. 175 ; 49 L. J. M. C. 47 ; 28 W. R. 416 ; 44 J. P. 394 ; distinguishing *Taylor* v. *Goodwin*, sup.).

V. VEHICLE : WHEELED CARRIAGE : LOCOMOTIVES : LOCOMOTIVE ENGINE : CART.

CARRIED.—"Goods carried into any Port in England or Wales in any ship," s. 6, 24 V. c. 10 ; *V. Dapueto* v. *Wyllie*, 43 L. J. Ad. 20 ; L. R. 5 P. C. 482.

CARRIER.—A "Carrier," as mentioned in 3 Car. 1, c. 1, means a Carrier of *Goods* (per Counsel in *Sandiman* v. *Breach*, 7 B. & C. 97 : *Va. Ex p. Middleton*, 3 B. & C. 164).

CARRY.—"To carry" a person, includes putting him in a position to be carried, and therefore placing a debtor on a coach for the purpose of conveying him to prison, was a carrying within s. 1, 32 G. 2, c. 28 (*Dewhurst* v. *Pearson*, 2 L. J. Ex. 143 ; 1 C. & M. 365 ; 3 Tyr. 242 ; 1 Dowl. 664).

CARRY AWAY.—*V.* TAKE AND CARRY AWAY.

CARRYING INTO EXECUTION.—An agreement compromising an action to which a Local Board is party, is not "a Contract·necessary for carrying the Act into execution" within s. 173, P. H. Act, 1875 (*A.-G.* v. *Gaskill*, 52 L. J. Ch. 163 ; 22 Ch. D. 537).

CARRY ON.—"The phrase 'Carrying on' implies a repetition or series of acts" (per Brett, L. J., *Smith* v. *Anderson*, 50 L. J. Ch. 52 ; 15 Ch. D. 247 : *Vf. Re Siddall*, 54 L. J. Ch. 682 ; 29 Ch. D. 1 : *Crowther* v. *Thorley*, 50 L. T. 43 ; 32 W. R. 350 : *Re Thomas*, 14 Q. B. D. 379).

A Railway Company "carries on business," ss. 60, 128, 9 & 10 V. c. 95, only at its principal office where the directors meet and the general business of the Company is transacted (*Minor* v. *Lond. & N. W. Ry.*, 26 L. J. C. P. 39 ; 1 C. B. N. S. 325 : *Shiels* v. *G. N. Ry.*, 30 L. J. Q. B. 331 ; 9 W. R. 739 : *Brown* v. *Lond. & N. W. Ry.*, 32 L. J. Q. B. 318 ; 4 B. & S. 326 : *Le Tailleur* v. *S. E. Ry.*, 3 C. P. D. 18). So, a Building Contractor "carries on business" where his general place of business is, and not at the locality where particular contracts are being executed (*Gorslett* v. *Harris*, 29 L. T. O. S. 75). But if the nature of a man's business be such that he must be personally moving about within a particular district, *e.g.*, an Apothecary,—that is carrying on business within that district within s. 128 of the same statute (*Mitchell* v. *Hender*, 23 L. J. Q. B. 273). A manufacturing joint-stock Company "dwells and carries on business" within the lastly mentioned section, at its place of manufacture and sale, and not at the registered office of the company (*Keynsham Lime Co.* v. *Baker*, 33 L. J. Ex. 41 ; 2 H. & C. 729).

To "carry on" a business means, primarily, to carry on one's *own* business ; therefore a salaried clerk does not "carry on business" at the office of his employer within the meaning of s. 12, Mayor's Court Procedure Act, 1857 (*Lewis* v. *Graham*, 20 Q. B. D. 784 ; 22 Ib. 1 ; 57 L. J. Q. B. 376 ; 58 Ib. 117 ; 36 W. R. 574 ; 37 Ib. 73 ; 59 L. T. 35). *Vh. Le Tailleur* v. *S. E. Ry.* (sup.).

A clerk in the Admiralty does not "carry on business" at his office within s. 40, London Small Debts Act (10 & 11 V. c. lxxi.) (*Buckley* v. *Hann*, 19 L. J. Ex. 151 ; 5 Ex. 43) : nor does a Deputy Sealer of the Court of Chancery (*Rolfe* v. *Learmouth*, 19 L. J. Q. B. 10 ; 14 Q. B. 196), nor a clerk in the Privy Council Office (*Sangster* v. *Cave*, 19 L. J. Ex. 313 ; nom. *Sangster* v. *Kay*, 5 Ex. 386), nor a partner in a mine on the cost-book principle, the business of which mine is wholly conducted by an agent (*Mitchell* v. *Hender*, sup.), *quà* s. 128, 9 & 10 V. c. 95 :—for the principle in these cases would seem to be that neither of the persons carried on "business" at all : *Va. Glennie* v. *Delmar*, 1 L. M. & P. 402.

But as a place where a Debtor's Summons could be served (R. 17, Bankry. Rules, 1870), it was held that a clerk "carried on business" at his employer's office (*Re Bowie, Ex p. Breull*, 50 L. J. Ch. 384 ; 16 Ch. D. 484 ; 29 W. R. 299).

But none of the foregoing cases apply when the question is, where are profits earned on which Income Tax is payable under 16 & 17 V. c. 34, s. 1 (*Erichsen* v. *Last*, 51 L. J. Q. B. 86 ; 8 Q. B. D. 414). In that case Jessel, M.R., said in his jdgmt. :—"There is no principle of law which decides what 'carrying on' trade is—a multitude of circumstances make up what is called 'carrying on' a trade ; for it is a compound fact made up of a variety of things. Now the facts of this case show that this is a Company with stations in this kingdom, with the ends of cables in this kingdom, and these cables are worked from here by the staff of the Company. There is an office in London, and the Company takes messages and sends them to foreign parts. There is, as it appears to me, a perfectly plain case of 'carrying on' trade here. A Company in this country which regularly undertakes the carrying of goods abroad for money as part of its ordinary business, carries on trade in this country, even though the whole of the carriage is done abroad. The mere fact that the Company enters into contracts in this country with English subjects for the right of carriage appears to me to be the same thing as if it made similar contracts for the sale of goods. Whether the contract is for carriage or for the right to transmit messages makes no difference. So if a Railway Company with a station at Dover and another at Calais, carries passengers from Dover to Calais as a regular practice, that would be a trading at Dover" (*Vf. Tischler* v. *Apthorpe*, 33 W. R. 548 ; 1 Times Rep. 344 : *Pomeroy* v.

Apthorpe, 56 L. J. Q. B. 155 : *Werle* v. *Colquhoun*, 57 L. J. Q. B. 326 ; 20 Q. B. D. 753). *V.* RESIDE.

As regards Covenants and Agreements *in Restraint of Trade*, the cases run a little fine.

An Agreement by A. not to "*carry on*" a *Business* "either in his own name or for his own benefit, or in the name or names, or for the benefit of any person," etc., is not broken by A. becoming an Agent for another person within the prescribed district (*Clarke* v. *Watkins*, 11 W. R. 319 : *Allen* v. *Taylor*, 39 L. J. Ch. 627 ; L. R. 10 Eq. 52 ; 19 W. R. 556). If, however, the agreement relates to a *Profession*,—*e.g.*, a Surgeon's,—the rule would be different, for the word "Profession" is much more emphatic than "Business :" carrying on a Trade, implies sharing in the profit or loss, but a person carries on a Profession when only acting as an Assistant to another (per Cotton, L.J., *Palmer* v. *Mallett*, 36 Ch. D. 411 ; 57 L. J. Ch. 226 ; 58 L. T. 64 ; 36 W. R. 460 : it is however to be observed that in that case, the words were shall not "directly or indirectly, and either alone or in partnership with, *or as assistant of*, any person . . . carry on the profession," &c.).

But if instead of, or in addition to, using the words "carry on," the restriction extends to "engage in" (*Rolfe* v. *Rolfe*, 15 Sim. 88 : *Vf.* ENGAGE IN), or "concerned or interested in" (*Newling* v. *Dobell*, 38 L. J. Ch. 111), or "concerned in" (*Jones* v. *Harrison*, 4 Ch. D. 636), then, though only relating to a Business, it will be broken by the agreeing party acting for another within the prescribed area, either as Assistant or Journeyman, and the same rule would obtain if the words of prohibition are, shall not "*carry on either as master or servant*" (*Proctor* v. *Sargent*, 10 L. J. C. P. 34 ; 2 M. & G. 20 : *Benwell* v. *Inns*, 26 L. J. Ch. 663 ; 24 Bea. 307).

Soliciting and supplying customers, or attending to patients, within the defined district, even without having any place of residence or business therein, is "carrying on" business there within a prohibiting agreement (*Turner* v. *Evans*, 22 L. J. Q. B. 412 ; 2 E. & B. 512 ; 2 D. G. M. & G. 740 : *Brampton* v. *Beddoes*, 13 C. B. N. S. 538 : *Mitchell* v. *Hender*, sup.). *V.* PRACTISE.

Where a Company is in liquidation and its business is being carried on thereunder with a view to its sale as a going concern, that is not a carrying on of the business by the Company within a contract by A. with the Company that no similar business should be carried on by A., so long as the Company carried on such a business (*Shorthorn Dairy Co.* v. *Hall*, 31 S. J. 479).

As to when a Banker "ceases" to carry on business ; *V. A.-G.* v. *Birkbeck*, 53 L. J. Q. B. 378 ; 12 Q. B. D. 605.

V. BUSINESS.

CARRY OUT.—The penalty imposed by s. 7, 6 & 7 W. 4, c. 37, if any seller of bread shall "*carry out or deliver*" bread without being provided with scales and weights, "refers only to a carrying out or delivery of bread by a person who is therein acting *as* a baker or seller of bread; and not to a carrying out or delivery by a person who, though in fact a baker or seller of bread, is, in carrying out or delivering the bread, acting merely from friendliness or the like, and not as such baker or seller of bread" (per Field, J., *Daniel* v. *Whitfield*, 54 L. J. M. C. 134; 15 Q. B. D. 408; 53 L. T. 471; 33 W. R. 905; 49 J. P. 694; 1 Times Rep. 574).

V. FOR SALE.

CARRY OVER.—To "Carry over" a Stock Exchange transaction is where the buyer, not wishing to pay for what he has bought on the day appointed, gets the settlement "carried over," or adjourned, to a subsequent settling-day; *Vh. Sachs* v. *Spielman*, W. N. (89) 103; 5 Times Rep. 487.

CART.—"Waggon, *Cart* or other such carriage," s. 7, 5 & 6 W. 4, c. 50;—"I think that this is a description of vehicles which carry heavy goods, and go slowly along the road. It cannot, in my opinion, extend to gigs, dog-carts, or gentlemen's carriages" (per Lush, J., *Danby* v. *Hunter*, 49 L. J. M. C. 16; 5 Q. B. D. 20; 44 J. P. 283). In that case it was held that a light spring cart used by the maker of agricultural implements for taking his wares to market, and in which he also drove out himself and family, and on which he paid tax under s. 18, 32 & 33 V. c. 14, was not a "Cart" within s. 7, 5 & 6 W. 4, c. 50.

V. LIGHT CART: TAXED CART: CARRIAGE.

CART ROAD.—A. conveyed the surface of lands reserving a "Waggon or Cart Road," 18 feet wide, to be at all times kept in repair at his own cost; held, that this reservation did not authorize A. to lay down a Railroad or Tramway (*Bidder* v. *N. Staffordshire Ry.*, 4 Q. B. D. 412).

CARUCATA.—"*Carucata terræ*, a ploughland, may containe houses, milles, pasture, medow, wood, &c." (Co. Litt. 86 b; *Va.* Ib. 5 a). *V.* PLOW-LAND: HIDE: OXGANGE.

CASE.—"In case of the Death;" *V.* DIE.

CASE OR CANISTER.—A linen or calico Bag is not "a Case or Canister" within s. 23, sub.-s. 2 (b), Metalliferous Mines Regn. Act, 1872, 35 & 36 V. c. 77 (*Foster* v. *Diphwys Casson Co.*, 56 L. J. M. C. 21; 18 Q. B. D. 428; 51 J. P. 470; 3 Times Rep. 301). "We should be violating the rules of construction if we were not to say that the words 'Case or Canister' explained one another (*Sv.* OR), and that 'Case' meant something in the nature of a 'Canister,'—something that is solid, substantial, covered over and calculated to prevent the escape of its contents and to resist their accidental ignition. The whole end and object of the Act is to preserve human life, and in placing the construction we do upon the rule in question, and holding that Case must be something in the nature of a Canister, we are construing it in accordance with its manifest intention and giving effect to the spirit of the Act" (per Coleridge, C.J., Ib.). "I confess it never occurred to me that 'Case' could mean a Bag. I always thought until the quotation of the definition in Dr. Johnson's Dictionary, that 'Case' meant something solid; but according to that definition a Net might be a 'Case'" (per Grove, J., Ib.).

CASH.—This is a stricter term than "Money." In *Beales* v. *Crisford* (13 L. J. Ch. 26; 13 Sim. 592), it was held that neither a Promissory Note payable to order, nor Long Annuities, nor Colombian Bonds came within "Cash or monies so called" (1 Jarm. 769, n.; *Vf.* Wms. Exs. 1194, n.). Bank of England Notes, and it would seem other Bank Notes, would pass under a bequest of "Cash" (*Miller* v. *Race*, 1 Burr. 452; 1 Sm. L. C. 491).

V. Money: In Cash.

CASH AGAINST BILL OF LADING.—*V. Ogg* v. *Shuter*, 44 L. J. C. P. 161; L. R. 10 C. P. 159.

CASH UNDER THE CONTROL OF THE COURT.—These words, occurring in s. 10 of the Law of Property Act, 1860 (23 & 24 V. c. 38) mean cash standing in the name of the Accountant-General in any cause or matter; and therefore include moneys paid into Court under the Lands C. C. Act, 1845, or under the Settled Estates Acts (*Ex p. St. John Baptist College*, 52 L. J. Ch. 268; 22 Ch. D. 93: over-ruling *Re Boyd*, 42 L. J. Ch. 506; 21 W. R. 667; and *Ex p. Rector of Kirksmeaton*, 51 L. J. Ch. 581; 20 Ch. D. 203); or money paid into Court under a Private Act and invested in Exchequer Bills (*Jackson* v. *Tyas*, 52 L. J. Ch. 830). *Vf.* Dan. Ch. Pr. 1765: *Re Wedderburn*, 47 L. J. Ch. 743; 9 Ch. D. 112: Ord. 22, R. 17, R. S. C., Nov. 1888.

CASH WITH OPTION OF BILL.—"'Cash less discount at a fixed rate, with option of Bill,' or *vice versâ*, 'Bill, with option of Cash less discount;'—in the former case, the seller can sue for the price of goods sold and delivered immediately on the buyer's refusal to accept at the date fixed. In the latter, the seller cannot sue for the price of the goods sold and delivered, until the due date of the bill drawn by him, even although the buyer has refused to accept it; but he may bring a special action against the buyer for non-acceptance of the bill" (Benj. 697, citing *Anderson* v. *Carlisle Horse Clothing Co.*, 21 L. T. 760).

CASTLE.—"By the name of a *castle* one or more manors may be conveyed: *et è converso*, by the name of a manor, &c., a castle may passe"

(Co. Litt. 5 a). "But by a Castle most commonly is signified no more but the house or building, and the parcel of ground inclosed wherein it doth stand" (Touch. 92 ; *Vf.* 2 Inst. 31 ; Mad. Baron. Anglic. 17). *V.* MANORS.

Note :—"No subject can build a Castle or house of strength imbattled" without license from the Crown (Co. Litt. 5 a).

CASUALTY.—*V.* FIRE.

CATTLE.—Bulls, Cows, Oxen, Steers, Bullocks, Heifers, Calves, Sheep and Lambs are "Cattle" (*Vh.* 14 G. 2, c. 1; 15 G. 2, c. 34). "The Legislature by the last Act says that it was not to be extended to Horses, Pigs or Goats, although all these are 'Cattle' (*Fletcher* v. *Sondes*, 3 Bing. 581). Yet Horses are 'Cattle' within the Black Act, 9 G. 1, c. 22 (*R.* v. *Paty*, 2 W. Bl. 721) ; and Bulls are not 'Cattle' within 3 G. 4, c. 71 (*Ex p. Hill*, 3 C. & P. 225)." Dwar. 636.

"Cattle," in s. 1, 28 & 29 V. c. 60, includes horses (*Wright* v. *Pearson*, L. R. 4 Q. B. 582 ; 33 J. P. 534), and, *semble*, pigs (*Child* v. *Hearn*, L. R. 9 Ex. 176 ; 43 L. J. Ex. 100). The latter case shows that "Cattle," as used in s. 68, 8 V. c. 20, includes pigs.

CATTLE GATE.—"'Cattlegate,' also called 'Beastgate.'—Sometimes the soil is vested in the owners as tenants in common in fee ; *R.* v. *Whixley*, 1 T. R. 137: *Va. Mellington* v. *Goodtitle*, Andr. 106, and on app. nom. *Bennington* v. *Goodtitle*, 2 Stra. 1084 ; a dictum in *Barnes* v. *Peterson*, 2 Stra. 1063 : *R.* v. *Watson*, 5 East, 480 ; where the beasts were turned out by such burgesses as chose to do so, according to a stint by a leet jury. Sometimes it is a mere right of pasture, the soil remaining in the lord of the manor ; *Lonsdale* v. *Rigg*, 11 Ex. 654 ; 1 H. & N. 923 ; 25 L. J. Ex. 73 ; 26 Ib. 196 : *V.* Wms. on Commons, 81 *et seq.*; Hall on Profits à Prendre, 23 *et seq.*" (Elph. 565.)

CATTLE SALESMAN.—A Farmer accustomed, for profit, to buy and sell more sheep than necessary to stock his farm, was held a "Cattle or Sheep Salesman" within the late Bankry. definition of "Trader" (*Ex p. Newall*, 3 Dea. 333).

CAUSA CAUSANS.—Is the "real effective cause of damage" (per Esher, M. R., *Pandorf* v. *Hamilton*, 55 L. J. Q. B. 548). *V.* CAUSED BY.

CAUSE.—"Cause," "is not a technical word signifying one kind or another, it is *causa jurisdictionis*, any suit, action, matter or other similar proceeding competently brought before, and litigated in, a Court" (per Selborne, L. C., *Re Green*, 51 L. J. Q. B. 40 ; nom. *Green* v. *Penzance*, 6 App. Ca. 657).

For the purposes of the Jud. Acts, "Cause," includes "any Action, Suit, or other Original Proceeding between a plaintiff and defendant, and any Criminal proceeding by the Crown" (s. 100, Jud. Act, 1873). *V.* ACTION.

A *Rule Nisi* against a Police Magistrate to hear an application for a Summons, is "a Cause or Matter *for Trial or Hearing*" within Sch. 52, Order as to Supreme Court Fees, 1884, and therefore the fee of £2 is payable on entering it at the Crown Office (*Ex p. Hasker*, 54 L. J. M. C. 94; 14 Q. B. D. 82); but an Appeal from Chambers is not such a Cause or Matter (*Ex p. Dudley*, 33 W. R. 751).

"Cause or Matter *relating to Real Estate*," Ord. 51, R. 1, R. S. C.; *V. Staines* v. *Staines*, 30 S. J. 502; W. N. (86) 113.

The "Cause" that under s. 83, subs. 4, Bankry. Act, 1869, had to be "shown" for the Removal of a Trustee, need not necessarily have amounted to dishonesty; unfitness, in the opinion of the Court, sufficed (*Ex p. Newitt*, 54 L. J. Q. B. 245; 14 Q. B. D. 177; 1 Times Rep. 98).

Cp. DUE CAUSE.

"Lawfull Cawse" to reject from the Communion, 1 Ed. 6, c. 1, s. 8;—*V. Jenkins* v. *Cook*, 45 L. J. P. C. 1; 1 P. D. 80.

"Cause or Matter," Ord. 39, R. 1, R. S. C.; *V. Matthews* v. *Ovey*, 53 L. J. Q. B. 439; 13 Q. B. D. 403: *Mason* v. *Wirral*, 4 Q. B. D. 459.

"For the *Same Cause*," s. 45, 24 & 25 V. c. 100; "The word 'Cause' may undoubtedly mean 'Act,' but it is ambiguous, and it may also, and perhaps with greater propriety, be held to mean 'Cause for the Accusation'" (per Byles, J., *R.* v. *Morris*, 36 L. J. M. C. 84; L. R. 1 C. C. 90); and, in accordance with that view, it was there held that a previous summary conviction for an assault under s. 42, was not for the "Same Cause" as a subsequent indictment for Manslaughter arising from the same assault. But an action for damages for an assault is for the "Same Cause,"—*i.e.* Same Offence,—as a previous conviction for the same assault (*Masper* v. *Brown*, 45 L. J. C. P. 203; 1 C. P. D. 97: *Holden* v. *King*, 46 L. J. Ex. 75).

V. CAUSE OF ACTION: CRIMINAL CAUSE: GOOD CAUSE.

CAUSE.—"To Cause;" *V.* INFLICT: *Vf.* CAUSED BY.

CAUSE AND EFFECT.—*V.* EFFECT.

CAUSE AND MATTER.—Stating in an Appeal Notice its "Cause and Matter," 49 G. 3, c. 68, s. 5;—*V. R.* v. *Oxfordshire Jus.*, 1 B. & C. 279.

CAUSE OF ACTION.—A "Cause of Action" is the entire set of facts that gives rise to an enforceable claim; the phrase comprises every fact which, if traversed, the plaintiff must prove in order to obtain judgment (per Esher, M.R., *Read* v. *Brown*, 58 L. J. Q. B. 120; 22 Q. B. D. 128).

Therefore, as used in s. 60 of the Act establishing the modern County

Courts (9 & 10 V. c. 95), this phrase, according to its natural construction, meant, the *whole* cause of action ; *e.g.*, the order, or other contract for, as well as the delivery of, the goods in a claim for goods sold and delivered (*Borthwick* v. *Walton*, 24 L. J. C. P. 83 ; 15 C. B. 501 ; 24 L. T. O. S. 271: *Aris* v. *Orchard*, 30 L. J. Ex. 21 ; 6 H. & N. 160 : *Va. Hernaman* v. *Smith*, 24 L. J. Ex. 175 ; 10 Ex. 659 : *Barnes* v. *Marshall*, 21 L. J. Q. B. 388 : *Fuller* v. *Mackay*, 22 L. J. Q. B. 415 ; 2 E. & B. 573).

So of "Cause of Action" in Mayor's Court Procedure Act, 1857, 20 & 21 V. c. clvii. (*Cooke* v. *Gill*, L. R. 8 C. P. 107). And when the plaintiff is an assignee from the original creditor, the assignment to him is part of his Cause of Action ; and, therefore, where a debt was entirely contracted outside the City of London, but an assignment of it to the plaintiff had been made in the City, it was held that part of the Cause of Action arose in the City, and that (under s. 12) the Mayor's Court had jurisdiction (*Read* v. *Brown*, sup.). It seems a little difficult to reconcile that decision with a previous decision under the same section, where it was held that the whole Cause of Action on a written agreement under the Stat. of Frauds arises as soon as the defendant has signed it (*Alderton* v. *Archer*, 54 L. J. Q. B. 12 ; 14 Q. B. D. 1). *Vf. Cowan* v. *O'Connor*, 57 L. J. Q. B. 401 ; 20 Q. B. D. 640 ; 58 L. T. 857 ; 36 W. R. 895.

The power of issuing a writ for service out of the jurisdiction when the "Cause of Action" arose within the jurisdiction (s. 18, Com. L. Pro. Act, 1852, 15 & 16 V. c. 76) has been superseded by Ord. 11, R. 1 (*e*), and Ord. 2, R. 4, R. S. C. ; but it may be useful, as a matter of construction, to observe that, after a singular conflict of decision between the old Common Law Courts, the rule laid down by the Common Pleas in *Jackson* v. *Spittal* (39 L. J. C. P. 321 ; L. R. 5 C. P. 542 ; 18 W. R. 1162) was ultimately adopted as the rule for all the Common Law Courts,—viz., that "Cause of Action" in the section cited did *not* mean the *whole* cause of action, but meant "the act on the part of the defendant which gave the plaintiff his cause of complaint" (*Vaughan* v. *Weldon*, 44 L. J. C. P. 64 ; L. R. 10 C. P. 47).

A "Cause of Action" does not arise out of a damage-causing tort, or out of a tort not actionable without special damage, until damage done ; and accordingly, the Statute of Limitations does not begin to run for such a tort until damage happens ; and each recurrence of a distinctly new damage (as distinguished from a development of an old one, *Fetter* v. *Beal*, 1 Raym. 339 ; 1 Salk. 11 : *Va. Clarke* v. *Yorke*, 52 L. J. Ch. 32), gives rise to a fresh cause of action (*Bonomi* v. *Backhouse*, 28 L. J. Q. B. 378 ; 34 Ib. 181 ; E. B. & E. 622 ; 9 H. L. Ca. 503 ; 9 W. R. 769 : *Whitehouse* v. *Fellowes*, 30 L. J. C. P. 305 ; 10 C. B. N. S. 765 ; 9 W. R. 556 : *Mitchell* v. *Darley Main Colly. Co.*, 53 L. J. Q. B. 471 ; 55 Ib. 529 ; 32 W. R. 947 : from which latter case it would seem that *Nicklin* v. *Williams*, 10 Ex. 227, is now of but little authority, whilst *Lamb* v. *Walker*, 47 L. J. Q. B. 451 ; 3 Q. B. D. 389, is over-ruled. *Va.* Add. T. 59, 60). And, still further, where the owner of a vehicle was himself injured in a collision, he was held not estopped from bringing an action for his personal injuries, by reason of having recovered judgment from the same defendant for the damage the collision had caused to the vehicle,—the personal injuries being unknown at the time action was brought for the damage to the vehicle : for each class of injuries and damage, in such a case, forms, with its common cause, a "Cause of Action" (*Brunsden* v. *Humphrey*, 53 L. J. Q. B. 476 ; 14 Q. B. D. 141 ; 32 W. R. 944).

CAUSE OF APPEAL.—*V.* DECISION.

CAUSE OR MATTER.—*V.* CAUSE.

CAUSE OR PERMIT.—A proprietor of a music-hall who engages a singer, but does not control what songs are to be sung, nevertheless "causes or permits" the singing of what songs are sung, within s. 20, Copyright Act, 5 & 6 V. c. 45 (*Monaghan* v. *Taylor*, 2 Times Rep. 685 : *Va. Marsh* v. *Conquest*, 17 C. B. N. S. 418 ; 33 L. J. C. P. 319). *V.* PERMIT.

CAUSE OR PROCURE.—The words in a covenant "do and execute, or *cause or procure* to be done or executed," all such acts as may be necessary for vesting property in trustees, "only mean that the covenantor would procure persons who were bound to obey his orders,—*e.g.* trustees,—to do such acts as were necessary" (per Kay, J., *Re De Ros*, 55 L. J. Ch. 75 ; 31 Ch. D. 81 ; 53 L. T. 524 ; 34 W. R. 36).

CAUSE SHEWN.—*V.* CAUSE.

CAUSE TO BE APPLIED.—Designs Copyright Act, 5 & 6 V. c. 100, s. 7 ; *V. Mallet* v. *Howitt*, W. N. (79) 107.

CAUSE TO BE TAKEN.—A person who supplies a woman with a drug, which is taken and intended to be taken by her in the absence of the person supplying it, "causes it to be taken" within s. 6, 1 V. c. 85 (replaced by s. 58, 24 & 25 V. c. 100), (*R.* v. *Wilson*, 26 L. J. M. C. 18 ; D. & B. 127 : followed in *R.* v. *Farrow*, D. & B. 164).

V. ADMINISTER.

CAUSED BY.—*In jure non remota causa sed proxima spectatur.* This maxim is paraphrased by Lord Bacon thus,—"It were infinite for the law to judge the causes of causes, and their impulsions one of another : therefore it contenteth itself with the *immediate* cause, and judgeth of acts by that ; without looking to any further degree" (Bac. Max., reg. 1 ; *Vf.* Broom's Max.). Accordingly, a Policy against Accidents other than those "*Caused by or Arising from* natural disease or weakness, or exhaustion consequent upon disease," will cover death by drowning, though the insured's fall into the water was the consequence of an epileptic fit; for the cause of death was drowning,—the fit was at most merely a *causa sine quâ non* (*Winspear* v. *Accident Insrce.*, 50 L. J. Q. B. 292; 6 Q. B. D. 42: followed in *Lawrence* v. *Acct. Insrce.*, 50 L. J. Q. B. 522; 7 Q. B. D. 216, in which case the words of exception were "Death arising from fits, or any disease"). So, in a case on a similar Policy, Huddleston, B., said, "'Caused by Accident,'—that is to say, immediately caused by accident" (*Re Isitt & Railway Passengers' Assrce.*, 58 L. J. Q. B. 195; 22 Q. B. D. 504). *V.* CAUSA CAUSANS: *Cp.* EFFECT.

CAUSEWAY.—*V.* FOOTPATH.

CAUSING.—A Railway Company carrying animals on their road, to a place within a district prohibited under the Contagious Diseases (Animals) Act, with knowledge of their destination, are guilty of "causing the Movement" of the animals, although they do not carry the animals further than a point outside the district, and do no act within it (*Mid. Ry.* v. *Freeman*, 53 L. J. M. C. 79; 12 Q. B. D. 629).

CAUTION.—Where a testator directed his trustees to use "great caution" in realizing his estate, it was held that the tenant for life was entitled to the income until conversion (*Scholefield* v. *Redfern*, 2 Dr. & Sm. 173: *Va. Mackie* v. *Mackie*, 5 Hare, 70). But where the direction was "to sail my ships for the benefit of the estate until they can be satisfactorily sold," the tenant for life was only entitled to 4 per cent. on the estimated value of the ships at the testator's death, the rest of their profits being carried to residue (*Brown* v. *Gellatly*, 2 Ch. 751).

CEASE.—"Ceased" is a strictly proper word to apply to the case where the *entire thing* has "ceased to be"—*e.g.*, as used in the phrase "any road which has . . . ceased to be a turnpike road" in s. 13, 41 & 42 V. c. 77 (*Lancashire Jus.* v. *Rochdale*, 53 L. J. M. C. 5; 8 App. Ca. 494:—and especially jdgmt of Lord Bramwell. *Vf. West Riding Jus.* v. *Sheffield*, 53 L. J. M. C. 41; 8 App. Ca. 781: *Newton-in-Makerfield* v. *Lancashire Jus.*, 54 L. J. M. C. 1; 13 Q. B. D. 623).

"Cease, determine and be void to all intents and purposes;" *V.* VOID.

"Cease *to carry on* the business of a Banker," s. 12, Bank Charter Act, 1844 (7 & 8 V. c. 32); *V. A.-G.* v. *Birkbeck*, 53 L. J. Q. B. 378; 12 Q. B. D. 605.

"Cease *to inhabit*" in a Condition; *V. Doe* d. *Shaw* v. *Steward*, 3 L. J. K. B. 141; 1 A. & E. 300; 3 N. & M. 372.

CELL: CELLA.—"A monastery appertaining to a larger; Spelm." (Elph. 565).

CEREMONIES.—*V.* Ornaments.

CERTAIN.—*V.* Certain Rent : Certain Time : Sums Certain : Twelve-month.

CERTAIN RENT.—"'*Certaine rent.*' A tenant holdeth of his lord certaine lands in socage, to pay yearely a paire of gilt spurs or five shillings in money at the feast of *Easter*. In this case the rent is uncertaine, and the tenant may pay which of them he will at the said feast" (Co. Litt. 90 b).

A Rent, the amount of which may fluctuate according to the happening of certain events, is not "uncertain," but is distrainable as Rent, even as against bankruptcy (*Ex p. Voisey, Re Knight,* 21 Ch. D. 442 ; 52 L. J. Ch. 121).

CERTAIN TIME.—" Certain Time," s. 28, 3 & 4 W. 4, c. 42, includes a certain event ; therefore where a written contract for goods stipulates for "Cash" payment, interest may be given from delivery (*Duncombe* v. *Brighton Club Co.*, 44 L. J. Q. B. 216 ; L. R. 10 Q. B. 371).

Vf. Re Blackburn Bg. Socy., 30 S. J. 254.

V. Sum Certain.

CERTIFIED.—"Certified Industrial School," s. 7, 29 & 30 V. c. 118 ; *V. R.* v. *West Derby,* L. R. 10 Q. B. 283 ; 44 L. J. Q. B. 98.

CERTIFY.—"The usual meaning of 'Certify' does not require anything written : otherwise why should parties ever expressly stipulate as to certifying in writing ?" (per Byles, J. *Roberts* v. *Watkins,* 32 L. J. C. P. 291 ; 14 C. B. N. S. 592 ; 11 W. R. 783) ; it was there held that an Architect's Certificate need not be in writing unless so stipulated.

CHALLENGE.—" *Challenge* is a word common as well to the English as to the French, and sometimes signifieth to claime, and the Latine word is *vendicare ;* sometime in respect of revenge to challenge into the field, and then it is called in Latine *vindicare* or *provocare ;* sometime in respect of partiality or insufficiency, to challenge in court persons returned on a jury. And seeing there is no proper Latin word to signify this particular kind of challenge, they have framed a word anciently written, *chalumniare,* and *columpniare,* and *calumpniare,* and now written *calumniare ;* and hath no affinity with the verbe *calumnior,* or *calumnia,* which is derived of that, for that is of a quite other sense, signifying a false accuser, and in that sense Bracton useth *calumniator* to be a false accuser : but it is derived of the old word *caloir* or *chaloir,* which in one signification is to care for or foresee. And for that to challenge jurors is the meane to care for or foresee, that an indifferent triall be had, it is called *calumniare,* to challenge, that is, to except against them that are returned to be jurors; and this is his proper signification" (Co. Litt. 155 b).

CHAMPERTY.—"Champerty is Maintenance in which the motive of the maintainor is an agreement that if the proceeding in which the maintenance takes place succeeds, the subject matter of the suit shall be divided between the plaintiff and the maintainor" (Steph. Cr. 97; *Vf.* Ib. 355, 356; Co. Litt. 368 b.; *V.* MAINTENANCE: Rosc. Cr. 720: *Guy* v. *Churchill*, 58 L. J. Ch. 345; 40 Ch. D. 481: *James* v. *Kerr*, 58 L. J. Ch. 355; 40 Ch. D. 449).

CHANCELLOR.—*V.* s. 12 (1), Interp. Act, 1889.

CHANCE-MEDLEY.—"Chance-medley, or *per infortunium*, is when one is slaine casually, and by misadventure, without the will of him that doth the act, whereupon death ensueth" (Co. Litt. 287 b).

CHAPEL.—"The legal meaning of the word 'Chapel' is a chapel of the Church of England" (per Grove, J., *Caiger* v. *St. Mary, Islington*, 50 L. J. M. C. 64).

As to diverting funds for purposes of, and trusts for maintaining a Chapel; *V.* Lewin, 531.

CHARACTER.—Fees and expenses voted to a Director of a Company, is a sum due to him "in his *Character* of a member" within subs. 7, s. 38, Comp. Act, 1862 (*Re Leicester Racecourse Co.*, 55 L. J. Ch. 206; 30 Ch. D. 629: *Cp.* CAPACITY). Qy., would fees definitely prescribed by Articles as payment for Directors' services be within the above words? A Managing Director's salary would not be within them, nor the Costs of a Solicitor who was also a Director (*Re Dale & Plant*, Times, 20 Dec., 1889).

V. GOOD CHARACTER.

CHARGE.—"The word 'Charge' has a wider meaning than the words 'Mortgage' or 'Lien:'" *e.g.*, in the definition of a Secured Creditor in the Bankry. Act, 1869 (per Cur., *Emanuel* v. *Bridger*, 43 L. J. Q. B. 99; L. R. 9 Q. B. 286; 22 W. R. 404; 30 L. T. 195: *Cp.* corresponding phrase in s. 168, Bankry. Act, 1883; *Va.* SECURED CREDITOR: SECURITY).

In *Emanuel* v. *Bridger*, sup., it was held that a Garnishee Order absolute was a "Charge" within s. 16 (5), Bankry. Act, 1869; and that was so even if the Order were only *nisi* (*Lowe* v. *Blackmore*, 44 L. J. Q. B. 155; L. R. 10 Q. B. 485; 23 W. R. 856: *Vf. Ex p. Jocelyn*, 47 L. J. Bank. 91; 8 Ch. D. 327; 26 W. R. 645; 38 L. T. 661: *Hall* v. *Pritchett*, 47 L. J. Q. B. 15; 3 Q. B. D. 215; 26 W. R. 95: *Re Stanhope Collieries Co.*, 48 L. J. Ch. 409; 11 Ch. D. 160; 27 W. R. 561; 40 L. T. 204). But to be now available in bankruptcy, an attachment of a debt must be completed by receipt of the money (s. 45, Bankry. Act, 1883). *Vf.* SECURITY.

"Charge *on Premises*," s. 257, P. H. Act, 1875 ; *V. Sunderland* v. *Alcock*, 51 L. J. Ch. 546. This is not a "Land Charge" requiring registration under 51 & 52 V. c. 52, Part IV. (*R.* v. *Holt*, 6 Times Rep. 104).

V. ABSOLUTE ASSIGNMENT : CHARGES : TOLL : IN CHARGE.

"To Charge ;" *V.* BIND.

CHARGE OF DEBTS.—As to what words will create a *Charge of Debts on Real Estate; V.* 2 Jarm. 582–601 ; and as to *Legacies*, Ib., 602–609. *Va.* IN THE FIRST PLACE.

CHARGE OR CONDUCT.—Of a vessel, 6 G. 4, c. 125, s. 70 ; *V. Beilby* v. *Scott*, 7 M. & W. 93 ; 10 L. J. Ex. 149.

CHARGE OR CONTROL.—As to meaning of person having "the charge or control of any signal," &c., in subs. 5, s. 1, Employers' Liability Act, 1880 (43 & 44 V. c. 42) ; *V. Gibbs* v. *G. W. Ry.*, 53 L. J. Q. B. 543 ; 12 Q. B. D. 208.

V. PERSON IN CHARGE : CONTROL.

CHARGE OR INCUMBER.—A covenant or condition not to "Charge or Incumber" prohibits a *direct* Charge or Incumbrance, and does not embrace something,—*e.g.* a Warrant of Attorney,—which may obliquely so operate (*Croft* v. *Lumley*, 25 L. J. Q. B. 73, 223 ; 27 Ib. 321; 6 H. L. Ca. 672) ; unless, indeed, that something be a mere contrivance to charge the property, and then it will be within the covenant or condition (*Doe* d. *Mitchinson* v. *Carter*, 8 T. R. 57, 300: *Croft* v. *Lumley*, sup.). *Croft* v. *Lumley* was a case on a Lease, and the prohibitive words of the covenant there were, "nor charge or incumber the said theatre . . . . by mortgaging the same, or granting any rent-charges or any other incumbrance or incumbrances whatsoever;" and it was held that a *bonâ fide* Warrant of Attorney, on which judgment had been entered up (1 & 2 V. c. 110, ss. 13, 19), was not a breach.

"Charge or Incumber" may sometimes be read "attempt to charge," &c. (*Blake* v. *Barnett*, 31 L. J. Ch. 898 ; 2 Dr. & Sm. 117, cited for this proposition by Fry, J., *Hurst* v. *Hurst*, 51 L. J. Ch. 421, on app., but not on this point, Ib. 729 ; 21 Ch. D. 278).

V. RESTRAINT ON ALIENATION.

CHARGE OR LIABILITY.—A Legacy "free from any Charge or Liability in respect thereof" is duty free (*Warbrick* v. *Varley*, 30 Bea. 241).

CHARGEABLE.—This word has substantially the same meaning as "payable" (per Hawkins, J., *Direct Spanish Telegraph Co.* v. *Shepherd*, 53 L. J. Q. B. 420 ; 13 Q. B. D. 202).

A Pauper is "chargeable" to his parish, s. 56, 7 & 8 V. c. 101, as soon as he is entitled to relief therefrom, but not "actually chargeable" till he gets such relief (*R.* v. *St. Clement Danes*, 32 L. J. M. C. 25 ; 3 B. & S. 143).

Rogue leaving wife "chargeable," s. 4, 5 G. 4, c. 83 ; *V. Heath* v. *Heape*, 26 L. J. M. C. 49.

In a Covenant relating to Rates, "chargeable" has a future meaning (*Scovell* v. *Gardiner*, 16 Ir. C. L. Rep. 318).

CHARGED.—The power, given by s. 29, 2 & 3 V. c. 71, to order restitution of "goods or money *charged* to be stolen or fraudulently obtained," relates only to goods or money respecting which such a charge has been specifically made (*R.* v. *D'Eyncourt*, 4 Times Rep. 455).

CHARGED UPON.—Sums "charged upon" land, s. 1, 3 & 4 W. 4, c. 27; *V. Payne* v. *Esdaile*, 58 L. J. Ch. 299 ; 13 App. Ca. 613 ; 37 W. R. 273 ; 59 L. T. 568 : S. 42, Ib. ; *V. Purcell* v. *Purcell*, 2 Dr. & War. 217.

CHARGED WITH.—*V.* SUBJECT TO ; CHARGE.

CHARGES.—An exceptional burden for structural works imposed by a Local Authority and ordinarily borne by the landlord pursuant to the P. H. Act, was held to be comprised in a covenant by a tenant to pay "all rates, taxes, charges, and assessments whatsoever, which now are or may be charged or assessed upon the said premises or any part thereof or upon any person or persons in respect thereof, land tax and property tax excepted" (*Hartley* v. *Hudson*, 48 L. J. Q. B. 751 ; 4 C. P. D. 367 : But *cp. Rawlings* v. *Biggs*, 47 L. J. C. P. 487 ; 3 C. P. D. 368). Where, however, the words of the covenant by the lessee were to pay "the sewer and main drainage rates . . . and other district rates and assessments whatsoever whether parliamentary, parochial or otherwise, which now are or which at any time during the said term shall be taxed, rated, *charged*, assessed, or imposed upon the said demised premises, or any part thereof, or upon or payable by the occupier or tenant in respect thereof ;"—it was held that such an exceptional burden made under the Metrop. Man. Act was not comprised (*Allum* v. *Dickinson*, 52 L. J. Q. B. 190 ; 9 Q. B. D. 632). *Hartley* v. *Hudson* was cited in *Allum* v. *Dickinson*, yet in the latter case the same judge (Lindley, J.) who decided *Hartley* v. *Hudson* said, that such an exceptional burden was "not a rate, charge or assessment imposed on the premises or on the occupier or tenant."

V. COSTS AND CHARGES : TOLLS.

CHARGES AND ALLOWANCES.—*V.* 1 Maude & P. 121, n. (*o*).

CHARITABLE PURPOSES.—A bequest for "Charitable" purposes, or for "Charities and other Public Purposes," is good (*Re Sutton*, 54 L. J. Ch. 613 ; 28 Ch. D. 464 ; 33 W. R. 519 : *Dolan* v. *Macdermot*, 3 Ch. 676), but a bequest "to be given in Private Charity" is not (*Ommaney* v. *Butcher*, 1 Turn. & R. 260). *Vf.* Tudor, Char. Trusts.

V. CHARITY : HUMANE : PURPOSE MERELY CHARITABLE.

The popular meaning of "Charitable Purposes" (and in such meaning the phrase is used in the Income Tax Act, 1842, s. 61, Sch. A. No. vi.) is where property or income is given to "be expended in assisting people to something considered by the donor to be for their benefit, and which assistance the donor intends shall be given to people who, in his opinion, cannot, in consequence of their poverty, obtain the benefit without his assistance; and where the intention of the donor to assist such poverty is the substantial cause of his gift" (per Esher, M. R., *R.* v. *Income Tax Commrs.*, 58 L. J. Q. B. 200; 22 Q. B. D. 296).

CHARITABLE USE.—As to what is a "Charitable Use" within the Mortmain and Charitable Uses Acts, 1888 (51 & 52 V. c. 42); *V.* Wms. Exs. 1074 *et seq.*; Tudor, Char. Trusts, ch. vi.

Land demised for a long term of years for the erection of a parish workhouse, is demised for a "Charitable Use" (*Webster* v. *Southey*, 36 Ch. D. 9; 56 L. J. Ch. 785; 56 L. T. 879; 35 W. R. 622; 3 Times Rep. 628).

CHARITY.—This "word in its widest sense denotes all the good affections men ought to bear towards each other; in its most restricted and common sense, relief of the poor. In neither of these senses is it employed in this (Chancery) Court. Here its signification is derived chiefly from the Statute of Elizabeth (43 Eliz. c. 4). Those purposes are considered charitable which that statute enumerates, or which by analogies are deemed within its spirit and intendment" (per Grant, M. R., *Morice* v. *Bishop of Durham*, 9 Ves. 405). The purposes enumerated by the Statute of Eliz. are "reliefe of aged impotent and poor people, maintenance of sicke and maymed soldiers and marriners, schooles of learninge, free schooles and schollers in universities, repaire of bridges, portes, havens, causwaies, churches, seabankes and highewaies, educac̄on and pfermente of orphans, reliefe stocke or maintenance for houses of correc̄con, mariages of poore maides, supportac̄on ayde and helpe of young tradesmen, handiecraftesmen and ps̄ons decayed, reliefe or redemption of prisoners or captives, aide or ease of any poor inhabitant concn̄inge payment of fifteenes, settinge out of souldiers and other taxes." This enumeration is continued in the Mortmain Act of 1888 (s. 13 (2), 51 & 52 V. c. 42); *V.* Tudor, Char. Trusts, 371; 1 Jarm. 205–250; Wms. Exs. 1059 *et seq.*, for collection of cases hereon; *Va. Beaumont* v. *Oliveira*, 38 L. J. Ch. 62, 239; 4 Ch. 309.

Poverty in the recipient is not necessary to enable him to receive the benefits of a Charity (*Pease* v. *Pattinson*, 55 L. J. Ch. 617; 32 Ch. D. 154; 54 L. T. 209; 34 W. R. 361).

Property purchased by a city ward out of its own moneys and for its own purposes, is not a "Charity" within s. 66, Charitable Trusts Act, 1853

(16 & 17 V. c. 137) (*Finnis to Forbes*, 53 L. J. Ch. 140, 141 ; 24 Ch. D. 587 ; 48 L. T. 813 ; 32 W. R. 55).

V. Endowment.

One who from "Charity" helps another in an action, is not guilty ot Maintenance, even though his "charity" be indiscreet; wisdom is not an ingredient of the word (*Harris* v. *Brisco*, 55 L. J. Q. B. 423 ; 17 Q. B. D. 504 ; 55 L. T. 14 ; 34 W. R. 729).

CHARITY COMMISSIONERS.—*V.* s. 12 (14), Interp. Act, 1889.

CHARITY ESTATE.—As to meaning of this phrase in s. 29, 18 & 19 V. c. 124 (Charitable Trusts Amendment Act, 1855) ; *V. Corporation of Sons of Clergy* v. *Sutton*, 29 L. J. Ch. 393, nom. *Corporation for Relief of Widows and Children of Clergy* v. *Sutton*, 27 Bea. 651 : *Royal Socy. & Thompson*, 17 Ch. D. 407 ; 50 L. J. Ch. 344 ; 44 L. T. 274 ; 29 W. R. 838 : *Finnis to Forbes*, 24 Ch. D. 587 ; 48 L. T. 813.

CHARITY PROPERTY.—The purposes to which, not the source from which, property is derived will determine whether or not it is "Charity Property," either generally or within ss. 5, 10, 11, City of London Parochial Charities Act, 1883 (46 & 47 V. c. 36) (*Re St. Botolph Without*, 56 L. J. Ch. 691 ; 35 Ch. D. 142 ; 56 L. T. 884 ; 35 W. R. 688 ; 3 Times Rep. 522, 553 : *A.-G.* v. *Eastlake*, 11 Hare, 205). An advowson, or other property not producing income, may be "Charity Property" within those sections (*Re St. Stephen's*, 57 L. J. Ch. 917 ; 39 Ch. D. 492 ; 59 L. T. 393 ; 36 W. R. 837).

CHASE.—"A Chase differs from a Forest, chiefly in that it is not subject to the forest laws (Chitty, Prerog. 137).

If the King, seised of a Forest, grants to another in fee ; the grantee has no Forest, because he has not the power to create judges or officers to hold forest courts ; but he has a Chase (4th Inst. 314).

By the grant, by a subject, of a Chase in his own land, not only the privilege but the land itself passes (Co. Litt. 5 b ; *V.* Wms. on Commons, 236 *et seq.*; Hall on Profits à Prendre, 325 ; 3 Cruise Dig. Tit. 27, s. 10, *et seq.*)." Elph. 566.

Cp. Park.

CHATTELS.—"'Chattels' is a French word and signifies Goods, which by a word of art we call *catalla*. Now Goods, or Chattels, are either personall or reall. Personall, as horse and other beasts, household stuffe, bowes, weapons and such like ; called personall, because for the most part they belong to the person of a man, or else for that they are to be recovered by personall actions. Reall, because they concerne the reality, as tearmes for yeares of lands or tenements, wardships, the interest of tenant by statute staple, by statute merchant, by elegit and such like" (Co. Litt. 118 b).

Chattels Real, as to what are; *V.* Wms. Exs. 676 *et seq.*, Pt. 2, Bk. 2, Ch. 1.

Chattels Personal are (1) Chattels Animate, (2) Chattels Vegetable, (3) Chattels Inanimate (Wms. Exs. 709); and *Vth.* at length Wms. Exs. 709 *et seq.*, Pt. 2, Bk. 2, Ch. 2.

"If one devise to J. S. all his 'Goods,' or all his 'Chattels,' by either of these is devised as much as by both of them" (Touch. 447 : *Vf.* Wms. Exs. 1184).

A bequest of "All other Chattels" may pass the residue (*Re Sharman* 38 L. J. P. & M. 47 ; L. R. 1 P. & D. 661).

V. ESTATE : GOODS AND CHATTELS.

A Dog is not a "Chattel" within s. 88, 24 & 25 V. c. 96, because, at Common Law, it is not the subject of Larceny (*R.* v. *Robinson,* 28 L. J. M. C. 58 ; Bell, C. C. 34) ; but a dog is "Goods" within s. 40, 2 & 3 V. c. 71 (*R.* v. *Slade,* 21 Q. B. D. 433).

CHAUNTRY: CANTARIA.—"A foundation for the maintenance of priests to say mass for the souls of the founder and his relations ; also a chapel or altar endowed for that purpose (*Adams & Lambert's Case,* 4 Rep. 104 b. ; Ducange ; Spelm.). In a grant by Henry 8th to the Earl of Arundel, the words *ecclesia collegiata*, *collegium,* and *cantaria* are used as synonyms ; *V. Norfolk* v. *Arbuthnot,* 4 C. P. D. 302 ; 48 L. J. C. P. 743" (Elph. 566).

CHEAP TRAIN.—"Cheap Train," ss. 6—10, Cheap Trains Act (7 & 8 V. c. 85) ; *V. North Lond. Ry.* v. *A.-G.,* 45 L. J. Ex. 315 ; 1 App. Ca. 148.

CHEAT.—To call a man a "Cheat," "Rascal," "Scoundrel," "Swindler," or "Villain," is not actionable, *per se* (per Pollock, C. B., *Barnett* v. *Allen,* 27 L. J. Ex. 412 ; 3 H. & N. 376 ; 31 L. T. O. S. 217).

CHEATING.—"Every one commits the misdemeanour called Cheating, who fraudulently obtains the property of another by any deceitful practice not amounting to felony, which practice is of such a nature that it directly affects, or may directly affect the public at large. But it is not Cheating within the meaning of this Article to deceive any person in any contract or private dealing by lies, unaccompanied by such practices as aforesaid" (Steph. Cr. 272). *Vf.* Arch. Cr. 535–557 ; Rosc. Cr. 393–395.

CHEQUE.—"A Cheque is a Bill of Exchange drawn on a Banker, payable on demand" (s. 73, Bills of Ex. Act, 1882). *V.* BILL OF EXCHANGE.

CHIEF CLERK.—*V.* CLERK.

CHIEF SECRETARY.—*V.* s. 12 (10), Interp. Act, 1889.

CHIEFEST AND DISCREETEST.—"Where the election (for a Charity) was given to the inhabitants and parishioners, or the major part of the '*chiefest and discreetest* of them,' it was held that by 'chiefest' was to be understood those who paid the church and poor rates; and by 'discreetest' those who had attained the age of 21" (Lewin, 87, citing *Fearon* v. *Webb*, 14 Ves. 13). *Vf.* PARISHIONER.

CHILD, CHILDREN.—"The word 'Child' in an Act of Parliament always applies exclusively to a legitimate child" (per Pollock, C. B. *Dickinson* v. *North Eastern Ry.*, 12 W. R. 52; 33 L. J. Ex. 91; *Vf. R.* v. *Maude*, 6 Jur. 646; 2 Dowl. N. S. 58; *Sv. R.* v. *Hodnett*, 1 T. R. 96; jdgmt. of Cotton, L. J., *Northwich* v. *St. Pancras*, 58 L. J. M. C. 73; 22 Q. B. D. 164).

So in a Will, or Deed, illegitimate children are not included in the word "Children;" unless, when the surrounding facts are ascertained and applied, some repugnancy or inconsistency, and not merely some violation of a moral obligation or of a probable intention, would result from their exclusion (*Dorin* v. *Dorin*, L. R. 7 H. L. 568; 45 L. J. Ch. 652; 23 W. R. 570: *V.* the rule stated in other, but similar, terms, 2 Jarm. 234, and *Vh. Re Ayle*, 1 Ch. D. 282; 45 L. J. Ch. 223: *Ellis* v. *Houston*, 10 Ch. D. 236. Consider the last case as to the inadmissibility of extrinsic evidence in such cases, which however was admitted in *Re Haseldine*, 31 Ch. D. 511; 34 W. R. 327).

Speaking generally, an illegitimate child will only be comprised in "children" when there is a *designatio personæ* (*Beachcroft* v. *Beachcroft*, 1 Mad. 430, stated 2 Jarm. 234: *Re Herbert*, 29 L. J. Ch. 870; 1 Jo. & H. 121: *Re Humphries*, 24 Ch. D. 691: *Milne* v. *Wood*, 42 L. J. Ch. 545: *Re Brown's Trusts*, 43 L. J. Ch. 84; L. R. 16 Eq. 239: *Megson* v. *Hindle*, 15 Ch. D. 198: *Re Bryon*, 55 L. J. Ch. 30; 30 Ch. D. 110: *Re Brown*, 58 L. J. Ch. 420). Thus in the Will of a bachelor "children" means his illegitimate children, for he can have no other (*Clifton* v. *Goodbun*, L. R. 6 Eq. 278; *Vth.* 2 Jarm. 237).

As to after-born illegitimate children the rule was thus stated by Ld. Chelmsford in *Hill* v. *Crook* (42 L. J. Ch. 712; L. R. 6 H. L. 265; 22 W. R. 137);—"No gift, however express, to unborn illegitimate children is allowed by law; nor under a gift, good as to illegitimate children as a class, will after-born illegitimate children be permitted to take." But in applying that rule there is "the essential distinction between a Deed and a Will for this purpose, in that a Deed operates from its execution and a Will from the death of the testator" (per Mellish, L. J., *Occleston* v. *Fullalove*, 43 L. J. Ch. 310; 9 Ch. 147; 22 W. R. 305): and it was accordingly held by the majority of the Court in that case (Selborne, L. C., diss.), that illegitimate children, sufficiently designated, born between the date of the Will and the death of the testator, could take (*Va. Eagleton* v. *Horner*, 4 Times Rep. 100; W. N. (87) 219: *Re Hastie*, 35 Ch. D. 728; 56 L. J. Ch. 792; 57 L. T. 168; 35 W. R. 692). The statement of the effect of *Occleston* v. *Fullalove*, by Jessel, M. R., in *Re Goodwin* (43 L. J. Ch. 258;

L. R. 17 Eq. 345), is not correct (*Re Bolton*, 55 L. J. Ch. 398 ; 31 Ch. D. 542 ; 34 W. R. 325), for "the law is clear that, however a man may wish to provide for illegitimate children he cannot do so by any means which involves an enquiry into the paternity, of which the law accepts no evidence except the fact of marriage" (per Bowen, L. J., *Re Bolton*) ; and therefore it was held in that case that the child of a reputed wife, *en ventre* at the testator's death, could not take under a bequest to his "child or children ;" *Vf.* as to testamentary gifts to Illegitimate Children, 2 Jarm. ch. 31 ; Wms. Exs. 1103.

What constitutes legitimacy is, however, rather a question of *status* than of construction. And it would seem to be now "settled that any person legitimate *according to the law of the domicil of his father at his birth*, is legitimate everywhere within the range of international law for the purpose of succeeding to *Personal* property" (per Kay, J., *Re Andros*, 52 L. J. Ch. 794 ; 24 Ch. D. 637 ; which case *V.* for discussion of the previous authorities and especially *Boyes* v. *Bedale*, 33 L. J. Ch. 283 ; 1 H. & M. 798, and *Re Goodman's Trusts*, 50 L. J. Ch. 425 ; 17 Ch. D. 266). So also persons who have the legal *status* of children by virtue of a foreign law applicable to their case, are "children" for the purpose of assessment to Legacy Duty (*V.* STRANGERS IN BLOOD). But a foreign status will not aid a person claiming to inherit land in England (*Birtwhistle* v. *Vardill*, 4 L. J. O. S. K. B. 190 ; 5 B. & C. 438 ; 2 Cl. & F. 571 ; 7 Ib. 895 ; 6 Bligh, N. S. 479 ; 9 Ib. 32 ; 6 Bing. N. C. 385).

"The words 'Child or Children' primarily mean issue in the first generation only—sons and daughters—to the exclusion of grandchildren or other remoter descendants" (per Ld. Blackburn, *Bowen* v. *Lewis*, 54 L. J. Q. B. 68 ; 9 App. Ca. 890 : *Oldham Case*, 1 O'M. & H. 160 : *Maund* v. *Mason*, L. R. 9 Q. B. 254 ; 43 L. J. M. C. 62 : *Moor* v. *Raisbeck*, 12 Sim. 123 : *Pride* v. *Fooks*, 28 L. J. Ch. 81 ; 3 D. G. & J. 252 : *Loring* v. *Thomas*, 30 L. J. Ch. 789 ; 1 Dr. & Sm. 497 : *Nicholson* v. *Kirk*, 29 S. J. 205 : Wms. Exs. 1102). But the context may show that these words have been used, by mistake, for "Descendants" or something else and so they would sometimes receive another construction than their ordinary one (*Morgan* v. *Thomas*, 51 L. J. Q. B. 556 : *Harley* v. *Mitford*, 21 Bea. 280 : *Re Smith*, 56 L. J. Ch. 771 ; 35 Ch. D. 558 ; 56 L. T. 878 ; 35 W. R. 663). But the mere fact that the word would be otherwise inoperative is not sufficient to widen its interpretation (*Nicholson* v. *Kirk*, sup.) ; *Vf.* as to testamentary gifts to Children, 2 Jarm. ch. 30 ; Wms. Exs. 1093 *et seq.*

Though the word "child" or "children," in its primary sense, is to be read as a word of purchase—as a designation of a person or persons (per Earl Cairns, *Bowen* v. *Lewis*, 54 L. J. Q. B. 63)—and to be confined to issue in the first degree, yet, *as regards Real Estate*, the context may convert it into a word of limitation and render it equivalent to "heirs of the body" and so create an entail (*Byng* v. *Byng*, 31 L. J. Ch. 470 ; 10 H. L. Ca. 171 : *Clifford* v. *Koe*, 5 App. Ca. 447) ; and if the devise be to " A. and his children," *he having none at the time of the devise*, the word " children " must be taken as a word of limitation and A. would take an entail (*Wild's Case*, 6 Rep. 17 ; reported also as *Anon.* in Gouldsborough, 139, pl. 47, and as *Richardson* v. *Yardley* in Moore, 397, pl. 519. For collection of cases on and discussion of *the Rule in Wild's Case ; V.* 2 Jarm. ch. 38 ; Wms. Exs. 1097 ; Hawk. 198 ; and *V. Bowen* v. *Lewis*, 54 L. J. Q. B. 55 ; 9 App. Ca. 890 ; 52 L. T. 189).

The principle of *Wild's Case* applies even where there is a child of A. *en ventre sa mère* at the death of the testator (*Roper* v. *Roper*, 36 L. J. C. P. 270 ; 37 Ib. 7 : *Sv. Grieve* v. *Grieve*, 36 L. J. Ch. 932 ; L. R. 4 Eq. 180).

V. ISSUE : OFFSPRING : BORN : NATURAL CHILDREN.

Note :—Property given to illegitimate children will be comprised in a *gift over* of property given to " Children " (*Smith* v. *Jobson*, 32 S. J. 662 ; 59 L. T. 397).

"Child under the age of 16," s. 35, 39 & 40 V. c. 61, means a child under that age at the time his parochial Settlement is being enquired into (*R.* v. *St. Mary, Islington*, 54 L. J. M. C. 110 ; Ib. 146 ; 15 Q. B. D. 95, 339, following *Madeley* v. *Bridgnorth*, 52 L. J. M. C. 71 ; 11 Q. B. D. 314 : *Va. Reigate* v. *Croydon*, 14 App. Ca. 465 ; 53 J. P. 580 ; 5 Times Rep. 716 : *West Derby* v. *Atcham*, 34 S. J. 10 : *Northwich* v. *St. Pancras*, 58 L. J. M. C. 73 ; 22 Q. B. D. 164 : *St. Pancras* v. *Norwich*, 56 L. J. M. C. 37 ; 18 Q. B. D. 521 ; 56 L. T. 311 ; 35 W. R. 547 ; 51 J. P. 343 : *V.* WIFE). As to the concluding words " and shall retain the Settlement," &c. ; *V. Dorchester* v. *Poplar*, 57 L. J. M. C. 78 ; 21 Q. B. D. 88 ; 59 L. T. 689 ; 36 W. R. 706 ; 52 J. P. 435, following *Highworth* v. *Westbury-on-Severn*, 57 L. J. M. C. 33 ; 20 Q. B. D. 597, and on these words, over-ruling *R.* v. *St. Mary, Islington*, sup. : But *Highworth* v. *Westbury-on-Severn* was afterwards reversed by H. L., 53 J. P. 580 ; 5 Times Rep. 716.

" Child," in s. 60, 24 & 25 V. c. 100, does not include a fœtus not matured enough to be born alive (*R.* v. *Berriman*, 6 Cox, C. C. 388).

Vh. Chitty, Eq. Ind. 7675–7678, 7710.

CHILDREN'S CHILDREN. — " I read the words ' Children's Children' (in Stat. of Distributions) as meaning ' Issue of Children' " (per North, J., *Re Natt, Walker* v. *Gammage*, 57 L. J. Ch. 798 ; 37 Ch. D. 517; 58 L. T. 722 ; 36 W. R. 548).

In a limitation of Realty ; *V. Hampton* v. *Holman*, 5 Ch. D. 183.

CHILDREN OF A. AND B.—*V.* 2 Jarm. 194 ; Hawk. 113 ; *Re Featherstone*, 22 Ch. D. 111; 52 L. J. Ch. 75.

"Children of A. & B. respectively;" *V. Fletcher* v. *Fletcher*, 9 L. R. Ir. 301.

CHILDREN OF THE WIFE.—This phrase in a Marriage Settlement of a husband's property, means children of the wife by that husband (*Dafforne* v. *Goodman*, 2 Vern. 362).

CHIMINAGE.—*V.* Way.

CHINA.—*V.* Plate.

CHOSE IN ACTION.—*Chose in Action* is the antithesis of *Chose in Possession.*

"According to my view, all personal things are either in possession or in action. The law knows no *tertium quid* between the two. 'No chattel,' says Lord Coke in *Fulwood's Case* (4 Rep. 65 a), 'either in action or possession shall go in succession,' as if the two alternatives were the only possible ones. 'Property in chattels personal,' says Blackstone, 'may be either in possession, which is when a man hath not only the right to enjoy, but hath the actual enjoyment of the thing; or else it is in action, where a man hath only a bare right without any occupation or enjoyment' (2 Com. 396); and so Lord Hardwicke in the great case of *Ryall* v. *Rowles* (1 Atk. 384), speaks of personal property, whether in possession or action, only as equivalent to all kinds of personal property. The expression *Choses in Suspense* is found in *Brooke's Abr.* in conjunction with *Choses in Action;* but, so far as I can understand, the two expressions are synonymous. It has been suggested that the expression *Choses in Action* was originally only applicable to debts; and that by a lax usage it has acquired a secondary and wider significance. I am not able to adopt this view. The article '*Choses in Action and Choses in Suspense*' in *Brooke's Abr.*, fo. 140, seems to show that as early as 5 Ed. 4 the expression was held to include the king's right to the marriage of his ward; in 9 Hen. 6, the property in deeds in the hands of a third person was considered as a Chose in Action; and in the 33 Hen. 8, the classification of *Choses in Action* into Real, Personal, and Mixed was recognized" (per Fry, L. J., *Colonial Bank* v. *Whinney,* 55 L. J. Ch. 593; 30 Ch. D. 261, a definition which, on appeal, was adopted by the H. L.). Accordingly it was held in that case that Shares in a Company are "Things in Action" within s. 44 (iii.), Bankry. Act, 1883 (56 L. J. Ch. 43; 11 App. Ca. 426; 55 L. T. 362; 34 W. R. 705, over-ruling *Ex p. Union Bank of Manchester, Re Jackson,* 40 L. J. Bank. 57; L. R. 12 Eq. 354; 19 W. R. 872; and jdgmt. of Lindley, L. J., in *Société Générale de Paris* v. *Tramways Co.,* 54 L. J. Q. B. 185; 14 Q. B. D. 424). *A fortiori* property in the Funds (*Dundas* v. *Dutens,* 1 Ves. jun. 196: *R.* v. *Capper,* 5 Price, 217, 263), a Life Policy (*Ex p. Ibbetson,* 8 Ch. D. 519), and a Debenture in a joint-stock company (*Ex p. Ransberg, Re Pryce,* 4 Ch. D. 685), are *Choses in Action;* so also is an undivided share in a partnership (*Ex p. Fletcher, Re Bainbridge,* 47 L. J. Bank. 70; 8 Ch. D. 218).

"Things in Action," s. 95, Companies Act, 1862, include Claims by the Liquidator against Directors for malpractices in reference to the property of a Co. (*Re Park Gate Wagon Co.,* 17 Ch. D. 234).

An Assignment of "all moneys now *or hereafter* standing to the credit of" A. at his banking account, is an assignment of a "legal Chose in

Action" within s. 25 (6), Jud. Act, 1873 (*Walker* v. *Bradford Bank*, 53 L. J. Q. B. 280; 12 Q. B. D. 511).

It is submitted that the definition established in *Colonial Bank* v. *Whinney* (sup.) is wide enough to embrace a claim to Damages for a Tort. Such a claim is surely property,—conceivably it may be a very valuable property, *e.g.* an infringement of a Patent. It is not in possession; and therefore, accepting the postulate in the definition of Fry, L. J., in *Colonial Bank* v. *Whinney*, it must be a chose in action. Yet, on the other hand, Blackstone says, "All property in action *depends entirely upon contracts* express or implied; which are the only regular means of acquiring a *Chose in Action*" (2 Com. 397).

Vf. as to the various meanings of "Chose in Action," Elphinstone's Intro. Conv. 2 Ed. 200 *et seq.*, and *V.* the subject of Choses in Action considered at large, Wms. Exs. 790 *et seq.*, Pt. 2, Bk. 3.

CHOSE IN SUSPENSE.—*V.* Chose in Action.

CHRISTIAN BROTHERS.—Gift for, good (*Hogan* v. *Byrne*, 13 Ir. Ch. Rep. 166).

CHRISTIAN BURIAL.—"There appears to be no clear authority as to what is meant by 'Christian Burial'; and as Bowen, J., held there was no evidence to go to the jury, the point was left undecided (Stafford Winter Assizes, 1879–80; 24 S. J. 245)." Stone, 169, 170.

CHRISTIAN NAME.—Where a document has to be authenticated by the Christian name of its signatory, a well known abbreviation,—*e.g.*, Wm. for William,—will suffice (*R.* v. *Bradley*, 30 L. J. Q. B. 180; 3 E. & E. 634: *Henry* v. *Armitage*, 53 L. J. Q. B. 111; 12 Q. B. D. 257).

CHRISTMAS DAY.—*V.* Michaelmas.

CHURCH.—"Church," s. 1, 5 G. 4, c. 36, includes the Chancel (*Rippin* v. *Bastin*, L. R. 2 A. & E. 386; 38 L. J. Ecc. 33).

CHURCHYARD.—Tombs in a churchyard are not within the word "Churchyard" as used in the Church Building Act, 49 G. 3, c. 108, s. 1; and a bequest for their repair is not saved by that Act (*Re Rigley*, 36 L. J. Ch. 147). *Vh. Re Vaughan*, 33 Ch. D. 187; 55 L. T. 547; 39 W. R. 104.

CIRCULARS.—"Circulars, Advertisements, or otherwise," s. 32, Patents, Designs, and Trade Marks Act, 1883, 46 & 47 V. c. 57; *V. Driffield Co.* v. *Waterloo Mills Co.*, 55 L. J. Ch. 391; 31 Ch. D. 638; 54 L. T. 210; 34 W. R. 360.

CIRCULATION.—A Bank-note "In Circulation," means a Note

which is passing from hand to hand as a negotiable instrument ; and when returned to the Bank (or any of its branches), it ceases to be "In Circulation" or "Outstanding" (*Bank of Africa* v. *Colonial Government*, 57 L. J. P. C. 66 ; 13 App. Ca. 215 ; 58 L. T. 427).

CIRCUMSTANCES.—*V.* SAME : SPECIAL : INSOLVENT CIRCUMSTANCES.

CITY.—"Every borough incorporate, that had a bishop within time of memory, is a citie, albeit the bishopricke be dissolved" (Co. Litt. 109 b).

CITY OF LONDON.—*V.* LONDON.

CIVIL DEBT.—A "Civil Debt" within s. 6 Summary Jurisdiction Act, 1879 (42 & 43 V. c. 49), is "a sum of money claimed to be due" before the commencement of the proceedings to recover it, and does not include a fine or penalty not due to anybody until the magistrate has adjudged its amount (*R.* v. *Paget*, 51 L. J. M. C. 9 ; 8 Q. B. D. 151. *Vf. Mellor* v. *Denham*, 49 L. J. M. C. 89 ; 5 Q. B. D. 467).

CIVIL PROCEEDING.—Is a process for the recovery of individual right or redress of individual wrong ; inclusive, in its proper legal sense, of suits by the Crown (*Bradlaugh* v. *Clarke*, 52 L. J. Q. B. 505 ; 8 App. Ca. 354).

A Quo Warranto is now a "Civil Proceeding" (s. 15, Judicature Act, 1884, 47 & 48 V. c. 61).

V. ACTION : CRIMINAL CAUSE : CRIMINAL SUIT.

CIVIL RIGHTS.—The "Property and Civil Rights" which by s. 92, British North America Act, 1867 (30 V. c. 3), are to be regulated by the Provincial Legislature include rights arising from contract, *e.g.*, Fire Insurance Policies : and such a contract is not a matter relating to "*Trade or Commerce*" within s. 91, and therefore to be regulated by the Dominion Legislature (*Citizens' Insrce.* v. *Parsons*, 51 L. J. P. C. 11 ; 7 App. Ca. 96 : *Vf.* as to "Trade or Commerce," *Severn* v. *The Queen*, 2 Sup. Ct. Can. Ca. 90). But an Act for the regulation of the sale of intoxicants relates to public order, and is not within the phrase "Property and Civil Rights," and is, therefore, within the competency of the Dominion Legislature. Such an Act "has in its legal aspect an obvious and close similarity to laws which place restrictions on the sale or custody of poisonous drugs or of dangerously explosive substances. These things, as well as intoxicating liquors can, of course, be held as property, but a law placing restrictions on their sale, custody or removal, on the ground that the free sale or use of them is dangerous to public safety, and making it a criminal offence punishable by fine or imprisonment to violate these restrictions, cannot properly be deemed a law in relation to property in the sense in which those words are used in the 92nd section . . . . Laws which make it a criminal offence for a man wilfully to set fire to his own house on the ground that such an act endangers the public safety, or to over-work his horse on the ground of cruelty to the animal, though affecting in some sense property and the right of a man to do as he pleases with his own, cannot properly be regarded as legislation in relation to property or to civil rights. Nor could a law which prohibited or restricted the sale or exposure of cattle having a contagious disease be so regarded. Laws of this nature designed for the promotion of public order, safety or morals, and which subject those who contravene them to criminal procedure and punishment belong to the subject of public wrongs rather than to that of civil rights" (per P. C. in *Russell* v. *The Queen,* 51 L. J. P. C. 81; 7 App. Ca. 829).

V. Direct Taxation.

CLAIM.—*V.* Debt, Claim, or Demand: Demand: Incumbrances.

"'Claim against the Crown for damages or compensation' (Crown Suits, Ordinance, 1876, s. 18, ii.), is an apt expression to include Claims arising out of Torts" (*A.-G. Straits Settlements* v. *Wemyss,* 57 L. J. P. C. 64; 13 App. Ca. 192; 58 L. T. 358).

Ord. 57, R. 5, R. S. C., does not mean that there should be a vague statement, but the "Claim" therein referred to should be precise and definite (*Hockey* v. *Evans,* 31 S. J. 231).

V. Sum Claimed.

CLAIMING UNDER.—As to who are persons "claiming by, from or under" a Covenantor; *V.* Elph. 491, 492; Dart, 884; Woodf. 677; Touch. 170–172.

V. Pretending to claim.

Semble, that a Trustee in Bankruptcy is not a person "Claiming through or under" the Bankrupt within s. 11, Com. L. Pro. Act, 1854 (*Pennell* v. *Walker,* 26 L. J. C. P. 9; 18 C. B. 651: *Piercey* v. *Young,* 14 Ch. D. 200).

CLASS.—"A number of persons are popularly said to form a 'Class' when they can be designated by some general name as 'children,' 'grand-children,' 'nephews'; but in legal language the question whether a gift is one to a class depends not upon these considerations, but upon the mode of gift itself, namely,—that it is a gift of an aggregate sum to a body of persons uncertain in number at the time of the gift, to be ascertained at a future time, and who are all to take in equal, or in some other definite, proportions, the share of each being dependent for its amount upon the ultimate number of persons" (1 Jarm. 268, 269).

CLAUSE.—A testator (obit 1836), devised realty to "E. Eley, her heirs and assigns for ever"; subsequently he obliterated "Eley, her heirs and assigns for ever," and re-wrote "Eley." Held, a revocation of a

"Clause" in the Will within s. 6, St. of Frauds (*Swinton* v. *Baily*, 48 L. J. Ex. 57 ; 4 App. Ca. 70).

CLEAN BILL OF LADING.—*V. Stephens* v. *Australasian Insrce.*, L. R. 8 C. P. 18 ; 42 L. J. C. P. 12 ; 1 Maude & P. 341.

CLEAR.—The gift of a "Clear" annuity or legacy exempts it from *Legacy Duty* (*Lethbridge* v. *Thurlow*, 21 L. J. Ch. 538 ; 15 Bea. 334 : *Banks* v. *Braithwaite*, 32 L. J. Ch. 35 ; 10 W. R. 612 : *Vf.* 1 Jarm. 187 n. ; Seton, 961 ; Watson, Eq. 1345). And this construction is not altered by a special direction that one annuity is to be "free of legacy duty," which direction is omitted as regards another annuity in the same Will (*Re Robins*, W. N. (88) 41 ; 32 S. J. 273). And even where an appointment of a residue of a fund would be regarded as a gift of a definite sum, a preceding appointment of part of such fund "of the Clear Value" of so much, will exempt that amount from liability to contribute to probate and legacy duty and testamentary expenses (*Re Currie*, 57 L. J. Ch. 743 ; 59 L. T. 200 ; 36 W. R. 752).

But in *Banks* v. *Braithwaite* (sup.), the direction was to retain so much consols "as should be sufficient to realize the clear yearly income of £150 ;" and the V.-C. decided that this income was *not* free of legacy duty ; for he said, "the amount (to be retained) having been arrived at, the dividends are then directed to be paid to the petitioner. The word 'clear' does not apply to that direction." *Va. Sanders* v. *Kiddell*, 5 L. J. Ch. 29 ; 7 Sim. 536 : *Pridie* v. *Field*, 19 Bea. 497 :—It has, however, been said that "this distinction does not seem to be tenable on principle" (1 Jarm. 187, citing *Wilks* v. *Groom*, 2 Jur. N. S. 798 : *Harper* v. *Morley*, 2 Jur. 653. *Va. Re Cole*, L. R. 8 Eq. 271).

The word "clear," alone, will scarcely exempt even a testamentary annuity from *Income Tax* (*Lethbridge* v. *Thurlow*, sup.) : but coupled with other apt words (in a Will, but not in a Deed) it would do so. *V.* Deductions.

"Clear *Profits*" of a Company ; *V. Re Alexandra Palace, Goodson's Case*, 51 L. J. Ch. 655 ; 21 Ch. D. 149.

"Clear *Sum* ;" *V. Re Currie*, W. N. (88) 154 ; 57 L. J. Ch. 743 ; 59 L. T. 200 ; 36 W. R. 752.

"By 'Clear *Yearly Rent*' is understood, a rent clear of all outgoings, &c., usually borne by the tenant ; but subject to such (*e.g.* Land Tax) as are borne by the landlord" (Dart, 137, citing *Tyrconnell* v. *Ancaster*, 2 Ves. sen. 500).

The "Clear *Yearly Value*" of a tenement within s. 27, Reform Act, 1832 (repealed, and s. 5, Rep. Peo. Act, 1884, 48 V. c. 3, substituted), means the annual amount which the tenement would ordinarily let at, deducting such rates, taxes and charges as may be payable by the landlord, but which generally are payable by a tenant ; but without deducting landlord's insurance or repairs (*Coogan* v. *Luckett*, 15 L. J. C. P. 159 ; 2 C. B. 182 ; 1 Lutw. 447 : *Colvill* v. *Wood*, 15 L. J. C. P. 160 ; 2 C. B. 210 ; 1 Lutw. 487). But for the purpose of a county vote the value of a freehold would be lessened by what the landlord would have to pay to keep it in repair under the letting, or in order to obtain a tenant at the amount of the agreed rent (*Hamilton* v. *Bass*, 22 L. J. C. P. 29 ; 12 C. B. 631). Indeed, in *Dobbs* v. *Grand Junc. Waterworks Co.* (53 L. J. Q. B. 50), *Colvill* v. *Wood* was treated as an exceptional decision on the particular statute to which it related ; and Lord Blackburn there said that as *Colvill* v. *Wood* had been acted upon so long it was too late to cast any doubt upon it. As to the meaning of "clear yearly value" in Scotland and Ireland, *quà* electoral qualification ; *V.* 48 V. c. 3, s. 11. *V.* NET : ANNUAL VALUE.

The phrase "Clear *Days*," means that the time is to be reckoned exclusive of both the first and last days (*Liffin* v. *Pitcher*, 1 Dowl. N. S. 767 : *V. quà* R. S. C., Ord. 64, R. 12).

Refreshers to Counsel may be allowed "for every *clear day*" subsequent to the first or other day or days of the trial of 5 hours each (Ord. 65, R. 48, R. S. C.),—that means every clear substantial portion of a day beyond a completed day or days of 5 hours each (per Grantham, J., at Chambers, in *Gibbs* v. *Barrow*, 30 S. J. 538).

CLERGYMAN.—A clergyman of the Church of England would undoubtedly come within the meaning of the word "clergyman ;" but "there are various authorities to show that a Roman Catholic Priest is, also, a Clergyman in Holy Orders" (per Stephen, J., *R.* v. *Haslehurst*, 53 L. J. M. C. 129).

"Rector, Vicar, or Curate, going to, or returning from, visiting any sick parishioner, or on other his parochial duty, *within his Parish*," *quà* exemption from Turnpike Toll, s. 32, 3 G. 4, c. 126, includes a curate temporarily acting, with the permission of the Bishop, though without his license (*Temple* v. *Dickinson*, 28 L. J. M. C. 10 ; 1 E. & E. 34), *secus*, if without the Bishop's permission (*Brunskill* v. *Watson*, L. R. 3 Q. B. 418 ; 37 L. J. M. C. 103 ; 32 J. P. 324, 692). "*Within his Parish*," defines the ambit of the clergyman's duties, not that of his exemption (*Temple* v. *Dickinson*, sup.). The exemption is not lost by the clergyman being accompanied by his wife and daughters (*Layard* v. *Ovey*, 37 L. J. M. C. 148 ; L. R. 3 Q. B. 415 ; 32 J. P. 293).

CLERK.—"*Clarke* (clerke)." *Clericus*, is twofold : *ecclesiasticus* (which Littleton here, s. 180, intendeth), and he is either secular or regular, so called because he is *servus et hæreditas domini :* and *laicus*, and in this sense is signified a pen-man, who getteth his living in some Court or otherwise by the use of his pen" (Co. Litt. 120 a).

The priority given in bankruptcy for payment of salary to a "Clerk"

(s. 40 (b) Bankry. Act, 1883), is not confined to trade clerks : it includes, *e.g.*, an architect's clerk (*Ex p. Gough*, M. & B. 417 ; 3 Dea. & C. 189).

A Banker's Clerk is properly described as " Clerk," for the purposes of the Bills of Sale Acts (*Lamb* v. *Bruce*, 45 L. J. Q. B. 538). *V.* GOVERNMENT CLERK.

The London Agent of a foreign Company is not its " Clerk " within Ord. 9, R. 8, R. S. C. ; the expression there, "*the* clerk or secretary," points to some definite individual whose knowledge may be taken to be the knowledge of the corporation (*Nutter* v. *Messageries Maritimes*, 54 L. J. Q. B. 528).

"A ' Clerk *or Servant*,' (*quà* Embezzlement), is a person bound either by express contract of service, or by conduct implying such a contract, to obey the orders and submit to the control of his master in the transaction of the business which it is his duty as such clerk or servant to transact " (Steph. Cr. 237, *V.* Ib. to p. 240 for cases in illustration).

Whatever called, a Clerk at the head of his department in a Bank, is a "*Chief* Clerk," s. 7, 9 G. 4, c. 23 (*R* v. *Greenland*, 36 L. J. M. C. 37 ; L. R. 1 C. C. 65).

CLIENT.—The description of a Vendor as "my client" or "your client" is not sufficient : *V.* PROPRIETOR.

In R. 6, Solicitors Gen. Remuneration Order, "Client" means *all* the clients (if more than one) for whom the solicitor is undertaking business (per Stirling, J., obiter, *Re Metcalfe*, 32 S. J. 60 ; 36 W. R. 137).

CLOCK.—*V.* OF THE CLOCK.

CLOSE.—"Close" is ambiguous, and may mean the quality or description of land, as well as the land itself (*Heath* v. *Milward*, 4 L. J. C. P. 292 ; 2 Bing. N. C. 98 ; 2 Sc. 160).

" Close," in a Declaration in Trespass, included the subsoil as well as the surface (*Cox* v. *Glue*, 17 L. J. C. P. 162 ; 5 C. B. 533).

CLOSE-HAULED.—"'Close-hauled' (in the Regulations for Preventing Collisions at Sea, 1879) is not confined to a vessel sailing as close as possible to the wind ; it may be applied to a vessel on a wind, although she may be able to luff a point or more without losing steerage-way " (1 Maude & P. 599, 600, citing, *Chadwick* v. *Dublin Steam Packet Co.*, 6 E. & B. 771).

CLOSELY ENTAILED.—A devise followed by a direction that the property should be "closely entailed," was cut down to a tenancy for life, remainder to the issue ; but the tenant for life was made unimpeachable for waste (*Woolmore* v. *Burrows*, 1 Sim. 512).

V. STRICT SETTLEMENT.

CLOTHES.—*V.* LINEN.

CLOUGH.—A valley (Co. Litt. 4 b.).

COAL MINES.—*V.* MINE.

COALS.—"Coals and Coal Mines;" *V.* SUBSOIL.

"Coals and Produce of any other Mines," includes Coke (*Bowes* v. *Ravensworth*, cited PRODUCE OF MINES).

"Coals exported;" *V.* EXPORTED.

COASTING TRADE.—"Ships employed in the *Coasting Trade* of the United Kingdom" (sub-s. 1, s. 379, Merchant Shipping Act, 1854, 17 & 18 V. c. 104), means ships continually or ordinarily so employed (*The Agricola*, 2 W. Rob. 10: *The Lloyds*, otherwise *The Sea Queen*, 32 L. J. P. M. & A. 197; B. & L. 359: *Vf.* 1 Maude & P. 277). *Cp.* TRADING.

COASTING VESSEL.—"A 'coasting vessel' would seem to mean a vessel that goes along the coast" (per Alderson, B., *Shepherd* v. *Hills*, 25 L. J. Ex. 9). But an Irish vessel trading between Belfast and London is not a coasting vessel within the Pilot Act, 52 G. 3, c. 39, s. 2 (*Davison* v. *Mekibben*, 6 Moo. 387); nor are vessels trading between England, and Guernsey and Jersey "coasting vessels" within the meaning of the Customs Acts, or of a Harbour Act (*Shepherd* v. *Hills*, 25 L. J. Ex. 6; 11 Ex. 55).

COASTWISE.—Goods brought from an Irish port to Bristol, are not brought "Coastwise" (*Battersby* v. *Kirk*, 5 L. J. C. P. 166; 2 Bing. N. C. 584).

COCK OF HAY.—An Indictment for setting fire to a "Cock" of Hay cannot be sustained under a Statute making it an offence to set fire to a "Stack" of hay. "We know that, popularly, a Cock of Hay, differs from a rick or stack. The small conical heap into which hay is formed temporarily in the field, to protect it from rain before it is completely saved, is commonly called a Cock of Hay; and in some districts it is called a lap cock, in others a field cock; while in other places it receives a different name. A Cock of Hay may, therefore, be any small heap of hay in the field, saved, or not completely saved; and may differ essentially from a stack or rick. A stack of hay, on the contrary, means a large heap of hay saved and made up, and protected from the weather, and the term is generally applied to that which has been drawn home from the field. Webster defines a Cock of Hay to be, 'a small conical pile, so shaped for shedding the rain, and called in England a cop; whilst a stack is a large conical pile, sometimes covered with thatch'" (per Fitzgerald, J., *R.* v. *M'Keever*, Ir. Rep. 5 C. L. 90, 91).

V. Stack.

COLEBERTI.—"*Coleberti*, often named in Domesday, signifieth tenants in free socage by free rent; and so it is expounded of record. *Radmans* and *radchemistres* (*rad*, or *rede* signifieth firme and stable) there also often named, these are *liberi tenentes qui arabant et herciebant ad curiam domini, seu falcabant, aut metebant*, because their estates are firme and stable; and they are many times called *sochemans* and *sokemanni*, because of their plough service" (Co. Litt. 5 b).

COLLATERAL.—The word "Collateral," *e.g.*, Collateral Security, means, side by side, "parallel," and, taken by itself, has no such meaning as "secondary," "auxiliary," "subsidiary," or "only to be made use of in aid" (*Early* v. *Early*, 49 L. J. Ch. 826 n.; 16 Ch. D. 214 n.: *Athill* v. *Athill*, 49 L. J. Ch. 821; 50 Ib. 123; 16 Ch. D. 211; 43 L. T. 581; 29 W. R. 309: *Bute* v. *Cunynghame*, 2 Russ. 275: *Leonino* v. *Leonino*, 48 L. J. Ch. 217; 10 Ch. D. 460. *Vh.* Dart, 921, 922).

For instances of Collateral Agreements between Landlord and Tenant, *V.* Woodf. 87.

COLLECTED.—"Levied or Collected;" *V.* Levy.

COLLECTOR.—A Cashier who deducts and forwards the contributions of members of a Friendly Society from their wages he has to pay, is a "Collector" of the Contributions within s. 30 Friendly Societies Act, 1875, 38 & 39 V. c. 60 (*Joyce* v. *Northumberland Miners' Socy.*, 4 Times Rep. 525).

COLLEGE.—"A 'College,' to be such in more than vulgar reputation, must have the 'countenance of a legal commencement;' a lawful erection and foundation. And it should seem that no one can found or incorporate a College within this realm, or assign, or license others to assign, temporal livings to it, but only the King himself. And reputative Colleges which had no lawful foundation, were held not to be given to the King by the Stat. 1 Edw. 6, unless they had the countenance of the King's Letters Patent, or might have had a legal commencement but for some error or imperfection in the penning or proceedings" (Dwar. 683, 684, citing *Adams and Lambert's Case*, 4 Rep. 108).

COLLIERY.—Besides its obvious meaning of a place where Coals are dug, "Colliery" "is a word sufficiently wide to include all contiguous and connected veins and seams of coal which are worked as one concern, without regard to the closes and pieces of ground under which they are carried (*V. Hodgson* v. *Field*, 7 East, 620). Indeed, it is apparently wide enough to include the engines and machinery in the contiguous and connected veins, as well as those veins themselves" (MacS. 25).

COLLISION.—Where a Bill of Lading exonerated the ship-owners from damage arising from "*Collision* and accidents, loss or damage from any act, neglect, or default whatsoever of the pilots, master or mariners or other servants of the company in navigating the ship;" it was held that "Collision" meant every collision however caused (*Chartered Mer. Bank of India* v. *Netherlands Steam Nav. Co.*, 52 L. J. Q. B. 220; 10 Q. B. D. 521).
V. DAMAGE BY COLLISION.

COLLUSION.—"Collusion," s. 30, Divorce Act, 20 & 21 V. c. 85, means an agreement between the parties wrongfully to withhold relevant facts from the Court (*Hunt* v. *Hunt*, 47 L. J., P. D. & A. 22; 39 L. T. 45: *Barnes* v. *Barnes*, L. R. 1 P. & D. 507; 37 L. J., P. & M. 4: *Bacon* v. *Bacon*, 25 W. R. 560: *Butler* v. *Butler*, Times, 18 Jan., 1890). *V.* CONNIVANCE.

COLONIAL.—"Colonial" *Goods*, even in a Colonial Statute or Regulation,—*e.g.* "Colonial Wine" in a New South Wales tariff of Railway Rates—mean the goods of any Colony (*Commrs. of Railways* v. *Hyland*, 56 L. J. P. C. 76; 56 L. T. 896).

In all Acts of Parliament passed after the 31st Dec. 1889, "the expression 'Colonial Legislature,' and the expression 'Legislature,' when used with reference to a BRITISH POSSESSION, shall respectively mean the authority, other than the Imperial Parliament or Her Majesty the Queen in Council, competent to make laws for a British Possession" (s. 18 (7), Interp. Act, 1889).

COLONIES.—"The word 'Colonies' in the statute—5 & 6 V. c. 49, s. 2—must extend to all Colonies, in the absence of a context to control it; and I can find here no such context" (per Turner, L.J., *Low* v. *Routledge*, 35 L. J. Ch. 116; 1 Ch. 42).

In all Acts of Parliament passed after the 31st Dec., 1889, "'Colony' shall mean any part of Her Majesty's Dominions exclusive of the BRITISH ISLANDS, and of BRITISH INDIA; and where parts of such Dominions are under both a central and a local legislature, all parts under the central legislature shall, for the purposes of this definition, be deemed to be one Colony" (s. 18 (3), Interp. Act, 1889).

COLOURABLE. — Is the reverse of BONÂ FIDE; and *V.* especially jdgmt. of James, L.J., *Etherington* v. *Wilson*, 45 L. J. Ch. 156; 1 Ch. D. 160.

COLOURABLY IMITATE.—*V.* COPY.

COMBE.—"*Combe, hope, dene, glyn, hawgh, howgh*, signifieth a valley" (Co. Litt. 5 b): *V.* DENE.

COME TO.—An instrument, fact, or thing, does not "Come to the Knowledge" of counsel, &c., within s. 3 (ii.), Conv. Act, 1882, simply because he knew it on a former occasion (*Re Cousins*, 55 L. J. Ch. 662 ; 31 Ch. D. 671 ; 54 L. T. 376 ; 34 W. R. 393).

A legacy to a married woman, unpaid before her desertion, "comes to" her after her desertion within s. 25, 20 & 21 V. c. 85 (*Re Coward & Adams*, 44 L. J. Ch. 384 ; L. R. 20 Eq. 179). *V.* Acquire.

"In case A. should come to *the possession* of the said estate"; held as not creating a Condition (*Edgeworth* v. *Edgeworth*, L. R. 4 H. L. 35) : come to an estate "in possession," *V. Hill* v. *Broughton*, 3 Bro. C. C. 180. *Vf.* Possession.

COMFORTABLE MAINTENANCE.—These words, in a provision by deed for the widows of officers in the East India Company coupled with a restriction on alienation, were held to vest the provision for the Separate Use of the beneficiaries (*Re Peacock*, 48 L. J. Ch. 265 ; 10 Ch. D. 490). *Vf.* Separate Maintenance.

COMING TO SETTLE.—13 & 14 Car. 2, c. 12 ; *V. R.* v. *Woolpit*, 5 L. J. M. C. 14 ; 4 A. & E. 205 ; 5 N. & M. 526.

COMMENCED.—An action is "commenced" by Writ or Originating Summons, and as soon as the same is sealed (*Galland* v. *Burton*, 30 Ch. D. 231 ; 54 L. J. Ch. 1131 : *Clarke* v. *Bradlaugh*, 51 L. J. Q. B. 1 ; 8 Q. B. D. 63).

"Any Action commenced," &c., s. 5, County Court Act, 1867, meant "Any action commenced in the High Court, and which could have been commenced in the County Court" (*Parsons* v. *Tinling*, 46 L. J. C. P. 230 ; 2 C. P. D. 119).

V. Set up.

COMMENCEMENT.—The "Commencement" of every Act of Parliament, means "the time at which the Act comes into operation" (s. 36 (1), Interp. Act, 1889). *Cp.* Passing. *V.* Day.

As to the common clause in Railway Acts giving compensation to landowners out of deposits (when the line is not opened in a certain time) for damages occasioned "by the Commencement, Construction, or Abandonment" of the railway ; *V. Re Potteries, Shrewsbury & N. Wales Ry.*, 53 L. J. Ch. 556 ; 25 Ch. D. 251. That case lays it down that this phrase is to be read disjunctively, and that the damages are to be ascertained by comparing the value of the land immediately before such commencement or construction or abandonment, with its value immediately after the happening of any of those three events.

"At the Commencement," s. 2, 23 H. 8, c. 15 ; *V. Doe* d. *Ellis* v. *Owens*, 11 L. J. Ex. 120 ; 9 M. & W. 455.

COMMENT.—*V.* Fair Comment.

COMMERCE.—"Trade or Commerce" ; *V.* Civil Rights.

COMMISSION.—*V.* Conducting : Free of Commission.

COMMISSIONERS OF WOODS AND FORESTS.—*V.* s. 12 (12), Interp. Act, 1889.

COMMISSIONERS OF WORKS.—*V.* s. 12 (13), Interp. Act, 1889.

COMMIT.—In dealing with the phrase "commit suicide," Pollock, C.B., in *Clift* v. *Schwabe* (17 L. J. C. P. 14 ; 3 C. B. 437), said, "The meaning of 'commit' in *Johnson* (with reference to this use of the word) is 'to perpetrate'—to do a fault—to be guilty of a crime ;" and "'perpetrate' is to commit, to act,—always in an ill sense." In the same case (p. 9, L. J.), Patteson, J., said,—"The word 'commit' is said always to be used in a bad sense—be it so :" but he proceeded to show that it is not always used in a *criminal* sense, and that view accords with the judgment of the majority of the Ex. Cham. in the case cited.

COMMITS.—This word in the Bankry. Act, 1883, is used in the present tense, not in relation to time, but as the present tense of logic, and means "shall have committed" an act of bankruptcy (*Ex p. Pratt*, 53 L. J. Ch. 613 ; 12 Q. B. D. 334 ; *V.* especially judgments by Bowen and Fry, L.JJ.).

COMMITTED : COMMITMENT : COMMITTAL.—The words "commitment," "committed," or "committal to prison," do not mean, as was held by Lush, J., "received into prison ;" but mean "when the order is made under which the person is to be kept in prison" (per Ld. Blackburn, *Mullins* v. *Surrey*, 51 L. J. Q. B. 149 : and per Ld. Penzance, Ib. 152) : and the words "period of committal" in s. 57, Prisons Act, 1877 (40 & 41 V. c. 21), mean that the expenses which (by the joint operation of that section and s. 4) are to be defrayed out of moneys to be provided by Parliament, are to be so paid from the time of the making out of the order of committal (*Mullins* v. *Surrey*, 51 L. J. Q. B. 145 ; 7 App. Ca. 1 : *Mews* v. *The Queen*, 52 L. J. M. C. 57 ; 8 App. Ca. 339). *V.* Imprisonment : Maintenance.

"Committed" will sometimes include *acts of omission, e.g.* as regards notice of action within a certain time "next after the fact committed," s. 109, Highway Act, 1835, 5 & 6 W. 4, c. 50 (*Holland* v. *Northwich*, 40 J. P. 517 ; 34 L. T. 137).

COMMITTED FOR TRIAL.—In all Acts of Parliament passed after the 31st Dec. 1889, "'Committed for Trial,' used in relation to any person shall, unless the contrary intention appears, mean, as respects England and Wales, committed to prison with the view of being tried before a judge and jury, whether the person is committed in pursuance of s. 22 or of s. 25 of the Indictable Offences Act, 1848, or is committed by a Court, Judge, Coroner, or other authority having power to commit a person to any prison with a view to his trial, and shall include a person who is admitted to bail upon a recognizance to appear and take his trial before a judge and jury" (s. 27, Interp. Act, 1889).

"Committed for trial at the Assizes;" *V. R.* v. *Johnson*, 10 A. & E. 740; 8 L. J. M. C. 99; 2 P. & D. 610.

COMMITTEE.—"The term 'Committee' means an individual, or body to which others have committed or delegated a particular duty, or who have taken on themselves to perform it, in the expectation of their act being confirmed by the body they profess to represent or act for" (per Pollock, C.B., *Reynell* v. *Lewis*, 16 L. J. Ex. 30; 15 M. & W. 526).

"I observed in the argument that, according to one's ordinary idea of the meaning of the word, a 'Committee' consists of more persons than one. But I was not right in saying that; because that is not *ex vi termini* the necessary meaning of the word 'Committee,' which simply means a person or persons to whom anything is committed" (per Kay, J., *Re Scottish Petroleum Co.*, 51 L. J. Ch. 845).

V. Provisional Committee.

COMMODITIES.—*V.* Advantages.

COMMON.—"'*Common of Pasture*'—*Communia*, it cometh of the English word common, because it is common to many; and thereupon and accordingly is here (s. 184) called by *Littleton* common of pasture, for that the feeding of beasts in the land wherein the common is to be had belongs to many" (Co. Litt. 122 a): *Vh.* Elph. 607—615; Pastures; Pasturage.

"There be also divers other commons, as of estovers, of turbary, of pischary, of digging for coles, minerals and the like" (Co. Litt. 122 a). *V.* Fishery.

"Common of Faldage;" *V.* Foldcourse.

And generally as to Commons; *V.* Wms. on Commons; Elton on Commons; Add. T. 255—263.

"The word 'Commons' means as often lands where rights of common are exercised, as common unenclosed open land where there are no commonable rights" (per Watson, B., *A.-G.* v. *Hanmer*, 27 L. J. Ch. 841).

V. Right of Common.

COMMON AND NOTORIOUS.—A person is not a "Common and Notorious" Depraver of the Common Prayer (Canons, 1603, No. 27), who, at solicitation, sends a friendly and private letter wherein the Common Prayer is depraved (*Jenkins* v. *Cook*, 45 L. J. P. C. 1; 1 P. D. 80). *V.* Deprave: Evil Liver.

COMMON BAWDY HOUSES.—"A Common Bawdy House is a house or room, or set of rooms, in any house kept for purposes of prostitution. And it is immaterial whether indecent or disorderly conduct is or is not perceptible from the outside" (Steph. Cr. 122). *Vf.* Arch. Cr. 1021, 1022 ; Rosc. Cr. 823.

COMMON BETTING HOUSES.—*V.* 16 & 17 V. c. 119, s. 1. Every Common Betting House is a COMMON GAMING HOUSE (Ib. s. 2). *Vf.* Arch. Cr. 1022.

COMMON CARRIERS.—*V.* NOT AS COMMON CARRIERS.

COMMON EMPLOYMENT.—As to when employées are engaged in a "Common Employment;" *V. Priestly* v. *Fowler,* 3 M. & W. 1 ; 7 L. J. Ex. 42 : *Johnson* v. *Lindsay,* 58 L. J. Q. B. 581.

COMMON FIELDS.—*V.* Elph. 566, 567.

COMMON FISHERY.—*V.* FISHERY.

COMMON GAMING HOUSE.—"Is a house in which a large number of persons are invited (whether publicly or privately) habitually to congregate for the purpose of gaming" (per Hawkins, J., *Jenks* v. *Turpin,* 53 L. J. M. C. 166 ; 13 Q. B. D. 505 : and *V.* that case for a collection of the authorities on this word. As to what is sufficient proof of a Common Gaming House, *V.* s. 2, 8 & 9 V. c. 109).

"A Common Gaming House is a house kept or used for playing therein at any game of chance, or any mixed game of chance and skill, in which (a) a bank is kept by one or more of the players, exclusively of the others ; or (b) in which any game is played the chances of which are not alike favorable to all the players, including among the players the banker or other person by whom the game is managed, or against whom the other players stake, play or bet" (Steph. Cr. 122, 123).

COMMON LODGING-HOUSE.—The phrase "Common Lodging House" in ss. 76–89, P. H. Act, 1875, held to include a house in which hawkers and other persons of an itinerant character were received at 6*d.* a night, and eating their meals at a common table in the kitchen (*Langdon* v. *Broadbent,* 42 J. P. 56, 67 ; 37 L. T. 434 ; 47 L. J. Q. B. 275, n. 11).

COMMON NUISANCE.—"A Common Nuisance is an act not warranted by law, or an omission to discharge a legal duty, which act or omission obstructs or causes inconvenience or damage to the public in the exercise of rights common to all Her Majesty's subjects. It is immaterial whether the act complained of is convenient to a larger number of the public than it inconveniences ; but the fact that the act complained of facilitates the lawful exercise of their rights by part of the public, may show that it is not a nuisance to any of the public" (Steph. Cr. ch. 19, *wh. V.* for instances of Common Nuisances). *Vf.* Arch. Cr. 1017–1050.

COMMON, Tenancy in.—*V.* TENANCY IN COMMON.

COMMON TO THE TRADE.—This phrase in s. 74 (1 b), Trade Marks Act, 1883, 46 & 47 V. c. 57, means "Open to the Trade" (*Re Wragg*, 29 Ch. D. 551; 54 L. J. Ch. 391: *Burland* v. *Broxburn Co.*, 58 L. J. Ch. 816; W. N. (89) 141). "In Common *Use*;" *V.* Ib.

COMMONLY UNDERSTOOD.—"Commonly understood," s. 241, 45 & 46 V. c. 50, means, "Commonly understood by any person comparing the Nomination Paper and the Burgess Roll" (*Moorhouse* v. *Linney*, 15 Q. B. D. 273: *Vf. R.* v. *Gregory*, 22 L. J. Q. B. 120; 1 E. & B. 600).

COMMOTE or **CONMOTE.**—"A commote is a great seigniory, and may include one or divers mannors" (Co. Litt. 5 a: *Vf.* Touch. 92; Elph. 567, 568).

COMMUTATION.—A "Commutation," *e.g.*, of Tithes, s. 42, 6 & 7 W. 4, c. 71, is to substitute one liability for another; therefore lands which were waste at the time of a Tithe Commutation Award but which were afterwards enclosed and so would have become titheable but for the Award, became liable to the per-acreage Tithe Commutation Rent Charge fixed by the award (*Trimmer* v. *Walsh*, 32 L. J. Q. B. 364; 4 B. & S. 40). In that case Cockburn, C. J., pointed out that "Commutation" was not to be confounded with "Apportionment," and Blackburn, J., distinguished it from "Compensation."

COMPANY.—Referring to the phrase "Company, Association or Partnership," in s. 4 Companies Act, 1862 (25 & 26 V. c. 89), James, L.J., said, "I believe the difference which was meant, as the difference according to the vernacular we use in these things between a Company or Association and an ordinary Partnership, is this: An ordinary *Partnership*, is a partnership composed of definite individuals bound together by contract between themselves to continue for some joint object either during pleasure or during a limited time; but the partnership is essentially composed of the persons originally entering into the contract with one another. A *Company* or *Association*—and I take the terms to be really synonymous—is an arrangement by which parties intend to have a partnership which will be constantly changing, that is to say, to have a succession of partnerships, a partnership to-day consisting of certain members, and to-morrow of some of those members only and some others who have come in; so that there will be a constant shifting of the partnership, a determination of the old and a creation of a new partnership, and always formed with the intention that, so far as they could by agreement between themselves, the new partnership should take upon itself the assets and liabilities of the old partnership—an object which as regards liability could not be effected in point of law by any arrangement between the persons themselves, unless the persons contracting with them by a *novatio* authorized the change, or unless by special provisions in the Acts of Parliament, sanction was given to such an arrangement. That is the sole distinction between Association and Partnership" (*Smith* v. *Anderson*, 50 L. J. Ch. 49; 15 Ch. D. 273). In that case, however, Brett and Cotton, L.JJ., suggest distinctions between "Company" and "Association."

V. INSURANCE COMPANY: TRADING AND OTHER PUBLIC COMPANIES.

COMPASSIONATE ALLOWANCE.—A "Compassionate Allowance" is a voluntary bounty, and not Income (*Re Webber*, *V.* INCOME).

COMPENSATION.—"Compensation" in Conditions of Sale; *V.* *Cordingley* v. *Cheesebrough*, 31 L. J. Ch. 617; 3 Giff. 496.

"Fair and Reasonable Compensation," *V.* REASONABLE.

"Making Compensation"; *V.* SATISFACTION.

V. COMMUTATION.

COMPETE.—An agreement "not directly or indirectly to enter into competition" in a business, is not confined to *active* competition; and a physician, having entered into such contract on the sale of his practice, is guilty of a breach if he attend a patient within the prohibited district, even though he was called in without any solicitation on his part, and though he recommended that some one else should be called in, and though it be proved that his vendee would not have been called in (*Rogers* v. *Drury*, 36 W. R. 496; 57 L. J. Ch. 504; 4 Times Rep. 98).

COMPETENT.—"Competent to dispose by Will of a Continuing Interest," s. 21, Succession Duty Act, 1853, means the quantity of the successor's interest in the property subject to duty, and does not refer to his mental capacity (*A.-G.* v. *Hallett*, 27 L. J. Ex. 89; 2 H. & N. 368); and the phrase includes the power (if executed) of a Tenant in Tail in possession to enlarge his estate to a fee simple (*Lilford* v. *A.-G.*, 36 L. J. Ex. 116; L. R. 2 H. L. 63).

Parties "Competent" to make admissions, s. 7, 21 & 22 Vict. c. 27, include Assignees in Bankruptcy, and Married Women (*Churchill* v. *Coller*, 1 N. R. 82); but not Infants (*Wilkinson* v. *Beal*, 4 Mad. 408).

COMPETITION.—*V.* COMPETE.

COMPLAINT.—An application to justices to settle compensation under s. 22, Lands C. C. Act, 1845, is not a "Complaint" within Jervis' Act, 11 & 12 V. c. 43 (*R.* v. *Hannay*, 44 L. J. M. C. 27: *R.* v. *Edwards*, 53 L. J. M. C. 149; 13 Q. B. D. 586: the latter case over-rules *Re Edmundson*,

21 L. J. M. C. 193 ; 17 Q. B. 67) ; nor are proceedings for enforcing a Rate a "Complaint" (*Sweetman* v. *Guest*, 37 L. J. M. C. 59 ; L. R. 3 Q. B. 262).

V. Information.

The filing an affidavit in support of a notice of motion to set aside an Award is a "Complaint" within 9 & 10 W. 3, c. 15, s. 2 (*Re Huddersfield & Jacomb*, 44 L. J. Ch. 96 ; 10 Ch. 92).

COMPLETE CARGO.—*V.* Cargo.

COMPLETION.—Where a contract for sale stipulates that interest on the unpaid purchase money shall be paid until "Completion," that means that interest shall be payable until the purchase money is paid (*Lewis* v. *S. W. Ry.*, 22 L. J. Ch. 209 ; 10 Hare, 113). In delivering judgment in that case, Turner, V.-C., said :—"The question is, what is the meaning of the words 'until the *completion* of the purchase'? Those words may no doubt import, and generally perhaps would be construed to refer to, the complete conveyance of the estate and final settlement of the business. But I do not think that is the only or necessary meaning of the words. They may mean, until the completion of the purchase by the purchaser, on whose part the purchase is completed, on the payment of the purchase money by him. . . . . Is it reasonable to construe the words as importing that interest is to be paid on the purchase money until the final completion of the purchase, although the purchase money itself might be paid long before? I think it would be unreasonable to put such a construction on the words, the more so when it is considered that interest is the compensation for the delay in the payment of the principal. That an agreement might be so expressed as to make interest on the purchase money payable up to the final completion of the purchase by the conveyance of the estate, although the purchase money itself was sooner paid, need not be denied ; but I think very strong words would be required for the purpose, and that the terms of this agreement do not warrant such a construction."

COMPLETION OF WORKS.—*V.* Works.

COMPOSITEURS.—*V.* Amiable Compositeurs.

COMPOSITION.—A "Composition with *Creditors*" is an arrangement between a Debtor and his Creditors, whereby the latter agree with the Debtor (and mutually amongst themselves) to receive, and the Debtor agrees to pay, an agreed proportion less than 20*s.* in the £, in satisfaction of the debts due or accruing due from the Debtor to his Creditors.

A *cessio bonorum* is not a "Composition with Creditors" disqualifying a member of a Local Board under R. 5, Sch. 2, P. H. Act, 1875 (*R.* v. *Cooban*, 56 L. J. M. C. 33). In that case Denman, J. (obiter), was of opinion that the "Composition" struck at by the Rule was one effected under the Bankry. Act, 1869 ; whilst Hawkins, J., was "inclined to think that this disqualifying Rule would include not only Compositions under the Bankry. Act, 1869, but also Private Compositions with Creditors by deed."

A "Composition" of a *Poor Rate* (proviso (1), s. 7, Rep. of the People Act, 1867, 30 & 31 V. c. 102), includes not only the case of an Owner paying less than the full amount by agreement, but also where he pays a less amount by Vestry Order under the Small Tenements Act (*Trotter* v. *Trevor*, 38 L. J. C. P. 51; L. R. 4 C. P. 502). *Vf. Mason* v. *Bennett*, 38 L. J. C. P. 48; L. R. 4 C. P. 502.

"Compositions," in exception to definition of "*Rent*," s. 1, 3 & 4 W. 4, c. 27; *V. Irish Land Commission* v. *Grant*, 10 App. Ca. 14.

COMPTABLE.—*V. Exchange Bank of Canada* v. *The Queen*, 55 L. J. P. C. 5; 11 App. Ca. 157; 54 L. T. 802.

CONCERN.—"Trade, Manufacture, Adventure, or Concern," Income Tax Act; *V.* TRADE.

CONCERNED IN.—A Shareholder in a Company, which Company has a contract with a Local Authority, would seem *not* to be "concerned in" that contract within s. 193, P. H. Act, 1875 (per Brett, M. R., *Todd* v. *Robinson*, 54 L. J. Q. B. 47; 14 Q. B. D. 739; 52 L. T. 120; 49 J. P. 278). But to do part of a work for another, knowing that that other has contracted with a Local Authority to do the work, is to be "concerned in" the bargain or contract for the work within R. 64, Sch. 2, of the Act just cited (*Nutton* v. *Wilson*, 58 L. J. Q. B. 443). *V.* and *cp.* INTERESTED IN.

Acting as a salaried servant, is being "concerned in" a business within a Covenant not to be concerned in such a business (*Hill* v. *Hill*, 55 L. T. 769; 35 W. R. 137; 51 J. P. 246; 3 Times Rep. 144: *Jones* v. *Heavens*, 4 Ch. D. 636).

The owner of a vessel who knowingly lets it to be employed in Smuggling, is "concerned in" the illegally unshipping of the goods, within s. 46, 8 & 9 V. c. 87 (*A.-G.* v. *Robson*, 20 L. J. Ex. 188; 5 Ex. 790). *V.* UNSHIPPING.

V. CARRY ON.

CONCERNING.—*V.* OF AND CONCERNING.

CONCLUSIVE.—*V.* FINAL AND CONCLUSIVE.

CONCLUSIVE EVIDENCE.—Anything which is duly prescribed as "Conclusive Evidence" of a fact, is absolute evidence of such fact, as well criminally as civilly, for all purposes for which it is so made evidence (*R.* v. *Levi*, 34 L. J. M. C. 174: *R.* v. *Robinson*, L. R. 1 C. C. 80). The phrase is also used in its largest sense in s. 51, Companies Act, 1862 (*Brynmawr Coal Co.*, W. N. (77) 45, cited Buckl. 173). *Vf. Barraclough* v. *Greenhough*, cited SUFFICIENT EVIDENCE, *wh. cp.*

CONDITION.—"A Condition is a clause of restraint in a deed, or a bridle annexed and joined to an estate,"—or transaction,—"staying and suspending the same, and making it uncertain whether it shall take effect or no" (Touch. 81), and it may be by parol. Thus an antecedent,—or as it would seem a contemporaneous,—parol agreement to repay by instalments a loan secured by a Bill of Sale, and thereby made otherwise payable, is a "Condition" within the words "Defeasance, Condition or Declaration of Trust" in the Bills of Sale Acts (s. 2, Act 1854, and subs. 3, s. 10, Act 1878), and as such must be written on the same paper or parchment as the Bill of Sale and registered with it (*Ex p. Southam,* 43 L. J. Bank. 39 ; L. R. 17 Eq. 578). But an agreement for the purpose of enlarging, or strengthening, the rights of the grantee of the Bill of Sale is not such a "Condition" (*Ex p. Collins,* 44 L. J. Bank. 78 ; 10 Ch. 367) ; nor is an agreement not to register (*Ex p. Popplewell,* 52 L. J. Ch. 39 ; 21 Ch. D. 73) ; nor, it would seem, a contemporary agreement letting on hire the goods to the grantor (*Ex p. McShane,* 29 S. J. 70).

V. DEFEASANCE : RESERVATION.

As to Devises and Bequests, on Condition ; *V.* 2 Jarm. ch. xxvii. ; Wms. Exs. 1264 *et seq.*

As to Estates upon Condition ; *V.* Co. Litt. l. 3, ch. 5.

As to Conditions in Deeds ; *V.* Elph. ch. xxix.

A Lease "upon Condition that" the lessee shall do certain things, amounts to a covenant by the lessee to do them (Elph. 411). "Conditions are most properly created by using the word 'Condition,' or the words 'On condition ;' but the word commonly and as effectually made use of, is, that of 'provided' (Touch. 122 ; Co. Litt. 146 b : *V.* PROVISO). The words 'Covenant' and 'Condition,' when used in an agreement, do not necessarily mean a Covenant under seal, or a Condition in the strict legal sense of the word, but may, in order to effectuate the intention of the parties, be construed to mean, 'Contract or Stipulation'" (Woodf. 181, citing *Hayne* v. *Cummings,* 16 C. B. N. S. 421). *Cp.* COVENANT.

"Condition," s. 12, 48 & 49 V. c. 72 ; *V. Walker* v. *Hobbs,* 23 Q. B. D. 458 ; 34 W. R. 63.

CONDITIONS.—Reasonable Conditions ; *V.* REASONABLE.

CONDITIONS AS PER CHARTER-PARTY.—"Other Conditions as per Charter-Party:" This phrase in a Bill of Lading does not bring in those clauses of the Charter-Party which are inconsistent with the Bill of Lading (*Gardner* v. *Trechmann,* 15 Q. B. D. 154 ; 54 L. J. Q. B. 515).

CONDONATION.—"Condonation" is a conclusion of fact, not of law ; and means the complete forgiveness and blotting out of a conjugal offence, followed by cohabitation,—the whole being done with the full knowledge of all the circumstances of the offence forgiven (*Peacock* v. *Peacock*, 27 L. J. P. & M. 71; 1 Sw. & Tr. 184 : *Keats* v. *Keats*, 28 L. J. P. & M. 57). Once accomplished, it has been said that Condonation is final (*Gandy* v. *Gandy*, 51 L. J. P. D. & A. 41; 7 P. D. 168 : *Rose* v. *Rose*, 52 L. J. P. D. & A. 25 ; 8 P. D. 98). In the latter case Jessel, M. R., said, —"I think that the notion of bygones being bygones is as important between husband and wife as between any other persons ;" and he scouted what he called "the old monkish doctrine" of Condonation being conditional on future fidelity ; but, almost simultaneously, the President of the P. D. & A. Div. laid it down that "the legal definition of Condonation is forgiveness upon condition that no matrimonial offence shall be committed in the future" (*Blandford* v. *Blandford*, 52 L. J. P. D. & A. 17; 8 P. D. 19: *Vf. Curtis* v. *Curtis*, 28 L. J. P. & M. 55 ; 1 Sw. & Tr. 192 ; 31 L. T. O. S. 272 : *Norris* v. *Norris*, 30 L. J. P. & M. 111).

CONDUCE.—"According to the received meaning of the word 'conduce,' I think that what has conduced an effect must in some sense have caused it, or contributed to it ; and the conducing cause must be such as, if not directly, at least indirectly, might at the time be contemplated as likely somehow to contribute to" that effect (per Campbell, C. J., *Cummington* v. *Cummington*, 28 L. J. P. & M. 102 ; 1 Sw. & Tr. 475); and accordingly it was held in that case that "Wilful Neglect or Misconduct" conducing to adultery (s. 31, Matrimonial Causes Act, 1857), means marital neglect or misconduct, and not such compulsory absence as is occasioned by a term of imprisonment. It means also such neglect or misconduct as has led up to the respondent's fall from virtue,—*i.e.* the first lapse (*St. Paul* v. *St. Paul*, 38 L. J. P. & M. 57; L. R. 1 P. & D. 739).

Vf., on the phrase cited, *Allen* v. *Allen*, 28 L. J. P. & M. 81: *Badcock* v. *Badcock*, 31 L. T. O. S. 268 : *Proctor* v. *Proctor*, 34 L. J. P. & M. 99 : *Dering* v. *Dering*, L. R. 1 P. & D. 531: *Davies* v. *Davies*, 32 L. J. P. & M. 111: *Hawkins* v. *Hawkins*, 54 L. J. P. D. & A. 94 ; 10 P. D. 177.

CONDUCIVE.—*V.* Incidental : Incidental or Conducive.

CONDUCT.—The "Conduct" of a Bankrupt which, under s. 28, Bankry. Act, 1883, has to be considered on his application for an Order of Discharge, is such as is described in s. 24 ; therefore his refusal to be medically examined, in order that a policy might be effected on his life so as to add value to a reversionary contingent interest dependent on his life, is not "Conduct" which can be so considered (*Re Betts*, 56 L. J. Q. B. 370 ; 19 Q. B. D. 39 ; 35 W. R. 530),—for the Court has no power to order him to submit to such an examination (*Re Garnett*, 55 L. J. Q. B. 77), and "the word 'Conduct' in s. 28 does not include general misconduct, —not, for example, immoral conduct such as a breach of promise of marriage" (per Lopes, L. J., *Re Betts*, sup.). *Re Betts*, nom. *Board* *of Trade* v. *Block*, affirmed in H. L., 58 L. J. Q. B. 113; 13 App. Ca. 570; 4 Times Rep. 770.

But s. 32, which provides for the removal of a Bankrupt's Disqualifications, is not affected by ss. 24, 28; and in order to obtain a certificate that his bankruptcy "was caused by *misfortune*, without any *misconduct* on his part," the Bankrupt must shew that it was caused by "misfortune,"—*i.e.*, something unforeseen which could not ordinarily be guarded against; and was not attributable to "misconduct,"—*i.e.*, conduct either legally or morally blameworthy (*Re Burgess*, 31 S. J. 593; 57 L. T. 200). In that case the bankruptcy had arisen through the bankrupt having been convicted of Libel, and sentenced to 3 months' imprisonment and to pay the costs of the prosecution.

V. Conducting: In the Conduct of a Suit: Charge or Conduct.

CONDUCTING.—As to the fee to Solicitors for "Conducting" a sale by Public Auction, within Sch. 1, Part 1, Remuneration Order; *V. Re Wilson*, 55 L. J. Ch. 627; 29 Ch. D. 790: *Re Sykes*, 56 L. J. Ch. 238: *Re Faulkner*, 56 L. J. Ch. 1011: *Newbould* v. *Bailward*, *Parker* v. *Blenkhorn*, 58 L. J. Q. B. 209; 37 W. R. 401. A lump sum paid to an Auctioneer for actually selling, is a "Commission" to him under R. 11, Sch. 1, Part 1, of that Order (*Newbould* v. *Bailward*, sup.: *Burd* v. *Burd*, 58 L. J. Ch. 170).

Conveying calves in a van, is not "Conducting *or Driving*" them, within the prohibition against doing so on the Lord's Day contained in the Islington Parish Act (*Triggs* v. *Lester*, L. R. 1 Q. B. 259: *V.* Driving).

CONFESSION.—A Judge's Order by consent, held to be a judgment by "Confession" within the proviso to 6 G. 4, c. 16, s. 108 (*Andrews* v. *Deeks*, 20 L. J. Ex. 127).

CONFIDE: CONFIDENCE.—*V.* Precatory Trust.

CONFIGURATION.—*V.* Shape.

CONFINE.—*V.* Impound.

CONFIRMED.—*V.* Required.

CONFISCATION.—"Confiscation must be an act done in some way on the part of the government of the country where it takes place, and in some way beneficial to that government; though the proceeds may not, strictly speaking, be brought into its treasury" (per Ellenborough, C. J., *Levin* v. *Allnutt*, 15 East, 269).

CONFLICT.—It seems that a difference between the provisions of a Settlement and those of the Settled Land Act, 1882, with respect to the person who is to exercise a particular power, is not a "Conflict" between the provisions of the Settlement and those of the Act, within s. 56, sub-s. 2 of the Act (*Re Newcastle,* 52 L. J. Ch. 645 ; 24 Ch. D. 138).

CONMOTE.—*V.* COMMOTE.

CONNECTED WITH.—*V.* BUSINESS CONNECTED WITH.

"In connexion with ;" *V. Lawson* v. *Wallasey,* 52 L. J. Q. B. 302 ; 11 Q. B. D. 229.

CONNIVANCE.—"Connivance," s. 30, 20 & 21 V. c. 85, is the willing consent to a conjugal offence in the sense of being an accessory before the fact, or a culpable acquiescence in a course of conduct reasonably likely to lead to the offence being committed (*Allen* v. *Allen,* 30 L. J. P. M. & A. 2 : *Glennie* v. *Glennie,* 32 L. J. P. M. & A. 17 : *Boulting* v. *Boulting,* 3 Sw. & Tr. 329 ; 12 W. R. 389 : *Gipps* v. *Gipps,* 33 L. J. P. M. & A. 161 ; 11 H. L. Ca. 1). *Vh.* Brown on Divorce, 3 Ed. 88 ; Dixon on Divorce, 181. *V.* ACCESSORY : COLLUSION.

CONQUEST.—"Conquest" when used as a verb active, and not as a noun, has a wide and flexible signification. Where a lady, by ante-nuptial Settlement, had conveyed to trustees whatever she might "conquest or acquire" during her marriage ; held, that those words passed property of every kind which came to her during the marriage by succession (*Diggens* v. *Gordon,* L. R. 1 H. L. Sc. 136). *V.* ACQUIRE.

CONSENT.—"Consent *or Agreement* in Writing," s. 3, 2 & 3 W. 4, c. 71 ; *V.* IN WRITING.

A reference under the Lands C. C. Act, 1845, is, *semble,* not a reference by "Consent" within s. 5 or s. 17, Com. L. Pro. Act, 1854 (*Ex p. Harper,* L. R. 18 Eq. 539 : *Re Dare Valley Ry.,* 4 Ch. 554 : *Rhodes* v. *Airedale Drainage Co.,* 43 L. J. C. P. 323 ; 45 Ib. 861 ; L. R. 9 C. P. 508 ; 1 C. P. D. 402 : *Re Harper and G. E. Ry.,* 20 Eq. 39 : *Bexley* v. *W. Kent Sewerage Bd.,* 51 L. J. Q. B. 456 ; 9 Q. B. D. 518). *V.* REFERENCE.

"It seems to be clear, that approbation subsequent to a marriage is not, in general, a sufficient compliance with a condition requiring 'Consent' ; but Ld. Hardwicke, in *Burleton* v. *Humfrey* (Amb. 256), took a distinction between the words 'Consent' and 'Approbation,' holding the latter to admit subsequent approval, where coupled with the former disjunctively ; but he decided the case principally on another ground ;—and in regard to the admission of subsequent consent the authority of the case has been questioned. *V. Clarke* v. *Parker,* 19 Ves. 21" (2 Jarm. 55 ; *Vf.* Watson, Eq. 1239). "Consent of Parents" means, parents *if any.* (Ib.).

Where there is a direction or agreement for the Conversion of Money into Land, and the Uses are exclusively applicable to realty, "the direction or agreement will be regarded as imperative though the Settlement require the purchase to be made *at the Request* of a person ; for the insertion of such a clause has been taken to mean, not that a conversion may not be effected *before*, but that it shall certainly be effected *after*, request. And the construction is the same, though the purchase be directed to be made with a person's *Consent* and *Approbation*" (Lewin, 948, and cases there cited).

The "*Free and Voluntary* Consent" (32 G. 2, c. 28, s. 1), necessary to authorize a Sheriff, &c., to carry a debtor to a tavern, &c., must have been an active consent, as distinguished from that consent which is said to be implied by silence (*Dewhurst* v. *Pearson*, 2 L. J. Ex. 143 ; 1 C. & M. 365 ; 3 Tyr. 242 ; 1 Dowl. 664) ; and where the officer was illegally carrying a debtor to gaol, and the debtor, to avoid being taken to gaol, consented to go to a tavern and there drew up a discharge agreement, the "Consent" so obtained was not "free and voluntary" (*Barsham* v. *Bullock*, 10 A. & E. 23 ; 2 P. & D. 241). *V.* VOLUNTARILY.

Covenant by Lessor not to "consent" to a certain trade on his other property ; *V. Stuart* v. *Diplock*, 34 S. J. 113.

V. WRITTEN CONSENT : IN WRITING : UNREASONABLY.

CONSEQUENCES.—The phrase in a Marine Insurance "Warranted free from all Consequences" of, *e.g.*, hostilities, extends only to the direct consequences of the excepted causes (*Ionides* v. *Universal Marine Insrce.*, 32 L. J. C. P. 170 ; 14 C. B. N. S. 259).

CONSIDERATION.—"In Consideration ;" *V.* PRECATORY TRUST.

CONSIGN.—*V. Phillips* v. *Briard*, 25 L. J. Ex. 235, 236.

CONSIGNEE PAYS CARRIAGE.—These words in a Consignment Note, do not relieve the consignor from his liability to the Carrier which the circumstances show he had contracted (*G. W. Ry.* v. *Bagge*, 54 L. J. Q. B. 599 ; 15 Q. B. D. 625).

CONSISTING.—This word in s. 4, Companies Act, 1862 (25 & 26 V. c. 89), means "for the time being consisting" (*Re Thomas, Ex p. Poppleton*, 54 L. J. Q. B. 336 ; 14 Q. B. D. 379).

"Consisting of ;" *V.* THAT IS TO SAY.

CONSOLS.—A Bequest of "Consols" will pass Three per Cents, if testator had no Consols (*Burbey* v. *Burbey*, 15 W. R. 479 : *V. Rowlatt* v. *Easton*, 11 W. R. 767).

V. FUNDS.

CONSPIRACY.—"When two or more persons agree to commit any crime, they are guilty of the misdemeanour called Conspiracy whether the crime is committed or not" (Steph. Cr. 37 : *Vf.* Arch. Cr. 1087–1095 ; Rosc. Cr. 423–437 : Wright on Conspiracy).

CONSTABLE.—"A constable is often taken in the law for a warder or keeper, as *Constabularius castri de Dover et 5. portuum*" (Co. Litt. 234 a, b).

CONSTITUTED.—If a Company, having a statutory constitution, has conferred on it, either by its special or a subsequent Act or series of Acts, power of constructing or working a railway, it is "a Company *constituted* by Act of Parliament . . . . *for the purpose of* constructing . . . . a Railway" within s. 3, Railway Companies Act, 1867, although the Railway made by the Company was not one of its fundamental objects and forms but a very small portion of its undertaking (*Re East and West India Dock Co.*, 57 L. J. Ch. 1053; 38 Ch. D. 576; 59 L. T. 237; 36 W. R. 849). *V.* RAILWAY COMPANY.

CONSTRUCTED.—Works "constructed," mean Works really constructed so as to be of use (*Bull* v. *Ventnor Harbour Co.*, W. N. (69), 12).

CONSTRUCTION.—Of a New Street; *V. Hendon* v. *Pounce*, 42 Ch. D. 602.

V. COMMENCEMENT.

CONSUETUDO.—*V.* CUSTOM.

CONSULAR OFFICER.—*V.* s. 12 (20), Interp. Act, 1889.

CONSUMED.—*V.* ON THE PREMISES.

CONSUMER OF WATER.—A "Consumer of Water," for the purposes of a Water Works Act, is "a person who either actually enjoys or is consuming water, or is entitled so to do and has intimated his intention so to do" (per Cotton, L. J., *Cooke* v. *New River Co.*, 57 L. J. Ch. 386; 38 Ch. D. 56; 58 L. T. 830; affd. H. L. 14 App. Ca. 698).

CONTAINING.—"The word 'containing' may easily admit of being construed as meaning 'inclusive of'; and not as in diminution of a general bequest" (per Sir S. Lushington in delivering jdgmt. of P. C. in *Henfrey* v. *Henfrey*, 6 Jur. 356; 2 Curt. 468; 4 Moo. P. C. C. 29; stated 1 Jarm. 175).

CONTEMPLATION. — "A Settlement in 'Contemplation' of marriage, is obviously an ante-nuptial Settlement" (per Selborne, L. C., *Re Sampson & Wall*, 53 L. J. Ch. 460; 25 Ch. D. 482: *Va. Re Leigh*, 58 L. J. Ch. 306; 40 Ch. D. 290). *V.* UPON.

CONTEMPT OF COURT.—*V.* CRIMINAL PRISONER.

CONTENTS.—A legacy of the "Contents of my house" is equivalent to a legacy of the goods "*in* my house." *V.* IN.

CONTENTS UNKNOWN.—"When there is a closed package and a representation as to its contents, the shipowner may accept the Bill of Lading, or may alter it, and if he adds, '*Contents Unknown*,' then, according to *Parsons on Shipping* (p. 198), the cases there cited, and *Jessel* v. *Bath* (36 L. J. Ex. 149 ; L. R. 2 Ex. 267), the meaning is, that he declines to accept the representation and merely accepts the package as it appears on the outside, but not the statement as to what is inside,—and he contracts to carry what really is inside" (per Brett, J., *Lebeau* v. *Gen. Steam Nav.*, 42 L. J. C. P. 1 ; L. R. 8 C. P. 88). The usual phrase in such a case is, "Weight, Contents and Value unknown." *Vh.* 1 Maude & P. 153, 154, 341, 342.

CONTESTED ELECTION.—"When a poll is demanded, the election commences with it, as being the regular mode of popular election ; the show of hands being only a rude and imperfect declaration of the sentiments of the electors" (per Sir Wm. Scott in *Antony* v. *Seger*, 1 Hag. Cons. Rep. 13). The phrase "contested election" in s. 68, Reform Act (2 W. 4, c. 45), also means an election carried to a poll (*Muntz* v. *Sturge*, 10 L. J. Ex. 234 ; 8 M. & W. 302). But now, for parliamentary or municipal honours, the hours appointed for the nomination are the time for the "election ;" which election is adjourned for a poll when more candidates are nominated than there are vacancies to be filled (35 & 36 V. c. 33, s. 1 ; Sch. 1, part 1, Rule 1).

CONTIGUOUS.—*V.* WATER AND SOIL.

CONTINGENCY.—Liability on a Contingency ; *V.* LIABILITY.

CONTINGENT.—Anything is "Contingent" when it is liable to failure on the happening or non-happening of an event, condition or state of things.

"A Contingent Remainder is a Remainder limited so as to depend on an event or condition, which may never happen or be performed, or which may not happen or be performed till after the determination of the preceding estate" (Fearne, Cont. Rem., 9 Ed. 3).

V. VEST.

CONTINUANCE.—"If a power be given to trustees to be exercised 'during the *continuance* of the trust,' it cannot be exercised after the time when the trust *ought* to have been completed, though, from the delay of the trustees, it happens that the trust has not in fact been executed" (Lewin, 605, citing *Wood* v. *White*, 2 Keen, 664 ; 4 M. & Cr. 460 ; 7 L. J. Ch. 203 ; 8 Ib. 209 : *Vf.* 2 Jarm. 299 ; and *Vf.* Lewin, 605, as to this word).

CONTINUATION.—This word is used in a technical sense on the Stock Exchange. It means to sell and to agree to re-buy the same amount of Stock at a future day at the same price, plus a sum for the accommodation. It is not a loan; but is a sale and an agreement for re-purchase. The original seller may perform his contract to re-buy, and if the Stock be not delivered to him he is entitled to damages for such non-delivery. On the other hand, he may make default, and then would be liable for such breach; but if the Stock has gone up in value there would be no damages; if, however, the value has gone down, the measure of damages would be the difference between the market value of the Stock at the time when the original seller ought to have re-bought it and the price at which, at the time of the sale, he agreed to re-buy it. In all these transactions the Stock remains the property of the original buyer until the original seller has completed the agreed re-purchase (*Bongiovanni* v. *La Société Génerale*, 54 L. T. 320; 2 Times Rep. 247).

CONTINUE.—To "Continue," in Stock Exchange phraseology; *V.* Continuation.

"Continue" as an equivalent of "Tarry;" *V.* Elope.

CONTINUE TO HOLD.—"Where trustees are authorized 'to continue to hold' special Investments, the power must, *primâ facie*, be held to apply to those trusts which are continuous; and the trustees may appropriate to a special continuous trust any of the investments which the settlor has authorised to be held" (Lewin, 326, citing *Fraser* v. *Murdoch*, 6 App. Ca. 855).

CONTINUING INTEREST.—"Continuing Interest," "Continuing charge on such Interest," s. 21, Sucn. Dy. Act, 1853; *V. Lilford* v. *A.-G.*, 36 L. J. Ex. 116; L. R. 2 H. L. 63.

CONTINUING TRUSTEE.—This is a phrase the meaning of which is not settled. Bacon, V.-C., decided that the term "Continuing Trustee" is not confined to one who remains after another has retired; but includes one who has made up his mind to retire, but who has not, as yet, executed a Deed evidencing his retirement (*Re Glenny*, 53 L. J. Ch. 417; 25 Ch. D. 611; 32 W. R. 457). But in so deciding, the decision of Kindersley, V.-C., in *Travis* v. *Illingworth* (34 L. J. Ch. 665; 2 Dr. & Sm. 344), was dissented from; a decision, however, which, notwithstanding *Re Glenny*, was adhered to by Pearson, J., in *Allen* v. *Norris* (53 L. J. Ch. 913; 27 Ch. D. 333), and per North, J., *Coates to Parsons* (56 L. J. Ch. 242: *Va.* Lewin, 664). The weight of judicial authority would, therefore, seem to be in favour of the proposition, that a retiring trustee is not a continuing trustee. But *Vh.* s. 31 (6), Conv. and L. P. Act, 1881; but even under that section a retiring trustee is not a "continuing" trustee unless it is shewn that he is competent and willing to act within its provisions (*Coates to Parsons*, sup.).

A trustee who has never acted and has declined to act is not a "surviving or continuing" trustee (*Nicholson* v. *Wright*, 26 L. J. Ch. 312; 5 W. R. 431). But it has been said that the decision in that case was a "narrow construction" (Sug. Pow. 886); and in *Pell* v. *De Winton* (2 D. G. & J. 13) Lord Cranworth said he was not prepared to follow it. In *Re Glenny*, sup., however, it was cited by Bacon, V.-C., apparently with approval. *Cp.* ACTING TRUSTEE: DECLINING TRUSTEE.

CONTRACT.—"In every Contract there must be *quid pro quo*, for *contractus est quasi actus contra actum*" (Co. Litt. 47 b). *V.* EVIDENCE OF A CONTRACT.

As to what contracts must be disclosed in a Company Prospectus so as to satisfy s. 38, Companies Act, 1867; *V.* notes on the section in Buckl.

"Contract, *Dealing or Transaction*," s. 49 (d), Bankry. Act, 1883; *V.* *Turquand* v. *Vanderplank*, 10 M. & W. 180: *Brewin* v. *Short*, 24 L. J. Q. B. 297; 5 E. & B. 227; 1 Jur. N. S. 798: *Ex p. Arnold, Re Wright*, 45 L. J. Bank. 130; 3 Ch. D. 71: *Stansfield* v. *Cubitt*, 27 L. J. Ch. 266; 2 D. G. & J. 222: *Re Curtoys*, 50 L. J. Ch. 691; 17 Ch. D. 653: *Hance* v. *Harding*, 57 L. J. Q. B. 403; 20 Q. B. D. 732; 59 L. T. 659; 36 W. R. 629. *Vf.* Yate Lee, 438—441; Wms. Bank. 211.

"Demands . . . arising otherwise than *by reason* of a contract," s. 31, Bankry. Act, 1869, include a sum found due from a Promoter of a Co., in respect of a secret profit (*Emma Co.* v. *Grant*, 50 L. J. Ch. 449; 17 Ch. D. 122; *Vf. Re Parkers*, 19 Q. B. D. 84). *V.* BY REASON.

"Action *founded on Contract*," s. 5, County Court Act, 1867;—an action is "founded on contract" when not arising out of a breach of a general duty, and when there would be no liability but for a contract (*Legge* v. *Tucker*, 26 L. J. Ex. 71; 1 H. & N. 500), and when it is directly, and not remotely, founded on such contract (*Pontifex* v. *Mid. Ry.*, 47 L. J. Q. B. 28; 3 Q. B. D. 23). Therefore an action against a Carrier for negligent loss of goods is "founded on Contract" (*Fleming* v. *Manchester, S. & L. Ry.*, 4 Q. B. D. 81: disapproving *Tattan* v. *G. W. Ry.*, 29 L. J. Q. B. 184; 2 E. & E. 844); but an action against a carrier for delivering goods to an insolvent consignee after notice of a stoppage *in transitu* is founded on Tort and not on contract, because the stoppage had put an end to the original contract of carrying (*Pontifex* v. *Mid. Ry.*, sup.). So negligent loss by a Cabman of his fare's luggage (*Baylis* v. *Lintott*, 42 L. J. C. P. 119; L. R. 8 C. P. 345), or negligent treatment of his customer's horse by a Livery-stable keeper (*Legge* v. *Tucker*, sup.), gives right to an action "founded on contract." *Cp.* TORT: *V.* FOUNDED ON.

"To contract a Marriage," read "to marry" (*Re M'Loughlin*, 1 L. R. Ir. 421).

CONTRACT IN WRITING.—*V.* IN WRITING.

CONTRACT OF SERVICE.—"Contract of Service, or a Contract personally to execute any *Work* or *Labour*," s. 10, Employers and Workmen's Act, 1875, 38 & 39 V. c. 90;—"I should say that the former employment would apply to the case of an employment for a certain *time*, and the latter to an employment for the performance of some specific *work*" (per Lopes, J., *Granger* v. *Aynsley*, 50 L. J. M. C. 51; 6 Q. B. D. 182; 29 W. R. 242; 45 J. P. 142).

CONTRACT TO SUPPLY.—An employer who retains out of his employees' wages so much a week for club-money and in consideration of which he is to supply medicine and medical attendance to his employees, "contracts to supply" such medicine, &c., within s. 23, Truck Act, 1 & 2 W. 4, c. 37 (*Cutts* v. *Ward*, 36 L. J. Q. B. 161; L. R. 2 Q. B. 357; 15 W. R. 445; 15 L. T. 614). *Vh.* Add. C. 1168.

CONTRACTED TO SELL.—A devise of an estate "which I have lately contracted to sell," has been held to pass merely the legal estate so as to enable the devisee to carry out the contract, but not to pass the purchase-money (*Knollys* v. *Shepherd*, 1 Jarm. 692). In view, however, of s. 30, Conv. & L. P. Act, 1881, it would be difficult to see how that ruling could be now supported; because the testator-vendor would, it is submitted, hold the estate as a trustee for the vendee, and if so the legal estate would, under the section cited, pass to the personal representatives of the vendor; and if that be so, then such a devise as that in *Knollys* v. *Shepherd* would now have no operation unless it be held to pass the vendor's beneficial interest in the contract, and with it the purchase money.

CONTRACTOR.—As a description of Occupation quà Bills of Sale Act; *V. Sharp* v. *McHenry*, 38 Ch. D. 428; 57 L. J. Ch. 961; 57 L. T. 606.

CONTRARY INTENTION.—Many modern Acts provide certain rules of construction unless a "Contrary Intention" be expressed.

V. As to this phrase:—In s. 43, Conv. and L. P. Act, 1881, jdgmt. by Fry, L. J., *Re Dickson, Hill* v. *Grant*, 29 Ch. D. 331; 54 L. J. Ch. 510; 52 L. T. 707; 33 W. R. 511: *Re Thatcher*, 53 L. J. Ch. 1050; 26 Ch. D. 426; 32 W. R. 679. In sub-s. 7, s. 31, same Act, *Cecil* v. *Langdon*, 54 L. J. Ch. 313.

In Locke King's Act (17 & 18 V. c. 113), Dart, 922, 923: *Re Fleck, Colston* v. *Roberts*, 57 L. J. Ch. 943; 37 Ch. D. 677; 58 L. T. 624; 36 W. R. 663.

In M. W. P. Act, 1882, *Harrison* v. *Harrison*, 58 L. J. P. D. & A. 28.

In the Wills Act (1 V. c. 26), *Re Portal to Lamb*, 54 L. J. Ch. 1012; 30 Ch. D. 50; 33 W. R. 71, 859: *Re Marsh*, 57 L. J. Ch. 639; 38 Ch. D. 630; 59 L. T. 595; 37 W. R. 10: *Re Phillips*, 41 Ch. D. 417: *Re Tarrant*,

W. N. (89) 146: *Re Wells*, 42 Ch. D. 646 : *Wilson* v. *Eden*, 21 L. J. Q. B. 385 ; 5 Ex. 752, and especially Lord Campbell's jdgmt. ; My.

CONTRIBUTION.—*V.* Subscription : Voluntary Contributions : Indemnity.

CONTROL.—To give or refuse assent to a certain proposed course, is to exercise a "Control" within s. 33, Tramways Act, 1870, 33 & 34 V. c. 78 (per Esher, M. R., *R.* v. *Croydon Tramways Co.*, 56 L. J. Q. B. 125 ; 18 Q. B. D. 39 ; 56 L. T. 78 ; 35 W. R. 299 ; 51 J. P. 420 ; 3 Times Rep. 32). "Control," s. 41, Reg. Ry. Act, 1868, "is confined to the control of the proceedings in the issue so long as they are actually going on, and does not extend to proceedings after judgment" (per Denman, J., *Birmingham Land Co.* v. *L. N. W. Ry.*, 58 L. J. Q. B. 588).

Whether a dog is "under the control of any person" within the Dogs Act, 1871 (34 & 35 V. c. 56), is a question of fact to be determined in each case by the justices ; but as a general rule a dog is not under such control unless muzzled or led (*Re Hay*, 31 S. J. 29 ; 3 Times Rep. 24).

"Under Proper Control or Destroyed," s. 2, Dogs Act, 1871 ; under this a dangerous dog may be ordered to be destroyed (*Pickering* v. *Marsh*, 43 L. J. M. C. 143).

V. Charge or Control : Custody.

CONTROVERSIES.—*V.* Quarrels.

CONVENIENCE.—A contract to pay at a person's "Convenience," means that the obligation to pay arises when he or his representatives are reasonably able to pay; the phrase is not equivalent to "at his will" or "pleasure" (*Crayshay* v. *Hornstedt*, 3 Times Rep. 426).

"Any *Court* convenient thereto," s. 65, Co. Co. Act, 1888, does not mean one that must be *near* to the Court of the district in which the defendant dwells, &c., but one which is "convenient" having regard to its facility to the parties (*Parsons* v. *Lakenheath School Bd.*, 58 L. J. Q. B. 371 ; 5 Times Rep. 497).

CONVENIENT.—"Convenient," as employed in the rubric at the end of the Anglican Marriage Service, should be construed in its strict and primary sense of "fit" or "proper,"—the secondary sense being a more modern one (*Blunt's Annotated Book of Common Pra.*, 6 Ed. 274 ; *Va. Mant's Prayer Book*, 468).

V. Just : Substantial.

CONVENIENT SPEED.—Trustees for sale are allowed a reasonable time for selling the property ; "and though the instrument creating the trust, direct them to sell '*with all convenient speed*,' that is no more than is implied by law, and does not render an immediate sale imperative " (Lewin, 424, citing *Buxton* v. *Buxton,* 1 M. & Cr. 80 : *Garrett* v. *Noble,* 3 L. J. Ch. 159 ; 6 Sim. 504 : *Fry* v. *Fry,* 28 L. J. Ch. 591 ; 27 Bea. 144 : *Va. Fitzgerald* v. *Jervoise,* 5 Mad. 25 : *Vickers* v. *Scott,* 3 M. & K. 500 : *Sculthorpe* v. *Tipper,* 41 L. J. Ch. 266 ; L. R. 13 Eq. 232 : *Turner* v. *Buck,* 43 L. J. Ch. 583 ; L. R. 18 Eq. 301 :—*Turner* v. *Buck* was considered in *Re Waters,* 42 Ch. D. 517) : and the construction is not different if the direction be to sell " with all convenient speed, *and within* 5 *years,*"—the direction in the last three words being directory only (Lewin, 424, citing *Pearce* v. *Gardner,* 10 Hare, 287 : *Va. Cuff* v. *Hall,* 1 Jur. N. S. 973 : *De La Salle* v. *Moorat,* 40 L. J. Ch. 44 ; L. R. 11 Eq. 8 : *Edwards* v. *Edmunds,* 34 L. T. 522). But trustees directed to sell " with all convenient speed," or " so soon as conveniently may be," are not arbitrarily to postpone the sale for an indefinite period (Dart, 63). Where property was directed to be sold " with all convenient speed," and proceeds to be paid to A., and no sale took place for 7 years, and A. had done acts of ownership in respect of the property ; held, that A. had elected to take as real estate (*Re Davidson, Martin* v. *Trimmer,* 11 Ch. D. 341).

A Charter-Party contained a clause that the ship should " with all Convenient Speed (on being ready), having liberty to take an outward cargo for owners' benefit direct or on the way, proceed to E., and there load a full cargo of cotton." The ship deviated to C. and arrived at E. a few days later than she would have done if she had gone there direct. The ship had not been taken up for any particular cargo, and a small loss in freight was the only result of this delay. Held, in an action against the freighter for not loading a cargo :—that the above clause was a stipulation and not a condition precedent, and that the delay afforded no justification to the freighter for refusing to load a cargo (*MacAndrew* v. *Chapple,* L. R. 1 C. P. 643 ; 35 L. J. C. P. 281 ; Har. & R. 745). " It seems to be now settled that delay by deviation is the same as a delay in starting ; and it is also settled, at any rate in this Court, that a delay or deviation which, as it has been said, goes to the whole root of the matter, deprives the charterer of the whole benefit of the contract, or entirely frustrates the object of the charterer in chartering the ship, is an answer to an action for not loading a cargo ; but that loss, delay, or deviation short of that gives an action for damages, but does not defeat the charter " (per Willes, J., S. C., L. R., 1 C. P. 648).

CONVENIENT TIME.—Where, under a Lease, the lessor is at liberty to view the premises at " Convenient Times," " I think he ought to give notice that he is coming ; and if he does not give notice, it is not to be considered a ' Convenient Time,' as it cannot be expected that where any business is carried on, they can allow the landlord to go all over the premises without they have previous notice of his coming " (per Denman, C. J., *Doe* d. *Wetherell* v. *Bird,* 6 C. & P. 200).

CONVENIENT WAY.—*V.* Way.

CONVERSION.—As to what words work a constructive conversion of property ; *V.* 1 Jarm. 584–597.

CONVERT.—It is stated that "a covenant not 'to convert' a Dwelling-house into a Shop, means a structural conversion, and not merely exposing goods for sale" (Woodf. 667, citing *Wilkinson* v. *Rogers*, 2 D. G. J. & S. 62 ; 12 W. R. 119, 284). But it would seem that that case supports the reverse of the proposition stated in Woodfall. It is only reported on an application for an interim injunction ; and in dissolving an injunction which had been granted by the M.R., the L.JJ. expressly reserved an actual decision till the hearing ; but they also intimated their opinion that the conversion into a shop might be effected without any structural change. Turner, L.J., said, "I think the premises may be 'converted' either by user, or by an alteration of structure." *V.* Shop.

CONVEY.—"The case of *Ex p. Shorland*, 7 Ves. 88, decided that a mere *gift by way of advancement* to a son, was not void by 1 Jac. 1, c. 15, s. 5, where the words used are, 'convey, or procure or cause to be conveyed'" (per Cave, J., *Re Player*, No. 2, 54 L. J. Q. B. 556).

V. Conveyance : Have or Convey.

CONVEY COALS.—*V.* Way.

CONVEYANCE.—By 2 & 3 Anne, c. 4, 5 & 6 Anne, c. 18 (quà West Riding), 6 Anne, c. 35 (quà East Riding), and 8 G. 2, c. 6 (quà North Riding), Deeds, *Conveyances* and Wills relating to lands in Yorkshire; and by 7 Anne, c. 20, Deeds, *Conveyances* and Wills relating to lands in Middlesex ; are to be registered. A simple *deposit of deeds* for the purpose of creating a charge, there being no writing at all accompanying, is not a Conveyance within these provisions (*Sumpter* v. *Cooper*, 9 L. J. O. S. K. B. 226 ; 2 B. & Ad. 223) ; because there is "nothing to register" (per Wood, V.-C., *Neve* v. *Pennell*, 33 L. J. Ch. 23).

But an Agreement to execute a mortgage, is a Conveyance within these provisions (*Re Wight's Mortgage Trust*, 43 L. J. Ch. 66 ; L. R. 16 Eq. 41 : *Neve* v. *Pennell*, 33 L. J. Ch. 19 ; 2 H. & M. 170 : *Wright* v. *Stansfeld*, 28 L. J. Ch. 183 ; 27 Bea. 8, over-ruled) ; and so also is a Further Charge though not under seal and though ancillary to a legal mortgage duly registered (*Moore* v. *Culverhouse*, 29 L. J. Ch. 419 ; 27 Bea. 639 : *Credland* v. *Potter*, 44 L. J. Ch. 169 ; 10 Ch. 8). In the last named case, Cairns, L. C., in giving judgment, said,—"There is no magic in the word 'Conveyance.' It means an instrument conveying from one person to another person an interest in land. By a Further Charge an interest is conveyed from one person to another. It gives the person who already has a mortgage a further interest in the land. Therefore a Further Charge is a Conveyance within the meaning of the Act." An Enfranchisement Deed is not a Conveyance of Copyholds within the exception in s. 17, 7 Anne, and ought, if of copyholds in Middlesex, to be registered (*R.* v. *Truro,* 57 L. J. Q. B. 577; 21 Q. B. D. 555 ; 59 L. T. 242 ; 36 W. R. 775).

By s. 6, subs. 2 of the Bankry. Act, 1869 (32 & 33 V. c. 71), a fraudulent "*Conveyance, Gift, Delivery or Transfer*" by a debtor of his property was an act of bankry. ;—a verbal charge on goods which are already in the hands of the chargee was not within either of these words (*Philps* v. *Hornstedt,* 42 L. J. Ex. 12 ; L. R. 8 Ex. 26 ; 1 Ex. D. 62) ; but if the charge were accomplished by a Deed (or other writing ?) it would be within them (*Woodhouse* v. *Murray,* 36 L. J. Q. B. 289 ; 38 Ib. 28 ; L. R. 2 Q. B. 634 ; 4 Ib. 27; 8 B. & S. 466 ; 9 Ib. 720). *V.* FRAUDULENT ASSURANCES.

For meaning of "Conveyance *on Sale,*" or "Conveyance," quà *Stamp Duty ; V.* ss. 70, 78, 33 & 34 V. c. 97; s. 15, 52 & 53 V. c. 42 ; and *Vth. Christie* v. *Inl. Rev.,* L. R. 2 Ex. 46 ; 36 L. J. Ex. 11 : *Thames Conservators* v. *Inl. Rev.,* 56 L. J. Q. B. 181; 18 Q. B. D. 279 ; 56 L. T. 198 ; 35 W. R. 274 : *Inl. Rev.* v. *Angus,* 23 Q. B. D. 579 ; 5 Times Rep. 697 : *Lewis* v. *Inl. Rev.,* 37 W. R. 509.

As to what "Conveyance" means for the purposes of the Conv. & L. P. Acts ; *V.* s. 2 (v.), Act, 1881. A Declaration vesting a Trust Estate is, for purposes of registration, a Conveyance (s. 34, sub-s. 4, Ib.).

"Convey," "Conveyance," in Trustee Acts ; *V.* Trustee Act, 1850, s. 2.

"Deed or Conveyance ;" *V.* DEED.

CONVICTED.—The word "convicted," or the "conviction" of a person accused, is equivocal. "In common parlance no doubt it is taken to mean, the verdict at the time of trial ; but in strict legal sense it is used to denote the judgment of the Court" (per Tindall, C. J., *Burgess* v. *Boetefeur,* 13 L. J. M. C. 126 ; 8 Scott, N. R. 194 ; 7 M. & G. 481), and, accordingly, it was there held that a person who pleaded guilty to keeping a brothel, on an indictment instituted under s. 5, 25 G. 2, c. 36, and who at a subsequent Sessions came up for judgment, was not "convicted" when he pleaded, but when judgment was pronounced. But if, under the same section, the plea of guilty be followed by an Order that defendant enter into recognizances to come up for judgment if called upon, he is then "convicted" (per Stephen, J., *Jephson* v. *Barker,* 3 Times Rep. 40). *Vf. Sutton* v. *Bishop,* 1 W. Bl. 665 ; 4 Burr. 2283 : *Lee* v. *Gansel,* Cowp. 1.

"'Convicted' has been often, according to many cases in the books, taken for 'attainted,' and therefore extends to a judgment upon demurrer ; which in *Foster's Case* was held to be a 'Conviction' within 23 Eliz." (Dwar. 683, citing *Foster's Case,* 11 Rep. 59).

"Upon Conviction" in s. 91, Elementary Education Act, 1870, 33 & 34

V. c. 75, means "upon Summary Conviction" (*R.* v. *Gaunt,* 50 L. J. M. C. 32; 29 W. R. 289; 45 J. P. 222).

"*Convicted of Felony,*" s. 14, 33 & 34 V. c. 29; This expression here describes a class of persons against whom the public ought to be guarded, and who ought not to be licensed to sell intoxicants, and means a person who shall be, or shall have been, "Convicted of Felony," and is equivalent to "Convicted Felon" (*R.* v. *Vine,* 44 L. J. M. C. 60; L. R. 10 Q. B. 195; nom. *Vine* v. *Leeds,* 39 J. P. 130, 213). *Cp.* PROHIBITED.

A person against whom a penalty has been recovered under s. 193, P. H. Act, 1875, is not a "Convicted *Offender*" within 22 V. c. 32 (*Todd* v. *Robinson,* 53 L. J. Q. B. 251; 12 Q. B. D. 530).

CONVICTION.—*V.* ORDER: CONVICTED.

"Under the firm Conviction;" *V.* PRECATORY TRUST.

CONVOY.—"A Convoy is a naval force, appointed by the Government, or by the commander of a station, to escort and protect merchant ships proceeding to certain parts" (1 Maude & P. 502, *wh. et seq. V.* as to the phrase "To Sail with Convoy").

"*Depart* with Convoy," means to sail with Convoy throughout the whole voyage (*Jeffery* v. *Legender,* 3 Lev. 321: *Va. Warwick* v. *Scott,* 4 Camp. 62).

"Sails with Convoy *and arrives*"; means that the ship is bound to sail with Convoy, but not to arrive with Convoy; and it is sufficient if the goods arrive, although they do not arrive safely, there being no warranty as to their condition. "Arrived" means "at the ultimate port of destination" (1 Maude & P. 559, citing *Kellner* v. *Le Mesurier,* 4 East, 396: *Va. Dalgleish* v. *Brooke,* 15 East, 295: *Leevin* v. *Cormac,* 4 Taunt. 483). *V.* ARRIVE.

"*Wait* for Convoy;"—"Where a ship was to sail with convoy, and demurrage was to be paid for every day beyond a certain number of days that she should 'wait for Convoy,' this was construed to mean that it was to be paid until the convoy was ready to sail, and not that the freighter was to be discharged on the arrival of the convoy at the port where the ship lay" (1 Maude & P. 409, citing *Lannoy* v. *Werry,* 4 Bro. Parl. c. 630).

COOPATURA.—"A thicket of wood; 4 Inst. 307; Spelm. *Coopertum*" (Elph. 568).

CO-OPERATION.—"Co-operation," which will give a title to Booty, must directly tend to produce the capture in question (*Banda and Kirwee Booty,* 35 L. J. Adm. 17).

COPARCENERS.—*V.* PARCENERS.

COPARTNERSHIP.—"Lord Hale and older writers use 'Copartnership' in the sense of 'Co-ownership,' but this is no longer customary:" (Lindl. 2). "Copartnership" is now synonymous with PARTNERSHIP; and therefore a member of an association which contemplates spiritual benefits, and not a division of profits, cannot be convicted, under s. 1, 31 & 32 V. c. 116, of embezzling the funds of a "Copartnership" (*R.* v. *Robson*, 55 L. J. M. C. 55; 16 Q. B. D. 137; 34 W. R. 276; 50 J. P. 488; 53 L. T. 823).

COPE.—*V.* HOWE.

COPPER.—"'Copper' applied to Coin, includes bronze or mixed metal, and every other kind of coin inferior in value to silver" (Steph. Cr. 310, stating s. 1, 24 & 25 V. c. 99).

Vf. Arch. Cr. 852.

COPY.—A served copy of the old writ of *Capias* which omitted the description of the defendant contained in the writ, was not a "Copy" of the writ within 2 W. 4, c. 39, s. 4 (*Cooke* v. *Vaughan*, 7 L. J. Ex. 219; 4 M. & W. 69).

The unintentional omission of the word "act" after "wilful" in an Innkeeper's copy of s. 1, 26 & 27 V. c. 41, renders it not a copy of that section, and its exhibition does not protect the innkeeper (*Spice* v. *Bacon*, 46 L. J. Ex. 713; 2 Ex. D. 463). *Semble*, an immaterial clerical error would be excused (Ib.).

Copy of a *Book*, s. 2, Copyright Act, 1842, 5 & 6 V. c. 45; *V. Warne* v. *Seebohm*, 57 L. J. Ch. 689; 39 Ch. D. 73; 58 L. T. 928; 36 W. R. 686, and cases there cited.

A Photograph is a copy of an *Engraving* within 8 G. 2, c. 13; 7 G. 3, c. 38; 17 G. 3, c. 57 (*Gambart* v. *Ball*, 32 L. J. C. P. 166; 14 C. B. N. S. 306: *Graves* v. *Ashford*, 36 L. J. C. P. 139; L. R. 2 C. P. 410); but a Pattern for Woolwork, though taken closely from, is not a copy of an Engraving within those statutes (*Dicks* v. *Brooks*, 49 L. J. Ch. 812; 15 Ch. D. 22).

"Copy or Colourably imitate" any *Painting*, *Drawing or Photograph*, s. 6, 25 & 26 V. c. 68; this includes a Photograph of an engraving of a painting (*Ex p. Beal*, 37 L. J. Q. B. 161; L. R. 3 Q. B. 387; 9 B. & S. 395).

COPYHOLD.—A devise of "Copyholds" will pass Customary Freeholds (*Roe* d. *Conolly* v. *Vernon*, 5 East, 83: *Doe* d. *Cook* v. *Danvers*, 7 East, 299; 1 Jarm. 798).

The provision in the Middlesex Registry Act (7 Anne, c. 20, s. 17) that it shall not extend to "any Copyhold Estates" does not extend to an Enfranchisement of Copyholds (*R.* v. *Truro*, 57 L. J. Q. B. 577; 21 Q. B. D. 555; 59 L. T. 242; 36 W. R. 775).

"Copyhold Ground Rent;" *V.* GROUND RENT.

CORN.—" It has been held that the word 'Corn,' in the Memorandum of a Policy of Marine Insurance, includes Malt, and also Peas and Beans, but not Rice" (1 Maude & P. 492 : *V. Moody* v. *Surridge,* 2 Esp. 633 : *Scott* v. *Bourdillion,* 2 Bos. & P. N. R. 213).

CORPORATE BUILDINGS.—*V.* BUILDING.

CORPORATION AGGREGATE.—" Corporation Aggregate," R. 8, Ord. 9, R. S. C., includes a Corporation established by foreign law, but having a residence in England (*Haggin* v. *Comptoir d'Escompte,* 58 L. J. Q. B. 508 ; 23 Q. B. D. 523).

CORRESPONDING.—*V.* LIKE.

CORROBORATED.—" Corroborated in some Material Particular," s. 4, Bastardy Laws Amendment Act, 1872, 35 & 36 V. c. 65. In an application in Bastardy the evidence of the mother is so corroborated if, by other evidence than hers, it is proved that the putative father was silent when taxed with the paternity (*V.* MATERIAL EVIDENCE), or said, that rather than pay he would go to America (*R.* v. *Piercey,* 18 L. T. O. S. 238), or if it is so proved that there had been acts of familiarity even though long antecedent, and having no direct relation to the actual begetting of the child (*Cole* v. *Manning,* 46 L. J. M. C. 175 ; 2 Q. B. D. 611 ; 41 J. P. 469), or that admissions had been made or money paid for the child by the putative father (*R.* v. *Berry,* 23 J. P. 81, 86).

CORRUPT, CORRUPTLY.—" To corrupt " a voter within the meaning of 2 G. 2, c. 24, meant to do an act of bribery which was completed by acceptance of the bribe, whether subsequently the voter voted or not (*Henslow* v. *Fawcett,* 3 A. & E. 51 ; 4 L. J. K. B. 147 ; 4 N. & M. 585).

To " corruptly " treat or do any other thing contrary to the Corrupt Practices Prevention Act, 1854 (17 & 18 V. c. 102), does not mean to do it " wickedly, or immorally, or dishonestly, or anything of that sort, but with the object and intention of doing that which the legislature plainly means to forbid " (per Blackburn, J., *Bewdley,* 1 O'M. & H. 19 ; 19 L. T. 676 ; see the cases hereon collected, Rogers, 13 Ed. 384 *et seq.*).

CORRUPT PRACTICES.—For definition of Corrupt Practices :

(*a.*) At Parliamentary Elections, *V.* Parl. Elec. Act, 1868 (31 & 32 V. c. 125), s. 3 ; Corrupt and Illegal Practices Prevention Act, 1883 (46 & 47 V. c. 51), ss. 3 and 33 (7), Sch. 3, Part 3.

(*b.*) At Municipal Elections, *V.* Municipal Elections (C. & I. P.) Act, 1884 (47 & 48 V. c. 70), s. 2, Sch. 3, Part 1.

Vh. Leigh & Le Marchant, ch. 1 ; Mattinson & Macaskie on Corrupt Practices, 2 Ed.

Vf. Arch. Cr. 1070 ; Rosc. Cr. 344.

COSCES.—*V.* BORDARII.

COST FREIGHT AND INSURANCE.—"The terms at a price 'to cover Cost Freight and Insurance,' payment by acceptance 'on receiving shipping documents,' are very usual, and are perfectly well understood in practice. The invoice is made out debiting the consignee with the agreed price (or the actual cost and commission, with the premiums of insurance, and the freight, as the case may be) and giving him credit for the amount of the freight which he will have to pay to the shipowner on actual delivery, and for the balance a draft is drawn on the consignee, which he is bound to accept (if the shipment be in conformity with his contract) on having handed to him the charter-party, bill of lading and policy of insurance. Should the ship arrive with the goods on board he will have to pay the freight, which will make up the amount he has engaged to pay. Should the goods not be delivered in consequence of a peril of the sea, he is not called on to pay the freight and he will recover the amount of his interest in the goods under the policy. If the non-delivery is, in consequence of some misconduct on the part of the master or mariners, not covered by the policy, he will recover it from the ship-owner. In substance, therefore, the consignee pays, though in a different manner, the same price as if the goods had been brought and shipped to him in the ordinary way" (per Blackburn, J., *Ireland* v. *Livingston*, L. R. 5 H. L. 406 ; 41 L. J. Q. B. 204).

A price C. F. I. does not necessarily include everything up to delivery ; and if the contract stipulates that the goods are "to be shipped," those are important words to show that the goods are at the buyer's risk as soon as placed on board, even though the price be quoted C. F. I. (*Wancke* v. *Wingren*, 58 L. J. Q. B. 519).

COSTS.—*V.* DAMAGES.

"Judgment with Costs ;" *V.* JUDGMENT.

COSTS AND CHARGES.—The "Costs and Charges of executing" a Will, do not include fines payable by devisees of copyholds (*Cole* v. *Jealous*, 5 Hare, 51).

V. IN THE CONDUCT OF A SUIT : MONEY COSTS, CHARGES AND EXPENSES.

COSTS IN THE CAUSE.—*V. Pugh* v. *Kerr*, 6 M. & W. 17 ; 9 L. J. Ex. 255.

COSTS OF EXECUTION.—*V.* EXECUTION.

COSTS OF SUMMONING JURY.—"Costs of summoning jury and expenses of witnesses" to be payable by a Railway on a Compensation

Assessment, *semble,* does not include the general costs of the enquiry (*R.* v. *Gardner*, 6 L. J. K. B. 130 ; 6 A. & E. 112 ; 1 N. & P. 308).

COSTS OF THE REFERENCE.—*V.* REFERENCE.

COSTS ONLY.—S. 49, Jud. Act, 1873 ; *V.* cases collected Ann. Pr., Ord. 65, R. 1.

COTTAGE.—" Cottage, *cotagium*, is a little house without land to it " (Co. Litt. 56 b.). " By the grant of a cottage, doth pass a little *dwelling* house that hath no land belonging to it " (Touch. 94) ; with which agrees the definition in *Doe* v. *Sotheron* (2 B. & Ad. 638), that, " A cottage is a small dwelling-house." In *Doe* d. *Hubbard* v. *Hubbard* (20 L. J. Q. B. 61 ; 15 Q. B. 227), it was held that the word " Cottage " was satisfied by a tenement partitioned off from a larger cottage and having a separate entrance, though not including an upper room under the same roof (1 Jarm. 781).

By 31 Eliz. c. 7, a lawful cottage must have had 4 acres of land attached to it, consequently Levancy and Couchancy was well alleged of a " Cottage," without more (*Emerton* v. *Selby*, 2 Ld. Raym. 1015 ; Salk. 169 : *Vth. Scholes* v. *Hargreaves*, 5 T. R. 46). But that statute was repealed by 15 G. 3, c. 32.

Cp. BORDARII.

COTUCAMI : COTARII : COTERELLI.—*V.* BORDARII.

COUCHANCY.—*V.* LEVANCY AND COUCHANCY.

COUNCIL.—" The Council of a borough," in s. 310, P. H. Act, 1875, as in other sections of the Act, means, " The Mayor, Aldermen and Burgesses acting by the Council " (*Hyde* v. *Bank of Eng.*, 51 L. J. Ch. 747 ; 21 Ch. D. 176).

COUNSEL.—*V.* AS COUNSEL SHALL ADVISE.

COUNSEL OR PROCURE.—" Fagin (ch. 47, *Oliver Twist*), after getting Sikes to say he would murder any one who should betray him, wakes up Noah Claypole and makes him tell Sikes that the girl Nancy had betrayed him, and, as Sikes rushes out in a passion, says, ' You won't be too violent, Bill ; I mean not too violent for safety.' I think that the whole conversation taken together would be evidence to go to a jury, that Fagin did ' counsel ' or ' procure ' the murder committed by Sikes, which would make him an accessory before the fact ; but if he had confined himself to merely telling Sikes what Claypole said he had heard, it would not have been enough " (Steph. Cr. 152, n).

Vf. Arch. Cr. 13, 14.

COUNT.—"Count, *i.e.*, *narratio*, cometh of the French word *conte*, which in *Latyne* is *narratio*, and is vulgarly called a declaration" (Co. Litt. 17 a). *Vf. Gell* v. *Burgess*, 18 L. J. C. P. 153 ; 7 C. B. 16.

COUNTERFEIT COIN.—"'Counterfeit Coin' means coin not genuine, but resembling or apparently intended to resemble, or pass for genuine coin ; and includes genuine coin prepared or altered so as to resemble or pass for a coin of a higher denomination" (Steph. Cr. 310, stating the definition in s. 1, 24 & 25 V. c. 99). A genuine coin, fraudulently reduced in weight by the removal of the milling and which has received a new milling in order to restore its appearance, is a counterfeit coin (*R.* v. *Hermann*, 48 L. J. M. C. 106 ; 4 Q. B. D. 284). *Vf.* Arch. Cr. 852.

COUNTING-HOUSE.—A "Counting-House" to qualify for the parliamentary franchise, s. 27, 2 W. 4, c. 45, need not consist of an entire building, or be structurally severed from the rest of the building of which it forms part (*Piercy* v. *Maclean*, L. R. 5 C. P. 252 ; 39 L. J. C. P. 115). *Note* :—This section repealed by 48 & 49 V. c. 3.

COUNTY.—"*Countie* is fetched from the French, and *shire* from the Saxon. For *scyran* in the *Saxon* tongue signifieth *partiri*, because everie countie or shire is divided and parted by certaine metes and bounds from another, and in *Latine* is called *comitatus à comitando*, for accompanying together" (Co. Litt. 50 a).

In Acts of Parliament passed since the end of 1850, "'County' shall be held to mean also County of a Town or of a City, unless such extended meaning is expressly excluded by words" (s. 4, 13 & 14 V. c. 21 ; s. 4, Interp. Act, 1889). "County" has this extended meaning in s. 38, 4 & 5 W. 4, c. 76 (*R.* v. *Pearce*, 49 L. J. M. C. 81 ; 5 Q. B. D. 386).

In every Act relating to Scotland, "Shire" or "County" includes a Stewartry (s. 7, Interp. Act, 1889).

The word "County" is used in s. 13, Highways and Locomotives Act, 1878 (41 & 42 V. c. 77), in its ordinary geographical sense ; and is not narrowed by the definition of "County" in s. 2, Highway Act, 1862, 25 & 26 V. c. 61 (*Over Darwen* v. *Lancashire*, 54 L. J. M. C. 51 ; 15 Q. B. D. 20 ; 51 L. T. 739). "County," s. 51, 15 & 16 V. c. 81 ; *V. R.* v. *East Looe*, 31 L. J. M. C. 245 ; 3 B. & S. 20.

"Counties, Ridings and Divisions ;" *V. Evans* v. *Stevens*, 4 T. R. 459 : *R.* v. *Isle of Ely*, 15 Q. B. 827 ; 19 L. J. M. C. 223.

COUNTY AUTHORITY.—The Recorder of a Borough when in session, is the "County Authority" over the roads extending from the County into the Borough, within s. 13, 41 & 42 V. c. 76 (*R.* v. *Dover*, 32 W. R. 876 ; 49 J. P. 86).

COUNTY BRIDGE.—*V. R.* v. *Chart*, 39 L. J. M. C. 107 ; L. R. 1 C. C. 237 : Glen on Highways, 90.

COUNTY COURT.—In Acts of Parliament passed since 1846, "the expression 'County Court' shall, unless the contrary intention appears, mean, *as respects England and Wales*, a Court under the County Courts Act, 1888" (s. 6, Interp. Act, 1889).

In all Acts passed after the 31st Dec. 1889, "'County Court,' shall, *as respects Ireland*, mean a Civil Bill Court within the meaning of the County Officers and Courts (Ireland) Act, 1877" (s. 29, Ib.).

COURSE.—"Of course legatee will give ;" *V.* PRECATORY TRUST.

"In the Course of his Trade ;" *V.* IN THE COURSE.

"Course," in Art. 22, Sailing Rules, refers to the direction of the vessel's head, and not to her speed (*The Beryl*, 9 P. D. 4 ; 53 L. J. P. D. & A. 75).

COURT.—"*Curia*, Court, is a place where justice is judicially ministered, and is derived *á cura, quia in curiis publicis curas gerebant*" (Co. Litt. 58 a).

The "Court," as defined in s. 4, Parliamentary Elections (Returning Officers) Act, 1875 (38 & 39 V. c. 84), does not exclusively mean the Judge, but includes also the Registrar, or other proper officer, in daily attendance, whose duty it is to bring the matter before the Judge (*R.* v. *Bloomsbury Co. Co.*, 55 L. J. Q. B. 443 ; 17 Q. B. D. 788 ; 54 L. T. 616).

COURT OF APPEAL.—*V.* s. 13 (2), Interp. Act, 1889.

COURT OF ASSIZE.—*V.* s. 13 (4), Interp. Act, 1889.

COURT OF CHANCERY.—*V. Re McClintock*, 10 Ir. Ch. Rep. 469.

COURT OF QUARTER SESSIONS.—*V.* s. 13 (14), Interp. Act, 1889.

COURT OF RECORD.—"When a case is made triable, or a penalty recoverable in a 'Court of Record,' the Supreme Court of Judicature alone, but not the Quarter Sessions, is intended" (Maxwell, 427, citing *Gregory's Case*, 6 Rep. 19 b ; 2 Hale, 29 ; Jenk. 228 : *Vf.* Co. Litt. 117 b, 118 a, 260 a).

V. RECORD.

COURT OF SUMMARY JURISDICTION.—"The Court of Summary Jurisdiction" to whom (s. 52 (2), Licensing Act, 1872) Notice of Appeal to Quarter Sessions had to be given, meant the Convicting Justices ; and a Notice directed to the Justices of the Division collectively, and served on their Clerk at his private residence, was not a compliance

(*Ex p. Curtis*, 47 L. J. M. C. 35 ; 3 Q. B. D. 13) ; and the principle of that case is still applicable to a demand for a special case under s. 33 (i) Summary Jurisdiction Act, 1879, 42 & 43 V. c. 49, and the Rule thereunder (*South Staffordshire W. Works Co.* v. *Stone*, 56 L. J. M. C. 122 ; 19 Q. B. D. 168 ; 57 L. T. 368 ; 36 W. R. 76 ; 51 J. P. 662 : *Lockhart* v. *St. Albans*, 57 L. J. M. C. 118 ; 21 Q. B. D. 188 ; 36 W. R. 800 ; 52 J. P. 420). *Note.*—But, generally, Notice of Appeal is now to be served on the Clerk to the Justices (s. 31 (2), Sum. Jur. Act, 1879 ; s. 6, Sum. Jur. Act, 1884).

For the statutory definition of "Court of Summary Jurisdiction," *V.* s. 50, Sum. Jur. Act, 1879, emended by s. 7 of the Sum. Jur. Act, 1884 ; but both of those enactments are now consolidated in s. 13 (11), Interp. Act, 1889. *Vh.* Archbold's Prac. Quarter Sess. 4 Ed. 640.

COURT OR JUDGE.—"It is well recognized that that phrase always includes a Judge at Chambers, unless there is some express enactment limiting the meaning of the phrase" (per Brett, M.R., *Dallow* v. *Garrold*, 54 L. J. Q. B. 78 ; 14 Q. B. D. 543 : *Vf. Ex p. Norris*, 17 Q. B. D. 731) ; but the phrase does not *per se* include a Master or District Registrar (*Lambton* v. *Parkinson*, 35 W. R. 545) ; or, possibly, a Judge at *Nisi Prius* (*Robson* v. *Lees*, 30 L. J. Ex. 235 ; 6 H. & N. 258).

Though by virtue of Ord. 54, R. 12, R. S. C., a Master may exercise the function of "the Court or a Judge" and decide an Interpleader in a summary manner under R. 8, Ord. 57 ; yet a Master is not included in the phrase "Court or a Judge" in R. 11 of the same Order (57), and accordingly there is an appeal from his decision under Ord. 54 R. 21 (*Bryant* v. *Reading*, 55 L. J. Q. B. 253 ; 17 Q. B. D. 128 ; 54, L. T. 524 : *Webb* v. *Shaw*, 55 L. J. Q. B. 249 ; 16 Q. B. D. 658).

COUSIN.—The word "Cousin," without a controlling context means First Cousin (*Stoddart* v. *Nelson*, 25 L. J. Ch. 116 ; 6 D. G. M. & G. 68 : *Stevenson* v. *Abingdon*, 31 Bea. 305 : *Burbey* v. *Burbey*, 6 L. T. 573 ; 2 Jarm. 152 ; Wms. Exs. 1109). In *Caldecott* v. *Harrison* (9 L. J. Ch. 331 ; 9 Sim. 457), Shadwell, V.-C., said, "I am quite willing to admit that the word 'Cousins' is sufficiently extensive to comprehend Cousins of every description, whether they are first cousins of any degree, or second cousins, or third cousins. That is the general meaning of the word 'Cousin.'" But that dictum was obiter ; and the actual decision in the case was that on the construction of the Will then before the Court, only first cousins were comprehended under the word "Cousins." It is therefore submitted that in view of the decisions in *Stoddart* v. *Nelson* and *Stevenson* v. *Abingdon*, sup., the dictum of V.-C. Shadwell cannot be relied on : *Va.* Obs. of Kay, J., *Wilks* v. *Bannister*, 54 L. J. Ch. 1141 ; 30 Ch. D. 512.

"Cousin," imports consanguinity. Yet, in a secondary sense, "Cousin" is often used to designate the husband or wife of a cousin (*Re Taylor*, *Cloak* v.

Hammond, 56 L. J. Ch. 173 ; 34 Ch. D. 255 ; 55 L. T. 649 ; 35 W. R. 186 ; *Cp.* NEPHEW). And as to the degree of kindred, *V.* Wms. Exs. 427.

V. SECOND COUSIN.

COUSIN GERMAN.—This is a synonym for FIRST COUSIN (*Saunderson* v. *Bailey*, 8 L. J. Ch. 18 ; 4 My. & C. 56).

COVENANT.—"Although the word 'Covenant,' in its strict sense, means an Agreement, *under seal*, that something has or has not already been done, or shall or shall not be done hereafter (Touch. 160, 162) ; it is sometimes, especially in Agreements, applied to any promise or stipulation, whether under seal or not (*Hayne* v. *Cummings*, 16 C. B. N. S. 421 ; 10 L. T. 341 : *Va. Brookes* v. *Drysdale*, 3 C. P. D. 52, where the word 'Covenant,' in an Agreement, was held to include a Proviso : *Severn and Clerke's Case*, 1 Leon. 122, where 'Covenants, Articles and Agreements,' in a Bond, included a Recital)." Elph. 407, 408 : *Vf. Holles* v. *Carr*, 3 Swanst. 647. *Cp.* CONDITION.

"The words 'Covenant, Grant and Agree' that A. should have the land for so many years, are apt words to make a Lease for years, and enure as a Lease" (*Whitlock* v. *Horton*, Cro. Jac. 91) ; so the word "Covenant" will of itself have a like effect (*Richards* v. *Sely*, 2 Mod. 80).

COVER.—A deposit of money as a "Cover" in Stock-Exchange dealings, seems to mean no more than a mere deposit as security in the ordinary sense (*Mundella* v. *Shaw*, 4 Times Rep. 253).

V. OPEN : INFAMOUS CONDUCT.

COVERED.—*V.* LAND COVERED WITH WATER.

COVERS.—In a Clause in a Railway Act enabling the Co. to charge "for providing Covers for minerals, goods, articles or animals," "providing covers" includes not only the supply of sheets, but the cost of the labour of covering the waggons with them (*Coxton* v. *N. E. Ry.*, 4 B. & Macn. 284).

COVERTURE.—*V.* DURING.

COWKEEPER.—A. had a farm of 104 acres cultivated so that no live stock was required to be kept by him on it ; he kept 4 cows solely for the purpose of making a profit by their milk and calves : Held, he was not a "Cowkeeper" within the late Bankruptcy definition of "Trader" (*Ex p. Dering, Re Cramp*, 16 L. J. Bank. 3 ; 1 D. G. 398 : *Vf. Bell* v. *Young*, 24 L. J. C. P. 66 ; 15 C. B. 524).

CRAFT.—*V. Tisdell* v. *Combe*, 7 L. J. M. C. 48 ; 7 A. & E. 788 : *Reed* v. *Ingham*, 23 L. J. M. C. 156 ; 3 E. & B. 889.

V. WHERRY.

CRAVE LEAVE TO REFER.—A Pleading which "craves leave to refer" to a document when produced, does not admit the document (*Barnard* v. *Wieland*, 30 W. R. 947).

CREDIBLE WITNESS.—The person to whom a bail-bond was assigned was not a "Credible Witness" of the assignment within 4 & 5 Anne, c. 16, s. 20 (*White* v. *Barrack*, 5 L. J. Ex. 167 ; 1 M. & W. 424).

As to who was a "Credible Witness" to the alteration of a Will within the Statute of Frauds ; *V. Hilliard* v. *Jennings*, Ld. Raym. 505 : *Holdfast* v. *Dowsing*, 2 Stra. 1253 : *Wyndham* v. *Chetwynd*, 1 W. Bl. 95.

CREDIT.—An undischarged bankrupt "Obtains Credit" for goods, within s. 31, Bankry Act, 1883, when he obtains them and does not pay their price ; although nothing may be said about credit, or any term of credit, at the time of the transaction (*R.* v. *Peters*, 55 L. J. M. C. 173 ; 16 Q. B. D. 636 ; 54 L. T. 545 ; 34 W. R. 399 ; 50 J. P. 631 ; 16 Cox, C. C. 36 : *R.* v. *Juby*, 3 Times Rep. 211).

CREDIT IN CASH.—"The words 'Credit in Cash,' mean 'hold at his command,' or 'pay to him'" (per Wilde, C.J., *Eddison* v. *Collingridge*, 19 L. J. C. P. 268).

CREDITOR.—The general meaning of "Creditor" is, a person to whom a debt is payable.

"In Bankry., 'Creditor' generally means a person entitled to prove in the bankry. (*Grace* v. *Bishop*, 25 L. J., Ex. 58 ; 11 Ex. 424 : *Re Poland*, 35 L. J. Bank. 19 ; 1 Ch. 356) ; and does not include a mere Receiver (*Re Sacker*, 58 L. J. Q. B. 4 ; 22 Q. B. D. 179).

"The word 'Creditor,' as used in s. 4 (g) of Bankry. Act, 1883, is not confined to persons who are creditors before they begin their action, but means Judgment Creditors" (per Selborne, L.C., *Re Faithfull, Ex p. Moore*, 54 L. J. Q. B. 190 ; 14 Q. B. D. 627). But though an Executor of the Judgment Creditor may serve a Bankry Notice under that section (*Re Woodall*, 53 L. J. Ch. 966 ; 13 Q. B. D. 479) ; yet an assignee cannot (*Ex p. Blanchett*, *Re Keeling*, 55 L. J. Q. B. 327 ; 17 Q. B. D. 303), nor can the Trustee in bankry of the judgment creditor (*Re Goldring, Ex p. Harper*, 58 L. J. Q. B. 3 ; 22 Q. B. D. 87 : *Re Connan*, 57 L. J. Q. B. 472). *Vf.* FINAL JUDGMENT.

"A *cestui que trust* is not a Creditor of his trustee, nor is a Trustee a creditor of his Co-trustee" (per Lindley, L.J., *Re Goldsmid, Ex p. Taylor*, 56 L. J. Q. B. 197 ; 18 Q. B. D. 295 ; 35 W. R. 148, citing *Re Wilkinson, Ex p. Stubbins*, 50 L. J. Ch. 547 ; 17 Ch. D. 58, and *Sinclair* v. *Wilson*, 24 L. J. Ch. 537 ; 20 Bea. 324).

The assignee of a debt rightfully using the name of his assignor is (*semble*) a "Creditor" for the purpose of presenting a petition for Winding-up a Co. under s. 82, Companies Act, 1862 (*Re Lond. & Birmn. Flint Glass & Alkali Co.*, 28 L. J. Bank. 17 ; 1 D. G. F. & J. 257 : *Paris Skating Rink Co.*, 5 Ch. D. 959).

But a creditor whose debt has been attached is not a "Creditor" within such section (*European Bankg. Co., Ex p. Baylis*, 35 L. J. Ch. 690; L. R. 2 Eq. 521); nor is a garnishee (*Re Combined Weighing Co.*, 34 S. J. 10); nor is a claimant for unliquidated damages (*Pen-y-van Colly. Co.*, 46 L. J. Ch. 390; 6 Ch. D. 477); nor an unpaid vendor of land, compulsorily taken, whose title remains unaccepted (*Re Milford Docks Co., Ex p. Lister*, 52 L. J. Ch. 774; 23 Ch. D. 292); nor will the untaxed costs of an arbitration constitute such a vendor a "creditor" (Ib.). *Note.*—The holder of a current Life Policy can petition under this section (ss. 2, 21, 33 & 34 V. c. 61). *Vf.* Buckl. 209.

"Creditors *and others*," 13 Eliz. c. 5;—"It is conceived that the words 'creditors and others' are wide enough to include any person who has a *legal* demand against the settlor, so that he may rank as a Creditor, although at the date of the settlement he may have no legal right to enforce it. The character of the claim, so long as it is a legal one, seems immaterial" (May on Fraudulent Conv. 2 Ed. 163). A mortgagee, fully secured, is not such creditor (*Lister* v. *Turner*, 5 Hare, 281: *Dolphin* v. *Aylward*, L. R. 4 H. L. 486; 23 L. T. 636), unless he relinquish (*Lister* v. *Turner*, sup.); but he is such creditor as regards so much of his debt as the mortgage does not cover (*Harman* v. *Richards*, 10 Hare, 81). *Vf.* May on Fraud. Conv., Part 2, ch. 8.

CREDITS.—*V.* Rights and Credits.

CRIMINAL CAUSE.—A Judgment in a "Criminal Cause or Matter," means "any decision by way of judicial determination of any question with regard to proceedings the subject matter of which is criminal, at whatever stage it arises" (per Esher, M.R., *Re Woodall*, inf.).

A Certiorari to quash a conviction for trespassing in pursuit of game on the ground that the justices' jurisdiction was ousted by a *bonâ fide* claim of right, is a "Criminal Cause or Matter" within s. 47, Jud. Act, 1873 (*R.* v. *Fletcher*, 46 L. J. M. C. 4; 2 Q. B. D. 43; 35 L. T. 538); so is an Order discharging a rule nisi for a certiorari to bring up an Order for restitution of property made under 24 & 25 V. c. 96, s. 100 (*R.* v. *Central Crim. Co.*, 56 L. J. M. C. 25; 18 Q. B. D. 314); so is an application for a Mandamus to Justices to state a case on a criminal information (*Brosman* v. *Roche*, 22 L. R. Ir. 334); so is a taxation of the costs of a successful defendant in a criminal information for libel (*R.* v. *Steel*, 46 L. J. M. C. 1; 2 Q. B. D. 37; 25 W. R. 34; 35 L. T. 534); or an Information for contravening By-Laws of a School Board (*Mellor* v. *Denham*, 49 L. J. M. C. 89; 5 Q. B. D. 467); or an Order to abate nuisance under P. H. Act, 1875 (*Ex p. Whitchurch*, 50 L. J. M. C. 99; 7 Q. B. D. 534); or a refusal of Bail (*R.* v. *Foote*, 52 L. J. Q. B. 528; 10 Q. B. D. 378); or an application for a certiorari under s. 3, Palmer's Act, 19 & 20 V. c. 16 (*R.* v. *Rudge*, 55 L. J. M. C. 112; 16 Q. B. D. 459; 34 W. R.

207) ; or, *à fortiori*, an Information for keeping a dog without a License (*R.* v. *Sullivan*, 8 Ir. R. C. L. 404 ; 19 S. J. 235). *Vf. Cattel* v. *Ireson*, 27 L. J. M. C. 167 ; E. B. & E. 91: *Parker* v. *Green*, 31 L. J. M. C. 133 ; 2 B. & S. 299 : *R.* v. *Hawkhurst*, 26 J. P. 772 ; 7 L. T. 268 : *Blake* v. *Beech*, 45 L. J. M. C. 111 ; 2 Ex. D. 335.

But an application for a *mandamus* to Election Commissioners to grant a witness a Certificate of Indemnity is not a "Criminal Cause" within the section (*R.* v. *Holl*, 7 Q. B. D. 575) ; nor is an application for excusal from an electoral Illegal Practice (*Ex p. Walker*, 58 L. J. Q. B. 190 ; 22 Q. B. D. 384) ; nor a *habeas corpus* in an Ecclesiastical Suit (*Ex p. Bell-Cox*, 20 Q. B. D. 1 ; 36 W. R. 209), *secus*, if the subject-matter of the proceedings against the prisoner be criminal (*Re Woodall*, 57 L. J. M. C. 71 ; 20 Q. B. D. 832 ; 36 W. R. 655 : *Sv. Re Keller*, 22 L. R. Ir. 158). An application to strike a Solicitor off the rolls on the ground of misconduct is not a "Criminal Cause or Matter" (*Re Hardwick*, 53 L. J. Q. B. 64 ; 12 Q. B. D. 148 ; 32 W. R. 191 ; *Vh.* CRIMINAL PRISONER), *secus*, of an imprisonment of an unqualified person for acting as a Solicitor (*Re Wall*, 32 S. J. 693). An Information for penalties on the revenue side of the old Court of Exchequer was not a "Criminal Cause" (*A.-G.* v. *Radloff*, 23 L. J. Ex. 240 ; 10 Ex. 84 ; 28 & 29 V. c. 104 ; and per Brett, M.R., *A.-G.* v. *Bradlaugh*, 54 L. J. Q. B. 215 ; 14 Q. B. D. 691) ; nor is an action to recover a penalty under 1 G. 1, st. 2, c. 13, s. 17, for voting in parliament without having taken the oath (*Miller* v. *Salomons*, 21 L. J. Ex. 161 ; 22 Ib. 169 ; 7 Ex. 475 ; 8 Ib. 778) ; nor an Information by the Attorney-General to recover penalties under the Parliamentary Oaths Act, 1866 (*A.-G.* v. *Bradlaugh*, 54 L. J. Q. B. 205 ; 14 Q. B. D. 667). *Vf. R.* v. *Barnardo*, 61 L. T. 547.

By s. 15, Jud. Act, 1884 (47 & 48 V. c. 61), *Quo Warranto* is a civil proceeding, "whether for purposes of appeal or otherwise."

CRIMINAL PRISONER.—A person summarily committed to prison for acting as a Solicitor without being qualified (s. 32, 6 & 7 V. c. 73), is a "Criminal Prisoner" within s. 4, Prisons Act, 1865 (28 & 29 V. c. 126) ; and is not a person "imprisoned under any Rule, Order or Attachment for *Contempt of Court*" within s. 41, Prisons Act, 1877 (40 & 41 V. c. 21) (*Osborne* v. *Milman*, 56 L. J. Q. B. 263 ; 18 Q. B. D. 471 ; 56 L. T. 808 ; 35 W. R. 397 ; 51 J. P. 437 ; 3 Times Rep. 452).

CRIMINAL PROCEEDING.—*V.* PROCEEDING : CRIMINAL CAUSE.

CRIMINAL PROSECUTION.—*V.* PROSECUTION.

CRIMINAL SUIT.—A proceeding to recover penalties for Non-Residence (under 1 & 2 V. c. 106, ss. 32, 114) is not a "Criminal Suit" within the Church Discipline Act, 3 & 4 V. c. 86, s. 23 (*Rackham* v. *Bluck*, 16 L. J. Q. B. 82 ; 9 Q. B. 691) ; nor is a proceeding under the Public

Worship Act, 1874 (*Harris* v. *Perkins*, 51 L. J. P. C. 83 ; 7 P. D. 31, 161) : *Secus*, as regards proceedings to examine the proofs of an ecclesiastical offence, for the purpose of deprivation (*Re Dean of York*, 2 Q. B. 1).

CROFT.—"A croft is a little close, or pightle, adjoining to a house, used either for pasture or arable, as the owner pleases. In many places such close is called a Ham" (Preston's addns. to p. 95, Touch.).

CROSSING.—"Crossing" a *Cheque* generally and specially ; *V.* ss. 76, 77, 78, Bills of Ex. Act, 1882 ; Not Negotiable. *Vf.* 19 & 20 V. c. 25 ; 21 & 22 V. c. 79, ss. 1, 3.

Ships "Crossing," Sailing Rules, No. 14 ; *V. Gen. Steam Navigation Co.* v. *Hedley*, 39 L. J. Adm. 20 ; L. R. 3 P. C. 44.

CROWN.—In every Act of Parliament, "references to the Sovereign reigning at the time of the passing of the Act or to the Crown shall, unless the contrary intention appears, be construed as references to the Sovereign for the time being ; and this Act shall be binding on the Crown" (s. 30, Interp. Act, 1889).

CROWN LANDS.—In Queensland Goldfields Act, 1874 ; *V. Osborne* v. *Morgan*, 58 L. J. P. C. 52.

In New South Wales Crown Lands Act, 1884 ; *V. Tearle* v. *Edols*, 58 L. J. P. C. 58.

CRUELLY.—"Cruelly ill-treat ;" *V.* Cruelty *to Animals*.

CRUELTY.—*Matrimonial Cruelty:* "Lord Stowell's judgment in *Evans* v. *Evans* (1 Hagg. Cons. R. 35) is the great authority on questions of legal cruelty. That very eminent judge, whom I may in some sense consider as a predecessor of my own, remarks on the mischiefs which would ensue from giving the sanction of law to the separation of man and wife too easily, or on the mere disinclination of one or both of the parties to live together. 'When people,' he continues, 'understand that they must live together, except for a very few reasons known to the law, they learn to soften by mutual accommodation that yoke which they know they cannot shake off ; they become good husbands and good wives from the necessity of remaining husbands and wives ; for necessity is a powerful master in teaching the duties which it imposes.' Lord Stowell refused to give any strict definition of cruelty. The causes which warrant separation 'must be grave and weighty, and such as show an absolute impossibility that the duties of the married life can be discharged. In a state of personal danger no duties can be discharged, for the duties of self-preservation must take place before the duties of marriage. What merely wounds the mental feelings is in few cases to be admitted, where it is not accompanied with bodily injury, either actual or menaced. Mere austerity of temper, petulance of manners, rudeness of language, a want of civil attention and accommodation, even occasional sallies of passion, if they do not threaten bodily harm, do not amount to legal cruelty; they are high moral offences in the marriage state undoubtedly, not innocent surely in any state of life, but still they are not that cruelty against which the law can relieve. Under such misconduct of either of the parties, for it may exist on one side as well as on the other, the suffering party must bear in some degree the consequences of an injudicious connection, must subdue by decent resistance, or by prudent conciliation, and if this cannot be done, both must suffer in silence. In the older cases of this sort, which I have had an opportunity of looking into, I have observed that the danger of life, limb, or health is usually inserted as the ground upon which the Court has proceeded to a separation. The Court has never been driven off this ground; it has always been jealous of the inconvenience of departing from it, and I have heard no one case cited in which the Court has granted a divorce without proof given of a reasonable apprehension of bodily hurt. I say an apprehension, because assuredly the Court is not to wait till the hurt is actually done; but the apprehension must be reasonable, it must not be an apprehension arising merely from an exquisite and diseased sensibility of mind.' Danger of life, limb, or health has continued in substance the rule upon which the Courts have acted; the phrase has sometimes been varied. Sir John Nicholl has used the expression, 'injury to person or to health;' which I am inclined to take in conjunction with Lord Stowell's expression, for there might be a great deal of suffering and brutal usage without coming strictly within the terms of the latter. There must, however, be bodily hurt (not trifling or temporary pain), or a reasonable apprehension of bodily hurt" (per Cresswell, J. O., *Tomkins* v. *Tomkins*, 1 Sw. & Tr. 170).

The following are acts of matrimonial cruelty:—Duress or threats tending to injury to health (*Kelly* v. *Kelly*, 39 L. J. P. & M. 28; 21 L. T. 564); or terrifying a wife into immorality (*Coleman* v. *Coleman*, 35 L. J. P. & M. 37); publicly outraging a wife's feelings by insulting language and assaulting her, even though no personal injury be inflicted (*Milner* v. *Milner*, 31 L. J. P. & M. 159); a violently intended, but futile, assault, or spitting on a wife (*D'Aguilar* v. *D'Aguilar*, 1 Hagg. Ecc. Supp. 776); habitual insult and violence of temper, inducing quarrels and producing physical suffering (*Knight* v. *Knight*, 34 L. J. P. & M. 112); knowingly or recklessly imparting a venereal disease (*Boardman* v. *Boardman*, L. R. 1 P. & D. 233: *Brown* v. *Brown*, Ib. 46; 35 L. J. P. & M. 13; as to cutaneous disease, *V. Chesnutt* v. *Chesnutt*, 1 Sp. Ecc. & Ad. 205); unreasonable denial of usual necessaries and comforts so as to affect health (*Dysart* v. *Dysart*, 3 N. C. 340: *Orme* v. *Orme*, 2 Add. 382); cruelty to children in the mother's presence, in order to wound her feelings, and to such an extent as probably to be injurious to her health (*Suggate* v. *Suggate*, 28 L. J. P. & M. 46: *Birch* v. *Birch*, 42 L. J. P. & M. 23).

But the following are *not* acts of matrimonial cruelty :

Drunkenness (*Scott* v. *Scott*, 29 L. J. P. & M. 64) ; debauching household servants (*Cousen* v. *Cousen*, 34 L. J. P. & M. 139) ; bad language (*Dysart* v. *Dysart*, sup.) ; debarring a wife from intercourse with her family (*Neeld* v. *Neeld*, 4 Hagg. Ecc. 269) ; sleeping in a separate bed (*D'Aguilar* v. *D'Aguilar*, sup.).

Vf. Dixon on Divorce, 98 *et seq.*

Cruelty is not excused by drunkenness or *delirium tremens* (*Marsh* v. *Marsh*, 28 L. J. P. & M. 13 ; 1 Sw. & Tr. 312 ; 7 W. R. 129) ; or ungovernable passion (*Curtis* v. *Curtis*, 27 L. J. P. & M. 73 ; 1 Sw. & Tr. 192) ; but insanity excuses (*Hall* v. *Hall*, 33 L. J. P. & M. 65 ; 3 Sw. & Tr. 349 : *White* v. *White*, 1 Sw. & Tr. 591).

Cruelty to Animals: If any person "cruelly beat, ill-treat, over-drive, abuse or torture" any domestic animal, that is an offence under s. 2, 12 & 13 V. c. 92. The cruelty under that section means, unreasonably inflicting unnecessary pain. Incensing Cocks to fight (*Bridge* v. *Parsons*, 32 L. J. M. C. 95 ; 3 B. & S. 382 ; 11 W. R. 424 ; 7 L. T. 784 ; 27 J. P. 117, 231), or cutting a Cock's comb in order to exhibit him as a Gamecock (*Murphy* v. *Manning*, 46 L. J. M. C. 211; 2 Ex. D. 311; 41 J. P. 130) is such cruelty ; and so it may be such cruelty to turn an animal which is already suffering into a field to graze, when it can only do so by giving itself additional pain (*Everitt* v. *Davies*, 26 W. R. 332 ; 42 J. P. 248 ; 38 L. T. 360). But the mere omission to kill a suffering animal is not such cruelty (Ib.) ; nor does the section include the merely unlawful killing an animal, or shooting it intending to kill it but leaving it to die in pain (*Powell* v. *Knight*, 26 W. R. 721; 42 J. P. 597; 38 L. T. 607), nor the sending parrots a ten-hours' railway journey without water (*Swan* v. *Sanders*, 50 L. J. M. C. 67; 29 W. R. 538 ; 45 J. P. 522 ; 44 L. T. 424), nor a painful operation *bonâ fide* believed to be proper, *e.g.*,—spaying sows, as they do in Sussex, to improve the flesh as human food (*Lewis* v. *Fermor*, 56 L. J. M. C. 45 ; 18 Q. B. D. 532 ; 56 L. T. 236 ; 35 W. R. 378 ; 51 J. P. 371). But in *Ford* v. *Wiley* (58 L. J., M. C. 145), the principle of *Lewis* v. *Fermor* was questioned, and it was held that dishorning cattle was within the section, although it might prevent them from goring each other, and made them graze better and fatten more quickly.

CURATE.—*V.* Clergyman.

CURRENT.—"'Current' applied to Coin, means coin coined in any of Her Majesty's mints, or lawfully current by virtue of any proclamation, or otherwise, in any part of Her Majesty's dominions, whether within the United Kingdom or without" (Steph. Cr. 310, abridging the definition in s. 1, 24 & 25 V. c. 99). *Vf.* Arch. Cr. 852.

"Current Coin," in Truck Act ; *V.* Payment.

CURTILAGE.—"A little garden, yard, field, or piece of void ground lying near and belonging to the messuage" (Touch. 94).

" 'A little croft or court or place of easement to put in cattle for a time, or to lay in wood, coal, or timber, or such other things necessary for household' (Fitzherbert on Surveying, ch. 1.) Spelman considers it to be 'the yard not the garden'; *see Curtilagium, Curtillum;* though it *may* be used for garden, he says: *V.* per Fairfax, 21 Ed. 4, 52, pl. 15; and per Frowike, Keilw. 57, pl. 7" (Elph. 569).

For a good example of what, in modern times, has been held to be part of the Curtilage of a house, *V. Marson* v. *Lond. Chatham & Dover Ry.*, 37 L. J. Ch. 483; L. R. 6 Eq. 101. *Va.* on this word, in s. 7, 33 & 34 V. c. 57, *Commrs. Inl. Rev.* v. *Goodfellow*, 45 J. P. 588.

Vf. Arch. Cr. 460–462; Rosc. Cr. 359, 368, 452.

CUSTODY. — "Custody or Control," s. 2, 36 V. c. 12, is large enough to enable the Court to commit the religious education of an Infant to the mother (*Condon* v. *Vollum*, 31 S. J. 575; 57 L. T. 154).

"Custody or Control" of Documents; *V. London & Yorksh. Bank* v. *Cooper*, 54 L. J. Q. B. 495; 15 Q. B. D. 7.

V. CARE: CONTROL: POSSESSION: PROPER CUSTODY.

CUSTOM.—"*Consuetudo* is one of the maine triangles of the lawes of England; those lawes being divided into Common Law, Statute Law, and Custome" (Co. Litt., 110 b.)

" 'This word *consuetudo* hath in law divers significations; 1. For the Common Law, as *consuetudo Angliæ;* 2. For Statute Law, as *contra consuetudinem communi concilio regni edit.;* 3. For Particular Customs, as Gavelkind, Borough English, and the like; 4. For Rents, Services, &c., due to the Lord, as *consuetudines et servitia*; 5. For Customs, Tributes or Impositions, &c., as *de novis consuetudinibus levatis in regno sive in terrâ sive in aquâ*; 6. Subsidies or Customs granted by common consent, that is, by authority of Parliament *pro bono publico*' (2 Inst. 58). *Consuetudo* signifies also Tolls, Murage, Frontage, Paviage, and such like newly granted by the King, (Co. Litt. 58 b). *V.* on this latter point, *Egremont* v. *Saul*, 6 A. & E. 924; 6 L. J. K. B. 205, and the cases there cited" (Elph. 569). In *Egremont* v. *Saul*, though the above passage from Co. Litt. was cited, it was held that "consuetudo" does not necessarily, or it should seem *primâ facie*, signify toll: *V.* TOLL.

"In 22 Ed. 1, 364 (Record Publ.) Customs are distinguished from Services as follows:—'Customs are things which are done, and demanded by reason of bodily service; Services are things which are demanded of the tenant by reason of the tenement which he holds of the demandant, to wit, rent, and things of that kind, or suit demanded by reason of the tenement' " (Elph. 569).

V. PRESCRIPTION: TOLL.

The word "Custom" in s. 2, Municipal Corporations Act (5 & 6 W. 4, c. 76) is not used in a technical sense, but is there equivalent to "Usage" (*Prestney* v. *Colchester*, 51 L. J. Ch. 805; 21 Ch. D. 111).

CUSTOM OF THE COUNTRY.—"The word 'Custom' as here used, does not mean a Custom in the strict legal signification of it; for that must be taken with reference to some defined limit or space, which is essential to every custom properly so called; but which does not exist here. What shall be considered in farming as a good and husbandlike manner must vary exceedingly according to soil, climate and situation. And, therefore, the 'Custom of the Country,' with reference to good husbandry, must be applied to the approved habits of husbandry in the neighbourhood, under circumstances of the like nature" (2 Platt, 279, citing *Legh* v. *Hewitt*, 4 East, 154). *Vf.* Woodf. 753—768.

CUSTOMARY.—*V.* USUAL AND CUSTOMARY MANNER.

CUSTOMARY EMPLOYMENT.—What is a person's "Customary Employment," *quà* a Friendly Society's Rules; *V. Manchester Law Clerks Society* v. *Wilson*, 4 Times Rep. 465.

CUSTOMARY FINES.—"Customary Fines, Fees, and other Dues and Payments," s. 20 (3), Settled Land Act, 1882; *V. Re Naylor and Spendla*, 34 Ch. D. 217; 56 L. J. Ch. 453; 56 L. T. 132; 35 W. R. 219.

CUSTOMARY MEASURE.—*V.* MEASURE.

CUSTOMARY RIGHTS.—A reservation in an agreement for a Lease of "all Customary Rights and Reservations" does not render the agreement void for uncertainty (*Parker* v. *Taswell*, 2 D. G. & J. 559; 6 W. R. 608; 31 L. T. O. S. 226).

CUTTING.—*V.* TEAR: WOUND.

DAMAGE.—"Neither in common parlance, nor in legal phraseology, is the word 'Damage' used as applicable to injuries done to the *person;* but solely as applicable to mischief done to *property*. We speak indeed of 'damages' as compensation for injury done to the person; but the term 'damages' is not employed interchangeably with the term 'injury' with reference to mischief wrongfully occasioned to the person" (per Cockburn, C. J., *Smith* v. *Brown*, 40 L. J. Q. B. 218). This definition, which reads so simple and clear, is nothing more than the central bone of contention in a series of cases distinguished by a remarkable conflict of judicial opinion, the last word in which has, at last, been spoken.

That conflict was over the very short words of s. 7 of the Admiralty Court Act, 1861 (24 V. c. 10) which says,—"The High Court of Admiralty shall have jurisdiction over *any claim for Damage* done by any ship." The question as to the meaning of "damage," unembarrassed by context, could hardly be presented in a more absolute way.

The Common Law Courts persistently (Blackburn, J., *hesitantly*) held that "Damage" in the section just quoted did not include injury to the person, or, still less, claims by surviving relatives for loss of life (*Smith* v. *Brown*, 40 L. J. Q. B. 214; L. R. 6 Q. B. 729: *James* v. *Lond. & S. W. Ry.*, 41 L. J. Ex. 89, 186; L. R. 7 Ex. 187, 287: *Simpson* v. *Blues*, 41 L. J. C. P. 128; L. R. 7 C. P. 290).

The exact contrary was, as persistently, held by the Admiralty Court and Privy Council (*The Sylph*, 37 L. J. Ad. 14; L. R. 2 A. & E. 24: *The Guldfaxe*, 38 L. J. Ad. 12; L. R. 2 A. & E. 325: *The Beta*, 38 L. J. Ad. 50; L. R. 2 P. C. 447: *The Explorer*, 40 L. J. Ad. 41; L. R. 3 A. & E. 289: *The Franconia*, 46 L. J. P. D. & A. 71; L. R. 2 P. D. 8).

When the point came before the Court of Appeal, the Equity members of the Court (James and Baggallay, L.JJ.) held that "Damage" did include personal injury and claims for loss of life; whilst their two brethren (Bramwell and Brett, L.JJ.), whose experience was at the Common Law Bar, went the other way (*Jeffrey* v. *Franconia*, 46 L. J. P. D. & A. 33; L. R. 2 P. D. 163: *Vf. The Alina*, 5 Ex. D. 227).

But the definition at the commencement of this article has now been authoritatively established by the House of Lords,—their lordships holding that a claim for loss of life under Lord Campbell's Act, is *not* a claim for "Damage" within s. 7 of the Admiralty Court Act (*Seward* v. *The Vera Cruz*, 54 L. J. P. D. & A. 9; 10 App. Ca. 59).

It may perhaps be added that Cockburn, C. J., was scarcely accurate in saying that "Damage" does not, in common parlance, include injury to the person; for St. Paul when on his voyage to carry his Appeal to Cæsar is thus reported,—"Sirs, I perceive that this voyage will be with hurt, and much *Damage*, not only of the lading and ship, *but also of our lives*" (Acts, xxvii. 10).

"Damage" may be controlled by the context and "*can* certainly mean personal injury," and therefore where a packet company issued a passenger's ticket containing a special provision respecting loss, damage or detention of luggage, and then, by a separate clause, dealing with passengers personally, obtained exemption for "*Loss or Damage*" from certain specified causes; it was held that that meant, injury to limb or life from the causes enumerated (*Haigh* v. *Royal Mail Steam Packet Co.*, 52 L. J. Q. B. 395; Ib. 640).

"*Making good all Damage*," s. 83 (6), Metrop. Building Act, 1855, 18 & 19 V. c. 122, provides for, and therefore only empowers, *structural* damage, not the invasion of a right of light (*Crofts* v. *Haldane*, 36 L. J. Q. B. 85; 8 B. & S. 194; L. R. 2 Q. B. 194).

"The feeling of anxiety is Damage" (per Cranworth, V.-C.) in reference to a covenant *quà* user (*Kemp* v. *Sober*, 1 Sim. N. S. 520); and so is invasion of privacy (*Manners* v. *Johnson*, 45 L. J. Ch. 404; 1 Ch. D. 673). *V.* Annoyance.

The "Damage" for which compensation is to be given under s. 68, Lands C. C. Act, 1845, for lands "injuriously affected," is such damage as would have given a right of compensation independently of that statute (*Caledonian Ry.* v. *Ogilvy*, 2 Macq. 229: *V.* Injuriously affected); and so of a Private Act incorporating the Lands C. C. Act (*Rhodes* v. *Airedale Commrs.*, 45 L. J. C. P. 861; 1 C. P. D. 402); and a similar construction was placed on the word "Damage" as used in s. 144, P. H. Act, 1848 (*Hall* v. *Bristol*, 36 L. J. C. P. 110; L. R. 2 C. P. 322).

As to this word in ss. 6, 16, Ry. C. C. Act, 1845; *V.* per Fry, L. J., *R.* v. *Poulter*, 57 L. J. Q. B. 138; 20 Q. B. D. 132; 58 L. T. 534; 36 W. R. 117; 52 J. P. 244: and as used in s. 308, P. H. Act, 1875; *V.* per Selborne, L. C., *Brierley Hill* v. *Pearsall*, 54 L. J. Q. B. 25; 9 App. Ca. 595.

"Damage," in s. 32, 24 & 25 V. c. 96, means direct, not consequential, injury (*R.* v. *Whiteman*, 23 L. J. M. C. 120).

"Damage" is often used in contracts of guarantee, *e.g.*, where one undertakes to shield another against the "costs, *damages*, and expenses" of actions that may be brought by third parties. If the verb of the guarantee is appropriate, an action may be brought on the guarantee before actual payment, as a liability to pay is, generally speaking, "damage" (*Spark* v. *Heslop*, 28 L. J. Q. B. 197; 1 E. & E. 563: *Randall* v. *Roper*, 27 L. J. Q. B. 266; E. B. & E. 84). *V.* Damages: Indemnify.

The phrase "*as little Damage as can be*" in the working clause of the

Ry. C. C. Act, 1845, applies not to what is done, but to the manner of doing it—the *modus operandi* (*R.* v. *E. & W. India Docks Co.*, 22 L. J. Q. B. 384; 2 E. & B. 474: *Fenwick* v. *E. Lond. Ry.*, 44 L. J. Ch. 602; L. R. 20 Eq. 544: *Biscoe* v. *G. E. Ry.*, L. R. 16 Eq. 636: *Pugh* v. *Golden Valley Ry.*, 12 Ch. D. 274).

DAMAGE BY COLLISION.—The jurisdiction given to County Courts, by Co. Co. Admiralty Jurisdiction Act, 1868, s. 3, sub-s. 3, in cases of "Damage by Collision," includes only, Damage by Collision by Ships (*Everard* v. *Kendall*, 39 L. J. C. P. 234; L. R. 5 C. P. 428); and does not include damage by a collision of a ship with something on shore (*Robson* v. *Owners of "Kate,"* 57 L. J. Q. B. 546; 21 Q. B. D. 13; 59 L. T. 557; 36 W. R. 910).

DAMAGE BY FIRE EXCEPTED.—*V.* REPAIR.

DAMAGE TO CARGO.—"The words 'Damage to Cargo,' s. 3, sub-s. 3, 32 & 33 V. c. 51, I think, obviously refer to cargo damaged whilst on board ship" (per Grantham, J., *Robson* v. *Owners of "Kate,"* 57 L. J. Q. B. 547; 21 Q. B. D. 13; 59 L. T. 557; 36 W. R. 910).

DAMAGE TO GOODS.—"Damage to any goods which is capable of being covered by insurance," in an exception in a Bill of Lading, includes a total loss or destruction, but not an abstraction, of goods (*Taylor* v. *Liverpool & Gt. Wn. Steam Co.*, 43 L. J. Q. B. 205; L. R. 9 Q. B. 546).

DAMAGES.—"'*Dammages.*' *Damna* in the common law hath a speciall signification for the recompense that is given by the jury to the plaintife or defendant (qy. demandant? *V.* Ritso's Intr. 119), for the wrong the defendant hath done unto him" (Co. Litt. 257 a). Costs are parcel of the Damages (Co. Litt. 257 a: *O'Loughlin* v. *Fogarty*, 5 Ir. L. R. 54).

Compensation under the Lands C. C. Act, 1845, for lands injuriously affected is not "Damages" within s. 140, Ry. C. C. Act, 1845 (*R.* v. *Edwards*, 53 L. J. M. C. 149; 13 Q. B. D. 586).

V. DAMAGE.

DANCING HOUSE.—*V.* PUBLIC DANCING HOUSE.

DANGER.—A lessee's covenant, in a Lease of a Public-house, that he will not do or suffer anything whereby the License "may be *in any Danger* of being suspended, discontinued or forfeited," is not broken by his being convicted of selling drink after hours, if the conviction is not indorsed on the License (per Charles, J., *Fleetwood* v. *Hull*, 58 L. J. Q. B. 341): the learned judge added,—"If the conviction had been endorsed on the License, a question might have arisen whether the License was or was not endangered. If two convictions had been endorsed, then the License would no doubt have been in danger, because a third conviction would, by s. 30, Licensing Act, 1872, forfeit the License."

DANGEROUS.—*V.* OFFENSIVE.

DANGERS.—" It has been held long ago that the words ' Dangers *of the Seas* ' are synonymous with PERILS OF THE SEAS " (per Esher, M.R., *Pandorf* v. *Hamilton*, 55 L. J. Q. B. 548). "' Dangers *and Accidents* of the Sea ' cannot have a narrower interpretation than ' Perils of the Sea ' " (per Ld. Herschell, *Wilson* v. *The Xantho*, 56 L. J. P. D. & A. 118; 12 App. Ca. 506 ; 57 L. T. 701 ; 36 W. R. 353 ; 6 Asp. 207).

The clause in a Charter-party excepting " Dangers and Accidents of the Sea " &c., applies only to the voyage and not to the whole Charter-party (*Smith* v. *Dart*, 54 L. J. Q. B. 121 ; 14 Q. B. D. 105 ; 52 L. T. 218 ; 33 W. R. 455).—Such an exception in a Bill of Lading does not limit the owner's implied warranty of seaworthiness (*The Glenfruin*, 54 L. J. P. D. & A. 49 ; 10 P. D. 103 ; 52 L. T. 769 ; 33 W. R. 826). *Vf.* 1 Maude & P. 353. *V.* NAVIGATION.

In a Contract of Affreightment, " the Court said that the words ' *Dangers of Roads* ' might be explained, by the context, to refer to Marine Roads where vessels lie at anchor, but that even supposing them to extend to roads on land, they could apply to such dangers only as were immediately caused by the condition of the roads ; such for instance as the over-turning of carriages " (1 Maude & P. 353, citing *Rothschild* v. *Roy. Mail Steam Packet Co.*, 7 Ex. 734 ; 21 L. J. Ex. 273).

DATE.—" Where a deed bears no date, or an impossible date, and in the deed reference is made to the ' Date,' that word must be construed ' Delivery ; ' but if the deed bears a sensible date, the word ' Date,' occurring in the deed, means the day of the date, and not that of the delivery " (Elph. 123, citing *Styles* v. *Wardle*, 4 B. & C. 908 ; 7 D. & R. 507 : *Vf.* Co. Litt. 46 b and Hargrave's note (8) thereon ; Woodf. 151). *V.* FROM THE DAY OF THE DATE.

DAUGHTER.—May be construed as a word of limitation ; *V.* 2 Jarm. 400 *et seq.*

" It cannot be said that the word ' Daughters ' is at all more appropriate to describe illegitimate daughters, than the word ' Children ' would be to describe illegitimate children " (per Wood, V.-C., *Re Herbert*, 29 L. J. Ch. 870 ; 1 J. & H. 123). And though in *Laker* v. *Hordern* (45 L. J. Ch. 315 ; 1 Ch. D. 644) Bacon, V.-C., held that a gift to " my daughters " meant existing illegitimate daughters, inasmuch as testator had always treated them as his daughters and had no legitimate children ; yet it has been submitted that that case cannot be supported and is undistinguishable from *Dorin* v. *Dorin* (2 Jarm. 234, n. (*o*) : *Va. Kelly* v. *Hammond*, 26 Bea. 36. For *Dorin* v. *Dorin* *V.* CHILDREN). *V.* SON : NEPHEW.

DAY.—"The *Jewes*, the *Chaldeans*, and *Babylonians* begin the day at the rising of the sun; the *Athenians*, at the fall; the *Umbri* in *Italy* beginne at midday; the *Ægyptians* and *Romanes* from midnight; and so doth the law of *England* in many cases" (Co. Litt. 135 a; *Vf.* Ib. 134 b). The English Day begins as soon as the clock begins to strike twelve p.m. of the preceding day (*Williams* v. *Nash*, 28 L. J. Ch. 886; 28 Bea. 93: s. 36 (2), Interp. Act, 1889).

V. DAYS.

DAY OF DATE.—*V.* FROM THE DAY OF THE DATE.

DAY OF HEARING.—This phrase in R. 104, Co. Co. Rules, 1867, which formerly regulated a demand for a jury, meant the day originally appointed for the hearing (*Fletcher* v. *Baker*, 43 L. J. Q. B. 112; L. R. 9 Q. B. 370: *R.* v. *Leeds Co. Co.*, 16 Q. B. D. 691).

V. RETURN DAY.

DAYS.—"The general rule of law is, that 'Days' mean consecutive days, *except Sunday is the first or last day;* but in mercantile cases it is sometimes otherwise, because mercantile contracts are to be construed with reference to mercantile usage" (per Alderson, B., *Brown* v. *Johnson*, Car. & M. 444).

"Where a certain number of days is to be allowed for the delivery of goods under a *Contract of Sale*, they are to be counted as consecutive days and *include Sundays*, unless the contrary be expressed, or an usage to that effect be shown. Extra day in Leap Year counts by itself and not reckoned as one with the previous day: 42 & 43 V. c. 59" (Benj. 674, citing *Brown* v. *Johnson*, 10 M. & W. 331; 11 L. J. Ex. 373: *Cochran* v. *Retberg*, 3 Esp. 121. *Note.*—The statute cited repeals 40 H. 3, which provided that the extra day in Leap Year *and the day preceding* should be reckoned as one day).

V. AT LEAST: CLEAR.

When Sunday, Christmas-day, &c., are to be "excluded,"—*e.g.* Parliamentary Elections Act, 1868, s. 49, Corrupt & Illegal Prac. Prev. Act, 1883, s. 40 (5), R. 3, Addl. Gen. Rules (Parliamentary), 1875,—all the Sundays, &c., of a prescribed sequence of days are to be eliminated in computing them (*Southampton Case, Pegler* v. *Gurney*, 19 L. T. 647; L. R. 4 C. P. 237, 238).

Where by the Bills of Ex. Act, 1882, "the time limited for doing any act or thing is less than 3 days, Non-business days are excluded" (s. 92). *V.* BUSINESS DAYS.

In a Charter-Party providing for Lay-days, "the word 'Days' alone, would mean days as reckoned in each particular port" (per Esher, M. R., *Neilson* v. *Wait*, 55 L. J. Q. B. 89; 16 Q. B. D. 70). *V.* DEMURRAGE DAYS: LAY DAYS: RUNNING DAYS: WORKING DAYS.

DAYS OF GRACE.—"Where a Bill (of Exchange) is not payable On Demand the day on which it falls due is determined as follows :

(1) Three days, called *Days of Grace*, are, in every case where the Bill itself does not otherwise provide, added to the time of payment as fixed by the Bill, and the Bill is due and payable on the last Day of Grace : Provided that

(a) When the last Day of Grace falls on Sunday, Christmas Day, Good Friday, or a day appointed by Royal proclamation as a Public Fast or Thanksgiving Day, the Bill is, except in the case hereinafter provided for, due and payable on the preceding business day ;

(b) When the last Day of Grace is a Bank Holiday (other than Christmas Day or Good Friday), under the Bank Holidays Act, 1871, and Acts amending or extending it, or when the last Day of Grace is a Sunday and the second Day of Grace is a Bank Holiday, the Bill is due and payable on the succeeding business day.

(2) Where a Bill is payable at a fixed period after date, after sight, or after the happening of a specified event, the time of payment is determined by excluding the day from which the time is to begin to run and by including the day of payment.

(3) Where a Bill is payable at a fixed period after sight, the time begins to run from the date of the acceptance if the Bill be accepted, and from the date of noting or protest if the Bill be noted or protested for non-acceptance, or for non-delivery."

(s. 14, Bills of Ex. Act, 1882): these provisions as to "Days of Grace" relate also to Promissory Notes (s. 89, Ib.).

DEAD.—Where there is a gift over to a prescribed class on the death of a tenant for life, and that is followed by a gift over to the same class—on the bankruptcy of the tenant for life "in the same manner as if he was *naturally* dead,"—this divesting would, it seems, rather apply to the tenant for life than to the class, so that the period for ascertaining the class would not be accelerated, and members of the class coming into being after the bankruptcy would be entitled to participate (*Re Bedson*, 54 L. J. Ch. 644 ; 28 Ch. D. 523).

V. Die.

DEAD BODY.—Leaving a living child in a secret place to die from exposure or want, is not a "secret disposition of the *Dead Body*" of the Child within s. 60, 24 & 25 V. c. 100 (*R.* v. *May*, 31 J. P. 356).

DEAD FREIGHT.—"The term 'Dead Freight' denotes an agreed sum to be paid in respect of space not filled according to charter, or damages provided for by a charter, in the event of the freighter not loading a full cargo" (1 Maude & P. 389, citing *Birley* v. *Gladstone*, 3 M. & S.

205 : *Phillips* v. *Rodie*, 15 East, 547 : *Pearson* v. *Göschen*, 17 C. B. N. S. 352 ; 33 L. J. C. P. 265 : *Vf. Gray* v. *Carr*, 40 L. J. Q. B. 257 ; L. R. 6 Q. B. 522).

DEAD RENT.—Dead Rent in a mining lease is "a rent payable whether the mines be worked or not." (Woodf. 382.)

DEAD STOCK.—*V.* LIVE AND DEAD STOCK.

DEALING.—"I take it that the strict definition of 'dealing' is 'distributing.' A Dealer is one who distributes" (per Alderson, B., *Allen* v. *Sharp*, 17 L. J. Ex. 212).

V. CONTRACT : TRADE OR DEALING : MUTUAL CREDITS.

DEAR : DEARLY-BELOVED.—As to the value of these expressions in devises, for the purpose of preventing a Resulting Trust to the heir ; *V.* 1 Jarm. 570.

V. BELOVED WIFE.

DEATH.—Where a life interest is to cease on the death or re-marriage of the tenant for life, and there is a gift over which (by an imperfection of language) is expressed to take effect on the happening of one only of those events, the gift over is read as taking effect at the termination of the life interest by either event (*Luxford* v. *Cheeke*, 3 Lev. 125 : *Bainbridge* v. *Cream*, 16 Bea. 25 : *Underhill* v. *Roden*, 45 L. J. Ch. 266 ; 2 Ch. D. 494 : *Re Stanford*, 56 L. J. Ch. 273 ; 34 Ch. D. 362 ; 55 L. T. 765 ; 35 W. R. 191 ; 1 Jarm. 802—804). *Note.*—These cases were followed doubtingly by Stirling, J., in *Re Tucker*, 56 L. J. Ch. 449 ; 56 L. T. 118 ; 35 W. R. 344 ; and followed, willingly, by Kay, J., in *Re Dear*, 58 L. J. Ch. 659.

"In case of death ;" *V.* Chitty, Eq. Ind. 8055, 8056.

V. DIE : AT HIS DEATH : AT THEIR DEATH.

DEBATES.—*V.* QUARRELS.

DEBENTURE.—This word seems to have originated from "Debentur mihi," with which various old forms of Acknowledgments commenced (per Chitty, J., *Levy* v. *Abercorris Co.*, 57 L. J. Ch. 204 ; 37 Ch. D. 260 ; 36 W. R. 411). In a previous case (*Edmonds* v. *Blaina Co.*, 56 L. J. Ch. 817 ; 36 Ch. D. 215 ; 57 L. T. 139 ; 35 W. R. 798), the same learned judge said, "So far as I am aware, the term 'Debenture' has never received any precise legal definition. It is, comparatively speaking, a new term. I do not mean a new term in the English language, because there is a passage in Swift (quoted in Latham's Dictionary), where the term 'Debenture' is used."

"No one seems to know exactly what 'Debenture' means" (Buckl. 153, citing *British India Steam Nav. Co.* v. *Inl. Rev.*, 50 L. J. Q. B. 517 ; 7 Q. B. D. 165, in which Grove, J., said,—this is "a word which has no definite signification in the present state of the English language:" *Re Florence Land Co., Ex p. Moor*, 48 L. J. Ch. 137; 10 Ch. D. 530). It should rather be said that no one has yet laid down an exhaustive definition of a Debenture. The *British India Steam Nav. Co.'s* case shows that it is not true to say that a Debenture is necessarily an obligation under seal, or a charge on any property. *Faute mieux*, it is suggested that a Debenture is a written Obligation or Acknowledgment in an impersonal form, and with conditions more elaborate than those of a Promissory Note, given by or for a Corporation or a Company to secure a sum of money. Thus, in the *British India Steam Nav. Co.'s* case, Lindley, J., said,—"Now, what the exact meaning of 'Debenture' is I do not know. I do not find any particular definition of it, and we know that there are various classes of instruments called 'Debentures.' You may have Mortgage Debentures, which are charges of some kind on property; you may have Debentures which are Bonds; you may have a Debenture which is nothing more than an Acknowledgment of debt; you may have an instrument, like this, which is something more—it is a statement by two Directors that a Company will pay. I think any instruments of that sort may be Debentures."

A Covering Deed by a Company would seem to be a "Debenture" within the exception in s. 17, Bills of Sale Act, 1882 (per Kay, J., *Ross* v. *Army & Navy Hotel Co.*, 55 L. J. Ch. 697; 34 Ch. D. 43; 35 W. R. 40; dissenting from decision of Field, J., in *Brocklehurst* v. *Railway Printing Co.*, W. N. (84) 71); and the Debentures based on such a deed would be within the section (*Ross* v. *A. & N. H. Co.*, sup.). An Agreement charging *the Undertaking* in favor of certain therein-named persons *pari passu* (*Edmonds* v. *Blaina Co.*, 56 L. J. Ch. 815; 36 Ch. D. 215; 35 W. R. 798), or in favor of an individual (*Levy* v. *Abercorris Co.*, 57 L. J. Ch. 202; 37 Ch. D. 260; 36 W. R. 411), is within the exception. But a charge on specific goods is not (*Re Cunningham*, 28 Ch. D. 682; 33 W. R. 387). *Vf.* Healey on Company Law, 2 Ed. 156: *Topham* v. *Greenside Co.*, 57 L. J. Ch. 583; 36 W. R. 464; 37 Ch. D. 281; 58 L. T. 274.

In Ireland it has been held that a Policy on the life of a debtor would pass, under a Will, as a "Debenture" (*Phillips* v. *Eastwood*, Ll. & Go. temp. Sugden, 270; 1 Jarm. 770); but, in England, Debenture Stock (into which Debentures had, since the Will, been converted) was held not to pass under bequest of "all my Debentures in the A. Ry." (*Re Lane*, 49 L. J. Ch. 768; 14 Ch. D. 856: *Sv. Dillon* v. *Arkins*, 17 L. R. Ir. 636).

DEBENTURE STOCK.—*V.* Part III., Companies Clauses Act, 1863 (26 & 27 V. c. 118).

DEBT.—A "Debt" is a sum payable in respect of a liquidated money demand.

But in s. 4, Bills of Sale Act, 1878, "Debt" is not confined to an existing debt; *V.* AUTHORITY OR LICENSE.

Interest which could only be given by way of damages, is not a "Debt" within s. 92, 1 & 2 V. c. 110 (*Ex p. Charman*, W. N. (87) 184: *Sv. Bermingham* v. *Burke*, 9 Ir. Eq. Rep. 86).

Costs of Execution are not part of "the Debt *owing*" within s. 6, (1) a, Bankry. Act, 1883 (*Salisbury* v. *Ray*, 8 C. B. N. S. 193; 29 L. J. C. P. 225: *Re Long*, 57 L. J. Q. B. 360; 20 Q. B. D. 316; 58 L. T. 664; 36 W. R. 346).

"Debt *provable* in Bankruptcy;" *V. Hardy* v. *Fothergill*, 13 App. Ca. 351; 58 L. J. Q. B. 44; 37 W. R. 177; 59 L. T. 273.

"All Debts *Owing or Accruing*," s. 61, Com. L. Pro. Act, 1854,—Ord. 45, R. 1, R. S. C.;—to obtain a Garnishee Order under this phrase there must be (1) a "Debt;" but (2) it may be either "Owing *or* Accruing."

1. *Johnson* v. *Diamond* (24 L. J. Ex. 217; 11 Ex. 73) is the first case on this phrase; and it was there held that money that might become payable under a Bond of Indemnity is not a "Debt." This case well illustrates the principle of what is a "Debt" within the phrase, viz. a liquidated money obligation for which, speaking generally, an action will lie (*Webster* v. *Webster*, 31 Bea. 393), but which obligation may be either legal or equitable (per Lindley, L.J., *Webb* v. *Stenton*, 52 L. J. Q. B. 588; 11 Q. B. D. 518; 48 L. T. 268); but for a Debt to be garnisheed it must be due to the judgment debtor alone and not jointly with some other person (*Macdonald* v. *Tacquah Co.*, 53 L. J. Q. B. 376; 13 Q. B. D. 535; 32 W. R. 760).

Therefore, neither of the following is a "Debt" within the phrase;—Damages, though after verdict, until judgment obtained (*Jones* v. *Thompson*, 27 L. J. Q. B. 234; E. B. & E. 63): verdict on a Marine Policy (*Dresser* v. *Johns*, 28 L. J. C. P. 281; 6 C. B. N. S. 429): unascertained claim on a Fire Policy (*Randall* v. *Lithgow*, 53 L. J. Q. B. 518; 12 Q. B. D. 525), or on a Notice to Treat under Lands C. C. Act, 1845 (*Richardson* v. *Elmit*, 2 C. P. D. 9): Moneys in the hands of a County Court Registrar (*Dolphin* v. *Layton*, 48 L. J. C. P. 426; 4 C. P. D. 130), or of a Clerk of the Peace (*D'Arcy* v. *Carragher*, 18 L. R. Ir. 317: *Sv.* 20 Ib. 189), or of the Police (*Jervis* v. *Peel*, 1 Times Rep. 206), or of a Trustee in Bankruptcy (*Boyse* v. *Simpson*, 8 Ir. C. L. Rep. 523: *Hunter* v. *Greensill*, 42 L. J. C. P. 55; L. R. 8 C. P. 24), or of a Liquidator (*Mack* v. *Ward*, W. N. (84) 16), or of a mortgagee as the surplus of a sale of the mortgaged property (*Chatterton* v. *Watney*, 50 L. J. Ch. 535; 17 Ch. D. 259; 44 L. T. 391): Moneys payable on a contingency (*Howell* v. *Metrop. Dist. Ry.*, 51 L. J. Ch. 158; 19 Ch. D. 508; 45 L. T. 707: *Richardson* v. *Elmit*, sup.): Rent, or instalments of an Annuity, not yet due (*Jones* v. *Thompson*, sup.; *Sv.* as to Annuities *Nash* v. *Pease*, 47 L. J. Q. B. 766): Trust income not in the hands of the Trustees (*Webb* v. *Stenton*, sup.; *V.* especially jdgmt., Lindley, L.J., over-ruling *Re Cowan*, 49 L. J. Ch. 402; 14 Ch. D. 638): Salary or

Pension not yet payable (*Hall* v. *Pritchett*, 47 L. J. Q. B. 15 ; 3 Q. B. D. 215 : *Booth* v. *Trail*, 53 L. J. Q. B. 24 ; 12 Q. B. D. 8 ; 49 L. T. 471 ; 32 W. R. 122) ; but the Half-pay of an Army Officer (*Birch* v. *Birch*, 52 L. J. P. D. & A. 88 ; 8 P. D. 163 : *Lucas* v. *Harris*, 18 Q. B. D. 127), or an Annual Gratuity from the East India Company under s. 93, 53 G. 3, c. 155 (*Innes* v. *East India Co.*, 25 L. J. C. P. 154 ; 17 C. B. 351), or a Custom-house or Revenue Officer's superannuation (45 & 46 V. c. 72, s. 3), or the Wages of Seamen (17 & 18 V. c. 104, s. 233), or Workmen (33 & 34 V. c. 30), are not attachable at all; nor are moneys held for a married woman who is restrained from anticipation (*Chapman* v. *Biggs*, W. N. (83) 92).

But, speaking generally, "money in the hands of a man who cannot refuse to pay it somehow or another, is a 'Debt,' and if so, it can be attached" (per Coleridge, C.J., *Booth* v. *Trail*, sup.). Therefore the over-due superannuation allowance of a retired Police Constable (*Booth* v. *Trail*), or County Court Judge (*Willcock* v. *Terrell*, 3 Ex. D. 323), or Civil Servant (*Sansom* v. *Sansom*, 48 L. J. P. D. & A. 25 ; 4 P. D. 69), or a commutation of a pension (*Crowe* v. *Price*, 22 Q. B. D. 429), are "Debts" and attachable. So is over-due Rent (*Mitchell* v. *Lee*, 36 L. J. Q. B. 154 ; L. R. 2 Q. B. 259) ; or an ascertained amount due on a Guarantee (*Bouch* v. *Sevenoaks &c. Ry.*, 48 L. J. Ex. 338 ; 4 Ex. D. 138) ; or proceeds of a Call on Shareholders, when made to provide for a debt due to the judgment debtor (*Ex p. Turner*, 2 D. G. F. & J. 354).

But a Garnishee Order does not make the Garnishor a "Creditor" of the Garnishee (*Re Combined Weighing Co.*, 34 S. J. 10), and therefore the amount garnished is not a "Debt" due to the garnishor which, in his hands, may be garnished (*Cooper* v. *Lawson*, 6 Times Rep. 34).

As to whether a Legacy can be attached, *V. Vyse* v. *Brown*, 13 Q. B. D. 199 ; Chitty's Arch. 14 Ed. 929 ; and *V.* Ib. 930 as to whether money in the hands of a Sheriff can be attached, but *cp. Dolphin* v. *Layton*, sup. As to when cheque has been given for the debt sought to be attached, *V. Cohen* v. *Hale*, 3 Q. B. D. 371 ; 47 L. J. Q. B. 496 : *Elwell* v. *Jackson*, 1 Times Rep. 454.

2. The phrase an "Accruing" Debt, was much discussed in *Webb* v. *Stenton* (sup. : *V.* especially jdgmt., Brett, M.R.). That case and *Jones* v. *Thompson*, much referred to in it, show that an "Accruing" does not mean a future debt, or one that very probably will soon arise. "It must be something which the law recognizes as a 'Debt'" (per Brett, M.R., *Webb* v. *Stenton*). It must therefore be "debitum in præsenti ;" but it may be "solvendum in futuro," and then it is an "Accruing" debt. Accordingly an actually existing debt, payable by instalments, not yet due, is an "Accruing Debt" and attachable (*Tapp* v. *Jones*, 44 L. J. Q. B. 127 ; L. R. 10 Q. B. 591). It seems a little difficult to reconcile with the reasoning of that case, the Irish decision that money secured by a current Promissory Note is not attachable as an "Accruing Debt" (*Pyne* v. *Kinna*, 11 Ir. R. C. L. 40).

"*Action for the recovery* of any Debt," s. 6, 7 & 8 V. c. 96 ; *V. Thomas* v. *Hudson*, 14 L. J. Ex. 283 ; 14 M. & W. 353.

"Debt incurred by Fraud or Breach of Trust ;" *V.* BREACH OF TRUST.

V. DEBTS : DEBTS DUE : DUE : ATTACHMENT FOR DEBT.

DEBT CLAIM OR DEMAND.—S. 1, 22 & 23 V. c. 49 ; *V. R.* v. *Stepney*, 43 L. J. M. C. 145 ; L. R. 9 Q. B. 383.

DEBT OR LIABILITY.—Alimony is not a "Debt or Liability" within s. 37, Bankry. Act, 1883 (*Linton* v. *Linton*, 54 L. J. Q. B. 529 ; 15 Q. B. D. 239).

Giving a Bill or Note for an existing debt, or giving a new Bill or Note for an old one, is "incurring" a "Debt or Liability" within s. 13 (1) Debtors Act, 1869 (*R.* v. *Pierce*, 56 L. J. M. C. 85 ; 56 L. T. 532 ; 51 J. P. 790).

V. INCAPABLE.

DEBT UPON RECORD.—Crown Dues recoverable "as a Debt upon Record," *e.g.*, Assessed Taxes under 5 & 6 W. 4, c. 20, s. 13, must be recovered by Scire Facias, Extent or Information, not in a popular action of Debt (*A.-G.* v. *Sewell*, 4 M. & W. 77 ; 7 L. J. Ex. 245).

DEBTOR.—The power to examine a "Debtor" as to what debts were due to him (s. 60, Com. L. Pro. Act, 1854) did not extend to a Corporation, to which, obviously, an oath could not be administered (*Dickson* v. *Neath & Brecon Ry.*, 38 L. J. Ex. 57 ; L. R. 4 Ex. 87. But now *V.* R. 32, Ord. 42, R. S. C.).

DEBTS.—"The expression in a Will, 'all my *just* Debts,' includes all the testator's debts whenever and wherever contracted, and therefore includes a debt contracted by him after the making of the Will, and contracted in a country other than that of his domicil, and secured upon property in that country" (Wms. Exs. 1719, citing *Maxwell* v. *Maxwell*, L. R. 4 H. L. 506 ; 39 L. J. Ch. 698). It also includes all Liabilities which the testator's personal estate would be liable to discharge (*V. Lomas* v. *Wright*, 2 My. & K. 769 ; 3 L. J. Ch. 68 : *Stone* v. *Parker*, 1 Dr. & Sm. 212 ; 29 L. J. Ch. 874 : *Alsop* v. *Bell*, 24 Bea. 469). And would not the construction be the same if the word "just" were omitted ?

The term "Debts" or "Just Debts" by law includes a Mortgage Debt ; and therefore a testamentary direction to pay "Debts" or "Just Debts" would include a mortgage debt in exoneration of the mortgaged property but for s. 1, 30 & 31 V. c. 69, which section has entirely done away with that reasoning (*Re Newmarch*, 48 L. J. Ch. 28 ; 9 Ch. D. 12 ; and especially jdgmt. of Jessel, M. R.).

Under a bequest of "Debts," a Bank Balance, and a bill of exchange deposited at the bankers, will pass (*Carr* v. *Carr*, 1 Mer. 541, n. : *Parker* v. *Marchant*, 12 L. J. Ch. 387 ; 1 Phill. 356) ; and so will an unascertained residuary personal estate to which the testator may be entitled at his decease (*Bainbridge* v. *Bainbridge*, 7 L. J. Ch. 4; 9 Sim. 16). The reasoning of the last case would seem to support the statement, that a share of a residuary estate, or a legacy to which a testator may be entitled at his decease, would pass under a bequest by him of "Debts." The bequest of a debt due on a particular security will pass only the principal, not arrears of interest (*Hamilton* v. *Lloyd*, 2 Ves. jun. 416). *Vf.* Wms. Exs. 1202–1204.

"The expression '*Debts due*' is sometimes used in bankry proceedings to include all demands which can be proved against a bankrupt's estate, although some of them may not be strictly debts at all" (per Mellish, L. J., *Ex p. Kempe*, 43 L. J. Bank. 52; 9 Ch. 383). *V.* In the Course.

The exemption from the Thellusson Act (39 & 40 G. 3, c. 98), of a provision for the payment of "Debts" applies as well to the debts of the grantor as to those of third persons (*Barrington* v. *Liddell*, 2 D. G. M. & G. 480; 22 L. J. Ch. 1), and also to contingent liabilities becoming debts after the testator's decease (*Varlo* v. *Faden*, 1 D. G. F. & J. 211; 29 L. J. Ch. 230).

V. Book Debts: Debt.

DEBTS DUE.—This phrase in s. 18, sub-ss. 1, 8, Bankry. Act, 1883, means all claims to which a debtor is liable and which are provable in his bankry. (*Flint* v. *Barnard*, 58 L. J. Q. B. 53; 22 Q. B. D. 90). *V.* Fairly Estimated.

Bequest of "Debts Due;" *V. Essington* v. *Vashon*, 3 Mer. 434: *Williams* v. *Williams*, 2 Bro. C. C. 87: *Devaynes* v. *Noble*, 1 Mer. 541: *Mayberry* v. *Brooking*, 25 L. J. Ch. 87; 2 D. G. M. & G. 673; 4 W. R. 155.

DECEASE.—*V.* Die.

DECEIVE.—It is hardly possible for any one now-a-days, to tell fortunes for money, without also intending "to *deceive or impose*" within s. 4, 5 G. 4, c. 83 (*Penny* v. *Hanson*, 18 Q. B. D. 478; 56 L. J. M. C. 41; 56 L. T. 235; 35 W. R. 379; 51 J. P. 167; 16 Cox, C. C. 173; 3 Times Rep. 409).

V. Calculated to deceive.

DECISION.—The "Decision" of a Local Authority, referred to in s. 268, P. H. Act, 1875, means its demand for payment of the expenses therein referred to (*R.* v. *Loc. Govt. Bd.*, 52 L. J. M. C. 4; 10 Q. B. D. 309).

"Cause of Appeal" in s. 269 (2), P. H. Act, 1875, has the same meaning as "Decision *of the Court*" in sub-s. 1 of the same section (*R.* v. *Barnet*, 45 L. J. M. C. 105; 1 Q. B. D. 558).

"Decision *or Order*" of a County Court in Bankry. (R. 143, Bankry. Rules, 1870) was perfect, *quâ* Appeal, when pronounced (*Ex p. Hookey*, 4 D. G. F. & J. 456: *Ex p. Whitton, Re Greaves*, 13 Ch. D. 881; 49 L. J. Bank. 31).

DECLARATION.—In all Acts of Parliament, "'Statutory Declaration,' shall, unless the contrary intention appears, mean a Declaration made by virtue of the Statutory Declarations Act, 1835" (s. 21, Interp. Act, 1889).

DECLARE.—In order to "declare such Admixture" (s. 3, 35 & 36 V. c. 74), it is sufficient to state that the article, *e.g.* mustard, is not sold as pure; it is not necessary to specify the nature and proportion of the substances admixed (*Pope* v. *Tearle*, 43 L. J. M. C. 129; L. R. 9 C. P. 499).

"Where a person by deed 'declares' that he will do a thing, it amounts to a covenant by him to do it" (Elph. 426, citing *Richardson* v. *Jenkins*, 1 Drew. 477).

V. Agreed and Declared: Acknowledge: Precatory Trust.

DECLARED.—*V.* Hereafter valued and declared.

DECLARING THE RIGHTS.—"Judgment or Order Declaring the Rights," R. 2 (1), Ord. 55, R. S. C.;—*V. Rolls* v. *Rolls*, 30 S. J. 201: *Re Brandram*, 25 Ch. D. 369; 53 L. J. Ch. 331: *Re Rhodes*, 31 Ch. D. 499: *Bates* v. *Moore*, 38 Ch. D. 381: *Re Evans*, 54 L. T. 527.

DECLINING TRUSTEE.—A person may be a "Declining Trustee" as well after having acted as if he has never accepted the trust (*Travis* v. *Illingworth*, 34 L. J. Ch. 664; 2 Dr. & Sm. 344: *Vh.* Lewin, 656). And the better opinion is that the phrase "if any Trustee shall *refuse* or *decline*" includes also one who disclaims (Lewin, 656; *Sv.* Ib. 647, 648). *Cp.* Continuing Trustee.

It has been held that a payment of the trust money into Court under the Trustee Relief Act, stamps the trustee with the character of a "Refusing or Declining Trustee" (Lewin, 656, citing *Re Williams*, 4 K. & J. 87); *Va.* Retiring Trustee.

DECORATIVE REPAIR.—*V.* Tenantable Repair.

DEDUCE.—"If we are to examine the word critically, it is quite clear that when you speak of deducing a title, as meaning to express either the delivery of the abstract or showing the deeds, it is not altogether an appropriate expression or strictly correct. *The deducing the Title*;—the appropriate use of that expression would be this: I deduce my title from my great-grandfather; I do not deduce my title by sending you a document or by showing you the deeds. By sending you the abstract and showing you the deeds, I show you *how* I deduce my title; but according to the strict meaning of the words 'Deducing the Title,' it is stating from whom or from what source the party draws forth his title" (per Kindersley, V.-C., *Oakden* v. *Pike*, 34 L. J. Ch. 622; 13 W. R. 673). *V.* Abstract.

The *ad val.* fee to Solicitors for "Deducing Title," and perusing and completing conveyance (Sch. 1, Part 1, Remn. Ord.) is payable if those three things are done, although the Solicitor may not have prepared the contract (per Fry, L. J., *Re Lacey,* 53 L. J. Ch. 289; 25 Ch. D. 301; 32 W. R. 233; 49 L. T. 755). There is no "Deducing Title" where purchaser gives notice that he requires no Abstract and accepts the vendor's title (*Re Lacey,* sup.), or where in fact no title is shown to the purchaser (*Re Harris, Powell* v. *Goodale,* 56 L. T. 477; 31 S. J. 365).

Cp. INVESTIGATING TITLE.

DEDUCTIONS.—"The Court always holds that *Income Tax* is not a Deduction" (per Wood, V.-C., *Turner* v. *Mullineux,* 1 J. & H. 334). In a contract touching the payment of taxes charged on premises, the incidence of the Income Tax cannot be shifted, not even in the case of an annuity which is payable "clear of all taxes and assessments" (ss. 73 & 103, 5 & 6 V. c. 35, *A.-G.* v. *Shield,* 28 L. J., Ex. 49; 3 H. & N. 834). But Wills are not mentioned in the sections just mentioned; and therefore in a Will it is competent, by apt words, to exonerate income from Income Tax (*Festing* v. *Taylor,* 32 L. J. Q. B. 41).

There are 2 classes of cases in reference to the question as to when a phrase in a Will giving an annuity without "deduction," will exonerate the annuitant from Income Tax:—

1. When the word "Deduction" is associated and construed with the word "Taxes."

2. When not.

1. A devise of a life interest in real estate accompanied with a direction to the Trustees "to pay and defray all taxes, parliamentary, parochial or otherwise, affecting" the same; held, that the Trustees were bound to pay the Income Tax (*Lovatt* v. *Leeds,* 31 L. J. Ch. 503; 2 Dr. & Sm. 62).

So a rent-charge payable to A. B. "without any deduction or abatement whatsoever on account of any taxes, charges, or assessments, already or to be hereafter taxed, charged, assessed, or imposed on the hereditaments or the said rent-charge, or the said A. B. in respect thereof by the authority of Parliament or otherwise however," is payable free of Income Tax (*Festing* v. *Taylor,* 3 B. & S. 217, 235; 31 L. J. Q. B. 36; 32 Ib. 41; 10 W. R. 246; 11 Ib. 70).

So too of an annuity or clear yearly sum given "free from all deductions in respect of any present or future taxes, charges, assessments, or impositions or other matter, cause, or thing whatsoever" (*Re Bannerman,* 51 L. J. Ch. 449; 21 Ch. D. 105).

So too, Bacon, V.-C., held that a testamentary gift of "a clear annual income" from which "no deduction shall be made for the legacy tax or any other matter, cause, or thing whatsoever," was payable free of Income Tax (*Peareth* v. *Marriott,* 51 L. J. Ch. 821. *V.* however, this case considered *inf.*)

2. But as was observed by Kay, J., in *Gleadow* v. *Leetham* (inf.) in all the three first named cases "the word 'deduction' was construed by the word

'taxes' which was associated with it." It is difficult to understand how that principle, or the case of *Wall* v. *Wall* (inf.) can be reconciled with *Peareth* v. *Marriott* (sup.); for the only mention of taxes in *Peareth* v. *Marriott* was "Legacy Tax," which is scarcely *ejusdem generis* with Income Tax, and was moreover there used in reference not only to the annuity but also to ordinary legacies; whilst in *Wall* v. *Wall*, "Taxes" was the controlling word in the clause. With the exception, however, of *Peareth* v. *Marriott*, the cases on this subject seem well to branch out into the two classes laid down in *Gleadow* v. *Leetham*. When *Peareth* v. *Marriott* went before the Court of Appeal on another point, the determination of which precluded the necessity of deciding the point now under discussion, at the end of his judgment Jessel, M.R., threw out a dictum from which it may be gathered that he considered the words in the Will in that case did *not* exonerate from income tax (52 L. J. Ch. 221; 22 Ch. D. 182). Assuming that dictum to be correct, *Peareth* v. *Marriott* would no longer form an exception, but would range amongst the cases here grouped in Class 2.

In *Wall* v. *Wall* (15 Sim. 513; 16 L. J. Ch. 305) a gift of an annuity to testator's widow "clear of all taxes and deductions," was held not exonerated from income tax, the maxim of the V.-C. being "the thing that is given is the thing that is to pay the tax."

So, too, of an annuity to testator's widow "free from legacy duty and other deductions" (*Sadler* v. *Rickards*, 4 K. & J. 302).

So, too, of an annuity "clear of every deduction," or "clear of legacy duty and every other deduction whatsoever," or "without any deduction for legacy duty or otherwise" (*Lethbridge* v. *Thurlow*, 15 Bea. 334; 21 L. J. Ch. 538).

So, too, of an annuity "payable without any deduction whatsoever" (*Abadam* v. *Abadam*, 33 Bea. 475; 33 L. J., Ch. 593; 12 W. R. 615).

So, too, of an annuity to testator's widow of a "clear yearly sum," "to be paid free from all deductions and abatements whatsoever" (*Gleadow* v. *Leetham*, 22 Ch. D. 269; 52 L. J. Ch. 102).

But an exception to the principle of the cases in Class 2 is where the testator has used the word "deduction" or a similar expression, with an obvious meaning that it should include and exonerate an annuitant from Income Tax, in which case the annuity would be exonerated (*Turner* v. *Mullineux*, sup.; which see explained in *Gleadow* v. *Leetham*, sup.).

Legacy Duty is a Deduction (36 G. 3, c. 52, s. 6): but

Succession Duty is not. And therefore where a person covenanted to pay, within twelve months after his death, £10,000 "free from all deductions whatsoever," only that sum was payable, and the payees, if any-one, had to provide for the Succession Duty (*Re Higgins*, 55 L. J. Ch. 235; 31 Ch. D. 142; 54 L. T. 199; 34 W. R. 81).

As to what expressions will exempt legatees from payment of Legacy Duty, *Vf.* n. (*p*), 1 Jarm. 186, 187; Watson, Eq. 1345, 1346.

"Free from all Deductions whatsoever, except Land Tax," in an Inclosure Act, did not include Corn Rent (*Mitchell* v. *Fordham*, 6 B. & C. 274.)

What are allowable "Deductions" under s. 17, Coal Mines Regulation Act, 1872, 35 & 36 V. c. 76 ; *V. Bourne* v. *Netherseal Co.*, 57 L. J. Q. B. 306 ; 20 Q. B. D. 606 ; 36 W. R. 405 ; 52 J. P. 453 ; affd. 14 App. Ca. 228.

V. TAXES : OUTGOINGS : LEGACY : SPECIFIC.

DEED.—"*'A deed,' factum.* This word (deed) in the understanding of the common law is an instrument written in parchment or paper, whereunto ten things are necessarily incident, viz. First, writing. Secondly, in parchment or paper. Thirdly, a person able to contract. Fourthly, by a sufficient name. Fifthly, a person able to be contracted with. Sixthly, by a sufficient name. Seventhly, a thing to be contracted for. Eighthly, apt words required by law. Ninthly, sealing. And tenthly, delivery. A deed cannot be written upon wood, leather, cloath, or the like, but onely upon parchment or paper, for the writing upon them can be least vitiated, altered, or corrupted" (Co. Litt. 35 b). As to the 9th of the above requirements (Sealing) it would seem that wax or a wafer must be used ; a mere circle enclosing the words "L. S.," or "place for seal," is insufficient (*Re Balkis Co.*, 36 W. R. 392 ; 58 L. T. 300 ; 4 Times Rep. 204). To a Deed Poll, the 5th and 6th of the above requirements would hardly be applicable ; and as to the difference between an Indenture and a Deed Poll, *V.* Co. Litt. 229 a ; and *Vth.* 2 Bla. Com. 295 ; 8 & 9 V. c. 106, s. 1.

"*Deed or Conveyance,*" *e.g.* in a clause prescribing mode of transfer of shares, is probably a synonym for the same thing, so that the transfer would have to be effected by deed (*Hibblewhite* v. *M'Morine*, 6 M. & W. 200 ; 9 L. J. Ex. 217 : *Société Générale de Paris* v. *Walker*, 13 App. Ca. 20).

Deed "*not otherwise charged;*" *V. Clayton* v. *Burtenshaw*, 5 B. & C. 41; 7 Dowl. & Ry. 800 : *Wilson* v. *Smith*, 12 M. & W. 401; 13 L. J. Ex. 113.

"Deed *or Writing;*" *V.* IN WRITING : INSTRUMENT IN WRITING.

DEEMED.—*V. De Beauvoir* v. *Welch*, 7 B. & C. 278.

DEEMED TO BELONG.—*V.* jdgmt. of Coleridge, C. J., *Milnes* v. *Huddersfield*, 53 L. J. Q. B. 12 ; 12 Q. B. D. 443.

DEEMED TO HAVE BEEN SURRENDERED.—S. 23, Bankry. Act, 1869 ; *V. Hill* v. *E. & W. India Dock Co.*, 9 App. Ca. 448 ; 53 L. J. Ch. 842 ; 51 L. T. 163 ; 32 W. R. 925 ; 48 J. P. 788 : and *Vth. Re Cock, Ex p. Shilson*, 20 Q. B. D. 346.

DEFAMATORY MATTER.—*V.* LIBEL.

DEFAULT.—"*Default* is a French word, and *defalta* is legally taken for non-appearance in Court" (Co. Litt. 259 b).

"'Default' would seem to embrace every failure by the defendant to perform his contract unless prevented by superior force over which he had no control, such as stress of weather" (per Fitzgerald, J., *Caffarini* v. *Walker*, 9 Ir. R. C. L. 437), or unless hindered by the plaintiff's non-performance of some condition precedent (*Randall* v. *Thorn*, W. N. (78) 150).

"Default is a purely relative term, just like Negligence. It means nothing more, nothing less, than not doing what is reasonable under the circumstances;—not doing something which you ought to do, having regard to the relations which you occupy towards the other persons interested in the transaction" (per Bowen, L. J., *Re Young & Harston*, 31 Ch. D. 174; 53 L. T. 837; 34 W. R. 84; 50 J. P. 245). There is therefore no longer a "Default," by a Trustee in Bankry (s. 102 (5), Bankry. Act, 1883), in paying money found due from him, after the money is paid, even though it be paid for him by a third party (*Re Tatum, Ex p. Harker*, 5 Times Rep. 574).

V. WILFUL DEFAULT.

"Act, Default, Permission or Sufferance;" *V.* PERMISSION.

"*Wrongful Act or Default*," s. 242, Merchant Shipping Act, 1854, does not include a mere error in judgment (*The Famenoth*, 7 P. D. 207).

A Covenant by a mortgagor for Quiet Enjoyment, "*after* Default," means only that, *before* default, the mortgagee is to rest on his own title as against strangers; and the Stat. of Limitations runs as against the mortgagee from the date of the mortgage (*Doe* d. *Roylance* v. *Lightfoot*, 11 L. J. Ex. 151; 8 M. & W. 553).

"A Covenant for Quiet Enjoyment against persons claiming '*by or through* his Default,' would, it appears, be broken by an entry by parties whose title he had it in his own power to bar;—*e.g.* if he were tenant in tail in possession, and the entry were made by remainderman (*Cavan* v. *Pulteney*, 2 Ves. 544);—and such a covenant has been held to extend to claims in respect of arrears of quit rent, although they accrued due before he acquired the estate (*V. Howes* v. *Brushfield*, 3 East, 491): the decision, however, is disapproved by Ld. St. Leonards (Sug. 602). But the omission by the covenantor to acquire from other parties a valid title, although he knew the defect, is not a 'Neglect or Default' within the meaning of such a covenant (*V. Woodhouse* v. *Jenkins*, 9 Bing. 431; 2 M. & Sc. 599: *Ireland* v. *Bircham*, 2 Sc. 207; 2 Bing. N. C. 90)." Dart, 885; *Va.* Elph. 488–490; 2 Platt, 311: *Vf.* NEGLECT OR DEFAULT.

"Negligence and Default," in a Bill of Lading or Contract for Towage; *V.* NEGLIGENCE.

"In Default of Issue," or "In Default of" objects of preceding limitation; *V.* DIE WITHOUT ISSUE.

V. IN DEFAULT: MAKING DEFAULT: FAILURE.

DEFAULT IN PAYMENT.—*V. Williams* v. *Stern*, W. N. (79) 214: *Thorn* v. *City Rice Mills*, 5 Times Rep. 172: PAYMENT.

DEFEASANCE.—"'*Defeasance,*' *Defeisantia,* is fetched from the French word *defaire, i.e.* to defeat or undoe" (Co. Litt. 236 b). "A Defeasance is a Condition relating to a deed, or to an obligation, recognizance, statute or the like, which being performed by the obligor, or recognisor, the act is disabled and made void as if it had never been done: which differeth from a Condition only in this, that this (a Condition) is always made at the same time and annexed to or inserted in the same deed; but that (a Defeasance) is always made in a deed by itself, and for the most part made after the deed whereunto it hath relation" (Touch. 396; *Vf.* 2 Bl. Com. 327, 342). "As I have always understood, a 'Defeasance' is something which defeats the operation of a deed or document. If it is contained in the same deed it is called a 'Condition'" (per Jessel, M. R., *Re Storey, Ex p. Popplewell,* 52 L. J. Ch. 42; 21 Ch. D. 73; cited with approval by Esher, M. R., *Blaiberg* v. *Beckett,* 56 L. J. Q. B. 36; 18 Q. B. D. 96; 55 L. T. 876; 35 W. R. 34).

Read strictly, the extracts just given from the *Touchstone* and from the jdgmt. of Sir Geo. Jessel, would seem to show that a Defeasance differs only from a Condition in the mode and manner of its creation. But that can hardly be so. A Defeasance defeats or puts an end to an instrument; a Condition restrains or qualifies it. And thus in the case cited, *Ex p. Popplewell,* Lindley, L. J., said: "The agreement,—*i.e.* a parol agreement not to register a Bill of Sale,—was obviously not a Defeasance. Was it a Condition?" A Defeasance therefore may, in the language of the *Touchstone,* be said to be a Condition; but it is a Condition of a special sort,—drastic but narrow in its operation.

A Policy deposited as a collateral security to a Bill of Sale, is not a "Defeasance or Condition" requiring registration under s. 10 (3), Bills of S. Act, 1878 (*Carpenter* v. *Deen,* W. N. (89) 186).

"Defeasance," in the prescribed form of a Bill of Sale (B. of S. Act, 1882), means the putting an end to the security by realizing the goods for the benefit of the mortgagee,—*e.g.* powers of lawful seizure and sale and reasonable appropriation of the proceeds (*Consolidated Credit Corp.* v. *Gosney,* 55 L. J. Q. B. 61; 16 Q. B. D. 24: *Lumley* v. *Simmons,* 55 L. J. Ch. 759; 34 W. R. 759). It "is not strictly a Defeasance, because the stipulation is in the same deed; it means a Condition in the nature of a Defeasance" (per Esher, M. R., *Blaiberg* v. *Beckett,* sup., *wh. Vh.*).

The *Touchstone,* in the passage already cited, says that a Defeasance "is always made *in a Deed* by itself." But it would seem that a Defeasance may be made without a deed. The Defeasance indorsed on a Warrant of Attorney to enter up judgment was generally under hand only (Chitty's Forms, 9 Ed. 490). But it would seem that there cannot be a Defeasance without a separate document (per Esher, M. R., *Blaiberg* v. *Beckett,* sup.). And so in *Ex p. Popplewell* (sup.), the Master of the Rolls said: "The agreement in question was a parol agreement. It cannot therefore be a

Defeasance." But a Condition may be by parol (*Ex p. Southam*, 43 L. J. Bank. 39 ; L. R. 17 Eq. 578).

V. CONDITION.

DEFECT.—" Defects in an estate may be either—

a. *Patent*,—that is, such as may be discovered by ordinary vigilance on the part of a purchaser ; *e.g.* the existence of an open footpath over the property (*Bowles* v. *Round*, 5 Ves. 508), or the ruinous state of buildings (*Grant* v. *Mint*, 9 Coop. 177 : *Keates* v. *Cadogan*, 10 C. B. 591 ; 20 L. J. C. P. 76 ; 16 L. T. O. S. 367) ; or,

b. *Latent*,—that is, such as the greatest attention (Sug. 333) would not enable him to discover ; *e.g.* the existence of defects in a ship's bottom when sold afloat (*V. Mellish* v. *Motteux*, Peake, N. P. 156)." Dart, 101, 102.

Unfitness or inadequacy for the purpose for which it is used is a "*Defect* in the condition" of Machinery within s. 1, Employers' Liability Act, 1880 (43 & 44 V. c. 42), though the machinery may be, in itself, perfect (*Heske* v. *Samuelson*, 53 L. J. Q. B. 45 ; 12 Q. B. D. 30 ; 49 L. T. 474). So is an unsound combination of sound Plant (*Cripps* v. *Judge*, 51 L. T. 182 ; 33 W. R. 35 ; 53 L. J. Q. B. 517 ; 13 Q. B. D. 583 : *Weblin* v. *Ballard*, 55 L. J. Q. B. 395 ; 17 Q. B. D. 122 ; 54 L. T. 532 ; 34 W. R. 455 ; 50 J. P. 597). But not a mere temporary obstruction, *e.g.* a substance negligently placed on a roadway (*McGiffen* v. *Palmer's Ship Building Co.*, 52 L. J. Q. B. 25 ; 10 Q. B. D. 5 : *Thomas* v. *Quartermaine*, 55 L. J. Q. B. 439 ; 17 Q. B. D. 414 ; 55 L. T. 360 ; 34 W. R. 741 : *Pegram* v. *Dixon*, 55 L. J. Q. B. 447) ; nor mere dangerousness when not used with ordinary care (*Walsh* v. *Whiteley*, 57 L. J. Q. B. 586 ; 21 Q. B. D. 371 ; 36 W. R. 876) ; nor insufficient packing of goods on a trolly (*Corcoran* v. *East Surrey Ironworks Co.*, 58 L. J. Q. B. 145).

The omission of the date of an accident from notice of injury under the Employers' Liability Act, 1880, is a "defect *or inaccuracy*" within s. 7 (*Carter* v. *Drysdale*, 53 L. J. Q. B. 557 ; 12 Q. B. D. 91 ; 32 W. R. 171), so also is the omission to state the cause of the injury if such omission be not misleading (*Stone* v. *Hyde*, 51 L. J. Q. B. 452 ; 9 Q. B. D. 76).

V. FORMAL : FAULTS.

DEFENCE.—"'*Defence*' commeth of the word *defendo*" (Co. Litt. 127 b) ; and as applied to a pleading it does not mean a "justification," which is the ordinary signification, but a "denial" (3 Bla. Com. 296, cited in Hargrave's note to Co. Litt. 127 b).

"Any Defence," s. 1, 31 & 32 V. c. 86 ; *V. Pellas* v. *Neptune Mar. Insrce.*, 48 L. J. C. P. 370 ; 5 C. P. D. 34.

DEFENDANT.—Notwithstanding that s. 100, Jud. Act, 1873, enacts that "Defendant," includes a person "served with notice of, or entitled to attend, any proceedings,"—the word does not include a person merely brought in as a Third-Party (*Eden* v. *Weardale Co.*, 54 L. J. Ch. 384; 28 Ch. D. 333; 33 W. R. 241: *Street* v. *Gover*, 46 L. J. Q. B. 582; 2 Q. B. D. 498). But when the Third-Party has been treated as an "Opposite Party" and has been ordered, at plaintiff's instance, to answer Interrogatories, he becomes a Defendant and entitled to an Order to interrogate the Plaintiff under Ord. 31, R. 1 (*Eden* v. *Weardale Co.*, 35 Ch. D. 287): *V.* OPPOSITE PARTY.

DEFINED CHANNEL.—Subterranean waters can only be the subject of riparian rights when flowing in Defined and Known Channels. "Defined," means a contracted and bounded channel, although the course of the stream may be undefined by human knowledge. "Known" means the Knowledge, by reasonable inference, from existing and observed facts in the natural or pre-existing condition of the surface of the ground. "Known" in this rule of law is not synonymous with "Visible," nor is it restricted to knowledge derived from exposure of the channel by excavation (*Black* v. *Ballymena Commrs.*, 17 L. R. Ir. 459).

DEFINITIVE.—"Definitive *Publication*" of an Order of the Charity Commrs., s. 8, 23 & 24 V. c. 136; *V. Ex p. Nicholls*, 34 L. J. Ch. 169.

"Definitive *Sentence;*" *V. Esnouf* v. *A.-G. Jersey*, 52 L. J. P. C. 26; 8 App. Ca. 304.

DEFORCEMENT.—"'*By wrong him deforces.*' *Deforciare* is a word of art, and cannot be expressed by any other word; for it signifieth, to withhold lands or tenements from the right owner" (Co. Litt. 331 b; *Va.* Ib. 277 b).

DEFRAUD.—*V.* INTENT TO DEFRAUD.

DELAY.—"Prosecute without Delay;" *V.* PROSECUTE.

V. WILFUL DELAY.

DELAY IN TRANSIT.—A delay by a carrier in not starting goods on their destination, is a "delay in transit" (*Brown* v. *Manchester S. & L. Ry.*, 51 L. J. Q. B. 599; 53 Ib. 124; 9 Q. B. D. 230; 8 App. Ca. 703: *Vh. Sheridan* v. *Mid. G. W. Ry., Ireland*, 24 L. R. Ir. 146).

DELFS.—"The word 'Delfs' probably means open pits or diggings" (*A.-G. for Isle of Man* v. *Mylchreest*, 48 L. J. P. C. 44; 4 App. Ca. 308).

DELINEATED.—In *Dowling* v. *Pontypool Ry.* (43 L. J. Ch. 761; L. R. 18 Eq. 714) the words "lands delineated upon the deposited plans," in the usual clause for compulsory acquirement of land, were considered at great length; and it was held that they were not limited to lands surrounded by lines on every side, but included lands so sketched, represented or shown that the owners would have notice that their property might be taken.

DELIVER.—*V.* Delivery : Carry Out.

DELIVERED.—Freight, on goods, *e.g.* cotton, at so much per cubic feet "delivered," is to be calculated on the measurement of the goods as put on board, and not when unloaded (*Gibson* v. *Sturge*, 10 Ex. 622 ; 24 L. J. Ex. 121 : *Buckle* v. *Knoop*, 36 L. J. Ex. 223 ; L. R. 2 Ex. 333).

DELIVERED IN EXECUTION.—Land is "actually delivered in execution," within s. 1, 27 & 28 V. c. 112, as soon as a sheriff under an *elegit* delivers it to the execution creditor (*Re Hobson*, 55 L. J. Ch. 754 ; 33 Ch. D. 493 ; 55 L. T. 255 ; 34 W. R. 786 : *Vf. Champneys* v. *Burland*, 19 W. R. 148 ; 23 L. T. 584), or as soon as a Receiver is appointed (*Hatton* v. *Haywood*, 43 L. J. Ch. 372 ; 9 Ch. 229 ; 30 L. T. 279 ; 22 W. R. 356 : *Anglo-Italian Bank* v. *Davies*, 47 L. J. Ch. 833 ; 9 Ch. D. 275 ; 27 W. R. 3 ; 39 L. T. 244 : *Ex p. Evans, Re Watkins*, 49 L. J. Bank. 7 ; 13 Ch. D. 252 ; 41 L. T. 565; 28 W. R. 127 : *Re Pope*, 55 L. J. Q. B. 522 ; 17 Q. B. D. 743 ; 55 L. T. 369 ; 34 W. R. 654, 693). *V.* Seizure.

An equitable leasehold interest cannot be "actually delivered in exon." (*Re Newcastle*, L. R. 8 Eq. 700).

Vh. Dan. Ch. Pr. 932 ; Fisher, 486.

DELIVERY.—The "Delivery" of an *Abstract of Title*, does not need, to make it complete, any offer of the deeds for examination. "An Abstract is delivered whenever a number of sheets of paper (call it what you will) is delivered to the purchaser, which contains, with sufficient clearness and sufficient fulness, the effect of every instrument which constitutes part of the title of the vendor" (per Kindersley, V.-C., *Oakden* v. *Pike*, 34 L. J. Ch. 622 ; 13 W. R. 673. *V.* Abstract).

Delivery of a *Bill of Exchange ; V.* s. 21, Bills of Ex. Act, 1882, and (of a Note) ss. 84, 89, Ib. Speaking generally, "Delivery," of a Bill or Note, "means transfer of possession, actual or constructive, from one person to another" (s. 2, Ib.).

Delivery of a Conveyance ; *V.* Conveyance.

Delivery of *Goods* to a tradesman so as to be exempt from distress ; *V. Clarke* v. *Milwall Dock Co.*, 55 L. J. Q. B. 378 ; 17 Q. B. D. 494 ; 54 L. T. 814 ; 34 W. R. 698 : and as to what is "Delivery" of goods on a Contract for Sale, *V.* Add. C. 948–951 ; Rosc. N. P. 470, 494–509.

"Delivery of a *Will*, means the same as publication ; and consists in executing it in the presence of two witnesses, and declaring it to be your Will. That is sufficient for the execution (by Will) of a Power requiring an instrument '*delivered*'" (per Romilly, M.R., *Smith* v. *Adkins*, 41 L. J. Ch. 628 ; L. R. 14 Eq. 402 : *Va. Mason* v. *Heywood*, 7 L. J. Ch. 145). *V.* Signed, Sealed and Delivered.

DEMAND.—"If a man release to another all maner of demands, this is the best release to him to whom the release is made, that he can have" (Litt. s. 508).

"'*Demand*,' *Demandum*, is a word of art, and in the understanding of the common law is of so large an extent, as no other one word in the law is, unlesse it be *clameum*, whereof Littleton maketh mention, Sect. 445." (Co. Litt. 291 b). But in *Parkins* v. *Hinde* (Cro. Eliz. 161), it was held that a lease by a parson at a rent to include "all Exactions and Demands" did not preclude the lessor from recovering his tithes; and the Court said, "that the words shall discharge the lessee of all rents and services, but not of suit at court, or such things as are not then in demand." *Vf. Stiles* v. *Miller*, Ow. 39; 1 Leon. 300.

V. INCUMBRANCES: ON DEMAND: LAWFULLY DEMANDED.

DEMERIT.—A power to punish according to a person's "Demerit," imports only that he shall be punished in the ordinary course of justice, by Indictment (4 Inst. 171; Dwar. 673).

DEMESNE.—"'Demains,' according to the common speech, are the Lord's chief manor place with the lands thereto belonging; *terræ dominicales*, which he and his ancestors have from time to time kept in their own manual occupation for the maintenance of themselves and their families; and all the parts of a manor, except what is in the hands of freeholders, are said to be demains. Copyhold lands have been accounted demains, because they that are the tenants thereof are judged in law to have no other estate but at the will of the lord; so that it is still reputed to be, in a manner, in the lord's hands; but this word is oftentimes used for distinction between those lands that the lord of the manor hath in his own hands, or in the hands of his lessees demised at a rack-rent, and such other land appertaining to the manor which belongeth to free or copyholders; Bract. lib. 4, tract. 3, c. 9: Fleta, lib. 5, c. 5" (Jacob, Law Dict., where it is said to be derived from *dominium*, and not, as some have supposed, from *de manu*. Cp. the Eng., 'in hand,' and Lat. *in manu* as used in the Civil Law).

"Britton, 205 b (Bk. III. ch. 15), says, 'Demeyne proprement est tenement qe chescun tient severalment en fee.'

"The Demesnes pass by a conveyance of the manor of which they form part (Touch. 92). It is therefore of importance on the sale of a manor to except any lands belonging to the vendor within the manor, which are not intended to be sold, as they may be demesne land.

"Kelham, Dict., gives *Demeigne*, *demenie*, *demeine*, meaning 'own,' a sense in which the word *demesne* (or some other form of the same word) is frequently used in the Year Books and other early documents. Prof. Skeat (Etym. Eng. Dict.) connects it with *dominium*, and says '*demesne*' is a false spelling, probably due to confusion with old Fr. *mesnee*, or *maisnie*, a household" (Elph. 570).

"*In his demesne as of fee*;" as to force of this expression, *V.* Co. Litt. 17 a.

DEMISE.—This word in a Lease implies an absolute covenant by the lessor for title and quiet enjoyment, unless there be an express qualifying covenant (Add. C. 1283 : Woodf. 172, 674, 675 : Dart, 636 : Elph. 422, 424). So also of a parol tenancy (*Bandy* v. *Cartwright*, 22 L. J. Ex. 285 ; 8 Ex. 913 : *Hall* v. *London Brewery*, 31 L. J. Q. B. 257 ; 2 B. & S. 737). But in the case of a lease or letting of Leaseholds this implied contract is limited to the duration of the lessor's interest (*Adams* v. *Gibney*, 6 Bing. 656 : *Penfold* v. *Abbott*, 32 L. J. Q. B. 67 ; 11 W. R. 169 : *Schwartz* v. *Locket*, 34 S. J. 80, 73).

"On the demise of a brewery, with the exclusive privilege of supplying ale, it would seem that no covenant can be implied with respect to such a privilege from the word 'demise'" (Woodf. 176, citing *Hinde* v. *Gray*, 1 M. & G. 195 ; 1 Sc. N. R. 123 ; 9 L. J. C. P. 253).

An instrument is not a Demise, although it contain the usual words of demise, if its contents show that such was not the intention of the parties (*Taylor* v. *Caldwell*, 32 L. J. Q. B. 164 ; 3 B. & S. 826).

DEMOLISH.—"Demolish or Pull Down or Destroy, or Begin to demolish, pull down or destroy," s. 11, 24 & 25 V. c. 97 ;—this phrase means a total destruction, "or the commencement of a demolition or destruction, the purpose being to effect a complete demolition and destruction if there is no interruption" (per Lindley, J., *Drake* v. *Foottit*, 50 L. J. M. C. 143 ; 7 Q. B. D. 201,—citing *R.* v. *Thomas*, 4 C. & P. 237 : *R.* v. *Price*, 5 Ib. 510 : *R.* v. *Batt*, 6 Ib. 329 : *R.* v. *Howell*, 9 Ib. 437 : *R.* v. *Adams*, Car. & M. 299). And a like meaning is to be given to "feloniously demolished, pulled down or destroyed, wholly or in part," in s. 2, 7 & 8 G. 4, c. 31 (*Drake* v. *Foottit*, sup.). A substantial destruction is a demolition, even though a small part of the building be left uninjured (*R.* v. *Langford*, Car. & M. 602) ; and that it was effected by fire is immaterial (*R.* v. *Harris*, Ib. 661).

V. DESTROY.

DEMURRAGE DAYS.—"Days are sometimes given in favour of the charterer which are called 'Demurrage Days.' Those are days beyond the 'Lay Days,' but during which the amount that he has to pay for the use of the ship is a fixed sum" (per Esher, M.R., *Neilsen* v. *Wait*, 16 Q. B. D. 70 ; 55 L. J. Q. B. 89).

V. DAYS.

DENARIATA TERRÆ.—An acre (Elph. 572, citing Spelm. *Fardella*) ; *Sv*. Elph. 598.

DENE.—"Some say that *dene* or *denne*, whereof *dena* commeth, is properly a valley or dale. *Dena silvæ*, and the like, as *drofden*, or *drufden*, or *druden*, signifieth a thicket of wood in a valley ; for *druf*, or *dru*, signifieth a thicket of wood, and is often mentioned in Domesday. And sometimes *dena* or *denna* signifieth, as *villa* and *denne*, a towne" (Co. Litt. 4 b: *V.* COMBE).

DENIZEN.—*V.* Co. Litt. 129 a.

DENOMINATIONAL FOUNDATION.—An endowed school having no instrument of foundation, or statutes or written regulations, is not a Denominational Foundation within 32 & 33 V. c. 56, s. 19, or 36 & 37 V. c. 87, s. 7 (*St. Leonards Trustees* v. *Charity Commrs.*, 54 L. J. P. C. 30; 10 App. Ca. 304).

DEODAND.—"'Whatever personal chattel is the immediate occasion of the death of any reasonable creature, which is forfeited to the King, to be applied to pious uses, and distributed in alms by his high almoner' (Jacob, Law Dict.: *V.* Spelm.; Chitty, Prerog. 153; 3rd Inst. cap. 9). For two curious examples in which a horse and a tree were deodands, *V.* Y. B. 30 & 31 Edw. I.; Record Publ. App. II., 528, 529" (Elph. 572).

DEPART.—"To Depart," in a Marine Insurance, means that "the ship should not only have broken ground on the day named, but that she should then be out of the port, or at sea" (1 Maude & P. 502, citing *Moir* v. *Royal Exchange Assrce.*, 4 Camp. 84; 3 M. & S. 461; 6 Taunt. 241). In *Van Baggen* v. *Baines* (23 L. J. Ex. 213; 9 Ex. 523), the case just cited was contrasted with that then under consideration in which the word used was LEAVE.

"Departs *out of England*," s. 4 (d), Bankry. Act, 1883; *V.* Yate Lee, 44, 45; Wms. Bank. 18; Robson, 139, 140; Baldwin, 57.

"Departs *from his dwelling-house*," s. 4 (d), Bankry. Act, 1883; *V.* Yate Lee, 46; Wms. Bank. 19; Robson, 140; Baldwin, 58.

DEPART THIS LIFE.—*V.* DIE.

DEPARTING UNITED KINGDOM.—A disqualification of Trustees on "departing the United Kingdom from whatever cause or motive, or under whatsoever circumstances," does not apply to a *temporary* absence abroad (*Re Moravian Socy.*, 26 Bea. 101; 4 Jur. N. S. 703).

DEPARTURE.—"A departure in pleading is said to be when the second plea containeth matter not pursuant to his former, and which fortifieth not the same, and thereupon it is called *decessus*, because he departeth from his former plea" (Co. Litt. 304 a).

DEPENDING.—*V.* PENDING.

DEPOSIT.—A "Deposit" is equivalent to an earnest, and is forfeited on breach by depositor of his agreement; even when the word is found in the following common collocation,—"as a Deposit and in part payment of the purchase money;" so that, on the contract going off, by reason of such breach, the deposit cannot be recovered back, unless there be circumstances which render it inequitable for the deposit to be retained by the depositee (*Howe* v. *Smith,* 53 L. J. Ch. 1055; 27 Ch. D. 89, which leaves *Palmer* v. *Temple,* 8 L. J. Q. B. 179; 9 A. & E. 508, of but little practical value. *Vf. Soper* v. *Arnold,* 14 App. Ca. 429). *V.* jdgmt. of Fry, L.J., in *Howe* v. *Smith,* for history and meaning of "Deposit."

V. LOAN.

DEPOSITED.—*V.* EXPOSE.

DEPRAVE.—"Common and notorious Depravers of the Book of Common Prayer," Canons 1603, No. 27; "The terms 'deprave or depraver,' in their more ancient signification, are now little used; but their meaning in the 16th century may be well collected from 1 Ed. 6, c. 1, where we find these expressions applied to the sacrament of the Holy Communion:—'Whatever person shall deprave, dispise or contempne the saide moste blessed Sacrament by any contemptuouse wordes, or by anny wordes of depravinge, dispisinge or reviling, shall suffer imprisonment'" (per Cairns, L. C., delivering jdgmt. of P. C. in *Jenkins* v. *Cook,* 45 L. J. P. C. 8; 1 P. D. 80). It was in that case held that a person who had published "Selections from the Old and New Testament," (omitting chapters and parts of chapters), as appropriate for family devotions, was not a "Depraver" of the Common Prayer within the Canon. *V.* COMMON AND NOTORIOUS.

DEPRIVED.—*V.* RELINQUISH.

DERIVATIVE LEASE.—As to whether "Derivative Lease" and "Underlease" are convertible terms; *V. Brumfit* v. *Morton,* 3 Jur. N. S. 1198; 30 L. T. O. S. 98.

V. UNDERLEASE.

DERIVE.—In determining that the Sucn. Dy. Act (*V.* SUCCESSION) does not apply to a *bonâ fide* sale, the vendor not being a Predecessor, from whom the interest of the purchaser "is derived" (*V.* s. 2), Jessel, M.R., said:—"How can you say that the interest of the purchaser is 'derived from' the vendor? He does not derive his interest from the vendor; he derives it from his own money which bought the property. You would not say, if you were talking of a horse you had bought, that you derived your interest in that horse from the horsedealer. You would say you bought it with your money" (*Fryer* v. *Morland,* 45 L. J. Ch. 820; 3 Ch. D. 675). In *Zetland* v. *Ld. Advocate* (3 App. Ca. 515), Ld. Hatherley said that "derived," in the section cited, "has somewhat of a metaphorical aspect. You have to say that the donor points to so many fountain heads, but he leaves it to the law to say which is to 'derive' the title to the interest under the settlement."

DESCENDANTS.—"'Descendants' mean children and their children and their children to any degree, and it is difficult to conceive any context by which the word 'Descendants' could be limited to mean children only" (per James, L. J., *Ralph* v. *Carrick*, 48 L. J. Ch. 808; 11 Ch. D. 873): and per Brett, L. J., in the same case,—"The *primâ facie* meaning of 'Descendants,' in ordinary parlance, is all descendants of any degree, and not only children, and I know of no authority for saying that in any legal document the word 'Descendants' is, merely because it is in collocation with the word 'parent,' to have any other meaning than it has in ordinary parlance." "Descendants" is, therefore, not in all respects an exact equivalent for ISSUE; though, generally speaking, and when unaffected by the context, it is so (2 Jarm. 101; *Va. Re Eyton*, W.N. (76) 142).

Notwithstanding the strong observation of James, L. J., just quoted, it had been previously held, under a bequest to "Descendants" of A., "in such proportions as each may be entitled," under the Statute of Distributions, that a child of A. took in exclusion of grand-children, "descendants" being there controlled by a context, a thing of which the L. J. thought it difficult to conceive (*Smith* v. *Pepper*, 27 Bea. 86, which case was not cited in *Ralph* v. *Carrick*. *Va. Craik* v. *Lamb*, 14 L. J. Ch. 84; 1 Coll. 489).

Vf. 2 Jarm. 98–100; Wms. Exs. 1117; Chitty, Eq. Ind. 7686: NAME.

DESCENT.—"'*Discents.*' This word commeth of the Latine word *discendere, id est, ex loco superiore in inferiorem movere*; and in legall understanding it is taken when land, &c., after the death of the ancestor, is cast, by course of law upon the heire, which the law calleth a discent" (Co. Litt. 237 a).

"Descent" is not always used in its strict legal sense; it may mean "a single step in the scale of genealogy" (*Bickley* v. *Bickley*, L. R. 4 Eq. 216; 36 L. J. Ch. 817).

DESCRIBED.—*V.* AS DESCRIBED.

DESCRIPTION.—*V.* NATURE.

The "Description" of a person is that which tells what he is; and where a statute requires that the name, place of abode, and description of a person be given, and only the name and place of abode is given, there is a total omission of the "description," not an "inaccurate description" (*R.* v. *Tugwell*, L. R. 3 Q. B. 704; 37 L. J. Q. B. 275; 9 B. & S. 367).

"To limit description of his workmen;" *V.* THREAT.

DESERTED: DESERTION: DESERT.—These words in the Matrimonial Causes Act, 1857 (20 & 21 V. c. 85: and *V.* ss. 16, 27, 31), mean continual absence from cohabitation, contrary to the will or without the consent of the party charging it, and without reasonable cause (*Ward* v. *Ward*, 27 L. J. P. & M. 63 ; 1 Sw. & Tr. 185 : *Cudlipp* v. *Cudlipp*, 27 L. J. P. & M. 64 : *Thompson* v. *Thompson*, Ib. 65 : *Haviland* v. *Haviland*, 32 L. J. P. M. & A. 65 : *Williams* v. *Williams*, 33 L. J. P. M. & A. 172 ; 3 Sw. & Tr. 547 : *Yeatman* v. *Yeatman*, 37 L. J. P. M. & A. 37 ; 1 P. & D. 489) : and there is no such consent if the separation be caused by ill-treatment (*Graves* v. *Graves*, 33 L. J. P. M. & A. 66 ; 3 Sw. & Tr. 350), or adultery (*Farmer* v. *Farmer*, 53 L. J. P. D. & A. 113 ; 9 P. D. 245 : *Garcia* v. *Garcia*, 57 L. J. P. D. & A. 101 ; 13 P. D. 216 ; 59 L. T. 524 ; 52 J. P. 584), or be obtained by fraud (*Crabb* v. *Crabb*, 37 L. J. P. & M. 42; 1 P. & D. 601; 16 W. R. 650); but merely living with another woman, and introducing her as wife, but without ceasing cohabitation with the real wife, is not desertion by a husband (*Ward* v. *Ward*, sup. : *Farmer* v. *Farmer*, sup.). So absconding, with the wife's consent, to escape a criminal prosecution, is not Desertion (*Townsend* v. *Townsend*, 42 L. J. P. & M. 71 ; L. R. 9 P. & D. 129) ; *secus*, where there is no such consent (*Drew* v. *Drew*, 57 L. J. P. D. & A. 64 ; 13 P. D. 97 ; 58 L. T. 923 ; 36 W. R. 927).

When husband and wife are living separate under an agreement to separate, there is no Desertion (*Crabb* v. *Crabb*, sup.: *Parkinson* v. *Parkinson*, 39 L. J. P. & M. 14 ; 2 P. & D. 25) ; but it must be a perfected agreement (*Nott* v. *Nott*, 36 L. J. P. & M. 10 ; 1 P. & D. 251), and with the real concurrence of the wife, and with some justification (*Dagg* v. *Dagg*, 51 L. J. P. D. & A. 19 ; 7 P. D. 17 ; 30 W. R. 431). Non-payment of an allowance under such an agreement will not convert separation into desertion (*Pape* v. *Pape*, 20 Q. B. D. 76 ; 57 L. J. M. C. 3 ; 36 W. R. 125). This last case was on "deserted," as used in s. 1, 49 & 50 V. c. 52 ; and Stephen, J., said :—"'Desertion,' at any rate, implies that the parties were living together at the time when the desertion took place."

Non-compliance with decree for Restitution of Conjugal Rights constitutes Desertion (47 & 48 V. c. 68 : *Vth. Bigwood* v. *Bigwood*, 57 L. J. P. D. & A. 80 ; 13 P. D. 89 ; 58 L. T. 642 ; 36 W. R. 928).

A *bonâ fide* offer to resume cohabitation will put an end to "Desertion," if made before the statutory two years have expired, otherwise not (*Cargill* v. *Cargill*, 27 L. J. P. & M. 69 : *Harris* v. *Harris*, 31 Ib. 6 ; 15 L. T. 448 : *Basing* v. *Basing*, 33 L. J. P. M. & A. 150 ; 3 Sw. & Tr. 516).

It was at one time suggested that "deserted," in s. 31, 20 & 21 V. c. 85, meant something equivalent to leaving the other party destitute (*Haswell* v. *Haswell*, 29 L. J. P. & M. 21 ; 1 Sw. & Tr. 502). That was obviously unsound, and has not been supported (*Yeatman* v. *Yeatman*, sup.).

By s. 21, 20 & 21 V. c. 85, "a wife deserted," in order to obtain a Magistrate's Protection Order, must be one who "is maintaining herself by her own industry or property." Desertion there means "not only that the husband has absented himself, but has left his wife unprovided for, and such desertion must continue at the time of making the Order ; and a *bonâ fide* offer of the husband to return and provide for his wife, would take away her right to have such an order made" (per J. O., in *Cargill* v. *Cargill*, sup.), even (as it should seem) though the separation had been caused by the husband's cruelty (*Vf. Henty* v. *Henty*, 33 L. T. 263 : *Stickland* v. *Stickland*, 25 W. R. 114).

"Desertion," s. 1, 49 & 50 V. c. 52, is a question of fact for the Justices (*R.* v. *Birwistle*, 58 L. J. M. C. 158).

But "Desertion" of a wife, in the statutes relating to Poor Law Removal, means no more than living apart. The meaning of the word in s. 3, 24 & 25 V. c. 55, "is that where the wife has been residing in a different place from her husband for a prolonged period, she shall be considered for poor law purposes as not being bound by the marriage tie, and as living apart" (per Cockburn, C.J., *R.* v. *Maidstone*, 49 L. J. M. C. 26 ; 5 Q. B. D. 31). Accordingly a married woman is none the less "deserted" by her husband within that section, because he allows and pays her 2s. 6d. a week (*R.* v. *St. Mary, Islington*, 39 L. J. M. C. 137 ; L. R. 5 Q. B. 445 ; 34 J. P. 646) ; nor even if the separation be caused by the wife's adultery (*R.* v. *Maidstone*, sup.), unless she take herself off in her husband's absence and without his consent (*R.* v. *Cookham*, 9 Q. B. D. 522).

To "Desert" a Ship "is used in the statute (s. 9, 7 & 8 V. c. 112) in a bad sense, and means abandoning the service without sufficient cause" (per Crompton, J., *Edward* v. *Trevellick*, 24 L. J. Q. B. 12 ; 4 E. & B. 59). *Vf. McDonald* v. *Jopling*, 7 L. J. Ex. 220 ; 4 M. & W. 285.

DESERVING.—A bequest to "Deserving" objects is bad, as being too indefinite ; but one to "Charitable and Deserving" objects is good, the sentence being governed by "Charitable" (*Re Sutton*, 54 L. J. Ch. 613 ; 28 Ch. D. 464 ; 33 W. R. 519). *Vf.*, as to "Deserving," *Re Wall, Pomeroy* v. *Willway*, 42 Ch. D. 510 ; 61 L. T. 357.

V. Relations.

DESIGN.—*V.* New Design.

DESIRABLE.—*V.* Opinion.

DESIRE.—*V.* Precatory Trust.

If a contracting party "shall desire" to terminate contract ; *V. Sun Insrce.* v. *Hart*, 58 L. J. P. C. 69.

DESIROUS OF BEING DISCHARGED.—Trustees who have paid their trust fund into Court thereby retire (*V.* Retiring Trustee), and cannot afterwards be treated as "desirous of being discharged," so as to execute a power of appointing new Trustees (*Re Bailey*, 3 W. R. 31).

DESIROUS OF WORKING.—An owner "desirous of working" minerals, s. 78, Ry. C. C. Act, 1845, means one who is really so desirous (*Mid. Ry.* v. *Robinson*, 6 Times Rep. 100 ; 37 Ch. D. 386 ; 57 L. J. Ch. 441).

DESPATCH. — *V.* POSSIBLE : PROMPT DESPATCH : USUAL DESPATCH : DUE DILIGENCE.

DESTINATION.—"Now what is meant by sending goods 'to their Destination?' It seems to me that it means sending them to a particular place, to a particular person who is to receive them there ; and not, sending them to a particular place without saying to whom" (per Brett, M. R., *Ex p. Miles*, 15 Q. B. D. 43).

DESTROY : DESTROYING.—The phrase "otherwise destroying" a Will so as to revoke it (s. 20, 1 V. c. 26), has to be read as *ejusdem generis* with the words immediately preceding it,—"burning, tearing,"—that is, there must be "destruction, in the proper sense of the word, of the substance or contents of the Will, or, at least, *complete* effacement of the writing, *e.g.*, by pasting over it a blank paper ; and not a 'destroying' in a secondary sense, as by cancelling or incomplete obliteration. These, unless they prevent the words, as originally written, from being apparent, —that is, apparent by looking at the Will itself,—are plainly excluded by the Statute. Glasses have been used for discovering what the words obliterated originally were" (1 Jarm. 142. *Vh. Cheese* v. *Lovejoy*, cited REVOKE : *Margary* v. *Robinson*, 56 L. J. P. D. & A. 44).

V. DEMOLISH : SPOIL.

DESTRUCTIVE.—Boiling Water held to be "Destructive *Matter*" within s. 5, 1 V. c. 85, repealed (*R.* v. *Crawford*, 2 C. & K. 129) ; but not a "Destructive *Substance*" within s. 29, 24 & 25 V. c. 100 (*R.* v. *Martin*, 62 Law Times, 372).

DETAIL.—*V.* "NATURE."

DETAIN.—"Detain ;" in Detinue, means that the defendant withholds the goods, and prevents plaintiff from having possession of them (*Clements* v. *Flight*, 16 M. & W. 42 ; 16 L. J. Ex. 11).

DETAINER.—*V.* FORCIBLE DETAINER.

DETAINMENTS.—*V.* RESTRAINTS OF KINGS.

DETENTION.—Hostile "Detention," in a Marine Insurance, is equivalent to SEIZURE (*Johnston* v. *Hogg*, 52 L. J. Q. B. 343 ; 10 Q. B. D. 432).

Where a contract for carriage exempts the carrier from damage by reason of "detention" of the goods, that means something which prevents the carrier from delivering at the proper time; and does not cover a wrongful detention by him (*Gordon* v. *G. W. Ry.*, 51 L. J. Q. B. 58; 8 Q. B. D. 44).

"Reasonable and Probable Cause" for detaining a Ship; *V.* REASONABLE CAUSE.

DETENTION BY DEFAULT.—*V.* DEFAULT.

DETENTION BY ICE: FROST.—"Detention by Ice not to be reckoned as laying days," in a Charter Party, means prevention of "access to the ship by reason of ice from any one of the storing places from which merchandize is to be conveyed direct to the ship" (per Willes, J., and adopted by Ex. Cham. in *Hudson* v. *Eve*, L. R. 3 Q. B. 415): and therefore where a ship was to proceed to Sulinah and there load grain or seed with a provision as to laying days for loading, "detention by ice not to be reckoned as laying days," and the port itself and sea immediately outside were free from ice, yet the River Danube, down which the grain had to be brought, was impeded with ice; it was held that there was a "detention by ice" within the meaning of the exception (*Hudson* v. *Eve*, 36 L. J. Q. B. 273; 37 Ib. 166; 8 B. & S. 639; 9 Ib. 480; L. R. 3 Q. B. 412). But *Hudson* v. *Eve* rather lays down an exception than a general rule; for the general rule is, that the conveyance of goods to the place of loading is no part of the loading. Accordingly where a ship had to proceed to Cardiff East Bute Dock, and there load, "detention by frost," &c., not to be reckoned as lay days; and the freighters' agents were prevented from getting the goods to the East Bute Dock by reason of the freezing over of the canal from their wharf to that dock, it was held that this time was to be reckoned as lay days (*Kay* v. *Field*, 52 L. J. Q. B. 17; 10 Q. B. D. 241: *Va. Grant* v. *Coverdale*, 53 L. J. Q. B. 462; 9 App. Ca. 470).

DETERMINABLE FUTURE TIME.—A Bill of Ex. (s. 11), or Promissory Note (s. 89), is payable at a "Determinable Future Time," within the Bills of Ex. Act, 1882, "which is expressed to be payable—

(1) At a fixed period after date or sight.

(2) On or at a fixed period after the occurrence of a specified event which is certain to happen, though the time of happening may be uncertain."

DETERMINATION.—"Determination" of an *Action; V. Burnaby* v. *Earle*, 43 L. J. Q. B. 209; L. R. 9 Q. B. 490.

"Determination" of a *Complaint*, s. 3, 20 & 21 V. c. 43; *V. Diss* v. *Aldrich*, 46 L. J. M. C. 183; 2 Q. B. D. 179; 41 J. P. 132: *West* v. *Potts*, 34 J. P. 760. *Vf.* Summary Jur. Act, 1879, 42 & 43 V. c. 49, s. 33.

The "Determination" of a *Term or Estate* is the same thing as its "Termination;" and does not mean premature extinction, but the coming to an end in any way whatever (*St. Aubyn* v. *St. Aubyn*, 30 L. J. Ch. 920; 1 Dr. & Sm. 611). To the same effect is the statutory interpretation of "Determination of Tenancy" for the purposes of the Agricultural Holdings Act, 1883, which by s. 61, "means the cesser of a contract of tenancy by reason of effluxion of time, or from any other cause;" and where a custom authorises the retention of part of a farm for a period beyond the prescribed term of letting, the "Determination of the Tenancy," quâ that Act, is not accomplished till that further period has expired (*R.* v. *Maconochie*, 34 S. J. 64. *Vh. Beavan* v. *Delahay*, 1 H. Bl. 5: *Knight* v. *Bennett*, 3 Bing. 366, 367).

"Sooner Determination," may be rejected as insensible; *V.* TERM.

DETERMINE.—*V.* HEAR.

DEVIATION.—In a Marine Insurance or Charter Party "Deviation" is any unexcused departure from the usual course of proceeding towards the terminus of the voyage (1 Arn. 446).

DEVICE.—To catch fish; *V.* PLACE.

DEVISE.—"The words 'Devise' and 'Bequeath' are terms of known use in our law, the former from Glanville's time and earlier. In their ordinary sense they signify the declaration of a man's will concerning the succession to *his own property* after his death. Such a 'devise' or 'bequest' operates (on subjects which either by common, or statute law, or custom can so be disposed of) by virtue of the Will, and of that alone. On the other hand, an Appointment under a *Limited* Power operates by virtue of the instrument creating the power; the execution, when valid, is read into, and derives its force from, that instrument. If the execution of the power must, or may, be by Will, it must be a Will duly executed and attested as such according to law, and the word 'Will' in the statute (Wills Act, 1 V. c. 26) extends to such a testamentary appointment. But, that condition being complied with, the execution operates in the same way after the death of the appointor as if the instrument were not testamentary. Before the Wills Act, the law as to *General* Powers was the same. 'A mere general devise or bequest, however unlimited in terms, would not comprehend the subject of the power unless it referred to the subject or the power itself, or generally to any power vested in the testator' (1 Sug. on Pow. 6 Ed. 385).

"It follows, we think, legitimately from these premises that the words 'devise or bequest' when used in the Wills Act without any indication of any intention that they should apply to Appointments under Powers, ought, *primâ facie*, to be understood in their ordinary sense, namely, as referring to a gift by Will of the testator's *own* property and nothing else" (per Selborne, L. C., in delivering the jdgmt. of the Court of App. in *Holyland* v. *Lewin*, 53 L. J. Ch. 530; 26 Ch. D. 266). It was accordingly held in that case (in approval of the rule in *Griffiths* v. *Gale*, 13 L. J. Ch. 286;

12 Sim. 354) that a testamentary exercise of a Limited Power of Appointment was not saved (by s. 33, Wills Act) from lapsing as regards children or issue of the appointor dying in his or her lifetime; but the Court pointed out that the case would have been different had the power been a general one, because s. 27 of the Wills Act makes the subject of a testamentary execution of a General Power part of the property of the testator. *Vf. Eccles* v. *Cheyne,* 2 K. & J. 676: *Freme* v. *Clement,* 50 L. J. Ch. 801; 18 Ch. D. 499: but *Freme* v. *Clement* was disapproved in *Holyland* v. *Lewin,* 26 Ch. D. 266.

"A Devise, or Legacy, is where a man in his testament doth give anything to another; the first of these terms is properly applied to the gift of lands and the last to the gift of goods or chattels; and therefore a devise is strictly said to be where a man in his testament doth give his lands to another after his decease; and a legacy is said to be where a man in his testament doth give any chattel to another to have after the death of the testator; but the word is promiscuously applied to the one and to the other" (Touch. 400. *Note.*—The word "Bequeath" does not seem to have been in use when the Touch. was written; and where we should now write "Bequest," the Touch. gives the word "Legacy"). It is still true that "Devise" and "Bequeath" may be used promiscuously, and that if a testator "Devise" goods they will pass, and so he may "Bequeath" lands or houses: that is to say, where the property dealt with is clear the intention will not be defeated because the wrong verb is used (*V. Whicker* v. *Hume,* 14 Bea. 518; 1 D. G. M. & G. 506; 21 L. J. Ch. 406: *Gyett* v. *Williams,* 2 J. & H. 436). But when the subject of the gift is expressed ambiguously the meaning will be aided by the verb. Thus, where a testator "gave, *devised,* and bequeathed" everything to A. for life, and after her death "gave, *devised* and bequeathed the whole of his *effects* which might be then remaining" to B., it was held that the realty passed (*Phillips* v. *Beal,* 25 Bea. 25: *Sv. Camfield* v. *Gilbert,* 3 East, 516). And on the other hand, where the testator "gave, *bequeathed* and disposed of" all his residuary "estate, effects, and property,"—words large enough to comprise realty,—yet there it was held that the realty did not pass, and in arriving at that conclusion the Court (*int. al.*) strongly relied on the absence of the word "Devise" from the operative words (*Coard* v. *Holderness,* 24 L. J. Ch. 388; 20 Bea. 147; *V.* 1 Jarm. 736, 737).

V. BEQUEATHED.

DEVISED.—*V.* AS DEVISED.

DEVOLUTION.—"Devolution of estate by operation of law," Ord. 17, R. 2, R. S. C.; *V. Wallis* v. *Smith,* 51 L. J. Ch. 577; 46 L. T. 473.

"Devolution by Law," in Sucn. Dy. Act; *V.* DISPOSITION.

DEVOLVE.—"To 'devolve' means to pass from a person dying to a person living ; the etymology of the word shews its meaning" (per Leach, M. R., *Parr* v. *Parr*, 1 Myl. & K. 648 ; 2 L. J. Ch. 167). *Vh. Swan* v. *Holmes*, 19 Bea. 476.

V. DEVOLUTION.

"Devolve upon ;" *V.* ACQUIRE.

DIE.—In the leading case of *Edwards* v. *Edwards* (21 L. J. Ch. 324 ; 15 Bea. 357), Romilly, M. R., propounded, from the prior decisions, four rules of construction for determining the meaning of a gift over in case of death :—

1. Where there is an immediate gift,—(as to a future gift, *V.* 2 Jarm. 756),—to A., and if he shall die, then to B.,—that means, if A. shall die during the life of the testator (*Va. Re Luddy,* 53 L. J. Ch. 21 ; 25 Ch. D. 394 : *Re Ross,* 32 S. J. 289) : and the consequence is, that on surviving the testator, A. will take an absolute interest and not a life interest with remainder to B.

2. Where there is a gift to A., and if he shall die *without leaving a child* or *without leaving issue* (as the case may be) then to B.,—that means, if *at any time,* whether before or after the death of the testator, A. shall die without leaving a child, &c., the gift over to B. will take effect.

3. Where there is a gift to A. for life, and after his decease to B., and if B. shall die, then to C.,—that means, if B. shall die before the death of A. the tenant for life, the gift over to C. will take effect, otherwise not : and if the tenant for life and B. should have died in testator's lifetime, then it would seem to follow that the gift over to C. will take effect on the death of the testator.

4. Where there is a gift to A. for life, and after his decease to B., and if B. shall die *without leaving a child,* or *without leaving issue* (as the case may be) then to C.,—that also means, if B. shall die before the death of A. the tenant for life, the gift over to C. will take effect, otherwise not.

These canons of construction, after having been followed for upwards of 20 years in a number of cases and pronounced by so high an authority as Lord Justice James as "very simple, intelligible and beneficial," came under review in the H. L. in *O'Mahoney* v. *Burdett* (44 L. J. Ch. 56 n. ; L. R. 7 H. L. 388), and in *Ingram* v. *Soutten* (44 L. J. Ch. 55 ; L. R. 7 H. L. 408). Their Lordships practically confirmed the first three propositions of *Edwards* v. *Edwards,* but disapproved of the fourth. Lord Hatherley in *O'Mahoney* v. *Burdett,* said,—"It seems to me that there is no reason for distinguishing the fourth rule from the second." That sentence, when the reasoning is closely followed, seems to sum up the *ratio decidendi* of the two cases in the House of Lords, with the result that the 2nd and 4th Rules of *Edwards* v. *Edwards* should be blended together into the following proposition :—

Where there is a gift to A. (whether preceded or not by a life estate) and if he shall die *without leaving a child* or *without leaving issue* (as the case may be), then to B.,—that means, if, *at any time*, A. should die without leaving a child, &c., the gift over to B. will take effect.

Vf. Olivant v. *Wright*, 1 Ch. D. 346 : *Besant* v. *Cox*, 6 Ch. D. 604 : *Re Hayward*, 51 L. J. Ch. 513 ; 19 Ch. D. 470 : *Re Parry*, 55 L. J. Ch. 237 ; 31 Ch. D. 130 ; 54 L. T. 229 ; 34 W. R. 353 ; and as to Rule No. 1, *Re Elliott*, 22 Ch. D. 236 ; 52 L. J. Ch. 222 ; Wms. Exs. 1266 ; 2 Jarm. ch. 48 ; and as to the Rules relating to words referring to Death coupled with a contingency, 2 Jarm. ch. 49.

As to supplying the complement to such elliptical phrases as "If I die," "If A. dies," or "In the event of A. dying ;" *V. Abbott* v. *Middleton*, 28 L. J. Ch. 110 ; 7 H. L. Ca. 68 ; 21 Bea. 143 : *Eastwood* v. *Lockwood*, 36 L. J. Ch. 573 ; L. R. 3 Eq. 487 : 1 Jarm. 488 ; 2 Ib. 21.

In the event of A. (a woman) "*not marrying or dying*," means if she shall die unmarried (*Hawkins* v. *Hawkins*, 4 L. J. Ch. 9).

"Dying," held not to import futurity ; *secus*, of "shall die" (*Coulthurst* v. *Carter*, 15 Bea. 421 ; 21 L. J. Ch. 555).

V. Dead.

DIE BY HIS OWN HANDS.—A life policy contained a proviso avoiding it (*int. al.*) in case the assured should "die by his own hands." The assured threw himself into the Thames and was drowned. The jury found that he intended to destroy his life and knew that he should thereby do so, but that, at the time of committing the act, he was not capable of judging between right and wrong :—Held, that he had died by his own hands, and that the policy was avoided (*Borrodaile* v. *Hunter*, 12 L. J. C. P. 225 ; 5 M. & G. 639).

V. Suicide.

DIE WITHOUT CHILDREN.—Read "without having had a child" (*Re Hambleton*, W. N. (84) 157).

DIE WITHOUT HAVING BEEN MARRIED.—*V.* Without having been married.

DIE WITHOUT ISSUE.—"In any devise, or bequest, of Real or Personal Estate the words '*Die without Issue*,' or '*Die without leaving Issue*,' or '*Have no Issue*,' or any other words which may import either a want, or failure, of Issue of any person in his lifetime or at the time of his death, or an indefinite failure of his issue, shall be construed to *mean a want or failure of issue in the lifetime or at the time of the death of such person ;* and not an indefinite failure of his issue, unless a contrary intention shall appear by the Will, by reason of such person having a prior estate tail, or of a preceding gift being, without any implication arising from such words, a limitation of an estate tail to such person or issue, or otherwise : Provided that this Act shall not extend to cases where such words as aforesaid import if no issue described in a preceding gift shall be born, or if there shall be no issue who shall live to attain the age or otherwise answer the description required for obtaining a vested estate by a preceding gift to such issue" (s. 29, 1 V. c. 26, which Act came into operation on 1st Jan., 1838).

"Thus if (in a Will since 1837) Real Estate be devised to A. and his heirs, or to A. indefinitely, with a limitation over to take effect on the death of A. without issue, or without having or leaving issue,—A. will not (as before) take an estate tail with remainder over, but an estate in fee, with an executory devise over in the event of his death without issue *living at his death.*

"So, if the devise be to A. for life, with a limitation over on his death without issue,—A. will not (as before) take an estate tail but an estate for life only, with the like executory devise over.

"Again, if Personal Estate be given to A., with a bequest over to B. upon the death of A. without issue,—the gift over will not (as before) be void for remoteness, but will take effect as a contingent executory bequest upon the death of A. without issue living at his death" (Hawk. 215 ; *V.* p. 216, Ib., as to whether such expressions as "In *Default*," or "On *Failure* of Issue" are within s. 29, Wills Act. *Vf.* as to effect of the section, 2 Jarm. 493–496, 532–535).

Prior to the Wills Act, just cited, the words "Die without issue" did not for all purposes mean the same as "Die without *leaving* issue." As applied to *Real Estate* these phrases were synonymous ; and imported an indefinite failure of issue (Hawk. 205, 213, and cases there cited), and were "exactly equivalent to 'on the extinction of the heirs of his body,' and that is held by implication to express an intention that the heirs of the body of the devisee for life shall take, and therefore these words give the devisee for life an estate tail" (per Ld. Blackburn, *Bowen* v. *Lewis*, 54 L. J. Q. B. 68 ; 9 App. Ca. 890, *wh. V.* as to the susceptibility of this construction to contextual variation, and for a very recent application of such rule of construction).

But in regard to *Personal Estate* a wide practical difference obtains, in Wills made prior to the Wills Act, as regards the phrases under consideration. Thus if in such a Will, Personalty be given to A. with a limitation over in the event of A. dying "Without Issue," that would mean an indefinite failure of issue, and A. would take the absolute interest, the gift over being void for remoteness (Hawk. 206) ; whilst if the words were "without *leaving* Issue" they would import a failure of issue *at the death of the person spoken of* and A. would take, subject to a contingent executory bequest over in the event of his dying without issue living at his death (*Forth* v. *Chapman*, 1 P. Wms. 663, and notes thereon, Tudor, L. C. Real Pro. 3 Ed. 682).

For a minute discussion of the construction of words importing failure of issue ; *V.* Jarm., chs. 40 and 41. *Va.* Watson, Eq., ch. 29, p. 1400.

V. Leaving.

"Where a *Remainder* is limited in 'default,' or 'for want' of the object or objects of the preceding limitation, these words mean, 'on the failure or determination of the prior estate or estates ;' and do not (as literally construed they would) render the ulterior estate contingent on the event of such prior object or objects not coming into existence. In short they signify all that is comprehended in the word 'Remainder,'—being merely an expression employed by the testator in carrying on the series of limitations" (1 Jarm. 800).

Vh. Chitty, Eq. Ind. 8056–8077.

DIFFERENCE.—A "Difference," in a contract, is a contention over a question of truth or fact, as distinguished from a non-agreement over a question of valuation (*Collins* v. *Collins,* 28 L. J. Ch. 184 ; 26 Bea. 306 : *Boss* v. *Helsham,* 36 L. J. Ex. 20 ; L. R. 2 Ex. 72 ; 4 H. & C. 645 : *V.* Arbitration).

"Differences," s. 11, Com. L. Pro. Act, 1854, includes a question of law (*Randegger* v. *Holmes,* L. R. 1 C. P. 679 : *Seligman* v. *Le Boutillier,* Ib. 681). *Vh. Randell* v. *Thompson,* 1 Q. B. D. 748 ; 45 L. J. Q. B. 713 : *Deutsche Springsteff Gesellschaft* v. *Briscoe,* 57 L. J. Q. B. 4.

"Difference," s. 33, Tramways Act, 1870 (33 & 34 V. c. 78) ; *V. R.* v. *Croydon Tramways Co.,* 56 L. J. Q. B. 125 ; 18 Q. B. D. 39 ; 56 L. T. 78 ; 35 W. R. 299 ; 51 J. P. 420 ; 3 Times Rep. 32.

V. Dispute.

DIFFICULT.—*V.* Inexpedient.

DILIGENCE.—*V.* Due Diligence.

DILIGENTLY.—*V.* Fairly.

DILUTE.—To "dilute" a drink means to make it less strong, whether by adding thereto a weaker drink or by adding water ; and therefore a Beer Retailer is (under s. 8 (2), 48 & 49 V. c. 51) guilty of "diluting" strong beer by mixing therewith a weaker beer (*Crofts* v. *Taylor,* 56 L. J. M. C. 137 ; 19 Q. B. D. 524 ; 57 L. T. 310 ; 36 W. R. 47 ; 51 J. P. 532, 789).

DIRECT.—*V.* Precatory Trust.

DIRECT TAXATION.—If, at the time of payment, the ultimate incidence of a tax is uncertain, the imposition is not "direct," but indirect taxation ; and therefore a Stamp Duty on exhibits to be used in an action, is not "Direct Taxation" within sub-s. 2, s. 92, British North America Act, 1867, and its imposition, by Act of Quebec, 44 V. c. 9, is *ultra vires* (*A.-G. Quebec* v. *Reed,* 54 L. J. P. C. 12 ; 10 App. Ca. 141) ; but a tax on Banks and Insurance Companies situate out of, but carrying on business in, the Province, is "Direct Taxation" (*Toronto Bank* v. *Lambe,* 56 L. J. P. C. 87).

V. Civil Rights.

DIRECTION.—"By his Direction ;" *V.* Refusal.

DIRECTION IN WRITING.—As used in s. 75, 24 & 25 V. c. 96; *V. R.* v. *Christian*, 43 L. J. M. C. 1; L. R. 2 C. C. R. 94.

DIRECTLY.—This word, as applied to the time of doing an act, would seem synonymous with IMMEDIATELY;—"It does not mean *instanter*" (per Cresswell, J., *Duncan* v. *Topham*, 8 C. B. 231; 18 L. J. C. P. 310); but "'directly' clearly means something different from a contract to be performed within a reasonable time" (per Coltman, J., Ib., 8 C. B. 230). *Va.* Add. C. 1188; Benj. 678; Blackb. 226; FORTHWITH.

The addition or omission of the words "Directly or Indirectly," to the offence of an Officer of a Corporation being "interested" in a contract with his Corporation, seems to be immaterial (*Todd* v. *Robinson*, 54 L. J. Q. B. 47; 14 Q. B. D. 739).

DIRECTLY AFFECTED.—"Parties directly affected by the appeal," Ord. 58, R. 2, R. S. C.; *V. Re Salmon, Priest* v. *Uppleby*, 5 Times Rep. 478. It is doubtful whether an Official Receiver is a party "directly affected" by a Bankry Appeal (*Re Webber*, 34 S. J. 144).

Person or Body Corporate "directly affected" who may appeal under s. 39, Endowed Schools Act, 1869, 32 & 33 V. c. 56; *V. Re Shaftoe's Charity*, 3 App. Ca. 872; 47 L. J. P. C. 98; 38 L. T. 793: *Re Sutton Coldfield Grammar School*, 7 App. Ca. 91; 51 L. J. P. C. 8; 45 L. T. 631; 30 W. R. 341: *Re Hemsworth Grammar School*, 12 App. Ca. 444; 56 L. T. 212; 35 W. R. 418; 3 Times Rep. 439. *Vf.* Tudor, Char. Trusts, 628–630.

DIRECTORS.—A Company's Articles, providing that "*the Directors*, whenever they may think fit, may call an extraordinary general meeting," do not authorise any of the directors, of their own authority, to call such a meeting; but mean that the Directors at a Board Meeting may do so (*Browne* v. *La Trinidad*, 57 L. J. Ch. 292; 37 Ch. D. 1; 58 L. T. 137; 36 W. R. 289).

A Promissory Note by "We, the Directors," &c., binds the makers personally (*Dutton* v. *Marsh*, L. R. 6 Q. B. 361; 40 L. J. Q. B. 175); so of a Building Society Deposit Note (*Richardson* v. *Williamson*, L. R. 6 Q. B. 276; 40 L. J. Q. B. 145).

DISABLE.—In an indictment for shooting, wounding, &c., "with intent to maim, disfigure, or disable," "'disable' is to do something which creates a permanent disability, and not merely a temporary injury" (Arch. Cr. 760). *Cp.* DISFIGURE.

"Wholly disabled;" *V.* WHOLLY.

DISABLED FROM ACTING.—As used in Sch. 2, R. 70, P. H. Act, 1875; *V. Fletcher* v. *Hudson*, 51 L. J. Q. B. 48; 7 Q. B. D. 611.

V. DISQUALIFIED.

DISADVANTAGE.—*V.* Undue Preference.

DISBURSEMENTS.—An unpaid liability, for Necessaries, incurred by a master of a *Ship*, is a " Disbursement " within s. 10 of the Admiralty Court Act, 1861, 24 V. c. 10 (*The Fairport*, 52 L. J. P. D. & A. 21 ; 8 P. D. 48) ; for which " Disbursement," however, he has no maritime lien (*The Sara*, 58 L. J. P. D. & A. 57 ; 14 App. Ca. 209, over-ruling *The Mary Ann*, 35 L. J. Adm. 6 ; L. R. 1 A. & E. 8, and the cases following it).

A payment of Probate Duty, is a " Disbursement " by a Solicitor within s. 37, Solicitors Act, 1843, 6 & 7 V. c. 73 (*Re Lamb*, 23 Q. B. D. 5 ; 58 L. J. Q. B. 455); but a payment as an agent,—*e.g.* hostile Costs,— is not (*Re Remnant*, 11 Bea. 603 ; 18 L. J. Ch. 374). The principles for determining what are a Solicitor's " Disbursements " were admirably laid down in the joint certificate of the Taxing Masters in *Re Remnant* (sup.), as follows:—

1. " Such payments as the Solicitor, in due discharge of the duty that he has undertaken, is bound to make so long as he continues to act as Solicitor, whether his client furnishes him with money for the purpose or with money on account, or not, as,—*e.g.* Fees of the Officers of the Court, Fees of Counsel, Expenses of Witnesses,—And also such payments in general business, not in suits, as the Solicitor is looked upon as the person bound by custom and practice to make, as,—*e.g.* Counsel's Fees on Abstracts and Conveyances, Payments for Registers in proving pedigree, Stamp Duty on Conveyances and Mortgages, Charges of Agents, Stationers or Printers employed by him—are by practice, and we think properly, introduced into the Solicitor's Bill of Fees and Disbursements.

2. "But payments which the Solicitor is not either by law bound to make, or by custom looked upon as the person to make, as,—*e.g.* Purchase-Moneys, or Interest thereon, Moneys paid into Court, Damages or Costs paid to Opponent parties, Bills due to the Solicitors of Trustees, Mortgagees or other parties, Legacy or Residuary Duties (*Va. Re Haigh*, 12 Bea. 307 ; 19 L. J. Ch. 79),—or other payments of a like description, which the Solicitor makes *as Agent* on the order of the client and not in discharge of his own duty or liability *as Solicitor*, are by practice, and we think properly, charged in the Cash Account.

3. "We also think that the question, whether such payments are Professional Disbursements or otherwise, is not affected by the state of the cash account between the solicitor and the client, and that, for instance, Counsel's Fees would not the less properly be introduced into the Bill of Costs as a Professional Disbursement, because the client may have given money expressly for paying them ; and that Purchase-Money or Damages would not be properly so introduced, notwithstanding the solicitor may have advanced the money out of his own funds."

V. Actual Costs and Expenses.

DISCHARGE.—Master or Mistress is not, without Justices' consent, to PUT AWAY or "in any way to *discharge*" a Parish Apprentice, s. 9, 56 G. 3, c. 139; but a mere agreement to discharge the Indentures on payment of a sum of money, is not a "Discharge" within the section, until actual payment (*R.* v. *Gwinear*, 3 L. J. M. C. 81; 1 A. & E. 152; 3 N. & M. 297).

DISCHARGING.—*V.* LOADING.

DISCLAIMER.—"*Disclaime, disclamare,* is compounded of *de* and *clamo,* and signifieth utterly to renounce" (Co. Litt. 102 a); *V. Doe* d. *Gray* v. *Stanion,* 5 L. J. Ex. 253; 1 M. & W. 695.

DISCLOSE: DISCLOSURE.—To "disclose" an offence, s. 6, 5 & 6 V. c. 39, is not to state it or confess to it; but to make the offence known for the first time (*R.* v. *Skeen,* 28 L. J. M. C. 91; Bell, C. C. 97).

"Disclose a Defence upon the merits," s. 27, Com. L. Pro. Act, 1852, means not merely to say there is a Defence, but to show what the nature of it is (*Whiley* v. *Wiley,* 27 L. J. C. P. 305; 4 C. B. N. S. 653: *Warrington* v. *Leake,* 25 L. J. Ex. 27; 11 Ex. 304).

V. FULL DISCLOSURE.

DISCONTINUANCE.—"'Discontinuance' is an ancient word in the law" (Litt. s. 592). "A discontinuance of estates in lands or tenements is properly (in legall understanding) an alienation made or suffered by tenant in taile, or by any that is seized in *auter droit,* whereby the issue in taile, or the heire or successor, or those in reversion or remainder, are driven to their action, and cannot enter" (Co. Litt. 325 a).

"Discontinuance of Possession," s. 3, 3 & 4 W. 4, c. 27; *V. Leigh* v. *Jack,* 5 Ex. D. 264; 49 L. J. Ex. 220.

V. DISPOSSESSION.

DISCOUNT.—In an Agreement to "underwrite" Shares at so much "Discount," "Discount" means "Commission," and the agreement does not mean that the shares are to be issued at a discount (*Re Licensed Victuallers' Assn.,* 58 L. J. Ch. 467; 42 Ch. D. 1; 5 Times Rep. 369).

V. UNDERWRITE.

DISCOVERED.—"Discovered or Opened," in a Lease of Mines; *V. Quarrington* v. *Arthur,* 11 L. J. Ex. 418; 10 M. & W. 335.

DISCOVERT.—For the purposes of the Stat. of Limitations respecting a personal tort, married women became "discovert" (s. 7, 21 Jac. 1, c. 16) by the operation of the M. W. P. Act, 1882 (*Lowe* v. *Fox,* 15 Q. B. D. 667; 54 L. J. Q. B. 561; affd. 12 App. Ca. 206).

DISCREETEST.—*V.* CHIEFEST AND DISCREETEST.

DISCRETION.—"Where something is left to be done according to the Discretion of the authority on whom the power of doing it is conferred, the discretion must be exercised honestly and in the spirit of the statute, otherwise the act done would not fall within the statute. 'According to his Discretion,' means, it is said, according to the rules of reason and justice, not private opinion (*Rooke's Case*, 5 Rep. 100 a: *Keighley's Case*, 10 Rep. 140 b: per Willes, J., *Lee* v. *Bude Ry.*, L. R. 6 C. P. 576; 40 L. J. C. P. 288); according to law and not humour; it is to be not arbitrary, vague and fanciful, but legal and regular (per Ld. Mansfield, *R.* v. *Wilkes*, 4 Burr. 2839); to be exercised not capriciously, but on judicial grounds and for substantial reasons (per Jessel, M. R., *Re Taylor*, 4 Ch. D. 160; 46 L. J. Ch. 400; and per Ld. Blackburn, *Doherty* v. *Allman*, 3 App. Ca. 728). And it must be exercised within the limits to which an honest man competent to the discharge of his office ought to confine himself (per Ld. Kenyon, *Wilson* v. *Rastall*, 4 T. R. 757); that is within the limits and for the objects intended by the legislature" (Maxwell, 147, 148, *wh.* to 151 *V.* for cases in illustration). *V.* MAY: OPINION.

The wide "Discretion" as to *Costs* given by R. 1, Ord. 65, R. S. C., and to the Ry. Commrs. by s. 28, 36 & 37 V. c. 48, does not authorise an order on the defendant to pay any part of the plaintiff's costs when the defendant has succeeded absolutely (*Foster* v. *G. W. Ry.*, 51 L. J. Q. B. 233; 8 Q. B. D. 515: *Dicks* v. *Yates*, 50 L. J. Ch. 809; 18 Ch. D. 76: *Witt* v. *Corcoran*, 45 L. J. Ch. 603; 2 Ch. D. 69: *Vh.* notes to R. 1, Ord. 65, Ann. Pr.).

The "free and unqualified discretion" to refuse or grant *Licenses*, which is given to Justices by the Beerdealers' Retail Licenses Act, 1882 (45 & 46 V. c. 34), is absolute as well as regards the renewal of an old, as the grant of a new, license (*R.* v. *Kay*, 52 L. J. M. C. 90; 10 Q. B. D. 213); so of their "discretion" under 9 G. 4, c. 61, s. 1 (*Sharpe* v. *Wakefield*, 22 Q. B. D. 239; 37 W. R. 187).

The Court will not, in the absence of misconduct, interfere with a "discretion" given to Trustees, as regards the mode of *Investment of Trust Funds* (*Brophy* v. *Bellamy*, 43 L. J. Ch. 183; 8 Ch. 798, and cases there cited: Lewin, 614): but during actual administration by the Court it may exercise a control (*Bethel* v. *Abraham*, 43 L. J. Ch. 180; L. R. 17 Eq. 24: *Brophy* v. *Bellamy*, sup.: *Re Gadd*, 52 L. J. Ch. 396; 23 Ch. D. 134).

A mere "discretion" as to investments will not authorize an investment on personal security (*Pocock* v. *Reddington*, 5 Ves. 794: *Potts* v. *Britton*, L. R. 11 Eq. 433: *Bethell* v. *Abraham*, sup.; Lewin, 316). Nor, *semble*, will a mere "discretion" justify Trustees in investing in unauthorised securities (*Bethel* v. *Abraham*, sup.): *secus*, if the power were exercisable in their "uncontrolled discretion" (*Re Brown*, 54 L. J. Ch. 1134; 29 Ch. D. 889). Where the words authorised investments "in such stock, funds, or shares as the trustees in their *absolute* discretion may think fit," the Court, acting for the protection of infants, refused to sanction an appropriation of securities for the satisfaction of a legacy, such securities being partly in Preference Stocks which were liable to be paid off, and were accordingly not of a permanent character (*Stewart* v. *Sanderson*, 39 L. J. Ch. 337; L. R. 10 Eq. 26).

Income, to be applied by Trustees "in their *uncontrolled and irresponsible* discretion," for the Maintenance of a husband or wife, or one of them, may, in the absence of *mala fides*, be all paid by them to the husband, though the wife is unable to live with him in consequence of his intemperate habits (*Tabor* v. *Brooks*, 48 L. J. Ch. 130; 10 Ch. D. 273).

"A *Devise* of property *to the discretion* of A. passes the fee, and does not merely confer a power; so a devise *at the disposition* of A. carries the fee. It is equivalent to a devise to A. *to give and sell at his pleasure.* There is no difference between a devise that A. shall do with the land *at* his discretion, and a devise of the land to A. *to do with it at* his discretion" (Sug. Pow. 104).

DISEASE.—For the purpose of furnishing an excuse for what would otherwise be a crime, "Voluntary Drunkenness is not regarded as a Disease affecting the mind; but Involuntary Drunkenness, and diseases caused by voluntary drunkenness, fall, so far as they affect the mind, within that term" (Steph. Cr. 22).

V. SICKNESS.

DISFIGURE.—In an indictment for an assault (24 & 25 V. c. 100, s. 18), to "disfigure" is to do some external injury which may detract from the personal appearance (Arch. Cr. 760).

Cp. DISABLE.

DISHONESTY.—*V.* FRAUD.

DISHONOURED.—A Bill of Exchange is dishonoured by *Non-Acceptance*—

"(*a*) When it is duly presented for Acceptance, and such an Acceptance as is prescribed by this Act is refused, or cannot be obtained; or

(*b*) When presentment for Acceptance is excused, and the Bill is not accepted"

(s. 43, Bills of Ex. Act, 1882).

A Bill, or Note, is dishonoured by *Non-Payment*—

"(*a*) When it is duly presented for payment, and payment is refused or cannot be obtained; or

(*b*) When presentment is excused and the Bill (or Note) is overdue and unpaid"

(ss. 47, 89 Ib.).

In a Notice of Dishonour to say that a Bill of Exchange has been "dishonoured," implies a due presentment (*Lewis* v. *Gompertz*, 9 L. J. Ex. 182; 6 M. & W. 399). *Cp.* HONOURED.

For the Rules as to Notice of Dishonour; *V.* ss. 48, 49, 50, Bills of Ex. Act, 1882.

DISMES.—"Dismes are Tithes" (Elph. 573).

DISORDERLY.—Disorderly *Houses;*—"The following houses are Disorderly Houses, that is to say, common bawdy houses, common gaming houses, common betting houses, disorderly places of entertainment" (Steph. Cr. 122). *Vf.* Arch. Cr. 1021.

Disorderly *Inn;*—"A Disorderly Inn is an Inn kept in a disorderly manner and suffered to be resorted to by persons of bad character for any improper purpose" (Steph. Cr. 125). *Vf.* Rosc. Cr. 821.

Disorderly *Person; V.* Idle and Disorderly Person.

Disorderly *Places of Entertainment; V.* 25 G. 2, c. 36, ss. 2, 4; 21 G. 3, c. 49, ss. 1, 2; stated Steph. Cr. 124, 125.

DISPATCH.—*V.* Despatch.

DISPLACE.—If a master agrees to make compensation if he "displace" his servant, he will be liable thereon if he voluntarily does anything that puts it out of his power to continue the employment,—*e.g.*, transfers his business (*Stirling* v. *Maitland*, 34 L. J. Q. B. 1; 5 B. & S. 840).

DISPONE.—As to the importance of "dispone" in the operative words of a Scotch Conveyance; *V. Alexander* v. *Kirkpatrick*, L. R. 2 H. L. Sc. 397.

DISPONER.—*V.* Settlor.

DISPOSAL.—A direction that a fund is to be at the "Disposal" of its donee, will generally negative the notion of a trust which might otherwise be gathered from the terms of the Will (*Lambe* v. *Eames*, 40 L. J. Ch. 447; 6 Ch. 597: *Re Adams and Kensington*, 27 Ch. D. 394: *Morrin* v. *Morrin*, 19 L. R. Ir. 37: but see these cases distinguished in *Re Haly*, 23 L. R. Ir. 130: *Vh.* 1 Jarm. 402).

So this word will sometimes cut down, or help to cut down, what, without it, might be an absolute gift. Thus where a testator gave his residue to his wife "for her own absolute use and benefit *and disposal*," with a gift over of what should "remain undisposed of" by her; it was held that the wife took a life interest with power of disposal by act *inter vivos* (*Re Pounder*, 56 L. J. Ch. 113; 56 L. T. 104). In the course of his jdgmt. in that case, Kay, J., said, "If he meant her to take absolutely there was no use in referring to 'Disposal.'" *Va. Espinasse* v. *Luffingham*, 3 J. & La. T. 186. The "Disposal," of chattels, may be perfected by gift and manual delivery (*Farington* v. *Parker*, L. R. 4 Eq. 116).

V. Dispose of: Disposition.

A bequest to a wife "to and for her own absolute use and disposal *during her life*" is an absolute gift and not one merely for life (*Re Bush*, W. N. (85) 61).

V. SOLE.

DISPOSE OF.—A Power enabling a woman "to dispose of" property "as she thinks fit," when following a life interest to her which she is restrained from alienating, would seem only exercisable by Will and not by writing *inter vivos* (*Archibald* v. *Wright*, 7 L. J. Ch. 120 ; 9 Sim. 161).

But a gift of real and personal estate to a wife, "for the term of her natural life, *to be disposed of* as she may think proper for her own use and benefit, according to the nature and quality thereof," and "in the event of her decease, *should there be anything remaining* of the said property or any part thereof," then, as to "the said part or parts thereof," over ; held, that the wife had no power of disposition by Will ; and that on her death the gift over took effect : the Court of Appeal also expressed a strong opinion that the wife took only a life estate in the property, with the power of enjoying the property in specie (*Re Thomson, Herring* v. *Barrow*, 49 L. J. Ch. 622 ; 14 Ch. D. 263 : *Sv. Re Mortlock*, 26 L. J. Ch. 671 ; 3 K. & J. 456 ; 30 L. T. O. S. 90).

"Dispose of" lands, ss. 127, 128, Lands C. C. Act, 1845, means "transfer ;" and does not relate to the mere application of the lands to a purpose other than that for which they were acquired (*Astley* v. *Manchester, S. & L. Ry.*, 27 L. J. Ch. 478 ; 2 D. G. & J. 453).

V. NEGOTIATE.

Not "to grant away, assign or let, charge or dispose of," in a covenant in a Lease ; *V. Croft* v. *Lumley*, 25 L. J. Q. B. 73, 223 ; 27 Ib. 321 ; 6 H. L. Ca. 672.

"Absolutely sell and dispose of ;" *V.* ABSOLUTELY SELL.

DISPOSITION.—"A devise *at the disposition* of A. carries the fee" (Sug. Pow. 104 : *Vf.* DISCRETION).

"Disposition" and "Devolution by Law" are contrasted in s. 2, Sucn. Dy. Act (*V.* SUCCESSION), and the Predecessor is determined by considering whether the Succession is by "Disposition" or by "Devolution by Law" (*Zetland* v. *Ld. Advocate*, 3 App. Ca. 505), in which case (p. 520) Selborne, L.C., said, that "*Devolution by Law* takes place whenever the title is such that an heir takes under it by descent from an 'Ancestor' according to the rules of law applicable to the descent of heritable estates." *Vf.* on "Disposition," *A.-G.* v. *Sibthorp*, 28 L. J. Ex. 9 : *Braybrooke* v. *A.-G.*, 9 H. L. Ca. 150 ; 31 L. J. Ex. 177 : *A.-G.* v. *Montefiore*, 21 Q. B. D. 461 ; 59 L. T. 534 ; 4 Times Rep. 658.

"Disposition" of realty, s. 4, 6 Anne (Ireland), c. 2 ; *V. Re O'Byrne*, 15 L. R. Ir. 189, 373.

DISPOSITIONS.—As to meaning of "Dispositions" of property within s. 153, Companies Act, 1862 ; *V. Re Oriental Bank*, 54 L. J. Ch. 322 ; 28 Ch. D. 634 ; 52 L. T. 167.

"Dispositions of Lands," s. 47, Fines and Recoveries Act, 3 & 4 W. 4, c. 74; *V. Bankes* v. *Small,* 36 Ch. D. 716; 56 L. J. Ch. 832; 57 L. T. 292; 35 W. R. 765; 3 Times Rep. 740.

DISPOSSESSION.—"Dispossession, or Discontinuance of Possession" (s. 3, Stat. Lim., 3 & 4 W. 4, c. 27), means the abandonment of possession by one entitled to it (*Rimington* v. *Cannon,* 22 L. J. C. P. 153; 12 C. B. 18), followed by actual possession by another (*Smith* v. *Lloyd,* 23 L. J. Ex. 194; 9 Ex. 562: *McDonnell* v. *McKinty,* 10 Ir. L. R. 514); ignorance on the part of the rightful owner that such adverse possession has been taken making no difference (*Rains* v. *Buxton,* 49 L. J. Ch. 473; 14 Ch. D. 537).

Acts of user which do not interfere, and are consistent, with the purpose to which the owner intends to devote the land, do not amount to Discontinuance of Possession by him (*Leigh* v. *Jack,* 5 Ex. D. 264; 49 L. J. Ex. 220, cited Rosc. N. P. 976, *wh. Vf.* hereon).

Small acts by the rightful owner will disprove "Dispossession or Discontinuance,"—*e.g.*, small repairs (*Leigh* v. *Jack,* sup.), or, as regards a boundary wall, an inscription claiming it (*Phillipson* v. *Gibbon,* 40 L. J. Ch. 406; 6 Ch. 428).

Vh. Watson, Eq. 574, 575.

V. Discontinuance.

DISPUTE.—A clause providing for an Arbitration "should any Dispute arise," includes Disputes of law as well as of fact (*Forwood* v. *Watney,* 49 L. J. Q. B. 447); and also a non-feazance, *e.g.*, the withholding a certificate (*Re Hohenzollern Co.,* 54 L. T. 596; 2 Times Rep. 294, 470).

A claim based on a non-agreement, as well as one based on an actual conflict *ad idem,* is a "Dispute" (*Clemson* v. *Hubbard,* 45 L. J. M. C. 69; 24 W. R. 312; 40 J. P. 725: *Grainger* v. *Aynsley,* 50 L. J. M. C. 51; 6 Q. B. D. 182; 29 W. R. 242; 45 J. P. 142: decided on ss. 3, 4, Emp. and Workm. Act, 1875, 38 & 39 V. c. 90).

As to meaning of "Dispute" for the purpose of the *Building Societies* Acts; *V.* 47 & 48 V. c. 41, s. 2, interpreted by *Western Suburban and Notting Hill Bg. Socy.* v. *Martin,* 55 L. J. Q. B. 382; 17 Q. B. D. 609; 54 L. T. 822; 34 W. R. 630; 2 Times Rep. 672: *Municipal Permanent Bg. Socy.* v. *Richards,* 39 Ch. D. 381; 58 L. J. Ch. 8. *V.* Capacity.

For the Building Society cases apart from legislative interpretation; *V.*, as regards Societies *Incorporated* under the Act of 1874, *Wright* v. *Monarch Bg. Socy.,* 46 L. J. Ch. 649; 5 Ch. D. 726: *Hack* v. *London Prov. Bg. Socy.,* 52 L. J. Ch. 541; 23 Ch. D. 106; 31 W. R. 392: *Municipal Bg. Socy.* v. *Kent,* 53 L. J. Q. B. 290; 9 App. Ca. 260: and, as regards *Unincorporated* Societies, *Mulkern* v. *Lord,* 48 L. J. Ch. 745; 4 App. Ca. 182; 27 W. R. 510: *Morrison* v. *Glover,* 19 L. J. Ex. 20; 4 Ex. 430: *R.* v. *Trafford,* 24 L. J. M. C. 20; 4 E. & B. 122: *Farmer* v. *Giles,* 30 L. J. Ex. 65; 5 H. & N. 753.

"Dispute" seems to have received no statutory interpretation for the purposes of the *Friendly Societies* Acts : *Vh. United Patriots Socy., Re Holt*, 48 L. J. M. C. 55 ; 4 Q. B. D. 29 ; 27 W. R. 339 ; 39 L. T. 622 : *Huckle* v. *Wilson*, 2 C. P. D. 410 ; 26 W. R. 98 : *Ex p. Wooldridge*, 26 J. P. 469 : *Jones* v. *Slee*, 32 Ch. D. 585 ; 55 L. J. Ch. 908 ; 55 L. T. 129 ; 34 W. R. 692 ; 2 Times Rep. 625.

"Dispute," s. 48, *Savings Bank* Act, 1863, 26 & 27 V. c. 87 ; *V. Re Cardiff Savings Bank*, 4 Times Rep. 10.

"Sum in Dispute ;" *V.* SUM CLAIMED.

V. DIFFERENCE.

DISPUTE AS TO THE AMOUNT.—A statutory direction to refer to arbitration any "Dispute as to the Amount," will be confined to questions of amount only, and will not embrace a case where the liability is in dispute (*R.* v. *Metropolitan Commrs. of Sewers*, 22 L. J. Q. B. 234 ; 1 E. & B. 694 : *Bradby* v. *Southampton*, 24 L. J. Q. B. 239 ; 4 E. & B. 1014 : *R.* v. *Burslem*, 29 L. J. Q. B. 242 ; 1 E. & E. 1077 : and *V.* per Willes, J., in the last case for obs. on *Bradford* v. *Hopwood*, 6 W. R. 818).

DISQUALIFIED.—*V. Lewis* v. *Carr*, 46 L. J. Ex. 314 ; 1 Ex. D. 484 : *Fletcher* v. *Hudson*, 51 L. J. Q. B. 48 ; 7 Q. B. D. 611.

DISSEISIN.—"*Disseisina* is a putting out of a man out of seisin, and ever implyeth a wrong. But dispossessing or ejectment, is a putting out of possession, and may be by right or by wrong" (Co. Litt. 153 b ; *Va.* Ib. 181 a).

DISTANCE.—By the Registration of Voters Act, 1843 (6 V. c. 18, s. 76), distances for the purposes of that Act are to be "measured in a straight line on the horizontal plane." That rule is now applicable to all Acts of Parliament passed since the 31st. Dec., 1889 (s. 34, Interp. Act, 1889). Indeed, without enactment, it would seem a universal rule for all Acts, without distinction (*Lake* v. *Butler*, 24 L. J. Q. B. 273 ; 25 L. T. O. S. 128 ; 19 J. P. 692).

A similar, though more amplified, rule obtains for the general measuring of distance. This rule was laid down by the Exchequer Chamber in *Mouflet* v. *Cole* (42 L. J. Ex. 8 ; L. R. 8 Ex. 32), wherein the prior authorities, somewhat conflicting, were cited ; and it is now established that, where there are no special controlling words, distance is not to be measured by the nearest available mode of access, but "as the crow flies," *i.e.*, by the shortest line that can be drawn from one place to another on a map without regard to the curvature or inequalities of the surface of the earth ; and where the distance is to be ascertained between houses, the measurement is to be taken from the nearest point of the one house to the nearest point of the other, without regard to where the doors are situated. *Vf. Duignan* v. *Walker*, 28 L. J. Ch. 867 ; Johns. 446.

For an example of a special provision for measuring distance; *V. Atkyns* v. *Kinnier*, 19 L. J. Ex. 132; 4 Ex. 776.

V. Traveller.

DISTINCT.—"Distinct *Properties*," *quà* Inhabited House Duty; *V. A.-G.* v. *Westminster Chambers Assn.*, 45 L. J. Ex. 886; 1 Ex. D. 469.

"Distinct" *Trusts*, s. 5, Conv. Act, 1882; *V. Re Hetherington*, 56 L. J. Ch. 174; 34 Ch. D. 211; 55 L. T. 806; 35 W. R. 285.

"*Separate* and Distinct *Building*," 59 G. 3, c. 50; *V. R.* v. *Henley-upon-Thames*, 6 L. J. M. C. 76; 6 A. & E. 294; 1 N. & P. 445.

"Separate and Distinct *Dwelling-House*," 6 G. 4, c. 57, s. 2; *V. R.* v. *Usworth*, 5 L. J. M. C. 139; 5 A. & E. 261; 6 N. & M. 811: *R.* v. *Wootton*, 3 L. J. M. C. 98; 1 A. & E. 232: *R.* v. *Ripon*, 14 L. J. M. C. 102; 7 Q. B. 225: *R.* v. *Husthwaite*, 21 L. J. M. C. 189: *R.* v. *Caverswall*, 8 L. J. M. C. 57; 10 A. & E. 270: *R.* v. *St. Lawrence*, 14 L. J. M. C. 56; 6 Q. B. 842.

DISTINCTIVE.—A "Distinctive" *Device*, Mark, etc. (s. 10, Trade Marks Registration Act, 1875, 38 & 39 V. c. 91; *V.* now Patents, Designs and Trade Marks Act, 1883, ss. 64, 67) "must be a Mark or Device of such kind as, in case of infringement, it shall be clear what it is that is being infringed, and that the mark is something distinct from all other marks used in the same class of goods" (per Lopes, L.J., *James* v. *Parry*, 55 L. J. Ch. 915; 33 Ch. D. 392; 55 L. T. 415; 35 W. R. 67); and that case establishes that a device or mark is none the less distinctive because it is a pictorial representation of the article; but colour alone will not make a device "distinctive" (*Re Hanson*, 57 L. J. Ch. 173; 37 Ch. D. 112; 57 L. T. 859; 36 W. R. 134). *Vf. Re Anderson*, 54 L. J. Ch. 1084; 26 Ch. D. 409: *Re Hudson*, 55 L. J. Ch. 531.

"Distinctive *Word*" in same section; *V. Re Palmer*, 21 Ch. D. 47; 24 Ib. 504; 51 L. J. Ch. 673: *Re Leonard and Ellis*, 26 Ch. D. 288; 53 L. J. Ch. 603: *Re Wood*, 32 Ch. D. 247: *Burland* v. *Broxburn Oil Co.*, 58 L. J. Ch. 816.

DISTRESS.—"A distress is one of the most ancient and effectual remedies for the recovery of rent. It is the taking, without legal process, cattle or goods as a pledge to compel the satisfaction of a demand, the performance of a duty, or the redress of an injury. The act of taking, the thing taken, and the remedy generally, having been called a Distress; an inaccuracy which the older text-writers usually avoided" (Woodf. 411).

A power in gross (apart from statute) to recover interest, gas rent or other sum by "Distress" will not confer the peculiar powers of a Landlord's Distress, which in bargains *inter partes* must be based on a tenancy (*Jolly* v. *Arbuthnot*, 28 L. J. Ch. 547; 4 D. G. & J. 224). And if a statute merely gives power to levy, *e.g.*, gas or water rent, by "Distress," that will not give a Landlord's Distress (*Ex p. Hill*, 46 L. J. Bank. 116;

6 Ch. D. 63); *secus*, if the statutory power is to levy "by the same means as landlords may recover rent in arrear" (*Ex p. Birmingham and Staffordshire Gas Co.*, 40 L. J. Bank. 52; L. R. 11 Eq. 615: *Re Peake*, 53 L. J. Ch. 977; 13 Q. B. D. 753). In the power to levy for Poor Rate "by *Distress* and sale of the offender's goods" (43 Eliz. c. 2, s. 4), "Distress" means "Execution;" and accordingly Beasts of the Plough may be taken thereunder (*Hutchins* v. *Chambers*, 1 Burr. 579).

The bailiff, and not the landlord, is the "*person making* any Distress" within s. 49, Agricultural Holdings Act, 1883 (46 & 47 V. c. 61), and is therefore entitled to the percentage prescribed by the statute (*Phillips* v. *Rees*, 38 W. R. 53; overruling *Coode* v. *Johns*, 55 L. J. Q. B. 475; 17 Q. B. D. 714; 55 L. T. 290; 35 W. R. 47).

"By any Distress, *Action or Suit*," s. 42, 3 & 4 W. 4, c. 27; *V.* By.

DISTRICT.—*V. Re Holton*, 31 L. T. O. S. 187.

DISTRICT OF ENGLAND.—Wales is a "District of England" within the Endowed Schools Act, 1869 (*Re Meyricke*, 41 L. J. Ch. 187; 553; L. R. 13 Eq. 269; 7 Ch. 500). *V.* England.

DISTURB.—*V.* Molest.

DISTURBANCE.—*V.* Interruption.

DITCH.—*V.* Drain.

DIVES' COSTS.—*V. Carson* v. *Pickersgill*, 54 L. J. Q. B. 484; 14 Q. B. D. 859.

DIVIDE: DIVIDED.—A testamentary gift "to be divided" between two or more, means an equal division and creates a tenancy in common (*Chapman* v. *Peat*, 1 Ves. sen. 542: *Ackerman* v. *Burrows*, 3 V. & B. 54). The word "Divide" is so strong in this connection that where the direction was "to pay, assign and divide" a sum to certain legatees "*as joint tenants*," yet Stuart, V.-C., held that a tenancy in common was created (*Booth* v. *Alington*, 27 L. J. Ch. 117). But for a consideration of the cases where the word "Divide" or "Divided" has itself been otherwise controlled by a context, *V.* 2 Jarm. 260-262.

The qualified exemption from Inhabited House Duty, given by s. 13, sub-s. 1, 41 V. c. 15, where a house is "divided into and let in different tenements," only applies where the house is structurally divided (*Yorkshire Insrce.* v. *Clayton*, 51 L. J. Q. B. 82; 8 Q. B. D. 421).

DIVIDEND.—"The word 'Dividend' carries no spell with it. Applicable to various subjects, it is not intelligible without knowing the matter to which it is meant as referring;" but its ordinary meaning is, share of profits (per Knight-Bruce, L.J., *Henry* v. *G. N. Ry.*, 27 L. J. Ch. 1; 1 D. G. & J. 606). A "Preference" Dividend is substantially interest, to this extent, that the failure of profits wherewith to pay it in one year will be made good out of any profits that may be made in a subsequent year (*Henry* v. *G. N. Ry.*, sup. : *Matthews* v. *G. N. Ry.*, 28 L. J. Ch. 375 ; 5 Jur. N. S. 284 ; 7 W. R. 233 ; 32 L. T. O. S. 355).

Profits in a *private* trading partnership, the deed of which provides that "Dividends" shall be made from time to time as the managing partners shall direct, are not "Dividends" within the *Apportionment Act*, 1870, 33 & 34 V. c. 35, s. 5 (*Jones* v. *Ogle*, 42 L. J. Ch. 334 ; 8 Ch. 192 ; 21 W. R. 239). From the language of the L. C. in that case, it would seem that no profits, except those arising in respect of a *Public* Company, can be "Dividends" within the meaning of the Act, or otherwise apportionable thereunder. *Vh.* the obs. of Malins, V.-C., in *Capron* v. *Capron*, 43 L. J. Ch. 677 ; L. R. 17 Eq. 288 : *Va. Re Cox*, 47 L. J. Ch. 735 ; 9 Ch. D. 159 : *Pollock* v. *Pollock*, 44 L. J. Ch. 168 ; L. R. 18 Eq. 329, correcting *Whitehead* v. *Whitehead*, L. R. 16 Eq. 528. Bonuses in a public company are "Dividends" within the Act, though only occasional and not strictly periodical (*Re Griffith*, 12 Ch. D. 655). *Vf.* PERIODICAL.

"Dividends ;" *V.* ANNUAL PROCEEDS : RENTS AND PROFITS.

"An *indefinite* gift (by Will) of the Dividends gives the absolute property of the Stock" (Wms. Exs. 1200, citing *Page* v. *Leapingwell*, 18 Ves. 463 : *Haig* v. *Swiney*, 1 Sim. & St. 487, 490 : *Southouse* v. *Bate*, 16 Bea. 132).

A Bequest, for life, of "Dividends" will not pass unreceived Dividends (*Shore* v. *Weekly*, 3 D. G. & Sm. 467 ; 18 L. J. Ch. 403 ; *Constable* v. *Bull*, 18 L. J. Ch. 302) ; nor will "Dividends" pass capitalized Dividends (*Ricketts* v. *Harling*, 23 L. T. 760). *Vf. Archibald* v. *Hartley*, 21 L. J. Ch. 399.

DIVINE SERVICE.—"Here note, that the almes and reliefe of poor people, being a worke of charity, is accounted in law divine service ; for what herein is done to the poor for God's sake, is done to God himself" (Co. Litt. 96 b).

DIVISION.—"County, Riding or *Division ;*" *V. Evans* v. *Stevens*, 4 T. R. 224, 459.

Gift over in case of death "before the division of my estate ;" *V. Re Collison*, 12 Ch. D. 834 ; 48 L. J. Ch. 720.

"Division," in a Bequest, unsuccessfully relied on to show that more than one person was meant (*Jodrell* v. *Seale*, Times, 16 Dec., 1889 ; W. N. (89) 230).

DIVORCE.—*V.* BIGAMY.

DO OR MAKE.—The words "Do or make Waste," Stat. of Marlebridge, 52 H. 3, c. 23, s. 2, in legal understanding in this place, as well as in the Stat. of Gloucester, 6 Ed. 1, c. 5, includes as well permissive Waste, which is waste by reason of omission or not doing, as Waste by reason of commission, as to cut down timber, trees, or prostrate houses and the like ; for he that suffereth a house to decay, which he ought to repair, doth the

Waste (2 Inst. 300, cited *Woodhouse* v. *Walker*, 49 L. J. Q. B. 611; 5 Q. B. D. 404). *Cp.* DONE.

V. WITHOUT IMPEACHMENT OF WASTE.

DO THE NEEDFUL.—As to the authority conferred by these words; *V. Dawson* v. *Lawley*, 4 Esp. 65.

DOCUMENTS.—An avouchment, whether written or printed, of the character or quality of a chattel is not a Document which, if false, would be a Forgery,—*e.g.* the false signature of an artist's name to a picture (*R.* v. *Cross*, D. & B. 460), or enclosing spurious goods in a wrapper imitating a trade-mark (*R.* v. *Smith,* 27 L. J. M. C. 225 ; D. & B. 566).

V. SHIPPING DOCUMENTS.

DOING.—"Doing" may create a covenant,—*e.g.* "Doing suit" (*Vyvyan* v. *Arthur*, 1 B. & C. 410), so of the phrase "Doing, Fulfilling and Performing" (*Boone* v. *Eyre*, 2 W. Bl. 1312).

DOLE.—"The share of any man in a lot meadow, or common meadow which is divided yearly and distributed by lots among the owners; *V.* Co. Litt. 4 a.; Spelm., *Dolae*; *Pratt* v. *Groome*, 15 East, 235; Elton on Commons, 31; Wms. on Commons, 90. The owner of a dole may have a freehold in the soil (Co. Litt. 4 a, 343 b); or he may have only vestura terræ (*Tenants of Owning's Case*, 4 Leon. 43). *Va.* as to lot meads, Wms. R. P., App. C" (Elph. 573).

DOMAIN.—*V.* DEMESNE.

DOMESTIC.—Books are articles of "domestic *use and enjoyment*" (*Cornwall* v. *Cornwall*, 10 L. J. Ch. 364 ; 12 Sim. 303).

Watering private horses, and washing private carriages is using the water for a "domestic *use or purpose*," within a Water Rating Act (*Busby* v. *Chesterfield Waterworks Co.*, 27 L. J. M. C. 174 ; E. B. & E. 176). Indeed it may be broadly laid down that "water used for the amenities of the house,—*e.g.* watering a pleasure-garden attached to and occupied with the house,—may be legitimately held to be used for domestic purposes" within the meaning of such an Act (per Smith, J., in delivering the jdgmt. of the Court in *Bristol Waterworks Co.* v. *Uren*, 54 L. J. M. C. 103 ; 15 Q. B. D. 637 : *Vf. Cooke* v. *New River Co.*, 14 App. Ca. 698).

DOMESTIC ANIMAL.—An animal (whether a quadruped or not, 17 & 18 V. c. 60, s. 3, and not absolutely *feræ naturæ*) which either by habit or special training lives in association with man is a "Domestic Animal." Thus linnets trained as decoy birds are domestic animals (*Colam* v. *Pagett*, 53 L. J. M. C. 64 ; 12 Q. B. D. 66 ; 48 J. P. 263 ; 32 W. R. 289), and so is a cock (*Bridge* v. *Parsons*, 32 L. J. M. C. 95 ; 3 B. & S.

382; 11 W. R. 424; 7 L. T. 784; 27 J. P. 231). Parrots may become, but young unacclimatised parrots are not, "Domestic Animals" (*Swan* v. *Sanders*, 50 L. J. M. C. 67; 29 W. R. 538; 45 J. P. 522; 44 L. T. 424); nor, *semble*, is a performing bear a domestic animal (28 S. J. 746).

DOMESTIC PURPOSES.—*V.* DOMESTIC.

DOMESTIC SERVANT.—*V. Jenner* v. *Turner*, W. N. (80) 170: SERVANT.

DOMICIL: DOMICILED.—A person's "Domicil" means, generally speaking, the place where he has his permanent home (*Whicker* v. *Hume*, 28 L. J. Ch. 396, 400; 7 H. L. Ca. 124: *A.-G.* v. *Rowe*, 31 L. J. Ex. 314, 320; 1 H. & C. 31). But "the word 'Domicil' has many meanings, according as it is used with reference to Succession, or for determining Rights of Belligerents, or ascertaining Trading Privileges" (per J. O., *Yelverton* v. *Yelverton*, 29 L. J. P. & M. 40; 1 Sw. & Tr. 574); *Vh.* Dicey on Domicil, App., Notes 1, 2 and 3; Foote on Private International Jurisprudence, ch. 2; Westlake on Private International Law, ch. 14.

"I would venture to suggest that the definition of an *acquired* domicile might stand thus:—'That place is properly the domicile of a person in which he has voluntarily fixed the habitation of himself and his family, not for a mere special and temporary purpose, but with a present intention of making it his permanent home, unless and until something (which is unexpected, or the happening of which is uncertain) shall occur to induce him to adopt some other permanent home'" (per Kindersley, V.-C., *Lord* v. *Colvin*, 4 Drew. 376; 28 L. J. Ch. 366).

The words "domiciled *in England*," in sub.-s. 1 (d), s. 6, Bankry. Act, 1883, mean domiciled in England as distinguished from Scotland or Ireland as well as from foreign countries (*Ex p. Cunningham, Re Mitchell*, 53 L. J. Ch. 1067).

A Joint-Stock Company is only "Domiciled or ordinarily resident within the jurisdiction" (Ord. 11, R. 1, R. S. C.), where its head office is (*Jones* v. *Scottish Acc. Insrce.*, 55 L. J. Q. B. 415; 17 Q. B. D. 421).

DOMINICALES TERRÆ.—*V.* DEMESNE.

DONE.—"Act done," s. 2, 35 G. 3, c. 101; *V. R.* v. *St. John, Hackney*, 4 L. J. M. C. 51; 4 N. & M. 336; 2 A. & E. 548.

An omission to do something which ought to be done in order to complete performance of a duty imposed upon a public body under an Act of Parliament, or the continuing to leave any such duty unperformed, amounts to "an act done or intended to be done" within the meaning of a clause requiring a Notice of Action (*Jolliffe* v. *Wallasey*, 43 L. J. C. P. 41 ; L. R. 9 C. P. 62 ; cited by Privy Council as laying down above definition, in *R.* v. *Williams*, 53 L. J. P. C. 71 : *Va. Wilson* v. *Halifax*, L. R. 3 Ex. 114 ; 37 L. J. Ex. 44). *Sv.* ACT : *Cp.* DO OR MAKE.

As to what is "done or intended to be done" under P. H. Act, 1875 (s. 264) ; *V. Ongley* v. *Chatham*, 3 Times Rep. 706 ; 4 Ib. 6 : under s. 106 Metrop. Man. Act, 1862 ; *V. Edwards* v. *St. Mary, Islington*, 58 L. J. Q. B. 165.

V. PURSUANCE.

DONE BY.—An act to be "done by" a person is, in general, well done by his agent (*R.* v. *Middlesex*, 20 L. J. M. C. 42 ; 1 L. M. & P. 621 : *Charles* v. *Blackwell*, 46 L. J. C. P. 368 ; 2 C. P. D. 151), unless it has to be done by HIMSELF.

DONEC.—*V.* QUAMDIU.

DOUBT.—"Do not doubt ;" *V.* PRECATORY TRUST.

DOWN.—*V.* DUNUM.

DRAIN.—The power which a Highway Authority has, under s. 67, 5 & 6 W. 4, c. 50, to make and cleanse "Ditches, Gutters, *Drains or Watercourses*," does not extend to a dumbwell or shaft into which surface-water is conducted by pipes, and from which it percolates away through the subsoil (*Croft* v. *Rickmansworth*, 58 L. J. Ch. 14 ; 4 Times Rep. 706). It was there conceded that such a dumbwell was not a "Ditch" or "Gutter ;" but the contention was that it was a "Drain or Watercourse ;" but in deciding in the negative Cotton, L. J., said, "I do not think the verb 'to drain' has anything to do with it." Fry, L. J., said, "I think 'a Drain or Watercourse' is applied to that sort of conveyance by which you direct the course of the water, and where you can follow the course of the water, and where you can correct any mischief which arises from an impediment to a flow of the water, where you can do the repairs ;" and Lopes, L. J., said, "I understand by a 'Drain' something conducting liquid away, and into and through which liquid may continuously pass ;" *V.* WATERCOURSE.

The word "Drain" in P. H. Act, 1875, means "Any Drain of and used for the drainage of one building only" (s. 4) ; *Vh. Acton* v. *Batten*, 54 L. J. Ch. 251 ; 28 Ch. D. 283 ; 52 L. T. 17 ; 49 J. P. 357.

As to the meaning of "Drain" in s. 250, Metrop. Local Man. Act, 1855 (18 & 19 V. c. 120) ; *V. Bateman* v. *Poplar*, 56 L. J. Ch. 149 ; 33 Ch. D. 360 ; 55 L. T. 374 ; 2 Times Rep. 860 ; 4 Ib. 137.

V. PUBLIC DRAIN : SEWER.

DRAMATIC.—By s. 2 of the Copyright Act, 1842 (5 & 6 V. c. 45), a "Dramatic Piece" means, "every tragedy, comedy, play, opera, farce, or other scenic, musical or dramatic entertainment." "These words comprehend any piece which could be called dramatic in its widest sense; any piece which, on being presented by any performer to an audience, would produce the emotions which are the purpose of the regular drama, and which constitute the entertainment of the audience" (per Denman, C. J., *Russell* v. *Smith*, 17 L. J. Q. B. 225; 12 Q. B. 217). Scenes and dresses are not essential to a "dramatic piece;" and such a composition as Mackay's Song of "The Ship on Fire" when sung with considerable expression was, in the case quoted, held to be a "dramatic piece." But in *Wall* v. *Taylor*, a composition called "Will o' the Wisp," the part of which that was called dramatic being a verse in which the performer departs from ordinary melody, and, in the words of the composition, "laughs, ha! ha! and laughs, ho! ho!" at which parts of the song some risibility by the performer ought to be indulged in, the learned judge (Day, J.), said that whether it was a "Dramatic Piece" was a question for the jury, but that that phrase would probably not include a performance where the performer merely exerted his vocal powers and did not resort to gesture or facial expression to endeavour to move the emotions of his audience:—there the jury found that "Will o' the Wisp" was not a "dramatic piece" (*Times*, 10 June, 1882): But it was obviously a "musical composition," and, being copyright, its unauthorized performance gave a right to the penalty provided by s. 2, 3 & 4 W. 4, c. 15, though it was not performed at a "place of dramatic entertainment;" for that condition attaches only to the representation of a dramatic piece and not to the performance of a musical composition (*Wall* v. *Taylor*, 51 L. J. Q. B. 547; 52 Ib. 558; 11 Q. B. D. 102: *Duck* v. *Bates*, 53 L. J. Q. B. 97, 338; 12 Q. B. D. 79).

A Pantomime is a "Dramatic Entertainment" within s. 2, 3 & 4 W. 4, c. 15 (*Lee* v. *Simpson*, 16 L. J. C. P. 105; 3 C. B. 871; 4 D. & L. 666).

V. Place: Entertainment.

DRAW OVER THE COUNTER.—*V. Modlen* v. *Snowball*, 4 D. G. F. & J. 145; 31 L. J. Ch. 44.

DRAWER.—Drawer of a Bill of Exchange; *V.* Bill of Exchange: and as to the liability of a Drawer, *V.* s. 55 (1), Bills of Ex. Act, 1882.

DRAWN.—Guarantee of all Bills of Ex. "drawn" by A., construed by Pollock, C. B., and Martin, B. (diss. Bramwell, B.), as referring to future Bills (*Broom* v. *Batchelor*, 25 L. J. Ex. 299; 1 H. & N. 255). *V.* Given.

DRENCH.—"Drenchs," in Domesday, "signifieth free tenants of a mannor" (Co. Litt. 5 b).

DRIFTWAY.—*V.* Way.

DRIVE: DRIVER: DRIVING.—To "drive" means "to make move;" *e.g.* to drive an ox, a steam-engine or a nail (per arg. of counsel in *Taylor* v. *Goodwin*, inf.)

A "Rider" of a horse or beast is included in the word "Driver," in the penal clause of 5 & 6 W. 4, c. 50, s. 78 (*Williams* v. *Evans*, 1 Ex. D. 277; 41 J. P. 151; 35 L. T. 864: over-ruling *R.* v. *Bacon*, 11 Cox, C. C. 540). *Cp.* RIDE.

The propulsion of a Bicycle by a person seated on, and carried by it, is "driving a Carriage" within the same section (*Taylor* v. *Goodwin*, 4 Q. B. D. 228; 48 L. J. M. C. 104; 27 W. R. 489; 43 J. P. 653).

Driving Cattle; *V.* CONDUCTING.

DRIVE AWAY.—*V.* TAKE AND CARRY AWAY.

DRUF or **DRU.**—*V.* DENE.

DRUNK.—*V.* ON THE PREMISES.

DRUNKEN PERSON.—The offence of selling intoxicants to a "drunken person" under s. 13, Licensing Act, 1872 (35 & 36 V. c. 94), is committed by a sale to a person who is drunk, although he show no indications of insobriety, and neither the license-holder nor his servants notice that he is drunk (*Cundy* v. *Le Cocq*, 53 L. J. M. C. 125; 13 Q. B. D. 207).

DUE.—A debt is still "due" notwithstanding that the Stat. of Limitations may have run against it, for that statute only bars the remedy and does not extinguish the debt; and in an Account asked for by the debtor he cannot avail himself of the statute (*Ex p. Cawley*, 34 S. J. 29).

Notwithstanding the Apportionment Act, 1870 (33 & 34 V. c. 35, s. 2), a testamentary direction to forgive a tenant "all rent or arrears of rent which may be due and *owing* from him at the time of my decease," only extends to the rent due at the quarter-day immediately preceding the testator's death (*Re Lucas*, 55 L. J. Ch. 101; 54 L. T. 30).

Gift over in event of death before a Share becomes "due *and payable;*" *V. Re Willmott*, 38 L. J. Ch. 275; L. R. 7 Eq. 532.

On a weekly hiring, wages are not "due" to a child, young person or woman, within s. 11, Employers and Workmen Act, 1875, until the end of the week; *secus*, of piece-work to be paid for weekly: "due" in this section means "earned" (*Warburton* v. *Heyworth*, 50 L. J. Q. B. 137; 6 Q. B. D. 1, distinguishing *Gregson* v. *Watson*, 34 L. T. 143).

But where Articles give a Company a lien upon a shareholder's shares for any moneys "due" from him, that means "presently payable," and gives no lien for a current Bill (*Re Stockton Iron Co.*, 45 L. J. Ch. 168; 2 Ch. D. 101).

V. DEBT: DEBTS DUE: FOUND: MONEY DUE: PAYABLE.

DUE ATTESTATION.—*V.* ATTEST.

DUE CAUSE.—The "Due Cause" which has to be shown for the removal of an Official Liquidator (s. 93, Comp. Act, 1862), is not *confined* to objections personal to the liquidator, but extends to any cause which renders it desirable, in the interest of the Company or the creditors, that the liquidator should be removed and another person substituted; and therefore a duly secured offer by a disputed creditor to pay in full the undisputed creditors of an insolvent Company if his nominee be appointed official liquidator, is "due cause" for removing an official liquidator already appointed, and appointing such nominee instead (*Re Adam Eyton, Lim.*, 36 Ch. D. 299; 57 L. J. Ch. 127; 3 Times Rep. 738).

And probably that rule would be applied to the interpretation of "due cause" as used in s. 141 of the same Act. No doubt *Sir John Moore Co.* (12 Ch. D. 325) decided that, under the latter section, "due cause shown" was not equivalent to "if the Court shall think," and pointed to some unfitness of the liquidator to be removed thereunder; yet the Court there said that they used the word "unfitness" "in a wide sense of the term." And as it seems difficult to read "due cause" differently in s. 141 from the way in which it is used in s. 93, it would seem that there would be an unfitness—a personal unfitness,—in retaining a liquidator under s. 141 if so doing would be inimical to the interests of the Company or its creditors. In that way, it is submitted, the two cases cited will stand together, and that both are applicable for determining what is "due cause" under each of the sections referred to (*Sv.* Buckl. 294, 295).

V. CAUSE: GOOD CAUSE: SPECIAL.

DUE COURSE.—*V.* HOLDER IN DUE COURSE: PAYMENT IN DUE COURSE.

DUE COURSE OF ADMINISTRATION.—A direction in a Will that on the death of a life tenant without children, a fund is to be disposed of "in a due course of administration" does not, on the event happening, give the fund to the next-of-kin according to the Statute, but the fund falls into the residue (*Scott* v. *Moore,* 13 L. J. Ch. 283; 14 Sim. 35; Wms. Exs. 1129).

DUE DILIGENCE.—A covenant to do a thing "with all due and reasonable diligence and despatch," is not excused from performance if it can be done; although the jury find that it cannot be done by any reasonable application of labour, diligence, skill, money or other means (*Jervis* v. *Tomkinson,* 26 L. J. Ex. 41; 1 H. & N. 195).

DUE INQUIRY.—*V.* INQUIRY.

DUE REGARD.—"Due Regard" to educational interests of persons entitled to privileges, s. 11, s. 39 (4), Endowed Schools Act, 1869, 32 & 33 V. c. 56; *V. Re Sutton Coldfield Grammar School,* 7 App. Ca. 91; 51

L. J. P. C. 8 ; 45 L. T. 631 ; 30 W. R. 341 : *Re Hodgson's School*, 3 App. Ca. 857 ; 47 L. J. P. C. 101 ; 38 L. T. 790 : *Ross* v. *Charity Commrs.*, 7 App. Ca. 463 ; 51 L. J. P. C. 106 ; 47 L. T. 172 : *Re Hemsworth Grammar School*, 12 App. Ca. 444 ; 56 L. T. 212 ; 35 W. R. 418 ; 3 Times Rep. 439. *Vf. Tudor Char. Trusts*, 605, 606.

DUFFER.—To charge a Pawnbroker with "duffing,"—*i.e.*, replenishing or doing up damaged pledges, and re-pledging them,—is actionable (*Hickinbotham* v. *Leach*, 11 L. J. Ex. 341 ; 10 M. & W. 361 ; 2 Dowl. N. S. 270).

DULY.—"Duly *administered* ;" *V.* PERJURY.

Sheriff "Duly *Arrested*," means that the Sheriff duly acted under authority enabling him, and was not a trespasser (*Butcher* v. *Steuart*, 12 L. J. Ex. 391 ; 11 M. & W. 857).

"Duly attested ;" *V.* ATTEST.

"Things duly *done*," within a saving clause of a repealing Act; *V. R.* v. *West Riding Jus.*, 45 L. J. M. C. 97 ; 1 Q. B. D. 220.

A clause in a Lease provided for its forfeiture if the lessee should be "duly *found and declared a bankrupt* ;" the lessee committed an act of bankruptcy and was found and declared a bankrupt, but the petitioning creditors were A. & B., whereas they should have been A. B. & C.; held, by Pollock, C. B. and Platt, B. (Parke, B., diss.), that the lessee was not "duly" found and declared bankrupt (*Doe* d. *Lloyd* v. *Ingleby*, 15 M. & W. 465).

"Duly honoured ;" *V.* HONOURED.

An applicant for an Off License under s. 8, 32 & 33 V. c. 27, need not reside in the premises and personally conduct the business there, in order to be "Duly Qualified" within sub-s. 4, Ib. (*R.* v. *Glamorgan*, 45 L. J. M. C. 57 ; 24 W. R. 343 ; 40 J. P. 150).

"Duly qualified ;" *Vf.* INFAMOUS CONDUCT.

DUM.—"*Dum* also maketh a limitation ; as if a lease be made, *dum sola fuerit*, or *dum sola et casta vixerit. Dummodo* is also a word of limitation ; as *dummodo solveret talem redditum*" (Co. Litt. 234 b).

DUNUM.—"*Dunum* or *duna* signifieth a hill or higher ground, and therefore commonly the townes that end in *dun*, have hills or higher grounds in them which we call downs. It commeth of the old French word *dun*" (Co. Litt. 4 b.).

DURESS.—As to what is Duress ; *V. Cummings* v. *Ince*, 17 L. J. Q. B. 105 ; 11 Q. B. 117, and authorities there cited : *Williams* v. *Bayley*, L. R. 1 H. L. 200 ; 14 L. T. 802. *Vf.* 2 Inst. 482 ; Dart, 1175.

DURING.—A contract for goods, to be shipped "during" specified months, implies a continuous act of shipping (per Lord Hatherley, *Bowes* v. *Shand*, 46 L. J. Q. B. 561 ; 2 App. Ca. 455).

An exception in a Charter-Party of Restraint, &c., "During the said *Voyage*," does not apply at the loading port (*Crow* v. *Falk*, 15 L. J. Q. B. 183 ; 8 Q. B. 467 : but this case disapproved in *Bruce* v. *Nicolopulo*, 11 Ex. 134).

As to meaning of "during" in s. 28, Municipal Corp. Act (5 & 6 W. 4, c. 76); *V.* jdgmt. of Bramwell, B., *Lewis* v. *Carr*, 46 L. J. Ex. 314 ; 1 Ex. D. 484.

"During the continuance ;" *V.* CONTINUANCE.

"'During *the Coverture:*' That is, during the continuance of the marriage. For to cover in *English*, is *tegere* in *Latine* ; and it is so called, for that the wife is *sub potestate viri*" (Co. Litt. 112 a ; *Va.* Ib. 32 a. ; 234 b.). A consideration of this reason seems to establish the proposition that coverture does not necessarily, and always, continue during the period that a wife retains her status of a married woman. She is only under coverture whilst she is *sub potestate viri.* Thus a covenant to settle a wife's property acquired "during the coverture" is not operative upon property acquired after a Judicial Separation (*Dawes* v. *Creyke*, 54 L. J. Ch. 1096 ; 30 Ch. D. 500 ; 53 L. T. 292 ; 33 W. R. 869 : *Waite* v. *Morland*, 38 Ch. D. 135 ; 57 L. J. Ch. 655 ; 59 L. T. 185 ; 36 W. R. 484) ; and on such a separation a restraint on alienation ceases (*Munt* v. *Glynes*, 41 L. J. Ch. 639 ; 20 W. R. 823), and the wife's *choses in action*, unreduced into possession, revert to her (*Johnson* v. *Lander*, 38 L. J. Ch. 229 ; L. R. 7 Eq. 228). Similar results follow whilst a Protection Order, under s. 21, Matrimonial Causes Act, 1857, is in operation (*Cooke* v. *Fuller*, 26 Bea. 99 : *Re Coward & Adams*, 44 L. J. Ch. 384 ; L. R. 20 Eq. 179. *Sv.* hereon *Ewart* v. *Chubb*, 45 L. J. Ch. 108 ; L. R. 20 Eq. 454 and *V. Cooke* v. *Fuller*, criticised in *Waite* v. *Morland*, sup.).

There is frequently great difficulty in construing the words "*during the coverture*" when those words occur in an ante-nuptial Marriage Settlement and the wife, *at the time of the marriage*, is possessed of other property than that mentioned in the Settlement. The question whether such other property is or is not comprised in the words is one the determination of which depends very much on the circumstances of each case and especially on the context. "The authorities seem to be such, upon the whole, as tend to show that the settlement should be taken to apply only to property which should come *in futuro* to the wife, and not to that which was hers before" (per Ld. Blackburn, *Williams* v. *Mercier*, 54 L. J. Q. B. 154 ; and his lordship there points out how easily a word or two may make all the difference). But in the same case (p. 152, Ib.) Selborne, L. C., makes the following observations :—"Then—*i.e.* where the covenant comprises property which the husband shall become entitled to 'in her right'—the question would be, whether the words, 'at any time during her now intended coverture' would apply. Surely you cannot exclude from the duration of the coverture the first moment of its inception any more than you can the last moment of its continuance. The moment that the marriage is complete by the performance of that which makes the parties husband and wife, that moment the coverture begins; and if at that moment he becomes entitled as her husband, in her right, I am totally unable to say that it is not *during* the intended coverture in a sense which the words will rightly, grammatically and reasonably bear" (*Williams* v. *Mercier*, 54 L. J. Q. B. 148; 10 App. Ca. 1; 52 L. T. 662; 33 W. R. 373; 49 J. P. 484, *wh. V.* for a discussion of the cases on this point; *V. Williams* v. *Mercier* distinguished, *Re Garnett*, 33 Ch. D. 300. *Vf. Re D'Estampes*, 53 L. J. Ch. 1117).

In *Re Edwards* (9 Ch. 97; 43 L. J. Ch. 265) the phrase "during the said intended coverture" was read into a covenant to settle contained in a Marriage Settlement; herein adopting *Dickinson* v. *Dillwyn* (39 L. J. Ch. 266; L. R. 8 Eq. 546) and *Carter* v. *Carter* (39 L. J. Ch. 268; L. R. 8 Eq. 551), and over-ruling *Stevens* v. *Van Voorst* (17 Bea. 305).

V. Entitled.

It has been said that "a *Lease* to one generally *during the coverture of* A. & B., would create but a tenancy at will, by reason of the uncertainty of the duration of the coverture" (Woodf. 158, citing Bac. Abr. tit. *Leases*, L. 3; *Sq.*).

"During *her life;*" Where on a *Separation* Arrangement, property is settled on, or an allowance is made to the wife "during her life," that means, generally, during her life if the separation shall last so long (*Nicol* v. *Nicol*, 54 L. J. Ch. 1042; 55 Ib. 437; 31 Ch. D. 524; 54 L. T. 470; 34 W. R. 283; 50 J. P. 468; 2 Times Rep. 280; which *V.* for a review of the previous cases, and especially for those in which the context has shown that the wife was to take during the whole period of her natural life, whether co-habitation be resumed or not). So of a Separation Order under s. 4, 41 & 42 V. c. 19 (*Haddon* v. *Haddon*, 18 Q. B. D. 778).

"During *Separation;*" A bequest to a wife "during such time as she may live apart from her husband" is void altogether; for the words quoted are part of the limitation of the gift and fixes its duration in an illegal way (*Re Moore*, 57 L. J. Ch. 936; 39 Ch. D. 116; 59 L. T. 681; 37 W. R. 83).

"During *their lives;*" The bequest of an annuity to more than one "During their natural lives" is joint, and does not lapse by the death of one in the lifetime of the testator, and the survivor will take the annuity for his own life (*Alder* v. *Lawless*, 32 Bea. 72).

"During *the Term,*" *V.* 2 Platt, 91–95; Woodf. 588, 678, 158. In a covenant in a Lease, "'During the said term' means during the whole term expressed to be granted, and not merely during the actual continuance of the term (*Evans* v. *Vaughan*, 4 B. & C. 261; 6 D. & R. 349: *Williams* v. *Burrell*, 1 C. B. 402; 14 L. J. C. P. 98; 9 Jur. 282); although it is otherwise where the covenant is implied by law" (Woodf. 678).

A covenant that lessee shall "during the term" hold discharged from tithes and to recoup him if same "recovered against him during the term," covers tithes for which action is brought against the lessee *after* the term (*Lanning* v. *Lovering,* Cro. Eliz. 916).

DUTCH TERMS.—*V.* On Dutch Terms.

DUTIES.—Where a lessee covenants to bear and pay all "Duties" respecting the premises demised, that word will comprise the expense of curing defective drainage under s. 96, P. H. Act, 1875 (*Budd* v. *Marshall,* 50 L. J. Q. B. 24; 5 C. P. D. 481; and *V.* that case cited, Taxes).

"If A. be accountable to B. and B. releaseth him all his duties, this is no barre in an action of account, for duties extend to things certaine, and what shall fall out upon the account is incertaine; and albeit the Latine word is *debita,* yet duties doe extend to all things due that are certaine, and therefore dischargeth judgments in personall actions, and executions also" (Co. Litt. 291 a.).

DWELL.—To "dwell," "dwelling," are expressions nearly equivalent to "Reside," "Residence." A person may "dwell" in two or more places (*Butler* v. *Ablewhite,* 28 L. J. C. P. 292); and a member of parliament residing in London for about 3 months in the year would "dwell" there, as well as at his country seat (*Bailey* v. *Bryant,* 28 L. J. Q. B. 86; 1 E. & E. 340). A man can, however, scarcely be said to "dwell" at his place of business (*Kerr* v. *Haynes,* 29 L. J. Q. B. 70: *Shields* v. *Rait,* 18 L. J. C. P. 120; 7 C. B. 116); still less in a prison in which he may be temporarily incarcerated (*Dunston* v. *Paterson,* 28 L. J. C. P. 97; 5 C. B. N. S. 267). But a Corporation can only "dwell" where it carries on business (*Taylor* v. *Crowland Gas Co.,* 24 L. J. Ex. 233; 11 Ex. 1; 3 W. R. 368); but that means the *principal* place where the business of the Corporation is carried on,—*e.g.* the Great Western Ry. Co. "dwells" at Paddington and not at every station on its lines of railway (*Adams* v. *G. W. Ry.,* 30 L. J. Ex. 124; 6 H. & N. 404; 9 W. R. 254. *Va. Shiels* v. *G. N. Ry.,* 30 L. J. Q. B. 331; 9 W. R. 739).

A manufacturing joint-stock Company "dwells and carries on business" within s. 74, County Courts Act, 1888, at its place of manufacture and sale, and not at the registered office of the company (*Keynsham Lime Co.* v. *Baker,* 33 L. J. Ex. 41; 2 H. & C. 729: *Aberystwith Promenade Pier Co.* v. *Cooper,* 35 L. J. Q. B. 44: *Baillie* v. *Goodwin,* 33 Ch. D. 605).

V. Carry On: Inhabit.

DWELLING-HOUSE.—A "Dwelling-house" is obviously a House with the super-added requirement that it is dwelt in or the dwellers in which are absent only temporarily, having *animus revertendi* and the legal ability to return (*Ford* v. *Barnes*, 55 L. J. Q. B. 24). "House" and "Dwelling-house" are used in their respective meanings in the Acts conferring the parliamentary franchise,—"House" in s. 27, Reform Act, 1832, and "Dwelling-house" in s. 3, sub-s. 2, Rep. People Act, 1867. The latter Act gives the franchise to one who for the prescribed time has been an "*inhabitant* occupier, as owner or tenant, of any dwelling-house." The word "inhabitant" here would seem to bring out more fully the meaning of the word "dwelling-house."

The difficulties experienced in determining the meaning of "Dwelling-house" as used in the Rep. People Act, 1867 (*Ellis* v. *Burch*, *Thompson* v. *Ward*, 40 L. J. C. P. 169; L. R. 6 C. P. 327: *Boon* v. *Howard*, 43 L. J. C. P. 115; 9 C. P. 277), are now, to some extent at least, set at rest by s. 5, 41 & 42 V. c. 26.

A Covenant prohibiting user otherwise than as a "*private* dwelling-house," would be broken by keeping the premises as an hotel or lodging-house; because although either would be a dwelling-house after a fashion, neither would be private (*Rolls* v. *Miller*, 53 L. J. Ch. 682, and especially jdgmt. of Lindley, L. J. *V.* PRIVATE DWELLING-HOUSE).

In Burglary, a "Dwelling-house" "means a permanent building in which the owner, or the tenant or any member of the family, habitually sleeps at night" (Steph. Cr. 247; for the cases *V.* Arch. Cr. 561–564; *Va.* 24 & 25 V. c. 96, s. 53). Lord Coke thought that Burglary might be committed in a church, "for ecclesia est domus mansionalis omnipotentis Dei" (3 Inst. 64); but Lord Hale thought—(he might possibly have spoken more decidedly)—that that opinion was only a quaint turn without any argument (1 Hale, 556; *V.* now 24 & 25 V. c. 96, s. 50).

"Dwelling-house" in s. 9, 18 & 19 V. c. 128, means the *building*, so that the 100 yards therein mentioned have to be measured from the walls of the dwelling-house itself (*Wright* v. *Wallasey*, 56 L. J. Q. B. 259; 18 Q. B. D. 783; 52 J. P. 4; 3 Times Rep. 525).

A Public-house in which a man has taken up his temporary abode (he having no other place of abode) is, *semble*, his "Dwelling-house" within s. 6 (d), Bankry. Act, 1883 (*Holroyd* v. *Gwynne*, 2 Taunt. 176), and certainly, for the purpose of this section, a "Dwelling-house" need not be an entire house, or a dwelling self-contained, or on a vertical plane as distinguished from a horizontal;—rooms which furnish a separate dwelling and are not mere lodgings, will suffice (*Re Hecquard*, W. N. (89) 187; 34 S. J. 96).

In a case of old fashioned pleading, proof that plaintiff was a lodger occupying two rooms in a house, was held not to support the averment that he was possessed of a "Dwelling-house" (*Monks* v. *Dykes*, 4 M. & W. 567; 8 L. J. Ex. 73).

In Rule 1, to the First and Second Cases of s. 100, Income Tax Act (5 & 6 V. c. 35), "Dwelling-house" means a house in which the person liable to pay Income Tax personally dwells; and therefore though a servant,—*e.g.* a Bank Manager,—for the purposes of a business, lives in a part of the business premises, nevertheless the value of the whole premises may be deducted in ascertaining the profits of the business liable to tax (*Russell* v. *Town & County Bank*, 58 L. J. P. C. 8). *V.* PROFITS.

But a Bank having a care-taker living in it, is an "*Inhabited* Dwelling-house" *quà* House Duty, s. 1, 14 & 15 V. c. 36 (*Chartered Mer. Bank of India* v. *Wilson*, 47 L. J. Ex. 153; nom. *Bank of India* v. *Wilson*, 3 Ex. D. 108); *secus*, of a Club not slept in at night (*Riley* v. *Read*, 48 L. J. Ex. 437; 4 Ex. D. 100). *V.* SERVANT, at end.

"Dwelling-house" in New River Co.'s Act, 1852, s. 35, means "any house which is so far adapted for the purposes which a dwelling-house is usually adapted to, as to require water for domestic purposes; and it is not necessary that all the house should be so adapted" (per Cotton, L. J., *Cooke* v. *New River Co.*, 57 L. J. Ch. 385; 38 Ch. D. 56; 58 L. T. 830; affd. in H. L. 14 App. Ca. 698).

DWELLING PLACE.—"Own Dwelling-place or Shop," s. 13, Markets and Fairs Clauses Act, 1847 (10 V. c. 14); *V. Ashworth* v. *Heyworth*, L. R. 4 Q. B. 316: *Fearon* v. *Mitchell*, 41 L. J. M. C. 170; L. R. 7 Q. B. 690: *McHole* v. *Davies*, 45 L. J. M. C. 30; 1 Q. B. D. 59: *Hooper* v. *Kenshole*, 46 L. J. M. C. 160; 2 Q. B. D. 127. *V.* SHOP.

DYE.—"'To dye Seeds,' means to give to seeds, by any process of colouring, dyeing, sulphur-smoking, or other artificial means, the appearance of seeds of another *kind*" (s. 2, 32 & 33 V. c. 112); but that does not include sulphur-smoking old clover seeds so as to make them look like young clover seeds, for the seeds do not thereby resemble another "kind" of seeds: *secus*, had the expression been "quality," or "kind or sort" (*Francis* v. *Maas*, 47 L. J. M. C. 83; 3 Q. B. D. 341). *V.* ADULTERATION: NATURE.

DYING.—*V.* DIE.

EACH.—A gift to "each" of two or more persons, or to "each of their respective heirs" (*Gordon* v. *Atkinson*, 1 D. G. & S. 478 : *Cp. Ex p. Tanner*, 24 L. J. Ch. 657; 20 Bea. 374 : *Vf.* 2 Jarm. 257), creates a tenancy in common.

As to effect of "each" in a contract or bond; *V. Mathewson's Case*, 5 Rep. 22 : *Collins* v. *Prosser*, 1 B. & C. 682 : *Armstrong* v. *Cahill*, 6 L. R. Ir. 440.

EARNEST.—For the derivation, history and effect of the "Earnest" of a Bargain; *V.* jdgmt. of Fry, L. J., in *Howe* v. *Smith*, 53 L. J. Ch. 1061; 27 Ch. D. 89. *Va.* Deposit.

"It is my Earnest *Hope* and I particularly request" non-alienation, when added to a devise in fee, does not qualify, but is repugnant to, the devise (*Hood* v. *Oglander*, 34 L. J. Ch. 528 ; 34 Bea. 513).

EARNINGS.—"Earnings and property," s. 21, 20 & 21 V. c. 85, mean honest earnings, not the wages of prostitution (*Mason* v. *Mitchell*, 34 L. J. Ex. 68 ; 3 H. & C. 528 ; 29 J. P. 119).

"Earnings," s. 2, M. W. P. Act, 1882 ; *V. Re Poole*, 46 L. J. Ch. 803; 6 Ch. D. 739.

EASEMENTS.—"Easements" in s. 2, Prescription Act (2 & 3 W. 4, c. 71), have been said to mean easements analogous to rights of way and water (per Erle, *Webb* v. *Bird*, 30 L. J. C. P. 387) ; but that dictum was disapproved by Selborne, L. C., in *Dalton* v. *Angus* (50 L. J. Q. B. 733, 734). An easement to be within the section must however be one of utility and benefit and not of mere amusement,—*e.g.* a prospect,—nor indefinite, such as the access of air to a windmill, a chimney, or to an open structure for storing timber (*Webb* v. *Bird*, 30 L. J. C. P. 384 ; 31 Ib. 335 ; 10 C. B. N. S. 268 ; 13 Ib. 841: *Bryant* v. *Lefever*, 48 L. J. C. P. 380 ; 4 C. P. D. 172: *Dalton* v. *Angus*, 50 L. J. Q. B. 689 ; 6 App. Ca. 740 : *Harris* v. *De Pinna*, 56 L. J. Ch. 344 ; 33 Ch. D. 238 ; 54 L. T. 770 ; 50 J. P. 486. *Vf.* Add. T. 269, 294 ; Rosc. N. P. 717).

The word "Easements" in s. 20, Artizans' and Labourers' Dwellings Improvement Act, 1875 (38 & 39 V. c. 36), means, easements of every kind (*Badham* v. *Marris*, 45 L. T. 579 ; 52 L. J. Ch. 237 : *Swainston* v. *Finn*, 52 L. J. Ch. 235).

Parliamentary running powers over a railway are not an "Easement" (per Jessel, M. R., *G. W. Ry.* v. *Swindon Ry.*, 52 L. J. Ch. 314, 317; *secus*, per Cotton, L. J., Ib. 320; *Va.* per Bowen, L. J., Ib. 321, 322: *V.* that case in the H. L. 53 L. J. Ch. 1075; 9 App. Ca. 787).

Vh. Gale on Easements; Watson, Eq. tit. "Easements," 139 *et seq.*

EAST INDIA STOCK.—*V.* the use of this phrase in s. 32, 22 & 23 V. c. 35, explained by s. 1, 30 & 31 V. c. 132.

EAST INDIES.—The Mauritius is not in the East Indies, nor is it an East Indian Island (*Robertson* v. *Clarke,* 1 Bing. 445).

EBB AND FLOW.—*V. A.-G.* v. *Chambers,* 4 D. G. M. & G. 206; 23 L. J. Ch. 662; 2 W. R. 636: *Ilchester* v. *Raishley,* cited NAVIGABLE.

ECCLESIASTICAL COMMISSIONERS.—*V.* s. 12 (15), Interp. Act, 1889.

ECCLESIASTICAL COURT.—*V. Re Green,* 51 L. J. Q. B. 25; 7 Q. B. D. 273; nom. *Green* v. *Penzance,* 6 App. Ca. 657.

ECCLESIASTICAL PURPOSE.—Marriage, when it takes place in a church, is an ecclesiastical function; and the solemnization of marriages is an "Ecclesiastical Purpose" within the New Parishes Acts, 1843 and 1856, 6 & 7 V. c. 37, s. 15; 19 & 20 V. c. 104, s. 14 (*Fuller* v. *Alford,* 52 L. J. Q. B. 265; 10 Q. B. D. 418); so is Burial (*Hughes* v. *Lloyd,* 58 L. J. Q. B. 122; 22 Q. B. D. 157).

EDITION.—In a contract between an author and a publisher, an "Edition" consists of so many copies as are issued to the public at a time; and, where the work is stereotyped, every fresh issue is a new Edition (*Reade* v. *Bentley,* 27 L. J. Ch. 254; 4 K. & J. 656). In that case Wood, V.-C., said (27 L. J. Ch. 259), "I apprehend the meaning of the word 'Editions,' is the putting forth the work *at successive periods;* and whether that is done by moveable type or by stereotype does not seem to me to make any substantial difference."

EDUCATION.—"Education" means training up the young in general learning; not teaching for a business or profession. Therefore the property of the Institution of Civil Engineers is not exempt (under. s. 11, subs. 3, Customs & Inl. Rev. Act, 1885, 48 & 49 V. c. 51) from assessment because used "for the promotion of Education" (*Re Institution of Civil Engineers,* 19 Q. B. D. 610; 20 Ib. 621; 56 L. J. Q. B. 576; 57 Ib. 353; 36 W. R. 523, 598; 3 Times Rep. 729). *V.* SCIENCE.

"Education *and* Learning," in a Charitable Bequest, read "Education *in* Learning" (*Whicker* v. *Hume,* 7 H. L. Ca. 124; 21 L. J. Ch. 406; 28 Ib. 396; 1 D. G. M. & G. 506; 14 Bea. 509).

EDUCATION DEPARTMENT.—*V.* s. 12 (6), Interp. Act, 1889.

EDUCATIONAL ENDOWMENT.—As used in s. 19 (1), Endowed Schools Act, 1869, 32 & 33 V. c. 56; *V. Re Holgate's School*, 56 L. J. P. C. 52.

EFFECT.—The "Effect" of a Cause, is anything which would not have happened but for that cause; and it is none the less an Effect of such a Cause, because it has been developed or accelerated by something supervening. Therefore where a Policy assured against "any injury *caused by* Accident or Violence . . . ., and if the assured should die from the *Effects* of such injury," and the assured met with an accident and died from pneumonia resulting from a cold the catching of which and its fatal result were due to the bad condition of his health which was the consequence of the injury caused by the accident;—Held, that the death resulted from "the Effects" of the injury (*Re Isitt and Railway Passengers' Assrce.*, 58 L. J. Q. B. 191; 22 Q. B. D. 504; 5 Times Rep. 194). *Cp.* CAUSED BY.

To *prosecute* a Replevin, within condition of Replevin Bond (or any other matter?) "*with* Effect," is to conduct it to a not unsuccessful termination (*Perreau* v. *Bevan*, 4 L. J. O. S. K. B. 177; 5 B. & C. 284: *Jackson* v. *Hanson*, 10 L. J. Ex. 396; 8 M. & W. 477); and such is the meaning even where a replevin is removed by the Defendant (*Tummons* v. *Ogle*, 25 L. J. Q. B. 403; 6 E. & B. 571); so that in no case can the death of the plaintiff be a breach (*Ormond* v. *Bierly*, Carth. 519: *Morris* v. *Matthews*, 11 L. J. Q. B. 57; 2 Q. B. 293). *Vf.* PROSECUTE.

"*Immaterial* to the Effect," in the Specification of a Patent; *V. Neilson* v. *Harford*, 11 L. J. Ex. 20; 8 M. & W. 806.

EFFECTIVE.—"Most proper and effective manner;" *V.* WORKABLE.

EFFECTS.—"The word 'Effects' (and even the word 'Goods' or 'Chattels') will, it seems, comprise the entire personal estate of the testator, unless restrained by the context within narrower limits" (1 Jarm. 751: *Va.* Wms. Exs. 1184: *Hodgson* v. *Jex*, 45 L. J. Ch. 388; 2 Ch. D. 122: *Re Shepheard*, 48 L. J. P. D. & A. 62: *Dunally* v. *Dunally*, 6 Ir. Ch. Rep. 540):—for an example of such a context, *V. Borton* v. *Dunbar*, 30 L. J. Ch. 8.

"Effects," standing alone, will *not* comprise Realty (1 Jarm. 724: *Henderson* v. *Farbridge*, 1 Russ. 479; cited 1 Jarm. 742: *Cross* v. *Wilks*, 35 Bea. 562: *Doe* d. *Haw* v. *Earles*, 16 L. J. Ex. 242; 15 M. & W. 457: *Belaney* v. *Belaney*, 2 Ch. 138; 35 Bea. 469; 36 L. J. Ch. 265: *Sv. Smyth* v. *Smyth*, 8 Ch. D. 561).

But in a case which came from British Honduras the P. C. said, "Their Lordships think that the word 'Effects' would pass land; and that word is certainly sufficient to pass a privilege of cutting logwood on a definite piece of land" (*A.-G. British Honduras* v. *Bristowe*, 50 L. J. P. C. 18; 6 App. Ca. 143).

"Effects" mean Realty (and it should seem nothing else) in such a phrase as Real Effects ; and "Effects" may include Realty if aided by a context ; *e.g.* (possibly) if the operative word be "Devise" (*Phillips* v. *Beal*, 25 Bea. 25 : *Sv.*, contra, *Camfield* v. *Gilbert*, 3 East, 516 : *V.* Devise : *Va. Stelfox* v. *Stelfox*, W. N. (74) 161: *Glover* v. *Chancellor*, W. N. (76) 152, wh. latter case dissents from *Doe* v. *Dring*, 2 M. & S. 454 : Rest. For full discussion of the cases on this contextual construction, *V.* 1 Jarm. 744–747, 749 ; Watson, Eq. 1319–1322). *Vf.* Temporal.

Bequest, *inter alia*, of "Effects" may carry moneys and book debts (*Re Parrott*, 53 L. T. 12 ; W. N. (85) 127) ; but a bequest of "Household Furniture and Effects" does not pass jewellery (*Northey* v. *Paxton*, 60 L. T. 30).

Bequest of Stock in Trade, Goodwill and "Effects," held to pass Trade Fixtures (*Pinder* v. *Pinder*, 18 W. R. 309).

As to "Effects" in a Marine Insurance ; *V. Duff* v. *Mackenzie*, 26 L. J. C. P. 313 ; 3 C. B. N. S. 16.

"Effects, Stock, Books and Book Debts," in an Assignment for the benefit of creditors by a Grocer and Farmer, will, under "Effects," convey the farm cattle (*Lewis* v. *Rogers*, 3 L. J. Ex. 326 ; 1 Cr. M. & R. 48 ; 4 Tyr. 872). In that case Lyndhurst, C. B., said, "'Effects' is *nomen generalissimum*, and the rule that it ought to be limited does not apply, because it precedes, instead of following, the enumeration of specific things."

"Effects *and Things*," in Partnership Articles, held equivalent to "Assets," and to include Goodwill (*Rolt* v. *Bulmer*, W. N. (78) 119 : *Reynolds* v. *Bullock*, Ib. 122 : *Hall* v. *Barrows*, 4 D. G. J. & S. 150 : *V.* Things) ; so of the phrase "other the Estate and Effects" (*Steuart* v. *Gladstone*, 47 L. J. Ch. 423 ; 10 Ch. D. 626 ; 38 L. T. 557).

V. Estate and Effects : Property and Effects.

EFFICIENTLY.—*V.* Fairly.

EFFORTS.—*V.* Utmost.

EGRESS.—*V.* Ingress.

EITHER.—Where there is a Devise to two, "but in case *either one* of them should die without children that share to go to the other," and both die without children, the property on the death of the one who died first goes to the other (*Drennan* v. *Andrew*, 36 L. J. Ch. 1 ; 1 Ch. 300).

In *Re Hill to Chapman* the question turned on the following phrase in a Will,—"in case of the death of either of them ;" on which Brett, M.R., observed, "I think the word 'either' means 'one,' and not 'the other'" (54 L. J. Ch. 597). So in *Sharp* v. *Sharp* (2 B. & Ald. 405 ; stated, Lewin, 655), a power to appoint new Trustees "in case *either*" of the appointed Trustees should die, &c., "either" was held to mean "some one" of the Trustees, not "all" of them.

V. One.

ELDEST.—The *primâ facie* meaning of "Eldest" is "Eldest, or First, born" (2 Jarm. 213 : *Bathurst* v. *Errington,* 46 L. J. Ch. 748 ; 2 App. Ca. 698 : *Meredith* v. *Treffry,* 48 L. J. Ch. 337 ; 12 Ch. D. 170). It is, however, sometimes construed as meaning the person already provided for.

Where provisions are made by any person, whether *in loco parentis* or not, for "younger children," by an instrument that does not make provision, or does not refer to or is not shown by extrinsic evidence to be connected with provisions already made, for the "eldest" child, the words "younger" and "eldest" are used in their primary meaning. On the other hand, where the provisions are made by a person *in loco parentis* for "younger" children, by an instrument which limits an estate to, or refers to, or is shown by extrinsic evidence to be connected with, an instrument limiting an estate to the "eldest" child, the word "eldest" is a designation of the person succeeding to the estate, *i.e.,* "provided for,"—and "younger," of the person not doing so, *i.e.,* "unprovided for" (Elph. 338 *et seq.*, and cases there cited in illustration and exception : *Vf.* 2 Jarm. 201 : and as to when the "eldest" and "younger" children are to be ascertained, 2 Jarm. 204–213. *Va.* Wms. Exs. 1094). But "*Livesey* v. *Livesey* (2 H. L. Ca. 419) is a decision of the H. L. that where you cannot read 'eldest son' as meaning son entitled to a particular estate, the words must have their literal signification" (per Kay, J., *Domvile* v. *Winnington,* 53 L. J. Ch. 786 ; 26 Ch. D. 382, in which case the word was construed literally).

"An eldest or only son, *primâ facie,* means one individual and not a series of persons" (per Kay, J., *Domvile* v. *Winnington,* sup.) ; and it was accordingly held in that case that when once a clause of exclusion has had its application, it has become satisfied and its operation exhausted.

It requires a strong context to construe "Eldest Son" as words of limitation, and so giving an estate tail to the person whose eldest son is referred to (*V.* discussion hereon, 2 Jarm. 407–410).

In *Thellusson* v. *Rendlesham* (28 L. J. Ch. 948 ; 7 H. L. Ca. 429), a case on the celebrated Thellusson Will, "Eldest"—in the phrase "Eldest Male Lineal Descendant,"—was construed prior in line, not senior by birth. In his judgment in that case Lord Wensleydale said,—"The 'eldest' Magistrate, or Officer, might not mean him who had lived the greatest number of years, nor even him who had filled the office for the longest time, for it might indicate rank only, and the 'Eldest Earl of England' would not mean him who was most advanced in years, but the eldest in point of family origin,—The Premier Earl."

"Eldest or Only Son *entitled in possession or remainder;*" *V. Carter* v. *Ducie,* W. N. (71) 236.

"*Become* Eldest Son ;" *V. Craven* v. *Errington, Bathurst* v. *Errington,* sup.
Vh. Chitty, Eq. Ind. 7678, 7710.

ELECTION.—*V.* Contested Election.

ELIGIBLE.—This word, as applied to the selection of persons, has two meanings, *i.e.*, "legally qualified," or "fit to be chosen" (per Ld. Chelmsford, *Baker* v. *Lee*, 30 L. J. Ch. 631 ; 8 H. L. Ca. 495).

V. Fit.

ELOPE.—"If the wife elope from her husband,—that is, if the wife leave her husband, and goeth away and tarrieth with her adulterer,—she shall lose her Dower until her husband, willingly without coertion ecclesiasticall be reconciled unto her" (Co. Litt. 32 a, b). "And if she goeth willingly with or to the avowtrer, this is a departure and a tarrying, albeit she remaineth not continually with the avowtrer" (Ib. 32 b.). *V.* Willingly.

ELSEWHERE.—A testamentary gift of all in a certain locality, "or elsewhere," includes the residuary personal estate (*Re Scarborough*, 30 L. J. P. M. & A. 85).

"The words 'the United Kingdom or elsewhere' (s. 2, Sch. D., Income Tax Act, 1853, 16 & 17 V. c. 34), by the alternative description, include the whole world" (per Fry, L.J., *Colquhoun* v. *Brooks*, 57 L. J. Q. B. 443 ; 21 Q. B. D. 52 ; 59 L. T. 661 ; 36 W. R. 657 ; 52 J. P. 645). But the decision of the majority of the Court of Appeal (affd. 14 App. Ca. 493) was the other way, and Esher, M.R., said,—"I do not think, when the Act is looked at, that 'Elsewhere' is meant to include every other part of the inhabited globe. There may be some outlying parts of the Queen's dominions which are not colonies, but over which the Queen exercises all sovereign rights, and therefore places in which Parliament has a right to exercise all its rights, and the words 'or elsewhere' may have been inserted by way of caution to include such places. I cannot think that they are meant to include all colonies which have their own Parliaments, nor all foreign countries."

V. Insured Elsewhere.

EMBARGO.—"An Embargo is an arrest laid on ships or merchandize by public authority, or an order prohibiting ships from putting to sea, and sometimes from entering ports" (Wood. 353).

EMBARRASS.—To "Embarrass," Ord. 19, R. 27, R. S. C., means to state in a party's pleading, matter that he is not entitled to make use of (per Jessel, M.R., *Heugh* v. *Chamberlain*, 25 W. R. 742 ; W. N. (77) 128 : *Va. Spurr* v. *Hall*, 46 L. J. Q. B. 693 ; 2 Q. B. D. 615 : *Berdan* v. *Greenwood*, 47 L. J. Ex. 628 ; 3 Ex. D. 251). A defence is not embarrassing by reason of alleging several inconsistent statements of fact (*Re Morgan*, 35 Ch. D. 492 ; 56 L. J. Ch. 603 ; 56 L. T. 503 ; 35 W. R. 705 ; affd. 39 Ch. D. 316).

EMBEZZLE.—"When a Clerk or a Servant, or person employed in the capacity of a clerk or servant, commits theft by converting any chattel, money, or valuable security delivered to or received, or taken into possession by him for or in the name or on account of his master or employer, his offence is called Embezzlement" (Steph. Cr. ch. 36, *wh. V.* hereon).

"The distinction between Embezzlement by a clerk or servant and other kinds of Theft is, that in other kinds of theft the property stolen is taken out of the possession of the owner, whereas in Embezzlement by a clerk or servant the property embezzled is converted by the offender whilst it is in the offender's possession on account of his master and before that possession has been changed into a mere custody" (Ib. 241).

Vf. Arch. Cr. 500–515; Rosc. Cr. 458–479.

EMBLEMENTS.—"Emblements" is the right which the occupier of land (or his personal representatives) has to reap in peace the crop which he sowed, when his occupation has been determined by his death or otherwise unexpectedly comes to an end from a cause beyond his control (Co. Litt. 55 a,—56 a). As to Emblements as between Heir and Executor, *V.* Wms. Exs. 715 *et seq.*; and as between Landlord and Tenant, *V.* Woodf. 749–752, and especially, in the latter connection, *V.* 14 & 15 V. c. 25, which in most cases substitutes the right of continued occupation for Emblements. *Va.* Dart, 235.

EMBRACERY.—"Everyone commits the misdemeanor called Embracery who by any means whatever except the production of evidence and argument in open Court, attempts to influence or instruct any juryman, or to incline him to be more favorable to the one side than to the other in any judicial proceeding, whether any verdict is given or not, and whether such verdict, if given, is true or false" (Steph. Cr. 88, 89). *Vf.* Rosc. Cr. 721; Co. Litt. 369 a.

EMOLUMENT.—*V.* Annual Emolument.

EMOLUMENTS.—*V.* Advantages.

The share of revenues which Canons have immemorially received in common with the rest of a Chapter, is "Emoluments" within s. 1, 4 & 5 W. 4, c. 90 (*Ecc. Commrs.* v. *Kildare*, 8 Ir. Ch. Rep. 93).

EMPLOY.—A contract "to employ" does not generally mean to find actual employment; it rather means, to retain and pay a person, whether employed or not, but if employed then to be employed in the work only in respect of which the contract is made. "Medical advisers may be employed at a salary to be ready in case of illness; members of theatrical establishments in case their labours should be needed; household servants in performance of their duty when their masters wish: in these and other similar cases the requirement of actual service is distinct from the employment by the party employing" (per Parke, B., delivering jdgmt. of the Ex. Cham. in *Elderton* v. *Emmens*, 17 L. J. C. P. 309; affd. 4 H. L. Ca. 624). *Vh. Whittle* v. *Frankland*, 2 B. & S. 49.

"In his employ:" *V.* Servant.

EMPLOYED.—"Person employed under the Post Office," s. 26, 7 W. 4 & 1 V. c. 36 ; "The term 'employed' in this statute, means 'engaged or occupied'" (per Parke, B., *R.* v. *Reason*, 23 L. J. M. C. 13 ; Dears. 226), and it was there held that a person who, at a post-master's request, gratuitously assisted him in sorting letters was within the section.

"Employed for the purpose or in the capacity of a Clerk or Servant," s. 68, 24 & 25 V. c. 96 ; a son who lived with and gratuitously assisted his father as Clerk to a Local Board, was held to have been "employed" by the father (*R.* v. *Foulkes*, 44 L. J. M. C. 65 ; L. R. 2 C. C. R. 150 ; 23 W. R. 696 ; 39 J. P. 501).

Solicitor "employed," s. 28, 23 & 24 V. c. 127 ; *V. Baile* v. *Baile*, W. N. (72) 45 : Recovered or Preserved.

The phrase "Employed in a Mine" in s. 18, Coal Mines Regulation Act, 1872 (35 & 36 V. c. 76), means employed *by the mine-owner* (*Hopkinson* v. *Caunt*, 54 L. J. Q. B. 284 ; 14 Q. B. D. 592).

"Persons employed on or about" a Mine, as this phrase is used in a Special Rule for the due management of the Mine, include those so employed who have discharged themselves whilst in the Mine, and the character of being so employed attaches to such until they get out of the Mine or until a reasonable time has elapsed before they are let out (*Higham* v. *Wright*, 46 L. J. M. C. 223 ; 2 C. P. D. 397).

V. Capital employed : Coasting Trade.

EMPOWER.—*V.* Precatory Trust.

EMPOWERED.—*V.* May : Shall and lawfully may.

EMPTY.—A Gale liable to be forfeited to the Crown for non-working, under s. 29, Dean Forest Act, 1838, is not *empty* till the Officer of the Crown has exercised the option to forfeit the gale (*James* v. *Young*, 53 L. J. Ch. 793 ; 27 Ch. D. 652).

ENABLING.—"In exercise of the power thereby reserved, and of all other powers enabling me in this behalf ;" as to the comprehensiveness of this phrase, *V. Southall* v. *Jones*, 28 L. J. P. & M. 112 ; 1 Sw. & Tr. 298.

ENCLOSED LANDS.—*V.* Inclosed Lands.

ENCLOSURE.—A permission,—*e.g.*, by a Lord of the Manor,—to occasionally erect a temporary circus on a small part of a Waste, is not an "Enclosure or Encroachment" on the Waste, within an Act for its free preservation (*Malvern Hill Conservators* v. *Foley*, 4 Times Rep. 672).

V. Parcel.

ENCROACHMENT.—*V.* Enclosure.

END.—When a person has to do a thing "at the End" of a period of time,—*e.g.*, claim "at the end of the year," repayment of Income Tax under s. 133. 5 & 6 V. c. 35,—that does not mean that he is to do it at any time, or within a reasonable time after such period ; "but it is to be done in the shortest time a person can do it if he has made every exertion which (in the particular case) he ought to have made" (per Esher, M.R., *R.* v. *Income Tax Commrs.*, 57 L. J. Q. B. 516 ; 21 Q. B. D. 313 ; 59 L. T. 455 ; 36 W. R. 776).

V. EXPIRATION : FOOT.

ENDANGER.—*V.* DANGER.

ENDEAVOURS.—*V.* UTMOST.

ENDORSE.—A direction to "endorse" anything on a document means, as a general rule, to write it on the *back* of the document (*Ackers* v. *Howard*, 55 L. J. Q. B. 278 ; 16 Q. B. D. 739 ; 54 L. T. 651 ; 34 W. R. 609 ; 50 J. P. 519 : which was a decision on R. 36, Ballot Act, 1872).

But this definition is not of universal application ; for it is not essential to the validity of an indorsement of a Bill of Exchange or Promissory Note that it should be on the back of the document ; it may equally well be on the face (Byles on Bills, 14 Ed. 171, citing *R.* v. *Bigg*, 1 Stra. 18 : *Ex p. Yates*, 27 L. J. Bank. 9 : *Yarborough* v. *Bank of England*, 16 East, 9). So s. 32 (1), Bills of Ex. Act, 1882, says that an Indorsement "must be written *on* the Bill itself." *Vf.* as to the requisites of an Indorsement of a Bill or Note, ss. 32 to 37 of that Act ; and as to liability of an Indorser, s. 55 (2).

ENDOW.—A bequest "to Endow" an institution does not offend the law of mortmain (*Edwards* v. *Hall*, 25 L. J. Ch. 82 ; 11 Hare, 1 ; 6 D. G. M. & G. 74). In that case Cranworth, L.C., in giving jdgmt. said,—"By the Endowment of a school, an hospital or a chapel, is commonly understood not the building, or providing a site for, a school or hospital or chapel ; but the providing of a fixed revenue for the support of those by whom the institutions are conducted." *Vf. Kirkbank* v. *Hudson*, 7 Price, 212 : Tudor, Char. Trusts, 410, 413 : 1 Jarm. 228, 230 : PROVIDE : FOUND : ERECT.

ENDOWMENT.—An "Endowment" is property, whether real or personal, devoted to some specific or particular purpose or trust ; and does not embrace property devoted to the general purposes of a Charity. Therefore the consent of the Charity Commissioners is not necessary to the sale of realty purchased by a Charity out of its general funds, or voluntary contributions (*Corporation for Relief of Widows and Children of the Clergy* v. *Sutton*, 27 Bea. 651, nom. *Corporation of the Sons of Clergy* v. *Sutton*, 29 L. J. Ch. 393 ; and nom. *Sons of Clergy Corporation* v. *Trustees of Stock Exchange*, 6 Jur. N. S. 84 : *Re Royal Socy. and Thompson*, 50 L. J. Ch. 344 ; 17 Ch. D. 407 ; 44 L. T. 274 ; 29 W. R. 838 : *Finnis to Forbes*, 24 Ch. D. 587 ; 48 L. T. 813).

An alternative bequest to "such other Charitable Endowment" as may be preferred, "must be taken to mean a *lawful* charitable endowment" and one not infringing the law of mortmain (per Wood, V.-C., *Salusbury* v. *Denton*, 26 L. J. Ch. 853 ; 3 K. & J. 529).

V. CHARITY : ENDOW : EDUCATIONAL ENDOWMENT.

ENEMY.—Pirates "are never recognized as Enemies, the word 'Enemy' applying to States" (1 Maude & P. 487).

The word "Enemies," or "King's Enemies," or "Queen's Enemies" in Bills of Lading and Charter Parties, is, probably, confined to the Enemies of the Sovereign of the stipulator ; it certainly includes them ; RESTRAINTS OF KINGS being generally added to comprise every other case of interruption by lawful authority (*Russell* v. *Niemann*, 34 L. J. C. P. 10 ; 17 C. B. N. S. 163). *Vf.* QUEEN'S ENEMIES.

ENFORCE OBEDIENCE.—A Rule requiring a Court to "enforce obedience" to its provisions, does not justify a committal without a previous Order requiring obedience (*Re Royle*, 50 L. J. Q. B. 656).

ENFRANCHISEMENT.—*V.* Litt. s. 204 ; Co. Litt. 137 a, b.

ENGAGE.—To "Engage" to do anything "has the same force as the word 'Covenant'" (per Parke, B., *Rigby* v. *G. W. Ry.*, 15 L. J. Ex. 62 ; 14 M. & W. 816).

ENGAGE IN.—A Patentee is, *semble*, "engaged in" business relating to the patented goods, so long as he receives royalties, even though he does not himself manufacture (*Re Ralph*, 53 L. J. Ch. 188 ; 25 Ch. D. 194).

V. CARRY ON.

ENGAGED IN WORKING.—"Engaged in Working" a Mine, s. 81, Companies Act, 1862, means, is, or has been engaged in working, or now or formerly engaged in working (*Re Silver Valley Mines*, 18 Ch. D. 472).

ENGAGEMENTS.—"All Engagements;" *V. Jones* v. *McCraw*, W. N. (71) 141.

"Money payable under any Engagement," in definition of "Personal property," s. 1, Sucn. Dy. Act, 1853 ; *V. A.-G.* v. *Montefiore*, 21 Q. B. D. 461 ; 59 L. T. 534 ; 4 Times Rep. 658.

ENGINE.—This word, derived from *ingenium*, includes a snare ; and a snare is accordingly within s. 3, Game Act, 1 & 2 W. 4, c. 32 (*Allen* v. *Thompson*, 39 L. J. M. C. 102 ; L. R. 5 Q. B. 336).

V. FIXED ENGINE : LOCOMOTIVE ENGINE.

ENGINEER.—*V.* PRINCIPAL ENGINEER.

ENGLAND.—"Except where the jurisdiction has been extended by an Act of Parliament, 'England,' and the sovereignty of the Queen, stop at low-water mark" (per Coleridge, C.J., *Harris* v. *The Franconia*, 46 L. J. C. P. 363 ; 2 C. P. D. 173 ; thus interpreting the decision in *R* v. *Keyn*, 46 L. J. M. C. 17 ; 2 Ex. D. 63).

"England," in an Act of Parliament, includes Wales and Berwick-upon-Tweed (20 G. 2, c. 42, s. 3) ; but not Scotland or Ireland (*Ex p. Cunningham, Re Mitchell*, 53 L. J. Ch. 1067).

V. DISTRICT OF ENGLAND.

ENGLISH CHANNEL DISTRICT.—For the Merchant Shipping Acts, "The English Channel District," comprises "the seas between Dungeness and the Isle of Wight" (s. 370 (2), 17 & 18 V. c. 104).

ENJOINED.—*V.* PRECATORY TRUST.

ENJOYED.—*V.* APPURTENANCES : HELD : ACTUALLY ENJOYED.

ENJOYMENT.—As to the meaning of an enjoyment under the Prescription Act, 2 & 3 W. 4, c. 71 ; *V.* Woodf. 700, citing *Cooper* v. *Hubbuck*, 12 C. B. N. S. 456 ; 31 L. J. C. P. 323 : *Beytagh* v. *Cassidy*, 16 W. R. 403 : *Battishill* v. *Reed*, 18 C. B. 696 ; 25 L. J. C. P. 290 : *Onley* v. *Gardiner*, 4 M. & W. 496.

V. ACTUAL : IMMEDIATE USE OR ENJOYMENT.

ENQUIRY.—*V.* INQUIRY.

ENTAIL.—As to what words create an Entail ; *V.* HEIRS.

ENTER.—"The word 'enter' (*quà* Burglary and Housebreaking) means, the entrance into the house of any part of the offender's body, or of any instrument held in his hand for the purpose of intimidating any person in the house, or of removing any goods ; but does not include the entrance of part of an instrument used to break the house open" (Steph. Cr. 248). *Vf.* Arch. Cr. 569 ; Rosc. Cr. 366.

ENTERED IN RELIGION.—"'*Entered and professed in religion.*' It is to be observed, that a man doth enter into religion at his first comming, and liveth under obedience ; but he is not professed, till a yeare be past, or some time of probation. And he is said to be professed, when he hath taken the habit of religion, and vowed three things, obedience, wilfull poverty, and perpetual chastity. And therefore our author saith here (s. 200), *entred and professed*" (Co. Litt. 131 b, 132 a).

ENTERING OR BEING.—This phrase, in the Game Acts (1 & 2 W. 4, c. 32, s. 30 ; 9 G. 4, c. 69, s. 1), constitutes but one offence (*R.* v. *Mellor*, 2 Dowl. P. C. 173), and means a personal and not a constructive entry, and does not include the mere sending a dog into a cover, or firing into it (*R.* v. *Pratt*, 24 L. J. M. C. 113 : *Mayhew* v. *Wardley*, 8 L. T. 504). *V.* SEARCH.

ENTERTAINMENT.—By the 23 V. c. 27, s. 6, a Refreshment-house requiring a license is a building "Kept open for public Refreshment, Resort, and *Entertainment.*" "Entertainment" as there used, means "not diversion or amusement, but the provision of food, drink and whatever else might be reasonably required for the *personal* comfort of guests" (*Taylor* v. *Oram*, 31 L. J. M. C. 252 ; 1 H. & C. 370) ; *e.g.*, cigars, coffee, ginger-beer or lemonade, the provision of which does not cease to be "Entertainment," because no seats are provided for their more comfortable consumption (*Muir* v. *Keay*, 44 L. J. M. C. 143 ; L. R. 10 Q. B. 594 : *Howes* v. *Inl. Rev.*, 45 L. J. M. C. 86 ; 46 Ib. 15 ; 1 Ex. D. 385).

In *Taylor* v. *Oram*, sup., Pollock, C.B., said that "Entertainment" in the section then being construed "refers to bodily not mental gratification ;" but he also said that, "with reference to some other Acts of Parliament, I should be strongly disposed to think the word meant amusement and gratification of some sort, other than food, meat and drink ;" and accordingly the prohibition in Bishop Porteous' Act (21 G. 3, c. 49), against the opening of places "for Public Entertainment or Amusement" on Sunday, is offended by an Aquarium (without a band of music) in connection with which is a museum, a reading-room (without newspapers), and a restaurant (*Terry* v. *Brighton Aquarium Co.*, 44 L. J. M. C. 173 ; L. R. 10 Q. B. 306 : *Warner* v. *Brighton Aq. Co.*, 44 L. J. M. C. 175 ; L. R. 10 Ex. 291). But a place duly and honestly registered as a place of public worship, in which no music but sacred is performed or sung, where nothing dramatic is introduced, where the discourses delivered are intended to be instructive, and contain nothing hostile to religion, where the objects of the promoters may be either to advance their own views of religion or to make science the handmaid of religion, is not used for "Public Entertainment or Amusement" within Porteous' Act (*Baxter* v. *Langley*, 38 L. J. M. C. 1 ; L. R. 4 C. P. 21).

A pantomime is a "*Dramatic Entertainment*" within s. 2, 3 & 4 W. 4, c. 15 (*Lee* v. *Simpson*, 16 L. J. C. P. 105 ; 3 C. B. 871 ; 4 D. & L. 666).

"Entertainment of the *Stage*," 10 G. 2, c. 28 ; Tumbling was not comprised herein (*R.* v. *Handy*, 6 T. R. 286). "Pepper's Ghost" is an "Entertainment of the Stage" within 6 & 7 V. c. 68, s. 23 (*Day* v. *Simpson*, 12 L. T. 386). *V.* STAGE PLAY.

ENTITLED.—The phrase "seized, or possessed of, or *entitled to*," very frequently occurs in Settlements and Wills, and other instruments where undefined property is dealt with by general words. Let us take the words in their order :—

"*Seized.*"—When you use the word "seized" it is obvious that this is the verb correlative with the Anglo-Norman noun "seizin." "Seizin" means the actual possession of an hereditament, and was that ceremony by which, in feudal times, the relationship of lord and vassal was consummated. A person acquires the seizin "either by his own entry, or by the possession of his own or his ancestor's lessee for years, or by receiving rent from a lessee of the freehold, or what is equivalent to corporal seizin in hereditaments that are incorporeal, such as the receipt of rent, a presentation to the church in case of an advowson and the like" (2 Bla. Com. 209; *Vf.* SEIZED). To speak, therefore, of an equitable seizin seems inaccurate,—seizin, by the force of the term, implying the legal, immediate, and corporeal possession of a corporeal hereditament, or the nearest approach thereto of an incorporeal hereditament.

"*Possessed of.*"—These words, when following "seized," as in the phrase under notice, seem to be coloured by that word so far as to be made to mean, having an interest in possession in the thing possessed. The action of the word "possessed" seems to be equivalent to that of "seized," the difference between the two consisting in the subjects on which they respectively operate. "Seized" applies to the legal interest in realty; "possessed of" applies to every other kind of property or interest *in possession, e.g.*, an equitable interest in realty, or a legal or equitable interest in goods, chattels, money deposited or invested, and other property, respecting which no seizin can be had (*V.* obs. of Kindersley, V.-C., *Wilton* v. *Colvin*, 25 L. J. Ch. 853, 854; 3 Drew. 617).

"*Entitled to.*"—These are the most comprehensive words of the phrase under notice. Under them will pass all kinds of property in which the person spoken of has any title at law or in equity; and this whether the property is in possession, reversion, or remainder (*Hughes* v. *Young*, 32 L. J. Ch. 137; *Va.* obs. of Kindersley, V.-C., *Archer* v. *Kelly*, 29 L. J. Ch. 912); but it seems that a mere contingent interest dependent on the happening of some future event will not be comprised in the words "entitled to" (*Atcherley* v. *Du Moulin*, 2 K. & J. 186, commented on by Wood, V.-C., *Hughes* v. *Young*, sup.).

In *Turner* v. *Gosset* (34 Bea. 593) the phrase "become entitled" in a bequest was, under the circumstances of that case, held to mean "become entitled in possession." It was held otherwise in *Hunter* v. *Hawke*, 29 S. J. 556. *Vf.* 2 Jarm. 202, notes (*b*) and (*g*). At p. 811, Ib., it is stated that, in gifts over on death before becoming "entitled," "the word 'entitled,' like 'vested,' points *primâ facie* to the right, and not to the possession." But the cases there cited (*Commrs. of Charitable Donations* v. *Cotter*, 1 Dr. & War. 498; 2 Dr. & Wal. 615: *Henderson* v. *Kennicott*, 18 L. J. Ch. 40; 2 D. G. & S. 492) were distinguished in *Re Noyce* (55 L. J. Ch. 114; 31 Ch. D. 75; 53 L. T. 688; 34 W. R. 147); and under the circumstances of that latter case, Bacon, V.-C., held that "entitled" meant "entitled in possession," and not "entitled in right" (*Va. Re Clinton*, L. R. 13 Eq. 295; 41 L. J. Ch. 191: *Jopp* v. *Wood*, 29 L. J. Ch. 406; 28 Bea. 53; 2 D. G. J. & S. 323: *Chorley* v. *Loveland*, 33 Bea. 189; 9 L. T. 596; 12 W. R. 187). *Vf.* Watson, Eq. 1228–1230.

"Entitled," in s. 2, Sucn. Dy. Act, 1853, means "entitled in possession" (per Jessel, M.R., *Fryer* v. *Morland*, 45 L. J. Ch. 817 ; 3 Ch. D. 675 : *Vh. De Rechberg* v. *Beeton*, 38 Ch. D. 192).

The privileges and educational advantages to which a class of persons is "entitled," and which are to be considered in any scheme abolishing or modifying them (s. 11, Endowed Schools Act, 1869, 32 & 33 V. c. 56) are legal rights, and not benefits merely enjoyed by permission or bounty (*Re Sutton Coldfield Grammar School*, 51 L. J. P. C. 8 ; 7 App. Ca. 91 ; 45 L. T. 631 ; 30 W. R. 341 : *Re Hemsworth Grammar School*, 12 App. Ca. 444 ; 56 L. T. 212 ; 35 W. R. 418 ; 3 Times Rep. 439).

The provision in s. 12, 11 G. 4 & 1 W. 4, c. 65, authorising the surrender of any Lease to which an infant is "entitled," applies as well to a lease where the infant is beneficially entitled as to one in which the legal interest is vested in him (*Re Griffiths*, 54 L. J. Ch. 742 ; 29 Ch. D. 248 ; 53 L. T. 262 ; 33 W. R. 728).

"So entitled," in s. 2, sub-s. 6, Settled Land Act, 1882, means entitled for life (*Re Atkinson*, 55 L. J. Ch. 49 ; affd. 31 Ch. D. 577 ; 54 L. T. 403 ; 34 W. R. 445. *Vth. Re Horne*, 39 Ch. D. 89).

In *Covenants to Settle*, the following canons have been extracted from the cases for the interpretation of such phrases as ;—

I. "*Is now* entitled."

II. "*Shall become* entitled."

I. "Where the covenant includes property to which the wife '*is now* entitled,' or 'at the time of the marriage shall be entitled,' all reversionary interests, whether vested or contingent, to which she is entitled at the date of the Settlement or Marriage, as the case may be, are bound."

II.—1. "Property to which the wife is entitled in possession at the date of the Settlement is not bound by the covenant, where the subject-matter of the covenant is described by words of future acquisition only (*e.g.*, 'shall become entitled') ; *Re Clinton*, L. R. 13 Eq. 295 ; 41 L. J. Ch. 191 :" *Sv. Williams* v. *Mercier*, cited DURING.

2. "In the absence of special words, a covenant to settle property to which the intended wife 'shall become entitled,' will be construed to mean 'shall become entitled *during the coverture* ;' *Re Edwards*, 9 Ch. 97 ; 43 L. J. Ch. 265 ; 22 W. R. 144, approving *Carter* v. *Carter*, L. R. 8 Eq. 551 ; 39 L. J. Ch. 268, and *Dickinson* v. *Dillwyn*, L. R. 8 Eq. 546 ; 39 L. J. Ch. 266 ; and over-ruling on this point *Stevens* v. *Van Voorst*, 17 Bea. 305." *Note.*—But this is a somewhat forced interpretation ; and where a reversion, belonging to the wife at the time of her marriage, fell into possession after her death, but during the husband's life, it was held to be bound by the husband's covenant, that covenant not, in terms, being confined to property coming to the wife "during the coverture" (*Fisher* v. *Shirley*, 34 S. J. 31 : Stirling, J., there said that the principle of *Re Edwards* was only applicable where the wife was the survivor).

3. "Property which the wife acquires in possession during coverture

and to which she had no title of any kind at the date of the marriage, is bound by the covenant, where the subject-matter of the covenant is described by words of future acquisition only ; *Re Clinton*, sup."

4. "Where a Vested Remainder or Reversionary Interest, to which the wife is entitled at the date of the Settlement, falls into possession during the coverture, it is bound by a covenant in which the property to be settled is described by words applicable to future acquisition only."

5. "Where a Vested Remainder or Reversionary Interest, to which the wife is entitled at the date of the settlement, does *not* fall into possession until after the determination of the coverture, it is not bound by a covenant in which the property to be settled is described by words applicable to future acquisition only."

6. "If the property be described by words of future acquisition only, and during the coverture the wife 'become entitled' to a Vested Remainder or Reversionary Interest, even though it does not fall into possession till after the termination of the coverture, it will be bound by the covenant."

7. "Where the property included in the covenant is described by words applicable to future acquisition only, property in which the wife has a Contingent Interest at the date of the settlement or of the marriage, is bound by the covenant if it fall into possession during the coverture, but not otherwise—(Obs. There may possibly be some doubt whether the rule applies where the contingent interest to which the wife was entitled at the time of the marriage vests in interest, but not in possession, during the coverture ; but probably the rule does apply)." (Elph. 510–523, where *V.* the authorities in support and illustration of the above propositions.) *Vf.* Watson, Eq., Ch. 10, p. 660 *et seq.* : DURING.

ENTITLED FOR THE TIME BEING.—This phrase in a power of maintenance has been held to mean "absolutely or presumptively entitled" (*Sidney* v. *Wilmer*, 25 Bea. 260).

"Mortgagor entitled for the time being *to possession*," s. 25 (5), Judicature Act, 1873 ; *V. Bennett* v. *Hughes*, 2 Times Rep. 715.

V. TIME BEING.

ENTITLED IN IMMEDIATE EXPECTANCY.—*V. Westcar* v. *Westcar*, 25 L. J. Ch. 866 ; 21 Bea. 328.

ENTITLED IN POSSESSION OR TO PAYMENT.—In a gift over on death before becoming "entitled in possession" (*Re Yates*, 21 L. J. Ch. 281,—"a most remarkable authority," per Malins, V.-C., *West* v. *Miller*, 37 L. J. Ch. 425), or "Entitled to the Payment" (*Re Williams*, 19 L. J. Ch. 46 ; 12 Bea. 317), or "to the receipt" (*Hayward* v. *James*, 29 L. J. Ch. 822 ; 28 Bea. 523) ; these phrases will generally mean "entitled in interest," and so receive a construction similar to that of PAYABLE ; *Vf.* 2 Jarm. 809.

V. POSSESSION.

ENTITLED TO BE ON BURGESS LIST.—S. 28, 5 & 6 W. 4, c. 76; *V. Ex p. Hindmarch*, L. R. 3 Q. B. 12; 37 L. J. Q. B. 58; 8 B. & S. 642.

ENTITLED TO REDEEM.—S. 15, Conv. & L. P. Act, 1881; *V. Teevan* v. *Smith*, 51 L. J. Ch. 621; 20 Ch. D. 724.

"Persons for the time being entitled to *the Equity of Redemption*," s. 5, Building Socs. Act, 6 & 7 W. 4, c. 32; *V. Hosking* v. *Smith*, 58 L. J. Ch. 367; 13 App. Ca. 582; 59 L. T. 565.

ENTITLED TO VOTE.—A dead man is not "entitled to vote;" and therefore to personate a dead elector is not Personation within s. 3, 14 & 15 V. c. 105 (*Whiteley* v. *Chappell*, 38 L. J. M. C. 51; L. R. 4 Q. B. 147; 32 J. P. 775); but if the words to be construed were "entitled, *or supposed to be* entitled" (54 G. 3, c. 93, s. 89), the case would be different (*R.* v. *Martin*, Russ. & Ry. 324: *R.* v. *Cramp*, Ib. 327). Referring to *R.* v. *Martin*, Lush, J. (in *Whiteley* v. *Chappell*), said, "If the Court had construed the words 'supposed to be entitled,' as 'alleged to be entitled,' there would be no difficulty in the judgment."

ENTIRE SERVICES.—A contract to render a person's "Entire Services," precludes him from accepting any other employment (*Woodworth* v. *Sugden*, 32 S. J. 742).

ENTREAT.—*V.* PRECATORY TRUST.

ENTRUST.—*V.* INTRUSTED.

ENTRY.—"Right to make Entry," s. 2, 3 & 4 W. 4, c. 27; *V. Re Lidiard and Jackson*, 58 L. J. Ch. 785.

V. FORCIBLE ENTRY.

EQUAL.—"Equal to Sample;" *V.* SAMPLE.

EQUALLY.—A testamentary gift to two or more, "equally," or "equally to be divided," or "in equal shares," or "equally amongst them," or "to be distributed in joint and equal proportions," creates a tenancy in common (2 Jarm. 257; Wms. Exs. 1469; Hawk. 112; Watson, Eq. 506). But this construction may be, though it rarely is, varied by the context (2 Jarm. 260–262: *Oakley* v. *Young*, 2 Eq. Abr. 536). *Vh.* Chitty, Eq. Ind. 7927, 7929.

EQUITABLE.—*V.* JUST AND EQUITABLE.

"Legal or Equitable" Debt; *V. Vyse* v. *Brown*, 13 Q. B. D. 199: DEBT.

"Equitable Execution:" It is not accurate to speak of the appointment of a Receiver as an "Equitable Execution;" it is not merely an execution, it is a relief judicially granted (*Re Shephard*, 38 W. R. 133).

Relief on "Equitable Grounds," s. 83, Com. L. Pro. Act, 1854, means Grounds depending on equity law, not equity practice (*Phelps* v. *Prothero*, 7 D. G. M. & G. 722; 25 L. J. Ch. 105).

ERECT.—"It has been much questioned whether a bequest of money to be applied in the 'Erection' of a school-house or other building, for charitable purposes, is bad as involving a trust to purchase. Lord Hardwicke considered that if the trustees could get a piece of ground given to them, so that land need not be purchased, the gift was good; but the contrary is now settled, and to make such a bequest valid, the testator must point to land already in mortmain, or he must forbid the purchase of land" (1 Jarm. 230), or declare his expectation or desire that land will be provided from other sources (*Philpott* v. *St. George's Hosp.*, 6 H. L. Ca. 338; 27 L. J. Ch. 70; 30 L. T. O. S. 15, over-ruling *Trye* v. *Gloucester*, 14 Bea. 173; 21 L. J. Ch. 81), or that the trust to "erect" or "build" is to wait till land be so otherwise provided (*Chamberlayne* v. *Brockett*, 8 Ch. 206; 42 L. J. Ch. 368: *Vth. Re White*, 33 Ch. D. 453: *Vf.* 1 Jarm. 206). *Vh.* Tudor, Char. Trusts, 409–412.

V. Endow: Found: Provide.

ERECTED.—Assignment of all Machinery and Fixtures whatsoever, "now erected, or set up, or standing, or being,—or which shall at any time hereafter be erected, or set up, or stand, or be,—in or upon the said lands, mills and premises, or any part thereof;" these words "are as comprehensive as could be devised to include the Machinery which is moved, as well as the moving Machinery" (per Campbell, L. C., *Haley* v. *Hammersley*, 30 L. J. Ch. 773, 774; 3 D. G. F. & J. 587).

ERECTION.—*V.* Building.

"Erection used in conducting the business of any Mine," s. 29, 24 & 25 V. c. 97; a scaffold erected at some distance *above the bottom* of a Mine, for the purpose of working a vein of coal on a level with the scaffold, is within these words (*R.* v. *Whittingham*, 9 C. & P. 234); and so is a wooden trough by means of which water is conveyed to, and for the purposes of, a Mine (*Barwell* v. *Winterstoke*, 19 L. J. Q. B. 206; 14 Q. B. 704; 15 L. T. O. S. 23).

ERRONEOUS.—*V.* Imperfect.

ERROR.—The phrase in Conditions of Sale of realty whereby a purchaser is precluded from compensation in respect of any "Error, Mis-statement or Omission" in the Particulars, only covers small errors, and will not deprive a purchaser of his right to compensation for such a mistake, as where 573 square yards have been represented as 753 square yards (*Whittemore* v. *Whittemore*, L. R. 8 Eq. 603: *Va. Ayles* v. *Cox*, 16 Bea. 23: *Portman* v. *Mill*, 2 Russ. 570: *Cordingley* v. *Cheesebrough*, 31 L. J. Ch. 617; 3 Giff. 496; 4 D. G. F. & J. 379: *Dimmock* v. *Hallett*, 36 L. J. Ch. 146; 2 Ch. 21: *Terry to White*, 55 L. J. Ch. 345; 32 Ch. D. 14; 34 W. R. 379). But in *Re Severne to Bird* (7 Aug. 1883), Kay, J., held that a purchaser who had bought under conditions similar to those in *Whittemore* v. *Whittemore* was not entitled to compensation for a mis-statement, whereby a cellar was wrongly stated to belong to the house described in the Particulars (*Va. Taylor* v. *Bullen*, 20 L. J. Ex. 21; 5 Ex. 779).

V. ADMEASUREMENTS.

"If the Vendor, on a sale of chattels, is not to be responsible for any defect or 'Error,' the stipulation will protect him from all unintentional misdescription and mis-statement" (Add. C. 996).

V. FAULTS : OMISSION : WRIT OF ERROR.

ESCHEAT.—"Escheat is a word of art, and signifieth properly when, by accident, the lands fall to the lord of whom they are holden, in which case we say the fee is escheated" (Co. Litt. 13 a : *Vf.* Ib. 92 b). If there is a mesne lord the escheat is to him ; if not, to the King (*V. A.-G. of Ontario* v. *Mercer*, 52 L. J. P. C. 84, 86 ; 8 App. Ca. 767 : *Vf. St. Catherine's Co.* v. *The Queen*, 14 App. Ca. 46).

ESQUIRE.—A Lessee and Manager of a Theatre is not properly described as "Esquire" for the purposes of the Bills of Sale Acts (*Ex p. Homann, Re Vining*, 39 L. J. Bank. 4 ; L. R. 10 Eq. 63).

"I do not agree with the proposition that an 'Esquire' cannot be a miller or a farmer. I would be slow to hold that this Statute (Com. L. Pro. Act, Ir. 1853, ss. 124, 125), was constructed to lay traps for persons registering their judgments and getting security. Am I to rule that the title meant was according to chivalry or ancient observances, or that the reasonable intendment of the world is what is referred to ?" (per Lynch, J., *Re Doughty*, Ir. Rep. 2 Eq. 237). But in referring to that case, Porter, M. R., said :—"As usual, Judge Lynch is again relied on as the champion of doubtful registrations" (*Spaddacini* v. *Treacy*, 21 L. R. Ir. 559).

ESSART.—*V.* ASSART.

ESTABLISH.—*V.* FOUND : NEWLY ESTABLISH.

ESTABLISHED CUSTOM.—*V.* Woodf. 767.

ESTATE.—"'State' or 'Estate' signifieth such inheritance, freehold, terme for yeares, tenancie by statute merchant, staple, elegit, or the like, as any man hath in lands or tenements, &c. And by the grant of his Estate, &c., as much as he can grant shall passe" (Co. Litt. 345 a : *Vh.* Elph. 204).

"'Estate,' is a *genus generalissimum*, predicable of two species that have their difference, whereby they are divided, that is, Estate Real, and Estate Personal. 'Estate Real,' is *genus subalternum* and has its species too ; that is Estate Real *in fee* or *for life*. And so is Estate Personal in like manner to be branched into Chattel Real and Chattel Personal ; and it has that difference of a chattel real, not because it is a real estate, but because it has a real extraction. If a man seized in fee make a lease for years, the lessee for years has a chattel real, because his estate is derived out of a real estate ; but still it is not a real estate" (per Holt, C. J., delivering jdgmt.

of Q. B., *Bridgewater* v. *Bolton,* 6 Mod. 107). "'Estate' comes from '*stando*,' because it is fixed and permanent, and imports the most absolute property that a man can have" in the thing of which it is spoken (Ib. 109).

"It is now (A.D. 1775) clearly settled, that the words 'all his Estate,'—in a Will,—will pass *every thing* a man has" (per Ld. Mansfield, *Hogan* v. *Jackson,* 1 Cowp. 306: *Vf.* 1 Jarm. 721 *et seq.*); but "all my freehold hereditaments and estate," will not pass copyholds (*Quennell* v. *Turner,* 20 L. J. Ch. 237; 13 Bea. 240).

"It appears to me to be perfectly clear that the word 'Estate,' before the new Wills Act, was a word sufficient to carry *the fee* if there was nothing at variance with that construction upon the whole of the Will. It would not be a word of the vigour and force of a gift to a man 'and his heirs;' but it would have the effect of carrying the fee equally, unless there was something in the context which led one to a different conclusion" (per Earl Cairns, *Bowen* v. *Lewis,* 54 L. J. Q. B. 62; 9 App. Ca. 890. The first case laying this down seems to have been *Bridgewater* v. *Bolton,* sup.).

"It has been long established that a devise of a testator's 'Estate' includes not only the *corpus* of the property, but the whole of his interest therein" (2 Jarm. 275, which, to p. 282, *V.* for cases illustrating and qualifying this proposition: *Vf.* 1 Jarm. 732–737: *Moore* v. *James,* W. N. (74) 80).

As to this word when used as one of description; *V.* 1 Jarm. 786, 788; Watson, Eq. 1318, 1319.

V. Temporal: Worldly Estate: Real Estate: Personal Estate: Estate and Effects.

As to the words of the *All the Estate Clause* ("Estate," "Right," "Title" and "Interest"), *V.* Co. Litt. 345 a; Elph. 204–209. This Clause may now safely be omitted from conveyances (s. 63, Conv. & L. P. Act, 1881).

ESTATE AND EFFECTS.—On the presentation of an Insolvency petition under 5 & 6 V. c. 16, all the "Estate and Effects" of the petitioner became vested in the Official Assignee. Choses in Action were included in those words (*Sayer* v. *Dufaur,* 17 L. J. Q. B. 50; 11 Q. B. 325). Denman, C. J., in giving judgment in that case said,—"The words 'Estate and Effects' are, at least, as strong as 'Personal Estate.'"

A devise of "all my Estate and Effects" will generally pass realty (*Stokes* v. *Salomons,* 20 L. J. Ch. 343; 9 Hare, 75). But "All Estate, Effects and Property whatsoever and wheresoever," has been held, by the context, not to pass realty (*Coard* v. *Holderness,* 24 L. J. Ch. 388; 20 Bea. 147), and especially such a phrase will not pass realty when occurring in a gift the qualifying word of which is "personal" (*Belaney* v. *Belaney,* 35 Bea. 469; 36 L. J. Ch. 265; 2 Ch. 138: *Jones* v. *Robinson,* 47 L. J. C. P. 673; 3 C. P. D. 344).

The Goodwill is included in "other the Estate and Effects" of a partnership (*Steuart* v. *Gladstone,* 47 L. J. Ch. 423; 10 Ch. D. 626). *Va.* Estate and Interest.

"Estate and Effects" as regards Probate Duty, s. 2, 55 G. 3, c. 184; *V. A.-G.* v. *Brunning,* 8 H. L. Ca. 243; 30 L. J. Ex. 379: *A.-G.* v. *Partington,* 6 L. T. 900: *A.-G.* v. *Ailesbury,* 12 App. Ca. 672.

Vh. Stein v. *Ritherdon,* W. N. (68) 65: *Charlton* v. *Charlton,* W. N. (71) 241: *Guthrie* v. *Walrond,* 52 L. J. Ch. 165; 22 Ch. D. 573: *Re Hotchkys, Freke* v. *Calmady,* 32 Ch. D. 408.

V. ESTATE: EFFECTS.

ESTATE AND INTEREST.—A contract for the sale of a person's "Estate and Interest" in a business property and in the business, will carry the GOODWILL (*Pearson* v. *Pearson,* 54 L. J. Ch. 32; 27 Ch. D. 145). *Va.* ESTATE AND EFFECTS.

"Estate or Interest in Land," s. 4, Public Works (New Zealand) Act, 1882; *V. Plimmer* v. *Wellington,* 9 App. Ca. 699; 53 L. J. P. C. 105: *Ramsden* v. *Dyson,* L. R. 1 H. L. 129.

ESTATE TAIL.—*V.* HEIRS.

ESTIMATED: ESTIMATION.—When Particulars of Sale state the property to be of an "Estimated" value, and an honest estimate has been made, no ground for compensation arises because the estimate is mistaken (*Re Hurlbalt & Chaytor,* 57 L. J. Ch. 421). *Cp.* ADMEASUREMENT.

The qualification of a quantity by the phrase "*By Estimation,*" is equivalent to MORE OR LESS (*Joliffe* v. *Baker,* 52 L. J. Q. B. 609; 11 Q. B. D. 255: Sug. V. & P. 559: Dart, 736).

ESTOPPEL.—"'Estoppe,' commeth of a French word *estoupe,* from whence the English word stopped, and it is called an estoppel, or conclusion, because a man's owne act or acceptance stoppeth or closeth up his mouth to allege or plead the truth; and *Littleton's* case here (s. 667) proveth this description" (Co. Litt. 352 a, where it is said Estoppel is of three kinds, *i.e.* Matter (1) of Record, (2) in Writing, (3) *in Paiis*).

ESTOVERS.—"By the grant of Estovers, will pass houseboote, hayboote, and plowboote. But if a man grant to me estovers out of his manor, I may not by this grant cut down any of the fruit trees within his manor" (Touch. 96).

V. BOTE.

ESTRAY.—*V.* Elph. 573.

ESTREPEMENT.—Waste, voluntary or permissive, by a tenant for life or years (Spelm.).

ET CETERA.—A bequest of "all my household furniture and effects, plate, glass, wearing apparel, *&c.,*" was held to pass the articles enumerated, and others *ejusdem generis,* but not the general residue (*Newman* v. *Newman,* 26 Bea. 220); and a like construction was given to the words "all my furniture, &c." (*Barnaby* v. *Tassell*, L. R. 11 Eq. 363). But though those cases were cited to Jessel, M.R., in *Chapman* v. *Chapman* (46 L. J. Ch. 104 ; 4 Ch. D. 800), he held that the general residue passed under a bequest, to the testator's widow, of "all my money, cattle, farming implements, *&c.*, she paying my brother the sum of £ ." *Vf. Gover* v. *Davis*, 30 L. J. Ch. 505 ; 29 Bea. 225 : *Dean* v. *Gibson*, 36 L. J. Ch. 657 ; L. R. 3 Eq. 713 : *Twining* v. *Powell*, 2 Coll. 262 ; 1 Jarm. 755, n. : *Mullally* v. *Walsh*, 3 L. R. Ir. 244.

The insertion of "&c." in some of the terms of an Agreement for a Lease, does not produce such uncertainty as to render the Agreement incapable of specific performance, if the material points are sufficiently stated (*Parker* v. *Taswell*, 27 L. J. Ch. 812 ; 2 D. G. & J. 559). On the sale of "GOODWILL, &c.," the "&c." carries the belongings of the Goodwill, *e.g.*, trade-marks (*Cooper* v. *Hood*, 28 L. J. Ch. 215).

V. OTHER.

EVASION.—"I never understood what is meant by an evasion of an Act of Parliament ; either you are within the Act of Parliament or not. If you are not within it you have a right to avoid it, to keep out of the prohibition ; if you are within it, say so, and then the course is clear" (per Cranworth, L.C., *Edwards* v. *Hall*, 25 L. J. Ch. 84).

EVASIVELY.—Pleading "evasively" (Ord. 19, R. 19, R. S. C.) is the converse of answering the POINT OF SUBSTANCE, *wh. V.* for cases hereon.

EVENT.—"Event" in the well-known phrase in arbitration agreements, and in the Rules of Court (Ord. 65, R. 1) that "the Costs shall follow the Event," is "a *nomen collectivum*, and may be said to be equivalent to 'Result,'" of which there may be more than one in the action or enquiry (per Bramwell, L.J., *Myers* v. *Defries*, 49 L. J. Ex. 270). "The Event is the outcome or the result of the trial, and although there may be one verdict and one judgment, still there may be more than one event" (per Baggallay, L.J., Ib. 271). "Event" in this phrase is therefore to be read, distributively, as "Events" (*Ellis* v. *Desilva*, 50 L. J. Q. B. 328 ; 6 Q. B. D. 521). The result of each distinct issue, in an action or an inquiry, is its "Event ;" the costs of which will go to the party who succeeds on it (*Myers* v. *Defries*, 49 L. J. Ex. 266 ; 5 Ex. D. 180 : *Ellis* v. *Desilva*, sup. : *Abbott* v. *Andrews*, 51 L. J. Q. B. 641 ; 8 Q. B. D. 648 : *Goutard* v. *Carr*, 53 L. J. Q. B. 55 ; 13 Q. B. D. 598 n. : *Hawke* v. *Brear*, 54 L. J. Q. B. 315 ; 14 Q. B. D. 841). Those costs mean the whole litigation relating to the "Event," including a wrong non-suit or verdict that has been set aside (*Creen* v. *Wright*, 46 L. J. C. P. 427 ; 2 C. P. D. 354 : *Field* v. *G. N. Ry.*, 47 L. J. Ex. 662 ; 3 Ex. D. 261). The general costs of a trial or an enquiry would, as a rule, in the one case follow the judgment and in the other would follow the general result, or balance, of the findings (*Goutard* v. *Carr*, sup.: *Lund* v. *Campbell*, 54 L. J. Q. B. 281; 14 Q. B. D. 821: *Shrapnel* v. *Laing*, 57 L. J. Q. B. 195; 20 Q. B. D. 334; 58 L. T. 705; 36 W. R. 297). But in *Myers* v. *Defries*, sup., Bramwell, L. J., said, "The costs of the writ, for instance, are necessarily incurred by the plaintiff if there is *an* event in his favour. Where *an* event is in the plaintiff's favour and where he gets costs, he will get the general costs of the cause; where, however, he recovers nominal damages and gets no costs, he will not have to pay any general costs to the other party" (49 L. J. Ex. 271). *Vf.* where there is a Counter-Claim, *Stooke* v. *Taylor*, 49 L. J. Q. B. 859; 5 Q. B. D. 569; dissenting from *Staples* v. *Young*, 2 Ex. D. 324; and distinguishing *Chatfield* v. *Sedgwick*, 4 C. P. D. 459.

"In the event of decease," in a Will, are (probably) words of futurity (per Kekewich, arg. *Re Webster*, 52 L. J. Ch. 768).

The death of a Copyhold Tenant, or the devolution of his title (during proceedings for Enfranchisement), would be an "Event" requiring Admittance within s. 1, 15 & 16 V. c. 51 (*Myers* v. *Hodgson*, 45 L. J. C. P. 603; 1 C. P. D. 609).

EVER.—*V.* For Ever.

EVERY.—In *Brown* v. *Jarvis* (29 L. J. Ch. 595; 2 D. G. F. & J. 168) a gift over "after the decease of *every* of them," *i.e.*, certain prior legatees, "every" was read "each." In that case Campbell, L.C., said, "Dr. Johnson tells us in his Dictionary that 'every' was formerly spelt 'Everich,' that is, Ever-each; and that the true meaning is, 'each one of all.' The word may be used in this sense, although other lexicographers may give another meaning to it." *V.* All and Every.

"Every *Dispute*," s. 22, Friendly Societies Act, 1875; *V. Morrison* v. *Glover*, 19 L. J. Ex. 20; 4 Ex. 430. *V.* Dispute.

"Every *Person*," 5 G. 4, c. 83, s. 43, does not apply to a deserted married woman who has not the means of supporting her children who have become chargeable to the parish (*Peters* v. *Cowie*, 46 L. J. M. C. 177; 2 Q. B. D. 131); nor did this phrase entitle a married woman to vote for municipal councillors under ss. 1 and 9, 32 & 33 V. c. 55 (*R.* v. *Harrald*, 41 L. J. Q. B. 173; L. R. 7 Q. B. 361).

"Every *Person*," having served in the Militia, should have freedom to set up a Trade (26 G. 3, c. 107), related only to persons exercising trades, and not to common labourers (*R.* v. *Gwenop*, 3 T. R. 135). So "Every Person" who impounds an animal is to feed it, s. 5, 12 & 13 V. c. 92, does not include the pound-keeper (*Dargan* v. *Davies*, 46 L. J. M. C. 122; 2 Q. B. D. 118); nor is an Innkeeper, whilst in his own inn after the same is closed, within the phrase "Every person found drunk on licensed premises," s. 12, 35 & 36 V. c. 94 (*Lester* v. *Torrens*, 46 L. J. M. C. 280; 2 Q. B. D. 403). But "Every Person" committed "for any offence or misdemeanour" to bear his own charges of being conveyed (3 Jac. 1, c. 10), includes deserters as well as ordinary criminals (*R.* v. *Pierce*, 3 M. & S. 62).

A penalty on "Every *Person*" concerned in an offence, may be recovered, for the same offence, against each person therein concerned (*R.* v. *Dean*, 13 L. J. Ex. 33; 12 M. & W. 39).

Devise to "Every *Son* during his life;" *V. Surtees* v. *Surtees*, L. R. 12 Eq. 400.

EVERYTHING.—"Under a bequest of 'Everything' in a house, Money and Bank Notes will pass" (Watson, Eq. 1327, citing *Popham* v. *Aylesbury*, Amb. 68: *Stuart* v. *Bute*, 11 Ves. 662: and as to the latter case *V.* Watson, Eq. 1328).

Vh. Re Methuen and Blore, 50 L. J. Ch. 464; 16 Ch. D. 696.

EVERY THING ELSE.—Held to include undisposed of realty in fee (*Wilce* v. *Wilce*, 9 L. J. O. S. C. P. 197; 5 Moo. & P. 682; 7 Bing. 664).

EVICTION.—"The word 'Eviction' has in latter times been understood to mean what formerly it was not intended to express. Formerly it meant what was expressed by the language of Pleading, 'evicted, expelled, removed, and put out,'—describing the different modes in which it might take place. 'Eviction,' from *evincere*, to evict or dispossess by course of law, was used originally when the person having the permanent title asserted it and expelled his tenant. But that sort of Eviction is not absolutely necessary in order to operate as a suspension of the rent, and the word is now used when that has been done which deprives the tenant of the enjoyment of the premises, and the rent is therefore suspended, and the right of the landlord to recover it is gone. The word 'Eviction' has come to have a popular meaning, and to be applied to every kind of expulsion in fact. Now, getting rid of the old notion of an Eviction, it may be taken to mean, not a mere trespass without anything more,—because, though every Eviction implies a Trespass, every Trespass does not amount to an Eviction,—but something of a more permanent character done by the landlord with the intention of depriving the tenant of the enjoyment of the whole or part of the demised premises. If that be shewn, the Eviction may be in various ways" (per Jervis, C.J., *Upton* v. *Townend*, 25 L. J. C. P. 51; 17 C. B. 30: *Vth. Wilson* v. *Burne*, 24 L. R. Ir. 20).

EVIDENCE.—For examples of what is "Evidence" in a Pleading, contrary to Ord. 19, R. 4, R. S. C.: *V. Davy* v. *Garrett*, 7 Ch. D. 473; 47 L. J. Ch. 218. *Cp.* MATERIAL FACTS.

"The Evidence" sufficient to justify an Election Court to order a prosecution, s. 28 (5), 47 & 48 V. c. 70, is the Evidence which has already been given before that Court in the enquiry out of which such prosecution is directed (*R.* v. *Shellard,* 58 L. J. M. C. 142).

V. CONCLUSIVE EVIDENCE : SUFFICIENT EVIDENCE : SATISFACTORY.

EVIDENCE OF A CONTRACT.—A document not intended to operate as a contract, but only used as proof of the existence of a previous contract, is not "Evidence of a Contract" and chargeable as an Agreement, within the Stamp Act (*Beeching* v. *Westbrook,* 10 L. J. Ex. 464 ; 8 M. & W. 411).

EVIL LIVER.—"An open and notorious Evil-Liver" who may be rejected from Communion (Rubric to Communion Office), is limited to one whose moral conduct, as distinguished from religious belief, is bad (*Jenkins* v. *Cook,* 45 L. J. P. C. 1 ; 1 P. D. 80); and, *semble,* such bad moral conduct must be "open and notorious :" *V.* COMMON AND NOTORIOUS.

EX QUAY OR WAREHOUSE.—"In a contract for the sale of goods 'Ex Quay or Warehouse,' there is an implied condition that the vendor shall give notice to the purchaser of the place of storage ; and until such notice has been given, the purchaser is not in default for non-acceptance" (Benj. 671, citing *Davies* v. *McLean,* 21 W. R. 264 ; 28 L. T. 113).

EXACTION.—"'Exaction' is a wrong done by an officer, or one pretending to have authority, in demaunding or taking any reward or fee for that matter, cause or thing for which the law alloweth not any fee at all. . . . 'Extortion' is where an officer demaundeth and wresteth a greater summe or reward than his just fee" (Termes de la Ley, *Exaction*). *V.* EXTORTION.

"Exactions ;" *V.* DEMAND.

EXACTLY.—An Insolvent was to have the benefit of the Act, 1 & 2 V. c. 110, though (s. 93) a debt was specified in his Schedule "not exactly," if error was "without any culpable negligence, or fraud, or evil intention ;" *V. Hoyles* v. *Blore,* 15 L. J. Ex. 28 ; 14 M. & W. 387.

EXAMINATIONS.—A Power to a Court to "take Examinations," or other accusation or proof, implies that it is to be done on oath (Dalt. c. 115, cited Dwar. 672).

EXCEPT.—A bequest of all testator's property "except" so much a year to A., gives A. an annuity in perpetuity (*Hill* v. *Potts,* 31 L. J. Ch. 380 ; 2 J. & H. 634). *V.* ANNUITY.

V. UNLESS.

EXCEPTING.—This word,—*e.g.,* a Lease, "excepting free passage" over premises demised,—may create a covenant (*Bush* v. *Cole*, Carth. 232 ; 12 Mod. 24 ; nom. *Bush* v. *Calis*, Show. 247 : *Cole's Case*, 1 Salk. 196).

EXCEPTION.—*V.* RESERVATION.

EXCESSIVE WEIGHT.—*V.* EXTRAORDINARY TRAFFIC.

EXCHANGE.—A Power of Sale or Exchange, authorises PARTITION.

EXCISABLE LIQUOR.—Beer is not now an "excisable liquor" (*Jones* v. *Whittaker*, 39 L. J. M. C. 139 ; L. R. 5 Q. B. 541 ; 22 L. T. 535 : 43 & 44 V. c. 20, s. 47), nor is Sweet Wine (*Lancashire* v. *Staffordshire Jus.*, 26 L. J. M. C. 171 ; nom. *R.* v. *Lancashire*, 7 E. & B. 839). *V.* BEER.

EXCLUDED.—Sunday "excluded ;" *V.* DAYS.

EXCLUSIVE OCCUPATION.—The ordinary Railway Station Bookstall does not have an "Exclusive Occupation" of any part of the platform, so as, thereby, to be rateable to the poor (*Smith* v. *Lambeth*, 10 Q. B. D. 327 ; 52 L. J. M. C. 1 ; 48 L. T. 57 ; 47 J. P. 244 : *Vf. R.* v. *Morrish*, 32 L. J. M. C. 245 ; 11 W. R. 960 ; 8 L. T. 697 ; 10 Jur. N. S. 71). As to rating advertising stations ; *V.* 52 & 53 V. c. 27.

EXCLUSIVELY.—A direction that a Charitable Bequest shall be paid "exclusively" out of pure personalty, implies marshalling the assets (*Wills* v. *Bourne*, L. R. 16 Eq. 487 ; 43 L. J. Ch. 89 : *Re Arnold*, 57 L. J. Ch. 682 ; 37 Ch. D. 637 ; 58 L. T. 469 ; 36 W. R. 424 : 1 Jarm. 237). *Cp.* RESERVE.

V. SCIENCE.

EXCURSION TRAIN.—*V.* PASSENGER TRAIN.

EXCUSE.—*V.* REASONABLE EXCUSE.

EXECUTED.—To speak of a Writ of Execution as "executed and levied" is to use synonymous terms signifying seizure (*Cheston* v. *Gibbs*, 13 L. J. Ex. 53 ; 12 M. & W. 111 ; *Vth. Congreve* v. *Evetts*, 10 Ex. 311 : *Vf. Whitmore* v. *Greene*, 13 L. J. Ex. 311 ; 13 M. & W. 112 : *Hall* v. *Wallace*, 10 L. J. Ex. 133 ; 7 M. & W. 353). *V.* TO BE EXECUTED : LEVY.

EXECUTION.—"'*Execution*,' *Executio*, and signifieth in law the obtaining of actual possession of any thing acquired by judgement of law, or by a fine executory levied, whether it be by the sherife or by the entry of the party" (Co. Litt. 154 a).

"Afore Execution *had*," 3 H. 7, c. 10, means before obtaining the fruits of Execution (*Newlands* v. *Holmes*, 11 L. J. Ex. 456 ; 4 Q. B. 858).

An "Execution" proceeds from a judgment, and does not include a distraint for rent or other cause (*Birmingham & Staffordshire Gas Co.*, *Re Fanshaw*, 40 L. J. Bank. 52 ; L. R. 11 Eq. 615 : *Ex p. Harrison*, *Re Peake*, 13 Q. B. D. 760) ; nor a Garnishee Order (per Coleridge, C.J., *Fellows* v

Thornton, 54 L. J. Q. B. 279 ; 14 Q. B. D. 335 ; 52 L. T. 389 ; 33 W. R. 258 ; but consider jdgmt. of Stephen, J., in that case) ; nor is a Charging Order under s. 14, 1 & 2 V. c. 110, an "Execution against the goods of a debtor," within s. 45, Bankry. Act, 1883 (*Re Hutchinson*, 55 L. J. Q. B. 582 ; 16 Q. B. D. 515 ; 54 L. T. 302 ; 34 W. R. 475 ; 3 Morr. 19).

As to what is a sufficient Execution entitling a Sheriff to Poundage ; *V. Bissicks* v. *Bath Colly. Co.* 46 L. J. Q. B. 611 ; 2 Ex. D. 459, and cases there cited. *Vf.* LEVY.

The "*Costs of Execution*" mentioned in s. 46 (1), Bankry. Act, 1883, do not include the Sheriff's poundage ; but under the same phrase in subs. 2 of the same section, such poundage is included (*Re Ludford*, 53 L. J. Q. B. 418 ; 33 W. R. 152 ; nom. *Re Ludmore*, 13 Q. B. D. 415). Expenses of reaping and harvesting growing crops, are not "Costs of Execution," though the selling value is thereby increased (*Re Woodham*, 57 L. J. Q. B. 46 ; 20 Q. B. D. 40 ; 58 L. T. 116 ; 36 W. R. 526).

As to the phrase "money, goods or chattels taken or intended to be taken *in execution* under any process," R. S. C., Ord. 57, R. 1, *b* ; *V. Smith* v. *Critchfield*, 54 L. J. Q. B. 366 ; 14 Q. B. D. 873.

V. DELIVERED IN EXECUTION : EQUITABLE.

EXECUTION OF STATUTORY POWERS.—By many statutes protection, absolute or qualified, is given for works done "in execution" of statutory powers. This means a careful and skilful execution, and no protection is afforded to carelessness or the absence of proper skilfulness (*Clothier* v. *Webster*, 31 L. J. C. P. 316 ; 12 C. B. N. S. 790).

V. IN PURSUANCE.

EXECUTOR.—*V.* PROPRIETOR.

EXECUTORS.—By what words Executors may be appointed, *V.* Wms. Exs. 243. An appointment of Executors would be revoked by a codicil naming a "sole Executor" (Ib. 251).

A substitutionary gift to the "Executors or Administrators" of a legatee in the event of his death in the testator's lifetime, does not vest the gift in the legatee's exors upon trust for his Next of Kin, but the exors take, and have to apply it, as part of the personal estate of the legatee (*Re Clay*, 54 L. J. Ch. 648 ; 52 L. T. 641 ; 32 W. R. 516 ; which distinctly over-rules *Palin* v. *Hills*, 1 Myl. & K. 470, *wh. V.* discussed Wms. Exs. 1148—1152 ; 2 Jarm. 114 : *Vf.* 2 Jarm. 117–120). A bequest to A. "*and* his exs., ads. and ass[s].," or to A. "*and* his representatives" will lapse by the death of A. in the testator's lifetime (Wms. Exs. 1212) ; *secus*, if it be to A. "and his *heirs*" (Ib. 1213), or to A. "*or* his exs.," &c. (Ib. 1216).

As to when a legacy to an Executor is conditional on his accepting office and acting ; *V.* Wms. Exs. 1286.

For the rules and cases on Limitations to "Executors," and the distinction between "Executors" and "Next of Kin," and as to whether and when "Executors and Administrators" may mean "Next of Kin," *V.* Elph. 312–316 ; Watson, Eq. 1406, 1407 ; Seton, 925 ; Chitty, Eq. Ind. 7690.

In *Graffiey* v. *Humpage* (1 Bea. 52 ; 8 L. J. Ch. 98), Langdale, M. R., said that "exors., admors. and assigns" cannot mean next of kin : Why not ? says Elph. 314.

As to construction of "Executors" in a Power ; *V.* Lewin, 603, 604, 656.

As to "By direction of the Exors." being a sufficient description of a vendor ; *V.* PROPRIETOR.

V. LEGAL PERSONAL REPRESENTATIVES : HEIRS, EXECUTORS, ADMINISTRATORS AND ASSIGNS.

EXECUTORSHIP EXPENSES.—This phrase is equivalent to "TESTAMENTARY EXPENSES" (*Sharp* v. *Lush*, 48 L. J. Ch. 231 ; 10 Ch. D. 468).

EXEMPTED.—The word "exempted" in s. 18, Sucn. Dy. Act, 1853, does not mean "free from," but means those legacies that were by the then existing Legacy Duty Acts expressly exempted from duty (*A.-G.* v. *Fitzjohn*, 27 L. J. Ex. 79 ; 2 H. & N. 465).

EXERCISE.—*V.* GAME.

"In Exercise ;" *V.* PURSUANCE.

"The Exercise of any of the powers of the Act," s. 308, P. H. Act, 1875 ; *V. Burgess* v. *Northwich*, 50 L. J. Q. B. 219 ; 6 Q. B. D. 264.

EXERCISED.—To "exercise" a business is the same thing as to carry it on. Business "exercised within the United Kingdom," s. 1, Income Tax Act, 16 & 17 V. c. 34 ; *V.* CARRY ON.

EXHAUSTED.—A Coal Gale is "exhausted" (1 & 2 V. c. 43, s. 61) when there is not enough coal left in it to make it worth working (*Ellway* v. *Davis*, 43 L. J. Ch. 75 ; L. R. 16 Eq. 294).

EXISTING.—"Existing Company ;" *V. Richmond W. W. Co.* v. *Richmond*, 45 L. J. Ch. 441 ; 3 Ch. D. 82.

A Conveyance subject to "existing Leases and Lettings" does not comprise parol unenforceable leases (*Rice* v. *O'Connor*, 11 Ir. Ch. Rep. 510).

EXONERATION.—A direction in a Will to pay debts "in aid of the personal and in exoneration of the real estate" (*Re Newmarch*, 48 L. J. Ch. 28 ; 9 Ch. D. 12), or, "in exoneration of the real estate" (*Re Rossiter*, 49 L. J. Ch. 36 ; 13 Ch. D. 355), will not exonerate the testator's mortgaged property from its primary liability to pay the mortgage debt.

As to Exoneration of Mortgaged Property before and since Locke King's Act ; *V.* 2 Jarm. 644–651 ; Wms. Exs. 1708 : and as to Exoneration of Personalty from debts ; *V.* 2 Jarm. 651–673 ; Wms. Exs. 1711.

EXPECTANT HEIR.—"Every person who is entitled either absolutely or contingently, to any reversion or remainder in a property or a portion, or who has the hope of succession to the property of an ancestor or relative, either by reason of his being the heir apparent or presumptive, or by reason merely of any supposed or presumed affection on the part of his ancestor or relative, is an Expectant Heir within the meaning of the rule" for setting aside catching bargains (Seton, 1367, citing *Beynon* v. *Cook*, 10 Ch. 391, n. *g.* : *Aylesford* v. *Morris*, 8 Ch. 497 : *Tyler* v. *Yates*, 6 Ch. 665 : *Tottenham* v. *Emmet*, 14 W. R. 3). *Vf. James* v. *Kerr*, 40 Ch. D. 449.

EXPECTATION.—Contracting debt without "reasonable or probable *Ground of Expectation* of being able to pay it" in s. 28, subs. 3 (c), Bankry. Act, 1883 ; *V. Ex p. White*, 14 Q. B. D. 600 ; 54 L. J. Q. B. 384 ; 33 W. R. 670.

EXPECTED TO ARRIVE.—*V. Bold* v. *Rayner*, 1 M. & W. 343 ; 5 L. J. Ex. 172 : *Smith* v. *Myers*, L. R. 7 Q. B. 139 ; 41 L. J. Q. B. 91. *V.* ARRIVE.

EXPEDIENT.—*V.* INEXPEDIENT.

EXPENSE.—A *Legacy* made "free of all expense," is duty free (*Gosden* v. *Dotterill*, 1 My. & K. 56).

"If a *Charter Party* provides that if the charterer gives certain directions respecting the vessel he will bear any expense which the vessel may incur in consequence of those directions, he is liable to pay only such expenses as are the natural consequence of the directions" (Wood, 167, citing *Sully* v. *Duranty*, 3 H. & C. 270 ; 33 L. J. Ex. 319).

"At Ship's Expense ;" *V.* RISK.

EXPENSES.—"Expenses" mean, actual disbursements, not allowances for loss of time (*Jones* v. *Carmarthen*, 10 L. J. Ex. 401 ; 8 M. & W. 605).

The kind of "Expenses," incidental to the stopping or diverting a highway, within s. 84, Highway Act, 1835, 5 & 6 W. 4, c. 50, are the expenses attending the view, the preparation of necessary plans and of structurally stopping or diverting the highway ; but not a solicitor's costs of taking the necessary legal steps in the matter (*United Land Co.* v. *Tottenham*, 53 L. J. M. C. 136 ; 13 Q. B. D. 640).

"Expenses of or incident to the making the Apportionment" of Tithes, s. 75, 6 & 7 W. 4, c. 71; *V. Hinchliffe* v. *Armitstead*, 11 L. J. Ex. 253 ; 9 M. & W. 155.

V. INCIDENTAL EXPENSES.

EXPENSES OF MANAGEMENT.—As to this phrase in s. 58 (ix), Settled Land Act, 1882 ; *V. Clarke* v. *Thornton*, 56 L. J. Ch. 304 ; 35 Ch. D. 307 ; 56 L. T. 294 ; 35 W. R. 603.

EXPIRATION.—"Expiration of the said term of years;" "'Expiration,' which is here used by similitude to things living, implies any end whatever. For as we signify by 'Expiration' the death of a man and his last end, whatever way it happens, so the word 'Expiration' being applied to an estate for years, may aptly enough signify the end of it, whatever way it be" (*Wrotesley* v. *Adams*, Plow. 198).

But when a consequence follows on the "Expiration" of a term, does that mean exclusively expiration by effluxion of the time? (*Vh.* jdgmt. of Coleridge, C.J., *Hall* v. *Comfort*, 56 L. J. Q. B. 187).

In this connection "to Expire" would seem rather to mean for the term to run itself out by effluxion of time or otherwise in due course, as distinguished from being forcibly put an end to—*e.g.* by forfeiture.

This apparently is the meaning put on the word in Ord. 3, R. 6, R. S. C.: for whilst speedy judgment for recovery of land may, under that Order, be obtained where the action puts an end to a tenancy created by an attornment in a mortgage deed (*Daubuz* v. *Lavington*, 53 L. J. Q. B. 283; 13 Q. B. D. 347: *Hall* v. *Comfort*, 56 L. J. Q. B. 185; 18 Q. B. D. 11; 55 L. T. 550; 35 W. R. 48); yet the Order is inapplicable to a case of forfeiture of a term (*Burns* v. *Walford*, W. N. (84) 31: *Mansergh* v. *Rimell*, W. N. (84) 34, cited Ann. Pr. 130). *V.* UNEXPIRED.

"At the expiration;" *V.* AT.

EXPLOSION.—*V.* *Stanley* v. *Western Insrce.*, 37 L. J. Ex. 73; L. R. 3 Ex. 71; 17 L. T. 513; 16 W. R. 369.

EXPLOSIVE.—Fog-signals are a "preparation or composition of an Explosive Nature," ss. 6 and 7, 23 & 24 V. c. 139 (*Bliss* v. *Lilley*, 32 L. J. M. C. 3; 7 L. T. 319).

EXPORT.—An inland town whence butter is sent direct to a foreign market, is not a "Place of Export" within 52 G. 3, c. 134, and 7 & 8 G. 4, c. 61 (*Hayes* v. *Dexter*, 13 Ir. C. L. Rep. 22).

EXPORTATION.—The words "Shipped for Exportation" are not, necessarily, restricted to an exportation to foreign countries, but may mean Exportation in its evident sense, *i.e.*, a carrying out of port, and thus include carrying commodities from one port to another within the Kingdom (*Stockton Ry.* v. *Barrett*, 11 Cl. & F. 590: *Vth.* Dwar. 648, 691).

EXPORTED.—"Exported" means "carried out;" therefore dues on "coals exported" from a Port are payable on coals to be consumed on board (*Muller* v. *Baldwin*, L. R. 9 Q. B. 457; 43 L. J. Q. B. 164).

V. IMPORTED.

EXPOSE.—Articles of food "Exposed for sale, or Deposited in any place for the purpose of sale," s. 116, P. H. Act, 1875 ; *V. R.* v. *White*, 49 L. J. M. C. 19 ; 5 Q. B. D. 15 ; 41 L. T. 524 ; 28 W. R. 168 ; 44 J. P. 87, 102 : *Newton* v. *Monkcom*, 58 L. T. 231 ; 4 Times Rep. 205.

V. Abandon : "Expose to Obvious Risk ;" *V.* Obvious.

EXPRESS.—"*Trains* to be sent express ;" *V. Rigby* v. *G. W. Ry.*, 15 L. J. Ch. 266 ; 2 Ph. 44.

"The words 'Express *Trust*' in this statute (3 & 4 W. 4, c. 27, s. 25) are used by way of opposition to trusts arising from implication, trusts resulting, or trusts by operation of law" (per Westbury, L.C., *Dickenson* v. *Teasdale*, 1 D. G. J. & S. 59 : *Vf.* per Kindersley, V.-C., *Petre* v. *Petre*, 1 Drew. 393) ; but an "Express Trust" may arise without the formal language usually employed in creating a Trust, and if a Trust clearly arises from the language of a document, an "Express Trust" will be created (*Salter* v. *Cavanagh*, 1 Dr. & Wal. 668 : *Patrick* v. *Simpson*, 24 Q. B. D. 128 ; 6 Times Rep. 23).

Trusts for sale and for application of purchase moneys in an ordinary mortgage, are not "Express Trusts" within the statute just cited (*Re Alison, Johnson* v. *Mounsey*, 11 Ch. D. 284 : *Chapman* v. *Corpe*, 27 W. R. 781). *Vh. Re Rowe*, 58 L. J. Ch. 703.

Cp. "Express Trusts" as used in s. 25 (2), Judicature Act, 1873, and in s. 10, 37 & 38 V. c. 57.

As to what are Express Trusts ; *Vf.* Lewin, 874.

EXPRESSLY NAMED.—A person,—*e.g.* an attorney to attest a Warrant of Attorney, s. 9, 1 & 2 V. c. 110,—is "named," or even "expressly named," by another if such other adopts a name that is suggested to him, for "expressly" does not mean "originally" (*Taylor* v. *Nicholl*, 6 M. & W. 91 ; 9 L. J. Ex. 78). *Vf.* Named.

EXPRESSLY PURCHASED.—S. 77, Ry. C. C. Act, 1845 ; *V. Errington* v. *Metrop. Distr. Ry.*, 51 L. J. Ch. 305 ; 19 Ch. D. 559.

EXPRESSLY REFER.—A condition that a General Power of Appointment is not to be executed by Will unless it "expressly refer" to the power or its subject-matter, will prevent the operation of s. 27, Wills Act, 1 V. c. 26 (*Re Phillips*, 58 L. J. Ch. 448 ; 41 Ch. D. 417 : *Phillips* v. *Cayley*, 58 L. J. Ch. 569 ; *Re Tarrant*, W. N. (89) 146. *Sv.* to the contrary, *Re Marsh*, 57 L. J. Ch. 639 ; 38 Ch. D. 630).

EXPRESSLY VARIED.—Where one Act incorporates another, except where "expressly varied" by the incorporating statute, it is not essentially necessary that there should be express words saying, this particular section or provision shall not apply. Express words are not required for that purpose ; but there must be something that indicates an express intention, that a particular provision in the prior statute shall not apply to the incorporating statute. A mere variation in the incorporating statute from the ordinary type and form of a general Act would not be sufficient to prevent the general clauses applying. A variation in the incorporating Act showing that a provision in the prior Act was inapplicable, would have the same effect as if that provision were expressly varied (per Blackburn, J., *Metrop. Dist. Ry.* v. *Sharpe*, 50 L. J. Q. B. 21). In that case it was held that s. 34, Lands C. C. Act, 1845, was not "expressly varied" by a special enactment as to arbitration which made no provision for costs (50 L. J. Q. B. 14 ; 5 App. Ca. 425).

EXTEND TO AND INCLUDE.—The words "shall extend to and include" (and so of the word "include" alone) in an Interpretation Clause, are wider and go further than the words "shall mean ;" and denote that, in addition to the popular meaning given to a word or phrase, such word or phrase shall also have the meanings given to it by the Interpretation Clause (per Baggallay, L.J. and Brett, M.R., *Portsmouth* v. *Smith*, 53 L. J. Q. B. 92 ; 13 Q. B. D. 184 : *Va. R.* v. *Elliott*, 41 L. J. Adm. 67 ; nom. *Dyke* v. *Elliott*, L. R. 4 P. C. 184).

EXTENDED.—S. 180 (9), P. H. Act, 1875 ; *V. Yeadon Case*, 58 L. J. Ch. 563 ; 41 Ch. D. 32 ; 60 L. T. 550.

EXTERNAL PARTS.—A covenant to repair the "External Parts" of a house includes a wall by which it adjoins to, and is divided from, another house,—the "External Parts" of premises being those which form the enclosure of them and beyond which no part of them extends (*Green* v. *Eales*, 2 Q. B. 225 ; 11 L. J. Q. B. 63 ; 1 G. & D. 468).

EXTINCT.—"'*Extinct*' commeth of the verbe *extinguere*, to destroy or put out ; and a rent is said to be extinguished, when it is destroied and put out" (Co. Litt. 147 b).

V. Suspense.

EXTINCTION.—"Where the title to any Succession shall be *accelerated* by the surrender or extinction of any prior interests," s. 15, Sucn. Dy. Act, 1853 ; *V. Ex p. Sitwell, Re Drury Lowe*, 21 Q. B. D. 466 ; 59 L. T. 539.

EXTINGUISHED.—*V.* Suspense : Extinct.

EXTORTION.—The offence of Extortion consists in a Public Officer "taking under colour of office from any person any money or valuable thing which is not due from him at the time when it is taken.

"If the illegal act consists in inflicting upon any person any bodily harm, imprisonment, or other injury not being extortion, the offence is called 'Oppression'" (Steph. Cr. 83). *V.* Exaction : Termes de la Ley, *Extortion.*

Vf. Arch. Cr. 468, 946 ; Rosc. Cr. 833 ; Co. Litt. 368 b.

EXTRAORDINARY EXPENSES.—S. 23, 41 & 42 V. c. 77 ; *V.* EXTRAORDINARY TRAFFIC.

EXTRAORDINARY TRAFFIC.—" What constitutes '*Excessive Weight*' or '*Extraordinary Traffic*' (within s. 23, 41 & 42 V. c. 77), must, to a great extent, depend upon the opinion of those (*i.e.*, the Justices) who know the neighbourhood" (per Grove, J., *Pickering* v. *Barry*, 51 L. J. M. C. 19 ; 8 Q. B. D. 59 ; 30 W. R. 246 ; 46 J. P. 215). In the same case, Lopes, J., in his jdgmt., said, " I think that the Legislature intended something Excessive in Weight or Extraordinary in Kind of Traffic, either,

1. As compared with what is usually carried over roads of the same nature in the neighbourhood, or

2. As compared with that to which the road in its ordinary and fair use may reasonably be subjected. It would not be sufficient to compare the Weight and Traffic complained of with the traffic usually carried on the particular road, because the traffic usually carried might be of the highest kind ; but surely the Legislature never intended that a man was not to use the road for carrying materials for building a dwelling-house, farm-house or barn, provided he used it in a reasonable way for those purposes. The comparison must be larger, and I think the definition I have given, if not exhaustive, will be found useful."

For cases illustrating clause 1 of Mr. Justice Lopes' definition ; *V. Aveland* v. *Lucas*, 5 C. P. D. 351 ; 49 L. J. C. P. 643 ; 28 W. R. 571 ; 43 J. P. 830 : *Savin* v. *Oswestry*, 44 J. P. 766 : *Williams* v. *Davis*, Ib. 347 : *Northumberland Whinstone Co.* v. *Alnwick*, Ib. 360 : *Wallington* v. *Hoskins*, 50 L. J. M. C. 19 ; 6 Q. B. D. 206 ; 29 W. R. 152 ; 45 J. P. 173 : *R.* v. *Ellis*, 8 Q. B. D. 466 ; 30 W. R. 613 (Traction Engine case) : *Ellis* v. *Maidstone*, 46 J. P. 295 : and *cp. Tunbridge* v. *Sevenoaks*, 33 W. R. 306 ; 49 J. P. 340, with *Raglan* v. *Monmouth Steam Co.*, 46 J. P. 598.

And as illustrating Clause 2 of the definition, *V. Pickering* v. *Barry*, sup., where Grove, J., whilst agreeing that using a road for carrying materials for the building of an ordinary dwelling-house would not be exceptional, said, "I do not mean to say that there might not be Excessive Weight or Extraordinary Traffic for an extraordinary building such as a College or Workhouse."

Unusual frequence of ordinary loads does not constitute " Extraordinary Traffic " (*R.* v. *Williamson*, 45 J. P. 505).

Vh. Stone, 353–355.

EXTRAVAGANCE.—*V.* UNJUSTIFIABLE EXTRAVAGANCE.

EY.—" *Ey*, *ing*, and *worth*, signifieth a watry place or water " (Co. Litt. 5 b).

F—FAC

F. C. S.—" Free of Capture and Seizure " (1 Maude & P. 449).

F. G. A.—" Free of General Average " (1 Maude & P. 449).

F. O. B.—" Free on Board." This expression throughout the whole of England, means that the seller is to put the goods on board at his own expense, but on account of, and thenceforward at the risk and as the property of, the purchaser ; and this is so whether the goods are specific or only a proportion of a quantity (*Cowas-jee* v. *Thompson*, 5 Moo. P. C. C. 173 : *Brown* v. *Hare*, 27 L. J. Ex. 372 ; 29 Ib. 6 ; 3 H. & N. 484 ; 4 Ib. 822 : *Inglis* v. *Stock*, 54 L. J. Q. B. 582 ; 10 App. Ca. 263 : Benj. 315 : Blackb. 362). In *Ex p. Rosevear Co., Re Cock* (11 Ch. D. 565), Bacon, C.J. in Bankry., said,—" Delivery 'free on board' only means, 'The price shall be that which we stipulate for, and you shall not have to pay for the wagons or carts necessary to carry (to the ship) ; we will bear all those charges and put it free on board the ship, the name of which you furnish.' "

F. P. A.—" Free of particular average " (1 Maude & P. 449).

" Where, in the Memorandum, the words 'Warranted free from Particular Average' are used, these words are not confined to losses arising from injury to the goods themselves, but amount to a warranty against any loss other than a total loss, or General Average ; and therefore, under a Marine Policy in the ordinary form on goods, the Underwriters are not liable for expenses incurred in relation to the goods unless such expenses are paid to avert a General Average loss, and are therefore recoverable under the Suing and Labouring Clause " (1 Maude & P. 493, citing *Meyer* v. *Ralli*, 1 C. P. D. 372, 373 ; 45 L. J. C. P. 741 : *Gt. Indian Peninsular Ry.* v. *Saunders*, 1 B. & S. 41 ; 30 L. J. Q. B. 218 ; 31 Ib. 206). *Vh. Hendricks* v. *Australasian Insrce.*, 43 L. J. C. P. 188 ; L. R. 9 C. P. 461 : *Stewart* v. *Merchants Mar. Insrce.*, 55 L. J. Q. B. 81 ; 16 Q. B. D. 619.

FABRICATE.—*V.* FALSELY ASSUMING TO ACT.

FACILITIES.—By s. 2, Ry. and Canal Traffic Act, 1854 (17 & 18 V. c. 31), Ry. and Canal Companies " shall, according to their respective powers, afford all reasonable *Facilities* " for receiving, forwarding, and delivering Traffic. The word " Facilities," here, does not mean merely facilities afforded by the management of traffic ; but a Company violates the Act " if (*having sufficient powers*) it keeps its platforms, booking-office, and other structures, at any station, in such a condition as to space and other arrangements as to cause dangerous or obstructive confusion, delay or other impediment to the proper reception, transmission, or delivery of the ordinary traffic of that station, whether consisting of passengers or of goods" (per Selborne, L.C., *S. E. Ry.* v. *Ry. Commrs.*, 50 L. J. Q. B. 206; 6 Q. B. D. 586). But refreshment-rooms, and covered platforms and carriage yards, even at places where invalids resort, are not "facilities" within the section (Ib.). *Vf. G. W. Ry.* v. *Ry. Commrs.*, 50 L. J. Q. B. 483; 7 Q. B. D. 182: *Brown* v. *G. W. Ry.*, 51 L. J. Q. B. 529; 9 Q. B. D. 744: *R.* v. *Ry. Commrs.*, 58 L. J. Q. B. 233; 22 Q. B. D. 642: *Nichol* v. *N. E. Ry.*, 4 Times Rep. 464. The section includes Facilities for Passengers (*Re Winsford Loc. Bd. and Cheshire Lines Committee*, Times 10 Feb. 1890).

FACT.—An action on a Distress for church rates is commenced within three calendar months "*after the Fact committed*" (53 G. 3, c. 127, s. 12), if brought within that time after the sale under the distress (*Collins* v. *Rose*, 5 M. & W. 194; 8 L. J. Ex. 273).

A recital that A. B. is seised in fee, is a "recital or statement of *a Fact*" (and not merely of a proposition of law); and if contained in a Deed 20 years old will be sufficient evidence of the truth of that fact within sub-s. 2, s. 2, Vendor & Purchaser Act, 1874 (37 & 38 V. c. 78), until the contrary is proved (*Bolton* v. *London School Board*, 47 L. J. Ch. 461; 7 Ch. D. 766).

"Question of Fact arising in the Action;" *V. Fennessey* v. *Clark*, 57 L. J. Ch. 398; 37 Ch. D. 184; 58 L. T. 289.

V. Material Facts: Perjury.

FACTOR.—"There are two extensive classes of mercantile agents, namely;—*Factors*, who are entrusted with the possession as well as the disposal of property; and *Brokers*, who are employed to contract about it without being put in possession" (Smith, Mer. Law, 9 Ed. 106, cited with approval by Brett, L.J., *Ex p. Dixon*, 46 L. J. Bank. 20; 4 Ch. D. 133; and by Chitty, J., *Stevens* v. *Biller*, 53 L. J. Ch. 249; 25 Ch. D. 31. *Vf.* as to "Factor," *A.-G.* v. *Trueman*, 13 L. J. Ex. 70; 11 M. & W. 694). *V.* Broker.

"Factors, Servants, or Assigns," in the Suing and Labouring Clause of a Marine Insurance; *V. Uzielli* v. *Boston Mar. Insrce.*, 15 Q. B. D. 11; 54 L. J. Q. B. 142.

FACTORY.—A "Factory," within s. 3, 30 & 31 V. c. 103, relates to trades carried on in covered buildings, and not to open-air processes, such as a Quarry, or Cement Works on a large piece of land (*Kent* v. *Astley*, 39 L. J. M. C. 3; 10 B. & S. 802; L. R. 5 Q. B. 19: *Redgrave* v. *Lee*, 43 L. J. M. C. 105; L. R. 9 Q. B. 363).

Vf. Palmer Ship-building Co. v. *Chaytor*, 38 L. J. M. C. 63; 10 B. & S. 177; L. R. 4 Q. B. 209.

Cp. s. 5, Factory and Workshop Act, 1871, 34 & 35 V. c. 104; and *Vth.* obs. Cockburn, C.J., in *Redgrave* v. *Lee*, sup.

FAIL.—"Fails to land and take delivery," s. 67, Mer. Shipping Act, 1862, need not imply a wilful default in the cargo owner (*Miedbrodt* v. *Fitzsimon*, 44 L. J. Adm. 25 ; L. R. 6 P. C. 306).

If Mine shall "fail," in a proviso for cesser in a Mining Lease, means (probably) if it shall become not WORKABLE, and (probably) does not refer to "exhaustion" (*Jervis* v. *Tomkinson*, 26 L. J. Ex. 44).

FAILURE.—"Failure, Neglect or Default" to perform an obligation ; *V. Lewis* v. *Swansea*, 4 Times Rep. 706.

V. DEFAULT.

FAILURE OF ISSUE.—*V.* DIE WITHOUT ISSUE.

FAIR.—Grant of a Fair "with all Liberties ;" *V.* WITH ALL LIBERTIES.

V. FAIR OR MARKET TOLLS.

FAIR AND REASONABLE.—"Fair and Reasonable *Compensation*," under 2nd par., s. 5, Agricultural Holdings (England) Act, 1883 ; *V.* Woodf. 779.

"Fair and Reasonable *Supposition*" of Right, s. 52, 24 & 25 V. c. 97 ; *V. White* v. *Feast*, L. R. 7 Q. B. 353 ; 41 L. J. M. C. 81 : *Va.* BONÂ FIDE.

FAIR AVERAGE QUALITY.—"If goods coming from a particular port are sold as being of 'a fair average quality,' a fair average quality of the various sorts of the article which comes from that port is meant, and not of the sorts which come from all parts of the world" (Wood. 354, citing *Jones* v. *Clarke*, 2 H. & N. 725 ; 27 L. J. Ex. 165).

FAIR COMMENT.—"A Fair Comment (excusing what would otherwise be a Libel) is a Comment which is either true, or which, if false, expresses the real opinion of its author (as to the existence of matter of fact, or otherwise), such opinion having been formed with a reasonable degree of care and on reasonable grounds" (Steph. Cr. 202).

"The nearest approach, I think, to an exact definition of the word 'fair,' is contained in the judgment of Tenterden, C.J., in *Macleod* v. *Wakley* (3 C. & P. 313), where he said,—'Whatever is fair and can be reasonably said of the works of authors or of themselves, as connected with their works, is not actionable, unless it appears, that, under the pretext of criticising the works, the defendant takes an opportunity of attacking the character of the author: then it will be a libel'" (per Bowen, L.J., *Merivale* v. *Carson*, 20 Q. B. D. 283).

Vh. an article, 84 L. T. 114.

FAIR OR MARKET TOLLS.—The duties which are usually paid at a fair or market are tolls, stallage, and pickage ; and this toll is a reasonable sum due to the owners of the fair or market upon the sale therein of things which are tollable (Gunning on Tolls, 44).

V. TOLL.

FAIR PRICE.—The "Fair Price,"—"agreed to be paid,"—referred to in s. 45, Agricultural Holdings Act, 1883 (46 & 47 V. c. 61), includes agreements for barter as well as for payments in cash (*London and Yorksh. Bank* v. *Belton*, 54 L. J. Q. B. 568; 15 Q. B. D. 457). In that case Coleridge, C.J., said,—"In ordinary colloquial language 'Price' does not always mean money, and 'fair price' is not necessarily an adequate sum of current coin: it may be used where the result of a transaction is that a man gave a fair equivalent for what he got." In the same case, Mathew, J., said, "I think that 'Fair Price' means Equivalent."

FAIR REPORT.—A Fair Report of a judicial proceeding, excusing what would otherwise be a Libel, is one that "is substantially accurate, and either complete or condensed in such a manner as to give a just impression of what took place;" but this does not extend to comments of the reporter or to observations of persons not entitled to take part in the proceedings (Steph. Cr. 206). The report may be "fair," although it contains only the speech of counsel and the summing-up of the judge (*Milissch* v. *Lloyd's*, W. N. (77) 36).

FAIR VALUATION.—When the terms of a contract, under which the produce of land is to be taken at a Fair Valuation, do not conclusively and clearly define what the parties mean by a "Fair Valuation," it will be a question of fact for the jury what is such a Valuation (*Cumberland* v. *Bowes*, 15 C. B. 348; 24 L. J. C. P. 46; 1 Jur. N. S. 236; 3 C. L. R. 149).

"It appears probable that a general agreement to sell 'at a Fair Valuation' may be enforced" (Dart, 257; *V.* cases there cited).

FAIRLY.—As to covenants "Fairly and Regularly," or "Diligently and Regularly," or "Uninterruptedly, Efficiently and Regularly," to work a Mine; *V.* MacS. 217, 233.

FAIRLY ESTIMATED.—The introduction of the adverb 'fairly' in the power to the Court to determine that a Liability in a Bankry shall not be proveable therein if it is incapable of being "fairly estimated" (s. 31, Bankry. Act, 1869; s. 37 (6), Bankry. Act, 1883), "involves the principle that all liabilities, subject to the express statutory exceptions, were intended to be included, but that in the one case where the Court should adjudicate that the liability was such that, at that time, it could not be 'fairly estimated,' then, and then only, should the liability continue" (per Halsbury, L.C., *Hardy* v. *Fothergill*, 58 L. J. Q. B. 45; 13 App. Ca. 351). *V.* DEBTS DUE: DEBT OR LIABILITY: INCAPABLE.

FAIRLY WORKABLE.—*V.* WORKABLE.

FAIRLY WROUGHT.—*V.* WROUGHT.

FAITOUR.—An evil doer (Termes de la Ley).

FALDAGE.—*V.* FOLDCOURSE : FRANKFOLDAGE.

FALESIA.—"*Falesia* is a bank or hill by the sea-side ; it commeth of *falaize*, which signifieth the same" (Co. Litt. 5 b).

FALL.—"Fall into Residue;" *V. Re Rhoades*, 29 Ch. D. 142 ; 54 L. J. Ch. 573: *Re Savage*, 50 L. J. Ch. 131, and *Re Ballance*, 42 Ch. D. 62, considering *Humble* v. *Shore*, 7 Hare, 247 ; 1 H. & M. 550 n.: *Lightfoot* v. *Burstall*, 1 H. & M. 546 ; 33 L. J. Ch. 188 : *Crawshaw* v. *Crawshaw*, 14 Ch. D. 817 ; 49 L. J. Ch. 662 : *Re Barker*, 15 Ch. D. 635.

FALSE DOCUMENT.—*V.* FORGERY.

FALSE PRETENCE.—An indictable "False Pretence," "means a false representation made either by words, by writing, or by conduct, that some fact exists or existed, and such a representation may amount to a false pretence, although a person of common prudence might easily have detected its falsehood by inquiry, and although the existence of the alleged fact was in itself impossible.

But the expression 'False Pretence' does not include—

(*a*) A promise as to future conduct not intended to be kept, unless such promise is based upon or implies an existing fact falsely alleged to exist ; or,

(*b*) Such untrue commendation or untrue depreciation of an article which is to be sold as is usual between sellers and buyers, unless such untrue commendation or untrue depreciation is made by means of a definite false assertion as to some matter of fact capable of being positively determined" (Steph. Cr. 265, and *V.* to p. 267 for cases in illustration). *Vf.* Arch. Cr. 535–556 ; Rosc. Cr. 490–525.

FALSE SWEARING.—"Every one commits a misdemeanor, who swears falsely before any person authorized to administer an oath upon a matter of public concern, under such circumstances that the false swearing if committed in a judicial proceeding would have amounted to perjury" (Steph. Cr. 95). *Cp.* PERJURY.

FALSE TRADE DESCRIPTION.—*V.* INTENT TO DEFRAUD.

FALSELY ASSUMING TO ACT.—"Merely filling up a Voting Paper without authority, and witnessing it as if signed by the voter, is not 'falsely assuming to act' in the name of the voter (*Bell* v. *Morson*, 43 J. P. 638). Signing a Voting Paper at an election for member of Board of Health, by direction of voter's wife who has been authorized by her husband to sign it, is not '*fabricating*' a vote (*Aberdare* v. *Hammett*, 39 J. P. 598). Nor is attesting a wife's signature of her husband's name to a Voting Paper for Guardians (*Wickham* v. *Phillips*, 47 J. P. 260)." Stone, 220.

FALSIFY.—"Note, that 'to falsifie,' in legall understanding, is to prove false,—that is, to avoyd, or, as Littleton here (s. 149) saith, to defeat, in Latine *falsare, seu falsificare, falsum facere*" (Co. Litt. 104 b).

"Liberty to Surcharge and Falsify;" *V.* Dan. Ch. Pr. 485.

FAMILY.—The primary legal meaning of "Family" is not equivalent to *familia* or *famille*, but means "Children" (per Jessel, M. R., *Pigg* v. *Clarke*, 45 L. J. Ch. 849; 3 Ch. D. 672). Therefore where there is a gift to the "Family" of a person who has *children* living at the Testator's death, the word means exclusively the children of that person and does not include grandchildren or great-grandchildren (*Barnes* v. *Patch*, 8 Ves. 604: *Re Parkinson*, 20 L. J. Ch. 224; 1 Sim. N.S. 242: *Burt* v. *Hellyar*, L. R. 14 Eq. 160; 41 L. J. Ch. 430: *Pigg* v. *Clarke*, sup.: *Re Muffett*, 56 L. J. Ch. 600; 56 L. T. 685; 51 J. P. 660; 3 Times Rep. 126); or wife, (*Re Hutchinson & Tennant*, 8 Ch. D. 540: *Re Muffett*, sup.); but an illegitimate child, treated and recognised as a child, would be entitled to participate as part of the "Family" (per James, L. J., *Lambe* v. *Eames*, 40 L. J. Ch. 448; 6 Ch. 597: *Humble* v. *Bowman*, 47 L. J. Ch. 62). *Sq*, Would the foregoing be the rule in a case where the person spoken of had children living at the date of the Testator's Will but none at his death? It should seem not; for a Will speaks as if executed immediately before death (1 V. c. 26, s. 24), and to construe "family" as "children" in the case supposed would be to work an intestacy.

The word "Family" may, however, be controlled by the context. Thus where a testator directed his business to be carried on by his wife and son "for the mutual benefit of my Family" it was held that the wife was included (*Blackwell* v. *Bull*, 5 L. J. Ch. 251; 1 Keen, 176). So the word "Family" may, by the context, be controlled to mean "Posterity or Descendants" generally, as in *Williams* v. *Williams* (20 L. J. Ch. 280; 1 Sim. N. S. 358; but whether a correct construction was adopted in that case was doubted by Jessel, M. R., in *Pigg* v. *Clarke*, 45 L. J. Ch. 852); or to mean "Heirs" or "Next of Kin" (per Cranworth, V.-C., *Williams* v. *Williams*, 20 L. J. Ch. 283: *V.* cases collected, Wms. Exs. 1129–1132); or "Heir" or "heir-at-law" or "Heirs of the body" (*Doe* d. *Chattaway* v. *Smith*, 5 M. & S. 126: *Wright* v. *Atkyns*, 19 Ves. 299: *Griffiths* v. *Evan*, 11 L. J. Ch. 219; 5 Bea. 241: *Lucas* v. *Goldsmid*, 30 L. J. Ch. 935; 29 Bea. 657; 2 Jarm. 91–93); or "Blood Relations" (*Re Macleay*, 44 L. J. Ch. 441; L. R. 20 Eq. 186); or "Relations" (2 Jarm. 95: *Snow* v. *Teed*, 39 L. J. Ch. 420; L. R. 9 Eq. 622) or relations by marriage (*McLeroth* v. *Bacon*, 5 Ves. 158); or even rejected as surplusage (*Robinson* v. *Waddelow*, 5 L. J. Ch. 350; 8 Sim. 134: *Sv.* this last case questioned in *Re Parkinson*, sup.), or as being too uncertain (Lewin, 133).

Obviously where the person spoken of is *single*, the word "Family" cannot be construed as meaning his or her "Children," and accordingly the statutory next of kin would in such a case be denoted, *quâ* personalty (*Cruwys* v. *Colman*, 9 Ves. 319); and probably the heir-at-law would take the realty. It is submitted that the construction would be the same if the person spoken of were married but never had a child; and possibly also if he had had a child, but none living either at the date of the Will or at the death of the Testator. So also, though less strongly, it is submitted that the construction would be the same if the person spoken of had had a child living at the date of the Will but none at the death of the testator.

Vf. Re Sibery, W. N. (68) 251 : *Re Norman*, W. N. (79) 175 : *Re Price*, W. N. (87) 216 ; and for a full consideration of this word 2 Jarm. 90–98 : *Va.* Watson, Eq. 1403 : Chitty, Eq. Ind. 7694 : and per Pearson, J., *Re Collins*, 55 L. J. Ch. 674.

As to when persons taking under it would take *per stirpes* and when *per capita*, *V.* Wms. Exs. 1519, 1520, n. (*q*).

FAMILY MANSION.—To an application, under Settled Estates Act, 1877, for an Order to sell two properties in one lot, it was objected that one of the properties was a Family Mansion. "The answer is, it is not. The whole property consists of a house and 165 acres, which were purchased in 1842, so that the whole is not sufficiently large to entitle it to be called a Family Mansion. There are only 165 acres of land, and it is not really a Family Mansion in the sense that there is anything in the shape of *pretium affectionis* about it at all" (per Jessel, M. R., *Re Spurway*, 48 L. J. Ch. 214 ; 10 Ch. D. 230 : *Cp.* "Principal Mansion House," s. 15, Settled Land Act, 1882).

FANCY BREAD.—*V.* French Bread.

FANCY WORD.—A "Fancy Word not in common use," as used in the Patents, Designs, and Trade-Marks Act, 1883 (46 & 47 V. c. 57, s. 64, subs. 1, c), "must either have, to ordinary English people to whom this Act of Parliament is addressed, no meaning,—like the word 'Eureka,' or the word 'AEILYTON,'—or, if it has any meaning at all, it must be obviously meaningless when used as a trade mark" (per Lindley, L.J. *Re Van Duzer*, 56 L. J. Ch. 377). "I think a word to be a 'Fancy Word' must be obviously meaningless as applied to the article in question. I think it must be a word fanciful in its application to the article to which it is applied in the sense of being so obviously and notoriously inappropriate as neither to be deceptive nor descriptive, nor calculated to suggest deception or description. Further than that, I think that the word must have an innate and inherent character of fancifulness which must not depend on evidence, and cannot be supported by evidence, to show that, in fact, it is neither deceptive nor descriptive or calculated to be deceptive or descriptive. What

I mean is that a fancy word, in my opinion, must speak for itself ; it must be a fancy word of its own inherent strength" (per Lopes, L.J., Ib. 378).

The following were held *not* such "Fancy Words ; "—

"Alpine" as applied to Cotton Embroidery (*Re Van Duzer*, 56 L. J. Ch. 370 ; 34 Ch. D. 623, disapproving *Re Alpine*, 54 L. J. Ch. 727 ; 29 Ch. D. 877) :

"Electric," as applied to Velveteen (*Re Van Duzer*, sup.) :

"Gem," as applied to Rifles (*Re Arbenz*, 35 Ch. D. 248 ; 56 L. J. Ch. 524 ; 56 L. T. 252 ; 35 W. R. 527. *Va.* per Cotton, L.J., *Re Van Duzer*, sup.) :

"Hand Grenade Fire Extinguisher" (*Re Harden Co.*, 55 L. J. Ch. 596 ; 54 L. T. 834) :

"Jubilee" as applied to Paper (*Towgood* v. *Pirie*, 56 L. T. 394 ; 35 W. R. 729) :

"Melrose," as applied to a Hair Restorer (*Re Van Duzer*, sup.):

"National Sperm," as applied to Candles (*Re Price Candle Co.*, 54 L. J. Ch. 210 ; 27 Ch. D. 681) :

"Reversi," as applied to a game (*Waterman* v. *Ayers*, 57 L. J. Ch. 893 ; 39 Ch. D. 29 ; 59 L. T. 17 ; 37 W. R. 110) :

"Self-Washer," as applied to Soap (*Lever* v. *Goodwin*, 31 S. J. 110) :

"Strathmore," as applied to Whisky (per Cotton, L.J., *Re Van Duzer*, sup., commenting on *Blair* v. *Stock*, 52 L. T. 123) :

"Zephyr Asiatic Walnut Pipe" (*Re Friedlander*, 30 S. J. 397).

Geographical and dictionary words might when very odd and uncommon have been "Fancy Words," but they should have been avoided and must have been "obviously meaningless" (*Re Van Duzer*, sup.)

Note.—S. 10, Patents, Designs and Trade-Marks Act, 1888, substitutes an amended clause for s. 64 in the prior Act. This amending clause omits the phrase "Fancy Word," &c., and substitutes for it "(d) An Invented Word or Invented Words ; or (e) A word or words having no reference to the character or quality of the goods, and not being a geographical name."

FARDELLA.—"Fardella ; Ferdella ; Fardendela ; Fardingdela ; Farding ; Ferdingel ; Farthindel ; Farundel ; Ferlingus—a Rood ; Spelm." (Elph. 574, *wh. Vf.* : *Va.* Termes de la Ley, *Fardingdeale*).

FARE.—*V.* His Fare.

FARM.—"The word 'Farm' or 'Ferme,' called in Latine *firma*, is a compound word and doth comprehend many things. And therefore by the grant of a Ferme, will pass a messuage and much land, meadow pasture, wood, &c., thereunto belonging or therewith used ; for this word doth properly signify a capital, or principal, messuage and a great quantity of demesnes thereunto appertaining. Also by the grant of all Farmes, or all Ferms, it seems leases for years do pass" (Touch. 93 ; *Va.* Co. Litt. 5 a : *Portman* v. *Mill*, 8 L. J. Ch. 161 ; 2 Russ. 570 ; 3 Jur. 356 : *Goodtitle* v.

Paul, 2 Burr. 1089 : *Goodtitle* v. *Southern*, 1 M. & S. 299 : *Wrotesley* v. *Adams*, Plow. 195 a : Termes de la Ley).

This definition treats the word " Farm " in its two-fold aspect :—

1. As a word of description :—

2. As an abstract phrase.

1. When a person speaks of his "Farm" *at* such a place, then the first part of the definition in the *Touchstone* applies, and as a word of description it is very strong. Thus in a devise of " my *freehold* farm and lands at" A., the word "farm" is the essential part of the description, and so much of the farm as is copyhold will pass as well as the freehold part (*Re Bright-Smith*, 55 L. J. Ch. 365 ; 31 Ch. D. 314 ; 54 L. T. 47 ; 34 W. R. 252) ; though perhaps if such a devise be accompanied with limitations inapplicable to leaseholds, leaseholds would not pass (*Hall* v. *Fisher*, 1 Coll. 47 : *Sv.* that case and also *Stone* v. *Greening*, 13 Sim. 390, questioned by Ld. Selborne in *Hardwick* v. *Hardwick*, 42 L. J. Ch. 636 ; L. R. 16 Eq. 168, and *Va. Re Bright-Smith*, sup. : FREEHOLD).

So a devise of " my farm " called Whiteacre, *in the occupation of A.*, will pass parts of Whiteacre Farm not in A.'s occupation (*Goodtitle* v. *Southern*, 1 M. & S. 299 : *Down* v. *Down*, 7 Taunt. 343) ; *secus*, if the words were "All those my lands at Whiteacre Farm in the occupation of A." (per Ld. Cranworth, *Slingsby* v. *Grainger*, 7 H. L. Ca. 283 ; 28 L. J. Ch. 617). *Va. Whitfield* v. *Langdale* (1 Ch. D. 61 ; 45 L. J. Ch. 177), where a devise of " All that my Farm called H. in the parish of L., containing by estimation 80 acres more or less, in the occupation of J. C.," passed a farm called H. in J. C.'s occupation, containing 175 acres of which 155 acres, partly freehold and partly copyhold, were in L, and the rest was situate in an adjoining parish.

2. When a person devises all his messuages, farms, and heredits, then it is not correct to say that Leases for years will pass. It is indeed said, on the authority of Co. Litt. 5 a, and *Doe* d. *Belasyse* v. *Lucan* (9 East, 448), that " the word ' Farm ' is construed, according to its obvious meaning, as including houses, lands and tenements of every tenure" (1 Jarm. 784). But in *Holmes* v. *Milward* (47 L. J. Ch. 522), the word came before the Court as part of a residuary devise of " manors, messuages, *farms*, lands, tithes, tenements, heredits and real estate as well copyhold as freehold." And in giving jdgmt. Fry, J., said,—"It is said that the word 'Farm' is an ambiguous word, and that it may as well mean the estate of the lessee as well as the estate of the lessor, and for that the case of *Lane* v. *Stanhope* (6 T. R. 345) has been pressed upon me. I have no hesitation in saying that where there is a gift of 'Farms,' with real estate, with limitations which import that the fee is given, that carries the interest in real estate only, and does not carry with it the leasehold interest in a farm. The word ' Farm ' undoubtedly may mean the interest of the lessor or lessee. Apparently, to refer to the old definition given in Plowden (pp. 132, 169, 195), it primarily and more naturally means the interest of the

lessor, but it may also mean the interest of the lessee. The emphatic meaning of the word 'Farm' is this. That it means lands which have not been held in hand by the owner, but granted out and occupied by another person. Where that is the case, the interest of the lessor or lessee may pass by the description of 'Farm;' but where it is contained in a devise of real estate upon limitations which import the fee, I have no hesitation in saying it carries the fee simple farms, *and fee simple farms only.*"

Vf. Arkell v. *Fletcher,* 10 Sim. 299.

But "Farm" is oftentimes used in other senses than those already stated; *e.g.* "Farmers," in Stat. Marlbridge, c. 23, mean Lessees, and sometimes "Farm" means a Rent reserved (*Wrotesley* v. *Adams,* Plow. 195: Termes de la Ley).

FARM BUILDING.—*V. Wiltshear* v. *Cottrell,* 22 L. J. Q. B. 177; 1 E. & B. 674.

FARM LET.—"To farm let;" as to origin of this phrase, *V.* 1 Platt, 2.

FARMER.—A farmer is one who cultivates his own land, or that of another, for his own profit;—he is not as such a tradesman; nor though he do the labour with his own hand is he a labourer (*R.* v. *Silvester,* 33 L. J. M. C. 79; nom. *R.* v. *Cleworth,* 4 B. & S. 927). *V.* FERMOR.

FARMING MAN.—*V. Reynolds* v. *Whelan,* 16 L. J. Ch. 434.

FARMING STOCK.—A bequest of "Farming Stock" includes not only all moveable property upon or belonging to the farm (Wms. Exs. 1193: *Harvey* v. *Harvey,* 32 Bea. 441), but also growing crops (per Jessel, M. R., *Re Roose, Evans* v. *Williamson,* 50 L. J. Ch. 197; 17 Ch. D. 696; 29 W. R. 230,—following *Cox* v. *Godsalve,* 6 East, 604 n.: *West* v. *Moore,* 8 East, 339: *Blake* v. *Gibbs,* 5 Russ. 12, n.: and dissenting from *Vaisey* v. *Reynolds,* 6 L. J. O. S. Ch. 172; 5 Russ. 12). In *Evans* v. *Williamson,* the M. R. said, "the reasoning of *Vaisey* v. *Reynolds* is quite untenable in the face of the previous decisions."

In *Brooksbank* v. *Wentworth* (3 Atk. 64) a bequest of "Stock on Farm" was held, on a context, to include a lessee's trade interest in a malt-house and a stock of malt.

Vh. Bryant v. *Easterson,* 5 Jur. N. S. 166.

FASTENED.—*V.* FIXED AND FASTENED.

FAULT.—*V.* DEFAULT.

FAULTS.—"With all faults," means all the faults that are consistent with a thing being what it is described (*Shepherd* v. *Kain,* 5 B. & Ald. 240; commented on in *Taylor* v. *Bullen,* 5 Ex. 779; 20 L. J. Ex. 23). Subject to that qualification a sale "with all Faults" will release the vendor from responsibility for honest mis-statements that are capable of being detected by a rigid examination (*Baglehole* v. *Walters*, 3 Camp. 154: *Pickering* v. *Dowson*, 4 Taunt. 779: *Taylor* v. *Bullen*, 20 L. J. Ex. 21; 5 Ex. 779: *Ward* v. *Hobbs*, 48 L. J. Q. B. 281; 4 App. Ca. 13; 27 W. R. 114; 40 L. T. 73; 43 J. P. 252).

In *Taylor* v. *Bullen* (sup.), a Ship was sold "without any allowance for deficiency in length, height, quantity, quality, *or any Defect or Error whatever*," and Pollock, C. B., said,—"The real meaning of the contract is this, and the defendant may be supposed to have used this language to the plaintiff:—'There is a vessel now lying at St. Katharine's Dock, I describe her as being the *Intrepid*, A. 1, and call her a teak-built barque; but I expressly give you notice that I do not mean to warrant anything; I point out what I mean, go and look at the Inventory of stores, examine and judge for yourself, but understand that you must take her with all her faults and without allowance for any defect or error whatever'" (5 Ex. 784; 22 L. J. Ex. 23).

But "with all faults" does not mean "with all frauds," and such a stipulation will not avail as against material representations that are false to the vendor's knowledge and fraudulently made by him, nor as against defects which he has fraudulently concealed, nor (probably) as against material defects within his knowledge but upon which he has been silent and which were undiscoverable by examination (Add. C. 996-998, and cases there cited. *Va.* Benj. 657; 1 Maude & P. 53, n. (*w*): *Freeman* v. *Baker*, 3 L. J. K. B. 17; 5 B. & Ad. 797).

FAVOUR.—"In favour or against any particular Company or person," s. 90, 8 V. c. 20; *V. Manchester S. & L. Ry.* v. *Denaby Colliery*, 54 L. J. Q. B. 103.

FEBRUARY.—*V.* NEXT.

FEE.—"Fee commeth of the French *fief* (*i.e.*) *prædium beneficiarium*, and legally signifieth inheritance" (Co. Litt. 1 b; *Vf.* Wright's Ten. 3: 1 Preston on Estates, 2 Ed. 42). "Fee in our legall understanding signifieth, that the land belongs to us and our heires, in respect whereof the owner is said to be seized in fee" (Co. Litt. 1 b). "So, if Fee (only) is mentioned, it shall be intended Fee-simple" (*Metcalfe's Case*, 11 Rep. 39 a).

V. FEE SIMPLE: TAIL.

FEE FARM.—*V.* Termes de la Ley.

FEE SIMPLE.—"Fee" "signifieth inheritance," "and simple is added, for that it is descendible to his heires generally, that is, simply, without restraint to the heires of his body, or the like. . . . This word (simple) properly excludeth both conditions and limitations, that defeat or abridge the fee" (Co. Litt. 1 b). *Vf.* Termes de la Ley.

Prior to the Conv. & L. P. Act, 1881, the apt and necessary word of limitation for conveying a fee simple *by Deed*, was "heirs" (Co. Litt. 8 b; Wms. R. P. ch. 3). That word still remains apt, though it is no longer necessary, "the words 'in fee simple' without the word 'heirs'" will suffice (s. 51, Conv. & L. P. Act, 1881).

But though the old rule had its influence on *Wills*, yet "a conviction that the rule is generally subversive of the actual intention of testators, always induced the Courts to lend a willing ear whenever a plausible pretext for a departure from it could be suggested" (2 Jarm. 268, *wh.* to p. 286, *V.* for a collection of the cases as to what words, in a Will, would pass the fee simple prior to the Wills Act). And now by s. 28 of that Act (1 V. c. 26), a simple devise of real estate will pass the fee without any words of limitation; unless a contrary intention shall appear.

It remains however that a *grant* to a man "and his heir," in the singular number, gives only a life estate (Co. Litt. 8 b; Touch. 106); and that in a conveyance to a Corporation Sole the limitation to create a fee simple, must be to the incumbent and his "successors" (Co. Litt. 8 b, 94 b), "but a fee will pass to a Corporation *Aggregate* without the word 'successors,' and sometimes to a Corporation Sole" (Hargr. n. to Co. Litt. 8 b, referring to Co. Litt. 94 b, Vin. Ab. *Estate*, L).

"*Seized* in Fee Simple or in Fee Tail in Possession," s. 8, 17 G. 3, c. 26 (Registration of Annuities Act); *V. Halsey* v. *Hales*, 7 T. R. 194.

A Power to Trustees to sell "the Fee Simple and Inheritance" of *Pews or Seats in a Church* only enables them to sell an easement, and does not enable them to sell the soil on which a Pew or Seat stands, so as to convey a Parliamentary Freehold (*Hinde* v. *Charlton*, 36 L. J. C. P. 79; L. R. 2 C. P. 104: *Brumfitt* v. *Roberts*, 39 L. J. C. P. 95; L. R. 5 C. P. 224).

FEEDING.—*V.* Pasture.

FELLOWS.—A bequest to "the Fellows and Demies of Magdalen College, Oxford," held void, it being uncertain whether the gift was charitable, or for individuals (*A.-G.* v. *Sibthorp*, 2 R. & M. 107).

FELON.—When a person, convicted of Felony, has suffered the punishment, it is actionable to call him a "Felon" (*Leyman* v. *Latimer*, 47 L. J. Ex. 470; 3 Ex. D. 352). A free pardon purges the offence (2 Hale, P. C. 278: *Hay* v. *Middlesex Jus.*, 34 S. J. 213; 6 Times Rep. 169). *V.* Convicted.

FELONY: FELONIOUSLY.—These are terms of art, which, in an Indictment, cannot be supplied by equivalent expressions (Co. Litt. 391 a: *Holford* v. *Bailey*, 18 L. J. Q. B. 109; 13 Q. B. 426: *R.* v. *Gray*, 33 L. J. M. C. 78; 1 L. & C. 365; 12 W. R. 350); but their redundant or inapt use would not vitiate (*R.* v. *Butterworth*, 25 L. T. 850).

In *Les Termes de la Ley* it is said of serious crimes,—"It seems that they are called Felonies, . . . of the ancient English word '*fell*' or 'fierce,' because that they are intended to be done with a cruell, bitter, fell, fierce or mischievous minde."

"Every crime, the perpetrator of which is, by any statute, ordained to have judgment of '*Life or Member*' is a Felony: although the word *Felony* be not contained in the statute" (Dwar. 673, citing 1 Inst. 391; 2 Inst. 434; 3 Inst. 91): but an offence is not made Felony if only prohibited "*under Pain of forfeiting Body and Goods*," or of being "*at the King's will* for Body, Lands and Goods" (Dwar. 673, citing 1 Inst. 391; 3 Inst. 145; Hob. 270).

"Felony," as respects Scotland; *V.* s. 28, Interp. Act, 1889.

FEMALE.—*V.* Male.

"Heirs Female," in Marriage Articles, mean daughters (Lewin, 114, citing *West* v. *Errissey*, 2 P. Wms. 349).

FEMALE LINE.—*V.* Male Line.

FENCE MONTH.—*V.* Termes de la Ley.

FENLAND.—"Fenland," in a contract description, implies its liability to usual fen land taxes (*Barraud* v. *Archer*, 2 Sim. 433; 2 Russ. & My. 751).

FERLINGUS.—*V.* Stadium.

FERMEHOLT.—In Lancashire, a farm (Co. Litt. 5 a).

FERMOR.—The term "Fermors" in the Stat. of Marlebridge (52 H. 3, c. 23, s. 2), comprehends all who hold by lease for life or lives or for years, by deed or without deed (2 Inst. 300, cited in *Woodhouse* v. *Walker*, 49 L. J. Q. B. 611; 5 Q. B. D. 404).

FERRY.—Is a common highway to all the Queen's subjects, usually across a large and deep river. It is "a liberty by prescription, or the King's grant, to have a boat for passage upon a river for carriage of horses and men for reasonable toll (Termes de la Ley, 388). Its termination must be in places where the public have rights,—as towns, or vills, or highways leading to towns or vills (per Abinger, C. B., *Huzzey* v. *Field*, 4 L. J. Ex. 243; 2 Cr. M. & R. 442: *Va. Newton* v. *Cubitt*, 12 C. B. N. S. 32; on app. 13 Ib. 864; 31 L. J. C. P. 246); or on ground that the owner of the ferry has a right to use: but he need not have the ownership of the soil at either end of the ferry (*Peter* v. *Kendal*, 6 B. & C. 703), nor need he have the ownership of the water (*Ipswich* v. *Brown*, Sav. 11, 14). *V.* the form of the King's grant in *Pim* v. *Curell*, 6 M. & W. 236. As to Ferries, *Va.* Woolrych on Ways, 363; Coulson & Forbes on the Law of Waters, ch. 8, 486: and *V.* the cases collected 7 Fisher, Dig. 786, Tit. *Way*" (Elph. 575). *Va. Letton* v. *Goodden*, 35 L. J. Ch. 427; L. R. 2 Eq. 123; 14 L. T. 296.

V. Opposition Ferry.

FICTITIOUS.—" Fictitious or Non-existing Person," s. 7 (3), Bills of Exchange Act, 1882 ; *V. Vagliano* v. *Bank of England,* 23 Q. B. D. 243 ; 58 L. J. Q. B. 27, 357..

" Illusory or Fictitious," Ord. 12, R. 12, R. S. C.; *V. Hoar* v. *Loe,* W. N. (84) 241: Ann. Pr.

FIDUCIARY CAPACITY.—An Admor who has received money under Letters of Admon., and who is ordered to pay it over in a suit for the recall of the grant, holds it "in a fiduciary capacity" within s. 4 (3), Debtors Act, 1869 (*Tinnuchi* v. *Smart,* 54 L. J. P. D. & A. 92 ; 10 P. D. 184) ; so of moneys in the hands of a Receiver (*Re Gent,* 58 L. J. Ch. 162 ; 40 Ch. D. 190), or Manager (*Marris* v. *Ingram,* 49 L. J. Ch. 123 ; 13 Ch. D. 338), or proceeds of sale in the hands of an Auctioneer (*Crowther* v. *Elgood,* 34 Ch. D. 691; 56 L. J. Ch. 416 ; 56 L. T. 415 ; 35 W. R. 369).

FILED.—" 'Filed,' held to be included in return of *non est inventus : Hunter* v. *Caldwell,* Easter Term, 1847 " (Dwar. 673).

FILICETUM.—"A brackie ground " (Co. Litt. 4 b) ; " or place where such things as fern grow " (Touch. 95).

FINAL AND CONCLUSIVE.—When a decision is " Final and Conclusive," an appeal is taken away (*Waterhouse* v. *Gilbert,* 54 L. J. Q. B. 440 ; 15 Q. B. D. 569 : *Bryant* v. *Reading,* 17 Q. B. D. 128 : *Lyon* v. *Morris,* 19 Q. B. D. 139 ; 56 L. J. Q. B. 378 ; 57 L. T. 324 ; 35 W. R. 707).

FINAL DECREE.—A Cognovit, by a defendant, was not to be enforced "until after Final Hearing" of a Chancery Suit, "and the Final Decree or Order to be pronounced thereon ;" at the Hearing the Decree was for the plaintiff, but defendant appealed ; held, that the appeal must be determined before there was a " Final Decree " (*Jones* v. *Reynolds,* 1 A. & E. 384 ; 3 N. & M. 465). *Cp.* FINAL JUDGMENT.

FINAL DIVISION.—The " Final Division " of a testator's estate, means the end of the dead year (*Spencer* v. *Duckworth,* 50 L. J. Ch. 774 ; 18 Ch. D. 634).

FINAL HEARING.—*V.* FINAL DECREE.

FINAL JUDGMENT.—" No Order, Judgment or other Proceeding can be *final* which does not at once affect the status of the parties, for whichever side the decision may be given ; so that if it is given for the plaintiff it is conclusive against the defendant, and if it is given for the defendant it is conclusive against the plaintiff" (per Brett, L.J., *Standard Discount Co.* v. *La Grange,* 3 C. P. D. 71). "Where any further step is necessary to perfect an Order or Judgment, it is not final but interlocutory" (per Baggallay, L.J., *Collins* v. *Paddington*, 5 Q. B. D. 370. *Vf.* *Metcalfe's Case*, 11 Rep. 38 a). *Cp.* FINAL DECREE.

For the purposes of the Bankry. Act, 1883, s. 4 (g), a judgment for default in pleading is "final" *quà* the taxed costs thereon, although it may provide for an enquiry as to damages which remains unexecuted (*Ex p. Moore, Re Faithfull*, 54 L. J. Q. B. 190; 14 Q. B. D. 627; 33 W. R. 438). *V.* CREDITOR.

But a mere *Order* cannot be a "Final Judgment," because it is not a Judgment at all, even though it put an end to the matter with which it deals. Thus an Order dismissing an action for *non pros* is not a Judgment, and costs thereon could accordingly not be due on a "Final Judgment" (*Cremetti* v. *Crom*, 48 L. J. Q. B. 337; 4 Q. B. D. 225: *Ex p. Strathmore, Re Riddell*, 20 Q. B. D. 512; 36 W. R. 532; 57 L. J. Q. B. 259; 58 L. T. 838); nor is a Garnishee Order absolute, a "Final Judgment" (*Ex p. Chinery*, 53 L. J. Ch. 662; 12 Q. B. D. 342; 32 W. R. 469); nor an Order for Costs (followed by taxation) on an action which has been stayed (*Ex p. Schmitz*, 53 L. J. Ch. 1168; 12 Q. B. D. 509; 50 L. T. 747; 32 W. R. 812); nor a "Balance Order" upon a contributory to a Company (*Ex p. Whinney, Re Sanders*, 13 Q. B. D. 476: *Ex p. Grimwade*, 55 L. J. Q. B. 495; 17 Q. B. D. 357); nor an Order for Alimony *pendente lite* (*Re Henderson*, 20 Q. B. D. 509; 36 W. R. 567; 57 L. J. Q. B. 258; 58 L. T. 835).

A judgment obtained by a deceased person is not "final" in the hands of his executor (within the cited Bankry. section), until leave to issue execution thereon has been obtained under R. 23 (a), Ord. 42, R. S. C. (*Ex p. Woodall*, 53 L. J. Ch. 966; 13 Q. B. D. 479; 32 W. R. 774: *Vf.* OBTAINED).

Under the R. S. C., Ord. 58, R. 15, the following are Final Judgments:—On Pleading admissions (*Emmet* v. *Emmet*, 13 Ch. D. 489); Default in Pleading (*Ex p. Moore, Re Faithfull*, sup.: *Sv. Gossett* v. *Campbell*, W. N. (77) 134); Foreclosure under Ord. 15 (*Smith* v. *Davies*, 55 L. J. Ch. 496; 54 L. T. 478; 31 Ch. D. 595); Findings by judge of Ch. D. on facts, the issues on which have *not*, at the commencement of the trial, been agreed shall be first tried (*Lowe* v. *Lowe*, 48 L. J. Ch. 383; 10 Ch. D. 432; distinguishing *Krehl* v. *Burrell*, 48 L. J. Ch. 252; 11 Ch. D. 146).

As to finality of Judgment in Ecclesiastical Cases; *V. Ridsdale* v. *Clifton*, 46 L. J. P. C. 27; 2 P. D. 276.

Final Judgment of a Foreign Court; *V. Re Henderson*, 57 L. J. Ch. 367; 37 Ch. D. 244; 58 L. T. 242.

V. FINAL ORDER: ORDER: FURTHER ORDER: INTERLOCUTORY: JUDGMENT.

FINAL ORDER.—The judgment of a Divisional Court on an appeal from a County Court in an Interpleader Issue, is a "Final Order" within Ord. 58, R. 3, R. S. C. (*Hughes* v. *Little*, 56 L. J. Q. B. 96; 18 Q. B. D.

32 ; 55 L. T. 476 ; 35 W. R. 36) ; so is an Order on Further Consideration (*Cummins* v. *Herron*, 46 L. J. Ch. 423 ; 4 Ch. D. 787 : unless action is not thereby concluded, *Re Johnson*, 42 Ch. D. 505) ; or an Order at a trial by jury depriving a successful party of his Costs (*Marsden* v. *Lancashire and Yorkshire Ry.*, 50 L. J. Q. B. 318; 7 Q. B. D. 641); or an Order on a Case stated by an Arbitrator, which provides that in one event the case is to be referred back, but in the other judgment is to be entered (*Shubrook* v. *Tufnell*, 9 Q. B. D. 621 ; 30 W. R. 740 ; distinguishing *Collins* v. *Paddington*, 5 Q. B. D. 370). *V.* INTERLOCUTORY.

An Appeal against an Order, in its nature "final," when made in Chambers, must be made within 21 days (s. 50, Jud. Act, 1873 : *Re Lewis*, 31 Ch. D. 623 ; 34 W. R. 420 : *Re Johnson*, 37 W. R. 765 ; 59 L. J. Ch. 99 : *Re Giles*, 34 S. J. 79).

V. FINAL JUDGMENT.

FINAL PORT.—A Marine Policy until the ship arrives "at her Final Port," covers her only until she arrives at her Port of Discharge ; and does not protect her while she is a seeking vessel from island to island (*Moore* v. *Taylor*, 3 L. J. K. B. 132 ; 1 A. & E. 25 ; 3 N. & M. 406).

FINAL SAILING.—"Final Sailing," in a Charter-party, means the final departure of the vessel from the port named, with her papers on board, and everything complete for the purpose, and with the view of proceeding on her voyage without intending to come back ; even though, without clearing the fiscal limits of the port, she may have been driven back to it by stress of weather (*Roelandts* v. *Harrison*, 23 L. J. Ex. 169 ; 9 Ex. 444 : *Hudson* v. *Bilton*, 26 L. J. Q. B. 27 ; 6 E. & B. 565 : *Price* v. *Livingstone*, 53 L. J. Q. B. 118 ; 9 Q. B. D. 679 : *Sailing-Ship "Garston" Co.* v. *Hickie*, 15 Q. B. D. 587).

V. SAIL.

FINALLY DETERMINED.—*V.* HEARD AND FINALLY DETERMINED.

FINANCIAL AGENT.—As a description of Occupation *quà* Bills of Sale Act ; *V. Sharp* v. *McHenry*, 38 Ch. D. 428 ; 57 L. J. Ch. 961 ; 57 L. T. 606.

FINANCIAL POSITION.—*V.* BUSINESS TRANSACTIONS.

FINANCIAL YEAR.—In all Acts of Parliament passed after the 31st Dec., 1889, "'Financial Year' shall, unless the contrary intention appears, mean,—as respects any matters relating to the Consolidated Fund or moneys provided by Parliament, or to the Exchequer, or to Imperial Taxes or Finance,—the twelve months ending the 31st day of March" (s. 22, Interp. Act, 1889).

FINDING.—" Finding unto the said apprentice sufficient Meat, Drink,

Lodgings and other Necessaries;" "finding" there means to supply gratis (*Abbott* v. *Bates*, 45 L. J. C. P. 117).

V. BEING.

FINDING A MASTER.—A trust to apply funds towards "finding a master" is well executed by applying part of the funds in rebuilding and repairing the school-room and school-house (*A.-G.* v. *Stamford*, 2 Sw. 592).

FINE.—"'*Fine*,' *finis*. Here (Litt. s. 194) signifieth a pecuniarie punishment for an offence, or a contempt committed againgst the King, and regularly to it imprisonment appertaineth. And it is called *finis*, because it is an end for that offence. And in this case a man is said *facere finem de transgressione*, &c., *cum rege*, to make an end or fine with the King for such a transgression. It is also taken for a summe given by the tenant to the lord for concord, and an end to be made. It is also taken for the highest and best assurance of lands, &c." (Co. Litt. 126 b).

V. AMERCIAMENT.

FINE AND RANSOM.—"The punishment of 'Fine and Ransom' is a single pecuniary penalty" (Maxwell, 427, citing Co. Litt. 127 a). *V.* RANSOM.

FINE ARTS.—*V.* SCIENCE.

FINE BARLEY.—*V.* BARLEY.

FINIS.—*V.* FINE.

FINLAND.—Gulf of Finland; *V.* BALTIC.

FIRE.—"Loss or damage occasioned by Fire," in a Fire Policy, are words to be construed as ordinary people would construe them. "They mean loss or damage either by ignition of the article consumed, or by ignition of part of the premises where the article is: in the one case there is a loss, in the other a damage, occasioned by Fire" (per Byles, J., *Everett* v. *London Assrce.*, 19 C. B. N. S. 133; 34 L. J. C. P. 301; 13 W. R. 862). "Fire" means, in this connection, an actual burning directly causing the injury, for *In jure non remota causa, sed proxima spectatur* (Bac. Max. Reg. 1).

Thus neither artificial nor solar heat (*Austin* v. *Drewe*, 6 Taunt. 436; 2 Marsh. 130: per Byles, J., *Everett* v. *London Assrce.*, sup.), nor lightning, nor an explosion of gunpowder or of fire-damp, or of a steam-engine, nor the discharge of ordnance, nor a projectile from either a volcano or a gun, is "Fire" within a Fire Policy, unless there be an actual setting on fire directly causing the injury insured against (*Everett* v. *London Assrce.*, sup.). *Vf.* Porter on Insurance, 109–112.

But "any loss resulting from an apparently necessary and *bonâ fide* effort to put out a fire, whether it be by spoiling the goods by water, or throwing the articles of furniture out of window, or even the destroying of a neighbouring house by an explosion for the purpose of checking the progress of the flames, in a word, every loss that clearly and proximately results, whether directly or indirectly, from the fire, is within the policy" (per Kelly, C.B., *Stanley* v. *Western Insrce.*, L. R. 3 Ex. 74 ; 37 L. J. Ex. 73 ; 17 L. T. 513 ; 16 W. R. 369). But, on the authority of some American cases, it has been stated that if a fire has not actually reached the premises whence articles are removed, the damage occasioned by such removal would not be occasioned by "Fire," even though the removal was under the reasonable apprehension that the fire would reach the premises in which the articles were (Porter, 119).

"Fire," in an exception to a covenant to repair, is not, in an open contract to sell the Lease, to be extended by adding "or other casualty" (*Crosse* v. *Morgan*, 60 L. T. 703 ; 37 W. R. 543).

V. Set Fire.

FIRE ON BOARD.—*V. Schmidt* v. *Royal Mail Steam-Ship Co.*, 45 L. J. Q. B. 646. "The protection afforded by the 26 G. 3, c. 86, s. 2, in cases of fire, was confined to cases in which the fire arose *on board* the ship, and, consequently, did not extend to a casual fire occurring on board a lighter employed by the shipowners to convey the goods from the shore to the ship" (1 Maude & P. 80, citing *Morewood* v. *Pollok*, 1 E. & B. 743 ; 22 L. J. Q. B. 250).

FIREARM.—V. Gun.

FIREWORKS.—In *Bliss* v. *Lilley* (32 L. J. M. C. 3 ; 7 L. T. 319) Wightman, J., held that Fog-Signals were "Fireworks" within ss. 6 and 7, 23 & 24 V. c. 139 ; but Cockburn, C.J., said that "'Fireworks' must refer to things that are made for amusement," and Blackburn, J., was of the same opinion. Cockburn, C. J., also asked,—"Take the case of a shell or a rocket used in war, could you call that a 'Firework ?'"

FIRM.—"The word 'Firm,' I believe, like many mercantile terms, is derived from an Italian word, which means simply 'Signature,' and it is as much the name of the house of business as John Nokes or Thomas Stiles is the name of an individual. The name of a Firm is a very important part of the Goodwill" (per Wood, V.-C., *Churton* v. *Douglas*, 28 L. J. Ch. 841 ; Johns. 174 ; 7 W. R. 365).

FIRMA BURGI.—*V.* Madox, *Firma Burgi ;* 1 Stubbs, Const. Hist., 4 Ed., 445 ; Elph. 575.

FIRST.—*V.* In the first place.

FIRST ACCRUED.—Within 12 years after the right of action "shall have first accrued," s. 1, Real Prop. Limitation Act, 1874, 37 & 38 V. c. 57 ; *Vh.* s. 3, 3 & 4 W. 4, c. 27, and, as to both sections, *V. Irish Land Commission* v. *Junkin*, 24 L. R. Ir. 40.

V. Accrue.

FIRST CHARGE.—A Debenture charging all the property, present and future, of a Company, and being a floating security, although expressed to be a "First Charge," will give a First Charge as against general creditors for the time being, but not as against a subsequent specific mortgagee, even if only equitable, whose security has been duly created (*Wheatley* v. *Silkstone Co.*, 54 L. J. Ch. 778; 29 Ch. D. 715).

FIRST COUSIN.—A person's first cousin is the child of his uncle or aunt; and only persons standing in that relationship to him will take under a gift to his "First Cousins;" first cousins once removed will not be comprised (*Sanderson* v. *Bailey*, 8 L. J. Ch. 18; 4 Myl. & Cr. 56: *Stoddart* v. *Nelson*, 25 L. J. Ch. 116; 6 D. G. M. & G. 68; *V.* 2 Jarm. 152), unless there be no first cousins properly so called (1 Jarm. 153; Wms. Exs. 1110).

V. Cousin: Second Cousin.

FIRST DISCLOSED.—*V.* s. 85, 24 & 25 V. c. 96: Disclose.

FIRST INVENTOR.—The grant of a Patent must be "to the true and First Inventor" (Stat. of Monopolies, 21 Jac. 1, c. 3). "It is a material question," says Tindal, C.J., "to determine whether the party who got the patent was the real and original inventor or not, because these patents are granted as a reward, not only for the benefit that is conferred upon the public by the discovery, but also to the ingenuity of the first inventor; and although it is proved that it is a new discovery so far as the world is concerned, yet, if anybody is able to show that, although that was new, the party who got the patent was not the man whose ingenuity first discovered it; that he had borrowed it from A. or B. (*Barber* v. *Walduck*, cited 1 C. & P. 567), or taken it from a book that was publicly circulated in England (*Vh. Stead* v. *Williams*, 7 M. & G. 818; 2 Webst. P. R. 126: *Heurteloup's Case*, 1 Webst. R. 553: *Plimpton* v. *Malcolmson*, 45 L. J. Ch. 505; 3 Ch. D. 531, 558: *Plimpton* v. *Spiller*, 47 L. J. Ch. 211; 6 Ch. D. 412: *Harris* v. *Rothwell*, 35 Ch. D. 416: *Re Avery*, 26 Ch. D. 307), and which was open to all the world; then, although the public had the benefit of it, it would become an important question whether he was the first and original inventor of it." There is nothing, however, to prevent him from employing his servants in assisting him to bring a design to perfection, or to work out an idea first suggested by him (*Minter* v. *Wells*, 1 Webst. R. 132), or from employing third persons for such a purpose (*Bloxam* v. *Elsee*, 1 C. & P. 558). He is still the true and first inventor. If there are two persons, actual inventors in this country, who invent the same thing simultaneously, he who first takes out the patent is the first and true inventor; and a person is also entitled to that title who patents an invention previously invented, but not sufficiently disclosed (*Plimpton* v. *Malcolmson*, sup.). The rule, it will be observed, is, he who is first *in* England is the first *for* England: and therefore if an invention be new *within the realm*, the person who introduces it is its first inventor, although it may previously have been practised abroad (*Edgeberry* v. *Stephens*, 2 Salk. 446 : *Plimpton* v. *Malcolmson*, sup.). The communication however made in England by one British subject to another, of an invention does not make the person to whom the communication is made the first and true inventor. If, therefore, a man makes an invention, and dies before he has taken out a patent for it, his representatives cannot take one out (*Marsden* v. *Saville Street Co.*, 3 Ex. D. 203).

Vf. Add. T. 512 *et seq.*; Lawson on Patents.

FIRST OPEN WATER.—In a contract of shipment; *V. Kemp* v. *Batt*, 5 Times Rep. 27.

FIRST PLACE.—*V.* IN THE FIRST PLACE.

FIRST PUBLICATION.—A mere reprint of a book, though called a new edition, is not "the First Publication" of itself or of the book of which it is a reprint, within s. 13, Copyright Act, 1842, 5 & 6 V. c. 45; *secus*, if the new edition is substantially a new work (*Thomas* v. *Turner*, 56 L. J. Ch. 56; 33 Ch. D. 292; 55 L. T. 534; 35 W. R. 177).

FIRST RATE BUILDING LOT.—*V. Dykes* v. *Blake*, 4 Bing. N. C. 463; 7 L. J. C. P. 282; 6 Sc. 320.

FIRST SON.—The "First Son," or "Child," means *primâ facie* the first-*born*. And in like manner if a child be designated by any other numeral,—such as "second," "third," &c.,—the reference is to the *order of birth*. But this construction may be varied by the context or circumstances (2 Jarm. 213–216; Elph. 352: *Va.* ELDEST).

FIRST VOYAGE.—"It seems that a 'First Voyage' is taken to be one entire trading voyage out and home, however long or indirect that voyage may be" (Wood. 354, citing *Fenwick* v. *Robinson*, 3 C. & P. 323: *Pirie* v. *Steele*, 8 C. & P. 200).

FISH.—Crayfish are "Fish" within s. 24, 24 & 25 V. c. 96 (*Caygill* v. *Thwaite*, 1 Times Rep. 386); and Oysters are "Fish" within 13 Ric. 2, St. 1, c. 19, and 17 Ric. 2, c. 9 (*Maldon* v. *Woolvet*, 12 A. & E. 13). From those cases, *semble*, shell fish are generally included in the word "Fish."

FISHERMAN.—As to what vessel may be called a "Fisherman;" *V. Shepherd* v. *Hills*, 25 L. J. Ex. 6; 11 Ex. 55.

FISHERY: PISCARY.—"There appears to be some confusion between the names given to Fisheries of different sorts. They are divided by Holt, C.J. (*Smith* v. *Kemp*, 2 Salk. 637; 4 Mod. 187; Carth. 285; Holt, 322; *Sv.* Skin. 342), into—

1. *Separalis Piscaria*, where he who has the Fishery is owner of the soil;

2. *Libera Piscaria*, which is where a mere Right of Fishing is granted; and

3. *Communis Piscaria.*

"But the term 'Several Fishery' is sometimes applied to a right of fishing in public waters, which may be exerciseable by many people, and the term 'Free Fishery' is sometimes applied to a several fishery, either in private or in public waters, and sometimes to a right of fishing in common with others (*V.* 6 Bac. Abr. tit. *Pischary*, and *Bloomfield* v. *Johnston*, Ir. R. 8 C. L. 68, 107, 108,—where Fitzgerald, B., after observing that, according to Blackstone (2 Com. 39), the name 'Free Fishery' is properly applicable only to a several fishery in public waters, said that, 'free fishery when used, as all admit it may be used, in the sense of a right of fishing not exclusive, is, if *in alieno solo*, not distinguishable from common of fishery.')

"In *Malcomson* v. *O'Dea* (10 H. L. Ca. 593), where the question related to a fishery granted by the Crown before Magna Charta, Willes, J. (delivering the unanimous opinion of the judges), said: 'Some discussion took place during the argument as to the proper name of such a fishery, whether it ought not to have been called in the pleadings (following Blackstone) a 'Free' instead of a 'Several' fishery. This is more of the confusion which the ambiguous use of the word 'free' has occasioned, from a period so early as that of the Y. B. 7 H. 7, fol. 13, down to the case of *Holford* v. *Bailey* (18 L. J. Q. B. 109; 13 Q. B. 426), where it was clearly shown that the only substantial distinction is between an exclusive right of fishery, usually called 'several,' sometimes 'free' (used as in 'free warren'), and a right in common with others, usually called 'common of fishery,' sometimes 'free' (used as in 'free port'). The fishery in this case is sufficiently described as a 'Several' Fishery, which means an exclusive right to fish in a given place, either with or without the property in the soil.'

"*Common of Fishery*, sometimes also called 'Free Fishery,' is the right of fishing in another man's water in common with the owner of the soil, and perhaps also with other persons who may be entitled to the same right (Wms. on Commons, 259). As this right is a *profit à prendre*, it cannot be claimed by the inhabitants of a parish (*Bland* v. *Lipscombe*, 24 L. J. Q. B. 155 n.; 4 E. & B. 713, n.); or of a parish and manor (*Allgood* v. *Gibson*, 34 L. T. 883; 25 W. R. 60).

"A *Common Fishery* (called by Hale, de Jur. Mar., cited 8 App. Ca. 177, 'A Public Common of Piscary'), which must be carefully distinguished from a Common of Fishery, is a Fishery which is free to all the public (*Benett* v. *Costar*, 8 Taunt. 183). It is submitted that a Common Fishery being a *profit à prendre*, can only exist in a tidal river or the sea (*Pearce* v. *Scotcher*, 9 Q. B. D. 162, and the cases there cited)." (Elph. 576–579, *wh. Vf.*). *Va.* Dart, 426, 427.

In a parish settlement case it has been held that a lease of a Fishery, with the sedge flags and rushes therein, passed the soil (*R.* v. *Old Alresford*, 1 T. R. 358). But as to whether the grant of a "Fishery," simpliciter, will pass the soil, *V.* Co. Litt. 4 b; Dart, 427, 428. But neither such a grant, nor the grant of a "Free Fishery," will exclude the grantor from the right to fish (*Bloomfield* v. *Johnston*, Ir. R. 8 C. L. 68); but a *reservation* of the right of fishing, means the exclusive right (*Paget* v. *Milles*, 3 Doug. 43). *Vf.* A: The.

As to implied grant of Fishery; *V. Devonshire* v. *Pattinson*, 57 L. J. Q. B. 189; 20 Q. B. D. 263; 58 L. T. 392; 52 J. P. 276.

FISHING.—*V.* Hunting.

FISHING MILL DAM.—A Dam built solely for milling purposes, and without any contrivances for catching fish, is not a "Fishing Mill Dam," within s. 4, 24 & 25 V. c. 109 (*Garnett* v. *Backhouse*, L. R. 3 Q. B. 30; 37 L. J. Q. B. 1; 8 B. & S. 490).

FISHING WEIR.—As to the interpretation of this word in Salmon Fishery Acts, 1861, 1865; *V. Rolle* v. *Whyte*, 37 L. J. Q. B. 105; L. R. 3 Q. B. 286; 8 B. & S. 116: *Leconfield* v. *Lonsdale*, 39 L. J. C. P. 305; L. R. 5 C. P. 657.

FIT.—"As may seem fit;" *V.* Opinion.

"A 'Fit' *Person* to execute an Office, is he,—'qui melius et sciat et possit, officium illud intendere.' 'This word *idoneus*,' says Ld. Coke, 'is oftentimes in law attributed to those who have any office or function; and he is said in law to be *idoneus*, apt and fit to execute his office, who has three things, Honesty, Knowledge and Ability: Honesty to execute it truly, without malice, affection or partiality; Knowledge to know what he ought duly to do; and Ability, as well in estate as in body, that he may intend and execute his office, when need is, diligently, and not for impotency or poverty neglect it'" (Dwar. 685).

V. Eligible: If they shall think fit: Think fit.

FIT TO BE.—An Action charging a serious Libel is "fit to be *prosecuted* in the High Court," and ought not to be remitted under s. 66, Co. Co. Act, 1888 (*Farrer* v. *Lowe*, 5 Times Rep. 234).

Where fraud and falsehood are alleged, the action is one eminently "fit to be *tried*" in the Superior Court (*Simpson* v. *Shaw*, 56 L. J. Q. B. 92; 56 L. T. 24; 3 Times Rep. 120: *Vh. Cherry* v. *Endean*, 55 L. J. Q. B. 292; 54 L. T. 763; 34 W. R. 458).

FITS.—*V.* Caused by.

FITTINGS.—"Fittings for Gas" in s. 14, Gasworks Clauses Act, 1847 (10 V. c. 15), includes all the apparatus for the supply or consumption of gas, including gas stoves used for heating (*Gaslight & Coke Co.* v. *Hardy*, 56 L. J. Q. B. 168; 17 Q. B. D. 619; 55 L. T. 585; 35 W. R. 50; 51 J. P. 6; 2 Times Rep. 851: *Same* v. *Smith*, 3 Times Rep. 15).

"Fixtures and *Fitting up*;" *V.* Fixtures.

FIXED AND FASTENED.—As applied to a Conveyance of Machines; *V. Metrop. Counties Assrce.* v. *Brown,* 28 L. J. Ch. 581; 26 Bea. 454. *Vf.* FIXTURES: PERSONAL CHATTELS.

"Affixed;" *V.* WINDOW.

FIXED ENGINE.—Stop Nets are "Fixed Engines" within the Salmon Fishery Acts (*Gore* v. *Commrs. for English Fisheries,* 40 L. J. Q. B. 252; L. R. 6 Q. B. 561). By ss. 4 and 11, Salmon Fishery Act, 1861 (24 & 25 V. c. 109), "Fixed Engines" are to include "all fixed implements for catching or facilitating the catching of fish," and "a net that is secured by anchors or otherwise temporarily fixed to the soil;" and by s. 39, Salmon Fishery Act, 1865 (28 & 29 V. c. 121), the phrase includes "any net or other implement for taking fish, fixed to the soil, *or made stationary* in any other way not being a fishing weir or fishing mill-dam." In the case cited Stop Nets were used in the following way:—The fisherman first steadied his boat athwart the current of the River Usk by pushing poles, lashed to either end of the boat, into the bed of the river in a slanting direction, and when the boat was steadied the net was put overboard. The net was about 30 feet wide at the mouth, tapering to a point. The net was distended by two light poles, called rames, about 22 feet long, tied together at the upper end with the tapered end of the net. The fisherman kept his hand upon this upper end when fishing, the rames being gradually distended until at their furthest end they stretched out the mouth of the net to its full width of 30 feet, and were kept distended by a stretcher. The net when used for fishing was lowered overboard in a slanting direction with its mouth to the current, until the two rames rested on the side of the boat at about 8 feet from their upper end. The net was kept steady in the water by the fisherman; and when he felt a fish he pulled the upper end of the rames down, using the side of the boat as a fulcrum, and so raised the mouth of the net out of the water and caught the fish: Held, that this was a "Fixed Engine" within the Acts cited, because the net was kept *stationary* by the rames being rested on the boat and the fisherman keeping his hand upon them. *Vf. Olding* v. *Wild,* 30 J.P. 295: *Holford* v. *George,* 37 L. J. Q. B. 185; 18 L. T. 817: and upon the phrase as defined in 24 & 25 V. c. 109, *Thomas* v. *Jones,* 34 L. J. M. C. 45; 5 B. & S. 916.

"'Fixed Engine,' shall include, in addition to the nets, fixed implements, engines, and devices respectively mentioned in 'The Salmon Fishery Acts, 1861 and 1865,' any net placed or suspended in any inland or tidal waters unattended by the owner or any person duly authorized by the owner to use the same for catching Salmon, and all engines, devices, machines, or contrivances (whether floating or otherwise) for placing or suspending such nets or maintaining them in working order or making them stationary" (s. 4, Salmon Fishery Act, 1873, 36 & 37 V. c. 71).

V. STATIONARY.

FIXED FURNITURE. — Looking-glasses, standing on chimney-pieces and nailed to the wall, and a Book-case standing on (but not fastened to) brackets and screwed to the wall, held within this phrase (*Birch* v. *Dawson*, 4 L. J. K. B. 49 ; 2 A. & E. 37; 4 N. & M. 22) ; but a Book-case merely placed in, but not fastened to, the wall, was held by Littledale, J., not "fixed furniture" (S. C., 6 C. & P. 658).

FIXED MOTIVE POWERS.—"Fixed Motive Powers," "Fixed Power Machinery," s. 5, Bills of Sale Act, 1878 ; *V. Topham* v. *Greenside Co.*, 57 L. J. Ch. 583 ; 37 Ch. D. 281; 58 L. T. 274 ; 36 W. R. 464.

FIXED PERIOD.—The Apportionment Act, 4 W. 4, c. 22, s. 2, provides for the apportionment of all Rents, Dividends, and other Payments "made payable, or coming due, at Fixed Periods ;" a Co.'s Dividends, out of profits to be divided half-yearly, were held payable at "Fixed Periods" (*Hartley* v. *Allen*, 27 L. J. Ch. 621; 31 L. T. O. S. 69 ; 6 W. R. 407). Wood, V.-C., doubted (but followed) that decision, but held that Ry. Dividends, where there was no obligation to pay them at any stated period, were not payable at "Fixed Periods" (*Re Maxwell*, 32 L. J. Ch. 333 ; 1 H. & M. 610; 11 W. R. 480). So Royalties on ore when obtained, are not so payable (*St. Aubyn* v. *St. Aubyn*, 30 L. J. Ch. 917; 1 Dr. & Sm. 611). *Vf. Harris* v. *Harris*, 11 W. R. 451.

V. now, as to Apportionment of Income, Apportionment Act, 1870, sub PERIODICAL : *Vf.* DIVIDEND.

FIXTURES.—"The word 'Fixtures' has no precise legal meaning ; it is not to be found in Termes de la Ley" (per Campbell, C. J., *Wiltshear* v. *Cottrell*, 22 L. J. Q. B. 179). It is "used by different writers to express different meanings ; but it is always applied to articles of personal nature which have been affixed to land. In its most extensive sense it means anything annexed to the *freehold* in such a manner as to become parcel of it" (Woodf. 620). But "the word 'Fixtures,' though properly applicable to something annexed to the freehold, is sometimes used in a larger sense,—*Sheen* v. *Rickie* (5 M. & W. 182 ; 8 L. J. Ex. 217), where it is said by Parke, B., it does not necessarily follow that the word 'Fixtures' must import things affixed to the freehold, nor has the word necessarily acquired that legal sense. It is a very modern word, and is generally understood to comprehend any article which a tenant has a power of removing" (per Coleridge, J., delivering jdgmt. of the Court in *Wiltshear* v. *Cottrell*, 22 L. J. Q. B. 177; 1 E. & B. 674. *Vf. Ex p. Barclay*, 5 D. G. M. & G. 403 ; 1 Jur. N. S. 1145 ; 26 L. T. O. S. 97; 4 W. R. 80 : *Gibson* v. *Hammersmith Ry.*, 32 L. J. Ch. 337; 11 W. R. 299 ; 8 L. T. 43).

As to what will pass under an Assignment of "Fixtures," *V. Southport Banking Co.* v. *Thompson*, 57 L. J. Ch. 114; 37 Ch. D. 64 ; 58 L. T. 143; 36 W. R. 113 : *Ex p. Fletcher*, 8 Ch. D. 218 : *Ex p. Brown*, 9 Ch. D. 389.

"Fixtures *and Fitting up*," will not pass Household Furniture (*Simmonds* v. *Simmonds*, 6 Hare, 352; 12 Jur. 8). *Cp.* PERSONAL CHATTELS.

Vf. as to Fixtures, Amos & Ferard on Fixtures (2 Ed.); Brown on Fixtures (3 Ed.); Woodf. 620–647; Wms. Exs. 733; Dart, 607, 608; Add. C. 247–252; notes to *Elwes* v. *Mawe*, 2 Sm. L. C. 182.

FLETH.—"Land is anciently called *Fleth*" (Co. Litt. 4 a).

FLOATING SECURITY.—As to the effect of this phrase in a Debenture; *V. Re Horne and Hellard*, 54 L. J. Ch. 919; 29 Ch. D. 736: *Va.* as to the effect of a Floating Charge on the property of a Company, Buckl. 152; Watson, Eq. 453, 454.

FLOTSAM.—*V.* Termes de la Ley, *Floatsam.*

FODDER.—From the moment produce is destined for food for cattle, it is "Fodder for Cattle" within a Turnpike exemption, *e.g.*, rye-grass or vetches cut and brought home at once, or turnips on their way to be boiled, or threshed barley on its way to be ground into meal; but not corn in the straw (*Clements* v. *Smith*, 30 L. J. M. C. 16; 3 E. & E. 238).

FOLDCOURSE.—"By the grant of a fouldcourse, lands and tenements may passe" (Co. Litt. 6 a; *Va.* Touch. 93).

"Here *fold-course* seems to be understood for land used as a *sheep-walk*; but the word has various other senses. Sometimes it signifies land to which is appurtenant the sole right of folding the cattle of others. Sometimes it means merely *such* right of folding. It is also used to denote the right of folding on another's land, which is called *common* of faldage. See in W. Jo. 375, and Cro. Car. 432, a case in which *common* of *faldage* was claimed; and 2 Ventr. 139, one in which the right of folding the cattle of others is prescribed for" (Hargrave's n. to above quotation from Co. Litt. 6 a).

"Foldcourse" has been recently defined as, "The right of a man to pasture his sheep on the commonable grounds of a manor or superior lordship, without being obliged to fold them in the lord's field" (Elph. 579, *wh. Vf.*). *Vh. Robinson* v. *Dhuleep Singh*, 11 Ch. D. 798; 48 L. J. Ch. 758.

Cp. FRANKFOLDAGE.

FOLLOW.—In a Marine Insurance, "The meaning of 'To follow Policy for £4,000. No. $\frac{3}{4246}$' is, that there being consecutive policies, any loss declared is to be borne first by the earlier policies, and that it is not till after the Policy No. $\frac{3}{4246}$ is exhausted, either by losses or declared adventures which have come in safe, that the underwriters on the policy which follows are to bear the balance of the loss, if any" (per Ld. Blackburn, *Inglis* v. *Stock*, 54 L. J. Q. B. 586; 10 App. Ca. 269).

"Costs to follow the event;" *V.* EVENT.

FOOD.—Baking Powder is not "Food," within s. 2, 38 & 39 V. c. 63

(per Bulwer, Recorder, *Warren* v. *Phillips*, 44 J. P. 61; 68 Law Times, 246).

FOOT.—As to the requirement in the Wills Act (1 V. c. 26) that a Will is to be signed "at the Foot or End thereof;" *V.* 15 V. c. 24, s. 1, and *Vth. Margary* v. *Robinson*, 56 L. J. P. D. & A. 42; 12 P. D. 8; 57 L. T. 281; 35 W. R. 350; 51 J. P. 407: *Hunt* v. *Hunt*, L. R. 1 P. & M. 209; 35 L. J. P. & M. 135.

FOOTPATH.—"Footpath or Causeway by the side of any road made or set apart for the use or accommodation of foot passengers," s. 72, Highway Act, 1835, 5 & 6 W. 4, c. 50; This only applies to a Footpath that is "by the side" of the road, and not to a mere footpath (*R.* v. *Pratt*, 37 L. J. M. C. 23; L. R. 3 Q. B. 64; 32 J. P. 246).

FOR.—"For," used with the active participle of a verb—*e.g.* a power "for making" Rules,—means, "for the purpose of" (*V.* jdgmt. of Westbury, L. C., *A.-G.* v. *Sillem*, 33 L. J. Ex. 213). So an unlicensed person does not fish "for" salmon (trout or char, 41 & 42 V. c. 39, s. 7) within s. 35, Salmon Fishery Act, 1865, unless he fishes for the purpose of catching salmon, &c. (*Marshall* v. *Richardson*, 58 L. J. M. C. 45); but the intent is immaterial *quâ* the offence (s. 36) of using (without license) an instrument other than rod and line "for catching" salmon, &c. (*Lyne* v. *Leonard*, 37 L. J. M. C. 55; L. R. 3 Q. B. 156).

For contrast between "for" and "subject to;" *V.* SUBJECT TO.

Sometimes "For" creates a Condition Precedent. "When one promises, agrees, or covenants to do one thing *for* another, there is no reason he should be obliged to do it till that thing, *for* which he promised to do it, be done; and the word 'for' is a Condition Precedent in such cases. But upon this head some diversities are to be observed. *First*, if there be a day set for the payment of money, or doing the thing which one promises, agrees, or covenants to do, *for* another thing, and that day happens to incur before the time the thing for which the promise, agreement or covenant is made, is to be performed by the tenor of the agreement; there, though the words be 'that the party shall pay the money,' or, 'do the thing *for* such a thing,' or, 'in consideration of such a thing,' after the day is past the other shall have an action for the money or other thing, although the thing, *for* which the promise, agreement, or covenant was made, be not performed; for it would be repugnant there to make it a Condition Precedent; and, therefore, they are in that case left to mutual remedies, on which, by the express words of the agreement, they have depended. *V.* 48 Edw. 3. 2, 3, cited in *Ughtred's Case*, 7 Rep. 10 b, where the diversity is taken when there are mutual remedies and not: it is thus put in that book: *Sir R. Pool* covenants with *Sir R. Tolcelser* to serve him with three Esquires in the wars of France. Sir R. Tolcelser covenants, *in consideration* of those services, to pay him so much money ; and there it is said, action will lie for the money without any services performed. But if you look into the book at large, you will find it was upon the diversity which I have taken ; for the Case in 48 Edw. 3. 2, 3 is, *R. Pool* covenants with *R. Tolcelser* to serve him with three Esquires in the wars of France, and *R. Tolcelser* covenanted with him to pay him so much for the service ; and it was further agreed, that twenty marks of the money should be paid in England, at a day certain, before they went for France, and the rest by quarterly payments, which might likewise incur before the service ; and upon action brought by *Sir R. Pool*, it was objected that the service was not performed ; but there was no room for that objection upon the diversity which I have taken, the money, by the agreement, being made payable at a day certain, before the service was to have been performed " (per Holt, C. J., *Thorp* v. *Thorp*, 12 Mod. 460, 461; 1 Ld. Raym. 662).

An obligation signed " for " or "*for and on behalf of*" another, makes that other, if anyone, liable ; not the signatory (*Aggs* v. *Nicholson*, 25 L. J. Ex. 348 ; 1 H. & N. 165) : but evidence is admissible to show that, by the custom of a market, a contract signed "*for and on account of* the owner" binds the signatory personally (*Pike* v. *Ongley*, 18 Q. B. D. 708 ; 56 L. J. Q. B. 373; 35 W. R. 534 ; 3 Times Rep. 549) ; and an unauthorised acceptance " for and on behalf of " another binds the acceptor personally (*West Lond. Commercial Bank* v. *Kitson*, 13 Q. B. D. 360 ; 53 L. J. Q. B. 345). *Vf.* as to signatures in a representative capacity of Bills of Exchange and Promissory Notes, s. 26, Bills of Ex. Act, 1882.

FOR ANY OTHER PURPOSE.—*Re Norris*, W. N. (83) 35, 65.

FOR DEBT.—*V.* Attachment for Debt.

FOR EVER.—Those words are useless or surplusage in a limitation by Deed of a fee, as in the not uncommon expression " his heirs and assigns *for ever* " (Litt. s. 1). In a Devise they would have passed the fee even before the Wills Act (2 Jarm. 328 ; Watson, Eq. 1370) : but they are not inconsistent with an estate tail (1 Jarm. 485, n. 2 ; Ib. 328, 391), and would sometimes create such an estate (*Good* v. *Good*, 7 E. & B. 295 ; 28 L. T. O. S. 266).

As to the value of " for ever " in a covenant for Renewal of a Lease, so as to give the right of perpetual renewal ; *V. Swinburne* v. *Milburn*, 54 L. J. Q. B. 6 ; 9 App. Ca. 844, and especially jdgmt. of Ld. Fitzgerald.

FOR SALE.—Bread is carried out " for sale," within s. 7, 6 & 7 W. 4, c. 37, if anything (including its being actually weighed in the presence of the *buyer*) remains to be done in reference to its sale (*Robinson* v. *Cliff*, 45 L. J. M. C. 109 ; 1 Ex. D. 294 : *Ridgway* v. *Ward*, 54 L. J. M. C. 20 ; 14 Q. B. D. 110) : *secus* if the bread has been bought in the seller's shop, weighed in the presence of the buyer, and merely sent by the seller to the house of the buyer for the latter's convenience (*Daniel* v. *Whitfield*, cited CARRY OUT).

"Supply gas for sale ;" *V.* SUPPLY.

FOR THE TIME BEING.—*V.* TIME BEING.

FOR WANT OF.—"In default," or "For want of" signifies "all that is comprehended in the word 'Remainder,' being merely an expression employed in carrying on the series of limitations" (1 Jarm. 800).

FORBEAR.—To "forbear" to press for immediate payment, means to give reasonable time ; which, though indefinite, is a sufficient consideration for a guarantee (*Oldershaw* v. *King*, 27 L. J. Ex. 120 ; 2 H. & N. 517 ; *Vth.* per Bowen, L.J., *Miles* v. *New Zealand Alford Estate Co.*, 32 Ch. D. 289 : *Coles* v. *Pack*, L. R. 5 C. P. 65 ; 39 L. J. C. P. 63 : *Crears* v. *Hunter*, 56 L. J. Q. B. 518 ; 19 Q. B. D. 341 ; 57 L. T. 554 ; 35 W. R. 821 : *V.* contra *Semple* or *Temple* v. *Pink*, 1 Ex. 74 ; 16 L. J. Ex. 237).

FORCE.—"'*With force and armes,' vi et armis.* Force, *vis*, in the common law is most commonly taken in ill part, and taken for unlawful violence, for *maximè paci sunt contraria vis et injuria.* And therefore *Britton* (116 a) said well, speaking in the person of the King, *nous volons, que touts gents pluis usent jugement que force.*

"*Arma*, Armes, in the common law signifieth anything that a man striketh or hurteth withall" (Co. Litt. 161 b).

"One or more may commit a force" (Ib. 257 a). An averment in a Statement of Claim that a trespass was committed *vi et armis*, would, it seems, not amount to an allegation of a breach of the peace (*Harvey* v. *Brydges*, 14 L. J. Ex. 272 ; 14 M. & W. 437).

V. BY FORCE.

FORCIBLE DETAINER.—"Everyone commits the misdemeanor called a Forcible Detainer who, having wrongfully entered upon any lands or tenements, detains such lands and tenements in a manner which would render an entry upon them for the purpose of taking possession forcible." (Steph. Cr. 55). *Vf.* Arch. Cr. 962–965 ; Rosc. Cr. 535–540.

FORCIBLE ENTRY.—"Everyone commits the misdemeanor called a Forcible Entry who, in order to take possession thereof, enters upon any lands or tenements in a violent manner, whether such violence consists in actual force applied to any other person, or in threats, or in breaking open any house, or in collecting together an unusual number of persons for the purpose of making such Entry. It is immaterial whether the person making such an entry had or had not a right to enter ; provided that a person who enters upon lands or tenements of his own, but which are in the custody of his servant or bailiff, does not commit the offence of Forcible

Entry" (Steph. Cr. 54, 55). *Vh. Lows* v. *Telford*, 45 L. J. Ex. 613; 1 App. Ca. 414.

Vf. Arch. Cr. 962–966; Rosc. Cr. 535–540; Co. Litt. 257 a, b.

FOREIGN.—*V. Commrs. of Railways* v. *Hyland*, 56 L. J. P. C. 76; 56 L. T. 896: Termes de la Ley, *Forrein.*

FOREIGN BILL.—*V.* INLAND.

FOREIGN BONDS.—This phrase will not, as a rule, include Colonial Bonds (*Hull* v. *Hill*, 4 Ch. D. 97; 25 W. R. 223). *Vf.* SECURITIES.

FOREIGN FUNDS.—*V.* FUNDS.

FOREIGN GOVERNMENT.—A Government is none the less a Government because it is a subordinate one; and therefore a power to invest in the Stocks or Funds of a "Foreign Government," will authorize an investment in the bonds or securities of any individual State of the United States, or of any of the separate kingdoms or governments of which the German Empire is composed (*Cadett* v. *Earle*, 5 Ch. D. 710; 46 L. J. Ch. 798. *Va. Ellis* v. *Eden*, 23 Bea. 543; 26 L. J. Ch. 533).

FOREIGN REFINED RAPE OIL.—*V. Nichol* v. *Godls*, 23 L. J. Ex. 314; 10 Ex. 191.

FOREIGN STATEMENT.—*V.* GENERAL AVERAGE AS PER FOREIGN STATEMENT.

FOREIGN WARRANT.—As to this phrase in s. 10, Extradition Act, 1870 (33 & 34 V. c. 52); *V. R.* v. *Ganz*, 51 L. J. Q. B. 419.

FORERA.—A headland (Spelm.).

FORESAID.—*V.* AFORESAID.

FORESHORE.—"The seashore up to the point of high water of medium tides, between spring and neap tides, is called the Foreshore; and is ordinarily and *primâ facie* vested in the Crown, subject to the rights of the Queen's subjects of fishing and navigation, not only in the sea, but in all tidal navigable rivers, and of passing over the foreshore itself; but it may belong to a subject, either by itself, or as part of a manor. *V.* the cases cited in Wms. on Commons, 265 *et seq.*: *A.-G.* v. *Burridge*, 10 Price, 350: *A.-G.* v. *Parmenter*, 10 Price, 378: *A.-G.* v. *Tomline*, 14 Ch. D. 58; 46 L. J. Ch. 654. *Va.* Co. Litt. 261a, note; Woolrych on Waters, 2 Ed. 23; Coulson & Forbes on Waters, 12; Chitty, Prerog. 207" (Elph. 580). As to *A.-G.* v. *Tomline*, *V.* per Esher, M. R., and Lopes, L. J., *West Norfolk Manure Co.* v. *Archdale*, 16 Q. B. D. 758, 760.

Vh. Moore on Foreshore and Sea Shore.

FOREST.—" Defined Spelm. *Foresta;* Manwood c. 1, s. 1; Termes de la Ley. A subject may hold a Forest by grant from the Crown (Co. Litt. 233 a); provided that the grant contains a provision that, on request made in Chancery, the grantee and his heirs shall have justices of the forest (4 Inst. 314. *V. Leicester Forest case,* Cro. Jac. 155).

" By the grant of a forest in a man's own ground, not only the privilege but the land itself passes (Co. Litt. 5 b; Touch. 96)." Elph. 580, *wh. Vf.*

Cp. CHASE : PARK.

FORESTALLER.—*V.* REGRATOR.

FORFEIT.—This word means not only an actual taking away of property on breach of a Condition, but also the doing or suffering a thing which creates a liability to such a deprival (*Re Levy,* 54 L. J. Ch. 968; 30 Ch. D. 119).

In that case, Kay, J., said :—" The word 'Forfeit,' the noun substantive, is defined in Dr. Johnson's Dictionary to be, 'Something lost by the commission of a crime; something paid for the expiation of the crime; a fine; a mulct.' By the same authority, the verb 'to forfeit' is defined to mean, 'to lose by some breach of condition; to lose by some offence.' He gives certain illustrations, as usual in his dictionary, and this is one: 'A father cannot alien the power he has over his child; he may perhaps to some degree forfeit it, but cannot transfer it.—Locke.' There forfeit is contrasted with 'lose.' Then 'forfeit,' the participial adjective, is defined to be, 'liable to penal seizure; alienated by a crime; lost either as to the right or possession, by breach of conditions.' Then he gives these fine lines of Shakespeare :—

> All souls that are, were forfeit once;
> And he that might the vantage best have took,
> Found out the remedy.
>
> *Measure for Measure.*

And again :—

> Beg that thou may'st have leave to hang thyself:
> And yet, thy wealth being forfeit to the state,
> Thou hast not left the value of a cord.
>
> *Merchant of Venice.*

Now clearly the word 'forfeit' does not merely mean that which is actually taken from the man by reason of some breach of condition, but includes also that which becomes *liable* to be so taken."

But " Forfeit" would seem to involve the idea of *permanent* loss or liability thereto. Thus s. 9, 11 G. 4 & 1 W. 4, c. 65 (repealing and re-enacting and extending 9 G. 1, c. 29), provides that an infant, feme covert or lunatic, shall not "forfeit" copyholds by non-appearance, &c.; but this does not take away the lord's right of seizure *quousque* (*Kensington* v. *Mansell,* 13 Ves. 240 : *Doe* d. *Twining* v. *Muscott,* 14 L. J. Ex. 185; 12 M. & W. 832 : *Dimes* v. *Grand Junction Canal,* 16 L. J. Q. B. 107;

9 Q. B. 469 : *Vf. King* v. *Dilliston*, Show. 31, 83 ; Salk. 386 ; 3 Mod. 222).

V. FORFEITURE.

FORFEITURE.—"Forfeiture," means "the loss of all interest" in the property spoken of (2 Bla. Com. 267 ; *Vf.* Co. Litt. 59 a).

"Forfeiture," in s. 1, 13 Eliz. c. 5, is not "intended only of a Forfeiture of an obligation, recognizance, or such like, but also of everything which shall by law be forfeit to the King or subject" (*Twyne's Case*, 3 Rep. 82).

"The words 'Forfeiture' and 'Breach of Condition' (in ss. 3, 4, of 3 & 4 W. 4, c. 27) are to be read in their largest sense; and to apply, whether the forfeiture gives a right to an estate under a conditional limitation, or whether it is a true forfeiture at law, and the gift over can only be taken advantage of by the heir or other person entitled in case of a forfeiture" (per Jessel, M. R., *Astley* v. *Essex*, 43 L. J. Ch. 819 ; L. R. 18 Eq. 290).

When a statute provides punishment by "Forfeiture," that "means Forfeiture to the Crown ; except when it is imposed for wrongful detention or dispossession, in which cases the forfeiture goes to the benefit of the party wronged" (Maxwell, 427, citing 1 Inst. 159 ; 11 Rep. 60).

V. FORFEIT : PENALTY OR FORFEITURE.

FORGERY.—"Forgery is making a false document with intent to defraud."

"To make a false Document is—

(*a.*) To make a document purporting to be what in fact it is not ;

(*b.*) To alter a document without authority in such a manner that if the alteration had been authorized it would have altered the effect of the document ;

(*c.*) To introduce into a document without authority, whilst it is being drawn up, matter which, if it had been authorized, would have altered the effect of the document ;

(*d.*) To sign a document—

1. In the name of any person without his authority, whether such name is or is not the same as that of the person signing ;
2. In the name of any fictitious person alleged to exist, whether the fictitious person is or is not alleged to be of the same name as the person signing ;
3. In a name represented as being the name of a different person from that of the person signing it, and intended to be mistaken for the name of that person ;
4. In the name of a person personated by the person signing the document, provided that the effect of the instrument

depends upon the identity between the person signing the document and the person whom he professes to be.

But it is *not* making a false Document—

(*a.*) To procure the execution of a document by fraud;

(*b.*) To omit from a document being drawn up matter which would have altered its effect if introduced, and which might have been introduced, unless the matter omitted qualifies the matter inserted;

(*c.*) To sign a document in the name of a person personated by the person who signs it, or in a fictitious name, provided that the effect of the instrument does not depend upon the maker's identity with the person personated, or on the correctness of the name assumed by him" (Steph. Cr. 285, 287, 288, *wh.* to p. 291, *V.* for cases in illustration).

Vf. Arch. Cr. 641, 682; Rosc. Cr. 541–595.

FORM.—*V.* In accordance with the Form: In the Form.

FORMAL.—Where the sealed copy of a Debtor's Summons stated the debt as £24 instead of £74, but the annexed Particulars of Demand stated the amount correctly, this was held a "Formal *Defect or Irregularity*" within s. 82, Bankry. Act, 1869 (*Ex p. Johnson*, 53 L. J. Ch. 309; 25 Ch. D. 112): so was an omission by a petitioning creditor to state in the petition his readiness to give up his security (*Ex p. Vanderlinden, Re Pogose*, 51 L. J. Ch. 760; 20 Ch. D. 289. *Note.*—s. 143 is the corresponding section in the Bankry. Act, 1883). But an omission (in a bankry. petition) to state the intent of a debtor's departure out of England is of the substance, and not merely "formal" (*Ex p. Coates, Re Skelton*, 5 Ch. D. 979).

So the signature of the Commissioner to a Trader Debtor's Summons (Sch. H. Bankry. Act, 1849) was an essential part of the document, and its omission from the served copy was fatal (*Ex p. Tindall*, 24 L. J. Bank. 18; 6 D. G. M. & G. 741). *Vf. Ex p. Rogers*, 15 Ch. D. 207: *Re Holt*, 11 Ch. D. 168.

V. Defect.

FORMATION EXPENSES.—Include Promotion Moneys paid to persons as commission for floating a Company (*Arkwright* v. *Newbold*, 50 L. J. Ch. 372; 17 Ch. D. 301).

FORMED.—A Company, Association or Partnership is not newly "formed," within s. 4, Companies Act, 1862, when it admits new members, if its continuing identity is practically preserved (*Shaw* v. *Simmons*, 53 L. J. Q. B. 29; 12 Q. B. D. 117).

It has been suggested that "formed" in this section means, "formed in this country" (Buckl. 4).

FORMER.—Covenant indemnifying against all "former" Titles and Incumbrances; *V. Lovell* v. *Lutterell*, Sav. 74: *Hamington* v. *Rydear*, 1 Leon. 92; Mo. 249, pl. 393; 1 And. 162, pl. 208; 10 Rep. 52 a, nom. *Haverington's Case*, Ow. 6. *V.* these cases stated, Platt on Covenants, 332, 333.

FORMING.—A school set back 80 feet from a street, and in the greater part hidden by houses between it and the street, but having a direct private access to the street, is a house "forming" part of a street within s. 105, Metrop. Man. Act, 1855 (*London School Board* v. *St. Mary, Islington*, 45 L. J. M. C. 1; 1 Q. B. D. 65). In that case, Cockburn, C.J., said,—"I think that whether a house is 'within' a street, or whether it is 'forming' or 'fronting' a street, is much the same thing."

V. Fronting: Within: and cp. the section above cited with s. 77, Metrop. Man. Act, 1862, where the words are "Bounding and abutting."

FORTHWITH.—Where a judge has to do a thing "forthwith" after the happening of something else, the word will have a different meaning according as the act to be done is,

1. Ministerial and demandable *ex debito justitiæ;* or
2. Judicial.

If the act comes within the first of these classes the word will mean, "forthwith *upon the application of the party entitled to have the act done.*" Thus a successful defendant in an assault summons is entitled, under s. 44, 24 & 25 V. c. 100, to a certificate of dismissal on applying for it (*Hancock* v. *Somes*, 28 L. J. M. C. 196: *Costar* v. *Hetherington*, 28 L. J. M. C. 198: over-ruling *R.* v. *Robinson*, 10 L. J. M. C. 9; 12 A. & E. 672).

Where, however, the act to be done is judicial and discretionary, "Forthwith" is synonymous with "Immediately" (*R.* v. *Francis*, Ca. temp. Hardwick, 115: *Grace* v. *Clinch*, 12 L. J. Q. B. 273; 4 Q. B. 606; 3 G. & D. 591: *Chaplin* v. *Levy*, 23 L. J. Ex. 200; 9 Ex. 673: *Hancock* v. *Somes*, sup.: *Heden* v. *Atlantic Royal Mail Steam Nav. Co.*, 29 L. J. Q. B. 191: per Cockburn, C.J., *R.* v. *Berkshire*, 27 W. R. 798).

V. Immediately.

In a *Contract*, and the ordinary transactions of life, "Forthwith" does *not* usually mean "Immediately" (*Roberts* v. *Brett*, 34 L. J. C. P. 241; 11 H. L. Ca. 337; 20 C. B. N. S. 148); but means "with all reasonable celerity" (per Tindal, C.J., *Burgess* v. *Boetefeur*, 7 M. & G. 494).

"I think the word 'forthwith' is to be construed according to circumstances. A covenant to insure a man's life, for instance, cannot be complied with in a moment. But where an act required to be done 'forthwith,' is one which is capable of being done without any delay, no delay can be permitted" (per Jessel, M.R., *Re Southam, Ex p. Lamb*, 51 L. J. Ch. 207; 19 Ch. D. 169; 30 W. R. 126). In that case an Appeal Notice in Bankry. was not sent to the country till the next day after the appeal was entered in London, and it was held not to have been sent "forthwith" (*Vth. Ex p. Williams*, 26 S. J. 345 : *Ex p. Hill, Re Darbyshire*, 53 L. J. Ch. 247).

"Forthwith" give Notice of Recognizances, s. 3, 8 V. c. 10 ; *V. Ex p. Lowe*, 15 L. J. M. C. 99 ; 3 Dowl. & L. P. C. 737 : *V. R.* v. *Price*, inf.

"Forthwith *proceed*" in a Charter-party ; *V. Hudson* v. *Hill*, 43 L. J. C. P. 273.

"A covenant 'forthwith' to put premises into *repair* must receive a reasonable construction, and it is not limited to any specific time ; therefore it is for the jury to say, upon the evidence, whether the defendant has done what he reasonably ought in performance of it" (Woodf. 588, citing *Doe* d. *Pitman* v. *Sutton*, 9 C. & P. 706).

"Forthwith" *replace* articles, comprised in a Bill of Sale, that may be destroyed or deteriorated, means that this should be done with as little delay as possible (per Hannen, Pr., *Furber* v. *Cobb*, 56 L. J. Q. B. 275 ; 18 Q. B. D. 494 ; 56 L. T. 689 ; 35 W. R. 398).

In an action against an Overseer for not giving a copy of a Rate "upon demand, forthwith," it was held that that meant within such time as the jury might think reasonable (*Tennant* v. *Bell*, 16 L. J. M. C. 31 ; 9 Q. B. 684). So the proprietor of a Lunatic Asylum is, by s. 72, 8 & 9 V. c. 100, to discharge his patient "forthwith" on the receipt of the order in that section mentioned ;—that is, the proprietor "has no discretion, but would be bound to release the patient 'forthwith' and against the patient's will, —not cruelly, as for instance, if it were raining heavily, but within such a time as a reasonable man would say was practicable" (per Esher, M.R., *Lowe* v. *Fox*, 54 L. J. Q. B. 563 ; 15 Q. B. D. 667 ; affd. 12 App. Ca. 206).

Where a consequence is "forthwith" to follow on an event, the word imperatively excludes a time within which something else may be done inconsistent with that consequence. Thus by s. 36, Municipal Corporations Act, 1882 (45 & 46 V. c. 50), a Town Council, on receiving the resignation of a person elected to a corporate office, is "forthwith" to declare that office vacant ; and therefore the resignation cannot be withdrawn (*R.* v. *Wigan*, 54 L. J. Q. B. 338 ; 14 Q. B. D. 908).

In a Notice, to a person charged criminally and out on bail to appear on pain of forfeiting his recognizance, "forthwith" means within a reasonable time from the service, and not from the date of the notice (*R.* v. *Price*, 8 Moo. P. C. C. 203).

Vf. Re Sillence, 7 Ch. D. 238 ; 47 L. J. Bank. 87 : *Ex p. Donnithorne*, 40 L. T. 660 : *Hyde* v. *Watts*, 13 L. J. Ex. 41 ; 12 M. & W. 254 : *Thomas* v. *Nokes*, L. R. 6 Eq. 521 : Benj. 679.

FORTUNE.—In a devise, "Fortune" includes realty and personalty (*Spearing* v. *Hawkes*, 6 Ir. Ch. Rep. 297).

V. SUBSTANCE : REASONABLE PORTION.

FORTUNES.—"Professing to tell fortunes," 5 G. 4, c. 83, s. 4 ; *V*

Penny v. *Hanson*, 56 L. J. M. C. 41 ; 18 Q. B. D. 478 ; 56 L. T. 235 ; 35 W. R. 379 ; 51 J. P. 167.

FOSSILS.—"The word 'Fossils' may, in a strict sense, apply to stones dug or quarried. Usually, however, it appears to apply only to metallic minerals" (MacS. 19, citing *Rosse* v. *Wainman*, 14 M. & W. 872, 873 ; 15 L. J. Ex. 67 ; affd. nom. *Wainman* v. *Rosse*, 2 Ex. 800).

FOTHER.—*V.* GORE.

FOULDCOURSE.—*V.* FOLDCOURSE.

FOUND.—Mineral "Found," means "ascertained to lie and be" (*Jowett* v. *Spencer*, 1 Ex. 647 ; 17 L. J. Ex. 367).

"No sufficient Distress *to be Found* on the demised premises," s. 2, 4 G. 2, c. 28 ; s. 210, Com. L. Pro. Act, 1852,—Goods are not so "to be found" if they are not so visible that a broker, using reasonable diligence, would be able to distrain them (*Doe* d. *Haverson* v. *Franks*, 2 C. & K. 678) ; nor if a distress be prevented by the outer door being locked (*Doe* d. *Chippendale* v. *Dyson*, 1 Moo. & M. 77 : *Doe* d. *Cox* v. *Roe*, 5 D. & L. 272 : *Hammond* v. *Mather*, 3 F. & F. 151).

The difference between "Found" and "*Frequenting*" as used in the Vagrant Act (5 G. 4, c. 83, s. 4), was pointed out in *R.* v. *Clark* (54 L. J. M. C. 66 ; nom. *Clark* v. *Reg.*, 14 Q. B. D. 92) ; where it was decided that a person "found" in a house, &c., for the purpose of committing a felony, could be convicted if only "found" there once ; but that the offence of "frequenting" a street, &c., for a like purpose is not shown to have been committed if the evidence does not show that the person was there more than once. *V.* FREQUENT.

"Found *committing*,"—*e.g.* in s. 63, 2 & 3 V. c. 47, s. 103 ; 24 & 25 V. c. 96,—applies to the case of persons who are taken *flagrante delicto* doing the specific act (*Simmons* v. *Millingen*, 15 L. J. C. P. 102 ; 2 C. B. 524 : *Vf. Roberts* v. *Orchard*, 33 L. J. Ex. 65 ; 2 H. & C. 769 ; 9 L. T. 737 : *Griffiths* v. *Taylor*, 46 L. J. C. P. 152 ; 2 C. P. D. 194 : *Downing* v. *Capel*, 36 L. J. M. C. 97 ; L. R. 2 C. P. 461).

"Found *offending*,"—*e.g.* 5 G. 4, c. 83, ss. 6, 11,—has a similar meaning ; so that a constable cannot, without a Warrant, arrest a man for having neglected to maintain his family (*Horley* v. *Rogers*, 29 L. J. M. C. 140 ; 24 J. P. 261). "Found *on*" licensed premises after hours (s. 25, 35 & 36 V. c. 94) would, *semble*, receive a similar interpretation.

"Found *drunk* on licensed premises," s. 12, 35 & 36 V. c. 94, means to be so found "in places where the public go, or which are open, and where the public may enter and consume drink" (per Mellor, J., *Lester* v. *Torrens*, 46 L. J. M. C. 281 ; 2 Q. B. D. 403) ; and therefore it was there held that an Innkeeper, in his own inn after the same is closed, cannot commit the offence.

"Found *to be due*," note (*d*), item 72, Court Fees Order, 1884, construed "found to have been received" (*Re Crawshay*, 57 L. J. Ch. 923; 39 Ch. D. 552; 59 L. T. 598).

"*To Found*," or "*to Establish*" a charity, such as a school, hospital or chapel, *primâ facie* involves the erection of a building for it; and a bequest for such a purpose is void as implying the bringing of lands into mortmain (*Hopkins* v. *Philipps*, 30 L. J. Ch. 671; 3 Giff. 182: *Tatham* v. *Drummond*, 34 L. J. Ch. 1; 2 H. & M. 262; 4 D. G. J. & S. 484: *Re Goldsmid, Mocatta* v. *A.-G.*, 34 S. J. 63; W. N. (89) 184. *Sv. quà* "establish," *Hartshorne* v. *Nicholson*, 27 L. J. Ch. 810; 26 Bea. 58: PROVIDE. *Vf.* 1 Jarm. 228, 229, 230). But a bequest "to Found a Charitable *Endowment*" is good (*Salusbury* v. *Denton*, 26 L. J. Ch. 851; 3 K. & J. 529: ENDOW: ERECT); and so is a bequest for "Supporting or Founding" ragged schools in a parish where such a school already exists (*Re Hedgman, Morley* v. *Croxon*, 8 Ch. D. 156: *V.* SUPPORT). *Cp.* NEWLY ESTABLISH.

FOUNDATIONS.—For Part II. Metrop. Man. Act, 1878, "Foundations" mean "the space immediately beneath the footings of a Wall" (s. 14).

FOUNDED ON.—A Motion is not in any way "founded on" an affidavit relating merely to procedure,—*e.g.* an affidavit of service,—so as to require copy of such affidavit to be served with notice of motion under Ord. 52, R. 4, R. S. C. (per Pearson, J., *Witham* v. *Witham*, 29 S. J. 707: *Schirges* v. *Schirges*, 30 S. J. 403; W. N. (86) 85). But in *Re Lysaght & ors.* (31 S. J. 233), North, J., declined to follow that interpretation.

Action may be said to be "Founded on Contract," or "Founded on Tort," *V.* s. 5, Co. Co. Act, 1867; s. 116 Co. Co. Act, 1888. In *Bryant* v. *Herbert* (47 L. J. C. P. 670; 3 C. P. D. 389; 26 W. R. 498; 49 L. T. 17) there was a curious conflict of opinion as to whether these are terms of art:—Bramwell, L. J., said, "They are plain English words, and are to have the meaning ordinary Englishmen would give them;" whilst Brett, L. J., said, "With the greatest deference to my learned brother, I do not think those words can be called plain English; for they seem to me to be technical terms." *V.* CONTRACT: TORT.

FOUNDER.—The "Founder" of an Endowment is the person or persons who originally created it; and "every accretion to the original subscriptions, which was not an endowment for any new and special purpose, must be taken to be upon the footing of the original foundation" (per Selborne, L. C., *St. Leonards Trustees* v. *Charity Commrs.*, 54 L. J. P. C. 31; 10 App. Ca. 304). Accordingly it was held in that case that mere subscribers to an endowment subsequent to its origination, are not "founders" within the Endowed Schools Acts, 1869, 1873 (32 & 33 V. c. 56, s. 19; 36 & 37 V. c. 87, s. 7).

"Founder," 17 Ric. 2, c. 1, a worker of metals by melting and casting (Termes de la Ley).

FOWL.—Fowls of the Warren are "of two sorts, viz., *Terrestres* and

Aquatiles. Terrestres of two sorts, *Silvestres*, and *Campestres :—Campestres*, as Partridge, Quaile, Raile, &c.; *Silvestres*, as Pheasant, Woodcocke, &c., *Aquatiles*, as Mallard, Herne, &c." (Co. Litt. 233 a).

"The word 'Fowl' comprehends all birds and poultry" (per Holt, C. J., *Keeble* v. *Hickeringill*, 11 East, 577).

V. WILDFOWL.

FOWLING.—*V.* HUNTING.

FRANCHISE.—"Franchise or Liberty.—A royal privilege belonging either to the Crown or to a subject by virtue of a grant from the Crown, either express, or implied from long enjoyment; Wms. on Commons, 228" (Elph. 581, *wh. Vf.*): "An immunity or exemption from ordinary jurisdiction" (Termes de la Ley).

FRANKALMOIGN.—"Our old bookes described frankalmoign thus; when lands or tenements were bestowed upon God, (that is) given to such people as are consecrated to the service of God" (Co. Litt. 94 b).

FRANKFOLDAGE.—"Frankfoldage—Faldagium—is the right of the lord of a manor, or other person, to have all the sheep within his manor, or within a certain vill or town or other district, folded at night on his land for the purpose of manuring it; *V.* Wms. on Commons, 274 *et seq.*" (Elph. 582, *wh. Vf.*).

Cp. FOLDCOURSE.

FRASSETUM.—"*Frassetum* signifieth a wood, or ground that is woodie" (Co. Litt. 4 b).

FRAUD.—"'Fraud,' in my opinion, is a term that should be reserved for something dishonest and morally wrong, and much mischief is, I think, done, as well as much pain inflicted, by its use where 'illegality' and 'illegal' are the really appropriate expressions" (per Wills, J., *Exp. Watson*, 57 L. J. Q. B. 613; 21 Q. B. D. 301; 59 L. T. 401; 36 W. R. 829; 52 J. P. 742).

"Fraud," in s. 26, subs. 4 (c), Patents, Designs and Trade-Marks Act, 1883 (46 & 47 V. c. 57), means something more than mistake or misconception, there must be some intention to commit a fraud on the petitioner, or otherwise to derive an unfair benefit (*Re Avery*, 36 Ch. D. 307; 56 L. J. Ch. 1007; 57 L. T. 506; 36 W. R. 249).

"Fraud," as used in s. 1, Sales of Reversions Act, 1867, 31 V. c. 4, "does not mean deceit or circumvention; it means an unconscientious use of the power arising out of the circumstances and conditions; and when the relative position of the parties is such as *primâ facie* to raise this presumption, the transaction cannot stand, unless the person claiming the benefit of it is able to repel the presumption by contrary evidence, proving it to have been, in point of fact, fair, just and reasonable" (per Selborne, L.C.,

Aylesford v. *Morris*, 42 L. J. Ch. 548 ; 8 Ch. 484 : *Vf. Fry* v. *Lane*, 58 L. J. Ch. 116 ; 40 Ch. D. 312).

V. Legal Fraud : Breach of Trust.

"Fraud *or Dishonesty*," in a Guarantee Policy ; *V. Ravenscroft* v. *Provident Clerks Assn.*, 5 Times Rep. 3.

FRAUDULENT ASSURANCE.—"Fraudulent Conveyance, Gift, Delivery or Transfer," s. 4 (b), Bankry. Act, 1883 ;—*Vh.* Yate Lee, 16–41 ; Wms. Bank. 7–17 ; Robson, 5 Ed. 147–167 ; Baldwin, 62–69. *Vh. Re Moroney*, 21 L. R. Ir. 27.

FRAUDULENT PREFERENCE.—A Fraudulent Preference "arises where the Debtor, in contemplation of bankry., that is, knowing his circumstances to be such as that bankry must be, or will be, the probable result, though it may not be the inevitable result, does, *ex mero motu*, make a payment of money, or a delivery of property, to a Creditor, not in the ordinary course of business, and without any pressure or demand on the part of the Creditor" (per Ld. Westbury, *Nunes* v. *Carter*, L. R. 1 P. C. 348 ; 36 L. J. P. C. 14 ; 15 W. R. 239).

For the cases hereon, *V.* Yate Lee, 419–432 ; Wms. Bank. 203–210 ; Robson, 167–177 ; Baldwin, 69–74 ; May, on Fraudulent Dispositions, 2 Ed. 101–106.

It is not a Fraudulent Preference to make a payment to revive a statute-barred debt that has not been treated as extinct (*Re Lane, Ex p. Gaze*, 58 L. J. Q. B. 373).

FRAUDULENT PURPOSE.—Taking a *fi. fa.* from a bailiff, under the impression that his authority to execute it depends on its possession, though not Larceny, is taking it "for a Fraudulent Purpose" within s. 96, 24 & 25 V. c. 96 (*R.* v. *Bailey*, 41 L. J. M. C. 61 ; L. R. 1 C. C. R. 347). *Vf.* Rosc. Cr. 992–996.

FRAUDULENTLY.—*V.* Knowingly.

FRAXINETUM.—"A wood of ashes is called *fraxinetum*, and passeth by that name" (Co. Litt. 4 b).

FREE.—*V.* Deductions : Expense : Outgoings.

"This adjective (*liber*) doth distinguish many things in law from others" (Co. Litt. 94 a, *wh. Vf.* hereon).

FREE ALONGSIDE.—*V. Perceval* v. *Lawes Manure Co.*, W. N. (80) 50.

FREE ALMS.—Grant, by the Sovereign, "In Free Alms for ever ;" *V. Re St. Alphage, London Wall*, 59 L. T. 64.

FREE AND CONVENIENT WAY.—*V.* Way.

FREE AND UNQUALIFIED DISCRETION.—*V.* DISCRETION.

FREE AND VOLUNTARY.—*V.* CONSENT.

FREE CUSTOMS.—*V.* CUSTOM : WITH ALL LIBERTIES.

FREE FISHERY.—*V.* FISHERY.

FREE FROM AVERAGE.—*V.* AVERAGE : F. P. A.

FREE FROM CAPTURE.—*V.* CAPTURE.

FREE GRAMMAR SCHOOL : FREE SCHOOL.—A Grammar School is, strictly, a School for teaching the Learned Languages (*A.-G.* v. *Whiteley*, 11 Ves. 241 : *Re Campden Charities*, 18 Ch. D. 310 ; 45 L. T. 152) ; but "*Writing and Arithmetic* may be well introduced into a scheme for the establishment or better regulation of a 'Free Grammar School.'" And so, *à fortiori*, of a "Free School" (Lewin, 536, and case there cited : *Vf.* Tudor Char. Trusts, 163).

FREE LAND.—"Free Land or Tenement to the value of 40/- by the year" to give qualification for a County Vote, 8 Hen. 6, c. 7 : *V. Dawson* v. *Robins*, 2 C. P. D. 38 ; 46 L. J. C. P. 62 : *Dodds* v. *Thompson*, 35 L. J. C. P. 97 ; L. R. 1 C. P. 133.

FREE LIBERTY.—The grant to a person, his heirs and assigns, of "Free Liberty, with servants or otherwise, to come upon lands and there to hawk, hunt, fish, and fowl," is a grant of license of profit, and not of a mere personal license of pleasure ; and therefore it authorizes the grantee, his heirs and assigns, to hawk, hunt, &c., by his servants (*Wickham* v. *Hawker*, 7 M. & W. 63 ; 10 L. J. Ex. 153). *V.* PROFIT À PRENDRE : SERVANTS.

FREE OF ALL OUTGOINGS.—*V.* OUTGOINGS.

FREE OF COMMISSION.—*V. Phillipps* v. *Briard*, 25 L. J. Ex. 233 : *Russell* v. *Griffith*, 2 F. & F. 118.

FREE OF DUTY.—*V.* DEDUCTIONS.

FREE OF EXPENSE AND RISK TO THE SHIP. — *V. Wright* v. *New Zealand Shipping Co.*, 4 Ex. D. 165.

FREE OF FREIGHT.—*V. Mer. & Exchange Bank* v. *Gladstone*, L. R. 3 Ex. 233 ; 37 L. J. Ex. 130 : FREIGHT.

FREE OF LEGACY DUTY.—*V.* LEGACY DUTY.

FREE ON BOARD.—*V.* F. O. B.

FREE PROFITS.—Synonymous with Net Profits (*Shaw* v. *Galt*, 16 Ir. C. L. Rep. 357). *V.* Net.

FREE PUBLIC HOUSE.—"The expression (in Particulars of Sale), 'Free Public House,' is a misdescription when the lease contains a covenant to take beer from the lessor" (Dart, 138, citing *Jones* v. *Edney*, 3 Camp. 285: *Modlen* v. *Snowball*, 31 L. J. Ch. 44; 29 Bea. 641; 4 D. G. F. & J. 143; 5 L. T. 299; 10 W. R. 24: *Vf.* Sug. V. & P. 23).

FREE USE.—*V.* Occupation: Use and Occupation.

FREE WARREN.—*V.* Warren.

FREEHOLD.—"'*Freehold.*' Here (Litt. s. 57) it appeareth that tenant in fee, tenant in taile, and tenant for life, are said to have a frank-tenement, a freehold, so called because it doth distinguish it from termes of yeares, chattels upon incertaine interests, lands in villenage, or customary or copyhold lands" (Co. Litt. 43 b).

Blackstone says (2 Com. 104), "Such an estate, *and no other*, as requires *actual possession* of the land is, legally speaking, freehold;" but "an estate of freehold, may, according to our modern ideas, be in possession, remainder or reversion" (n. Watkins on Conveyancing, 8 ed. 63).

Butler (n. 1 Co. Litt. 266 b) says, "The word *freehold* is now generally used to denote an estate for life, in opposition to an estate of inheritance." In olden times "the word *freehold* always imported the whole estate of the feudatory, but varied as that varied" (Ib.). When more than an estate for life is intended, "it is now more accurate to say, 'Freehold and Inheritance'" (n. Watkins on Conv. 64). *V.* Inheritance.

Devise of "my property, whether freehold or personal, wheresoever situate," comprises copyholds, "freehold" being construed "real" (*Reeves* v. *Baker*, 23 L. J. Ch. 599; 18 Bea. 372).

So Leaseholds will pass under a devise of "freeholds" where there are no freeholds (1 Jarm. 676); and when "freehold" is shown to be a misdescription it will be rejected (Ib. 785; *V.* Farm). *Vf.* Watson, Eq. 1361.

Vh. Early v. *Rathbone*, W. N. (88) 64; 57 L. J. Ch. 652; 58 L. T. 517.

Semble, it is not a misdescription, in Conditions of Sale, to describe Customary Freeholds as "Freehold" (*Wadmore* v. *Toller*, 6 Times Rep. 58).

FREIGHT.—"Freight," as used in a policy of Marine Insurance, "imports the benefit derived from the employment of the ship" (per Ld. Tenterden, *Flint* v. *Flemyng*, 1 B. & Ad. 48).

"'Freight' is the value of the use of the ship" (per Day, J., *Gayner* v. *Sunderland*, Cab. & El. 295).

"In my opinion nothing is Freight unless there is involved in it a contract to carry; for Freight is a sum payable in respect of a contract to carry, and if there is no contract to carry, then, although the sum to be paid may be called Freight, it is not in point of law Freight within the rule that the mortgagee is entitled to the accruing freight" (per Mellish, L.J., *Keith* v. *Burrows*, 2 C. P. D. 167 ; 46 L. J. C. P. 460 ; affd. by H. L. 2 App. Ca. 636 ; 46 L. J. C. P. 801).

"Freight, according to the dictionaries, includes (1) the Cargo ; (2) the actual Transport from one place to another ; (3) the Hire of the ship, or part of it, or the charge for the transport of goods therein. *It may by extension include the Passengers,* or even *Passage Money,* as, for instance, upon a question arising upon the now abandoned maxim that 'Freight is the mother of Wages,' or upon a question of sale or capture or abandonment, because the Passage Money is equally with the Freight of goods an incident or accessory of the ship. Accordingly, Chancellor Kent (3 Com. 7 Ed. 296) states that, 'Freight, in the common acceptation of the term, means the price for the actual transportation of goods by sea from one place to another ; but in its more extensive sense it is applied to all rewards or compensation paid for the use of ships, including the transportation of passengers.' And he refers to *Giles* v. *The Cynthia* (1 Peters, Adm. 206), in which the question arose upon a claim to wages. And in *Mullow* v. *Backer* (5 East, 321) Lawrence, J., said, 'Foreign writers consider Passage-Money the same as Freight ;' and Lord Ellenborough added, 'Except for the purpose of lien, it seems the same thing'" (per Willes, J., *Denoon* v. *Home and Col. Assrce.*, 41 L. J. C. P. 168 ; L. R. 7 C. P. 348). *Vh. Sweeting* v. *Darthez*, 23 L. J. C. P. 131 ; 14 C. B. 538 ; *Williams* v. *North China Insrce.*, 1 C. P. D. 757.

There is no loss of "Freight," if, having been earned, the charterers are entitled to, and do, withhold it as a mulct or forfeit (*Inman Co.* v. *Bischoff*, 52 L. J. Q. B. 169 ; 7 App. Ca. 670).

V. BACK FREIGHT : DEAD FREIGHT : FREE OF FREIGHT : PAYING FREIGHT : VALUE OF THE SHIP AND FREIGHT.

FREIGHT IN ADVANCE SUBJECT TO INSURANCE.—"This, in a Charter-Party, does not mean that the insurance is to be a condition precedent to the recovery of the freight ; but merely that the insurance premium is to be deducted from the freight" (1 Maude & P. 365, citing *Jackson* v. *Isaacson*, 3 H. & N. 405 ; 27 L. J. Ex. 392 : *Vh.* per Manisty, J., *Rodoconachi* v. *Milburn*, 17 Q. B. D. 322).

FREIGHT PAYABLE HERE.—*V. Lidgett* v. *Perrin*, 11 C. B.N.S. 362 ; stated 1 Maude & P. 365, n. (*h*).

V. HE OR THEY PAYING FREIGHT : ON PAYMENT OF FREIGHT.

FRENCH BREAD.—"French or Fancy Bread or Rolls," s. 4, 6 & 7 W. 4, c. 37 ;—"At the time this Act was passed (A.D. 1836), there was Household Bread, which consisted of ordinary loaves and which any poor or ignorant purchaser would expect to get of the right weight ; and there was also bread called 'Fancy Bread,' which, according to my recollection of that time, was made of a fine quality of flour, and was made in the shape of a long roll, and a person in buying bread of that description would not expect to get the weight so accurately as if he were buying a Household loaf. Then, taking that view of the matter, and seeing that it was more according to the shape of loaf than anything else, the Legislature, it seems to me, enacted that bread should be sold by weight, *i.e.*, all ordinary bread ; and then it was provided that nothing should prevent any baker selling bread 'usually sold' under the denomination of 'French or Fancy Bread or Rolls' without previously weighing the same. My opinion is that that meant such bread as, at the time the legislature passed the Act, was sold under the denomination of 'French or Fancy Bread,' which, I think, as a matter of fact, bore these different *shapes* which have been referred to" (per Blackburn, J., *Aërated Bread Co.* v. *Grigg*, 42 L. J. M. C. 119 ; L. R. 8 Q. B. 355 ; 37 J. P. 388 ; 28 L. T. 187 ; an opinion acquiesced in by the whole Court and therein dissenting from the opinion that it is the exceptional *quality* of the bread which constitutes it "French or Fancy" which had been given by the majority of the Court, Lush & Hayes, JJ., Hannen, J., diss., in *R.* v. *Wood*, 38 L. J. M. C. 144 ; L. R. 4 Q. B. 599 ; 33 J. P. 823).

Tinned Loaves, made crusty all round but with same ingredients as ordinary bread, except that carbonic acid gas is forced into it, is not "French or Fancy Bread" within the section (*Aërated Bread Co.* v. *Grigg*, sup.).

V. By Weight.

FREQUENT: FREQUENTING.—To "frequent" a place is to frequently go there, or to be in the habit of going there, *e.g.*, to frequent a public-house. Therefore a conviction cannot be sustained under the Vagrant Act (5 G. 4, c. 83, s. 4), for "frequenting" a street, &c., with intent to commit felony, where the evidence does not show that the person has been there more than once (*R.* v. *Clark*, 54 L. J. M. C. 66 ; 14 Q. B. D. 93 ; 52 L. T. 136 ; 33 W. R. 226 ; 49 J. P. 246 ; 1 Times Rep. 109). "He must in fact be seen hanging about the street" (per Grove, J., Ib.).

V. Found.

To "frequent a *Market*," seems to mean the principal market in which the person deals (*Stephens* v. *Derry*, 16 East, 147 : *Reeves* v. *Stroud*, 1 Dowl. P. C. 399 : *Double* v. *Gibbs*, 1 Dowl. P. C. 583 ; 2 L. J. Ex. 87 : *Jenks* v. *Taylor*, 5 L. J. Ex. 263 ; 1 M. & W. 578).

FRESH FORCE.—*V.* Termes de la Ley.

FRESH STEP.—An Appearance to a Writ, is a "Fresh Step" within R. S. C., Ord. 70, R. 2 (*Mulckern* v. *Doerks*, 53 L. J. Q. B. 526 ; 51 L. T. 296, 429 ; 33 W. R. 14).

FRESH SUIT.—*V.* Termes de la Ley.

FRESH TAXES.—A covenant in a Lease to pay "all Fresh Taxes," would seem, primarily, to mean all new taxes (*Watson* v. *Atkins*, 3 B. & Ald. 647).

FRIEND.—In a contract of sale for "my Friend," the Vendor is not sufficiently described; *V.* PROPRIETOR.

FRIENDS AND RELATIONS.—A Power to Appoint amongst "Relations *and* Friends," or "Relations *or* Friends," is the same as one to RELATIONS (*Gower* v. *Mainwaring*, 2 Ves. sen. 87, 110: Sug. Pow. 654: *Re Caplin*, 34 L. J. Ch. 578; 2 Dr. & Sm. 527).

"The next and most faithful Friends" to whom Administration is to be granted, 31 Edw. 3, st. 1, c. 11, means "next-of-blood" (*Hersloe's Case*, 9 Rep. 39 b); and property directed by Will to "*revert*" to "my Friends" will go to the testator's kindred,—either his heirs-at-law or next-of-kin—(*Coogan* v. *Hayden*, 4 L. R. Ir. 585). In that case, Dowse, B., citing Schmidt's Shakespeare Lexicon, p. 456, said, "Friends" is sometimes used for "near Relations, particularly parents."

FRIPERER.—"'Friperer' is used, 1 Jac. c. 21, for a kind of Broker" (Termes de la Ley).

FRITH.—*V.* FRYTHE.

FRIVOLOUS OR VEXATIOUS.—As to this phrase as used in Ord. 25, R. 4, R. S. C.; *V. Darlow* v. *Scratton*, 29 S. J. 131: *Metropolitan Bank* v. *Pooley*, 10 App. Ca. 210; 54 L. J. Q. B. 449: *Willis* v. *Beauchamp*, 11 P. D. 63: *Burstall* v. *Beyfus*, 26 Ch. D. 35; 32 W. R. 418; 53 L. J. Ch. 565: *Lawrance* v. *Norreys*, 39 Ch. D. 213: *Mittens* v. *Foreman*, 58 L. J. Q. B. 40: *Barrett & Elers, Limd.* v. *Day*, Times, 5 Feb. 1890.

FROM.—When an act has to be done "from" or "within" two times, *e.g.* "from 6 to 8 weeks,"—the time for doing it is some period fairly between those times (per Brett, J., *Ashworth* v. *Redford*, 43 L. J. C. P. 58; nom. *Ashforth* v. *Redford*, L. R. 9 C. P. 22).

V. AFTER: AT AND FROM: FROM THE DAY OF THE DATE: SAY.

A bequest to a Class "from S. downwards," includes S. (*Lett* v. *Osborne*, 51 L. J. Ch. 910).

FROM AND AFTER.—The expression "From and after the death" is "generally regarded as being equivalent merely to 'Remainder'" (1 Jarm. 816, commenting on *Andrew* v. *Andrew*, 45 L. J. Ch. 232; 1 Ch. D. 410: *Vf. Jull* v. *Jacobs*, 3 Ch. D. 703, 713: *Ferguson* v. *Ferguson*, 17 L. R. Ir. 560: *Re Jobson*, 34 S. J. 155: 1 Jarm. 806).

"From and after" death, controlled by context in *Rhodes* v. *Rhodes*, 51 L. J. P. C. 53; 7 App. Ca. 192.

It is said that under a reversionary lease, which incorrectly recites an existing lease to A., habendum "from and after the *said* lease," the term commences immediately ; but that if it were "from and after *the* lease to A.," the term commences on expiration of lease to A. (Elph. 139, *wh. Vf.*).

V. AFTER : first par. AT : AT AND FROM.

FROM ANY CAUSE WHATEVER.—As to effect of Condition of Sale giving interest if delay in completion take place "from any cause whatever;" *V.* Dart, 143, 144, 719–723.

FROM HENCEFORTH.—A lease to begin "From henceforth" or "From the making hereof," "shall begin in the day on which it is delivered, for the words of the Indenture are not of any effect till the deliverie, and thereby from the making, or from henceforth, take their first effect" (Co. Litt. 46 b). *Vf. Llewelyn* v. *Williams*, Cro. Jac. 258 : *Pope* v. *Skinner*, Hob. 72 : *Clayton's case*, 5 Rep. 1 a : *Cornish* v. *Cawsy*, Aleyn, 75 ; 2 Platt, 55.

Cp. FROM THE DAY OF THE DATE.

An enactment "'from henceforth,' '*de cœtero*,' does not necessarily imply a new law; as may be seen upon the doubts arising on the Stat. Merton, c. 2" (Dwar. 685 ; *Vf. Ib.* Ch. 11).

FROM HIS WORK.—A man is not on his way "From his Work," within the meaning of the Rules of a Friendly Society, who after leaving his work goes to a public-house and there stays for 4 hours, and, getting drunk there, meets with an accident on his way home (*Joyce* v. *Northumberland Miners' Society*, 4 Times Rep. 525.)

FROM THE DAY OF THE DATE.—A term limited to commence "from the day of the date," or "from the date" of the instrument, or from a certain day, will be taken to include or exclude that day, according to the context and subject-matter (*Williams* v. *Nash*, 28 L. J. Ch. 886 ; 28 Bea. 93 : *Ammerman* v. *Digges*, 12 Ir. C. L. Rep. App. i. : Elph. 124 ; 2 Platt, 54–57 ; Woodf. 150 ; and cases there cited : *Vh.* Co. Litt. 46 a). *V.* DATE.

"The general understanding is, that terms for years last during the whole anniversary of the day from which they are granted. Indeed, if this were otherwise, the last day, on which rent is almost uniformly made payable, would be posterior to the lease." (Per Denman, C. J., *Ackland* v. *Lutley*, 9 A. & E. 879 ; 8 L. J. Q. B. 164 ; 1 P. & D. 636).

Cp. FROM HENCEFORTH.

FROM THE DECK.—"Where a cargo was sold 'From the Deck,' it was held to mean that the seller should pay all that was necessary in order to enable the buyer to remove the cargo from the deck" (Benj. 638, citing *Playford* v. *Mercer*, 22 L. T. 41).

FROM TIME TO TIME.—"The words 'From time to time' are words which are constantly introduced where it is intended to protect a person who is empowered to act from the risk of having completely discharged his duty when he has once acted, and therefore not being able to act again in the same direction." The meaning of the words "From time to time" is, that after once acting, the donee of the power may act again;—and either independently of, or by adding to, or taking from or reversing altogether his previous act (per Ld. Penzance, *Lawrie* v. *Lees*, 51 L. J. Ch. 214; 7 App. Ca. 19. *Vf. Re Sutton Coldfield Grammar School*, 51 L. J. P. C. 8; 7 App. Ca. 91).

Expenses payable "from time to time," s. 81, Ry. C. C. Act. 1845; *V. Whitehouse* v. *Wolverhampton Ry.*, L. R. 5 Ex. 6; 39 L. J. Ex. 1.

Va. Market Harborough v. *Kettering*, 42 L. J. M. C. 137; L. R. 8 Q. B. 308.

It seems to be considered that the words "from time to time," or "and so *toties quoties*," added to a covenant for renewal of a lease, creates the right to a perpetual renewal (1 Platt, 712, citing *Furnival* v. *Crew*, 3 Atk. 83; 9 Mod. 446: *Iggulden* v. *May*, 7 East, 242: *Maxwell* v. *Ward*, 11 Price, 3; 13 Ib. 674; McClel. 458: *Atkinson* v. *Pilsworth*, 1 Vern. & Scriv. 156. *Sv. Baynham* v. *Guy's Hospital*, 3 Ves. 295).

FRONT OF.—By a local Act power was given of rating to the extent of 1*s*. per yard "of the length *in front of*" buildings. A county prison with its garden and grounds abutted at its entrance, at its back, and at both its sides on to public ways: held, that "the words 'in front of' mean that part of the gaol which would be frontage if there were doors and windows in it, and therefore that that part of the gaol which abuts on public ways in the front, back and sides of the gaol is to be considered liable to be rated" (per Pollock, C.B., *Bedfordshire Jus.* v. *Bedford Improvement Commrs.*, 21 L. J. M. C. 227; 7 Ex. 658). *Vf. Governors of Bedford Infirmary* v. *Bedford Improvement Commrs.*, 21 L. J. M. C. 229; 7 Ex. 768.

V. FRONTING.

FRONTING.—Premises "*fronting, adjoining or abutting*" on a street, and as such chargeable with expense of road-making under s. 150, P. H. Act, 1875, need not be absolutely contiguous (*Wakefield* v. *Lee*, 1 Ex. D. 336: *Newport* v. *Graham*, 9 Q. B. D. 183); but must have direct access thereto (*Williams* v. *Wandsworth*, 53 L. J. M. C. 187; 13 Q. B. D. 211: *Lightbound* v. *Higher Bebington*, 54 L. J. M. C. 130; 55 Ib. 94; 14 Q. B. D. 849; 16 Ib. 577).

V. BOUNDING: FRONT OF: FORMING: WITHIN.

FROST.—*V.* DETENTION BY ICE.

FRUIT.—"The term 'Fruit,' in legal acceptation, is not confined to the produce of those trees which in popular language are called *fruit* trees; but applies also to the produce of oak, elm, and walnut trees. In the old books the lessee is stated to have an interest in the trees in respect of the shade for cattle, and the fruit thereof" (per Bayley, J., *Bullen* v. *Denning*,

5 B. & C. 847). In *Liford's Case* (11 Rep. 48 a), it is laid down that the lessee shall have the young of all birds that breed in the trees and the fruits. *Va. Berry* v. *Heard*, Cro. Car. 242 ; Com. Dig. tit. Biens, H. Trees : TREES.

FRUSTUM.—"*Frustum* signifieth a parcell" (Co. Litt. 5 b). In the 4th ed. Co. Litt., this word is spelt "frustrum."

FRYTHE.—"*Frythe* is a plaine betweene woods ; and so is *lawnd* or *lound*" (Co. Litt. 5 b).

"Frith, or Frydd, (in Wales) a close : *A.-G.* v. *Reveley*, printed for private circulation (in Linc. Inn Library)" (Elph. 582).

FUGITIVE CRIMINAL.—The Extradition Act, 1870 (33 & 34 V. c. 52, s. 26) defines a "Fugitive Criminal" as "any person accused or convicted of an extradition crime committed within the jurisdiction of any foreign state, *who is in* or who is suspected of being in some part of her Majesty's dominions." The words italicised show that the idea of flight from justice is not necessarily involved ; and accordingly, for the purposes of the statute, the phrase "fugitive criminal" includes a person who being in England (and not in any sense fleeing) commits an offence abroad,—*e.g.*, a false pretence by means of sending a letter (*R.* v. *Nillins*, 53 L. J. M. C. 157).

FULFILLING.—*V.* DOING.

FULL.—*V.* IN FULL.

FULL AGE.—"'*Full age*,' regularly is one and twenty yeares" (Co. Litt. 78 b).

Quà Parliamentary Franchise ; *V. Hargreaves* v. *Hopper*, 45 L. J. C. P. 105 ; 1 C. P. D. 195.

FULL AND COMPLETE CARGO.—*V.* CARGO.

FULL CONFIDENCE.—*V.* PRECATORY TRUST.

FULL CONSIDERATION.—"Full and Valuable Consideration" in Mortmain Acts, 9 G. 2, c. 36, s. 2, and now 51 & 52 V. c. 42, s. 4 (5) : *V.* interpretation, s. 10 (iv.), lastly cited Act ; *Vh.* Tudor, Char. Trusts, 394, 395.

Discharge of a burden on real estate in the event of the same being sold or charged "for a Full or Valuable Consideration ;" *V. Redman* v. *Rymer*, 5 Times Rep. 287.

V. VALUABLE.

FULL COSTS.—"Full Costs," 17 Car. 2, c. 17, s. 3, mean ordinary costs (*Jamieson* v. *Trevelyan*, 24 L. J. Ex. 74 ; 10 Ex. 748).

FULL DISCHARGE.—"Full Discharge" of a prisoner "from custody, without any adjudication," s. 37, 1 & 2 V. c. 110 ; *V. Basham* v. *Smith*, 22 Bea. 190.

FULL DISCLOSURE.—*V. Fawcett* v. *Whitehouse*, 1 R. & M. 132: and per Jessel, M.R., *Dunne* v. *English*, L. R. 18 Eq. 535.

V. DISCLOSE.

FULL INTEREST ADMITTED.—A Marine Policy containing the term "Full Interest Admitted," is void under 19 G. 2, c. 37, s. 1 (*Berridge* v. *The Man On Insrce.*, 18 Q. B. D. 346).

V. WITHOUT BENEFIT OF SALVAGE.

FULL NOTE.—"Full Notes of Evidence;" *V.* NOTE.

FULL OPPORTUNITY.—*V.* OPPORTUNITY.

FULL SALARIES.—A bequest to employées of "Full Salaries" for a stated period, means that the salaries are to be calculated free from incidental deductions either by custom of trade or illness, or anything of that sort, but does not exempt the legatee from legacy duty (per North, J., *Re Marcus*, 56 L. J. Ch. 830; 57 L. T. 399; W. N. (87) 168).

FULL SATISFACTION.—*V.* SATISFACTION.

FULLEST PRACTICABLE EXTENT.—*V.* WORKABLE.

FULLY ESTATED.—Condition to keep Leaseholds for Lives "fully estated" with lives; *V. Blake* v. *Peters*, 32 L. J. Ch. 200; 1 D. G. J. & S. 345.

FUNDED PROPERTY.—*V.* IRISH FUNDED PROPERTY.

FUNDS.—"The Funds," or "Government Funds" or "The Public Funds" (which expressions are synonymous, per Ld. Cranworth, *Slingsby* v. *Grainger*, 7 H. L. Ca. 280; 28 L. J. Ch. 617), generally means funded securities guaranteed by the English Government, *i.e.*, Consols, Reduced Annuities, Long Annuities, or any other of the English Funds (*Howard* v. *Kay*, 27 L. J. Ch. 448); but does not include Foreign Bonds guaranteed by England (*Burnie* v. *Getting*, 2 Coll. 324), nor Bank Stock (*Slingsby* v. *Grainger*, 8 D. G. M. & G. 385; 7 H. L. Ca. 273; 28 L. J. Ch. 616), nor East India Stock, under 3 & 4 W. 4, c. 85 (*Brown* v. *Brown*, 4 K. & J. 704), nor even unfunded Exchequer Bills (*Johnson* v. *Digby*, 8 L. J. O. S. Ch. 38); unless there is nothing more appropriate to answer the bequest (*Mangin* v. *Mangin*, 16 Bea. 300). *V.* CONSOLS.

As to Irish Government debentures; *V. Ridge* v. *Newton*, 2 Dr. & War. 239.

"*Foreign* Funds" mean securities for which the faith of a foreign government is directly pledged (*Ellis* v. *Eden*, 23 Bea. 543; 26 L. J. Ch. 533: *Cadett* v. *Earle*, 5 Ch. D. 710; 46 L. J. Ch. 798); but scarcely includes the bonds of an undertaking,—*e.g.*, a railway,—which are to be paid off by a sinking fund which is guaranteed by a foreign government (*Re*

Langdale, L. R. 10 Eq. 39 : *Va. Ellis* v. *Eden*, sup.). *V.* FOREIGN BONDS : FOREIGN GOVERNMENT.

Vh. 1 Jarm. 770 n. ; Wms. Exs. 1197 ; Lewin, 322.

FUNDUS.—"*Quod olim dicebatur fundus nunc manerium dicitur*" Co. Litt. 5 a). A little further on, in same page, it is said, "anciently *fundus* signified a fearme, and sometime land."

FUNERAL EXPENSES.—What are, and what may be allowed for ; *V.* Wms. Exs. 972 *et seq.*

FURLONG.—*V.* STADIUM.

FURNISH.—*V.* PROVIDE.

FURNISHES THE SUPPLY.—A Water Company "furnishes the supply" of water within s. 62, P. H. Act, 1875, when its mains are laid in such a position as regards a house as will reasonably enable the owner to connect it with the mains (*Southend Water W. Co.* v. *Howard*, 53 L. J. Q. B. 354 ; 13 Q. B. D. 215).

FURNITURE.—"It has been held that the habit of hiring Furniture in Hotels is so notorious that the doctrine (of reputed ownership) does not apply. It has not yet been declared what is meant by 'Furniture ;' but the custom is such that it does not allow any one to think that anything used in the business of the hotel is within the reputed ownership of the hotel-keeper" (per Brett, M.R., *Re Parker*, 54 L. J. Q. B. 244 ; 14 Q. B. D. 636).

A Bequest of "Furniture" may pass pictures (*Cremorne* v. *Antrobus*, 5 Russ. 312 ; 7 L. J. O. S. Ch. 88).

V. HOUSEHOLD : FIXED FURNITURE : GOODS AND CHATTELS.

"It has been held that *Ballast* is not part of the Furniture of a Merchant Ship" (1 Maude & P. 53, n. (*x*), citing Molloy, B. 2, c. 1, s. 8 : *Kynter's Case*, 1 Leon. 46). *V.* TACKLE. But *Provisions*, for the use of the crew, are covered by a policy on the ship "and Furniture" (*Brough* v. *Whitmore*, 4 T. R. 206 : *Va. Hill* v. *Patten*, 8 East, 373).

FURS.—Hat bodies made partly of the soft parts of rabbit skins and partly of sheep's wool, are not "Furs" within s. 1, Carriers' Act, 1830 (*Mayhew* v. *Nelson*, 6 C. & P. 58).

FURTHER.—In *Doe* d. *Wickham* v. *Turner* (2 D. & Ry. 398), the Will was in the following words,—"I give unto H. W. a messuage or tenement now in the possession of W. *Item*, I give *further* unto my nephew H. W. half part of my garden, and £100 stock in the 4 per cent. Bank Annuities ; I give, *further*, my yard, stables, cowhouse, and all other outhouses in the said yard, my sister M. W. to have the interest and profits during her natural life ;"—and the Court read in the words "to him" after the second "*further*," so that H. W. was held entitled to the yard, &c. *Vh.* 1 Jarm. 490, 491.

"Further or other Valuable *Consideration*," s. 16, 17 & 18 V. c. 83 ; *V. Re Bolton*, L. R. 5 Ex. 82 ; 39 L. J. Ex. 51.

"Further *Consideration Money*," in reddendum of a Mining Lease ; *V. Barrs* v. *Lea*, 33 L. J. Ch. 437.

"To further :" A testamentary gift "to further" the teaching of certain doctrines, does not offend against the Mortmain Act (*Re Moseley*, 4 Times Rep. 301).

FURTHER CHARGE.—*V.* CONVEYANCE.

FURTHER EVIDENCE.—"Further Evidence," Ord. 58, R. 4, R. S. C., means Evidence not used in the Court below (*Re Chennell*, 47 L. J. Ch. 583 ; 8 Ch. D. 492).

FURTHER ORDER.—A Decree directing periodical payments in a certain way "until further order," is final as to the rights of the parties, and temporary only as to the sources and mode of payment (*Peareth* v. *Marriott*, 52 L. J. Ch. 221 ; 22 Ch. D. 182).

FUTURE.—Read as "former" (*Pasmore* v. *Huggins*, 25 L. J. Ch. 251 ; 21 Bea. 103).

As to the value of this word in construing a covenant, in a Marriage Settlement, to settle after-acquired property ; *V.* jdgmt. of Lindley, L. J., *Re Garnett*, 55 L. J. Ch. 779 ; 33 Ch. D. 300 ; 55 L. T. 562 : *Re Michell*, 9 Ch. D. 5 ; 48 L. J. Ch. 50.

"Future *Cargo* ;" *V. Langton* v. *Horton*, 11 L. J. Ch. 299 ; 1 Hare, 549.

An Agreement to pay an Agent a commission on the sale or letting of goods "at any Future *Date*," is not valid for all time, but only for a reasonable time ; and a County Court Judge having held that such an agreement made in Feb. 1883 might be determined in Sept. 1884, it was held his decision was final, the question being one of fact (*Houghton* v. *Orgar*, 1 Times Rep. 653).

The words "or other future *Estate or Interest*" (s. 3, Stat. Lim. 3 & 4 W. 4, c. 27), comprehend all executory devises (per Tindal, C.J., *James* v. *Salter*, 3 Bing. N. C. 554). *Vf. Doe* d. *Johnson* v. *Liversedge*, 13 L. J. Ex. 61 ; 11 M. & W. 517 : *Lewis* v. *Rees*, 3 K. & J. 132 : *Astley* v. *Essex*, L. R. 18 Eq. 290 ; 43 L. J. Ch. 817 : *Jumpsen* v. *Pitchers*, 13 Sim. 327 : *Doe* d. *Corbyn* v. *Bramston*, 3 A. & E. 63.

A covenant to settle all such "Future *Fortune*" as may be acquired or succeeded to, embraces property the title to which was in existence at the date of the covenant, but the enjoyment of which was not acquired till afterwards (*Grafftey* v. *Humpage*, 1 Bea. 46 ; 8 L. J. Ch. 98).

GABEL.—"Here note for the better understanding of ancient records, statutes, charters, &c., *gabel*, or *gavell*, *gablum*, *gabellum*, *gabellettum*, *galbellettum*, and *gavillettum*, doe signifie a rent, custome duty, or service, yeelded or done to the king or any other lord" (Co. Litt. 142 a). *Vf.* Termes de la Ley, *Gable;* Elph. 582.

GAIN.—Business Companies, of more than 20 persons, for "the acquisition of Gain" must be registered (s. 4, Companies Act, 1862, 25 & 26 V. c. 89). "'Gain,' means exactly acquisition. Therefore the expression here is, 'the acquisition of acquisition.' Gain is something obtained or acquired. It is not limited to pecuniary gain. In fact, we should have to put the word 'pecuniary' to show it. It is not 'gains,' but 'gain,' in the singular. Commercial profits, no doubt, if acquired are gain; but I cannot find any word limiting it simply to a commercial profit. I take the word as referring to a Company which is formed to acquire something, as distinguished from a Company formed for spending something and in which the individual members are simply to give something away or to spend something, and not to gain anything" (per Jessel, M. R., *Re Arthur Average Assn.*, 44 L. J. Ch. 572; 10 Ch. 546: *Vf. Smith* v. *Anderson*, 50 L. J. Ch. 39; 15 Ch. D. 247: *Crowther* v. *Thorley*, 50 L. T. 43: *Re Siddall*, 54 L. J. Ch. 682). A diminution of a loss, is a "Gain" within the meaning of the section (*Re Padstow Assrce.*, 51 L. J. Ch. 344; 20 Ch. D. 137).

V. Gains: Business: Hire.

"Arable Land (which anciently is called *hyde and gaine*)" (Co. Litt. 85 b).

"Beasts that *gain* his land;" *V.* Beasts: Termes de la Ley, *Gainage.*

GAINS.—"Although in the Income Tax Act (5 & 6 V. c. 35, s. 100), 'profits' and 'gains' are really equivalent terms, yet the use of the word 'Gains' in addition to the word 'Profits' furnishes an additional argument for excluding the contention that you are to introduce into the word 'Profits' some ideas connected, not with the nature of the thing, but with the manner and rule of its application. What are the 'Gains' of a trade? If it could be reasonably contended that the word 'Profits' in these (Income Tax) Acts has reference to some advantage which the persons carrying on the concern are to derive from it, it might be said, perhaps, that the same argument might have been raised upon the word 'Gains';

but, to my mind, it is reasonably plain that the 'Gains' of a trade are that which is gained by the trading, for whatever purpose it is used—whether it is gained for the benefit of a community or for the benefit of individuals. Whether the benefit is to be obtained by dividends, or whether it is to be obtained by lightening and diminishing public burdens, it is all the same" (per Selborne, L. C., *Mersey Docks* v. *Lucas*, 53 L. J. Q. B. 7; 8 App. Ca. 891; 49 L. T. 781; 32 W. R. 34; 48 J. P. 212).

V. PROFITS.

GALE.—From GABEL comes "'Gale,' still used for the taking of a mine in the West of England. To *gale* a mine, to acquire the right of working it; and *gale* is the common word in Ireland for a payment of rent, or for the rent due at a certain term; Wedgwood, Dict. Eng. Etym., *Gabel*" (Elph. 582). *Vf.* Wood on Dean Forest, 6, 94; s. 1, Dean Forest Act, 1861, 24 & 25 V. c. xl.

GAMBLER.—*V.* PROFESSED GAMBLER.

GAME: Animals.—"The word 'Game' is an indefinite word, and seems at various times to have had various meanings; to have at one time included one thing, at one time another; to have had at one time a wider, and at another time a narrower signification" (per Erle, C.J., *Jeffryes* v. *Evans*, 34 L. J. C. P. 263; 19 C. B. N. S. 264).

Under 9 G. 4, c. 69 (s. 13), and under the Game Laws Amendment Act, 1831 (1 & 2 W. 4, c. 32, s. 2), "Game" includes "Hares, pheasants, partridges, grouse, heath or moor game, black game and bustards;"—a definition which, it will be observed, does not include rabbits (*Spicer* v. *Barnard*, 28 L. J. M. C. 176; 1 E. & E. 874: *Padwick* v. *King*, 29 L. J. M. C. 42; 7 C. B. N. S. 88).

Under the Poaching Prevention Act (25 & 26 V. c. 114), "Game" includes "Hares, pheasants, partridges, eggs of pheasants and partridges, woodcocks, snipes, rabbits, grouse, black or moor game, and eggs of grouse, black or moor game" (s. 1).

"Bird of Game" in s. 4, Act 1831, means English Bird of Game (*Guyer* v. *The Queen*, 58 L. J. M. C. 81); but extends throughout the section to *live* birds (*Loome* v. *Baily*, 30 L. J. M. C. 31; 3 E. & E. 444).

V. ENTERING OR BEING: SEARCH.

GAME: Lawful.—A Foot-race is a "lawful game" (*Batty* v. *Marriott*, 17 L. J. C. P. 215; 5 C. B. 818). So are Billiards (*Parsons* v. *Alexander*, 24 L. J. Q. B. 277; 5 E. & B. 263), Dominoes, Chess or Draughts (*R.* v. *Ashton*, 22 L. J. M. C. 1; 1 E. & B. 286). So Cards would seem, *per se*, not unlawful (*Patten* v. *Rhymer*, 29 L. J. M. C. 189).

V. GAMING.

Subscriptions or contributions for any plate, prize or sum of money, to be awarded to the winner "of any lawful game, sport, pastime, or exercise," are legal (*V.* proviso to s. 18, Gaming Act, 8 & 9 V. c. 109). But a match for so much a side is a wager and not within this proviso (*Diggle* v. *Higgs*, 2 Ex. D. 422 : *Trimble* v. *Hill*, 5 App. Ca. 342 : over-ruling *Batty* v. *Marriott*, sup.).

V. SUBSCRIPTION.

GAME, Sport, Pastime or Exercise.—Gambling by tossing with coins, if not a "game," is a "pastime or exercise" within s. 17, Gaming Act, 8 & 9 V. c. 109 (*R.* v. *O'Connor*, 15 Cox, 3 ; and as to what is a "Game" within the section, *V. R.* v. *Hudson*, 29 L. J. M. C. 145 ; Bell, C. C. 263).

GAMING.—"To game," is to play at any game, whether of skill or chance, for money or money's worth ; and the act is not less gaming because the game played is not in itself unlawful (*R.* v. *Ashton*, 22 L. J. M. C. 1 ; 1 E. & B. 286 : *Patten* v. *Rhymer*, 29 L. J. M. C. 189 : *Parsons* v. *Alexander*, 24 L. J. Q. B. 277 ; 5 E. & B. 263 : *Bew* v. *Harston*, 47 L. J. M. C. 121 ; 3 Q. B. D. 454 ; 26 W. R. 915 ; 42 J. P. 808 : *Dyson* v. *Mason*, 58 L. J. M. C. 55 ; 22 Q. B. D. 351 ; 5 Times Rep. 230). In view of the "serious doubts" expressed by Cockburn, C. J., in *Bew* v. *Harston*, sup., the clause in the above definition expressed in the words "whether of skill or chance" cannot be regarded as absolutely settled by authority.

An innkeeper is guilty of an offence against his license prohibiting "any gaming whatsoever," and he or any licensed person is guilty of suffering "any gaming" within s. 17, Licensing Act, 1872 (35 & 36 V. c. 94), if he permits, even his private friends, to play at cards or other games of chance for money or money's worth, however small the stakes (*Foot* v. *Baker*, 6 Sc. N. R. 301 ; 5 M. & G. 335 ; 11 J. P. 444 : *Patten* v. *Rhymer*, sup.). And convictions against licensed persons for allowing games of skill,—such as ten pins, skittles, skittle-pool, "puff and dart,"—to be played for money or money's worth have been supported (*Danford* v. *Taylor*, 33 J. P. 277 : *Luff* v. *Leaper*, 36 J. P. 54 : *Dyson* v. *Mason*, sup. : *Bew* v. *Harston*, sup.).

V. SUFFER : UNLAWFUL GAMING.

GAMING HOUSE.—*V.* COMMON GAMING HOUSE.

GAMING OR WAGERING CONTRACTS.—The Act (8 & 9 V. c. 109, s. 18) which renders null and void, "all contracts or agreements by way of *gaming or wagering*," means contracts or agreements *for* wagers ; and relates only to contracts which are themselves by way of wagering (per Cleasby, B., in *Beeston* v. *Beeston*, 45 L. J. Ex. 232 ; 1 Ex. D. 13). Therefore an agreement between two persons that one shall make bets for the other, is not a contract "by way of gaming or wagering." And, accordingly, money won and received by a betting agent may be recovered from him by his principal (*Beeston* v. *Beeston,* sup. : *Bridger* v. *Savage,* 15 Q. B. D. 363 ; 54 L. J. Q. B. 464 ; 53 L. T. 129 ; 33 W. R. 891 ; 49 J. P. 725) ; and the agent may recover from his principal all moneys paid in pursuance of a betting agency (*Rosewarne* v. *Billing,* 33 L. J. C. P. 55 ; 15 C. B. N. S. 316 : *Bubb* v. *Yelverton, Ker's Claim,* 19 W. R. 739 ; 24 L. T. 822 : *Bubb* v. *Yelverton, Steel & Nicholl's Claim,* 39 L. J. Ch. 428; L. R. 9 Eq. 471 : *Re Lister,* 47 L. J. Bank. 100 ; 8 Ch. D. 754). And, "if a person employs another to bet for him in his (the agent's) own name, an authority to pay the bets if lost is coupled with the employment; and although *before the bet is made* the employment and authority are both revocable,—the moment the employment is fulfilled by the making of the bet, the authority to pay it if lost becomes irrevocable," and the liability of the principal is, consequently, irrevocable (per Hawkins, J., *Read* v. *Anderson,* 52 L. J. Q. B. 219 ; 13 Q. B. D. 779 : *Vth. Lilley* v. *Rankin,* 56 L. J. Q. B. 248 : *Cohen* v. *Kittell,* 58 L. J. Q. B. 241 ; 22 Q. B. D. 680 : *Seymour* v. *Bridge,* 54 L. J. Q. B. 347 ; 14 Q. B. D. 460 : *Perry* v. *Barnett,* 54 L. J. Q. B. 351, 446 ; 15 Q. B. D. 388). *Vh.* 5 & 6 W. 4, c. 41.

GARBLE.—*V.* Termes de la Ley.

GARDEN.—In *R.* v. *Hodges* (Moo. & M. 341), the jury (after being directed by Parke, J.), found that a piece of ground chiefly used to grow grafted seedling pear-trees for sale (though there were also a few currant and raspberry bushes on it, and a crop of potatoes and cabbages had in the preceding summer been grown amongst the pear-trees), was not a "Garden," but was a "Nursery Ground" only, within s. 43, 7 & 8 G. 4, c. 29. *Vf. Ex p. Hammond,* 14 L. J. Bank. 14 ; D. G. 93 ; 9 Jur. 358.
V. Market Garden.

GAS.—Under a Fire Insurance excepting damage by explosion "except explosion *by Gas,*" the insurer is not liable for an explosion of Gas created incidentally by the chemicals used in the works of the insured (*Stanley* v. *Western Insrce.,* 37 L. J. Ex. 73 ; L. R. 3 Ex. 71 ; 17 L. T. 513 ; 16 W. R. 369). In that case Kelly, C.B., said,—"Strictly and philosophically speaking it is Gas ; but so are the component parts of the water of the ocean in their strict, philosophical and physical sense. But it appears in this case, and, without any statement to that effect, we know of our own knowledge, that though steam and vapour and substances of that description which find their way into the atmosphere strictly speaking are Gas, they do not pass in ordinary parlance by the name of Gas. Therefore construing the Policy on the principle that these parties expressed themselves in the ordinary language, not only of men of business but even of scientific men when dealing with matters of this description, I think that *the Company were not to be liable for any explosion unless occasioned by Illuminating Gas.*"

GATEWAY.—By a grant of "the exclusive use" of a "Gateway" (with defined dimensions), not merely a right of way, but the right to use the gateway for all lawful purposes passed (*Reilly* v. *Booth*, 34 S. J. 250). *V.* WAY.

GAVEL-ERTH: GAVEL-RIP.—*V.* BENERTH.

GENERAL.—*V.* SPECIFIC.

GENERAL AVERAGE.—"The term 'General Average' is used indiscriminately, sometimes to denote the kind of loss which gives a claim to general average contribution, and sometimes to denote such contribution itself; in order to prevent confusion it is better to use the term General Average Loss when speaking of the former, and General Average Contribution when speaking of the latter" (2 Arnould on Mar. Insrce, 1 Ed. 877; *Va.* 2 Ib., 5 Ed. 812; Lowndes, 210, n. (*p.*); Maude & P. 425 *et seq.*).

V. GENERAL AVERAGE CONTRIBUTION: G. A. LOSS: G. A. SACRIFICE: PARTICULAR AVERAGE: AVERAGE.

GENERAL AVERAGE CONTRIBUTION.—"The object of General Average Contribution is to indemnify the person making the general average sacrifice against so much of the loss caused directly thereby as does not fall to his own proportionate share" (per Bowen, L.J., *Svensden* v. *Wallace*, 53 L. J. Q. B. 393; 13 Q. B. D. 84: affd. 54 L. J. Q. B. 497; 10 App. Ca. 404).

GENERAL AVERAGE LOSS.—"A General Average Loss may be defined to be a loss arising out of extraordinary sacrifices made, or extraordinary expenses incurred, for the joint benefit of ship and cargo" (per Brett, M.R., *Svensden* v. *Wallace*, 13 Q. B. D. 74; 53 L. J. Q. B. 387, citing Arnould on Mar. Insrce.: *Svensden* v. *Wallace*, affd. 10 App. Ca. 404; 54 L. J. Q. B. 497).

GENERAL AVERAGE PER FOREIGN STATEMENT.—"Policies on Cargoes destined to foreign ports sometimes contain a provision that the underwriter is 'to pay General Average as per Foreign Statement if so made up,' or to the like effect. Where this is inserted, the underwriters are bound by a foreign adjustment in accordance with the law in force where it is made, although its effect may be to treat as General Average, what, according to English law, would be Particular Average" (1 Maude & P. 492, n. (*g*), citing *Harris* v. *Scaramanga*, L. R. 7 C. P. 481; 41 L. J. C. P. 170: *Hendricks* v. *Australasian Insrce.*, L. R. 9 C. P. 460; 43 L. J. C. P. 188: *Mavro* v. *Ocean Mar. Insrce.*, L. R. 9 C. P. 595; 10 Ib. 414; 44 L. J. C. P. 229).

In the lastly cited case, *Mavro* v. *Ocean Mar. Insrce.*, Cockburn, C.J., said, "In a policy of Marine Insurance 'General Average as per Foreign Statement' appears to be this: the underwriter is only to be liable for a general average, but what is general average is to be determined by the law of the foreign place to which the ship is bound."

GENERAL AVERAGE SACRIFICE.—"A General Average

Sacrifice is an extraordinary sacrifice, voluntarily made in the hour of peril for the common preservation of ship and cargo" (per Bowen, L.J., *Svensden* v. *Wallace,* 53 L. J. Q. B. 393; 13 Q. B. D. 84: affd. 54 L. J. Q. B. 497; 10 App. Ca. 404).

GENERAL CONTRACTORS.—"General Contractors," as one of the objects of a Company as stated in its Memorandum, will be controlled by the other objects in association with which the phrase is used (*Ashbury Co.* v. *Riché,* 44 L. J. Ex. 185; L. R. 7 H. L. 653).

GENERAL EXPENSES.—S. 229, P. H. Act, 1875; *V. Lancashire & Yorkshire Ry.* v. *Bolton,* 5 Times Rep. 610.

GENERAL INTEREST.—The mere question as to whether a particular person has committed perjury, or whether otherwise there be a question of individual character, is not "of General or Public Interest" so as to justify an order for costs on the higher scale under s. 5, 45 & 46 V. c. 57 (*R.* v. *City of London Court,* 56 L. J. Q. B. 79; 18 Q. B. D. 105; 55 L. T. 736; 35 W. R. 123).

V. PUBLIC INTEREST.

GENERAL LINE OF BUILDINGS.—"General Line of Buildings," s. 75, Metrop. Man. Act, 1862; *V. Barlow* v. *St. Mary Abbott,* 55 L. J. Ch. 680; 11 App. Ca. 257; 55 L. T. 221; 34 W. R. 521; 50 J. P. 691.

The decision of the Superintending Architect as provided in the section cited, is conclusive as to the General Line of Buildings (*Spackman* v. *Plumstead,* 54 L. J. M. C. 81; 10 App. Ca. 229). *Vf. Gilbert* v. *Wandsworth,* 5 Times Rep. 31.

GENERAL OR QUARTER SESSIONS.—This phrase, 3 & 4 W. & M. c. 11; s. 6, 8 & 9 W. 3, c. 30; s. 4, 17 G. 2, c. 38; s. 14, 5 G. 4, c. 83; means, even in London and Middlesex, the Quarter Sessions only (*R.* v. *London Jus.,* 15 East, 632: *R.* v. *Middlesex Jus.,* 12 L. J. M. C. 134; 4 Q. B. 807).

V. QUARTER SESSIONS.

GENERAL WORDS.—General Words in a Conveyance are not to be construed as merely passing Easements, but must be construed "like any other words with reference to what the words are intended to mean" (per Fry, J., *Willis* v. *Watney,* 51 L. J. Ch. 181: *V.* YARDS).

Sometimes the phrase "General Words" refers to those just mentioned, and sometimes describes a class of things,—*e.g.* "personal estate" (Elph. 186, n.).

As to the effect of express words upon rights conferred by s. 6, Conv. & L. P. Act, 1881; *V. Birmingham Bank* v. *Ross,* 57 L. J. Ch. 601; 38 Ch. D. 295; 59 L. T. 609; 36 W. R. 914.

GENERALLY.—"And *generally* do all such acts and things *in relation to* his property . . . as may be reasonably required:"—This obligation on a bankrupt (prescribed by s. 24 (2), Bankry. Act, 1883), does not require him to submit to a medical examination with a view to an insurance on his life, and thereby the better to realize a contingent reversionary interest belonging to him (*Board of Trade* v. *Block,* 58 L. J. Q. B. 113 ; 13 App. Ca. 570 ; 4 Times Rep. 770 : *Vf.* CONDUCT). Fry, L.J., when that case (nom. *Re Betts,* 56 L. J. Q. B. 370 ; 19 Q. B. D. 39) was in the Court of Appeal, said, "The most anxious desire is exhibited by the legislature to prevent its special words limiting the generality of its general words, by its use of the word 'generally,'" and therefore that the bankrupt was bound to submit to the examination ; but in the H. L., Halsbury, L. C., dissented from that view, and said that the examination was not an act "in relation to" the bankrupt's property.

GENTLEMAN.—"According to Sir T. Smith, this title is applied generally to those who have nothing to do, and can 'live idly'" (per Pollock, C.B., *Allen* v. *Thompson,* 25 L. J. Ex. 250 ; 1 H. & N. 15: *Va. Spaddacini* v. *Treacy,* 21 L. R. Ir. 553).

Therefore, for the purposes of the Bills of Sale Acts, neither of the following is correctly described as "Gentleman ;"—

A Clerk in the Audit Office (*Allen* v. *Thompson,* sup.),

An Attorney or an Attorney's Clerk (*Tuton* v. *Sanoner,* 27 L. J. Ex. 293 ; 3 H. & N. 280 : *Brodrick* v. *Scale,* 40 L. J. C. P. 130 ; L. R. 6 C. P. 98),

An Attorney's Clerk out of regular employment, but engaged in making out bills for a firm of solicitors (*Beales* v. *Tennant,* 29 L. J. Q. B. 188),

A Buyer of Silks (*Adams* v. *Graham,* 12 W. R. 282; 33 L. J. Q. B. 71).

But each of the following has been held to be correctly described as "Gentleman," *quà* B. of S. Acts ;—

One who has never had an occupation (*Gray* v. *Jones,* 13 C. B. N. S. 743),

A Medical Student who had, for a short time, acted as a surgeon's assistant but for 6 months had been in no business (*Bath* v. *Sutton,* 27 L. J. Ex. 388 ; nom. *Sutton* v. *Bath,* 3 H. & N. 382),

A Coal Agent who, having been dismissed, was, at the time, out of employ (*Morewood* v. *South Yorkshire Ry.,* 28 L. J. Ex. 114; 3 H. & N. 798 : *Va. London & Westminster Loan Co.* v. *Chase,* 31 L. J. C. P. 314; 12 C. B. N. S. 730),

A person who had been, but had ceased to be, a Proctor's Clerk and was occasionally collecting debts, but who lived chiefly on an allowance from his mother (*Smith* v. *Cheese,* 45 L. J. C. P. 156 ; 1 C. P. D. 60).

"Gentleman" is an insufficient description of a deponent to the fitness of a new trustee (*Re Orde,* 52 L. J. Ch. 832 ; 24 Ch. D. 271).

"Gentleman," in a description of a transferee of Shares ; *V. Re Humber Iron Co., Williams' Case,* 1 Ch. D. 576.

GET.—To "Get" Minerals (or to "Get Materials," s. 4, 5 & 6 W. 4, c. 50), is, it seems, synonymous with to "Win" them (*Ramsden* v. *Yeates,*

50 L. J. M. C. 135; 6 Q. B. D. 583; 29 W. R. 628; 44 L. T. 612: *Vh. Jowett* v. *Spencer*, 17 L. J. Ex. 367; 1 Ex. 647). *V.* WIN: WORKABLE.

GIFT.—"This word (Gift), importing no more than the transferring of the property of a thing from one to another, is of larger extent than a Feoffment, which is always applied to an immoveable thing; for this is often applied to moveable things also" (Touch. 227).

Conveyance by gift, *donatio*, was formerly the apt mode for creating an entail (Ib., 228, in note by Hilliard to 6 Ed.). For full information on the history of the use and the effect of the word "Give" in Conveyances of Real Property, *V.* note 1 to 384 a, Co. Litt. 18 Ed. by Harg. & Butl. But now in Deeds, executed after the 1st Oct., 1845, "Give" will not imply any covenant in law in respect of any tenement or hereditament except so far as it may do so by force of some special Act of Parliament (s. 4, 8 & 9 V. c. 106). The late Mr. Joshua Williams stated that he was "not aware of any Act of Parliament by force of which the word 'Give' implies a covenant" (Wms. R. P. 368: *Vf.* Dart, 635).

V. GRANT: CONVEYANCE.

GILD.—"'Gild' hath divers significations, as sometimes a Tribute, other times an Amercement, thirdly a Fraternity or Company . . . by the King's license" (Termes de la Ley).

GILD AND SILVER.—"'Gild' and 'Silver,' as applied to coin, include casing with gold or silver respectively, and washing and colouring by any means whatsoever with any wash or materials capable of producing the appearance of gold or silver respectively" (Steph. Cr. 310, stating s. 1, 24 & 25 V. c. 99).

GIN.—"Gin," sold simply as such, must not be reduced more than 35 degrees under proof (Sale of Food and Drugs Act Amendment Act, 1879, 42 & 43 V. c. 30, s. 6); but there is no offence in selling it when reduced below that standard, if the purchaser have notice that it is sold "as diluted spirits. No alcoholic strength guaranteed" (*Gage* v. *Elsey*, 52 L. J. M. C. 44; 10 Q. B. D. 518: *Webb* v. *Knight*, 46 L. J. M. C. 264; 2 Q. B. D. 530).

In Mining, "a 'Gin' is a windlass fixed in the ground, and worked *by a horse* for the purpose of drawing materials from the mine" (MacS. 246, n. 8; *Cp.* WIMSEY).

GIRDLAND.—The Saxon name for YARD-LAND: "the Saxons called it *girdland*, and now the *g* is turned to a *y*" (Co. Litt. 5 a).

GIVE.—*V.* GIVEN: GIFT: GRANT.

GIVEN.—Goods "*given* in parochial relief," s. 77, 4 & 5 W. 4, c. 76, mean goods gratuitously supplied for the purpose of parochial relief, though only by way of loan (*Davies* v. *Harvey*, 43 L. J. M. C. 121; L. R. 9 Q.B.433).

Notice to be "given," may be oral, *V.* SERVED; if by post, *V.* BY POST.

"Given," as a participle, is doubtful in its tense,—it may refer to the past or the future; as in a guarantee made "in consideration of the credit given by A. to B," on which Pollock, C.B., and Martin, B. (diss. Bramwell, B.), decided that there was a good consideration stated, because "given" referred to future credit (*Broom* v. *Batchelor*, 25 L. J. Ex. 299; 1 H. & N. 255). Pollock, C.B. said,—"the word 'given' is indefinite in point of time. It is, no doubt, a perfect participle; but it may mean perfect past, perfect present, or perfect future:" and he seems to have thought the latter its *primâ facie* meaning. On the other hand, Bramwell, B., said,—"'Given' is a participle, and, *primâ facie*, it must have its primary meaning, namely, 'already given.'" *V.* May be.

GLASS.—S. 1, Carriers' Act, 1830; *V. Owen* v. *Burnett*, 2 Cr. & M. 353; 4 Tyr. 133: *Glover* v. *Lond. & S. W. Ry.*, 37 L. J. Q. B. 57; L. R. 3 Q. B. 25.

GLEBE.—"Glebe" as used in Church Building Act, 43 G. 3, c. 108; *V. Re Randell*, 57 L. J. Ch. 899; 38 Ch. D. 213; 58 L. T. 626; 36 W. R. 543.

GLYN.—*V.* Combe.

GOD.—*V.* Act of God.

GOD'S LAW.—The degrees of consanguinity within which marriages are prohibited by "God's Law," as mentioned in 32 H. 8, c. 38, are those enumerated in 25 H. 8, c. 22, and 28 H. 8, c. 7 (*R.* v. *Chadwick*, 17 L. J. M. C. 33; 11 Q. B. 173).

GODLY LEARNING.—In a Deed made in 1549, a trust for the promotion of "Godly Learning," means that the instruction to be given is to be in conformity with the doctrines of the Protestant Church of England as by law established (*Re Ilminster School*, 2 D. G. & J. 535; nom. *Baker* v. *Lee*, 30 L. J. Ch. 625; 8 H. L. Ca. 495).

"If land or money be given for maintaining '*the Worship of God*' (*A.-G.* v. *Pearson*, 3 Mer. 409), or the promotion of '*Godly Learning*' (*Re Ilminster School*, sup.), and nothing more is said, the Court will execute the trust in favour of the established form of religion; and dissenters cannot be appointed trustees" (Lewin, 533, citing *Re Stafford Charities*, 25 Bea. 28; 27 L. J. Ch. 381: *Re Ilminster School*, sup.: *A.-G.* v. *Clifton*, 32 Bea. 596). It was however held in the lastly cited case, that the instruction was open to scholars of every denomination.

GODLY PREACHERS.—A bequest to "Godly Preachers of Christ's Holy Gospel," may be explained by parol (*Shore* v. *Wilson*, 9 Cl. & F. 356; 11 Sim. 592; 7 Jur. 781).

GOING TO.—In reference to the phrase of "going to or returning from" certain places and duties, that so frequently recurred in the clause giving exemptions from Turnpike Tolls (s. 32, 3 G. 4, c. 126), it may be useful to call attention to *Harrison* v. *Brough* (6 T. R. 706), where a horse ridden by its owner to *fetch* cattle from pasture, was held not be within such an exemption, under "Cattle going to or returning from pasture," or "Horses *attending* cattle returning from pasture."

GOLD.—"Gold," s. 1, 30 & 31 V. c. 90, does not mean pure gold, but merely what in common parlance is called gold (*Young* v. *Cook*, 47 L. J. M. C. 28; 3 Ex. D. 101).

V. Metals.

GOOD.—The phrase "*good* consideration" is sometimes used as synonymous with "*meritorious* consideration," which is good-for-nothing (Wms. P. P. 67). But in the statutes of Elizabeth, the one (13 E. c. 5) for the protection of creditors, and the other (27 E. c. 4) for the protection of purchasers,—"good" means *valuable* consideration (*Twyne's Case*, 3 Rep. 81, 83: *Vf. Re Moroney*, 21 L. R. Ir. 54). Yet the quantum of value required by the latter of those statutes is very different from that required by the former. Under 27 E. c. 4, the valuable consideration, if genuine, will not be put into the judicial scales to be weighed as against the property conveyed; and therefore the obligation of the lessee's covenants is a "good" consideration for the assignment of leaseholds so far as the 27 E. is concerned (*Price* v. *Jenkins*, 46 L. J. Ch. 805; 5 Ch. D. 619: *Re Lulham*, 53 L. J. Ch. 928; 32 W. R. 1013; 33 Ib. 788: *Va. Schreiber* v. *Dinkel*, 54 L. J. Ch. 241: *Harris* v. *Tubb*, 42 Ch. D. 79). But the doctrine of *Price* v. *Jenkins* does not apply, even as regards the 27 E., if leaseholds be transferred by sub-demise at a merely nominal rent (*Shurmur* v. *Sedgwick*, 53 L. J. Ch. 87; 24 Ch. D. 597); and in no case is it applicable to the 13 E. c. 5, which was passed to prevent creditors being defeated or delayed, and in view of that statute, a consideration, though valuable, will not be "good" if substantially out of proportion to the property conveyed (*Ridler* v. *Ridler*, 52 L. J. Ch. 343; 22 Ch. D. 74: *Green* v. *Paterson*, 32 Ch. D. 104: *Va. Twyne's Case*, 3 Rep. 83: May on Fraudulent Dispositions, 2 Ed. 257–260). *V.* Valuable.

A bequest for the "good" of a place is a valid charitable bequest (*A.-G.* v. *Lonsdale*, 1 Sim. 105: *Va. A.-G.* v. *Webster*, L. R. 20 Eq. 483).

GOOD BARLEY.—*V.* Barley.

GOOD CAUSE.—The "Good Cause" which will enable the Judge to deprive a successful litigant of his costs in an action tried with a jury (Ord. 65, R. 1, R. S. C.) involves the idea of misconduct on his part in or in relation to the litigation, and whether any such "Good Cause" exists is a question on which an appeal lies (*Jones* v. *Curling*, 53 L. J. Q. B. 373; 13 Q. B. D. 262). But if any "good cause" exists, the Court of Appeal will not (probably cannot, *Huxley* v. *West Lond. Extn. Ry.*, inf.) interfere with the exercise of the Judge's discretion (*Williams* v. *Ward*, 55 L. J. Q. B.

566). Mis-statements, inviting the litigation, made by the successful litigant, is "Good Cause" for depriving him of costs (*Sutcliffe* v. *Smith,* 2 Times Rep. 881 : *Vf. Pool* v. *Lewin,* 1 Ib. 165 : *Harnett* v. *Vise,* 5 Ex. D. 307), and so is the making of an extravagant claim (*Huxley* v. *West Lond. Extn. Ry.,* 14 App. Ca. 26 ; 58 L. J. Q. B. 305 ; 60 L. T. 642).

A letter "Without Prejudice" cannot be looked at to show such "Good Cause" (*Walker* v. *Wilsher,* 58 L. J. Q. B. 501 ; 37 W. R. 723 ; 5 Times Rep. 649).

Vh. Obs. of Jessel, M.R., *Cooper* v. *Whittingham,* 49 L. J. Ch. 752 ; 15 Ch. D. 501 : *Pool* v. *Lewin,* 1 Times Rep. 165 ; and *V.* those cases cited per Brett, M.R., *Felix* v. *Gordon,* 1 Times Rep. 97. *Va. Pearman* v. *Burdett-Coutts,* 3 Times Rep. 719 : *Rooke* v. *Czarnikow,* 4 Ib. 669 : *Macgregor* v. *Clay,* 4 Ib. 715 : *Moore* v. *Gill,* 4 Ib. 738 : *Myers* v. *Financial News,* 5 Ib. 42 : *Beckett* v. *Stiles,* 5 Ib. 88 : *Wilts Bank* v. *Hammond,* 5 Ib. 196 : *Barnes* v. *Maltby,* 5 Ib. 207 : *Wood* v. *Cox,* 5 Ib. 272 : *Marriage* v. *Wilson,* 53 J. P. 120.

The corresponding phrase in Ireland is "Special Cause," s. 53, 40 & 41 V. c. 57 : *V.* SPECIAL.

V. CAUSE : DUE CAUSE.

GOOD CHARACTER.—A certificate that an applicant for a license is of "Good Character" is not false because he is cohabiting with a woman without being married to her (*Leader* v. *Yell,* 33 L. J. M. C. 231 ; 16 C. B. N. S. 584). In that case Erle, J., said :—"'Character' must mean the estimation in which a man is held by those who are acquainted with him. You cannot pry into the secrets of a man's conduct ; if you could do so, there might be many circumstances which would palliate the cohabitation."

GOOD CONDITION.—The question as to what is "Good Condition" of a demised premises, is "to be viewed with regard to the class of tenement to which the demised one belongs" (per Fry, J., *Saner* v. *Bilton,* 47 L. J. Ch. 270 ; 7 Ch. D. 815).

GOOD FAITH.—"In Good Faith," s. 48 (2), Bankry. Act, 1883,—*i.e.,* that a person taking a preference from a bankrupt "must not be conscious himself of an intention to favour one creditor above another" (per Ld. Hatherley, *Butcher* v. *Stead,* L. R. 7 H. L. 849 ; 44 L. J. Bank. 134).

"In Good Faith," in s. 46 (3), Ib., would seem to mean, innocent of the knowledge, and of the means of knowledge, that there is an adverse bankruptcy (*Lucas* v. *Dicker,* 49 L. J. C. P. 415 ; 50 Ib. 190 ; 5 C. P. D. 150 ; 6 Q. B. D. 84).

"A thing is to be deemed to be done in Good Faith, within the meaning of this Act, where it is in fact done *honestly,* whether it is done negligently or not" (s. 90, Bills of Ex. Act, 1882). "That section is obviously founded on the distinction pointed out in *Jones* v. *Gordon* (47 L. J. Bank. 1; 2 App. Ca. 616; 37 L. T. 477), by Ld. Blackburn, between the case of a person who was 'honestly blundering and careless,' and the case of a person who has acted not honestly, that is, not necessarily with the intention to defraud, but not with an honest belief that the transaction was a valid one, and that he was dealing with a good Bill. Ld. Blackburn there, with regard to the person on whom the onus of proof lies in such a case, says,—'If the facts and circumstances are such that the jury, or whoever has to try the case, came to the conclusion that he was not honestly blundering and careless, but that he must have had a suspicion that there was something wrong, and that he refrained from asking questions because he thought in his own mind—'I suspect there is something wrong, and if I ask questions and make further enquiry, it will be no longer my suspecting it, but my knowing it, and then I shall not be able to recover,'—I think that is dishonesty.' I think that that is the dishonesty to which the Act refers where the word 'honestly' is used" (per Denman, J., *Tatam* v. *Hasler*, 23 Q. B. D. 345 ; 58 L. J. Q. B. 433).

V. Boná fide.

GOOD SAFETY.—*V.* Safety.

GOOD TITLE.—"Good Title," in a contract for sale of realty, means such a title as will be forced on a purchaser in an action for specific performance, and as would be an answer to an action of ejectment by any claimant (*Jeakes* v. *White*, 21 L. J. Ex. 265 ; 6 Ex. 873).

GOODS.—"If one devise to J. S. all his 'Goods,' or all his 'Chattels' by either of these is devised as much as by both of them" (Touch. 447 : *Vf.* Wms. Exs. 1184 : Goods and Chattels).

The jurisdiction given to County Courts (by s. 2, 32 & 33 V. c. 51) to try claims arising "in relation to the carriage of *Goods* in any ship" is confined to claims respecting merchandize, and does not include claims respecting personal luggage (*R.* v. *City of London Court*, 53 L. J. Q. B. 28 ; 12 Q. B. D. 115 ; 51 L. T. 197).

Though a dog, not being the subject of Larceny at Common Law, is not a "Chattel" within s. 88, 24 & 25 V. c. 96 (*R.* v. *Robinson*, 28 L. J. M. C. 58 ; Bell, C. C. 34) ; yet a dog is "Goods" within s. 40, 2 & 3 V. c. 71 (*R.* v. *Slade*, 57 L. J. M. C. 120 ; 21 Q. B. D. 433 ; 59 L. T. 640 ; 37 W. R. 141 ; 52 J. P. 599 ; 4 Times Rep. 777).

Certificates of Ry. Stock are not "Goods" within the Factors Act, 5 & 6 V. c. 39 (*Freeman* v. *Appleyard*, 32 L. J. Ex. 175).

In s. 16, Stat. of Frauds, "Goods" includes Leaseholds ; and it has been suggested that it bears a similarly wide meaning in s. 1, Mercantile Law Amendment Act, 1856, which is *in pari materiâ* (Elphinstone & Clark on Searches, 69). *Cp.* Goods, Wares and Merchandize.

V. Chose in Action.

"Goods, Materials or Provisions ;" *V.* Use.

"Goods or Burden ;" *V.* Burden.

"Goods supplied ;" *V.* Supplied.

GOODS AND CHATTELS.—These words are synonymous (Wms. P. P. Intro. Ch.). A *Bequest* of all testator's "Goods and Chattels" "doth pass all his estate, active and passive (except land of inheritance and free-hold estates and such things as depend thereon,) as Leases for years, Gold, Silver, Plate, Household Stuff, Cattle, Corn, Debts and the like; and if one devise to J. S. all his 'goods' or all his 'chattels,' by either of these is devised as much as by both of them" (Touch. 447). But in such a connection as a bequest of "*Furniture,* goods and chattels," the latter words would pass only such things as are *ejusdem generis* with "Furniture," and would not include jewellery, guns, tricycles and scientific instruments (*Manton* v. *Tabois,* 54 L. J. Ch. 1008; 30 Ch. D. 92), still less a sum of money (*Gibbs* v. *Lawrence,* 30 L. J. Ch. 170: *Vf. Lamphier* v. *Despard,* 2 Dr. & War. 59; *Timewell* v. *Perkins,* 2 Atk. 103: *Roberts* v. *Kuffin,* Ib. 113: *Smart* v. *Bute,* 11 Ves. 656). *Growing Crops,* as between exor and heir, or between the exor and remainder-man, and in most other respects, are looked upon as "Chattels" (Wms. Exs. 713-715; but *Vth.* the obs. of Brett, J., *Brantom* v. *Griffits,* 45 L. J. C. P. 592). *Vf.* as to this phrase in Wills, 1 Jarm. 751 *et seq.;* Wms. Exs. 1184.

But on the other hand whilst a *Grant,* by deed *inter vivos,* of all one's "Goods and Chattels" comprises generally speaking such property as would pass by a similar bequest (Touch. 97); yet such a grant does *not* comprise *Leases for Years* (*Portman* v. *Willis,* Cro. Eliz. 386; and *Vh. Harrison* v. *Blackburn,* 34 L. J. C. P. 109; 17 C. B. N. S. 678, qualifying *Ringer* v. *Cann,* 7 L. J. Ex. 108; 3 M. & W. 343); nor *Choses in Action* (Touch. 98: Add. T. 422: but qy. would this be so, now that Choses in Action are assignable? *V.* note to p. 97, 6 Ed. Touch.); "nor *Things of Pleasure,* such as hawks, hounds, &c." (Add. T. 422). This last negative is possibly founded, though not so stated, on the dictum at p. 98, Touch.; but Termes de la Ley (*Catals*) says, that Hawks and Hounds are not accounted "catals," "*for they are feræ naturæ.*"

Equally under Deed or Will, "Goods and Chattels" would pass property whether held in severalty or in common (Touch. 98).

Though the Touchstone says that "Debts" pass by a bequest of "Goods and Chattels," yet *Vh. Hertford* v. *Lowther,* 7 Bea. 1; 13 L. J. Ch. 41, and cases cited in the judgment. "*Choses in Action* were held to be included in the expression 'Goods and Chattels' in all the Bankruptcy Acts from the time of James I. downwards," (per Lindley, L.J., *Colonial Bank* v. *Whinney,* 55 L. J. Ch 590, a statement not affected by the reversal of the judgment in that case by the H. L. 56 Ib. 43; 11 App. Ca. 426; 55 L. T. 362; 34 W. R. 705); but the same expression in 13 Eliz. c. 5, s. 1, did not include Choses in Action (*Dundas* v. *Dutens,* 1 Ves. jun. 196. *V.* 1 & 2 V. c. 110, s. 12).

A newspaper has been held to be within "Goods and Chattels" in a Bankruptcy Act (*Re Baldwin, Ex p. Foss,* 27 L. J. Bank. 17); so of a Trade Mark (*Ex p. Young,* Sebastian, Tr. Mark Ca. 537).

"Goods and Chattels," 13 Eliz. c. 5, "are words of very extensive signification, and undoubtedly comprise both property tangible, and property which is not tangible" (per Turner, L. J., *Re Baldwin*, 27 L. J. Bank. 22 ; 2 D. G. & J. 230).

"Money, Goods or Chattels," Ord. 57, R. 1, R. S. C., authorising Interpleader Issue, includes, in "Chattels," Choses in Action, *e.g.*, Shares (*Robinson* v. *Jenkins*, 34 S. J. 210 ; 6 Times Rep. 158.).

"In an indictment *Bills of Exchange or Promissory Notes* ought not in strict propriety to be described as 'Chattels.' But for almost all purposes, they are comprehended under the general words 'Goods and Chattels,' or either of them, and as such are forfeitable to the Crown, and may be the subject of reputed ownership or fraudulent transfer" (Byles, 4, and cases there cited).

"By the Common Law, no estate of inheritance or freehold is comprehended under these words *bona* or *catalla*" (Co. Litt. 118 b).

In the frequent phrase "Goods, Chattels and EFFECTS," the last word is the most comprehensive.

V. CHATTELS : GOODS : HOUSEHOLD.

GOODS, WARES AND MERCHANDIZES.—When the substance of a contract is a chattel or chattels to be sold and delivered by one party to the other, the subject matter is within "Goods, Wares and Merchandizes" as used in s. 17, Stat. of Frauds (*Atkinson* v. *Bell*, 8 B. & C. 277 : *Lee* v. *Griffin*, 30 L. J. Q. B. 252 ; 1 B. & S. 272). Therefore a contract to supply a properly fitting set of artificial teeth is within the phrase, for "there can hardly be said to be more skill in fitting teeth than in fitting a pair of breeches" (per Crompton, J., *Lee* v. *Griffin*, sup.). But if the substance of the contract be work and labour,—*e.g.*, an Artist painting a picture, a Solicitor preparing a deed, or a Printer printing a book, or an Engineer making plans and models for an intended patent—then the subject matter is not within this phrase (*Clay* v. *Yates*, 25 L. J. Ex. 237 ; 1 H. & N. 73 : *Lee* v. *Griffin*, sup. : *Grafton* v. *Armitage*, 15 L. J. C. P. 20 ; 2 C. B. 336). So again though Fixtures are not within the phrase (*Hallen* v. *Runder*, 3 L. J. Ex. 260 ; 1 Cr. M. & R. 266 : *Lee* v. *Gaskell*, 45 L. J. Q. B. 540 ; 1 Q. B. D. 700) ; yet "Timber and Growing Crops are so, because the clear intention being that they shall be severed, they are taken, by a fiction of law, as being actually severed" (per Cockburn, C.J., *Lee* v. *Gaskell*, sup., referring to *Smith* v. *Surman*, 9 B. & C. 561 : *Parker* v. *Staniland*, 11 East, 362 : *Mayfield* v. *Wadsley*, 3 B. & C. 357 ; *Vf.* Rosc. N. P. 285). *A fortiori* trees felled, are within the phrase (*Acraman* v. *Morrice*, 19 L. J. C. P. 57 ; 8 C. B. 449).

Choses in action are not within this phrase (Benj. Part ii. Ch. ii.: per Denman, C.J., *Humble* v. *Mitchell*, 9 L. J. Q. B. 30); therefore neither Shares in a Joint-Stock Company (*Humble* v. *Mitchell*, 9 L. J. Q. B. 29 ; 11 A. & E. 205), or in a Canal Company (*Latham* v. *Barber*, 6 T. R. 76), or in a

Railway (*Bowlby* v. *Bell,* 16 L. J. C. P. 18 ; 3 C. B. 284), or in a Mining Company (*Watson* v. *Spratley,* 24 L. J. Ex. 53 ; 10 Ex. 222) are included therein ; nor are the Bonds or Certificates of Foreign Stock (*Heseltine* v. *Siggers,* 18 L. J. Ex. 166 ; 1 Ex. 856), or the Certificates of ordinary Stock or Shares (*Freeman* v. *Appleyard,* 32 L. J. Ex. 175).

Shares are not "Goods, Wares or Merchandize," within the exemption of Agreements from Stamp Duty (*Knight* v. *Barber,* 16 L. J. Ex. 18 ; 16 M. & W. 66).

As to that phrase as used in the Eau Brink Act, 35 G. 3, c. 77 ; *V. Coulton* v. *Ambler,* 14 L. J. Ex. 10 ; 13 M. & W. 403.

V. STONE.

GOODWILL.—"'Goodwill' may be taken in the words of Ld. Eldon (in *Cruttwell* v. *Lye,* 17 Ves. 335), 'as the probability that the old customers will resort to the old place'" (per Cotton, L.J., *Pearson* v. *Pearson,* 54 L. J. Ch. 41 ; 27 Ch. D. 145). The "Goodwill" of a business means, every affirmative advantage,—as contrasted with negative advantage,—that has been acquired in carrying on the business, whether connected with the premises of the business, or its name or style, and everything connected with or carrying with it the benefit of the business (per Wood, V.-C., *Churton* v. *Douglas,* 28 L. J. Ch. 845 ; John. 174 ; 7 W. R. 365 : following *Cruttwell* v. *Lye,* sup. ; Ld. Eldon's order in *Cook* v. *Collingridge,* Jac. 607 ; *V.* 27 Bea. 456 n : *Kennedy* v. *Lee,* 3 Mer. 441. *Vf. Johnson* v. *Helleley,* 34 L. J. Ch. 179 ; 2 D. G. J. & S. 446 : *Shakle* v. *Baker,* 14 Ves. 468). "The name of a FIRM is a very important part of the Goodwill" (per Wood, V.-C., *Churton* v. *Douglas,* sup.) ; and therefore the vendor of a goodwill must not carry on business in the name appertaining to such goodwill or hold out his new enterprise as the old business (Ib.).

But in the absence of express restriction, the Vendor may, notwithstanding the sale of his "Goodwill," continue to deal with his old customers (*Leggott* v. *Barrett,* 51 L. J. Ch. 90 ; 15 Ch. D. 306 ; 28 W. R. 962 : over-ruling the contrary proposition by Jessel, M.R., in *Ginesi* v. *Cooper,* 49 L. J. Ch. 601 ; 14 Ch. D. 596) : and although the weight of authority is against his being allowed to *solicit* the custom of the old customers (per Ld. Romilly, M.R., *Labouchere* v. *Dawson,* 41 L. J. Ch. 427 ; L. R. 13 Eq. 322 ; 20 W. R. 309 : per Jessel, M.R., and Brett, L.J., *Leggott* v. *Barrett,* sup. : per Lush and Lindley, L.JJ., *Walker* v. *Mottram,* 51 L. J. Ch. 108 ; 19 Ch. D. 355 ; 30 W. R. 165 : per Fry, J., *Mogford* v. *Courtenay,* 29 W. R. 864 : and per Kay, J., and Lindley, L.J., *Pearson* v. *Pearson,* 54 L. J. Ch. 32 ; 27 Ch. D. 145 ; 32 W. R. 1006 :—as opposed to the doubts of James, L.J., in *Leggott* v. *Barrett,* sup., and to the jdgmts. of Baggallay and Cotton, L.JJ., in *Pearson* v. *Pearson,* sup.) ; yet as the judgments last referred to were those of a majority of the Court of Appeal which definitely and in terms over-ruled *Labouchere* v. *Dawson,* the doctrine of that latter case is no longer law, and, as a result, the Vendor of a Goodwill may, in the absence of express restriction, solicit his old customers to deal with him in regard to any new business he may start. *Vh. Vernon* v. *Hallam,* 56 L. J. Ch. 115 ; 34 Ch. D. 748.

The sale of a Goodwill by a Trustee in Bankry carries no implied restriction as against the bankrupt (*Walker* v. *Mottram,* sup.).

The term " Goodwill " seems inapplicable to a business,—*e.g.* that of a Solicitor,—depending upon personal trust and confidence (*Austen* v. *Boys,* 27 L. J. Ch. 243, 714 ; 2 D. G. & J. 626 ; 24 Bea. 598 : *Va.* per Jessel, M.R., *Arundell* v. *Bell,* 52 L. J. Ch. 537). And however that may be, clients' papers are not included in the sale of the " Goodwill " of a solicitor's business (*James* v. *James,* 33 S. J. 366).

Vh. Allan on Goodwill : Art., 34 S. J. 294.

V. Et Cetera : Plant : Share : Effects.

GORE.—" ' Gore, Fother, or Pyke.—Parcels in the common fields ; ' and they are called so, because they be broad in the one end and a sharp pyke in the other end ' " (Elph. 583, and authorities there cited).

GORS: GORT: GUORT.—*V.* Gurges.

GOTTEN.—*V.* Get: Mineral Gotten.

GOVERNING BODY.—*V.* Interpretation of " Governing Body " of an Endowed School as given in s. 7, 32 & 33 V. c. 56, controlled by context in *Christ's Hospital* v. *Charity Commrs.,* 62 L. T. 10.

GOVERNMENT.—A legacy to " Government " for the public benefit is to be disposed of under the sign manual of the Crown (*Newland* v. *A.-G.,* 3 Mer. 684 ; Wms. Exs. 1155).

V. Foreign Government.

GOVERNMENT CLERK.—A Clerk in the Admiralty is properly described as " Government Clerk," for purposes of Bills of Sale Acts (*Grant* v. *Shaw,* 41 L. J. Q. B. 305 ; L. R. 7 Q. B. 700).

GOVERNMENT SECURITIES.—Where a trust authorized investments " in the purchase of *Government* or East India Stocks or funds, Exchequer Bills or any other easily convertible securities," the word " Government " does not necessarily mean the British Government (per Jessel, M.R., *Sykes* v. *Beadon,* 48 L. J. Ch. 530; 11 Ch. D. 170). But a bequest of " Government Stock or Securities," will not include Indian Government, or Colonial, securities (*Re Hamilton,* 34 S. J. 251 ; 6 Times Rep. 173).

" Government Security " does not apply to Exchequer Bills (*Ex p. Chaplin,* 3 Y. & C. 397: *Knott* v. *Cottee,* 16 Bea. 77; 16 Jur. 752 : *Vf. Matthews* v. *Brise,* 6 Bea. 239 ; 12 L. J. Ch. 263) ; but the contrary was held in *Ex p. S. E. Ry.* (9 Jur. 650).

Vh. Lewin, 334 ; Watson, Eq. 1326.

V. Funds : Foreign Government : *Cp.* Public Securities.

GOVERNOR.—*V.* s. 18 (6), Interp. Act, 1889.

GRACE.—*V.* Days of Grace.

GRAIN.—"Other Grain," in a Charter-party; *V. Warren* v. *Peabody*, 19 L. J. C. P. 43; 8 C. B. 800.

GRAMMAR SCHOOL.—*V.* Free Grammar School.

GRANDCHILD.—Notwithstanding the opinion of Lord Northington to the contrary (*Hussey* v. *Berkley*, 2 Eden, 196), it seems now settled that *great* grand-children are not included in the word "grandchildren" (*Orford* v. *Churchill*, 3 Ves. & B. 59; stated and commented on, Wms. Exs. 1107: *Va. Arnold* v. *Congreve*, 1 R. & My. 209: *Sv. Strutt* v. *Finch*, 7 L. J. O. S. Ch. 176). A grand-child *by marriage* is not within the word (*Hussey* v. *Berkley*, sup.).

V. Child.

GRANGE.—"By the name of Grange, *Grangia*, a house or edifice, not onely where corne is stored up like as in barnes, but necessarie places for husbandrie also, as stables for hay and horses, and stables and sties for other cattell, and a *curtilage;* and the close wherein it standeth shall passe; and it is a French word and signifieth the same as we take it" (Co. Litt. 5 a; *V.* Spelm.). "Where land, meadow, and pasture, &c., belonging to such houses are called altogether by the name of a Grange, there perhaps by this word the whole may pass" (Touch. 93). "*V. Ognel's Case* (4 Rep. 48 b), where a farm was called Crewelfield Grange. In Lincolnshire and some of the northern counties every solitary farmhouse is called a grange: Tomlin's Law Dict." (Elph. 583).

GRANT.—"This word is taken largely, where any thing is granted or passed from one to another. And in this sense it doth comprehend feoffments, bargains and sales, gifts, leases, charges and the like; for he that doth give, or sell, doth grant also. And thus it is sometimes in writing or by deed, and sometimes it is by word without writing. But the word being taken more strictly and properly, it is the grant, conveyance, or gift by writing, of such an incorporeal thing *as lieth in grant, and not in livery,* and cannot be given or granted by word only without deed. Or it is the grant by such persons as cannot pass any thing from them but by deed, as the King, bodies corporate, &c. And this albeit it may be made by other words, yet it is most commonly made by this word (grant) as being most proper to this purpose" (Touch. 228). As regards that part of the above definition which is italicised, it is to be observed that, since the 1st Oct., 1845, all corporeal hereditaments (as well as those incorporeal) "lie in grant as well as in livery" (s. 2, 8 & 9 V. c. 106).

S. 49, Conv. & L. P. Act, 1881, contains the following clause;—"The word 'Grant' is not necessary in order to convey tenements or hereditaments, corporeal or incorporeal."

For the history of the use and effect of the words "Grant," and "Give," in Conveyances; *V.* n. 1 to 384 a, Co. Litt. 18 Ed., by Harg. & Butl.: *Clarke* v. *Samson*, 1 Ves. sen. 100: *Va.* Lewin, 441. But now in Deeds executed after the 1st Oct., 1845, "Grant" will not imply any covenant in law in respect of any tenement or hereditament except so far as it may do so by force of some special Act of Parliament (s. 4, 8 & 9 V. c. 106)—*e.g.* in Conveyances *by* Companies under Lands C. C. Act, 1845 (s. 132, 8 & 9 V. c. 18); or in Conveyances *to* the Governors of Queen Anne's Bounty (s. 22, 1 & 2 V. c. 20); or the words "grant, bargain and sell" in a Bargain and Sale registered under the Registry Acts for Yorkshire (6 Anne, c. 35, ss. 30, 34; 8 G. 2, c. 6, s. 35; replaced as from 1 Jan., 1885, by 47 & 48 V. c. 54).

V. GIFT.

Not "to grant away, assign or let, charge or dispose of," in a Covenant in Lease; *V. Croft* v. *Lumley*, 25 L. J. Q. B. 73, 223; 27 Ib. 321; 6 H. L. Ca. 672.

GRATUITY.—*V.* HANDSOME GRATUITY.

GRAVA.—"*Grava* signifieth a little wood, in old deeds, and *hirst* or *hurst* a wood; and so doth *holt* and *shawe*" (Co. Litt. 4 b).

GREAT CAUTION.—*V.* CAUTION.

GREAT MEN.—The exemption from Tithes of "Great Men or Noble Men" in 31 H. 8, c. 12, s. 16, did not comprise an ecclesiastical Magnate, *e.g.*, a Dean; for "Great Men" there, being in association with "Noblemen," comprise only Great Men of a "noble" kind (*Warden of St. Paul's* v. *The Dean*, 4 Price, 65).

GREATER.—*V.* THREE TIMES GREATER.

GREE.—Satisfaction for an offence (Termes de la Ley, citing 1 Ric. 2, c. 15).

GREEN HEWE.—A synonym for VERT (Termes de la Ley).

GREEN TEA.—*V. Roberts* v. *Egerton*, 43 L. J. M. C. 135; L. R. 9 Q. B. 494.

GRIEVANCE.—*V.* ANNOYANCE.

GRIEVED.—*V.* AGGRIEVED.

GRIEVOUS BODILY HARM.—*V.* INFLICT.

GROSS.—"Gross *Value* is different from Value. It is, though a convenient, an inaccurate expression, like 'gross profits.' The difference between what a thing costs and the larger sum it sells for is not profit, if the buying and selling are attended with expense to the trader. Value is net value" (per Ld. Bramwell, *Dobbs* v. *Grand Junc. Waterworks Co.*, 53 L. J. Q. B. 52 ; 9 App. Ca. 49).

In an Act authorising a Waterworks Company to levy rates on "the *Gross sum assessed to the Poor Rate* of the premises" they supply, that means the gross estimated rental, and not the rateable value (*Bristol Waterworks Co.* v. *Uren*, 54 L. J. M. C. 97 ; 15 Q. B. D. 637).

"*The Gross Estimated Rental*" for the purpose of the Union Assessment Committee Act, 1862 (25 & 26 V. c. 103), is "the rent at which the hereditament might reasonably be expected to let from year to year, free of all usual tenant's rates and taxes, and tithe commutation rent charge, if any" (s. 15).

"*The Gross Value*," for the purpose of the Valuation (Metropolis) Act, 1869 (32 & 33 V. c. 67), means "the annual rent which a tenant might reasonably be expected (taking one year with another) to pay for an hereditament, if the tenant undertook to pay all usual tenant's rates and taxes, and tithe commutation rent-charge (if any), and if the landlord undertook to bear the costs of the repairs and insurance, and the other expenses (if any) necessary to maintain the hereditament in a state to command that rent" (s. 4). As to the application of this section to a School Board school ; *V. R.* v. *London School Board*, 55 L. J. M. C. 169 ; 17 Q. B. D. 738 ; 55 L. T. 384 ; 34 W. R. 583 ; 50 J. P. 419.

V. Annual Value.

A thing or right "*In Gross*," is independent of anything else : *e.g.*, a Sum of Money in Gross as distinct from a Rent (Touch. 80), or a Common in Gross, as distinct from a Common Appendant or Appurtenant.

"Gross *Negligence*," "is the same thing as 'Negligence,' with the addition of a vituperative epithet" (per Rolfe, B., *Wilson* v. *Brett*, 11 M. & W. 115, 116 ; cited with approval by Willes, J., *Grill* v. *General Iron Screw Colliery Co.*, 35 L. J. C. P. 330 ; L. R. 1 C. P. 600 ; affd. 37 L. J. C. P. 205 ; L. R. 3 C. P. 476). Referring to this phrase, Erle, C.J., said (35 L. J. C. P. 324, 325), "I advisedly abstained from using a word to which I can attach no definite meaning ; and no one, as far as I know, ever was able to do so." *Vf. McCawley* v. *Furness Ry.*, 42 L. J. Q. B. 4 ; L. R. 8 Q. B. 57 : 1 Sm. L. C. 223.

GROUND.—"Same Ground ;" *V.* Same.

"Equitable grounds ;" *V.* Equitable.

GROUND RENT.—"By the expression 'Ground Rent,' if unexplained, is to be understood a rent less than the rack-rent of the premises : its proper meaning is the rent at which land is let for the purpose of improvement by building (*Stewart* v. *Alliston*, 1 Mer. 26 : *Sv. Bartlett* v. *Salmon*, 6 D. G. M. & G. 33 ; 26 L. T. O. S. 82 ; 4 W. R. 32 ; and *Vf. Lecoy* v. *Mogford*, 2 Jur. N. S. 1084 ; 4 W. R. 805) : but the expression is very carelessly used" (Dart, 138 : *V.* Sug. V. & P. 28, 29 : *Evans* v. *Robins*,

1 H. & C. 302 ; 2 Ib. 410 ; 31 L. J. Ex. 465 ; 33 Ib. 68 ; 6 L. T. 897 ; 10 W. R. 776 : *Langford* v. *Selmes*, 3 K. & J. 220). *V.* SECURED.

By a Devise of "Ground Rent," "not only the rent, but the reversion will pass" (1 Jarm. 797).

By a devise of "*Copyhold* Ground Rent," a copyhold estate held to pass (*Walker* v. *Shore*, 19 Ves. 387).

By a bequest of "*Leasehold* Ground Rent," not only the reserved rent, but also the reversionary leasehold interest, held to pass (*Kaye* v. *Laxon*, 1 Bro. C. C. 76).

GUARANTEED.—This word in a Charter Party "has no technical meaning. It is no more than 'I have promised;' and means probably that the ship shall be ready"—(or whatever be the thing guaranteed),—"provided she be not prevented by the excepted perils" (per Willes, J., *Barker* v. *M'Andrew*, 34 L. J. C. P. 194 ; 18 C. B. N. S. 759 ; cited with approval by Esher, M.R., *Nottebohm* v. *Richter*, 56 L. J. Q. B. 33 ; 18 Q. B. D. 66 ; 35 W. R. 300).

"Guaranteed," as a Trade Name ; *V. Symington* v. *Footman*, W. N. (87) 70 ; 56 L. T. 696.

GUARDIANS.—"Board of Guardians;" *V.* s. 16 (1), (3), Interp. Act, 1889.

GUEST.—An innkeeper's "Guest" is a TRAVELLER, who, by himself, or his beast, has been, however temporarily, accepted to, and remains under, hospitality within an Inn or its curtilage (*Calye's Case*, 1 Sm. L. C. 141, and cases there collected: *Strauss* v. *County Hotel Co.*, 53 L. J. Q. B. 25 ; 12 Q. B. D. 27 : Add. C. 303).

GUILD.—*V.* GILD.

GUN.—For the purposes of the Gun License Act, 1870 (33 & 34 V. c. 57), "Gun," includes a Firearm of any description, and an Air-gun or any other kind of gun from which any shot, bullet, or other missile can be discharged (s. 2). A small Toy Pistol is a "Firearm" within this definition (*Campbell* v. *Hadley*, 40 J. P. 756).

GURGES.—"*Gurges*, a deepe pit of water, a gors or gulfe, consisteth of water and land ; and therefore by the grant thereof by that name the soile doth passe . . . . In Domesday it is called *guort*, *gort*, and *gors* plurally : as for example, *de* 3 *gorz mille anguillæ*" (Co. Litt. 5 b : *Vf.* Termes de la Ley, *Gors*). "By the name of *Stagnum* a pool, or *Gurges* a gulf, the water, land, and fish in the water will pass" (Touch. 95).

This word is also used for "Weir" (Spelm. Gloss. *Gors*) ; and *V.* "Gurgites," "Gors," and "Wears" discussed by Willes, J., *Malcomson* v. *O'Dea*, 10 H. L. Ca. 619. *Vf.* Elph. 583 : KIDEL.

GUTTER.—*V.* DRAIN.

HAB—HAL

HABENDUM.—"When a man limits a thing before the Habendum, and afterwards says, *habendum* for years, or for Life, or in Fee, and does not name the thing in the Habendum, it shall be referred to the thing mentioned before the Habendum, and it is not necessary to repeat the thing again in the Habendum" (*Wrotesley* v. *Adams*, Plow. 196). *V.* To have and to hold.

HABITABLE REPAIR.—*V.* Repair.

HÂC RE.—*V.* In hâc re.

HACKNEY CARRIAGE.—"I think that a Hackney Carriage is a Carriage exposed for hire to the public, whether standing in the public street, or exposed for public use in a private gateway. The test is whether the Carriage is held out for the general accommodation of the public" (per Lush, J., *Bateson* v. *Oddy*, 43 L. J. M. C. 131 ; 30 L. T. 712 ; 22 W. R. 703). *Vh.* 1 & 2 W. 4, c. 22, s. 4 ; 6 & 7 V. c. 86, s. 2 : *Skinner* v. *Usher*, 41 L. J. M. C. 158 ; L. R. 7 Q. B. 423 : *Case* v. *Storey*, L. R. 4 Ex. 319 ; 38 L. J. M. C. 113. Ply.

For the purpose of the Excise License, a Public Omnibus is a "Hackney Carriage," and liable only to the lower duty of 15*s.* (*Hickman* v. *Birch*, 24 Q. B. D. 172 ; 6 Times Rep. 104).

HAD.—"Had" sometimes means "obtained," *e.g.*, "afore Execution had ;" *V.* Execution.

HAGA.—"In Domesday, a house in a city or burrough is called *haga ;* other houses are called there, *mansiones, mansura,* and *domus ;* and in an ancient plea concerning Feversham in Kent, *hawes* are interpreted to signifie *mansiones.* In Normans French it is called *mesiul,* or *mesuil*" (Co. Litt. 5 b).

HAIA.—A Park (4 Inst. 294 ; Spelm.) ; also a net for catching coneys (Ib.).

HALF A YEAR.—A "Half a year" is not the same as "Six months" (*V.* Six Months), but means half the days of a year. "'Half a yeare' containeth 182 dayes ; for the odde houres, in legall computation, are rejected" (Co. Litt. 135 b). But in Woodf. (348), a half-year is stated to be 183 days.

V. By Law.

HALF-YEARLY.—Where a Leasing Power provided that the rents should be reserved by "Half-yearly" payments, it was held that this required a division of the rent into, as nearly as may be, two *equal* half-yearly payments; and that, therefore, a Lease reserving rent at the Feast of St. Philip and St. James (1 May), and St. Michael (29 Sep.), was not valid (*Doe* d. *Harries* v. *Morse*, 3 L. J. Ex. 70; 4 Tyr. 185; 2 Cr. & M. 247; cited in the jdgmt. in *Doe* d. *Douglas* v. *Lock*, 4 L. J. K. B. 118).

V. Yearly: Quarterly.

HALYMOTE.—*V.* Elph. 584.

HAM.—"Properly a house; 4 Inst. 294: a vill; a piece of ground shaped like the ham of the leg; Spelm." (Elph. 584, *wh. Vf.*). *Va.* Croft.

HAMLET.—Hamlet is "in common acceptation used for a vill (per Kenyon, C.J., *King* v. *Morris*, 4 T. R. 552). Spelman (Gloss., *Hamel*) and Holt, C.J. (*Anon.*, 12 Mod. 546, pl. 912), consider it to be *a part* of a vill. The distinction seems to be that a Vill has a constable and a Hamlet has none (*R.* v. *Hewson*, 12 Mod. 180; sub nom. *Chorley's Case*, Holt, 153; 1 Salk. 175: *R.* v. *Horton*, 1 T. R. 374, 376)." (Elph. 584.)

HAND.—*V.* His Hand.

HANDICRAFT.—*Quâ* Workshop Regulation Act, 1867, 30 & 31 V. c. 146, "'Handicraft' shall mean any Manual Labour exercised by way of Trade or for purposes of Gain in or incidental to the making any Article or part of an Article, or in or incidental to the altering, repairing, ornamenting, finishing or otherwise adapting for sale any Article" (s. 4). Making straw plait, by a child under the age of 8 years and who is being taught such plaiting, is a "Handicraft" within this definition (*Beadon* v. *Parrott*, 40 L. J. M. C. 200; L. R. 6 Q. B. 718). *Cp.* Handicraftsman.

V. Manual Labour.

HANDICRAFTSMAN.—Is a skilled workman (per Brett, L.J., *Morgan* v. *Lond. Gen. Omnibus Co.*, 53 L. J. Q. B. 352; 13 Q. B. D. 832).

This word is, probably, synonymous with Artificer. *Cp.* Handicraft.

HANDSOME GRATUITY.—A request by a testator that a "handsome gratuity" should be given his executor, is void for uncertainty (*Jubber* v. *Jubber*, 9 Sim. 503).

But a promise to make a "Handsome Present" for services rendered, is evidence on which the promisee may recover reasonable recompense for those services (*Jewry* v. *Busk*, 5 Taunt. 302).

HARBOUR.—To "harbour,"—*e.g.*, thieves, ss. 10, 11, Prevention of Crimes Act, 1871, 34 & 35 V. c. 112,—means to give persons shelter, or to permit them to congregate, even though it be only to take part in a "friendly lead" for the purpose of raising a legitimate subscription (*Marshall* v. *Fox*, L. R. 6 Q. B. 370 ; 19 W. R. 1108 ; 24 L. T. 751). An Innkeeper would, probably, be said to "harbour" a thief by permitting him to participate in a "free-and-easy."

Cp. ASSEMBLE.

"A Harbour, in its ordinary sense, is a place to shelter ships from the violence of the sea, and where ships are brought for commercial purposes to load and unload goods. The quays are a necessary part of a Harbour" (per Esher, M.R., *R.* v. *Hannam,* 2 Times Rep. 234).

HARD PINCH.—"Hard Pinch," of metals so as to make them cohere, in a Patent Specification ; *V. Betts* v. *Menzies*, 30 L. J. Q. B. 81 ; 31 Ib. 233 ; 10 H. L. Ca. 117.

HATH.—The Bedford Level Act, 15 Car. 2, c. 17, s. 15, provides that none shall be qualified as Governor or Bailiff that "hath" not 400 acres, or more, in the Level ; held, that a mere legal estate qualifies (*Childers* v. *Childers*, 26 L. J. Ch. 743 ; 1 D. G. & J. 482 ; 3 Jur. N. S. 1277). In that case Knight Bruce, L. J., said,—"'Hath' must be taken as equivalent to the French word 'ait' in old statutes, *e.g.*, 2 Hen. 5, c. 3, and 8 Hen. 6, c. 7."

HAVE.—A devise to children "who have Issue," means who have Issue when the Will takes effect (*Doe* d. *Burton* v. *White*, 18 L. J. Ex. 59 ; 2 Ex. 797).

A devise of "the lands which *I have*," speaks from the death, and not the date of the Will, and therefore includes lands acquired after the Will (*Doe* d. *York* v. *Walker*, 12 M. & W. 591) ; and on the balance of the authorities (and, *semble*, of good sense), that larger interpretation would not be narrowed to the date of the Will, if the phrase were "the lands which I *now* have" (*Castle* v. *Fox*, L. R. 11 Eq. 542 ; 40 L. J. Ch. 302 : *Miles* v. *Miles*, 35 Bea. 192 ; 35 L. J. Ch. 315 ; L. R. 1 Eq. 462 : *Cox* v. *Bennett*, L. R. 6 Eq. 422 : *Wedgwood* v. *Denton*, 40 L. J. Ch. 526 ; L. R. 12 Eq. 290 : *Saxton* v. *Saxton*, 13 Ch. D. 359 ; 49 L. J. Ch. 128 : *Backwell* v. *Child*, 1 Amb. 260 : *Struthers* v. *Struthers*, 5 W. R. 809 : *Re Russell*, 51 L. J. Ch. 401 ; 19 Ch. D. 432 : *Sv.* per contra, *Cole* v. *Scott*, 19 L. J. Ch. 63 ; 1 M. & G. 518 : *Emuss* v. *Smith*, 2 D. G. & S. 722). *Vf.* NOW : *Cp.* MY.

HAVE ADJUDGED.—A statement in a Justice's Order that "we have adjudged" means "we do now adjudge" (*R.* v. *Moulden*, or *Maulden*,

6 L. J. O. S. M. C. 76 ; 8 B. & C. 78 : *R.* v. *St. Nicholas, Leicester*, 4 L. J. M. C. 97 ; 3 A. & E. 79 ; 4 N. & M. 624).

HAVE AND TO HOLD.—These words which, as is well known, are the commencement of the HABENDUM in a conveyance, mean, "*to have* an estate of inheritance and *to hold* the same of some superior lord" (Co. Litt. 6 a).

HAVE HAD.—"Have had a child;" *V.* BORN.

HAVE OR CONVEY.—"Have in his possession or Convey anything suspected of being stolen or unlawfully obtained," s. 24, 2 & 3 V. c. 71;—"Have" here is read as *ejusdem generis* with "convey," and therefore the phrase does not apply to the possession of a building, but is confined to the class of offences contemplated by s. 66, 2 & 3 V. c. 47 (*Hadley* v. *Perks*, 35 L. J. M. C. 177 ; L. R. 1 Q. B. 444 ; 7 B. & S. 375 ; *V.* KEEP).

HAVE OR KEEP.—*V.* KEEP.

HAVING.—"Every person having *Manors*," &c., may make Wills, 34 H. 8, c. 5 ; "This word 'having' imports two things, sc. Ownership and Time of Ownership ; for he ought to have the land at the time of the making of his Will, and the statute gives such person *having*, &c." the authority thereby conferred (*Butler & Baker's Case*, 3 Rep. 30 a).

The words "Die without *having Issue*" are equivalent to DIE WITHOUT ISSUE (*Lee's Case*, 1 Leon. 385 : *Cole* v. *Goble*, 22 L. J. C. P. 148 ; 13 C. B. 445 : *Eastwood* v. *Lockwood*, 36 L. J. Ch. 573 ; L. R. 3 Eq. 487). *Cp.* LEAVING.

"Having *or Conveying*" anything suspected of being stolen, s. 24, 2 & 3 V. c. 71 : *V. Hadley* v. *Perks*, 35 L. J. M. C. 177 ; L. R. 1 Q. B. 444 ; 7 B. & S. 375.

"Having or Taking" bote for repair ; *V.* BEING.

HAWES.—*V.* HAGA.

HAWGH OR HOWGH.—*V.* COMBE.

HAWKER.—A person who goes from the town in which he resides and takes a room at another town and there sells goods which are brought direct from the town of his residence, was a "Hawker, Pedlar, Petty Chapman, or other trading person going from town to town" within s. 6, 50 G. 3, c. 41 (*Manson* v. *Hope*, 31 L. J. M. C. 191 ; 2 B. & S. 498 ; *Vf.* TRADING PERSON).

But the 50 G. 3, c. 41 and the other Acts relating to Hawkers are now consolidated and repealed by the Hawkers Act, 1888 (51 & 52 V. c. 33), which, by s. 2, provides that "'Hawker' means any person who travels with a horse or other beast bearing or drawing burden, and goes from place to place or to other men's houses carrying to sell or exposing for sale any goods, wares, or merchandise, or exposing samples or patterns of any goods, wares, or merchandise to be afterwards delivered, and includes any person who travels by any means of locomotion to any place in which he does not usually reside or carry on business, and there sells or exposes for sale any goods, wares, or merchandise in or at any house, shop, room, booth, stall, or other place whatever hired or used by him for that purpose."

Semble, a single act of selling does not make a Hawker (*R.* v. *Little*, 1 Burr. 609).

Vh. Termes de la Ley, *Haukers.*

HAWKING.—*V.* HUNTING.

HAZARDOUS.—*V.* RASH AND HAZARDOUS.

HE OR THEY PAYING FREIGHT.—"It is now well settled that the usual clause in Bills of Lading engaging the Master to deliver goods to the consignees or assignees '*he or they paying freight,*' is introduced for the benefit of the Master only, and does not cast upon him the duty of obtaining at his peril the freight from the consignees at the time of the delivery" (1 Maude & P. 386, 387, citing *Weguelin* v. *Cellier*, L. R. 6 H. L. 286; 42 L. J. Ch. 758).

HEAD OFFICER.—*V.* OFFICER.

HEALTH.—That is injurious to health which makes sick people worse, —*e.g.* an offensive smell (*Malton Loc. Bd.* v. *Malton Manure Co.*, 49 L. J. M. C. 90; 4 Ex. D. 302).

HEAR: HEARING.—To "hear" a cause or matter means, to hear and determine it. And "unless there be something which by natural intendment, or otherwise, would cut down the meaning, I apprehend there can be no doubt that the Legislature, when they direct a particular cause to be heard in a particular Court, mean that it is to be heard and finally disposed of there. And further, when they say that it is to be heard—(meaning heard and finally disposed of)—in a particular Court, they mean, unless there is something in the context which either by natural interpretation or by necessary implication would cut it down, that in all matters which are not provided for that Court is to follow its ordinary procedure" (per Ld. Blackburn, *Re Green*, 51 L. J. Q. B. 44); or, as Selborne, L. C., put it in the same case, "Hearing" includes not only its necessary antecedents, but also its necessary or proper consequences (Ib. 40; nom. *Green* v. *Penzance*, 6 App. Ca. 657).

But sometimes to "hear" is not quite the same as to "hear and determine" (per Denman, C. J., *R.* v. *Warwickshire Jus.*, 4 L. J. M. C. 62; 4 N. & M. 370; 2 A. & E. 768).

"Hear and determine;" *V.* Termes de la Ley, *Oyer and Terminer.*

When power is given "to hear and determine" an Offence, the condition is implied that the accused be first cited by summons, and have an opportunity of defence (Dwar. 671, 672).

When two or more are to "hear and determine," they must sit together, not separately (Burn's Justice, Introd. xxiv., cited Dwar. 670).

"Hearing of any Motion or Summons," s. 46, Com. L. Pro. Act, 1854, includes an application for a Rule *nisi* (*Morgan* v. *Alexander*, 44 L. J. C. P. 167; L. R. 10 C. P. 184, distinguishing *Thomas* v. *Stutterheim*, 5 W. R. 6).

There is a "Hearing" of a Summons before Justices, s. 27, 9 G. 4, c. 31, if the defendant attends on the return day and claims and obtains its dismissal, the complainant having withdrawn complaint and not appearing (*Bradshaw* v. *Vaughton*, 30 L. J. C. P. 93; 9 C. B. N. S. 103; 25 J. P. 102: *Tunnicliffe* v. *Tedd*, 17 L. J. M. C. 67; 5 C. B. 553; 12 J. P. 249: *R.* v. *Stamper*, 10 L. J. M. C. 73; 1 Q. B. 119). To avoid the rule in these cases *quà* the effect of a Certificate of Dismissal in a case of assault or battery, the Hearing must be "upon the merits" (s. 44, 24 & 25 V. c. 100).

V. Day of Hearing.

HEARD AND FINALLY DETERMINED.—A provision that certain matters shall be "heard and finally determined" by an inferior Court, does not oust the supervision of the High Court (*R.* v. *Plowright*, 3 Mod. 95: 2 Hawk. P. C., c. 27, s. 23; cited Maxwell, 153).

HEIR-LOOMS.—"In some places chattels as Heire-loomes (as the best bed, table, pot, pan, cart, and other dead chattels moveable) may go to the heire" (Co. Litt. 18 b).

"Heir-looms are such goods and personal chattels as shall go *by special custom* to the heir along with the inheritance, and not to the executor or administrator of the last proprietor. The termination 'loom' is of Saxon origin, in which language it signifies a limb or member: so that Heir-loom is nothing else but a limb or member of the inheritance" (Wms. Exs. 726, *wh. et seq. Vf.*).

The popular and familiar sense of the word "Heir-looms," is "things directed to descend by way of inheritance" (per Westbury, L.C., *Byng* v. *Byng*, 31 L. J. Ch. 472; 10 H. L. Ca. 183). *V.* article on Heir-looms, 8 S. J. 282: *Va. Scarsdale* v. *Curzon*, 29 L. J. Ch. 249: Watson, Eq. 255.

HEIR *under this my Will.*—Construed as the Residuary Legatee (*Rose* v. *Rose*, 17 Ves. 347). *V. Thomason* v. *Moses*, 5 Bea. 77.

HEIRS: HEIR.—The word "heir" means the person born or begotten in wedlock, of human shape, in allegiance to the Crown, and who, according to the English Canons of Descent, is entitled to the undevised freehold estates of inheritance of a deceased person (Co. Litt. 7 b–8 b; 2 Bla. Com. 246–251). For the Canons of Descent relating to persons dying before 1 Jan., 1834, *V.* 2 Bla. Com., ch. 14; and relating to persons dying since that date, *V.* 3 & 4 W. 4, c. 106 (Inheritance Act), and Wms. R. P., ch. 4. The tenures by Gavelkind (Litt., s. 210; Co. Litt. 140 a; 2 Bla. Com. 84; Wms. R. P. 105) and Borough English (Litt. s. 211; Co. Litt. 140 b; 2 Bla. Com. 83; Wms. R. P. 107) are exceptions as regards the descent of freehold estates. Copyhold estates descend to the person who is heir according to the particular custom of the manor (Litt. ss. 73, 77; 2 Bla. Com. 97; Wms. R. P. 303).

So if, by Will, a person be appointed or recognized as "heir" to the testator, that will amount to a devise in fee of testator's undisposed of realty; *V.* Acknowledge.

Where a devise is made of property held in Gavelkind or according to Borough English, or of Copyholds to A. for life, with remainder to the "Right Heirs" of A. (when words of purchase), or to the "heirs" of A. (by words of purchase), the heir at common law will take (*Re Garland*, 47 L. J. Ch. 711; 9 Ch. D. 213: *Sladen* v. *Sladen*, 31 L. J., Ch. 775; 2 J. & H. 369: Co. Litt. 10 a, and Hargrave's n. (4) thereon: *Va. De Beauvoir* v. *De Beauvoir*, 15 Sim. 163; 15 L. J. Ch. 305; 3 H. L. Ca. 524: 2 Jarm. 78; Lewin, 824; Watson, Eq. 1373). But if the phrase "heirs" be one of limitation, then the heir according to the peculiar tenure will take (Co. Litt. 10 a, and Hargrave's n. (3) thereon: Co. Litt. 27 a: *Doe* d. *Eustace* v. *Easley*, 4 L. J. Ex. 87; 1 Cr. M. & R. 823).

"Heirs" is, *primâ facie*, a word of limitation, so that a devise or conveyance of realty to "A. and his heirs" merely limits or defines the estate that is taken by A., but gives no indefeasible interest to his heirs (Wms. R. P. 120; Watson, Eq. 199, 1371 *et seq.*). The well-known *Rule in Shelley's Case* (1 Rep. 94; for a defence of which, *V.* jdgmt. of Earl Cairns, *Bowen* v. *Lewis*, 54 L. J. Q. B. 63, 64; 9 App. Ca. 890), is probably the most conspicuous example of the application of this principle, laying down, as it does, the proposition that when A. takes an estate of freehold, and, by the same document, an estate is limited, either mediately or immediately, to his heirs in fee or in tail, the word "heirs" merely limits the estate of A., which he can dispose of, by the appointed means, to the exclusion of his heirs, who can only take as heirs in the event of A. making no effectual disposition of the property (Wms. R. P. 211, 215). But the first estate of freehold must be of the same quality as the limitation, *i.e.*, both must be legal or both equitable; otherwise *Shelley's Case* will not apply (per Turner, L. J., *Re Wynch*, 23 L. J., Ch. 930; 5 D. G. M. & G. 188; and *V.* obs. of Cranworth, L. C., therein): and in a Will (even where the first estate and the imitation are alike in quality) the context may control "heirs" to be read as a word of purchase, and then *Shelley's Case* would not apply (*Jordan* v. *Adams*, 29 L. J. C. P. 180 ; 30 Ib. 161 ; 6 C. B. N. S. 748). For a neat statement of the Rule in *Shelley's Case*, *V.* Goodeve, Real Pro. 2 Ed. 219 *et seq.*, and for an elaborate discussion of it, *V.* Jarm., Ch. 36 ; Watson, Eq. 217–221 ; Elph. 238, 242–246.

"There is no case which establishes that you may not apply the Rule in *Shelley's Case* to a *gift of Personalty*" (per Bacon, V.-C., *Comfort* v. *Brown*, 48 L. J., Ch. 318 ; 10 Ch. D. 146) ; in that case a blended gift of freeholds and leaseholds was made to A. for life, to remainders (which failed), and on their failure to "the Right Heirs of A. for ever," and it was held that A. took an absolute interest in the leaseholds as well as the freeholds.

When the words are to "A. and his heir" (in the singular number), the heir would probably take by purchase as *persona designata*, and that construction would be conclusively established if the words were followed by a limitation to the heirs of the heir (*Greaves* v. *Simpson*, 33 L. J., Ch. 641).

Vf. as to words under which the "heir" would take as purchaser, 2 Jarm., ch. 28 ; *Va.* as to the use of "heir" (in the singular), Watson, Eq. 200, 208.

A grant to A. "and his heir," in the singular number, gives only a life estate (Co. Litt. 8 b; Touch. 106).

As to the construction of a *Power* to a person's "heirs ;" *V.* Lewin, 601, 602.

When the word "heirs" is found in conjunction with words of procreation, defining the class of heirs,—*e.g.* "to A. and the heirs of his body,"—this will create an *Entail* in the person whose heirs are referred to (Litt. ss. 14–34, and Coke thereon ; 2 Bla. Com. 113–115). In *Deeds* (prior to the Conv. & L. P. Act, 1881) there could be no entail unless there were a designation of the body or bodies out of whom the heirs were to issue (Litt., s. 31 ; 2 Bla. Com. 115) ; but by s. 51 of that Act it will be sufficient, in Deeds executed after the 31st Dec. 1881, to create an entail to use the words "in tail," "in tail male," or "in tail female," as the case may be. In *Wills*, words of procreation were never absolutely necessary, the intention of the testator being regarded, though technical words were absent : thus, a devise "to A. and his heirs male," or to "A. and his heirs lawfully begotten," would, as they now will, create an entail (Co. Litt. 27 a ; 2 Bla. Com. 115 ; for a collection of cases hereon, *V.* 2 Jarm. ch. 35–40 ; Watson, Eq. 207, 1371 *et seq.* : *Va. Nanfan* v. *Legh*, 7 Taunt. 85: *Webb* v. *Hearing*, Cro. Jac. 415: *Mortimer* v. *Hartley*, 20 L. J. Ex. 132). So "the rule is established that if a testator expresses an intention that A. shall have an estate for life, and on the failure of the heirs of the body of A., the estate shall go over, the effect is that an estate tail is given to A. by necessary implication, as otherwise all the subsequent limitations would be too remote" (per Ld. Blackburn, *Bowen* v. *Lewis*, 54 L. J. Q. B. 69 ; 9 App. Ca. 890, citing *Roddy* v. *Fitzgerald*, 6 H. L. Ca.

823 : *Jesson* v. *Wright*, 2 Bli. 1 : *Doe* v. *Gallini*, 3 L. J. K. B. 71 ; 5 B. & Ad. 621).

As to the sometimes difficult question, whether the person forming the stock of an entail is to take an estate for life, or in tail ; *V. Chamberlayn* v. *Chamberlayn*, 6 E. & B. 625 ; 25 L. J. Q. B. 187, 357 ; 27 L. T. O. S. 238 : *Towns* v. *Wentworth*, 11 Moo. P. C. 526 ; 31 L. T. O. S. 274 : *Jordan* v. *Adams*, 29 L. J. C. P. 180 ; 30 Ib. 161 ; 6 C. B. N. S. 748 : *Jenkins* v. *Clinton*, 26 Bea. 108 ; nom. *Jenkins* v. *Hughes*, 30 L. J. Ch. 870.

Of course the word "heirs" is used inappropriately as indicating the successors to *Personal Property;* and when so used—when used as a word of substitution—it means, next of kin according to the Statute of Distributions (*Doody* v. *Higgins*, 2 K. & J. 729 ; 25 L. J. Ch. 773 ; 27 L. T. O. S. 281: *Low* v. *Smith*, 25 L. J. Ch. 503 ; 2 Jur. N. S. 344 : *Neilson* v. *Monro*, 27 W. R. 936 : *Re Newton's Trusts*, 37 L. J. Ch. 23 ; L. R. 4 Eq. 171 : *Stannard* v. *Burt*, 52 L. J. Ch. 355). But, like the use of the word "heir" as regards realty (*Greaves* v. *Simpson*, sup.), so "heir," or "heirs," as regards personalty, may be used as a designation ; and then the person answering the designation will take. Thus, where there was a bequest in remainder of personalty coupled with a devise of freehold, copyhold and leasehold property, and the personalty with the rest was to go to testator's "own right heirs for ever" (*De Beauvoir* v. *De Beauvoir*, 15 L. J. Ch. 305 ; 15 Sim. 163 ; 3 H. L. Ca. 524) ; or in the case of a bequest of personalty in remainder to testator's "next heir-at-law" (*Southgate* v. *Clinch*, 27 L. J. Ch. 651 ; 31 L. T. O. S. 263) ; or to be equally divided between the "heirs" of three specified persons (*Re Rootes*, 29 L. J. Ch. 868 ; 1 Dr. & Sm. 228); or to go to the "lawful heir or heirs" of the tenant for life (*Smith* v. *Butcher*, 48 L. J. Ch. 136 ; 10 Ch. D. 113),—in all these cases the heir-at-law took as *persona designata*. (But *cp. Re Russell*, 53 L. J. Ch. 400 : *Vf.* Wms. Exs. 1113 ; Watson, Eq. 1373.)

And on this principle of the heir taking as a person designated, a bequest of personalty "to A. *and his heirs*" will not lapse by the death of A. in testator's lifetime (Wms. Exs. 1213).

But in *Roberts* v. *Edwards* (12 W. R. 33 ; 33 L. J. Ch. 369 ; 33 Bea. 259), "heirs," in a bequest of personalty, was read as "children :" *Sv. Smith* v. *Butcher*, sup.

In *Re Walton* (25 L. J. Ch. 569 ; 8 D. G. M. & G. 173), where there was a gift in remainder of personalty to children "or their heirs or assigns," the latter words were rejected as surplusage ; but in *Wingfield* v. *Wingfield* (47 L. J. Ch. 768 ; 9 Ch. D. 658), a *mixed gift* of real and personal property in remainder to "brothers and sisters then living *or their heirs*" was read distributively, so as to mean heirs-at-law, as regards the realty and statutory next of kin (including widows), as regards the personalty —a construction which was followed in *Keay* v. *Boulton* (54 L. J. Ch. 48 ; 25 Ch. D. 212).

A bequest of personalty in terms which, if applied to real estate, would create an entail, vests the property absolutely in the first taker (Wms. Exs. 1111, and cases there cited: *Va. Re Barker*, 52 L. J. Ch. 565).

In like manner, if "heirs" be used in connection with a legacy as merely a word of limitation, the legatee takes an absolute interest (*Re Russell*, 53 L. J. Ch. 400).

As to a Limitation in Marriage Articles of chattels to "the heirs of the body;" *V.* Lewin, 115.

As to when there is a Resulting Trust to the Heir; *V.* 1 Jarm. ch. 18.

Vh. Chitty, Eq. Ind. 7696.

V. HEIRS OF THE BODY : NEXT OF KIN : FEE SIMPLE.

HEIRS AND ASSIGNS.—A reservation in a Lease to a Lessor, "his heirs and assigns," attaches, as a general rule, to the reversion, so that whoever is entitled, for the time being, to the reversion, is also entitled to the reservation (*Dynevor* v. *Tennant*, 57 L. J. Ch. 1078; 13 App. Ca. 279; 59 L. T. 5).

V. ASSIGNS.

HEIRS, EXORS., ADMORS. AND ASSIGNS.—This phrase means all persons claiming or to claim under the person to whom it refers whether by Deed, Will or otherwise: *Vh.* Hatherley, L. C., *Pride* v. *Bubb*, 41 L. J. Ch. 109; 7 Ch. 64.

HEIRS MALE: HEIRS FEMALE.—*V.* MALE : FEMALE : HEIRS.

HEIRS OF THE BODY.—"'Heirs of the body' and 'Issue' are far from being synonymous expressions. The former are properly words of limitation, whereas the latter term is in its primary sense a word of purchase. In several cases the Court appears to have ordered a strict settlement from the use of the term 'Issue,' where had the expression been 'Heirs of the body,' the estate would probably have been construed an estate tail" (Lewin, 120, and cases there cited).

Vf. ISSUE : HEIRS.

"If in *Marriage Articles* the real estate of the husband or the wife be limited to the *heirs of the body*, or the *issue*, of the contracting parties or either of them, or to the heirs of the body, or issue and their heirs, so that 'heirs of the body' or 'issue,' if taken in their ordinary legal sense, would enable one or other of the parents to defeat the provision intended for the children, these words will then be construed in equity to mean 'first and other sons;' and the settlement will be made upon them successively in tail as purchasers" (Lewin, 113, and cases there cited).

HELD.—"Held or Enjoyed therewith;" *V. Williams* v. *Phillips*, 51 L.J. Q. B. 102; 8 Q. B. D. 437: *Roe* v. *Siddons*, 22 Q. B. D. 224.

In the Pauper Settlement Act of 59 G. 3, c. 50, house or building "held," is used as distinguished from land "occupied:" *Vh. R.* v. *Stow Bardolph*, 1 B. & Ad. 222 : *R.* v. *North Collingham*, 1 B. & C. 578 : *R.* v. *Tonbridge*, 6 Ib. 88 : *R.* v. *Great Bolton*, 8 Ib. 71: *R.* v. *Wainfleet*, Ib. 227.

"The true meaning of the word 'held,'—shares held,—in s. 40, Companies Act, 1867, is simply that the contributory has had his name upon the register as the holder of the shares for the period in question" (per Chitty, J., *Re Wala Wynaad Mining Co.*, 52 L. J. Ch. 88; 30 W. R. 915).

HENCEFORTH.—*V.* FROM HENCEFORTH.

HERBAGE.—If a man grant "vesturam terræ," "the land itselfe shall not passe, because hee hath a particular right in the land: for thereby he shall not have the houses, timber-trees, mines, and other reall things parcell of the inheritance, but he shall have the vesture of the land, (that is) the corne, grasse, underwood, sweepage, and the like, and hee shall have an action of trespasse *quare clausum fregit.* The same law, if a man grant *herbagium terræ*, hee hath a like particular right in the land, and shall have an action *quare clausum fregit;* but by grant thereof and liverie made, the soile shall not passe, as is aforesaid" (Co. Litt. 4 b; on wh. passage *V.* Hargrave's note, *Va.* Elph. 585 : *Cp.* PASTURES). *Vf.* Cowell, Interp.; Jacob, Law. Dict.

"Spelman (*Herbagium*) restricts *vestura terræ* to that which is taken by the mouths of animals; but '*Sweepage,*' in the passage cited from Co. Litt., appears to mean 'by mowing'" (Elph. 586).

V. PASTURAGE.

HEREAFTER.—*V.* TO BE BORN.

HEREAFTER BORROW.—The power given, s. 3, 12 & 13 V. c. 87, to Turnpike Commrs of setting apart a sinking fund to pay off moneys they should "hereafter borrow," relates to further moneys borrowed for some fresh purpose, and not to moneys borrowed at a cheaper rate to supply the place of a prior loan (*Chatham* v. *Rochester Commrs.*, 35 L. J. M. C. 81; L. R. 1 Q. B. 24).

HEREAFTER VALUED AND DECLARED.—In a Marine Insurance, "The meaning of to be 'hereafter valued and declared' is, that if the insured has several adventures, all within the description in the policy, out, he may select at his pleasure which is to be protected by the policy, and on his giving notice of such a selection to the insurers, the policy is as if it had named that adventure from the beginning" (per Ld. Blackburn, *Inglis* v. *Stock*, 10 App. Ca. 269; 54 L. J. Q. B. 586).

HEREBY AGREED AND DECLARED.—*V.* AGREED AND DECLARED.

HEREBY SETTLED.—*V. Leman* v. *Saffery*, W. N. (72) 26.

HEREDITAMENT.—"The word 'Hereditament' is of as large extent as any word, for whatsoever may be inherited, be it corporeal or incorporeal, real, personal or mixt, is an hereditament" (Touch. 91;—a definition almost verbally copied from Co. Litt. 6 a. *Vf.* Co. Litt. 16 a, 383 a, b). "'Hereditament' is defined in the text-books of authority to signify all such things, whether corporeal or incorporeal, which a man may have to him and his heirs by way of inheritance, and which, if they be not otherwise bequeathed, come to him who is next of blood, and not to exors or admors as chattels do" (per Wilde, C. J., *Lloyd* v. *Jones*, 17 L. J. C. P. 206; 6 C. B. 81). "The most comprehensive words of description applicable to Real Estate are *Tenements* and *Hereditaments;* as they include every species of realty, as well corporeal as incorporeal" (1 Jarm. 777), *e.g.* an Advowson (*Westfaling* v. *Westfaling*, 3 Atk. 460: *Crompton* v. *Jarratt*, 54 L. J. Ch. 1109; 30 Ch. D. 298: *Vf.* AT). *Vh.* Wms. R. P. 5, 12; Watson, Eq. 193.

This large meaning, however, may be cut down by a context. And in the present state of the authorities it is a question whether "Hereditament," in the definition of "Land" as prescribed by s. 3, Lands C. C. Act, 1845, is or is not confined to a corporeal hereditament. That definition says that, for the purposes of that Act, "Land" shall extend to "Messuages, Lands, Tenements and Hereditaments *of any tenure*." Leaning on the three latter words Cranworth, L. C., in *Pinchin* v. *Lond. & Blackwall Ry.* (24 L. J. Ch. 417; 5 D. G. M. & G. 851; 1 K. & J. 34) said,—"Looking at the whole context, the conclusion to which I have come is, that a 'hereditament' there means a corporeal hereditament: a hereditament which may be the subject of tenure," which a right of way, or other easement not actually attached to land or buildings to be purchased,—*e.g.* a right of Common in gross—cannot be. But in *G. W. Ry.* v. *Swindon & Cheltenham Ry.* (53 L. J. Ch. 1075; 9 App. Ca. 787), Lord Bramwell ("with profound respect for that most learned, able and accurate lawyer," Lord Cranworth) was of a directly opposite opinion; whilst, in the same case, Lord Fitzgerald, though not apparently with much energy, adhered to the doctrine of *Pinchin* v. *Lond. & Blackwall Ry.*; whereas Lord Watson took a middle course, and whilst agreeing generally with Lord Bramwell, observed (53 L. J. Ch. 1083) that the word is "in many of the leading clauses of the Act of 1845, limited, by reason of the context, to corporeal hereditaments." It should be added that the actual decision in the *G. W. Ry.* v. *Swindon & Cheltenham Ry.* scarcely proceeded on the exact meaning of "Hereditament." *Vh. R.* v. *Cambrian Ry.*, L. R. 6 Q. B. 422.

So Market Tolls are not rateable under a power to rate "land, house, shop, warehouse, or other building, tenement or hereditament" (*Colebrooke* v.

Tickell, 5 L. J. K. B. 180 ; 4 A. & E. 916 ; 6 N. & M. 483) ; but where a similar collocation was followed by "meadow and pasture ground excepted," it was held that a Gas Company was rateable as occupiers of the land in which its pipes were placed (*R.* v. *Shrewsbury Gas Co.*, 1 L. J. M. C. 18 ; 3 B. & Ad. 216) ; so of Tithes under 6 & 7 W. 4, c. 96 (*R.* v. *Capell*, 9 L. J. M. C. 65 ; 12 A. & E. 382).

On the other hand, "Hereditament" may include leaseholds. Thus in s. 56, County Courts Act, 1888 (which restricts the jurisdiction of the Co. Co.), "Hereditament" is used, "not to describe the quantum of interest, but the thing itself which is the subject-matter of the interest" (per Bowen, L. J.), and leaseholds are within the restriction (*Tomkins* v. *Jones*, 58 L. J. Q. B. 222 ; 22 Q. B. D. 599 ; 37 W. R. 328 ; 5 Times Rep. 302 : *Vf. Chew* v. *Holroyd*, 22 L. J. Ex. 95 ; 8 Ex. 249 : *Moore* v. *Denn*, 2 Bos. & P. 251).

"Hereditament" in Mortmain Act ; *V.* Interest in Land.

"Hereditament," s. 4, Valuation (Metropolis) Act, 1869, 32 & 33 V. c. 67 ; *V. R.* v. *St. George's*, 41 L. J. M. C. 30 ; L. R. 7 Q. B. 90.

V. Incorporeal Hereditament : Tenement.

Prior to the Wills Act (1 V. c. 26) a devise of "Hereditaments," without words of limitation, carried only an estate for life (2 Jarm. 284).

HEREIN : HEREINAFTER.—"A direction in a Will that the legacy duty on the legacies '*herein*' given shall be paid out of the estate, does not extend to legacies given by Codicil, even though the Codicil is directed to be taken as part of the Will (*Early* v. *Benbow*, 2 Coll. 355 : *Va.*, as to 'herein,' *Radburn* v. *Jervis*, 3 Bea. 450: *Fuller* v. *Hooper*, 2 Ves. sen. 242 : *Jauncey* v. *A.-G.*, 3 Giff. 308 ; 10 W. R. 129 ; 5 L. T. 374). *Secus*, where legacies generally are given duty free (*Byne* v. *Currey*, 3 L. J. Ex. 177 ; 2 Cr. & M. 603 ; 4 Tyr. 478 : *Va. Williams* v. *Hughes*, 27 L. J. Ch. 218 ; 24 Bea. 474)." 1 Jarm. 187.

"Where a testator, by his Will, charges his lands with the payment of the legacies 'hereinafter' bequeathed, the charge does not extend to legacies bequeathed by a codcil" (1 Jarm. 95 ; *Vf.* Ib. 90, 186 : *Edmunds* v. *Low*, 26 L. J. Ch. 432 ; 3 K. & J. 318 ; 5 W. R. 444).

HERETOFORE.—"Now or heretofore held or enjoyed ;" *V. Roe* v. *Siddons*, 22 Q. B. D. 224.

HERIOT.—"This dutie to the lord is very ancient ; for in the lawes before the Conquest it is said, *sive quis incuria, sive morte repentinâ, fuerit intestat' mortuus, dominus tamen nullam rerum suarum partem (præter eam quæ jure debetur herioti nomine) sibi assumito.* In the Saxon tongue it is called *heregeat*, as much to say (as I take it) as the lord's best ; for *here* is Lord, and *geat* is Best" (Co. Litt. 185 b). *Vf.* Termes de la Ley, *Hariot.*

As to the use of "Heriots" in 3 & 4 W. 4, c. 27 ; *V.* Sug. R. P. Statutes, 2 Ed. 17, 18 : *Owen* v. *De Beauvoir*, 16 M. & W. 547, 566.

HERITABLE AND PERSONAL SECURITY.—*V. Knox* v. *Mackinnon*, 13 App. Ca. 753.

HÉRITIER.—"Héritier," "Autres Héritiers" in the Civil Code of Lower Canada; *V. Herse* v. *Dufaux*, 42 L. J. P. C. 1; L. R. 4 P. C. 468.

HERMIT.—*V.* RECLUSE.

HIDE: HYDE.—"One plow-land, *carucata terræ*, or a hide of land, *hida terræ* (which is all one), is not of any certaine content, but as much as a plough can by course of husbandrie plow in a yeere. And therewith agreeth *Lambert verbo Hide.* And a plow-land may containe a messuage, wood, meadow, and pasture, because that by them the plowmen and the cattell belonging to the plow are maintained" (Co. Litt. 69 a.; *Va.* Ib. 5 a., 86 b; *Vf.* Elph. 587). *V.* KNIGHT'S FEE: PLOW-LAND: CARUCATA.

A Hide, speaking generally, would seem to be four times as much as an OXGANGE, because the latter is as much as an ox can till, and a JUGUM (or half a plow-land) as much as two oxen can till.

HIGH AND LOW WATER-MARK.—The space between "high and low water mark" means medium high and low water mark, *i.e.* half way between the spring tide and neap tide high and low water-marks respectively (*Webber* v. *Richards*, 10 L. J. Q. B. 203; 1 G. & D. 114).

HIGH COURT.—*V.* s. 13 (3), Interp. Act, 1889.

HIGH TREASON.—"Every one commits High Treason who forms and displays by any overt act, or by publishing any printing or writing, an intention to kill or destroy the Queen, or to do her any bodily harm, tending to death or destruction, maim or wounding, imprisonment or restraint" (Steph. Cr. 40). So also to LEVY WAR against the Queen or ADHERING TO THE QUEEN'S ENEMIES is High Treason. *Vf.* Steph. Cr. 40–44: Arch. Cr. 828–843.

HIGHWAY.—S. 5, Highway Act, 1835, 5 & 6 W. 4, c. 50; *V. R.* v. *Chart*, 39 L. J. M. C. 137; L. R. 1 C. C. R. 237.

"*Highway repairable by the inhabitants at large,*" s. 150, P. H. Act, 1875; *V. Austerberry* v. *Oldham*, 55 L. J. Ch. 633; 29 Ch. D. 750; 53 L. T. 543; 33 W. R. 807; 49 J. P. 532: *Gibson* v. *Preston*, L. R. 5 Q. B. 218; 10 B. & S. 942; 39 L. J. Q. B. 131: *Hirst* v. *Halifax*, L. R. 6 Q. B. 181; 40 L. J. M. C. 43.

"Street not being a Highway," s. 69, P. H. Act, 1848, held not to include a piece of ground dedicated, by user, as a public road (*Healey* v. *Batley*, 44 L. J. Ch. 642; L. R. 19 Eq. 375).

V. STREET (at end).

HIMSELF.—When a person "himself" has to do a thing he cannot do it by an agent (*Monks* v. *Jackson*, 46 L. J. C. P. 162 ; 1 C. P. D. 683). So where (by s. 38 (1), 46 & 47 V. c. 51) power is given to a person, reported guilty of electoral malpractices, of being heard, "by Himself," before the Court enquiring into the Municipal Election at which such malpractices are alleged to have taken place, he cannot appear by Counsel or Solicitor (*Hereford Case, R.* v. *Jones*, 23 Q. B. D. 29 ; 37 W. R. 508 ; 5 Times Rep. 411).

V. Done by : His Hand.

HIRE.—Is it acting "for hire" within s. 11, 6 & 7 V. c. 68, to represent a stage play at an evening party, the actor being, of course, paid by the host and not by the spectators? It would seem not (s. 16). In *Fredericks* v. *Payne* (32 L. J. M. C. 16), Bramwell, B., said, "The acting was 'for hire' whether payment was made at the door or any other place."

Rowing on Thames for "Hire or Gain," Thames Waterman's Act, 1859, 22 & 23 V. c. cxxxiii., means for the purpose of obtaining a direct reward for rowing (*Showell* v. *Skittrell*, 6 Times Rep. 120 ; nom. *Skittrell* v. *Showell*, 59 L. J. M. C. 26 : *Tadhunter* v. *Buckley*, 7 L. T. 273). *Vh. R.* v. *Tibble*, 4 E. & B. 888.

HIRST OR HURST.—*V.* Grava.

HIS.—"If a man be seized of land in fee simple, or for life, and have an estate in it for years, by statute merchant, a staple, elegit, or the like ; and he grant all his estate, or all his right, or all his title, or all his interest of and in the land ; by this grant all his estate, and as much as he is able to grant, doth pass" (Touch. 98 : *Vh.* per St. Leonards, C., *Drew* v. *Norbury*, 3 J. & La T. 284 ; 9 Ir. Eq. 171, 524) ; but when a person has a beneficial interest and also one as a trustee, it is a question of construction as to whether he means to pass both interests, or only one and which one (*Stronge* v. *Hawkes*, 4 D. G. M. & G. 186 : *Rooper* v. *Harrison*, 2 K. & J. 112 ; *Vh.* Elph. 205–209).

"When A. demises to B. for the term of *his* life, the word 'his' would, in ordinary construction, apply to B. as the last antecedent. But instances perpetually occur where that word is used, and does not refer to the last party named" (per Taunton, J., *Doe* d. *Pritchard* v. *Dodd*, 5 B. & Ad. 693).

HIS FARE.—"Without having previously paid His Fare," s. 103, 8 V. c. 20 ; "His Fare" here means the fare by the train, and for the class of carriage, in which the passenger travels ; therefore a traveller wrongfully travelling 2nd Class with a 3rd Class Ticket has not paid "his fare," though he has paid "a fare" (*Gillingham* v. *Walker*, 29 W. R. 896 ; 44 L. T. 715 ; 45 J. P. 470 : *Vh. Langdon* v. *Howells*, 48 L. J. M. C. 133 ; 4 Q. B. D. 337 ; 27 W. R. 657 ; 43 J. P. 717).

HIS HAND.—A letter written by a bankruptcy trustee's solicitor in his own name disclaiming a Lease; held not a due Disclaimer by the trustee, under s. 23, Bankry. Act, 1869, because it was not a "Writing under his (*i.e.* the Trustee's) hand" (*Wilson* v. *Wallani*, 49 L. J. Ex. 437; 5 Ex. D. 155). *V.* HIMSELF.

HOLD OUT.—Will not "hold himself out, nor seek to induce others to believe;" *V. Wolmerhausen* v. *O'Connor*, 36 L. T. 921.

HOLD OVER.—*V.* WILFULLY HOLD OVER.

HOLDER.—*V.* HELD: IN HIS OWN RIGHT.

"'Holder,' of a Bill or Note, means, the Payee or Indorsee of it," "who is in possession of it, or the bearer thereof" (s. 2, Bills of Ex. Act, 1882); and every Holder of a Bill or Note "is *primâ facie* deemed to be a HOLDER IN DUE COURSE" (s. 30 (2), Ib.). As to the rights of the Holder, *V.* s. 38, Ib.

HOLDER FOR VALUE.—"Every indorsee of a Bill has his own title, and that of each intermediate party; and if he or any of such parties gave value for the bill, without fraud, he is a Holder for Value" (per Abinger, C. B., *Isaac* v. *Farrer*, 1 M. & W. 69; 5 L. J. Ex. 96). *V.* BONÂ FIDE.

The phrase "Bonâ fide Holder for Value, without Notice," *quâ* Bills and Notes, is now superseded by the phrase HOLDER IN DUE COURSE.

HOLDER FOR THE TIME BEING.—"The words 'Holder for the time being,'—in a Debenture,—are, in my opinion, identical with the words 'to Bearer'" (per Malins, V.-C., *Re Marseilles Imperial Land Co.*, 40 L. J. Ch. 96).

V. BEARER.

HOLDER IN DUE COURSE.—A "Holder in Due Course" of a Bill of Ex., "is a Holder who has taken a Bill, complete and regular on the face of it, under the following conditions, namely;

(a) That he became the Holder of it before it was overdue, and without notice that it had been previously dishonoured, if such was the fact:

(b) That he took the Bill in Good Faith and for Value, and that at the time the Bill was negotiated to him he had no notice of any defect in the title of the person who negotiated it.

(2) In particular the title of a person who negotiates a Bill is defective within the meaning of this Act, when he obtained the Bill, or the Acceptance thereof, by fraud, duress, or force and fear, or other unlawful means, or for an illegal consideration, or when he negotiates it in breach of faith, or under such circumstances as amount to a fraud.

(3) A Holder (whether for Value or not) who derives his title to a Bill through a Holder in Due Course, and who is not himself a party to any fraud or illegality affecting it, has all the rights of that Holder in Due Course as regards the Acceptor and all parties to the Bill prior to that Holder"

(s. 29, Bills of Ex. Act, 1882): and so of a Promissory Note (s. 89, Ib.).

Vf. as to presumption of VALUE and GOOD FAITH, s. 30, Ib.; and as to subs. 2 of that section, *V. Tatam* v. *Hasler,* 58 L. J. Q. B. 432; 23 Q. B. D. 345.

HOLDING.—Where Articles of a Company gave a power to demand a poll to "Shareholders qualified to vote and *holding* in the aggregate" a stated number of shares; held that "themselves" must be read in before "holding," so that the required number could not be made up by proxies (*R.* v. *Government Stock Investment Co.*, 47 L. J. Q. B. 478; 3 Q. B. D. 442).

V. IN HIS OWN RIGHT.

HOLIDAYS EXCEPTED.—By a Charter-Party, a vessel was "to be loaded in L. in 14 days, and to be discharged, weather permitting, at not less than 25 tons per working day (holidays excepted);"—held, that though "holidays" are not included in "working day," yet that the exception related only to the discharge as its last antecedent, and that the loading was to be done in 14 days including Sundays (*Niemann* v. *Moss,* 29 L. J. Q. B. 206).

HOLME.—"*Holme,* or *hulmus,* signifieth an isle or fenny ground" (Co. Litt. 5 a).

HOLT.—*V.* GRAVA.

HOLY ORDERS.—*V.* CLERGYMAN.

HOMAGE.—Termes de la Ley, *Homage; Homage auncestral.*

HOME.—*V.* AT HOME.

HOME FARM.—S. 21, Land Law (Ireland) Act, 1881, 44 & 45 V. c. 49; *V. Hamilton and Sharpe,* 20 L. R. Ir. 224.

HOMESOKEN.—To be quit of Amerciaments (Termes de la Ley).

HOMICIDE.—"Homicide, as it is legally taken, is when one is slaine with a man's will, but not with malice prepensed" (Co. Litt. 287 b: *Vf.* Termes de la Ley).

"Homicide is the killing of a human being by a human being. A child becomes a human being within the meaning of this definition, when it has completely proceeded in a living state from the body of its mother, whether it has or has not breathed, and whether the navel string has or has not been divided; and the killing of such a child is homicide, whether it is killed by injuries inflicted before, during, or after birth. A living child in its mother's womb, or a child in the act of birth, even though such child may have breathed, is not a human being within the meaning of this definition, and the killing of such a child is not homicide" (Steph. Cr. 151 ; *Vf.* Ib. Ch. 23). *V.* KILLING.

Vf. Arch. Cr. 711 ; Rosc. Cr. 634.

HONEST.—"Honest Persons," for trustees, in a charitable trust deed made in 1549 ; *V. Baker* v. *Lee*, 30 L. J. Ch. 625 ; 8 H. L. Ca. 495.

"Honestly ;" *V.* GOOD FAITH.

HONOUR.—"By the name of an Honor which a subject may have, divers mannors and lands may passe" (Co. Litt. 5 a : *Vf.* Termes de la Ley ; Touch. 92 ; Elph. 558).

"*Acceptance* for Honour, supra protest ;" *V.* ss. 65, 66, 67, Bills of Ex. Act, 1882.

"*Payment* for Honour, supra protest ;" *V.* s. 68, Ib.

HONOURED.—In a guarantee of a promissory note if it be not "duly honoured and paid," "'duly honoured,' means no more than duly paid when due. 'Honoured' means payment at maturity" (per Parke, B. *Walton* v. *Maskell*, 14 L. J. Ex. 56 ; nom. *Walton* v. *Mascall*, 13 M. & W. 457). *Cp.* DISHONOURED.

HOO.—*V.* HOWE.

HOPE.—*V.* PRECATORY TRUST : EARNEST : COMBE.

HORSE DEALER.—*V. Allen* v. *Sharp*, 17 L. J. Ex. 209; 2 Ex. 352.

HOSPITAL.—A "Hospital" is an eleemosynary institution and, strictly speaking, there is no legal Hospital unless it be incorporated and the persons benefited are themselves the corporation (*Sutton's Hospital*, 10 Rep. 31 a) ; "and of these Hospitals some be eligible, some donative, and some presentable" (Co. Litt. 342 a).

But referring to this definition the Court of Ex. in *Colchester* v. *Kewney* (35 L. J. Ex. 206) said,—"It seems rather more reasonable to hold that the word (in the exemption from Land Tax in s. 25, 38 G. 3, c. 5) is used in a popular sense only, and that any institution which, though not in a strictly legal, might in a popular sense be called a Hospital, might claim exemption. But some doubts arise whether even upon this view this Institution (the Wandsworth Royal Victoria Patriotic Asylum) would be a 'Hospital,' by which word we understand, rather an Institution for the relief of the sick or aged than for the maintenance and education of children." *V.* that jdgmt. affirmed, 36 L. J. Ex. 172 ; L. R. 2 Ex. 253 ; 16 L. T. 463.

"I apprehend that even a Hospital would not be the less entitled to exemption under this Act (Income Tax Act, 5 & 6 Vict. c. 35, s. 60, Sch. A. No. VI.) because, in order to diminish its expense, certain fees were taken from certain richer patients who might choose to obtain the benefit of the Hospital for payment. As to '*Almshouse*,' there, it would be impossible to suppose a case in which anybody except poor almsmen or almswomen would take the benefit of such an institution" (per Denman J., *Blake and London Corpn.*, 56 L. J. Q. B. 152; 18 Q. B. D. 437; 35 W. R. 212; 51 J. P. 71; affd. 56 L. J. Q. B. 424; 19 Q. B. D. 79; 35 W. R. 791). A self-supporting Lunatic Asylum, though founded by subscription, is not within this exemption as a "Hospital" (*Needham* v. *Bowers*, 21 Q. B. D. 436).

V. Public School.

In *Colchester* v. *Kewney* (sup.), it was held that no Hospital is, under s. 25, 38 G. 3, c. 5, exempt from Land Tax unless founded before 38 G. 3, c. 60.

"Hospitals of London;" *V.* London.

HOSPITALITY.—A gift for "Hospitality or Charity," is void for uncertainty (*Re Hewitt*, 53 L. J. Ch. 132: *Re Jarman*, 47 L. J. Ch. 675; 8 Ch. D. 584).

HOSTEL.—*V.* Inn: Hotel.

HOTCHPOT.—"This word is in English a pudding; for in this pudding is not commonly put one thing alone, but one thing with other things together" (Litt. s. 267). "*Hutspot*, or *Hotspot*, is an old Saxon word, and signifieth so much as Littleton here speaks. And the French use *hotchpot* for a commixion of divers things together. It signifieth here metaphorically *in partem positio*. In English we use to say *hodgepodge*, in Latine *farrago* or *miscellaneum*" (Co. Litt. 177 a). *Vf.* Termes de la Ley; 2 Bla. Com. 190, 517; Wms. Exs. 1505 *et seq.*: and as to effect of a Hotchpot Clause in a Will, *V. Fox* v. *Fox*, 40 L. J. Ch. 182; L. R. 11 Eq. 142.

In a Settlement pursuant to Articles, a Hotchpot Clause will not be inserted unless it be expressly directed (*Lees* v. *Lees*, Ir. R. 5 Eq. 549: *Svth. Miller* v. *Gulson*, 13 L. R. Ir. 408).

HOTEL.—"Hotel" is not to be confounded with the old word "Hostel" which is a synonym for Inn.

An "Hotel" is a place where lodgings are let and where provisions are, to some extent, supplied (*Smith* v. *Scott*, 1 L. J. C. P. 143; 9 Bing. 14: *Gibson* v. *King*, 12 L. J. Ex. 9; 10 M. & W. 667); that the lodgings are let to invalids, makes no difference (*Re Jones, Ex p. Thorne*, 45 L. J. Bank. 158; 3 Ch. D. 357). These were decisions on "Keepers of Hotels" in the late Bankry definition of "Trader." In *Smith* v. *Scott*, Tindal, C. J., said,—"It is clear that the word 'Hotel' is not used in the sense of the old word 'Hostel,' for that means what is now termed an 'Inn;' and as the word 'Inn' immediately precedes, it could scarcely have been intended to designate the same thing by both. The modern word is introduced from the French, and rather implies a house to which people resort for lodgings, than for the sort of entertainment procured only at an Inn." In that case a Lodging-house Keeper who procured and supplied, at a small profit, provisions for her lodgers,—such provisions being kept separately for the individuals for whom they were respectively procured,—was the keeper of an "Hotel:" and in *Gibson* v. *King* (sup.) it was held that a Boarding-house was, *à fortiori*, an "Hotel" within the definition.

HOUR.—In relation to the hour up to which a vendor can make a valid delivery on the last day fixed by the contract; *V. Startup* v. *Macdonald*, 6 M. & G. 593; 12 L. J. Ex. 477: *Va.* REASONABLE HOUR.

HOUSE.—"'*House*,' *Mese*, or *Maison* called in legall Latine *Messuagium*, containeth (as hath beene said) the buildings, curtelage, orchard and garden" (Co. Litt. 56 a, 56 b; in the margin it is added "Six acres of land may be parcell of a house"). "By the grant of a messuage, or house, *mesuagium*, the orchard, garden and curtilage doe passe; and so an acre or more may passe by the name of a house" (Co. Litt. 5 b). To this passage Mr. Hargrave has the following Note (1);—"*Contra* as to the garden, Keilw. 57. Mo. 24. Dal. in N. Bendl. 29. But see acc. *post*, 56 a and b. Plowd. 171. 2 Co. 32. 2 Saund. 401. S. P. adj. acc. in case of a devise. 3 Leon. 214, and Cro. Eliz. 89. See acc. 2 Cha. Cas. 27. See further Litt. Rep. 6, where the Court held that the devise of a messuage was not sufficient to pass two acres four miles distant from the messuage, though occupied with it. In Keilw. 57, a difference is taken between *messuage* and *domus*; and it is there said that *messuage* extends to the *curtilage*, though not to the *garden*, but that *domus* only comprehends buildings. Also in some of the cases cited, particularly that from Plowden, the grant was of a *messuage* with the *appurtenances*; on which *latter* word some stress seems to have been laid:" *Vth.* Elph. 588. *Sv.* MESSUAGE for authorities, in addition to Co. Litt. sup., that that word and "House" are synonymous, and that the distinction between them (which distinction seems to have been started by Frowike, C. J., Keilw. 57, pl. 7: *Va. Thomas* v. *Lane*, 2 Cha. Cas. 26) is not to be relied on.

"By the grant of a House, the Estovers appendant thereunto will pass" (Touch. 89), also "the doors, windows, locks and keys do pass as parcel of it, albeit at the time of the grant they be actually severed from the house," also "the ground whereon it doth stand doth pass" (Ib. 90). *Vf.* Woodf. 139, 140.

For the cases as to what will pass on a Devise of "House;" *V.* 1 Jarm. 779–782.

A "House" is a structure of a permanent character (1 Hale, 557), structurally severed from other tenements (and usually, *but not necessarily*, under its own separate roof) that is used, or may be used, for the habitation of man, and of which the holding (as distinct from lodgings) is independent (*Evans and Finch's Case*, Cro. Car. 473 ; W. Jones, 394 : *Yorkshire Insrce.* v. *Clayton*, 8 Q. B. D. 421 ; 51 L. J. Q. B. 82 : *Chapman* v. *Royal Bank of Scotland*, 50 L. J. Q. B. 670 ; 7 Q. B. D. 136 : *R.* v. *Usworth*, 5 L. J. M. C. 139 ; 5 A. & E. 261 ; 6 N. & M. 811 : *Cook* v. *Humber*, 31 L. J. C. P. 73 ; 11 C. B. N. S. 41, with which last case compare, *Wilson* v. *Roberts*, 31 L. J. C. P. 78 ; 11 C. B. N. S. 50, *Henrette* v. *Booth*, 33 L. J. C. P. 61 ; 15 C. B. N. S. 500, and *Cuthbertson* v. *Butterworth*, 38 L. J. C. P. 98 ; L. R. 4 C. P. 523 : *Nunn* v. *Denton*, 14 L. J. C. P. 43 ; 7 M. & G. 66 ; 1 Lut. 178 : *Daniel* v. *Coulsting*, 14 L. J. C. P. 70 ; 7 M. & G. 122 ; 1 Lut. 230 : *Monks* v. *Dykes*, 8 L. J. Ex. 73 ; 4 M. & W. 567). It is not necessary that a "House," if adapted for residential purposes, should be actually dwelt in (*Daniel* v. *Coulsting*, sup.). It is true that in *Surman* v. *Darley* (14 L. J. M. C. 145 ; 14 M. & W. 181) Pollock, C.B., in commencing his judgment said,—"We all think that the term 'houses' *primâ facie* means dwelling-houses ;" but there the phrase to be construed was, "houses of the *inhabitants*" (in a Rating Act applicable to a particular district), and it was held that Covent Garden Theatre was not such a "house." But, besides that the word "houses" was there coloured by its context "inhabitants," it could scarcely be contended that the Theatre had ever been adapted for residential purposes, so that the proposition above stated on the authority of *Daniel* v. *Coulsting*, that a "house," as such, need not be actually dwelt in, would seem unimpeached.

Notwithstanding the language used by Grove, J., in *Caiger* v. *St. Mary, Islington* (50 L. J. M. C. 63), it would seem that the decisions which have been pronounced on "Houses" as used in the 18 & 19 V. c. 120, s. 105, are in accordance with the principle just stated ; for a Church consecrated according to the rites of the Established Church (as it never can be legally used as a habitation) is *not* a "house" thereunder (*Angell* v. *Paddington*, 37 L. J. M. C. 171 ; L. R. 3 Q. B. 714 ; 9 B. & S. 496 : *G. E. Ry.* v. *Hackney*, 52 L. J. M. C. 105 ; 8 App. Ca. 687) ; but a Dissenting Chapel, merely registered as a place of worship, without any dedication in perpetuity, and over the vestry of which are rooms forming the residence of the care-taker and his family, *is* such a "house" (*Caiger* v. *St. Mary, Islington*, 50 L. J. M. C. 59 : *Wright* v. *Ingle*, 55 L. J. M. C. 17 ; 16 Q. B. D. 379 ; 54 L. T. 511 ; 34 W. R. 220 ; 50 J. P. 436 ; 2 Times Rep. 143).

"House" in s. 92, Lands C. C. Act, 1845, "comprises all that would pass by a Grant of a house" (per Wood, V.-C., *St. Thomas' Hospital* v. *Charing Cross Ry.*, 1 J. & H. 404) : and, therefore, the word "House" there, comprises not only the curtilage, but also the garden and all that is necessary to the enjoyment of the *house*,—as distinct from what is merely subsidiary to the personal use and enjoyment of a particular *occupier*,—

whether attached to the main building or not, even though purchased subsequently to the erection of the main building (Lloyd on Compensation, 5 Ed. 24 : Dart, 245 : *St. Thomas' Hospital* v. *Charing Cross Ry.*, 30 L. J. Ch. 395 ; 1 J. & H. 400 ; 4 L. T. 13 ; 9 W. R. 411 : *Marson* v. *Lond. Chat. & D. Ry.*, 37 L. J. Ch. 483 ; L. R. 6 Eq. 101 ; L. R. 7 Eq. 546 ; 18 L. T. 317), and two tenements, internally inter-communicated, may form only one "House" (*Harvie* v. *S. Devon Ry.*, W. N. (74) 195). For the other cases hereon, and as to what is "Part of a House" within the section ; *V. Kerferd* v. *Seacombe Ry.*, 36 W. R. 431 ; 57 L. J. Ch. 270 ; 58 L. T. 445 ; 4 Times Rep. 228 : *Littler* v. *Rhyl Imp. Commrs.*, W. N. (78) 219 : *Treadwell* v. *L. & S. W. Ry.*, W. N. (84) 233 : *Barnes* v. *Southsea Ry.*, 27 Ch. D. 536 : Lloyd on Comp., 5 Ed. 24–27 ; Woolf & Middleton on Comp., 204–207 ; 1 Jarm. 778, 779 n. (*o*) ; Dart, 245–247 ; Seton, 1417, 1418.

A Workhouse is a "House" within Water Works Clauses Act, 1847, 10 V. c. 17 (*Liskeard Un.* v. *Liskeard W. Works*, 7 Q. B. D. 505). *V.* PUBLIC PURPOSES.

"House," in Inhabited House Duty Act, 48 G. 3, c. 55 ;—*V. A.-G.* v. *Westminster Chambers Assn.*, 45 L. J. Ex. 886 ; 1 Ex. D. 469.

Trade Fixtures, though covenanted to be left, are not,—(but, *semble*, ordinary tenant's fixtures are),—within the phrase "*house or other buildings*" in s. 83, 14 G. 3, c. 78 (*Ex p. Gorely*, 34 L. J. Bank. 1).

Two houses with a common yard, water-closet and ash-pit, are not one "house" for the purpose of value in a covenant contained in a building lease (*Snow* v. *Whitehead*, 53 L. J. Ch. 885 ; 27 Ch. D. 588).

"Part of a house" is now a "House," &c., for the purposes of the Reform Act, 1832, if "separately occupied for the purpose of any trade, business, or profession" (s. 5, 41 & 42 V. c. 26). *Vth. Thompson* v. *Ward*, *Ellis* v. *Burch*, L. R. 6 C. P. 327.

V. DWELLING-HOUSE : THE HOUSE.

"House," as a word of limitation or substitution, "is considered as synonymous" with FAMILY (2 Jarm. 91). *Sq.*

HOUSEHOLD.—This word is frequently used in bequests as a qualifying adjective : *e.g.*, "household,"—*Furniture ; Goods ; Stuff ; Effects ; Property.*

Of these Household *Furniture*, and Household *Goods* (1 Jarm. 757 n.), and Household *Stuff* (Touch. 447) are synonyms. Either phrase will include all personal chattels that may contribute to the use or convenience of the householder or the ornament of the house, such as Plate (*Sv. Jesson* v. *Essington*, Pre. Ch. 207), Linen, China (both useful and ornamental), and Pictures, also Prize Medals, Coins or Trinkets, if framed and hung or otherwise disposed for household ornament (Wms. Exs. 1191 ; 1 Jarm. 757 n. ; Touch. 447 : *Field* v. *Peckett*, 30 L. J. Ch. 813 ; 29 Bea. 573 :

Re Londesborough, 50 L. J. Ch. 9) ; or the Clock of the house, if not a fixture (*Slanning* v. *Style,* 3 P. Wms. 336) ; but qy. as to a Bust (*Willis* v. *Curtois,* 1 Bea. 195).

But the Touch-Stone lays it down (p. 447) that a bequest of Household *Stuff* will *not* comprise "Apparel, Books, Weapons, Tools for Artificers, Cattle, Victuals, Corn, Plow-geere, and the like ;" a restriction equally applicable to Household "Goods" or "Furniture" (*Slanning* v. *Style,* 3 P. Wms. 334 : *Bridgman* v. *Dove,* 3 Atk. 202 : *Kelly* v. *Powlet,* Ambl. 611 : *Porter* v. *Tournay,* 3 Ves. 311). But in *Ouseley* v. *Anstruther* (10 Bea. 462), and *Hutchinson* v. *Smith* (11 W. R. 417) Books, and (in the latter case) Consumable Stores (Wines) passed by force of the general intention of the Will although there was no more appropriate word to carry them than "Furniture." On the other hand, in *Manton* v. *Tabois* (54 L. J. Ch. 1008 ; 30 Ch. D. 92), a bequest of "Furniture, *Goods and Chattels*" was held not to include Jewellery, Guns, Pistols, Tricycles, or Scientific Instruments. *V.* GOODS AND CHATTELS.

In *Peto* v. *Grissell* (5 L. J. Ch. 286) and *Paton* v. *Sheppard* (10 Sim. 186), Shadwell, V.-C., held that Tenant's Fixtures in a leasehold house passed as "Household Furniture :" but Jessel, M. R., refused to follow that ruling (*Finney* v. *Grice,* 48 L. J. Ch. 247 ; 10 Ch. D. 13).

"Household *Effects*" (*V.* EFFECTS) will comprise all that Household "Furniture," "Goods," or "Stuff" would carry ; and it will also comprise Books and Consumable Stores, and also Weapons if kept for domestic defence (*Cole* v. *Fitzgerald,* 1 Sim. & Stu. 189 ; 3 Russ. 301). By the case lastly cited it was also determined that the term "Household Effects" included a pair of pistols, lathes and apparatus for turning, with a quantity of ivory, mahogany, &c., a sawing machine, a vice and anvil, a copying-machine and an organ, and a hay-stack if retained exclusively for home consumption (*Va. Re Labron,* inf.) ; but that it did not include a pony or a cow, or some fowling-pieces that apparently were not used for domestic defence. Whether the V.-C. decided that a parrot was included, is a matter of dispute between the reporters (*V.* note, 3 Russ. 301). In *Re Labron,* Kay, J., decided that a bequest of "Household Effects" would carry hay-ricks, chicken and sheep-troughs, store pigs, poultry and carriages that were on the grounds (40 acres in extent) appertaining to the dwelling-house of the testator (29 S. J. 147) ; but not a horse, cows, or sheep (Ib., on a second application, 1 Times Rep. 248).

Articles of a "household" nature will pass under that description, although they may never have been used by the testator, nor even kept in his house (*Pellew* v. *Horsford,* 25 L. J. Ch. 352).

Neither of the terms now under definition will include Articles of Trade (*Pratt* v. *Jackson,* 2 P. Wms. 302 : *Le Farrant* v. *Spencer,* 1 Ves. sen. 97 : *V.* note, 24 L. J. Ch. 526 ; Wms. Exs. 1191 : *Sv. Manning* v. *Purcell,* 24 L. J. Ch. 522 ; 2 Sm. & G. 284 : *Fitzgerald* v. *Field,* 1 Russ. 427) ; nor Farming Stock (*Stone* v. *Parker,* 29 L. J. Ch. 874 : 1 Dr. &

Sm. 212); nor Articles exclusively of Personal Ornament (*Tempest* v. *Tempest*, 2 K. & J. 635). *V.* In or about.

"Household *Property*," held to include Leaseholds (*Harris* v. *Darley*, W. N. (73) 137).

HOUSEHOLDER.—"Householder," (*e.g.* in s. 8, 26 G. 3, c. 38) though it be not of so strict a sense as "Housekeeper," will not include a lodger or temporary inmate, but it will include a partner daily resorting to his firm's counting-house in the place referred to, the dwelling-part of which counting-house is occupied by a servant of the firm (*R.* v. *Hall*, 1 B. & C. 123).

HOUSEKEEPER.—*V.* Householder.

HOWE.—"*Howe, hoo, knol, law, pen, and cope* signifyeth a hill" (Co. Litt. 5 b).

HULMUS.—*V.* Holme.

HUMAN BEING.—*V.* Homicide.

HUMANE AND CHARITABLE PURPOSES.—A testator bequeathed £1000 to a lunatic asylum thereafter to be instituted "for the humane and charitable purposes of that institution." An asylum afterwards built under statutory compulsory powers, and maintained by compulsory rates, was held not entitled to the bequest (*Lechmere* v. *Curtler*, 24 L. J. Ch. 647).

HUNDRED.—"A grant of the Hundred by a subject passes only the franchises and not his lands within the Hundred: per King, C., *Bays* v. *Bird*, 2 P. Wms. 400" (Elph. 589; *wh. Vf.*)

"Hundred or Tithing;" *V. R.* v. *Milland*, 1 Burr. 577.

HUNDRED, PER.—Evidence of usage is admissible to show that "per Hundred" in a contract means some other figure than 100;—*e.g.* six score (*Smith* v. *Wilson*, 1 L. J. K. B. 194; 3 B. & Ad. 728).

HUNTING.—The grant or reservation of "Hunting, Shooting, Fishing and Sporting" includes all things generally hunted, shot, fished, or sported after, in contradistinction to small birds and things of a similar character, *e.g.*, rats and sparrows (per Willes, J., *Jeffryes* v. *Evans*, 34 L. J. C. P. 261; 19 C. B. N. S. 264). That case decided that rabbits would be included in such a reservation. It also decided that a covenant for quiet enjoyment in such a grant or reservation, does not imply any undertaking restricting the ordinary use of the land: *Va. Gearns* v. *Baker*, 44 L. J. Ch. 334; 10 Ch. 355.

The *Grant* of a right to sport without more, would probably be held not to exclude the grantor (*Bloomfield* v. *Johnston*, 8 Ir. R. C. L. 68); *secus*, of a *Reservation* of the right (*Paget* v. *Milles*, 3 Doug. 43). *V.* A.

"The liberty of Fowling has been decided to be a profit à prendre, and may be prescribed for as such (*Davies' Case*, 3 Mod. 246). The liberty to Hawk is one species of *ancupium* (Manwood, c. 18, s. 10, p. 107), the taking of birds by hawks, and seems to follow the same rule. The liberty of Fishing appears to be of the same nature; it implies, that the person who takes the fish, takes for his own benefit; it is Common of Fishing. The liberty of Hunting is open to more question, as that does not of itself import the right to the animal when taken; and if it were a license given to one individual either on one occasion, or for a time, or for his life, it would amount only to a mere personal license of pleasure, to be exercised by the individual licensed" (per Parke, B., *Wickham* v. *Hawker*, 10 L. J. Ex. 159, 160; 7 M. & W. 72); but even in the latter case if the grant were to the grantee "his heirs *and assigns*," or to be exercised by him or his "servants" it would be a profit à prendre (Ib.) *V.* FREE LIBERTY: PROFIT À PRENDRE: SERVANTS.

HUSBAND.—A gift to A. (a woman) for life,—remainder, "in trust for any husband with whom she may intermarry, if he shall survive her:"—Held, that a man whom A. had married but from whom she had been divorced and who survived her, was entitled as A.'s "Husband," although he had married again before her death (*Re Bullmore*, 52 L. J. Ch. 456; 22 Ch. D. 619). But in *Hitchins* v. *Morrieson* (40 Ch. D. 32; 37 W. R. 91), Kay, J., said he should certainly have decided *Re Bullmore* otherwise, and refused to follow and apply it to a similar bequest in which however the word was "Wife" instead of "Husband." *V.* WIFE.

A gift to an unmarried woman for life, remainder to her Husband in fee, gives a vested remainder in fee to her *first* husband (*Radford* v. *Willis*, 41 L. J. Ch. 19; 7 Ch. 7).

Vh. Chitty, Eq. Ind. 7709.

V. WIDOW: NEXT OF KIN.

HUSBANDRY.—*V.* SERVANT IN HUSBANDRY: TRADE.

I—IF

I HAVE.—*V.* Have : Now.

I PROMISE.—" Where a Note runs ' I promise to pay,' and is signed by two or more persons, it is deemed to be their joint and several Note" (s. 85 (2) Bills of Ex. Act, 1882).

I WILL BE READY.—*V.* Ready.

I WILL SEE YOU PAID.—These words amount, *primâ facie*, to an original and independent agreement to pay, as distinguished from a guarantee for payment (*Birkmyr* v. *Darnell,* 1 Salk. 27 ; 1 Sm. L. C. 335 : *Lakeman* v. *Mountstephen,* 43 L. J. Q. B. 188 ; L. R. 7 H. L. 17).

ICE.—*V.* Detention by Ice.

IDLE AND DISORDERLY PERSONS.—*V.* 5 G. 4, c. 83, s. 3 ; 34 & 35 V. c. 108 ; Steph. Cr. 129.

IF.—*V.* When.

" If," in a stipulation, will generally create a Condition Precedent (*Bromfield* v. *Crowder,* 1 B. & P. N. S. 313, 326 : *Festing* v. *Allen,* 12 M. & W. 289 : *Duffield* v. *Duffield,* 3 Bli. N. S. 260, 331).

" If " may create a Reservation; *e.g.* of Mines and minerals in an Inclosure Act, under these words, "*If* the lord shall enter on any inclosure for the purpose of getting any Coals or other Minerals" (*Micklethwait* v. *Winter,* 20 L. J. Ex. 313 ; 6 Ex. 644).

IF FROM ANY CAUSE.—*V.* Any.

IF NECESSARY.—A defendant under terms to take " Short Notice of Trial, if necessary," is not entitled to full notice, if the plaintiff, using reasonable diligence, is unable to give it (*Drake* v. *Pickford,* 15 M. & W. 607 ; 15 L. J. Ex. 346 : *Pretty* v. *Nauscawen,* 43 L. J. Ex. 3 ; L. R. 9 Ex. 42).

V. Necessary.

IF POSSIBLE.—*V.* Possible.

IF REQUIRED.—*V.* Required.

IF SUFFICIENT WATER.—*V.* Sufficient Water.

IF THEY SHALL THINK FIT.—*V. R.* v. *Boteler*, 33 L. J. M. C. 101 ; 4 B. & S. 959 : *R.* v. *Adamson*, 45 L. J. M. C. 46 ; 1 Q. B. D. 201 : Maxwell, 149, 150.

In such a phrase as "may *if they shall see fit*" the words italicised seem surplusage (*Julius* v. *Bishop of Oxford*, 5 App. Ca. 228).

V. May : Discretion : Think fit.

ILL.—The power (s. 17, 11 & 12 V. c. 42) to read a deposition if the deponent is "so ill as not to be able to travel," may arise if the source of illness is pregnancy (*R.* v. *Wellings*, 47 L. J. M. C. 100 ; 3 Q. B. D. 426 : *cp.* Sickness), or paralysis of speech (*R.* v. *Cockburn*, 26 L. J. M. C. 136 ; Dears. & B. 203) ; but not in a case of mere nervousness at the thought of appearing in court (*R.* v. *Farrell*, 38 J. P. 390), or absence abroad (*R.* v. *Austin*, 25 L. J. M. C. 48 ; Dears. 612). *Vh. R.* v. *Stephenson*, 31 L. J. M. C. 147 ; L. & C. 165.

V. Disease.

ILLEGAL PAYMENTS.—(a) At Parliamentary Elections; *V.* Corrupt and Illegal Practices Prevention Act, 1883 (46 & 47 V. c. 51), ss. 13–21 :

(b) At Municipal Elections ; *V.* Municipal Elections (C. & I. P.) Act, 1884 (47 & 48 V. c. 70), ss. 9–18.

Vh. Leigh & Le Marchant, Ch. 3 ; Mattinson & Macaskie, Ch. 2.

ILLEGAL PRACTICES.—(a) At Parliamentary Elections; *V.* Corrupt and Illegal Practices Prevention Act, 1883 (46 & 47 V. c. 51), ss. 7–12.

(b) At Municipal Elections; *V.* Municipal Elections (C. & I. P.) Act, 1884 (47 & 48 V. c. 70), ss. 4–8.

Vh. Leigh & Le Marchant, Ch. 2 ; Mattinson & Macaskie, Ch. 2.

ILLEGITIMATE CHILD.—*V.* Child : Natural Children.

ILL-TREAT.—*V.* Cruelty *to Animals.*

ILLUSORY.—*V.* Fictitious.

IMITATE.—*V.* Copy.

IMMEDIATE APPROACH.—"Immediate Approach" to a Railway Bridge ; *V. Waterford Ry.* v. *Kearney*, 12 Ir. C. L. Rep. 224.

IMMEDIATE ARREST.—*V. R.* v. *Curran*, 3 C. & P. 397 : *Hanway* v. *Boultbee*, 1 Moo. & R. 15 : Immediately.

IMMEDIATE EXPECTANCY.—*V.* Entitled in im. exp.

IMMEDIATE POSSESSION.—In an agreement for a Lease, the words "Immediate Possession, if required" do not fix the commencement of the term; and if it be not otherwise fixed there is no contract (*Rock Portland Cement Co.* v. *Wilson*, 52 L. J. Ch. 214).

IMMEDIATE USE OR ENJOYMENT.—"'Occupier,' shall include every person in the Immediate Use or Enjoyment of any hereditaments rateable under this Act, whether corporeal or incorporeal," 1 & 2 V. c. 56, s. 124; *V. Callan* v. *Armstrong*, 16 L. R. Ir. 33.

IMMEDIATELY.—"The word 'Immediately,' although in strictness it excludes all mean Times, yet to make good the Deeds and Intents of Parties it shall be construed such convenient Time as is reasonably requisite for doing the Thing" (*Pybus* v. *Mitford*, 2 Lev. 77). "The Court cannot say it absolutely excludes all *mesne* acts" (*R.* v. *Francis*, Ca. temp. Hardwick, 115): but "Immediately" implies that the act to be done should be done with all convenient speed (per Rolfe, B., *Thompson* v. *Gibson*, 10 L. J. Ex. 243; 8 M. & W. 281).

Thus as regards a Judge's Certificate which any particular statute says shall be given "immediately," that "does not mean ten minutes, or a quarter or half an hour; but such a lapse of time as excludes the possibility of other business intervening to alter the impression made on the judge's mind" (per Abinger, C. B., Ib.). *V.* as to granting Judge's Certificates "immediately," under the various statutes: (Costs) *Thompson* v. *Gibson*, sup.: *Gillett* v. *Green*, 10 L. J. Ex. 124; 7 M. & W. 347: *Spain* v. *Cadell*, 10 L. J. Ex. 313; 8 M. & W. 131: *Page* v. *Pearce*, 10 L. J. Ex. 434; 8 M. & W. 677: *Shuttleworth* v. *Cocker*, 10 L. J. C. P. 1; 2 Sc. N. S. 47: *Nelmes* v. *Hedges*, 2 Dowl. N. S. 350: *Grace* v. *Clinch*, 12 L. J. Q. B. 273; 4 Q. B. 606: *Jones* v. *Williams*, 14 L. J. Ex. 76; 13 M. & W. 420: *Forsdike* v. *Stone*, 37 L. J. C. P. 301; L. R. 3 C. P. 607: (Special Jury) *Christie* v. *Richardson*, 12 L. J. Ex. 86; 10 M. & W. 688: *Skipper* v. *Skipper*, 29 L. J. P. M. & A. 133.

V. DIRECTLY: FORTHWITH.

So where a statute requires anything to be done "Immediately," that is the same thing as "Forthwith;" and implies "speedy and prompt action and an omission of all delay; in other words, that the thing to be done should be done as quickly as is reasonably possible" (per Cockburn, C. J., *R.* v. *Berkshire Jus.*, 48 L. J. M. C. 137; 4 Q. B. D. 469: *Va. R.* v. *Aston*, 19 L. J. M. C. 236; 1 L. M. & P. 491). So where on an Appeal to Quarter Sessions recognizances are required to be entered into "Immediately" after notice of appeal, that raises a question of fact which the Sessions are to determine having regard to all the circumstances of each case; and if they, fairly exercising their judgment, say that a lapse of a week is *not* too long (*Re Blues*, 5 E. & B. 291), or that one of four days *is* too long, their determination is final (*R.* v. *Berkshire Jus.*, sup.).

"May be *immediately apprehended* without a Warrant and *forthwith taken*" before a Justice, s. 103, 24 & 25 V. c. 96; Whether this power is properly exercised, is a question for the jury, who should give effect to "Immediately" and "Forthwith" according to the principle just stated (*Griffiths* v. *Taylor, Thatcher* v. *Taylor*, 46 L. J. C. P. 152; 2 C. P. D. 194).

Similarly where a power to seize goods is given by a Bill of Sale if the grantor does not "Immediately" upon demand make a prescribed payment, that means that the payment is to be made within a reasonably quick and prompt time after the demand, of which the jury are to judge having regard to the circumstances of the time and place of making the demand, including time to enquire into the authority of the person making the demand if it be not made by the creditor himself (*Toms* v. *Wilson*, 32 L. J. Q. B. 33, 382; 4 B. & S. 455; 11 W. R. 117; 7 L. T. 421: *Brighty* v. *Norton*, 32 L. J. Q. B. 38; 11 W. R. 167: *Massey* v. *Sladen*, 38 L. J. Ex. 34; L. R. 4 Ex. 13). *Cp.* INSTANTLY.

A similar rule would apply where a person is to perform an act "Immediately" after an Award (18 E. 4, 22, cited *Butler & Baker's Case*, 3 Rep. 28 b, 34).

V. ON DEMAND: POSSIBLE: REASONABLE.

IMMEDIATELY ADJOINING LAND.—*V.* ADJOINING OWNER.

IMMOVEABLES.—A devise of all testator's "Immoveables" passes leases, rents, grass and the like; but not debts (Touch. 447). *V.* MOVEABLES.

IMPEACHED.—"Impeached, affected or incumbered in title, estate or otherwise howsoever;" *V. Clifford* v. *Hoare*, 43 L. J. C. P. 225; L. R. 9 C. P. 362: AFFECT.

IMPEACHMENT OF WASTE.—*V.* WITHOUT IMPEACHMENT OF WASTE.

IMPENDING.—A legal proceeding is "impending" when a recourse to it is pressingly necessary in order to ascertain a right or a status (*Grimston* v. *Turner*, 18 W. R. 724).

V. PENDING.

"Impending *Danger*," Board of Trade Regulations for Steam Trams (No. 3); *V. Jolly* v. *North Staffordshire Tramway Co.*, Times, 27 July, 1887: *Downing* v. *Birmingham & Mid. Trams*, 5 Times Rep. 40.

IMPERFECT.—An "Imperfect or Erroneous" Valuation, within s. 11, Copyhold Act, 1887, 50 & 51 V. c. 73, includes a case where the valuation is too low; "Erroneous" is not confined to a valuation "erroneous in principle" (*R.* v. *Land Commrs.*, 23 Q. B. D. 59; 58 L. J. Q. B. 313; 5 Times Rep. 445).

IMPERIL.—Where a man, acting for a married woman with whom he was living, took a Lease of a Public-house and agreed with the landlord that he would do nothing whereby the License might be "imperilled," and handed the Lease and endorsed the License to the woman who carried on the business, and afterwards, having quarrelled with the woman, the man left her with an intention to abandon the premises and did not return, and the woman continued to carry on the business; it was held that, only 3 days having elapsed since the man left, he had not then done anything to "imperil" the License so as to justify the landlord to re-enter under a clause of forfeiture:—had the landlord allowed time to elapse sufficient to enable the woman to obtain a transfer of the license, and she had neglected to do so, possibly the result would have been different (*Moore* v. *Robinson*, 48 L. J. Q. B. 156).

IMPLEMENT.—"Implements;" *V.* Termes de la Ley, *Implements:* MATERIALS.

IMPLEMENT OF HOUSEBREAKING.—Common door-keys, or a pair of pincers, may be such Implements within s. 58, 24 & 25 V. c. 96 (*R.* v. *Oldham*, 21 L. J. M. C. 134; 2 Den. 472).

IMPLEMENT OF HUSBANDRY.—"'Implements of Husbandry,' in 3 G. 4, c. 126, s. 32, shall be deemed to include Threshing Machines" (s. 4, 14 & 15 V. c. 38); and a Steam Engine used for working a Threshing Machine (*semble*, or any other Implement of Husbandry) is part of the Machine, and within the exemption from Turnpike Toll, though unconnected with the machine at the time of passing through the Toll-gate, and though capable of being used for other purposes (*R.* v. *Matty*, 27 L. J. M. C. 59; 8 E. & B. 712).

IMPORT FOR SALE.—As to "importing for sale" a printed book contrary to s. 17, Copyright Act, 1842 (5 & 6 V. c. 45); *V. Cooper* v. *Whittingham*, 49 L. J. Ch. 752; 15 Ch. D. 501: *Va.* that case for the distinction drawn by Jessel, M. R., between "import for sale" and "*knowingly* sell, publish or expose to sale" as provided in the section cited; *Vf.* Watson, Eq. 127.

IMPORTED.—The 48 G. 3, c. civ, s. 33, imposed a duty on all goods "imported into or exported from Berwick Harbour." The harbour extended from Berwick Bridge down the Tweed to the sea, but not above the Bridge. Goods were brought up the river in a sea-going vessel, which, having first used the Harbour Commissioners' rings and posts in order to moor the vessel while lowering the masts, passed through Berwick Bridge and unloaded her cargo about 200 yards above the Bridge and beyond the limits of the Harbour:—Held, that these goods were not "imported into" the Harbour, and as such liable to duty (*Wilson* v. *Robertson*, 24 L. J. Q. B. 185; 4 E. & B. 923).

V. EXPORTED.

IMPORTUNITY.—"Importunity," (to invalidate a Will), "in its correct legal acceptation, must be in such a degree as to take away from the testator free agency; it must be such importunity as he is too weak to resist; such as will render the act no longer the act of the deceased; nct the free act of a capable testator." (Wms. Exs. 46, citing *Kindleside* v. *Harrison,* 2 Phillimore, 551, 552.)

IMPOSE.—*V.* DECEIVE.

IMPOSED.—As used in a covenant to pay rates, &c. "imposed" means imposed by compulsion; and, therefore, where a lessor covenanted to pay the rates, taxes, and impositions which might be "imposed" on the demised premises, it was held that he was not liable to the Water Rate (*Badcock* v. *Hunt,* 58 L. J. Q. B. 134; 22 Q. B. D. 145).

V. RATE.

IMPOSITIONS.—"Impositions," in the collocation in a lessee's covenant to pay "Taxes, Rates, Assessments, and Impositions," means Impositions of a nature similar to that of Taxes, Rates, and Assessments and does not comprise an exceptional burden imposed by a local authority and ordinarily to be borne by the landlord (*Tidswell* v. *Whitworth,* 36 L. J. C. P. 103; L. R. 2 C. P. 326). In the argument of *Crosse* v. *Raw* (43 L. J. Ex. 145) counsel said that "Impositions" was as extensive a word as "OUTGOINGS;" but that is not borne out by *Tidswell* v. *Whitworth.*

V. DEDUCTIONS: DUTIES: OUTGOINGS: TAXES.

IMPOST.—*V.* Termes de la Ley.

IMPOTENT.—*V.* SICK.

IMPOUND.—To "impound or otherwise secure" a Distress, 11 G. 2, c. 12, implies its being put in an enclosed place (per Tindal, C. J., *Thomas* v. *Harries,* 1 M. & G. 702; 9 L. J. C. P. 308; 1 Scott, N. R. 524). *V.* SECURE.

A document is impounded when it is ordered by a Court to be kept in the custody of its officer.

IMPOUND OR CONFINE.—The penalty provided by 12 & 13 V. c. 92, s. 5, on "every person who shall impound or confine" animals and then fail to supply them with proper food and water, applies to the person at whose instance they are detained, and does not extend to the poundkeeper who, in keeping the animals, only does what he is obliged to do (*Dargan* v. *Davies,* 46 L. J. M. C. 122; 2 Q. B. D. 118; 41 J. P. 468).

IMPRIMIS.—*V.* IN THE FIRST PLACE.

IMPRISONMENT.—When a statute provides punishment by "Commitment" or "Imprisonment," without stating its commencement, it commences immediately (*Foggassas' Case, Bonham's Case,* Plow. Com. 17 b, and 8 Rep. 119 ; *cp.* 11 & 12 V. c. 43, s. 25) ; but if there be no limit to its duration, the prisoner must remain at the discretion of the Court (Dwar. 674, citing Dalt. 410).

IMPROPER.—"'Improper' really means 'wrongful,'—that is otherwise than by inevitable accident" (per Brett, M.R., *The Warkworth,* 53 L. J. P. D. & A. 66).

IMPROPER NAVIGATION.—"'Improper Navigation,' within the meaning of this deed (one between owners for their mutual indemnity), is something improperly done with the ship or part of the ship in the course of the voyage . . . . an omission properly to navigate the ship" (per Willes, J., *Good* v. *London Steamship Owners Assn.*, L. R. 6 C. P. 569) ; and accordingly it was there held that damage to cargo from water, caused by the bilge-cock and sea-cock being negligently left open, was damage from "Improper Navigation."

"Improper Navigation" within subs. 4, s. 54, Merchant Shipping Act Amendment Act, 1862 (25 & 26 V. c. 63), may result as well from structural defect in the vessel or from its gear being out of order, as from the negligence of those on board (*The Warkworth,* 53 L. J. P. D. & A. 4, 65 ; 9 P.D. 20, 145 : *Carmichael* v. *Liverpool Sailing-Ship Assn.*, 56 L. J. Q. B. 208, 428 ; 19 Q. B. D. 242 ; 57 L. T. 550 ; 35 W. R. 793 ; 3 Times Rep. 636).

But neither in a document *inter partes,* nor in the statute cited, does damage to cargo, caused by its being placed in a badly cleansed hold, arise from "Improper Navigation ;" such damage arises rather from "Improper Stowage" (*Canada Shipping Co.* v. *British Shipowners Assn.*, 22 Q. B. D. 727 ; 58 L. J. Q. B. 462 ; 38 W. R. 87 ; 5 Times Rep. 700).

V. NAVIGATION.

IMPROPER STOWAGE.—*V. Canada Shipping Co.* v. *British Shipowners Assn.*, cited IMPROPER NAVIGATION.

IMPROVE.—" Utmost endeavours to improve," in a covenant in a Lease; *V. Croft* v. *Lumley,* 25 L. J. Q. B. 73, 223 ; 27 Ib. 321 ; 6 H. L. Ca. 672.

V. REPAIR.

IMPROVEMENT.—*V.* WINDOW.

IMPURE.—*V.* PURE.

IN.—"If one grant all his goods *in* such a place ; by this grant nothing doth pass but the goods that are in such a place at the time of the grant, and not any other goods that shall be there afterwards" (Touch. 98).

A legacy of the goods, or of certain classes of goods, "in" a house or other place, will comprise all the goods of the kind indicated the usual locality of which is in such house or other place, though they may at the time be actually somewhere else, if they have only been removed from their usual locality for a temporary purpose, *e.g.*, at testator's banker's for safe custody (*Re Johnson*, 53 L. J. Ch. 645 ; 26 Ch. D. 538 : Wms. Exs. 1333). But in *Heseltine* v. *Heseltine* (3 Madd. 276) it was held that a gift of "the chattels *in* my house at Doctors' Commons" did not pass the furniture in testator's house in Bedford Square, where he subsequently removed, though they were in his house at Doctors' Commons at the date of his Will. *Vf. Spencer* v. *Spencer*, 21 Bea. 548.

A bequest of all testator's property "in" a particular country, county or other locality will include all the *Debts* due to him from persons resident in such locality (*Nisbet* v. *Murray*, 5 Ves. 149 : *Tyrone* v. *Waterford*, 29 L. J. Ch. 486 ; 1 D. G. F. & J. 613 : *Arnold* v. *Arnold*, 4 L. J. Ch. 123 ; 2 M. & K. 365 : *Horsfield* v. *Ashton*, 2 Jur. N. S. 193, 355 : *Guthrie* v. *Walrond*, 52 L. J. Ch. 165 ; 22 Ch. D. 573 : *Cp. Jones* v. *Sefton*, cited IN OR ABOUT).

But an Advowson is not properly described as being situate "in," or "at," a place, and it will not, *primâ facie*, pass under such general words as "heredits situate in" a particular place ; though if the grantor or testator had no other hereditament in that place, it might pass, and so, if the context favoured its inclusion (*Crompton* v. *Jarratt*, 54 L. J. Ch. 1109 ; 30 Ch. D. 298, and cases there cited).

As to what passes under a general description of property "in" or "at" a place ; *V. Crompton* v. *Jarratt*, sup. : *Rooke* v. *Kensington*, 2 K. & J. 753 ; 25 L. J. Ch. 795 : *Early* v. *Rathbone*, 57 L. J. Ch. 652 ; 58 L. T. 517 : AT.

In *Doe* d. *Humphreys* v. *Roberts* (5 B. & Ald. 407), there was a devise of all testator's messuage or dwelling-house in High Street in the town of H., and all and every his buildings and hereditaments "*in*" *the same street :* the testator had only one house in High Street, but behind it he had two cottages fronting Bakehouse Lane ; there was no thoroughfare through that lane, the only entrance into it being from the High Street : it was held that the two cottages passed under the Will, and Holroyd, J., said, "The only way to these cottages was through the High Street, and there was no thoroughfare through Bakehouse Lane. If there had been an opening from the High Street to these cottages alone, they would clearly be 'in' the street, and I can see no difference from the circumstance of there being other houses in the court." *V.* WITHIN.

V. NEAR.

"*In his Trade or Business*" (s. 44 (iii), Bankry. Act, 1883), "means, not necessarily visibly in his trade or business, but acquired for the purposes of the business and used for those purposes" (per Lindley, L.J., *Colonial Bank* v. *Whinney*, 55 L. J. Ch. 591 ; 30 Ch. D. 261 :—*V.* that case reversed by H. L. on another point, 56 L. J. Ch. 43 ; 11 App. Ca. 426 ; 55 L. T. 362 ; 34 W. R. 705. *Vf. Re Jenkinson*, 54 L. J. Q. B. 601 ; 15 Q. B. D. 441).

A contract for goods, to be paid for "in," or "within," a *stated period*, gives the buyer the right to call for delivery at any reasonable time within that period without tendering the price, which is only payable at the expiration of the period (*Spartali* v. *Benecke*, 19 L. J. C. P. 293; 10 C. B. 212: *Vh.* Blackb. 226).

IN ACCORDANCE WITH THE FORM.—Bills of Sale as Security for Money, must be "in accordance with the Form" prescribed in the Sch. to Bills of S. Act, 1882 (*V.* s. 9). In *Re Barber, Ex p. Stanford* (55 L. J. Q. B. 344; 17 Q. B. D. 269; 54 L. T. 894; 34 W. R. 507), it was pointed out in the jdgmt. of Esher, M.R. and Cotton, Lindley, Bowen, and Lopes, L.JJ., that the words of that section did not say that a Bill of Sale was to be "*in* the Form" prescribed, but "*in accordance with* the Form;" and it was added, "the distinction can scarcely be accidental:" the phrase means "*substantially* in accordance with the form" (per Day, J., *Consolidated Credit Corp.* v. *Gosney*, 55 L. J. Q. B. 62; 16 Q. B. D. 24; 54 L. T. 21; 34 W. R. 106).

But still the requirement that a document must be "in Accordance with the Form" prescribed is one of stringent obligation; as those who did not pay due heed to it in the Act cited, have found to their cost. *Vh. Liverpool Investment Soc.* v. *Richardson*, 55 L. J. Q. B. 455 n.; 2 Times Rep. 602, *Svth. Re Cleaver*, 55 L. J. Q. B. 455: *Melville* v. *Stringer*, 53 L. J. Q. B. 482; 13 Q. B. D. 392; 50 L. T. 774; 32 W. R. 890: *Hetherington* v. *Groome*, 53 L. J. Q. B. 576; 13 Q. B. D. 789; 51 L. T. 412; 33 W. R. 103: *Sibley* v. *Higgs*, 54 L. J. Q. B. 525; 15 Q. B. D. 619; 33 W. R. 748: *Parsons* v. *Hargreaves*, 55 L. J. Q. B. 408; 17 Q. B. D. 336; 34 W. R. 717: *Calvert* v. *Thomas*, 56 L. J. Q. B. 470; 19 Q. B. D. 204; 57 L. T. 441; 35 W. R. 616: *Macey* v. *Gilbert*, 57 L. J. Q. B. 461: *Kelly* v. *Kellond*, or, *Thomas* v. *Kelly*, 58 L. J. Q. B. 66; 13 App. Ca. 506. *Cp.* with last case, *Re Burdett*, 57 L. J. Q. B. 263; 20 Q. B. D. 310. *Vf. Blankenstein* v. *Robertson*, 6 Times Rep. 178: Reed on Bills of Sale Acts, 7 Ed. 131–144.

The obligation of the phrase is so exigent that if a transaction by way of security on chattels cannot, from its nature, be made "in Accordance with the Form," it ought not to be made at all (*Ex p. Parsons*, 55 L. J. Q. B. 137; 16 Q. B. D. 532; 53 L. T. 897; 34 W. R. 329: *Hughes* v. *Little*, 56 L. J. Q. B. 96; 18 Q. B. D. 32; 55 L. T. 476; 35 W. R. 36).

V. In the form.

IN ADDITION.—*V.* Addition.

IN AID.—Where a testator charged his general realty "*in aid of my personal estate* and in exoneration of my other personal estate, with the payment of all my just debts, funeral and testamentary expenses,"—it was held that this did not amount to a direction to pay a mortgage debt on realty specifically devised (*Re Newmarch*, 48 L. J. Ch. 28; 9 Ch. D. 12: *Buckley* v. *Buckley*, 19 L. R. Ir. 555: Debts).

IN BLOOD.—The addition of "In Blood" to "Next-of-kin," makes the latter phrase stronger against a widow taking under it (*Re Fitzgerald*, 58 L. J. Ch. 662 ; 37 W. R. 552).

IN CASE.—*V.* WHEN.

IN CASE OF NEED.—"Referee in case of Need," of a Bill of Exchange, is a person to whom the Holder may resort if the Bill is dishonoured (s. 15, Bills of Ex. Act, 1882).

IN CASE OF THE DEATH.—*V.* DIE.

IN CASH.—A statutory requirement that things,—*e.g.* Shares in a Company under s. 25, Companies Act, 1867—shall be paid for "In Cash," is satisfied not only by actually handing over the amount in moneys counted, but by anything that would sustain a plea of payment in point of law, as distinguished from mere accord and satisfaction ; and therefore if there be *money due* to the person who has to make the payment and that money be set-off against what he has to pay, that will be a payment "In Cash" (*Spargo's Case*, 8 Ch. 407 ; 42 L. J. Ch. 488 : *Fothergill's Case*, 8 Ch. 270; 42 L. J. Ch. 481 : *White's Case*, 12 Ch. D. 517 ; 48 L. J. Ch. 820 : *Kent's Case*, 39 Ch. D. 259 : *Re Jones & Co.*, 41 Ch. D. 159 ; 58 L. J. Ch. 582). But the debt must be presently payable (*Re Land Development Assn.*, 57 L. J. Ch. 977 ; 39 Ch. D. 259 ; 59 L. T. 449 ; 36 W. R. 818). *Vh.* Buckl. 525.

V. CASH.

IN CHARGE.—"In Charge," s. 126, subs. 2, 38 & 39 V. c. 55 ; *V. Tunbridge Wells* v. *Bishopp*, 2 C. P. D. 187.

IN CIRCULATION.—*V.* CIRCULATION.

IN COMMON USE.—*V.* COMMON TO THE TRADE.

IN CONFIDENCE.—*V.* PRECATORY TRUST.

IN DANGER.—*V.* DANGER.

IN DEFAULT.—An Owner "in Default," s. 150, P. H. Act, 1875, does not include a person who was owner when the notice to do the work was given, but who has ceased to be owner before completion of the works by the Local Authority (*R.* v. *Swindon*, 48 L. J. M. C. 119 ; 4 Q. B. D. 305).

V. DIE WITHOUT ISSUE.

IN EXECUTION.—*V.* PURSUANCE.

IN FULL.—Agreement to pay rent "in full," s. 103, 5 & 6 V. c. 35 ; *V. Lamb* v. *Brewster*, 48 L. J. Q. B. 421 ; 4 Q. B. D. 220.

Sending a cheque "in full *of all demands*," even though the cheque be kept and placed to credit, does not, of itself, amount to an Accord and Satisfaction (*Day* v. *McLea*, 22 Q. B. D. 610 ; 58 L. J. Q. B. 293 ; 60 L. T. 947 ; 5 Times Rep. 379).

"In full *for the voyage;*" *V. Sweeting* v. *Darthez*, 23 L. J. C. P. 131 ; 14 C. B. 538.

IN HÂC RE.—Solicitor "In hâc re ;" *V.* jdgmt. of Turner, L. J., *Holman* v. *Loynes*, 23 L. J. Ch. 534.

IN HIS CAPACITY OR CHARACTER.—*V.* CAPACITY : CHARACTER.

IN HIS DEMESNE AS OF FEE.—*V.* DEMESNE.

IN HIS OWN RIGHT.—Holding Shares "in his own right," *quà* qualification of Director, does not mean holding beneficially (*Pulbrook* v. *Richmond Mining Co.*, 48 L. J. Ch. 65 ; 9 Ch. D. 610 ; 27 W. R. 377). In that case Jessel, M. R., said, "the Company cannot look behind the Register as to the beneficial interest." But in *Bainbridge* v. *Smith* (41 Ch. D. 462 ; 37 W. R. 594), Cotton, L. J. (*obiter*) dissented from that view, whilst Lindley, L. J., said that that conventional meaning had been acted upon so long that he was not prepared to disturb it (*Vth. Re Bainbridge*, 34 S. J. 154, 155 ; W. N. (89) 228). *Vh.* 33 S. J. 624 : *Va. Gill* v. *Continental Union Gas Co.*, 41 L. J. Ex. 176 ; L. R. 7 Ex. 332.

Vf. Re Blakely Ordnance Co., 46 L. J. Ch. 367.

IN HIS TRADE OR BUSINESS.—This phrase, in s. 44 (iii) Bankry. Act, 1883, does not comprise property unconnected with a bankrupt's trade or business, although mortgaged by him to secure a trade account (*Re Jenkinson*, 54 L. J. Q. B. 601 ; 15 Q. B. D. 441 : *Vf. Colonial Bank* v. *Whinney*, 55 L. J. Ch. 585 ; 56 Ib. 43 ; 30 Ch. D. 261 ; 11 App. Ca. 426).

V. TRADE : BUSINESS AS A TRADER.

IN LIEU OF.—Bequest "in lieu of ;" *V. Barclay* v. *Maskelyne*, 5 Jur. N. S. 12 : *Cooper* v. *Day*, 3 Mer. 154 : *Hill* v. *Walker*, 4 K. & J. 166.

V. INSTEAD OF : LIEU AND SUBSTITUTION.

IN LIKE MANNER.—*V.* AFORESAID.

IN LOCO PARENTIS.—*V.* LOCO PARENTIS.

IN MANNER AFORESAID.—*V.* AFORESAID.

IN OPEN COURT.—*V.* OPEN.

IN OPERATION.—V. OPERATION.

IN OR ABOUT.—In *Re Labron* (29 S. J. 147), Kay, J., held that residuary bequest of household furniture, plate, books, . . . and other household effects "in or about" testator's dwelling-house—included hay-ricks, chicken and sheep-troughs, store pigs, poultry and carriages that were on the grounds (40 acres in extent) appertaining to the dwelling-house. *Cp. Fitzgerald* v. *Field*, inf. : *V.* HOUSEHOLD.

A bequest of all corn &c., "in or about" a Mill, held not to include a cargo of wheat consigned to the testator but which, in due course of transit, did not reach the mill till after his death (*Lane* v. *Sewell*, W. N. (74) 51).

And there would appear to be no difference, in such a connection as the foregoing, between "in *or* about," and in "*and* about." Thus in *Gower* v. *Gower* (Ambl. 612 ; 2 Eden, 201) the Running Horses (Race-horses ?) of a nobleman were held to be included in a bequest of goods and chattels "which should be in and about his dwelling-house and out-houses" (*Vth. Porter* v. *Tournay*, 3 Ves. 314). But a Money Bond and a sum of Cash (found in an iron chest in testator's house) were held not to pass under a bequest of such parts of personal estate "as should be in and about his house" (*Jones* v. *Sefton*, 4 Ves. 166), the short reason given by Loughborough, L.C., being, "there is no annexation." No such consideration as that is however to be discerned in *Fitzgerald* v. *Field* (1 Russ. 427), wherein the words "household furniture, &c., and utensils in and about my house," were held not to pass farming utensils on lands occupied by testator along with his house.

"In or about," as used in stating a date ; *V. R.* v. *St. Paul's, Covent Garden*, 14 L. J. M. C. 109 ; 7 Q. B. 232.

IN OR AS OF.—*V.* AS OF.

IN OR NEAR.—*V.* NEAR : IN SIVE JUXTA.

IN PORT.—*V. Hunter* v. *Northern Insrce.*, 13 App. Ca. 717.

IN POSSESSION.—*V.* POSSESSION : COME TO.

IN PURSUANCE.—*V.* PURSUANCE.

IN QUESTION.—*V.* MATTER.

IN RECEIPT.—"In receipt of the *Profits* of such land or such rent," s. 3, Stat. Lim. 3 & 4 W. 4, c. 27 :—"The expression 'in receipt of the profits of any land' is used in this Act in conjunction with the words 'in possession of the land,' to denote, not the receipt of rent from a tenant, but the receipt of the actual proceeds of the land" (Sug. R. P. Statutes, 2 Ed. 47. *V. Grant* v. *Ellis*, 11 L. J. Ex. 228; 9 M. & W. 113 : upon which case, *V. Irish Land Commission* v. *Grant*, 10 App. Ca. 26).

IN REGULAR TURNS OF LOADING.—*V.* TURN.

IN RELATION TO.—*V.* RELATING: RELATION: GENERALLY.

IN RESPECT OF.—"An offence in respect of the commission of which," s. 17 (1) Summary Jurisdiction Act, 1879; *V. Williams* v. *Wynne*, 57 L. J. M. C. 30; 58 L. T. 283; 52 J. P. 343.

IN SEARCH.—"In Search, or Pursuit, of Game;" *V.* SEARCH.

IN SIVE JUXTA.—*V. A-G.* v. *Horner*, 54 L. J. Q. B. 227; 55 Ib. 193; 14 Q. B. D. 245; 11 App. Ca. 66: NEAR.

IN THAT BEHALF.—"'In that behalf,' is a phrase of wide signification" (per Pollock, C. B., *Garby* v. *Harris*, 21 L. J. Ex. 160).

IN THE CAUSE.—*V.* COSTS IN THE CAUSE.

IN THE CONDUCT OF A SUIT.—Matters done before action brought or after judgment recovered, were not "In the conduct of a suit," within s. 36, Co. Co. Act, 1856, 19 & 20 V. c. 108 (*Druiff* v. *Joel*, 51 L. J. Q. B. 490; nom. *Re Emanuel*, 9 Q. B. D. 408: *Vth. Re Dod & Co., Ex p. Lamond*, 21 Q. B. D. 242). *V.* CONDUCTING.

IN THE COURSE.—"Debts due to the bankrupt in the Course of his Trade" (s. 44, iii, Bankry. Act, 1883) mean in *connection* with his trade (*Ex p. Rensberg, Re Pryce*, 4 Ch. D. 685).

IN THE FIRST PLACE.—In some of the cases reliance seems to have been placed on such words as "*Imprimis*," "*In the first place*," and "*First*" in determining whether a direction to pay Debts charged the realty; but it seems now tolerably well settled that such phrases "are merely introductory words of form, denoting the commencement of the testamentary act; or, if they have any meaning, only denote the order of payment, not the fund out of which payment is to be made" (2 Jarm. 588), nor do they imply priority of payment (*Nash* v. *Dillon*, 1 Moll. 236). *Vf.* 2 Jarm. 587–590, for a discussion of the cases hereon; *Va.* Watson, Eq. 32.

"In the first place," "In the next place;" *V. Re Hardy*, 50 L. J. Ch. 241; 17 Ch. D. 798.

IN THE FORM.—Where a statute says that a thing shall be "in the Form" prescribed, that means that the form must be strictly and literally followed (*Henry* v. *Armitage*, 53 L. J. Q. B. 111; 12 Q. B. D. 257. *V.*, on this phrase in R. 2 of Rules of Nov. 1842, under 5 & 6 V. c. 116, *Re Russell* and *Re Fry*, 28 L. T. O. S. 343: *Re Hendrie*, 31 Ib. 14: *Re Pollastrini*, 7 L. T. 171: *Re Edwards*, 28 L. T. O. S. 258). *Secus*, where the words "or to the like effect" are added (*Henry* v. *Armitage*, sup.). Where the words are IN ACCORDANCE WITH THE FORM, the obligation to comply with the Form is strict ; though, probably, not so strict as where "in the Form" is used.

IN THE SAME MANNER.—*V.* AFORESAID.

IN THIS PARTICULAR.—*V.* PARTICULAR.

IN TRUST.—The phrase "In trust" or "On trust" may frequently be read as, "entrusted to :" *e.g.*, in a floating fire policy by a carrier or warehouseman on "goods *in trust* or on commission" (*Waters* v. *Monarch Co.*, 25 L. J. Q. B. 102 ; 5 E. & B. 880 : *Lond. & N. W. Ry.* v. *Glyn*, 28 L. J. Q. B. 188 ; 1 E. & E. 652 : *cp. North British Co.* v. *Moffatt*, 41 L. J. C. P. 1 ; L. R. 7 C. P. 25 : *Martineau* v. *Kitching*, 41 L. J. Q. B. 227 ; L. R. 7 Q. B. 436).

Property held "In Trust for an Industrial Society" shall vest in the Society on registration, s. 6, 25 & 26 V. c. 87 ; *V. Queensbury Industrial Society* v. *Pickles*, 35 L. J. Ex. 1 ; 3 H. & C. 857 ; L. R. 1 Ex. 1.

Property held "In Trust for an Infant," s. 43, Conv. & L. P. Act, 1881 ; *V. Re Dickson, Hill* v. *Grant*, 54 L. J. Ch. 510 ; 29 Ch. D. 331 : *Re Smith, Henderson-Roe* v. *Hitchins*, 58 L. J. Ch. 860.

A Royal Warrant granting booty "In Trust" to be distributed, does not transfer the booty or create a trust (*Kinloch* v. *Indian Secretary*, 51 L. J. Ch. 885 ; 7 App. Ca. 619).

V. UPON TRUST.

IN TURN TO DELIVER.—*V.* TURN.

IN VALUE.—Where a statute prescribes that something may be done by a Majority "In Value" of creditors, the value of the securities held by such creditors as are secured is not to be deducted from the amounts of their debts (*Whittaker* v. *Lowe*, 35 L. J. Ex. 44 ; L. R. 1 Ex. 74 ; 4 H. & C. 109).

IN VESTRY ASSEMBLED.—*V.* PARISHIONER.

IN WRITING.—"*An Agreement* in Writing" between Solicitor and Client as to costs, s. 4, 33 & 34 V. c. 28, must be signed by both parties (*Ex p. Munro, Re Lewis*, 45 L. J. Q. B. 816 ; 1 Q. B. D. 724). The meaning of "In Writing," in such a connection, is "that the terms agreed to should be ascertained in writing, to which the signatures of both parties should be attached" (per Coleridge, C. J., *Ib.*).

"*Contract* duly made in Writing," s. 25, Companies Act, 1867 ; "'Duly made in writing,' means, I suppose, signed by the contracting party" (per Jessel, M.R., *Firmstone's Case*, 44 L. J. Ch. 618 ; L. R. 20 Eq. 524), or, rather, by both the contracting parties (*Re New Eberhardt Co.*, 59 L. J. Ch. 73 ; 6 Times Rep. 56 ; 38 W. R. 97). *Vf.* as to what is a "Contract" within this phrase, *Firmstone's Case*, and *Re New Eberhardt Co.*, sup.; *Crickmer's Case*, 10 Ch. 614; 44 L. J. Ch. 595: *Anderson's Case*, 7 Ch. D. 104; 47 L. J. Ch. 273: *Forde's Case*, 30 Ch. D. 153; 54 L. J. Ch. 724: Buckl. 530.

"I think that the expression 'Contract in Writing,' in s. 1, Bovill's Act, 28 & 29 V. c. 86, means, 'Contract in Writing signed by the parties'" (per Jessel, M.R., *Pooley* v. *Driver*, 46 L. J. Ch. 467; 5 Ch. D. 458); and accordingly an unsigned Contract was held not within the section. *Vf.* Rosc. N. P. 501; Watson, Eq. 792.

A "*Consent or Agreement...by Deed or Writing*," which, under s. 3, Prescription Act (2 & 3 W. 4, c. 71), will prevent the acquisition of an easement for Light, need only be signed by the licensee, by or through whom the easement is claimed (*Bewley* v. *Atkinson*, 49 L. J. Ch. 153; 13 Ch. D. 283: *Mitchell* v. *Cantrill*, 37 Ch. D. 61).

"*Consent* in Writing of the Author," s. 2, 3 & 4 W. 4, c. 15; *V.* *Eaton* v. *Lake*, 57 L. J. Q. B. 227; 20 Q. B. D. 378; 59 L. T. 100; 36 W. R. 277.

V. Instrument in Writing: Note: Signed: Writing.

INABILITY.—"Inability," and "Incapable," to act, in regard to Trustees, seem convertible terms; and mean a personal impossibility of acting (*e.g.* from age or infirmity, *Re Lemann*, 22 Ch. D. 633; 52 L. J. Ch. 560), as distinguished from unfitness (*V.* Unfit).

In *Withington* v. *Withington* (16 Sim. 104), it was held that a Trustee did not become "incapable" to act by residing abroad (*Va. Re Harrison*, 22 L. J. Ch. 69); but in *Mesnard* v. *Welford* (22 L. J. Ch. 1053; nom. *Mennard* v. *Welford*, 1 Sm. & G. 426), Stuart, V.-C., said,—"How *can* Mr. Welford perform the duties of a trustee of property situate at Somers Town and in Paddington, if he is a resident in New York? I think that a trustee domiciled at New York can hardly be *capable* of acting as a trustee of the property in question." But it has been said that this "seems scarcely in harmony with correct principle (residence abroad being rather a question of *unfitness*, than incapacity), and cannot be reconciled with other authorities (*Withington* v. *Withington*, sup.: *Re Harrison*, sup.: *Va. Re Watts*, 9 Hare, 106; 20 L. J. Ch. 337: *O'Reilly* v. *Alderson*, 8 Hare, 104). And the Court has since intimated an opinion that Incapacity, means *personal* incapacity (*Re Bignold*, 7 Ch. 223; 41 L. J. Ch. 235)." Lewin, 658, 659.

A temporary absence would clearly not be "inability" or "incapacity" (*Re Moravian Socy.*, 26 Bea. 101; 4 Jur. N. S. 703).

V. Incapable: Inexpedient: Unsound Mind.

INACCURACY.—*V.* Defect.

INALIENABLE.—"Even if there were no authority to the effect that the word 'inalienable' (in a gift to a married woman) amounts to a restraint on anticipation, I should be prepared so to hold; but there is ample authority—*Steedman* v. *Poole,* 6 Hare, 193 : *Spring* v. *Pride,* 10 Jur. N. S. 646, 647, and other cases" (per Bowen, L.J., *Harrison* v. *Harrison,* 58 L. J. P. D. & A. 32; 13 P. D. 186).

INAPPRECIABLE.—An "inappreciable" abstraction of water from a stream, has been suggested to mean, so "inconsiderable an amount as to be incapable of value or price" (per Talfourd, J., *Embrey* v. *Owen,* 20 L. J. Ex. 212 ; 6 Ex. 353) ; on which Parke, B., in delivering the jdgmt. of the Court of Exchequer, said,—"We are not prepared to say that the learned judge was correct in the interpretation of 'inappreciable' when connected with 'quantity ;' nor are we sure that he was not. The word 'unappreciable,' or 'inappreciable,' is one of a new coinage, not to be found in Johnson's Dictionary, Richardson's or Webster's. The word 'appreciate' first appears in the edition of Johnson by Todd, in 1827, with the explanation, 'To estimate and value.'" *Vth.* per Bowen, L.J., *Brunsden* v. *Humphrey,* 14 Q. B. D. 150.

INATTENTION.—*V.* Mismanagement.

INCAPABLE.—"Debt or Liability incapable of being fairly estimated," s. 31, Bankry. Act, 1869 ; s. 37 (6), Bankry. Act, 1883 ;—The liability of a bankrupt contributory for future calls to a Limited Co. which goes into liquidation pending his bankruptcy, is not so "incapable" (*Re Mercantile Mar. Insrce.,* 53 L. J. Ch. 593 ; 25 Ch. D. 415); nor is an Annuity terminable on a second marriage (*Ex p. Blakemore,* 46 L. J. Bank. 118 ; 5 Ch. D. 372). *V.* Fairly Estimated.

A Mayor is "incapable *of acting,*" s. 36, 5 & 6 W. 4, c. 76, whether the incapacity be physical, or legal, *e.g.*, when he is a candidate for election as Town Councillor and is thus disqualified from acting as Returning Officer (*R.* v. *Owens,* 2 E. & E. 86 ; 28 L. J. Q. B. 316 : *R.* v. *White,* 36 L. J. Q. B. 267 ; 8 B. & S. 587 ; L. R. 2 Q. B. 557) : so of an Alderman, under s. 72, 3 & 4 V. c. 108 (*Fanagan* v. *Kernan,* 8 L. R. Ir. 44).

V. Inability : Unfit : Legal Incapacity.

INCENDIARISM.—In a Fire Policy, a condition that it does "not cover any loss or damage occasioned by or in consequence of *Incendiarism,*" includes any act of incendiarism, wherever committed, *e.g.*, in the adjoining house, which directly causes the loss (*Walker* v. *London & Prov. Insrce.,* 22 L. R. Ir. 572).

INCIDENTAL.—"*Costs* of and incident to all Proceedings in the Supreme Court," Ord. 65, R. 1, R. S. C. ; *V. Re Chennell,* 47 L. J. Ch. 583 ; 8 Ch. D. 492.

On a sale under the Settled Land Act, 1882, by a tenant for life, the costs of the concurrence of his mortgagee are not costs "of or incidental to" the sale, within s. 21 (x) of the Act (*Cardigan* v. *Curzon Howe,* 58 L. J. Ch. 177, 436 ; 40 Ch. D. 338 ; 41 Ib. 375—explaining, but not following, *Re*

Beck, 52 L. J. Ch. 815 ; 24 Ch. D. 608 ; and considering *Re Sebright*, 56 L. J. Ch. 169 ; 33 Ch. D. 429). *Vf. Re Llewellin*, 57 L. J. Ch. 316 ; 37 Ch. D. 317 ; 58 L. T. 152 ; 36 W. R. 347 : *Re Stamford*, 43 Ch. D. 84.

"Costs of and incident to any proceeding" in Bankruptcy, s. 105 (1), Bankry. Act, 1883, do not include the debtor's solicitor's attendance at a meeting of creditors to confirm an arrangement (*Re Strand*, 53 L. J. Q. B. 563 ; 13 Q. B. D. 492).

"*Services* incidental to the duty or business of a carrier," include, *primâ facie*, station and siding accommodation, weighing, checking, clerkage, watching and labelling (*Hall* v. *L. B. & S. Ry.*, 15 Q. B. D. 505 ; 17 Ib. 230); but not taking waggons to and from a private siding, or allowing heavy goods to be left on the carrier's land (*Lancashire & Yorkshire Ry.* v. *Gidlow*, 45 L. J. Ex. 625 ; L. R. 7 H. L. 517).

INCIDENTAL OR CONDUCIVE.—As to the meaning of this phrase in a Memorandum of Association of a Joint Stock Co.; *V. Simpson* v. *Westminster Palace Hotel Co.*, 29 L. J. Ch. 561 ; 2 D. G. F. & J. 141, 146, 152 ; 8 H. L. Ca. 712 : *Joint Stock Discount Co.* v. *Brown*, L. R. 3 Eq. 150 : *Baglan Hall Colliery Co.*, 5 Ch. 346, 356 : *Leifchild's Case*, L. R. 1 Eq. 231, 235 : *Taunton* v. *Royal Insrce*, 33 L. J. Ch. 406 ; 2 H. & M. 135 : *Studdert* v. *Grosvenor*, 33 Ch. D. 538 : *London Financial Assn.* v. *Kelk*, 53 L. J. Ch. 1025 ; 26 Ch. D. 107 : *Re Faure Electric Accumulator Co.*, 58 L. J. Ch. 48 ; 40 Ch. D. 141.

A *Gratuity* may be within this phrase, if for the benefit of the Company as, *e.g.*, tending to secure able officers (*Henderson* v. *Bank of Australasia*, 58 L. J. Ch. 197 ; 40 Ch. D. 170) ; secus, of a mere subscription, *e.g.* to the Imperial Institute (*Tomkinson* v. *S. E. Ry.*, 35 Ch. D. 675).

INCIDENTAL EXPENSES.—The costs of a Rule to return a fi. fa. are not "Incidental Expenses" to the execution (*Hutchinson* v. *Humbert*, 8 M. & W. 638 ; 10 L. J. Ex. 418).

V. Expenses.

INCLOSED LANDS.—The words "Inclosed Lands," in ss. 97, 98, Turnpike Act, 3 G. 4, c. 126, are used in their popular sense, as denoting lands which are actually inclosed within fences (*Tapsell* v. *Crosskey*, 10 L. J. Ex. 188 ; 7 M. & W. 441).

Vf. Allaway v. *Wagstaff*, 29 L. J. Ex. 51 ; 4 H. & N. 681.

INCLOSURES.—*V.* Old Inclosures : Enclosure.

INCLUDE.—*V.* Extend to and include.

INCLUDING.—*V.* Namely.

INCOME.—"Income" signifies "what comes in" (per Selborne, L.C. *Jones* v. *Ogle*, 42 L. J. Ch. 336). It "is as large a word as can be used" to denote a person's receipts (per Jessel, M.R., *Re Huggins*, 51 L. J. Ch.

938) ; and will therefore for the purpose of s. 90, Bankry. Act, 1869, and now of s. 53 (2), Bankry. Act, 1883, include the retiring pension of a Colonial Judge notwithstanding that such pension has to be voted every year (*Re Huggins*, 52 L. J. Ch. 935 ; 21 Ch. D. 85 : *Va. Re Currie*, 26 S. J. 563) ; but it will not include a voluntary allowance even though made from public funds (*Ex p. Wicks*, 50 L. J. Ch. 620 ; 17 Ch. D. 70 : *Re Webber*, 56 L. J. Q. B. 209 ; 18 Q. B. D. 111 ; 55 L. T. 816 ; 35 W. R. 308 ; 3 Times Rep. 138), nor, seeing that the word in the sections mentioned is used in association with the word " Salary," will it for the purpose of those sections include prospective personal earnings (*Ex p. Benwell, Re Hutton*, 54 L. J. Q. B. 53 ; 14 Q. B. D. 301 ; 51 L. T. 677 ; 33 W. R. 242).

V. SALARY.

A Devise of the " Income " of realty may pass the property itself (*V.* RENTS AND PROFITS : USE AND OCCUPATION); but the ordinary acceptation of " Income," in a devise or bequest, is annual income (*Re Little, Mather* v. *Roddy*, W. N. (81) 138).

" Income," s. 43, Conv. & L. P. Act, 1881 ; *V. Re Dickson, Hill* v. *Grant*, 54 L. J. Ch. 510 ; 29 Ch. D. 331 ; 52 L. T. 707 ; 33 W. R. 511.

" Income " in a Building Society's Rules, read as including all the incomings of whatever nature (*Re West Riding Socy.*, 6 Times Rep. 16 ; 59 L. J. Ch. 197).

" Income," s. 4, St. John's, New Brunswick, Assessment Act (31 V. c. 36), means the balance of gain over loss in any financial year (*Lawless* v. *Sullivan*, 50 L. J. P. C. 33 ; 6 App. Ca. 373) ; but where Commrs are, by statute, authorized to receive certain moneys, and at the same time directed to pay a portion to another body, the gross sum received is to be deemed the " Income " of the Commrs. (*R.* v. *Southampton Commrs.*, L. R. 4 H. L. 449 ; 39 L. J. Q. B. 253).

INCOME TAX.—As to what words will relieve a recipient of income from Income Tax ; *V.* DEDUCTIONS.

INCOMING TENANT.—The Trustee in a bankruptcy is not, as such, the " Incoming Tenant " of the bankrupt's premises (per Cotton, L.J., *Re Peake*, 53 L. J. Ch. 977 ; 13 Q. B. D. 753).

INCONVENIENCE.—*V.* ANNOYANCE : UNNECESSARY INCONVENIENCE.

INCORPOREAL HEREDITAMENT.—" A right issuing out of a thing corporate, whether real or personal, or concerning or annexed to, or exercisable within the same. It is not the thing corporate itself, which may consist in lands, houses, jewels or the like ; but something collateral thereto, as a rent issuing out of those lands or houses, or an office relating to those jewels " (Kerr's Blackstone, 4 Ed. Vol. 2, p. 16, cited and applied by Cotton, L.J., *Re Christmas*, 55 L. J. Ch. 880).

Mixed Incorporeal Hereditaments are Reversions, Remainders, and Executory Interests (Wms. R. P., Part ii. chs. 1, 2, and 3).

There are three kinds of pure Incorporeal Hereditaments :—

1. *Appendant:*
   e.g., Seigniories ; manorial Rights of Common ; Advowson (appendant to a manor) ;
2. *Appurtenant:*
   e.g., Rights of Common, of Way, or of Light annexed to land and arising by grant or prescription ;
3. *In gross:*
   e.g., Seigniories severed from a manor ; Rent-Seck ; Rent-Charge ; Common in Gross ; Advowsons (generally) ; Tithes ; Titles of Honour ; Offices.

V. Wms. R. P., Part ii. ch. 4.

Poor Rates, being charged in respect of the occupation of land, may reasonably be considered as Incorporeal Hereditaments within the Statute of Mortmain (*Re Christmas*, 55 L. J. Ch. 878 ; 33 Ch. D. 332 ; 55 L. T. 197 ; 33 W. R. 779 ; 50 J. P. 759).

"Incorporeal Hereditament," in s. 2, subs. 10 (i), Settled Land Act, 1882, is not to be restricted to incorporeal hereditaments of a saleable or alienable character, but extends to an hereditary dignity, whether such dignity does or does not concern lands or a place ; so that the Court, under s. 37, has power to order a sale of chattels devolving with the title (*Re Rivett-Carnac's Will*, 54 L. J. Ch. 1074 ; 30 Ch. D. 136 ; 53 L. T. 81 ; 33 W. R. 837 : *Re Aylesford's Estate*, 32 Ch. D. 162).

INCORRIGIBLE ROGUE.—*V.* 5 G. 4, c. 83, s. 5 ; Steph. Cr. 132. *V.* ROGUE AND VAGABOND.

INCREASE.—A mortgage of "all the Issue, *Increase*, and Progeny of the sheep," does not, under the word "Increase," include additions to the flock made by purchase, but means the natural increase or offspring of the original sheep mortgaged (*Webster* v. *Power*, 37 L. J. P. C. 9 ; L. R. 1 P. C. 150).

INCUMBENT.—"'*Incumbent*' commeth from the verb *incumbo*, that is, to be diligently resident, *id est*, *obnixê operam dare;* and when it is written *encumbent*, it is falsely written, for it ought to be *incumbent*, as *Littleton* doth here (s. 180). And therefore the law doth intend him to be resident on his benefice" (Co. Litt. 119 b). *Vf.* Termes de la Ley.

"Incumbent or Minister," ss. 32, 52, Burials Act, 1852, 15 & 16 V. c. 85 ; *V. Stewart* v. *West Derby Burial Bd.*, 34 Ch. D. 314 ; 56 L. J. Ch. 425 ; 56 L. T. 380 ; 35 W. R. 268.

V. MINISTER.

INCUMBER.—*V.* CHARGE OR INCUMBER.

INCUMBRANCE.—"Incumbrance *affecting*" an estate, 18 G. 2, c. 20, includes a Sequestration on a Benefice (*Pack* v. *Tarpley*, 8 L. J. M. C. 93; 9 A. & E. 468; 1 P. & D. 478).

The phrase "Incumbrances affecting the *Inheritance*" in s. 21 (ii) Settled Land Act, 1882, means Incumbrances affecting the land sold or any other land comprised in the Settlement (*Re Chaytor*, 53 L. J. Ch. 312; 50 L. T. 88; 32 W. R. 517; 25 Ch. D. 651: *Re Stamford*, 43 Ch. D. 95); but it only includes incumbrances in the ordinary sense, *e.g.* Mortgages, Portions, &c.; and does not include sums which, if he lives sufficiently long, will be payable by the tenant for life, or which, at any rate, affect him as much as those in remainder, *e.g.* charges for a Drainage Loan effected prior to the Act (*Re Knatchbull*, 54 L. J. Ch. 154, 1168; 27 Ch. D. 349; 29 Ib. 588; 33 W. R. 10, 569; 51 L. T. 695; 53 Ib. 284. *Vf.* that case as to application of Capital to Drainage under s. 25 (i) of the S. L. Act. *Re Knatchbull*, followed in *Re Leinster*, 23 L. R. Ir. 160).

"Incumbrances, *Claims and Demands*," in the ordinary covenant against Incumbrances whether express or implied under s. 7 (a) Conv. & L. P. Act, 1881, include apportioned assessment under the Public Health Act, 1875 (*Re Bettesworth and Richer*, 37 Ch. D. 535: *Vth. Re Boor*, 40 Ch. D. 577); but not those under s. 77, Metrop. Man. Act, 1862 (*Egg* v. *Blayney*, 57 L. J. Q. B. 460; 21 Q. B. D. 107; 59 L. T. 65; 36 W. R. 893; 52 J. P. 517).

V. Charge or Incumber: Prior Incumbrancer.

INCUR.—*V.* Debt or Liability.

INCURRED.—Though a contract with a Local Authority may not be obligatory on them by reason of its not being under seal (s. 174 (1), P. H. Act, 1875: *Hunt* v. *Wimbledon Loc. Bd.*, 48 L. J. C. P. 207; 4 C. P. D. 48: *Young* v. *Royal Leamington Spa*, 8 App. Ca. 517), yet if street work be done for a Local Authority and they recognize their liability and pay for such work, though there be no contract under seal, such payments are "expenses *incurred*" and may be recoverable against owners under s. 150, P. H. Act, 1875 (*Bournemouth Commrs.* v. *Watts*, 54 L. J. Q. B. 93; 14 Q. B. D. 87).

But the phrase "have incurred expenses" (s. 257, Ib.) means at least, that the local authority has paid those expenses, or become liable to pay them, as distinguished from estimated expenses (*West Ham* v. *Grant*, 58 L. J. Ch. 121).

INDEBTED.—As to the meaning of this word in Art. 10, Table A, Companies Act, 1862; *V.* Buckl., 412, 413.

INDECENT.—A prostitute accosted four men in the Haymarket, for the purposes of her trade, and in each case put her arm into that of the man and walked by his side until he threw her off; the Middlesex Sessions held she had not behaved in an "indecent manner" within s. 3, 5 G. 4, c. 83 (*R.* v. *De Ruiter*, 44 J. P. 90).

INDEMNIFY.—A contract to "indemnify," implies that the contractee must pay before he sues on the contract (*Collinge* v. *Haywood*, 8 L. J. Q. B. 98 ; 9 A. & E. 633). *Secus*, where the contract is to be "answerable," or "responsible" (*Spark* v. *Heslop*, 28 L. J. Q. B. 197 ; 1 E. & E. 563).

V. Damage.

INDEMNITY.—An "Indemnity" is a *contract*, express or implied, to indemnify, and the liability under which is coterminous with the liability it is intended to cover (*Pontifex* v. *Foord*, 53 L. J. Q. B. 321 ; 12 Q. B. D. 152 : *Catton* v. *Bennett*, 53 L. J. Ch. 685 ; 26 Ch. D. 161 : *Speller* v. *Bristol Steam Nav. Co.*, 53 L. J. Q. B. 322 ; 13 Q. B. D. 96 : *Carshore* v. *N. E. Ry.*, 29 Ch. D. 344 : *Birmingham Land Co.* v. *Lond. & N. W. Ry.*, 34 Ch. D. 272 ; inf.: *Tritton* v. *Bankart*, 56 L. J. Ch. 629 ; 56 L. T. 306 ; 35 W. R. 474).

Therefore the covenants by an underlessee, in precisely similar terms to those of the original lease, are not an "Indemnity" by the underlessee to the original lessee within the Third Party Procedure (R. S. C. Ord. 16, R. 48) ; because the effect in such a case, even of the same words, would vary according to the age of the house, or the condition of the demised premises, at the time each obligation was undertaken (*Pontifex* v. *Foord*, sup. ; distinguishing *Hornby* v. *Cardwell*, 51 L. J. Q. B. 89 ; 8 Q. B. D. 329 ; 45 L. T. 781 ; 30 W. R. 263. *Vf. Tritton* v. *Bankart*, sup.). And so a right to damages for breach of contract, is not a right to an "Indemnity" within the rule (*Birmingham Land Co.* v. *Lond. & N. W. Ry.*, 34 Ch. D. 261 ; 56 L. J. Ch. 956 ; 55 L. T. 699 ; 35 W. R. 173 ; 3 Times Rep. 179).

So an allegation by one defendant against a co-defendant, that the contract sued on was induced by the co-defendant's false representation, will not well found a claim for "Contribution or Indemnity" under Ord. 16, R. 55 (*Catton* v. *Bennett*, sup.).

V. "Contracts of Indemnity," Add. C. Bk. 2, ch. 4.

INDIA.—*V.* British India.

INDIAN ISLAND.—*V.* East Indies.

INDICTMENT.—"I think it is clear that in old times the word 'Indictment' included any charge made by an inquest which had power to make the inquiry, and that when the charge made by them was reduced into writing, it was called an 'Indictment.' And the reason of the thing is, that in all charges of felony the preliminary step is that 12 men should be sworn to make the inquiry. The ordinary case is that of Grand Jurors. They are sworn, and when they find some charge it is reduced into writing, and becomes a record of the Court. In practice it is brought to them in the shape of a Bill, and they write upon the back of it either, 'A True Bill' or 'No Bill' ; but when it is thus in the shape of a record, it appears in the present tense, 'the Jurors &c. present,' as in the old times they would have come into Court, and would have said, 'We present,' &c., and their presentment would afterwards have been put into writing. The Coroner has authority to make an inquiry by the jury upon the dead body ; but the accusation by such jury is equally an accusation as that of the grand jury, and the judgment upon the one is like a judgment upon the other" (per Blackburn, J., *R.* v. *Ingham,* 33 L. J. Q. B. 189; 5 B. & S. 257). It was accordingly held in that case that "Indictment" generally includes an Inquisition, and does so within s. 6, 24 & 25 V. c. 100.

But "Indictment" does not include an Information, *e.g.* in the proviso to s. 7, 26 V. c. 29 (*R.* v. *Slator,* 51 L. J. Q. B. 246 ; 8 Q. B. D. 267 : INFORMATION).

Vh. s. 30, 14 & 15 V. c. 100.

INDIFFERENT.—Commissioners of Sewers to be appointed under 23 H. 8, c. 5, are to be "substantial and indifferent persons" (s. 1); "Indifferent," "that is persons who have no interest in the matter with which they are dealing" (per Coleridge, C.J., *R.* v. *Essex Commrs. of Sewers,* 14 Q. B. D. 578).

INDIRECT TAXATION.—*V.* DIRECT TAXATION.

INDIRECTLY.—*V.* DIRECTLY.

INDORSE.—*V.* ENDORSE.

INDORSED.—"The claim *indorsed*" on a Writ, s. 26, 19 & 20 V. c. 108, meant a claim for a liquidated money demand ; for at the date of the act that was the only kind of claim that could be "indorsed ;" and therefore there was no power under that section to remit an action to the County Court where *damages* for breach of contract were claimed, although the claim as indorsed on the writ did not exceed £50 (*Knight* v. *Abbott,* 52 L. J. Q. B. 131 ; 10 Q. B. D. 11 : *Vf. Mackay* v. *Bannister,* 16 Q. B. D. 174).

INDORSEMENT.—*V.* ENDORSE.

INDUSTRIAL SCHOOL.—*V.* CERTIFIED.

INEVITABLE.—An "Inevitable Accident" will not comprise "anything arising from the acts or defaults of either of the contracting parties." This phrase does not apply to anything known when the deed or contract is executed (*Jervis* v. *Tomkinson,* 26 L. J. Ex. 41 ; 1 H. & N. 195; 4 W. R. 683); nor does it apply to anything which either party might have avoided, and it is immaterial upon which of them the burden lies of providing against it (per Fry, J., *Saner* v. *Bilton,* 47 L. J. Ch. 270 ; 7 Ch. D. 815 : approved in *Manchester Bonding Warehouse Co.* v. *Carr,* 49 L. J. C. P. 809; 5 C. P. D. 507 : *Vf. The Buckhurst,* 51 L. J. P. D. & A. 10 ; 6 P. D. 152).

V. PERILS OF THE SEA.

"An influx of Brine is, probably, in a Lease of Salt Mines, an 'Inevitable Accident'" (MacS. 244, n. 1, citing *Jervis* v. *Tomkinson*, sup.).

INEXPEDIENT.—Where a Power of appointing new Trustees was exerciseable by husband and wife jointly, but the wife had obtained a judicial separation and the husband was living in Australia, North, J., held that it was "*inexpedient or difficult*," within s. 32, Trustee Act, 1850, to exercise the power without the assistance of the Court, and accordingly made the appointment (*Re Somerset*, 31 S. J. 559). So of a Trustee permanently residing abroad (*Re Bignold*, 41 L. J. Ch. 235; 7 Ch. 223; 20 W. R. 345), or incapacitated through age or infirmity (*Re Lemann*, 22 Ch. D. 633; 52 L. J. Ch. 560; 48 L. T. 389; 31 W. R. 520). *V.* INABILITY: UNFIT.

INFAMOUS CONDUCT.—For a medical man to publish in a popular form, directions to enable women to prevent conception (*Allbutt* v. *Gen. Medical Council*, 23 Q. B. D. 400; 37 W. R. 771), or to allow his name to be used as a "Cover" for an unqualified person (*Leeson* v. *Gen. Medical Council*, Times, 23 Dec., 1889; 38 W. R. 303) may be regarded as "Infamous Conduct in a professional respect," within s. 29, 21 & 22 V. c. 90. In the latter case it was held that to state in the notice that the offender had acted so as to enable the other to charge "as if he were *duly qualified*," was sufficient, because in that connection, "duly qualified" had reference to a medical qualification.

INFANGTHEEFE.—The privilege "that Theeves taken within your demesne or fee convicted of thefts, shall be judged in your court" (Termes de la Ley). *Cp.* OUTFANGTHEEFE.

INFERIOR COURT.—The London Lord Mayor's Court is an Inferior Court (*London* v. *Cox*, 36 L. J. Ex. 225; L. R. 2 H. L. 239: *wh. V.* for an extraordinarily elaborate and learned opinion by Willes, J. which was adopted by the H. L., and in which, as Ld. Cranworth said, the subject-matter of Inferior Courts was investigated "with a care and attention rarely equalled"). The Mayor's Court is also within "any other Inferior Court" as used in s. 45, Jud. Act, 1873 (*Appleford* v. *Judkins*, 47 L. J. C. P. 615; 3 C. P. D. 489; 38 L. T. 801; 26 W. R. 734).

INFLICT.—To "inflict *Grievous Bodily Harm*," s. 20, 24 & 25 V. c. 100, means "the *direct* causing of some grievous injury to the body itself with a weapon, as by a cut with a knife, or without a weapon, as by a blow with a fist or by pushing a person down." Poisoning, whether of the ordinary kind or by animal infection, is not within the phrase. "If a man by a grasp of the hand infects another with small pox, it is impossible to trace out in detail the connection between the act and the disease, and it would, I think, be an unnatural use of language to say that a man by such an act 'inflicted' small-pox on another. It would be wrong in interpreting an Act of Parliament to lay much stress upon etymology; but I may just observe that 'inflicting' is derived from *infligo*, to which, in Facciolati's Lexicon, three Italian and three Latin equivalents are given, all meaning 'to strike,'—viz. *dare, ferire*, and *percutere*, in Italian, and *infero, impingo*, and *percutio* in Latin" (per Stephen, J., *R.* v. *Clarence*, 58 L. J. M. C. 18, 19 ; 22 Q. B. D. 23). And in accordance with the reasoning of Stephen, J. it was held (by a majority) in the case cited, that knowingly suffering from a venereal disease and yet having connection with, and imparting the disease to, one of the opposite sex who is ignorant that the embracer is so suffering, is not to "inflict grievous Bodily Harm" within the section ; nor is it an "*Assault occasioning Actual Bodily Harm*" within s. 47 of the same statute : and whether the parties are married or not is immaterial for the purpose of this construction. But Hawkins, J., delivered a strong judgment against the conclusion at which the majority of the Court arrived ; and in the course of that judgment said that, in his opinion, "Inflict," "Cause," and "Occasion," were used as synonymous terms in the sections (and their cognates) then under discussion. *Vh. Hegarty* v. *Shine*, 4 L. R. Ir. 288.

Vh. R. v. *Martin*, cited MALICE : Following that case, where a woman had been so terrified by her husband that she attempted to get out of the window but, when partially out, her daughter caught hold of her and was preventing her from falling, when the husband ordered the daughter to let go which she accordingly did, and in consequence the woman fell into the street and broke her leg, there it was held that the injury was "inflicted" by the husband within the section cited (*R.* v. *Halliday*, 6 Times Rep. 109 ; 34 S. J. 129).

INFLUENCE.—*V.* UNDUE INFLUENCE.

INFORMALITY.—To quash an Order for "Informality" does not exclusively mean for something informal appearing on the face of the Order ; it may mean nothing more than that the decision to quash did not proceed upon the merits (*R.* v. *Cottingham*, 4 L. J. M. C. 65).

INFORMATION.—"'Information' is of a two-fold character, one granted by the Queen's Bench at the relation of a private person, and the other laid by the Attorney-General, *ex proprio motu*, as the officer of the Crown" (per Denman, J., *R.* v. *Slator*, 51 L. J. Q. B. 246 ; 8 Q. B. D. 267. *Vf.* 3 Burn's Justice, 30 Ed. 2). *Cp.* INDICTMENT.

The foregoing definition relates to an Information in the High Court. There is also an Information leading to a Justice's Summons or Warrant for an offence punishable upon a summary conviction ; and in this connection "Information" is used as distinguished from "Complaint" leading to an Order for the payment of money or otherwise (ss. 1, 8, 9 & 10, 11 & 12 V. c. 43 : *Vh.* Stone, Tit. "Procedure," "Practice"). *V.* COMPLAINT.

V. WHOSOEVER WILL GIVE INFORMATION.

INFRINGEMENT.—"Infringement of his Patent," proviso to s. 32, 46 & 47 V. c. 57 ; *V. Barrett* v. *Day*, W. N. (90) 36 ; Times, 5 Feb. 1890.

ING.—*V.* Ey.

INGIURIE GRAVI.—These words (Art. 46, Ordinance of Malta, No. 5, 1867) leave a large discretion to the tribunal having to consider the facts; and words, as well as acts, designed to wound the feelings of the party complaining may amount to "Ingiurie Gravi" (*Sant* v. *Sant*, 43 L. J. P. C. 73; L. R. 5 P. C. 542). *V.* Injury.

INGRESS.—A grant of a Right of "*Ingress, Egress and Regress*," is a grant of a right of way from the *locus a quo* to the *locus ad quem*, and from the *locus ad quem* forth to any other spot to which the grantee may lawfully go, or back to the *locus a quo* (*Somerset* v. *G. W. Ry.*, 46 L. T. 883).

INHABIT.—"The word 'inhabit' simply means to dwell in" (per Cave, J., in delivering jdgmt. of the Court in *Atkinson* v. *Collard*, 55 L. J. Q. B. 23; 16 Q. B. D. 254; 53 L. T. 670; 34 W. R. 75; 50 J. P. 23: *V.* that case and *Adams* v. *Ford*, 55 L. J. Q. B. 13, and *Stribling* v. *Halse*, 55 L. J. Q. B. 15, as to meaning of the word in Rep. Peo. Act, 1884, 48 V. c. 3, s. 3). Qy.—would it not be more accurate to say that "inhabit" implies the place where a person usually sleeps? *Cp.* Dwell: *V.* Cease: Serve.

Power to Rate persons who "Inhabit or Occupy;" *V. Donne* v. *Martyr*, 8 B. & C. 62: *Cp.* Occupied.

INHABITANT.—"Inhabitants," "Takes in housekeepers, though not rated to the poor, also persons who are not housekeepers, as for instance, such as who have gained a Settlement and by that means have become Inhabitants" (per Hardwicke, L. C. *A.-G.* v. *Parker*, 3 Atk. 577; 1 Ves. sen. 43). *Cp.* Parishioner: Ratepayer: and for a comparative analysis of the cases on "Inhabitants" and "Parishioners," *V.* Tudor, Char. Trusts, 867–870.

An "Inhabitant" of a place, speaking generally, is one who has his permanent home there (*R.* v. *Mitchell*, 10 East, 511); but the word has no definite legal meaning, its signification varying according to the subject matter (*R.* v. *Mashiter*, 6 L. J. K. B. 121; 6 A. & E. 153; 1 N. & P. 314), or, sometimes, according to usage (*R.* v. *Sandford*, 6 L. J. K. B. 126; 1 N. & P. 328; nom. *R.* v. *Davie*, 6 A. & E. 374).

"Inhabitant" in s. 1, 43 Eliz. c. 2, means a person, who, by himself, family or servants, resides and sleeps in the parish (*R.* v. *Nicholson*, 12 East, 330: *R.* v. *North Curry*, 4 B. & C. 953): and therefore a person who is lessee of a stall in a market and comes there only on market days to sell his wares, is not rateable to the Poor Rate, as an "Inhabitant" (*Holledge's Case*, 1 Bott. 134. *Vf.* Arch. P. L. 721: *Donne* v. *Martyr*, 8 B. & C. 62). So of the liability of an "Inhabitant" to serve as constable (*R.* v. *Adlard*, 4 B. & C. 772).

But when the object of an Act is to impose a burden on property, then "Inhabitants" will (probably) generally include all holders of rateable property in the district; but not mere dwellers therein, *e.g.*, servants (*R.* v. *North Curry*, sup.: *Vf.* Maxwell, 77, 78).

A person who qualifies as a vestryman as being an "Inhabitant," *semble*, need not sleep as well as reside in the parish (*Wilson* v. *Sunderland*, 34 L. J. M. C. 90).

A legacy for the benefit of the "Inhabitants" of a place would seem a good charitable bequest (*A.-G.* v. *Clarke*, Amb. 422), as one to the "Poor Inhabitants" certainly is, under which the persons to be benefited are those poor inhabitants who are not in receipt of parochial relief (Ib. : Wms. Exs. 1155).

In *Rogers* v. *Thomas* (2 Keen, 8), a gift "to the Inhabitants of Tawleaven Row, Sethney" took effect as a *designatio personarum*.

A Grant to or Prescription by the "Inhabitants" of a place is too vague and not good (Touch. 237) ; unless the Grant be by the Crown and then it erects the Inhabitants into a Corporation (*Willingale* v. *Maitland*, 36 L. J. Ch. 64 ; L. R. 3 Eq. 103 : *wh.* case see explained by *Chilton* v. *London*, 47 L. J. Ch. 433 ; 7 Ch. D. 735). Towards end of the jdgmt. of Jessel, M.R., in the latter case *V.* obs. as to what would be the meaning of "Inhabitant" in such a Crown Grant : *Va. Rivers* v. *Adams*, 48 L. J. Ex. 47 ; 3 Ex. D. 361 : *Re St. Alphage, London Wall*, 59 L. T. 614.

"Inhabitant *Householder* ;" *V. Rutter* v. *Chapman*, 10 L. J. Ex. 495 ; 8 M. & W. 1.

"Inhabitant *Occupier*," s. 3, 30 & 31 V. c. 102, as explained by s. 5, 41 & 42 V. c. 26 ;—*V. Bradley* v. *Baylis*, 51 L. J. Q. B. 183 ; 8 Q. B. D. 195. *Vf. Stribling* v. *Halse*, 16 Q. B. D. 246 ; 55 L. J. Q. B. 15 : *Hogan* v. *Sterrett*, 20 L. R. Ir. 344.

A Municipal Bye-Law prohibiting things to the "annoyance of *any of the Inhabitants*," does not mean to "any one," but means a reasonable number, of the Inhabitants (*Booth* v. *Howell*, 5 Times Rep. 449).

INHABITED DWELLING-HOUSE.—*V.* DWELLING-HOUSE.

INHERIT.—"Inherit" held to mean succession by descent (*East* v. *Twyford*, 9 Hare, 729).

INHERITANCE.—"This word (Inheritance) is not only intended where a man hath lands or tenements by descent of inheritage, but also everie fee simple or taile which a man hath by his purchase may be said an inheritance, because his heires may inherit him" (Litt. s. 9 ; *Vth.* Co. Litt. 16 a, 383 b). *V.* Termes de la Ley, *Enheritance* : FREEHOLD.

A devise of an "Inheritance," apart from the Wills Act, carries the fee (2 Jarm. 283 ; *Sv.* Note thereto). So too of an appointment by Will of "*Trustees of Inheritance*, for the execution hereof," for that phrase is equivalent to "Trustees of my inheritance" or "Trustees to inherit my estate for the execution of this my Will" (2 Jarm. 394, citing *Trent* v. *Hanning*, 1 B. & P. N. R. 116 ; 10 Ves. 495 ; 7 East, 97 : *Va.* Lewin, 215).

"By inheritance ;" *V. Wilkinson* v. *Bewicke*, 22 L. J. Ch. 781 ; 3 D. G. M. & G. 937.

INHERITOR.—This word may be used in the sense merely of "Taker" (per Knight-Bruce, L.J., *Boys* v. *Bradley*, 22 L. J. Ch. 621; 10 Hare, 389; 4 D. M. & G. 58).

INJURE.—"An intent to 'injure,' in strictness, means more than an intent to do harm. It connotes an intent to do wrongful harm" (per Bowen, L.J., *Mogul Co.* v. *McGregor*, 58 L. J. Q. B. 479; 23 Q. B. D. 598). *Vf.* MALICE.

INJURIOUS TO HEALTH.—"An offensive smell which makes sick people worse must, more or less, interfere with the health of robust people;" and is therefore "injurious to health" generally (per Stephen, J., *Malton Loc. Board* v. *Malton Manure Co.*, 49 L. J. M. C. 93; 4 Ex. D. 302). *V.* NUISANCE.

INJURIOUSLY AFFECTED.—"Injuriously affected by the execution of the works," s. 68, Lands C. C. Act, 1845;—The complex meaning of this phrase has, probably, never been more clearly explained than by Bramwell, B., in *McCarthy* v. *Metrop. Bd. of Works* (42 L. J. C. P. 93, 94; L. R. 8 C. P. 208, 209), as follows:—

1. "The word 'Injuriously,' does not mean 'Wrongfully' affected. What is done is rightful under the powers of the Act. It means 'Hurtfully' or 'Damnously' affected. As where we say of a man that he fell and injured his leg, we do not mean that his leg was wronged, but that it was hurt. We mean he fell, and his leg was injuriously (that is to say), hurtfully affected. At the same time I am clearly of opinion that to entitle the parties interested to compensation, the injury or hurt must be such as could not lawfully be inflicted except by the powers of the Act."

2. "The words of the section shew this: The lands must be 'injuriously affected by reason of the *exercise*, as regards such lands, *of the powers of the Act*.' The act, therefore, injuriously affecting must be one which would be wrongful but for the Statute."

In accordance with the first branch of this definition it is settled that no injury can be embraced in this phrase unless it would have been an actionable wrong but for the Act authorising it (*Rickett* v. *Metrop. Ry.*, L. R. 2 H. L. 175; 36 L. J. Q. B. 205; 15 W. R. 937; 16 L. T. 542: *McCarthy* v. *Metrop. Bd. of Works*, L. R. 7 H. L. 243; 43 L. J. C. P. 385; 23 W. R. 115; 31 L. T. 182). But in *Re Stockport Ry.* (33 L. J. Q. B. 251; 10 L. T. 426), it was held, as an exception to this rule, that non-actionable nuisances might be the subject of compensation if done on land that had, by the nuisance maker, been compulsorily acquired from the person complaining and whose other land was affected by such nuisances. After a long litigation the ruling in the *Stockport Ry. Case* has been upheld by the H. L. (*Cowper-Essex* v. *Acton*, 14 App. Ca. 153; 58 L. J. Q. B. 594).

In accordance with the second branch of the definition, the injury must be done whilst the powers of the Act are being exercised, as distinguished from the authorised user of the thing which the Act authorises. Therefore, *e.g.*, though damages may be recovered against a Railway Company for injury caused by vibration, smoke and noise caused by their trains during the *construction* of their line, because such damage is caused by reason of the exercise of their powers ; yet they are not liable for such damages occasioned by their trains *after their line is completed*, because then they are only using the thing that their Act has authorised (*Brand* v. *Hammersmith Ry., Hammersmith Ry.* v. *Brand*, L. R. 2. Q. B. 223 ; L. R. 4 H. L. 171 ; 36 L. J. Q. B. 139 ; 38 Ib. 265 ; 16 L. T. 101 ; 21 Ib. 238 ; 15 W. R. 437 ; 18 Ib. 12).

The following are examples of how land may be "injuriously affected" so as to give right to compensation under the section :—Narrowing (*Beckett* v. *Mid. Ry.*, 37 L. J. C. P. 11 ; L. R. 3 C. P. 82 ; 17 L. T. 499 ; 16 W. R. 221), or obstructing a Highway which is the proximate access to the land in question (*Caledonian Ry.* v. *Walker*, 7 App. Ca. 259 ; 30 W. R. 569 ; in which case Selborne, L.C., questioned whether a mere change of gradient would carry compensation, and *Vth. R.* v. *Eastern Counties Ry.*, 2 Q. B. 347 ; 11 L. J. Q. B. 66 ; 1 G. & D. 589 ; 2 Rail. Ca. 736) : Interference with a Right of Way, though only of a temporary nature (*Ford* v. *Metrop. Ry.*, 55 L. J. Q. B. 296 ; 17 Q. B. D. 12 ; 54 L. T. 718 ; 34 W. R. 426 ; 50 J. P. 661) : Darkening Ancient Lights (*Eagle* v. *Charing Cross Ry.*, 36 L. J. C. P. 297 ; L. R. 2 C. P. 638 ; 15 W. R. 1016 ; 16 L. T. 593) : so of Modern Lights when ancient ones are darkened with them (*Gower's-Walk Schools* v. *Lond. Tilbury & Southend Ry.*, 24 Q. B. D. 326 ; 6 Times Rep. 120) : Obstructing access to a water frontage (*McCarthy* v. *Metrop. Bd. of Works*, sup.: *Buccleuch* v. *Metrop. Bd. of Works*, 41 L. J. Ex. 137 ; L. R. 5 H. L. 418 ; 27 L. T. 1 : *Lyon* v. *Fishmongers' Co.*, 46 L. J. Ch. 68 ; 1 App. Ca. 662 ; 25 W. R. 165 : *North Shore Ry.* v. *Pion*, 59 L. J. P. C. 251 : *Sv. Falls* v. *Belfast Ry.*, 12 Ir. L. R. 233) : Inundation caused by raising the level of a stream (*R.* v. *North Mid. Ry.*, 2 Rail. Ca. 1) : Damage caused by insufficient drainage or protection of a Railway (*R.* v. *North Union Ry.*, 1 Rail. Ca. 729).

But land is *not* "injuriously affected" in the following cases :—Diversion of Traffic by interference with a Highway, and not being the immediate access to the land in question (*Rickett* v. *Metrop. Ry.*, sup.), or which Highway is an access to a Ferry (*Hopkins* v. *G. N. Ry.*, 46 L. J. Q. B. 265 ; 2 Q. B. D. 224 ; 36 L. T. 898) : Level Crossing (*Caledonian Ry.* v. *Ogilvy*, 2 Macq. 229).

Note.—The dictum of Chelmsford, L. C., in *Rickett* v. *Metrop. Ry.* (sup.) that land to be "injuriously affected" must have *permanent* damage done to it, is not supported (*Ford* v. *Metrop. Ry.*, sup.).

Vf. Lloyd on Compensation, 5 Ed. 109–134 ; Woolf. & Middleton on Comp. 120–129.

INJURY.—Loss of condition to cattle through want of food and water, is "Injury" to them within s. 7, 17 & 18 V. c. 31 (*Allday* v. *G. W. Ry.*, 34 L. J. Q. B. 5; 5 B. & S. 903: *Sheridan* v. *Midland Great Western Ry*, 24 L. R. Ir. 161.

V. Annoyance: Loss: Ingiurie Gravi.

INJURY TO PROPERTY.—Means "a substantial physical injury to property" (per Field, J., *Goodhand* v. *Ayscough*, 52 L. J. Q. B. 99; 10 Q. B. D. 71).

INJUSTICE.—"Without Injustice to Creditors," s. 18 (11), Bankry. Act, 1883; *V. Re Moon*, 56 L. J. Q. B. 496; 19 Q. B. D. 669; 35 W. R. 743.

INLAND.—Demesne land (Elph. 590, citing Spelm.; *Sv.* other references given by Elph.).

An Inland *Bill of Exchange* was defined in *Amner* v. *Clark* (2 Cr. M. & R. 471) as a Bill both drawn and payable in Great Britain; and now such a Bill, "is a Bill which is, or on the face of it purports to be, (a) both drawn and payable within the British Islands, or (b) drawn within the British Islands upon some person resident therein. Any other Bill is a Foreign Bill.

"For the purposes of this Act, 'British Islands' mean any part of the United Kingdom of Great Britain and Ireland, the islands of Man, Guernsey, Jersey, Alderney, and Sark, and the islands adjacent to any of them being part of the dominions of Her Majesty.

"(2) Unless the contrary appear on the face of the Bill the holder may treat it as an Inland Bill" (s. 4, Bills of Ex. Act, 1882).

So of Promissory Notes (s. 89, Ib.).

INMATES.—*V.* Termes de la Ley.

INN.—An Inn or Hostel may be defined to be a house in which travellers, passengers, wayfaring men, and other such like casual guests are accommodated with victuals and lodgings and whatever they reasonably desire, for themselves and their horses, at a reasonable price, while on their way (*V. R.* v. *Luellin*, 12 Mod. 445: *Thompson* v. *Lacy*, 3 B. & Ald. 283. 1 Burn's Jus., *Alehouse*, 30 Ed. 64). A Refreshment-bar, though part of a duly licensed premises, is not an Inn (*R.* v. *Rymer*, 46 L. J. M. C. 108; 2 Q. B. D. 136: *Strauss* v. *County Hotel Co.*, 53 L. J. Q. B. 25; 12 Q. B. D. 27); nor is an ordinary Coffee-house (*Doe* v. *Laming*, 4 Camp. 77); nor is a Boarding-house (*Dansey* v. *Richardson*, 3 E. & B. 144): but a London Coffee-house where beds as well as provisions are provided would seem to be an Inn (*Thompson* v. *Lacy*, sup.). *Va.* 1 Sm. L. C. 142; Add. C. 297, 298.

For the purpose of the Act limiting the liability of an Innkeeper, an "Inn" means "any Hotel, Inn, Tavern, Public-house, or other place of refreshment, the keeper of which is now by law responsible for the goods and property of his guests" (26 & 27 V. c. 41, s. 4).

V. Hotel: Victualling-House: Guest.

INNOCENT SHIPPERS.—*V. Brooking* v. *Maudslay*, 57 L. J. Ch. 1001 ; 38 Ch. D. 636 ; 58 L. T. 852 ; 36 W. R. 664.

INNOCENTLY ACTED.—*V. Wood* v. *Burgess*, 59 L. J. M. C. 11.

INQUIRY.—An "Inquiry" in an action is not limited to what a man can see with his own eyes ; it signifies a judicial inquiry with witnesses ; therefore in a Reference "for Inquiry and Report" under s. 56, Jud. Act, 1873, the Referee may, and it is the invariable practice to, hear counsel and witnesses (*Wenlock* v. *River Dee Co.*, 19 Q. B. D. 155 ; 56 L. J. Q. B. 589 ; 57 L. T. 320 ; 35 W. R. 822).

A "*Due* Inquiry," s. 29, 21 & 22 V. c. 90, means to give its subject-matter a fair hearing (*Allbutt* v. *Gen. Medical Council*, 23 Q. B. D. 400 ; 37 W. R. 771 : *Leeson* v. *Gen. Medical Council*, Times, 23 Dec. 1889 ; 38 W. R. 303).

INSIST.—A Power to rescind a Contract of Sale, if purchaser shall make Requisitions "and shall *insist* thereon," cannot be exercised until a fair attempt has been made to answer the Requisitions (*Greaves* v. *Wilson*, 25 Bea. 290 ; 27 L. J. Ch. 546) ; in this connection "persist" is synonymous with "insist" (*Mawson* v. *Fletcher*, 39 L. J. Ch. 583 ; L. R. 10 Eq. 212). *Cp.* UNWILLING.

INSOLVENT.—"An 'Insolvent' in ordinary acceptation, is a person who cannot pay his debts" (per Parke, B., *Parker* v. *Gossage*, 5 L. J. Ex. 4 ; 2 Cr. M. & R. 617 ; T. & G. 105).

A person is an "Insolvent," within a clause of forfeiture, who enters into a Composition Deed which recites his inability to pay his creditors in full (*Billson* v. *Crofts*, 42 L. J. Ch. 531 ; L. R. 15 Eq. 314), or who (under the Bankry. Act, 1869) presented a petition for liquidation under which a composition was accepted (*Nixon* v. *Verry*, 54 L. J. Ch. 736; 29 Ch. D. 196). It is indeed broadly stated that "where 'Insolvency' is made a cause of forfeiture, it is not generally necessary that the legatee should have taken the benefit of any Act for the relief of insolvent debtors. It is enough that he is unable to pay his debts in full" (2 Jarm. 37). "As to the meaning of the word 'Insolvent' it is now settled that it is not a technical term, but simply means a person who is incapable of paying his debts" (per Wood, V.-C., *Re Muggeridge*, 29 L. J. Ch. 288 ; Joh. 625), or the being liable to more debts than he can pay (*Biddlecombe* v. *Bond*, 5 L. J. K. B. 47 ; 4 A. & E. 332 ; 5 N. & M. 621) ; but insolvency is not shewn by proving non-payment on demand of one debt (*Doe* d. *Gatehouse* v. *Rees*, 7 L. J. C. P. 184 ; 4 Bing. N. C. 384 ; 6 Sc. 161).

But where the phrase is, shall become "*bankrupt or otherwise insolvent*," "insolvent" (it may very plausibly be contended) should be read as *ejusdem generis* with "bankrupt" (per Blackburn, J., *R.* v. *Saddlers' Co.*, 32 L. J. Q. B. 340 ; 10 H. L. Ca. 404 : *Parker* v. *Gossage*, sup.). The question as to "Insolvent" arose in *R.* v. *Saddlers' Co.* on the following Bye-Law of the Saddlers' Co.,—"that no person who has been a Bankrupt, or become otherwise Insolvent, shall hereafter be admitted a member of the Court of Assistants, unless it be proved, to the satisfaction of the Court, that such person, after his bankruptcy or insolvency, has paid his creditors in full, or shall have established a fair and honourable character for the seven years subsequent." The H. L., having regard chiefly to the need of some definite time from which to calculate this 7 years, held that "become otherwise Insolvent" meant notorious or avowed insolvency, *e.g.* a public stoppage in business, or calling creditors together and obtaining time or terms of indulgence or entering into a deed of composition: *V.* jdgmt. of Westbury, L. C.

A Company becoming "Insolvent" as regards the return of a parliamentary deposit; *V. Re Bradford Tramway Co.*, 46 L. J. Ch. 89; 4 Ch. D. 18.

INSOLVENT CIRCUMSTANCES.—"'In Insolvent Circumstances' has always been held to mean, not merely being behind the world, if an account were taken, but insolvency to the extent of being unable to pay just debts in the ordinary course of trade and business" (per Willes, J., *R.* v. *Saddlers' Co.*, 32 L. J. Q. B. 345; 10 H. L. Ca. 404. *Vf. Teale* v. *Younge*, McCl. & Y. 497).

Vf. Insolvent.

INSTANT.—"Although an instant *est unum indivisibile tempore quod non est tempus nec pars temporis, ad quod tamen partes temporis connectuntur*, and that *instans est finis unius temporis et principium alterius*; yet in consideration of law there is a prioritie of time in an instant," so that a surviving joint tenant takes and is preferred before the devisee of his companion (Co. Litt. 185 b). *Vf.* Termes de la Ley, *Instant.*

INSTANTLY.—"Instantly" does not, at least in a Bill of Sale, seem a more intense word than "Immediately" (*Massey* v. *Sladen*, 38 L. J. Ex. 34; L. R. 4 Ex. 13).

Indeed in *R.* v. *Brownlow* (9 L. J. M. C. 15; 11 A. & E. 119; 3 P. & D. 52), it was said that "Instantly" had no definite meaning; there a Coroner's Inquisition stated an explosion on a Thames steamer from the effects of which A. B. "instantly died," and the Inquisition was quashed for not averring with sufficient distinctness the time of the death.

INSTEAD OF.—The words "Instead of," "In lieu of," though naturally implying some, need not necessarily mean a total, substitution. Thus a gift by a Codicil "instead of" one in the Will, may be read "instead of so much of the gift in the Will only as is incompatible with the Codicil" (1 Jarm. 177, 178, citing *Doe* d. *Murch* v. *Marchant*, 13 L. J. C. P. 59; 6 M. & G. 813; 7 Sc. N. R. 644: *Hill* v. *Walker*, 4 K. & J. 168: *Butler* v. *Greenwood*, 22 Bea. 303: *Barclay* v. *Maskelyne*, 5 Jur. N. S. 12). *Vf. Ex p. Drew*, W. N. (71) 184.

A fund provided by statute "in lieu of" other means of payment, may become the primary fund (*R.* v. *St. Saviour's, Southwark,* 7 L. J. M. C. 59 ; 7 A. & E. 925 ; 3 N. & P. 126).

Buildings "in lieu of," mean "in the place of" (*Boyer* v. *Bancroft,* W. N. (83) 67).

V. ADDITION : LIEU AND SUBSTITUTION.

INSTITUTED.—A proceeding "instituted," means one commenced ; therefore where, to a petition for restitution of conjugal rights, the answer charged adultery, there was no "action, suit or proceeding . . . . *instituted* in consequence of adultery" within s. 4, 14 & 15 V. c. 99 (*Blackborne* v. *Blackborne,* 37 L. J. P. & M. 73 ; L. R. 1 P. & M. 563). *V.* PROCEEDING.

INSTITUTION.—*V.* ADMISSION.

"Societies and Institutions ;" *V.* SOCIETIES.

INSTROKE.—"The right of 'Instroke' is the right of conveying Minerals from a demised mine to the surface through a pit or shaft in an adjoining mine. It is the converse right to that of 'Outstroke ;' which is the right of conveying Minerals from an adjoining mine to the surface through a pit or shaft in the demised mine" (MacS. 231, *wh.* to p. 239, *Vf.*).

INSTRUCT.—*V.* TEACH AND INSTRUCT.

INSTRUMENT.—An "Instrument" is a formal legal writing. "The words, 'Instrument of foundation or statutes' s. 19, 32 & 33 V. c. 56, and s. 7, 36 & 37 V. c. 87, point with great distinctness to written instruments" (per Selborne, L. C., *St. Leonards Trustees* v. *Charity Commrs.,* 54 L. J. P. C. 31 ; 10 App. Ca. 304 ; 51 L. T. 305 ; 33 W. R. 756).

A Power by "Deed, *Instrument* or Will" is well executed by a mere writing which is neither a Deed nor a Will (*Brodrick* v. *Brown,* 1 K. & J. 328). *V.* WRITING : INSTRUMENT IN WRITING.

Orders of Court are not "Instruments" within s. 2, Apportionment Act, 4 & 5 W. 4, c. 22 (*Jodrell* v. *Jodrell,* 38 L. J. Ch. 507 ; L. R. 7 Eq. 461).

"Instrument," in the phrase "Bond, Covenant or Instrument" in the Schedule to the Stamp Act, 1870, means an Instrument of the same nature as "Bond" or "Covenant" with which it is associated, *i.e.,* one for securing payment of money (*Thames Conservators* v. *Inl. Rev.,* 56 L. J. Q. B. 181 ; 18 Q. B. D. 279 ; 56 L. T. 198 ; 35 W. R. 274).

"Instruments" of a Ship ; *V.* TACKLE.

V. TESTAMENT.

INSTRUMENT OF GAMING.—A machine used for registering bets at a race is an "Instrument of Gaming" (*Tollet* v. *Thomas,* 24 L. T. 509).

Money is not an "Instrument of Gaming" (*Watson* v. *Martin,* 34 L. J. M. C. 50 ; 28 J. P. 775 : *Hirst* v. *Molesbury,* 40 L. J. M. C. 76 ; L. R. 6 Q. B. 130 ; 23 L. T. 555).

INSTRUMENT IN WRITING.—Where by a Company's Articles

a Transfer of Shares may be by an "Instrument in Writing," a Deed is not necessary, even though the Company's uniform practice has required one (*Re Tahiti Cotton Co., Ex p. Sargent*, L. R. 17 Eq. 273 ; 43 L. J. Ch. 425 : *Ortigosa* v. *Brown*, 47 L. J. Ch. 168 ; 38 L. T. 145. *Vh.* Buckl. 429).

Semble, an "Instrument in Writing" does not necessarily require to be signed by the party making it (per Parke, B., *Hunter* v. *Parker*, 10 L. J. Ex. 288 ; 7 M. & W. 322).

As to the execution of a Power by Deed or "Instrument in Writing ;" *V.* WRITING.

Submission to arbitration by "Deed or Instrument in Writing," s. 17, Com. L. Pro. Act, 1854 ; *V. Re Dawdy and Hartcup*, 54 L. J. Q. B. 574 ; 15 Q. B. D. 426 : SUBMISSION.

V. IN WRITING : INSTRUMENT.

INSTRUMENTALITY.—Under s. 28, 23 & 24 V. c. 127, a Solicitor is entitled to a charge for his costs on property recovered or preserved through his "instrumentality." "Suppose that a Solicitor is employed in a hotly contested action, and prepares the whole case of the plaintiff down to the moment of trial, and that just before the trial the plaintiff changes his solicitor, and then, owing to the exertions of the solicitor formerly employed, he succeeds in the action. Can it possibly be said that that success is not owing to the 'instrumentality' of the discharged solicitor ?" (per Kay, J., *Re Wadsworth*, 54 L. J. Ch. 640 ; 29 Ch. D. 517 ; 52 L. T. 613 ; 33 W. R. 558). *V.* RECOVERED OR PRESERVED.

INSUFFICIENT.—"Insufficient" Sureties for Costs, s. 8, Parl. Elec. Act, 1868 (31 & 32 V. c. 125),—does not mean general incapacity of entering into a suretyship, but insufficiency for the purpose of the Act ; therefore a Recognizance for Costs signed by an election petitioner is "insufficient" and may be amended by a deposit of money under s. 9 ; and, *semble*, that this would be so if the Recognizance were signed by an infant or married woman (*Pease* v. *Norwood*, L. R. 4 C. P. 235 ; 38 L. J. C. P. 161). *V.* that case, and especially jdgmt. of Bovill, C.J., for discussion of contrast as to when such a Recognizance is "insufficient" and amendable, and "*invalid*" and altogether void.

V. ON BEHALF.

INSURANCE COMPANY.—"Insurance Company" whose premiums may be deducted from Income Tax (s. 54, 16 & 17 V. c. 34 ; 16 & 17 V. c. 91), must be a Co. in the United Kingdom, and a Co. according to English law (*Colquhoun* v. *Heddon*, 6 Times Rep. 153 ; 34 S. J. 196).

INSURED.—*V.* NOT INSURED.

INSURED ELSEWHERE.—As a Condition in a Fire Policy ; *V. Australian Agricultural Co.* v. *Saunders*, 44 L. J. C. P. 391 ; L. R. 10 C. P. 668.

INTAKE MEASURE OF QUANTITY DELIVERED.—*V. Spaight* v. *Farnworth*, 5 Q. B. D. 115 ; 49 L. J. Q. B. 346 ; cited and stated 1 Maude & P. 380, 381.

INTENDED.—A part of a Building Estate was sold to A. under restrictive covenants as to user and occupation, and in the Conditions of Sale and also in the recitals to the conveyance to A. it was stated that "it is intended" that the other parts of the Estate should, in the hands of the respective purchasers thereof, be subject to similar covenants, but the vendor entered into no covenant in that behalf with A. ; held, that "intended" amounted, if not to a covenant, yet to an implied agreement by the vendor, and that he could be restrained by A. from selling the remaining parts of the Estate free from the restrictive covenants, so as to contravene the building scheme thereby contemplated (*Mackenzie* v. *Childers*, 43 Ch. D. 265 ; 59 L. J. Ch. 188 ; 34 S. J. 142 : *Vf. Collins* v. *Castle*, 57 L. J. Ch. 76 : *Sheppard* v. *Gilmore*, Ib. 6 : *Spicer* v. *Martin*, 58 L. J. Ch. 309).

INTENDED HUSBAND.—A clause restraining alienation of a married woman's separate estate being applicable to all her covertures, unless expressly limited (*Re Gaffee*, 19 L. J. Ch. 179 ; 1 Mac. & G. 541), the phrase, in a Marriage Settlement, that separate estate is to be enjoyed by the lady "independently of her said intended husband" is not enough to confine the restraint clause to that particular coverture (*Hawkes* v. *Hubback*, 40 L. J. Ch. 49 ; L. R. 11 Eq. 5 : *Shafto* v. *Butler*, 40 L. J. Ch. 308 ; 19 W. R. 595). *Vh.* Elph. 299, 300.

INTENDED TO BE DONE.—*V.* DONE.

INTENT TO DEFRAUD.—To use a False Trade Description with "Intent to Defraud," s. 2 (1), Merchandize Marks Act, 1887, does not mean "with intent to cheat," for as good Goods may be supplied under a false, as under a true, Description ; an intention to represent the Goods as being manufactured by some one other than the real manufacturer brings a case within the section (*Starey* v. *Chilworth Gunpowder Co.*, 59 L. J. M. C. 13 ; nom. *Starcy* v. *Chilworth Gunpowder Co.*, 6 Times Rep. 95 : *Wood* v. *Burgess*, 59 L. J. M. C. 11).

INTENTS.—"Void to all intents and purposes ;" *V.* VOID : ALL INTENTS AND PURPOSES.

INTEREST.—"*Interesse* is vulgarly taken for a terme or chattle reall, and more particularly for a future tearme ; in which case it is said in pleading that he is possessed *de interesse termini*. But *ex vi termini*, in legall understanding, it extendeth to estates, rights and titles, that a man hath of, in, to, or out of lands ; for he is truly said to have an interest in them : and by the grant of *totum interesse suum* in such lands, as well reversions as possessions in fee simple shall passe" (Co. Litt. 345 b ; *Vh.* Elph. 205).

"Where the 'Interest' or 'Produce' of a *Fund* is bequeathed to a legatee, or in trust for him, *without any limitation as to continuance*, the principal will be regarded as bequeathed also" (Wms. Exs. 1199, 1200, and cases there cited); but this "is not a very strong rule," and "it is always a question of construction whether the testator did or not intend to give more than a life interest" (per Parker, V.-C., *Blann* v. *Bell*, 21 L. J. Ch. 813; 5 D. G. & S. 663: *Va. Wetherell* v. *Wetherell*, 32 L. J. Ch. 476; 1 D. G. J. & S. 134; 4 Giff. 51). *V.* PRODUCE.

"*All* my Interest;" *V. Manton* v. *Tabois*, 30 Ch. D. 92; 54 L. J. Ch. 1008; 53 L. T. 289; 33 W. R. 832: *Scott* v. *Best*, 6 L. R. Ir. 7.

"Interest," s. 38 (2) *c*, Customs & Inl. Rev. Act, 1881, 44 & 45 V. c. 12; *V. A.-G.* v. *Heywood*, 56 L. J. Q. B. 572; 19 Q. B. D. 326; 57 L. T. 271; 35 W. R. 772.

V. RIGHT AND TITLE: RENTS AND PROFITS: SHARE.

INTEREST IN LAND.—By the construction put upon the *Mortmain Act* (9 G. 2, c. 36; repealed but its provisions re-enacted by the Mortmain and Charitable Uses Act, 1888), no Interest in Land can be given by Will to charitable uses. For the very numerous and frequently conflicting cases defining what is an Interest in Land within these provisions, *V.* Tudor, Char. Trusts, 398–409; Wms. Exs. 1062–1074; 1 Chit. Stat. 3 Ed. 486; Seton, 599, 600.

In *Jervis* v. *Lawrence* (52 L. J. Ch. 244; 22 Ch. D. 202), Bacon, V.-C., said, "I believe there is a fault that has been committed in a great many of these cases." Many of the cases came under review in *Attree* v. *Hall* (47 L. J. Ch. 863; 9 Ch. D. 337), which decided that a Railway Debenture is not an interest in land. The principle of that case as stated by Jessel, M. R., *Re Harris* (49 L. J. Ch. 687; 15 Ch. D. 561), is that in order to create an interest in land, within the Statute of Mortmain, the land must be affected directly. *In re Harris* decided that Bonds charged on Police Rates under 3 & 4 V. c. 88, and now payable by justice's precept under 7 & 8 V. c. 33, are pure personalty. *Va.* the effect of *Attree* v. *Hall*, and *Re Harris*, (sup.), on the cases prior thereto, discussed and applied by Bacon, V.-C., in *Jervis* v. *Lawrence* (sup.). In the last case the learned judge illustrated his position by the following (perhaps questionable) reasoning, "A man who has a power of distress has no interest in the land. *A landlord or lessor, while the lease subsists, has no interest in the land*;" but only his right of distress. It was in that case held that Bonds created under the Act for the improvement of the Norland Estate, in St. Mary Abbot's, Kensington (6 V. c. xxxiii.), and which were secured by a rate levied upon owners or occupiers on the estate and enforceable against them by action or distress, did not create an interest in land, but were pure personalty. So a Charge binding assets of a Building Society is not an Interest in Land within the Mortmain Act; but a charge on municipal rates, or on a legacy payable out of realty and personalty, is (*Walmsley* v. *Rice*, 29 S. J. 256). Money secured by mortgage of real estate is such an interest in land (*Re Watts*, 55 L. J. Ch. 332, discussing

Re Harris, sup.), and so is a share of proceeds of realty the time for selling which has not arrived (*Brook* v. *Badley*, 36 L. J. Ch. 741 ; 3 Ch. 672). Whether Statutory Duties, Tolls or Dues are an interest in land within the Statute of Mortmain depends on the particular provisions of the Act by which they are authorised (*Re Christmas*, 55 L. J. Ch. 878 ; 33 Ch. D. 332 ; 55 L. T. 197 ; 34 W. R. 779; 50 J. P. 759, in which *V. Knapp* v. *Williams*, 4 Ves. 430 n., commented on and explained. *Vf. Re David, Buckley* v. *Lifeboat Inst.*, 43 Ch. D. 27 ; 59 L. J. Ch. 87 ; 60 L. T. 786).

By s. 4 of the *Statute of Frauds* (29 Car. 2, c. 3) no contract for the sale of lands, tenements or hereditaments or "any interest in or concerning them" is valid, unless evidenced by a signed writing. For the cases on that provision, *V.* Add. C. 159 *et seq.* ; Woodf. 86, 87 ; Rosc. N. P. 285. These decisions have gone to the length of establishing that a right to shoot game and take it away for one's own benefit is an "Interest in Land" within the St. of Frauds (*Webber* v. *Lee*, 51 L. J. Q. B. 486 ; 9 Q. B. D. 315, which *V.* for cases establishing the contrary as regards contracts for Board and Lodging, use of a Graving-Dock, Shares in a Cost-book Mine, and an Opera Box). So the sale of standing buildings to be taken down and cleared away in 2 months is of an "Interest in Land" (*Lavery* v. *Pursell*, 57 L. J. Ch. 570 ; 39 Ch. D. 508 ; 58 L. T. 846 ; 37 W. R. 163). *Vf. McManus* v. *Cooke*, 56 L. J. Ch. 662; 35 Ch. D. 681; 56 L. T. 900; 35 W. R. 754 ; 51 J. P. 708 : *Gray* v. *Smith*, 43 Ch. D. 208 ; 58 L. J. Ch. 803 ; 38 W. R. 310.

"Lands" or an Interest in Land within s. 3, Lands C. C. Act, 1845, includes an equitable interest (*Martin* v. *Lond. Chatham & Dover Ry.*, 35 L. J. Ch. 795 ; 1 Ch. 501 ; 14 W. R. 880 ; 14 L. T. 814) ; but not a contract for purchase (*Tasker* v. *Small*, 7 L. J. Ch. 19 ; 3 M. & Cr. 63 : and see that case cited in the judgment of Erle, C. J., in *Bird* v. *G. E. Ry.*, 34 L. J. C. P. 371; 13 W. R. 991; 19 C. B. N. S. 267). A right of shooting by an agreement not under seal, is not an interest in land within the L. C. C. Act, nor (probably) would it be so if granted by deed (*Bird* v. *G. E. Ry.*, sup.). *V.* HEREDITAMENT. A quarterly tenant, after notice to quit duly given, has no "interest in land" entitling him to notice under s. 18, L. C. C. Act, 1845 (*Syers* v. *Metrop. Board of Works*, 36 L. T. 277).

A right of support, or of light, is not an "Interest in Land" within s. 19, *Artisans' and Labourers' Dwellings Improvement Act*, 1875 (38 & 39 V. c. 36) ; but is an "easement" upon the servient tenement within s. 20 of that Act (*Barham* v. *Marris*, 45 L. T. 579 ; 52 L. J. Ch. 237 : *Swainston* v. *Finn*, 52 L. J. Ch. 235).

A life interest in part of the proceeds of the sale of land is an "Interest" in land within s. 9, *Dower Act*, 1833, 3 & 4 W. 4, c. 105 (*Re Thomas*, 56 L. J. Ch. 9 ; 34 Ch. D. 166 ; 55 L. T. 629 :—following dictum of Jessel, M. R., *Lacey* v. *Hill*, 44 L. J. Ch. 215 ; L. R. 19 Eq. 346).

"Interest in Land," s. 13, 1 & 2 V. c. 110 ; *V. Thomas* v. *Cross*, 34 L. J. Ch. 580 ; 2 Dr. & Sm. 423.

INTEREST IN LEASE.—Sale of ; *V.* Lease.

INTEREST IN THE NATURE OF REAL ESTATE.—*V.* Real Estate.

INTEREST OF MONEY.—Sch. D. Income Tax Act, 1853, 16 & 17 V. c. 34 ; *V. Clerical Med. & Gen. Life Assrce.* v. *Carter*, 58 L. J. Q. B. 224 ; 22 Q. B. D. 444.

INTEREST OR CHARGE.—"Interests and Charges having priority to the Settlement," s. 20 (2), Settled Land Act, 1882 ; *V. Grainge* v. *Wilberforce*, 5 Times Rep. 436.

INTERESTED.—*V.* Person interested : Party interested.

INTERESTED IN.—"Interested in" a business or bargain seems a little wider expression than "concerned in."

A person is "interested in" a Contract if he be a shareholder in a Company who has that contract (*Dimes* v. *Grand Junc. Canal Co.*, 3 H. L. Ca. 759). That construction still applies as regards officers and servants of Local Authorities in respect of s. 193, P. H. Act, 1875 (*Todd* v. *Robinson*, 54 L. J. Q. B. 47 ; 14 Q. B. D. 739 ; 52 L. T. 120 ; 49 J. P. 278). An officer of a Local Authority who lets rooms to the Board is "concerned or interested in a Bargain or Contract" within that section (*Burgess* v. *Clark*, 14 Q. B. D. 735) ; and a Town Surveyor who takes out the quantities for a contract for which he is paid by the contractor, is "interested in" the contract (*Whiteley* v. *Barley*, 57 L. J. Q. B. 643 ; 21 Q. B. D. 154 ; 36 W. R. 823 ; 52 J. P. 595 : *R.* v. *Ramsgate*, 58 L. J. Q. B. 352 : *R.* v. *Whiteley*, 58 L. J. M. C. 164).

Cp. Concerned in.

As regards Municipal Corporations, *V.* proviso to s. 28, 5 & 6 W. 4, c. 76, and s. 5, 32 & 33 V. c. 55.

"Interested in" an Award ; *V. Carr* v. *Metrop. Bd. of Wks.*, 49 L. J. Ch. 272 ; 14 Ch. D. 807.

V. Carry on : Concerned : Party interested : Person interested.

INTERFERE.—"The words 'interfere with or affect any Settlement' (s. 19, M. W. P. Act, 1882), means, invalidate or render inoperative any Settlement" (per Lindley, L. J., *Re Armstrong*, 57 L. J. Q. B. 557 ; 21 Q. B. D. 264 ; 36 W. R. 772 : *Re Onslow*, 57 L. J. Ch. 941 ; 39 Ch. D. 622 ; 59 L. T. 308 ; 36 W. R. 883).

V. Affect : Unnecessary Interference.

INTERLINEATION.—"Interlineation," s. 21, 1 V. c. 26, is not confined to something written between lines ; it includes something put into one of the lines, but written *on* the line (per Hannen, P., *Bagshawe* v. *Canning*, 52 J. P. 583).

INTERLOCUTORY.—An Interlocutory *Judgment* determines the right to recover, but not how much. *Vh.* Ord. 13, R. 5, R. S. C.

The following are Interlocutory *Orders* within Ord. 58, R. 15, R. S. C.:—Leave to sign immediate judgment under Ord. 14 (*Standard Discount Co.* v. *La Grange*, 47 L. J. C. P. 3 ; 3 C. P. D. 67) ; Order on Summons by Creditors and Claimants in an Administration or Winding-up (*Lewis* v. *Lewis*, 34 W. R. 40, 420 ; 54 L. T. 199 : *Lewis* v. *Williams*, 31 Ch. D. 623 : *Pheysey* v. *Pheysey*, 12 Ch. D. 305) ; Order to work out rights given by a Final Judgment (*Blakey* v. *Latham*, 43 Ch. D. 23) ; Order on a Case stated by an Arbitrator for his guidance prior to making Award (*Collins* v. *Paddington*, 49 L. J. Q. B. 264 ; 5 Q. B. D. 368 : *Sv. Shubrook* v. *Tufnell*, 9 Q. B. D. 621 ; 30 W. R. 740 : *V.* FINAL ORDER) ; Findings on Interpleader Issues (*McAndrew* v. *Barker*, 47 L. J. Ch. 340 ; 7 Ch. D. 701) ; Findings by a judge of the Ch. D. on distinct issues of fact which at the commencement of the trial have been agreed shall be first tried, *secus* if issues not so settled (*Krehl* v. *Burrell*, 48 L. J. Ch. 252 ; 11 Ch. D. 146 : *Lowe* v. *Lowe*, 48 L. J. Ch. 383 ; 10 Ch. D. 432) ; Order discharging rule *nisi* for Prohibition (*R.* v. *Local Board*, 26 S. J. 545) ; Opinion of Q. B. D. on Case stated from Quarter Sessions (*Peterborough* v. *Wilsthorpe*, 53 L. J. M. C. 33 ; 12 Q. B. D. 1).

Note.—On Appeals, "any doubt which may arise as to what Decrees, Orders or Judgments are Final, and what are Interlocutory, shall be determined by the Court of Appeal" (s. 12, Judicature Act, 1875).

"Interlocutory Order," s. 25 (8), Jud. Act, 1873, is not confined to an Order made between writ and final judgment, but means an Order other than final judgment ; and, therefore, a Receiver may be appointed under that section after final judgment (*Smith* v. *Cowell*, 6 Q. B. D. 75 ; 50 L. J. Q. B. 38 ; *Vth. Manchester and Liverpool Bank* v. *Parkinson*, 22 Q. B. D. 175).

Cp. FINAL JUDGMENT : FINAL ORDER.

INTERMEDDLE.—A provision that "no Court shall intermeddle" with an inferior Court, does not oust the supervision of the High Court (*R.* v. *Moreley*, 2 Burr. 1041 : *Vth. Re Heaphy*, 22 L. R. Ir. 513).

INTERMENT.—Re-interment of human remains is not an "Interment" of bodies, within s. 44, 15 & 16 V. c. 85 (*Scadding* v. *St. Pancras*, W. N. (89) 45, 120).

INTERPLEADER.—Interpleader Issue ; *V.* ACTION.

"Proceedings in Interpleader," s. 120, County Co. Act, 1888 ; *V. Lumb* v. *Teal*, 58 L. J. Q. B. 298 ; 22 Q. B. D. 675.

INTERRUPTION.—The "Interruption" which defeats a prescriptive right under s. 4, 2 & 3 W. 4, c. 71, is an adverse obstruction by the owner of the servient tenement, not a mere discontinuance of user by the claimant himself (*Carr* v. *Foster*, 3 Q. B. 581 ; 11 L. J. Q. B. 284 ; 2 G. & D. 753 ;

6 Jur. 837 : *Cooper* v. *Straker*, 58 L. J. Ch. 26 ; 40 Ch. D. 21 : and *Vh. Bennison* v. *Cartwright*, 33 L. J. Q. B. 137 ; 5 B. & S. 1 : *Arkwright* v. *Gell*, 8 L. J. Ex. 201 ; 5 M. & W. 203 : *Flight* v. *Thomas*, 8 Cl. & F. 231 : Dart, 432). *V.* ACTUALLY ENJOYED.

"The words 'Interruption,' 'Disturbance,' and the like, in the covenant for Quiet Enjoyment, mean lawful interruptions and disturbances only" (Elph. 483) ; but the covenant may be so worded as to extend to tortious acts, *e.g.*, if against all "claiming or *pretending to claim*" (*Chaplin* v. *Southgate*, 10 Mod. 384 ; nom. *Southgate* v. *Chaplin*, 1 Com. Rep. 230 : *V. Hunt* v. *Allen*, Winch. 25).

INTERVAL.—Where an "Interval" of so many days has to elapse between two events, *e.g.*, two meetings, the days are *clear* days, and have to be reckoned exclusive of both the days between which the interval is to elapse (*Re Railway Sleepers Co.*, 54 L. J. Ch. 720 ; 29 Ch. D. 204) ; but if the interval, in a Company's meetings, be less than 14 clear days, the defect does not concern creditors (*Re Miller's Dale Co.*, 31 Ch. D. 211).

V. CLEAR : NOT LESS.

INTERVENTION.—Plaintiffs, house agents, were instructed by Defendant to offer a house for sale, at a commission of 2½ per cent. on the purchase money if they found a purchaser, but to receive £1 1s. 0d. only if sale made "without their Intervention." A., who had observed that the house was for sale, but had not then seen over it, called on Plaintiffs, and obtained a Card to View the house, and also other houses, the terms being written by Plaintiff's clerk on the back of the Card. A. went to the house, but thought the price asked (£2200) too high, and went away. A. had no further communication with Plaintiffs ; but he subsequently renewed his negotiation with a friend of Defendant's, and became the purchaser for £1700 ; held, that there was evidence for a jury that A. had become the purchaser "through the Intervention" of the Plaintiffs, who were consequently entitled to the commission. At the trial, the Judge put the following question to A., "Would you, if you had not gone to the Plaintiffs' office and got the Card, have purchased the house ?" and, over-ruling an objection by Defendant's counsel, received this answer, "I should think not :" *Semble*, that the answer was properly received (*Mansell* v. *Clements*, L. R. 9 C. P. 139).

INTESTATE.—*V.* LEFT.

INTIMIDATE.—As to Electoral Intimidation ; *V.* Leigh & Le Marchant, 4 Ed. 30–38.

It is to "intimidate," within s. 7, subs. 1, Conspiracy & Protection of Property Act, 1875 (38 & 39 V. c. 86), to tell a Master that he should not employ a Workman not belonging to a Trades Union (*Shelbourne*

v. *Oliver*, 30 J. P. 213), or to say to a Workman, "If you leave the town quietly we shall not hurt you" (*Hodgson* v. *Graveling*, 31 J. P. 115), or to "picket" Workmen (*R.* v. *Bauld*, Stone, 465): but there is no Intimidation in bonâ fide, and in answer to enquiries, communicating a Society rule as to the number of apprentices a Master might take (*Wood* v. *Bowron*, 31 J. P. 21). *Vf.* Stone, 465.

INTO.—The employment of a Humber pilot is not compulsory upon a vessel which is being towed from one dock to another in the port of Hull, as it is not, under such circumstances, passing "*into or out of*" the port within s. 22, Hull Pilot Act, 2 & 3 W. 4, c. cv. (*The Maria*, L. R. 1 A. & E. 358).

V. Through.

INTRODUCE BUSINESS.—*V. Neck* v. *Andrews*, 1 Times Rep. 607.

INTRUSION.—"Intrusion first properly is, when the ancestor dyed seized of any estate of inheritance expectant upon an estate for life, and then tenant for life dyeth, and between the death and the entry of the heire an estranger doth interpose himselfe and intrude.

"Secondly, he that entreth upon any of the king's demesnes, and taketh the profits, is said to intrude upon the king's possession.

"Thirdly, when the heire in ward entreth at his full age without satisfaction for his marriage, the writ saith, *quod intrusit*" (Co. Litt. 277 a, b).

INTRUSTED.—Factors Act, 6 G. 4, c. 94, s. 2; *V. Phillips* v. *Huth*, 10 L. J. Ex. 65; 6 M. & W. 572: *Hatfield* v. *Phillips*, 11 L. J. Ex. 425; 9 M. & W. 647; 14 Ib. 665; 12 Cl. & F. 343. *Vth.* s. 4, 5 & 6 V. c. 39; 1 Sm. L. C. 822.

V. Agent Intrusted.

INVALID.—*V.* Insufficient.

INVENTED WORD.—*V.* Fancy Word.

INVENTION.—*V.* New Manufacture.

INVENTOR.—*V.* First Inventor.

INVENTORY.—An "Inventory" is a detailed list of goods, enumerating them with reasonable particularity according to the well understood usage of business men; and the word is so used in s. 4, Bills of Sale Act, 1882 (*Witt* v. *Banner*, 20 Q. B. D. 114; 57 L. J. Q. B. 141; 58 L. T. 34; 36 W. R. 115; 3 Times Rep. 759: *Carpenter* v. *Deen*, 23 Q. B. D. 566; 33 S. J. 590; 5 Times Rep. 647). *V.* Specific.

Vh. Termes de la Ley, *Inventary*.

INVEST.—In a Will a Trust for Sale may be implied from a trust "to invest" (*Affleck* v. *James*, 17 Sim. 121).

V. Accumulation.

INVESTED BY ME.—A Bequest of the income of a certain sum "invested by me" in a particular way, is specific (*Kermode* v. *Macdonald*, 35 L. J. Ch. 358 ; 37 Ib. 879 ; L. R. 1 Eq. 457 ; 3 Ch. 584).

INVESTIGATING TITLE.—If a purchaser's solicitor has in any way inquired into the vendor's title, he is entitled to the scale fee for "investigating title" provided by Sch. 1, Part 1, Remuneration Ord.; and this though no Abstract or Evidence of Title be delivered by the vendor or though "the investigation took only 5 minutes instead of 10 days" (per Kay, J., *Ex p. London Corp.*, 56 L. J. Ch. 308 ; 34 Ch. D. 452 ; 35 W. R. 211 ; 56 L. T. 13 : *Ex p. Ferguson to Buckley*, 21 L. R. Ir. 396, 397).

Cp. "Deducing Title ;" *V.* Deduce.

INVESTING.—"Investing" member of a Building Society; *V. Re Norwich and Norfolk Bg. Socy.*, 45 L. J. Ch. 785.

INVESTMENTS.—Foreign Government Bonds will pass under a bequest of "Investments" (*Arnould* v. *Grinstead*, 21 W. R. 155).

INWARDS.—"Trading Inwards ;" *V.* Trading.

I. O. U.—An I. O. U. not given in acknowledgment of a debt due, nor as the result of an account stated between the parties, is not evidence under a count on an account stated (*Lemere* v. *Elliott*, 30 L. J. Ex. 350 ; 6 H. & N. 656).

IRISH FUNDED PROPERTY.—Government Debentures, held not to pass under a bequest of "Irish Funded Property" (*Ridge* v. *Newton*, 4 Ir. Eq. R. 389 ; 2 Dr. & War. 239 ; 1 Con. & L. 381).

IRISH VALUATION ACTS.—*V.* s. 24, Interp. Act, 1889.

IRON.—In a Marine Insurance was this clause,—"Warranted no Iron or ore or phosphate cargoes, exceeding the net register tonnage, across the Atlantic ;"—Held, that Steel was included in the word "Iron" (*Hart* v. *Standard Mar. Insrce.*, 22 Q. B. D. 499 ; 58 L. J. Q. B. 284 ; 60 L. T. 649).

IRREGULARITY.—*V. Ex p. Johnson*, 53 L. J. Ch. 309 ; 25 Ch. D 112 : Formal : Informality.

IRRESPONSIBLE.—"In their absolute and irresponsible discretion ;" *V.* Discretion.

IS.—"*Is* of full age," in s. 6, Rep. People Act, 1867 (30 & 31 V. c. 102), means being of full age at or before the end of the year of qualification (*Hargreaves* v. *Hopper*, 45 L. J. C. P. 105 ; 1 C. P. D. 195). In this connection "is" was read "was."

ISLE.—"By the name of an isle, *insula*, many manors, lands and tenements may passe" (Co. Litt. 5 a : *Vf.* Touch. 92).

ISSUE.—This is a word of flexible meaning ;—

1. Its legal meaning is "Descendants :"
2. Its popular meaning is "Children."

(Per Jessel, M. R., *Morgan* v. *Thomas*, 51 L. J. Q. B. 556 ; 9 Q. B. D. 643 ; and per James and Brett, L.JJ., *Ralph* v. *Carrick*, 48 L. J. Ch. 807, 808, 809 ; 11 Ch. D. 873) : and it may be used in different clauses of the same instrument in different senses (*Carter* v. *Bentall*, 9 L. J. Ch. 303 ; 2 Bea. 551 : *Re Warren*, 53 L. J. Ch. 787 ; 26 Ch. D. 208).

In its popular meaning it is a designation of persons ; whilst in its technical import it is generally a word of limitation.

In devises of *Real Estate*, "Issue" is a word of limitation which, when uncontrolled by the context, is equivalent to, but more flexible than "heirs of the body" (*Sv.* Heirs of the body) ; so that a devise to A. "and his Issue" will generally give to A. an estate tail (*Roddy* v. *Fitzgerald*, 6 H. L. Ca. 823 : *Bowen* v. *Lewis*, 54 L. J. Q. B. 55 ; 9 App. Ca. 890 : *Sandes* v. *Cooke*, 21 L. R. Ir. 445 : *Woodhouse* v. *Herrick*, 24 L. J. Ch. 649 ; 1 K. & J. 352 : *Vf.* 2 Jarm. 414 *et seq.* : *Williams* v. *Williams*, 33 W. R. 118 ; W. N. (84) 198 : *Whitelaw* v. *Whitelaw*, 5 L. R. Ir. 120).

But where there is a manifest indication in a Will, made since 1838, that the Testator intended A. to take a life interest in realty, a subsequent limitation to the "Issue" of A. would be construed as words of purchase, and the "Issue" would be entitled to take subject to the life interest and the word would frequently, if not generally, be construed as "Children" (*Ralph* v. *Carrick*, 11 Ch. D. 882, 885 : *Morgan* v. *Thomas*, 51 L. J. Q. B. 289, 556 ; 9 Q. B. D. 643. *V.* the latter case for a collection of the cases on Wills made prior to 1838 shewing the care the Courts took to construe a devise, where "issue" mentioned, as an entail when the words superadded were insufficient to carry the fee ;—a reason which, as was observed by the M. R. in the case just quoted, does not exist as regards Wills made since the Wills Act, 1 V. c. 26).

It has been said that a bequest of *Personal Property* to "A. and his Issue" will give to A. the absolute interest (Wms. Exs. 1114). But the rule would seem to be better stated thus :—"The rule that 'Issue' is *primâ facie* a word of limitation does not extend to bequests of personal estate (*Knight* v. *Ellis*, 2 Bro. C. C. 570 : *Ex p. Wynch*, 5 D. G. M. & G. 188 ; 1 Sm. & G. 427 ; 22 L. J. Ch. 750 ; 23 Ib. 930). If it be clear that the testator intended to make such a disposition of personal estate as would in the case of real estate amount to an estate tail, the first taker will take the absolute interest ; but it is not the case that every expression which would create an estate tail in real estate, will be held to indicate the same intention in the case of personal estate ; . . . and slight circumstances would probably be held to shew an intention that the issue should take in remainder after a life interest in the parent" (Hawk. 197, 198 : *V.* this point elaborately treated, 2 Jarm. 567–581).

But the question frequently occurs in cases where "Issue" are entitled in remainder as under *words of purchase,* whether the word means "Descendants" according to its legal rendering and so include grandchildren and remoter issue or whether it should be confined to children in the first generation. Upon this branch of the meaning of the word "Issue" it is conceived that there could be no difference between a devise of real, and a bequest of personal estate ; and then we come to this proposition,—When the phrase "Issue" is employed in a Will (and *a fortiori* in a Deed, *Harrison* v. *Symons,* 14 W. R. 959) as a word of purchase or as a description of a class, it will, in its ordinary import, comprise all those who can claim as Descendants of the person whose issue are indicated, *i.e.,* grandchildren and great grandchildren and so on, as well as children ; and in order to restrain this primary legal sense of the word, a clear intention to do so must appear upon the instrument (Wms. Exs. 1116, and cases there cited). The rule hereon has also been thus stated,—"The word *Issue,* though its popular sense is said to be 'Children,' is technically and when not restrained by the context, co-extensive and synonymous with *Descendants,* comprehending objects of every degree" (2 Jarm. 101).

"But it is, I think, settled by the case of *Pruen* v. *Osborne* (11 Sim. 132), that as a general rule, when you find a gift to a person, and then a gift to the issue of that person, such issue to take only the *parent's* share, the word 'Issue' is cut down to mean 'Children'" (per James, L. J., *Ralph* v. *Carrick,* 48 L. J. Ch. 807 ; 11 Ch. D. 873 : the leading case on this point is *Sibley* v. *Perry,* 7 Ves. 522, but of that case Brett, L. J., said, in *Ralph* v. *Carrick,* "I should have no objection to be present at the funeral of *Sibley* v. *Perry,*" 48 L. J. Ch. 809) ; and a similar construction will obtain if a similar collocation of parent and issue occur in a Deed (*Barraclough* v. *Shillito,* 53 L. J. Ch. 841). But where there is a gift over, the meaning of "Issue," even when collocated with "Parent," will frequently be widened to mean "Descendants" (*Ross* v. *Ross,* 20 Bea. 645 : *Ralph* v. *Carrick,* sup.).

If the construction of "Issue" should be "Descendants" distributively. they will take *per capita* and, failing words of severance, as joint tenants (*Davenport* v. *Hanbury,* 3 Ves. 258 : *Hobgen* v. *Neale,* 40 L. J. Ch. 36 ; L. R. 11 Eq. 48 : *Hume* v. *Lloyd,* 47 L. J. Ch. 775 ; 26 W. R. 828 : 2 Jarm. 101 ; Wms. Exs. 1519, 1520, n. *q*).

In the following cases "Issue" was read as "*Children :*"—*Sibley* v. *Perry,* sup. : *Pruen* v. *Osborne,* sup. : *Barraclough* v. *Shillito,* sup. : *Heasman* v. *Pearse,* 41 L. J. Ch. 705 ; 7 Ch. 275 : *Martin* v. *Holgate,* 35

L. J. Ch. 789 ; L. R. 1 H. L. 175 : *Bryden* v. *Willett*, L. R. 7 Eq. 472 : *Re Dreweatt*, W. N. (68) 106 : *Re Hall*, W. N. (71) 136 : *Grove* v. *Marshall*, W. N. (72) 43 : *Buckingham* v. *Sellick*, W. N. (72) 136 : *Morgan* v. *Thomas*, sup. : *Re Hopkin*, 47 L. J. Ch. 672 ; 9 Ch. D. 131 : *Re Smith*, 58 L. J. Ch. 661 : *Re Mullis*, 27 S. J. 585 : *Fairfield* v. *Bushell*, 32 Bea. 158 : *Lanphier* v. *Buck*, 34 L. J. Ch. 650 ; 2 Dr. & Sm. 484 : *Maynard* v. *Wright*, 26 Bea. 285 : *Smith* v. *Horsfall*, 25 Bea. 628 : *Slater* v. *Dangerfield*, 16 L. J. Ex. 51 ; 15 M. & W. 263 : *Cursham* v. *Newland*, 7 L. J. Ex. 212 ; 4 M. & W. 101 : *Re Handcock*, 23 L. R. Ir. 34.

In the following cases "Issue" was read as "*Descendants* :"—*Hobgen* v. *Neale*, sup. : *Re Warren*, 53 L. J. Ch. 787 ; 26 Ch. D. 208 : *Waldron* v. *Boulter*, 22 Bea. 284.

Vf. McGregor v. *McGregor*, 1 D. G. F. & J. 63 : 2 Jarm. 101–107 ; Wms. Exs. 1114 ; Watson, Eq. 1391–5 ; Hawk. 189–198 ; Prior on Issue ; Chitty, Eq. Ind. 7719–7726, 7907.

V. CHILDREN : OFFSPRING : DESCENDANTS.

"Issue *Male*," means sons (*Fitzherbert* v. *Heathcote*, cited 4 Ves. 794), or sons of sons (*Lambert* v. *Peyton*, 8 H. L. Ca. 1) : "Issue *Female*," means daughters (*Sussex* v. *Temple*, 1 Ld. Raym. 310). *Note* :—In *Blackwell* v. *Hale* (1 Ir. C. L. Rep. 612), "Issue Male" was read "Heirs Male."

ISSUE of Bank Notes.—The word "Issue" (of Bank Notes) "means the delivery of the Notes to persons who are willing to receive them in exchange for value in gold, in bills or otherwise, the person who delivers them being prepared to take them up when they are presented for payment" (per Stephen, J., delivering jdgmt. of the Court, *A.-G.* v. *Birkbeck*, 53 L. J. Q. B. 382 ; 12 Q. B. D. 605).

ISSUE of Bills of Ex. or Promy. Notes.—"Issue" of a Bill or Note, "means the first delivery of a Bill or Note, complete in form, to a person who takes it as a Holder" (s. 2, Bills of Ex. Act, 1882).

ISSUE of Debentures.—To "issue" a Debenture, s. 17, Bills of Sale Act, 1882, means its "delivery over by the Company to the person who has the charge" (per Chitty, J., *Levy* v. *Abercorris Co.*, 37 Ch. D. 264).

ISSUE of Orders.—By s. 161, Metropolis Loc. Management Act, 1855 (18 & 19 V. c. 120), Overseers, to whom an Order of a District Board of Works "is issued," have to levy the amount mentioned therein. "The *issuing* of the Order is not effected by sending the precept by the Clerk of the Board to the Overseers, but by the putting of the hands and seal of the Board to the document" (per Stephen, J., *Glen* v. *Fulham*, 54 L. J. M. C. 12 ; 14 Q. B. D. 328 ; 51 L. T. 856 ; 33 W. R. 165 ; 49 J. P. 519 : but *cp.* jdgmt. of Day, J., Ib.).

ISSUE of Shares.—The word "Issue" in s. 25, Companies Act, 1867, means putting the shareholder in complete possession of his share, a conclusion which is one more of fact than of law on a consideration of all the circumstances. It is not necessarily either the allotment of the shares or delivery of the share certificate which constitutes "Issue" within this section (*Blyth's Case*, 4 Ch. D. 140 : *Clarke's Case*, 8 Ch. D. 635 ; 47 L. J. Ch. 696 : *Pool's Case*, 35 Ch. D. 581 : *Vh.* Buckl. 532).

ISSUED.—"Execution Issued," 3 G. 4, c. 39, s. 2 ;—The Court refused to read this as Execution either "levied" or "executed" (*Green* v. *Wood*, 14 L. J. Q. B. 217 ; 7 Q. B. 178).

Foreign Security "issued" in the United Kingdom, s. 2 (1), 34 V. c. 4 ; s. 21, 48 & 49 V. c. 51 ; *V. Grenfell* v. *Inl. Rev.*, 45 L. J. Ex. 465 ; 1 Ex. D. 242.

ISSUES.—*V.* RENTS AND PROFITS.

IT SHALL BE LAWFUL.—*V.* MAY ; and obs. of Jessel, M. R., in *Emden* v. *Carte*, 51 L. J. Ch. 373 ; 19 Ch. D. 311 : *Va. Re Newport Bridge*, 29 L. J. M. C. 52 (on s. 32, Trustee Act, 1850) : *Re Morgan*, 32 S. J. 272, 273.

Vh., in a direction to Trustees to renew Leaseholds, Lewin, 365.

IT SHALL SUFFICE.—"There is no doubt that in many cases these words standing alone, and unexplained by a context, would be quite consistent with something different from, larger or smaller, more or less numerous, more or less costly, than what is mentioned, being supplied.

"Here, however (Rubric to Communion Office as to the Bread), the sentence commences with the introduction : 'To take away all occasion of dissension and superstition which any person hath or might have concerning the Bread, *it shall suffice, &c.* These words seem to their Lordships to make it necessary that that which is to take away the occasion of dissension and superstition should be something definite, exact and different from what had caused the dissension and superstition. If not, the occasion of dissension remains, and the superstition may recur. 'To suffice,' it must be as here described. What is substantially different will not 'suffice'" (per Cairns, L. C., delivering jdgmt. of P. C., *Ridsdale* v. *Clifton*, 46 L. J. P. C. 63 ; 2 P. D. 276). It was accordingly there held that a Communion Wafer was not allowed by the words "it shall suffice that the Bread be such as is usual to be eaten."

ITEM.—As an adverb is synonymous with LIKEWISE.

JAMPNA.—*V.* JUNCARIA.

JETTISON.—" 'Jettison,' in its largest sense, signifies any throwing overboard; but, in its ordinary sense, it means throwing overboard for the preservation of the ship and cargo, and most jurists treat of it in this sense under the head of general average" (per Abbott, C. J., *Butler* v. *Wildman*, 3 B. & Ald. 400). *V.* Termes de la Ley, *Jetsam*.

JEWELS.—On the context, and having regard to the circumstances of the testatrix, the word "Jewels" was held by Lyndhurst, L.C., as specially comprising diamonds,—*e.g.* diamond necklace, cross, and rings,—so that a direction to sell "Jewels" took effect on such diamonds; and that accordingly (and in competition with the word "Jewels"), diamond rings did not pass under the words "the remainder of my rings" (the testatrix having specifically given one diamond ring), nor did a valuable diamond necklace and cross pass under "necklaces of every description" (*A.-G.* v. *Harley*, 5 Russ. 173; 7 L. J. O. S. Ch. 31. *Note.*—It is suggested that it will be seen, on reference to the reports, that the statement of the judgment in this case is erroneously given in Wms. Exs. 1204, in that it is there stated that the L. C. held that the diamond necklace, &c., "were *not* to be sold;" the "not" here should, it is suggested, be placed between the words "did" and "pass").

A bag of Coins held not to pass under a bequest of "Jewellery" (*Sudbury* v. *Brown*, 4 W. R. 736). Masonic Orders and filigree ornaments passed as "Jewels" (*Brooke* v. *Warwick*, 12 Jur. 912; 2 D. G. & S. 425).

JOINT.—Where a husband is liable for the ante-nuptial debts of his wife, and he and she are sued jointly, the judgment "shall be a *joint* judgment against the husband personally, and against the wife as to her separate property" (s. 15, M. W. P. Act, 1882): but "what the word 'joint' means in this sentence is not clear" (per Lindley, L. J., delivering the judgment of the Court of Appeal, *Beck* v. *Pierce*, 58 L. J. Q. B. 518). From the decision in that case, "joint" would seem without meaning in the sentence cited.

JOINT AND EQUAL.—A direction that the subject of a gift shall "be distributed in *joint and equal* proportions" creates a tenancy in common (2 Jarm. 257, citing *Ettricke* v. *Ettricke*, Amb. 656).

JOINT AND SEVERAL.—*V.* JOINTLY AND SEVERALLY.

JOINT CAPTORS.—For the purposes of Booty, "Joint Captors" are those who, not being the actual captors, have assisted, or are taken to have assisted, the actual captors by conveying either encouragement to them, or intimidation to the enemy (*Banda and Kirwee Booty,* 35 L. J. Adm. 17).

JOINT LIVES.—A gift to two or more for their "joint lives" and then over, will generally mean "for their joint lives and the lives or life of the survivors or survivor of them" and then over (*Townley* v. *Bolton,* 2 L. J. Ch. 25; 1 My. & K. 148: *Smith* v. *Oakes,* 14 Sim. 122: *Moffat* v. *Burnie,* 23 L. J. Ch. 591: *Sv. Grant* v. *Winbolt,* 23 L. J. Ch. 282. *Vf.* 2 Jarm. 542; Elph. 283).

JOINT STOCK COMPANY.—Institution "in the Nature of a Joint Stock Company," proviso to s. 30, 17 & 18 V. c. 112, does not comprise an Institution the rules of which do not permit of any dividend, division or bonus among its members (*Re Bristol Athenæum,* 59 L. J. Ch. 116; 43 Ch. D. 236).

JOINT TENANCY.—"A limitation, either at Common Law or in a Conveyance to Uses [or in a Will], of estates of the same nature to several, either nominatim or as a class, without more, makes them joint tenants. The estate must begin at the same time if the conveyance is at Common Law, but this is immaterial if it be under the Statute of Uses" (Elph. 279, *wh. V.*: *Vh.* 2 Jarm. ch. 32).

Cp. TENANCY IN COMMON.

JOINT TENANTS.—"The expression 'as Joint Tenants' is, no doubt, a technical expression" (per Stuart, V.-C., *Booth* v. *Alington,* 27 L. J. Ch. 117); but the decision in that case shows that a gift to two or more "as joint tenants" may be controlled by a context so that, notwithstanding that expression, a tenancy in common may be created.

JOINTLY.—*V.* SEIZED JOINTLY.

A gift to two or more "jointly *and between* them" is a tenancy in common (*Perkins* v. *Baynton,* 1 Bro. C. C. 118: *Richardson* v. *Richardson,* 14 Sim. 526).

JOINTLY AND SEVERALLY.—"If a man grants *proximam advocationem,* or makes a Lease for years of land to two 'jointly and severally,' these words 'severally' are void, and they are joint tenants" (*Slingsby's Case,* 5 Rep. 19 a: *Vth. White* v. *Tyndall,* 13 App. Ca. 275). *V.* SEVERALLY.

Where a Note signed by three persons was in the following words,—"For value received we the subscribers *jointly and severally* promise to pay Messrs. B. or order, for the Boston Glass Manufactory," it was held, in America, that the words "jointly and severally" showed that it was a personal undertaking (*Bradlee* v. *Boston Glass Manufactory*, 16 Pick. 347); in citing which case, Bramwell, B., said,—"I infer that, but for those words, it would have been held that the Note bound the Company" (*Aggs* v. *Nicholson*, 25 L. J. Ex. 349).

V., as to a "joint and several" Note of Hand, Byles, 8: "joint and several" Contracts, Add. C. 38–40: "joint and several" Partnership Debts and Property, per Cairns, L.-C., *Kendall* v. *Hamilton*, 4 App. Ca. 504; 48 L. J. C. P. 705; 41 L. T. 418: *Cambefort* v. *Chapman*, 19 Q. B. D. 229: *Pilley* v. *Robinson*, 20 Ib. 155: *Re Hodgson*, 31 Ch. D. 177: *Badeley* v. *Consolidated Bank*, 34 Ch. D. 536: Watson, Eq. 822, 823; Lindl. 369, ch. 4.

JOINTURE.—*V.* By Way of: Termes de la Ley, *Joynture.*

JONCARIA.—*V.* Juncaria.

JOURNEYMAN.—*V. Lowther* v. *Radnor*, cited Labourer.

JUDGE.—"The words 'Judges' and 'Justices' cannot mean any but the Judges and Justices of the Courts at Westminster" (per Littledale, J., *Wardroper* v. *Richardson*, 1 A. & E. 75). "The words 'Judge or Judges' certainly mean a Judge or Judges of the Superior Courts" (per Parke, B., *Elsley* v. *Kirby*, 12 L. J. Ex. 97; 9 M. & W. 536).

Notwithstanding Ord. 54, R. 12, and Ord. 35, R. 6, R. S. C., "Judge," in s. 49, Jud. Act, 1873, means only a Judge of the High Court (*Foster* v. *Edwards*, 48 L. J. Q. B. 767: *Svth. Bryant* v. *Reading*, 17 Q. B. D. 131).

"Unless *the Judge* certify," s. 5, County Court Act, 1867;—This meant "the Judge who tried the case;" *e.g.*, a County Court Judge to whom it was remitted (*Taylor* v. *Cass*, L. R. 4 C. P. 614), or an Undersheriff on a Writ of Inquiry (*Craven* v. *Smith*, L. R. 4 Ex. 146). But now *V.* s. 116, Co. Co. Act, 1888.

V. Court or Judge.

"To judge" a matter, s. 29, 21 & 22 V. c. 90, means, generally, to come to a conclusion on it (*Allbutt* v. *Gen. Medical Council*, 23 Q. B. D. 400; 37 W. R. 771: *Leeson* v. *Gen. Medical Council*, Times, 23 Dec., 1889; W. N. (89) 227).

JUDGMENT.—A "Judgment" is the sentence of the law pronounced by the Court upon the matter contained in the record (*Vh.* Co. Litt. 39 a, 168 a).

"Judgment or Order," s. 19, Jud. Act, 1873; a Judge's Certificate,—*e.g.*, for Special Jury, or allowing Counsel, or under 3 & 4 V. c. 24, or under s. 31, Patents Act, 1883,—is neither a "Judgment" nor an "Order" (*Haslam Co.* v. *Hall*, 32 S. J. 288; 4 Times Rep. 350); nor is a Certificate under s. 31, 46 & 47 V. c. 57 (*Haslam Co.* v. *Hall*, 57 L. J. Q. B. 352; 20 Q. B. D. 491; 59 L. T. 102; 36 W. R. 406).

A Judgment against a Married Woman, though in the form laid down in *Scott* v. *Morley* (20 Q. B. D. 120; 57 L. J. Q. B. 43; 36 W. R. 67), is none the less a "Judgment" within Ord. 45, R. 1, R. S. C. (*Holtby* v. *Hodgson*, 59 L. J. Q. B. 46; 34 S. J. 28; W. N. (89) 186; 6 Times Rep. 24).

"Judgment," as used in s. 47, Jud. Act, 1873, and especially when read in connection with s. 19, Jud. Act, 1875, does not merely mean the final judgment in criminal cases, but is there used in its larger sense, as including *any decision* in such cases; such as taxation of costs, refusal to quash a magisterial conviction for trespass in pursuit of game, or refusing to admit to bail, or to grant a certiorari (*R.* v. *Steel*, 46 L. J. M. C. 1; 2 Q. B. D. 37; 25 W. R. 34; 35 L. T. 534: *R.* v. *Fletcher*, 46 L. J. M. C. 4; 2 Q. B. D. 43; 35 L. T. 538: *R.* v. *Foote*, 52 L. J. Q. B. 528; 10 Q. B. D. 378: *R.* v. *Rudge*, 16 Q. B. D. 459; 55 L. J. M. C. 112; 34 W. R. 207; 2 Times Rep. 243). *V.* Criminal Cause.

A Conviction is a "Judgment" within s. 7, 12 & 13 V. c. 45 (*R.* v. *Biggins*, 26 J. P. 437).

An Assessment under s. 68, Lands C .C. Act, 1845, is not equivalent to a Judgment, so as to carry interest (per Collier, Co. Co. Judge, *Evans* v. *Lond. & N. W. Ry.*, 31 S. J. 333: *V.* Sums Certain).

A Foreclosure Judgment is not included in the word "Judgment" as used in s. 18, Middlesex Registry Act (7 Anne, c. 20), and will not be ordered to be registered thereunder (*Burrows* v. *Holley*, 31 S. J. 379).

Where a Rule for a Prohibition is made absolute without pleadings, there is no "Judgment" giving right to costs under 1 W. 4, c. 21 (*Ex p. Everton*, 40 L. J. C. P. 201; 19 W. R. 927; L. R. 6 C. P. 245; following *R.* v. *Kealing*, 1 Dowl. 440; *Svth. Wallace* v. *Allan*, 23 W. R. 703).

"Judgment *with Costs*" means only such costs as have been incurred through the adversary's act (per Esher, M.R., *Stumm* v. *Dixon*, 22 Q. B. D. 529; 60 L. T. 560).

V. Order: Final judgment.

JUDGMENT CREDITOR.—A petitioner in a Divorce Suit is not a "Judgment Creditor," within s. 103, Bankry. Act, 1883, *quà* damages recovered against the Co-Respondent (*Re Fryer*, 55 L. J. Q. B. 478; 17 Q. B. D. 718; 55 L. T. 276; 34 W. R. 766).

JUDICIAL DOCUMENT.—"Judicial Document authorising the arrest of a person accused of crime," interpreting "Warrant," s. 26. Extradition Act, 1870, 33 & 34 V. c. 52; *V. R.* v. *Ganz*, 51 L. J. Q. B. 419; 9 Q. B. D. 93.

JUDICIAL PROCEEDING.—Statements made extra-judicially to a magistrate with a view to asking his advice are not a Judicial Proceeding (*M'Gregor* v. *Thwaites*, 3 B. & C. 24). *Vf.* Perjury.

JUGUM.—" Jugum terræ in Domesday containeth halfe a plow-land " (Co. Litt. 5 a); and " is as much as two oxen can till, and by the grant of half a plow-land may pass meadow and pasture " (Touch. 93). *V.* HIDE.

JUNCARIA.—" By the grant of *omnes juncarias* or *joncarias*, the soile where rushes do grow doth passe; for *jonc* in French is a rush, whereof *joncaria* commeth . . . . And *jampna* commeth of *jonc* and *nower*, a waterish place, and is all one in effect with *joncaria* " (Co. Litt. 5 a).

JUNIOR.—" Junior,"—*e.g.*, Tom Brown, Junr.,—is no part of a man's name; to add " Junior " to the signature of a Nominator at a County Council Election, if that be his ordinary mode of signing, does not invalidate the signature (*Gledhill* v. *Crowther*, 23 Q. B. D. 136; 58 L. J. Q. B. 327).

JURISDICTION.—*V.* WITHIN THE JURISDICTION.

JUST.—" There is always some difficulty in understanding the meaning of the term 'just;' but I am putting a favourable construction on it if, in this case—(*i.e.*, on the phrase " just and reasonable " in s. 7, Ry. and Canal Traffic Act, 1854)—I construe it as meaning 'to the advantage of the customer' " (per Cave, J., *Brown* v. *Manchester, S. & L. Ry.*, 51 L. J. Q. B. 601: *V.* S. C., 52 L. J. Q. B. 132; 53 Ib. 124; 9 Q. B. D. 230; 10 Ib. 250; 8 App. Ca. 703).

" Just," in such a connexion as " Just *Cause* " for a Court to do anything, " does not add much weight, though it may add a little. It means some substantial reason must be shewn " (per Jessel, M.R., *Ex p. Cocks*, *Re Poole*, 52 L. J. Ch. 65; 21 Ch. D. 397).

Disqualification from bankruptcy or notorious insolvency, is a " just and reasonable " provision in the Bye-Laws of a City Company (*R.* v. *Saddlers' Co.*, 32 L. J. Q. B. 337; 10 H. L. Ca. 404).

V. REASONABLE.

In ascertaining what is a " Just *or Convenient* " case in which the Court should grant an interlocutory Mandamus or Injunction or appoint a Receiver (s. 25 (8), Jud. Act, 1873), regard should be had to what is " Just " according to settled legal principles, as well as to what is " Convenient " (*Beddow* v. *Beddow*, 47 L. J. Ch. 588; 9 Ch. D. 89). For cases hereon *V. quà Injunctions*, Ann. Pr. Ord. 50, R. 6, R. S. C. and *quà Receivers*, Ib. R. 16.

" Just Debts;" *V.* DEBTS.

As to when it is " Just *and Equitable* " that an Order should be made to wind up a Company, s. 79 (5), Companies Act, 1862; *V. Re German Date Coffee Co.*, 20 Ch. D. 169; 51 L. J. Ch. 564: Buckl. 202.

JUST ALLOWANCES.—This term in a Redemption Order includes,—Payments in discharge of Legacies (*Nightingale* v. *Lawson*, 1 Cox, 23); Counsel's Opinions and procuring directions (*Fearns* v. *Young*, 10 Ves. 184); Dower deductions (*Graham* v. *Graham*, 1 Ves. sen. 262); Partnership Business Expenses (*Brown* v. *De Tastet*, Jac. 284, 289: *Cook* v. *Collingridge*, Ib. 607, 621); But not taxed costs of a solicitor accountable for rents received by him as Plaintiff's steward (*Jolliffe* v. *Hector*, 12 Sim. 398); *V.* the foregoing cases cited from Daniel, Ch. Pr. by Jessel, M.R., in *Wilkes* v. *Saunion* (47 L. J. Ch. 151; 7 Ch. D. 188), which case decided that expenses of taking and holding possession of a mortgaged ship, advertising her sale, and effecting insurances, came under "Just Allowances." So do all necessary repairs; but not repairs beyond what are necessary, nor substantial improvements (*Tipton Green Colliery* v. *Tipton Moat Colliery*, 47 L. J. Ch. 152; 7 Ch. D. 192). So the expense of defending the title is within the phrase (*Godfrey* v. *Watson*, 3 Atk. 518). *Vf.* hereon Dan. Ch. Pr. 1054; Seton, 1079–1081; Fisher, 861–868; Coote, 814, 871–6; MacS. 84, 538.

JUST BEFORE.—In a plea justifying the shooting a dog, that "just before" the defendant shot the dog it was worrying the defendant's sheep,—"just before" was construed as "at the time when," or as implying that the dog had attacked the sheep and was about to renew the attack (*Kellett* v. *Stannard*, 2 Ir. C. L. Rep. 156). *Vh. Janson* v. *Brown*, 1 Camp. 41.

JUSTICE.—"Necessary for the purposes of Justice," Ord. 37, R. 5, R. S. C.; *V. Re Mysore Mining Co.*, 58 L. J. Ch. 731.

JUSTLY.—"To act justly" (*Mussoorie Bank* v. *Raynor*, 51 L. J. P. C. 72; 7 App. Ca. 321), or "to do Justice" to Relations (*Re Bond*, *Cole* v. *Hawes*, 4 Ch. D. 238; 46 L. J. Ch. 488), do not create a PRECATORY TRUST.

JUXTA.—*V.* IN SIVE JUXTA.

KEEP.—"'To keep *in good repair,*' pre-supposes the putting into it, and means that during the whole term the premises shall be in good repair" (per Rolfe, B., *Payne* v. *Haine*, 16 M. & W. 546 : Woodf. 589). *V.* REPAIR : KEEPING SAME IN REPAIR.

"To keep" a *place* or thing, involves the idea of having over it the immediate control, of a character more or less permanent. Thus the landlord of a brothel wholly let out in rooms to different tenants at weekly rents, and who has no control over the premises except that of determining the tenancies, does not "keep" the brothel (*R.* v. *Stannard*, 33 L. J. M. C. 61 ; L. & C. 349 : *Va. R.* v. *Barrett*, 32 L. J. M. C. 36 ; L. & C. 263: Steph. Cr. 122 : Stone, 724 : *Sv. Halligan* v. *Ganly*, 19 L. T. 268). And to "keep" a place for a particular purpose, involves the idea that it is used for that purpose on more than one occasion ; but the how many or how frequent those occasions must be, is a question of fact to be determined in each case (*Marks* v. *Benjamin*, 5 M. & W. 568 ; 9 L. J. M. C. 20),—*e.g.* Place "opened, kept or used" for illegal Betting, s. 1, 16 & 17 V. c. 119 ; *Vth. R.* v. *Cook*, 13 Q. B. D. 377.

The words "have" and "keep" are not, *per se*, synonyms in the phrase "*to have or keep*." Therefore the proprietor of an unlicensed theatre incurs the penalty prescribed by s. 2, Theatres Regulation Act (6 & 7 V. c. 68), by permitting it to be used, if only for a single occasion, for the public performance of stage plays (*Shelley* v. *Bethell*, 53 L. J. M. C. 16 ; 12 Q. B. D. 1) ; yet it would seem that the person to whom such occasional permission may be given would neither "have" nor "keep" the theatre (*R.* v. *Strugnell*, 35 L. J. M. C. 78 ; L. R. 1 Q. B. 93).

But under the 12 G. 3, c. 61, s. 11, the word "have" as used in the phrase to "have or keep" gunpowder was held to be synonymous with "keep," because in s. 18 of that Act there is the phrase "have and convey," and the word "have" was held to refer in each section to the word with which in each place it was associated : and therefore a carrier having only the temporary custody of the prohibited quantity of gunpowder was not liable to the penalty imposed by s. 11 (*Biggs* v. *Mitchell*, 31 L. J. M. C. 163 ; 2 B. & S. 523 : *Vth.* per Coleridge, C.J., *Foster* v. *Diphwys Casson Co.*, 18 Q. B. D. 432). *V.* CASE OR CANISTER : HAVE OR CONVEY.

As to keeping a place for Bull-baiting, &c., within s. 3, 12 & 13 V. c. 92, *V. Clarke* v. *Hague*, 29 L. J. M. C. 105 ; and as to the phrase "Open, keep or use" a house for unlawful gaming, s. 4, 17 & 18 V. c. 38 ; *V. Jenks* v. *Turpin*, 53 L. J. M. C. 161; 13 Q. B. D. 505.

KEEP HOUSE.—"Begins to keep house," s. 4 (d), Bankry. Act,

1883; *V.* Yate Lee, 50–53; Wms. Bank. 19; Robson, 142–144; Baldwin, 58.

KEEP OUT OF THE WAY.—*V.* 1 Maude & P. 599.

KEEPER.—Is, one who keeps. *V.* KEEP.

KEEPING SAME IN REPAIR.—A devise of realty to A. for life, he "keeping the same in repair," gives the remainderman a right of action against the exors of A. if the property is allowed to go out of repair; and the measure of damages is the sum reasonably necessary to put the property in that state of repair in which A. ought to have left it (*Woodhouse* v. *Walker*, 49 L. J. Q. B. 609; 5 Q. B. D. 404; 42 L. T. 770: *Re Williames*, 52 L. T. 41: *Batthyany* v. *Walford*, 33 Ch. 630, 631). *Vh. Re Cartwright*, cited WASTE at end. *Vf.* REPAIR.

KELP-SHORE.—"Kelp-Shore," probably, includes the land between high and low-water mark; but where a conveyance of land "with the Kelp-Shore" gave metes and bounds which clearly excluded the land between high and low-water mark, it was held that such land was not included, and that parol evidence could not be received to show that it was included (*Boyle* v. *Mulholland*, 10 Ir. C. L. Rep. 150).

KIDEL: KIDDLE.—"Kidels is a proper name for open weirs whereby fish are caught" (2 Inst. 38). "Weirs (kidelli, or gurgites) were the means usual in ancient times for appropriating and enjoying several fisheries in tidal waters" (per Selborne, L.C., *Neill* v. *Devonshire*, 8 App. Ca. 144). *V.* GURGES.

KILL.—"Killing is causing the death of a person by an act or omission but for which the person killed would not have died when he did, and which is directly and immediately connected with his death. The question whether a given act or omission is directly and immediately connected with the death of any person is a question of degree dependent upon the circumstances of each particular case" (Steph. Cr. 151, 152). *Vf.* Arch. Cr. 712–731.

V. HOMICIDE: MANSLAUGHTER: MURDER.

KIND.—*V.* DYE.

KINDRED: KIN.—Neither husband nor wife is of "kin" to the other (Wms. Exs. 1123, 1124); but persons related by the half-blood are of "kin" equally with those of the whole-blood (Ib. 1124).

The Statutes of Distribution (22 & 23 Car. 2, c. 10; 1 Jac. 2, c. 17, s. 7), furnish the best rules that can be observed for limiting the extent of this word (*Carr* v. *Bedford*, 2 Rep. in Chanc. 146).

V. NEXT OF KIN.

KING'S ENEMIES.—*V.* ENEMY.

KING'S PLEASURE.—*V.* AT THE KING'S PLEASURE.

KING'S WILL.—"At the King's will for Body, Lands and Goods;" *V.* FELONY.

KNIGHT'S FEE.—"There is great diversity of opinions concerning the contents of a knight's fee, that is, how much land goeth to the livelyhood of a knight. For some say that a knight's fee consisteth of eight hides, and everie hide containeth an hundred acres, and so a knight's fee should containe 800 acres. Others say that a knight's fee containeth 680 acres. Others say, that an oxgange of land containeth 15 acres, and eight oxgangs make a plowland; by which account a plowland containes 120 acres; and that *virgata terræ,* or a yardland, containeth 20 acres. But I hold that a knight's fee, an hide or plowland, a yardland or oxgange of land, doe not containe any certaine number of acres; but a knight's fee is properly to be esteemed according to the qualitie and not according to the quantitie of the land, that is to say, by the value and not by the content" (Co. Litt. 69 a). *V.* HIDE.

"The word 'Knight's fee' is a compound word, and may comprehend many things. And therefore by the grant of this may pass land, meadow and pasture as parcel of it. And sometimes by this, doth pass so much land as to make a knight's fee. And some say it doth contain 8 hides of land. And it seems also that a manor may pass by this name if it be usually called so" (Touch. 92, 93). In Hilliard's note to this passage it is said, "In different ages a Knight's fee was estimated at several values, 2 Inst. 596:" and "probably it does not contain any certain number of acres" (Elph. 590, *wh. V.* for further references).

KNOL.—*V.* HOWE.

KNOW.—"Well Know;" *V.* PRECATORY TRUST.
"Know of or be privy to;" *V.* PERMIT.

KNOWINGLY.—As to the importance of the presence, or absence, of this word in statutory definitions of offences; *V. Mullins* v. *Collins,* 43 L. J. M. C. 67; L. R. 9 Q. B. 292: *Cundy* v. *Le Cocq,* 53 L. J. M. C. 125; 13 Q. B. D. 207, and cases cited in the latter case. From the observations of Stephen, J., in *Cundy* v. *Le Cocq,* it would seem that the maxim, *Actus non facit reum nisi mens sit rea* is not nearly as robust as it once was: "the Act of Parliament must be looked at to see what knowledge is necessary to complete the criminal act." "Knowingly" ought not to be read into a statutory offence "unless it is clear that the legislature intended some such qualification" (per Cave, J., *Betts* v. *Armstead,* 57 L. J. M. C. 101; 20 Q. B. D. 771; 58 L. T. 811; 36 W. R. 720; 52 J. P. 471). But how that clear intention is to be ascertained,—(by trained minds, to say nothing of the common herd),—is not very apparent. Thus in *R.* v. *Tolson,*

(23 Q. B. D. 168; 58 L. J. M. C. 97; 37 W. R. 716), nine judges read the word into s. 57, 24 & 25 V. c. 100; whilst five judges declined to do so: the practical point which the majority decided in that case being that a married person, who re-marries, is not guilty of Bigamy if he or she, in good faith and on reasonable grounds, believes that his or her wife or husband is dead at the time of such re-marriage, and this notwithstanding the proviso in the section which, in terms, excepts from Bigamy a re-marriage after a seven years' absence. The following observations of Stephen, J., in the case just cited may be usefully added:—"Crimes are in the present day much more accurately defined by statute or otherwise than they formerly were. The mental element of most crimes is marked by one of the words '*Maliciously*,' '*Fraudulently*,' '*Negligently*,' or '*Knowingly*' [should it not be added "wilfully?"]; but it is the general,—I might, I think, say the invariable,—practice of the Legislature to leave unexpressed some of the mental elements of crime. In all cases whatever, competent age, sanity, and some degree of freedom from some kinds of coercion are assumed to be essential to criminality, but I do not believe they are ever introduced into any statute by which any particular crime is defined."

It is not necessary to show that the seller of an Article of Food,—*e.g.*, Milk,—in an altered state (s. 9, 38 & 39 V. c. 63), knew that it had been altered (*Pain* v. *Boughtwood*, 6 Times Rep. 167; 54 J. P. 68; 59 L. J. M. C. 45; 34 S. J. 214). *V.* MILK.

V. SUFFER; Stone, 653, 654; Maxwell, 115.

"Knowingly *issuing*" Fraudulent Prospectus (s. 38, Companies Act, 1867), means intentionally issuing it (*Twycross* v. *Grant*, 2 C. P. D. 469; 46 L. J. C. P. 636).

"Knowingly *sell*, publish or expose to sale" any printed book contrary to s. 17, Copyright Act, 1842, 5 & 6 V. c. 45; *V. Cooper* v. *Whittingham*, 49 L. J. Ch. 752; 15 Ch. D. 501.

V. MALICE: NEGLIGENTLY: WILFULLY.

KNOWLEDGE.—"Come to the Knowledge;" *V.* COME TO.

"Notice and Knowledge;" *V.* NOTICE.

V. NOT TO MY KNOWLEDGE.

KNOWN CHANNEL.—*V.* DEFINED CHANNEL.

LABOUR.—"The expression used" (in the definition of "Workman" in the Employers and Workmen Act, 1875, and Employers' Liability Act, 1880), "is not 'manual *Work*,' but 'manual *Labour*;' for many occupations involve the former but not the latter, such as telegraph clerks, and all persons engaged in writing" (per A. L. Smith, J., *Cook* v. *N. Metrop. Tramways Co.*, 18 Q. B. D. 684; 56 L. J. Q. B. 309; 56 L. T. 448; 57 Ib. 476; 35 W. R. 577; 51 J. P. 630); in which case it was held that the Driver of a Tram-car, though engaged in manual *work*, is not engaged in manual *labour*, and is, therefore, not a "Workman" within the Acts cited. *V.* WORKMAN: MANUAL LABOUR.

V. TROUBLE: LABOURER.

LABOURER.—"A 'Labourer' is a man who digs and does other work of that kind with his hands. A Carpenter or a Bailiff or a Parish Clerk is not called a Labourer" (per Brett, L. J., *Morgan* v. *Lond. Gen. Omnibus Co.*, 53 L. J. Q. B. 353; 13 Q. B. D. 832).

So, under s. 1, 20 G. 2, c. 19, a man in possession was not a "Labourer" (*Bramwell* v. *Penneck*, 7 B. & C. 536; 1 M. & R. 409). Neither would "Labourer" include a skilled Artizan; "there being, as I take it, a known distinction between a Journeyman in any art, trade, or mystery, or other workman employed in the different branches of it, and a Labourer" (per Ellenborough, C. J., *Lowther* v. *Radnor*, 8 East, 124).

V. LABOUR: SERVANT: WORKMAN: ARTIFICER.

It is doubtful whether the word "Labourer" in the Sunday Act (29 Car. 2, c. 27) extends to an Agricultural Labourer (*R.* v. *Silvester*, 33 L. J. M. C. 79, nom. *R.* v. *Cleworth*, 4 B. & S. 927; nom. *Cleworth* v. *Leigh Jus.*, 12 W. R. 375). That case decided that a Farmer is not a Labourer within the Act, even though he work with his own hands.

LACE.—As used in s. 1, Carriers Act, "Lace" does not include Machine-made Lace (s. 1, 28 & 29 V. c. 94); but it includes a piece of valuable lace framed for an exhibition (*Treadwin* v. *G. E. Ry.*, L. R. 3 C. P. 308; 37 L. J. C. P. 83).

LACERTA.—*V.* SALIVA.

LACHES.—"*Laches, or lasches,* is an old French word for slacknesse or negligence, or not doing" (Co. Litt. 380 b; *Va.* Ib. 246 b; Termes de la Ley.)

LACTARIUM: LACTITIUM.—*V.* VACCARIA.

LADIES' OUTFITTER.—What amounts to a breach of a covenant not to carry on the business of a "Ladies' Outfitter;" *V. Stuart* v. *Diplock*, 59 L. J. Ch. 142; 34 S. J. 113.

LADY DAY.—*V.* MICHAELMAS.

LAGAN.—*V.* TERMES DE LA LEY.

LAME DUCK.—"'Lame Duck' would be actionable if applied to a person on the Stock Exchange, because there it has acquired a particular meaning" (per Watson, B., *Barnett* v. *Allen*, 27 L. J. Ex. 412; 3 H. & N. 376; 31 L. T. O. S. 217).

LAMMAS LANDS.—"Lands belonging to the owner in fee simple, who is absolutely the owner in fee simple, to all intents and purposes for half the year; and the other half of the year he is still the owner in fee simple, subject to a right of pasturage over the land by other people" (per Jessel, M. R., *Baylis* v. *Tyssen Amhurst*, 46 L. J. Ch. 721; 6 Ch. D. 507). Lammas lands were formerly opened to the right of pasturage on the 1st August; but, since the 2nd September, 1752, the right commences eleven days later, *i.e.*, 12th August (24 G. 2, c. 23, s. 5).

LAND.—"To land;" *V.* LANDED.

LAND: LANDS.—Though the word "Land" anciently meant "whatsoever may be plowed" (Co. Litt. 4 a), and signified "nothing but arable land" (Touch. 91); yet in and since the time of Lord Coke, and now, it "comprehendeth any ground, soile or earth whatsoever" (Co. Litt. 4 a; *Va.* Touch. 91); whether of freehold or of copyhold tenure (*Doe* d. *Clarke* v. *Ludlam*, 7 Bing. 275; *Vf.* 1 V. c. 26, s. 26). But as regards Leaseholds, the law prior to Jan. 1, 1838, was that "if a man hath Lands in fee, and Lands for yeers, and deviseth all his Lands and Tenements, the Fee simple Lands passe only and not the Lease for yeers: And if a man hath a Lease for yeers, and no Fee simple, and deviseth all his Lands and Tenements, the Lease for yeers passeth; For otherwise the Will should be meerly void" (*Rose* v. *Bartlett*, Cro. Car. 293: *Vf. Thompson* v. *Lawley*, 2 B. & P. 303: *Swift* v. *Swift*, 29 L. J. Ch. 121; 1 D. G. F. & J. 160: 1 Jarm. 667–672). But since the date mentioned, a Will of "Lands," *primâ facie* includes all kinds of leaseholds (1 V. c. 26, s. 26: *Wilson* v. *Eden*, 11 Bea. 237; 14 Ib. 317; 16 Ib. 153; 17 L. J. Ch. 459; 21 L. J. Q. B. 385; 5 Ex. 752; 18 Q. B. 474: *Prescott* v. *Barker*, 43 L. J. Ch. 498; 9 Ch. 174: *Butler* v. *Butler*, 54 L. J. Ch. 197; 28 Ch. D. 66: *Re Davison*, 58 L. T. 304. *Vf.* 1 Jarm. 673).

"Land or other hereditaments of whatever tenure," Locke King's Act, 1877, 40 & 41 V. c. 34, includes Leaseholds (*Re Kershaw*, 57 L. J. Ch. 599; 37 Ch. D. 674; 58 L. T. 512; 36 W. R. 413).

V. REAL ESTATE.

"Land," or "Lands," not only means the surface of the ground, but also everything (except gold or silver mines, *Mines Case*, 1 Plow. 336, 336 a), on or under it, for *cujus est solum ejus est usque ad cœlum* (Co. Litt. 4 a; Touch. 91; 2 Bla. Com. 18. Ld. Coke calls the earth "the suburbs of heaven"). But though a devise of "Lands" will generally carry the houses on it, "yet, of course, this does not hold where the testator evidently uses the term in contradistinction to 'house.' As where A., having a messuage at L., and a messuage and lands at W., devised his house at L., with all other his lands, meadows, pastures, with their appurtenances lying in W., the house at W. was held not to pass" (1 Jarm. 777, citing *Ewer* v. *Hayden*, Cro. Eliz. 476, 658; 2 And. 123: *Va. Re Portal to Lamb*, 54 L. J. Ch. 1012; 30 Ch. D. 50; 33 W. R. 859; 53 L. T. 650).

Tithes (*Ritch* v. *Sanders*, Styles, 261), or a Fee-Farm Rent (*Inchley* v. *Robinson*, 2 Leon. 165, pl. 218) may pass under a devise of "Lands" when there is nothing else on which it can operate: *Sq.* as to Rent-Charge or Rent-Seck (*West* v. *Lawday*, 11 H. L. Ca. 375). So Running Water may, by a context, pass under the name of "land" (*Canham* v. *Fish*, 2 Cr. & J. 126; 2 Tyrw. 155): but the Touchstone says (p. 91), "Rents, Advowsons, and such like things," do not pass under this word (*Va. Westfaling* v. *Westfaling*, 3 Atk. 460).

"The word 'Lands' has often been extended to include Trusts" (Lewin, 721); and money to be laid out in land "will pass, by the cestui que trust's Will, under the general description of all the testator's *lands*" (Ib. 940, 941, citing *int. al. Guidot* v. *Guidot*, 3 Atk. 256: *Rashleigh* v. *Master*, 1 Ves. jun. 201: *Chandler* v. *Pocock*, 15 Ch. D. 491: *Re Greaves*, 23 Ch. D. 313; 52 L. J. Ch. 753).

In all Acts of Parliament since 1850, "Land" includes "messuages, tenements and hereditaments, houses and buildings of any tenure, unless where there are words to exclude houses and buildings, or to restrict the meaning to tenements of some particular tenure" (13 & 14 V. c. 21, s. 4: *Vf.* s. 3, Interp. Act, 1889).

In the great Clauses Consolidation Statutes of 1845, the word "Lands" extends to "messuages, lands, tenements, and hereditaments of any tenure" (8 V. cc. 16, 18 & 20). In the contemporary Consolidation Statutes for Scotland, the definition is, "houses, lands, tenements, and heritages of any description or tenure" (8 V. cc. 17 & 19). As to the first of these definitions, *V. G. W. Ry.* v. *Swindon Ry.*, 53 L. J. Ch. 1075; 9 App. Ca. 787; 32 W. R. 957; 48 J. P. 821: HEREDITAMENT.

For the purposes of the Conv. & L. P. Act, 1881, "'Land,' unless a contrary intention appears, includes land of any tenure, and tenements and hereditaments, corporeal or incorporeal, and houses and other buildings, also an undivided share in land" (s. 2, ii). In *Re Lake & Taylor*, *Spain* v. *Mowatt* (33 W. R. 597), Pearson, J., seems to have held that a share of an equitable interest in an agreement for a lease is within that definition.

For the purposes of the Settled Land Act, 1882, "*Land*" includes incorporeal hereditaments, also an undivided share in land" (s. 2, subs. 10, i), and under that definition a Baronetcy or other title is "Land" (*Re Rivett-Carnac*, 54 L. J. Ch. 1074 ; 30 Ch. D. 136 : *Re Aylesford*, 55 L. J. Ch. 523; 32 Ch. D. 162 ; 54 L. T. 414 ; 34 W. R. 410).

As to what "Land" includes under,

(a) Judgments Act, 1864 (27 & 28 V. c. 112, s. 2) ; *V.* Dart, 545.

(b) Lighting & Watching Act (3 & 4 W. 4, c. 90, s. 33); *V. R.* v. *Mid. Ry.*, 44 L. J. M. C. 137 ; L. R. 10 Q. B. 389.

(c) Metrop. Local Man. Acts, 1855, 1862 ; *V. Higgins* v. *Harding*, L. R. 8 Q. B. 7 ; 42 L. J. M. C. 31 : *Wright* v. *Ingle*, W. N. (85) 210.

(d) Sale by Auction Act, 1867 (30 & 31 V. c. 48, s. 5) ; *V.* the section.

(e) Satisfied Terms Act (8 & 9 V. c. 112) ; *V.* Dart, 329, 330.

(f) Statutes of Limitations (3 & 4 W. 4, c. 27 ; 37 & 38 V. c. 57); *V.* Dart, 433, 434, 454.

(g) Trustee Act, 1850 (13 & 14 V. c. 60, ss. 13–15) ; *V.* Dart, 657 n.

(h) Vendor & Purchaser Act, 1874 (37 & 38 V. c. 78) ; *V.* Dart, 160.

And as to what "Land" includes in a Contract for Sale ; *V.* Dart, 128–130.

V. INTEREST IN LAND : RECOVERY OF LAND : SOIL.

LAND CHARGE.—*V.* CHARGE.

LAND COVERED WITH WATER.—These words in s. 55, Local Gov. Act, 1858, 21 & 22 V. c. 98, include a wet dock (*R.* v. *Newport Dock Co.*, 31 L. J. M. C. 266 : *R.* v. *Birmingham Waterworks*, 1 B. & S. 84).

Land is "not the less Land for being covered with water" (per Patteson, J., *R.* v. *Leeds & Liverpool Navigation Co.*, 7 A. & E. 685 ; 7 L. J. M. C. 41 ; 2 N. & P. 540).

In *R.* v. *Regent's Canal Co.* (6 B. & C. 720) the expression in the Act incorporating the Company was, "Lands, whether covered with water or not."

LAND NOT SETTLED.—This phrase includes unsettled reversion of settled land (1 Jarm. 654).

LAND OF LIKE QUALITY.—*V.* LIKE.

LAND ONLY USED AS RAILWAY.—*V.* RAILWAY.

LAND TAX REDEEMED.—As to what is a sufficient recital in a title deed of the redemption of Land Tax, within a Condition of Sale, making such a recital evidence ; *V. Buchanan* v. *Poppleton*, 27 L. J. C. P. 210 ; 4 C. B. N. S. 20.

LAND USED FOR BUILDING PURPOSES.—*V.* BUILDING PURPOSES.

LANDED.—"All risk of Craft until safely *landed;*" *V. Houlder* v. *Merchants' Mar. Insrce.*, 55 L. J. Q. B. 420 ; 17 Q. B. D. 354 ; 55 L. T. 244 ; 34 W. R. 673.

Stones shot from boats on to a harbour shore, below high-water mark, where they remain until shipped for exportation, are not "landed" within an Act enabling Commrs to levy tolls on goods "landed" within their harbour (*Harvey* v. *Lyme Regis*, 38 L. J. Ex. 141 ; L. R. 4 Ex. 260).

LANDLORDS.—Same Distress "as Landlords;" *V.* DISTRESS.

LANDS CLAUSES ACT.— *V.* s. 23, Interp. Act, 1889.

LANNEMANNI.—*V.* ALODIUM.

LAPSE.—*V. Prior* v. *Mackinnon*, W. N. (70) 117.

LARCENY.—*V.* THEFT.

LARGEST.—In Conditions of Sale relating to who shall have the custody of the deeds, the "largest Lot," means, largest in extent, not in value (*Griffiths* v. *Hatchard*, 23 L. J. Ch. 957 ; 1 K. & J. 17) : and in this connection, "Lot" means single lot, and not the aggregation of more than one (*Scott* v. *Jackman*, 21 Bea. 110 : *Sv. Re Doherty*, 15 L. R. Ir. 247). *Vh.* Sug. V. & P. 34.

LAST.—"Last *Defence*," Ord. 23, R. 1, R. S. C. ; Where the plaintiff added new defendants after Answer, the "last Answer," (Cons. Ord. 33, R. 10, 1), was held to mean the last Answer of the *original* defendants (*Bertolacci* v. *Johnstone*, 13 L. J. Ch. 99 ; 2 Hare, 632).

"Last *Place of Abode* ;" *V. R.* v. *Evans*, 19 L. J. M. C. 151 ; nom. *Ex p. Jones*, 1 L. M. & P. 357 : *R.* v. *Damarell*, L. R. 3 Q. B. 50 ; 37 L. J. M. C. 21 ; 8 B. & S. 659 : *R.* v. *Davis*, 22 L. J. M. C. 143 ; 1 Bail C. C. 191 : *R.* v. *Higham*, 26 L. J. M. C. 116 ; 7 E. & B. 557 : *R.* v. *Brown*, 24 J. P. 5 : *R.* v. *Smith*, L. R. 10 Q. B. 604 ; 23 W. R. 523 ; 39 J. P. 292, 322. "Last *known* place of abode ;" *V. Hanrott* v. *Evans*, 4 Times Rep. 128. *V.* PLACE : USUAL PLACE OF ABODE.

"Last *Port ;*" *V. Price* v. *Livingstone*, 53 L. J. Q. B. 118 ; 9 Q. B. D. 679.

A sole trustee is "the last surviving or continuing *Trustee*" within s. 31, Conv. & L. P. Act, 1881 (per Pearson, J., *Re Shafto*, 29 S. J. 372).

"Last *Will*." "My last Will dated," &c., giving date of the first Will ; held to mean the last Will in fact, the date given being rejected as a mistake (*Re Ince*, 46 L. J. P. D. & A. 30 ; 2 P. D. 111 : *Re Steele*, 37 L. J. P. & M. 72, *n.* : *Re Wilson*, Ib.: *Thomson* v. *Hempestall*, 1 Rob. 783 ; 13 Jur. 814). And, generally speaking, "Last Will," means the one latest in date, though there may be two or more Wills all speaking from the death of the testator (*Pettinger* v. *Ambler*, 35 L. J. Ch. 389; L. R. 1 Eq. 510; 35 Bea. 321).

"This is my last Will and Testament" does not, of itself, revoke a former Will (*Cutto* v. *Gilbert*, 9 Moo. P. C. 131 : *Freeman* v. *Freeman*, 5 D. G. M. & G. 704 ; 23 L. J. Ch. 838) ; but may be confirmatory proof of an intention to revoke (*Plenty* v. *West*, 16 Bea. 173 ; 22 L. J. Ch. 185 ; 1 W. R. 3). *Vf. Re Petchell*, L. R. 3 P. & M. 153 ; 43 L. J. P. & M. 22.

LAST MENTIONED.—*V. Ashton* v. *Brevitt*, 14 M. & W. 106 ; 14 L. J. Ex. 297.

LAST PAST.—In a deed, a day "now last past" means, last preceding the day of the delivery, not of the date (*Steele* v. *Mart*, 4 B. & C. 272).

LATE.—*V.* SOMETIME.

LATELY.—Devise of cottages and premises "which I have *lately* purchased;" *V. Cave* v. *Harris*, 57 L. J. Ch. 62 ; 57 L. T. 768 ; 36 W. R. 182.

LATENT DEFECT.—*V.* DEFECT.

LAW.—*V.* BY LAW.

LAW or LAWE.—"*Cope* signifieth a hill, and so doth *lawe ;* as *stanlawe* is *saxeus collis*" (Co. Litt. 4 b). *V.* HOWE.

LAW DAY.—"'Law-day' signifies a Leet or Sheriffes tourne" (Termes de la Ley). "Law-day or lage-day was properly any day of open court, and commonly used for the more solemn courts of a county or hundred" (Hilliard's n. to Touch. 92, citing Cow. Interp. *Vf.* Elph. 591). *V.* MANOR.

LAW LIBRARY.—Under a bequest of "Law Library, and Books of Antiquity," Dugdale's Monasticon, Domesday Book, and State Trials passed (*Wallace* v. *Bayldon*, 4 L. J. O. S. Ch. 74).

LAWFUL.—"It shall be lawful ;" *V.* MAY.

LAWFUL CAUSE.—"The priest shall not without Lawful Cause deny the Communion," s. 8, 1 Edw. 6, c. 1 ; such cause is that the person is an open and notorious Evil Liver (*Jenkins* v. *Cook*, 45 L. J. P. C. 1; 1 P. D. 80). *V.* DEPRAVE : EVIL LIVER.

Whether a Coroner's absence is "from any Lawful or Reasonable Cause," s. 1, 6 & 7 V. c. 83, is a question for the judge ; and it includes taking a necessary vacation, though a good part of it be spent in shooting (*R.* v. *Johnson*, 42 L. J. M. C. 41 ; L. R. 2 C. C. R. 15).

V. REASONABLE CAUSE.

LAWFUL GAME.—*V.* GAME, *Lawful.*

LAWFUL HEIRS.—A limitation to "lawful heirs" will not, standing alone, create an entail, but gives the fee (2 Jarm. 325, and cases there cited). *Cp.* LAWFULLY BEGOTTEN.

And a gift of Personalty in remainder to a person's "lawful heir or heirs," does not mean his next of kin, but means "the person or persons who, either together or separately, take the fee simple of an intestate" (per Jessel, M. R., *Smith* v. *Butcher*, 48 L. J. Ch. 136; 10 Ch. D. 113). *V.* HEIRS, p. 346.

V. LEGAL HEIRS.

LAWFUL ISSUE.—*V. Re Corlass*, 45 L. J. Ch. 118; 1 Ch. D. 460.

LAWFUL TRADE.—In *Havelock* v. *Hancill* (3 T. R. 277) a marine insurance against loss "'in Lawful Trade,' was construed, 'during employment *by the owner* in lawful trade,'—that is, by limiting the condition to acts of the owner" (per Cotton, L. J., *Cory* v. *Burr*, 51 L. J. Q. B. 472; 9 Q. B. D. 463; affd. 52 L. J. Q. B. 657; 8 App. Ca. 393).

Vf. Manning v. *Clement*, 7 Bing. 362.

LAWFULLY BEGOTTEN.—A limitation in a Will to "heirs lawfully begotten," creates an entail (*Nanfan* v. *Legh*, 7 Taunt. 85, cited by Parke, B., *Mortimer* v. *Hartley*, 20 L. J. Ex. 132: *Vf.* 2 Jarm. 325: *Mayhew* v. *Cattermole*, W. N. (78) 153).

Cp. LAWFUL HEIRS: LEGITIMATE HEIR. *V.* TO BE BORN.

LAWFULLY DEMANDED.—If a Lease in its clause of *Re-entry* on non-payment of rent, does not dispense with demand, or makes the right of re-entry conditional on the rent being "demanded" or on its being "*lawfully* demanded," such demand must be made by the landlord, or by his agent duly authorised; and it must be made (1) of the precise rent due and payable to save the forfeiture, (2) on the exact day on which it became so due and payable, (3) at a convenient hour before sunset, and (4) at the appointed place, if any appointed, and if not, then at the most notorious place of the demised premises, *e. g.* if there be a dwelling-house it must be made there and at its front door (Rosc. N. P. 938, and cases there cited). When however *a half-year's rent* is in arrear, then *V.* Com. L. Pro. Act, 1852, s. 210, which makes similar provisions to those contained in 4 G. 2, c. 28, s. 2.

But a *Power of Distress* conditional on the rent being "demanded," does not need the demand to be made in the strict way above stated (*Maund's Case*, 7 Rep. 28 b); nor even if the condition require the rent to be "*legally* demanded" (*Thorp* v. *Hart*, 30 S. J. 469). If indeed such a power were made conditional on the rent being "*lawfully* demanded," it is submitted that such a phrase would not import into the condition the technicalities of demand required at Common Law prior to re-entry for non-payment.

In *Thorp* v. *Hart* (sup.), Chitty, J., finding that the power of distress was only conditional on the rent being "*legally* demanded," refused to say that that meant all that the cases had decided must be done prior to re-entry for default in payment after the rent had been "*lawfully* demanded." And that was enough for the decision in *Thorp* v. *Hart*. But having regard to the different character of a forfeiture as compared with a distress, it is difficult to believe that the strictness of the one would be applied to the other, even if the power of distress were not to be exercised until after the rent had been "*lawfully* demanded." It seems indeed not free from doubt whether *any* demand of rent is needed prior to distress, even though the Lease give power to distrain on default of payment of rent after demand (Bac. Ab. Rent, J., cited by Chitty, J., in *Thorp* v. *Hart*, sup.).

LAWND or LOUND.—*V.* Frythe.

LAWRENCE.—*V.* St. Lawrence.

LAY DAYS.—"Days which are given to the charterer in a Charter-party either to load or unload without paying for the use of the ship are 'Lay Days.'" "The Lay Days are described as days for loading and unloading, and they are sometimes called Lay Days and sometimes Working Days" (per Esher, M. R., *Neilsen* v. *Wait*, 16 Q. B. D. 70; 55 L. J. Q. B. 89). *Vh. Pyman* v. *Dreyfus*, 24 Q. B. D. 152.

V. Days: Working Days.

LAY OUT.—*V.* New Street.

LEA.—"*Lea* or *ley* signifieth pasture" (Co. Litt. 4 b).

LEAD.—Reward for such information as shall "lead to" the apprehension and conviction of a criminal; *V. Tarner* v. *Walker*, L. R. 2 Q. B. 301; 35 L. J. Q. B. 179.

LEAD AWAY.—*V.* Take and carry away.

LEAKAGE AND BREAKAGE.—"'Not accountable for Leakage,'—is frequently inserted in Bills of Lading, and in such case the owners are not answerable for loss by leakage, unless it is proved that the leakage was caused by the negligence of the master and crew" (1 Maude & P. 356, citing *The Helene*, Br. & L. 429: *Phillips* v. *Clark*, 2 C. B. N. S. 156; 26 L. J. C. P. 168).

An exception of damage arising from "Rust, Leakage and Breakage," does not include rust, leakage or breakage caused by the carelessness of the shipowner or his servants in stowing (*Phillips* v. *Clark*, sup.: *The Nepoter*, L. R. 2 A. & E. 375; 38 L. J. Adm. 63: *Czech* v. *Gen. Steam Nav. Co.*, 37 L. J. C. P. 3; L. R. 3 C. P. 14: *The Chasca*, 44 L. J. Adm. 17; L. R.

4 A. & E. 446 : and per Lindley, L. J., *Chartered Mercantile Bank of India* v. *Netherlands Steam Nav. Co.*, 52 L. J. Q. B. 230 ; 10 Q. B. D. 521) ; and the primary and natural meaning of the exception is that the shipowner will not be answerable if the thing comprised in the Bill of Lading shall *itself* rust, leak or break, and therefore it furnishes him no protection against his liability to compensate for consequential damage happening to that thing by reason of some other thing rusting, leaking or breaking (*Thrift* v. *Youle*, 46 L. J. C. P. 402 ; 2 C. P. D. 432).

LEASE.—"A Lease doth properly signify a demise or letting of lands, rent, common, or any hereditament unto another for a lesser time than he that doth let it hath in it. For when a lessee for life or years doth grant over all his estate or time unto another, this is more properly called an Assignment than a Lease" (Touch. 266 : *Vf. Beardmore* v. *Wilson*, 38 L. J. C. P. 91 ; L. R. 4 C. P. 57; 17 W. R. 54 : Woodf. 124) : but "the word 'Lease' does not in law import a written instrument" (per Abinger, C. B., *Bridgland* v. *Shapter*, 5 M. & W. 381 ; 8 L. J. Ex. 246 : *Va. Bicknell* v. *Hood*, 5 M. & W. 107, 108 ; 8 L. J. Ex. 193), except, it may perhaps be added, in those cases where, by statute, a writing is required.

"The definition of 'Lease' given in s. 14 (3), Conv. & L. P. Act, 1881, does not appear to include an *Agreement* for a lease" (per Esher, M. R., *Coatsworth* v. *Johnson*, 55 L. J. Q. B. 221 : *Vf.* per Charles, J., *Swain* v. *Ayres*, 20 Q. B. D. 585 ; 52 J. P. 500), and certainly does not include a tenancy from year to year (*Swain* v. *Ayres*, 21 Q. B. D. 289 ; 57 L. J. Q. B. 428 ; 36 W. R. 798).

As to what is a "Lease or Tack" for purposes of Stamp Act, 1870 ; *V. Thames Conservators* v. *Inl. Rev.*, 56 L. J. Q. B. 181; 18 Q. B. D. 279 ; 56 L. T. 198 ; 35 W. R. 274.

The Scale Fee for "Lease," Sch. 1, Part 2, Solicitors' Remuneration Order (under 44 & 45 V. c. 44), includes a Preliminary Agreement (*Re Emanuel & Simmonds*, 55 L. J. Ch. 710 ; 33 Ch. D. 40), and negotiations for the Lease actually granted (*Re Field*, 54 L. J. Ch. 661 ; 29 Ch. D. 608) ; but not abortive negotiations with persons not the actual lessee (*Re Marten*, 58 L. J. Ch. 478 ; 41 Ch. D. 381).

The word "Lease" has the same force in implying a covenant as DEMISE.

A title under an Underlease for the original term less (say) 3 days, satisfies a contract by a vendor to sell "all his Interest in the Lease" (*Waring* v. *Scotland*, 57 L. J. Ch. 1016 ; 36 W. R. 756) ; *secus*, if the contract be "for the Residue" of the original term (*Madeley* v. *Booth*, 2 D. G. & S. 718). So a contract which represents a property as held under a "Lease" when it is held under an Underlease for the original term less 2 days, will not be enforced against the purchaser (*Re Beyfus & Masters*, 39 Ch. D. 110, disapproving dictum of Jessel, M. R., in *Camberwell & S. Lond. Bg. Socy.* v. *Holloway*, 13 Ch. D. 760).

LEASEHOLD.—Property held on a Lease for Life, is properly described as "Leasehold" *quà* Parliamentary Qualification (*Jones* v. *Jones*, L. R. 4 C. P. 422 ; 38 L. J. C. P. 43).

LEASEHOLD GROUND RENT.—*V.* GROUND RENT.

LEASEHOLD INTEREST.—A Lease of Chattels is not a "Leasehold Interest" (*Sheffield Waggon Co.* v. *Stratton*, 48 L. J. Ex. 35).

LEASEHOLD SECURITY.—A power to invest in "Leasehold Securities" does not authorize the lending of trust money on a short term,—*e.g.* one for 14 years (*Pince* v. *Beattie*, 9 Jur. N. S. 1119).

LEAST.—*V.* AT LEAST.

LEAVE.—"To leave" at the end of a term certain things comprised in a lease,—*e.g.*, Pillars in a Mine,—does not assume that there will be any power to remove those things and afterwards to restore them (per Bacon, V.-C., *Mostyn* v. *Lancaster*, 51 L. J. Ch. 702 ; 23 Ch. D. 583 ; 31 W. R. 3, 686 ; 46 L. T. 648 ; 48 Ib. 715).

"If tenant leaves the house," implies, in a condition for a payment to the tenant on that event, that the tenant shall "leave" on a legal termination of his tenancy (*Lucas* v. *Rideout*, L. R. 3 H. L. 153).

A Power "to leave" property, signifies, *ex vi termini*, a disposition *by Will* (*Doe* v. *Thorley*, 10 East, 438 : *Moore* v. *Ffolliot*, 19 L. R. Ir. 504 : *Vf. Archibald* v. *Wright*, 7 L. J. Ch. 120 ; 9 Sim. 161 : Sug. Pow. 210).

"To Leave" a port,—(in a Charter-Party),—does not mean that the ship is to "sail on her voyage" therefrom ; "leave" in such a connection has no other than its ordinary signification of "going away from" (*Van Baggen* v. *Baines*, 23 L. J. Ex. 213 ; 9 Ex. 523).

LEAVING.—Though this word, in such a phrase as "dying without leaving children" "obviously points at the period of death" (2 Jarm. 199) ; yet, in a gift over, it frequently means "HAVING" or "having had."

Thus if property, real or personal, be given by Will or limited by Settlement to the children of A., the shares to vest in them on a given event which has no reference to their surviving A., but there is a gift over on the death of A. without "leaving" a child, &c.,—the word "leaving" will be construed "having," or "having had," in order not to defeat the vested interests which A.'s children who may have predeceased him, may have acquired under the terms of the gift (*Maitland* v. *Chalie*, 6 Mad. 243 : *Re Thompson*, 5 D. G. & S. 667 : *Kennedy* v. *Sedgwick*, 3 K. & J. 540 : *Marshall* v. *Hill*, 2 M. & S. 608 : *Ex p. Hooper*, 1 Drew. 264 : Hawk. 217). This is sometimes called the Rule in *Maitland* v. *Chalie*.

But the interpretation of "having" or "having had" has not always been confined to the protection of vested interests of children. Thus in *Wight* v. *Hight* (12 Ch. D. 751), where there was a devise to A. absolutely, with a gift over "after her decease without *leaving* any issue," it was held that the devise to A. became indefeasible upon her having a child (*V.* that case criticised 2 Jarm. 825, and it is now over-ruled: *Re Ball*, 58 L. J. Ch. 232; 40 Ch. D. 11. *V.* generally as to meaning of "Leaving," 2 Jarm. 200, 823–827).

If however a gift be introduced by words importing contingency,—such as a gift to the children of A. "in case he *shall leave* any child or children,"—the word has its natural construction and means "leave living at his death" (*Bythesea* v. *Bythesea*, 23 L. J. Ch. 1004: *Young* v. *Turner*, 30 L. J. Q. B. 268; 1 B. & S. 550).

But to construe "leaving" as "having" or "having had" is to do violence to the language; and such a construction will only be adopted within the lines distinctly laid down by the cases, or where there is a real ambiguity (*Re Hamlet, Stephen* v. *Cunningham*, 38 Ch. D. 183; 39 Ib. 426; 57 L. J. Ch. 1007; 58 Ib. 242; where *V.* the authorities hereon reviewed). In *Re Hamlet*, it was said that the addition of such words as "her surviving" or "at her death," makes it much more difficult to construe "Leaving" as "having" or "having had."

"Die without leaving *Issue Male*;" *V. Re Ball, Slatterley* v. *Ball*, 40 Ch. D. 11; 58 L. J. Ch. 232: *Clay* v. *Coles*, 57 L. T. 682.

Devise to A. "and the Heir Male of his body, and the heirs and assigns of such heir male," but if A. should "die without leaving *any* Son," gives A. an estate for life, with a contingent remainder in fee to the person (if any) who at A.'s death should be the heir male of his body, with a limitation over if there should be no such heir (*Chamberlayne* v. *Chamberlayne*, 25 L. J. Q. B. 357; 6 E. & B. 625).

V. DIE: DIE WITHOUT ISSUE: DIE WITHOUT CHILDREN.

LEAVING A WIDOW.—"Shall die leaving a Widow;" *V. Hood* v. *Hood*, W. N. (69) 237.

LEET.—*V.* Elph. 592.

LEFT.—A bequest of what shall "remain," or "be left" at the decease of the prior legatee, or of what the legatee is possessed of at the time of death, or of "what he does not want," or "does not spend," or "can transfer," or "can save," or "of what remains undisposed of," or of the "bulk" of certain property, or a gift over of the whole legacy in case of the death of the prior legatee "intestate," is void for uncertainty (1 Jarm. 362, 363, and cases there cited).

But where the Will gives to A. a limited interest with a power of disposal of the corpus, and this is followed by a gift over of what "remains," or is "remaining" at the death of A., or of what "remains undisposed of," or other like expression, the gift over will take effect upon such of the property as A. may not have disposed of by act *inter vivos* (*Re Pounder*, 56 L. J. Ch. 113 ; 56 L. T. 104 : *Re Thomson*, 49 L. J. Ch. 622 ; 14 Ch. D. 263 : *Re Stringer*, 46 L. J. Ch. 633 ; 6 Ch. D. 1). In *Re Pounder*, Kay, J., said that "Remaining" was equivalent to "Remaining undisposed of." *Vf.* WHAT IS LEFT.

Notice to be "left ;" *V.* SERVED.

"Left an Orphan ;" *V.* ORPHAN.

LEGACY.—"The plain import of the word 'Legacies,' includes both specific and pecuniary legacies ; " "Residue is not a legacy in the ordinary sense of the term" (per Romilly, M.R., *Ward* v. *Grey*, 29 L. J. Ch. 75, 76 ; 26 Bea. 485) : *V.* LEGATEE.

"Under a charge of 'Legacies,' Annuities will generally be included ; unless the testator manifests an intention to distinguish them, as by sometimes using both words" (2 Jarm. 609 : *Cf. Gaskin* v. *Rogers*, L. R. 2 Eq. 284 : Wms. Exs. 1202 n. : Seton, 961).

"A direction to pay 'Legacies' free of duty, will not generally include the proceeds of realty directed to be sold (*White* v. *Lake*, L. R. 6 Eq. 188) ; but, probably, would include legacies payable out of such proceeds (*Hodges* v. *Grant*, 36 L. J. Ch. 935 ; L. R. 4 Eq. 140) ; " 1 Jarm. 187. Such a direction applies to specific, as well as pecuniary legacies (*Re Johnson*, 53 L. J. Ch. 645 ; 26 Ch. D. 538).

"Legacy," *primâ facie*, has reference to personalty only (*Windus* v. *Windus*, 26 L. J. Ch. 185 ; 6 D. G. M. & G. 549 : *Gethin* v. *Allen*, 23 L. R. Ir. 241) ; but, contextually, it may extend to realty (*Hardacre* v. *Nash*, 5 T. R. 716 : 1 Jarm. 743 : *V.* RESIDUARY LEGATEE).

V. PECUNIARY LEGACIES : DEVISE.

A bequest of a share of proceeds arising from the sale of real and leasehold properties is a "Legacy" within s. 65, County Court Acts, 9 & 10 V. c. 95, s. 65 ; 13 & 14 V. c. 61, s. 1 ; Co. Co. Act, 1888, s. 58 (*Pears* v. *Wilson*, 20 L. J. Ex. 381 ; 6 Ex. 833) ; so, *semble*, of a bequest conditional on good conduct (per Campbell, C.J., *Re Fuller*, 2 E. & B. 575, 576 ; 22 L. J. Q. B. 415 ; 21 L. T. O. S. 166). But where there are active trusts to be exercised in respect of the fund bequeathed (*Phillips* v. *Hewston*, 25 L. J. Ex. 133 ; nom. *Hewston* v. *Phillips*, 11 Ex. 699 : *Va. Beard* v. *Hine*, 10 W. R. 45), or where so much a week is to be paid by a person taking a benefit under the Will (*Longbottom* v. *Longbottom*, 22 L. J. Ex. 74 ; 8 Ex. 203), there is no "Legacy" within the meaning of these sections.

A direction in a Will that a Solicitor Trustee may make professional charges, is a "Legacy" within s. 15, Wills Act (1 V. c. 26), so that if he be one of the attesting witnesses the direction is void (*Re Barber*, 55 L. J. Ch. 373 ; 31 Ch. D. 665 : *Re Pooley*, 58 L. J. Ch. 1 ; 40 Ch. D. 1).

LEGACY DUTY.—A direction in a Will that all legacies are "to be *paid*, free of Legacy Duty," will apply to all the specific legacies of chattels as well as to the pecuniary legacies; but not to the Succession Duty in respect of a bequest of leaseholds (*Re Johnson*, 53 L. J. Ch. 645; 26 Ch. D. 538).

As to what words will exempt a legatee from payment of Legacy Duty; *V.* 1 Jarm. 186, 187.

LEGAL ESTATE.—As to what words vest the legal estate in Trustees; *V.* Jarm. ch. 34.

LEGAL FRAUD.—In the general acceptation of the phrases, there would seem no real difference between "Legal Fraud" and "Fraud" (*Derry* v. *Peek*, 14 App. Ca. 337; 58 L. J. Ch. 864; 38 W. R. 33; 61 L. T. 265; 5 Times Rep. 625).

Vh. Joliffe v. *Baker*, 52 L. J. Q. B. 609; 11 Q. B. D. 255: *Glasier* v. *Rolls*, 42 Ch. D. 436: FRAUD.

LEGAL HEIRS.—*V. Low* v. *Smith*, 25 L. J. Ch. 503; 2 Jur. N. S. 344: *Re Dixon*, 47 L. J. P. D. & A. 57; 4 P. D. 81: HEIRS: LAWFUL HEIRS.

LEGAL INCAPACITY.—A woman, as such, is subject to a "Legal Incapacity" to vote for a Member of Parliament, within s. 3 (1), Representation of the People Act, 1867 (*Chorlton* v. *Lings*, 38 L. J. C. P. 25; L. R. 4 C. P. 374: *Va. Beresford-Hope* v. *Sandhurst*, 58 L. J. Q. B. 316; 23 Q. B. D. 79).

V. INCAPABLE.

LEGAL MORTGAGE.—A "Legal Mortgage" means a *first* mortgage. This is unquestionably so as regards land, because it is only the first mortgage which can grant the legal estate in the land. But where a person had agreed to give a "Legal Mortgage" of a *Ship* it was contended that this did not necessarily mean a first mortgage, because (by the Merchant Shipping Act, 1854, 17 & 18 V. c. 104, ss. 66, 70) even a first mortgage would not pass the legal interest in a ship. It was, however, held in that case that even as regards a ship the expression "Legal Mortgage" generally means a first mortgage (*Thompson* v. *Clerk*, 7 L. T. 269; 11 W. R. 23).

LEGAL MERCHANDIZE.—Under the words "Other Legal Merchandize" in a Charter-party, the charterer is at liberty to ship any lawful article he pleases (due regard being had to the safety of the vessel), but is bound to pay the same amount of freight as the vessel would have earned if loaded within the terms of the Charter (*Cockburn* v. *Alexander*, 18 L. J. C. P. 74; 6 C. B. 791).

LEGAL NOTICE.—A "Legal Notice,"—*e. g.* "Legal Notice to Quit," s. 50, Co. Co. Act, 1856, s. 138, Co. Co. Act, 1888,—means a Notice provided by law, as distinguished from one prescribed by contract (*Friend* v. *Shaw*, 57 L. J. Q. B. 225 ; 20 Q. B. D. 374 ; 36 W. R. 236 ; 58 L. T. 89). *V.* By Law : Notice to Quit.

LEGAL OR EQUITABLE DEBT.—*V. Vyse* v. *Brown*, 13 Q. B. D. 199 : Debt.

LEGAL OR NEXT OF KIN.—*V. Harris* v. *Newton*, 46 L. J. Ch. 268.

V. Next of Kin.

LEGAL PERSONAL REPRESENTATIVES. — *V.* Legal Representatives.

LEGAL PROCEEDINGS.—In *Smith* v. *Manchester* (53 L. J. Ch. 96 ; 24 Ch. D. 611), it was held that a Winding-up Petition was not a legal proceeding within Articles of Association empowering directors to direct "Legal Proceedings" to be prosecuted on behalf of the Company.

LEGAL PROCESS.—*V.* Process.

LEGAL REPRESENTATIVES.—The primary meaning of "Representatives," "Legal Representatives," "Personal Representatives," or "Legal Personal Representatives," is "Executors or Administrators" in their official capacity (*Stockdale* v. *Nicholson*, 36 L. J. Ch. 793 ; L. R. 4 Eq. 359 and cases therein cited : 2 Jarm. 120 ; Wms. Exs. 1132–1134 ; Chitty, Eq. Ind. 7690), but that meaning may be controlled by the context. Thus in a gift to nephews and nieces, living on the happening of an event, "or their legal personal representatives *share and share alike*," the phrase "legal personal representatives" means Next of Kin (*King* v. *Cleaveland*, 4 D. G. & J. 477 ; 26 Bea. 26, 166 ; 28 L. J. Ch. 835, 74, 76 : *Va. Walker* v. *Camden*, 17 L. J. Ch. 488 ; 16 Sim. 329). The phrase "Legal Representatives," and such like phrases will generally mean next of kin, and not exors or admors, when the individuals so indicated are to take beneficially (*Briggs* v. *Upton*, 7 Ch. 376 ; 41 L. J. Ch. 33 : 2 Jarm. 111 *et seq.* ; Wms. Exs. 1136, 1137 : *Jacob* v. *Catling*, W. N. (81) 105 : *V.* Executors).

Where such a phrase as "Legal Representatives" would be held to mean next of kin, that would, it has been said, generally imply next of kin according to the Statute of Distribution and would include a wife, but not a husband (2 Jarm. 125 ; Wms. Exs. 1141–1143). But *Booth* v. *Vicars* (13 L. J. Ch. 147 ; 1 Coll. 6) cited on this point in Wms. Exs. was, in *Stockdale* v. *Nicholson* (sup.), thus dealt with by Malins, V.-C., in his judgment :—"In the case of *Booth* v. *Vicars*, Lord Justice Knight Bruce held that it was the next of kin, *according to the statute*, who took ; but I think the authorities since that decision are so clear that a gift to the next of kin, as a class, gives a joint tenancy to the *nearest of kin.*" But as the point had only been slightly argued he invited further discussion, upon which Counsel, whose interest it was to argue the other way, said that he considered the question had been so clearly settled by *Withy* v. *Mangles* (10 L. J. Ch. 391 ; 10 Cl. & F. 215 ; 4 Bea. 358) and other cases that it would be hopeless to argue it.

V. PERSONAL REPRESENTATIVES : NEXT PERSONAL REPRESENTATIVES : NEXT OF KIN.

LEGAL RIGHTS.—S. 32, Patent, Designs and Trade Marks Act, 1883 (46 & 47 V. c. 57) ; *V. Kurtz* v. *Spence,* 55 L. J. Ch. 919 ; 33 Ch. D. 579 ; 55 L. T. 317 ; 35 W. R. 26 : *Svth. Challender* v. *Royle,* 36 Ch. D. 425.

LEGALLY DEMANDED.—*V.* LAWFULLY DEMANDED.

LEGATEE.—Where a testator directed "every legatee" to make a per centage contribution "out of their legacies," it was held that legatees of chattels and annuities, as well as ordinary pecuniary legatees, were included and also (on the context) the residuary legatees (*Ward* v. *Grey,* 29 L. J. Ch. 74 ; 26 Bea. 485).

V. LEGACY : RESIDUARY LEGATEE.

LEGISLATURE.—*V.* COLONIAL.

LEGITIMATE HEIR.—A limitation to A. "and his Legitimate Heir or Legitimate Heirs" passes a fee simple, as the words of the limitation are not to be construed as "heirs of the body lawfully begotten" (*Re Co-operative Wholesale Socy. & Kershaw,* W. N. (86) 45). *V.* LAWFULLY BEGOTTEN : LAWFUL HEIR.

LESS.—*V.* NOT LESS.

A covenant in a Mining Lease to pay certain royalties where "less than" a stated quantity is gotten, is applicable to a case where none is gotten (*Jervis* v. *Tomkinson,* 26 L. J. Ex. 41 ; 1 H. & N. 195).

"Less than," read as "Not exceeding" (*Garby* v. *Harris,* 21 L. J. Ex. 160 ; 7 Ex. 591).

LESSEE.—"Lessee," s. 14 (1). Conv. & L. P. Act, 1881, includes an Assignee of a Lease (*Cronin* v. *Rogers,* Cab. & El. 348).

LESSEN.—*V.* AFFECT.

LESWES.—*V.* PASTURES.

LET.—As an operative word in a Lease, "let" is synonymous with DEMISE (*Hart* v. *Windsor,* 12 M. & W. 68, 85 ; 13 L. J. Ex. 135, 136 : *Mostyn* v. *West Mostyn Co.,* 1 C. P. D. 152 ; 45 L. J. C. P. 405).

V. ASSIGN : UNDERLEASE.

"Let *into possession*;" *V.* *Wheeler* v. *Tootel*, 36 L. J. Ch. 221; L. R. 3 Eq. 571.

"Let to be used for Pasture;" *V.* PASTURE.

LEVANT AND COUCHANT.—Levancy and Couchancy, for the purpose of estimating the number of Cattle which a commoner has the right to depasture on an unstinted common, means the *capability* of the commonable tenement to maintain, during the winter, by its summer produce, the cattle claimed to be depastured (*Scholes* v. *Hargreaves*, 5 T. R. 46 : *Mellor* v. *Spateman*, 1 Wms. Saund. 343 : *Rogers* v. *Benstead*, Camb. Sum. Ass. 1727, cor. Lord Raymond, C. J., MS., Serj. Leeds, quoted by Bayley, J., *Cheesman* v. *Hardham*, 1 B. & Ald. 711); but the cattle need not be actually fed on the commonable tenement, or from its produce (*Carr* v. *Lambert*, 34 L. J. Ex. 66; 3 H. & C. 499 : *Robertson* v. *Hartopp*, 6 Times Rep. 126).

LEVEL.—Oral evidence may be given to explain this word as used in a Mining Lease (*Clayton* v. *Gregson*, 4 L. J.. K. B. 161; 5 A. & E. 302; 6 N. & M. 694).

LEVIED.—*V.* LEVY.

LEVY.—By s. 1, 29 Eliz. c. 4, a Sheriff became entitled to poundage on the amount of goods which he should "levy" under a *fi. fa.*; "levy" there, means to seize the goods and turn them into money; and, therefore, where the debt and costs were paid before seizure (*Coles* or *Colls* v. *Coates*, 9 L. J. Q. B. 232; 11 A. & E. 826; 3 P. & D. 511), or where the *fi. fa.* was, after seizure but before sale, set aside for irregularity (*Miles* v. *Harris*, 31 L. J. C. P. 361; 6 L. T. 649), there was no "Levy;" *secus*, where the writ was set aside after sale (*Bullen* v. *Ansley*, 6 Esp. 111), or where a sale was prevented by a compromise between the parties (*Alchin* v. *Wells*, 5 T. R. 470).

But *Alchin* v. *Wells* only related to civil proceedings; and under s. 3, 3 G. 1, c. 15, the amount "*levied or collected*" for the Crown, on which poundage was chargeable was the amount actually obtained, although such amount was the result of a compromise (*R.* v. *Robinson*, 4 L. J. Ex. 319; 2 Cr. M. & R. 334); but on the other hand, the poundage under this latter statute was payable on the amount "levied *or collected*," and therefore, *semble*, if the amount was paid before seizure, the poundage was payable (*R.* v. *Jetherell*, Parker, 177 : *Vth.* per Denman, C. J., *Coles* v. *Coates*, sup.).

"Levied," in a Declaration for a False Return of *nulla bona*, imported not only a seizure and a sale under the plaintiff's *fi. fa.*, but also that the sheriff had in his hands the proceeds (*Drewe* v. *Lainson*, 9 L. J. Q. B. 69; 11 A. & E. 529; 3 P. & D. 245).

V. EXECUTED.

LEVY WAR.—"Every one commits High Treason who levies war against the Queen in any of her dominions. The expression 'to levy war' means—(a) Attacking in the manner usual in war the Queen herself or her military forces, acting as such by her orders, in the execution of their duty; (b) Attempting by an insurrection of whatever nature by force or constraint to compel the Queen to change her measures or counsels, or to intimidate or overawe both Houses or either House of Parliament; (c) Attempting by an insurrection of whatever kind to effect any general public object.

"But the expression 'to levy war against the Queen,' does not include any insurrection against any private person for the purpose of inflicting upon him any private wrong, even if such insurrection is conducted in a warlike manner" (Steph. Cr. 41).

Vf. Arch. Cr. 834–839.

LIABILITY.—*V.* Charge or Liability; Debts.

"Liability," for purpose of Proof in Bankruptcy; *V.* s. 37 (8) Bankry. Act, 1883. *Vh. Hardy* v. *Fothergill*, 56 L. J. Q. B. 363; 58 Ib. 44; 13 App. Ca. 351; nom. *Morgan* v. *Hardy*, 18 Q. B. D. 646. *V.* Fairly Estimated.

"Do not admit liability;" *V. G. W. Ry.* v. *McCarthy*, 56 L. J. P. C. 33; 12 App. Ca. 218; 56 L. T. 582; 35 W. R. 429; 51 J. P. 532.

"Liabilities," in a Building Society's Rules, include sums payable to Investing Members (*Re West Riding Bg. Socy.*, 59 L. J. Ch. 197; 6 Times Rep. 160).

LIABILITY TO CEASE.—In a Charter-Party, the cases shew "that the plain meaning of the words 'liability to cease' is not that the liability should cease to accrue, but that the liability should cease to be enforced" (per Cleasby, B., *Francesco* v. *Massey*, L. R. 8 Ex. 104; 42 L. J. Ex. 76, 77: *Vf. Kish* v. *Cory*, L. R. 10 Q. B. 561; 44 L. J. Q. B. 205).

LIABLE.—For an instance as to the practical value of this word; *V. James* v. *Young*, 53 L. J. Ch. 796; 27 Ch. D. 652.

"Liable to pay" a Solicitor's Bill and so entitled to tax it, s. 38, 6 & 7 V. c. 73; *V. Re Barber*, 15 L. J. Ex. 9; 14 M. & W. 720.

An Owner is "liable" to pay rates within s. 19, Poor Rate Assessment and Collection Act, 1869, 32 & 33 V. c. 41, whether he is so by agreement with the overseers under s. 3, or by vestry order under s. 4, or by agreement with the occupier (*Barton* v. *Birmingham*, 48 L. J. C. P. 87).

"Liable, by reason of any contract or promise, to a demand in the nature of damages," s. 153, Bankry. Act, 1861; *V. Johnson* v. *Skafte*, L. R. 4 Q. B. 700; 38 L. J. Q. B. 318.

"Liable to contribute in whole or in part to the County Rate," s. 117, 5 & 6 W. 4, c. 76; *V. R.* v. *Monck*, 2 Q. B. D. 544; 46 L. J. M. C. 251.

V. Liability: Not liable.

LIBEL.—"The word 'Libel' means—

(*a*) The offence defined in this Article.

(*b*) Anything by the publication of which the offence is committed.

"Everyone commits the misdemeanour called Libel who maliciously publishes defamatory matter of any person, or body of persons, definite and small enough for its individual members to be recognized as such, in or by means of anything capable of being a Libel in the second sense of the word. The publication of a libel on the character of a dead person is not a misdemeanour unless it is calculated to throw discredit on living persons." (Steph. Cr. 197 ; *Vf.* Ib. 200–206 ; Arch. Cr. 975 ; Rosc. Cr. 695–716.)

"*Defamatory Matter* is matter which, either directly or by insinuation or irony, tends to expose any person to hatred, contempt or ridicule" (Steph. Cr. 198).

A similar definition obtains for the purposes of an action for Libel (Rosc. N. P. 784 ; Add. T. ch. 6, s. 1).

LIBERALITY.—*V.* Benevolence.

LIBERTY.—*V.* Franchise : With all Liberties.

LIBERTY OF WORKING.—Where an owner conveys lands to a singular successor or other person, reserving the "Liberty of working the Coal" in these lands, he must be taken to have reserved the Estate of coal (unless there were clear words in the deed qualifying that right of property) with which he stands vested by infeftment at the date of the conveyance (*Hamilton* v. *Dunlop*, 10 App. Ca. 813).

LIBERTY TO APPLY.—The rule that an Order carries with it "Liberty to apply" though not expressly reserved, only relates to an Order which is not one of a final nature (*Penrice* v. *Williams*, 23 Ch. D. 353 ; 52 L. J. Ch. 593).

LIBERTY TO CALL.—When a Bill of Lading, or Charter-party, gives "Liberty to call at any Ports" on the voyage, that means that the ship must call at the ports in their geographical order ; but when the liberty is "to call at any Ports *in any order*," then the ship may go backwards and forwards from the Ports of call as long as she does not deviate from the ordinary track of the voyage (per Esher, M. R., *Leduc* v. *Ward*, 20 Q. B. D. 475 ; 36 W. R. 537 ; 57 L. J. Q. B. 379 ; 58 L. T. 908 ; 4 Times Rep. 313).

LIBRATA TERRÆ.—240 acres (Elph. 592, *wh. Vf.*).

LICENSE.—A letter whereby the owner of goods authorises another to take immediate possession of them and afterwards to sell them, and out of the proceeds to deduct money due to him from the owner, to pay certain accounts, and to pay over the balance to the owner, is a "*License* to take possession of personal chattels as security for any debt" within s. 4, Bills of Sale Act, 1878, and is a Bill of Sale by way of security for money within the Bills of Sale Act, 1882 (*Re Townsend, Ex p. Parsons*, 55 L. J. Q. B. 137 ; 16 Q. B. D. 532 ; 53 L. T. 897 ; 34 W. R. 329).

V. AUTHORITY OR LICENSE.

LICENSED PREMISES.—"Licensed Premises," s. 12, 35 & 36 V. c. 94, means premises open to the public for the sale of drink under the provisions of the Act, and therefore a publican may get tipsy on his own premises after hours, without becoming liable under this section (*Lester* v. *Torrens*, 46 L. J. M. C. 280 ; 2 Q. B. D. 403).

LIEN.—A Lien—(without effecting a transference of property *ad rem*)—is the right to retain possession of a thing until a claim be satisfied ; and it is either particular or general. For the different sorts of lien and the cases thereon *V.* Add. C.; Rosc. N. P.

By s. 184, Bankry. Act, 1849, the rights of creditors holding "any Mortgage of or Lien upon any part of the property" of a bankrupt were preserved ; and that "referred to cases in the nature of mortgages or liens by some conveyance or contract, or course of dealing which is the same as contract, where some property in (Qy., right to possession of ?) the thing passed ;" and at all events the word "Lien" referred to something different from the mere binding of goods by delivery of a *fi. fa.* to the sheriff, or by the seizure of bills or notes under 1 & 2 V. c. 110, s. 12, or by the defendant being bound by a garnishee order (per Campbell, C. J., in delivering the jdgmt. of the Q. B. in *Holmes* v. *Tutton*, 24 L. J. Q. B. 351 ; 5 E. & B. 67 : *Cf. Tilbury* v. *Brown*, 30 L. J. Q. B. 46 : *Turner* v. *Jones*, 26 L. J. Ex. 262 ; 1 H. & N. 878).

Thus though a "Lien" is a "Security," yet the former word is much too narrow to comprise all that may be comprehended under the latter.

V. SECURITY : CHARGE.

LIEU AND SUBSTITUTION.—A bequest in a Codicil, "in lieu of" or "in substitution for," one in the Will, is to be taken with all the accidents and conditions of the original bequest (*Shaftesbury* v. *Marlborough*, 7 Sim. 237 ; 2 Myl. & K. 111 : *Re Boddington*, 53 L. J. Ch. 477 ; nom. *Boddington* v. *Clairat*, 25 Ch. D. 685).

V. ADDITION : IN LIEU OF : INSTEAD OF.

LIFE.—"During Life ;" *V.* DURING.

"Life or Member ;" *V.* FELONY.

LIGEANCE.—"Ligeance is the true and faithful obedience of a liegeman or subject to his liege lord, or soveraigne" (Co. Litt. 129 a).

LIGHT CART.—An ordinary farmer's cart without springs, if driven with reins, is a "Light Cart" within s. 132, 3 G. 4, c. 126 (*Morton* v. *Freeman*, 26 J. P. 215).

LIGHT AND UNJUST.—*V.* UNJUST.

LIGHTER.—*V.* WHERRY.

LIGHTS.—*V.* WITH ALL ITS LIGHTS.

LIKE.—"The like" is not equivalent to "the same." Therefore, where a sum of money was settled to A. for life, and in default of appointment to her next-of-kin, as if she had died intestate, and the Settlement contained a covenant that her after-acquired property should be settled "upon the like trusts, intents and purposes," it was held that, in default of appointment, after-acquired realty went to her heir-at-law, personalty to her next-of-kin (*Brigg* v. *Brigg*, 54 L. J. Ch. 464).

V. SAME : SIMILAR.

"In like *Manner*;" *V.* AFORESAID.

Business of a "like *Nature;*" *V. Re Empire Assrce.*, L. R. 4 Eq. 341 ; 36 L. J. Ch. 663.

"Like *Penalty*," means a Penalty of a like amount, recoverable in a like way (per Selborne, L. C., *Bradlaugh* v. *Clarke*, 52 L. J. Q. B. 507 ; 8 App. Ca. 357).

"Like *Proceedings*" in s. 21, Highway Act, 1864, includes all proceedings contained in s. 85, Highway Act, 1835, and also those proceedings designated by the general name of appeal to Quarter Sessions given by s. 88 (*R.* v. *Surrey Jus.*, L. R. 5 Q. B. 87 ; 39 L. J. M. C. 49).

S. 101, Regent's Canal Act, 52 G. 3, c. 195, provided that the land belonging to the Company should be rated "in like manner as lands of a like *Quality*," *i.e.*, as open land which never could be built upon, but which perhaps might have some enhanced value from its proximity to the Canal and adjoining buildings, as applicable to any purpose except for building (*Regent's Canal Co.* v. *St. Pancras*, 47 L. J. M. C. 37 ; 3 Q. B. D. 73).

"With the like *Remainder* over in default of Issue, *similar to* and in all respects *corresponding with;*" *V. Surtees* v. *Hopkinson*, 36 L. J. Ch. 305 ; L. R. 4 Eq. 98.

"Like *Trusts*, intents and purposes," in a Settlement ; *V. Brigg* v. *Brigg*, 54 L. J. Ch. 464.

LIKEWISE.—When a clause begins with "Likewise," or "Item," it is, generally speaking, to be read independently of the former clause, as a fresh departure, and starting upon a new disposition (1 Jarm. 831, 832, citing *Lethieullier* v. *Tracy*, 3 Atk. 774 ; Amb. 204 : *Pearson* v. *Rutter*, 3 D. G. M. & G. 398 : *Boosey* v. *Gardener*, 5 D. G. M. & G. 122).

"It is not, however, to be assumed that whenever the word 'Item' or 'Likewise' begins a sentence, it creates a complete severance of all that follows from the previously-expressed contingency. It cannot be put higher than this, that such expressions make a *primâ facie* case for the disconnexion, which the context of the Will may either maintain or rebut" (1 Jarm. 832, 833); and where there is a devise, *e.g.*, for life, upon condition, and that is followed by another devise of the same estate, commencing with "Likewise," such other devise will, probably, be construed as subject to the same condition as the prior devise (*Paylor* v. *Pegg*, 24 Bea. 105, stated 1 Jarm. 833).

V. ALSO.

LIMIT.—S. 43, Sanitary Act, 1872, 35 & 36 V. c. 79, provides that any "Limit" of rating imposed by a Local Act shall not apply to that Act; "Limit" there does not include "Exemption," and, therefore, property exempted by a Local Act was held not rateable under the Sanitary Act (*Walton* v. *Walford*, L. R. 10 Q. B. 180; 44 L. J. Q. B. 74: *R.* v. *Wexford*, 18 L. R. Ir. 132).

"To Limit;" *V.* THREAT.

LINE.—*V.* MALE LINE: LINEAL.

LINE OF BUILDINGS.—*V.* GENERAL LINE OF BUILDINGS.

LINE OF RAIL.—*V.* RAIL.

LINEAL.—The expressions "Lineal Descent," "Lineally descended," indicate, *primâ facie*, a direct line of descent from father to son (*V.* hereon note to *Craik* v. *Lambe*, 1 Coll. 491); but under the peculiar circumstances of that case, yet still with difficulty, Knight-Bruce, V.-C., held that collateral next-of-kin were meant by "Relations by *Lineal Descent*" (14 L. J. Ch. 84; 1 Coll. 489). Again in *Boys* v. *Bradley* (22 L. J. Ch. 623; 4 D. G. M. & G. 58), the same learned judge, when L. J., said, "Whatever may be the range of the word 'Lineal,' considered by Mr. Collyer in his note to *Craik* v. *Lambe*, to speak of a man's collateral kindred, as related to him in any line, is *not* an improper use of language, but equally allowable with the genealogical *transversa linea* of the civil lawyers." *Vf.* 2 Jarm. 99.

"The eldest *male* lineal descendant" is inapplicable to a male person claiming in part through a female (*Oddie* v. *Woodford*, 7 L. J. Ch. 117; 3 My. & C. 584: *Vh.* 2 Jarm. 69).

V. STRANGERS IN BLOOD.

LINEN.—"Under this term, without qualification, table and bed linen, and every article to which that general word can be applied, will pass. But where there is a bequest of 'all linen and *clothes* of all kinds,' it has been held that only body linen will pass" (Wms. Exs. 1205, citing *Hunt* v. *Hort*, 3 Bro. C. C. 311).

LIQUIDATED DAMAGES.—Where parties to a contract agree that, in the event of default by either, a sum stated shall be paid as "Liquidated Damages;" the primary meaning of that phrase is, that the sum named has been "assessed between the parties" (per Cotton, L. J., *Wallis* v. *Smith*, 52 L. J. Ch. 154), as the damages to be paid by the party in default. Sometimes, however, the Courts hold that the sum so named shall be treated as a penalty, and be irrecoverable (*Magee* v. *Lavell*, L. R. 9 C. P. 107, and especially per Coleridge, C. J.); but the tendency of modern decisions is to hold contracting parties to the bargains they make, and the clear meaning of the words they use (*Wallis* v. *Smith*, 52 L. J. Ch. 145; 21 Ch. D. 243; and the cases there cited: *Vf.* Add. C. 1110–1118: *Green* v. *Price*, 14 L. J. Ex. 225; 13 M. & W. 695. In *Dickson* v. *Lough*, 18 L. R. Ir. 529, O'Brien, J., said,—"Sir Geo. Jessel, in *Wallis* v. *Smith*, fell foul of the ruling in *Magee* v. *Lavell*, as he fell foul of many other things, for which reason those fell foul of him who came after him; and in his contempt for authority he went so far as to say there was no authority for it").

"*Un*liquidated Damages," s. 31, Bankry. Act, 1869; this phrase did not include a sum found due from a Promoter of a Co., in respect of a secret profit (*Emma Co.* v. *Grant*, 50 L. J. Ch. 449; 17 Ch. D. 122), nor a patentee's right to an account of profits made by an infringer (*Watson* v. *Holliday*, 52 L. J. Ch. 543).

LITERATURE.—*V.* SCIENCE.

LITTLE DAMAGE.—"As little damage as can be;" *V.* DAMAGE.

LIVE AND DEAD STOCK.—"The words 'Live and Dead Stock' have never occurred alone in a bequest, consequently their import in the abstract could not have received a legal interpretation. Since, however, the term 'Stock' is of extensive meaning, and not rendered less so by the prefatory words 'Live and Dead,'—expressions that merely distinguish such part of the personal estate as is inanimate from that which is animate,—it is not improbable that a Court might interpret the word 'Stock,' under those circumstances, as synonymous with 'Property,' and sufficient to pass the whole of a testator's personal estate" (Rop. 274). It is however submitted that it would need a context, and probably a strong one, to warrant so large an interpretation, and that the primary meaning of "Live and Dead Stock" is that which was put on the phrase in *Porter* v. *Tournay* (3 Ves. 311), viz. "out-of-door Stock;" indeed in that case the M. R. said, that that would be the interpretation of the phrase "if those words stood alone." But where the bequest was of "all testator's furniture, linen, plate, pictures, carriages, horses, and *other Live and Dead Stock*," Wood, V.-C., considering that "other" referred to all the previous words of the sentence and that the testator evidently meant to include every stock and store he had about his house, held that Books and Wines passed under the bequest. He said,

"The words 'Dead Stock' might apply to in-door things. The expression 'Stock of Wines' was common; but 'Stock of Books' was not heard so often" (*Hutchinson* v. *Smith*, 11 W. R. 417; 8 L. T. 602: *Rudge* v. *Winnall*, 12 Bea. 357).

Vf. Randall v. *Russell*, 3 Mer. 190: *Hardman* v. *Johnson*, Ib. 347: *Burbidge* v. *Burbidge*, 37 L. J. Ch. 47; 16 W. R. 76; 17 L. T. 138.

V. STOCK.

LIVE AND RESIDE.—A condition in a gift of a house that the donee shall "*Live* and Reside" therein, does not seem more exigent than if it said nothing about living and only required residence: *V.* RESIDE. In *Fillingham* v. *Bromley* (T. & R. 530), Ld. Eldon said,—"Suppose the devisee had been an M.P., and had a house in London, would you say he did not *live and reside* at J.?" It would seem that "live" in that question adds nothing to its point.

LIVELIHOOD.—In *Stephens* v. *Derry* (16 East, 147), a man who lived with his wife in Middlesex, the wife carrying on a business there as a milliner, acted as clerk to a solicitor in London, and it was held that he was not within the London Court of Requests Act (39 & 40 G. 3, c. 104) as a person "seeking his livelihood" in London; inasmuch as he did not get his *whole* livelihood there; the trade which he carried on by his wife, being, in fact, *his* trade. *Va. Jenks* v. *Taylor*, 5 L. J. Ex. 263; 1 M. & W. 578.

LIVING.—"Now the word 'Living' is ambiguous. It is sufficient to pass the Advowson. On the other hand it may be restricted to a single Presentation: the law does not determine which is its meaning, and the point must be ascertained from the context" (per Wood, V.-C., *Webb* v. *Byng*, 2 K. & J. 674; aff. 10 H. L. 171: *V.* note on this case, 2 Jarm. 286).

"A Power to Appoint to Children *living* at the parent's decease, includes a child in *ventre sa mère* at that time (*Beale* v. *Beale*, 1 P. Wms. 244). This point has been otherwise decided (*Pierson* v. *Garnett*, 2 Bro. C. C. 38, 63); but the law is now perfectly settled (*Clarke* v. *Blake*, 2 Bro. C. C. 320; 2 H. Bl. 399: *Va. Thellusson* v. *Woodford*, 4 Ves. 226: *Hale* v. *Hale*, Prec. Ch. 50);" Sug. Pow. 673.

V. BORN.

Bequest on Condition of "Being" or "Living in England," or "residing in this country;" *V. Woods* v. *Townley*, 23 L. J. Ch. 281; 11 Hare, 314: *Dale* v. *Atkinson*, 3 Jur. N. S. 41.

Bequest to A. for life, remainder to "her children living;" held, that children of A. living at the death of testator took vested interests (*Hodgson* v. *Smithson*, 26 L. J. Ch. 110; 21 Bea. 354).

"Who shall be living;" *V. Penny* v. *Clarke*, 29 L. J. Ch. 370; 1 D. G. F. & J. 425; Johns. 619.

V. THEN LIVING.

LIVING WITH ME.—The phrase "living with me" in a bequest to servants does not mean "living in my house" but means "living in my service" (per Turner, V.-C., in *Blackwell* v. *Pennant*, 22 L. J. Ch. 155 ; 9 Hare, 551).

V. Servant.

LOAD: LOADING.—To "load" a *Cargo* is actually to put it on board; and circumstances which prevent the cargo from being brought to the place of loading, are not "accidents preventing the loading" within an exception in a charter-party relieving from charges for demurrage (*Grant* v. *Coverdale*, 53 L. J. Q. B. 462 ; 9 App. Ca. 470 ; 51 L. T. 472 ; 32 W. R. 881 : *Stephens* v. *Harris*, 57 L. J. Q. B. 203 ; 4 Times Rep. 11).

The words "*loading or discharging*" as used in s. 41, Merchant Shipping Act Amendment Act, 1862 (25 & 26 V. c. 63) are employed in their general sense, and are not confined to loading or discharging cargo, but will (*int. al.*) comprise taking in coals to enable the ship to carry on her voyage (*The Winston*, 52 L. J. P. D. & A. 72 ; 53 Ib. 69 ; 9 P. D. 85 ; 51 L. T. 183).

"Loading excepted;" *V. Lister* v. *Van Haansbergen*, 45 L. J. Q. B. 495 ; 1 Q. B. D. 269.

"Loading *in Turn*;" *V. Taylor* v. *Clay*, 9 Q. B. 713 ; 16 L. J. Q. B. 44.

V. Ready to Load : Port.

"Load," and "Unload," in a *Railway Act*, are used in their ordinary sense, and do not cover station accommodation, and the like (*Kempson* v. *G. W. Ry.*, 4 B. & Macn. 426).

LOAD IN USUAL AND CUSTOMARY MANNER.—*V.* Usual and Customary Manner.

LOAD WITH USUAL DESPATCH OF PORT.—*V.* Usual Despatch.

LOAN.—A loan at interest to a Building Society from its bankers, secured by deposit of title deeds, and made by allowing over-draughts, is a "Loan" within s. 15, 37 & 38 V. c. 42 (*Looker* v. *Wrigley*, 9 Q. B. D. 397).

A rule of a Building Society merely stating that the Society is established for the purpose of raising by subscriptions and "Deposits on Loans" a fund for advances, confers a power to borrow by receiving deposits on loans (*Re Mutual Aid Bg. Society*, 54 L. J. Ch. 493 ; 29 Ch. D. 182).

LOCAL ACT OF PARLIAMENT.—"Local and Personal" Act is "Local, in being confined to local limits, and Personal, as affecting a particular description of persons only, as distinguished from that of all the Queen's subjects" (per Parke, B., delivering jdgmt. of the Court, *Richards* v. *Easto*, 15 L. J. Ex. 167 ; 15 M. & W. 251), which case shews that an Act may be "Local and Personal" although some of its objects are public. *Vf. Cock* v. *Gent*, 13 L. J. Ex. 24 ; 12 M. & W. 234.

LOCAL GOVERNMENT REGISTER OF ELECTORS.—*V.* s. 17 (3), Interp. Act, 1889.

LOCAL INVESTIGATION.—*V.* PROLONGED EXAMINATION.

LOCAL MEAN TIME.—*V.* OF THE CLOCK: TIME.

LOCAL MEASURE.—*V.* MEASURE.

LOCAL TRAFFIC.—*V. Midland Ry.* v. *Manchester, &c. Ry.*, W. N. (70) 117.

LOCO PARENTIS.—"What is the meaning of a person *in loco parentis?* I cannot do better than refer to the definition of it given by Lord Eldon in *Ex p. Pye* (18 Ves. 140), referred to and approved by Lord Cottenham in *Powys* v. *Mansfield* (3 M. & Cr. 359, 367; 7 L. J. Ch. 9). Lord Eldon says it is a person, '*meaning* to put himself *in loco parentis,*—in the situation of the person described as the lawful father of the child.' Upon that Lord Cottenham observes,—'But this definition must, I conceive, be considered as applicable to those parental offices and duties to which the subject in question has reference, *viz.*, to the office and duty of the parent to make provision for the child. The offices and duties of a parent are infinitely various, some having no connection whatever with making a provision for a child; and it would be most illogical, from the mere exercise of any of such offices or duties by one not the father, to infer an intention of such person to assume also the duty of providing for the child.' So that a person *in loco parentis* means a person taking upon himself the duty of a father of a child to make a provision for that child" (per Jessel, M. R., *Bennet* v. *Bennet*, 10 Ch. D. 477: *Vf. Montagu* v. *Sandwich*, 32 Ch. D. 537: per Kay, J., *Re Hamlet*, 38 Ch. D. 190: Wms. Exs. 1343: Elph. 350)

LOCOMOTIVE.—A tricycle capable of being propelled by the feet, or by steam as an auxiliary, or by steam alone, but going along without noise or escape of steam or anything to frighten or cause danger beyond any ordinary tricycle, is a "Locomotive propelled by steam or by other than animal power" within s. 38, Highways and Locomotive (Amendment) Act, 1878, 41 & 42 V. c. 77 (*Parkyns* v. *Preist*, 50 L. J. Q. B. 648; 7 Q. B. D. 313; 30 W. R. 13; 45 J. P. 452).

V. CARRIAGE: LOCOMOTIVE ENGINE.

LOCOMOTIVE ENGINE.—A steam-crane fixed on a trolly, and propelled by steam along a set of rails when it is desired to move it, is not a "Locomotive Engine" within s. 1 (5) Employers' Liability Act, 1880, 43 & 44 V. c. 42 (*Murphy* v. *Wilson*, 52 L. J. Q. B. 524).

V. RAILWAY.

LODGER.—"Generally speaking, a lodger is a person whose occupation is of part of a house, and subordinate to, and in some degree under, the control of a landlord or his representative, who either resides in or retains the possession of or dominion over the house generally, or over the outer door, and under such circumstances that the possession of any particular part of the house held by the lodger does not prevent the house generally being in the possession of the landlord.

"Where a landlord resides in part of a house, and there is an outer door from the street, and he, by himself or his servants, has the control of this outer door, and undertakes the care or control of rooms let to other persons and the access to them, and those rooms themselves have not anything in the nature of an outer door, and are not structurally severed from the rest of the house, there could be little hesitation in saying that an occupier of those rooms, being part of the house, is only a *Lodger*. On the other hand, if there be no real outer door to the street, and neither the landlord nor his servants, nor any one representing him, occupies any part of the premises, or exercises any control over any part of them, and the rooms occupied by another person are structurally severed from the rest of the house and have an outer door to the general landing or staircase, and no one but such tenant has or exercises any care or control over the room or that outer door, as a general proposition, the person so occupying those rooms could not properly be said to be a lodger.

"It is always important in determining whether a man is a lodger, to see whether the owner of the house retains his character of master of the house, and whether he occupies a part of it by himself or his servants, and at the same time retains the general control and dominion over the whole house, and this he may do though he do not personally reside on the premises."

The foregoing definition is taken from the judgment of Bovill, C. J., in *Thompson* v. *Ward* (40 L. J. C. P. 188; L. R. 6 C. P. 360, 361), and it seems closely applicable for determining who *as Lodger* is entitled to the *Parliamentary Franchise*. Perhaps a Lodger for the purpose of that franchise may be generally and briefly defined to be,—One who occupies apartments, whether furnished or not, in another man's dwellinghouse, and who, besides the benefit of that occupation, is entitled to domestic service, or otherwise to participate (more or less) in the general œconomy of the house. If the rooms are, so to speak, self-sufficient, they would seem to confer the Household Franchise as being a "part of a house . . . separately occupied as a dwelling" (s. 5, Registration Act, 1878, 41 & 42 V. c. 26: *Vf. Ancketill* v. *Baylis*, 52 L. J. Q. B. 104; 10 Q. B. D. 577: *Bradley* v. *Baylis*, 51 L. J. Q. B. 183; 8 Q. B. D. 195: *Hogan* v. *Sterrett*, 20 L. R. Ir. 344: *Thompson* v. *Ward*, sup.: and the cases cited in those cases. *V.* also LODGINGS).

But the object of the *Lodgers' Protection Act* (34 & 35 V. c. 79), is "to protect persons who are in the house under contract subordinate to that of the tenant, and who are in no direct relation to the landlord of the premises" (per Grove, J., *Phillips* v. *Henson*, 47 L. J. Q. B. 276); and therefore it was there held that an under-tenant who lodges—*i.e., semble*, resides, —in a house, under an agreement rendering him independent of its general œconomy, is none the less a Lodger within the meaning of the last-named Act (*Phillips* v. *Henson*, 47 L. J. Q. B. 273; 3 C. P. D. 26): though probably he would be a Householder for the purpose of the parliamentary franchise. Still even for the purpose of the Lodgers' Protection Act there must be a retention by the immediate landlord of the claimant-lodger of some such dominion over the house as the master of a house let in lodgings usually has (*Morton* v. *Palmer*, 51 L. J. Q. B. 7). In that case Brett, L. J., after noticing that the Act gives no definition of a "Lodger," proceeded to say,—"I am of opinion that the word 'Lodger' must be taken to mean a lodger according to the understanding of that word by the majority of persons conversant with the modes of letting and occupying houses in this country to lodgers and under-tenants. The Courts have at various times given some tests which help to decide whether a person is a lodger or an under-tenant. I will refer to two tests which have been given. The first given by Mr. Justice Maule in *Toms* v. *Luckett* (17 L. J. C. P. 27; 5 C. B. 23), contains the fundamental proposition, which is as follows:—'Where the owner of a house takes in a person to reside in a part of it, though such person has the exclusive possession of the rooms appropriated to him, and the uncontrolled right of ingress and egress, yet, *if the owner retains his character of master of the house*, the individual so occupying part of it occupies as a lodger only.' It is clear, therefore, that if all that has been done is for the owner or lessee of a house to give a man the house to live in on certain terms, that man may be a tenant or an under-tenant; but it cannot be said that the lessor has taken him in to lodge with him. It does not follow that a man who has been taken in to lodge with another should live at the table or sleep in the room of that other. He may very well have the exclusive use of part of the house. A further test was given by Mr. Justice Blackburn in *Allan* v. *Liverpool* (43 L. J. M. C. 69; L. R. 9 Q. B. 180), where he said:—'A lodger in a house, although he has the exclusive use of rooms in the house in the sense that nobody else is to be there, and though his goods are stowed there,'—by which I understand him to mean that the rooms may be unfurnished,—'yet he is not in exclusive occupation in that sense, because the landlord is there, for the purpose of being able, as landlords commonly do in the case of lodgings, to have his own servants to look after the house and the furniture, and has retained to himself the occupation,'—that is, of the house,—'though he has agreed to give the exclusive occupation,'—that is, of the rooms,—'to the lodger.' It follows that the person who takes in another to lodge must retain power in and dominion over the house, as the master of a house usually does in this country. It is not absolutely necessary that he should live or sleep in the house: he may live elsewhere and yet reserve power in and dominion over the house, such as a master of a house does in this country usually have. If, however, he goes away, if he gives up all power of dealing with the house as master, then I do not think it is possible to say that he takes another person in to lodge with him." Cotton, L. J., in the same case said :—" I think that a 'Lodger' is a man living in a house owned by or leased by another person, and to some extent living there with that other person." *Vf. Ness* v. *Stephenson*, 9 Q. B. D. 245 : *Heawood* v. *Bone*, 13 Q. B. D. 179 ; 51 L. T. 125 ; 32 W. R. 752 ; 48 J. P. 710.

Lodger or " Person Lodging " in licensed premises, s. 10, Licensing Act, 1874 ; *V. Pine* v. *Barnes*, 57 L. J. M. C. 28 ; 20 Q. B. D. 221 ; 58 L. T. 520 ; 36 W. R. 473 ; 52 J. P. 199.

LODGINGS.—For the purposes of the parliamentary franchise the term " Lodgings " includes " any apartments or place of residence, whether furnished or unfurnished, in a dwellinghouse " (s. 5, 41 & 42 V. c. 26).

V. LODGER.

LODGING-HOUSE.—*V.* COMMON LODGING-HOUSE.

LONDON.—" London," in a contract, means strictly and properly, the *City* of London, and not the metropolis in its popular sense (*Mallan* v. *May*, 14 L. J. Ex. 48 ; 13 M. & W. 511). So in *R.* v. *Lewen* (1 Sid. 405), there was a conviction for perjury for swearing that a person in Southwark was in London : but this latter case " would be scarcely followed in the present day " (per Romilly, M. R., *Wallace* v. *A.-G.*, 33 L. J. Ch. 316).

" The London Right " of a drama means the whole right of representation in London (*Taylor* v. *Neville*, 47 L. J. Q. B. 254) ; but in that case no definition of " London " was attempted, though it is obvious that it was accepted not in the restricted sense of *Mallan* v. *May*, sup., but rather in a popular sense as embracing all the theatres which are usually called London Theatres.

In a Will where there was a bequest to the " Hospices de Londres," the Will being French and being made by an Englishman, who had resided all his life in France and who in his Will referred to his notary as " de Londres " (who however carried on business at Saville Row and had no place of business or residence in the City), Romilly, M. R., refused to follow *Mallan* v. *May* and *R.* v. *Lewen* (sup.), and practically adopted Sir Wm. Petty's definition by which, writing in 1686, he defined " London " as, " The housing within the Walls, with the Liberties thereof, Westminster and the Borough of Southwark, and so much of the built ground in Middlesex and Surrey whose houses are contiguous unto, or within call of those before mentioned " (*Wallace* v. *A.-G.*, 12 W. R. 506 ; 33 L. J. Ch. 314 ; 33 Bea. 384 ; 10 L. T. 51 : *Va. Beckford* v. *Crutwell*, 5 C. & P. 242 ; 1 M. & Ro. 187). *V.* HOSPITAL.

For statutory definition of the "City of London;" *V.* 11 & 12 V. c. clxiii. s. 262.

V. Metropolis: London District.

LONDON DISTRICT.—For the purposes of the London Coal and Wine Duties (abolished as to Coals, 52 & 53 V. c. 17), "London District" was defined as, "so much of the several Counties of Middlesex, Surrey, Kent, Herts, Essex, Bucks, and Berks, as shall be situate within the Metropolitan Police District; and shall include the Cities of London and Westminster" (24 & 25 V. c. 42, s. 3).

For the Merchant Shipping Acts, "The London District" comprises "the waters of the Thames and Medway as high as London Bridge and Rochester Bridge respectively, and also the seas and channels leading thereto or therefrom as far as Orfordness, to the north, and Dungeness, to the sonth; so nevertheless that no Pilot shall be hereafter licensed to conduct Ships both above and below Gravesend" (s. 370 (1), 17 & 18 V. c. 104).

LONDON GAZETTE.—A single sheet from the *London Gazette* containing a notice, is not proof that such notice has appeared in the *Gazette* (*R.* v. *Lowe*, 52 L. J. M. C. 122).

LONDON RIGHT.—The "London Right" of a Drama, means the right of its representation in London (*Taylor* v. *Neville*, 47 L. J. Q. B. 254). *V.* London.

LONG.—Possession to give a prescription at Common Law must be "*long*, continual and peaceable" (Co. Litt. 113 b). "As to 'long,' Lord Coke says it is the time given by law, which in England is the 'time whereof there is no memory of man to the contrary' . . . . . namely the time of Richard I. (A.D. 1189)" (per Ld. Blackburn, *Dalton* v. *Angus*, 50 L. J. Q. B. 740; 6 App. Ca. 810, 811).

LONG WEIGHT.—*V.* Ton.

LOOSE.—To "turn loose" cattle on a thoroughfare (s. 54, 2 & 3 V. c. 47), means to allow cattle to be there without any control at all, and does not apply to cattle turned out under the care of a boy (*Sherborn* v. *Wells*, 32 L. J. M. C. 179; 3 B. & S. 784). *Cp.* Lying About.

LORD CHANCELLOR.—*V.* s. 12 (1), Interp. Act, 1889.

LORD LIEUTENANT.—*V.* s. 12 (9), Interp. Act, 1889.

LOSS.—The word "Loss" in the exemption clause in the Carriers Act (s. 1, 11 G. 4 & 1 W. 4, c. 68), does not comprise all cases where the owner of the article suffers damage from the neglect of the carrier to carry.

It means such loss as the abstraction of a parcel by a stranger, or by the carrier's servant, not amounting to a felonious act; or by the carrier or his servants losing a parcel in its transit, or mislaying it so that it cannot be found when it ought to be delivered (*Hearn* v. *Lond. & S. W. Ry.*, 24 L. J. Ex. 181; 10 Ex. 801: *Vf. Harris* v. *G. W. Ry.*, 45 L. J. Q. B. 729; 1 Q. B. D. 515: *Skipwith* v. *G. W. Ry.*, 4 Times Rep. 589: *Roche* v. *Cork Ry.*, 24 L. R. Ir. 250).

It is, however, "immaterial whether the loss is temporary or absolute" (per Lopes, J., *Millen* v. *Brasch*, 51 L. J. Q. B. 166; 10 Q. B. D. 142; confirmed, on this point, on appeal, 52 L. J. Q. B. 127); but in the case of a temporary loss, the carrier will not be protected against an unreasonable detention after the goods have been found (*Hearn* v. *Lond. & S. W. Ry.*, sup.: *Millen* v. *Brasch*, sup.).

"It has been held, that, in construing a Bottomry Bond, 'Loss' (of a Ship) means a loss by going to the bottom of the sea" (per Martin, B., *Broomfield* v. *Southern Insrce.*, L. R. 5 Ex. 196; 39 L. J. Ex. 186: *Vf. The Great Pacific*, L. R. 2 P. C. 516; 38 L. J. Adm. 14, 45.)

"Personal injury is not 'Loss;' because a limb may be broken without being lost. The word 'Injury' would certainly be more apt" (per Brett, M.R., in delivering jdgmt. of the Court, *Haigh* v. *Royal Mail Steam Packet Co.*, 52 L. J. Q. B. 643).

V. Damage: Freight: Total Loss: Partial Loss.

"Loss," in s. 20, Artizans' Dwellings Act, 1875, 38 & 39 V. c. 36; *V.* Rights.

LOST OR NOT LOST.—When money for the carriage of goods by sea is payable at the port of destination, "Ship lost or not lost," and the ship is wrecked upon the voyage, the shipowner has no lien upon the goods, although the money to be paid for carriage is described as "Freight" (*Nelson* v. *Protection Assn.*, 43 L. J. C. P. 218).

A stipulation in a Charter-Party that freight should be paid in advance, vessel 'Lost or not Lost," does not prevent the charterer from recovering back the freight as damages from the ship-owner upon a loss of the vessel owing to negligence (*Gt. Indian Pen. Ry.* v. *Turnbull*, 53 L. T. 325; 33 W. R. 874).

LOT.—*V.* Largest.

LOT MEADS.—*V.* Dole.

LOTHERWIT.—"'Lotherwit,' that is, that you may take amends of him which doth defile your bond-woman without your license" (Termes de la Ley).

LOTTERY.—"In *Webster's Dictionary* a Lottery is defined to be,—'A distribution of prizes by lot or chance,'—and a similar definition is given in *Johnson*. Such definitions are, in our opinion, correct; and in such sense we think the word is used in s. 2, 42 G. 3, c. 119" (per Hawkins, J., in delivering jdgmt. of the Court in *Taylor* v. *Smelten*, 52 L. J. M. C. 101; 11 Q. B. D. 207). And accordingly it was held in that case that selling packets of good tea at prices worth the money, but in each packet of which (as publicly and truly stated) was a coupon entitling the purchaser to receive the prize (whatever it might turn out to be) mentioned on such coupon, was a "lottery" within the statute. *Vf. Morris* v. *Blackman*, 2 H. & C. 912; 28 J. P. 199: *R.* v. *Harris*, 10 Cox, C. C. 352.

LUGGAGE.—*V.* Ordinary Luggage: Personal Luggage.

LUNATIC.—"Lunatic," s. 114, 8 & 9 V. c. 100, means, "every Insane Person, and every person being an Idiot or Lunatic, or of Unsound Mind;" imbecility arising from natural causes,—*e.g.*, intemperance or old age,—would constitute "unsoundness of mind" within that section (*R.* v. *Shaw*, 37 L. J. M. C. 112; L. R. 1 C. C. R. 145). *V.* Unsound Mind.

LUPULICETUM.—"Where hoppes grow" (Co. Litt. 4 b): "a hopyard or place where hops do grow" (Touch. 95).

LYING ABOUT.—Cattle, &c., may be "lying about" a Highway, s. 25, 27 & 28 V. c. 101, although under the control of a keeper (*Lawrence* v. *King*, L. R. 3 Q. B. 345; 37 L. J. M. C. 78; 9 B. & S. 325). *Cp.* Loose.

LYNCHES: LINCES.—"The banks between the terraces formed where a common field is on a hill-side by ploughing, so as to turn the sod down hill; also the terraces themselves: Seebohm, Eng. Vill. Comm. 5" (Elph. 592).

MACHINE.—"Machine" includes the Engine that works it; *V.* Implement of Husbandry.

MADE.—An Objection to the renewal of License, made privately to Justices before they come to Court, is not an "Objection made" within s. 42, 35 & 36 V. c. 94 (*R.* v. *Merthyr Tydvil*, 14 Q. B. D. 584; 54 L. J. M. C. 78).

A Receiving Order in Bankruptcy is "made" when it is pronounced, not when it is afterwards formally drawn up and signed (*Re Manning*, 55 L. J. Ch. 613; 30 Ch. D. 480; 54 L. T. 33; 34 W. R. 111).

An Order by a Chancery Judge in Chambers is made, not when it is pronounced, but when it is signed and entered, or otherwise perfected (*Heatley* v. *Newton*, 19 Ch. D. 326; 51 L. J. Ch. 225).

A Poor Rate is "made" when it is signed by the Parish Officers, and allowed by the Justices (*Jones* v. *Bubb*, L. R. 4 C. P. 468; 38 L. J. C. P. 57).

V. Acknowledge.

Building "made or suffered to continue;" *V. Pearson* v. *Kingston*, 35 L. J. M. C. 36; 3 H. & C. 921.

MADE WINES.—*V.* Sweets.

MADRAS COTTON.—*V. Azemar* v. *Casella*, 36 L. J. C. P. 263; L. R. 2 C. P. 677.

MAGNATES.—*V.* Great Men.

MAIM.—"'*Mayhem*,' *mahemium, membri mutilatio, or obtruncatio*, commeth of the French word *mehaigne*, and signifieth a corporall hurt, whereby hee loseth a member, by reason whereof hee is lesse able to fight; as by putting out his eye, beating out his fore-teeth, breaking his skull, striking off his arme, hand, or finger, cutting off his legge or foot, or whereby he loseth the use of any of his said members" (Co. Litt. 288 a). "And the law hath so appropriated this word *mayhem*, which our author here (s. 194) useth, to this offence, as *mayhemavit* cannot be expressed by any other word, as *mutilavit, truncavit*, or *detruncavit*, or the like" (Ib. 126 a, b). *Vh.* Termes de la Ley, *Maihim* or *Maime*.

"A Maim is bodily harm whereby a man is deprived of the use of any member of his body, or of any sense which he can use in fighting, or by the loss of which he is generally and permanently weakened; but a bodily injury is not a Maim merely because it is a disfigurement" (Steph. Cr. 142).

In shooting with intent to maim (24 & 25 V. c. 100, s. 18), "to Maim is to injure any part of a man's body which may render him, in fighting, less able to defend himself, or annoy his enemy" (Arch. Cr. 760).

MAIN ROAD.—*V. Lancashire* v. *Rochdale*, 53 L. J. M. C. 5; 8 App. Ca. 494; 32 W. R. 65; 49 L. T. 368; 48 J. P. 20: *West Riding* v. *Sheffield*, 53 L. J. M. C. 41; 8 App. Ca. 781; 32 W. R. 253: *Newton-in-Makerfield* v. *Lancashire Jus.*, 54 L. J. M. C. 1; 56 Ib. 17; 13 Q. B. D. 623; 15 Ib. 25; 33 W. R. 488; 48 J. P. 406.

V. CEASED: TURNPIKE ROAD.

MAIN TIMBERS.—*V.* TIMBERS.

MAINLY.—*V.* PASTURE.

MAINTAIN.—To "Maintain and repair" a Road, does not include lighting it (*County Road Trustees* v. *Fleming*, W. N. (86) 180).

"Work and Maintain" a Railway; *V. Sevenoaks T. & M. Ry.* v. *Lond. Chatham & Dover Ry.*, 48 L. J. Ch. 513; 11 Ch. D. 625.

V. MAINTENANCE: REPAIR.

MAINTENANCE.—Maintenance is of two kinds:

1. Maintenance of an Action;
2. Maintenance of Persons, Corporeal Things, or Documents.

1. In the judgment in *Bradlaugh* v. *Newdegate* (52 L. J. Q. B. 454; 11 Q. B. D. 1), Coleridge, C. J., said that perhaps the fullest and completest definition of "Maintenance" was to be found in *Termes de la Ley*, which is as follows,—"Maintenance is where any man giveth or delivereth to another, that is plaintife or defendant in any action, any sum of money or other thinge for to maintaine his plee, or else maketh extreame labour for him, when he hath nothing therwith to doe; then the party grieved shal have against him a Writ, called a Writ of Maintenance." *Va.* same judgment for collection of other definitions of "Maintenance" and their application to the case then before the Court (*Vf.* Steph. Cr. 97, 355; Co. Litt. 368 b). But to assist a suit *out of charity* is not Maintenance, even though the charity be not discreet (*Harris* v. *Brisco*, 55 L. J. Q. B. 423; 17 Q. B. D. 504; 55 L. T. 14; 34 W. R. 729). *V.* CHAMPERTY.

2. By s. 4, Prisons Act, 1877 (40 & 41 V. c. 21), the "Maintenance" of Prisons and Prisoners is to be defrayed out of moneys provided by Parliament; and by s. 57, "the maintenance of a prisoner" "includes all such necessary expenses incurred in respect of a prisoner for food, clothing, custody, safe conduct and removal from one place of confinement to

another or otherwise" from the time the Order of Committal is made out until his death or discharge; and includes the cost of his conveyance from where he is committed to his place of confinement, and the cost of his food, &c., when in a lunatic asylum during the term of his imprisonment (*Mullins* v. *Surrey*, 51 L. J. Q. B. 145; L. R. 7 App. Ca. 1: *Mews* v. *The Queen*, 52 L. J. M. C. 57; 8 App. Ca. 339), or, if after imprisonment the prisoner be sent to a Reformatory School, the cost of suitable clothing prior to his admission there (*Prison Commrs.* v. *Liverpool*, 49 L. J. Q. B. 431; 5 Q. B. D. 332).

V. COMMITMENT; PRISONER.

As to what words will create a Trust for Maintenance of *Children; V.* Lewin, 137, 138.

A power to a wife to appoint for her "Maintenance and Support" enables her to appoint the corpus (*Re Heginbotham*, W. N. (84), 179).

As to the power of Trustees to apply income of an Infant's property for or towards his Maintenance, Education or Benefit; *V.* s. 43, Conv. & L. P. Act, 1881, and *Vth. Re Wells*, 43 Ch. D. 281; 59 L. J. Ch. 113.

Education is included in the phrase "Maintenance and Support" as applied to children (*Re Breed*, 45 L. J. Ch. 191; 1 Ch. D. 226).

Semble, that words giving income for the "Maintenance and Support" of a wife and children, are sufficient to create a separate use in the wife (*Austin* v. *Austin*, 46 L. J. Ch. 92; 4 Ch. D. 233).

The restoration of a *Highway* that has been completely destroyed, or so damaged as not to be restorable except at a very large outlay, is not within the parochial obligation, or a statutory power, requiring or enabling its "Maintenance" (*R.* v. *Paul*, 2 Moo. & R. 307: *R.* v. *Bamber*, 13 L. J. M. C. 13; 5 Q. B. 279: *R.* v. *Hornsea*, 23 L. J. M. C. 59; 1 Dears. C. C. 291); nor is converting a macadamised road into one paved with sets of granite, "Maintenance" within s. 13, 41 & 42 V. c. 77 (*Leek* v. *Stafford Jus.*, 57 L. J. M. C. 102; 20 Q. B. D. 794; 36 W. R. 654; 52 J. P. 403), for (as there remarked by Bowen, L. J.), "Maintenance," in that section, is identical with "Repair." But the restoration, at a cost of £341, of 252 yards of a highway rendered impassable by a landslip (*R.* v. *Greenhow*, 45 L. J. M. C. 141; 1 Q. B. D. 703), or, on the other hand, the removal of an obstruction occasioned by a heavy fall of snow (*Amesbury* v. *Wilts Jus.*, 52 L. J. M. C. 64; 10 Q. B. D. 480), are matters of "Maintenance." *V.* MAINTAIN.

A bequest for the "Maintenance" of an *Institution* is not against the Mortmain Act (*Kirkbank* v. *Hudson*, 7 Price, 221): *Va.* SUPPORT.

Terms for the "Maintenance *of the Security*," as used in the prescribed Form of a *Bill of Sale* (Bills of S. Act, 1882), mean such terms as may maintain the title to, or otherwise preserve the goods comprised in a Bill of Sale or for rendering the document effective as a security (*Vh. Re Morritt*, 56 L. J. Q. B. 139; 18 Q. B. D. 222; 56 L. T. 42; 35 W. R. 277: *Furber* v. *Cobb*, 18 Q. B. D. 494; 56 L. J. Q. B. 273; 56 L. T. 689; 35 W. R.

398 : *Goldstrom* v. *Tallerman*, 18 Q. B. D. 1 ; 35 W. R. 68 ; 56 L. J. Q. B. 22 ; 55 L. T. 866 : *Hammond* v. *Hocking*, 12 Q. B. D. 291 ; 53 L. J. Q. B. 205 ; 50 L. T. 267) : but an addition to a power of sale exonerating a purchaser from enquiring as to whether default has been made, is a provision for the relief of the purchaser and not a "Maintenance" of the security (*Blaiberg* v. *Beckett*, 56 L. J. Q. B. 35 ; 18 Q. B. D. 96 ; 55 L. T. 876 ; 35 W. R. 34. *Vf. Bianchi* v. *Offord*, 17 Q. B. D. 484 ; 55 L. J. Q. B. 486) ; nor is giving the grantee larger rights than the Act would confer, such a "Maintenance" (*Calvert* v. *Thomas*, 56 L. J. Q. B. 470 ; 19 Q. B. D. 204 : *Watson* v. *Strickland*, 56 L. J. Q. B. 595 ; 19 Q. B. D. 391 ; 35 W. R. 769 : *Lyon* v. *Morris*, 19 Q. B. D. 139 ; 56 L. J. Q. B. 378 ; 57 L. T. 324 ; 35 W. R. 707 : *Macey* v. *Gilbert*, 57 L. J. Q. B. 461).

MAJORITY.—*V.* MINORITY.

MAKE.—" Make and Prosecute ; " *V.* PROSECUTE.
V. MADE : DO OR MAKE.

MAKE COMPLAINT.—*V.* COMPLAINT.

MAKE GOOD.—To "Make Good" damage done to property, means to restore the property to the condition in which it was immediately before the damage ; and not that pecuniary compensation be given (*Wells* v. *Ody*, 5 L. J. Ex. 199 ; 1 M. & W. 452 : *Crofts* v. *Haldane*, 36 L. J. Q. B. 85 ; 8 B. & S. 194 ; L. R. 2 Q. B. 194).

MAKE SALE.—*V.* NEGOTIATE.

MAKE VOID.—*V.* AFFECT.

MAKER.—Maker of a Promy. Note ; *V.* PROMISSORY NOTE : and as to the liability of a Maker ; *V.* s. 88, Bills of Ex. Act, 1882.

MAKING.—*V.* FROM HENCEFORTH.

MAKING COMPENSATION. — " Making Compensation," or " Satisfaction ; " *V.* SATISFACTION.

MAKING DEFAULT.—" The purchaser making default " to pay interest ; *Vh. Denning* v. *Henderson*, 17 L. J. Ch. 8 ; 1 D. G. & S. 689. *V.* WILFUL DEFAULT.

MALE.—" In order to entitle a person to *inherit* by the description of ' Heir Male,' or ' Heir Female ' of the body, it is essential, not only that the claimant be of the prescribed sex but, that such person trace his or her descent *entirely* through the male or female line, as the case may be. Thus, it is laid down by *Littleton* (s. 24) that,—' If Lands be given to a man and to the heirs male of his body, and he hath issue a daughter, who has issue a son, and dieth, and after the donee die ; in this case the son of the daughter shall not inherit by force of the entail : for whoever shall inherit by force of a gift in tail made to the heirs male, ought to convey his descent *wholly by heirs male*.' It is otherwise, however, in the case of gifts to the heir male or female by words of *purchase*" (2 Jarm. 68, *wh. et seq. Vh.*).

V. MALE LINE.

MALE CHILDREN.—Held, MALE DESCENDANTS (*Bernal* v. *Bernal*, 7 L. J. Ch. 115 ; 3 My. & C. 559).

MALE DESCENDANTS.—In *Bernal* v. *Bernal* (7 L. J. Ch. 115 ; 3 My. & C. 559) a devise to "Male Descendants" was confined to males claiming through males ; *Vth.* 2 Jarm. 69 ; Wms. Exs. 1118: MALE: MALE LINE.

MALE LINE : MALE LINEAL.—"The phrase 'linea masculina' properly means a line commencing with a male and continued through males" (per Earl Selborne, *D'Amico* v. *Trigona*, 58 L. J. P. C. 23).

"'Male Lineal' has been construed to mean as though it were one word signifying,—'male in a line of males.' With this construction I entirely agree ; and I agree that it may be read as though it were a compound word,—'Male-Line'" (per Bramwell, B., *Thellusson* v. *Rendlesham*, 28 L. J. Ch. 953 ; 7 H. L. Ca. 429).

But though the *primâ facie* meaning of "In the Male Line," "Male Lineal," may be a Male in a Line of Males, yet such meaning will readily yield to a context (*Boys* v. *Bradley*, 22 L. J. Ch. 617 ; 25 Ib. 593 ; 10 Hare, 389 ; nom. *Sayer* v. *Bradly*, 5 H. L. Ca. 873). Whether the phrase means *ex parte paternâ* is doubtful :—*cp.* jdgmt. of Wood, V.-C., with that of Knight-Bruce, L. J., in the case just cited. The latter learned judge said,—"The expression 'Female Line' is one habitually, I believe, used less strictly than the phrase 'Male Line.' The idiom of the English language seems to authorise me to designate all his maternal kindred as his relatives in the Female Line, whether related to his mother on her father's side, or otherwise ; but not to authorise an equally free application of the term 'Male Line.' When a correct speaker says that one person is related to another in the Male Line we understand him to mean that they are the *agnati* of the Roman Law ; that is *cognati per virilis sexûs personas cognatione conjuncti* :" and he added he did not think, in that case, that it would be safe to construe "In the Male Line" as equivalent to *ex parte paternâ*. The case, however, did not turn on this question ;—the phrase there to be construed being, "The *Nearest of Kin* in the Male Line, in preference to the Female Line," a collocation which, with the other provisions of the Will, led the V.-C., the L. JJ., and the H. L., unanimously to the conclusion that the (bachelor) testator's only surviving sister was entitled in preference to a remoter relative who was a male claiming kinship with the testator through an unbroken line of males. *Vh.* 2 Jarm. 110, 68, 69.

V. MALE : LINEAL.

MALE SERVANT.—A man being employed as a yardsman and farm labourer did such groom-work as his master, a farmer, required, but this only occupied a small portion of the man's time; held that the employer was not bound to take out a license for him, as the man was not a "Male Servant" within s. 19, 32 & 33 V. c. 14, but came within the exceptions in s. 5, 39 V. c. 16 (*Yelland* v. *Winter*, 34 W. R. 121; 2 Times Rep. 117).

MALICE: MALICIOUS: MALICIOUSLY.—"The word 'Malice' is satisfied by the thing being done with knowledge of the plaintiff's right, and with intent to interfere with it 'maliciously' or, which is the same thing, 'with notice' (per Crompton, J., *Lumley* v. *Gye*, 2 E. & B. 224; 22 L. J. Ex. 9). The effect of Malice is adopted by Sir W. Erle, and so long ago as by Ld. Holt in *Keeble* v. *Hickeringill* (11 Mod. 75; *Va.* 11 East, 574). 'Suppose,' he says, 'the defendant had shot in his own ground; if he had occasion to shoot it would have been one thing; but to shoot on purpose to damage the plaintiff is another thing and a wrong.' In truth, I have never known this rule doubted" (per Esher, M. R., *Mogul Co.* v. *McGregor*, 58 L. J. Q. B. 477). In the same case Bowen, L. J., said,—"The terms 'maliciously,' 'wrongfully,' and 'injure,' are words all of which have accurate meanings well known to the law, but which also have a popular and less precise signification. An intent to 'injure,' in strictness, means more than an intent to harm. It connotes an intent to do wrongful harm. 'Maliciously,' in like manner means and implies an intention to do an act which is wrongful, to the detriment of another. The term 'wrongful' imports in its term the infringement of some right."

The word "Malice,' "seldom has any meaning except a misleading one. It refers not to intention but to motive; and in almost all legal inquiries intention, as distinguished from motive, is the important matter. Another objection to it is that its popular meaning is not barely ill will, but an ill will which it is immoral to feel. No one would describe legitimate indignation as 'Malice'" (Steph. Cr. 204, n. 3: *Vf.* the learned author's jdgmt. in *R.* v. *Tolson*, 23 Q. B. D. 168; 58 L. J. M. C. 97; 37 W. R. 716: KNOWINGLY).

But a "Malicious Damage" is something illegally and unreasonably done for mischief's sake; and scarcely comprises a thing done in the exercise of a right that is reasonably believed to exist (*R.* v. *Jenner*, 7 L. J. O. S. M. C. 79).

"Where any person wilfully does an act injurious to another without lawful excuse" he does it maliciously (per Ld. Blackburn, *R.* v. *Pembliton*, 43 L. J., M. C. 91; L. R. 2 C. C. R. 122) even though it be a piece of foolish mischief which results in injury, *e.g.* causing panic by putting out the lights in a place where people are assembled (*R.* v. *Martin*, 51 L. J. M. C. 36 : 8 Q. B. D. 54 ; 30 W. R. 106 ; 46 J. P. 228 : *Vh.* INFLICT). So "it is common knowledge that when one person has a malicious intent against another and in carrying it out injures a third person, he is guilty of malice against the person he has injured ; he has general malice, and that is enough to support the general allegation of malice" (per Coleridge, C. J., *R.* v. *Latimer*, 55 L. J. M. C. 136 ; 17 Q. B. D. 359 ; 54 L. T. 768).

V. WILFUL AND MALICIOUS.

MALICE AFORETHOUGHT.—"Malice Aforethought, means any one or more of the following states of mind preceding or co-existing with the act or omission by which death is caused, and it may exist where that act is unpremeditated.

(a.) An intention to cause the death of, or grievous bodily harm to, any person, whether such person is the person actually killed or not ;

(b.) Knowledge that the act which causes death will probably cause the death of, or grievous bodily harm to, some person, whether such person is the person actually killed or not ; although such knowledge is accompanied by indifference whether death or grievous bodily harm is caused or not, or by a wish that it may not be caused ;

(c.) An intent to commit any felony whatever ;

(d.) An intent to oppose by force any officer of justice on his way to, in, or returning from the execution of the duty of arresting, keeping in custody, or imprisoning any person whom he is lawfully entitled to arrest, keep in custody, or imprison, or the duty of keeping the peace, or dispersing an unlawful assembly, provided that the offender has notice that the person killed is such an officer so employed.

"The expression '*Officer of Justice*' in this clause includes every person who has a legal right to do any of the acts mentioned, whether he is an officer or a private person.

"Notice may be given, either by words, by the production of a warrant, or other legal authority, by the known official character of the person killed, or by the circumstances of the case" (Steph. Cr. 158, 159 ; *Vf.* Ib. 364*et seq.*).

Vf. Arch. Cr. 715.

MAN OF STRAW.—To write, or speak, of a person in trade that he is a "Man of Straw," is to impute insolvency (*Eaton* v. *Johns*, 11 L. J. Ex. 150 ; 1 Dowl. N. S. 602).

MANAGEMENT.—*V.* CARE OR MANAGEMENT, *Addenda*.

MANAGER.—"A Manager, in ordinary talk, is a person who has the management of the whole affairs of the Company ; not an agent who is to do one thing, or a servant who is to obey orders and do another, but a

Manager who is entrusted with power to manage the whole of the affairs" (per Blackburn, J., *Gibson* v. *Barton*, 44 L. J. M. C. 86; L. R. 10 Q. B. 329). *V.* that case as to "Manager" as used in s. 27, Companies Act, 1862.

MANILLA HEMP.—*V. Jones* v. *Just*, 37 L. J. Q. B. 89; L. R. 3 Q. B. 197; 9 B. & S. 141.

MANNER AND FORM.—*V.* TENOR.

MANOR.—"'This word *Manor* is a word of large extent, and may comprehend many things (*Hill* v. *Grange*, Plowd. 168). And therefore by the grant of a Manor, without the words of *cum pertinentiis*, do pass demesnes, rents and services (Co. Litt. 310 b, 319 b), lands, meadows, pastures, woods, commons, advowsons appendant (*Ive's Case*, 5 Rep. 11 b), villains regardant, courts baron, and perquisites thereof, that are in truth at the time of the grant parcel of the manor. But nothing that in truth is not parcel of the manor, albeit it be so reputed, will pass by the grant of the manor; and therefore if one have a manor, and after purchase the Law-day (*i.e.* the Leet), or a warren to it, and then he grant away the manor,—hereby the law-day, or the warren will not pass (Dy. 30 b, pl. 209). And yet if by union time out of mind [or for a short period] they have gotten a reputation of appendancy, perhaps by the grant of the manor *cum pertinentiis*, these things may pass (Plowd. 168 a). By the grant of a manor also divers towns (Co. Litt. 5 a) [the land in divers towns] may pass. An honor also may pass by this name. And so also may a castle or a hundred. And one manor also, that is parcel of another manor, may pass by the grant of that manor whereof it is parcel' [viz. the seignory of the inferior manor] *Marsh and Smith's Case*, 1 Leon. 26. Touch. 92; Cro. Eliz. 38. *Va.* Co. Litt. 58 a: *Darell* v. *Wybarne*, Dy. 207 a, pl. 14. The freehold interest in the copyhold passes; *Delacherois* v. *Delacherois*, 11 H. L. Ca. 62; 13 W. R. 24; 10 L. T. 884; 4 N. R. 501.

"By a grant of a '*Reputed* Manor,' the freehold interest in the waste does not pass, nor does any specific tenement of the grantor; *Doe* d. *Clayton* v. *Williams*, 12 L. J. Ex. 429; 11 M. & W. 803.

"By 'Manor' a Reputed Manor may pass in a Deed, but not in a Fine or Recovery; *Mallet* v. *Mallet*, Cro. Eliz. 524, 707: *Finch's Case*, 6 Rep. 64 a: *Treswallen* v. *Penhules*, 2 Rol. Rep. 66" (Elph. 593–595, *wh. Vf.*).

By grant of a Manor its unsevered Mines would pass (MacS. 203).

V. CASTLE.

A Devise of a Manor, with all Courts, &c., extends to the demesne lands of the Manor (*Hicks* v. *Sallit*, 1 W. R. 226; 2 Eq. Rep. 818).

Prior to the Wills Act (1 V. c. 26) a devise of a "Manor" without words of limitation, only gave a life estate (*Paice* v. *Archb. Canterbury*, 14 Ves. 364); but such a devise comprised the devisor's copyholds, though acquired after the making of the Will (*Roe* d. *Hale* v. *Wegg*, 6 T. R. 708), and Escheats (*Delacherois* v. *Delacherois*, sup.).

As to what will pass under a Conveyance of a "Manor," executed since 31 Dec., 1881; *V.* s. 6, Conv. & L. P. Act, 1881.

MANSION.—*V.* FAMILY MANSION: HAGA.

"'Mansion' is in our law most commonly taken for the chief messuage or habitation of the Lord of a Mannor,—the Mannor House where he doth most remain or continue, his Capitall Messuage, as it is called" (Termes de la Ley, *Mansion*).

"Mansion-house, garden and premises," in a Devise; *V. Lethbridge* v. *Lethbridge*, cited PREMISES.

MANSLAUGHTER.—"Manslaughter is unlawful homicide without malice aforethought" (Steph. Cr. 158; *Vf.* Ib. ch. 24, 362–383). *V.* HOMICIDE.

"Homicide, which would otherwise be murder, is not murder, but manslaughter, if the act by which death is caused is done in the heat of passion; caused by provocation, unless the provocation was sought or voluntarily provoked by the offender as an excuse for killing or doing bodily harm" (Steph. Cr. 161, *wh. Va.* as to what is Provocation within this definition).

Vf. Arch. Cr. 14, 711–716; Rosc. Cr. 723–742.

MANSURA.—*V.* HAGA.

MANUAL LABOUR.—As to "Manual Labour" within s. 8, Employers' Liability Act, 1880 (43 & 44 V. c. 42); *V. Shaffers* v. *Gen. Steam Nav. Co.*, 52 L. J. Q. B. 260; 10 Q. B. D. 356. The duties of an Omnibus Conductor (*Morgan* v. *Lond. Gen. Omnibus Co.*, 53 L. J. Q. B. 352; 13 Q. B. D. 832; 32 W. R. 759; 48 J. P. 503; dissenting from *Wilson* v. *Glasgow Tramways Co.*, 5 Sess. Ca. 4th series, 981), or those of the Driver of a Tram-car (*Cook* v. *North Metrop. Trams Co.*, 18 Q. B. D. 683; 56 L. J. Q. B. 309; 56 L. T. 448; 57 Ib. 476; 35 W. R. 577; 3 Times Rep. 523), do not involve manual labour.

V. LABOUR: WORKMAN: HANDICRAFT.

MANUFACTORY.—As to what is a "Manufactory" within s. 92, Lands C. C. Act, 1845; *V. Gibson* v. *Hammersmith Ry.*, 32 L. J. Ch. 337; 11 W. R. 299; 8 L. T. 43: *Barker* v. *North Staffordshire Ry.*, 2 D. G. & S. 55; 12 Jur. 589: *Dakin* v. *Lond. & N. W. Ry.*, 3 D. G. & S. 414; 13 L. T. O. S. 156; 13 Jur. 579: *Furniss* v. *Mid. Ry.*, L. R. 6 Eq. 473: *Sparrow* v. *Oxford, Worcester & Wolverhampton Ry.*, 2 D. G. M. & G. 94; 19 L. T. O. S. 131; 16 Jur. 703: *Richards* v. *Swansea Improvement Co.*, 9 Ch. D. 425; 38 L. T. 833; 26 W. R. 764: *Reddin* v. *Metrop. Bd. of Works*, 31 L. J. Ch. 661; 4 D. G. F. & J. 532; 10 W. R. 764; 7 L. T. 6: *Benington* v. *Metrop. Bd. of Works*, 54 L. T. 837; 50 J. P. 740. *Va.* Lloyd on Comp. 28–30; Dart, 247; Seton, 1418.

MANUFACTURE.—"The word 'Manufacture' in the Statute of

Monopolies (21 Jac. 1, c. 3), must be construed in one of two ways. It may mean the machine when completed, or the mode of constructing the machine" (per Parke, B., *Morgan* v. *Seaward*, 6 L. J. Ex. 156 ; 2 M. & W. 558). "The word 'Manufacture,'" said Abbott, C. J., in *R.* v. *Wheeler* (2 B. & Ald. 349), "has been generally understood to denote, either a thing made which is useful for its own sake, and vendible as such, as a medicine, a stove, a telescope and many others ; or to mean an engine or instrument, or some part of an engine or instrument, to be employed either in the making of some previously known article, or in some other useful purpose, as a stocking frame, or a steam engine for raising water from mines ; or, it may, perhaps, extend also to a new process to be carried on by known implements or elements acting upon known substances, and ultimately producing some other known substance, but producing it in a cheaper or more expeditious manner, or of a better or more useful kind. No mere philosophical or abstract principle can answer to the word 'Manufactures.' Something of a corporeal and substantial nature,—something that can be made by man from the matters subjected to his art and skill, or at the least some new mode of employing practically his art and skill, is required to satisfy the word."

V. NEW MANUFACTURE.

MANUFACTURING PROCESS.—*V.* ARTICLE.

MANUMISSION.—*V.* Litt. s. 204 ; Co. Litt. 137 a, b ; Termes de la Ley.

MARETTUM.—"This word *marettum* is derived of *mare* the sea, and *tego*, and properly signifieth a moorish and gravelly ground, which the sea doth cover and overflow at a full sea, and lyeth betweene the high water marke and low water marke, *infra fluxum et refluxum maris*" (Co. Litt. 5 a).

MARINER.—"Any Mariner or Seaman, *being at Sea*" may make a Nuncupative Will (Stat. of Frauds, s. 22 ; Wills Act, 1 V. c. 26, s. 11).

The term "Mariner or Seaman" here includes *merchant* seamen (*Morrell* v. *Morrell*, 1 Hagg. Ecc. 51 : *Re Milligan*, 2 Robert. 108 ; 13 Jur. 1011 : *Re Parker*, 2 Sw. & Tr. 375 ; 5 Jur. N. S. 553 : *Re Thompson*, 5 Notes of Ecc. Cases, 596) ; and includes also the whole profession, as well of the Royal Navy as of the merchant service, from the highest officer to a common seaman (*Re Hayes*, 2 Curt. 338).

"At Sea :" An Admiral of a Naval Station, living on shore and who made his Will at his house, held not within this phrase (*Euston* v. *Seymour*, cited 2 Curt. 339 ; 3 Ib. 530), and so it was held of a seaman who was in a British port whose vessel did not sail for several days after he had made the alleged Will (*Re Corby*, 18 Jur. 634). But a seaman stationed at

Portsmouth on board a training ship was held to be "at Sea" (*Re MacMurdo*, 16 W. R. 283), and a seaman who, being in harbour, went on shore and there was so severely injured that he died, was held to be "at Sea" (*Re Lay*, 2 Curt. 375). A test seems to be, was the seaman "in expeditione?" and therefore (following *Re Lay*), it was held that a Seaman engaged with the enemy and on board ship, but in a River beyond the flux and reflux of the tide, was "at Sea" within the phrase under consideration (*Re Austen*, 17 Jur. 284; 2 Robert. 611). *Vf.* Wms. Exs. 119: AT SEA.

MARISCUS.—"He that granteth *omnes mariscos suos*, all his fennes or marish grounds doe passe. *Mariscus* is derived of the French word *mares* or *marets*" (Co. Litt. 5 a).

MARK.—*V.* OUTWARD MARK.

MARKET.—"Market (anciently written *mercat*, Fr., *mercatus*, L.), a public time and appointed place of buying and selling; also purchase and sale" (Wharton, Law Lex.). A market may be granted without metes and bounds (*A.-G.* v. *Horner*, 54 L. J. Q. B. 227; 55 Ib. 193; 14 Q. B. D. 245; 11 App. Ca. 66). *Vh.* WITH ALL LIBERTIES.

MARKET GARDEN.—A market-gardener and nurseryman occupied a piece of land upon which were built 16 green-houses built on brick foundations, and which practically covered the surface of the land and in which the occupier grew fruit and vegetables for sale in his business: held, that it was a "Market Garden" or "Nursery Ground" within s. 211, subs. 1 (b), P. H. Act, 1875 (*Purser* v. *Worthing*, 56 L. J. M. C. 78; 18 Q. B. D. 818; 35 W. R. 682; 51 J. P. 596; 3 Times Rep. 509, 637).

V. GARDEN: MARKET GARDENER.

MARKET GARDENER.—A tenant of 130 acres, under a farming lease, who grew annually 20 acres of green peas and 12 acres of young potatoes, the produce of which he sold by forwarding the same from time to time to salesmen in London, was held not to be a "Market Gardener" within the late Bankruptcy definition of "Trader" (*Ex p. Hammond*, 14 L. J. Bank. 14; D. G. 93; 9 Jur. 358).

V. MARKET GARDEN.

MARKET VALUE.—In a contract for the sale of goods, "Market Value" means the price in the market to an ordinary customer, irrespective of the particular contract (*Orchard* v. *Simpson*, 2 C. B. N. S. 299).

MARKETABLE SECURITY.—"Marketable Security," *quà* Stamp Acts, means, "a Security of such a description as to be capable of being sold in any stock market in the United Kingdom" (s. 2 (10), Stamp Act, 1870).

MARRIAGE.—*V.* Solemnization.

Cesser of a life interest on death or re-marriage; *V.* Death.

MARRIAGE SETTLEMENT.—"A 'Marriage Settlement' is well understood to be a Deed executed in consideration of a marriage about to take place" (per Hill, J., *Foster* v. *Fowler*, 5 Jur. N. S. 99); and therefore (unless made in pursuance of an ante-nuptial agreement), a post-nuptial Settlement of personal chattels is not a "Marriage Settlement" which, under s. 4, Bills of Sale Act, 1878, is exempt from registration (*Fowler* v. *Foster*, 28 L. J. Q. B. 210; 5 Jur. N. S. 99: *Ashton* v. *Blackshaw*, 39 L. J. Ch. 205; L. R. 9 Eq. 510): but "there is no doubt that a post-nuptial Settlement, in pursuance of an ante-nuptial Agreement, is a 'Marriage Settlement' and within that exemption" (per Bowen, L.J., *Courcier* v. *Bardili*, 27 S. J. 276: *Vf.* Rosc. N. P. 1152).

MARRY.—"If she shall marry;" *V.* Death.

"Being Married," "Marries;" *V.* Bigamy.

MARSHALL.—Marshalling Assets; *V.* Tudor, Char. Trusts, 58–66.

MARTINMAS.—*V.* Michaelmas.

MASTER.—"Master," R. 21, Ord. 54, R. S. C., includes a Registrar of the Probate Divorce and Admiralty Div. (*Re Patrick*, 14 P. D. 42; 58 L. J. P. D. & A. 36; 60 L. T. 343). *Vf.* R. 1, Ord. 71.

V. Finding a Master.

MATERIAL ALTERATION.—"When a Deed is altered in a Point material, by the Plaintiff himself or by any Stranger without the Privity of the Obligee, be it by Interlineation, Addition, Rasing, or by drawing of a Pen through a Line, or through the midst of any material Word, the Deed thereby becomes void: as if a Bond is to be made to the Sheriff for Appearance, &c., and in the Bond the Sheriff's name is omitted, and after the Delivery thereof his Name is interlin'd, either by the Obligee or a Stranger without his Privity, the Deed is void: So if one make a Bond of £10 and after the Sealing of it another £10 is added which makes it £20, the Deed is void: So if a Bond is rased, by which the first word can't be seen, or if it is drawn with a Pen and Ink through the Word, although the first Word is legible, yet the Deed is void" (*Pigot's Case*, 11 Rep. 27 a: Touch. 68, 69: *Swiney* v. *Barry*, 1 Jones, 109).

The Touchstone (p. 68) thus particularises what is a *material* alteration in a Deed:—"As if it be in a deed of grant, in the name of the grantor, grantee, or in the thing granted, or in the limitation of the estate; or if it be in an obligation when the word [heirs] shall be inserted, or the sum increased, or in the date of either or the like."

But the execution of a Deed of Arrangement by Creditors, *after* its registration under 50 & 51 V. c. 57, is not to make a Material Alteration in the deed, and does not render the deed void (*Re Batten, Ex p. Milne*, 58 L. J. Q. B. 333 ; 22 Q. B. D. 685 ; 37 W. R. 499).

The alteration of a date in a Bill of Exchange, whereby its due date would be accelerated (*Master* v. *Miller*, 4 T. R. 320; affd. 5 T. R. 367 ; 2 H. Bl. 141 ; 1 Anst. 225 ; 1 Sm. L. C. 825), or the alteration of the number of a Bank of England Note (*Suffell* v. *Bank of Eng.*, 51 L. J. Q. B. 401 ; 7 Q. B. D. 270 ; 9 Ib. 555 : *Leeds Bank* v. *Walker*, 11 Q. B. D. 84), is material (and so probably of the numbers on bonds which have to be drawn by lot ; but not of a number put on a Bill of Ex. or Cheque ; per Jessel, M. R., in *Suffell* v. *Bank of Eng.*, sup.). Erasing the crossing of a Cheque is not a material alteration of the Cheque (*Simmons* v. *Taylor*, 27 L. J. C. P. 45, 248 ; 4 C. B. N. S. 463). *V.* now as to alterations in Bills of Ex., Bills of Ex. Act, 1882, ss. 63, 64.

As to what verbal alteration in a Sale Note or other Contract is material ; *V. Powell* v. *Divett*, 15 East, 29 : *Mollett* v. *Wackerbarth*, 17 L. J. C. P. 47 ; 5 C. B. 181. It is probably safe to say that only such an alteration is material as would alter the business effect of the instrument if used for any ordinary business purpose for which such an instrument or any part of it is used (*V.* jdgmt. of Brett, L. J., and *cp.* that of Jessel, M. R., in *Suffell* v. *Bank of Eng.*, sup.). To put a seal against the signature to a contract which was not under seal, is a material alteration of the contract (*Davidson* v. *Cooper*, 12 L. J. Ex. 467 ; 13 Ib. 276 ; 11 M. & W. 778 ; 13 Ib. 343).

MATERIAL EVIDENCE.—"Material Evidence in support of the Promise of Marriage," s. 2, 32 & 33 V. c. 68 ;—Evidence of silence when a man is taxed with such a promise is "Material Evidence" in its support (*Bessela* v. *Stern*, 46 L. J. C. P. 467 ; 2 C. P. D. 265 ; 42 J. P. 197). In that case Bramwell, L. J., said,—"I rather fancy it has somewhere been said that the word 'Material' makes no difference in the meaning of the section."

V. Corroborated.

MATERIAL FACTS.—The "Material Facts" that are to be stated in Pleadings (Ord. 19, R. 4, R. S. C.), may, and generally should, include the consequences, or motives, of the matter relied on as well as those pertinent to that matter itself ; *e.g.*—seduction and imparting venereal disease, in an action for Breach of Promise of Marriage (*Millington* v. *Loring*, 50 L. J. Q. B. 214 ; 6 Q. B. D. 190 ; 29 W. R. 207), or of malicious motives in Defamation (*Glossop* v. *Spindler*, 29 S. J. 556) ; but not damages (*Wood* v. *Durham*, 57 L. J. Q. B. 547 ; 21 Q. B. D. 501 ; 59 L. T. 142 ; 37 W. R. 222).

The following are examples of what are "Material Facts" within the Rule ;—

In Defamation the precise words complained of (*Harris* v. *Warre*, 48 L. J. C. P. 310 ; 4 C. P. D. 125) ; in a Defence to Defamation the facts relied on to show justification or privilege (*Belt* v. *Lawes*, 51 L. J. Q. B. 359); the purport of documents when such are relied on (*Philipps* v. *Philipps*, 4 Q. B. D. 127; 48 L. J. Q. B. 135; 27 W. R. 436); in Ejectment, when the claim is by devolution, the material steps showing title (Ib. *Davis* v. *James*, 53 L. J. Ch. 523; 26 Ch. D. 778; 32 W. R. 406; 50 L. T. 115; *sv. Evelyn* v. *Evelyn*, 28 W. R. 532: and as to the Defence, *V. Danford* v. *McAnulty*, 52 L. J. Q. B. 652; 8 App. Ca. 456); in a Right of Way case, the termini and general course of the Way and whether claim arises by prescription or grant (*Harris* v. *Jenkins*, 52 L. J. Ch. 437; 22 Ch. D. 481; 31 W. R. 137); in Negligence, inevitable accident (*Winchilsea* v. *Beckly*, 2 Times Rep. 300); in Negligence, under Employers' Liability Act, the knowledge by the master of the danger and the want of such knowledge by the servant (*Griffiths* v. *London & St. K. Docks Co.*, 53 L. J. Q. B. 504; 13 Q. B. D. 260); in Donatio Mortis Causâ, the actual facts attending the gift (*Re Parton*, 30 W. R. 287). *Vf.* Ann. Pr.

Cp. EVIDENCE: *V.* FACT: PERJURY.

MATERIAL PARTICULAR.—*V.* CORROBORATED.

MATERIALLY ALTERED.—Transfer of an Endowment if a School should become "materially altered in discipline, numbers or other circumstances;" *V. London School Bd.* v. *Faulconer*, 48 L. J. Ch. 41; 8 Ch. D. 571.

V. MATERIAL ALTERATION.

MATERIALS.—"*Materials, Tools, or Implements* to be used by such artificer in his trade or occupation, if such artificer be employed in mining," s. 23, Truck Act, 1 & 2 W. 4, c. 37;—Wooden Props or "Sprags," though neither "Tools, or Implements," are "Materials" within these words (*Cutts* v. *Ward*, 36 L. J. Q. B. 161; L. R. 2 Q. B. 357; 15 W. R. 445; 15 L. T. 614).

"'Implements,' is used for things of necessary use in any trade or mystery, which are implyed in the practice of the said trade, or without which the worke cannot be accomplisht. And so also for furniture of houshold with which the house is filled. And in that sense you shall finde the word often in Wils and Conveyances of moveables" (Termes de la Ley, *Implements*).

MATERNÂ.—*Ex p. maternâ*;—*V.* NEXT OF KIN.

MATTER.—*V.* CAUSE.

"Matter" contrasted with "Substance;" *V.* DESTRUCTIVE.

"Matter" of an Agreement, *quà* Stamp Act; *V. Doe* d. *Marlow* v. *Wiggins*, 12 L. J. Q. B. 177; 4 Q. B. 367; 3 G. & D. 504: *Marlow* v. *Thompson*, 1 Dowl. N. S. 575.

"Matter *in Question*," Ord. 31, R. 12, R. S. C.; *V. Penrice* v. *Williams*, 23 Ch. D. 353; 52 L. J. Ch. 593. *V.* QUESTION.

"Matter," Ord. 37, R. 5, R. S. C.; *V. Mysore Mining Co.*, 58 L. J. Ch. 731.

"Matter *not being an Action*," Ord. 54, R. 15, R. S. C.; *V. Re Fawsitt, Galland* v. *Burton*, 54 L. J. Ch. 1131; 30 Ch. D. 231.

An Originating Summons is a "Matter" within s. 43, Trustee Act, 1850 (*Re Jones*, 59 L. J. Ch. 157; 61 L. T. 554).

Exception of "*Matters or Things* done at any time before the passing of this Act," s. 1, 6 & 7 V. c. 73; *V. Doe* d. *Potts* v. *Jinders*, 14 L. J. Q. B. 245; 2 Dowl. & L. 986.

MAURITIUS.—*V.* East Indies.

MAY.—Though dicta of eminent judges may be cited to the contrary, it must be the plainest conclusion of common sense that "may," "it shall be lawful," "it shall and may be lawful," "empowered," "shall hereby have power," "shall think proper," and such like phrases, give, in their ordinary meaning, an enabling and discretionary power. "They are potential and never (in themselves) significant of any obligation" (per Ld. Selborne, *Julius* v. *Bishop of Oxford*, 49 L. J. Q. B. 585). "They confer a faculty or power, and they do not of themselves do more than confer a faculty or power;" and therefore, where the point in question is not covered by authority, "it lies upon those who contend that an *obligation* exists to exercise this power, to shew in the circumstances of the case something which according to the principles I have mentioned creates this obligation" (per Cairns, L. C., Ib. 578, 579; 5 App. Ca. 214; 42 L. T. 546; 28 W. R. 726).

Julius v. *Bishop of Oxford* (sup.) may now be regarded as the leading case on the principles therein referred to by Lord Cairns for construing as obligatory, phrases which in their ordinary meaning are merely enabling. His Lordship in that case gathers those principles into the following proposition:—

"Where a power is deposited with a public officer for the purpose of being used for the benefit of persons (1) who are specifically pointed out, and (2) with regard to whom a definition is supplied by the Legislature of the conditions upon which they are entitled to call for its exercise, that power ought to be exercised, and the Court will require it to be exercised" (49 L. J. Q. B. 580; 5 App. Ca. 214).

And the following supplemental proposition may be gathered from the judgment of Lord Blackburn in the same case:—

Enabling words are construed as compulsory whenever the object of the power is to effectuate a legal right: and if the object of the power is to enable the donee to effectuate a legal right, then it is the *duty* of the donee of the power to exercise the power when those who have the right call upon him to do so.

"May," and such enabling words as those above referred to, therefore group themselves into two classes according as they impose or give;—

I. An Obligatory Duty;

II. A Discretionary or Enabling Power.

I. In the following cases, which all seem to come well within the principles to which form and substance were given by *Julius* v. *Bishop of Oxford*, enabling words have been held to impose

An Obligatory Duty:—

Where by the joint effect of 13 Eliz. c. 7, s. 2, and 1 Jac. 1, c. 15, s. 3, the Lord Chancellor "shall have full power and authority" to issue a bankrupt commission (*Backwell's Case*, 1 Vern. 152 : *V.* a concise statement of this case in the judgment of Lord Blackburn in *Julius* v. *Bishop of Oxford*, sup.) :

Where it was declared by 14 Car. 2, c. 12, s. 18, that constables and others, out of purse in enforcing the poor-law, "together with the churchwards and overseers of the poor and other inhabitants of the parish, shall hereby have power and authority" to make a rate to reimburse the constables and others (*R.* v. *Barlow*, 2 Salk. 609 : *V.* this case also stated in Lord Blackburn's judgment in *Julius* v. *Bishop of Oxford*, sup.) :

Where, by 8 & 9 W. 3, c. 11, s. 8, a plaintiff in an action on a bond or for a penal sum "may" assign as many breaches as he shall think fit, the statute being for the benefit of defendants (*Roles* v. *Rosewell*, 5 T. R. 538 : *Hardy* v. *Bern*, cited Ib. 540 : *Plomer* v. *Ross*, 5 Taunt. 386) :

Where a power was granted by royal charter to the steward and suitors of a manor enabling them to hear and determine civil suits (*R.* v. *Steward of Havering-atte-Bower*, 5 B. & Ald. 691) :

Where, by 56 G. 3, c. lv., "it shall be lawful" for the wardens, &c., to raise a rate to pay the increased stipends of two chaplains and the schoolmaster of St. Saviour's, Southwark (*R.* v. *St. Saviour's, Southwark*, 7 L. J. M. C. 59 ; 1 N. & P. 496 ; 7 A. & E. 925) :

Where, by 7 W. 4 & 1 V. c. 78, s. 24, "it shall be lawful" for the King's Bench to enquire into the title of a claimant (whose claim has been rejected in the revision court) to have his name inserted in the Burgess Roll (*R.* v. *Harwich*, 8 A. & E. 919 ; *Sv.* s. 47 (2), Municipal Corporations Act, 1882) :

Where, by 2 & 3 V. c. 84, s. 1, "it shall be lawful" for two justices to summon overseers to a special sessions for their contribution to their union, "and if the justices at such sessions shall think fit" to issue warrant of distress (*R.* v. *Boteler*, 4 B. & S. 959 ; 33 L. J. M. C. 101) :

Where by 5 & 6 V. c. 54, s. 7, the Tithe Commissioners were "empowered" to confirm invalid agreements respecting tithes when a fair equivalent given (*R.* v. *Tithe Commrs.*, 14 Q. B. 459 ; 19 L. J. Q. B. 177) :

Where, by 7 & 8 V. c. 110, s. 66, judgments against certain joint-stock companies "shall and may" take effect and be enforced against the shareholders (*Hill* v. *London and County Assurance*, 1 H. & N. 398 ; 26 L. J. Ex. 89, overruling *Thompson* v. *Universal Salvage Co.*, 3 Ex. 310 ;

An Obligatory Duty:—

18 L. J. Ex. 242 : and see judgments in *Morisse* v. *Royal British Bank*, 1 C. B. N. S. 67 ; 26 L. J. C. P. 62) :

Where, by 7 & 8 V. c. 113, s. 13, execution "may be issued by leave of the Court" (against a shareholder in a joint-stock bank) on motion by a judgment creditor, and that "it shall be lawful" for such Court to make absolute or discharge such rule (*Morisse* v. *Royal British Bank*, sup.) :

Where, by Jervis' Act (11 & 12 V. c. 42), s. 9, justices "may if they think fit" issue summons or warrant (*R.* v. *Adamson*, 1 Q. B. D. 201 ; 45 L. J. M. C. 46) :

Where by Public Health Act, 1848 (11 & 12 V. c. 63) s. 89, a local board of health "may" make rates to pay charges within that section (*R.* v. *Rotherham*, 8 E. & B. 906 ; 27 L. J. Q. B. 156 : *Worthington* v. *Hulton*, L. R. 1 Q. B. 63 ; 35 L. J. Q. B. 61 ; cited by Ld. Blackburn, in *Julius* v. *Bishop of Oxford*, sup.) :

Where by the Winding Up Act (11 & 12 V. c. 45), s. 73, "it shall be lawful" for a judge to restrain an action against a contributory to a Company unless Master's permission to proceed obtained and the debt proved before the Master (*Marson* v. *Lund*, 13 Q. B. 664) :

Where by a Private Act it was declared that "it shall be lawful" for a Railway Company to construct bridges *of a certain height and span* (*R.* v. *Caledonian Ry.*, 16 Q. B. 19 ; 20 L. J. Q. B. 150) :

Where, by 13 & 14 V. c. 61, s. 13, a Judge "may" order costs of an action in a Superior Court (under certain defined conditions) though for an amount which might have been sued for in the County Court (*Macdougall* v. *Paterson*, 21 L. J. C. P. 27 ; 11 C. B. 755 : *Crake* v. *Powell*, 21 L. J. Q. B. 183 ; 2 E. & B. 210 : *Asplin* v. *Blackman*, 21 L. J. Ex. 78 ; 7 Ex. 386 : over-ruling the previous decisions in the Exchequer of *Jones* v. *Harrison*, 20 L. J. Ex. 166 ; 6 Ex. 328 : *Palmer* v. *Richards*, 20 L. J. Ex. 323 ; 6 Ex. 335 ; *Vh.* s. 4, 15 & 16 V. c. 54) :

Where by the Companies Act, 1862 (25 & 26 V. c. 89), s. 79, a Company "may" be wound up by the Court (*Bowes* v. *Hope Socy.*, 11 H. L. Ca. 389 ; 35 L. J. Ch. 574) :

Where by s. 211, P. H. Act, 1875, power is given of rating the owner of property instead of the occupier, but at a reduced estimate, and when that estimate is in respect of tenements whether occupied or not, then the assessment "may" be on one half an occupier's rating (*R.* v. *Barclay*, 51 L. J. M. C. 47 ; 8 Q. B. D. 486).

II. In the following cases the words now under consideration have been held to confer,

A Discretionary or Enabling Power:—

Where, by 43 G. 3, c. 59, s. 2, "it shall and may be lawful" for justices in Quarter Sessions to widen county bridges (*Re Newport Bridge*, 29 L. J. M. C. 52 ; 2 E. & E. 377) :

A Discretionary or Enabling Power:—

Where, by 1 W. 4, c. 22, s. 4, "it shall be lawful" for the Courts to order examination of witnesses before a Master within the jurisdiction or to issue commission for the examination of witnesses out of the jurisdiction (*Ducket* v. *Williams*, 9 L. J. O. S. Ex. 177 : *Castelli* v. *Groome*, 21 L. J. Q. B. 308 ; 18 Q. B. 490) :

Where by Church Discipline Act (3 & 4 V. c. 86), s. 3, "it shall be lawful" for a bishop to issue a commission to enquire as to the conduct of clerks in holy orders within his diocese (*R.* v. *Chichester*, *Bp.*, 29 L. J. Q. B. 23 ; 2 E. & E. 209 : *Julius* v. *Oxford*, *Bp.*, sup. : secus under 37 & 38 V. c. 85 ; *R.* v. *London*, *Bp.*, 58 L. J. Q. B. 385 ; 24 Q. B. D. 213) :

Where, by s. 125 (4) Bankry. Act, 1883, the Court "may" transfer an Administration Action to a Bankry. Court (*Re Baker*, *Nichols* v. *Baker*, 34 S. J. 317) :

Where, by the Attorney and Solicitors Act (6 & 7 V. c. 73), s. 37, "it shall be lawful" for the Court or judge to order the delivery up of documents in possession of a solicitor upon an application under that section for taxation of costs (*Ex p. Jarman*, 46 L. J. Ch. 485 ; 4 Ch. D. 835) :

Where, by Order 65, R. 48, R. S. C., the taxing master "may allow" Refreshers to Counsel (*Smith* v. *Wills*, 29 S. J. 684) :

Where, by Companies Clauses Act, 1845 (8 & 9 V. c. 16), s. 97, directors "may" contract on behalf of a Company by writing and under their common seal (per Turner, L.J., *Wilson* v. *West Hartlepool Ry.*, 34 L. J. Ch. 250) :

Where, by Acts obtained in 1846 and 1849, it was recited that it would be for the local and public advantage that a certain railway should be made and that "it shall be lawful" for the projecting Company to make it (per Exch. Chamber in *York. & North Mid. Ry.* v. *The Queen*, 22 L. J. Q. B. 225 ; 1 E. & B. 858, reversing the judgment of the Queen's Bench, 22 L. J. Q. B. 41 ; 1 E. & B. 178 : *Va. R.* v. *Lancashire & Yorkshire Ry.*, 1 E. & B. 228 : *R.* v. *G. W. Ry.*, 1 E. & B. 253, 874, and jdgmt. of Manisty, J., in *S. E. Ry.* v. *Ry. Commrs.*, 49 L. J. Q. B. 277 ; 5 Q. B. D. 217, reversed on appeal, 6 Q. B. D. 586) :

Where, by Com. L. Pro. Act, 1852, s. 40, "it shall be lawful" for a husband, in an action for injury to his wife, to add thereto claims in his own right (*Brockbank* v. *Whitehaven Junction Ry.*, 31 L. J. Ex. 349 ; 7 H. & N. 834) :

Where, by Com. L. Pro. Act, 1854, s. 64, a Judge, if a garnishee disputes his liability, "may" (instead of ordering execution) order that judgment creditor shall be at liberty to proceed against the garnishee by writ (*Wise* v. *Birkenshaw*, 29 L. J. Ex. 240) :

Where, by 18 & 19 V. c. 128, s. 4, a vacancy in a Burial Board "may" be filled up by the Board, in case vestry shall, for one month, neglect to supply the vacancy (*R.* v. *South Weald*, 5 B. & S. 391 ; 33 L. J. M. C. 193) :

Where, by the Sunday and Ragged Schools (Exemption from Rating)

Act, 1869 (32 & 33 V. c. 40), s. 1, the rating authority "may" exempt from rating a Sunday or Ragged School (*Bell* v. *Crane*, 42 L. J. M. C. 122; L. R. 8 Q. B. 481).

Note.—In *Castelli* v. *Groome*, sup., it was contended in argument that the words there should be construed imperative, as being governed by *R.* v. *Havering-atte-Bower*, sup., and it has since been urged that *Castelli* v. *Groome* is an inconsistent decision (Wilberforce, 202).

But in the earlier case the question was as to the right to sue at all and which right was inherent in suitors without distinction of mode; but in *Castelli* v. *Groome* the question was as to the mode of taking evidence in certain cases,—a mode by no means the usual and necessarily a costly one. It would therefore seem that *Castelli* v. *Groome* is peculiarly within the canon of *Julius* v. *Bishop of Oxford*, and like *Wise* v. *Birkenshaw*, sup., was a case in which enabling words should receive their ordinary meaning.

In *Ex p. Jarman*, and *R.* v. *South Weald*, sup., the enabling nature of the words would scarcely need adventitious aid; but in each case it was pointed out that the enabling words under discussion were found in sections which for other purposes employed imperative words.

Undetermined.

In *Davies* v. *Evans* (51 L. J. M. C. 132; 9 Q. B. D. 238), the magistrates decided that the power under 35 & 36 V. c. 65, s. 4, whereby justices "may if they see fit" commit a putative father for disobedience to a bastardy order, gave a discretion which they refused to exercise; and on appeal the Court was equally divided, Huddleston, B., holding that the power was obligatory, Grove, J., holding that it was discretionary.

It is doubtful whether "may" as used in s. 4, Removal of Wrecks Act, 1877 (40 & 41 V. c. 16), makes it obligatory on a Harbour Authority to remove wrecks that have sunk within the area of its jurisdiction. During the argument of *The Douglas*, Brett, L.J., indicated that "may" should here be read as "must," and apparently to a like effect was the judgment of Cotton, L.J. (7 P. D. 151; 51 L. J. P. D. & A. 89). But in *Dormont* v. *Furness Ry.* (52 L. J. Q. B. 331; 11 Q. B. D. 496), Kay, J., hesitated to follow the lead as indicated, rather than positively ruled, in *The Douglas*, and based his decision for the plaintiff on another ground.

V. SHALL: SHALL AND LAWFULLY MAY: *Vf.* Maxwell, 286–303: Wilberforce, 193–206.

"May," like "Shall," may denote futurity, *e.g.* a gift to the children of the members of a class "who *may die* in my lifetime," would not include children of a member of such class who was already dead at the date of the Will (*Re Hotchkiss*, 38 L. J. Ch. 631; L. R. 8 Eq. 643).

MAY BE.—Guarantee of "any balance that may be due," construed by Pollock, C. B., and Martin, B. (diss. Bramwell, B.) as referring to a future balance (*Broom* v. *Batchelor*, 25 L. J. Ex. 299 ; 1 H. & N. 255). Pollock, C. B., said,—" 'May be' is, in my judgment, clearly future. I have been unable to find direct authority in any Dictionary ; but in *Cruden's Concordance of the Bible*, from sixty to eighty references are given, and the expression 'may be' is found in various parts of the Bible, nine out of ten of which have manifestly a reference to the future, and not to the past or present, and not one is necessarily future. As far as I can bring my knowledge of the English language to bear upon the subject, 'may be' is much oftener used with reference to the future than the past or the present." On the other hand Bramwell, B., said,—" 'May be' is the present tense, and, *primâ facie*, means, 'now may be.' It is occasionally used in the future tense, no doubt, as, for instance, 'may be due to-day,' or 'may be due to-morrow. I apprehend you may use it to indicate future applications ; but in that case it must be understood as applied in the present tense. A thing 'may be black,' or 'it may be fit to eat,' or 'it may be fit to cook.' If you use the words 'may be,' without indicating the time, to my mind the expression applies to the present, or, more correctly, not to a question with reference to the future." *V.* GIVEN.

MAYOR ELECT.—*V.* OUTGOING ALDERMAN.

MEADOWS.—" If a man grant *omnia prata sua*, all his meadowes, the land itselfe of that kinde passeth" (Co. Litt. 4 b).

"In general, where meadow or pasture land is named, it must be understood of *ancient* meadow or pasture" (Woodf. 139, citing *Tresham* v. *Lamb*, 2 Brownl. & Gold. 46 : *Gunning* v. *Gunning*, Show. 354. But this deduction from the cases has been questioned, *V.* Elph. 596).

MEAN.—*V.* EXTEND TO AND INCLUDE.

MEAN OF TWO LONDON CHEMISTS.—*V. Heyworth* v. *Knight*, 33 L. J. C. P. 298 ; 17 C. B. N. S. 298.

MEAN TIME.—*V.* OF THE CLOCK : TIME.

MEANS.—A judgment-debtor was ordered to pay the debt by £5 a month ; and subsequently he received (by £5 a week) £60 as a voluntary gift from his brother. Cave, J., refused to commit, being of opinion that gifts are not " Means to pay " within s. 5, subs. 2, Debtors Act, 1869 (32 & 33 V. c. 62). The Court of Appeal upheld the decision ; but on the ground that there had been no evidence of the circumstances of the debtor other than the receipt of the £60 ; and both Cotton and Lindley, L.JJ., were of opinion that "Means" had no relation to their source (*Koster* v. *Park*, 54 L. J. Q. B. 389 ; 14 Q. B. D. 597). *Vh. Chard* v. *Jervis*, 51 L. J. Q. B. 442 ; 9 Q. B. D. 178.

"Acts, Means," &c. ; *V.* ACTS.

MEASE: MESE.—A Messuage (Spelm.; Termes de la Ley).

MEASURE.—A "Measure," within 41 & 42 V. c. 49, is a Vessel ordinarily used as a Measure;—the material of which it is made, is immaterial (*Washington* v. *Young*, 19 L. J. Ex. 348; 5 Ex. 403: *R.* v. *Aulton*, 30 L. J. M. C. 129; 3 E. & E. 568). As to selling by the "Glass;" *V. Craig* v. *McPhee*, 10 Sess. Ca. (4 Ser.) 51; 48 J. P. 115.

"Local or Customary Measure," s. 19, Ib.;—*V. Hughes* v. *Humphreys*, 23 L. J. Q. B. 356; 3 E. & B. 954: *Jones* v. *Giles*, 23 L. J. Ex. 292; 24 Ib. 259; 10 Ex. 119; 11 Ib. 393.

For the old and modern *Measures of Land; V.* Elph. 596–602.

MEASUREMENT.—*V.* Admeasurement.

Measurement of Distance; *V.* Distance.

V. Weight and Measurement.

MECHANIC.—Probably this word is synonymous with Artificer. *Va. Jackson* v. *Hill*, 13 Q. B. D. 618; 48 J. P. 488.

V. Workman.

MEDALS.—This word, in a bequest, will pass curious pieces of current coin kept by the testator with his medals (*Bridgman* v. *Dore*, 3 Atk. 202; Wms. Exs. 1205).

MEDICAL.—The meaning of the term "Medical or Surgical Assistance" in the Medical Relief Disqualification Removal Act, 1885 (48 & 49 V. c. 46), "depends upon the nature of the service rendered, and not necessarily upon the person who renders it" (per Pollock, B., *Honeybone* v. *Hambridge*, 56 L. J. Q. B. 48; 18 Q. B. D. 418; 56 L. T. 365; 35 W. R. 520; 51 J. P. 103); and it was accordingly there held that it included the attendance of a Mid-wife.

MEDICAL CORPORATION.—The Apothecaries Hall, Dublin, is a Medical Corporation within s. 3, Medical Act, 1886, 49 & 50 V. c. 48 (*A.-G. Ireland* v. *Apothecaries Hall*, 21 L. R. Ir. 253).

MEDICINE.—"Medicine dispensed by a registered person," s. 17, Pharmacy Act, 1868, 31 & 32 V. c. 121; *V. Berry* v. *Henderson*, L. R. 5 Q. B. 296; 39 L. J. M. C. 77.

V. Poison.

MEET.—*V.* Seem meet.

MEET TOGETHER.—*V.* Assemble.

MEETING.—One swallow does not make a summer, nor does the presence of one shareholder constitute a "Meeting" (*Re Sanitary Carbon Co.*, W. N. (77) 223). "The word 'Meeting' implies a concurrence, or coming face to face, of at least two persons" (per Coleridge, C. J., *Sharpe* v. *Dawes*, 46 L. J. Q. B. 104; 2 Q. B. D. 26; 25 W. R. 66: 36 L. T. 188). There is accordingly, and speaking generally, no "Meeting" of Shareholders or other bodies if only one attends; though "no doubt in a particular statute the word might be used in a special sense, so that the attendance of one might satisfy it" (per Coleridge, C. J., *Sharpe* v. *Dawes*, sup.).

"Present at the Meeting," 5 & 6 W. 4, c. 50 s. 18;—a power to determine questions by vestrymen so present, does not preclude the common law right to demand a poll (*R.* v. *How*, 33 L. J. M. C. 53: *R.* v. *D'Oyly*, 12 A. & E. 139: *R.* v. *St. Mary, Lambeth*, 8 Ib. 356; 9 L. J. M. C. 113: *White* v. *Steel*, 31 L. J. C. P. 265; 12 C. B. N. S. 383).

MEMBER.—"Life or Member;" *V.* FELONY.

"Members," s. 199, Companies Act, 1862, does not necessarily mean Shareholders (*Re South London Fish Market*, 39 Ch. D. 324; 37 W. R. 3; 59 L. T. 210).

MEMORANDUM.—*V.* NOTE.

MENIAL SERVANT.—A "Menial Servant" is a subordinate domestic servant (not always, though generally, an indoor servant) whose service brings him into close proximity to his master, and thus rendering it to the interest of both master and servant that the contract should be determinable before the end of the year of service (per Erle, C. J., *Nicoll* v. *Greaves*, 33 L. J. C. P. 261).

A Head Gardener is a menial servant (*Nowlan* v. *Ablett*, 4 L. J. Ex. 155; 2 Cr. M. & R. 54); so is a Huntsman (*Nicoll* v. *Greaves*, sup.); so is a general handy man, though partly paid by perquisites (*Johnson* v. *Blenkensopp*, 5 Jur. 870).

But a Governess is not a menial servant (*Todd* v. *Kerrich* or *Kellage*, 8 Ex. 151; 22 L. J. Ex. 1); nor is a Housekeeper of a large hotel (*Lawler* v. *Linden*, Ir. Rep. 10 C. L. 188).

In *Lawler* v. *Linden*, sup., Lawson, J., said,—"We have had an interesting disquisition as to the derivation of the word 'mœnia,' and it has received a Saxon, a Latin, and a Greek origin. If I were to offer an opinion I should say that the word 'mœnia' has nothing to do with it. Johnson derives it from the Saxon word *meiny*, which occurs in Chaucer and Shakespeare." *Vth.* Eversley on Domestic Relations, 910 n. (*a*).

V. SERVANT.

MERCHANDIZE.—*V.* GOODS, WARES AND MERCHANDIZES: STONE.

"Other legal Merchandize," in a Charter-party; *V. Cockburn* v. *Alexander*, 18 L. J. C. P. 74: *Vf. Warren* v. *Peabody*, 19 L. J. C. P. 46; 8 C. B. 800.

"Merchandize in trust or on commission for which the assured are responsible," in a Fire Policy; *V. North British and Mer. Insrce* v. *Moffatt*, L. R. 7 C. P. 25; 41 L. J. C. P. 1.

MERCHANT.—A merchant of, or in, an article, is one who buys and sells it. A manufacturer who confines himself to selling his own manufactures is not a "Merchant" (*Josselyn* v. *Parson*, 41 L. J. Ex. 60; L. R. 7 Ex. 127). In that case Bramwell, B., said that even where a man sells goods not of his own manufacture but sells only one class of those goods, he is not a Merchant. He said, "I think a Porter Merchant is a man who deals in all or many sorts of porter, not one only." The decision in the case was that a man travelling for a Brewer did not offend against a bond whereby he was prohibited from travelling "for any Porter, Ale or Spirit Merchant."

MERCHANTS' ACCOUNTS.—The exception in the Statute of Limitations, 21 Jac. 1, c. 16, s. 3, relating to Merchants' Accounts, applies only to the Action of Account, or, *semble*, to an action for not accounting. It does not apply to an action for the several items of which the account is composed, or for the general balance (*Inglis* v. *Haigh*, 10 L. J. Ex. 406; 8 M. & W. 769).

MERCHANT'S RISK.—Goods carried "at Merchant's Risk" and properly jettisoned, give rise to a claim by the charterers for a general average contribution (*Burton* v. *English*, 53 L. J. Q. B. 133; 12 Q. B. D. 218).

MERE ACCOUNT.—*V.* ACCOUNT.

MERELY CHARITABLE.—*V.* PURPOSE.

MESIUL: MESUIL.—*V.* HAGA.

MESNE.—*V.* Termes de la Ley.

MESSUAGE.—This word is synonymous with (Co. Litt. 5 b; Touch. 94; per Bullen, J., *Scholes* v. *Hargreaves*, 5 T. R. 46), or, at least, as comprehensive as HOUSE.

"The distinction suggested in the early cases between *Messuage* and *House* in regard to the greater comprehensiveness of the former is not to be relied on; and it is clear that even the word 'Messuage' would not now be held to carry land beyond a homestead or orchard, though contiguous to or enjoyed with it" (1 Jarm. 779). It may, however, be added that where under special circumstances, the word "House" would carry land or buildings beyond its own ambit, a like result would follow if the word "Messuage" were employed. *Vf.* 1 Jarm. 778, 779; Elph. 602: *Hibon* v. *Hibon*, 32 L. J. Ch. 374; 8 L. T. 195; 11 W. R. 455.

A Mill will pass by the name of a Messuage (*Hill* v. *Grange*, 1 Plowd. 170 a).

" All that my Messuage," being partly freehold and partly leasehold, and of which leasehold part testator afterwards acquired the fee,—passed the fee of the entirety (*Miles* v. *Miles*, L. R. 1 Eq. 462 ; 35 L. J. Ch. 315 ; 14 W. R. 272 ; 13 L. T. 697).

METAL.—"The word 'Metals' taken in its ordinary sense does not include the precious metals,"—*i.e.* gold or silver (per Parke, J., *Casher* v. *Holmes*, 2 B. & Ad. 597).

"'Metal' is a word of less extensive meaning than 'Mineral.' All Metals are Minerals ; but all Minerals are not Metals" (MacS. 18) ; and the same learned author proceeds to adopt the definition in Johnson's Dictionary as follows ;—" We understand by the term 'Metal' a firm, heavy and hard substance, opake, fusible by fire, and concreting again when cold into a solid body such as it was before, which is malleable under the hammer and is of a bright glossy and glittering substance where newly cut or broken."

METROPOLIS.—By the Metrop. Man. Act, 1855 (18 & 19 V. c. 120), s. 250, the "Metropolis," for the purposes of that Act, is defined as,

The City of London :—

and the parishes and places mentioned in Schedules A., B. and C. to that Act,—as follows,—

Schedule A.

The Parishes of St. Marylebone, St. Pancras, Lambeth, St. George Hanover Square, Islington St. Mary, Shoreditch St. Leonard :

The Parishes of Paddington, St. Matthew Bethnal Green, St. Mary Newington, Camberwell, St. James Westminster, St. James and St. John Clerkenwell, Chelsea, Kensington St. Mary Abbott, St. Luke Middlesex, St. George the Martyr Southwark, Bermondsey, St. George in the East, St. Martin in the Fields, Hamlet of Mile End Old Town, Woolwich, Rotherhithe, St. John Hampstead.

Schedule B.

Whitechapel District,—The Parishes of St. Mary Whitechapel, Christchurch Spitalfields, St. Botolph without Aldgate Middlesex, and Holy Trinity Minories, The Precinct of St. Katherine, Hamlet of Mile End New Town, Liberty of Norton Folgate, Old Artillery Ground, District of Tower :

Westminster District,—The Parishes of St. Margaret, St. John the Evangelist :

Greenwich District,—The Parishes of St. Paul Deptford including Hatcham, St. Nicholas Deptford, Greenwich :

Wandsworth District,—The Parishes of Clapham, Tooting Graveney, Streatham, St. Mary Battersea (excluding Penge), Wandsworth, Putney including Roehampton :

Hackney District,—The Parishes of Hackney, St. Mary Stoke Newington :

St. Giles District,—The Parishes of St. Giles in the Fields, St. George Bloomsbury :

Holborn District,—The Parishes of St. Andrew Holborn above Bars, St. George the Martyr and St. Sepulchre Middlesex,—Saffron Hill, Hatton Garden, Ely Rents and Ely Place, The Liberty of Glasshouse Yard :

Strand District,—The Parishes of St. Anne Soho, St. Paul Covent Garden, St. John the Baptist Savoy (or Precinct of the Savoy), St. Mary-le-Strand, and St. Clement Danes, The Liberty of the Rolls :

Fulham District,—The Parishes of St. Peter and St. Paul Hammersmith, Fulham :

Limehouse District,—The Parishes of St. Anne Limehouse, St. John Wapping, and St. Paul Shadwell, The Hamlet of Ratcliffe :

Poplar District,—The Parishes of All Saints Poplar, St. Mary Stratford-le-Bow, St. Leonard Bromley :

St. Saviour's District,—The Parishes of Christchurch, St. Saviour (including the Liberty of the Clink) :

Plumstead District,—The Parishes of Charlton next Woolwich, Plumstead, Eltham, Lee, Kidbrooke :

Lewisham District,—The Parishes of Lewisham including Sydenham Chapelry, and the Hamlet of Penge :

Rotherhithe and St. Olave District,—The Parishes of Rotherhithe, St. Olave, St. Thomas Southwark, St. John Horsleydown.

Schedule C.

The Close of the Collegiate Church of St. Peter :
The Charter House :
Inner Temple :
Middle Temple :
Lincoln's Inn :
Gray's Inn :
Staple Inn :
Furnival's Inn.

And any Parish adjoining, containing not less than 750 rated inhabitants, to which the Act may be extended by Order in Council (s. 249).

The foregoing definition is adopted for the purposes of the following Statutes :—

The Metropolis *Management* Amendment Act, 1862 (25 & 26 V. c. 102, s. 112) ;

The Metropolitan *Building* Act, 1855 (18 & 19 V. c. 122, s. 4) ;

The Metropolis *Gas* Act, 1860 (23 & 24 V. c. 125, s. 4) ;

The Metropolis *Water* Act, 1871 (34 & 35 V. c. 113, s. 3 : for the definition in the previous Metropolitan Water Act see 15 & 16 V. c. 84, s. 29) ;

The Metropolitan *Fire Brigade* Act, 1865 (28 & 29 V. c. 90, s. 2);

The *Slaughter Houses, &c.* (Metropolis), Act, 1874 (37 & 38 V. c. 67, s. 12);

The Highways and Locomotives (Amendment) Act, 1878 (41 & 42 V. c. 77, s. 38); and

The Local Government Act, 1888 (51 & 52 V. c. 41, s. 100).

For the purposes of the Metropolitan *Open Spaces* Act, 1877 (40 & 41 V. c. 35, s. 6), the "Metropolis" means all parishes and places mentioned in Schedules A., B., and C. to the Metrop. Man. Act, 1855. (Observe,—This does not include the City of London and any parish annexed to the Metropolitan Board of Works by Order in Council).

The Artizans and Labourers Dwellings Act (31 & 32 V. c. 130, s. 3), provides that the "Metropolis," for its purposes, shall not include the City of London or the Liberties thereof, but shall include all other Parishes or Places within the jurisdiction of the Metropolitan Board of Works: and that definition is adopted for the purposes of The Artizans and Labourers Dwellings Improvement Act, 1875 (38 & 39 V. c. 36, s. 31).

The Infant Life Protection Act, 1872 (35 & 36 V. c. 38, 1st Sch.), provides that, for the purposes of that Act, the "Metropolis" shall include all Parishes and Places in which the Metropolitan Board of Works have power to levy a Main Drainage Rate, exclusive of the City of London and the Liberties thereof.

The Metropolitan *Interments* Act, 1852 (15 & 16 V. c. 85, s. 53 and Schedule), contains a special definition of "Metropolis" for the purposes of that Act.

V. LONDON.

METROPOLITAN POLICE DISTRICT.—*V.* definition, 10 G. 4, c. 44, s. 4 and Sch.; 2 & 3 V. c. 47, s. 2; and 24 & 25 V. c. 42, s. 3.

MICHAELMAS.—When "Michaelmas" or "the Feast of St. Michael" is mentioned as a date, it means New Michaelmas, 29th September; not 11th October according to the Old Style (*Doe* d. *Spicer* v. *Lea,* 11 East, 312). So "Martinmas" means the 11th November, not the 23rd (*Smith* v. *Walton,* 1 L. J. C P. 85; 8 Bing. 235; 1 Moo. & Sc. 380). So "Lady Day" means the 25th March, not the 6th April (*Doe* d. *Hall* v. *Benson,* 4 B. & Ald. 588). So, of course, "Christmas Day" means the 25th December, not the 6th January.

The two firstly cited cases show that in a Deed or a Pleading parol evidence was not admissible to show that the date by the Old Style was meant; but that rule was otherwise on an agreement by parol (*Doe* d. *Hall* v. *Benson,* sup.).

The Act (on which the above decisions proceeded) for regulating the commencement of the Year and rectifying the Julian Calendar (24 G. 2, c. 23), takes operation from the 1st January, 1752; so that in documents prior to that date the Feast dates above referred to would be construed according to the Old Style.

MILITARY SERVICE.—A vessel despatched to furnish and lay for the French Government a telegraphic cable along the French coast between Cherbourg and Verdun, and which cable, though valuable to such Government in a military sense, was chiefly intended for commercial purposes and not to subserve the military service of France, was held not to have been despatched to be employed "in the *Military or Naval Service*" of France within s. 8, Foreign Enlistment Act, 1870, 33 & 34 V. c. 90 (*The International,* 40 L. J. Adm. 1; L. R. 3 A. & E. 321). *Cp.* NAVAL SERVICE.

V. ACTUAL MILITARY SERVICE.

MILITES REGIS.—*V.* TAINI.

MILK.—"Milk, commercially speaking, means skimmed milk" (per Mathew, J., *Lane* v. *Collins,* 54 L. J. M. C. 76; 14 Q. B. D. 193). It was accordingly held in that case that the sale of milk which had been deprived of 60 per cent. of its butter fat was not an offence within s. 6, Sale of Food and Drugs Act, 1875 (38 & 39 V. c. 63); but selling skimmed milk as "milk," is an offence under s. 9 of that Act (*Pain* v. *Boughtwood,* 24 Q. B. D. 353; 59 L. J. M. C. 45; 54 J. P. 68; 34 S. J. 214: *Vf.* KNOWINGLY). *V.* NATURE.

MILL.—"By the grant of a Mill, the millstone doth pass, albeit at the time of the grant it be actually severed from the mill" (Touch. 90: *Vf. Place* v. *Fagg,* 4 M. & Ry. 277).

Looms, standing upon a loom-foot and removable at pleasure, do not "belong" to a mill, within a contract for its sale "with all machinery, &c., belonging to the said Mill" (*Hutchinson* v. *Kay,* 26 L. J. Ch. 457; 23 Bea. 413). *Vf. Burt* v. *Haslett,* 25 L. J. C. P. 201; 18 C. B. 162: *Cosby* v. *Shaw,* 23 L. R. Ir. 181: BELONGING.

MILL DAM.—*V.* FISHING MILL DAM.

MINE: MINES: MINERALS.—"The primary meaning of the word '*Mine,*' standing alone, is an underground excavation made for the purpose of getting minerals (*Bell* v. *Wilson,* 35 L. J. Ch. 337; 1 Ch. 303; 14 L. T. 115; 14 W. R. 493: *Vf. Listowel* v. *Gibbings,* 9 Ir. C. L. Rep. 223). In Leases and similar documents it is commonly used in a slightly different sense. For instance, 'all that mine, vein or seam of coal,'—&c. There the word includes the stratum of the minerals as well as the excavation made to win it. '*Minerals,*' on the other hand, means primarily all substances,—other than (*and underneath*) the agricultural surface of the ground,—which may be got for manufacturing or mercantile purposes, whether from a mine, as the word would seem to signify; or such as stone or clay, which are got by open working as decided in *Mid. Ry.* v. *Checkley* (36 L. J. Ch. 380; L. R. 4 Eq. 19; 15 W. R. 671; 16 L. T. 260), and

Rosse v. *Wainman* (15 L. J. Ex. 67; 14 M. & W. 859). The particular signification of each of these words may be varied largely by the context" (per Kay, J., *Mid. Ry.* v. *Haunchwood Co.,* 51 L. J. Ch. 778; 20 Ch. D. 552; 46 L. T. 301; 30 W. R. 640: approved in *Mid. Ry.* v. *Robinson,* 57 L. J. Ch. 441; affd. in H. L. 6 Times Rep. 100); or indeed by the kind of document in which they are found (*Menzies* v. *Breadalbane,* 1 Shaw, App. 225: *Glasgow* v. *Farie,* 58 L. J. P. C. 33; 13 App. Ca. 657; 37 W. R. 627; 60 L. T. 274, and especially jdgmt. of Halsbury, L. C., in the latter case).

The words "and underneath" italicised in the above definition by Mr. Justice Kay are not to be found in the extract just given, and are added, with submission, in order to complete the primary meaning of the word "Minerals." Thus in *Hext* v. *Gill* (41 L. J. Ch. 761; 7 Ch. 699; 26 L. T. 502; 27 Ib. 291; 20 W. R. 959), Mellish, L. J., said the word "'Minerals' includes every substance which can be got from *underneath* the surface of the earth for the purpose of profit." (The *ipsissima verba* of that definition were adopted by Fry, J., in *A.-G.* v. *Tomline,* 46 L. J. Ch. 657). And so in *Tucker* v. *Linger* (52 L. J. Ch. 941; 8 App. Ca. 508; 32 W. R. 40), Ld. Blackburn said it was "by no means clear" that Flints in a flinty district, that were turned up by ploughing and lying on the surface, would be "Minerals" within a reservation in a Lease: and qy., is an Ancient Boat,—for centuries embedded in the soil several feet below the surface but not fossilised or petrified,—a "Mineral" within a like reservation?—Chitty, J., was of opinion that it was not (*Elwes* v. *Brigg Gas Co.,* 55 L. J. Ch. 734; 33 Ch. D. 562).

"Minerals" is by far a more general word than "Mines" (per Mellish L. J., in *Hext* v. *Gill,* sup.); in which case, however, the same learned judge said that "Mines" may possibly extend to open workings or even not apply to workings at all. But in *Darvill* v. *Roper* (24 L. J. Ch. 779; 3 Drew. 294; 3 W. R. 467; 25 L. T. O. S. 302), Kindersley, V.-C., said, "Mining, is when you begin on the surface, and, by sinking shafts, you work underground in a horizontal direction, making a tunnel as you proceed, and leaving a roof overhead." But "putting the word 'Mines' before 'Minerals,'—as in the ordinary phrase 'Mines and Minerals,'—does not alter the more extended meaning of the word 'Minerals'" (per Mellish, L. J., *Hext* v. *Gill,* sup.; *Va. Mid. Ry. Co.* v. *Haunchwood Co.,* sup.: jdgmt. Ld. Macnaghten in *Glasgow* v. *Farie,* sup.). *Vf.* hereon MacS. 1–19, and Ib. 15–17 for a discussion of the cases in which the *primâ facie* meaning of "Mines and Minerals" has been restricted by the context.

In s. 78, Ry. C. C. Act, 1845, "Mines" ought to receive the widest possible construction short of straining the language; the word there is not confined to minerals got by underground workings (*Mid. Ry.* v. *Robinson,* 37 Ch. D. 386; 57 L. J. Ch. 441; affd. in H. L., 15 App. Ca. 19; 6 Times Rep. 100).

The following have been held to be "Minerals:"—

Brick Clay, in a Reservation by deed (*Jersey* v. *Neath,* 22 Q. B. D.

555; 58 L. J. Q. B. 573), or under s. 77, Ry. C. C. Act, 1845, and whether got underground or by open workings (*Mid. Ry.* v. *Haunchwood Co.*, sup.: *Loosemore* v. *Tiverton and North Devon Ry.*, 51 L. J. Ch. 570; 22 Ch. D. 25; 30 W. R. 628; 47 L. T. 151: *Mid. Ry.* v. *Miles*, 55 L. J. Ch. 745; 33 Ch. D. 632; 55 L. T. 428; 35 W. R. 76: *Dixon* v. *Cal. Ry.*, 5 App. Ca. 820; 43 L. T. 513; 29 W. R. 249). *Cp. Glasgow* v. *Farie* and *Church* v. *Inclosure Commrs.*, inf.:

China Clay (*Hext* v. *Gill*, sup.):

Coal and Ironstone (*Bell* v. *Wilson*, sup.: *Mid. Ry.* v. *Robinson*, sup.):

Coprolites (*A.-G.* v. *Tomline*, 46 L. J. Ch. 654; 5 Ch. D. 750):

Freestone and Limestone got by open workings, as within s. 77, Ry. C. C. Act (*Dixon* v. *Cal. Ry.*, sup.: *Sv. Menzies* v. *Breadalbane*, inf.: *Listowel* v. *Gibbings*, inf.):

Granite (*A.-G.* v. *Welsh Granite Co.*, 1 Times Rep. 549).

Stone got by quarrying (*Mid. Ry.* v. *Checkley*, sup.: *Bell* v. *Wilson*, sup.: *Rosse* v. *Wainman*, sup.: *Micklethwait* v. *Winter*, 20 L. J. Ex. 313; 6 Ex. 644; 17 L. T. O. S. 185):

Vf. MacS. 12, where it is said, on the authority chiefly of the above cases, that "Minerals" include "every kind of Stone, Flint, Marble, Slate, Brick Earth, Chalk, Gravel and Sand; provided only that these articles are under the surface and do not lie loosely upon it." *Va.* Seton, 1652.

The following have been held *not* to be Minerals:—

Boat, ancient and embedded, but unpetrified (*Elwes* v. *Brigg Gas Co.*, sup.):

Brine formed by the percolation of rain-water through rock salt, *quà* subs. 3, s. 4, Settled Estates Act, 1877, 40 & 41 V. c. 18 (*Re Dudley*, 26 S. J. 359):

Clay and Sand, under the Act of Settlement (1703) of the Isle of Man whereby tenants were confirmed in their customary estates, "saving always all mines and minerals of what kind and nature soever, quarries and delfs of flag, slate or stone" (*A.-G.* v. *Mylchreest*, 48 L. J. P. C. 36; 4 App. Ca. 294; 40 L. T. 764). (In that case the Court said,—"The words 'quarries and delfs of flag, slate or stone' appear to be used to describe open workings and the specified substances got by such workings, as distinguished from mines properly so called, and mineral substances usually got by underground works"):

Clay Subsoil, *quà* s. 18, Waterworks Clauses Act, 1847 (10 V. c. 17), as incorporated in a Scotch Act (*Glasgow* v. *Farie*, 13 App. Ca. 657; 37 W. R. 627; 60 L. T. 274; 58 L. J. P. C. 33: *Va. Church* v. *Inclosure Commrs.*, 31 L. J. C. P. 201; 11 C. B. N. S. 664. *Cp. Hext* v. *Gill* and *Mid. Ry.* v. *Haunchwood Co.*, sup.):

Freestone Quarry, in a reservation in a Feu in Scotland (*Menzies* v. *Breadalbane*, 1 Shaw, App. 225: *Sv. Dixon* v. *Cal. Ry.*, sup.):

Limestone, in Ireland (*Listowel* v. *Gibbings*, 9 Ir. C. L. Rep. 223).

In view of the doctrine that "*Coal Mines*" in 43 Eliz. c. 2, was confined to mines of coal so that mines of other minerals were not thereunder rateable to the Poor Rate (*Leadsmelting Co.* v. *Richardson*, 3 Burr. 1341; 1 W. Bla. 389; 1 Bott. 159: *Morgan* v. *Crawshay*, 40 L. J. M. C. 202; L. R. 5 H. L. 304), it was held that Stone Quarries or Lime Works (*R.* v. *Alberbury*, 1 East, 534; 1 Bott. 210), Slate Works (*R.* v. *Woodland*, 2 East, 164; 1 Bott. 212), and a potter's Clay pit (*R.* v. *Brown*, 8 East, 528), were not mines at all, but only gave additional value to the rateable land wherein they were; unless, indeed, the material was obtained by underground mining works (*R.* v. *Sedgley*, 2 B. & Ad. 65; 9 L. J. O. S. M. C. 61: *R.* v. *Brettell*, 3 B. & Ad. 424; 1 L. J. M. C. 46: *R.* v. *Dunsford*, 2 A. & E. 568; 4 L. J. M. C. 59). In the last case Denman, C. J., said,—"The principle established is, that the *mode* of obtaining the material, and not the nature of the material itself, is to be considered in order to come to a decision whether it constitutes a Mine or not." *Vf.* jdgmt. of Ld. Watson in *Glasgow* v. *Farie* (sup.).

For the purpose of the Settled Land Act, 1882 (45 & 46 V. c. 38), "Mines and Minerals, mean Mines and Minerals whether already opened or in work or not, and include all minerals and substances in, on or under the land obtainable by under-ground or by surface working" (s. 2, subs. 10, iv.).

Note.—Where in a conveyance there was a reservation to the vendor of mines and minerals, "with full liberty to search for, dig, bore, sink, win, work, lead and carry away the same," it was held that the working must be by under-ground mining and not from the surface (*Bell* v. *Wilson*, sup.). *Va.* *Proud* v. *Bates*, 34 L. J. Ch. 406; 12 L. T. 565.

Note further.—Gold and Silver Mines are part of the prerogative of the Crown (*Mines Case*, 1 Plow. 336, 336 a: *A.-G. British Columbia* v. *A.-G. Canada*, 58 L. J. P. C. 91; 14 App. Ca. 295).

V. With all Mines.

MINE OR PART OF A MINE.—*V.* Part.

MINER.—*V.* Practical Working Miner.

MINERAL GOTTEN.—"Mineral contracted to be gotten," s. 17, 35 & 36 V. c. 76, includes Slack as well as Large Coal (*Netherseal Co.* v. *Bourne*, 59 L. J. Q. B. 66).

MINERAL PROPERTY.—"All erections made upon or affixed to the solum of the surface land, in virtue of the powers conferred upon the miner by the 5th Custom in the Act, constitute 'Mineral Property' as defined in s. 2, 14 & 15 V. c. xciv" (per Ld. Watson, *Wake* v. *Hall*, 52 L. J. Q. B. 500; 8 App. Ca. 207; 31 W. R. 585; 48 L. T. 834; *Va.* per Ld. Fitzgerald, S. C.).

MINISTER.—A Bishop is included in the word "Minister," as used in the Rubrics relating to the celebration of the Holy Communion (*Read* v. *Bishop of Lincoln*, 14 P. D. 148).

"The word 'Minister' is general, and may apply to any person who has the cure of souls in the district" (per Blackburn, J., *R.* v. *Allen*, 42 L. J. Q. B. 37 ; L. R. 8 Q. B. 69) ; which case decides that a Perpetual Curate, as well as a Rector or Vicar, is a "Minister" entitled to appoint a churchwarden within the meaning of a custom founded on the 89th of the Canons of 1603.

"Minister," in s. 68, 5 & 6 W. 4, c. 76, is "used in its most general signification" (per Littledale, J., *R.* v. *Liverpool*, 7 L. J. Q. B. 134 ; 8 A. & E. 176 ; 3 N. & P. 280) ; and it was there held that a Lecturer in Holy Orders at St. John's, Liverpool, who occasionally assisted its regular Incumbent in the services, though not "*the* Minister" of the Church, was yet *a* "Minister" of it, within the section.

V. INCUMBENT : REGULAR CLERGYMAN : REGULAR MINISTER.

MINORITY.—A gift of income "during Minority" may, on a context, mean until the beneficiaries attain some other age than 21, if such other age be clearly indicated (*Milroy* v. *Milroy*, 13 L. J. Ch. 266 ; 14 Sim. 48 ; 1 Jarm. 845). *Vf. Weddell* v. *Munday*, 6 Ves. 341 : *Hart* v. *Tulk*, 2 D. G. M. & G. 300

As to accumulations during "Minority ;" *V.* 1 Jarm. 304.

MISAPPLICATION.—"Misapplication" of public funds, s. 44, 7 W. 4 & 1 V. c. 78, only covers cases of corrupt practices or of shewing illegal favour (*R.* v. *Norwich*, 30 W. R. 752).

"Wilfully waste or misapply ;" *V.* WILFUL WASTE.

MISAPPROPRIATE.—"Misappropriate," means the wrongful conversion of or dealing with anything, by the person to whom it has been intrusted (*Vh.* Steph. Cr. 275–278, summarising and stating 24 & 25 V. c. 96, ss. 75–80).

MISBEHAVIOUR.—"Misbehaviour in his Office," s. 6, 23 & 24 V. c. 116 ; *V. Re Ward*, 30 L. J. Ch. 775. *Cp.* MISDEMEAN.

MISCONDUCT.—*V.* CONDUCT : CONDUCE : MISFORTUNE : WILFUL MISCONDUCT.

MISDEMEAN.—"Misdemean himself in his Office," s. 6, 1 W. & M. c. 21 ; *V. Wildes* v. *Russell*, L. R. 1 C. P. 722 ; 35 L. J. M. C. 241 ; H. & R. 689. *Cp.* MISBEHAVIOUR.

MISDEMEANOUR.—The absolute refusal of a Bankrupt's Discharge when "the Debtor has committed *any* Misdemeanour under Part 2 of the Debtors Act, 1869" (s. 2 (3), 50 & 51 V. c. 66), is restricted to any such Misdemeanour as may be committed "in any matter connected with, or arising out of the bankruptcy ;" the words quoted are to be read into the provision (*Re Brocklebank*, 58 L. J. Q. B. 375).

"Misdemeanour," as respects Scotland ; *V.* s. 28, Interp. Act, 1889.

MISFEASANCE.—This word, in s. 165, Companies Act, 1862 (25 & 26 V. c. 89), means "'Misfeasance in the nature of a Breach of Trust:' it must be an act resulting in loss to the Company. The section does not give the Court power to fine a Director for misconduct. It gives no new rights, but simply provides a summary mode of enforcing rights which must otherwise have been enforced by action" (Buckl. 378 *et seq.*).

MISFORTUNE.—A thing caused by "Misfortune," is where it arises through something unforeseen which cannot ordinarily be guarded against (*Re Burgess*, 57 L. T. 200; 35 W. R. 702; *Vf.* CONDUCT).

Bankruptcy "caused by Misfortune without any Misconduct," s. 32 (2 b), Bankruptcy Act, 1883; *V. Re Campbell*, 20 Q. B. D. 816; 59 L. T. 194; 36 W. R. 582.

"Misfortune," in a plea that the plaintiff contributed to the "Misfortune" complained of, is not ambiguous (*Smith* v. *McAuley*, Ir. Rep. 8 C. L. 525).

MISMANAGEMENT.—"'Mismanagement' and 'Inattention' are not synonymous. The one is active, the other passive; the one denotes commission, the other omission" (per Vaughan, B., *Brooks* v. *Blanshard*, 2 L. J. Ex. 281; 1 C. & M. 779; 3 Tyr. 844).

MISPRISION.—Misprision of *Felony*;—"Everyone who knows that any other person has committed Felony and conceals or procures the concealment thereof, is guilty of Misprision of Felony" (Steph. Cr. 104, 105). *Vf.* Rosc. Cr. 420.

Misprision of *Treason*;—"Every one who knows that any other person has committed High Treason, and does not within a reasonable time give information thereof to a Judge of Assize, or a Justice of the Peace, is guilty of Misprision of Treason" (Steph. Cr. 104).

Vh. Termes de la Ley, *Misprision.*

MISSING SHIP.—*V. Stribley* v. *Imperial Mar. Insrce.*, 45 L. J. Q. B. 396; 1 Q. B. D. 507.

MISSIONARY PURPOSES.—A trust for "Missionary Purposes," is void for vagueness (*Scott* v. *Brownrigg*, 9 L. R. Ir. 246).

MISTAKE.—Mistake of Fact; *V. Withington* v. *Herring*, 5 Bing. 442.

V. BONÂ FIDE.

MIS-STATEMENT.—*V.* ERROR.

MIXTURE.—*V.* PROPER MIXTURE.

MODERATE SPEED.—"Moderate Speed" in Art. 13, Regulations for Preventing Collisions at Sea, is a relative term, depending upon the circumstances: it means that a Vessel is to reduce her speed so far as she can, consistently with keeping steerage way (*The Zadok*, 9 P. D. 114; 53 L. J. P. D. & A. 72); and a sailing ship going in a dense fog is not to go at a greater speed than is enough to keep her under control (*The Beta*, 9 P. D. 134).

MODERATE TERMS.—An agreement to sell goods on "Moderate Terms" satisfies the Statute of Frauds *quà* price (*Aschcroft* v. *Morrin*, 4 M. & G. 450).

MOIETY.—"Although the proper meaning of 'Moiety' is a *half* part, it is here, in my opinion, used by the testator, who seems to have been an ill-educated person, in the sense of an *equal* part or share. I am not aware of any judicial opinion having been expressed on the meaning of this or a similar word; in the Imperial Dictionary, I find one of its meanings given as, a part or share as distinguished from a half part" (per Chatterton, V.-C., *Morrow* v. *M'Conville*, 11 L. R. Ir. 252). In that case the testator had made provision for three separate moieties, adding "the several moieties to be arranged by the executors."

A devise of "My Moiety," even before 1 V. c. 26, would generally pass the fee (2 Jarm. 285).

MOLEST: MOLESTATION.—"Molestation," in contravention of a covenant in a Separation Deed, is an act done by the person contracting (or contracted for), or her or his authorised agent. It must be an act the natural tendency of which is to injure or annoy the covenantee. The mere adultery of a wife, even though she have a bastard child, is not a "Molestation" by her of her husband. But adultery might be done under such circumstances of aggravation towards the covenantee as would amount to Molestation; *e.g.*, if a wife caused her bastard child to be called by her husband's name, or by one of his titles, and (especially) if she held out that such child was her husband's son and heir, that would amount to "Molestation" of the husband (*Fearon* v. *Aylesford*, 53 L. J. Q. B. 410; 54 Ib. 33; 12 Q. B. D. 539; 14 Ib. 792).

A suit for Judicial Separation is not a breach of a covenant not to "Molest or Disturb" (*Thomas* v. *Everard*, 30 L. J. Ex. 214; 6 H. & N. 448).

Picketing,—*i.e.* besetting workmen not in a strike,—with a view to prevent them from working; held "Molestation" under s. 1 (3), 34 & 35 V. c. 32, repealed (*R.* v. *Druitt*, 16 L. T. 855). So a threat by workmen to combine to strike as against other workmen was a "Molestation" within s. 3, 6 G. 4, c. 129 (*Walsby* v. *Anley*, 30 L. J. M. C. 121). *Vth.* 22 V. c. 34: *Va.* THREAT.

As to an agreement with a tenant "not to molest, disturb or raise the rent;" *V.* Woodf. 90, 91, citing *Kusel* v. *Watson*, 11 Ch. 129; 48 L. J. Ch.

413; 27 W. R. 714: *Wood* v. *Davis,* 6 L. R. Ir. 50: *Roberts* v. *Tregaskis,* 38 L. T. 176.

MONEY, COSTS, CHARGES AND EXPENSES.—"When the legislature mentions 'Money, Costs, Charges and Expenses' (s. 18, 1 & 2 V. c. 110), it means money decreed or ordered to be paid, together with the costs, charges and expenses to be ascertained in the usual way by the officers of the Court. It is unnecessary to decide the further point; but I am of opinion, that, with respect to costs, it is enough if they are ascertained by the officer of the Court, and that it is not necessary that there should be any order to pay after they are taxed" (per Parke, B., *Jones* v. *Williams,* 10 L. J. Ex. 257; 8 M. & W. 349).

V. Costs and Charges.

MONEY: MONEYS.—The natural meaning of a gift of "Money" or "Moneys," as established by the authorities and when unaffected by a context, is that it will only include, "Cash in the house and at bankers and any other money belonging to the testator at law. Any sums actually due and really payable,—sums in fact which he had a right to receive on demanding them,—would pass; but income not payable until a future time would not pass. Arrears due under a Settlement would therefore pass, but the apportioned parts of current dividends would not pass" (per Selborne, L.C., *Byrom* v. *Brandreth,* 42 L. J. Ch. 826; L. R. 16 Eq. 475).

According to this definition "the term Moneys" is equivalent to "Ready Money at Call" (per Pearson, J., *Re Townley,* 53 L. J. Ch. 518).

But in *Williams* v. *Williams* (47 L. J. Ch. 857; 8 Ch. D. 789), Baggallay, L. J., cited with approval a dictum of Wood, V.-C., in *Langdale* v. *Whitfield* (27 L. J. Ch. 795; 4 K. & J. 426), that *primâ facie* a bequest of "Moneys" "will be confined to Ready Money actually in Hand." *Vf. Dunally* v. *Dunally,* 6 Ir. Ch. Rep. 540: *Dillon* v. *McDonnell,* 7 L. R. Ir. 335: Cash: Money Due.

The meaning of the word "Money" in a Will, will, however, generally depend upon the context—if there is any that can explain it—and upon the surrounding circumstances (per Kay, J., *Re Cadogan,* 53 L. J. Ch. 209; 25 Ch. D. 154; 32 W. R. 57; cited Possessed of). But from the observations of the learned judge in that case it would seem that there is no middle course between holding "Money" to its natural sense, and construing it as meaning "the Personal Estate." And it would seem to follow that if the word is employed so that it could not be considered as having so wide a meaning as "Personal Estate," then it must be restricted to its natural sense. *Sv. Re Townley,* 53 L. J. Ch. 516.

When "Money" is bequeathed charged with debts or funeral expenses, that affords "a strong inference that the testator considered himself as disposing of that property which by law was subject to those charges," namely his personal estate or (as the case may be) his residuary personal estate (per Leach, M. R., *Kendall* v. *Kendall,* 4 Russ. 371; a doctrine adopted by Langdale, M. R., in *Rogers* v. *Thomas*, 2 Keen, 13: *Va. Williams* v. *Williams*, *Re Cadogan*, sup., and *Re White*, 51 L. J. P. D. & A. 40; 7 P. D. 65).

On the other hand if a bequest of "Money" is *followed* by other legacies, whether pecuniary or specific, then "Money" will generally be restricted to the natural meaning of the word (*Lowe* v. *Thomas*, 23 L. J. Ch. 453, 616; 5 D. G. M. & G. 315: *Byrom* v. *Brandreth*, sup.: *Re Cadogan*, sup.).

The use of the word "Moneys" (in the plural) *e.g.* "*all* my moneys,"—is a circumstance, though it is submitted a slight one, favouring the larger interpretation (*Re Townley*, 53 L. J. Ch. 516).

Besides the cases already cited on this word, *V. Dowson* v. *Gaskoin*, 2 Keen, 18; 6 L. J. Ch. 295: *Stratton* v. *Hillas*, 2 Dr. & War. 51: *Waite* v. *Combes*, 5 D. G. & S. 676; 21 L. J. Ch. 814, in which it was held that "Money" included the undisposed-of personal estate: and *Va. Larner* v. *Larner*, 26 L. J. Ch. 668; 3 Drew. 704: *Collins* v. *Collins*, L. R. 12 Eq. 455, in which the word was confined to its literal and natural meaning.

Vf. PRINCIPAL MONEY: RESIDUE: 1 Jarm. 768 n. (*e*): Wms. Exs. 1194: Watson, Eq. 1324, 1325: Chitty, Eq. Ind. 7819-7825, 7854.

As to the phrase "*Money Due*," *V. Stephenson* v. *Dowson*, 10 L. J. Ch. 93; 3 Bea. 342: and consider how that case is affected by s. 24, 1 V. c. 26.

V. MONEY DUE: READY MONEY: SECURITIES FOR MONEY.

"Moneys," in a Declaration against a Sheriff for not levying "the whole of the moneys" under a fi. fa., held to embrace not only the debt but also all the items endorsed on the writ (*Slade* v. *Hawley*, 14 L. J. Ex. 217; 13 M. & W. 757).

"Money," s. 135, Com. L. Pro. Act (Ireland) 1853, includes the Suitors Fee Fund (*Quinn* v. *O'Keeffe*, 10 Ir. C. L. Rep. 393).

MONEY DUE.—A bequest of "Money *due*" obviously differs from one of MONEY. "Money due" points to debts or to moneys arising under a contractual obligation. Under a bequest of "Money due" will pass moneys payable on the termination of testator's own life (*Petty* v. *Willson*, 4 Ch. 574; 17 W. R. 778), and damages for breach of contract to which he was entitled, though the amount be ascertained in an action by his executor after his death (*Bide* v. *Harrison*, 43 L. J. Ch. 86; L. R. 17 Eq. 76; 29 L. T. 451); but not money for a service uncompleted at testator's death (*Stephenson* v. *Dowson*, 10 L. J. Ch. 93; 3 Bea. 342).

"I think it very likely that the words, 'Sums of money due and owing,' might extend beyond what were strictly debts. It might possibly, under the particular circumstances of certain Wills, be held to include any sum which could be recovered either at law or in equity" (per Mellish, L. J., *Martin* v. *Hobson*, 42 L. J. Ch. 342; 8 Ch. 401; 21 W. R. 376; 28 L. T. 427); but in that case it was held that such phrase did not comprise an unascertained share in certain partnership assets to which the testatrix was entitled as one of the next of kin of her son.

A bequest to testator's *debtor* of "All Moneys due" from him, means, if there be cross accounts, the balance (*Ganly* v. *Dowling*, 5 L. R. Ir. 628).

"Money due *on a mortgage*," will not pass a sum merely *charged* on property (*Poulett* v. *Hood*, 35 L. J. Ch. 253 ; L. R. 5 Eq. 115 ; 35 Bea. 234 ; 13 L. T. 783 ; 14 W. R. 298) : *Sr. Brown* v. *Brown*, 6 W. R. 613. *V.* MONEY ON MORTGAGE.

V. DUE.

MONEY, GOODS or CHATTELS.—*V. Robinson* v. *Jenkins*, cited GOODS AND CHATTELS, towards end.

MONEY IN HAND.—"There is no real difference between 'Money in Hand' and 'Ready Money'" (per Lyndhurst, L. C., *Parker* v. *Marchant*, 12 L. J. Ch. 387). *V.* READY MONEY.

MONEY IN THE FUNDS.—Foreign Bonds guaranteed by England not included herein (*Burnie* v. *Getting*, 2 Coll. 324 : *V.* FUNDS).

V. Grant v. *Mussett*, 8 W. R. 330 : 2 L. T. 133.

MONEY ON MORTGAGE.—Prior to the Conv. & L. P. Act, 1881, a bequest of "Money on Mortgage" passed also the fee in the mortgaged property (*Doe* d. *Guest* v. *Bennett*, 20 L. J. Ex. 323 ; 6 Ex. 892 : *Re Arrowsmith*, 27 L. J. Ch. 704). But that Act, since it came into operation, has superseded this ruling (s. 30).

V. MONEY DUE : MORTGAGE.

MONEY PAID.—*V.* PAID : PAYMENT : TRULY SET FORTH.

MONEY RECEIVED.—Agreement to pay Commission on "Money Received ;" *V. Fisher* v. *Drewett*, 48 L. J. Ex. 32 ; W. N. (78) 151.

MONEY VALUE.—The reservation, in a Lease for 500 years dated in 1647, of a silver penny, if demanded, is a "Rent having no money value" within s. 65, Conv. & L. P. Act, 1881 (*Chapman to Hobbs*, 54 L. J. Ch. 810 ; 29 Ch. D. 1007).

MONEY'S WORTH.—Marriage is not a "valuable consideration in *Money or Money's Worth*" within s. 17, Sucn. Dy. Act, 1853 (*Floyer* v. *Bankes*, 33 L. J. Ch. 1 : *V.* obs. of Westbury, L. C., in that case on the meaning of this phrase).

V. PECUNIARY CONSIDERATION.

MONITION.—"'Monition' (which is sometimes itself called an ecclesiastical censure) is described in the books as of a 'preparatory' nature, that is (as I understand the term) as a warning or command to be followed in case of disobedience by some coercive sanction" (per Selborne, L. C., *Mackonochie* v. *Penzance*, 50 L. J. Q. B. 611 ; 6 App. Ca. 424 ; cited in *Enraght* v. *Penzance*, 51 L. J. Q. B. 510 ; 7 App. Ca. 240).

MONTH.—"A Month, *mensis*, is regularly accounted in law 28 dayes, and not according to the solar month, nor according to the Kalendar, unlesse it be for the account of the laps in a *quare impedit*" (Co. Litt. 135 b). "A Month, in law, is a lunar month, or 28 days, unless otherwise expressed; not only because it is always one uniform period, but because it falls naturally into a quarterly division by weeks" (2 Bla. Com. 141). "In legal proceedings, the word 'Months,' means lunar months, unless the contrary appear to be the meaning from the subject-matter to which that term is applied" (per Bayley, J., *Johnstone* v. *Hudleston*, 4 B. & C. 932). "In the instance, indeed, of a *quare impedit*, the computation of time is by calendar months, but that depends on the words of an Act of Parliament, *tempus semestre*. But for all other purposes, and in all Acts of Parliament, where 'Months' are spoken of without the word 'Calendar,' and nothing is added from which a clear inference can be drawn that the legislature intended calendar months, it is understood to mean lunar months" (per Kenyon, C. J., *Lacon* v. *Hooper*, 6 T. R. 224). *Sv.*, as to Acts of Parliament since 1850, 13 & 14 V. c. 21, s. 4; Interp. Act, 1889, s. 3.

"Month," means lunar month, "unless there is admissible evidence of an intention in the parties using the word to denote calendar month. If the context shows that calendar month was intended, the Judge may adopt that construction (*Lang* v. *Gale*, 1 M. & S. 111: *R.* v. *Chawton*, 10 L. J. M. C. 55; 1 Q. B. 247). If the surrounding circumstances, at the time the instrument was made, show that the parties intended to use the word, not in its primary or strict sense, but in some secondary meaning, the Judge may construe it, from such circumstances, according to the intention of the parties (*Goldshede* v. *Swan*, 16 L. J. Ex. 284; 1 Ex. 154: *Walker* v. *Hunter*, 15 L. J. C. P. 12; 2 C. B. 324: Bacon's Maxims, 10, and the examples there given: *Mallan* v. *May*, 14 L. J. Ex. 48; 13 M. & W. 511: *Beckford* v. *Crutwell*, 1 Moo. & R. 187; 5 C. & P. 242). If there is evidence that the word was used in a sense peculiar to a trade, business, or place, the jury must say whether the parties used it in that peculiar sense (*Smith* v. *Wilson*, 1 L. J. K. B. 194; 3 B. & Ad. 728: *Grant* v. *Maddox*, 16 L. J. Ex. 227: *Jolly* v. *Young*, 1 Esp. 186)." (Per Denman, C. J., *Simpson* v. *Margitson*, 17 L. J. Q. B. 81; 11 Q. B. 23);—in which case it was held that the conduct of the parties was not, by itself, admissible evidence to vary the primary meaning of "Month."

"In a *Contract* at law 'Month' means a lunar month, unless there is admissible evidence of an intention in the parties using the word to denote a calendar month" (Sug. V. & P. 257; *Va.* Dart, 492).

On the question being suggested by counsel for the plaintiff as to whether so many "Months'" credit, for goods sold and delivered, meant Calendar or Lunar Months, Pollock, C. B., said:—"In Legal matters a 'Month' means a Lunar month; but in *Commercial matters* a 'Month' always means a Calendar month. In Bills of Exchange, Promissory Notes, Invoices, Times of Credit, and everything else relating to commercial matters it is so; and I know of no instance to the contrary" (*Hart* v. *Middleton*,

2 C. & K. 10). But it is to be observed that this is a nisi prius ruling on a point not, apparently, taken by defendant's counsel and one on which, in the result, the case did not turn.

"The word 'Month,' although at common law it generally means a lunar month, is in *Mercantile Contracts* understood to mean a calendar month (*R.* v. *Chawton*, 10 L. J. M. C. 55; 1 Q. B. 247, 250: *Hart* v. *Middleton*, sup.: *Webb* v. *Fairmaner*, 7 L. J. Ex. 140; 3 M. & W. 474). And the Court will look at the context in all cases, to see whether a calendar month was not intended, and, if so, will adopt that construction (*Simpson* v. *Margitson*, sup.: *Webb* v. *Fairmaner*, sup.)" (Benj. 674). It is submitted that the first part of this definition is not established by the cases cited; and that though in *Mercantile* Contracts "Month" might be read "Calendar month" more readily than in other contracts, yet that as a matter of law there is no difference between them, and that the proposition above cited from Sug. V. & P. correctly states the law as applicable to *all* Contracts. Yet at p. 230, Blackb., citing *Hart* v. *Middleton*, sup., it is said, "The word 'Month' means a lunar month in legal matters; but in *Commercial* matters it always means a calendar month, unless the context shows differently." And again in Maude & P. 293, it is stated (on the authority of *Jolly* v. *Young* and *Simpson* v. *Margitson*, sup.), that "in Charter-Parties, *as in other mercantile contracts*, the expression 'A Month' is construed to mean a calendar month." But on the other hand, and also citing *Simpson* v. *Margitson*, it is stated in Woodf. 224, "Month *in any legal document* means lunar month, unless calendar month be specified, or there be admissible evidence to show that a calendar month was intended." (*Va.* as to Agreement for hire of Furniture, *Hutton* v. *Brown*, W. N. (81) 116; 45 L. T. 343.) But again, per contra, it is said that where a term (in an agreement between landlord and tenant) "is for Months, without specifying whether lunar or calendar, the latter must now be understood" (Watson, Eq. 544), and for that proposition 13 & 14 V. c. 21, s. 4, is cited; though it would be probably difficult to show how that Statute operates on Leases.

In Bills of Exchange or Promissory Notes, "Month" means a calendar month (s. 14 (4), Bills of Ex. Act, 1882). So also in *Matters Ecclesiastical* (*Catesby's Case*, 6 Rep. 62 a). So *quà* period allowed for redemption in a Foreclosure Decree (Fisher, 952; Coote, 1107). And so also in *Proceedings in the Supreme Court* (Ord. 57, R. 1, R. S. C.), or in the *County Court* (Ord. 52, Co. Co. Rules, 1889); and so as regards a stipulation for a "Six Months'" Notice to Quit (*V.* SIX MONTHS), and in calculating the time for performance of conditions (*Franco* v. *Alvares*, 3 Atk. 346).

"Month," in the rule that a Domestic Servant may be discharged by a month's notice or payment of a month's wages, means a calendar month,—the wages being the money wages and not including board wages (*Gordon* v. *Potter*, 1 F. & F. 644).

In *Acts of Parliament* passed before the end of the year 1850, "Month," unless otherwise specially interpreted, means lunar month (2 Bla. Com.

141: *Lacon* v. *Hooper*, 6 T. R. 224): in all Acts passed since that date "Month," "unless words be added showing lunar month to be intended," means calendar month (13 & 14 V. c. 21, s. 4; *Vf.* s. 3, Interp. Act, 1889).

For the American view of the meaning of "Month;" *V.* Burrill's Law Dict.

V. Calendar Month: Twelve-month.

MORA.—"*Mora* is derived of the English word moore, and signifieth a more barren and unprofitable ground than marshes, dangerous for any cattell to go there, in respect of myrie and moorish soyle, neither serves it for getting of turves there" (Co. Litt. 5 a).

MORE OR LESS.—"'About,' and 'More or less,' seem to be words of general import, and I should have much difficulty in saying that evidence ought to be received to ascertain their meaning" (per Littledale, J., *Cross* v. *Elgin*, 2 B. & Ad. 106).

Where goods are sold as "about" a certain quantity, or "thereabouts," or "*more or less*," these words are intended to provide only for a small difference between the numbers; and the purchaser is not bound to accept 350 tons on a bargain for "about 300 tons, more or less;" at least, unless it be shown that a large excess was contemplated (*Cross* v. *Elgin*, sup.). So a tender of 2700 stones of wool is not warranted by a contract for "2300 stones, 100 stones more or less" (*Macdonald* v. *Longbottom*, 28 L. J. Q. B. 293; 29 Ib. 256; 1 E. & E. 977, 987). But in *Cockerell* v. *Aucompte* (26 L. J. C. P. 194; 2 C. B. N. S. 440), it was held that the delivery of 127 tons of coal was according to a contract for "100 tons, more or less." In *Morris* v. *Levison* (45 L. J. C. P. 409; 1 C. P. D. 155), it was held that an allowance of 3 per cent. either way would be a fair estimate for satisfying the word "about" (*V.* especially jdgmt. of Brett, J.). *Vf. Reuter* v. *Sala*, 48 L. J. C. P. 492; 4 C. P. D. 239: *Tamvaco* v. *Lucas*, 28 L. J. Q. B. 150, 301; 1 E. & E. 581: *Beckh* v. *Page*, 28 L. J. C. P. 164, 341; 5 C. B. N. S. 708; 7 Ib. 861: *Bourne* v. *Seymour*, 24 L. J. C. P. 202; 16 C. B. 337: *Moore* v. *Campbell*, 10 Ex. 323; 23 L. J. Ex. 310.

Where the Defendant instructed the Plaintiffs to buy for him 500 tons of sugar, "50 tons more or less of no moment if you are enabled to get a suitable vessel," and the Plaintiffs bought 400 tons, parcel by parcel, according to the usage of the market, and could buy no more at the price named, it was held that the Defendant was not bound to accept the 400 tons, as the usage could not affect the express order (*Ireland* v. *Livingston*, 39 L. J. Q. B. 282; L. R. 5 Q. B. 516; reversed on another ground, 41 L. J. Q. B. 201; L. R. 5 H. L. 395). *Sv. Johnston* v. *Kershaw*, 36 L. J. Ex. 44; L. R. 2 Ex. 82.

A contract to supply the whole of a specified article required for a specified work, is not controlled and limited by the addition of an estimate of a specified quantity "more or less" (*Tancred Co.* v. *Steel Co. of Scotland*, Times, 8th March, 1890).

Vh. Blackb. 215–222 : Benj. 682, 683 : SAY : THEREABOUTS.

"The words 'More or Less' or 'Thereabouts,' in a Contract for Sale of Realty, will only cover a moderate excess or deficiency, and will never be suffered to be the instrument of fraud" (Add. C. 891 : *Va.* Dart, 736). They would cover 5 out of 41 acres (*Winch* v. *Winchester*, 1 V. & B. 375), but not 100 out of 349 acres (*Portman* v. *Mill*, 8 L. J. Ch. 161 ; 3 Jur. 356 ; 2 Russ. 570). *Va. Gell* v. *Watson*, 3 Mad. 225 ; 2 S. & S. 402 ; Sug. V. & P. 325 : *Leslie* v. *Tompson*, 9 Hare, 268, 273 ; 20 L. J. Ch. 561 ; 15 Jur. 717 ; 17 L. T. O. S. 277.

"More or Less" in a Devise of Realty ; *V. Whitfield* v. *Langdale*, 1 Ch. D. 61 ; 45 L. J. Ch. 177, cited FARM.

MORTALITY.—"The word 'Mortality' may, under certain circumstances, include every description of death, every termination of life to which mortals are subject. It applies generally, however, to that description of death which is not occasioned by violent means" (per Bayley, J., *Lawrence* v. *Aberdein*, 5 B. & Ald. 112. *Vf. Gabay* v. *Lloyd*, 3 B. & C. 793).

MORTGAGE : MORTGAGES.—The ordinary meaning of a "Mortgage" is a conveyance of freehold, copyhold, or leasehold property with a proviso for redemption to secure an advance : and does not include a statutory charge on Turnpike Tolls (*Cavendish* v. *Cavendish*, 55 L. J. Ch. 144 ; 30 Ch. D. 227 : *Poulett* v. *Hood*, 35 L. J. Ch. 253 ; L. R. 5 Eq. 115 ; 35 Bea. 234 : *V.* REAL SECURITY).

A security created by a trust for sale is a "Mortgage" within the Statutes of Limitation, 3 & 4 W. 4, c. 27, s. 28, replaced by s. 7, 37 & 38 V. c. 57 (*Locking* v. *Parker*, 8 Ch. 30 ; 42 L. J. Ch. 257 : *Re Alison, Johnson* v. *Mounsey*, 11 Ch. D. 284).

An Equitable Charge, is not a "Mortgage" within the Act against Clandestine Mortgages, 4 & 5 W. & M. c. 16 (*Kennard* v. *Futvoye*, 29 L. J. Ch. 553 ; 2 Giff. 81).

Compare the definition of "Mortgage" as given in the Conv. & L. P. Act, 1881 (s. 2, vi.), in Ld. St. Leonards Act (22 & 23 V. c. 35, s. 25), and in the Stamp Act, 1870 (33 & 34 V. c. 97, s. 105).

For the purposes of the Acts which, in an administration of a deceased's estate, throw the burden of mortgage debts on the mortgaged property, "the word 'Mortgage' shall be deemed to extend to any Lien for unpaid Purchase Money" (s. 2, 30 & 31 V. c. 69).

A bequest of "Mortgages" prior to the Conv. & L. P. Act, 1881, and if uncontrolled by context, passed the legal estate in the mortgaged hereditaments (1 Jarm. 699) ; but *V.* s. 30 of that Act as regards testator's dying after 31 Dec. 1881.

"That the benefit of a mortgage will pass by the word 'Mortgages,' collocated with other personal chattels, is perfectly clear" (1 Jarm. 692).

Vh. Fisher, ch. 1 ; Coote, ch. 1 : Co. Litt. 205 a.

V. CHARGE : LEGAL MORTGAGE : MONEY ON MORTGAGE : MONEY DUE.

MORTGAGEE.—"For the Mortgagee" is a sufficient description of a Vendor ; *V.* PROPRIETOR.

MORTGAGOR ENTITLED TO REDEEM.—This phrase in s. 15, Conv. & L. P. Act, 1881, means, the mortgagor, or other the person under him who has the right to a Reconveyance (*Teevan* v. *Smith*, 51 L. J. Ch. 621 ; 20 Ch. D. 724 : *Va. Kinnaird* v. *Trollope*, 39 Ch. D. 636 : *Alderson* v. *Elgey*, 26 Ch. D. 567). But the section is modified by s. 12, Conv. Act, 1882.

MOSSES.—In a fee-farm grant it was held that the words "All Mosses," as used in the fee-farm grant and controlled by its context, meant all places in which turf, or matter in the course of becoming turf, was found, including the soil of such places. Per Palles, C. B. :—Though the word "Turbary" would *primâ facie* mean "a right to cut turf," qy., whether the word "Turbaries" might not, according to the context, more properly mean "places in which turf may be cut" (*Quinn* v. *Shields*, Ir., Rep. 11 C. L. 254). *V.* TURBARY.

MOST DESERVING.—*V.* NEAREST.

MOST PROPER AND EFFECTIVE MANNER.—*V.* WORKABLE.

MOST RENT.—*V.* Sug. Pow. 791.

MOTHER.—As to whether the expression "Mother of my children," will, contextually, let in illegitimate children ; *V. Beachcroft* v. *Beachcroft*, 1 Mad. 430, stated and discussed 2 Jarm. 234–236.

MOTHER'S SHARE.—In a substitutionary gift to children of their "Mother's Share," held, that what was meant was, the share which the mother would have taken had she survived the period of distribution (*Re Hunter*, L. R. 1 Eq. 295).

MOUTH OF THE THAMES.—*V.* THAMES.

MOVEABLES.—A bequest of all testator's "Moveables" "doth pass all his personal goods, both quick and dead, which either move themselves,—as horses, sheep, and the like ; or may be moved by another,—as plate, household stuff, corn in the garners and barns or in the sheaf, &c., also all bonds and especialties ; and by a devise of *Immoveables* do pass leases, rents, grass and the like, but not any of those things that do pass by the devise of Moveables : but Debts will not pass by either of these devises" (Touch. 447). It will be observed that here there is a difference drawn between "Bonds and Especialties" and "Debts"—the latter, *i.e.*, as it would seem, Simple Contract Debts—not passing under "Moveables." The reason would seem to be because that which creates a Bond or Specialty Debt can be carried about,—*i.e.* is moveable. But that also is true of a Bill of Ex. or Pro. Note ; yet the money secured by such a document would be a mere debt, and therefore, according to the definition in the Touch-Stone would not be comprised in a bequest of "Moveables." *Sed qy.*

In *Steignes* v. *Steignes* (Mos. 296) it was held that "Moveables" did not comprise a sum of South Sea Stock ; but that was simply because the word was controlled by a context.

In citing that case it is stated at p. 755, 1 Jarm., that "the word, if unrestrained by the context, would take in the whole *purely* personal estate." What is meant by this is shewn in a note at p. 4, Ib., where it is shewn that Leaseholds are not "Moveables," and where this word is discussed and distinguished from the large acceptation of "Personal Estate." But even so, it is difficult to reconcile the statement that "the whole purely personal estate" is comprised in "Moveables," seeing that the Touch-Stone says that Debts are not within that word.

Money is a "Moveable" (*Swinfen* v. *Swinfen*, 29 Bea. 207).

MOVEMENT.—*V.* CAUSING.

MULTIPLE.—"This term may be understood in a restricted sense so as to comprehend only multiples numerically expressed, such as 10 pounds, 100 pounds, &c.; or generally all multiples, however expressed, such as a Stone, a Hundredweight, a Ton, or any other weight, such as a 'Weigh,' a 'Tod,' or a 'Hobbet,' supposing these words to be in use for expressing multiples of the pound avoirdupois" (per Maule, J., in delivering jdgmt. of Ex. Cham., *Giles* v. *Jones*, 24 L. J. Ex. 261 ; 11 Ex. 393). *V.* TON.

MULTITUDE.—"Multitude of people," Litt. s. 431,—"a multitude here spoken of (as some have said) must be ten or more. *Multitudinem decem faciunt.* And so (say they) it is said *de grege hominum.* But I could never read it restrained by the common law to any certaine number, but left to the discretion of the judges" (Co. Litt. 257 a). *Cp.* ASSEMBLY.

MUNICIPAL BOROUGH.—*V.* s. 15 (1), (2), Interp. Act, 1889.

MUNITION AND FURNITURE.—*V. Gale* v. *Laurie*, 5 B. & C. 156 ; FURNITURE.

MURAGE.—"'Murage' is a toll or tribute levied for the repairing or building of publike walls" (Termes de la Ley).

MURDER.—"Murder is when one is slaine with a man's will, and with malice prepensed or forethought . . . . Murder commeth of the Saxon word *mordren*" (Co. Litt. 287 b: *Vf.* Termes de la Ley). But the person slain must be another person than the slayer (4 Bla. Com. 195); therefore Suicide is not Murder (*R.* v. *Burgess*, 32 L. J. M. C. 55); but if two agree to kill each other and one only is killed, the survivor is guilty of Murder (*R.* v. *Alison*, 8 C. & P. 418: *R.* v. *Dyson*, Russ. & R. 523).

"Murder is unlawful homicide with malice aforethought" (Steph. Cr. 158; *Vf.* Ib. ch. 24, 362–383).

"Murder" is a term of art (*Holford* v. *Bailey*, 18 L. J. Q. B. 113; 13 Q. B. 430, 446: *R.* v. *Gray*, 33 L. J. M. C. 78; L. & C. 365).

Vf. Arch. Cr. 704–739; Rosc. 746–808.

V. HOMICIDE: MALICE AFORETHOUGHT: SUICIDE.

MUSICAL COMPOSITION.—*V. Russell* v. *Smith*, 17 L. J. Q. B. 225; 12 Q. B. 217: *V.* DRAMATIC PIECE.

MUST NOT.—"If the landlord of a house let out in separate tenements lives in the house, he *must not* return the names of the occupiers of tenements in that house" (last par. of Form A, Sch. 2, Part ii. Registration Act for England, 1885, 48 V. c. 15). "Must not" means the same as "Need not" in the corresponding Form provided for Ireland, *i.e.* Form No. 34, 48 V. c. 17 (per Porter, M. R., *Hogan* v. *Sterrett*, 20 L. R. Ir. 349).

V. NEED NOT.

MUTUAL ACCOUNTS.—"'Mutual Accounts,' by which are meant not where one only of two parties has received money and made payments on account of the other, but where each of two parties has received and paid on account of the other" (Seton, 777).

MUTUAL CREDITS.—"Mutual Debts and Credits," s. 50, 6 G. 4, c. 16; *V. Alsager* v. *Currie*, 12 M. & W. 756; 13 L. J. Ex. 203.

"Mutual Credits and Dealings," s. 39, Bankry. Act, 1869; *V. Jack* v. *Kipping*, 9 Q. B. D. 113; 51 L. J. Q. B. 463: *Peat* v. *Jones*, 8 Q. B. D. 147; 51 L. J. Q. B. 128: *Booth* v. *Hutchinson*, L. R. 15 Eq. 30; 42 L. J. Ch. 492. *Vh.* 26 S. J. 575.

MY.—If a testator refers to his possessing any particular and definite thing,—*e.g.* "My Estate at A.," "My ring," "My horse,"—it seems that the contrary intention referred to by the Wills Act (1 V. c. 26) is manifested, and the Will, *quà* such bequest, speaks from its date and the gift is specific: but where the bequest is generic, of that which may be increased or diminished,—*e.g.* Consols,—the Act requires something more to indicate such contrary intention than that the subject-matter should be preceded by "My;" and accordingly, *quà* such a bequest, the Will would speak from the death of the testator (*Goodlad* v. *Burnett*, 1 K. & J. 341:

Re Gibson, L. R. 2 Eq. 669 ; 35 L. J. Ch. 596 : *Vh.* 1 Jarm. 329–332, and as to the old rule, Ib. 320–329). But on the authority of *Miles* v. *Miles* (L. R. 1 Eq. 462 ; 35 L. J. Ch. 315 ; 13 L. T. 697 ; 14 W. R. 272) it has been stated that " the use of the pronoun ' My,' in the description of the thing given, is not sufficient evidence of an intention that the Will shall not speak as from the date of the death " (Dart, 309). *Cp.* Now : Have.

My *Property* at R.'s bank ; " *V. Re Prater*, 37 Ch. D. 481 ; 57 L. J. Ch. 342 ; 58 L. T. 784 ; 36 W. R. 561.

" All my Land at S. ; " *V. Re Portal & Lamb*, 27 Ch. D. 600 ; 30 Ib. 50 ; 54 L. J. Ch. 1012 ; 53 L. T. 650 ; 33 W. R. 859.

So as regards the objects of the gift. " My son " of a particular name, means the son of that name at the date of the Will, and him only (1 Jarm. 323).

" My *house*," where there are two answering the description given ; *V. Gardiner* v. *Jewers*, W. N. (72) 35.

Bequest of " All My " *property* will pass property subject to a General Power of Appointment (*Chandler* v. *Pocock*, 50 L. J. Ch. 380 ; 16 Ch. D. 648).

V. Watson, Eq. 1330.

" My *own Heirs* whatsoever ; " *V. Gordon* v. *Gordon*, 7 App. Ca. 713.

" My *Wife*," " My *Children*," as a *designatio personæ ; V. Pratt* v. *Mathew*, 25 L. J. Ch. 409 ; 22 Bea. 328 : *Re Petts*, 29 L. J. Ch. 168 ; 27 Bea. 576 : *Vf.* Child. " My Sons " as a class ; *V.* Son.

NAME.—" Sometimes it is made part of the description or qualification of a devisee or legatee, that he be of the testator's *Name*. The word 'name' so used, admits of either of the following interpretations :—

1. As designating one whose name answers to that of the testator (which seems to be the more obvious sense) ;

2. As denoting a person of the testator's family,—the word 'name' being, in this case, synonymous with 'Family' or 'Blood.'

The former, as being the more natural construction, prevails in the absence of an explanatory context ; and such is most indisputably its meaning when found in company with some other term or expression which would be synonymous with 'name' if otherwise construed" (2 Jarm. 141, *wh.*, to p. 146, *V.* for discussion of the cases).

A woman losing the "Name" by marriage, loses her right to be classed as one of the "Name ;" but not so a person who assumes another name by license or Act of Parliament (Ib. 144).

" Descendants who shall bear the Name of ;" *V. Re Roberts*, 19 Ch. D. 520 ; 50 L. J. Ch. 265.

NAMED.—" The strict and accurate meaning of this word 'named' is (as stated by Kindersley, V.-C., *Re Holmes*, 1 Drew. 321; 22 L. J. Ch. 393), 'mentioned *nominatim*, if not by all their names, by some at least, either their Christian or their surnames'" (per Stirling, J., *Jodrell* v. *Seale*, W. N. (89), 230 ; 34 S. J. 129). "Named" is sometimes used, but only in a secondary sense, as meaning "mentioned" or "referred to" (Ib.).

V. Expressly Named.

NAMELY.—" A difference, in grammatical sense, in strictness exists between the words 'namely' and 'including.' 'Namely' imports interpretation, *i.e.*,—indicates what is included in the previous term ; but 'Including' imports addition, *i.e.*,—indicates something not included" (2 Jarm. 229). As to how far a *videlicet* is restrictive, *V. Fisher* v. *Hepburn*, 14 Bea. 626 ; 1 Jarm. 753, 759 : as to its antecedent, *V. Harrington* v. *Pole*, Dy. 77 b, pl. 38 ; cited, Hob. 173.

In *Smith* v. *Walton* (1 L. J. C. P. 85 ; 8 Bing. 235 ; 1 Moo. & Sc. 380), the explanatory phrase was "*To Wit ;*" and it was there held, on a Pleading, that the phrase " Martinmas, to wit, on the 23rd November, 1830," meant Martinmas, the 11th November, according to the New Style, and that the *videlicet* did not enable the Court to read the date as the 23rd Nov. *V.* MICHAELMAS.

V. THAT IS TO SAY.

NARROW CHANNEL.—*V.* 1 Maude & P. 603, n. (*y*).

NATIONAL DEBT COMMISSIONERS.—*V.* s. 12 (17), Interp. Act, 1889.

NATIVE BORN.—There is no distinction between "Native-Born" as used in the French Extradition Treaty, and "Natural-Born" as used in the Extradition Act (*Re Guerin*, 37 W. R. 269).

NATIVE OYSTER.—*V. Whitstable Free Fishers* v. *Elliott*, W. N. (88) 27.

NATURAL CHILDREN.—As to when illegitimate children are sufficiently designated by the words "Natural Children;" *V. Bentley* v. *Blizard*, 4 Jur. N. S. 652: *Worts* v. *Cubitt*, 2 W. R. 633; 19 Bea. 421: *Vf.* CHILD.

NATURALLY.—"Naturally dead;" *V.* DEAD.

NATURE.—"Nature of the *Action*;" *V. Smith* v. *Hailey*, 42 L. J. Ex. 5; L. R. 8 Ex. 16.

"Specifying the Nature *and Detail* of such other Expenses," s. 14, Regulation of Railways Act, 1873, 36 & 37 V. c. 48; these words require a Railway Co. to state what terminal charges they undertake to perform with regard to the particular traffic, and how much they charge for each of such services; and this obligation is not discharged by merely giving a list of services performed and the total amount of the charge therefor (*Colman* v. *G. E. Ry.*, 4 B. & Macn. 108; 26 S. J. 534).

The "Nature" of an *Invention* which has to be stated in the provisional specification; this does not confine the complete specification to minute agreement with the provisional specification the object of which is to set forth fairly, though it may be roughly, the "Nature" of the Invention for which a patent is sought (*United Telephone Co.* v. *Harrison*, 51 L. J. Ch. 705; 21 Ch. D. 720, in which the prior cases are collected: *Vf. Liddell* v. *Vickers*, 39 Ch. D. 92).

V. JOINT STOCK COMPANY.

The "Nature of *Qualification*," entitling a person to be on an Electoral List, means those facts which bring him within some one of the qualifying franchises; and therefore a Successive Occupation is a qualification of a nature different from an occupation of one property during the whole of the qualifying period (*Foskett* v. *Kaufman*, 55 L. J. Q. B. 1; 16 Q. B. D. 279; 54 L. T. 64; 34 W. R. 90; 50 J. P. 484; 1 Colt, 466; following *Bartlett* v. *Gibbs*, 13 L. J. C. P. 40; 5 M. & G. 81). The distinction between the substantial "Nature" of the Qualification (which the Revising Barrister has not an inherent power to amend) and the verbal "*Description*" of it (within such power), is shown by a comparison between the cases just cited and *Friend* v. *Towers* (52 L. J. Q. B. 109 ; 10 Q. B. D. 87), *Dashwood* v. *Ayles* (55 L. J. Q. B. 8 ; 16 Q. B. D. 295 ; 53 L. T. 588 ; 34 W. R. 53 ; 50 J. P. 132 ; 1 Colt, 486), and *Minifie* v. *Banger* (55 L. J. Q. B. 10 ; 16 Q. B. D. 302 ; 53 L. T. 590 ; 50 J. P. 131; 1 Colt, 493). In the first of these latter cases "house" was amended into "dwelling-house," and in the two last cases "tenement" was amended into "dwelling-house." *Vf. Wilson* v. *Buchanan*, 20 L. R. Ir. 213 : *Melaugh* v. *Chambers*, Ib. 286 : *Alexander* v. *Burke*, 22 L. R. Ir. 595 : *Birks* v. *Allison*, 32 L. J. C. P. 51; 13 C. B. N. S. 12 : *Howitt* v. *Stephens*, 28 L. J. C. P. 105; 5 C. B. N. S. 30.

"Nature, Substance and *Quality* of the Article demanded," s. 6, Sale of Food and Drugs Act, 1875, 38 & 39 V. c. 63, means the Nature or Quality according as the Article is ordinarily understood in the trade dealing with it ; therefore when tincture of opium was demanded and a tincture was supplied one-third less in strength than the article according to the recognised standard (*i.e.*, the British Pharmacopœia) ; held that the Article supplied was not of the "Nature or Quality" demanded (*White* v. *Bywater*, 19 Q. B. D. 582 ; 51 J. P. 821; 3 Times Rep. 631) ; but skimmed milk is a good supply for a demand of "milk" within this section (*V.* MILK). *V.* ARTICLE DEMANDED : PREJUDICE OF PURCHASER.

"Any Writing in the Nature of a *Will*" means the same as a Will (Sug. Pow. 230).

NAVAL SERVICE.—"Naval Service of a Foreign State," s. 8 (4), Foreign Enlistment Act, 1870, 33 & 34 V. c. 90, does not merely mean a service in or directly connected with some warlike naval operation, but includes, *e.g.*, the employment of an English tug to tow a prize to the captor's waters (*R.* v. *Elliott, The Gauntlet*, 41 L. J. Adm. 65 ; nom. *Dyke* v. *Elliott*, L. R. 4 P. C. 184). *Cp.* MILITARY SERVICE.

NAVIGABLE.—Land may properly be said to be covered with "Navigable" water although at different times of short duration dry portions of the land may be seen. When, however, such portions of the land are dry for days together, this excludes the notion of navigability. The legal and technical meaning of "Navigable," requires not only that navigation should be possible, but also that there should be ebb and flow of the tide (*Ilchester* v. *Raishley*, 38 W. R. 104 ; 61 L. T. 477). *V.* EBB AND FLOW.

NAVIGATED.—*V.* WORKED AND NAVIGATED.

NAVIGATING WITHIN.—"The words 'Navigating within' in the Merchant Shipping Act, 1854, s. 379, mean 'Being within ;' and, therefore, a vessel belonging to the Port of London, not carrying passengers and coming from the west, is not bound to employ a licensed pilot when she is within the limits of the Port of London" (1 Maude & P. 278, citing *The*

Stettin, Br. & L. 199 ; 31 L. J. P. M. & A. 208). In that case Dr. Lushington said,—"Though I do not deny that the word 'Navigating' alone is a doubtful expression, yet, coupled with the word 'within,' it appears to me to negative voyages beyond the limits, and to be confined to those within the limits." *Cf. General Steam Nav. Co.* v. *British & Colonial Steam Nav. Co.*, 37 L. J. Ex. 194 ; 38 Ib. 97 ; L. R. 3 Ex. 330 ; 4 Ib. 238.

NAVIGATION.—"Navigation," is, "the science or art of conducting a ship from one place to another. This includes the supply of necessary implements and skilful mariners. The instruments are useless without the skilful mariners, and conversely, navigation includes two things,—the supply of the instruments or organs of the ship, and the living instruments, or seamen. If either of these is wanting by the negligence of the owner, or of those for whom he is responsible, there is Improper Navigation" (per Fry, L. J., *The Warkworth*, 53 L. J. P. D. & A. 66 ; 9 P. D. 145 : *Vf. Good* v. *London Steamship Assn.*, L. R. 6 C. P. 563 ; 20 W. R. 33 : *Carmichael* v. *Liverpool Sailing-Ship Assn.*, 56 L. J. Q. B. 208 ; 56 L. T. 863).

"Cases have decided that the word 'Navigation,' for some purposes, includes a period when the ship is not in motion ; as, for instance, when she is at anchor" (per Denman, J., *Hayn* v. *Culliford*, 3 C. P. D. 417 ; 47 L. J. C. P. 759 ; affd., 4 C. P. D. 182 ; 48 L. J. C. P. 372).

Canting over in port is a "Danger or Accident of Navigation" (*Laurie* v. *Douglas*, 15 M. & W. 746) : so damage "caused by the bad navigation of another ship, is a 'Danger of Navigation.' Where, however, the loss is brought about by the shipowner's own servants, that is not a 'Danger of Navigation,' for the danger there is a danger arising from the shipowner having employed inefficient or negligent servants" (per Esher, M. R., *Garston Ship. Co.* v. *Hickie*, 56 L. J. Q. B. 40 ; 18 Q. B. D. 17 ; 55 L. T. 879 ; 35 W. R. 33).

This word as used in 7 & 8 G. 4, c. lxxv, "seems to be used as synonymous with rowing" (per Coleridge, J., *Tisdell* v. *Coombe*, 7 L. J. M. C. 48).

V. Improper Navigation : Perils of the Sea : Dangers.

NEAR.—"In or near," in the Grant of a Market ; *V. A.-G.* v. *Horner*, 54 L. J. Q. B. 227 ; 55 Ib. 193 ; 14 Q. B. D. 245 ; 11 App. Ca. 66.

In his judgment in that case, Brett, M.R., is reported (54 L. J. Q. B. 230) to have said,—"A distinction was attempted to be drawn between the words 'next' and 'near ;' but I can see none ;" *Sv. R.* v. *Harvey*, 1 W. Bl. 19 ; and as "Next" is synonymous with Nearest, can it also be said that "near" is the equivalent of "nearest" ?

"In or near the Parish or Division," 43 Eliz. c. 2, is directory (*R.* v. *Loxdale*, 1 Burr. 447).

"As near as ;" *V.* So far as.

NEAR RELATIONS.—*V.* Relations.

NEAR THERETO AS SHE MAY SAFELY GET.—"It appears from *Parker* v. *Winlow* (27 L. J. Q. B. 49 ; 7 E. & B. 942), *Bastifell* v. *Lloyd* (31 L. J. Ex. 413 ; 1 H. & C. 388), and *Dahl* v. *Nelson* (50 L. J. Ch. 411 ; 12 Ch. D. 568 ; 6 App. Ca. 38) that when the Charter-Party provides that a ship shall go to a harbour named, or 'as near thereto as she can safely get,'—the primary object is to get to the place named, and the alternative condition does not arise unless the cause which prevents the immediate arrival of the ship at the place named, is such that it cannot be got rid of by the ship-owner by reasonable means and within a reasonable time, having regard to the nature and object of the voyage ; and further, that if the cause of detention be the arrival of the vessel during the low tides, her having to wait for the tides to increase is one of the ordinary incidents of navigation, and the ship-owner must submit to the delay so occasioned" (per North, J., *Horsley* v. *Price,* 52 L. J. Q. B. 605 ; 11 Q. B. D. 244 : *Vf. Schilizzi* v. *Derry,* 24 L. J. Q. B. 193 ; 4 E. & B. 873 : *Shield* v. *Wilkins,* 19 L. J. Ex. 238 ; 5 Ex. 305 : *The Alhambra,* 50 L. J. P. D. & A. 36 ; 6 P. D. 68 : *Castel* v. *Trechman,* 1 Cab. & El. 276 : 1 Maude & P. 296, 317, 320, n. *f*). "The words 'as near thereto as she can safely get,' must receive a reasonable, and not a literal, application" (per Pollock, B., *Nielsen* v. *Wait,* 14 Q. B. D. 522 ; affd. 16 Q. B. D. 67). *Vf. Capper* v. *Wallace,* 49 L. J. Q. B. 350 ; 5 Q. B. D. 163 : *Pyman* v. *Dreyfus,* 24 Q. B. D. 152 ; 59 L. J. Q. B. 13.

V. Safe Port.

NEARER.—In estimating whether a proposed new Highway is "nearer" than an old one which is proposed to be diverted (s. 89, 5 & 6 W. 4, c. 50), "nearer" does not mean nearer as between two arbitrary points, but as between the terminus *à quo* and the terminus *ad quem,—i.e.,* the point where the proposed diversion begins, and the point where it ends (*R.* v. *Shiles,* 10 L. J. M. C. 157 ; 1 Q. B. 919 ; but that case dissented from in *R.* v. *Phillips,* L. R. 1 Q. B. 648).

NEAREST.—"Nearest" is synonymous with Next (*Smith* v. *Campbell,* 19 Ves. 400). In *Griffiths* v. *Evan* (11 L. J. Ch. 219 ; 5 Bea. 241), a power of appointment of realty to the "nearest Family" of the donee of the power, was held to mean his heir-at-law.

"Nearest of Blood," "Nearest of Kin ;" *V.* Next of Kin.

"Nearest of Kin in the Male Line, in preference to the Female Line ;" *V.* Male Line.

"Nearest Relations ;" *V.* Relations.

"Nearest Relative in the Male Line ;" *V. Woolmore* v. *Burrows,* 1 Sim. 529.

"Nearest and Most Deserving Male Cousin, and a regular Power of the Family ;" *V. Power* v. *Quealy,* 2 L. R. Ir. 227 ; 4 Ib. 20.

"Nearest "*Common Sewer,*" s. 61, 11 & 12 V. c. clxiii., means the one practicably nearest, not the one literally nearest (*Bathard* v. *London Sewers Commrs.*, 54 J. P. 135).

V. NEAR : NEXT OF KIN.

NECESSARIES.—"Necessaries," in a Master's covenant in an *Apprentice Indenture*, includes Clothing and Washing (*Abbott* v. *Bates*, 45 L. J. C. P. 117) ; and in that case it was found that there was no custom with Horse Trainers giving the word a restricted meaning, and, held, that had there been such a custom it would be inapplicable because inconsistent with the terms of the contract.

The "Necessaries" for which an *Infant* may contract liability are not confined to such articles as are necessary for the support of life ; but extend to such articles as are reasonably fit to maintain the particular person in his state, station and degree (Add. C. 124, 125, and cases there cited), and are suitable to his fortune and circumstances (Rosc. N. P. 598, and cases there cited) ; and (among such circumstances) regard must be had as to whether he was already sufficiently supplied with the kind of article in respect of which the liability was contracted (*Barnes* v. *Toye*, 53 L. J. Q. B. 567 ; 13 Q. B. D. 410 ; 33 W. R. 15 : *Johnstone* v. *Marks*, 35 W. R. 806 ; 19 Q. B. D. 509 ; 57 L. J. Q. B. 6).

Shipping Necessaries :—

"The general rule is, that the Master may bind his Owners for necessary repairs done, or supplies provided, for the ship. It was contended that this liability of the owners was confined to what was absolutely necessary. I think that rule too narrow, for it would be extremely difficult to decide, and often impossible in many cases, what is absolutely necessary. If, however, the jury are to enquire only what is necessary, there is no better rule to ascertain that, than by considering what a prudent man, if present, would do under circumstances in which the agent, in his absence, is called upon to act. I am of opinion, that whatever is fit and proper for the service on which a vessel is engaged, whatever the owner of that vessel as a prudent man would have ordered, if present at the time, comes within the meaning of the term 'Necessary,' as applied to those repairs done or things provided for the ship by order of the Master for which the Owners are liable" (per Abbott, C.J., *Webster* v. *Seekamp*, 4 B. & Ald. 354).

"The expression 'Necessaries Supplied' in 3 & 4 V. c. 65, s. 6, which gave the Admiralty Court jurisdiction over foreign ships, though it is not to be restricted to things absolutely and immediately necessary for a ship in order to put to sea (*The Perla*, Swab. 354), must still be confined to things directly belonging to the ship's equipment necessary at the time, and under the existing circumstances, for the service on which the ship is engaged (*The Alexander*, 1 Wm. Rob. 361). But the insurance of a vessel is something quite extraneous to its equipment for sea ; and however prudent it may be for an owner to insure, it is prudence exercised for his own protection, and not for the requirements of the vessel, which is the sense in which the word 'Necessaries' is used in the statute" (per Hannen, P., *The Henrich Bjorn*, 52 L. J. P. D. & A. 84; 8 P. D. 151; reversed on app. without, *semble*, affecting the dictum just cited, 10 P. D. 44; 11 App. Ca. 270; 54 L. J. P. D. & A. 33; 55 Ib. 80).

"I shall hold that 'Necessaries' means primarily indispensable Repairs, —Anchors, Cables, Sails, when immediately necessary; and also Provisions; but, on the other hand, does not include things required for the Voyage, as contra-distinguished from things necessary for the ship" (per Dr. Lushington, *The Comtesse de Frègeville*, Lush. 332). The latter part of this definition was not followed by Sir R. Phillimore in *The Riga* (41 L. J. Adm. 39; L. R. 3 A. & E. 516), where he held (citing opinion of Abbott, C. J., sup.), that there was no distinction between Necessaries for the Ship and Necessaries for the Voyage.

Coals and a Screw Propeller, for a steamer, are Necessaries (*The West Friesland*, Swa. 454: *The Flecha*, 1 Spk. 441), so is Insurance of Freight and, *semble*, Brokerage Charges (*The Riga*, sup.); *secus*, expenses of witnesses (*The Bonne Amélie*, L. R. 1 A. & E. 19; 35 L. J. Adm. 115: *Va. Gunn* v. *Roberts*, L. R. 9 C. P. 331; 43 L. J. C. P. 233), or payments for Averages (*The Aaltje*, L. R. 1 A. & E. 107).

Vf. 1 Maude & P. 99, 157.

NECESSARILY.—Justices' Clerks Fees, held "Expenses necessarily incurred" in carrying out 5 & 6 W. 4, c. 76, within s. 92, Ib. (*R.* v. *Gloucester*, 13 L. J. Q. B. 233; 5 Q. B. 862).

NECESSARY.—"Necessary *Apparatus*." *V.* REGULATE.

A necessary *Easement* is one necessary for the enjoyment of the property as it stood at the time when such property was acquired under the title in virtue of which the easement is claimed (*Pyer* v. *Carter*, 1 H. & N. 916; 26 L. J. Ex. 258, commented on in *Morland* v. *Cook*, L. R. 6 Eq. 252; dissented from in *Wheeldon* v. *Burrows*, 12 Ch. D. 31; and approved in *Watts* v. *Kelson*, 6 Ch. 166: *Vf.* Gale on Easements, 5 Ed. 131; Elph. 189, 190). *Cp.* APPARENT EASEMENT.

"*Expenses* (if any) necessary to maintain hereditaments in a state to command such rent," in definition of Annual Value in s. 1, 6 & 7 W. 4, c. 96, include Drainage Works for a Farm (*R.* v. *Gainsborough*, 41 L. J. M. C. 1; L. R. 7 Q. B. 64). *V.* ANNUAL VALUE.

"Necessary *for the Purposes of Justice*," Ord. 37, R. 5, R. S. C.; *V. Re Mysore Mining Co.*, 58 L. J. Ch. 731.

An exception, in a contract for sale of an estate, of "Necessary *Land* for making a Railway," renders the contract void for uncertainty (*Pearce* v. *Watts*, 44 L. J. Ch. 492; L. R. 20 Eq. 492).

A fund applicable to the "Reparations, Ornaments and other Necessary *Occasions*" of a Parish Church may be applied (probably under either of the words "Reparations" or "Ornaments," and certainly under "Necessary Occasions") in the building of a spire to the Church, although the Church has not previously had a spire (*Re Palatine Estate Charity*, 39 Ch. D. 54; 36 W. R. 732; 57 L. J. Ch. 751; 58 L. T. 925; 4 Times Rep. 499). So a gift for the "Reparation" of a building may be applied in erecting a new one (*A.-G.* v. *Wax Chandlers' Co.*, L. R. 6 H. L. 1; 42 L. J. Ch. 425; 28 L. T. 681; 21 W. R. 361).

"Necessary *Outgoings*" deductible from the annual value of a Succession (s. 22, 16 & 17 V. c. 51) mean, "permanent charges made on the occupier of the property,—such as repairs, poor rates, highway, sewer and county rates, drainage-rates and the like;" but Income Tax or Commission to agent is not included (*Re Elwes*, 28 L. J. Ex. 46; 3 H. & N. 719: *Re Cowley*, L. R. 1 Ex. 288).

"Necessary *or Proper* Party," Ord. 11, R. 1 (*g*) R. S. C.; The party to be served hereunder if "proper," need not also be "necessary" (*Sykes* v. *Scholfield*, 28 S. J. 477). *Vh. Massey* v. *Heynes*, 57 L. J. Q. B. 521; 21 Q. B. D. 330; 36 W. R. 834: Ann. Pr.

"Necessary," in the phrase "Necessary *Repairs*," neither adds to nor takes away from the meaning (per Jessel, M. R., *Truscott* v. *Diamond Rock Co.*, 51 L. J. Ch. 260; 20 Ch. D. 251).

"Necessary *Wayleave*;" *V.* WAY.

"Necessary *Work* connected therewith," s. 46, Ry. C. C. Act, 1845; *V. Waterford Ry.* v. *Kearney*, 12 Ir. C. L. Rep. 224.

The power given by s. 96, P. H. Act, 1875 enabling justices to order the doing of *Works* "necessary" for the abatement of a nuisance, does not extend "to whatever the Local Sanitary Authority thinks necessary" (per Stephen, J., *Ex p. Whitchurch*, 50 L. J. M. C. 42; 6 Q. B. D. 545); and accordingly it was there held that an Order to supply a particular kind of closet was bad. But an Order to do such specified things as may be necessary to prevent the recurrence of the nuisance,—*e.g.* to remove a closet from the middle to the outside of a house, or specifying the works necessary to be done to abate a nuisance,—is within the power (*Ex p. Saunders*, 52 L. J. M. C. 89; 11 Q. B. D. 191: *R.* v. *Llewellyn*, 13 Q. B. D. 681: *Whitaker* v. *Derby*, 55 L. J. M. C. 8); and indeed unless the Order does specify what is required to be done it will be bad (*R.* v. *Wheatley*, 55 L. J. M. C. 11; 16 Q. B. D. 34; 54 L. T. 680; 34 W. R. 257; 50 J. P. 424).

"Necessary" Works, s. 46, P. H. Act, 1848; *V. Swanston* v. *Twickenham*, 48 L. J. Ch. 623; 11 Ch. D. 838.

The Surveyor is the proper person to determine what Sewers and Water Mains are "necessary" under ss. 16, 54, P. H. Act, 1875 (*Lewis* v. *Weston-super-Mare*, 58 L. J. Ch. 39; 40 Ch. D. 55; *wh. V.* for a discussion of "Necessary" in this connection).

Where a party has a contractual right to demand such things as he may "*think necessary*,"—*e.g.* to ask for further proof or information,—this does not enable him to act capriciously, it only embraces such things as he may reasonably require (*Braunstein* v. *Accidental Insrce.*, 31 L. J. Q. B. 17; 1 B. & S. 782).

An act is not "necessary" within s. 16, Ry. C. C. Act, 1845, merely because it would be economical to the Company (*R.* v. *Wycombe Ry.*, L. R. 2 Q. B. 310 : *Fenwick* v. *East Lond. Ry.*, L. R. 20 Eq. 544 ; 44 L. J. Ch. 602 : *Pugh* v. *Golden Valley Ry.*, 12 Ch. D. 274).

"Necessary to be dug or carried away or used," s. 77, Ry. C. C. Act, 1845 ; *V.* per Fry, J., *Loosemore* v. *Tiverton Ry.*, 51 L. J. Ch. 574, 575 ; 22 Ch. D. 33, 34 ; 30 W. R. 628 ; 47 L. T. 151 : *Jamieson* v. *North Brit. Ry.*, 6 Scot. L. R. 188.

"Necessary to make a *Separate Valuation*," s. 76, 32 & 33 V. c. 67 ; *V. A.-G.* v. *Westminster Chambers Assn.*, 45 L. J. Ex. 886 ; 1 Ex. D. 469.

V. If Necessary.

NECESSITOUS.—*V.* Relations.

NECESSITY.—Baking rolls on a Sunday is not a "Work of Necessity" within the exception in s. 1, Sunday Act, 29 Car. 2, c. 7 (*Crepps* v. *Durden*, 2 Cowp. 640), nor is baking bread in the ordinary course of a baker's business (*R.* v. *Younger*, 5 T. R. 451 : *Va.* 34 G. 3, c. 61) ; but baking dinners for customers is (*R.* v. *Cox*, 2 Burr. 787 : *R.* v. *Younger*, 5 T. R. 449). Whether haymaking (and indeed it should seem any other work not covered by authority) is of "necessity" is a question of fact on which the finding of Justices is conclusive (*R.* v. *Cleworth*, 4 B. & S. 927).

NECKLACES.—Where a testatrix gave her "Necklaces of every description" to A. and her "Pearls" to B.,—held that a Pearl Necklace passed to A. (*A.-G.* v. *Harley*, 5 Russ. 173 ; 7 L. J. O. S. Ch. 31).

NEED.—*V.* In case of need.

NEED NOT.—This phrase does not mean "must not ;" and therefore though by sub-s. 2, s. 1, M. W. P. Act, 1882, a husband "need not" be joined in actions by or against his wife, yet he *may* be joined, especially so where the wife is a defendant in an action of tort (*Seroka* v. *Kattenburg*, 17 Q. B. D. 177 ; 55 L. J. Q. B. 375 ; 54 L. T. 649 ; 34 W. R. 542).

V. Must not.

NEEDFUL.—*V.* Do the needful.

NEGATIVE PREGNANT.—*V.* Termes de la Ley, *Negativa pregnans*: R. 19, Ord. 19, R. S. C.

NEGLECT.—To "neglect" doing, "is the omission to do some duty which the party is able to do" (per Patteson, J., *King* v. *Burrell*, 12 A. & E. 468).

A prisoner was convicted on an Indictment charging him with Neglect to provide food and clothing for his child, but omitting to allege ability ;—held, that the ability to provide was implied in the word "Neglect" (*R.* v. *Ryland*, 37 L. J. M. C. 10 ; L. R. 1 C. C. R. 99).

V. Wilful Neglect.

NEGLECT OR DEFAULT.—"A 'Neglect' and a 'Default' (in a Covenant for Quiet Enjoyment) seems to imply something more than the mere want of discretion with respect to the covenantor's own interests; something like the breach of a duty or legal obligation existing at the time; those words, in their proper sense, implying the not doing some act to secure his title which he ought to have done, and which he had the power to do; and the not preventing or avoiding some danger to the title which he might have prevented—or avoided" (per Tindal, C. J., *Woodhouse* v. *Jenkins*, 9 Bing. 441, 442). *Vf.* DEFAULT: Sug. V. & P. 602–604.

NEGLECT OR MISCONDUCT.—*V.* CONDUCE.

NEGLIGENCE.—"Negligence" is not an affirmative word; "it is a negative word; it is the absence of such care, skill and diligence as it was the duty of the person to bring to the performance of the work which he is said not to have performed" (per Willes, J., *Grill* v. *General Iron Screw Collier Co.*, 35 L. J. C. P. 330).

"Negligence is the omitting to do something that a reasonable man would do, or the doing something which a reasonable man would not do" (per Alderson, B., *Blyth* v. *Birmingham Water Works Co.*, 25 L. J. Ex. 212; 11 Ex. 781). Accordingly it was there held that a Water Works Co. were not liable for injuries occasioned by one of their plugs bursting through an extraordinary frost.

Where in a Bill of Lading, or Contract for Towage, the owners of the vessel contract themselves out of liability for "negligence or default" of themselves or their servants, they will be protected from the consequences of breaking any express statutory rule in the same way as they would be for the breach of the general law (*The United Service*, 52 L. J. P. D. & A. 18).

V. GROSS.

NEGLIGENCE OR DEFAULT OF MASTER OR MARINERS.—*V.* 1 Maude & P. 358, citing *The Duero*, L. R. 2 A. & E. 393; 38 L. J. Adm. 69: *Steel* v. *State Line Co.*, 3 App. Ca. 72.

NEGLIGENTLY.—When "Negligently" is a part of the definition of an offence, it implies that the act constituting the offence shall have been done, or caused, by the alleged offender himself; proof that it was done by the alleged offender's servant, without more, will not bring the charge home (*Chisholm* v. *Doulton*, 58 L. J. M. C. 133). *Cp.* KNOWINGLY.

NEGOTIABLE.—"Negotiable Instrument," s. 90, Com. L. Pro. (Ireland) Act, 1856, includes a Bank Note (*M'Donnell* v. *Murray*, 9 Ir. C. L. Rep. 495).

V. NOT NEGOTIABLE.

NEGOTIATE.—"(1) A Bill is negotiated when it is transferred from one person to another in such a manner as to constitute the transferee the Holder of the Bill.

(2) A Bill payable to Bearer, is negotiated by Delivery.

(3) A Bill payable to Order, is negotiated by the Indorsement of the holder, completed by delivery" (s. 31, Bills of Ex. Act, 1882): and so of a Note (s. 89, Ib.).

Vf. subs. 4 & 5 of s. 31, Ib.; and as to requisites of an Indorsement ss. 32 to 37, Ib.

A Power of Attorney "to negotiate, make sale, dispose of, assign and transfer" a Promissory Note, does not authorise its being pledged (*Jonmenjoy Coondoo* v. *Watson*, 53 L. J. P. C. 80; 9 App. Ca. 561); had the word "negotiate" stood alone it might have included a pledge (S. C., 53 L. J. P. C. 84): and if a power to "indorse" be included in the enabling words, that would authorize a pledge (*Bank of Bengal* v. *Macleod*, 5 Moo. Ind. App. 1).

NEIGHBOUR.—Who is my neighbour? How ought he to behave to me? and, How ought I to behave to him? *V.* Mac S. chs. 14–17.

NEIGHBOURING.—A covenant prohibiting anything that may be an ANNOYANCE, &c., to the "neighbouring or adjoining" property, is not restricted, so as only to prevent annoyance to the occupiers of property belonging to the covenantee (*Tod-Heatley* v. *Benham*, 58 L. J. Ch. 83; 40 Ch. D. 80).

NEPHEW: NIECE.—Is the child of a person's brother or sister, whether such brother or sister be of the whole or only of the half-blood (*Grieves* v. *Rawley*, 22 L. J. Ch. 625; 10 Hare, 63). "I have no doubt that the primary meaning, of 'Nephew' or 'Niece,' is 'Child of Brother or Sister'" (per Jessel, M.R., *Wells* v. *Wells*, 43 L. J. Ch. 681; L. R. 18 Eq. 504; 22 W. R. 893; 31 L. T. 16).

Accordingly a great-nephew or great-niece, is not included in a testamentary gift to "nephews and nieces" (*Shelley* v. *Bryer*, Jac. 207: *Falkner* v. *Butler*, 1 Amb. 514: *Crook* v. *Whitley*, 26 L. J. Ch. 350; 7 D. G. M. & G. 490), nor a great grand-nephew in a gift to "grand-nephews" (*Waring* v. *Lee*, 8 Bea. 247): but these extended meanings may be gathered from a context (*Weeds* v. *Bristow*, 35 L. J. Ch. 839; L. R. 2 Eq. 333; 14 L. T. 587; 14 W. R. 726), though not easily (*Thompson* v. *Robinson*, 29 L. J. Ch. 280; 27 Bea. 486). *Vf.* Wms. Exs. 1108; 2 Jarm. 152.

"As regards the term 'Nephew' and 'Niece,' popular language has attached a meaning which includes nephews and nieces *by marriage*; but I do not think there is any such popular usage with regard to the term 'Cousin'" (per Bowen, L.J., *Re Taylor*, *Cloak* v. *Hammond*, 56 L. J. Ch. 173; 34 Ch. D. 255; 55 L. T. 649; 35 W. R. 186. *Vf. Grant* v. *Grant*, 39 L. J. C. P. 140, 272; 39 L. J. P. & M. 17; L. R. 2 P. & D. 8; L. R. 5 C. P. 380, 727; 18 W. R. 951. But in *Wells* v. *Wells*, sup., Jessel, M.R., questioned *Grant* v. *Grant*, adding however that it was not a question of law, but of the English language." *Grant* v. *Grant* was also questioned by Malins, V.-C., in *Merrill* v. *Morton*, 17 Ch. D. 382 ; 50 L. J. Ch. 249 ; 29 W. R. 394 ; 43 L. T. 750).

If a testator has no nephews and nieces of his own and no possibility of any, his wife's nephews and nieces would take under a bequest to his "Nephews and Nieces" (*Sherratt* v. *Mountford*, 42 L. J. Ch. 688 ; 8 Ch. 928 ; 21 W. R. 818 ; 29 L. T. 284 : *Hogg* v. *Cook*, 32 Bea. 641 : *Adney* v. *Greatrex*, 38 L. J. Ch. 414 ; 17 W. R. 637 ; 20 L. T. 647) ; and so of a bequest to nephews and nieces "*on both sides*" (*Frogley* v. *Phillips*, 30 Bea. 168 ; 3 D. G. F. & J. 466 ; 3 L. T. 718). *Vh. Smith* v. *Lidiard*, 3 K. & J. 252.

"*All and every* my Nephews and Nieces ;" *V. Re Goodall*, W. N. (88) 69.

A Residuary bequest to "all my Nephews and Nieces," held (there being legitimate nieces), not to include an illegitimate niece who, in a previous part of the Will, had been spoken of as testator's "niece" (*Re Brown*, 58 L. J. Ch. 420. *Va. Re Hall*, 56 L. J. Ch. 780 ; 35 Ch. D. 551 ; 57 L. T. 42 ; 35 W. R. 797).

NET.—"*Annual* Net Value ;" *V. R.* v. *Wislow*, 5 A. & E. 260 ; 5 L. J. M. C. 122.

"Net *Annual Value ;*" *V. R.* v. *Liverpool*, 20 L. J. M. C. 35 : ANNUAL VALUE.

A direction to sell goods "at such a price as will *realize*" so much "Net *Cash*," does not mean that the goods are necessarily to be sold for ready money ; though possibly, in the absence of a trade custom, that might be the construction if the direction were simply to sell for so much "Net Cash" (*Boden* v. *French*, 20 L. J. C. P. 143 ; 10 C. B. 886).

"Net *Moneys* ;" *V. Court* v. *Buckland*, 45 L. J. Ch. 214 ; 1 Ch. D. 605.

A commission payable to an agent on "Net *Proceeds*," is only payable on the actual sum which reaches the pocket of the principal after deducting all charges, expenses, and bad debts (*Caine* v. *Horsfall*, 17 L. J. Ex. 25 ; 1 Ex. 519 : *Vf. Bower* v. *Jones*, 8 Bing. 65).

"Net *Profits*" of a Company ; *V. Lambert* v. *Neuchatel Asphalte Co.*, 51 L. J. Ch. 882. Net profits is the sum divisible after discharging, or making provision for, every outgoing properly chargeable against the period, whether a year or less, for which the profits are to be calculated (per Kekewich, J., *Glasier* v. *Rolls*, 42 Ch. D. 453).

"When a party stipulates to receive a 'Net *Rent*,' that means a rent clear of all deductions to which it would otherwise be liable ; the covenant to pay land tax and sewers rate must, therefore, be a usual covenant in a lease reserving a certain Net rent" (per Tenterden, C. J., *Bennett* v. *Wormack*, 7 B. & C. 628 ; 3 C. & P. 96 ; 6 L. J. O. S. K. B. 175). The principle of that case would seem to extend to all landlord's taxes, except property tax, where net rent is stipulated for. *Va. Barrett* v. *Bedford*, 8 T. R. 602.

Similarly a direction to Trustees to permit A. to receive "*Net* Rents and Profits" vests the legal estate in the trustees, for they must take the gross rents, and, after paying the charges thereon, hand over the net rents (*Barker* v. *Greenwood*, 8 L. J. Ex. 5; 4 M. & W. 421).

"Net *Rental*" simply means the profit rent,—*i.e.* the difference between the gross rent paid by under-tenants, and the head rents and annual fines (*Re Barnewall*, Ir. Rep. 1 Eq. 308).

V. CLEAR.

NEW BUILDING.—Where a small building erected against the wall of a yard belonging to a house is taken down and re-erected in another part of the yard, the old materials being re-used, and portions of the old wall of the yard being used as two sides of the re-erection,—such a re-erection is a "New Building" within s. 34, Local Government Act, 1858 (21 & 22 V. c. 98), and of bye-laws made thereunder (*Hobbs* v. *Dance*, 43 L. J. M. C. 21; L. R. 9 C. P. 30). But where the proprietor of a house, yard, coach-house, and stable, pulled down the coach-house and stable and erected a building partly upon their site and partly upon the yard, with rooms over—the ground-floor opening into the yard and also into a back street, but the access to the rooms over the ground-floor was by a covered way from the old house,—the object of the new works being to increase the accommodation of the old house which had been converted into an hotel;—this was held not to be a "New Building" within the meaning of the Act just cited (*Shiel* v. *Sunderland*, 30 L. J. M. C. 215; 6 H. & N. 796).

Under s. 157, subs. 2, P. H. Act, 1875, a moveable structure used as a butcher's shop was held a "New Building" (*Richardson* v. *Brown*, 49 J. P. 661).

As to what is a "New Building" seems chiefly a question of fact (*James* v. *Wyrill*, 48 J. P. 725).

NEW DESIGN.—"Design, signifies something in the nature of a picture, or drawing, or diagram,—something to be applied to a subject-matter of manufacture. It may be applied to pottery ware, to calico printing, to worsted, and to a great many other things" (per Crompton, J., *Harrison* v. *Taylor*, 29 L. J. Ex. 3; 4 H. & N. 815); "I apprehend the word 'Design' imports configuration" (per Byles, J., Ib.).

Whether a Design was "New *and* Original," s. 2, 5 & 6 V. c. 100, was a question for the jury; and not to be withdrawn from them because the Design was composed of a simple combination of two sizes of a previously well-known pattern (*Harrison* v. *Taylor*, sup.). And so, under s. 47, Patents, &c., Act, 1883, 46 & 47 V. c. 57, for a Design to be "New *or* Original" it must be "either substantially novel, or substantially original, having regard to the nature and character of the subject-matter" (per Fry, L. J., *Le May* v. *Welch*, 54 L. J. Ch. 283; 28 Ch. D. 35; *Vf. Re Read and Greswell*, 58 L. J. Ch. 624).

NEW HOUSE.—*V. Barlow* v. *St. Mary Abbott*, 53 L. J. Ch. 899; 27 Ch. D. 362; 32 W. R. 966; reversed on another point, 11 App. Ca. 257; 55 L. J. Ch. 680; 34 W. R. 521.

NEW LICENSE.—New Alehouse License; *V. R.* v. *Smith*, 48 L. J. M. C. 38. *Vf.* RENEWAL.

NEW MANUFACTURE.—A new combination of materials previously in use, producing a new, better, or cheaper article than that previously produced by the old method, is a "New Manufacture" or "Invention," within the Patent laws (*Crane* v. *Price*, 12 L. J. C. P. 81; 4 M. & G. 580; 5 Sc. N. S. 338).

V. MANUFACTURE.

NEW PARISH.—The Vestry of any "New Parish," s. 5, 20 & 21 V. c. 81; *V. Cronshaw* v. *Wigan*, 42 L. J. Q. B. 137; L. R. 8 Q. B. 217.

NEW STREET.—For the purposes of s. 157, P. H. Act, 1875, a street becomes a "*New* Street" on its acquiring the character of a "Street" in the ordinary meaning of that word (*V.* STREET); and therefore a way, which would not ordinarily be called a "Street" but which has been included in that word by force of s. 4 of the Act, becomes a "New" Street when buildings are erected by its side in such a mode as to give it a street character (*Robinson* v. *Barton*, 51 L. J. Ch. 467; 52 Ib. 5; 53 Ib. 226; 21 Ch. D. 621; 8 App. Ca. 798; 48 J. P. 276; 50 L. T. 57).

As to when a street is laid out and is "new," reference may be made to the judgment of Brett, L. J., in the case just cited; for although the judgment of the learned judge was reversed by the H. L., that reversal proceeded on a ground that left untouched the value of the following observations:—

"New streets may be made under different circumstances. You may have the whole land on both sides belonging to one owner. Then he makes a plan; he has an intention in his mind, and he has a plan drawn. But that does not begin the street. To my mind that is not *laying out* the street within the meaning of the Act of Parliament. The Act of Parliament does not care what people do upon paper. It cares about what they do in point of fact, and upon the land. When would such an owner *begin* to lay out and form a street? To my mind he would do so when he built his first house, having the intention to go on to make a street. He would have begun to lay out and to form a street then; and it would then from that moment begin to be a street. But streets are formed in another way. Supposing that along the line of that which would eventually be considered a street there are a great many owners. There is not any one of them who would make a plan for the whole; but it may be clear that all of them are intending to build there, and to build, having regard to a roadway—if there is an existing roadway, certainly having regard to that. Then how will those people lay out and form a street? Why, each of them, by what he does on his own land, would be laying out and forming a street. Which of them begins? I should say the one who begins first in point of time begins to form a street; and if you find that there are several proprietors along a line each of whom is letting it be known, so that the tribunal comes to the conclusion that each of them intends to build not absolutely in a line, but in the same direction, why then the tribunal would have the right to say that there is a common intention amongst all these people to build in a particular course. When they have done so, that course will produce a street, and therefore the first of them who in virtue of that, not consensus, but of a common idea, begins to build, and begins to form and lay out that street—he and all others are subject to the jurisdiction of the Board. There is another case which my Lord has alluded to,—where there shall be several proprietors along a long line, but no tribunal could say that there ever was at the same time an intention amongst them all to build,—that is to say, that one man at the end of the street may have that intent, but the others have not shown by any act that they have any intent at all; they have not laid out their land as building land, they have not advertised it as building land—they have done nothing to show that intent. Then the street really forms itself, as it were, by continuous action or successive action without any common intent. Then you have to wait until you can see by the course of building that there is that common intent. The moment you see *that*, you come to the conclusion that it is a street, and that it is begun to be formed."

As to "New Streets" within the Metrop. Local Man. Acts; *V. Pound* v. *Plumstead*, 41 L. J. M. C. 51; L. R. 7 Q. B. 183: *St. Mary Islington* v. *Barrett*, L. R. 9 Q. B. 278; 43 L. J. M. C. 85: *Dryden* v. *Putney*, 1 Ex. D. 223; 40 J. P. 263: *Williams* v. *Powning*, 47 J. P. 486; 48 L. T. 672: *L. B. & S. Ry.* v. *St. Giles, Camberwell*, 48 L. J. M. C. 184; 4 Ex. D. 239: *A.-G.* v. *Wandsworth Bd. of Wks.*, 6 Ch. D. 539; 46 L. J. Ch. 771: *St. John's Hampstead* v. *Hoopel*, 54 L. J. M. C. 147; 15 Q. B. D. 652: *St. John's Hampstead* v. *Cotton*, 16 Q. B. D. 475.

Vh., generally, *Evans* v. *Newport*, 59 L. J. M. C. 8; 24 Q. B. D. 264.

NEW SUCCESSION.—"Any title not conferring a New Succession," s. 15, 16 & 17 V. c. 51; *V. A.-G.* v. *Cecil*, L. R. 5 Ex. 263.

NEW TENANT.—"New Tenant or Occupier" of licensed premises, s. 14, 9 G. 4, c. 61, is not restricted to a tenant next in succession to the licensed occupier, but embraces any succeeding tenant applying during the currency of the license (*Re Todd*, 47 L. J. M. C. 89; 3 Q. B. D. 407).

NEWLY ESTABLISH.—A slaughter-house newly built, and afterwards let to butchers;—held, "newly established" *by the Owners* within s. 64, P. H. Act, 1848 (*Liverpool Cattle Market Co.* v. *Hodson*, 36 L. J. M. C. 30; L. R. 2 Q. B. 131; 8 B. & S. 184). *Cp.* FOUND.

NEWLY FORMED.—*V.* Formed.

NEWSPAPER.—The Newspaper Libel and Registration Act, 1881 (44 & 45 V. c. 60, s. 1), contains, for its purposes (and, *semble*, it may be of general utility), the following definition;—"The word 'Newspaper' shall mean any paper containing public news, intelligence, or occurrences or any remarks or observations therein, printed for sale, and published in England or Ireland periodically or in parts or numbers at intervals not exceeding 26 days between the publication of any two such papers, parts or numbers." This definition is a partial adoption of the definition in Sch. A, 6 & 7 W. 4, c. 76; *Vth. A.-G.* v. *Bradbury*, 21 L. J. Ex. 12; 7 Ex. 97.

Is a Newspaper a Book? *V.* Book.

NEXT.—"Next," "is only an abbreviation of the word 'nearest'" (per Knight-Bruce, V.-C., *Booth* v. *Vicars*, 1 Coll. C. C. 9; 13 L. J. Ch. 147; and *V.* that case and also *Stockdale* v. *Nicholson*, 36 L. J. Ch. 793; L. R. 4 Eq. 359, for illustrations as to the effect of "next" in such a phrase as Next Personal Representatives). "The word 'next' means nearest or nighest; not in the sense of propinquity alone, as for example, three persons on three chairs, one in the midst, those on each side of the middle one are equally near, each 'next' to the centre one. But it signifies also order, or succession, or relation as well as propinquity" (per Kindersley, V.-C., *Southgate* v. *Clinch*, 27 L. J. Ch. 654).

"Next *Quarter Sessions*" for a pauper Settlement Appeal, 13 & 14 Car. 2, c. 12, s. 2, means "next practically possible, in order that the appellants might have the possibility of exercising their right" (per Erle, C. J. delivering jdgmt. of the Court, *R.* v. *Sussex*, 34 L. J. M. C. 71; 4 B. & S. 966: *Vf.* cases therein cited); so of a Poor Rate Appeal under s. 4, 17 G. 2, c. 38 (*R.* v. *Surrey*, 50 L. J. M. C. 10; 6 Q. B. D. 100).

"Next before some suit or action;" *V.* Some.

As to the phrase "day *next appointed*" for holding brewster sessions, in the Sunday Closing (Wales) Act, 1881 (44 & 45 V. c. 61, s. 3); *V. Richards* v. *Macbride*, 51 L. J. M .C. 15; 8 Q. B. D. 119. The Court in that case refused to read that phrase as though it ran the "next day appointed."

Where a *Contract for Sale* of reversionary interests was signed on the 15th Dec., 1885, and the day of completion was therein fixed for "the 28th of December *next*," and if not then completed interest to run on the unpaid purchase money from that day; it was held that the day appointed for completion was the 28th Dec., 1885,—*i.e.*, that "next" was in that connection equivalent to "instant," for that "the 28th of Dec. *next*" was to be read as one noun substantive and meant the next 28th Dec. following the 15th Dec., 1885,—*viz.*, the 28th Dec., 1885 (*Dawes* v. *Charsley*, 30 S. J. 401; W. N. (86) 78: *V.* this case cited, Dart, n. 142, 143). So also, where an Award dated 13th Oct., 1840, directed money to be paid "on the 28th Oct. next," "next" was read "instant" (*Brown* v. *Smith*, 8 Dowl. 867).

"The 29*th February* next," means the 29th February in the next Leap Year (*Chapman* v. *Beecham*, 3 Q. B. 723 ; 12 L. J. Q. B. 42 ; 3 G. & D. 71).

"On the   of," any named month, "next ensuing" means, *semble*, some day of that month next happening (*Chapman* v. *Beecham*, sup).

"*The next two months*," in the Iron Trade ; *V*. *Bissell* v. *Beard*, 28 L. T. 740.

NEXT AVOIDANCE.—The gift of the "Next Avoidance" of a Living, was in *Hatch* v. *Hatch* (20 Bea. 105), construed as the next at the testator's disposal.

The words "Next Avoidance of, or Presentation to, any Benefice,"—12 Anne, st. 2, c. 12, s. 2,—refer only to chattel interests and do not extend to freehold estates, and therefore the purchase of an estate for life in an Advowson is not Simony within the statute (*Walsh* v. *Bp. of Lincoln*, 44 L. J. C. P. 244 ; L. R. 10 C. P. 518 ; 32 L. T. 471 ; 23 W. R. 829).

NEXT ENTITLED.—"Next entitled in Remainder ;" *V*. *Turton* v. *Lambarde*, 29 L. J. Ch. 361 ; 1 D. G. F. & J. 495.

NEXT FRIEND.—"Here (Litt. s. 123) *friend* (amy) is taken for the next of blood" (Co. Litt. 88 a).

NEXT HEIR.—In an executory devise to the "Next Heir" of A., the person is meant who shall fill the character of true heir to A. (*Doe* d. *Knight* v. *Chaffey*, 17 L. J. Ex. 154 ; 16 M. & W. 664).

Under a bequest of personalty to testator's "next heir-at-law,"—the heir, and not the next of kin, is the person entitled (*Southgate* v. *Clinch*, 27 L. J. Ch. 651 ; 31 L. T. O. S. 263).

And so in a devise, "Next Heir" may mean a person, and not the heir general (*Baker* v. *Wall*, 1 Raym. 185, cited 2 Jarm. 76). And such a phrase would be one of purchase and not of limitation (*Re Parry*, 55 L. J. Ch. 239 ; 31 Ch. D. 130 ; 54 L. T. 229 ; 34 W. R. 353).

V. Heirs.

NEXT MALE KIN.—"Next male kin," does not indicate a single individual, but a class of persons. (*Re Chapman*, W. N. (83) 232).

NEXT OF KIN.—"The expressions 'Nearest of Kin,' 'Nearest of Blood,' and 'Next of Kin,' are synonymous" (Seton, 925) ; so of "Next of Kindred."

The primary and proper meaning of "Next of Kin" is, the nearest in proximity of blood (whether of the whole or half-blood), living at the death of the person whose next of kin are spoken of (*Withy* v. *Mangles*, 10 L. J. Ch. 391 ; 4 Bea. 358 ; 10 Cl. & F. 215 : *Collingwood* v. *Pace*, 1 Vent. 424 : *Brown* v. *Wood*, Aleyn, 36 : *Moss* v. *Dunlop*, Johns. 490 : *Bullock* v. *Downes*, 9 H. L. Ca. 1 : *Re Webber*, 17 Sim. 221 ; 19 L. J. Ch. 445 :

Halton v. *Foster*, 3 Ch. 505 ; 37 L. J. Ch. 547 : *Heron* v. *Stokes*, 4 Ir. Eq. Rep. 296 : *Mortimore* v. *Mortimore*, 47 L. J. Ch. 134 ; 48 Ib. 470 ; 4 App. Ca. 449, nom. *Mortimer* v. *Slater*, 7 Ch. D. 322 : Wms. Exs. 1123–1128 : 2 Jarm. 108, 124, 129 : Watson, Eq. 1404).

Where however there is an express or implied reference to the Statutes of Distribution (or to intestacy, *Garrick* v. *Camden*, 14 Ves. 372), or the word "heirs" is used as a limitation of personalty and is therefore construed as "next of kin," or the phrase "next of kin" is coloured by association with the word "heirs,"—*e.g.*, a gift of realty and personalty to the "heirs or next of kin" of A.,—in those cases the *statutory* next of kin are entitled (*Doody* v. *Higgins*, 25 L. J. Ch. 773 ; 2 K. & J. 729 ; 27 L. T. O. S. 281 : *Re Thompson*, 48 L. J. Ch. 135 ; 9 Ch. D. 607 : *Vf.* 2 Jarm. 109).

A husband is obviously not of kin to his wife nor a wife to her husband ; and, further, neither would be entitled under a limitation to the statutory "Next of Kin" of the other (*Garrick* v. *Camden*, 14 Ves. 372 : *Re Parry*, *Leak* v. *Scott*, 32 S. J. 645 : *Milne* v. *Gilbert*, 23 L. J. Ch. 828 ; 2 D. G. M. & G. 715 ; 5 Ib. 510 : In Blood. *Cp.* Legal Representatives, and *Vf.* 2 Jarm. 125).

A child illegitimate by the law of England but having the status of legitimacy in a foreign country where his or her parent is domiciled, is one of the "next of kin" of such parent within the Stat. of Distribution, 22 & 23 Car. 2, c. 10 (*Re Goodman*, 50 L. J. Ch. 425 ; 17 Ch. D. 266 ; disapproving *Boys* v. *Bedale*, 33 L. J. Ch. 283 ; 1 H. & M. 798 : *Vf. Re Grove*, 40 Ch. D. 216 ; *Re Andros*, 24 Ib. 637).

Under a bequest to next of kin "*ex parte Maternâ*," a person who is next of kin on the father's, as well as the mother's, side will be entitled (*Gundry* v. *Pinniger*, 21 L. J. Ch. 405 ; 14 Bea. 94 ; 1 D. G. M. & G. 502), unless expressly excluded (*Say* v. *Creed*, 5 Hare, 580) ; and a direction that one line is to take "in preference" to another, does not exclude the latter, but only postpones it (*Boys* v. *Bradley*, 10 Hare, 399 ; 4 D. G. M. & G. 58 ; nom. *Sayer* v. *Bradly*, 5 H. L. Ca. 892, 900 ; nom. *Sayers* v. *Boys*, 25 L. J. Ch. 593).

A devise to "nearest of kin *by way of heirship*," means the heir though he be not next of kin (*Williams* v. *Ashton*, 1 J. & H. 115). But a gift of personalty to "the heirs or next of kin" of A., goes to his statutory next of kin (*Re Thompson*, 48 L. J. Ch. 135 ; 9 Ch. D. 607) ; because, as was pointed out in that case by Jessel, M.R., "next of kin" was there used in connection with "heirs," and as "heirs" (as regards succession to personalty) means statutory next of kin, and as the testatrix meant both descriptions to apply to the one class, that class was the statutory next of kin. *V.* Heirs.

Lineal descendants of children,—*e.g.*, grandchildren,—are not comprised in "Next of Kindred" as that phrase is used in ss. 6 & 7, Stat. of Distribution, 22 & 23 Car. 2, c. 10, for such descendants are provided for in the phrase "legal representatives" of children in s. 6, and the word "no child," in s. 7, should be read " no child either in person or in its descendants : " Therefore where such descendants take (even where they are all in the same degree) they take by representation, *per stirpes* (per North, J., *Re Natt, Walker* v. *Gammage*, 57 L. J. Ch. 797 ; 37 Ch. D. 517 ; 58 L. T. 722 ; 36 W. R. 548 ; following Ld. Hardwicke's last opinion in *Lockyer* v. *Wade*, Barnard, Ch. 444 ; 1 Hargrave's Jurisconsult Exercitationes, 271 ; Burton's Compendium, 7 Ed. 438 ; Joshua Williams' n. on Watkins on Descents, 4 Ed. 259 ; and *Re Ross*, 41 L. J. Ch. 130 ; L. R. 13 Eq. 286 : and rejecting the text of Watkins on Descents ; Toller on Exors., 375 ; Wms. Exs. 1503). Where, however, collaterals take under the phrase "Next of Kindred," they take *per capita* (*Davers* v. *Dewes*, 3 P. Wms. 40 : *Lloyd* v. *Tench*, 2 Ves. sen. 213).

" Legal or Next of Kin ; " *V. Harris* v. *Newton*, 46 L. J. Ch. 268.

In construing a Limitation (common in a *Settlement of a Wife's Property*), to Wife for life, remainder to Husband for life, remainder to *Wife's statutory Next of Kin*, the exact words of each case will of course have to be considered to determine at whose death the Next of Kin are to be ascertained, in the event of the Husband surviving. Romilly, M. R., favoured the death of the Husband as the proper period (*Pinder* v. *Pinder*, 28 Bea. 44 ; 29 L. J. Ch. 527 : *Chalmers* v. *North*, 28 Bea. 175), and so, apparently, does Kay, J. (*Re Beach, Clarke* v. *Hayne*, 42 Ch. D. 529 ; 59 L. J. Ch. 195 ; 37 W. R. 667); but Pearson, J. (*Druitt* v. *Seaward*, 31 Ch. D. 234 ; 55 L. J. Ch. 239 ; 34 W. R. 180) and Stirling, J. (*Re Bradley*, 58 L. T. 631) favoured the death of the Wife as the proper period for ascertaining the class : *Vh.* 33 S. J. 697.

Vh. Chitty, Eq. Ind. 7729–7739.

NEXT PERSONAL OR LEGAL REPRESENTATIVES.— Under a gift to a person's "next Personal Representatives," or "next Legal Representatives," his nearest of kin, in blood, will take (*Booth* v. *Vicars*, 13 L. J. Ch. 147 ; 1 Coll. C. C. 6 : *Withy* v. *Mangles*, 10 L. J. Ch. 391 ; 10 Cl. & F. 215 : *Stockdale* v. *Nicholson*, 36 L. J. Ch. 793 ; L. R. 4 Eq. 359).

NEXT PRESENTATION.—*V.* NEXT AVOIDANCE ; 2 Vin. Ab. *Advowson* (B).

NEXT QUARTER SESSIONS.—*V.* NEXT.

NEXT SURVIVING SON.—*V. Eastwood* v. *Lockwood*, 36 L. J. Ch. 573 ; L. R. 3 Eq. 487.

NIECE.—*V.* NEPHEW.

NIGHT.—" As to what is reckoned Night, and what Day, for this purpose (Burglary) : antiently the day was accounted to begin only at sunrising, and to end immediately upon sunset ; but the better opinion seems to be, that if there be daylight or *crepusculum* enough, begun or left, to discern a man's face withal, it is no burglary. But this does not extend to moonlight; for then many midnight burglaries would go unpunished: and besides the malignity of the offence does not so properly arise from its being done in the dark, as at the dead of night; when all creation, except beasts of prey, are at rest; when sleep has disarmed the owner, and rendered his castle defenceless" (4 Bla. Com. 224: *Vf.* Co. Litt. 135 a).

But now for all purposes relating to Larceny and other similar offences including Burglary, "Night" means from 9 p.m. to 6 a.m. (24 & 25 V. c. 96, s. 1); and a similar definition applies as regards the phrase "in the night," in s. 11, 14 & 15 V. c. 19; *V.* s. 13 thereof. But under the Poaching Act, night-time begins the first hour after sunset, and ends the last hour before sunrise (s. 12, 9 G. 4, c. 69).

Qy. What is the definition of "Night" as used in s. 56, Highway Act, 1835 (5 & 6 W. 4, c. 50), and in s. 10, Gasworks Clauses Act, 1847 (10 V. c. 15)?

NO INSTRUCTIONS.—A tender to a clerk whose reply is, he has "No Instructions," and his master is out, is good (*Finch* v. *Boning,* 4 C. P. D. 143); *secus,* had the reply been. "No Authority" (Ib. *Bingham* v. *Allport,* 1 N. & M. 398).

NOBLEMEN.—*V.* Magnates.

NOISOME.—*V.* Offensive: Noxious.

NOISY.—A Concertina is a "Noisy Instrument" within a Municipal Bye-Law (*Booth* v. *Howell,* 5 Times Rep. 449).

V. Offensive.

NOKA.—A half virgate, generally 7½ acres (Elph. 605).

NOMINATE.—In an agreement for reference, a provision that each party shall "nominate" a referee means, not only naming him, but also the communication of the nomination to the other party (*Tew* v. *Harris,* 17 L. J. Q. B. 2; 11 Q. B. 7).

V. Acknowledge.

NOMINATED.—The person nominated by an instrument creating a trust, as the person to appoint new trustees, is the person "nominated" for the purposes of s. 31, Conv. & L. P. Act, 1881, though the event on which such new appointment becomes necessary was not contemplated at the date of the instrument (*Re Walker,* 53 L. J. Ch. 135; 24 Ch. D. 698).

NOMINEE.—*V. Urquhart* v. *Butterfield,* 56 L. J. Ch. 938; W. N. (87), 102, 228, 239.

NON-BUSINESS DAYS.—*V.* Business Days.

NON-CULTIVATION.—" 'Non-Cultivation' will not let in evidence of bad cultivation" (Dwar. 688, citing no authority).

NONE EFFECT.—"Void & of None Effect;" *V.* VOID.

NON-EXISTING.—*V.* FICTITIOUS.

NOT AS COMMON CARRIERS.—"We hold not as Common Carriers, but as Warehousemen, at Owner's sole risk, and subject to usual warehouse charges;" *V. Mitchell* v. *Lancashire & Yorkshire Ry.*, L. R. 10 Q. B. 256; 44 L. J. Q. B. 107.

NOT BEFORE DEVISED.—"A devise of lands, 'not before devised,' or 'not before disposed of,' carries the reversion in lands which the testator had previously devised for life" (1 Jarm. 655).

NOT EXACTLY.—*V.* EXACTLY.

NOT EXCEEDING.—A sum "not exceeding;" *V. Palmer* v. *Newell,* W. N. (72) 9: *Vf. R.* v. *St. George's, Southwark,* 56 L. J. Q. B. 652; 19 Q. B. D. 533; 35 W. R. 841; 52 J. P. 6.

NOT INSURED.—"Please send the marbles not insured,"—in a direction to a Carrier; *V. North Staffordshire Ry.* v. *Peek,* 10 H. L. Ca. 473; 32 L. J. Q. B. 241.

NOT LESS.—Where time is to be computed as "not less" than a given number of days, that means clear days (*Chambers* v. *Smith,* 13 L. J., Ex. 25; 12 M. & W. 2: *Re Railway Sleepers Co.*, 54 L. J. Ch. 720; 29 Ch. D. 204: *Sv. Re Miller's Dale Co.*, 31 Ch. D. 211).

V. CLEAR: SAY.

NOT LIABLE.—Bequest of Farming Effects to wife for life, remainder to children, with a direction that the wife should "not be liable to account for any diminution" in the effects; held, that the wife took absolutely (*Breton* v. *Mockett,* 47 L. J. Ch. 754; 9 Ch. D. 95).

NOT NEGOTIABLE.—"Where a person takes a crossed cheque which bears on it the words 'Not Negotiable,' he shall not have, and shall not be capable of giving, a better title to the cheque than that which the person from whom he took it had" (s. 81, Bills of Ex. Act, 1882).

The protection given to a Banker by the latter part of s. 12, Crossed Cheques Act, 1876, repd. by Bills of Ex. Act, 1882, was not confined to a cheque which, under the first part of the section, had "not negotiable" in its crossing (*Matthieson* v. *London & County Bank,* 48 L. J. C. P. 529; 5 C. P. D. 7). *Vh.*, now, ss. 80, 82, Bills of Ex. Act, 1882.

NOT OTHERWISE CHARGED.—*V.* DEED.

NOT SETTLED.—A devise of lands, "Not Settled," or "Out of Settlement," or "Not by him formerly settled or thereby disposed of," will pass an unsettled reversion in fee, of lands of which a lesser estate or interest is in settlement (1 Jarm. 654, 655).

V. UNSETTLED ESTATE.

NOT TO BE.—An agreement "*not to be* performed within the space of one year from the making thereof" (s. 4, St. of Frauds), means one which, you can see from its terms, *cannot* be so performed (*Peter* v. *Compton*, Skinner, 353; 1 Sm. L. C. 359: *Boydell* v. *Drummond*, 11 East, 142: *Souch* v. *Strawbridge*, 2 C. B. 808; 15 L. J. C. P. 170: *McGregor* v. *McGregor*, 57 L. J. Q. B. 591; 21 Q. B. D. 424; 37 W. R. 45; 52 J. P. 772). The last case shows that *Davey* v. *Shannon* (48 L. J., Ex. 459; 4 Ex. D. 81) was not well decided. *V.* YEAR.

Vf. McManus v. *Cooke*, 56 L. J. Ch. 662; 35 Ch. D. 681; 56 L. T. 900; 35 W. R. 754; 51 J. P. 708.

NOT TO MY KNOWLEDGE.—Where a proper Requisition on Title is made on a question of fact, "an answer by the seller's solicitor, 'not to his knowledge,' is not satisfactory; he should apply to his client for information before he answers the inquiry, and, if necessary, search amongst the title deeds" (Sug. V. & P. 416).

NOT WORTH THE EXPENSE.—*V.* WORTH THE EXPENSE.

NOTE.—"Note or Memorandum in Writing," s. 17, Stat. of Frauds; For the numerous cases on this phrase, *V.* Add. C. 172; Rosc. N. P. 475; Benj. 185–218; Blackb. 44–65. A Telegram is within the phrase (*Godwin* v. *Francis*, L. R. 5 C. P. 295; 39 L. J. C. P. 121).

"The only difference between an 'Agreement' and the 'Note' of an Agreement is that, in the one instance a formal agreement is meant; and in the other, something not so particular in form and technical accuracy, but still containing the essentials of the agreement" (per Cockburn, C. J., *Williams* v. *Lake*, 29 L. J. Q. B. 3). *V.* AGREEMENT.

V. WRITING.

"Full Notes *of Evidence*," s. 76 (7), 43 V. c. 25 (Canada), may be well taken in short-hand (*Riel* v. *The Queen*, 10 App. Ca. 675).

NOTICE.—"Notice," is a direct and definite statement of a thing, as distinguished from supplying materials from which the existence of such thing may be inferred (*Vh.* per Parke, B., *Burgh* v. *Legge*, 5 M. & W. 420; 8 L. J. Ex. 258: *Vallee* v. *Dumergue*, 18 L. J. Ex. 398; 4 Ex. 290).

The "Notice" prior to action, to be given under the Employers' Liability Act, 1880 (43 & 44 V. c. 42), must be in writing, because the words of s. 7 are only appropriate to a written document (*Moyle* v. *Jenkins*, 51 L. J. Q. B. 112; 8 Q. B. D. 116; 30 W. R. 324); and such notice "should be one and single, delivered at one and the same time, containing in it at one and the same time all the incidents which the statute has made a condition precedent to the right to maintain an action" (per Coleridge, C. J., *Keen* v. *Milwall Dock Co.*, 51 L. J. Q. B. 278 ; 8 Q. B. D. 482 ; so by the other members of the Court). *Keen* v. *Milwall Dock Co.* is an instance of an insufficient notice. *Clarkson* v. *Musgrave*, 51 L. J. Q. B. 525 ; 9 Q. B. D. 386 : *Stone* v. *Hyde*, 51 L. J. Q. B. 452 ; 9 Q. B. D. 76 : *Carter* v. *Drysdale*, 53 L. J. Q. B. 557; 32 W. R. 171, furnish instances of sufficient notices.

The "Notice" to be given to a prisoner of an intention to take a deposition under s. 6, 30 & 31 V. c. 35, must be written (*R.* v. *Shurmer*, 55 L. J. M. C. 153 ; 17 Q. B. D. 323 ; 55 L. T. 126 ; 34 W. R. 656 ; 50 J. P. 743) ; so of a Notice of Distress under 2 W. & M. sess. 1, c. 5, s. 2 (*Wilson* v. *Nightingale*, 15 L. J. Q. B. 309 ; 8 Q. B. 1034) ; though in neither case is writing expressly prescribed.

V. SERVED.

"Notice" of Suspension (s. 4 (h), Bankry. Act, 1883), must be a definite statement of suspension or intention to suspend (*Ex p. Gibson, Re Lamb*, inf.: *Re Crook*, 24 Q. B. D. 320 ; 6 Times Rep. 147) ; and cannot be inferred from a conversation, or even from a meeting of Creditors called by a circular from the debtor, and at which a statement showing his insolvency is produced (*Ex p. Oastler*, 54 L. J. Q. B. 23 ; 13 Q. B. D. 471; 33 W. R. 126 : *Ex p. Jones*, 29 S. J. 357 : *Sv. Ex p. Gibson, Re Lamb*, 55 L. T. 817; W. N. (87) 12 ; affd. 4 Morr. 25).

"Notice" of a Co.'s 2nd meeting, s. 51, 25 & 26 V. c. 89 ; *V. Alexander* v. *Simpson*, 59 L. J. Ch. 137.

"Notice" in s. 24 (3), Jud. Act, 1873, includes Notice to a Defendant by including him in a Counter-claim (*Dear* v. *Sworder*, 4 Ch. D. 482 ; 46 L. J. Ch. 100).

"Notice" is used in s. 3, Conv. Act, 1882, "in its strict legal sense" (per Chitty, J., *Re Cousins*, 55 L. J. Ch. 664 ; 31 Ch. D. 671; 54 L. T. 376 ; 34 W. R. 393).

The "Notice" mentioned in s. 1, 27 & 28 V. c. 39 (the giving of which is a condition precedent to an Assessment Committee hearing objection to a Valuation List), means only the notice to be given by the objecting party to the Committee (*R.* v. *Langriville*, 54 L. J. Q. B. 124).

Cp. definition of Notice in MALICE AFORETHOUGHT.

"*Notice and Knowledge*," of an infirmity in a Negotiable Instrument, means not merely express notice, but knowledge, or the means of knowledge to which the party wilfully shuts his eyes,—a suspicion in the mind of the party, and the means of knowledge in his power wilfully disregarded (per Parke, B., *May* v. *Chapman*, 16 M. & W. 355 : *Vf. Raphael* v. *Bank of England*, 17 C. B. 161; 25 L. J. C. P. 33 ; 1 Sm. L. C. 519).

"Notice" and "Knowledge" contrasted ; *V.* jdgmts. of Ld. Blackburn and Selborne, L. C., *Mildred* v. *Maspons*, 53 L. J. Q. B. 38, 40 ; 8 App. Ca. 888.

NOTICE TO QUIT.—A "Notice to Quit" is a Notice (which generally speaking may be written or verbal) which on its expiry does, of itself and in accordance with the subsisting contract, put an end to a relationship of Landlord and Tenant.

Under Ord. 3, R. 6, R. S. C., a Writ may be specially indorsed where a tenancy has been determined "by Notice to Quit," though such tenancy be only created by an Attornment in a Mortgage Deed (*Daubuz* v. *Lavington,* 53 L. J. Q. B. 283 ; 13 Q. B. D. 347 ; 51 L. T. 206 : *Hall* v. *Comfort,* 56 L. J. Q. B. 185 ; 18 Q. B. D. 11 ; 55 L. T. 550 ; 35 W. R. 48) ; but a Notice demanding possession on a Forfeiture, is not a "Notice to Quit" under that Rule (*Burns* v. *Walford,* W. N. (84) 31 : *Mansergh* v. *Rimmell,* Ib. 34).

Nor is a Notice demanding possession on a Forfeiture, a "*Legal* Notice to Quit" within s. 50, Co. Co. Act, 1856, s. 138, Co. Co. Act, 1888 (*Friend* v. *Shaw,* 57 L. J. Q. B. 225 ; 20 Q. B. D. 374 ; 58 L. T. 89 ; 36 W. R. 236 : *V.* LEGAL NOTICE) ; nor is it a "*Regular* Notice to Quit" within s. 1, 1 G. 4, c. 87 (*Doe* d. *Cundey* v. *Sharpley,* 15 L. J. Ex. 341; 15 M. & W. 558) ; nor would a Notice demanding possession of a tenant holding over after surrendering his term be within the last phrase (*Doe* d. *Tindal* v. *Roe,* 2 B. & Ad. 922 ; 1 Dowl. 143).

NOTORIOUS.—*V.* COMMON AND NOTORIOUS.

NOTWITHSTANDING.—"'Anything in this Act to the contrary notwithstanding ;' is equivalent to saying that the Act shall be no impediment to the measure, and precisely corresponds to the words in the second saving of the Stat. of Uses, 27 H. 8, c. 10, 'as if this Act had not been made'" (Dwar. 683, citing *Cheinie's Case ; Cecil's Case,* 7 Rep. 20).

NOW.—"The word 'Now,'—'any property I *now possess* '—would pass all the property possessed by the testator at *the time of his death* " (per Kay, J., *Re Portal to Lamb,* 53 L. J. Ch. 1163,—reversed without affecting this proposition, 54 L. J. Ch. 1012 ; 30 Ch. D. 50,—citing *Wagstaff* v. *Wagstaff,* 38 L. J. Ch. 528 ; L. R. 8 Eq. 229 : *Re Ord,* 12 Ch. D. 22 : *Everett* v. *Everett,* 47 L. J. Ch. 367 ; 7 Ch. D. 428 : *Goodlad* v. *Burnett,* 1 K. & J. 341 : *Re Otley and Ilkley Committee,* 34 L. J. Ch. 596 ; 34 Bea. 525. *Sv.* Wms. Exs. 225). It will, however, be observed that this interpretation is based on the rule embodied in s. 24, Wills Act (1 V. c. 26), which says that every Will "with reference to the *real estate and personal estate* comprised in it," shall speak from the death. *Vf.* HAVE.

For other purposes,—*e.g.,* ascertaining persons or classes, or for fixing a particular description of property, 1 Jarm. 332–334,—"It may be stated, as a general rule, that wherever a testator refers to an actually existing state of things, his language is referential to *the date of the Will,*—and not to his death, as this is then a prospective event. Such, it is clear, is the construction of the word 'Now,' or any other expressions pointing at present time" (1 Jarm. 318 : *Va.* 154, Ib., where it is said that a testamentary "gift to children ' now *living* ' applies to such as are in existence *at the date of the Will* and those only ").

So " now *occupied by A.*" are words of description and relate to the date of the Will (*Hutchinson* v. *Barrow*, 30 L. J. Ex. 280 ; 6 H. & N. 583). *Vf. Cole* v. *Scott*, 19 L. J. Ch. 63 ; 1 Mac. & G. 518 : *Sv.*, as to that case, HAVE.

" I now *Possess ;* " *V. Hepburn* v. *Skirving*, 4 Jur. N. S. 651.

But in the case of a *Residuary* Gift, " Now " does not always have the effect of making the gift speak from the date of the Will (*Miles* v. *Miles*, 35 L. J. Ch. 315 ; 35 Bea. 192 ; L. R. 1 Eq. 462 ; 14 W. R. 272 ; 13 L. T. 697 : *Cox* v. *Bennett*, L. R. 6 Eq. 422 : *Saxton* v. *Saxton*, 49 L. J. Ch. 128 ; 13 Ch. D. 359 ; 41 L. T. 648 ; 28 W. R. 294. *Vf.* Dart, 309).

" Now *and in future ;* " *V. Weller* v. *Stone*, 54 L. J. Ch. 497.

" Now *are*," in a tenant's agreement " to leave the premises in the same state and condition as they now are," may properly be taken as referring to the commencement of the tenancy (*White* v. *Nicholson*, 11 L. J. C. P. 264; 4 M. & G. 95 ; 4 Sc. N. S. 707).

" Now *born ;* " *V.* BORN ; 1 Jarm. 423, 2 Ib. 184, 222.

An assignment of all household goods and other estate and effects of or to which the assignor is " now *possessed or entitled*," or " belonging or due " to him, will not pass a contingent interest under a Will (*Pope* v. *Whitcombe*, 3 Russ. 124 : *Re Wright*, 15 Bea. 367).

" Now *paid ;* " as to when this is a true setting forth of the consideration of a Bill of Sale (s. 8, B. of S. Acts, 1878, 1882) ; *V. Ex p. Allam ; Re Munday*, 14 Q. B. D. 43 : *Hamlyn* v. *Betteley*, 5 C. P. D. 327 ; 49 L. J. C. P. 465 : *Ex p. Hunt, Re Cann*, 13 Q. B. D. 36. The last case distinguished *Ex p. Firth ; Re Cowburn*, 19 Ch. D. 419 ; 51 L. J. Ch. 473. *Vf. Re Hockaday*, 4 Morr. 12 : Rosc. N. P. 1154 ; Watson, Eq. 714.

" Now last past ; " *V.* LAST PAST.

" Now *let at ;* " *V.* USUALLY.

" Now *in the Port of A. ;* " these words, in a Charter-Party, import a warranty (*Behn* v. *Burness*, 32 L. J. Q. B. 204 ; 3 B. & S. 751) ; so do the words " Now *on Passage* " (*Gorrisen* v. *Perrin*, 27 L. J. C. P. 29 ; 2 C. B. N. S. 681).

Devise of messuage " wherein D. now *resides ;* " *V. Otley and Ilkley*, sup.

" Now *residing ;* " *V. Re Lyon*, W. N. (79) 20.

NOXIOUS.—The penalty imposed by s. 64, P. H. Act, 1848 (11 & 12 V. c. 63), for newly establishing, without license, " the business of a blood-boiler, bone-boiler, fell-monger, slaughterer of cattle horses or animals of any description, soap-boiler, tallow-melter, tripe-boiler, or other *noxious or offensive* business, trade or manufacture," was, on the *ejusdem generis* principle, restricted to trades that dealt with substances which are, or must necessarily become, in themselves, noxious or offensive ; and brick-making was not necessarily prohibited (*Wanstead* v. *Hill*, 32 L. J. M. C. 135 ; 13 C. B. N. S.

479 ; 11 W. R. 368). In that case it was also pointed out that all the enumerated trades involve the collection of large quantities of animal matter, which brick-making does not. *Vf. Bamford* v. *Turnley,* cited NUISANCE.

V. OFFENSIVE.

A thing is "Noxious," ss. 58, 59, 24 & 25 V. c. 100, if capable of doing harm, and if noxious as administered ; although innoxious if differently administered (*R.* v. *Cramp,* 49 L. J. M. C. 44 ; 5 Q. B. D. 307 ; 28 W. R. 701 ; 42 L. T. 442 ; 44 J. P. 70, 411. *Vf. R.* v. *Hennah,* 13 Cox, 547 : *R.* v. *Perry,* 2 Ib. 223 : *R.* v. *Blakeman,* 12 Ib. 463 : *R.* v. *Isaacs,* 32 L. J. M. C. 52 ; L. & C. 220). *V.* POISON.

NUISANCE.—"'Nusauns' is where any man levieth any wall, or stoppeth any water, or doth any thing upon his owne ground, to the unlawfull hurt or annoyance of his neighbour" (Termes de la Ley).

"I do not think that the 'Nuisance' for which an action will lie is capable of any legal definition, which will be applicable to all actions and useful in deciding them. The question so entirely depends on the surrounding circumstances,—the place, where,—the time, when,—the alleged nuisance, what,—the mode of committing it, how,—and the duration of it, whether temporary or permanent, occasional or continual,—as to make it impossible to lay down any rule of law applicable to every case, and which will be also useful in assisting a jury to come to a satisfactory conclusion. It must at all times be a question of fact with reference to all the circumstances of the case. Most certainly, in my judgment, it cannot be laid down as a legal proposition, or doctrine, that anything which, under any circumstances, lessens the comfort or endangers the health or safety of a neighbour, must necessarily be an actionable nuisance. That may be a nuisance in Grosvenor Square which would be none in Smithfield Market. That may be a nuisance at mid-day which would not be a nuisance at mid-night. That may be a nuisance which is permanent and continual, which would be no nuisance if temporary or occasional only. A clock striking the hour, or a bell ringing for some domestic purpose, may be a nuisance if unreasonably loud and discordant, of which the jury alone must judge ; but although not unreasonably loud, if the owner, from some whim or caprice, made the clock strike the hour every ten minutes, or the bell ring continually, I think that a jury would be justified in considering it to be a very great nuisance. In general, a kitchen chimney, suitable to the establishment to which it belonged, could not be deemed a nuisance ; but if built in an inconvenient place or manner, on purpose to annoy the neighbours, it might very properly be treated as one. The compromises that belong to social life, and upon which the peace and comfort of it mainly depend, will furnish an indefinite number of examples in which some apparent natural right is invaded, or some enjoyment abridged to provide for the more general convenience or necessities of the whole community" (per Pollock, C. B., *Bamford* v. *Turnley*, 31 L. J. Q. B. 292 ; 3 B. & S. 62 ; 6 L. T. 721). In that case it was held that Brickmaking may be so carried on as to be an actionable Nuisance : *Va. Beardmore* v. *Tredwell*, 31 L. J. Ch. 892 ; 3 Giff. 683 ; 7 L. T. 207 : *Cavey* v. *Lidbetter*, 32 L. J. C. P. 104 ; 13 C. B. N. S. 470 : *Boreham* v. *Hall*, W. N. (70) 57. *Sv. Wanstead* v. *Hill*, cited Noxious. A "Nuisance" is, "an inconvenience materially interfering with the ordinary comfort physically of human existence, not merely according to elegant or dainty modes and habits of living, but according to plain and sober simple notions among the English people" (per Knight-Bruce, V.-C., *Walter* v. *Selfe*, 4 D. G. & S. 322 ; 20 L. J. Ch. 435. This definition was approved in *Tod-Heatley* v. *Benham*, inf.). *Vf. Bendelow* v. *Wortley*, 57 L. J. Ch. 762 ; 57 L. T. 849 ; 36 W. R. 168 : *Reinhardt* v. *Mentasti*, 42 Ch. D. 685 ; 58 L. J. Ch. 787 : *Truman* v. *L. B. & S. Ry.*, 55 L. J. Ch. 354 ; 11 App. Ca. 45 : *Metrop. Asylum District* v. *Hill*, 6 App. Ca. 193 ; 50 L. J. Q. B. 353 : Rosc. N. P. 669–680 : Add. T. 332 *et seq.*

In the ordinary Covenant against "Nuisance, Injury or Annoyance," it would seem that the words are used in the order of their relative extent ; for a Nuisance is also an "Injury" and "Annoyance," whilst there may be an "Annoyance" without its constituting a "Nuisance," or creating any very definite "Injury." "Unless the nuisance complained of is one for which an indictment would lie, or an action could be maintained, it is no Nuisance within the terms" of such a covenant (per Bacon, V.-C., *Harrison* v. *Good*, 40 L. J. Ch. 300 ; L. R. 11 Eq. 338 ; 24 L. T. 263 ; 19 W. R. 346) ; and, accordingly, it was there held that the establishment of a National School, with playground, for boys, in the immediate neighbourhood of valuable residential properties, was not a "Nuisance," though it would be an "Annoyance," and, probably, an "Injury." But in *Tod-Heatley* v. *Benham* (58 L. J. Ch. 83 ; 40 Ch. D. 80 ; 37 W. R. 38), Lindley, L. J., referring to *Harrison* v. *Good*, said, "I am not by any means sure that the V.-C. did not put on the word 'Nuisance' in that covenant too restricted an interpretation ;" and Bowen, L. J., said that that interpretation was "a matter that may be doubted." *Vf. Jenkins* v. *Jackson*, 58 L. J. Ch. 124 ; 40 Ch. D. 71.

V. Annoyance.

A "Nuisance," under s. 8, Nuisances Removal Act, 1855 (18 & 19 V. c. 121), must have been one that was injurious to health (*G. W. Ry.* v. *Bishop*, 41 L. J. M. C. 120 ; L. R. 7 Q. B. 550). But, as used in the corresponding section in the P. H. Act, 1875 (s. 114), Stephen, J., was of opinion that the word "Nuisance" was not confined to something that was injurious to health (*Malton Local Board* v. *Malton Manure Co.*, 49 L. J. M. C. 90 ; 4 Ex. D. 302) ; which latter case was followed in *Bishop Auckland Sany. Authy.* v. *Bishop Auckland Iron Co.* (52 L. J. M. C. 38 ; 10 Q. B. D. 138, *quâ* subs. 4, s. 91 of the P. H. Act, 1875). As used in the same Act in s. 47, subs. 1, the section against keeping any swine or pigstye "so as to be a *Nuisance*,"—the word was held to be used in its general and popular sense, and as not necessarily implying injury to health (*Banbury* v. *Page*, 51 L. J. M. C. 21; 8 Q. B. D. 97).

"Nuisance," s. 19, Sanitary Act, 1866, 29 & 30 V. c. 90, includes an overcrowded house, though occupied by one family only (*Rye* v. *Payne*, 44 L. J. M. C. 148). *Vf.* as to the section, *Barnes* v. *Akroyd*, 41 L. J. M. C. 110; L. R. 7 Q. B. 474: *Norris* v. *Barnes*, 41 L. J. M. C. 154; L. R. 7 Q. B. 537.

V. PURPRESTURE.

NULL AND VOID.—*V.* VOID.

NUMMATA TERRÆ.—A synonym with DENARIATA TERRÆ (Elph. 605).

NURSE CHILD.—A child under the age of seven years is accounted a Nurse Child (*Dumbleton* v. *Beckford*, 2 Salk. 470: *Re Cumner* v. *Milton*, Ib. 528).

NURSERY GROUND.—*V.* GARDEN: MARKET GARDEN.

OATH.—In Acts of Parliament passed since the end of 1850, "the words 'Oath,' 'Swear,' and 'Affidavit,' shall include Affirmation, Declaration, Affirming and Declaring, in the case of persons by law allowed to declare or affirm instead of swearing" (s. 4, 13 & 14 V. c. 21; *Vf.* s. 3, Interp. Act, 1889).

"Proof made upon oath" (s. 32, Solicitors Act, 1843, 6 & 7 V. c. 73),—"I think that admits proof on affidavit, but is not confined to it" (per Esher, M. R., *Osborne* v. *Milman*, 56 L. J. Q. B. 264).

V. PERJURY.

OBEDIENCE.—"In Obedience" to Rules, Bye Laws, or Particular Instructions, s. 1 (4), 43 & 44 V. c. 42; *V. Whately* v. *Holloway*, 6 Times Rep. 190.

V. ENFORCE OBEDIENCE.

OBJECTION.—"Objection made:" *V.* MADE.

OBJECTS OF VERTU.—*V.* VERTU.

OBLATIONS.—*V.* OFFERINGS.

OBLIGATION.—"'Obligation,' is a word of his owne nature of a large extent: but it is commonly taken in the common law, for a bond containing a penalty, with condition for payment of money or to do or suffer some act or thing, &c., and a bill is most commonly taken for a single bond without condition" (Co. Litt. 172 a).

V. Ryland v. *Delisle*, 38 L. J. P. C. 67; L. R. 3 P. C. 17.

OBLIGE.—*V.* BIND.

OBLITERATE: OBLITERATING.—As to revocation of a Will by "obliterating" the same under the Stat. of Frauds (29 Car. 2, c. 3); *V.* 1 Jarm. 133–139. Since the Wills Act (1 V. c. 26, s. 20), an obliteration in a Will is inoperative unless it be executed like a Will or the words erased are no longer "apparent," *i.e.*, apparent by looking at the Will itself, in doing which the assistance of glasses may be used (1 Jarm. 142).

OBOLATA TERRÆ.—Half an acre, or half a square perch (Elph. 605, citing Spelm., *Fardella; Obolata*).

OBSERVANCE OR PERFORMANCE.—"A negative cannot be *performed*" (Co. Litt. 303 b), referring to which proposition Fry, J., said, "the word 'performance' is not applicable to negative covenants" (*Evans* v. *Davis*, 48 L. J. Ch. 225), and in another report of that case (10 Ch. D. 757) that learned judge amplified his meaning thus,—"I have always understood that 'Non-Observance' refers to the negative covenants, and 'Non-Performance' to the affirmative covenants." And so Brett, L. J., in delivering the jdgmt. of the Court of Appeal in *Hyde* v. *Warden* (47 L. J. Ex. 127 ; 3 Ex. D. 82) said that the Court were prepared to hold that the forfeiture there "being only in the event of the lessee wilfully failing or neglecting to *perform* any of the covenants, does not apply to a breach of a negative covenant."

That is all clear, but in support of that proposition, *West* v. *Dobb* (39 L. J. Q. B. 193 ; L. R. 5 Q. B. 460) was cited. But in *West* v. *Dobb* the words of forfeiture were, in case the lessee "should fail in the *observance* or performance of any or either of the covenants or agreements" on his part ; and, assuming the correctness of the dictum of Fry, J., above stated, a negative covenant would be within the word "observance." This latter word seems, however, not to have been observed. Nor indeed was the point necessary for the decision in *West* v. *Dobb*. Kelly, C. B., speaking for himself and Channell, B., merely said, "the proviso *seems* to refer only to a failure in the performance of an affirmative covenant ;" but Montague Smith, J., said, "I think it quite unnecessary to put a construction upon the words 'Observance or Performance of the covenant.'"

OBSTACLE.—*V.* Unavoidable Obstacle.

OBSTRUCT.—To omit (after notice) to remove an obstruction is to "wilfully obstruct the free passage of a highway," within s. 72, Highway Act, 1835, 5 & 6 W. 4, c. 50 (*Gully* v. *Smith*, 53 L. J. M. C. 35 ; 12 Q. B. D. 121 ; 48 J. P. 309 : *Sv. R.* v. *Lordsmere*, 50 J. P. 388). So, *à fortiori*, is it such an obstruction to leave unlighted at night large stones on a road under repair (*Fearnley* v. *Ormsby*, 4 C. P. D. 136 ; 27 W. R. 823 ; 43 J. P. 384) ; or to leave on the side of a highway anything calculated to frighten horses going along it (*Harris* v. *Mobbs*, 3 Ex. D. 268 ; 27 W. R. 154 ; 39 L. T. 164 : *Wilkins* v. *Day*, 12 Q. B. D. 110 ; 48 J. P. 6).

But an obstruction within this section must involve an interference with the surface of the highway ; and therefore trees and underwood growing over and across a road is not such an obstruction (*Walker* v. *Horner*, 45 L. J. M. C. 34 ; 1 Q. B. D. 4 ; 39 J. P. 773). But if trees or underwood grow *across* a road in such a way as to send a growth up from their roots through the surface of the road, then, *semble*, that would be within *Gully* v. *Smith*, sup.

A custom, *e.g.* for a Fair, may justify such an obstruction (*R.* v. *Smith*,

4 Esp. 109 : *Elwood* v. *Bullock,* 13 L. J. Q. B. 330 ; 6 Q. B. 383) ; but not a private user (*Gerring* v. *Barfield,* 28 J. P. 615 ; 11 L. T. 270).

Changing a Signal, or stretching out the arm as a Signal, so as to cause a Railway Train to go more slowly, is to "obstruct" it within s. 36, 24 & 25 V. c. 97 (*R.* v. *Hadfield,* 39 L. J. M. C. 131 ; L. R. 1 C. C. R. 253 : *R.* v. *Hardy,* 40 L. J. M. C. 62 ; L. R. 1 C. C. R. 278).

"Obstruction," 6 G. 4, c. 129 ; *Vth.* 22 V. c. 34 : *Va.* MOLEST.

OBTAIN.—The primary meaning of "obtain" a Patent is the original obtaining from the Crown : but a context (*e.g.*, as in s. 1, 5 & 6 W. 4, c. 83) may make it to mean "the becoming possessed, either by original grant, by assignment or by any other title" (*Russell* v. *Ledsam,* 14 L. J. Ex. 357 ; 16 Ib. 145 ; 14 M. & W. 588 ; 16 Ib. 633 ; 1 H. L. Ca. 687 : *Vf. Spilsbury* v. *Clough,* 11 L. J. Q. B. 109 ; 2 Q. B. 466).

"The word 'obtains' (in s. 88, 24 & 25 V. c. 96) means an obtaining by the offender from the owner, with an intent on the part of the offender to deprive the owner permanently and entirely of the thing obtained ; and it includes cases in which things are obtained by a contract which is obtained by a false pretence, unless the obtaining under the contract is remotely connected with the false pretence" (Steph. Cr. 267). *Vf.* Rosc. Cr. 449.

"Obtains Credit ;" *V.* CREDIT.

OBTAINED.—A final judgment is not "obtained" (within the meaning of s. 4 (*g*), Bankry. Act, 1883) by anyone except the successful party to the action himself, or his personal representatives, who for this purpose are in fact the same *persona* (*Ex p. Woodall,* 53 L. J. Ch. 966 ; 13 Q. B. D. 479 ; 32 W. R. 774). An assignee of a judgment debt is not within the phrase (*Re Keeling, Ex p. Blanchett,* 55 L. J. Q. B. 327 ; 17 Q. B. D. 303 ; 34 W. R. 538).

V. FINAL JUDGMENT.

But the assignee of a judgment debt is a person who has "obtained" the judgment for the purpose of getting a Garnishee Order under Ord. 45, R. 1, R. S. C. (*Goodman* v. *Robinson,* 18 Q. B. D. 332 ; 56 L. J. Q. B. 392 ; 55 L. T. 811 ; 35 W. R. 274).

OBVENTIONS.—*V.* OFFERINGS.

OBVIOUS.—An "Obvious" *Imitation* within s. 58, Patents Registration Act, 1883, does not mean obvious to the uneducated or unskilled eye, but obvious to a judge or jury sitting as experts (*Mitchell* v. *Henry,* 15 Ch. D. 181 : *Grafton* v. *Watson,* 50 L. T. 420 ; 51 Ib. 141).

A person exposes himself to "Obvious *Risk*" of injury, within an exception in an Accident Policy, (1) if the Risk is obvious to him at the time he exposes himself to it, or (2) if it would be obvious if he were paying reasonable attention to what he is doing (*Cornish* v. *Accident Insrce.,* 58 L. J. Q. B. 591 ; 38 W. R. 139).

V. APPARENT.

OCCASION.—*V.* Inflict.

"Necessary Occasions" of a Church; *V.* Necessary.

OCCASIONED.—An injury to a horse is not "occasioned" by plunging (within a Carrier's exemption) if the animal is made to plunge by actionable negligence (per FitzGibbon, L. J., *Sheridan* v. *Mid. Great Western Ry.*, 24 L. R. Ir. 173).

OCCUPANT.—*V.* Co. Litt. 41 b.

OCCUPATION: OCCUPANCY.—Occupation or occupancy is said to arise out of "the actual possession and manurance of the land" (Vin. Abr. "Occupancy," H. *Vf.* Co. Litt. 249 b).

"Occupation" and "Possession" are used in contrast in ss. 18 & 26, Reform Act, 1832 (2 W. 4, c. 45); and whilst under the latter section an owner of a Rent-charge in fee would be entitled to qualify for a county vote, after having been for the prescribed time in the actual "possession" of the rent-charge, yet if being only entitled for life he is, by the circumstances, driven to claim as for its "actual and *bonâ fide* occupation" under s. 18, then he will fail because a Rent-charge is incapable of such occupation (*Druitt* v. *Christchurch*, 53 L. J. Q. B. 177; 12 Q. B. D. 365). *V.* Actual.

"'Occupation,'"—(as a condition in a devise)—"is not living and residing" (per Ld. Eldon, *Fillingham* v. *Bromley*, T. & R. 536); and if in any given case it means "residing," that does not involve a continual personal living in the house (*V.* Residence). And so a devise of the "Free Use" (*Cook* v. *Gerrard*, 1 Saund. 181, 186 e), or of the "Use and Occupation" (*Whittome* v. *Lamb*, 13 L. J. Ex. 205; 12 M. & W. 813: *Rabbeth* v. *Squire*, 24 L. J. Ch. 203; 19 Bea. 70; 4 D. G. & J. 406: *Mannox* v. *Greener*, L. R. 14 Eq. 456) of land, passes an estate with the right to let or assign it, and is not confined to a personal use and occupation, unless the context clearly calls for that limited construction (*Maclaren* v. *Stainton*, 27 L. J. Ch. 442; 4 Jur. N. S. 199: *Stone* v. *Parker*, 29 L. J. Ch. 874). *Vh.* 1 Jarm. 798: *R.* v. *Eatington*, 4 T. R. 181, cited Elph. 605. Occupied: Reside: Use and Occupation.

"Occupation" *quà* Inhabited House Duty; *V. Bent* v. *Roberts*, 3 Ex. D. 66.

"Occupation" *quà* Poor Rate; *V. Smith* v. *Lambeth*, 52 L. J. M. C. 1; 10 Q. B. D. 327: *Taylor* v. *Pendleton*, 56 L. J. M. C. 146; 19 Q. B. D. 288; 57 L. T. 530; 35 W. R. 762; 51 J. P. 613: Beneficial.

OCCUPIED.—Permitting persons to use small portions of land, for growing potatoes, is a breach of a stipulation in a Lease of a Farm not to "suffer to be occupied by any other person," without consent (*Greenslade* v. *Tapscott*, 3 L. J. Ex. 328; 1 Cr. M. & R. 59; 4 Tyr. 566).

"Premises occupied" by a grantor of a Bill of Sale, s. 7, 17 & 18 V.

c. 36, meant not merely premises of which he is tenant, but premises actually under his control (*Robinson* v. *Briggs*, 40 L. J. Ex. 17 ; L. R. 6 Ex. 1).

V. OCCUPATION : HELD : INHABIT.

OCCUPIER.—The tenant, though absent, is, speaking generally, the "Occupier" of premises (*R.* v. *Poynder*, 1 B. & C. 178), but a servant, or other person who may be there *virtute officii*, is not an Occupier (*Clarke* v. *St. Mary, Bury St. Edmunds*, 26 L. J. C. P. 12 ; 1 C. B. N. S. 23 : *Bent* v. *Roberts*, 47 L. J. Ex. 112 ; 3 Ex. D. 66 : *R.* v. *Spurrell*, 35 L. J. M. C. 74 ; L. R. 1 Q. B. 72).

For cases on Betting Houses Act ; *V.* PLACE.

"Occupier," Ground Game Act, 1880, 43 & 44 V. c. 47 ; *V. Saunders* v. *Pitfield*, 4 Times Rep. 233.

If an owner is driving his cattle, or if, *with his consent*, his cattle are being driven, along a road leading to a Level Crossing on a Railway, such an owner is an "Occupier" of the road, and therefore of "*Adjoining Land*" to the Railway within s. 68, 8 V. c. 20 (*Vh.* s. 47) ; but if the cattle are being driven *without the owner's consent* he is not such an "Occupier" (per Esher, M. R., *Charman* v. *S. E. Ry.*, 57 L. J. Q. B. 598 ; 21 Q. B. D. 524 ; 37 W. R. 8 : *Manchester, S. & L. Ry.* v. *Wallis*, 14 C. B. 213 ; 23 L. J. C. P. 85). *V.* ADJOINING OWNER.

V. TENANT : OCCUPIED : OCCUPATION : Art. 54 J. P. 100.

OCCUPY.—Power "to Occupy"; *V.* OCCUPATION : RESIDE.

OF.—"Of," as meaning "belonging to," *e.g.*, "Burial Ground *of* any Parish," s. 18, 18 & 19 V. c. 128, means one that is parish property, not one that is merely *in* the parish (*R.* v. *St. John, Westgate*, 31 L. J. Q. B. 205 ; 2 B. & S. 703).

"Of" a place, imports dwelling ; and is ordinarily taken to mean that the person spoken of dwells at the place named (Dwar. 675 : *Sv.* per Littledale, J., *R.* v. *Toke*, 8 A. & E. 232 ; 7 L. J. M. C. 74 ; 3 N. & P. 323).

"My estate of A. ;"—In a devise in these words it was held, that "of" was equivalent to "at," and that the devise could not, by extrinsic evidence, be extended to property out of, though contiguous to, A. (*Doe* d. *Chichester* v. *Oxenden*, 3 Taunt. 147). But for this construction it has been suggested that "the distinction between a devise of 'my estate *of* A.,' and a devise of 'my estate *called* A.' is not very perceptible" (1 Jarm. 428 ; CALLED).

"Of" is sometimes the equivalent of AFTER,—*e.g.*, "within 21 days *of* the execution," s. 3, 17 G. 3, c. 26 (*Ex p. Fallon*, 5 T. R. 283 : *Williams* v. *Burgess*, 10 L. J. Q. B. 10 ; 12 A. & E. 635).

OF AND CONCERNING.—"Of and concerning the premises,"

in an Arbitrator's Award; *V. Dunn* v. *Warlters*, 9 M. & W. 296; 11 L. J. Ex. 188: *Perry* v. *Mitchell*, 12 M. & W. 802; 14 L. J. Ex. 88.

OF COURSE.—*V.* Precatory Trust.

OF RIGHT.—*V.* Right.

OF THE BODY.—"The distinction between heirs *of* the body, and heirs *on* the body, must be attended to: where 'heirs *of* the body of the husband begotten by him *on* the body of the wife' are spoken of, the heirs intended are the heirs of the body of the husband, but they are restricted by the words 'on the body of the wife' to a particular class of the heirs of the body of the husband, namely, those that he has by her. 'Heirs begotten by the husband *of* the body of the wife,' means 'heirs of the body of the wife,' but they are restricted to the heirs begotten by the husband. On the other hand, 'heirs begotten by the husband *on* the body of the wife,' means the heirs of their two bodies, because the word 'heirs' is not applied to the one more than the other" (Elph. 235; *wh. Vf.*).

OF THE CLOCK.—This expression indicates "Mean as opposed to Solar Time, but a question might arise as to whether it means Local Mean Time or the Mean Time commonly observed at any given place. London Time, or, as it is called, Railway Time, is now very generally observed, and there is a difference of more than 20 minutes between London and Cornwall. Local Mean Time is the natural meaning" (Steph. Cr. 247, n. 2). *Vh. Curtis* v. *Marsh*, 28 L. J. Ex. 36; 3 H. & N. 866; 4 Jur. N. S. 1112: Time.

OFFENCE.—Contempt of Court in a civil action is not an "Offence" within s. 19, Extradition Act, 1870, 33 & 34 V. c. 52 (*Pooley* v. *Whetham*, 50 L. J. Ch. 236; 15 Ch. D. 435).

Semble, that the non-payment by an Overseer of a sum certified by the Poor Law Auditor as due from him is not an "Offence" within s. 99, 4 & 5 W. 4, c. 76 (*R.* v. *Master*, 38 L. J. M. C. 73; L. R. 4 Q. B. 285; 10 B. & S. 42).

"Offence," in s. 15, Copyright Act, 5 & 6 V. c. 45, is not co-extensive with "Offence" in s. 26 (*Hogg* v. *Scott*, 43 L. J. Ch. 705; L. R. 18 Eq. 444).

Vh. Biggs v. *G. E. Ry.*, W. N. (68) 173.

OFFENSIVE.—In construing a covenant not to carry on any "Offensive" Trade, or Business on premises demised, much will depend on the situation of the premises; and in construing such a covenant it is particularly worthy of consideration, whether such trade as that complained of was carried on there at the time of the demise; and, *semble*, that a trade carried on there at the time of the demise would not be within the covenant (per Tindal, C. J., *Gutteridge* v. *Munyard*, 7 C. & P. 129); and the words "any other offensive trade" must be read as *ejusdem generis* with those they follow (*Doe* d. *Wetherell* v. *Bird*, 4 L. J. K. B. 52; 2 A. & E. 161; 4 N. & M. 285). Neither a Private Lunatic Asylum (*Doe* d. *Wetherell* v. *Bird*, sup.), nor a Hospital for curing diseases which may be infectious (*V.* per Lindley, L. J., *Tod-Heatley* v. *Benham*, 58 L. J. Ch. 91; 40 Ch. D. 80), nor the business of a Licensed Victualler (*Jones* v. *Thorne*, 1 B. & C. 715), nor that of a Lucifer Match Deposit (*Hickman* v. *Isaacs*, 4 L.T. 285), is an "Offensive" Business within such a covenant. In the last case the words were "*Noisome* or Offensive;" and Cockburn, C. J., asked if the word "Dangerous" were in the covenant, and getting a negative reply, said to counsel arguing for a breach, "then you cannot make anything of your point."

The business of a Butcher, though in carrying it on beasts are slaughtered on the premises, is not, necessarily, an "Offensive, *Noisy or Noisome*" trade within such a covenant (*Cleaver* v. *Bacon*, 4 Times Rep. 27).

V. Noxious: Nuisance.

OFFERINGS.—"Offerings: Oblations: Obventions.—Explained in 1 Phil. Ecc. Law (Ed. 1873) 1596, citing Com. Dig. tit. *Prohibition*, G. 11; Ayliffe's Parergon, 11. *Va.* 16 Vin. Ab. 77, tit. *Offerings*" (Elph. 605).

OFFICE.—As to what is an "Office" within s. 3, Betting Act, 1853, 16 & 17 V. c. 119; *V. Shaw* v. *Morley*, 37 L. J. M. C. 105; L. R. 3 Ex. 137; 19 L. T. 15: *Bows* v. *Fenwick*, 43 L. J. M. C. 107; L. R. 9 C. P. 339.

As to what is an "Office" held so as to disqualify as a Director, under a Company's Articles; *V. Iron Ship Coating Co.* v. *Blunt*, 37 L. J. C. P. 273; L. R. 3 C. P. 484.

As to what is an "Office" so as to entitle its holder to compensation on its abolition; *V. R.* v. *Local Govt. Bd.*, L. R. 9 Q. B. 148; 43 L. J. Q. B. 49; 22 W. R. 315: *R.* v. *Carmarthen*, 9 L. J. Q. B. 25; 11 A. & E. 9; 3 P. & D. 35.

"Accepted" Office; *V.* Accepted.

OFFICER.—Neither a Banker (*Re Imperial Land Co.*, 39 L. J. Ch. 331; L. R. 10 Eq. 298), nor a Solicitor (*Re Great Wheal Polgooth Co.*, 53 L. J. Ch. 42: *Re Great Western Coal Co.*, 55 L. J. Ch. 494; 31 Ch. D. 496; 54 L. T. 531; 34 W. R. 516; 2 Times Rep. 293, explaining *Ex p. Valpy & Chaplin*, 7 Ch. 289: *Va. Brown* v. *Thames & Mersey Insrce.*, 43 L. J. C. P. 112), is an "Officer" of a Joint Stock Company within either s. 165, Companies Act, 1862, or (as it would seem) s. 38, Companies Act, 1867. A Trustee is not an "Officer" within the latter section (*Cornell* v. *Hay*, 42 L. J. C. P. 137; L. R. 8 C. P. 328), but he may be within the former (*British Guardian Co.*, W. N. (80) 63).

Its Solicitor is not an "Officer" of a Body Corporate within s. 50, Com. L. Pro. Act, 1854 (*Brown* v. *Thames & Mersey Insrce.*, sup.).

A Union Chaplain or Doctor, is an "Officer" within s. 46, Poor Law Amendment Act, 1834, 4 & 5 W. 4, c. 76 (*R.* v. *Braintree Union*, 10 L. J. M. C. 76; 1 Q. B. 130: *R.* v. *Haslehurst*, 53 L. J. M. C. 127; 13 Q. B. D. 253; 51 L. T. 95; 32 W. R. 877; 48 J. P. 774).

An Architect to a School Board, is an "Officer" within Rule 7, Sch. 3, Elementary Education Act, 1870, 33 & 34 V. c. 75 (*Scott* v. *Clifton School Bd.*, 1 Cab. & El. 435).

The London Agent of a Foreign Company is not its "*Head* Officer" within Ord. 9, R. 8, R. S. C. (*Nutter* v. *Messageries Maritimes*, 54 L. J. Q. B. 527: *Haggin* v. *Comptoir d'Escompte*, 23 Q. B. D. 519. *Vf. Mackreth* v. *Glasgow & S. W. Ry.*, 42 L. J. Ex. 82; L. R. 8 Ex. 149, on same phrase in s. 16, Com. L. Pro. Act, 1852).

The Clerk to stipendiary Magistrates appointed under 53 G. 3, c. 72, is not an "Officer of a Borough, County or Division of a County" within s. 2, 5 & 6 V. c. 111 (*R.* v. *Manchester*, 16 L. J. Q. B. 27; 9 Q. B. 458).

The Bankruptcy Act, 12 & 13 V. c. 106, s. 113, which imposed a penalty on "any Officer" detaining a bankrupt after production of his protection; held, not to apply to the gaoler or governor of a prison, but only to the Officer who actually arrested the bankrupt (*Myers* v. *Veitch*, 38 L. J. Q. B. 316; L. R. 4 Q. B. 649).

OFFICER OF JUSTICE.—*V.* MALICE AFORETHOUGHT.

OFFICIATE.—To "Officiate as a Clergyman" means the public performance of the service of the Established Church, *in accordance with the laws regulating it* (per Hardwicke, L. C., *Trebec* v. *Keith*, 2 Atk. 498).

V. REGULAR CLERGYMAN.

OFFSPRING.—"When a man uses the terms 'Offspring,' 'Issue' or 'Descendants,' they are vague expressions which no doubt, on the particular context, may mean 'Children,' or remote descendants; but, *primâ facie*, it can hardly be supposed to mean 'Children' when that simple word is so obvious a one to use. The word 'Offspring,' in its proper and natural sense extends to any degree of lineal descendants and has the same meaning as 'Issue'" (per Kindersley, V.-C., *Young* v. *Davies*, 32 L. J. Ch. 373; 2 Dr. & Sm. 167; 9 Jur. N. S. 399: *Va. Thompson* v. *Beasley*, 24 L. J. Ch. 327; 3 Drew. 7; 2 Jarm. 101 n.). *V.* ISSUE.

In *Lister* v. *Tidd* (29 Bea. 618), "Offspring" was construed "Children," to the exclusion of grandchildren.

OFTEN.—*V.* AS OFTEN AS.

OLD INCLOSURES.—This phrase is, ordinarily, equivalent to "Old Inclosed Land," or "Old Closes;" and in that ordinary sense itis used in s. 62, Inclosure Act, 1845, 8 & 9 V. c. 118 (*Hornby* v. *Silvester*, 57 L. J. Q. B. 558 ; 20 Q. B. D. 797 ; 59 L. T. 666 ; 36 W. R. 679 ; 52 J. P. 468). "I find the term, 'Ancient Inclosures' and 'Old Inclosures' almost invariably used in private Inclosure Acts to denote inclosed lands in the ordinary sense of the words" (per Lopes, L.J., Ib.).

V. Inclosed Lands.

OLD RENT.—*V.* Accustomed Rent.

OMISSION.—An "Omission" to perform a duty involves the idea that the person to act is aware that performance is required or needful (*Lond. & S. W. Ry.* v. *Flower*, 45 L. J. C. P. 54 ; 1 C. P. D. 77).

V. Error.

OMITTED.—An "Omitted" Interest in Lands, s. 124, Lands C. C. Act, 1845, is one (as the section says) omitted "by mistake ;" *Vth. Thomas* v. *Barry Dock Co.*, 5 Times Rep. 360.

ON.—Where there is a devise to A. in fee, and if he "dies without issue," then, "*at*," or "*on*," or "*upon*" his death, over ;—A. takes an estate in fee with an executory devise over in case he leaves no issue living at his death (*Doe* d. *King* v. *Frost*, 3 B. & Ald. 546 : *Ex p. Davies*, 21 L. J. Ch. 135 ; 2 Sim. N. S. 114 : *Parker* v. *Birks*, 24 L. J. Ch. 117; 1 K. & J. 156 : *Coltsmann* v. *Coltsmann*, L. R. 3 H. L. 121 ; in this last case the words were "die without heirs of the body"). But if the phrase is "*after*" his death, over,—that is not quite so strong (per Wood, V.-C., *Parker* v. *Birks*, 1 K. & J. 165), pointing, as it does, less precisely to the moment of his death ; and accordingly the construction, in the latter case, will frequently give A. an estate tail (*Walter* v. *Drew*, 1 Comyn, 372 : *Doe* d. *Cock* v. *Cooper*, 1 East, 229 : *Jones* v. *Ryan*, 9 Ir. Eq. 249 : *Vf.* 2 Jarm. 516–522).

"If an estate be vested in trustees upon trust for A. for life, and '*on the decease of A.*' to sell,—the trustees have no power to sell during the life of A., however beneficial it may be to the parties interested in the trust (*Johnstone* v. *Baber*, 8 Bea. 233 : *Blacklow* v. *Laws*, 2 Hare, 40 : *Mosley* v. *Hide*, 17 Q. B. 91; 20 L. J. Q. B. 539 : *Want* v. *Stallibrass*, L. R. 8 Ex. 175 ; 42 L. J. Ex. 108). But if an estate be devised to A. for life and after her decease to trustees upon trust to sell 'as soon as conveniently may be after *the testator's decease*,'—the trustees, with the concurrence of A., can make a good title (*Mills* v. *Dugmore*, 30 Bea. 104)." Lewin, 430.

The power to grant Alimony "*On any such Decree*," s. 32, Matrimonial Causes Act, 1857, 20 & 21 V. c. 85, "if not confined to the time of making the Decree, must mean shortly after" (per Jessel, M. R., *Robertson* v. *Robertson*, 8 P. D. 96 ; 48 L. T. 591; 31 W. R. 652).

V. At : Upon : After : Passing.

ON ACCOUNT OF.—*V.* For.

ON ALLOTMENT.—Payment on Shares "on Allotment," means "as and when allotted" (*Browne* v. *Pickering*, 4 Times Rep. 726).

ON ATTAINING.—*V.* ATTAIN.

ON BEHALF.—Where security is to be given "On behalf" of a person,—*e.g.* for costs that may become payable by an Election Petitioner, s. 6 (4), Parl. Elec. Act, 1868, 31 & 32 V. c. 125,—it cannot be given by the person himself (*Pease* v. *Norwood*, L. R. 4 C. P. 235; 38 L. J. C. P. 161); *V.* INSUFFICIENT.

"For and on behalf;" *V.* FOR.

ON BOARD.—*V.* FIRE ON BOARD.

A Bequest of Goods "on board" a ship, may pass goods on board at the date of the Will, but removed thence at the testator's death (*Chapman* v. *Hart*, 1 Ves. sen. 271).

ON DEMAND.—"In general where money is payable *on demand*, the law holds that the debtor is bound to find out the creditor and pay him" (per Blackburn, J., *Toms* v. *Wilson*, 32 L. J. Q. B. 37): and this the debtor is liable to do at once. Therefore a Promissory Note payable "on demand" is payable the instant the note is signed: no demand is necessary prior to bringing an action, and the Statute of Limitations will run from its date (*Norton* v. *Ellam*, 6 L. J. Ex. 121; 2 M. & W. 461: and *V. Maltby* v. *Murrells*, 29 L. J. Ex. 377: *Re Bethell*, 34 Ch. D. 566).

But the reason of the cases last cited seems to come from the peculiar stringency of the Law Merchant by which "the debtor is bound to have the money ready on demand" (per Blackburn, J., *Brighty* v. *Norton*, 32 L. J. Q. B. 40). For in other cases the general rule is, that where a right or duty arises on demand of something else, an actual demand must be made and a reasonable time given for compliance before that right or duty will arise. Thus if, by a Bill of Sale or other document, a power to seize goods be given, if the grantor or other donor of the power does not "immediately upon demand" pay a certain sum, such power will not arise until demand made and subsequent default be made after a reasonable time given to get the money and make the payment; and the word "immediately," or even such a phrase as "instantly on demand and without delay on any pretence whatsoever," will not alter that construction (*Toms* v. *Wilson*, 32 L. J. Q. B. 33, 382; 4 B. & S. 442; 11 W. R. 117: *Brighty* v. *Norton*, 32 L. J. Q. B. 38; 3 B. & S. 305; 11 W. R. 167: *Massey* v. *Sladen*, 38 L. J. Ex. 34; L. R. 4 Ex. 13: *Moore* v. *Shelley*, 52 L. J. P. C. 35; 8 App. Ca. 285; 48 L. T. 918): and a premature seizure will give rise to a claim for substantial damages (*Massey* v. *Sladen*, and *Moore* v. *Shelley*, sup.).

So even in the case of a Promissory Note, if it be payable at a certain time *after* demand, an actual demand must be made before action brought, and the Statute of Limitations will only run from such demand (*Thorpe* v. *Booth,* Ry. & Moo. 388). *Vf.* as to Bills and Notes "On Demand," ss. 10, 86, 89, Bills of Ex. Act, 1882.

V. AT SIGHT : IMMEDIATELY.

If a power of distress be given on default of payment of rent "if demanded," the demand need not be accompanied with the formalities required for re-entry on non-payment of rent (*Maund's Case*, 7 Rep. 28 b); and a like rule obtains where such a power is made conditional on the rent being "legally demanded" (*Thorp* v. *Hart*, 30 S. J. 469). From the citation, in the judgment in the last case, of Bac. Ab. (Rent, I.), it would seem doubtful whether a power of distress may not be exercised without a prior demand even though the Lease makes it conditional on a demand being made.

Officer distraining for Rates to return overplus "On Demand," s. 2, 27 G. 2, c. 20; *V. Charinton* v. *Johnson*, 14 L. J. Ex. 299; 13 M. & W. 856.

V. LAWFULLY DEMANDED.

ON DUTCH TERMS.—Marine Policy "to pay all claims and losses on Dutch terms, and according to statement made up by official dispacheur in Holland;" *V. Hendricks* v. *Australasian Insrce.*, 43 L. J. C. P. 188; L. R. 9 C. P. 460.

ON GOODS.—In a Marine Insurance; *V. Mackenzie* v. *Whitworth,* 1 Ex. D. 36.

ON MARRIAGE.—Read "at 21 or marriage" (*Lang* v. *Pugh,* 1 Y. & C. Ch. 718: *Vf.* 1 Jarm. 488, and cases there cited).

ON PAYMENT OF FREIGHT.—"The meaning of the words 'on Payment of Freight' in Bills of Lading and Charter Parties, is not that freight is to be paid either immediately before or immediately after the delivery of the cargo, but that the two acts are to be concurrent, and the Master may demand payment of the freight each day on the cargo delivered" (1 Maude & P. 153, citing *Black* v. *Rose,* 2 Moo. P. C. C. N. S. 277: *Paynter* v. *James*, L. R. 2 C. P. 348). *V.* PAYING FREIGHT.

ON SALE.—"On Sale or Trial," "On Sale or Return;" *V.* SALE OR TRIAL.

ON THE ACCOUNT.—"On the Account of his master or employer," s. 68, 24 & 25 V. c. 96; *V. R.* v. *Cullum,* 28 L. T. 571: *R.* v. *Gale,* 46 L. J. M. C. 134; 2 Q. B. D. 143; 41 J. P. 119.

ON THE BODY.—*V.* OF THE BODY.

ON THE PREMISES.—A Beer Retailer, having only an Off License, placed a bench just outside his street door and his customers sat on the bench whilst drinking the ale he supplied; held that the ale was sold "to be consumed on the premises" (*Cross* v. *Watts*, 32 L. J. M. C. 73; 13 C. B. N. S. 239; 27 J. P. 7, 18); but ale handed through a window to a customer who called for it and drank part of it whilst standing on the highway, was held not to have been sold "to be consumed on the premises," though he drank the remainder of the ale whilst sitting on the window-sill of the house (*Deal* v. *Schofield*, 37 L. J. M. C. 15; L. R. 3 Q. B. 8; 8 B. & S. 760; 31 J. P. 724). *Sv.* now hereon s. 6, 35 & 36 V. c. 94.

ON THE SHORE.—The phrase "on the shore of any sea or tidal water" in s. 458, Merchant Shipping Act, 1854 (17 & 18 V. c. 104) means, according to its nautical interpretation, near the shore, not hard and fast on the shore (*The Leda*, Swabey, 40: *The Mac*, 51 L. J. P. D. & A. 81).

V. KELP-SHORE.

ONCE.—"If a statute requires some act to be done periodically and recurrently once in a certain space of time,—*e.g.* the inspection of the boilers of steamers 'once in 6 months,'—it would, probably, be understood to mean that not more than six months should elapse between the two acts. It would not be satisfied by dividing the year into two equal periods and doing the act once in the beginning of the first, and once at the end of the second period (*Virginia and Maryland Steam Nav. Co.* v. *U. S.*, Taney & Campbell's Maryland Rep. 418)". Maxwell, 423.

ONE.—"It has often been laid down that if a devise be to '*one*' of the sons of J. S. (*he having several sons*) the devise is void for uncertainty, and cannot be made good" (1 Jarm. 370; *Sv.* Watson, Eq. 1298). So an appointment of "either one" of testator's three sisters as sole executrix (*Re Blackwell*, 46 L. J. P. D. & A. 29; 2 P. D. 72), or of "any two" of his sons as exors (*Re Baylis*, 31 L. J. P. M. & A. 119; 2 Sw. & Tr. 613) is void.

But a devise "to *one* of my cousin A.'s daughters that shall marry with a Norton within 15 years" has been held to mean the daughter who shall *first* marry a Norton, and consequently a good devise (*Bate* v. *Amherst*, T. Raym. 82: *Vth. Smithwick* v. *Hayden*, 19 L. R. Ir. 497); and in *Ashburner* v. *Wilson* (19 L. J. Ch. 330; 17 Sim. 204), a remainder, after certain estates for life, "to *a* son of James Wilson, in marriage, his heirs and assigns," was construed as giving an estate in fee to the first-born son of James Wilson. *Vf.* 1 Jarm. 433, n. *x*.

"When an Act of Parliament gives Power or Interest to one person certain, by that express designation of *one*, all others are excluded, although such statute be in the affirmative" (*Foster's Case*, 11 Rep. 59 a; *Vf.* Ib. 64).

"Where a statute appoints a conviction to be 'on the Oath of one Witness,' this ought not to be by the single oath of the Informer; for if the same person shall be allowed to be both prosecutor and witness, it would induce profligate persons to commit perjury for the sake of the reward" (Dwar. 672, citing 2 Ld. Raym. 1545).

"By one Broker or more," 57 G. 3, c. 93, Sch.; here the singular number does not repeal s. 2, 2 W. & M. c. 5, requiring the employment of two sworn appraisers (*Allen* v. *Flicker,* 9 L. J. Q. B. 42 ; 10 A. & E. 640).

ONE DAY.—Notice of Taxation given before 9 o'clock, p.m. of one day for the day following at 12, held "One Day's Notice" within the Rule of Trinity Term, 1 W. 4, s. 12 (*Edmunds* v. *Cates,* 4 M. & W. 66).

ONE TIME.—A covenant to settle property which may "at any one time" be acquired, means "from one and the same source" (Elph. 526, citing *Hood* v. *Franklin,* L. R. 16 Eq. 496 : *Re Hooper,* 13 W. R. 710 ; 11 Jur. N. S. 479). But it is added, "In neither of these cases had the wife any interest in either fund at the date of the Settlement. But in *Mackenzie's Settlement* (2 Ch. 345 ; 36 L. J. Ch. 320), where the wife was entitled at the date of the Settlement to two different reversions which fell into possession at the same instant, it was held that, in estimating the *value* for the purpose of the covenant, the aggregate value of the two shares, and not the value of each share separately, must be taken." So in *St. Leger* v. *Magniac* (W. N. (80) 183), it was held that "at one time" included sums of money coming from different sources, but falling into possession at the same time, *e.g.*, the death of the wife's mother.

ONEROUS.—"Onerous Act," "Onerous Covenant," s. 55 (1), Bankry. Act, 1883 ; *V. Re Maughan, Ex p. Monkhouse,* 54 L. J. Q. B. 128 ; 14 Q. B. D. 956 : *Re Cock, Ex p. Shilson,* 57 L. J. Q. B. 169 : *Re Gee,* 59 L. J. Q. B. 16.

ONLY.—"In trust *only* for E. W. (a married woman), her exs., ads. and assns.," is not a trust for her separate use (*Spirett* v. *Willows,* 34 L. J. Ch. 365 ; 1 Ch. 520).

OPEN.—"In Open *Court,*" s. 5 (1*a*), Debtors Act, 1869, means "what any one would take to be a Court, with the usual accompaniments of the jury-box, the witness-box, the judge's seat, and seats for solicitors, counsel and others" (per Coleridge, C. J.) and does not include the private room of a County Court Judge, though often used by him for hearing causes (*Kenyon* v. *Eastwood,* 57 L. J. Q. B. 455).

An "open *Cover,*" is a proposal to insure, before the goods to be insured are shipped (*Bhugwandass* v. *Netherlands Insrce.,* 14 App. Ca. 83). *V.* Cover.

To "open" Licensed Premises for the sale of drink ; *V. Cates* v. *South,* 1 L. T. 365 ; 23 J. P. 823 : *Overton* v. *Hunter,* 1 L. T. 366 ; 23 J. P. 808 : 37 & 38 V. c. 49, s. 30.

"Open, *keep, or use*" a place for Betting ; *V.* Use.

An "open *Place,*" for the sale of goods, means "open" to the public, not to the sky (per Bowen, arg. *Hooper* v. *Kenshole*, 46 L. J. M. C. 162). *V.* KEPT.

"Open and Public Place;" *V.* PLACE.

V. FIRST OPEN WATER.

OPENED.—Place "opened, kept or used" for illegal betting, s. 1, 16 & 17 V. c. 119; *V. R.* v. *Cook*, 13 Q. B. D. 377: KEEP.

V. DISCOVERED.

OPENING.—A bequest for "Opening New Schools" is not against the Mortmain Act (*Crafton* v. *Frith*, 20 L. J. Ch. 198).

OPERATION.—If a Company is not dissolved, it is "in Operation" within s. 7 (5) Companies Act, 1880 (43 V. c. 19), although it is not carrying on business (*Re Financial Corporation*, 27 S. J. 199). *Vh. Re Outlay Assrce.*, 56 L. J. Ch. 448; 34 Ch. D. 479; 56 L. T. 477; 35 W. R. 343.

"By operation of Law;" *V.* DEVOLUTION.

OPINION.—"In the Opinion of the *Court* or a Judge," s. 57, Jud. Act, 1873, means according to the *judgment* of the Court or Judge, which judgment is subject to appeal (*Ormerod* v. *Todmorden Co.*, 51 L. J. Q. B. 348; 8 Q. B. D. 664). So a decision that it is "desirable" to try without a jury under R. 4, Ord. 36, R. S. C., is appealable (*Re Martin*, 51 L. J. Ch. 683; 20 Ch. D. 365; explaining jdgmt. of James, L. J., *Ruston* v. *Tobin*, 10 Ch. D. 558, 565, and approving *Golding* v. *Wharton Co.*, 1 Q. B. D. 374).

The "Opinion" of a Bishop that proceedings should not be taken under the Public Worship Regulation Act, 1874 (37 & 38 V. c. 85), has to be stated with "the Reason of his Opinion" (s. 9); this does not give him an absolute discretion; his Reasons may be examined on an application for a Mandamus (*R.* v. *London Bp.*, 24 Q. B. D. 213; 58 L. J. Q. B. 385: *Cp. Julius* v. *Oxford Bp.*, 49 L. J. Q. B. 577; 5 App. Ca. 214; 42 L. T. 546; 28 W. R. 726).

V. DISCRETION.

OPPORTUNITY.—A prisoner present, when a statement is taken down against him under s. 6, 30 & 31 V. c. 35, and who is not in any way hindered from cross-examining the witness, has "full opportunity" to do so within the meaning of the section, even though he be not told he may do so (*R.* v. *Shurmer*, 55 L. J. M. C. 153; 17 Q. B. D. 323; 55 L. T. 126; 34 W. R. 656; 50 J. P. 743).

OPPOSITE.—A. conveyed to B. a piece of land with a house (No. 7, Windsor Terrace) on the west side of a road, and covenanted that no building (except monuments and tombs) should be erected on any part of the land belonging to him (A.) "lying on the east side of the said Terrace *and opposite* to the plot of land thereby conveyed;" held, that the covenant applied only to that part of A.'s land which was "opposite" to, and of the same width as,—*i.e.*, " immediately opposite,"—the piece conveyed (*Patching* v. *Dubbins*, 23 L. J. Ch. 45 ; Kay, 1). Wood, V.-C., in his affirmed jdgmt., said,—" The word ' Opposite ' is not, *ex vi termini*, necessarily confined to land precisely opposite, between parallel lines drawn from the sides of the plot conveyed. If the words had been ' the land opposite ' only, it would have been merely a word of description, showing the particular position of the land in question."

OPPOSITE PARTY.—A Third-party, who has obtained leave to resist the plaintiff's claim under Ord. 16, R. 53, R. S. C., is an " Opposite Party" to the plaintiff within Ord. 31, R. 1, and is liable to be interrogated (*MacAllister* v. *Bishop of Rochester*, 49 L. J. C. P. 443 ; 5 C. P. D. 194 : *Eden* v. *Weardale Co.*, 56 L. J. Ch. 178 ; 34 Ch. D. 223 ; 35 W. R. 235) ; but as to when he becomes a " Defendant," within such Rule, so as to be entitled to deliver Interrogatories, *V.* DEFENDANT.

A defendant to a counter-claim, who was not a party to the original action, is not an " Opposite Party," to his co-defendant to the counter-claim who was the plaintiff in the original action (*Molloy* v. *Kilby*, 15 Ch. D. 162 ; 29 W. R. 127 : *Marshall* v. *Langley*, W. N. (89) 222). *Vf.* PARTY.

OPPOSITION FERRY.—*V. Dixon* v. *Curwen*, W. N. (77) 4. *V.* FERRY.

OPPRESSION.—*V.* EXACTION : EXTORTION.

OPTION.—*V.* CASH WITH OPTION OF BILL.

OR.—" Or " is, *primâ facie*, an alternative or substitutionary word (Litt., s. 732 : per Parke, B., *Elliott* v. *Turner*, 15 L. J. C. P. 49 ; 2 C. B. 446). It is, however, " not always disjunctive. It is sometimes interpretative, or expository, of the former word ; *' balivam, vel jurisdictionem.'* Stat. Marlbridge " (Dwar. 689 : *Vf. Hills* v. *London Gas Co.*, 5 H. & N. 312 ; 29 L. J. Ex. 409 ; *Sv. Hills* v. *Evans*, 31 L. J. Ch. 466). In the power in the Infants' Settlement Act, 1855 (18 & 19 V. c. 43, s. 1), to make a Settlement " upon *or* in contemplation of " marriage, the words " in contemplation of " are not expository of " upon ; " for the " or " has its natural disjunctive effect of presenting to the view two distinct things (per Selborne, L. C., *Re Sampson & Wall*, 53 L. J. Ch. 460 ; 25 Ch. D. 482 : *Vth. Seaton* v. *Seaton*, 13 App. Ca. 68).

A bequest to be applied " to any charitable *or* benevolent purpose," or to be expended " in acts of hospitality *or* charity," is void, for the vice of uncertainty taints so much of the bequest as is not charitable, whilst the alternative " or " contra-distinguishes that part from so much of the bequest as is charitable (*Morice* v. *Bishop of Durham*, 9 Ves. 399 ; 10 Ves. 522 : *Ellis* v. *Selby*, 4 L. J. Ch. 69 ; 5 Ib. 214 ; 7 Sim. 352 ; 1 Myl. & C. 286 : *Re Jarman*, 47 L. J. Ch. 675 ; 8 Ch. D. 584 : *Re Hewitt*, 53 L. J. Ch. 132 : *Re Sutton*, 54 L. J. Ch. 613 ; 28 Ch. D. 464 : 1 Jarm. 215–217). *V.* AND.

So, "if a man give lands to one, to have and to hold to him *or* his heires, he hath but an estate for life, for the uncertaintie" (Co. Litt. 8 b.; *Va.* Touch. 106).

In a testamentary gift to a class "or" their heirs, issue, children, or descendants, the word "or" is substitutionary (*Re Sibley,* 46 L. J. Ch. 387; 5 Ch. D. 494: *Re Webster*, 52 L. J. Ch. 767; 23 Ch. D. 737).

But sometimes "Or" is used as an introduction to a substitutional bequest, and then it is synonymous with "In case of" (2 Jarm. 758: *V.* DIE).

An alternative bequest is good, *e.g.*, a gift to A. B. "of £50 *or* £100," the option being with the legatee (1 Jarm. 359, citing *Seale* v. *Seale,* 1 P. Wms. 290: *Haggar* v. *Neatby,* 23 L. J. Ch. 455; Kay, 379: *Phillipps* v. *Chamberlaine,* 4 Ves. 50). But qy. where the *person* to take is in the alternative (*V.* 1 Jarm. 372, 375, 376).

"It appears to be now established that where there is a bequest 'to A. *or* his personal representatives,' or 'to A. *or* his heirs,' the word 'or,' generally speaking, implies a substitution, so as to prevent a lapse" (Wms. Exs. 1215, 1216). Secus, where the gift is "to A. *and* his exs., ads. and assns." (Wms. Exs. 1212); but when "to A. *and his heirs,*" there is no lapse (Ib. 1213).

Where there are alternative times or modes for the performance of an act, and nothing is said as to the person who is to exercise the option, that option is with the person by whom the act is to be performed. Thus, on a sale at 6 "or" 9 months' credit, the purchaser, by not paying at the end of the 6 months, elects not to pay till the expiration of 9 months, and the price cannot be recovered till then (*Price* v. *Nicholson,* 5 Taunt. 333): so of a loan (*Reed* v. *Kilburn Socy.*, 44 L. J. Q. B. 126; L. R. 10 Q. B. 264). *Vf. Alexander* v. *Vanderzee,* L. R. 7 C. P. 530: *Ashworth* v. *Redford,* 43 L. J. C. P. 57; nom. *Ashforth* v. *Redford,* L. R. 9 C. P. 20.

So, a lease for 7, 14 "or" 21 years is not void, but gives the *lessee* an option to determine the lease at the end of the 7th or 14th year (*Dann* v. *Spurrier,* 3 B. & P. 399: *Doe* d. *Webb* v. *Dixon,* 9 East, 15: *Price* v. *Dyer,* 17 Ves. 356: *Goodright* d. *Hall* v. *Richardson,* 3 T. R. 462: *Powell* v. *Smith,* 41 L. J. Ch. 734; L. R. 14 Eq. 85).

A Power to appoint to certain persons "or" their children, gives a discretion (*Longmore* v. *Broom,* 7 Ves. 124).

The power given to Justices by s. 3, Licensing Act, 1872 (35 & 36 V. c. 94), to inflict a fine "or" to imprison, is in the alternative; and "or" is not to be read "or in default of paying the fine:" therefore, a conviction imposing a fine or, in default of payment, imprisonment, is bad (*Re Brown,* 47 L. J. M. C. 108; 3 Q. B. D. 545: *Re Clew,* 51 L. J. M. C. 140; 8 Q. B. D. 511). *Cp.* CASE OR CANISTER: RATED OR ASSESSED.

The power to Justices to order a person to comply with specified health requisitions, "*or otherwise to abate the nuisance,*" gives the Justices the alternative, and does not compel them to make an alternative Order (*Whitaker* v. *Derby,* 55 L. J. M. C. 8; 50 J. P. 357; 2 Times Rep. 68;

dissenting from *Ex p. Whitchurch*, 6 Q. B. D. 545 ; 50 L. J. M. C. 41. *Va. Ex p. Saunders*, 11 Q. B. D. 191 ; 52 L. J. M. C. 89 : *R.* v. *Llewellyn*, 13 Q. B. D. 681).

"Or," as used in a Patent Specification ; *V. Elliott* v. *Turner*, sup. : *Hills* v. *London Gas Co.*, and *Hills* v. *Evans*, sup. : *Beard* v. *Egerton*, 3 C. B. 97 ; 8 Ib. 165 ; 15 L. J. C. P. 270 ; 19 Ib. 36.

OR read as AND, and vice versâ.—"You will find it said in some cases that 'or' means 'and'; but 'or' never does mean 'and.'" (So also 'and' never does mean 'or'). "There is a context which shows that 'or' is used for 'and,' by mistake. Suppose a man said, 'I give the black *cow* on which I usually ride to A. B.,' and he rode on a black *horse.* Of course the horse would pass, but I do not think even a modern annotator of cases would put in the marginal note 'cow' means 'horse.' You correct the wrong word by the context" (per Jessel, M. R., *Morgan* v. *Thomas*, 51 L. J. Q. B. 557 ; 9 Q. B. D. 643).

Still, "it is an ancient rule of construction (the principle of which, however, would not be extended at the present day) to avoid disinheriting issue, that if real estate be devised to A. in fee simple with a limitation over in the event of A. dying under 21 *or* without issue, the word 'or' will be read 'and,' and the gift over will be construed to take effect only in the event of A. dying under twenty-one *and* without issue (*Soulle* v. *Gerrard*, Cro. Eliz. 525 : *Fairfield* v. *Morgan*, 2 B. & P. N. R. 38 : *Right* v. *Day*, 16 East, 69 : *Eastman* v. *Baker*, 1 Taunt. 174) :" Hawk. 203. *Vf.* 1 Jarm. 505–507 ; *Johnson* v. *Simcox*, 31 L. J. Ex. 38 ; 7 H. & N. 344. But if the first estate is less than the fee simple, the rule just stated will not apply (*Mortimer* v. *Hartley*, 20 L. J. Ex. 129 ; 6 Ex. 47 : *Cooke* v. *Mirehouse*, 34 Bea. 27).

Besides that rule there is probably no other general rule which could with practical utility be relied on, for sanctioning the change of "Or" to "And," or the converse (*Sv.* 1 Jarm. 505–524, where this change of words is elaborately treated : *Va.* Watson, Eq. 1316–1318). Whenever such a construction is adopted there must be some violence done to the language which only a context can justify.

In the following cases, "Or" *read as* "And :"—*Read* v. *Snell*, 2 Atk. 645 : *Fowler* v. *Paget*, 7 T. R. 509 : *Harris* v. *Davis*, 1 Coll. 416 : *Morris* v. *Morris*, 17 Bea. 198 : *Shand* v. *Kidd*, 19 Bea. 310 : *Maude* v. *Maude*, 22 Bea. 290 : *Bentley* v. *Meech*, 25 Bea. 197 : *Maynard* v. *Wright*, 26 Bea. 285: *Greated* v. *Greated*, 26 Bea. 621 ; 28 L. J. Ch. 756: *Hawksworth* v. *Hawksworth*, 27 Bea. 1 : *Cooke* v. *Mirehouse*, 34 Bea. 27 : *Greenway* v. *Greenway*, 29 L. J. Ch. 601 ; 2 D. G. F. & J. 128 ; 1 Giff. 131 : *Parkin* v. *Knight*, 15 L. J. Ch. 209 ; 15 Sim. 83 : *G. W. Ry.* v. *Bishop*, 41 L. J. M. C. 120 ; L. R. 7 Q. B. 550 (but *Vth. Malton Local Board* v. *Malton Manure Co.*, 49 L. J. M. C. 90 ; 4 Ex. D. 302, and *Bishop Auckland Loc. Bd.* v. *Bishop Auckland Iron Co.*, 52 L. J. M. C. 38) : *Metrop. Bd. of Works* v. *Steed*, 51 L. J. M. C. 22 ; 8 Q. B. D. 445 : *Re Philps*, L. R. 7 Eq. 151 : *Holland* v. *Wood*, L. R. 11 Eq. 91.

Vf. Wms. Exs. 1089 ; Co. Litt. 99 b.

In the following cases " OR " *not read as* " AND : "—*Mersey Docks* v. *Henderson,* 4 Times Rep. 703 : *Prim* v. *Smith,* 20 Q. B. D. 643 ; 57 L. J. Q. B. 336 ; 58 L. T. 606 ; 36 W. R. 530 : *Re Huggins,* 58 L. J. Q. B. 207 ; 22 Q. B. D. 277 : *Re Clew,* 51 L. J. M. C. 140 ; 8 Q. B. D. 511 : *Re Sanders,* L. R. 1 Eq. 675 : *Simpson* v. *Holliday,* 35 L. J. Ch. 811 ; L. R. 1 H. L. 315 : *Wingfield* v. *Wingfield,* 47 L. J. Ch. 768 ; 9 Ch. D. 658 : *Re Stroud,* W. N. (75) 148 : *Wright* v. *Frant,* 32 L. J. M. C. 204 ; 4 B. & S. 118 : *R.* v. *Phillips,* 35 L. J. M. C. 217 ; 7 B. & S. 593 ; L. R. 1 Q. B. 648 (overruling *R.* v. *Shiles,* 10 L. J. M. C. 157 ; 1 Q. B. 919) : *Harrington* v. *Ramsay,* 22 L. J. Ex. 326 ; 8 Ex. 879 : *R.* v. *Pocock,* 15 L. J. M. C. 132 ; 8 Q. B. 729 : *Green* v. *Wood,* 14 L. J. Q. B. 217 ; 7 Q. B. 178.

In the following cases " AND " *read as* " OR : "—*Brownsword* v. *Edwards,* 2 Ves. sen. 243 : *Waterhouse* v. *Keen,* 6 D. & R. 257: *Townsend* v. *Read,* 30 L. J. M. C. 245 ; 10 C. B. N. S. 317 : *Stapleton* v. *Stapleton,* 21 L. J. Ch. 434 ; 2 Sim. N. S. 212 : *Townsend* v. *Kingston,* 6 Ir. Eq. Rep. 118.
Vf. Wms. Exs. 1089.

In the following cases " AND " *not read as* " OR : "—*Twyne's Case,* 3 Rep. 80 a : *Doe* d. *Usher* v. *Jessop,* 12 East, 288 : *Grey* v. *Pearson,* 26 L. J. Ch. 473 ; 6 H. L. Ca. 61 : *Seccombe* v. *Edwards,* 28 Bea. 440 : *Reed* v. *Braithwaite,* L. R. 11 Eq. 514 ; 40 L. J. Ch. 355 : *Re Kirkbride,* L. R. 2 Eq. 400 : *Barker* v. *Young,* 33 L. J. Ch. 279 ; 33 Bea. 353 : *Oldfield* v. *Dodd,* 22 L. J. Ex. 144 ; 8 Ex. 578 : *Re Sanders,* L. R. 1 Eq. 675.

WHERE BOTH WORDS USED.

When a contract specifies that it is to be performed during "and or" two or more months, that means during either both or all those months (*Bowes* v. *Shand,* 46 L. J. Q. B. 564).
Vh. Chitty, Eq. Ind. 7647–7658.

OR, read as NOR.—*V. Metrop. Bd. of Works* v. *Steed,* 51 L. J. M. C. 22 ; 8 Q. B. D. 445.

ORDELF.—" 'Ordelfe' is where any claimes to have the Ore that is found in the soile or ground " (Termes de la Ley).

ORDER.—An Order (as contrasted with a Judgment) is a judicial or ministerial direction or conclusion on matters outside the record.

An opinion by the Q. B. D. (under s. 11, 12 & 13 V. c. 45), on a Case stated from Quarter Sessions, though not a "Judgment," is an "Order" within s. 19, Jud. Act, 1873, and it is interlocutory (*Walsall* v. *Lond. & N. W. Ry.,* 48 L. J. M. C. 65 ; 4 App. Ca. 30 : *Peterborough* v. *Wilsthorpe,* 53 L. J. M. C. 33 ; 12 Q. B. D. 1: *Holborn* v. *Chertsey,* 15 Q. B. D. 76 ; 54 L. J. Q. B. 137) ; *secus,* as regards such an opinion on a Special Case stated by an Arbitrator when in the reference (made by consent before the Jud. Acts) the parties agreed that neither party should bring error (*Jones* v. *Victoria Dock Co.,* 2 Q. B. D. 314).

A refusal to transfer Bankry. proceedings under R. 16, Bankry. R., 1883, is an appealable "Order" under s. 104, Bankry. Act, 1883 (*Ex p. Gillibrand, Re Walker*, W. N. (84) 159).

But the settlement by Justices of compensation under s. 22, Lands C. C. Act, 1845, is not an "Order," or Conviction within Jervis' Act, 11 & 12 V. c. 43, s. 1 (*R.* v. *Edwards*, 53 L. J. M. C. 149; 13 Q. B. D. 586; over-ruling *Re Edmundson*, 21 L. J. M. C. 193; 17 Q. B. 67).

The mere entry by a County Court Registrar of an Order of Commitment, is not an "Order" (*Harris* v. *Slater*, 57 L. J. Q. B. 539; 21 Q. B. D. 359; 37 W. R. 56).

V. JUDGMENT: FINAL JUDGMENT: TO ORDER.

In a commercial sense, "Order,"—*e.g.* in an agreement to pay commission on "Orders,"—means a binding contract to take a commodity (*Field* v. *Manlove*, 5 Times Rep. 614).

ORDER AND DIRECT.—*V.* PRECATORY TRUST.

ORDER OF ADJUDICATION.—"Order of Adjudication," as defined by s. 42 (2), Bankry. Act, 1883, to include "an Order for the Administration of the estate of a deceased person," is confined to Orders made under s. 125, and does not include a Chancery Administration Order (*Re Fryman*, 57 L. J. Ch. 862; 38 Ch. D. 468; 58 L. T. 872; 36 W. R. 631).

ORDER OF COURSE.—"An Order of Course, means an Order made on an *ex parte* application, and to which a party is entitled as of right on his own statement, and at his own risk" (Ann. Pr. Ord 62, R. 18).

ORDERED.—Goods "ordered to be given in Parochial Relief," s. 77, 4 & 5 W. 4, c. 76; *V. Davies* v. *Harvey*, 43 L. J. M. C. 121; L. R. 9 Q. B. 433.

ORDINARY CALLING.—Enlisting is not part of the "Ordinary Calling" of a soldier within s. 1 of the Sunday Act (29 Car. 2, c. 7); for the ordinary duty of a soldier is to attend drill and fight the battles of his country (*Wolton* v. *Gavin*, 16 Q. B. 48; 20 L. J. Q. B. 73); nor is the giving by a tradesman of a guarantee for the fidelity of an intended employé (*Norton* v. *Powell*, 4 M. & G. 42; 11 L. J. C. P. 202). Nor is it within a farmer's "ordinary calling" to hire out a stallion to cover a mare (*Scarfe* v. *Morgan*, 7 L. J. Ex. 324; 4 M. & W. 270); or to employ labourers (*R.* v. *Whitnash*, 7 B. & C. 596; 6 L. J. O. S. M. C. 26; 1 M. & R. 452). Selling horses is not within the "ordinary calling" of any one except he be a horse-dealer (*Drury* v. *Defontaine*, 1 Taunt. 131: *Fennell* v. *Ridler*, 5 B. & C. 406; 8 D. & R. 204: as to these cases, *V.* per Park, J., *Smith* v. *Sparrow*, 4 Bing. 88). *V.* WORLDLY LABOUR.

ORDINARY COURSE.—As to the phrase, "Transfers of goods in the Ordinary Course *of Business*" in s. 4, Bills of Sale Act, 1878; *V. Re Hall*, 54 L. J. Q. B. 43; 14 Q. B. D. 386; 51 L. T. 795; 33 W. R. 228: *Re Cunningham, Ex p. Attenborough*, 28 Ch. D. 682.

When a Notice is to be considered as served when "in the Ordinary Course *of Post*" it would be delivered, the onus is on the sender to show that there is an Ordinary Course of Post at the place and to the person addressed (*Lewis* v. *Evans*, 44 L. J. C. P. 41; L. R. 10 C. P. 297: *Hudson* v. *Louth*, 6 L. R. Ir. 69: *Doogan* v. *Colquhoun*, 20 L. R. Ir. 361: *Chillis* v. *Cox*, 4 Times Rep. 114).

"Ordinary *Way of his Trade*," s. 11, subs. 14, 15, Debtors Act, 1869; *V. Ex p. Brett*, 45 L. J. Bank. 17; 1 Ch. D. 151.

ORDINARY LUGGAGE.—As regards the contract of carriage, this has the same meaning as PERSONAL LUGGAGE.

ORDINARY OUTGOINGS.—The Cost of Drainage Works under s. 73, 18 & 19 V. c. 120, is within a direction to deduct "Ordinary Outgoings" from the income of a tenant for life; and is certainly so if such outgoings be expressed to be for "taxes *or otherwise*" (*Re Crawley, Acton* v. *Crawley*, 54 L. J. Ch. 652; 28 Ch. D. 431).

V. OUTGOINGS.

ORDINARY TRAIN.—A Train having a special object other than the ordinary traffic and purposes of the particular Railway, going faster and stopping much less frequently than the usual trains thereon, is not an "Ordinary Train" within a Special Act (*Turner* v. *Lond. & S. W. Ry.*, 43 L. J. Ch. 430; L. R. 17 Eq. 561). *Va.* "Special Train," sub SPECIAL.

ORDINARY WAY OF.—*V.* ORDINARY COURSE.

ORDNANCE MAP.—*V.* s. 25, Interp. Act, 1889.

ORIGINAL DESIGN.—*V.* NEW DESIGN.

ORIGINAL HOLDER.—*V. Re Oriental Bank* (54 L. J. Ch. 481; 1 Times Rep. 273), in which it was held, on the construction of a clause in the Charter of that Bank, that "Original Holder" of shares did not mean the first allottee, but meant the immediate transferor to the person holding the shares at the time when the phrase became operative,—*i.e.*, in that case, the winding-up of the Company.

ORIGINAL SUBJECT.—"Original Subject of the cause or matter," s. 24 (3), Judicature Act, 1873; *V. Barber* v. *Blaiberg*, 51 L. J. Ch. 509; 19 Ch. D. 473; 30 W. R. 362.

ORIGINALLY.—By the Blackheath Court of Requests Act (6 & 7 W. 4, c. 120, s. 22), that Court had no jurisdiction over debts "for any sum being the balance of an account *originally exceeding*" £5. "The meaning of the term 'originally' in this clause is somewhat obscure and has not been judicially decided; but we think it is to be understood to apply to a case where credit was given at one time for an amount exceeding £5, either in one or different sums, although afterwards the credit might have been reduced under that sum by part payments before the commencement of the suit in the superior Court" (per Parke, B., *Pope* v. *Banyard,* 7 L. J. Ex. 183; 3 M. & W. 424). And under another statute (2 W. 4, c. 65, s. 10), it was settled that a claim which at its inception exceeded the stated amount, "originally" exceeded it, though reduced by payment below such amount before action brought (*Green* v. *Bolton,* 4 Bing. N. C. 308: *Elsley* v. *Kirby,* 12 L. J. Ex. 96; 9 M. & W. 536).

When passengers, travelling upon branch lines to the termini of the main line, have to await the arrival of a train upon the main line to reach their destination, the terminus of the main line from which the train started is "the place from which the Train *originally started*" (*Barry* v. *Midland G. W. Ry.,* 1 C. L. Ir. Rep. 130).

ORIGINATE.—*V. Best* v. *Stonehewer,* 34 L. J. Ch. 349; 34 Bea. 66; 2 D. G. J. & S. 537.

ORNAMENTAL TIMBER.—*V. Ford* v. *Tynte,* 2 D. G. J. & S. 127: *Magennis* v. *Fallon,* 2 Molloy, 590. *Vf.* TIMBER.

ORNAMENTS.—As to what are the proper "Ornaments" in the Church Services; *V. Westerton* v. *Liddell,* Moore, Special Rep. 187: *Martin* v. *Mackonochie,* 38 L. J. Ecc. 1; L. R. 2 P. C. 365; L. R. 4 A. & E. 279: *Sumner* v. *Wix,* 39 L. J. Ecc. 25; L. R. 3 A. & E. 58: *Clifton* v. *Ridsdale,* 1 P. D. 316: *Ridsdale* v. *Clifton,* 46 L. J. P. C. 27; 2 P. D. 276: *Masters* v. *Durst,* 45 L. J. P. C. 51; 1 P. D. 123, 373: *Elphinstone* v. *Purchas,* 39 L. J. Ecc. 28; L. R. 3 A. & E. 66; nom. *Hebbert* v. *Purchas,* 40 L. J. Ecc. 33; L. R. 3 P. C. 605: *Boyd* v. *Phillpotts,* 44 L. J. Ecc. 1; L. R. 4 A. & E. 297: *Phillpotts* v. *Boyd,* L. R. 6 P. C. 435: *White* v. *Bowron,* 43 L. J. Ecc. 7; L. R. 4 A. & E. 207.

"Ornaments and other Necessary Occasions;" *V.* NECESSARY.

Bequest of "Ornaments;" *V.* PERSONAL ORNAMENTS.

ORPHAN.—Though Johnson defines an Orphan as "a child who has lost father, or mother, or both;" yet where there was a bequest to A. until 21, "provided she be left an Orphan, unprovided for, and lives with part of my family," it was held, by Wood, V.-C., that though A.'s mother was dead, yet as her father was alive and as on him lay the obligation of providing for A., she was not an "Orphan" as contemplated by the bequest (*Guilmette* v. *Mossop,* 7 L. T. 190).

A charitable gift for the "Orphans" of a place is good (*A.-G.* v. *Comber,*

2 Sim. & St. 93 : *Russell* v. *Kellett*, 3 Sm. & G. 264 ; 26 L. T. O. S. 193 ; 2 Jur. N. S. 132).

OTHER.—" 'Other,' ought to be other in Nature Quality and Person" (*Mildmay's Case*, 1 Rep. 177). So a power to appoint "any other Person" a new Trustee, excludes the donee of the Power, and he cannot appoint himself (*Re Skeats*, 58 L. J. Ch. 656).

But "Where general words follow particular ones, the rule is to construe them as applicable to persons *ejusdem generis*" (per Tenterden, C. J., *Sandiman* v. *Breach*, 7 B. & C. 99). This rule has been "acted upon in all times, but nowhere more clearly stated than by Lord Tenterden in *Sandiman* v. *Breach*" (per Denman, C. J., *Kitchen* v. *Shaw*, 7 L. J. M. C. 16 ; 6 A. & E. 729) ; and it is therefore sometimes called Lord Tenterden's Rule, which *quà* the word "Other" may perhaps be more fully stated thus :—Where a statute, or other document, enumerates several classes of persons or things, and immediately following and classed with such enumeration the clause embraces "other" persons or things,—the word "other" will generally be read as "other such like," so that the persons or things therein comprised may be read as *ejusdem generis* with, and not of a quality superior to, or different from, those specifically enumerated. The principle of this rule as regards statutes was explained by Kenyon, C. J., in *R.* v. *Wallis* (5 T. R. 379), wherein he said that if the legislature had meant the general words to be applied without restriction it "would have used only one compendious word."

But very frequently the word receives its wide and larger interpretation of "every other sort or kind." It is perhaps impossible to lay down any workable rule to determine which of these two interpretations the word should receive in any case not already covered by authority. Therefore, it would seem to be the most practically useful way to range, as far as possible, the cases into their two classes of interpretation :—

I. *Ejusdem generis ;*

II. Unrestrictedly Comprehensive.

Ejusdem Generis.

I. The Sunday Act (29 Car. 2, c. 7), from the readiness with which it may be apprehended, and because it was in *Sandiman* v. *Breach* (decided upon that statute) that Lord Tenterden gave his celebrated expression to the rule, may well be placed as the leading example of the application of the *ejusdem generis* interpretation of "Other." That Act enacts that "no tradesman, artificer, workman, laborer, or *other Person* whatsoever," shall exercise his ordinary calling on the Lord's Day ; but neither an Attorney nor Solicitor (*Peate* v. *Dickin*, 4 L. J. Ex. 28 ; 1 Cr. M. & R. 422 ; 5 Tyr. 116), Farmer (*R.* v. *Silvester*, 33 L. J. M. C. 79 ; nom. *R.* v. *Cleworth*, 4 B. & S. 927), nor a Stage-Coachman (*Sandiman* v. *Breach*,

7 B. & C. 96; 5 L. J. O. S. K. B. 298), is comprised within the phrase "other person" in that enactment. (Note. This construction of the Sunday Act is not only remarkable because it stands at the head of the numerous modern cases on the word "Other," but also because the words in that Act are "or other person *whatsoever*," and it might well have been held that "whatsoever" would have widened the meaning of "other," so as to give the latter word an unrestrictedly comprehensive meaning. Nor can the narrowing of the word "other" in the Sunday Act be attributed to any judicial unwillingness to enforce the statute; for *Sandiman* v. *Breach* was decided only three years after the Court which decided it had declared that that statute "ought to receive a liberal construction, being for the better observance of the Lord's Day:" Per Cur., *Ex p. Middleton*, 3 B. & C. 164):—

So the power to examine a judgment debtor or "any *other Person*," in aid of execution (Ord. 42, R. 32, R. S. C.), does not authorize the examination of a stranger to the record; and the phrase only means that if the judgment debtor be a corporation, any of its officers may be examined (*Irwell* v. *Eden*, 56 L. J. Q. B. 446; 18 Q. B. D. 588; 56 L. T. 620; 35 W. R. 511; 3 Times Rep. 535).

So the words "or other *Agent*," in s. 75, Larceny Act, 1861, must be read as *ejusdem generis* with "Banker, Merchant, Broker, Attorney," with which they are there associated (*R.* v. *De Portugal*, 55 L. J. Q. B. 567; 34 W. R. 42).

Abstracts of Title are not within the scale of fees for "perusing Deeds, Wills, and other Documents," provided in the first part of Sch. 2 of the Solrs. Remuneration Ord. (*Re Parker*, 54 L. J. Ch. 959; 29 Ch. D. 199; 52 L. T. 686; 33 W. R. 541). *Vh. Ex p. O'Hagan*, 19 L. R. Ir. 99: *Re Robertson*, 19 Q. B. D. 1.

A *Conveyance* of described lands "and all other the Freehold Heredits" of the grantor "in the several parishes of D., W. & C., in the county of York;" held, not to pass an advowson of a church at D. (*Crompton* v. *Jarratt*, 54 L. J. Ch. 1110; 30 Ch. D. 298: *Svth. Early* v. *Rathbone*, 57 L. J. Ch. 652). So a mortgage by the Secretary of a Building Society to the Society, to secure subscriptions (on an advance), fines, "and other Moneys," does not secure moneys embezzled (*Bailes* v. *Sunderland Bg. Socy.*, 55 L. T. 808; 51 J. P. 310; 3 Times Rep. 97).

A *Bill of Sale* by a yearly tenant of a dwelling-house, of all his household goods, furniture and other household effects, in and about the house, "and *all other his Personal Estate whatsoever*," does not pass his interest in the house (*Harrison* v. *Blackburn*, 34 L. J. C. P. 109; 17 C. B. N. S. 678). But, probably, if the Bill of Sale had included growing crops (per Byles, J., in *Harrison* v. *Blackburn*), or without that, if the document had been an Assignment for the benefit of Creditors, the interest in the tenancy

Ejusdem Generis:—

of the premises would have passed (*Ringer* v. *Cann*, 7 L. J. Ex. 108; 3 M. & W. 343).

A *Proviso for Reduction of Rent* in case of "fire, flood, storm, tempest, or *other Inevitable Accident*," does not apply to damage arising from faulty construction of the premises (*Saner* v. *Bilton*, 47 L. J. Ch. 267; 7 Ch. D. 815: *Manchester Bonding Warehouse Co.* v. *Carr*, 49 L. J. C. P. 809; 5 C. P. D. 507). *V.* INEVITABLE.

The sale of a British ship by licitation is not a Transmission of it "by any lawful means *other than a transfer*," within s. 58, Merchant Shipping Act, 1854 (17 & 18 V. c. 104), as the word "other" in that phrase comprehends only transmissions of the same nature as those previously enumerated in that section (*Chasteauneuf* v. *Capeyron*, 51 L. J. P. C. 37; 7 App. Ca. 127).

"*All other Perils*," in a Marine Insurance, covers only such perils as are *ejusdem generis* with the enumerated perils (*Thames & Mersey Mar. Insrce.* v. *Hamilton*, 12 App. Ca. 484; 56 L. J. Q. B. 626. *Vf.* the cases there cited).

The Act (11 G. 2, c. 19, ss. 8, 9), for extending the Common Law right of Distress, and which enables a landlord to distrain upon "all sorts" of growing "corn and grass, hops, roots, fruits, pulse, or *other Product* whatsoever," does not include trees, shrubs and plants growing in a nursery garden (*Clark* v. *Gaskarth*, 8 Taunt. 431: *Clark* v. *Calvert*, 3 Moo. 114: and see *R.* v. *Hodges*, Moo. & M. 341, which is a similar decision, as regards the offence created by 7 & 8 G. 4, c. 29, s. 38).

"Any way or *other Easement*" in the Prescription Act (2 & 3 W. 4, c. 71, s. 2) does not include a right of wind or air (*Webb* v. *Bird*, 30 L. J. C. P. 384; 31 Ib. 335; 10 C. B. N. S. 268; 13 Ib. 841).

"*Other Building*" to qualify for the parliamentary franchise under s. 27, Reform Act, 1832 (2 & 3 W. 4, c. 45) must be something substantial and *ejusdem generis* with the preceding words, "house, ware-house, counting-house, shop" (*Powell* v. *Boraston*, 34 L. J. C. P. 76; 18 C. B. N. S. 175; H. & P. 170: *Morrish* v. *Harris*, L. R. 1 C. P. 155, nom. *Norrish* v. *Harris*, 35 L. J. C. P. 101: *Powell* v. *Farmer*, 34 L. J. C. P. 71); and so, of the same phrase in s. 3, 2 & 3 W. 4, c. 71 (*Harris* v. *De Pinna*, 33 Ch. D. 238).

In Rating Acts, where power is given to rate enumerated classes of corporeal property (*e.g.*, lands, houses) and "*other Tenements or Hereditaments*," these latter words will generally be confined to *corporeal* tenements or hereditaments, and will not extend to Tithes (*R.* v. *Neville*, 15 L. J. M. C. 33; 8 Q. B. 452: which case seems practically to have over-ruled *Powell* v. *Bull*, 1 Comyn, 265, and *R.* v. *Skingle*, 1 Stra. 100); or Market-Tolls (*R.* v. *Mosley*, 2 B. & C. 226: *Colebrooke* v. *Tickell*, 5 L. J. K. B. 180; 4 A. & E. 916); or the Street Mains of a Gas, or Water, Company (*R.* v.

Ejusdem Generis:—

Manchester Waterworks Co., 1 B. & C. 630 ; 3 D. & R. 20 : *East London Waterworks Co.* v. *Mile End Old Town*, 17 Q. B. 512 : *Chelsea Waterworks Co.* v. *Bowley*, 17 Q. B. 358 ; 20 L. J. Q. B. 520 : but see *R.* v. *Shrewsbury Gas Co.*, p. 548, *post*). So where (by s. 33, 3 & 4 W. 4, c. 90) the rating of "houses, buildings and Property (other than land)" was to be triple that of land, it was held that "property" did not include a canal and towing-path (*R.* v. *Neath Canal Nav.*, 40 L. J. M. C. 193 ; L. R. 6 Q. B. 707).

The duties on metals exported or imported into the port of Arundel and imposed by the Schedule to 6 G. 4, c. clxx., which enumerated Copper, Iron, Lead, Brass, Pewter and Tin, and concluded with an assessment "on all other Metals not enumerated," were held not to apply to gold or silver (*Casher* v. *Holmes*, 9 L. J. O. S. K. B. 280 ; 2 B. & Ad. 592).

The penalty imposed by the Turnpike Act (3 G. 4, c. 126, s. 121) for hauling "any timber or stone or other Thing otherwise than upon wheeled carriages," is confined to heavy substances injurious to roads, like timber or stone, and does not extend to straw (per Crompton and Mellor, JJ., Cockburn, C.J., dub., *Radnorshire* v. *Evans*, 33 L. J. M. C. 100 ; 3 B. & S. 400).

The Act (7 & 8 G. 4, c. lxxv., s. 37) imposing a penalty for the navigation of the Thames by unqualified persons with "any wherry, lighter or *other Craft*," does not include a steam-tug carrying neither passengers nor goods (*Reed* v. *Ingham*, 23 L. J. M. C. 156 ; 3 E. & B. 889). But s. 57 of the same statute, enabling the Corporation to make bye-laws for the navigation "of *Boats*, *Vessels* and *other Craft*," does extend to steam vessels (*Tisdell* v. *Combe*, 7 L. J. M. C. 48 ; 7 A. & E. 788).

The penalty imposed by s. 64, P. H. Act, 1848 (11 & 12 V. c. 63) for newly establishing, without a licence, "the business of a blood-boiler, bone-boiler, fell-monger, slaughterer of cattle, horses or animals of any description, soap-boiler, tallow-melter, tripe-boiler *or other Noxious or Offensive business, trade or manufacture*," was restricted to trades that dealt with substances which are or must necessarily become, in themselves, noxious or offensive; and brick-making, *per se*, was not prohibited (*Wanstead* v. *Hill*, 32 L. J. M. C. 135 ; 13 C. B. N. S. 479).

The penalty imposed by s. 3, Hosiery Manufacture (Wages) Act (37 & 38 V. c. 48) for making deductions from wages "for frame rent and standing *or other Charges*," does not include fines for misconduct (*Willis* v. *Thorp*, 44 L. J. Q. B. 137 ; L. R. 10 Q. B. 383).

So the penalties for fishing without licence in the Severn Fishery District,—(defined by the Secretary of State's certificate to be "So much of the River Severn and of the Rivers Vyrynw and Teme, and of *all other Tributaries* of the said River Severn as is situate" in certain counties, &c.)—are only applicable to such tributaries of the Severn as are like Vyrynw and Teme, *i.e.*, those that are *direct* tributaries (*Merricks* v. *Cadwallader*, 51 L. J. M. C. 20).

A builder employed by a building owner is not entitled to notice of

Ejusdem Generis:—

action under s. 108, Metrop. Bg. Act, 1855 (18 & 19 V. c. 122), which requires such a notice to be given to "any district surveyor or other Person" (*Williams* v. *Golding*, 35 L. J. C. P. 1; L. R. 1 C. P. 69; H. & R. 18: cp. *R.* v. *Doubleday*, p. 547, *post*).

It has been stated that when words descriptive of the rank of persons or things are used in a descending order according to rank, and general words (such as "other" persons or things) are superadded, that word will not include persons or things of a higher rank or importance than the highest named, if there be any lower species to which they can apply (Maxwell, 417, 418; *wh. V.* and *Va.* Wilberforce, 183, 184, for cases on early statutes illustrating this rule). The case of *Ex p. Hill* (3 C. & P. 225), which decided that the 3 G. 4, c. 71, which punished cruelty to any "horse, mare, gelding, mule, ass, ox, cow, heifer, sheep, or other Cattle," did not include a Bull, was certainly a remarkable decision; but it may be doubted whether it, or the rule just stated, which it is supposed to illustrate, is of much practical value at the present day.

For other cases of the application of the *ejusdem generis* interpretation of the word "Other;" *V. Lowther* v. *Radnor*, 8 East, 113: *Kitchen* v. *Shaw*, 7 L. J. M. C. 14; 6 A. & E. 729: *Bramwell* v. *Penneck*, 6 L. J. O. S. M. C. 47; 7 B. & C. 536,—on 20 G. 2, c. 19, s. 1; 6 G. 3, c. 25, s. 4, and 4 G. 4, c. 34, s. 3: *Midgley* v. *Richardson*, 15 L. J. Ex. 257; 14 M. & W. 595: *Hedley* v. *Fenwick*, 3 H. & C. 349, on Enclosure Acts: *R.* v. *Hall*, 1 B. & C. 237,—on 9 Anne, c. 20: *R.* v. *Spratley*, 25 L. J. Q. B. 257; 6 E. & B. 363,—on Municipal Act, 5 & 6 W. 4, c. 76, ss. 32, 142: and *R.* v. *Dickenson*, 26 L. J. M. C. 204; 7 E. & B. 831, on a Bye-law made under that Act: and *Ward* v. *Folkstone Waterworks Co.*, 24 Q. B. D. 334,—on a Local Waterworks Act.

Va. Alms.

Unrestrictedly Comprehensive.

II. It seems the better opinion, in view of modern authorities, that the *ejusdem generis* principle of construing the word "other" is not, in general, applicable in the construction of *Wills*. No doubt in *Hotham* v. *Sutton*, 15 Ves. 326 (which was a Will case), Ld. Eldon said, "The doctrine appears now to be settled in this Court, that the words 'other effects,' in general, mean effects *ejusdem generis*;" but he did not in that case apply the doctrine, but rather seized upon an exception of money out of "other effects" as a reason for giving that latter phrase its full meaning after allowing the express exception. And so although in Wms. Exs. (p. 1188) it is stated that the *ejusdem generis* rule is applicable even to Wills, yet, it is added, "this rule is not of universal application." Whilst at p. 757, 1 Jarm., it is said that the rule "seems scarcely to accord" with the recent decisions there, *et seq.*, very elaborately stated (*Va.* Theobald, 176, 177). If, indeed, the rule exists at all for the purpose of construing Wills, it is at least subject to so many exceptions and may so easily be displaced

Unrestrictedly Comprehensive:—

by very small expressions, that it is probably safe to say that the *ejusdem generis* principle has practically so slender a value, *quà* Wills, as to be inappreciable; and that therefore when general words, such as "other," occur in a Will they must be construed according to the circumstances of each case. Thus in *Hodgson* v. *Jex* (45 L. J. Ch. 388; 3 Ch. D. 122), it was held that a bequest of "all my furniture, plate, linen, and *other Effects*," comprised all the residuary personal estate of the testator; and so of a bequest of "All my Wines and other Property" (*Arnold* v. *Arnold*, 4 L. J. Ch. 123; 2 My. & K. 365; *Vf. Bernard* v. *Minshull*, 28 L. J. Ch. 649; Johns. 276: 1 Jarm. 751, 754, n.: ET CETERA).

It would also seem that the *ejusdem generis* rule of interpretation has but little, if any, value in statutes conferring discretionary powers on the judiciary or such like public functionaries. Thus the power to remit to the County Court actions for "Malicious Prosecution, Illegal Arrest, Illegal Distress, Assault, False Imprisonment, Libel, Slander, Seduction, *or other action of Tort*," in cases where the plaintiff has no visible means of paying costs (s. 10, Co. Co. Act, 1867; *Sv.* now Co. Co. Act, 1888, s. 66), seems to have applied to all actions of tort without limitation (*Clapham* v. *Oliver*, 30 L. T. 365; 22 W. R. 655).

So the power given by s. 7 of the County Rate Act, 1852 (15 & 16 V. c. 81), to a County Assessment Committee to summon "overseers, constables, assessors, collectors, and any *other Persons* whomsoever" to produce documents relating to values of property, &c., is not confined to officials, but extends to all persons whomsoever (*R.* v. *Doubleday*, 3 E. & E. 501); *Cp. Williams* v. *Goldring*, p. 546, *ante*.

The words "any *other Article or Thing*" in s. 37, Prisons Act, 1865 (28 & 29 V. c. 126), which makes it felony to facilitate the escape of a prisoner by conveying to the prison "any mask, dress, or other disguise, or any letter, or any other Article or Thing," mean any other article or thing of any kind, sort or description whatsoever, *e.g.* a crow-bar (*R.* v. *Payne*, 35 L. J. M. C. 170; L. R. 1 C. C. R. 27). *Note.*—The Court in that case gave as a reason for its judgment that all the prior statutes on the subject had included a crow-bar, but its omission should, it is submitted, have rather had a contrary effect. The decision would, perhaps, be better based if the word "or," after the word "letter," were construed as altogether disconnecting "article or thing" from the preceding enumerations.

A power to rescind a Contract "from any other *Cause* whatever," includes any reasonable cause (*Sun Insrce.* v. *Hart*, 58 L. J. P. C. 69).

The penalty imposed by s. 3, Nuisances Removal Act, 1863 (26 & 27 V. c. 117), for preventing Inspectors from entering any "slaughter-house, shop, building, market or other Place" extends to "every species of premises," *e.g.*, a yard (*Young* v. *Gattridge*, 38 L. J. M. C. 67; L. R. 4 Q. B. 166).

V. PLACE as to meaning of "*other* place."

By a Private Town Act the Trustees were empowered to rate occupiers of all "shops, malt-houses, granaries, warehouses, coach-houses, yards, gardens, garden-ground, stables, cellars, vaults, wharfs, and other Buildings and *Hereditaments*" within certain limits, "*meadow and pasture-ground excepted.*" This exception was held to take the words "other hereditaments" out of the *ejusdem generis* rule, so that the mains of a Gas Company were rateable (*R.* v. *Shrewsbury Gas Co.*, 1 L. J. M. C. 18 ; 3 B. & Ad. 216 ; *Va.* as to the value of an exception in controlling the construction, *Hotham* v. *Sutton*, 15 Ves. 326: ALMS : and *Cp. R.* v. *Manchester Water Works Co.*, and other cases, pp. 544, 545, *ante*).

"Other Legal Merchandize ;" *V.* LEGAL MERCHANDIZE.

Vh. Cork and Bandon Ry. v. *Goode*, 22 L. J. C. P. 198 ; 13 C. B. 826.

OTHER SONS.—In a gift to second, third, fourth, and all and every "other Sons" of A., the first son though not mentioned is not excluded, but rather the word "other," "*ex vi termini*, includes the first" (per Ld. Brougham, *Langston* v. *Langston*, 8 Bligh, N. S. 167; 2 Cl. & F. 194, cited 2 Jarm. 215, 216). In *Locke* v. *Dunlop* (39 Ch. D. 387; 57 L. J. Ch. 1010 ; 3 Times Rep. 628), Stirling, J., held, on the context, that "other son" had reference to futurity, and included only those sons who should be born after his sons who were in existence at the date of his Will.

OTHER THAN.—"Other than" creates an Exception (*Wrotesley* v. *Adams*, 1 Plow. 195).

V. BESIDES.

OTHER THE ISSUE.—In *Allgood* v. *Blake* (41 L. J. Ex. 217 ; 42 Ib. 101 ; L. R. 7 Ex. 339 ; 8 Ib. 160), the words (at the end of a series of limitations in tail special) "to the use of all and every Other the Issue," were read, not as excluding those before mentioned, but rather, as completing a provision for all the issue and as thus creating a vested remainder in tail general.

OTHER TRUSTEE.—"Where four Trustees were appointed originally, and the power was to the surviving or continuing or *other* Trustee to appoint new Trustees, it was held that the survivor of the four trustees who desired himself to be discharged, could, by force of the words 'other Trustee,' appoint four new trustees in the place of himself and three others" (Lewin, 665, citing *Camoys* v. *Best*, 19 Bea. 414).

OTHERS OR OTHER.—Not read as "Survivors or Survivor ;" *V. Re Hagen*, 46 L. J. Ch. 665. *V.* SURVIVOR.

OTHERWISE.—Speaking generally, "Otherwise" when following an enumeration, should receive an *ejusdem generis* interpretation much in the same way as OTHER. As to this general rule "no authority is necessary" (per Cleasby, B., *Monck* v. *Hilton*, 46 L. J. M. C. 167), and Pollock, B., says (Ib. 168) " the principle upon which this rule is founded is thoroughly established." *Va.* per Dowse, B., *Haren* v. *Archdale*, 12 L. R. Ir. 318. But it is a general rule which, in the case of "Otherwise," is not unfrequently found inapplicable.

Vernon's Case (4 Rep. 1 a) is the leading authority on this word ; and there it was decided that the proviso, contained in s. 9, 27 Hen. 8, c. 10, enabling a wife to take or reject hereditaments given to her "for term of her life *or otherwise in jointure*," extended to an estate in fee simple : but the judgment says, "for *nota*, this word 'otherwise' is not indefinite, but 'otherwise *in jointure*'" (4 Rep. 3 a).

By s. 1, Jervis' Act (11 & 12 V. c. 43), Justices may issue a summons in cases where they have authority to make "any Order for the Payment of any Money *or otherwise:*" an order for the demolition of a building under a local Improvement Act is within these words and must therefore (by s. 11) be made within 6 months after the completion of the building (*Morant* v. *Taylor*, 45 L. J. M. C. 78 ; 1 Ex. D. 188 ; 40 J. P. 101).

S. 4 of the Vagrant Act (5 G. 4, c. 83), makes it an offence "pretending or professing to tell fortunes, or using any subtle craft, means or device by Palmistry *or otherwise* to deceive." "Reading this as a whole I should take the word 'otherwise,' not as limiting the earlier words, but as enlarging the word 'palmistry,' and providing against the professing to tell fortunes or using craft, means or devices to deceive, whether by palmistry or by contrivance to deceive other than palmistry, *provided they are of the same general character as is indicated by the earlier words of the section*" (per Pollock, B., *Monck* v. *Hilton*, 46 L. J. M. C. 169). Accordingly pretended spiritualism is within the offence (*Monck* v. *Hilton*, 46 L. J. M. C. 163 ; 2 Ex. D. 268 ; 25 W. R. 373 ; 41 J. P. 214). But a trick of legerdemain is not (*Johnson* v. *Fenner*, 33 J. P. 740) ; for, "in such a case no peculiar power is pretended, like telling fortunes or palmistry, to impose upon the credulous" (per Cleasby, B., in *Monck* v. *Hilton*, 46 L. J. M. C. 167). *Vf. Ex p. A.-G.*, 41 J. P. 118 : *R.* v. *Middlesex Jus.*, Ib. 629 : *Re Slade*, 36 L. T. 402.

Though under the County Courts Act, 1867 (30 & 31 V. c. 142, s. 7), an action in the High Court for an amount exceeding £50, but reduced by payment *after action brought*, could not be remitted to the County Court under the words of the section "reduced by payment, an admitted set-off, or otherwise" (*Osborne* v. *Homburg*, 45 L. J. Ex. 65 ; 1 Ex. D. 48 ; 24 W. R. 161 : *Walesby* v. *Goulston*, L. R. 1 C. P. 567 : *Foster* v. *Usherwood*, 47 L. J. Ex. 30 ; 3 Ex. D. 1; 37 L. T. 389 ; 26 W. R. 91: *Va.* Co. Co. Act, 1888, s. 65, and thereon *Hodgson* v. *Bell*, 6 Times Rep. 211; 24 Q. B. D. 302 ; 38 W. R. 325), yet, after issue joined, such an action, however subsequently reduced below £50, could be remitted under s. 26, Co. Co. Act, 1856 (19 & 20 V. c. 108), because in that section the words are "reduced by *payment into Court*, payment, an admitted set-off or otherwise," and as "payment into Court" must refer to something after action brought, the words "or otherwise" received their natural meaning (*Gray* v. *Hopper*, 36 W. R. 746 ; 21 Q. B. D. 246 ; 57 L. J. Q. B. 505). *V.* REDUCED BY PAYMENT.

A provision in a Private (Borough) Improvement Act that nothing therein contained should affect any right which the Corporation might have "under the Municipal Corporation Acts, or otherwise," is not confined to Acts similar in kind to the Municipal Corporation Acts, but extends to all Acts (*Taylor* v. *Oldham*, 46 L. J. Ch. 108 ; 4 Ch. D. 395).

"A *Power to Appoint*, 'by Will or otherwise,' of course authorises an appointment by Deed" (Sug. Pow. 211, citing *Irwin* v. *Farrer*, 19 Ves. 86: *Van* v. *Barnett*, Ib. 110).

A *Condition of Sale* empowered a vendor to vacate the sale if any objection were made "as to the abstract of title, or the evidence thereof, or the conveyance, or as to compensation or indemnity *or otherwise ;*" and Westbury, L. C., held that the word "otherwise" would comprehend all other subjects as to which there might be an objection or a claim made by the purchaser (*Cordingley* v. *Cheesebrough*, 31 L. J. Ch. 621 ; 3 Giff. 496 ; 4 D. G. F. & J. 379 : *Vf.* jdgmt. of Esher, M. R., *Terry to White*, 55 L. J. Ch. 347; 32 Ch. D. 14 ; 34 W. R. 379). So in the ordinary Power to Trustees to apply capital in or towards "the Advancement or Preferment *or otherwise for the benefit*" of a person, the words italicised are not restricted by "advancement" or "preferment" (*Lowther* v. *Bentinck*, 44 L. J. Ch. 197; L. R. 19 Eq. 167: in this case Jessel, M.R., said, "When I find the words 'or otherwise,' I am bound to say I don't know what is *ejusdem generis*"). So a direction to make deductions, from the income of a tenant for life, for all ordinary outgoings for "Taxes *or otherwise*," was held to include cost of drainage works under s. 73, 18 & 19 V. c. 120 (*Re Crawley*, 54 L. J. Ch. 652 ; 28 Ch. D. 431).

A gift of real estate, to hold "*for ever or otherwise*," according to the respective natures and tenures thereof, held to include leaseholds for years (*Swift* v. *Swift*, 29 L. J. Ch. 121; 1 D. G. F. & J. 160).

Where a party to an Action has to satisfy the Court of any matter "by Affidavit *or otherwise*," that means by affidavit or any other sufficient means (*Shelford* v. *Louth Ry.*, 4 Ex. D. 317; 28 W. R. 407).

An Admission "either on the Pleadings *or otherwise*" (Ord. 32, R. 6, R. S. C.), may be in an affidavit (*Freeman* v. *Cox*, 47 L. J. Ch. 560 ; 8 Ch. D. 148 : *Porrett* v. *White*, 55 L. J. Ch. 79 ; 31 Ch. D. 52: *Laudergan* v. *Feast*, 55 L. J. Ch. 505 ; 54 L. T. 369), or even in a letter before action (*Hampden* v. *Wallis*, 54 L. J. Ch. 1175 ; 27 Ch. D. 251; 32 W. R. 977). "Jessel, M.R., used to say that one admission is as good as another" (per Chitty, J., Ib.).

"Though an Indictment will not lie for an offence newly created by statute where another method of prosecution is appointed, yet if the statute gives a recovery by Action of Debt, Bill, Plaint, Information, '*or Otherwise*,' it authorizes a proceeding by way of Indictment" (Dwar. 673).

As to "Dividends, Profits *or otherwise*," subs. 7, s. 38, Companies Act,

1862; *V. Re Leicester Racecourse Co.*, 55 L. J. Ch. 206 ; 30 Ch. D. 629 ; 53 L. T. 340 ; 34 W. R. 14.

"Circulars, Advertisements *or otherwise*," s. 32, Trade Marks Act, 1883, has a general interpretation (*Driffield & East Riding Linseed Co.* v. *Waterloo Mills Co.*, 31 Ch. D. 638 ; 55 L. J. Ch. 391 ; 54 L. T. 210 ; 34 W. R. 360).

On the other hand :—

The provision in the Wills Act (1 V. c. 26, s. 20), for revoking a Will by "burning, tearing *or otherwise destroying*" it, the words italicised have to be read as *ejusdem generis* with "burning, tearing ;" *V.* DESTROY.

So the phrase in s. 53, Towns Improvement Clauses Act (10 & 11 V. c. 34), relating to streets not theretofore Paved and Flagged, "or otherwise made good," refers to a process *ejusdem generis* with paving and flagging ; *i.e.* otherwise made into an artificial road in a manner similar to that in which a road is made by paving and flagging (per Brett, M.R., *Portsmouth* v. *Smith*, 53 L. J. Q. B. 92 ; 13 Q. B. D. 184 ; in H. L., 54 L. J. Q. B. 473 ; 10 App. Ca. 364).

So the phrase "*otherwise engaged in Manual Labour*" (s. 10, Employers and Workmen Act, 1875, 38 & 39 V. c. 90), following, as it immediately does, an enumeration of employments exclusively manual, embraces only "people who are ordinarily known in the English language as working people who exercise manual labour" (per Brett, L.J.), and does not include an omnibus conductor (*Morgan* v. *Lond. Gen. Omnibus Co.*, 53 L. J. Q. B. 352 ; 13 Q. B. D. 832 : *Va.* per Smith, J., *Cook* v. *N. Metrop. Tramways*, 18 Q. B. D. 684).

The direction in the Act, which is the foundation of the modern Poor Law (43 Eliz. c. 2), that the Poor Rate is to be raised "*weekly or otherwise*," means "that it is to be raised at the outside annually" (per Esher, M.R., *R.* v. *Christopherson*, 55 L. J. M. C. 5 ; 16 Q. B. D. 7; 53 L. T. 804 ; 34 W. R. 86 ; 50 J. P. 212).

And perhaps one of the most instructive decisions as to the meanings of "Otherwise" is that of Cave, J., in *Ex p. Tidswell* (56 L. J. Q. B. 548 ; 57 L. T. 416 ; 35 W. R. 669), wherein he analysed the use of the word in several of the sections of the M. W. P. Act, 1882, and as a result held that in s. 3 a loan from a wife to her husband for the purpose "of any trade or business carried on by him—*or otherwise*," means trade or business carried on by him or otherwise in partnership with others or as agent, &c., and that therefore a wife is entitled to prove in competition with the general creditors of her husband for a loan advanced for private purposes wholly unconnected with trade or business.

OUT OF.—Where a testator directed his legatees to contribute to A. a percentage "out of their legacies," Romilly, M.R., said, "I doubt whether the testator intended by the words 'out of' to point to any particular description of legatees who were to contribute" (*Ward* v. *Grey,* 29 L. J. Ch. 75 ; 26 Bea. 485).

V. INTO.

OUT OF SETTLEMENT.—*V.* NOT SETTLED ; UNSETTLED ESTATE.

OUT OF THE BUSINESS.—A provision in Partnership Articles that moneys that might be due to a retiring partner shall be paid "out of the Business by the continuing or surviving partners" by annual instalments, does not mean that the source of such payment is to be restricted to the Business from time to time carried on by such continuing or surviving partners, but means that such moneys are to be paid by such partners as partners and becomes a personal obligation on them (*Beresford* v. *Browning,* 45 L. J. Ch. 36 ; 1 Ch. D. 30). "The word 'Business' there, is evidently the Capital" (per Jessel, M. R., Ib.).

V. BUSINESS.

OUT OF THE PROFITS.—An agreement to pay an annual sum "out of the Profits" of a business, refers to *net* profits (per Parke, B., *Bond* v. *Pittard,* 3 M. & W. 357; 7 L. J. Ex. 78).

V. PROFITS.

OUT OF THE REALM.—*V.* REALM.

OUT OF THE RENTS.—A devise of an Annuity for life to be paid "out of Rents and Profits" which prove insufficient to keep down the Annuity, does not entitle the annuitant to a continuing charge upon the rents and profits after his death until the arrears are satisfied, but only to the rents and profits during his life (*Wormald* v. *Muzeen,* 50 L. J. Ch. 776 : *Stelfox* v. *Sugden,* Johns. 234 : on the latter case, *V. Bell* v. *Bell,* Ir. Rep. 6 Eq. 239).

OUTFANGTHEEFE.—"'Outfangtheefe,' that is, that theeves or felons of your Land or Fee, out of your land or fee, taken with felony or stealing, shall be brought back to your Court, and there judged" (Termes de la Ley). *Cp.* INFANGTHEEFE.

OUTFIT.—"'Outfit,' is, correctly speaking, that portion of the ship's furniture or apparel which ordinarily perishes, or is consumed in the course of her voyage, as provisions for the crew, spare ropes, and the like" (Lowndes on Average, 11).

"'Outfit' (in a fishing voyage) differs materially from what is comprehended under the term 'Goods'" (per Ellenborough, C. J., *Hill* v. *Patten,* 8 East, 375).

OUTFITTER.—*V.* LADIES' OUTFITTER.

OUTGOING ALDERMAN.—An Outgoing Alderman though Mayor

Elect and though he has done everything to qualify him to act as Mayor, is still "an Outgoing Alderman" and disqualified to vote in the election of Aldermen under s. 60 (2), Municipal Corporation Act, 1882 (*Hounsell* v. *Suttill*, 56 L. J. Q. B. 502 ; 19 Q. B. D. 498 ; 57 L. T. 102 ; 36 W. R. 127 ; 51 J. P. 440).

OUTGOINGS.—The word "Outgoings," in a Covenant to bear burdens "is of the largest possible signification" (per Brett, L. J., *Budd* v. *Marshall*, 50 L. J. Q. B. 26) ; but at the same page Bramwell, L.J., speaks of the word as "an awkward one ;" "but the word 'Outgoings' is certainly as strong as DUTIES" (per Grove, J., *Aldridge* v. *Ferne*, 55 L. J. Q. B. 588). "'An Outgoing' means something that has gone out, an expense that some one has been at" (per Bramwell, B., *Crosse* v. *Raw*, 43 L. J. Ex. 144 ; L. R. 9 Ex. 209) ; and it was accordingly held in that case that the expense of sanitating a house, under s. 10, Sanitary Act, 1866 (29 & 30 V. c. 90), was an outgoing within a lessee's covenant to pay "taxes, rates, assessments, and outgoings." So the expenses of street paving under the Metrop. Man. Acts are within a lessee's covenant to pay "outgoings of every description for the time being payable either by the landlord or tenant" in respect of the premises (*Aldridge* v. *Ferne*, 55 L. J. Q. B. 587 ; 17 Q. B. D. 212 ; 34 W. R. 578, in *wh. Hill* v. *Edward*, W. N. (85) 32 was doubted). *Va. Batchelor* v. *Bigger*, 60 L. T. 416.

So under an agreement for a lease at a rent "free of all outgoings," the tenant has to pay land tax and tithe rent-charge, and the landlord is entitled to have a covenant to that effect inserted in the lease (*Parish* v. *Sleeman*, 1 D. G. F. & J. 326 ; 29 L. J. Ch. 96 ; 1 L. T. 506 ; 8 W. R. 166 ; 6 Jur. N. S. 385. *Vf.* TAXES : SCOT).

A paving assessment under the Manchester General Improvement Act, 1851, is an "Outgoing" within a Contract for *Sale of a House* which provides that "all rents, rates, taxes, and outgoings shall be received and discharged by the vendor up to the time of completion" (*Midgley* v. *Coppock*, 4 Ex. D. 309 ; 48 L. J. Q. B. 674 ; 28 W. R. 161). So also is a liability for works done by a Local Board and chargeable on an owner by virtue of ss. 150, 257, P. H. Act, 1875, although the assessment by the Board may not be made until after the date fixed for completing the contract for sale (*Re Furtado & Jeffries*, 27 S. J. 466) : *Secus*, of expenses of paving under s. 77, Metrop. Man. Act, 1862, under vendor's implied covenant (*Egg* v. *Blayney*, 21 Q. B. D. 107). But where, in a *Deed of Gift*, the tenant for life was to pay all "Outgoings" during his life ; it was held that that word did not comprise expenses of making up a road abutting on the premises comprised in the deed, which work had been done by a Local Board in the lifetime of the tenant for life and on his non-compliance with their notice, but which expenses had not been assessed by the Loc. Bd. until after the death of the tenant for life (*Re Boor*, 58 L. J. Ch. 285 : *Vh. Re Bettesworth & Richer*, 57 L. J. Ch. 749 ; 37 Ch. D. 535.)

On a *Sale of Leaseholds* in which all "Outgoings" are to be cleared by the Vendor to date of completion, the vendor must pay a proportionate part of the rent reserved by the lease under which the premises are held (*Lawes* v. *Gibson,* 35 L. J. Ch. 148 ; L. R. 1 Eq. 135 ; 13 L. T. 316 ; 14 W. R. 25).

A *Bequest of Leaseholds* "free of all Outgoings and payments except the annual and other rent" payable in respect of it, means that the testator's estate must pay the rent, taxes, and other payments in respect of the property up to his death ; and after that time the legatee takes the property subject to the rents and the liability to perform the covenants (*Re Taber, Arnold* v. *Kayess,* 51 L. J. Ch. 721).

V. ORDINARY OUTGOINGS : DEDUCTIONS : NECESSARY.

OUTSTANDING.—*V.* CIRCULATION.

OUTSTROKE.—*V.* INSTROKE.

OUTWARD MARK.—For a tradesman to place on a wire-blind to a front window such letters as "H. B. & Co., late S. B. & Co.," with similar letters on a roller-blind and on a brass-plate fixed on the front railings, is to make an "Outward Mark or Show of Business" within a restrictive covenant in a lease (*Evans* v. *Davis,* 10 Ch. D. 747 ; 48 L. J. Ch. 223).

OUTWARDS.—"Trading Outwards;" *V.* TRADING.

OVER.—*V.* THROUGH.

OVERPLUS.—"Overplus," as used in 2 W. & M. sess. 1, c. 5, s. 2, means what remains after payment of the rent and the reasonable charges of the Distress (*Lyon* v. *Tomkies,* 1 M. & W. 603 : *Knight* v. *Egerton,* 7 Ex. 407).

A bequest of "Overplus" usually includes whatever shall turn out to be the Overplus (*Shaw* v. *Bull,* 12 Mod. 593 ; stated and commented on, 1 Jarm. 729 : *Page* v. *Leapingwell,* 18 Ves. 463 : *Beverley* v. *A.-G.,* 27 L. J. Ch. 66 ; 6 H. L. Ca. 310). *Cp.* RESIDUE : REMAINDER : SURPLUS.

OVERRATE.—To "Over-rate," "in its strictest signification, means a rating by way of excess, and not one which ought not to have been made at all" (per Parke, B., *Allen* v. *Sharp,* 17 L. J. Ex. 214 ; 2 Ex. 352) ; but that learned judge, and the Court, held that the word in s. 24, 43 G. 3, c. 99 (giving appeal for an "over-rating"), had a far wider interpretation.

OVERSEER.—*V. Caunter* v. *Addams,* 33 L. J. C. P. 68 ; 15 C. B. N. S. 512 : *Green* v. *Mepham,* 48 L. J. C. P. 92 : s. 101, 6 V. c. 18.

OVERT.—A Lease, under a Power requiring accustomed clauses, was objected to because, in the clause of re-entry, if there were no distress on the premises, it omitted to say (as previous leases had said), no "Overt" distress; but the Court decided against the objection, and (per Denman, C.J.), said: "The law recognises a difference between a *Pound* Overt and a *Pound* Covert; but as to *Distress*, the law does not affix any meaning to the word 'Overt.' Is 'Overt' to be confined to what may be seen by walking over the lands and farm-yard, without going into any inclosed buildings? or does it extend to what may be seen by opening the outer doors of a house or other building, or what may be seen by opening inner doors, or by opening cupboards, chests, and boxes which are not concealed and have no locks, or various other shades of being less 'Overt'?" (*Doe* d. *Douglas* v. *Lock*, 4 L. J. K. B. 119; 2 A. & E. 705).

OVERTAKEN.—A ship is "being overtaken by another," within Art. 11, Regulations for Preventing Collisions at Sea, when the other vessel is going faster than, and coming nearer to her in such a position that her lights cannot be seen by the approaching ship (*The Main*, 55 L. J. P. D. & A. 70; 11 P. D. 132; 55 L. T. 15; 34 W. R. 678; 2 Times Rep. 689, and the cases there cited).

OWELTY.—*V.* Termes de la Ley.

OWING.—*V.* DEBT: DUE: MONEY DUE.

OWN DWELLING-PLACE.—*V.* DWELLING-PLACE.

OWN HANDS.—*V.* DIE BY HIS OWN HANDS.

OWN HEIRS.—*V.* MY.

OWN PROFIT.—Goods are supplied by a Poor Law Guardian "for his own profit," 55 G. 3, c. 137, s. 6; 4 & 5 W. 4, c. 76, s. 77, if supplied by his partner, even though it be without his knowledge (*Davies* v. *Harvey*, 43 L. J. M. C. 121; L. R. 9 Q. B. 433).

OWN RIGHT.—*V.* IN HIS OWN RIGHT.

OWN RISK.—Passenger travelling "at his Own Risk;" *V. McCawley* v. *Furness Ry.*, L. R. 8 Q. B. 57: RISK.

OWN SOLE USE.—For the purpose of giving a married woman a Separate Use, "own" does not seem to give any additional force to "sole" (*Re Tarsey*, 35 L. J. Ch. 452; L. R. 1 Eq. 561). *V.* SOLE.

OWN USE AND BENEFIT.—A limitation to A., "his exors or admors, *to and for his and their own use and benefit*," does not, under the italicised words, give the exors or admors any beneficial interest; they simply take the property as part of A.'s estate (*Hames* v. *Hames*, 2 Keen, 646; 7 L. J. Ch. 123: *Meryon* v. *Collett*, 8 Bea. 386; 14 L. J. Ch. 369).

OWNER.—The "Owner" or "Proprietor" of a property is the person in whom (with his or her assent), it is for the time being beneficially vested, and who has the occupation, or control, or usufruct of it: *e.g.*, a lessee is, during the term, the owner of the property demised (*V.* jdgmt. of Bramwell, L. J., *Eglinton* v. *Norman*, 46 L. J. Q. B. 559 : *Va. Chauntler* v. *Robinson*, 4 Ex. 163 ; 19 L. J. Ex. 170 : *Lister* v. *Lobley*, 6 L. J. K. B. 200 ; 7 A. & E. 124). So, in *Cook* v. *Humber* (31 L. J. C. P. 75), Erle, C. J. speaks of the "occupation" necessary to the franchise, under s. 27, Reform Act, 1832 (2 W. 4, c. 45), as equivalent to the "actual exercise of the rights of the Owner of a house in possession." But in *Re Crawley, Acton* v. *Crawley* (54 L. J. Ch. 654 ; 28 Ch. D. 431), Pearson, J., said, "the Owner—that is, the person entitled to the rack-rent."

"Owner" is a sufficient description of a vendor of property, in an Agreement for Sale ; *V.* PROPRIETOR.

"Owner" of Goods, held to mean the *Importer*, for the purpose of duties, under a Royal Charter, on goods brought beyond seas into the Tyne (*Newcastle Pilots* v. *Hammond*, 18 L. J. Ex. 417 ; 4 Ex. 285).

Under the *Metropolitan Building Act*, 1855, 18 & 19 V. c. 122, ss. 3, 73, the lessee for years, and not the lessor, of a chapel or house, is its "owner" (*Mourilyan* v. *Labalmondiere*, 30 L. J. M. C. 95 ; 1 E. & E. 533 : *Hunt* v. *Harris*, 34 L. J. C. P. 249 ; 19 C. B. N. S. 13) : nor, under a building agreement, is the ground landlord the "owner" of the buildings, within ss. 3, 51 (*Evelyn* v. *Whichcord*, 27 L. J. M. C. 211 ; E. B. & E. 126 : *Canwell* v. *Hanson*, 41 L. J. M. C. 8 ; nom. *Caudwell* v. *Hanson*, L. R. 7 Q. B. 55) : nor is the incumbent of a district church the "owner" of it within ss. 3, 69–74 (*R.* v. *Lee*, 48 L. J. M. C. 22 ; 4 Q. B. D. 75 : *Vf. Chorlton-upon-Medlock* v. *Walker*, 12 L. J. Ex. 88 ; 10 M. & W. 742). The "owner" who is liable for surveyor's charges, under s. 51, is the person answering that description at the time the service is rendered (*Tubb* v. *Good*, 39 L. J. M. C. 135 ; L. R. 5 Q. B. 443).

"Owner," s. 250, *Metrop. Man. Act*, 1855 ; *V. London School Bd.* v. *St. Mary, Islington*, 1 Q. B. D. 65 ; 45 L. J. M. C. 1.

As to the phrase "Owner of land bounding or abutting on" a new street, in s. 77, *Metrop. Man. Act*, 1862; *V. Holland* v. *Kensington*, 36 L. J. M. C. 105 ; L. R. 2 C. P. 565 : *Plumstead Bd. of Works* v. *British Land Co.*, L. R. 10 Q. B. 203 ; 44 L. J. Q. B. 38 : *Williams* v. *Wandsworth Bd. of Works*, 53 L. J. M. C. 187 ; 13 Q. B. D. 211 ; 32 W. R. 908 ; 48 J. P. 439 : *Wright* v. *Ingle*, 55 L. J. M. C. 17 ; 16 Q. B. D. 379 ; 54 L. T. 511 ; 34 W. R. 220 ; 50 J. P. 436.

"Owner," s. 3, *Artizans Dwellings Act*, 1868, 31 & 32 V. c. 130 ; *V. R.* v. *St. Marylebone*, 57 L. J. M. C. 9 ; 20 Q. B. D. 415 ; 58 L. T. 180 ; 36 W. R. 271 ; 52 J. P. 534.

Under the *Public Health Act*, 1875, ss. 150, 257, the phrase "owner in default" means the person who is owner at the time of the completion by the local authority of the works the expenses of executing which are sought to be recovered (*R.* v. *Swindon*, 48 L. J. M. C. 119 ; 4 Q. B. D. 305 ;

27 W. R. 732 ; 43 J. P. 431). *Vh. Bowditch* v. *Wakefield*, 40 L. J. M. C. 214 ; L. R. 6 Q. B. 567 : *Peek* v. *Waterloo*, 33 L. J. M. C. 11 ; 2 H. & C. 709 : *Wallsend* v. *Murphy*, 6 Times Rep. 29.

What Mr. Justice Blackburn called the "rough" interpretation of "Owner" in the *Nuisances Removal Act*, 1855 (18 & 19 V. c. 121) has been made still wider by s. 4, P. H. Act, 1875, apparently for the purpose of getting rid of *Cook* v. *Montagu* (41 L. J. M. C. 149 ; L. R. 7 Q. B. 418) : as to "Owner" under Nuisances Removal Act, 1855, *V. Blything* v. *Warton*, 32 L. J. M. C. 132 ; 3 B. & S. 352.

"Owner" in s. 65, *Highway Act*, 1835 (5 & 6 W. 4, c. 50), means the person in occupation, who may be either the actual owner, or else only the occupying tenant (*Woodard* v. *Billericay*, 48 L. J. Ch. 535 ; 11 Ch. D. 214 ; 27 W. R. 594 ; 43 J. P. 224).

The occupier is an "Owner of Lands and Buildings" within s. 33, *Town Police Clauses Act*, 1847, 10 & 11 V. c. 89 (*Lewis* v. *Arnold*, 44 L. J. M. C. 68 ; L. R. 10 Q. B. 245).

An "Owner" within s. 3, *Lands C. C. Act*, 1845, is "any person or corporation who, under the provisions of that or the special Act, would be enabled to sell and convey lands to the promoters of the undertaking." *Vh. Chauntler* v. *Robinson*, 4 Ex. 163 ; 19 L. J. Ex. 170 : *R.* v. *Kerrison*, 1 M. & S. 435 : *Bullard* v. *Harrison*, 4 M. & S. 387 : *Russell* v. *Shenton*, 3 Q. B. 449. "It would appear, although there has been some doubt on the subject, that a *tenant* of a farm is an Owner, so as to entitle him to sue for penalties under s. 54" (Lloyd on Compensation, 5 Ed. 229, citing *Mann* v. *G. Southern & Western Ry.*, 9 Ir. C. L. R. 105 : *Collinson* v. *Newcastle Ry.*, Walford on Railways, 99). As to the construction of "Owner" in s. 76 ; *V. Ex p. Winder*, 46 L. J. Ch. 572 ; 6 Ch. D. 696 : *Douglass* v. *Lond. & N. W. Ry.*, 3 K. & J. 173 : *Wells* v. *Chelmsford*, 49 L. J. Ch. 827 ; 15 Ch. D. 108.

"Owner," s. 54, *Ry. C. C. Act*, 1845 ; *V. Mann* v. *G. Southern & Western Ry.*, 9 Ir. C. L. Rep. 105.

The "Owner of the Prior Estate" who, under s. 22, *Fines and Recoveries Act* (3 & 4 W. 4, c. 74), is the Protector of a Settlement, is "the real substantial owner of the estate,—that is to say,—the person who has the beneficial interest in the land" (per James, L. J., *Re Dudson*, 47 L. J. Ch. 632 ; 8 Ch. 8, 628 : *Va. Re Ainslie*, 54 L. J. Ch. 8 ; 51 L. T. 780 ; 33 W. R. 148).

"Owner," s. 64, *Irish Landed Estates Act* (21 & 22 V. c. 72) ; *V. Grier* v. *Grier*, L. R. 5 H. L. 688.

"Owner" in the *Merchant Shipping Act*, 1854 (17 & 18 V. c. 104), in s. 169 at least if not all through that Act, does not mean the registered owner of a ship if he has parted with all control over it ; but "must be restrained to such actual owner for the time being of the ship, as either himself, or by his master or other authorized agent, manages and controls her" (*Meiklereid* v. *West*, 45 L. J. M. C. 91 ; 1 Q. B. D. 428 ; 40 J. P. 708). A person who has paid a deposit on purchase of a share in a ship, but who has not been registered, is not an "Owner" within s. 147 (*Hughes* v. *Sutherland*, 7 Q. B. D. 160; 50 L. J. Q. B. 567).

The "Owner" of a Wreck within s. 56, *Harbours Act*, 1847 (10 & 11 V. c. 27) is the person who was the owner when the right to remove it first accrued to the harbour master (*Eglinton* v. *Norman*, 46 L. J. Ex. 557).

"Owner," s. 13, *Metalliferous Mines Regulation Act*, 1872 (35 & 36 V. c. 77); *V. Evans* v. *Mostyn*, 47 L. J. M. C. 25 ; 2 C. P. D. 547 : *Arkwright* v. *Evans*, 49 L. J. M. C. 82.

V. True Owner.

OWNER OF A LIMITED INTEREST IN LAND.—*V. Landowners' West of England Co.* v. *Ashford*, W. N. (80) 205.

OWNER IN DEFAULT.—*V. Re Bettesworth & Richer*, 57 L. J. Ch. 749 ; 37 Ch. D. 535 ; 58 L. T. 796 ; 36 W. R. 544 ; 52 J. P. 740 : *Va.* Owner, sub P. H. Act, 1875.

OWNER'S RISK.—Goods carried at "Owner's Risk," means, at the risk of the owner, *minus* the liability of the carrier for the misconduct of himself or servants (per Bramwell, L. J., *Lewis* v. *G. W. Ry.*, 47 L. J. Q. B. 134 ; 3 Q. B. D. 195) ; and a stipulation that goods shall be carried "at owner's risk," only exempts the carrier from the ordinary risks of the transit and does not cover the carrier's negligent delay (*Robinson* v. *G. W. Ry.*, 35 L. J. C. P. 123) ; even though less than the usual freight be charged (*D'Arc* v. *Lond. & N. W. Ry.*, L. R. 9 C. P. 325).

Vf. McCawley v. *Furness Ry.*, L. R. 8 Q. B. 57 : *Stewart* v. *Lond. & N. W. Ry.*, 33 L. J. Ex. 199.

OXGANGE.—"*Una bovata terræ*, an oxgange, or an oxgate of land, is as much as an ox can till ;" but, like *carucata*, it "may containe meadow, pasture, and wood necessary for such tillage" (Co. Litt. 5 a. ; *Vf.* Touch. 93 : *Sv.* Elph. 564). *V.* Hide : Knight's Fee.

OYER AND TERMINER.—The Court of Queen's Bench (and now the Q. B. D.), is a Court of "Oyer and Terminer," *e.g.*, in s. 20, 11 & 12 V. c. 42 (*R.* v. *Eyre*, 37 L. J. M. C. 159 ; L. R. 3 Q. B. 487).

PA—PAI

P.A.—*V.* Particular Average.

PACKAGE.—*V.* Parcel.

PACKER.—"This is a term well understood in London, and means a person employed by merchants to receive, and (in some instances) to select, goods for them from manufacturers, dyers, calenderers, &c., and pack the same for exportation" (Arch, Bankry. 11 Ed. 37).

PAID.—A testamentary direction that all legacies are to be "*paid*" free of Legacy Duty, will be read as including the idea of satisfaction, transfer or delivery; so that chattels, stock, or shares, the subject of a specific legacy, will, like payment of a pecuniary legacy, have to be delivered or transferred free of duty to the legatee (*Ansley* v. *Cotton*, 16 L. J. Ch. 55: *Re Johnston, Cockerell* v. *Essex*, 53 L. J. Ch. 645; 26 Ch. D. 538; 32 W. R. 634).

A testamentary direction that Debts are to be "paid" (whether Legacies are also mentioned or not) prevents the presumption that a legacy to a Creditor is in satisfaction of his claim (*Re Huish, Bradshaw* v. *Huish*, 43 Ch. D. 260; disapproving *Edmunds* v. *Low*, 3 K. & J. 318; 26 L. J. Ch. 432).

Articles of a Co. which empower the declaration of Dividends "to be paid" to Members, do not authorize the issue of Bonds for Dividends (*Wood* v. *Odessa Water W. Co.*, 42 Ch. D. 636; 58 L. J. Ch. 628; *Hoole* v. *G. W. Ry.*, 3 Ch. 262).

V. To be paid: Payable: Payment.

A Bill of Sale "truly sets forth its consideration" (s. 8, B. of S. Act, 1882), if the money therein stated to be "paid" did not actually pass in cash, but was a sum owing by the grantor to the grantee for unpaid purchase-money of the chattels therein comprised (*Ex p. Bolland*, 52 L. J. Ch. 113; 21 Ch. D. 543; 31 W. R. 102). *V.* Truly set forth.

In a Charter-Party agreeing to pay the highest sum proved to have been paid, "paid" may be read as meaning "contracted to be paid" (*Gether* v. *Capper*, 15 C. B. 701).

Stamp on Security for money to be "lent, advanced, or *paid*," Sch. 55 G. 3, c. 184; *V. Wroughton* v. *Turtle*, 11 M. & W. 561; 13 L. J. Ex. 57.

V. Payment.

PAIN.—"Under pain of forfeiting Body and Goods;" *V.* Felony.

PAINTING.—A "Painting," is a pictorial work in colours the object and value of which are artistic. Hence original trade models and working designs, though carefully painted by hand and skilfully designed, are not

"Paintings" within the Carriers Act (*Woodward* v. *Lond. & N. W. Ry.*, 47 L. J. Ex. 263; 3 Ex. D. 121). Nor (per Hawkins, J., in the same case) would such models or designs be "Original Paintings" within the Copyright Act, 25 & 26 V. c. 68.

When it is doubtful whether a pictorial work is a "Painting" or not, the question is for the jury, like as it is on the other things enumerated in the Carriers Act, *e.g.* SILK.

V. PICTURE.

PALMISTRY.—*V. Monck* v. *Hilton*, 46 L. J. M. C. 163; 2 Ex. D. 268; 25 W. R. 373; 41 J. P. 214.

PANEL.—"'*Pannell*' is an English word, and signifieth a little part; for a pane is a part, and a pannell is a little part; as a pannell of wainscot, a pannell of a saddle, and a pannell of parchment wherein the jurors' names be written and annexed to the writ. And a jury is said to be impannelled, when the sheriffe hath entered their names into the pannell, or little peece of parchment, *in pannello assisæ*" (Co. Litt. 158 b.).

PANNAGE.—All the definitions "agree that the Right of Pannage is simply a right granted to an owner of pigs (he is generally entitled to some land; as a rule it was granted to the owners of land of some kind who kept pigs) to go into the wood of the grantor of the right, and to allow the pigs to eat the acorns or beech mast which fell upon the ground. That is what the right has always been defined to be. The pigs have no right to take a single acorn or any beech mast off the tree, either by themselves or by the hands of those who drive them, who might reach them or knock them down. There is not even a right to shake the tree. It is only a right to eat those things which fell" (per Jessel, M. R., *Chilton* v. *London*, 47 L. J. Ch. 435; 7 Ch. D. 562: *Vf.* Jacob, Law Dict.; Termes de la Ley; Elph. 606). *V.* PASTURES.

As to the rateability of Herbage and Pannage; *V. Bute* v. *Grindall*, 1 T. R. 338: *Jones* v. *Maunsell*, 1 Doug. 302.

PANNELL.—*V.* PANEL.

PAPER.—"Paper," is a manufactured substance composed of fibres,—(whether vegetable or animal),—adhering together, in form consisting of sheets of various sizes and of different thicknesses, used for writing or printing or other purposes to which flexible sheets are applicable (*A.-G.* v. *Barry*, 28 L. J. Ex. 211; 4 H. & N. 470).

PARALLEL.—In the Specification of a Patent for a Horse-clipping machine, "Parallel" was construed in its popular sense of going side by side, and not in its purely mathematical sense (*Clarke* v. *Adie*, 2 App. Ca. 423; 46 L. J. Ch. 598).

PARAMOUNT. — "'Paramount'" is a word compounded of two

French words (*par* and *monter*), and it signifies in our law, the highest lord of the fee" (Termes de la Ley, *Paramount;* referring further to Fitz. N. B. 135).

PARCEL.—Paintings, exceeding the value of £10, laid upon one another without any covering or tie in a waggon which has sides but no top, is a "Parcel or Package" within ss. 1, 2, Carriers Act, 11 G. 4 & 1 W. 4, c. 68 (*Whaite* v. *Lancashire & Yorkshire Ry.*, 43 L. J. Ex. 47; L. R. 9 Ex. 67; 22 W. R. 374).

"Packed Parcel" as contrasted with "Enclosure" or "Enclosed Parcel," for the purpose of carriage; *V. Crouch* v. *G. N. Ry.*, 25 L. J. Ex. 137; 11 Ex. 742.

PARCENERS.—"Many times parceners are called coparceners" (Co. Litt. 164 b). As to description and division of Parceners; *V.* Ib. 163 a, *et seq.;* Termes de la Ley, *Parceners.*

PARENT: PARENTS.—The ordinary sense of the word "Parent" is father or mother (*Sibley* v. *Perry*, 7 Ves. 530: *Vf.* ISSUE: 2 Jarm. 103–105); but it may mean any lineal ancestor (*Ross* v. *Ross*, 20 Bea. 645: "I have tried hard to understand that part of the judgment in *Ross* v. *Ross* that deals with the shifting meaning of the word 'Parent.'" Per Brett, L.J., *Ralph* v. *Carrick*, 48 L. J. Ch. 809).

Where there is a Condition in Restraint of Marriage without the consent of "Parents," a surviving parent may give the consent (*Dawson* v. *Oliver-Massey*, 45 L. J. Ch. 519; 2 Ch. D. 753; 34 L. T. 120: *Booth* v. *Meyer*, 38 L. T. 125. *Vh. Re Brown*, 18 Ch. D. 61: CONSENT).

PARISH.—In all Acts of Parliament passed since 1866, "'Parish' shall, unless the contrary intention appears, mean, as respects England and Wales, a place for which a separate Poor Rate is or can be made, or for which a separate Overseer is or can be appointed" (s. 5, Interp. Act, 1889).

Residence for 3 years "in any Parish" so as to confer a pauper settlement under s. 34, 39 & 40 V. c. 61, means "any one Parish," not two or more Parishes in the same Union (*Plomesgate* v. *West Ham*, 50 L. J. M. C. 51; 6 Q. B. D. 576).

"Parish . . not under any Local Authority," s. 32, Elementary Education Act, 1876, 39 & 40 V. c. 79: *V. R.* v. *Vane*, 51 L. J. M. C. 114.

"Parish *or Place*," s. 1, 3 & 4 V. c. 61; *V. Preston* v. *Buckley*, 39 L. J. M. C. 105; L. R. 5 Q. B. 391: and as to same phrase in s. 15, same statute; *V. Smith* v. *Redding*, 35 L. J. M. C. 202; 7 B. & S. 360; L. R. 1 Q. B. 489: *Rice* v. *Slee*, L. R. 7 C. P. 378.

"Parishes *or Places*," s. 20, 3 G. 4, c. 72; *V. Craven* v. *Sanderson*, 7 A. & E. 880; 7 L. J. Q. B. 81; 2 N. & P. 641.

"Parish separately maintaining its own Highways," s. 32, 25 & 26 V. c. 61; *V. R.* v. *Central Wingland*, 46 L. J. M. C. 282; 2 Q. B. D. 349.

Extra-parochial places, deemed Parishes, for rating purposes, by 20 V. c. 19.

V. VILL.

Property "belonging" to a Parish; *V.* BELONGING.

PARISHIONER.—"'Parishioner' is a very large word, and takes in not only Inhabitants of the parish, but persons who are occupiers of land, that pay the several rates and duties, though they are not resiant, nor do contribute to the ornaments of the church" (per Hardwicke, L.C., *A.-G.* v. *Parker*, 3 Atk. 577: *Vf. Etherington* v. *Wilson*, 45 L. J. Ch. 153; 1 Ch. D. 160: *Batten* v. *Gedye*, 41 Ch. D. 507). *Cp.* INHABITANT.

"Parishioners *and Inhabitants*" of a parish,—"*i.e.* the Parishioners being Inhabitants of the parish" (Lewin, 86).

In regard to persons to execute a Trust, "the expression '*Parishioners and Inhabitants*' is, in itself, extremely vague, and has never acquired any very exact and definite meaning" (Lewin, 86, 87); but even without qualifying words,—*e.g.* CHIEFEST AND DISCREETEST,—"Parishioners and Inhabitants" would be generally confined to those paying scot and lot; yet, if the phrase stand alone, it may easily, and with no better warrant than constant usage, be read as *Housekeepers*, whether paying scot and lot, or not (Lewin, 87, 88).

"By 'Parishioners and Inhabitants *in Vestry assembled*,' are meant the persons who by the existing law constitute the Vestry" (Lewin, 87, n. (*a*), citing *Re Hayle*, 31 Bea. 139; 31 L. J. Ch. 612: *Va. Etherington* v. *Wilson*, sup.).

V. cases hereon discussed, Tudor, Char. Trusts, 867–870: 40 J. P. 225.

PARK.—"*Parke*, this should be written *parque*, which is a French word, and signifieth that which we vulgarly call a Parke, of the French word *parquer*, to imparke, to inclose. It is called in *Domesday*, *Parcus*. In law it signifieth a great quantity of ground inclosed, priviledged for wild beasts of chase by prescription or the King's grant. . . . A forest and a chase are not, but a parke must be, inclosed" (Co. Litt. 233 a). "To a lawful park three things are required: (1) a Liberty either by grant or prescription; (2) Inclosure by pale, wall or hedge; (3) Beasts savage of the park: 2 Inst. 199" (Elph. 606). The right of a Parker to kill unyielding trespassers in his Park (21 Ed. 1, De Malefactoribus in Parcis), was only incident to a strictly legal Park (1 Hale, 491; 3 Dyer, 326 b).

By the grant of a "Park," "not onely the priviledge, but the land itselfe passes" (Co. Litt. 5 b).

PARLIAMENTARY.—"A 'Parliamentary' Tax is one that is imposed *directly* by Act of Parliament" (per Parke, B., *Palmer* v. *Earith*,

14 L. J. Ex. 257; 14 M. & W. 428). Land Tax is a "parliamentary" tax (*Manning* v. *Lunn*, 2 C. & K. 13 : *Christ's Hospital* v. *Harrild*, 2 M. & G. 707; 3 Scott, N. R. 126) : but a Sewers Rate is not (*Waller* v. *Andrews*, 3 M. & W. 312 ; 7 L. J. Ex. 68 : *Palmer* v. *Earith*, sup.) ; nor a Local Improvement Rate (*Bedford Union* v. *Bedford Imp. Commrs.*, 21 L. J. M. C. 229 ; 7 Ex. 777) ; nor a rate made, under a Local Act, for Repair of a Bridge *ratione tenuræ* (*Baker* v. *Greenhill*, 11 L. J. Q. B. 161; 2 G. & D. 435 ; 3 Q. B. 148) ; nor a County Rate which, by statute, was to be levied and paid out of the Poor Rate (*R.* v. *Aylesbury*, 9 Q. B. 261). *Vf.* Woodf. 556 : *cp.* PAROCHIAL.

PARLIAMENTARY BOROUGH.—*V.* s. 15 (3), Interp. Act, 1889.

PARLIAMENTARY ELECTION.—*V.* s. 17 (1), Interp. Act, 1889.

PARLIAMENTARY REGISTER OF ELECTORS.—*V.* s. 17 (2), Interp. Act, 1889.

PAROCHIAL BUSINESS.—In country parishes the Poor Rate Collector's Office will, generally, be the "Place for transacting Parochial Business," within the provision as to serving Notices in s. 101, 6 V. c. 18 (*Green* v. *Mepham*, 48 L. J. C. P. 92).

PAROCHIAL FUNDS.—*V.* PUBLIC PAROCHIAL FUNDS.

PAROCHIAL RELIEF.—Parochial Relief, speaking generally and also as disqualifying a person from being an elector (s. 36, Reform Act, 2 & 3 W. 4, c. 45), means the receipt of any benefit, service or needful thing at the cost of, or by persons employed and paid by, the parish to or for the presumptive voter, or his wife or child under 16 not being blind, or deaf, or dumb (4 & 5 W. 4, c. 76, s. 56) ; and such relief to a wife or child would still be parochial relief to the husband or father though he did not at the time require parochial assistance and did not authorise his wife to apply for it (*Bewdley*, 1 O'M. & H. 176). Of course the supply of nutriment is such relief. And so also is the supply of a coffin or the payment of funeral expenses (*Oldham*, 1 O'M. & H. 159, 160, 161 : *Vf.* Rogers, 134). So charitable parish labour at a price exceeding the value of the work done, is parochial relief (*Magarrill* v. *Whitehaven*, 55 L. J. Q. B. 38 ; 16 Q. B. D. 242 ; 53 L. T. 667 ; 34 W. R. 275 ; 49 J. P. 743).

Excusal from payment of poor-rate on the ground of poverty is not receiving parochial relief (*Mashiter* v. *Dunn*, 18 L. J. C. P. 13 ; 6 C. B. 30 ; 2 Lutw. 112), in which case Maule, J., said,—"A man is not receiving parochial relief because he does not pay the rate, any more than I receive money from a beggar, because I do not give him any when he asks me."

Nor is relief by way of loan under s. 58, 4 & 5 W. 4, c. 76, disqualifying (*Oldham,* 1 O'M. & H. 161). And though Medicine from, or Medical Attendance by, the parish doctor is parochial relief (*Oldham,* sup.); yet that kind of relief does not now disqualify a person from being registered as a parliamentary or municipal voter (48 & 49 V. c. 46, ss. 2, 4; *V.* MEDICAL; but s. 2 excludes its application to elections of guardians); and statutory exceptions from what would otherwise be parochial relief are also made, so that no "right or privilege" shall be lost by reason of Parochial Vaccination (30 & 31 V. c. 84, s. 26), and so that no "franchise, right or privilege" shall be lost by reason of School Fees being paid for poor persons by the guardians (39 & 40 V. c. 79, s. 10).

V. ALMS: RELIEF.

PAROCHIAL TAX.—Neither Land Tax (*Waterloo Bridge Co.* v. *Cull,* 29 L. J. Q. B. 10; 1 E. & E. 213), nor a Sewers Rate (*Waller* v. *Andrews,* 3 M. & W. 312; 7 L. J. Ex. 68: *Palmer* v. *Earith,* 14 M. & W. 428; 14 L. J. Ex. 256), nor an Improvement Rate by virtue of a local act (*Bedford Union* v. *Bedford Imp. Commrs.,* 21 L. J. M. C. 229; 7 Ex. 777), nor a rate made, under a Local Act, for Repair of a Bridge *ratione tenuræ* (*Baker* v. *Greenhill,* 11 L. J. Q. B. 161; 2 G. & D. 435; 3 Q. B. 148) is a "Parochial" Tax. But a County Rate, levied and paid out of the poor rate, is Parochial (*R.* v. *Aylesbury,* 9 Q. B. 261). *Vf.* Woodf. 556: *Cp.* PARLIAMENTARY.

V. PAROCHIAL RELIEF: ALMS.

PARSON.—"'*Parson,*' *Persona.* In the legall signification it is taken for the rector of a church parochiall, and is called *persona ecclesiæ,* because he assumeth and taketh upon him the parson of the church, and is said to be seised *in jure ecclesiæ*" (Co. Litt. 300 a, b).

"'Parson impersonee,' is he that is in possession of a Church Appropriate, or Presentative, for so it is used in both cases in Dyer, 40 b and 221 b" (Termes de la Ley).

PARSONAGE.—*V.* RECTORY.

PART.—A "part" of a *Drama* within the Copyright Act (3 & 4 W. 4, c. 15, s. 2) does not mean a particle of it, but a substantial or material part (*Chatterton* v. *Cave,* 47 L. J. C. P. 545; 3 App. Ca. 483).

Part of a "*House*" or "*Manufactory*" within s. 92, Lands C. C. Act, 1845; *V.* HOUSE: MANUFACTORY.

Part of a "House," *quà* Reform Act; *V.* HOUSE.

"Part of a *Mine,*" within the Coal Mines Regulation Act, 1872 (35 & 36 V. c. 76), means "a part having a separate system of ventilation, which, by the terms of the statute, is a separate mine" (per Day, J., *Wales* v. *Thomas,* 55 L. J. M. C. 61; 16 Q. B. D. 340; 55 L. T. 400; 50 J. P. 516; 2 Times Rep. 53).

As to "part of a *Street;*" *V. Mile-End Old Town* v. *Whitechapel Union* 45 L. J. M. C. 75; 46 Ib. 138.

A Power of Sale of "*any Part*" of an estate would, probably, authorize the sale of the whole of it (*Rendlesham* v. *Meux*, 14 Sim. 249: *V. Cooke* v. *Farraud*, 7 Taunt. 122. *Vf.* ANY).

A Devise of "*my* Part," even before the Wills Act, would generally carry the fee (2 Jarm. 285: *Woodhouse* v. *Herrick*, 1 K. & J. 352; 24 L. J. Ch. 649; 3 W. R. 303).

PART WITH.—*V.* ASSIGN: UNDERLEASE.

PARTIAL LOSS.—"This expression includes both a deterioration of all or any part of, and a total destruction of a part of, the subject of insurance" (Wood. 359, citing 2 Phillips, No. 1422. *Vf.* Park on Mar. Insrce., Ch. VI., 8 Ed. 215; Maude & P. 525 *et seq.*).

V. TOTAL LOSS: LOSS: TRANSHIPMENT.

PARTICATA TERRÆ.—A Rood (Elph. 606).

PARTICIPATE.—Where beneficiaries are to "participate" in a trust property, and there is no direction as to the shares to be taken, they take as tenants in common, in equal shares and proportions (*Liddard* v. *Liddard*, 29 L. J. Ch. 619; 28 Bea. 266). In *Robertson* v. *Fraser* (40 L. J. Ch. 776; 6 Ch. 696), Hatherley, L.C., said, "the word 'participate' clearly implied a sharing or division, and a tenancy in common was the natural consequence."

PARTICULAR.—"If a Condition of Sale provide compensation for any mistake in the description of the lots or for any error or misstatement 'in this particular,' the latter words will be construed 'in these particulars,' so as to embrace an error in the Particulars" (Sug. V. & P. 15, citing *White* v. *Cuddon*, 8 Cl. & F. 766; 4 Y. & C. Ex. 25; Sug. Real Prop. Law, 591).

PARTICULAR AVERAGE.—*V. G. Indian Peninsular Ry.* v. *Saunders*, 30 L. J. Q. B. 218; 31 Ib. 206; 1 B. & S. 41; 2 Ib. 266: *Kidston* v. *Empire Mar. Insrce.*, 35 L. J. C. P. 250; 36 Ib. 156; L. R. 1 C. P. 535; 2 Ib. 357: 1 Maude & P. 426, n. (*y*).

V. GENERAL AVERAGE: AVERAGE: F. P. A.

PARTICULAR CHARGES.—*V. Kidston* v. *Empire Mar. Insrce.*, 35 L. J. C. P. 250; 36 Ib. 156; L. R. 1 C. P. 535; 2 Ib. 357.

PARTICULAR PROVISION.—As to this phrase in s. 59, 6 G. 4, c. 125, and in s. 370 (3), Merchant Shipping Act, 1854; *V. The Killarney*, Lush. 427; 30 L. J. P. M. & A. 41: *Hadgraft* v. *Hewith*, L. R. 10 Q. B.

350 ; 44 L. J. M. C. 140 : *The Hankow*, 4 P. D. 197 ; 48 L. J. P. D. & A. 29 : *Vf.* 1 Maude & P. 261, n. (*s*) : TRINITY HOUSE OUTPORT DISTRICTS.

PARTITION.—"It is clear that a Power to make Partition of an Estate will not authorize a Sale or Exchange of it ; but it has frequently been a question amongst conveyancers, whether the usual Power of Sale and Exchange does not authorize a Partition, and several partitions have been made, by force of such powers, under the direction of men of eminence" (Sug. Pow. 856). The learned author proceeds to discuss *Abell* v. *Heathcote* (4 Bro. C. C. 278 ; 2 Ves. jun. 98) : *McQueen and Farquhar* (11 Ves. 467) : *A.-G.* v. *Hamilton* (1 Mad. 214), and *Bradshaw* v. *Fane* (3 Drew. 534 ; 2 Jur. N. S. 247 ; 25 L. J. Ch. 413) ; but his conclusion is (p. 857), —"Until the question shall receive further decision, it can scarcely be considered clear that a Power to Exchange will authorize a Partition." That further decision was, however, furnished in *Re Frith and Osborne* (3 Ch. D. 618 ; 45 L. J. Ch. 780), in which Jessel, M.R., reviewed all the authorities hereon, and, without hesitation, ruled that a Partition may be effected through a Power of Sale and Exchange.

PARTNERSHIP.—"An agreement that something shall be attempted with a view to gain, and that the gain shall be shared by the parties to the agreement, is the grand characteristic of every partnership" (Lindl. 1) ; and "to use the word 'partnership' to denote a society not formed for gain is to destroy the value of the word" (Ib. 2).

For a discussion of the various definitions of "Partnership ;" *V. Pooley* v. *Driver*, 46 L. J. Ch. 466 ; 5 Ch. D. 458 : *Badeley* v. *Consolidated Bank*, 34 Ch. D. 536 ; 38 Ib. 238.

V. COMPANY : COPARTNERSHIP.

A bequest of all "my share right and interest" in a partnership, does not include a debt due to the testator from the partnership (*Re Beard*, 57 L. J. Ch. 887 ; 58 L. T. 629 ; 36 W. R. 519).

PARTY.—"Signed by the Party to be charged therewith," ss. 4, 17, St. of Frauds ;—"Party" there is not to be construed *party* as to a deed, but person in general (Sug. V. & P. 129, citing 3 Atk. 503).

"Party" read "Person" in *Barlow* v. *Osborne*, 20 L. J. Ch. 308 ; 6 H. L. Ca. 556.

The word "Party" in the latter part of s. 40, Chancery Procedure Act, 1852 (15 & 16 V. c. 86) means "person ;" so that when an affidavit by any "person" has been filed under that statute it cannot be withdrawn for the purpose of preventing the cross-examination of that person whether he be a "party" to the cause or not (*Re Quartz Hill Gold Mining Co.*, 51 L. J. Ch. 940 ; 21 Ch. D. 642, upholding *Clarke* v. *Law*, 2 K. & J. 28 ; 4 W. R. 35 ; and setting at rest the doubt expressed by Ld. Selborne in *Pike* v. *Dickinson*, 21 W. R. 862). But in s. 17, Com. L. Pro. Act, 1860 (23 & 24 V. c. 126), the word "Parties" means only the litigant parties and does not include the Sheriff (*Smith* v. *Darlow*, 53 L. J. Ch. 696; 26 Ch. D. 605; 32 W. R. 665).

For the purposes of the Judicature Acts and Rules, "Party," unless controlled by context, "includes every person served with notice of, or attending, any proceeding, although not named on the record" (Jud. Act, 1873, s. 100; *Vth. Fraser* v. *Burrows*, 46 L. J. Q. B. 501; 2 Q. B. D. 624: *Burstall* v. *Fearon*, 31 W. R. 581).

A Third-party, who has appeared, is a "Party" within Ord. 31, R. 12, R. S. C. (*MacAllister* v. *Bishop of Rochester*, 49 L. J. C. P. 443; 5 C. P. D. 194); but the Next Friend of an infant is not (*Re Corsellis*, 52 L. J. Ch. 399; 31 W. R. 414: *Dyke* v. *Stephens*, 55 L. J. Ch. 41; 30 Ch. D. 189; 33 W. R. 932: in the latter case Pearson, J., refused to follow *Higginson* v. *Hall*, 48 L. J. Ch. 250; 10 Ch. D. 235, because there the application was unopposed, or *Crowe* v. *Bank of Ireland*, 19 W. R. 910).

A co-plaintiff or co-defendant is within this Rule, and also within R. 3, Ord. 50, "so long as there is some right between" him and others on the same side of the record "which may be adjusted; but it does not so apply when there is no right to be adjusted" (per Esher, M.R., *Shaw* v. *Smith*, 56 L. J. Q. B. 175; 18 Q. B. D. 193; 56 L. T. 40; 35 W. R. 188, explaining *Brown* v. *Watkins*, 55 L. J. Q. B. 126; 16 Q. B. D. 125; 34 W. R. 293: *Vh. Whitham* v. *Whitham*, 28 S. J. 456). *V.* Opposite Party.

"Parties," s. 36, 9 G. 4, c. 22; *V. Ranson* v. *Dundas*, 6 L. J. C. P. 137; 3 Bing. N. C. 123, 180, 556.

"*All parties*," in s. 24, Metropolis Water Act, 1871 (34 & 35 V. c. 113), means "all persons" (*East Lond. W. W. Co.* v. *St. Matthew, Bethnal Green*, 55 L. J. Q. B. 571; 17 Q. B. D. 475; 54 L. T. 919; 35 W. R. 37; 50 J. P. 820).

Vh. Termes de la Ley, *Parties*.

V. Person.

PARTY AGGRIEVED.—*V.* Aggrieved.

PARTY BY LAW ENABLED TO DECLARE SUCH TRUST.—This phrase, in s. 7, Statute of Frauds, means the owner of the beneficial interest in the property to be affected (*Dye* v. *Dye*, 13 Q. B. D. 147; 53 L. J. Q. B. 442), whether such property be real (*Tierney* v. *Wood*, 19 Bea. 330; 23 L. J. Ch. 895: *Kronheim* v. *Johnson*, 7 Ch. D. 60; 47 L. J. Ch. 132: *Dye* v. *Dye*, sup.), or personal (*Bridge* v. *Bridge*, 16 Bea. 315; 22 L. J. Ch. 189: *Ex p. Pye*, 18 Ves. 140). *Vh.* Lewin, 57.

PARTY INTERESTED.—"Party interested," s. 39, Solicitors Act, 1843, 6 & 7 V. c. 73, means a party under a trust created by Deed, Will, or under an Intestacy (*Re Leadbitter*, 48 L. J. Ch. 242; 10 Ch. D. 388).

Money paid into Court to the account of the "Party interested" under Lands C. C. Act, 1845; *V. Re Winder*, 46 L. J. Ch. 572; 6 Ch. D. 696,

Incumbrancers upon the shares of persons entitled in common to real estate, are " Parties Interested in the property " within the Partition Act, 1868, so as to be able, adversely to the persons entitled to the equity of redemption, to claim a sale under the Act (*Davenport* v. *King*, W. N. (83) 133).

V. PERSON INTERESTED : INTERESTED IN.

PARTY LIABLE.—As to this phrase in s. 5, 3 & 4 W. 4, c. 42 ; *V. Roddam* v. *Morley*, 1 D. G. & J. 1 ; 26 L. J. Ch. 438 : *Toft* v. *Stephenson*, 1 D. G. M. & G. 28 ; 21 L. J. Ch. 129 ; 7 Hare, 1 : *Pears* v. *Laing*, L. R. 12 Eq. 41 ; 40 L. J. Ch. 225 : *Coope* v. *Cresswell*, 2 Ch. 112 ; 35 L. J. Ch. 496 ; 36 Ib. 114.

PARTY OR PRIVY.—Though a covenant that the covenantor has not done, permitted, or suffered anything preventing him from conveying, is not broken by his having assented to what he could not prevent, yet if the words " or been party or privy to " were added, there would be a breach in such a case (*Hobson* v. *Middleton*, 6 B. & C. 295 ; 9 D. & R. 249. *Vh.* Elph. 490 ; Dart, 885, 886 ; Sug. V. & P. 603, 604). *Vh. Clifford* v. *Hoare*, 43 L. J. C. P. 225 ; L. R. 9 C. P. 362 : PERMIT.

PARTY STRUCTURE.—*V. Major* v. *Park Lane Co.*, L. R. 2 Eq. 453.

PARTY TO THE SUIT.—" Generally speaking, the Crown is not bound under the terms 'Party to the suit' " (per Alderson, B., *A.-G.* v. *Donaldson*, 11 L. J. Ex. 340 ; 10 M. & W. 117, citing *R.* v. *Tuchin*, 2 Ld. Raym. 1066).

A Next Friend is not a "Party to the Suit," and therefore was not within the proviso to 6 & 7 V. c. 85, as a " party " "individually named in the Record " (*Sinclair* v. *Sinclair*, 14 L. J. Ex. 109 ; 13 M. & W. 640). *V.* PARTY.

PARTY-WALL.—" 'Party-wall' may be used in four different senses:—

" *First.*—A wall of which the two adjoining owners are tenants in common : *Wiltshire* v. *Sidford*, 1 M. & R. 404 : *Cubitt* v. *Porter*, 8 B. & C. 257 : *Stedman* v. *Smith*, 26 L. J. Q. B. 314 ; 8 E. & B. 1 : *Standard Bank, British S. America* v. *Stokes*, 47 L. J. Ch. 554 ; 9 Ch. D. 68 : *Watson* v. *Gray*, 49 L. J. Ch. 243 ; 14 Ch. D. 192. This is the most common and primary meaning of the term ; per Fry, J., *Watson* v. *Gray*, sup.

" *Second.*—A wall divided longitudinally into two strips, one belonging to each of the neighbouring owners. In this case the owners are not tenants in common, even if the wall was erected at their joint expense (*Matts* v. *Hawkins*, 5 Taunt. 20) : but where there has been a common user of the wall erected at the common expense, that, in the absence of any other evidence, is sufficient evidence for a jury to find that the wall is held by the two parties as tenants in common ; *Cubitt* v. *Porter*, and *Standard Bank, B. S. America* v. *Stokes*, sup.

" *Third.*—A wall which belongs entirely to one of the adjoining owners, but is subject to an easement or right in the other to have it maintained as a dividing wall between the two tenements. The term is so used in the Metrop. Bg. Act, 18 & 19 V. c. 122, s. 3 : *Knight* v. *Pursell*, 49 L. J. Ch. 120 ; 11 Ch. D. 412. Such a wall may be a party-wall for some part of its height, and above that height the separate property of one of the adjoining owners (*Weston* v. *Arnold*, 43 L. J. Ch. 123 ; 8 Ch. 1084) ; and in the same way such a wall may be laterally a party wall for such distance as it is used by both owners and no further ; *Knight* v. *Pursell*, sup.

" *Fourth.*—A wall divided longitudinally into two moieties, each moiety being subject to a cross-easement in favour of the owner of the other moiety. This meaning is suggested in the note to *Wiltshire* v. *Sidford*, sup.

" The cases are collected in 5 Fisher, Dig. 990 *et seq.*; and *V.* Hunt on Boundaries, Ch. 5 " (Elph. 606, 607).

PASCUUM.—*V.* Pastures.

PASS.—" Every indorsee of a Bill of Lading to whom the property in the goods shall *pass*," s. 1, 18 & 19 V. c. 111 ; *V. Sewell* v. *Burdick*, 54 L. J. Q. B. 156 ; 10 App. Ca. 74.

PASS AND REPASS.—" Pass and Repass," in a local Turnpike Act, held to mean going and returning over the road once only (*Armstrong* v. *Hunt*, 34 J. P. 823).

PASSAGE.—" Now on Passage ;" *V.* Now.

" Passage *or Place* which now is, or hereafter may be built upon, or in building," in a Local Paving Act, 55 G. 3, c. xxv., s. 3, does not include a Bridge, forming part of a public highway, and which was built over a canal, and had walls 4 to 5 feet high on either side (*Arnell* v. *Regent's Canal Co.*, 23 L. J. C. P. 155 ; 14 C. B. 564).

PASSENGER.—The wife and father-in-law of a Captain of a vessel, who were on the vessel and being carried by it to a place to which they wished to go, but who were being so carried by the captain's invitation without the knowledge of the owners, held not to be " Passengers " within s. 379, Merchant Shipping Act, 1854 (*The Lion*, 17 W. R. 993). From that case it would seem that payment of a fare is not a necessary test of what is a " Passenger ;" any one (other than the officers and crew) being carried by a ship, and towards whom the owners have, during the voyage, any obligation or duty, would, probably, be a " Passenger " within the section.

PASSENGER'S RISK.—*V. Stewart* v. *Lond. & N. W. Ry.*, 33 L. J. Ex. 199. *V.* OWNER'S RISK.

PASSENGER SHIP.—"Passenger Ship," *quà* s. 52, Passengers Act, 1855, and s. 15, Act 1863, signifies "every description of sea-going Vessel carrying one or more passenger or passengers on any voyage from any place in Her Majesty's Dominions to any place whatever" (s. 2, 52 & 53 V. c. 29).

"The Passengers Acts (1855, 1863, 1870, 1872) do not extend to Queen's ships, or to ships in the service of the Admiralty; but their provisions chiefly apply to 'Emigrant Passenger Ships,' that is, to every description of sea-going vessel, whether British, or Foreign, or Colonial, carrying, on any voyage from the United Kingdom to any place out of Europe and not in the Mediterranean Sea, or on certain Colonial voyages described in the Act (1855, ss. 95–99), more than 50 passengers, or a greater number of passengers when the ship is propelled by sails, than in the proportion of one statute adult (*i.e.*, one person of the age of 12 or upwards, or two persons between the ages of 1 and 12) to every 33 tons of the registered tonnage, or, when the ship is propelled by steam, a greater number than in the proportion of one statute adult to every 20 tons registered tonnage" (1 Maude & P. 712; *Vth. Ellis* v. *Pearce*, E. B. & E. 431; 27 L. J. M. C. 257).

PASSENGER TRAIN.—"A 'Passenger Train,' *primâ facie*, is a train advertised to take passengers generally,—people travelling from place to place,—upon the terms and in the manner *ordinarily* applicable to such passengers" (per Selborne, L.C., *Burnett* v. *G. N. of Scotland Ry.*, 54 L. J. Q. B. 535; 10 App. Ca. 147).

Accordingly, in that case (the defendant company having agreed that all their passenger trains should regularly stop at Crathes), it was held that Queen's Messenger trains and Post Office trains, which ran only whilst the Queen was staying at Balmoral, but which were advertised in the Company's time-tables, and by which, to some extent, ordinary passengers could travel, were "Passenger Trains;" but (diss. Ld. Bramwell) that Excursion trains were not.

PASSING.—The date of the "Passing" of an Act "are common English words, which have a fixed meaning in our language and law,—they mean the time when the Royal Assent is given to a Bill which has passed both Houses of Parliament" (per James, L.J., *Ex p. Rashleigh, Re Dalzell*, 45 L. J. Bank. 31; 2 Ch. D. 9), and that is also the date of its COMMENCEMENT where it provides no other commencement (33 G. 3, c. 13; s. 36 (1), Interp. Act, 1889). *Vh. Hall* v. *L. B. & S. Ry.*, 55 L. J. Q. B. 328; 17 Q. B. D. 233: *Ings* v. *Lond. & S. W. Ry.*, 38 L. J. C. P. 8; L. R. 4 C. P. 20: *Wood* v. *Hunt*, 38 L. J. C. P. 10, n. 8; L. R. 4 C. P. 18, n. 2. But where there is a date named in the Act for it to come into operation, and a thing prohibited by it is completed before that date, then the phrase "after the passing" would seem to mean "after the Act shall come into operation" (*Wood* v. *Riley*, 37 L. J. C. P. 24; L. R. 3 C. P. 26).

Where an Act comes into operation on a stated day, it becomes law as soon as the clock begins to strike twelve on the previous night (*Tomlinson* v. *Bullock*, 48 L. J. M. C. 95; 4 Q. B. D. 230: s. 36 (2), Interp. Act, 1889).

"Passing over the same portion of the Line," s. 90, 8 V. c. 20; *V.* SAME.

PASTIME.—*V.* GAME, p. 320.

PASTORAL.—*V.* AGRICULTURAL.

PASTURAGE.—A right of "Common Pasturage and Herbage," only authorizes taking what can be taken by the mouth or bite of cattle, and not to cut or carry away any part of the growth of the soil (*De la Warr* v. *Miles*, 50 L. J. Ch. 754; 17 Ch. D. 535).

"Right of Pasturage usually enjoyed;" *V. Musgrave* v. *Inclosure Commrs.*, L. R. 9 Q. B. 162.

PASTURE.—"Any Holding *let* to be used *wholly or mainly* for the purpose of Pasture," s. 58 (3), Land Law (Ireland) Act, 1881, 44 & 45 V. c. 49; *V. Westropp* v. *Elligott*, 9 App. Ca. 815; 14 L. R. Ir. 319: *Battersby* v. *Nicholson*, 22 L. R. Ir. 38: *Holmes* v. *Lauder*, Ib. 47.

PASTURES.—"If a man doth grant all his pastures, *pasturas*, the land itselfe imployed to the feeding of beasts doth passe, and also such pastures or feedings as he hath in another man's soile. *Leswēs* or *lesues*, is a Saxon word, and signifieth pastures. Between *pastura* and *pascuum*, the legall difference is, that *pastura* in one signification containeth the ground itselfe called pasture. *Pascuum*, feeding, is wheresoever cattell are fed, of what nature soever the ground is" (Co. Litt. 4 b: *Vh.* Elph. 607–615). *Cp.* HERBAGE: *V.* MEADOWS.

"Pasture;"—"Pasture is a general name for herbage, acorns, mast and nuts, and for leaves and flowers, and for all things comprised under the name of Pannage" (Britton, l. 2, ch. 24, 1 Nichols, Ed. 371; *Va.* Bracton, l. 4, c. 38, fol. 222; Fleta, l. 4, c. 19). *V.* PANNAGE.

V. COMMON.

PATENT DEFECT.—*V.* DEFECT.

PATENTEE.—A description on a manufacturer's label as "Patentee," held to be equivalent to describing the article as "patent" (*Nixey* v. *Roffey*, W. N. (70), 227).

PATERNA.—"Ex parte Paternâ;" *V.* NEXT OF KIN.

PATRIMONY.—"Patrimony" is not necessarily restricted to property derived directly from a father (*Green* v. *Giles*, 5 Ir. Ch. Rep. 25).

PAVEMENT.—A footway made up with gravel and kerbed, but not paved with stone or flagged, is a "Pavement" within s. 78, Metrop. Man. Act, 1855 (*St. John's, Hampstead* v. *Hoopel*, 15 Q. B. D. 652; 54 L. J. M. C. 147; 1 Times Rep. 584).

PAY TO.—*V.* PERMIT.

PAYABLE.—Where there is a gift to a remainderman on attaining 21 or marrying, but to go over in case of his death before his share becomes "payable," this word will generally be read as "vested" (*Emperor* v. *Rolfe*, 1 Ves. sen. 208).

It frequently happens that "A money fund is given to a person for life, and after his decease, to his children at majority or marriage, with a gift over in the event of any of the objects dying before their shares become *payable*. In such cases it becomes a question whether the word 'payable' is to be considered (1) as referring to the age or marriage (or any other such circumstance affecting the personal situation of the legatee), on the arrival or happening of which the shares are made 'payable,' or (2) to the actual period of distribution; in other words, whether the shares vest absolutely at the majority or marriage of the legatees,—*in the lifetime of the legatee for life*; or whether the vesting is postponed to the period of such majority or marriage, *and the death of the legatee for life*. As the latter construction exposes the legatees to the risk of losing the testator's provision in the event of their dying in the lifetime of the legatee for life,—although they may have reached adult or even advanced age and may have left numerous descendants,—the Courts have strongly inclined to hold the word 'Payable' to refer to the majority or marriage of the legatees, especially if the testator stood towards the legatees in the parental relation.

"And where (as often happens) the question has arisen under Marriage Settlements, the leaning to this construction is strongly aided by the occasion and design of the instrument, whose primary object obviously is, to secure a provision for the issue of the marriage. In Wills, the point, like all others, depends solely upon the intention to be collected from the context" (2 Jarm. 799, *wh.* to p. 808, *V.* for cases illustrating and qualifying these propositions: *Vf. Wakefield* v. *Maffet*, 55 L. J. Ch. 4; 10 App. Ca. 422; 53 L. T. 169: *Partridge* v. *Baylis*, W. N. (81) 81).

"It is presumed that if upon the true construction of the Will 'payable' applies to the age or marriage of the legatee, the construction will not be varied by the accident of the legatee for life dying before the majority or marriage of the legatee in remainder; but that the interest of the latter will remain liable to defeasance during minority or until marriage.

"But if no time is specified—(or, can be collected as specified?),—for payment, the word 'payable' in the gift over will be held to refer to the death of the tenant for life, and the legatee in remainder must survive him in order to take.

"If an *immediate* legacy is given without specifying a time for payment, and is given over in case the legatee dies before it becomes payable, the word 'payable' can only have reference to the death of the testator. And even where a legacy (whether immediate or after a prior life estate) is directed to be paid at a particular age, and is given over in case the legatee dies before it becomes 'payable,' the gift over takes effect if the legatee dies before the testator, although he may have attained the age" (2 Jarm. 808, 809). *Vf.* Watson, Eq. 1228–1230.

"*Due* and Payable;" *V. Re Wilmot,* 38 L. J. Ch. 275; L. R. 7 Eq. 532.

V. RECEIVED.

PAYEE.—"Purchaser, Payee, or Incumbrancer," at end of s. 92, Bankry. Act, 1869;—*V. Butcher* v. *Stead,* 44 L. J. Bank. 129; L. R. 7 H. L. 839. In the corresponding section (48 (2)) of the Bankry. Act, 1883, this phrase is varied to "any person making title through or under a creditor of the bankrupt."

PAYING.—The usual preface in a Lessor's Covenant for Quiet Enjoyment,—viz., the Lessee "paying the rent hereby reserved and performing the covenants on his part herein contained,"—does not make such payment or performance a condition precedent to the performance by the lessor of his covenant (*Hays* v. *Bickerstaffe,* 2 Mod. 34; Vaugh. 118: *Dawson* v. *Dyer,* 5 B. & Ad. 584; 2 N. & M. 559: *Edge* v. *Boileau,* 55 L. J. Q. B. 90; 34 W. R. 103. *Vh.* Woodf. 678, note *n*). In his successful argument in *Hays* v. *Bickerstaffe,* Pemberton, Serjt., said: "The words 'Paying and Yielding' make no condition, nor was it ever known that for such words the Lessor entered for non-payment of rent; and there is no difference between these words and 'Paying and Performing,' *Bennet's Case* in B. R.: *Duncomb's Case,* Owen, 54." In a previous part of his argument he admitted that "the word 'Paying,' in some cases, may amount to a condition; but that is where, without such construction, the party could have no remedy."

V. YIELDING AND PAYING.

"Paying a Dividend;" *V.* STOCKS.

PAYING FREIGHT.—"Paying Freight and all other conditions as per Charter-Party," in a Bill of Lading signed by consignees as agents, will not make such consignees liable for demurrage due under the terms of the Charter-Party (*Steamship County of Lancaster* v. *Sharpe,* 59 L. J. Q. B. 22; 24 Q. B. D. 158, explaining *Wegener* v. *Smith,* 24 L. J. C. P. 25; 15 C. B. 285). *V.* ON PAYMENT OF FREIGHT.

PAYMENT.—A "payment ought to be reall, and not in shew or appearance" (Co. Litt. 209 b).

"'Payment' is not a technical word: it has been imported into law proceedings from the Exchange and not from law treatises. It does not necessarily mean payment in satisfaction and discharge, but may be used in a popular sense" (Dwar. 675, citing *Maillard* v. *Argyle*, 6 M. & G. 40).

A payment may generally be made by the mere transfer of figures in an account without any money passing (*Eyles* v. *Ellis*, 4 Bing. 112 : *Bodenham* v. *Purchas*, 2 B. & Ald. 39 : *Hills* v. *Mesnard*, 16 L. J. Q. B. 306 ; 10 Q. B. 266) ; or by payment to a third person (*Waller* v. *Andrews*, 3 M. & W. 312 : *Bramston* v. *Robins*, 4 Bing. 11) ; or by acceptance of goods (*Cannan* v. *Wood*, 2 M. & W. 465 ; nom. *Canning* v. *Wood*, 6 L. J. Ex. 112 : *Hooper* v. *Stephens*, 4 A. & E. 71) ; or (conditionally) by bill or note (*V.* cases collected Rosc. N. P. 621) ; or by sending a cheque by post in compliance with a request for a cheque (*Norman* v. *Ricketts*, 31 S. J. 124).

"Payment," s. 41, Solicitors Act, 6 & 7 V. c. 73 ; *V. Re Street*, 39 L. J. Ch. 495 ; L. R. 10 Eq. 165 : *Re Stogdon*, 56 L. J. Ch. 420 ; 56 L. T. 355 ; 51 J. P. 565. What are a Solicitor's "Disbursements ;" *V.* DISBURSEMENTS.

A receipt for a Peppercorn Rent is not a receipt for a "Payment" within s. 3 (4), Conv. & L. P. Act, 1881 (*Re Moody and Yates*, 54 L. J. Ch. 886 ; 30 Ch. D. 344 ; 33 W. R. 785). In that case, Brett, M.R., said that the subsection was not applicable where rent is reserved in kind ; "the words, 'the receipt for the last payment due for rent under the lease,' apply only when there is to be a payment of money."

A payment to take a case out of a Statute of Limitation must be by, or on behalf of, the person liable to make it (*Chinnery* v. *Evans*, 11 H. L. Ca. 115 ; 11 L. T. 69 : *Cockburn* v. *Edwards*, 51 L. J. Ch. 46 ; 18 Ch. D. 449 : *Harlock* v. *Ashberry*, 51 L. J. Ch. 394 ; 19 Ch. D. 539 : *Lewin* v. *Wilson*, 55 L. T. 410 : *Re Frisby*, 59 L. J. Ch. 94 ; 43 Ch. D. 106).

An Order to deposit money in Court to abide a subsequent Order, is not one for the "*payment* of a Sum of Money" within s. 4, Debtors Act, 1869, and it may be enforced by attachment (*Lynch* v. *Lynch*, 54 L. J. P. D. & A. 93 ; 10 P. D. 183 : *Bates* v. *Bates*, 58 L. J. P. D. & A. 85 ; 14 P. D. 17 ; 60 L. T. 125) ; *Secus*, as regards an Order to pay Taxed Costs (*Hewitson* v. *Sherwin*, L. R. 10 Eq. 53).

"Reduced by Payment or otherwise," s. 65, Co. Co. Act, 1888 ; *V.* OTHERWISE, p. 549 : REDUCED BY PAYMENT.

The deduction of Fines from the wages of an ARTIFICER is not a "Payment otherwise than in the Current Coin of the Realm," within s. 9, Truck Acts, 1 & 2 W. 4, c. 37; 50 & 51 V. c. 46 (*Redgrave* v. *Kelly*, 37 W. R. 543); *secus*, of a merely colourable payment (*Gould* v. *Haynes*, 59 L. J. M. C. 9). *Vh. Archer* v. *James*, 31 L. J. Q. B. 153 ; 2 B. & S. 61 ; 1 L. T. 26.

V. PAID : UNPAID.

PAYMENT FOR HONOUR.—Payment for Honour, supra protest; *V.* s. 68, Bills of Ex. Act, 1882.

PAYMENT IN CASH.—*V.* In Cash.

PAYMENT IN DUE COURSE.—"Payment in Due Course," of a Bill or Note, means payment made at or after the maturity of the Bill or Note, to the Holder thereof in Good Faith, and without notice that his title to the Bill or Note is defective (ss. 59, 89, Bills of Ex. Act, 1882) : *Vf.* s. 59.

PEACEABLY AND QUIETLY.—In a covenant for quiet enjoyment "'Quietly' does not mean 'undisturbed by noise.' When a man is quietly in possession it has nothing whatever to do with noise. 'Peaceably and Quietly' means, without interference,—without interruption of the possession" (per Kekewich, J., *Jenkins* v. *Jackson*, 58 L. J. Ch. 124 ; 40 Ch. D. 71 : *wh. V.* for discussion of *Shaw* v. *Stenton*, 27 L. J. Ex. 253 ; 2 H. & N. 858, as explained by *Sanderson* v. *Berwick*, 53 L. J. Q. B. 559 ; 13 Q. B. D. 547. *Vf. Robinson* v. *Kilvert*, 41 Ch. D. 88). *V.* Quiet Enjoyment.

PEARLS.—*V.* Necklaces.

PECUNIARY CONSIDERATION.—The exémption from registration of annuities contained in s. 8, 17 G. 3, c. 26 (repealed), for "any Voluntary Annuity granted without regard to *Pecuniary Consideration*," was held to comprise the case of a grantee giving up his business to the grantor (*Crespigny* v. *Wittenoom*, 4 T. R. 790 : *Hutton* v. *Lewis*, 5 T. R. 639), or the assignment of a leasehold interest (*James* v. *James*, 2 B. & B. 702), or where the consideration was a transfer of stock (*Cumberland* v. *Kelley*, 1 L. J. K. B. 172 ; 3 B. & Ad. 602). But Bank Notes (*Wright* v. *Reed*, 3 T. R. 554 : *Cousins* v. *Thompson*, 6 T. R. 335 : *Morris* v. *Wall*, 1 B. & P. 208), Cheques (*Pool* v. *Cabanes*, 8 T. R. 328), and Bills of Exchange or Promissory Notes (*Rumball* v. *Murray*, 3 T. R. 298), were held to be "Pecuniary Consideration" within the section.

Under 53 G. 3, c. 141 (which replaced 17 G. 3, c. 26), it was held that the surrender of a life interest in a sum of money and of a contingent interest in the corpus, was not a "Pecuniary Consideration" (*Evatt* v. *Hunt*, 22 L. J. Q. B. 348 ; 2 E. & B. 374, following *Blake* v. *Attersoll*, 2 L. J. O. S. K. B. 193 ; 2 B. & C. 875).

V. Money's Worth.

PECUNIARY LEGACIES.—"If you find simply the word 'Legacy' used, and a direction to apportion property amongst the legatees, there,—unless there be something apparent on the face of the Will which shows that the testator has not used the word in its ordinary legal signification,—it will include annuitants. The expression 'Pecuniary Legatees' in itself, I do not think, would go further than this—it would exclude specific legatees, that is, legatees of mere chattels, but it would have no effect in excluding, *primâ facie*, annuitants from taking the same benefit as they would have taken if the word had been 'Legatees' instead of 'Pecuniary

Legatees'" (per Wood, V.-C., *Gaskin* v. *Rogers*, L. R. 2 Eq. 291 : in which case, however, Annuitants were excluded, by a context, from participating in a residue given to persons " taking pecuniary legacies ").

V. Legacy.

PEDIGREE.—" The term ' Pedigree ' embraces not only general questions of descent and relationship, but also the particular facts of *birth*, *marriage* and *death*, and the *times* when, either absolutely or relatively, these events happened, provided such facts are required to be proved for some genealogical purpose " (Taylor on Evidence, s. 642).

PEN.—*V.* Howe.

PENAL.—" A penal law is a statute which imposes a penalty " (per Parke, B., *Spencer* v. *Swannell*, 7 L. J. Ex. 75 ; 3 M. & W. 162). In that case it was held that an action of debt upon 2 & 3 Ed. 6, c. 13, was a penal action within the 4th clause 21 Jac. 1, c. 4.

PENALTY.—Where an Act gives a power to inflict a " Penalty *or Forfeiture*," such words " clearly relate to a sum inflicted " (per Groves, J., in *Ex p. Elsdon*, inf.) ; and a power to appeal with respect to any " Penalty or Forfeiture " does not embrace an Order for demolition of buildings (*Ex p. Elsdon*, 51 L. J. M. C. 94 ; 9 Q. B. D. 41 : *Va. Bermondsey* v. *Johnson*, 42 L. J. M. C. 67 ; L. R. 8 C. P. 441).

A liability created by a Ry. Co.'s Bye-Law for non-production by a passenger of his ticket is, *semble*, a " Penalty or Forfeiture " under Ry. C. C. Act, 1845, s. 145 (*Brown* v. *G. E. Ry.*, 46 L. J. M. C. 231 ; 2 Q. B. D. 406).

" *Right*, or Penalty ; " *V.* Right.

PENDING.—A legal proceeding is " pending " as soon as commenced (on *wh. V.* 5 Rep. 47, 48 ; 7 Ib. 30), and until it is concluded, that is,—so long as the Court having original cognizance of it, can make an order on the matters in issue, or to be dealt with, therein.

The issue of a citation, for Dissolution of a voidable Marriage, though only issued 7 days before the 5 & 6 W. 4, c. 54 received the royal assent, constituted a suit " depending " at the passing of the Act (*Sherwood* v. *Ray*, 1 Moore, P. C. 353 ; 1 Curt. 173).

A Liquidation under the Bankruptcy Act, 1869, was " pending " (within No. 292 of the Rules made in pursuance thereof) until the Receiver was discharged (*Ex p. Jefferey*, 43 L. J. Bank. 27 ; 9 Ch. 144 ; 22 W. R. 57 : *Ex p. McHenry*, 53 L. J. Ch. 27 ; 24 Ch. D. 35 : *Vh. Ex p. Hooper, re Elliott*, 8 Ch. D. 53) ; and Composition Proceedings were " pending " until the composition was fully paid (*Re Lund*, 18 S. J. 343). So, as regards the old Insolvent Debtors Court, a matter was " pending " within s. 4, 32 & 33 V. c. 83, if some proceeding therein might still have been taken (*Re Clagett, Fordham* v. *Clagett*, 20 Ch. D. 637 ; 30 W. R. 857).

As to the meaning of this word, as used in s. 169 (3), Bankry. Act, 1883; *V. Ex p. Pratt*, 53 L. J. Ch. 613; 12 Q. B. D. 334.

As to what is a *Cause or Proceeding* "pending" within s. 24 (5), Jud. Act, 1873; *V. Hart* v. *Hart*, 50 L. J. Ch. 697; 18 Ch. D. 670: 30 W. R. 8: *Marshall* v. *Marshall*, 48 L. J. P. D. & A. 49; 5 P. D. 19: *Va.* Ann. Pr. 13. For the purposes of s. 24 (7), Jud. Act, 1873, a Cause is "pending," even after final judgment, so long as such judgment remains unsatisfied (*Salt* v. *Cooper*, 50 L. J. Ch. 529; 16 Ch. D. 544).

So, speaking generally, an Unsatisfied Judgment is a "Depending Suit" (*Howell* v. *Bowers*, 2 Cr. M. & R. 621).

So the Quebec Act, 43 & 44 V. c. 49, saving suits then "pending," applies to proceedings taken in execution of a final judgment (*Redfield* v. *Wickham*, 57 L. J. P. C. 94; 13 App. Ca. 467; 58 L. T. 455).

An action for Infringement of a Patent is not, after judgment, a "pending" action within s. 18 (10), Patents Act, 1883, although an appeal from the judgment is pending (*Cropper* v. *Smith*, 54 L. J. Ch. 287; 28 Ch. D. 148). As to pending "legal proceeding" in the same section; *V. Re Hall*, 21 Q. B. D. 137; 57 L. J. Q. B. 494; 59 L. T. 37; 36 W. R. 892.

"Suit or Matter *actually* pending," s. 17, Charitable Trusts Act, 1853, means pending at the time of the application (*Re Lister's Hospital*, 6 D. G. M. & G. 187; 26 L. T. O. S. 192; 4 W. R. 156); and when a Final Order has been made, the Petition is no longer "actually pending" (*Re Jarvis' Charity*, 1 Dr. & Sm. 97; 5 Jur. N. S. 724; 7 W. R. 606. *Va. Re Ford's Charity*, 3 Drew. 324). *Vh.* Tudor's Char. Trusts, 336, 480.

As to a "pending" *Election; V. Davies* v. *Stone*, 36 J. P. 390: *R.* v. *Pyne*, 37 Ib. 363.

V. IMPENDING.

PENSION.—Surplus moneys of a Pension which (by an Order under s. 53, Bankry. Act, 1883) are in the hands of a Trustee in Bankruptcy, are "Pension" within s. 141, Army Act, 1881; but otherwise of Commutation Money (*Crowe* v. *Price*, 58 L. J. Q. B. 215; 22 Q. B. D. 429; 37 W. R. 424. *V.* that case for the other authorities as to sequestration of a Pension).

PEOPLE.—In a Marine Insurance, "People" means the People of all nations in their respective collective capacities, and not bodies of insurgents acting in opposition to their rulers. It means the governing power of the country; therefore if a corn vessel is seized and detained by a hungry mob, or a party of rebels, that is not a detention by "the People" (*Nesbitt* v. *Lushington*, 4 T. R. 783: *Va. Rotch* v. *Edie*, 6 Ib. 413: 1 Maude & P. 487).

PER CAPITA.—A distribution *per capita* is when the members of a class take the fund distributable among them in equal shares. Its opposite is PER STIRPES.

PER CWT.—In the Hop Trade, a contract for the sale of a stated number of pockets of hops at so many shillings, means that that is the price "per cwt." (*Spicer* v. *Cooper*, 1 Q. B. 424; 10 L. J. Q. B. 241; 1 G. & D. 52).

PER HUNDRED.—*V.* HUNDRED.

PER MY ET PER TOUT.—*Vh.* Co. Litt. 186 a.

PER PROCURATION.—The expression "Per Procuration" does not always necessarily mean that the act is done under procuration. All that it means is this, "I am an agent, not acting on any authority of my own in the case, but authorised by my principal to enter into this contract" (per Pollock, C. B., *Smith* v. *M'Guire*, 27 L. J. Ex. 468; 3 H. & N. 554).

A signature of a Bill of Exchange or Promissory Note "by Procuration, operates as notice that the Agent has but a limited authority to sign, and the Principal is only bound by such signature if the Agent, in so signing, was acting within the actual limits of his authority" (ss. 25, 89, Bills of Ex. Act, 1882, codifying *Stagg* v. *Elliott*, 31 L. J. C. P. 260; 12 C. B. N. S. 373). *V.* s. 26, Ib. as to when an Agent is personally responsible on his signature.

PER STIRPES.—Where a distribution of property amongst a class embracing descendants "is to be *per stirpes*, the principle of representation will be applied through all degrees, children never taking concurrently with their parents (*Ralph* v. *Carrick*, 11 Ch. D. 873; 48 L. J. Ch. 801). In a case (*Robinson* v. *Shepherd*, 32 Bea. 665, on app. 10 Jur. N. S. 53), where the gift was 'to the descendants of A. and B. per stirpes,' Sir J. Romilly, M. R., thought A. and B. were the stirpes in the first instance to be considered, so that the primary division should be into two parts. But Ld. Westbury held that you must look to the number of families or stirpes descended either from A. or B., and existing at the testator's death, and divide the fund primarily into a corresponding number of parts. However, in a subsequent case, the M. R. acted on his own opinion, which appears to have been acquiesced in (*Gibson* v. *Fisher*, L. R. 5 Eq. 51; 37 L. J. Ch. 67: *Va. Booth* v. *Vicars*, 1 Coll. 6; 13 L. J. Ch. 147). If the gift were to the descendants of *one* person, per stirpes, it must necessarily be dealt with on Ld. Westbury's principle" (2 Jarm. 100). In *Re Wilson* (53 L. J. Ch. 130; 24 Ch. D. 664), North, J., endeavoured to reconcile *Gibson* v. *Fisher* with *Robinson* v. *Shepherd*; but added, "if I had to choose between them I should follow *Robinson* v. *Shepherd* in preference to *Gibson* v. *Fisher*." In *Re Wilson* the bequest was upon the determination of a prior estate to such cousins (children of 6 named aunts and uncles), and such issue of predeceased cousins, living at the period of distribution, as should attain the age of 21 years, or should die under that age, leaving issue, "to take if more than one in a course of distribution, *according to the stocks*, and not to the number of individuals," and it was held that under that phrase the property was not divisible into 6 parts, but into 16;

because the cousins (16 in number), and not the aunts aud uncles, were the "stocks."

Vh. Watson, Eq. 1409.

Vf. as to when a distribution is to be made *per stirpes*, and when *per capita*, 2 Jarm. 101, 107, 112, 122, 194 ; Wms. Exs. *n.* 1519.

PEREMPTORY.—A "Peremptory" Order for time to plead means, that the Order is final, unless special circumstances are shown for a further extension (*Falck* v. *Axthelm*, 24 Q. B. D. 176 ; 34 S. J. 141).

PEREMPTORY SALE.—*V.* WITHOUT RESERVE.

PERFORMANCE.—*V.* OBSERVANCE OR PERFORMANCE : REPRESENTING OR PERFORMING : PERFORMED.

PERFORMED.—No agreement "that is not to be performed" within one year from its making is valid unless evidenced by a signed writing (s. 4, Stat. of Frauds, 29 Car. 2, c. 3). This means, (1) a complete performance ; (2) by one of the parties. A contract which contemplates more than a year for its performance is within the statute, though it may be defeasible within the year : and, on the other hand, a contract which does not in terms contemplate more than a year for its performance is not within the statute, because it may exceed that limit (*Vh.* Add. C. 170–172 ; Rosc. N. P. 468, 469).

PERFORMING.—*V.* DOING : PAYING.

PERILS OF THE ROAD.—*V.* DANGERS.

PERILS OF THE SEA.—"I am of opinion that 'Perils of the Sea' is a phrase having the same meaning in Bills of Lading and Charter Parties, as in Policies of Insurance" (per Ld. Bramwell, *Hamilton* v. *Pandorf*, 12 App. Ca. 527 ; 57 L. J. Q. B. 28, 29 ; 6 Asp. 212 ; 57 L. T. 726 ; 36 W. R. 369 : *Va. Wilson* v. *The Xantho*, 56 L. J. P. D. & A. 116 ; 12 App. Ca. 503 ; 57 L. T. 701 ; 36 W. R. 353 ; 6 Asp. 207).

"I think the definition of 'Perils of the Sea,' of Lopes, L. J., in this case very good :—'It is a Sea Damage, occurring at Sea, and nobody's fault.' What is the 'Peril'? It is that the ship or goods will be lost or damaged, but it must be 'Of the Sea'" (per Ld. Bramwell, *Hamilton* v. *Pandorf*, 12 App. Ca. 526, 527 ; 57 L. J. Q. B. 24).

But in view of the decision of the H. L. in *Wilson* v. *The Xantho* (sup.), it is suggested, with the greatest diffidence in a matter on which the greatest authorities have differed, that Ld. Justice Lopes' definition should be thus amended,—"A 'Peril of the Sea' is a Sea Damage, *undesignedly* occurring at Sea."

For, the broad principle of *Wilson* v. *The Xantho* seems to be, that a Collision, which popularly would be called accidental, is a "Peril of the

P P 2

Sea," though brought about by the negligence of one of the vessels, or even (possibly) of both of them. The consequences, indeed, would vary according as there might be negligence ; but those varying consequences would arise not from a varying interpretation of "Perils of the Sea," but because other, and varying, considerations would come into play. Thus, *e.g.*, as regards a Bill of Lading, the ship-owner, in the case of a Collision, could rely on the exception if his vessel were not in fault, because he and those for whom he is answerable would have done nothing to deprive him of its benefit ; but if his vessel were in fault, he could not so rely, not because "Perils of Sea" would have changed meaning, but because something else (his vessel's negligence), by a paramount obligation, would have rendered him liable on the ground that the author of a mischief cannot avail himself of his own wrong. *Note.—Woodley* v. *Michell* (11 Q. B. D. 47 ; 52 L. J. Q. B. 325 ; 31 W. R. 651) is over-ruled by *Wilson* v. *The Xantho.*

Vf. as to Collisions, *Lloyd* v. *Gen. Iron Screw Collier Co.*, 33 L. J. Ex. 269 ; 3 H. & C. 284 : *Grill* v. *Gen. Iron Screw Collier Co.*, 35 L. J. C. P. 321 ; 37 Ib. 205 ; L. R. 1 C. P. 600 ; 3 Ib. 476 ; H. & R. 654.

As to whether a loss by Sea-Worms or Barnacles is a "Peril of the Sea," *V.* jdgmt. of Esher, M. R., *Pandorf* v. *Hamilton*, 17 Q. B. D. 679 ; 55 L. J. Q. B. 550.

Vh. Abbott on Shipping, 12 Ed. 329 : ACCIDENT : DANGERS.

Loss by Pirates is a Peril of the Sea (*Vh.* jdgmt. of Bowen, L. J., *Pandorf* v. *Hamilton*, 55 L. J. Q. B. 553). So are losses "by the Swell of the Tide in a dry harbour ; by the Wilful but not barratrous Act of the Crew in throwing the ballast overboard ; or by a Stranding rendered necessary by leakage produced by the careless loading of the cargo" (1 Maude & P. 355, and cases there cited). Neither Fire nor Lightning is a Peril of the Sea (per Ld. Bramwell, *Hamilton* v. *Pandorf*, 12 App. Ca. 527).

Direct damage done to cargo by Rats is not a Peril of the Sea (*Laveroni* v. *Drury*, 22 L. J. Ex. 2 ; 8 Ex. 166) ; but damage caused by the incursion of sea-water through a Rat-hole is a Peril of the Sea, and, if the shipowner has not been guilty of neglect or default he may rely on the exception (*Hamilton* v. *Pandorf*, sup.).

In view of recent decisions, before referred to, the following can now hardly be regarded as a perfectly accurate statement of English law :—

"The phrase 'Perils of the Sea' whether understood in its most limited sense as importing a loss by natural accidents peculiar to that element, or whether understood in its more extended sense as including inevitable accidents occurring upon that element, must still in either case be understood to include such losses only to the goods on board as are of an extraordinary nature or arise from some irresistible force, or from inevitable accident or some overwhelming power which cannot be guarded against by the ordinary exertions of human skill and prudence. Hence it is that if the loss occurs by a Peril of the Sea which might have been avoided by the exercise of any reasonable skill or diligence at the time when it occurred, it is not deemed to be, in the sense of the phrase, such a loss by the Perils of the Sea as will exempt the carrier from liability, but rather a loss by the gross negligence of the party " (Story on Bailments, 512 a).

The general words, in a Marine Insurance, whereby "all *other* Perils," &c., are insured against, do not cover such a thing as the bursting of the air-chamber of a donkey-pump, whether it occur negligently or accidentally, for such a peril is not *ejusdem generis* with those enumerated (*Thames and Mersey Insrce.* v. *Hamilton,* 12 App. Ca. 484 ; 56 L. J. Q. B. 626 ; disapproving *West India and Panama Telegraph Co.* v. *Home and Col. Mar. Insrce.,* 50 L. J. Q. B. 41 ; 6 Q. B. D. 51).

PERIODICAL.—A " Periodical *Work* " within the *Copyright Act,* 1842 (5 & 6 V. c. 45), is "a work that comes out from time to time and is miscellaneous in its articles " (*Brown* v. *Cooke,* 16 L. J. Ch. 142) ; but a newspaper was held not a " Periodical " within ss. 18, 19 of that Act (*Cox* v. *Land and Water Journal Co.,* 39 L. J. Ch. 152 ; L. R. 9 Eq. 324) ; but in *Walter* v. *Howe* (50 L. J. Ch. 621 ; 17 Ch. D. 708), *Cox* v. *Land &c. Co.* was not followed, and the " Times " newspaper was held to be a " Periodical Work " within the sections. *V.* BOOK.

" Periodical *Payments,*" apportionable under the *Apportionment Act,* 1870 (33 & 34 V. c. 35, s. 2), "must be payments occurring periodically, that is, at fixed times from some antecedent obligation, and not at variable periods at the discretion of individuals " (per Selborne, L. C., *Jones* v. *Ogle,* 42 L. J. Ch. 337 ; 8 Ch. 192 ; 21 W. R. 239) ; therefore it was held in that case that profits in a private trading partnership were not within the phrase. *V.* DIVIDEND.

" Periodical Payments," s. 2, 47 & 48 V. c. 68 ; *V. Theobald* v. *Theobald,* 15 P. D. 26.

"Annuities or Periodical *Sums* charged upon land," s. 1, 3 & 4 W. 4, c. 27 ; *V. Payne* v. *Esdaile,* 58 L. J. Ch. 299 ; 13 App. Ca. 613 ; 37 W. R. 273 ; 59 L. T. 568.

PERJURY.—" Perjury is an assertion upon an oath duly administered in a judicial proceeding, before a competent Court, of the truth of some matter of fact, material to the question depending in that proceeding, which assertion the assertor does not believe to be true when he makes it, or on which he knows himself to be ignorant.

" In this definition, the word '*Oath*' includes every Affirmation which any class of persons are by law permitted to make in place of an oath.

" The expression '*duly administered,*' means administered in a form binding on his conscience, to a witness legally called before them, by any Court, Judge, Justice, Officer, Commissioner, Arbitrator, or other person who by the law for the time being in force, or by consent of the parties, has authority to hear, receive and examine evidence. The fact that a person takes an oath in any particular form is a binding admission that he regards it as binding on his conscience.

"The expression '*Judicial Proceeding*,' means a proceeding which takes place in or under the authority of any Court of Justice, or which relates in any way to the administration of justice, or which legally ascertains any right or liability. A proceeding may be judicial although the person accused in it was brought before the Court, by which the proceeding is held, by an irregular warrant.

"The word '*Fact*,' includes the fact that the witness holds any opinion or belief.

"The word '*Material*' means of such a nature as to affect in any way, directly or indirectly, the probability of any thing to be determined by the proceeding, or the credit of any witness, and a fact may be material although evidence of its existence was improperly admitted" (Steph. Cr. 93, 94).

Vf. Arch. Cr. 920, 940 ; Rosc. Cr. 836–864.

Cp. False Swearing.

PERMANENT INVESTMENT.—Applications for "Permanent Investment," R. 2 (7), Ord. 55, R. S. C. ; *V. Ex p. Jesus College*, W. N. (84) 37 : *Ex p. Bethlehem and Bridewell Hospitals*, 30 Ch. D. 541 ; 54 L. J. Ch. 1143.

PERMISSION.—"Act, Default, Permission or Sufferance ;" *V. Draper* v. *Sperring*, 30 L. J. M. C. 225 ; 10 C. B. N. S. 113 : Permit : Suffer : Default.

PERMISSIVE WASTE.—*V.* Voluntary Waste.

PERMIT.—A devise of realty to trustees with a simple trust to pay { or, and } "permit and suffer, A. to receive the rents" gives the legal estate to A. (*Doe* d. *Leicester* v. *Biggs*, 2 Taunt. 109 : *Vf.* 2 Jarm. 293 ; Lewin, 216. *Sv.* Lewin, 212, as to the difference between "pay to *and* permit" and "pay to *or* permit"). But the rule does not apply where the direction is to permit the receipt of the "clear," or "net," rents (*White* v. *Parker*, 4 L. J. C. P. 178 ; 1 Bing. N. C. 573 : *Barker* v. *Greenwood*, 8 L. J. Ex. 5 ; 4 M. & W. 421), or where the trustees have duties to perform regarding the legal estate, for in such cases it will be in the trustees notwithstanding the words referred to (*Re Tanqueray-Willaume to Landau*, 51 L. J. Ch. 434 ; 20 Ch. D. 465. *Vf.* 2 Jarm. 294).

In a clause of Forfeiture on alienation, the word "Permit" means the same as Suffer (per James, L. J., *Ex p. Eyston*, 47 L. J. Bank. 63 ; 7 Ch. D. 145).

"'Permitting and Suffering,' (in a Covenant) do not bear the same meaning as *Knowing of and being Privy to* ;'—the meaning of them is that the covenantor should not concur in any act over which he had control" (per Bayley, J., *Hobson* v. *Middleton*, 6 B. & C. 303 ; *Vth.* Sug. V. & P. 603, 604) : nor does that phrase mean "to hinder and forbid" (per Lopes, L. J., *Hall* v. *Ewin*, 36 W. R. 86 ; 37 Ch. D. 74 ; 57 L. J. Ch. 95 ; 57 L. T. 831).

Vf. Roffey v. *Bent*, L. R. 3 Eq. 759 : *Re Ryan*, 19 L. R. Ir. 24 : Elph. 490: PARTY OR PRIVY.

"Will not permit any *Sale by Public Auction;*" *V. Toleman* v. *Portbury*, (41 L. J. Q. B. 98 ; L. R. 7 Q. B. 344 ; 26 L. T. 292 ; 20 W. R. 441), where it was held that a sale in which the lessee took no part, but which was made under a Bill of Sale he had given, was not "permitted" by him, and accordingly there was no breach of the covenant.

The phrase "permit and suffer" the hirer of a cabin in a ship to stow baggage in the hold, imports that the hirer shall make some request for space (*Corbyn* v. *Leader*, 6 C. & P. 32 ; 10 Bing. 275 ; 3 Moore & S. 751).

"So far as the law will permit;" *V.* SO FAR AS.

V. CAUSE OR PERMIT : PERMISSION : SUFFER : USE OR PERMIT : PROVIDED THE FUNDS PERMIT.

PERMITTING.—"Wind, Weather, and Tide permitting;" *V. Hawes* v. *S. E. Ry.*, 54 L. J. Q. B. 174 ; 52 L. T. 514.

V. AT ALL TIMES OF TIDE.

PERPETRATE.—*V.* COMMIT.

PERPETUAL ADVOWSON.—A devise of a "Perpetual Advowson," prior to the Wills Act (1 V. c. 26), only passed a life estate (*Pocock* v. *Bp. of Lincoln*, 3 Brod. & B. 27). *Cp.* LIVING.

PERQUISITES.—"Profits arising to the lord from his Court Baron above the yearly revenue, such as fines in respect of copyholds ; Perkins, 20, 21. *Perquisitum* is also used in the sense of purchase : Spelm., *Perquisitum* ; Bracton, l. 2, c. 30, num. 3" (Elph. 615, 616).

"Perquisites are advantages and profits that come to a Manor by casualty, and not yearely, as Escheats, Hariots, Reliefes, Waifes, Estraies, Forfeitures, Amerciaments in Courts, Wards, Marriages, goods and lands purchased by villeines of the same manor, fines of copiholds, and divers other like things that are not certaine, but happen by chance, sometimes more often than at other times. See Perkins, 20 and 21" (Termes de la Ley).

PERSIST.—*V.* INSIST.

PERSON.—*Primâ facie* the word "Person," in a public statute, includes a Corporation as well as a natural person (per Selborne, L. C., *Pharmaceutical Socy.* v. *Lond. & Provincial Supply Assn.*, 49 L. J. Q. B. 736 ; 5 App. Ca. 857 : *Vf.* ss. 2, 19, Interp. Act, 1889).

"The word 'Person' may very well include both a natural person (a human being), and an artificial person (a corporation). I think that in an Act of Parliament, unless there be something to the contrary, probably, (I would not like to pledge myself to that) it ought to be held to include both. I have equally no doubt that in common talk, in the language of men (not speaking technically), a 'Person' does not include a corporation. Nobody in common talk, if he were asked who is the richest person in London, would answer, The London and North Western Ry. Co. It is plain that in common speech 'Person' would mean a natural person. In technical language it may include the other, but which meaning it has in any particular Act, must depend on the context subject-matter. I do not think that the presumption that it includes an artificial person,—a Corporation,—(*if the presumption does arise*)—is at all strong. Circumstances, and indeed very slight circumstances, in the context might show which way the word is to be construed in an Act of Parliament. And I am quite clear about this, that whenever you can see the object of the Act requires that 'Person' shall have the more extended sense or the less extended sense, then you should apply the word in that sense and construe the Act accordingly" (per Ld. Blackburn, Ib.).

The case from which the definitions just given have been taken shows that "Person" as used in ss. 1 and 15, Pharmacy Act, 1868 (31 & 32 V. c. 121) does not include a Corporation.

The Attorney-General, acting *ex officio*, is not a "Person" within the Statute of Limitation, 3 & 4 W. 4, c. 27; but an action by him on behalf of the poor of a parish may be statute barred, as these constitute "a class of persons" within s. 1 (*A.-G.* v. *Magdalen Coll.*, 23 L. J. Ch. 844; 18 Bea. 223: *Magdalen Coll.* v. *A.-G.*, 26 L. J. Ch. 620; 6 H. L. Ca. 189). The Ecclesiastical Commrs. are "persons" within ss. 1, 2 of the Act just cited, except in cases where they claim (by virtue of s. 57, 3 & 4 V. c. 113) through an Ecclesiastical Corporation (*Ecclesiastical Commrs.* v. *Rowe*, 49 L. J. Q. B. 771; 5 App. Ca. 736).

A Corporation is not a "Person" within the Mortmain Act, 9 G. 2, c. 36, s. 1 (*Walker* v. *Richardson*, 6 L. J. Ex. 229; 2 M. & W. 882), nor so as to become a Common Informer (*St. Leonards Shoreditch* v. *Franklin*, 47 L. J. C. P. 727; 3 C. P. D. 377).

By the Melbourne Harbour Trust Act a "Person" includes a Corporation, and this was held to include Commissioners appointed under the Act (*Union Steamship Co.* v. *Melbourne Harb. Commrs.*, 53 L. J. P. C. 59; 50 L. T. 337; 9 App. Ca. 365).

So where trustees of a Will had power to grant leases to "any person or persons" they should think fit, Chitty, J., held that this authorized them to grant a lease to a Limited Company (*Re Jeffcock*, 51 L. J. Ch. 507).

So where a Railway Act provided that "any person" acting in pursuance of it should be entitled to Notice of Action, it was held the Company itself was included (*Boyd* v. *Lond. & Croydon Ry.*, 7 L. J. C. P. 241; 4 Bing. N. C. 669; 6 Sc. 461).

"Person" in s. 20, Trustee Act, 1850, does not mean person beneficially entitled (*Re Dickson*, W. N. (72) 223).

"Persons belonging to a Ship;" *V.* BELONGING.

"Person by whose act, &c.," Nuisance arises; *V.* BY WHOSE ACT.

"Person nominated ;" *V.* Nominated.

"Person residing ;" *V.* Residing.

"Person" running away and leaving children parochially chargeable, s. 4, 5 G. 4, c. 83, does not include a married woman deserted by her husband, and, *semble,* does not include a married woman at all (*Peters* v. *Cowie,* 46 L. J. M. C. 177 ; 2 Q. B. D. 131).

Women are comprised in, and entitled to vote under, the phrase "every Person of full age," s. 22, Towns Improvement (Ireland) Act, 1854 (*R.* v. *Crosthwaite,* 17 Ir. C. L. Rep. 157).

V. Any : Every : Other : Party.

PERSON ENTITLED TO ANY REVERSION.—Held by Fry, J., that the words in s. 8, Prescription Act (2 & 3 W. 4, c. 71), "person entitled to any Reversion expectant on the determination" of a tenancy for life, are not limited to an owner of the whole reversion, but include a tenant at will to such an owner (*Laird* v. *Briggs,* W. N. (80) 205).

PERSON ENTITLED TO EQUITY OF REDEMPTION.—*V.* Entitled to redeem.

PERSON ENTITLED TO VOTE.—*V.* Entitled to vote.

PERSON IN CHARGE.—A Pilot, by "compulsion of law," was not a "Person in Charge," within s. 33, Merchant Shipping Act, 1862 (*The Queen,* L. R. 1 A. & E. 354 ; 38 L. J. Adm. 39). *Note.*—This section repealed by s. 33, Mer. S. Act, 1873, and s. 16 of that Act substituted, *wh. Vh. Vf.* 1 Maude & P. 286.

V. Charge or Control.

PERSON INTERESTED.—"Person interested," s. 14, Regulation of Railways Act, 1873 (36 & 37 V. c. 48), includes any person who makes out, by proper evidence, that the Rates which he seeks to have dissected are really and substantially competitive Rates with his own (per Wills, J. and Price, Commr.) ; and (per Peel, Commr.) includes all persons who have a *bonâ fide* interest in knowing how the particular Rates, which are the subject of their application, are made up (*Pelsall Co.* v. *Lond. & N. W. Ry.,* 23 Q. B. D. 536 ; 61 L. T. 257).

"Person interested in the Minerals" of an abandoned Mine, and liable to fence the shaft (s. 13, 35 & 36 V. c. 77), includes owners in fee who have leased the Mine, reserving a royalty on the minerals produced (*Evans* v. *Mostyn,* 47 L. J. M. C. 25 ; 2 C. P. D. 547).

The Trustees of a Friendly Society, held not within "any Person interested" in the matter of an application for altering its Rules, within s. 41, 18 & 19 V. c. 63 (*Hull* v. *Macfarlane,* 27 L. J. C. P. 41 ; 2 C. B. N. S. 796).

V. Party interested.

PERSON MAKING ANY DISTRESS.—*V.* Distress.

PERSONAL.—For examples of this word qualifying the whole of a testamentary gift, so as to exclude realty therefrom ; *V. Belaney* v. *Belaney*, 35 Bea. 469 ; 36 L. J. Ch. 265 ; 2 Ch. 138 : *Jones* v. *Robinson*, 47 L. J. C. P. 673 ; 3 C. P. D. 344.

PERSONAL ACT OF PARLIAMENT.—*V.* Local Act of Parliament.

PERSONAL ACTION.—*V. A.-G.* v. *Churchill*, 8 M. & W. 192 ; 10 L. J. Ex. 314.

PERSONAL CHATTELS.—The definition, *quà* Bills of Sale, of "Personal Chattels," given by s. 7, Bills of S. Act, 1854, is superseded by that given by s. 4, Bills of S. Act, 1878. Under the former, Growing Crops (unsevered, *Ex p. National Mercantile Bank*, 16 Ch. D. 104 ; 50 L. J. Ch. 231), were not "Personal Chattels" (*Brantom* v. *Griffits*, 46 L. J. C. P. 408 ; 2 C. P. D. 212) : but they are included in the latter "when separately assigned or charged ;" and so of Fixtures.

The fixed machinery and all the essential parts of the fixed machinery of a building were part of the realty, and were not "Personal Chattels," under Bills of S. Act, 1854 (*Longbottom* v. *Berry*, 39 L. J. Q. B. 37 ; L. R. 5 Q. B. 123 : *Holland* v. *Hodgson*, 41 L. J. C. P. 146 ; L. R. 7 C. P. 328 : *Sheffield Bg. Socy.* v. *Harrison*, 54 L. J. Q. B. 15 ; 15 Q. B. D. 358) ; *secus*, as respects machines only fixed for occasional convenience, and not for the permanent improvement of the building (*Waterfall* v. *Penistone*, 26 L. J. Q. B. 100 ; 6 E. & B. 876 ; 27 L. T. O. S. 252 : *Vth. Walmsley* v. *Milne*, 29 L. J. C. P. 97 ; 7 C. B. N. S. 115).

PERSONAL ESTATE.—The "Personal Estate and Effects," or, its equivalent, the "Personal Property" of an individual may perhaps be broadly defined to be, all his property other than that which, if he died intestate, would go to his heir. Either of these phrases includes all a person's Goods and Chattels, Moneys, Choses in Action, Leases for Years, Funded Property and Shares (Wms. R. P. Introd. Ch. : Wms. Exs. Pt. 2, Bk. 2, Ch. 1 and 2 : *Va. Butler* v. *Butler*, 54 L. J. Ch. 197; 28 Ch. D. 66). New River Shares however are realty (*Drybutter* v. *Bartholomew*, 2 P. Wms. 127: *Buckeridge* v. *Ingram*, 2 Ves. jun. 652 : *Bligh* v. *Brent*, 6 L. J. Ex. Eq. 58 ; 2 Y. & C. Ex. 268). But Chelsea Water Works Shares have been held to be personalty (*Bligh* v. *Brent*, sup.). Sometimes Canal Shares have been held to be realty (Wms. Exs. 817, 818).

For the purposes of the Wills Act (1 V. c. 26), "Personal Estate" extends to "Leasehold estates and other chattels real, and also to moneys, shares of government and other funds, securities for money (not being real estates), debts, choses in action, rights, credits, goods, and all other property whatsoever which by law devolves upon the exor. or admor., and to any share or interest therein" (s. 1).

"Personal Estate" in s. 2, 24 & 25 V. c. 114, is not confined to moveables, but comprises also leaseholds (*Re Watson*, 35 W. R. 711).

But the context may restrict the wide meaning of "Personal Estate." Thus in *Harrison* v. *Blackburn* (34 L. J. C. P. 109 ; 17 C. B. N. S. 678), a Bill of Sale of the grantor's household goods, stock in trade, and all other goods, chattels and effects in or about his dwelling-house, "and all other his *personal estate* whatsoever," did not pass the term he had in his dwelling-house (*cp. Ringer* v. *Cann*, 7 L. J. Ex. 108 ; 3 M. & W. 343).

So "where a testator shows by his Will that he uses the term 'Personal Estate' as contradistinguished from 'leaseholds,' occurring in the same bequest, and he afterwards by a codicil directs a charitable legacy to be payable out of his 'personal estate,' the expression is considered as used in the same restricted and peculiar sense as in his Will ; and the legacy is payable out of the pure personalty and is therefore good" (1 Jarm. 239, citing *Wilson* v. *Thomas*, 3 My. & K. 549 ; 3 L. J. Ch. 144). But it has been said (Elph. 178), "no general rule can be laid down as to whether leaseholds will pass by a general description of 'Personal Property.' The principal cases are *Ringer* v. *Cann*, 3 M. & W. 343 ; 7 L. J. Ex. 108 : *Doe* d. *Farmer* v. *Howe*, 9 L. J. Q. B. 352 : *Hopkinson* v. *Lusk*, 34 Bea. 215 : *White* v. *Hunt*, L. R. 6 Ex. 32 ; 40 L. J., Ex. 23."

On the other hand the expression "Personal Estate" may be widened by a context so as to include realty (*Doe* d. *Tofield* v. *Tofield*, 11 East, 246, stated 1 Jarm. 748 : *Vf. Cadman* v. *Cadman*, 41 L. J. Ch. 468 ; L. R. 13 Eq. 470). But in such phrases as "Personal Estate and Property," or "Personal Property, Estate and Effects," the word "Personal" will generally over-ride the whole (1 Jarm. 748 n. and cases there cited : *Vf.* per Mansfield, C.J., in *Hogan* v. *Jackson*, 1 Cowp. 306 : *Va. Jones* v. *Robinson*, 47 L. J. C. P. 673 ; 3 C. P. D. 344).

So, "if a testator direct his *lands to be sold,* and afterwards add a general bequest of all his 'Personal Estate' (*Maugham* v. *Mason*, 1 V. & B. 410 : *Smith* v. *Harding*, W. N. (74) 101: *Va. Gibbs* v. *Rumsey*, 2 V. & B. 294), or appoint a person '*Residuary Executor*' (*Berry* v. *Usher*, 11 Ves. 87), any part of the proceeds of the sale that is undisposed of will not form part of the residuary fund in the first case, or pass to the residuary executor in the second ; for nothing, properly speaking, is a testator's 'Personal Estate' but what possesses that character at the moment of his decease" (Lewin, 159, *wh. Vf.* as to cases where the special language employed requires a different construction).

V. Estate : Personalty.

PERSONAL GOODS.—For examination of this phrase as used Co. Litt. 185 b ; *V. Re Butler*, 57 L. J. Ch. 643 ; 38 Ch. D. 286.

PERSONAL LUGGAGE.—"Personal" means the same thing as "Ordinary Luggage" (*Hudston* v. *Mid. Ry.*, 38 L. J. Q. B. 213; L. R. 4 Q. B. 366; 10 B. & S. 504; 17 W. R. 705).

"Whatever the passenger takes with him for his personal use or convenience, according to the habits or wants of the particular class to which he belongs, either with reference to the immediate necessities or to the ultimate purpose of the journey, must be considered as Personal Luggage. This would include, not only all articles of apparel, whether for use or ornament, but also the gun-case or the fishing apparatus of the sportsman, the easel of the artist on a sketching tour, or the books of the student, and other articles of an analogous character the use of which is personal to the traveller, and the taking of which has arisen from the fact of his journeying. On the other hand, the term 'Ordinary Luggage' being thus confined to that which is personal to the passenger, and carried for his use and convenience, it follows that what is carried for the purpose of business, such as merchandize or the like, or for larger or ulterior purposes, such as articles of furniture or household goods, would not come within the description of Ordinary Luggage, unless accepted as such by the carrier" (per Cockburn, C. J., in delivering the judgment of the Q. B. in *Macrow* v. *G. W. Ry.*, 40 L. J. Q. B. 304; L. R. 6 Q. B. 612).

The cases of *Cahill* v. *Lond. & N. W. Ry.* (31 L. J. C. P. 271; 13 C. B. N. S. 818; 10 W. R. 391), *G. N. Ry.* v. *Shepherd* (21 L. J. Ex. 286; 8 Ex. 30), and *Belfast & Ballymena Ry.* v. *Keys* (9 H. L. Ca. 556), establish that Articles of Merchandize cannot be considered as personal luggage: and, by a parity of reasoning, it has been held, at the Liverpool Co. Co., that samples and accounts are not personal luggage of a Commercial Traveller (*Bayley* v. *Lancashire & Yorkshire Ry.*, 18 S. J. 301); neither are documents carried by a Solicitor for use in a cause in which he is professionally engaged (*Phelps* v. *Lond. & N. W. Ry.*, 34 L. J. C. P. 259; 19 C. B. N. S. 321; 13 W. R. 782): and though in *Macrow* v. *G. W. Ry.*, sup., it was laid down that an easel of an Artist on a sketching tour would be his personal luggage, yet in *Mytton* v. *Mid. Ry.* (28 L. J. Ex. 385; 4 H. & N. 615; 7 W. R. 737), it was held that the sketches of an artist are not such luggage. But a chronometer is, it seems, luggage for a Master Mariner (*Le Conteur* v. *Lond. & S. W. Ry.*, 35 L. J. Q. B. 40; L. R. 1 Q. B. 54).

A child's rocking-horse is not personal luggage (*Hudston* v. *Mid. Ry.*, sup.); and though, probably, bedding for a passenger's own use on a journey might be held "personal luggage," yet bedding intended for the passenger's household when permanently settled would not (*Macrow* v. *G. W. Ry.*, sup.).

PERSONAL ORNAMENTS.—A question arose on this phrase as used in the Will of Dr. John Willis (physician to George III.). He possessed an ivory Tooth-pick Case with a portrait of his father in the centre, a gold Pencil-Case, a silver Lip-salve Box, a gold Eye-glass, a Pocket-book and a

Case of Instruments which he usually carried about his person. Langdale, M. R., decided that the pocket-book and case of Instruments were not "Personal Ornaments." But as to the other things he said,—"The question seems to be whether a thing that is ornamental and capable of being applied to useful purposes, is, or is not, to be considered as an Ornament. There are some things of no personal use, a common ring, for instance, which may be set round with diamonds and be of extreme value, and yet of no use, except as an ornament; but it may be said, if you convert that into a signet-ring and seal letters with it, in consequence of that useful purpose to which it is applied, it becomes an article of utility as well as of ornament. A shirt-pin is equally useful. A pencil-case certainly is useful as containing the pencil. The inclination of my opinion is, that though those things were capable of being connected with personal *use*, yet they were considered as personal ornaments in the sense in which the testator intended them. If you come to a minute definition, they may not be so; but at the same time they may be put in such a form and appearance that the ornamental part is paramount to the useful part, and consequently they might pass as "Ornaments" (*Willis* v. *Curtois*, 1 Bea. 196). In the report of this case in the Law Journal (8 L. J. Ch. 106) the learned M. R. is reported to have said,—"I do not think that the tooth-pick case or the silver lip-salve box passed under the Will." As the matter was settled between the parties, no decision was given except as to the pocket-book and case of instruments.

V. TRINKETS.

PERSONAL PROPERTY.—*V.* PERSONAL ESTATE: REAL OR PERSONAL PROPERTY.

PERSONAL REPRESENTATIVE.—This is synonymous with LEGAL REPRESENTATIVES.

An executor (though he has not taken probate) of a surviving trustee, is such trustee's "Personal Representative" within s. 25, 13 & 14 V. c. 60 (*Re Ellis*, 24 Bea. 426); so also is one of the next of kin though not an executor (*Re Stroud*, W. N. (74) 180).

"Personal Representatives," held, contextually, to mean Descendants of Children of testatrix (*Rainford* v. *Knowles*, 59 L. T. 359).

V. NEXT PERSONAL REPRESENTATIVES.

PERSONALLY.—*V.* APPEAR: CONTRACT OF SERVICE.

PERSONALTY.—A direction to pay a Charitable Bequest out of the "Personalty" means the PURE Personalty (*Nickisson* v. *Cockill*, 3 D. G. J. & S. 622; 11 W. R. 353, 1082: *Roberts* v. *Jones*, W. N. (80) 96).

PERSONATE.—To "personate" means "to pretend to be a person" (per Crompton, J., *R.* v. *Hague*, inf.); and the offence of personating a voter is complete as soon as a person has, to the proper officer, falsely represented himself as the person entitled to vote, even though he stop short of voting (*R.* v. *Hague*, 33 L. J. M. C. 81 ; 4 B. & S. 715).

As to Personation,

1. To obtain money ; *V.* 24 & 25 V. c. 98, s. 34 ;—
2. Of Stock-holders ; *V.* 33 & 34 V. c. 58, s. 21 ; of India Stock-holders, *V.* 26 & 27 V. c. 73, s. 111 ; and of holders of Joint-Stock Co.'s Stock, *V.* 30 & 31 V. c. 131, s. 35 ;—
3. In giving recognizance &c. ; *V.* 24 & 25 V. c. 98, s. 34 ;—
4. In fraud of the Admiralty ; *V.* 28 & 29 V. c. 124, s. 8.

Vf. Arch. Cr. 698–702 ; Rosc. Cr. 490–492.

PETITIONER.—S. 2, 28 & 29 V. c. 27, provides that when the Committee of either House of Parliament on a Private Bill decides that the preamble is proved, and reports that the promoters have been vexatiously subjected to expense by the opposition of any petitioner against the same, then the Committee may order such Petitioner to pay costs to the promoters ; there, "Petitioner" only includes the person appearing on the petition as the petitioner, and the Committee cannot go behind the petition and award costs against a person not appearing on the petition as Petitioner on the ground that he was in fact the real Petitioner (per Bowen & Fry, L.JJ., Esher, M. R., diss., *Mallet* v. *Hanly*, 18 Q. B. D. 787 ; 56 L. J. Q. B. 384 ; 35 W. R. 601 ; 3 Times Rep. 497).

PETTY SESSIONAL.—"Petty Sessional Court ;" *V.* s. 13 (12), Interp. Act, 1889.

"Petty Sessional Court House ;" *V.* s. 13 (13), Ib.

PICKAGE.—*V.* STALLAGE AND PICKAGE.

PICLE.—"Picle : Pickle : Pightel : Pitle : Pigtle.—A little close ; Spelm. *Pictellum*" (Elph. 616).

"'Picle,' or 'Pitle,' seems to come from the Italian (*Piccolo, Parvus*), and it signifies with us a little small close or inclosure" (Termes de la Ley).

PICTURE.—Its frame is part of a "Picture," as that word is used in the Carriers Act (*Henderson* v. *Lond. & N. W. Ry.*, L. R. 5 Ex. 90 ; nom. *Anderson* v. *Lond. & N. W. Ry.*, 39 L. J. Ex. 55. *Sc. Treadwin* v. *G. E. Ry.*, 37 L. J. C. P. 83 ; L. R. 3 C. P. 308). *V.* PAINTING.

V. VERTU.

PILOTAGE DUES.—The 10*s.* 6*d.* per day to which a licensed pilot, taken, without his consent, to sea or beyond the limits of his pilotage district, in any ship, is entitled by 17 & 18 V. c. 104 (Merchant Shipping Act, 1854), s. 357, are not "Pilotage Dues" for which the ship-brokers are liable under s. 363 (*Morteo* v. *Julian*, 4 C. P. D. 216 ; 48 L. J. M. C. 126).

PINCH.—*V.* HARD PINCH.

PIPES.—"The Pipes" in s. 35, Waterworks C. C. Act, 1847 (10 & 11 V. c. 17), are the water *Mains*, and do not include Service-pipes by which water is conducted into houses (*Milnes* v. *Huddersfield*, 56 L. J. Q. B. 1; 11 App. Ca. 511; 55 L. T. 617; 34 W. R. 761; 50 J. P. 676).

PIRACY.—"Piracy by the law of nations is, Taking a ship on the high seas or within the jurisdiction of the Lord High Admiral from the possession or control of those who are lawfully entitled to it, and carrying away the ship itself, or any of its goods, tackle, apparel, or furniture, under circumstances which would have amounted to Robbery if the Act had been done within the body of an English County. It is doubtful whether persons cruising in armed vessels, with intent to commit piracies, are pirates or not" (Steph. Cr. 73, 74). *Vf.* Ib. 74–76, 78; Arch. Cr. 484–488; Rosc. Cr. 867–871.

PIRATES, ROVERS AND THIEVES.—*V.* 1 Maude & P. 487.

A Pirate "signifieth a rover at sea" (Co. Litt. 391 a).

Pirates "certainly take by force and not by stealth" (per Pollock, C. B., *Rothschild* v. *Royal Mail Steam Packet Co.*, 21 L. J. Ex. 276; 7 Ex. 734).

V. ROBBERS: THIEVES.

PISCARY.—*V.* FISHERY.

PITS AND VEINS.—As to what would pass under a devise of "Pits and Veins;" *V. Brown* v. *Whiteway*, 8 Hare, 145, and *Vth.* MacS. 2, n. 7.

PLACARD.—*V.* BILL.

"'Placard' is a word used in the statutes of 33 H. 8, c. 6, and 2 & 3 Ma. c. 9, and it signifies a license to use unlawful games or to shoot in a gunne" (Termes de la Ley).

PLACE.—The word "Place" is generally found in conjunction with other words which give it a colour, and is usually controlled by its context.

In the Vagrant Act (5 G. 4, c. 83), s. 4, it is, *inter alia*, declared an act of vagrancy to play or bet "in any street, road, highway, *or other open and public place*," and in the amplified version of that enactment contained in s. 3 of the Vagrant Act Amendment Act, 1873 (36 & 37 V. c. 38), the words defining the locality of the offence are identical with those just quoted: Held, that a Railway Carriage in transit on a railway is an "Open and Public Place" within those sections (*Langrish* v. *Archer*, 52 L. J. M. C. 47; 10 Q. B. D. 44; 31 W. R. 183; 47 L. T. 548; 47 J. P. 295); but the conviction must shew that the carriage was in actual transit at the time of the commission of the offence (*Ex p. Freestone*, 25 L. J. M. C. 121; 1 H. & N. 93; 20 J. P. 376).

"*Open* Place to which *the public* have or are permitted to *have access*," s. 3, 36 & 37 V. c. 38; *V. Turnbull* v. *Appleton*, 45 J. P. 469: *Hirst* v. *Molesbury*, L. R. 6 Q. B. 130; 40 L. J. M. C. 76.

An Inn Skittle-alley, used for the sale of manufactured goods, is an "*Open* Place" within a Local Market Act prohibition against selling outside a Market, and is not a "Shop" within an exception thereto (*Hooper* v. *Kenshole*, 46 L. J. M. C. 160; 2 Q. B. D. 127). *V.* SHOP.

In the phrase "At some *Standing or Place* appointed," s. 33, 6 & 7 V. c. 86, "Place" means "public street or road" (*Skinner* v. *Usher*, 41 L. J. M. C. 158; L. R. 7 Q. B. 423).

By s. 4, Vagrant Act, already cited, it is an act of vagrancy to indecently expose the person "in any street road or public highway, or in the view thereof, or in any *Place of Public Resort* with intent to insult a female," or for a suspected person or reputed thief to frequent any river, &c., "or any *Place of Public Resort*." Within these words a private house in which a sale by Public Auction is being held, is a "Place of Public Resort" (*Sewell* v. *Taylor*, 29 L. J. M. C. 50; 7 C. B. N. S. 160; 1 L. T. 37; 23 J. P. 792); so is the platform of a Railway Station (*Ex p. Davis*, 26 L. J. M. C. 178; 21 J. P. 280); and so (probably) is the inside of an omnibus (*R.* v. *Holmes*, 22 L. J. M. C. 122; Dears. 207); or a public urinal (*R.* v. *Harris*, 40 L. J. M. C. 67; L. R. 1 C. C. R. 282; 24 L. T. 74); or the roof of a house (*R.* v. *Thallman*, inf.): or, indeed, any place where a number of persons may be affected by the criminal act (*R.* v. *Thallman*, 33 L. J. M. C. 58; 12 W. R. 88; L. & C. 326: *R.* v. *Saunders*, 45 L. J. M. C. 11; 1 Q. B. D. 15: *R.* v. *Wellard*, 54 L. J. M. C. 14; 14 Q. B. D. 63: Steph. Cr. 115).

A curious contrast to *Sewell* v. *Taylor* (sup.), and as shewing how exactly similar words are controlled into a different meaning by the context, is furnished by s. 2 of the Act for regulating Theatres, 6 & 7 V. c. 68. It is thereby provided that it shall not be lawful "to have or keep any house or other *Place of Public Resort*" for the public performance of stage plays without a license; and it was held that a booth used by strolling players is not within those words (*Davys* v. *Douglas*, 28 L. J. M. C. 193; 4 H. & N. 180. *Va. Fredericks* v. *Howie*, 31 L. J. M. C. 249; 1 H. & C. 381). It will be observed that in the section just mentioned the phrase "place of public resort" occurs in conjunction with the word "house," and that both are controlled by the verbs "have *or keep*." Accordingly the kind of "Place" intended is one of a permanent character. But in the very same Act (s. 11) it is provided that no person shall, for hire, act "in any Place, not being a patent theatre or duly licensed as a theatre;" and the Court held (apparently rejecting the force of the word "place" being found in conjunction with "patent theatre") that a booth used by strolling players is within s. 11 (*Fredericks* v. *Payne*, 32 L. J. M. C. 14: *Tarling* v. *Fredericks*, 21 W. R. 785; 28 L. T. 814; 38 J. P. 197). The curious consequence is reached that whilst it is not unlawful to have or keep an unlicensed moveable booth in which, for hire, stage plays may be acted, yet it is unlawful for any one so to act therein.

A "Place of *Dramatic Entertainment*" within s. 2, 3 & 4 W. 4, c. 15, is not confined to those places,—*e.g.*, a regular theatre,—that are ordinarily or habitually used for representing the drama for profit; but means a place adapted, for the time being, for the representation of a dramatic piece to an audience of a public, or quasi public character, as distinguished from one that is merely domestic, internal, and private; and though a money charge for admission would, probably, conclusively shew the audience to be a public one, yet such a charge is not an essential element in this definition (*Russell* v. *Smith*, 17 L. J. Q. B. 229; 12 Q. B. 217: *Duck* v. *Bates*, 53 L. J. Q. B. 97, 338; 12 Q. B. D. 79). It was accordingly held in the latter case that a room at Guy's Hospital fitted up for the play of "Our Boys," with theatrical scenery at the expense of the Governors, the actors being all unpaid, and the entertainment being for the amusement of the medical staff, nurses, and patients of the Hospital, and of the friends of the Governors and actors, all of whom were admitted by ticket obtained privately without payment, was not,—though it was very near the line,—a "Place of Dramatic Entertainment" within the lastly cited statute; for though the place had been adapted for the drama, the audience was merely domestic.

In *Duck* v. *Bates* (sup.), Brett, M.R., said that Patteson, J., must have been putting a jocular illustration in saying,—"When *Punch* is performed in the street, the street becomes a place of scenic entertainment" (*Russell* v. *Smith*, 17 L. J. Q. B. 227).

V. Dramatic Piece.

S. 3 of the Betting Houses Act, 1853 (16 & 17 V. c. 119), creates a prohibition against keeping or using any "house, office, room, or place" for betting: and, within that section, a large umbrella temporarily fixed into the ground by means of its spiked, telescopic handle, so as to form a tent, is a "Place" (*Bows* v. *Fenwick*, 43 L. J. M. C. 107; L. R. 9 C. P. 339; 22 W. R. 804); so is a wooden box on which the betting-man stands, and which temporarily rests on a spot in "the Ring" of a Racecourse (*Galloway* v. *Maries*, 51 L. J. M. C. 53; 8 Q. B. D. 275; 30 W. R. 151; 45 L. T. 763; 46 J. P. 326); so is an enclosed yard or ground, whether roofed over or not, and however large its dimensions (*Shaw* v. *Morley*, 37 L. J. M. C. 105; L. R. 3 Ex. 137: *Eastwood* v. *Miller*, 43 L. J. M. C. 139; L. R. 9 Q. B. 440; 22 W. R. 799: *Haigh* v. *Sheffield*, 44 L. J. M. C. 17; L. R. 10 Q. B. 102; 39 J. P. 230). But such a "Place" must, during its use, be an "ascertained" place, and the habitual standing, or using a table, under a tree in Hyde Park does not make it a "Place" for betting (per Bramwell, B., Mellor, J., and Piggott, B., *Doggett* v. *Catterns*, 34 L. J. C. P. 159; 19 C. B. N. S. 765); for a person using the shelter of a tree in public property like Hyde Park, has no right to use it for betting (per Pollock, C.B., Channell, B., and Blackburn, J., in *Doggett* v. *Catterns*: and *V.* jdgmt. of Lush, J., in *Eastwood* v. *Miller*, sup.). Habitual user, indeed, has in the Betting Act no value either way; for whilst *Doggett* v. *Catterns* shows that such a user will not convert a mere standing into a "place," neither, on the other hand, is habitual user of the essence of a "place" (*Haigh* v. *Sheffield*, sup.). It comes almost to this, that any piece of ground appropriated, by its owner or occupier for the time being, for the purposes of betting is a "place" within the statute (per Lopes, J., *Galloway* v. *Maries*, 51 L. J. M. C. 56). But the ground must be so appropriated, and must be an ascertained place; and therefore betting *ambulante*, in an enclosed field where races are going on, is not within the statute (*Snow* v. *Hill*, 54 L. J. M. C. 95; 14 Q. B. D. 588; 33 W. R. 476; 49 J. P. 149). *Vf. Henretty* v. *Hart*, 13 Sess. Ca. 10. USE.

A "Place" within which the offence of bull-baiting, cock-fighting, &c., can be committed within s. 3, *Cruelty to Animals Act*, 1849, 12 & 13 V. c. 92, must be one kept or used for the purpose (*Clarke* v. *Hague*, 29 L. J. M. C. 105; 2 E. & E. 281: *Morley* v. *Greenhalgh*, 32 L. J. M. C. 93; 3 B. & S. 374: *Coyne* v. *Brady*, 12 Ir. C. L. 577; 9 L. T. 30). *V.* AFORESAID. As to effect of s. 2, *V. Bridge* v. *Parsons*, 32 L. J. M. C. 95; 11 W. R. 424; 27 J. P. 231.

In Ireland it has been held that a *cart moving along the street* was within the phrase "*Any Place*" as used in s. 116, P. H. Act, 1875, so as to justify the seizure of diseased meat therein (*Daly* v. *Webb*, Ir. Rep. 4 C. L. 309). This seems a strong order. *Vh. Young* v. *Gattridge*, L. R. 4 Q. B. 166; 38 L. J. M. C. 67.

"Place *of Abode*" usually means the Place of Residence; "in Johnson's Dictionary 'Abode' is defined to be 'Habitation, Dwelling, Place of Residence,' and 'Residence' is defined to be 'Place of abode, Dwelling.' A man's residence, where he lives with his family and sleeps at night, is always his Place of Abode in the full sense of that expression" (per Campbell, C. J., *R.* v. *Hammond*, 21 L. J. Q. B. 153; 17 Q. B. 772).

"Place *of Abode*" occurs frequently in the Forms provided by the Acts for the *Registration of Voters* (6 V. c. 18; 41 & 42 V. c. 26). What is a person's Place of Abode within the meaning of these Acts is "rather a question of fact than of law" (per Erle, C. J., *Courtis* v. *Blight*, 31 L. J. C. P. 48; 5 L. T. 450). That case related to an Objector's place of abode: and *Vth. Sheldon* v. *Flatcher*, 17 L. J. C. P. 34; 5 C. B. 17. The place of abode of a person entitled to vote, need only be described in an Overseer's List where the person has one, and it may be given as "travelling abroad" where the facts warrant that statement (*Walker* v. *Payne*, 15 L. J. C. P. 38; 2 C. B. 12; 1 Lutw. 324). In a *Notice of Action*, or other such like document, a Solicitor's "Place of Abode" would be sufficiently given by his business address (*Roberts* v. *Williams*, 5 L. J. M. C. 23; 2 Cr. M. & R. 561; 5 Tyr. 583; 4 Dowl. 486).

V. RESIDE: USUAL PLACE OF ABODE: LAST.

A Warehouse is a "*Place*" within s. 10, 17 G. 3, c. 56 (*R.* v. *Edmundson*, 28 L. J. M. C. 213). *V.* TENEMENT.

"Place of Entertainment;" *V.* ENTERTAINMENT.

"Place of Export;" *V.* EXPORT.

"Place for transacting Parochial Business;" *V.* PAROCHIAL BUSINESS.

"Place of Religious Worship;" *V.* USUAL PLACE OF RELIGIOUS WORSHIP.

"Passage or Place;" *V.* PASSAGE.

"Place *opened, kept, or used*" for any purpose; *V.* KEEP: USE.

V. PARISH: PORT OR PLACE.

PLACE, To.—A Device for catching fish will be "placed" within the meaning of s. 15, Salmon Fishery Act, 1873 (36 & 37 V. c. 71), by merely raising the shuttles of a weir constructed in 1838, and so using a grating, that had always been part of the weir, as a trap to catch fish, that being the intended use of such grating from the time of the construction of the weir (*Briggs* v. *Swanwick*, 52 L. J. M. C. 63; 10 Q. B. D. 510). That seems an extraordinary decision; how can a thing be "placed" to catch, when it is simply *moved* so that something else may catch?

An agreement "to place" *Shares* in a Company is not equivalent to an agreement to take them, and the contractor is thereby liable, not as a contributory, but only in damages for breach of contract (*Gorrissen's Case*, 42 L. J. Ch. 864; 8 Ch. 507). *V.* UNDERWRITE.

PLACE OUT.—"Place out" a Parish Apprentice, recital to s. 9, 56 G. 3, c. 139; *V.* PUT AWAY.

PLAINTIFF.—For the purposes of the Jud. Acts this word includes "every person asking any relief (otherwise than by way of counter-claim as a defendant) against any other person by any form of proceeding, whether the same be taken by action, suit, petition, motion, summons, or otherwise" (s. 100, Jud. Act, 1873). Therefore, as used in Ord. 31, R. S. C., it includes Petitioner, and a Petitioner for the revocation of a Patent is not an exception (*Re Haddan*, 54 L. J. Ch. 126; 51 L. T. 190; 33 W. R. 96).

PLAN.—The "Plan" to be submitted to a Local Authority of works to be done, does not mean something merely showing "method" or "manner," but means a "map," or its equivalent, which will enable the Authority to judge whether what is proposed shall be allowed to proceed; and therefore under s. 31, 10 V. c. 17, the position and depth of proposed pipes ought to form part of the "Plan" (*Edgeware* v. *Colne Valley Water Co.*, W. N. (77) 154).

PLANT.—A legacy of "Plant and Goodwill" passes the house of business held at rack-rent (*Blake* v. *Shaw*, 8 W. R. 410; Johns. 732).

Is a horse "Plant" within s. 1 (1), Employers' Liability Act, 1880?—

V. jdgmt. Lopes, L. J., *Yarmouth* v. *France*, 57 L. J. Q. B. 17; 18 Q. B. D. 685.

V. PRODUCT.

PLANTATION.—The devise of a "Plantation" will, it seems, pass also the stock, implements, utensils, &c., upon it (*Lushington* v. *Sewell*, 1 Sim. 435, cited Wms. Exs. 1206).

PLATE.—"Plate," will not pass plated articles where the testator is possessed of solid silver ones (*Holden*, or *Holder* v. *Ramsbottom*, 4 Giff. 205; 11 W. R. 302; 7 L. T. 735).

In *Field* v. *Peckett* (30 L. J. Ch. 813; 29 Bea. 573), it was held that "Plate and China" would carry snuff-boxes of gold, silver and china.

Vf. Domvile v. *Taylor*, 32 Bea. 604.

PLEADING.—For the purposes of the Jud. Acts, "'Pleading' shall include any Petition or Summons, and also shall include the Statements in writing of the Claim, or Demand of any Plaintiff, and of the Defence of any Defendant thereto, and of the Reply of the Plaintiff to any Counter-claim of a Defendant" (s. 100, Jud. Act, 1873). But this does not repeal s. 9, 23 & 24 V. c. 38; and therefore though an ordinary "Pleading" does not now require signature of Counsel (Ord. 19, R. 4), yet a Petition for the advice of the Court must be so signed (*Re Boulton*, 30 W. R. 596).

The endorsement on a Writ was not a "Pleading" within Ord. 40, R. 11, R. S. C. 1875 (*Wallis* v. *Jackson*, 52 L. J. Ch. 384; 23 Ch. D. 204); nor is a specially endorsed Writ a "Pleading" under Ord. 64, R. 11, R. S. C. 1883 (*Murray* v. *Stephenson*, 19 Q. B. D. 60; 56 L. J. Q. B. 647; 56 L. T. 720; 35 W. R. 666).

"Mode of Pleading;" *V.* PRACTICE.

PLEASURE.—A devise to A. *to give and sell at his pleasure*, carries the fee (Sug. Pow. 104; *Vf.* DISCRETION).

A Head Master of Eton, Winchester, Eton College, or Winchester College, holding his office "*at the pleasure*" of the Governing Body (s. 13, 31 & 32 V. c. 118), is dismissible without cause assigned; and such a dismissal, if *bonâ fide*, cannot be impeached (*Hayman* v. *Rugby School*, 43 L. J. Ch. 834; L. R. 18 Eq. 28); *semble*, if cause assigned, it may be enquired into.

PLIGHT.—"Plight is an old English word, and here (s. 357, Litt.) signifieth not only the estate but the habit and quality of the land, and extendeth to rent charges, and to a possibility of dower. *Vide* Sect. 289, where Plight is taken for an estate or interest of and in the land itself, and extendeth not to a rent charge out of the land" (Co. Litt. 221 b).

PLOUGHING.—In a Reference for Valuation of "Ploughing and Sowing," all expenses incidental to the preparation of land for sowing are included (*Branscombe* v. *Rowcliffe*, 18 L. J. C. P. 38 ; 6 C. B. 523). *Va.* that case for what was allowed for "Ploughing."

PLOW-LAND : PLOUGHLAND.—"'Plow-land' and a 'Hide of land' are *synonyma,* and are collective words. And, therefore, by the grant of *Carucatam* or *Hidam terræ,* or of a plow-land, or a hide of land, may pass 100 acres of land, meadow and pasture, and the houses thereupon ; but it doth properly intend as much land as one plow can till in a year" (Touch. 93). *V.* HIDE : CARUCATA : JUGUM.

PLUNDER.—"Whosoever shall *plunder* or steal any part of any ship or vessel which shall be in distress ;" s. 64, 24 & 25 V. c. 96—"I do not know that this word 'plunder' has any special legal signification" (Steph. Cr. 255, n. 5) ; *Vf.* Arch. Cr. 439, 440.

PLY.—To "ply" a Passenger Steamer, within s. 318, Merchant Shipping Act, 1854, means to "ply for hire" (*R.* v. *Ipswich Jus.*, 5 Times Rep. 405).

A Hackney Carriage "plies *for hire,*" within s. 7, 32 & 33 V. c. 115, if it solicits passengers in a Railway Station (*Clark* v. *Stanford,* 40 L. J. M. C. 151 ; L. R. 6 Q. B. 357 : *Allen* v. *Tunbridge,* 40 L. J. M. C. 197 ; L. R. 6 C. P. 481) : *secus,* under the previous (repealed) Act, 1 & 2 W. 4, c. 22 ; because in that Act the offence of unlicensed plying was restricted to a public street or place, which a Railway Station is not (*Case* v. *Storey,* L. R. 4 Ex. 319 ; 38 L. J. M. C. 113). *V.* HACKNEY CARRIAGE.

POINT.—A sailor's "Point" is not a mathematical point at the end of a promontory ; it is the whole of the promontory. "The Point begins where a vessel having to go round it, either up or down the river, would, if there were nothing in the way, be obliged to use her steerage for the purpose of continuing her course, and that it ends where the necessity, if there were nothing in the way, of using the steerage in order to go round, ceases." "*Rounding*" a Point "begins from the time when, if there were nothing in the way, a vessel would have to begin to use her steerage to go round, and that the rounding ends at the same place that I before stated, where, if there were nothing in the way, she would cease using her steerage for the purpose of going round, and would then be straight for her opposite course" (per Brett, M. R., *The Margaret,* 53 L. J. P. D. & A. 18 ; 9 P. D. 47 ; 50 L. T. 447 ; 32 W. R. 564 ; 5 Asp. 204).

POINT OF SUBSTANCE.—As to what is "the Point of Substance" in a Pleading within Ord. 19, R. 19, R. S. C. ; *V. Thorp* v. *Holdsworth,* 3 Ch. D. 637 ; 45 L. J. Ch. 406 : *Collette* v. *Goode,* 7 Ch. D. 842 ; 47 L. J. Ch. 370 : *Byrd* v. *Nunn,* 7 Ch. D. 284 ; 47 L. J. Ch. 1 ; 26 W. R. 101 : *Tildesley* v. *Harper,* 10 Ch. D. 393 ; 48 L. J. Ch. 495 ; 27 W. R. 249 : *Green* v. *Sevin,* 49 L. J. Ch. 166 ; 13 Ch. D. 589. And *cp. Rutter* v. *Tregent,* 48 L. J. Ch. 791 ; 27 W. R. 902 ; 12 Ch. D. 758, and *Harris* v. *Gamble,* 7 Ch. D. 877 ; 47 L. J. Ch. 344, with *Smith* v. *Gamlen,* W. N. (81) 110.

POISON.—" With regard to the meaning of the term 'Poison' (s. 58, 24 & 25 V. c. 100), there are certain things which have acquired the name of Poisons; and as to these, possibly, if a small quantity only were administered, the administration might come with the statute" (per Stephen, J., *R.* v. *Cramp*, 49 L. J. M. C. 45; 5 Q. B. D. 307; 28 W. R. 701; 42 L. T. 442; 44 J. P. 70, 411). But in the same case Coleridge, C. J., said, "A 'Poison' is defined to be that which, *when administered*, is injurious to health or life." And surely that must be the test. It is submitted that nothing is a Poison, unless regard be had to its administration, *e.g.*, Strychnine is a deadly poison, or a valuable medicine, according to how and how much taken. *V.* MEDICINE: NOXIOUS.

For the purposes of the Pharmacy Act, 1868, 31 & 32 V. c. 121, the following are by s. 2 and Sch. A., deemed Poisons:—Arsenic and its preparations; Prussic Acid; Cyanides of Potassium and all metallic cyanides; Strychnine and all poisonous vegetable alkaloids and their salts; Aconite and its preparations; Emetic Tartar; Corrosive Sublimate; Cantharides; Savin and its Oil; Ergot of Rye and its preparations; Oxalic Acid; Chloroform; Belladonna and its preparations; Essential Oil of Almonds, unless deprived of its Prussic Acid; Opium and all preparations of Opium or of Poppies.

Death "by Poison,"—*e.g.*, in an exception in a Life or Accident Policy,—is none the less so because the poison is taken accidentally (*Cole* v. *Accident Insrce.*, 5 Times Rep. 370).

POLICY HOLDER.—"Policy Holder," s. 14, 33 & 34 V. c. 61, includes covenantees under a deed by which an Insurance Co. guarantees the payment of annuities (*Re Sovereign Life Assrce.*, 58 L. J. Ch. 811).

POOL.—"*Stagnum*, in English a poole, doth consist of water and land, and therefore by the name of *stagnum*, or a poole, the water and land shall passe also" (Co. Litt. 5 a, b). *V.* GURGES.

POOR.—A trust for the benefit of "the Poor" of a locality does not, as a general rule, include those who are receiving Parochial Relief (*A.-G.* v. *Exeter Corp.*, 3 Russ. 395; 6 L. J. O. S. Ch. 50: *A.-G.* v. *Clarke*, 1 Amb. 422: *A.-G.* v. *Wilkinson*, 1 Bea. 370: *A.-G.* v. *Gutch*, Reg. Lib. A., 1830, fo. 2720: 1 Jarm. 209: Lewin, 531, 532. *V.* jdgmt. *St. Nicholas, Deptford* v. *Sketchley*, 17 L. J. M. C. 22, 23: *Sv.* RELIEF). A charity for the benefit of "Poor Boys," was held *not confined* to those poor boys who required parish relief or to the boys of persons requiring such relief (*Canterbury Gdns.* v. *Canterbury Corp.*, 31 L. J. Ch. 810).

V. POOREST; RELATIONS.

A trust of impure personalty, "to give it to the Poor as the trustees may think fit," is void as against the statutes of Mortmain (*Re Clark, Husband* v. *Martin*, 54 L. J. Ch. 1080).

Sometimes "Poor" is used as a term of endearment (*Anon.*, 1 P. Wms. 327; *Vth.* 2 Jarm. 126, 127).

POOR INHABITANTS.—*V.* INHABITANT.

POOR LAW UNION.—*V.* s. 16 (2), (4), Interp. Act, 1889.

POOR RELATIONS.—*V.* RELATIONS.

POOREST.—In order that a gift "for the relief and use of the poorest of my kindred" may be good as a charitable bequest, the word "poorest" must mean "poor" or "very poor," and not "the least wealthy of a number of wealthy persons" (*A.-G.* v. *Northumberland*, 47 L. J. Ch. 569 ; 7 Ch. D. 745 ; 26 W. R. 586 ; 38 L. T. 245 : disapproving dictum of Wickens, V.-C., in *Gillam* v. *Taylor*, 42 L. J. Ch. 674 ; L. R. 16 Eq. 581). *Vf.* Tudor, Char. Trusts, 5, 103.

V. POOR : RELATIONS.

PORCA TERRÆ.—"By the name of *selio* or *porca terræ*, doth pass a Ridge of land, which is sometimes longer, and sometimes shorter" (Touch. 95). *V.* SELION.

PORCARIA.—"Fleta maketh mention of *porcaria*, a swinestye" (Co. Litt. 5 b).

PORK BUTCHER.—*V.* BUTCHER.

PORT.—The word "Port" in a Charter-party is to be understood in its popular, or business, or commercial sense ; it does not in such a document necessarily mean the port as defined for revenue or pilotage purposes (*Sailing-Ship "Garston" Co.* v. *Hickie*, 15 Q. B. D. 580 : in which case tests for determining the business meaning of "Port" were considered). *Vf. Price* v. *Livingstone*, 9 Q. B. D. 679.

Insurance on a Ship "at and from her Port of Lading in North America to Liverpool." She took in part of her cargo at K., in New Brunswick, and sailed thence to B., in the same province, seven miles distant on the same bay of the sea. She there completed her cargo, and then returned to K., to receive provisions, &c., after which she sailed for England, and was lost on the voyage. B. was not in the way from K. to Liverpool, B. and K. were situate on creeks opening in the bay, and were spoken of by some persons as ports, but neither of them had a custom-house. They had custom-house officers and were under the jurisdiction of the custom-house of St. John, New Brunswick ; Held, that after the ship had begun to load at K., that was her port of lading ; that the term 'Port of Lading' in the policy did not allow of her afterwards going to B., and that her doing so was a deviation (*Brown* v. *Tayleur*, 4 A. & E. 241 ; 5 L. J. K. B. 57 ; 5 N. & M. 472). "There must be a nonsuit in this case, unless we are prepared to say, that 'Port' is equivalent to 'Ports' or 'Port or Ports.' But I think we are not at liberty here to construe the word with reference to custom-house regulations, but must consider it *as merely indicating a place*" (per Coleridge, J., S. C., 4 A. & E. 250 ; 5 L. J. K. B. 60). *Vf*

Harrower v. *Hutchinson*, 39 L. J. Q. B. 229 ; 10 B. & S. 469 ; L. R. 5 Q. B. 584.

In the warranty of freedom from seizure in Port *of Discharge*, "the word 'Port' is not to be taken in its narrow or strict legal sense, but rather as meaning the place of discharge agreed upon by the assured and underwriters" (1 Maude & P. 507 ; and cases there cited).

V. Safe Port : Port or Place.

PORT CHARGES.—"Port Charges, Pilotages, and other expenses at the Port," in a charter-party, do not include coals supplied at a port into which a steamer has been obliged to put in consequence of the breakdown of her machinery (*The Durham City*, 14 P. D. 85 ; 58 L. J. P. D. & A. 46).

PORT OR PLACE.—*V. Hull Dock Co.* v. *Priestley*, 4 B. & Ad. 178 ; 1 N. & M. 85 ; with *wh. cp. Tennant* v. *Swansea Harbour Trustees*, 3 Times Rep. 128.

PORTION.—"Portion" is synonymous with Share ; and a bequest of a legatee's "Portion" will not, without an auxiliary context, pass an accrued share (2 Jarm. 711, 712).

"Portions *for Children*," s. 2, Thellusson Act, 39 & 40 G. 3, c. 98 :—"Portions for Children are, I think, generally understood to be sums of money secured to them out of property springing from or settled upon their parents ; and although there may, no doubt, be cases in which provisions for children out of property in which the parents take no interest may well be called 'Portions,' I think that such provisions should only receive that designation where the nature or context of the instrument gives them that character. Where there is a gift to children both of capital and income, and there is nothing in the nature or context of the instrument to impress upon the gift the character of a Portion, I do not think it could be called a 'Portion' in the ordinary sense of the word, or ought to be so considered within the meaning of this Act" (per Turner, V.-C., *Jones* v. *Maggs*, 22 L. J. Ch. 91 ; 9 Hare, 605 : *Vf.* the cases there cited, and *Va.* Watson, Eq. 8).

PORTIONIBUS.—This word is properly employed to mean a portion of the Tithes of one parish claimed by the Rector of another parish (*Scarlet* v. *Lucton School*, 4 Cl. & F. 1 ; 10 Bligh, N. S. 592).

PORTRAIT.—A Portrait is the pictorial presentment, taken from life or from "reasonable materials from which a likeness may be framed," of a person (or it may be of more than one person), the chief object of the picture being the preservation of a life-like resemblance of the countenance ; and it is not less a "Portrait" because accompanied by subordinate accessories more or less of an ideal character (*Leeds* v. *Amherst*, 14 L. J. Ch. 73 ; 13 Sim. 459, in which case the word, and even its derivation, are treated with a wealth of learning and illustration not a little unusual in a case on which the L. C. said, "nothing but Mr. Bethell's talent and ingenuity could have thrown any doubt"). In that case Lord Lyndhurst in the course of his judgment said,—"I may be permitted to say this, that if a picture is painted *after a man's death*, and meant to represent him, if there is nothing affording the materials for the portrait, it is completely an ideal picture, and cannot properly be called a Portrait ; but if there are reasonable materials from which a likeness may be framed, I do not consider it less a portrait, though painted after the death of an individual, than if painted during his lifetime" (14 L. J. Ch. 81).

Qy., Would a likeness of an animal,—*e.g.*, a horse,—come within the meaning of "Portrait" ? (*V.* obs. of Shadwell, V.-C., in *Leeds* v. *Amherst*, 14 L. J. Ch. 75).

POSSESSED OF.—As to whether the use of the word "possess," in any of its inflections, will limit a general testamentary gift to personalty,—*e.g.*, in such a phrase as "all I am possessed of ;" *V.* ALL.

"Moneys I die possessed of ;" *V. Re Greaves*, 23 Ch. D. 313 ; 52 L. J. Ch. 753 : *Petty* v. *Willson*, 4 Ch. 574 ; 17 W. R. 778 : *Chapman* v. *Reynolds*, 28 Bea. 221 ; 29 L. J. Ch. 594 ; 8 W. R. 403.

"Money of which I am possessed ;" *V. Re Cadogan*, 25 Ch. D. 154 ; 32 W. R. 57 ; 53 L. J. Ch. 209, following *Prichard* v. *Prichard*, L. R. 11 Eq. 232 ; 40 L. J. Ch. 92, and dissenting from *Larner* v. *Larner*, 3 Drew. 704 ; 26 L. J. Ch. 668 ; 5 W. R. 513. MONEY.

Property, as mentioned in a Settlement, which a wife during the coverture may become "possessed of ;" *V. Wilton* v. *Colvin*, 25 L. J. Ch. 850 ; 3 Drew. 617 : and *Vth. Archer* v. *Kelly*, 6 Jur. N. S. 814.

V. ENTITLED.

POSSESSION.—"Possession is said two waies, either actuall possession, or possession in Law.

"Actuall Possession, is when a man entreth in deed into lands or tenements to him descended, or otherwise.

"Possession in Law, is when lands or tenements are descended to a man, and hee hath not as yet really, actually, and in deed entred into them : And it is called Possession in Law because that in the eye and consideration of the law, he is deemed to be in possession, forasmuch as he is tenaunt to every man's action that will sue concerning the same lands or tenements" (Termes de la Ley, *Possession*).

Sometimes "in Possession," in relation to an estate, will be construed as "vested" (*Foley* v. *Burnell*, 1 Bro. C. C. 274 ; 4 Bro. P. C. 319 : *Martelli* v. *Holloway*, 42 L. J. Ch. 26 ; L. R. 5 H. L. 532).

But, generally, where an estate or interest in realty is spoken of as being "in Possession," that does not, primarily, mean the actual occupation of the property; but means the present right thereto or to the enjoyment thereof, as distinguished from Reversion, Remainder or Expectancy as illustrated by the old conveyancing phrase,—"In possession, reversion, remainder or expectancy." In this sense the word is employed at the commencement of s. 58, Settled Land Act, 1882 (*Re Morgan*, 53 L. J. Ch. 85; 24 Ch. D. 114), and in s. 2, sub-s. 5, same Act (*Re Atkinson*, 31 Ch. D. 577). *Va.* COME TO.

Probably, also, when personal property is being dealt with by way of settlement, the word "Possession" would receive a similar interpretation, and especially so in those cases where the property,—*e.g.*, Consols,—would be incapable of physical possession. But "in general, in technical language, one is said to be possessed of goods when he has the property, and an immediate right to have the goods dealt with as he will" (Blackb. 334). Yet obviously the word,—and peculiarly so when used as regards personalty,—is one largely dependent on the context (*Vh.* Blackb. 334).

In the *Mortmain Act* (9 G. 2, c. 36, s. 1) "take effect in possession," means "giving the right to possession" (1 Jarm. 220, citing *Fisher* v. *Brierley*, 10 H. L. Ca. 159; 32 L. J. Ch. 281).

"Possession" to be given *on Completion of a Purchase*, does not, of itself, mean "Personal Occupation;" and, if the property be tenanted, putting the purchaser into the receipt of the rent will be giving him "Possession" (*Lake* v. *Dean*, 28 Bea. 607; *Vth.* Sug. V. & P. 8: *V.* COMPLETION); *secus*, if the phrase be "Actual Possession" (*Royal Bristol Bg. Society* v. *Bomash*, 56 L. J. Ch. 840; 35 Ch. D. 390; 57 L. T. 179). "Possession," in this connexion, means Possession with a good title shewn (*Tilley* v. *Thomas*, 3 Ch. 61).

"Possession" as used in s. 2251, Civil Code of Lower Canada; *V.* *Dunn* v. *Lareau*, 57 L. J. P. C. 108.

V. ACTUAL.

As to what acts will take goods out of the "*Apparent Possession*" of a grantor, for the purpose of the *Bills of Sale Act*, 1878; *V. Gough* v. *Everard*, 32 L. J. Ex. 210; 2 H. & C. 1; 11 W. R. 702: *Ex p. Homann, Re Vining*, 39 L. J. Bank. 4; L. R. 10 Eq. 63: *Ex p. Lewis, Re Henderson*, 6 Ch. 626: *Davies* v. *Jones*, 7 L. T. 130: *Robinson* v. *Briggs*, 40 L. J. Ex. 17; L. R. 6 Ex. 1: *Ex p. Saffery, Re Brenner*, 16 Ch. D. 668: *Gibbons* v. *Hickson*, 55 L. J. Q. B. 119; 53 L. T. 910; 34 W. R. 140: *Ex p. Mutton, Re Cole*, 41 L. J. Bank. 57; L. R. 14 Eq. 178: *Ex p. Jay, Re Blenkhorn*, 43 L. J. Bank. 122; 9 Ch. 697. The last case decides that the "Apparent Possession" will remain in the grantor unless much more be done to take it from him than would be necessary with reference to the doctrine of reputed ownership. If in fact the grantor keeps possession he is none the less in apparent possession because his act is wrongful (*Ancona* v. *Rogers*, 46 L. J. Ex. 121; 1 Ex. D. 285); or because he occupies as the salaried servant of the grantor (*Pickard* v. *Marriage*,

45 L. J. Ex. 594 ; 1 Ex. D. 364). *Vf. Cookson* v. *Swire*, 54 L. J. Q. B. 249 ; 9 App. Ca. 653.

As to the meaning of the word "Possession" in the *Reputed Ownership Clause* of the Bankruptcy Act, 1883, s. 44 ; *V.* Baldwin, 206 ; Wms. Bank. 179 ; Robson, ch. 23 ; Yate Lee, 367.

V. OCCUPATION.

"Possession," *quâ* the *Criminal Law* and Offences against Property, has been thus defined :—

"A moveable thing is said to be in the possession of a person when he is so situated with respect to it that he has the power to deal with it as owner to the exclusion of all other persons, and when the circumstances are such that he may be presumed to intend to do so in case of need.

"A moveable thing is in the possession of the husband of any woman, or the master of any servant, who has the custody of it for him, and from whom he can take it at pleasure. The word '*Servant*' here, includes any person acting as a servant for any particular purpose or occasion.

"The word '*Custody*,' means such a relation towards the thing as would constitute Possession if the person having custody had it on his own account.

"If a servant receives anything for his master from a third person, not being a fellow-servant, he has the Possession as distinguished from the Custody of it, until he has put it into his master's possession, by putting it into a place or thing belonging to his master, or by some other act of the same sort, whether the servant himself has or has not the custody of that place or thing.

"If a servant receives anything belonging to his master from a fellow-servant who has received it from their common master, such thing continues to be in the Possession of the master, unless the servant who delivered it, delivered it with the intention to pass the property therein to the servant to whom it is delivered, having authority to do so from the master.

"If a servant receives anything belonging to his master from a fellow-servant who has received it on the master's account, and has done no act to put it into the master's possession, it is in the Possession of the servant who so receives it, and not in his Custody merely" (Steph. Cr. 210, 211).

As to meaning of "fraudulently allure, &c., a woman, under the age of 21 years, *out of the Possession* and against the will of her father or mother," s. 53, 24 & 25 V. c. 100 ; *V. R.* v. *Burrell*, 33 L. J. M. C. 54 ; L. & C. 354. And as to a similar use of "Possession" in s. 55 of the same Act ; *V. R.* v. *Manktelow*, 22 L. J. M. C. 115 ; Dears. 159 : *R.* v. *Timmins*, 30 L. J. M. C. 45 : *Vf.* TAKE.

Possession of *Unwholesome Meat*, s. 117, P. H. Act, 1875 ; *V. Newton* v. *Monkcom*, 58 L. T. 231 ; 4 Times Rep. 205.

POSSESSION OR POWER.—As to the meaning and requirements of this phrase in an Affidavit of Documents ; *V.* Ann. Pr., notes to Ord. 31, R. 13, R. S. C.

POSSESSIONS.—The word "Possessions," in the 5th case, Sch. D., s. 100, Income Tax Act, 5 & 6 V. c. 35, includes a Trade or Business, and is to be taken in the widest sense, as denoting all property that may be a source of income (*Colquhoun* v. *Brooks*, 59 L. J. Q. B. 53 ; 61 L. T. 518).

V. PROFITS.

POSSIBLE.—Where a manufacturer undertakes to supply an article "*as soon as* possible," that means with all reasonable promptitude, regard being had to the manufacturer's means of business, and the orders he has already in hand (*Attwood* v. *Emery*, 26 L. J. C. P. 73 ; 1 C. B. N. S. 110 : *Va.* Add. C. 1188 ; Blackb. 226 : *Sv. Hydraulic Engineering Co.* v. *McHaffie*, 4 Q. B. D. 670 ; and *Vth.* Benj. 678).

So where a local Act modified the then law requiring furnaces to consume their own smoke, by enacting that they should do so "*as far as* possible," this was held to mean "as far as possible consistently with carrying on the manufacture in question" (*Cooper* v. *Woolley*, L. R. 2 Ex. 88 ; 36 L. J. M. C. 27 ; 15 L. T. 539. *Note.*—The general phrase hereon now is, "as far as *practicable* ;" s. 91, proviso 2, P. H. Act, 1875).

V. IMMEDIATELY : PRACTICABLE : REASONABLE.

"To load with all *possible Despatch ;*" *V. Hudson* v. *Clementson*, 25 L. J. C. P. 234 ; 18 C. B. 213.

"*If* possible ;" *V. Wilson* v. *Kynock*, W. N. (77) 164.

POST.—*V.* BY POST : ORDINARY COURSE.

POST LETTER.—The definition of "Post Letter," in s. 47, Post Office Act, 1837 (1 V. c. 36), does not include a letter not posted in the proper course, but put by a Post Official amongst letters so posted, as a trap for a suspected person (*R.* v. *Shepherd*, 25 L. J. M. C. 52 ; Dears. 606). *Vf.* Rosc. 881.

POSTMASTER-GENERAL.—*V.* s. 12 (11), Interp. Act, 1889.

POST-OFFICE.—A covenant to use demised premises as a "Post-Office" only, is not broken by issuing therefrom Inland Revenue Licenses (*Wadham* v. *Postmaster-General*, 24 L. T. 545).

POSTER.—*V.* BILL.

POSTHUMOUS CHILD.—*V.* Wms. Ex. 1101.

POUND.—*V.* Co. Litt. 47 b.

POWER.—"Power to appoint," s. 27, 1 V. c. 26, means, "Power to appoint, *by the Will in question*" (*Phillips* v. *Cayley*, 43 Ch. D. 222 ; 59 L. J. Ch. 177). *V.* EXPRESSLY REFER.

"Shall hereby have Power ;" *V.* MAY.

"According to their respective Powers ;" *V.* FACILITIES.

"Powers in anywise enabling;" *V.* Enabling.

"Right, Power or Privilege;" *V.* Right.

V. Possession or Power.

P. P.—As used in a sporting match; *V. Daintree* v. *Hutchinson*, 11 L. J. Ex. 186; 10 M. & W. 85.

PRACTICABLE.—"All Practicable Speed;" *V. Nicholls* v. *Hall*, 42 L. J. M. C. 105; L. R. 8 C. P. 322.

"As far as Practicable," s. 91, proviso 2, Public Health Act, 1875; *V. Cooper* v. *Woolley*, L. R. 2 Ex. 88; 36 L. J. M. C. 27; 15 L. T. 539: Possible.

V. Reasonably Practicable.

PRACTICAL WORKING MINER.—A man who has been a working miner, but who is, and for 8 years has been, employed above ground as a check-weigher, is not a "Practical Working Miner" within Rule 38, s. 49, Coal Mines Regulation Act, 1887, 50 & 51 V. c. 58 (*Indian* v. *Colquhoun*, Times, 18 Jan., 1890).

PRACTICE.—The "Practice" of a Court, when that word is used in its ordinary and common sense, denotes the Rules that make or guide the *cursus curiæ*, and regulate procedure within the walls or limits of the Court itself, and does not involve or imply anything relating to the extent or nature of its jurisdiction; and, therefore, the Queen's Remembrancer's Act (22 & 23 V. c. 21, s. 26), enabling the now abolished Barons of the Exchequer to frame Rules for making "the process, *Practice*, and mode of pleading" on the Revenue side of the Court uniform with that on the Plea side, did not give those learned judges the power they assumed to exercise, of giving an appeal in Revenue cases (*A.-G.* v. *Sillem*, 33 L. J. Ex. 209; 10 H. L. Ca. 704).

PRACTISE.—A solicitor holding a country certificate, and whose office is in the country, does not "act or practise" in London, within s. 59, Stamp Act, 1870, by attending one taxation at the central office (*Re Horton*, 8 Q. B. D. 434; 51 L. J. Q. B. 309).

PRATA.—*V.* Meadows.

PRAYER.—"What is Prayer? Barrow says it is not only supplication, but adoration" (per Byles, J., *Baxter* v. *Langley*, 38 L. J. M. C. 5).

So, though "bequests for Prayers for the Soul of the testator are void as superstitious" (Tudor's Char. Trusts, 23, and cases there cited), yet, *semble*, a bequest to say Prayers for the living, or to offer Thanksgiving for the Dead in the sense at the end of the Prayer for the Church Militant, would be good (*Re Michel*, 28 Bea. 39; 29 L. J. Ch. 547; 2 L. T. 46; 8 W. R. 299; 6 Jur. N. S. 573).

PRECARIÆ.—Precariæ, or Benework, or Boonwork, is "special work done by a tenant at the request of his lord, as distinguished from fixed services; Seebohm, 78 ; Spelm. *Precariæ siccæ* are 'boon days without allowance of drink'; Domesday of St. Paul's (Cam. Soc.), notes, cxxiv. *Precariæ* is also used in the sense of Benefices (feuds) ; 2 Palgr. Eng. Commonwealth, ccv" (Elph. 616, 563).

PRECATORY TRUST.—"It has long been settled that words of Recommendation, Request, Entreaty, Wish or Expectation, addressed to a devisee or legatee, will make him a trustee for the person or persons in whose favour such expressions are used" (1 Jarm. 385. *Va.* Lewin, 130) : but "it is essential that there should be (1) a *certain* subject, and (2) a *certain* object of the trust to be so created" (per Wood, V.-C., *Bernard* v. *Minshull,* Johns. 285, 286 ; 28 L. J. Ch. 649). *V.* Judgment in that case for an explanation as to these two essential certainties. *Va. Knight* v. *Knight,* 3 Bea. 148 ; 9 L. J. Ch. 354, for a full discussion of this doctrine before and by Langdale, M.R. *Vf. Cowman* v. *Harrison,* 22 L. J. Ch. 993.

"The doctrine of thus construing expressions of Recommendation, Confidence, Hope, Wish and Desire into positive and peremptory commands, is not a little difficult to be maintained, upon sound principles of interpretation of the actual intention of the testator." "Accordingly we find, of late, a more strict and uniform requisition of definiteness, in regard to both the subject-matter and the objects of the intended trust, than can be traced in some of the earlier, and a few of the more modern, adjudications" (1 Jarm. 391) ; and the strong disposition now is "to give to the words of Wills their natural and ordinary sense, unless it is clear that they are designed to be used in a peremptory sense" (Sto. 339).

Each of the following phrases in Wills has been held to create a Precatory Trust.

"**Advise** him to settle" (*Parker* v. *Bolton,* 5 L. J. Ch. 98).

"Well **Assured**" (*Macey* v. *Shurmer,* 1 Atk. 389 ; 1 Amb. 520. *V. Ray* v. *Adams,* 3 My. & K. 237).

"Have full **Assurance** and confident **Hope**" (*Macnab* v. *Whitbread,* 17 Bea. 299).

"**Authorise** and **Empower**" (*Brown* v. *Higgs,* 4 Ves. 708 ; 5 Ib. 495 ; 8 Ib. 561 ; 18 Ib. 192 : and *V. Griffiths* v. *Evan,* 11 L. J. Ch. 219 ; 5 Bea. 241).

"**Beg**" (*Corbet* v. *Corbet,* Ir. Rep. 7 Eq. 456).

"In the full **Belief**" (*Fordham* v. *Speight,* W. N. (75) 140).

"Most heartily **Beseech**" (*Meredith* v. *Heneage,* 1 Sim. 553).

"**Confide**" (*Griffiths* v. *Evan,* 11 L. J. Ch. 219 ; 5 Bea. 241 : and *V. Shepherd* v. *Nottige,* 2 J. & H. 766).

"Have the fullest **Confidence**" (*Shovelton* v. *Shovelton,* 32 Bea. 143 ;

Re Downing, 60 L. T. 140 : *Wright* v. *Atkyns*, 17 Ves. 255 ; 19 Ib. 299 : *Webb* v. *Wools*, 21 L. J. Ch. 625 ; 2 Sim. N. S. 267 : *Palmer* v. *Simmonds*, 2 Drew. 225 : *Curnick* v. *Tucker*, L. R. 17 Eq. 320 : *Le Marchant* v. *Le Marchant*, L. R. 18 Eq. 414). *Secus*, where the words expressing "confidence" are preceded by an absolute gift (*Re Adams*, 52 L. J. Ch. 758 ; 24 Ch. D. 199 : *Va. Lambe* v. *Eames*, 40 L. J. Ch. 447 ; 6 Ch. 597 : *Re Hutchinson & Tenant*, 8 Ch. D. 540 : *Mussoorie Bank* v. *Raynor*, 51 L. J. P. C. 72 ; 7 App. Ca. 321).

"In **Consideration** the legatee has promised to give" (*Clifton* v. *Lombe*, 1 Amb. 519).

"Under the firm **Conviction**" (*Barnes* v. *Grant*, 26 L. J. Ch. 92 ; 2 Jur. N. S. 1127).

"**Of Course** the legatee will give" (*Robinson* v. *Smith*, 6 Mad. 194 : *Sv. Lechmere* v. *Lavie*, 2 My. & K. 198).

"**Declare**;" *V.* "Will and Declare," *post.*

"**Desire**" (*Harding* v. *Glyn*, 1 Atk. 469 : *Mason* v. *Limbury*, cited *Vernon* v. *Vernon*, Amb. 4 : *Trott* v. *Vernon*, 2 Vern. 708 : *Pushman* v. *Filliter*, 3 Ves. 7 : *Brest* v. *Offley*, 1 Ch. Rep. 246 : *Bonser* v. *Kinnear*, 2 Giff. 195 : *Cary* v. *Cary*, 2 Sch. & Lef. 189 : *Cruwys* v. *Colman*, 9 Ves. 319 : *Va. Shaw* v. *Lawless*, L. & G. t. Sug. 154. *V.* on the contrary *Re Diggles*, 32 S. J. 608).

"**Direct**;" *V.* "Order and Direct," *post.*

"Do **not Doubt**" (*Parsons* v. *Baker*, 18 Ves. 476 : *Taylor* v. *George*, 2 V. & B. 378 : *Malone* v. *O'Connor*, Ll. & G. 465 : and *V. Sale* v. *Moore*, 1 Sim. 534).

"**Empower**;" *V.* "Authorize and Empower," *sup.*

"**Entreat**" (*Prevost* v. *Clarke*, 2 Mad. 458 : *Meredith* v. *Heneage*, 1 Sim. 553, 555 : and *V. Taylor* v. *George*, 2 V. & B. 378).

"**Hope**" (*Harland* v. *Trigg*, 1 Bro. C. C. 142 : and *V. Paul* v. *Compton*, 8 Ves. 380 : *V.* "Assurance and Hope," *sup.*). *Sv. Eaton* v. *Watts*, L. R. 4 Eq. 151.

"Well **Know**" (*Bardswell* v. *Bardswell*, 7 L. J. Ch. 268 ; 9 Sim. 323 : *Nowlan* v. *Nelligan*, 1 Bro. C. C. 489 : *Briggs* v. *Penny*, 21 L. J. Ch. 265 ; 3 Mac. & G. 546 ; 3 D. G. & S. 525 : *Sv.* obs. on *Briggs* v. *Penny* in *Stead* v. *Mellor*, 46 L. J. Ch. 880 ; 5 Ch. D. 225 ; 36 L. T. 498).

"**Order and Direct**" (*Cary* v. *Cary*, 2 Sch. & Lef. 189).

"**Recommend**" (*Tibbits* v. *Tibbits*, Jac. 317; 19 Ves. 656 : *Horwood* v. *West*, 1 L. J. O. S. Ch. 201; 1 S. & S. 387: *Paul* v. *Compton*, 8 Ves. 380 : *Malim* v. *Keighley*, 2 Ves. jun. 333, 529 : *Malim* v. *Barker*, 3 Ves. 150 : *Meredith* v. *Heneage*, 1 Sim. 553 : *Kingston* v. *Lorton*, 2 Hogan, 166 : *Cholmondeley* v. *Cholmondeley*, 14 Sim. 590 : *Hart* v. *Tribe*, 23 L. J. Ch. 462 ; 18 Bea. 215 : *White* v. *Briggs*, 15 L. J. Ch. 182 ; 15 Sim. 33). "That 'recommend' may amount to a command and create a binding trust is certain. It is equally certain that the word is susceptible of a different interpretation. It must depend upon the language of the particular instrument in which this word is found, in which of the two senses it is to be taken" (per Knight Bruce, V.-C., *Johnson* v. *Rowlands*, 17 L. J. Ch. 438 ; 2 D. G. & S. 356).

"**Request**" (*Pierson* v. *Garnet*, 2 Bro. C. C. 38 : *Eade* v. *Eade*, 5 Mad. 118 : *Moriarty* v. *Martin*, 3 Ir. Ch. Rep. 26 : *Bernard* v. *Minshull*, 28 L. J. Ch. 649 ; Johns. 276 : *Va. House* v. *House*, W. N. (74) 189).

"**Trusting**" (*Irvine* v. *Sullivan*, 38 L. J. Ch. 635 ; L. R. 8 Eq. 673).

"**Trusting and Confiding**" (*Wade*, or *Wood* v. *Cox*, 5 L. J. Ch. 361; 6 Ib. 366 ; 1 Keen, 317; 2 My. & C. 684 : *Pilkington* v. *Boughey*, 12 Sim. 114).

"**Well Know**;" *V.* "Know," sup.

"**Will**" (*Eales* v. *England*, Pr. Ch. 200: *Clowdsley* v. *Pelham*, 1 Vern. 411).

"**Will and Declare**" (*Gray* v. *Gray*, 11 Ir. Ch. Rep. 218).

"**Will and Desire**" (*Birch* v. *Wade*, 3 V. & B. 198 : *Forbes* v. *Ball*, 3 Mer. 437).

"**Wish and Desire**" (*Liddard* v. *Liddard*, 29 L. J. Ch. 619 ; 28 Bea. 266). *Sv. Stead* v. *Mellor*, inf.

"**Wish and Request**" (*Foley* v. *Parry*, 5 Sim. 138 ; 2 My. & K. 138 : *Re Hutchings*, W. N. (87) 217).

But either of the foregoing (or such like) phrases might easily be controlled the other way by a context ; for, in the present day, there is probably no construction more dependent on, or more easily liable to be affected by, the general tenor of the instrument than one from which a precatory trust is to be gathered. "I fully agree with Lord Justice James in what he said in *Lambe* v. *Eames* (40 L. J. Ch. 447; 6 Ch. 597), that when you come to read the older authorities you can only arrive at the conclusion that they created trusts in numbers of cases where trusts were never intended" (per Pearson, J., *Re Adams*, 52 L. J. Ch. 761 ; 24 Ch. D. 199).

Words of entreaty when coupled with discretionary words (*White* v. *Briggs*, 15 L. J. Ch. 182 ; 15 Sim. 33 : *Williams* v. *Williams*, 20 L. J. Ch. 280 ; 22 Ib. 639 ; 17 Bea. 156 : *Hart* v. *Tribe*, 23 L. J. Ch. 462 ; 18 Bea. 215 : *Eaton* v. *Watts*, L. R. 4 Eq. 151: *Re Bond, Cole* v. *Hawes*, 4 Ch. D. 238 ; 46 L. J. Ch. 488 : *Lambe* v. *Eames*, 40 L. J. Ch. 447; 6 Ch. 597), or with an absolute gift (*Re Adams*, 52 L. J. Ch. 758 ; *Re Moore*, 55 L. J. Ch. 418), do *not* create a precatory trust. In the case lastly cited the words were, "They are hereby ENJOINED to take care of my nephew J. J. N. C. as may seem best in the future." So "feeling confident that she will ACT JUSTLY" does not create Precatory Trust (*Mussoorie Bank* v. *Raynor*, 51 L. J. P. C. 72 ; 7 App. Ca. 321) ; nor a desire that the fund will be distributed "AGREEABLY TO MY WISHES" (*Stead* v. *Mellor*, 46 L. J. Ch. 880 ; 5 Ch. D. 225 ; 36 L. T. 498).

Note.—The doctrine of precatory trusts, though usually arising on Wills, is applicable to transactions *inter vivos* (*Liddard* v. *Liddard*, 29 L. J. Ch. 619; 28 Bea. 266: *Wheeler* v. *Smith*, 29 L. J. Ch. 194; 1 Giff. 300): and on the subject of Precatory Trusts generally, *V.* Lewin, 130 *et seq.*; 1 Jarm. 385 *et seq.*

PRECEDING TWELVE MONTHS.—As to this phrase in s. 46, Valuation (Metrop.) Act, 1869; *V. R.* v. *East & W. India Docks Co.*, 53 L. J. M. C. 97; 13 Q. B. D. 364; 51 L. T. 97; 48 J. P. 564.

PREDECESSOR.—In Sucn. Dy. Act, 1853; *V. A.-G.* v. *Braybrooke*, 9 H. L. Ca. 150; 31 L. J. Ex. 177: *A.-G.* v. *Floyer*, 9 H. L. Ca. 477; 31 L. J. Ex. 404: *A.-G.* v. *Smythe*, 9 H. L. Ca. 497; 31 L. J. Ex. 404: *Charlton* v. *A.-G.*, 4 App. Ca. 427; 49 L. J. Ex. 86: *A.-G.* v. *Mitchell*, 50 L. J. Q. B. 406; 6 Q. B. D. 548: *Re O'Neill*, 20 L. R. Ir. 73: *Re Barker*, 30 L. J. Ex. 404; 7 H. & N. 109: *Re Ramsay*, 30 L. J. Ch. 849; 30 Bea. 75: *Re Lovelace*, 28 L. J. Ch. 489; 4 D. G. & J. 340.

V. Succession: Ancestor: Disposition.

PREFERENCE.—*V.* Fraudulent Preference: Undue Preference.

PREFERENCE DIVIDEND.—*V.* Dividend.

PREFERMENT.—*V. Lowther* v. *Bentinck*, 44 L. J. Ch. 197; L. R. 19 Eq. 167: Advancement.

PREFERRED.—In the power given by s. 98, 5 & 6 W. 4, c. 50, to the Court before whom a Highway Indictment shall be "preferred" to award Costs, "preferred" means "tried" (*R.* v. *Pembridge*, 12 L. J. Q. B. 47; 3 Q. B. 901; 3 G. & D. 5).

PREJUDICE. — *V.* Annoyance: Undue Preference: Without Prejudice.

PREJUDICE OF PURCHASER.—A purchaser who *knows* that the article which he buys is not of the nature, substance and quality demanded by him, has not had the article sold to him to his "Prejudice" within s. 6, Sale of Food and Drugs Act, 1875 (38 & 39 V. c. 63); even though no label is delivered to him pursuant to s. 8 (*Sandys* v. *Small*, 47 L. J. M. C. 115; 3 Q. B. D. 449; 26 W. R. 814; 42 J. P. 550). But "Prejudice" here does not mean pecuniary prejudice, or injury from taking unwholesome food; it means the prejudice which the person buying sustains as a customer in getting, *without his knowledge*, an article different from that demanded; and it is immaterial that he buys only for analysis or with money other than his own (*Hoyle* v. *Hitchman*, 48 L. J. M. C. 97; 4 Q. B. D. 233; 27 W. R. 487; 43 J. P. 431; adopting the principle on which *Sandys* v. *Markham*, 41 J. P. 53, was remitted to be re-stated: *Vh.*

s. 2, 42 & 43 V. c. 30). *Vf. Horder* v. *Grainger*, 44 J. P. 188 : *Kirk* v. *Coates*, 55 L. J. M. C. 182 ; 16 Q. B. D. 49 ; 34 W. R. 296 ; 50 J. P. 148 ; 54 L. T. 178.

V. ARTICLE DEMANDED.

The principle of *Sandys* v. *Small* (sup.), is applicable to the sale of spirits diluted below the standard prescribed by s. 6 of the Sale of Food and Drugs Act Amendment Act, 1879, 42 & 43 V. c. 30 (*Gage* v. *Elsey*, 52 L. J. M. C. 44 ; 10 Q. B. D. 518).

It is not necessary to show the seller's guilty knowledge (*Betts* v. *Armstead*, 57 L. J. M. C. 100 ; 20 Q. B. D. 771 ; 58 L. T. 811 ; 36 W. R. 720 ; 52 J. P. 471).

PREMISES.—The *Premises* of a *Deed* are all the foreparts of the deed before the *Habendum* (Touch. 75). The word "Premises" in fact signifies what has gone before ; and therefore may with propriety be used in relation to any preceding subject or subjects. Thus where a testator devised a certain messuage and the furniture in it, to A. for life and after his decease he gave "the said messuage and premises" to B., the latter devise was held to carry the furniture as well as the messuage (*Sanford* v. *Irby*, 4 L. J. O. S. Ch. 23 : *Va. Doe* v. *Meakin*, 1 East, 456 : *Fitzgerald* v. *Field*, 1 Russ. 427).

But frequently property is spoken of as "Premises," without a preceding description or mention of it. Thus where a testator gave permission to A. to occupy a "mansion, house, garden *and premises*" rent-free ; it was held that the word "premises" meant, "premises in immediate connection with the mansion and without the occupation of which, the mansion could not be conveniently occupied and enjoyed" (per Turner, L. J., *Lethbridge* v. *Lethbridge*, 31 L. J. Ch. 741 ; 4 D. G. F. & J. 35). A park of 100 acres adjoining the Mansion-house was accordingly, in that case, held to be included in the word "Premises" (30 L. J. Ch. 388) ; *secus*, as regards the Home Farm, though it was contiguous to the Mansion-house and was in hand at the death of the testator (31 L. J. Ch. 737). In such a connection "Premises" is as nearly as possible synonymous with APPURTENANCES (*Read* v. *Read*, W. N. (66) 386 ; 15 W. R. 165). *Vf. Doe* d. *Hemming* v. *Willetts*, 18 L. J. C. P. 240 ; 7 C. B. 709 : 1 Jarm. 778.

"Premises" in Factory Acts ; *V.* FACTORY.

"Premises," s. 22, P. H. Act, 1875, means, "premises in the state in which they are ;—not at the time the grant was made, the Act passed or the arrangements come to ;—but, it means, the premises in all time according to the state in which they are at the time" (per North, J., *New Windsor* v. *Stovell*, 54 L. J. Ch. 117 ; citing *Newcomen* v. *Coulson*, 46 L. J. Ch. 459 ; 5 Ch. D. 133 : *Finch* v. *G. W. Ry.*, 5 Ex. D. 254).

"Premises" in s. 257, P. H. Act, 1875, is used in the sense defined by s. 4, and accordingly the charge created by s. 257 is on the respective interests of every owner for the time being in proportion to the value of his interest (*Birmingham* v. *Baker*, 17 Ch. D. 782).

PREPARED.—Under a Condition of Sale that the conveyance is "to be *prepared and completed* at the *vendor's* expense," the vendor is only liable to pay for the costs of the actual work done in such preparation and completion under Sch. 2, Rem. Ord., and is not liable for the Scale Fee on the amount of purchase money under Sch. 1 (*Re Thackeray*, 34 S. J. 64).

PREROGATIVE.—"*Littleton* speaketh of the king's prerogative but twice in all his bookes, viz., here (s. 125), and sect. 178, and in both places as part of the laws of *England*. *Prærogativa* is derived of *præ*, *i.e. ante*, and *rogare*, that is, to aske or demand beforehand, whereof commeth *prærogativa*, and is denominated of the most excellent part; because though an act hath passed both the houses of the lords and commons in parliament, yet before it be a law, the royall assent must be asked or demanded and obtained, and this is the proper sense of the word. But legally it extends to all powers, preheminences, and priviledges which the law giveth to the Crowne" (Co. Litt. 90 b).

PRESBYTERIAN.—*V. A.-G.* v. *Bunce*, 37 L. J. Ch. 697; L. R. 6 Eq. 563: *A.-G.* v. *Anderson*, 57 L. J. Ch. 543; 58 L. T. 726; 36 W. R. 714.

PRESCRIBED LIMITS.—This phrase in s. 13, Markets and Fairs Act, 1847, 10 & 11 V. c. 14, means the boundaries of the borough to which the local Act relates, and not the limits of the market (*Casswell* v. *Cook*, 31 L. J. M. C. 185; 11 C. B. N. S. 637). *Vf. Llandaff Market Co.* v. *Lyndon*, 8 C. B. N. S. 515; 6 Jur. N. S. 1344.

PRESCRIPTION.—"Prescription is a title taking his substance of use and time allowed by the law. In the common law a prescription, which is personall, is for the most part applied to persons. . . . And a custome, which is locall, is alledged in no person, but laid within some mannor or other place" (Co. Litt. 113 a, b; *wh. V.* for illustration of this distinction); *V.* CUSTOM.

PRESENCE.—The subscription of the attesting witnesses of a Will has to be done in the "Presence" of the Testator (1 V. c. 26, s. 9). This means that he must be corporeally in such a position as to be able to see the witnesses subscribe, and mentally capable of knowing what they are doing (1 Jarm. 86–88, *wh. V.* for cases hereon). By the same section a testator is to sign his Will in the "presence" of two or more witnesses; and that also means "that the witnesses should see *and be conscious* of the act done" (per Dr. Lushington, *Hudson* v. *Parker*, 1 Rob. Ecc. 24), but that requirement is complied with if, in fact, it has been so done—even though the witnesses may not be aware that the document is a Will or that what they saw the testator write was his signature (*Smith* v. *Smith*, 35 L. J. P. & M. 65 ; L. R. 1 P. & D. 143).

PRESENT.—*V.* FUTURE.
"Handsome Present ;" *V.* HANDSOME GRATUITY.

PRESENT AT.—*V.* MEETING.

PRESENT RIGHT TO RECEIVE.—This phrase in s. 40, 3 & 4 W. 4, c. 27, means an *immediate* right without waiting for the happening of any future event (*Farran* v. *Beresford*, 10 Cl. & F. 319, 334).

As to the same phrase, in s. 13, 23 & 24 V. c. 38 ; *V. Re Johnson, Sly* v. *Blake*, 29 Ch. D. 964.

As used in s. 8, Real Property Limitation Act, 1874, 37 & 38 V. c. 57 ; *V. Hornsey* v. *Monarch Bg. Socy.*, 59 L. J. Q. B. 105 ; W. N. (89) 187.

PRESENT TIME.—*V.* AT THE PRESENT TIME.

PRESENTATION.—"The word 'Presentation' may have many meanings according to the context or as circumstances require, and it may mean either 'shewing' or 'delivering over'" (per Jervis, C. J., *Bartlett* v. *Holmes*, 22 L. J. C. P. 185 ; 13 C. B. 630). In that case the vendor's memorandum of contract was to deliver 1,000 tons of pig iron "on the presentation of this document," and it was held that there, "Presentation" meant "delivering over."

In ecclesiastical law "Presentation is derived *à præsentando* . . . and is the act of the patron offering his clerke to the bishop of that diocesse, to bee instituted to such a church, in these or the like words directed to the bishop, *Præsento vobis* A. B. *clericum meum ad ecclesiam de* Dale, &c." (Co. Litt. 120 a).

PRESENTLY ANSWER.—*V.* ANSWER.

PRESERVATION.—To restrain a lessee of a mine from allowing damage by ceasing to pump, is "Preservation" within R. 3, Ord. 50, R. S. C. (*Strelley* v. *Pearson*, 15 Ch. D. 113 ; 49 L. J. Ch. 406 ; 28 W. R. 752 ; 43 L. T. 155 : *Vf. Pollini* v. *Gray*, 12 Ch. D. 438).

PRESERVED.—*V.* RECOVERED OR PRESERVED.

PRESS.—"The finishing process of a Press," in a Patent Specification ; *V. Barber* v. *Grace*, 17 L. J. Ex. 122 ; 1 Ex. 339.

PRESSURE.—Merely paying money under protest to suit one's own convenience is not paying under "Pressure" (*Re Harrison*, 16 L. J. Ch. 170 ; 10 Bea. 57 : *Re Boycott*, 29 Ch. D. 571 ; 52 L. T. 482 ; 34 W. R. 26 : and *V.* especially latter case hereon).

PRESUMED.—"Admeasurements are presumed to be correct;" *V.* ADMEASUREMENT: *Cp.* ESTIMATED.

PRETENCED.—A "Pretenced" title within 32 H. 8, c. 9, s. 2, is one purely fictitious (*Kennedy* v. *Lyell*, 15 Q. B. D. 491). Formerly a right of entry disannexed from actual possession, however good and true it might be, was a pretenced title within the statute (Co. Litt. 369 a: *Partridge* v. *Strange*, 1 Plowd. 88: *Doe* d. *Williams* v. *Evans*, 14 L. J. C. P. 237: 1 C. B. 717): but as a right of entry, formerly incapable of being conveyed, may now be conveyed (8 & 9 V. c. 106, s. 6), it is not, as such, a pretenced title within the statute of Henry 8 (*Jenkins* v. *Jones*, 51 L. J. Q. B. 438; 9 Q. B. D. 128; 46 L. T. 795; 30 W. R. 668).

"'Pretensed Right or Title' is where one is in possession of lands or tenements, and another who is out of possession, claimeth it, and sueth for it" (Termes de la Ley, *Pretensed Right or Title*).

"Buying or selling a *pretended* title is buying or selling lands, of which the title is known to be in dispute, below the value which they would have if the title was not in dispute, and to the intent that the buyer may carry on the suit in place of the seller" (Steph. Cr. 97).

PRETENDING TO CLAIM.—"A covenant that the lessee shall quietly enjoy against all claiming 'or pretending to claim' a right in the premises, extends to all interruptions, be the claim legal or not, provided it appear that the disturber do not claim under the lessee himself" (Woodf. 681, citing *Chaplin* v. *Southgate*, 10 Mod. 384; 1 Comyn, 230: *Va. Ibbett* v. *De la Salle*, 6 H. & N. 233; 30 L. J. Ex. 44).

PREVIOUSLY OFFERED.—"The sum *previously offered*" in s. 51, Lands C. C. Act, 1845, means, the sum mentioned in the notice for a jury given under s. 38 (*R.* v. *Smith*, 53 L. J. Q. B. 115; 12 Q. B. D. 481; 32 W. R. 275).

PRICE.—*V.* FAIR PRICE.

PRIMAGE.—"This is a small payment made by the owner or consignee of the goods to the Master for his care and trouble, which varies in amount according to the particular trade in which the Ship is engaged" (1 Maude & P. 121).

PRIME BACON.—*V. Yates* v. *Pym*, 6 Taunt. 446; 2 Marsh. 141: 1 Sm. L. C. 597.

PRINCIPAL ENGINEER.—As to who is the "Principal Engineer" of a Ry. Co., within a clause referring disputes for arbitration; *V. Re Wansbeck Ry.*, L. R. 1 C. P. 269.

PRINCIPAL IN FIRST DEGREE.—"Whoever actually commits, or takes part in the actual commission of a crime, is a Principal in the First Degree, whether he is on the spot when the crime is committed or not; and if a crime is committed partly in one place and partly in another, every one who commits any part of it at any place is a principal in the first degree" (Steph. Cr. 29). "Whoever commits a crime by an innocent agent is a Principal in the First Degree" (Ib.).

"The general definition of a Principal in the First Degree is, one who is the actor or actual perpetrator of the fact" (Arch. Cr. 9).

PRINCIPAL IN THE SECOND DEGREE.—"Whoever aids or abets the actual commission of a crime, either at the place where it is committed, or elsewhere, is a Principal in the Second Degree in that crime.

Mere presence on the occasion when a crime is committed does not make a person a Principal in the Second Degree, even if he neither makes any effort to prevent the offence or to cause the offender to be apprehended, but such presence may be evidence for the consideration of the jury of an active participation in the offence.

When the existence of a particular intent forms part of the definition of an offence, a person charged with aiding or abetting the commission of the offence must be shown to have known of the existence of the intent on the part of the person so aided" (Steph. Cr. 30).

Vf. Arch. Cr. 9; Rosc. Cr. 181.

PRINCIPAL MONEY.—A testator possessed of a small amount of cash, but of considerable other property both real and personal, gave as follows,—"I desire that the income arising from my Principal Money shall be paid to my wife, while unmarried, for the support of herself and the education of my children, and at her death or on her marriage to be divided between them;" held, that all the personalty, including leaseholds, passed, but not the realty (*Prichard* v. *Prichard*, 40 L. J. Ch. 92; L. R. 11 Eq. 232; 24 L. T. 259).

V. MONEY.

PRINCIPAL SUM.—Where a Covenant of Indemnity is given as a collateral security for principal and interest secured by a mortgage, and to the covenant there is a proviso that "no greater Principal Sum shall be ultimately recoverable under or by virtue hereof than the Principal Sum of," *e.g.* £3000,—the phrase "Principal Sum" in such a proviso does not mean "no greater sum in respect of the principal secured by the mortgage," but means the amount to be recovered under the indemnity: so that if, after realizing the property mortgaged, there remain, *e.g.* £2047 7*s.* 6*d.* due for arrears of interest and £6175 for principal in respect of the mortgage debt, the amount recoverable under the Indemnity is not the £3000 plus the arrears of interest, but the £3000 and no more (*Miller* v. *Miller*, cases filed in H. L. Sess. 1886).

As to the phrase "Principal Sum" in a Power of Appointment; *V. Samuda* v. *Lousada,* 7 Bea. 243.

PRIOR INCUMBRANCER.—A judgment creditor is a "Prior Incumbrancer" within the proviso to s. 42, 3 & 4 W. 4, c. 27 (per Ld. St. Leonards in *Henry* v. *Smith*, 2 Dr. & War. 381): but outstanding charges assigned to a trustee for a purchaser of the equity of redemption are not within the exception (*Chinery* v. *Evans*, 11 H. L. Ca. 115); nor is a tenant for life such a "prior incumbrancer" as regards a creditor of a remainderman (*Vincent* v. *Going*, 1 J. & La T. 697).

PRISAGE.—"'Prisage' is that part or portion that belongs to the King of such merchandizes as are taken at sea by way of lawfull prize. And this word you shall finde in the statute of 31 Eliz. c. 5."

"Prisage *of Wines*, mentioned in the statutes of 1 H. 8, c. 5, is a Custome by which the King out of every barke laden with wine under forty Tunne, claimes to have two tun at his own-price." (Termes de la Ley).

PRISON.—*V. Prison Commrs.* v. *Cl. of Peace for Middlesex*, 51 L. J. Q. B. 433; 9 Q. B. D. 506.

PRISON AUTHORITY.—This term first became a *nomen juris* on the passing of the Prison Act, 1865 (per Ld. Watson, *Mullins* v. *Treasurer of Surrey*, 51 L. J. Q. B. 150; 7 App. Ca. 1: and *Vf.* that case hereon).

PRISONER.—A "Prisoner," Prisons Act, 1877 (40 & 41 V. c. 21), is "any person committed to prison on remand, or for trial, safe custody, punishment or otherwise" (s. 57): and such a person does not cease to be a "prisoner" by reason of being removed to a lunatic asylum during the term of punishment (*Mews* v. *The Queen*, 52 L. J. M. C. 57; 8 App. Ca. 339).

V. Maintenance.

A Charity for the "relief or redemption of Prisoners or Captives" (43 Eliz. c. 4)," does not include prisoners for crime, as poachers, *Thrupp* v. *Collett*, 26 Bea. 125. A bequest for such a purpose is against public policy and void" (1 Jarm. 208).

PRIVATE CHARITY.—*V.* Charitable Purposes.

PRIVATE DEBTS.—*V. Re Fleck, Colton* v. *Roberts*, 57 L. J. Ch. 943; 37 Ch. D. 677; 58 L. T. 624; 36 W. R. 663.

PRIVATE DWELLING-HOUSE.—A covenant requiring a house to be used as a "Private" dwelling-house only, is broken by its being used as a school or dancing academy (*Wickenden* v. *Webster*, 25 L. J. Q. B. 264; 6 E. & B. 387), or as an institution for educating the daughters of missionaries, or as a club (*German* v. *Chapman*, 47 L. J. Ch. 250 ; 7 Ch. D. 271 ; 37 L. T. 685 ; 26 W. R. 149), or as an hotel or lodging-house (*Rolls* v. *Miller*, 53 L. J. Ch. 682 ; 27 Ch. D. 71), or by using it as an office for receiving orders, putting a trade-blind in one of the windows, *e.g.*, "Coal Office" (*Wilkinson* v. *Rogers*, 2 D. G. J. & S. 62 ; 10 Jur. N. S. 5, 162 ; 12 W. R. 119, 284 : *Va. Evans* v. *Davies*, 10 Ch. D. 747 ; 48 L. J. Ch. 223 ; 39 L. T. 391 ; 27 W. R. 285) : but a public auction of the furniture of the house is not a breach of such a covenant (*Reeves* v. *Cattell*, 24 W. R. 485. *Vf.* AUCTION).

An art studio erected away from the housé in such a way as not to be an adjunct thereto, is a breach of a covenant that only "private dwelling-houses" shall be erected (*Patman* v. *Harland*, 17 Ch. D. 353 ; 50 L. J. Ch. 642 ; 44 L. T. 728 ; 29 W. R. 707) ; so is the erection of a wall (*Bowes* v. *Law*, L. R. 9 Eq. 636 ; 39 L. J. Ch. 483 ; 22 L. T. 267 ; 18 W. R. 640) ; *secus*, of a stable with a bedroom over it (*Russell* v. *Baber*, 18 W. R. 1021).

V. DWELLING-HOUSE.

PRIVILEGE.—"Privilege, Servitude or Eastment ;" *V. Ramsay* v. *Blair*, 1 App. Ca. 701.

"Right, Power or Privilege ;" *V.* RIGHT.

"'Priviledges' are liberties and franchises granted to an Office, Place, Towne or Mannor, by the King's great charter, letters patents, or Act of Parliament : as Toll, Sake, Socke, Infangtheefe, Outfangtheefe, Turne, Ordelfe, and divers such like" (Termes de la Ley, *Priviledges*).

PRIVY.—*V.* PARTY : Termes de la Ley, *Privie or Privites.*

PRIVY COUNCIL.—*V.* s. 12 (5), Interp. Act, 1889.

PRIVY TO.—*V.* PERMIT.

PROBABLE.—*V.* REASONABLE AND PROBABLE CAUSE : REASONABLE EXPECTATION.

PROCEED TO SEA.—*V. Rodriques* v. *Melhuish*, 10 Ex. 110 : *Wood* v. *Smith*, L. R. 5 P. C. 451 ; 43 L. J. Adm. 11 : *The Cachapool*, 7 P. D. 217.

PROCEED WITH ALL CONVENIENT SPEED.—*V.* CONVENIENT SPEED.

PROCEEDING.—"Any Proceeding," s. 89, Jud. Act, 1873, is equivalent to "any Action," and does not mean any step in an action (*Pryor* v. *City Offices Co.*, 52 L. J. Q. B. 362 ; 10 Q. B. D. 504). But in R. 13, Ord. 64, R. S. C., "Proceeding" is obviously used as meaning a step in an action ; *i.e.*, *semble*, a step "towards," and not "after," judgment (*Houlston* v. *Woodward*, Law Notes, 1885, p. 15).

"Any other Proceeding in the Action," Ord. 26, R. 1, R. S. C., means any Proceeding with a view to continuing the action (*Spincer* v. *Watts*, 58 L. J. Q. B. 383 ; 61 L. T. 711).

"Proceeding," s. 53, Judicature Act (Ireland), 1877 ; *V. Cassidy* v. *O'Loghlen*, 4 L. R. Ir. 731.

An Action is a "Proceeding" within s. 13, 14 & 15 V. c. 99 (*Richardson* v. *Willis*, 42 L. J. Ex. 15 ; L. R. 8 Ex. 69) ; and the word "Proceeding" in s. 6, Ry. & Canal Traffic Act, 1854 (17 & 18 V. c. 31), includes an action (*Manchester, S. & L. Ry.* v. *Denaby Colliery*, 54 L. J. Q. B. 103 ; 14 Q. B. D. 209).

A Counter-Claim is a "Proceeding" within the Condition of a Bond (*Norman* v. *Bolt*, Cab. & El. 77).

"Proceedings," in s. 84, Co. Co. Act, 1888, apply to all Proceedings that may be brought in a Co. Co., including Administration Proceedings (*R.* v. *Bloomsbury Co. Co.*, 24 Q. B. D. 309 ; 34 S. J. 231).

The power given by s. 85, Companies Act, 1862, to restrain "any Action, Suit, or *other Proceeding*" against a Company in liquidation, extends to quasi-criminal Proceedings, *e.g.*, for recovering penalties for neglecting to publish Statement, Form D., or Annual List of Members, or to make yearly statement of revenue (*Re Briton Medical Assrce.*, 55 L. J. Ch. 416 ; 32 Ch. D. 503 ; 54 L. T. 152 ; 34 W. R. 390).

Going to sale under a *fi. fa.* executed by seizure, is a "Proceeding" within the same section (*Re Perkins Beach Lead Mining Co.*, 7 Ch. D. 371 : *Re Artistic Colour Printing Co.*, 49 L. J. Ch. 526 ; 14 Ch. D. 502).

The Taxation of Costs is a "Proceeding" within the phrase, "no actions, suits, executions, attachments, or other proceedings," shall be continued or commenced without leave (*R.* v. *Lond., Chatham & D. Ry.*, L. R. 3 Q. B. 170 ; 37 L. J. Q. B. 75).

A Debtor's Summons, under the Act of 1869, was a "Proceeding" in Bankry (*Ex p. Johnson*, 53 L. J. Ch. 309) ; but Conveyancing business in a Bankry is not a "Proceeding" in it, so as to limit the solicitor's costs by the three-fifths rule, if the assets do not exceed £300 (*Re Parfitt*, 58 L. J. Q. B. 428).

An Arbitration, under Lands C. C. Act, 1845, is not a "Proceeding *in a Court of Justice*," within s. 28, Solicitors Act, 1860, 23 & 24 V. c. 127 (*Macfarlane* v. *Lister*, 57 L. J. Ch. 92 ; 37 Ch. D. 88 ; 58 L. T. 201).

An Examination of a witness, under s. 115, Companies Act, 1862, is not a "Proceeding" in a matter (*Re Grey's Brewery*, 53 L. J. Ch. 262 ; 25 Ch. D. 400 : *Re Norwich Equitable Fire Assrce.*, 54 L. J. Ch. 254) ; nor is a Meeting of creditors for confirming or rejecting a scheme of arrangement of a debtor's affairs, "a Proceeding in Court," within subs. 1, s. 105, Bankry. Act, 1883 (*Re Strand*, 53 L. J. Q. B. 563 ; 13 Q. B. D. 492).

The phrase "other Legal Proceeding," in s. 18, subs. 10, Patents Act, 1883, refers to a proceeding for the revocation of a patent (*Cropper* v. *Smith*, 54 L. J. Ch. 287 ; 28 Ch. D. 148).

A Power of Attorney to commence, &c., "actions, suits, or other Proceedings," confers authority to sign a Bankruptcy Petition (*Ex p. Wallace*, 54 L. J. Q. B. 293 ; 14 Q. B. D. 22) ; and in like manner, the power given to an Official Liquidator (s. 95, Comp. Act, 1862), to bring or defend "any action, suit, or prosecution, or other legal Proceeding," includes the power to serve a Bankry Notice (*Re Winterbottom*, 56 L. J. Q. B. 238 ; 18 Q. B. D. 446 ; 56 L. T. 168).

A "*Criminal* Proceeding" is a far larger term than "Criminal Prosecution" (*Yates* v. *The Queen*, 54 L. J. Q. B. 258 ; 14 Q. B. D. 648).

V. Action : Criminal Cause : Pending.

"Proceeding *in the Cause;*" *V. Ball* v. *Stanley*, 9 L. J. Ex. 161 ; 6 M. & W. 398.

"Proceeding," s. 7, Friendly Societies Act, 1858, 21 & 22 V. c. 101 ; *V. Roberts* v. *Page*, 45 L. J. Q. B. 601 ; 1 Q. B. D. 476.

Proceedings by Poor Law Guardians against a husband, to compel him to maintain a child which, although born of his wife in wedlock, he refuses to maintain, on the ground that he is not its father, are not "Proceedings instituted in *consequence of Adultery*," within s. 3, Evidence Further Amendment Act, 1869, 32 & 33 V. c. 68 (*Nottingham* v. *Tomkinson*, 4 C. P. D. 343 ; 48 L. J. M. C. 171). *V.* Instituted.

PROCEEDS.—Money paid under protest is the "Proceeds" of goods and chattels taken under a *fi. fa.* within Ord. 57, R. 1 b, R. S. C. (*Smith* v. *Critchfield*, 54 L. J. Q. B. 366 ; 14 Q. B. D. 873).

"Proceeds of such Sale," s. 1, 9 Anne (Ireland), c. 8 ; *V. Re M'Carthy*, 7 L. R. Ir. 473 : *Davidson* v. *Allen*, 20 Ib. 16.

V. Rents and Profits : Sale.

PROCESS.—"'Proces' are the writs and precepts that go upon the originall . . . . But in actions personals, as in Debt, Trespasse or Detinue, the Processe is a distresse" (Termes de la Ley, *Proces*).

"Process" is the doing of something in a proceeding in a civil or criminal Court ; and that which may be done without the aid of a Court is not a "Process." Therefore, a distraint, whether for rent or any other payment, and whether the right of distress be given by the Common Law or Statute (or, as it should seem, by any other authority), is not a "Process," nor is it "an Execution or other Legal Process" within s. 13, Bankry. Act, 1869, or within the substituted section (s. 10) of the Bankry. Act, 1883 (*Blackamore's Case*, 8 Rep. 157 a : *R.* v. *Crisp*, 1 B. & Ald. 287 : 3 Bla. Com. 3, 6, 7 : *Ex p. Birmingham & Staffordshire Gas Co., Re Fanshaw*, 40 L. J. Bank. 52 ; L. R. 11 Eq. 615 : *Re Peake, Ex p. Harrison*, 53 L. J. Ch. 977 ; 13 Q. B. D. 753) : but a Writ of Sequestration is such a

Process (*Re Browne*, 40 L. J. Bank. 46 ; nom. *Ex p. Hughes*, L. R. 12 Eq. 137).

V. Practice.

"All the steps taken in an execution—the seizure and the sale—are, in the natural meaning of the word, comprehended in the term 'Process'" (per Lynch, J., *Re Delahoyd*, 11 Ir. Ch. Rep. 407).

A mere notice, though headed with the name of a County Court, is not a "Process" within s. 57, 9 & 10 V. c. 95 (*R.* v. *Castle*, 30 L. T. 188) ; but such a notice, especially if it also has the Royal Arms and (without authority) professes to bear the signature of the Registrar, is a "False Colour or Pretence" of such "Process" (*R.* v. *Evans*, 26 L. J. M. C. 92 ; Dears. & B. 236 : *R.* v. *Richmond*, 28 L. J. M. C. 188).

A Trader-Debtor's Summons was not a "Process" (*Re Dobson*, 8 Ir. Ch. Rep. 391), nor an Adjudication in Bankruptcy thereon (*Re Kerr*, 1 L. R. Ir. 67 : *Re M'Veigh*, 5 Ib. 177) ; nor is a Petition in Bankruptcy (*Ex p. Walker*, *Re Haywood*, 6 D. G. M. & G. 752 : *Ex p. Treherne*, *Re Saunders*, 2 D. G. F. & J. 661 : *Ex p. Hills*, 3 D. G. & J. 476, n.).

PROCURATION.—*V.* Per Procuration.

PROCURE.—Gifts, &c., "to endeavour to procure the return" of a Member of Parliament, s. 2, subs. 3, 17 & 18 V. c. 102, are Bribery, though given only on a test ballot, and to secure a person being adopted as the candidate of a particular party (*Britt* v. *Robinson*, L. R. 5 C. P. 503 ; 23 L. T. 188 ; nom. *Brett* v. *Robinson*, 39 L. J. C. P. 265).

"Procure himself to be arrested, or his goods, &c., attached, sequestered, or taken in execution," 6 G. 4, c. 16, s. 3 ; 12 & 13 V. c. 106, s. 67 :—This old Act of Bankruptcy imported an intent *on the part of the alleged bankrupt* to defeat or delay his creditors, and did not include a *fi. fa.* on a default judgment (*Gibson* v. *King*, C. & M. 458), or on a Warrant of Attorney (*Gore* v. *Lloyd*, 12 M. & W. 463 ; 13 L. J. Ex. 366). In the latter case Abinger, C.B., said,—"It might just as well be argued, that any step which any defendant voluntarily takes in a cause, is a procuring of the judgment and execution against him, as that the giving of this warrant of attorney, and the entering up judgment upon it, was a procuring by this person of his goods to be taken in execution."

Commission on Loan "procured ;" *V. Fisher* v. *Drewett*, 48 L. J. Ex. 32 : *Green* v. *Lucas*, 33 L. T. 584.

V. Cause or Procure : Counsel or Procure.

PROCUREMENT.—*V.* Acts.

PRODUCE.—"The 'Produce' of *Capital* employed in Trade is, all that the Capital produces ; *i.e.*, whether in the shape of interest or profits allowed" (per Wood, V.-C., *Johnston* v. *Moore*, 27 L. J. Ch. 455, 456) ;

and accordingly a direction to pay to A. for life "the Rents, Dividends, and Produce" of an estate consisting partly of Capital in a partnership, will give to A. the profits on that Capital, so long as the Capital is properly employed in the business of partnership (Ib.: *Howe* v. *Dartmouth*, 7 Ves. 137). *V.* INTEREST.

In a *Charter-Party* containing an agreement to ship at A. "a full cargo of Produce," "Produce" means "anything produced by the country in the neighbourhood of the port of lading, and being an ordinary subject of importation" (per Maule, J., *Warren* v. *Peabody*, 19 L. J. C. P. 46; 8 C. B. 800).

PRODUCE OF MINES.—"The expression 'Produce' of Mines or Minerals does not necessarily mean Produce in its native state: Coke may be such Produce, although by combustion its chemical nature is changed" (MacS. 19, citing *Bowes* v. *Ravensworth*, 15 C. B. 518, 523; 24 L. J. C. P. 73; 3 W. R. 241; 24 L. T. O. S. 257).

PRODUCT.—"Corn, Grass, *or other Product*" growing on land, 11 G. 2, c. 19; young trees are not distrainable under these words (*Clark* v. *Gaskarth*, 8 Taunt. 431). *V.* OTHER.

"*Plant*, Root, Fruit or *Vegetable Production* growing in a garden, orchard, nursery-ground, hot-house or conservatory," s. 42, 7 & 8 G. 4, c. 29, does not include young fruit trees (*R.* v. *Hodges*, Moo. & M. 341).

PROFANENESS.—"Profaneness" in 21 G. 3, c. 49, is used in the classical sense of "non-religious" (per Denman, as Counsel, in *Baxter* v. *Langley*, 38 L. J. M. C. 5).

PROFESSED EXERCISE.—*V.* PURPORTING.

PROFESSED GAMBLER.—"The phrase 'Professed Gambler' would not, *per se*, be actionable" (per Watson, B., *Barnett* v. *Allen*, 27 L. J. Ex. 412; 3 H. & N. 376; 31 L. T. O. S. 217). *V.* BLACK.

PROFESSED IN RELIGION.—*V.* ENTERED IN RELIGION.

PROFESSION.—*V.* CARRY ON.

PROFESSIONAL CHARGES.—In a clause that a Solicitor Trustee may make "the Usual Professional Charges,"—though accompanied by a special direction that he shall be entitled to the same remuneration for all business done, attendances, time, and trouble as if (not being a Trustee) he were employed by the Trustees,—the Solicitor Trustee is only entitled to charge for business of a strictly professional character (*Re Chapple, Newton* v. *Chapman*, 27 Ch. D. 584). But where a testator directed that a Solicitor Trustee might make "the Usual Professional, or other proper and reasonable charges for all business done and time expended in relation to the trusts of the Will, whether such business should be usually within the business of a Solicitor or not;" held, that a Solicitor Trustee might charge for business not strictly of a professional character (*Re Ames, Ames* v. *Taylor*, 25 Ch. D. 72).

PROFIT.—As to phrase "Sewers made by any person for his *Own Profit*," &c., s. 13, P. H. Act, 1875; *V. Acton* v. *Batten*, 54 L. J. Ch. 251; 28 Ch. D. 283: *Bonella* v. *Twickenham*, 57 L. J. M. C. 1; 20 Q. B. D. 63; 58 L. T. 299; 36 W. R. 50; 52 J. P. 356.

V. PROFITS.

PROFIT À PRENDRE.—The leading case on whether a grant is (1) a Personal License of Pleasure, or (2) a Profit à Prendre, is *Norfolk* v. *Wiseman*, Year Book, 12 Hen. 7, 25; 13 Hen. 7, 13, pl. 2: *Vh. Wickham* v. *Hawker*, 10 L. J. Ex. 153; 7 M. & W. 72. *V.* FREE LIBERTY: HUNTING: SERVANTS.

PROFIT CHARGES.—*V.* USUAL AGENCY TERMS.

PROFITABLE.—*V.* BENEFICIAL.

PROFITS.—The Profits of a Company are not such sum as may remain after the payment of every debt, but are the excess of ordinary receipts over expenses properly chargeable to revenue account (*Mills* v. *Northern Ry. of Buenos Ayres Co.*, 5 Ch. 621, 631: *Vh. Birch* v. *Cropper, Re Bridgewater Nav.*, 14 App. Ca. 525: *Lee* v. *Neuchatel Co.*, 58 L. J. Ch. 409; Buckl. 486; which latter *V.* as to working out a profit and loss account).

So under the Income Tax Act (5 & 6 V. c. 35, ss. 60–100), the "Profits" assessable "is the amount got from the property (or business) *minus* the cost of getting it" (per Jessel, M.R., *Mersey Docks* v. *Lucas*, 51 L. J. Q. B. 116; 32 W. R. 34: *Vf. Erichsen* v. *Last*, 51 L. J. Q. B. 86; 8 Q. B. D. 414: *Russell* v. *Town and County Bank*, 58 L. J. P. C. 8). The decision in *Mersey Docks* v. *Lucas* also laid down that excess of earnings over expenditure was "Profits," even though such excess had to be applied in reduction of a past debt. Nor (apart from express exemption) is it material, for the purpose of the Income Tax, that the "Profit" is earned by a Public Company, or by a Board—(*e.g.*, Burial Board)—on behalf of parochial ratepayers (*Mersey Docks* v. *Lucas*, 51 L. J. Q. B. 114; 53 Ib. 4; 8 App. Ca. 891: *Paddington Burial Board* v. *Inl. Rev.*, 53 L. J. Q. B. 224; 13 Q. B. D. 9), or by a Hospital charging its richer, for the benefit of its poorer, patients (*St. Andrew's Hosp.* v. *Shearsmith*, 31 S. J. 608). After a remarkable conflict of judicial opinion, and ultimately by the decision of the H. L. (Lords Blackburn and Fitzgerald; Lord Bramwell diss.), it has been ruled that bonuses by an Insurance Company to participating policy-holders are "Profits" chargeable with Income Tax (*Last* v. *London Assrce.*, 55 L. J. Q. B. 92; 10 App. Ca. 438; 32 W. R. 233: *Svth. New York Insrce.* v. *Styles*, 14 App. Ca. 381; 61 L. T. 201. *Va. Mersey Loan Co.* v. *Wootton*, 4

Times Rep. 164 : *Gresham Assrce.* v. *Styles*, 24 Q. B. D. 500). *V.* CARRY ON, p. 109 : ELSEWHERE.

As to interest on a Company's Investments ; *V. Clerical Med. & Gen. Insrce.* v. *Carter*, 58 L. J. Q. B. 224 ; 22 Q. B. D. 444 ; 37 W. R. 346.

V. POSSESSION.

In the case of Mines the cost of sinking pits is not, generally speaking, deductible from the gross Profits (*Coltness Co.* v. *Black*, 51 L. J. Q. B. 626 ; 6 App. Ca. 315) ; nor repayments out of royalties in respect of antecedent losses (*Broughton Co.* v. *Kirkpatrick*, 54 L. J. Q. B. 268 ; 14 Q. B. D. 491).

Costs of collecting are not deductible from Manorial Rates and Dues (*Norfolk* v. *Lamarque*, 24 Q. B. D. 485 ; 59 L. J. Q. B. 119 ; 34 S. J. 196).

An allowance from the Curates' Augmentation Fund is not "Profits or Gains" assessable to Income Tax (*Turner* v. *Cuxson*, 58 L. J. Q. B. 131 ; 22 Q. B. D. 150).

When trustees, under the powers of a Will, postpone the sale of their testator's business, the net profits realized by their carrying on the business will belong to the person to whom "the Rents, *Profits*, and Income" of the testator's estate are, by the Will, to be paid during postponement of conversion (*Re Chancellor*, 53 L. J. Ch. 443 ; 26 Ch. D. 42).

"Profits" of a Partnership include the rise in value of Partnership Assets (*Robinson* v. *Ashton*, 44 L. J. Ch. 542 ; L. R. 20 Eq. 25).

"If a man seised of lands in fee, by his deed granteth to another the 'profit' of those lands, to have and to hold to him and his heires, and maketh livery *secundum formam chartæ*, the whole land itself doth passe ; for what is the land but the profits thereof ; for thereby vesture, herbage, trees, mines, and all whatsoever parcel of that land doth passe" (Co. Litt. 4 b).

But a Bequest of the Profits of Leaseholds was held to pass only the profits accruing from the death of the testator (*Tissen* v. *Tissen*, 1 P. Wms. 503).

In *Gordon* v. *Rutherford* (T. & R. 373 ; 2 L. J. O. S. Ch. 50) a direction as to a son sharing in the Profits of testator's business was held not to be operative until after the son was admitted to partnership in the business.

In an Order, against an innocent occupier, to account for "*Rents and Profits*," the latter word means, profits in the nature of rent and as arising from the land, and not such profits as may have been made by carrying on a business,—*e.g.*, a colliery,—upon the land (*Re Morewood, Errington* v. *Morewood*, 29 S. J. 320 ; W. N. (85) 51).

V. ADVANTAGES : GAINS : RENTS AND PROFITS : OUT OF THE PROFITS : IN RECEIPT.

PROHIBITED.—A Penalty on smuggling "Prohibited" goods, may extend to goods prohibited by a subsequent statute (*A.-G.* v. *Saggers*, 1 Price, 182). *Cp.* "Convicted of Felony," sub CONVICTED : FELON.

PROHIBITED DEGREES.—The "prohibited degrees of consanguinity or affinity" within which marriages are now absolutely void by s. 2, 5 & 6 W. 4, c. 54, are those enumerated in 25 H. 8, c. 22, and 28 H. 8, c. 7 (*R.* v. *Chadwick*, 17 L. J. M. C. 33; 11 Q. B. 173).

PROLONGED EXAMINATION.—"Cause or matter requiring any *Prolonged Examination* of documents or accounts, or any *Scientific* or *Local Investigation*," s. 57, Jud. Act, 1873; s. 14 (*b*), Arbitration Act, 1889;—An action to recover Damages for abstracting and heating water from a river is not within these words (*Ormerod* v. *Todmorden Mill Co.*, 51 L. J. Q. B. 348; 8 Q. B. D. 667); nor, speaking generally, is an action for Constructive Total Loss of a Vessel (*Hamilton* v. *Merchant Mar. Insrce.*, 58 L. J. Q. B. 544): but a complicated Builder's Bill, wherein many items are disputed, is within them (*Ward* v. *Pilley*, 49 L. J. Q. B. 705; 5 Q. B. D. 427).

PROMISSORY NOTE.—"A Promissory Note is an Unconditional Promise in Writing made by one person to another, signed by the maker, engaging to pay, ON DEMAND, or at a fixed or DETERMINABLE FUTURE TIME, a SUM CERTAIN in money to, or to the order of, a specified person, or to bearer" (s. 83, *Bills of Ex. Act*, 1882). That section further provides that,

"An instrument in the form of a Note payable to maker's order is not a Note within the meaning of this section unless and until it is indorsed by the maker.

"A Note is not invalid by reason only that it contains also a pledge of collateral security with authority to sell or dispose thereof."

The provisions of the Act relating to Bills of Exchange apply, generally, to Promissory Notes (s. 89).

Cp. BILL OF EXCHANGE.

"The term 'Promissory Note' means and includes any document or writing (except a bank-note) containing a promise to pay any sum of money" (s. 49 (1), *Stamp Act*, 1870). A document is not within that definition unless it contains a promise to pay a definite and ascertained sum of money, which promise is substantially the whole contents of the document (*Mortgage Insrce.* v. *Inl. Rev.*, 57 L. J. Q. B. 630; 21 Q. B. D. 352; 36 W. R. 833).

PROMOTER.—"First, Cockburn, C.J., in *Twycross* v. *Grant* (46 L. J. C. P. 636; 2 C. P. D. 469), defined a Promoter to be 'one who undertakes to form a Company with reference to a given project, and to set it going, and who takes the necessary steps to accomplish that purpose.' Bowen, L.J., in *Whaley Bridge Printing Co.* v. *Green* (49 L. J. Q. B. 326: 5 Q. B. D. 109), says,—'The term, Promoter, is a term not of law but of business, usefully summing up in a single word a number of business operations, familiar to the commercial world, by which a Company is generally brought into existence.' Then Lindley, L.J., in *Emma Silver Mining Co.* v. *Lewis* (48 L. J. C. P. 504 ; 4 C. P. D. 396), says,—'With respect to the word Promoter, we are of opinion that it has no very definite meaning. As used in connection with Companies the term, Promoter, involves the idea of exertion for the purpose of getting up and starting a Company, or what is called floating it, *and also the idea of some duty towards the Company imposed by or arising from the position which the so-called Promoter assumes towards it.*' All this is by no means satisfactory" (per Bacon, V.-C., *Re Great Wheal Polgooth Co.*, 53 L. J. Ch. 46 ; 49 L. T. 20 ; 32 W. R. 107 ; 47 J. P. 710). Referring to the passage in the judgment of Lindley, L.J., which is italicised in the above extract, the V.-C. went on to observe, "That is the most satisfactory of all these varying definitions that I have been able to find."

Vf. Buckl. 542 : *Lydney Iron Co.* v. *Bird*, 55 L. J. Ch. 387 ; 33 Ch. D. 85 ; 55 L. T. 558 ; 34 W. R. 749 : *Re Coal Economising Gas Co*, 44 L. J Ch. 323 ; 1 Ch. D. 182 : *Rooney* v. *Palmer*, 9 Ir. L. R. 327.

"'The Promoters of the Undertaking,' shall mean the parties (whether Company, Undertakers, Commissioners, Trustees, Corporations, or Private Persons) by the Special Act empowered to execute the Works or Undertaking" (s. 2, Lands C. C. Act, 1845).

"Promoters," of a Tramway, s. 42, Tramways Act, 1870, 33 & 34 V. c. 78 ; *V. Re Pontypridd Tramways Co.*, 58 L. J. Ch. 536.

PROMOTION MONEY.—*V.* Formation Expenses.

PROMOTION OF.—*V.* Godly Learning.

PROMPT DISPATCH.—"Prompt Dispatch in loading," in a Charter-party ; *V. Elliott* v. *Lord*, 52 L. J. P. C. 23.

PROOF.—The 17 V. No. 22 (New South Wales), s. 1, provides, whenever a person executing a Power of Attorney, declares that such Power shall continue in force until notice of his death or of revocation shall have been received by the Attorney, then a Solemn Declaration by the Attorney that he has not received notice of revocation, by death or otherwise, shall, if made immediately before or after acting, "be Conclusive Proof of such non-revocation" in favour of a purchaser for value without notice ; that means, that such Declaration is Conclusive Proof of non-revocation, in favour of such a purchaser, even though the Attorney had notice of revocation at the time of acting on the Power (*Mutual Provident Socy.* v. *Macmillan*, 59 L. J. P. C. 22). *Cp.* ss. 8, 9, Conv. Act, 1882.

PROPER.—"Shall think proper ;"—*V.* May ; *Va.* jdgmt. Cockburn, C. J., *S. E. Ry.* v. *Ry. Commrs.*,'49 L. J. Q. B. 289 ; 5 Q. B. D. 217 : *Sv.* same case reversed on App. 6 Q. B. D. 586.

V. Reasonable and Proper.

PROPER AND WORKMANLIKE.—A covenant, in a Mining Lease, to work in "a Proper and Workmanlike Manner," though open to parol evidence to explain its local meaning, does not, *primâ facie,* mean in such a manner only as shall be most advantageous to the lessor ; "but it means in such a manner as shall not be simply an attempt to get out of the earth as much mineral as can be got for the particular purpose of the lessee, regardless of any ordinary or workmanlike proceeding" (per Hatherley, L. C., *Lewis* v. *Fothergill,* 5 Ch. 108).

PROPER CLAUSES AND POWERS.—The phrase "Proper *Clauses*" in an *Agreement for a Lease* does not seem quite synonymous with "Usual Clauses." In *Edie* v. *Addison* (52 L. J. Ch. 82, 83), Pearson, J., said,—"Then it is said that the word is 'proper,' not 'usual.' But that argument seems to me to have great weight on behalf of the plaintiff; because a clause against underletting *which might have been proper with regard to a publican to whom the house was to be let,* would be manifestly improper with regard to Mr. Eadie, who was known to be a brewer and to have no intention whatever of going into the trade of a publican." Accordingly specific performance of an agreement to lease, with "proper clauses," a Public-house to a Brewer who it was known was not going to occupy it himself, was decreed without a clause against underletting. But could such a clause be insisted on even if the intended lessee were an occupying publican ? Can "proper" in such a case really be distinguished from "usual" ?

V. Usual, and especially the cases of *Church* v. *Brown,* and *Hodgkinson* v. *Crowe* there cited.

A power to appoint New Trustees is "a Proper and Reasonable *Power*" (*Lindow* v. *Fleetwood,* 6 Sim. 152) ; but a power of Sale or Exchange is not (Lewin, 128, 129, citing *Brewster* v. *Angell,* 1 Jac. & W. 625 : *Horne* v. *Barton,* Jac. 437). *Vf.* as to "Proper Powers" in a Settlement, Settled Land Act, 1882, ss. 3, 4, 6, *et seq.* ; Conv. & L. P. Act, 1881, ss. 42, 66 : and *Vth.* Lewin, 129.

V. Necessary.

PROPER CONTROL.—*V.* Control.

PROPER CUSTODY.—Of Documents ; *V.* Taylor on Evidence, ss. 659–667.

PROPER ENTAIL.—As to effect of direction for "a Proper Entail ;" *V.* Lewin, 118.

PROPER MIXTURE.—A proviso exonerating a Lessee of Iron Mines from working them if the iron-stone therein found will not "with a Proper Mixture," make good common pig-iron, does not mean that the "Proper Mixture" should necessarily be procurable on the premises (*Foley* v. *Addenbrooke*, 14 L. J. Ex. 169 ; 13 M. & W. 174).

PROPER PARTY.—"Necessary or Proper Party to an Action," Ord. 11, R. 1 (*g*), R. S. C. ; *V. Massey* v. *Heynes*, 21 Q. B. D. 330 ; 57 L. J. Q. B. 521 ; 36 W. R. 834 : *Sykes* v. *Scholfield*, 28 S. J. 477 : Ann. Pr.

PROPERTY.—"Property" is the generic term for all that a person has dominion over. Its two leading divisions are (1) Real and (2) Personal ; *Vh.* Mr. Joshua Williams' treatises on these two topics.

But care must be taken to distinguish between "Property" and "Power." "The power of a person to appoint an estate to himself, is no more his 'Property' than the power to write a book or to sing a song" (per Fry, L. J., *Re Armstrong*, 55 L. J. Q. B. 579).

"'Property,' is the most comprehensive of all terms which can be used, inasmuch as it is indicative and descriptive of every possible interest which the party can have" (per Langdale, M.R., *Jones* v. *Skinner*, 5 L. J. Ch. 90). *Vf. Morrison* v. *Hoppe*, 4 D. G. & S. 234 ; 15 Jur. 737.

A gift by Will of all the testator's "Property" will pass everything belonging to him at his death (or over which he had a general power of appointment, 1 V. c. 26, s. 27) whether real or personal property (per Knight Bruce, L. J., *Tyrone* v. *Waterford*, 29 L. J. Ch. 486 ; 1 D. G. F. & J. 613) : and in that case it was decided that a testamentary gift of "all my property in the County of N——" passed debts due to testator in respect of collieries in that county. Even such a collocation as a bequest of moneys at a bank and "all my wines *and property*" does not narrow down the latter word to things *ejusdem generis* (*Arnold* v. *Arnold*, 4 L. J. Ch. 123 ; 2 My. & K. 365 : *Va. Gover* v. *Davis*, 30 L. J. Ch. 505 ; 29 Bea. 222). But a bequest of "*Personal Estate and Property*" whatsoever and wheresoever, was held by Wood, V.-C., not to pass realty (*Buchanan* v. *Harrison*, 31 L. J. Ch. 74 ; 1 J. & H. 662 : *Va. Belaney* v. *Belaney*, 36 L. J. Ch. 265 ; 35 Bea. 469 ; 2 Ch. 138). *Vf.* 1 Jarm. 728 ; Wms. Exs. 1189, 1190. *V.* All : In.

As to the word "Property" in s. 2, *Sucn. Dy. Act* ; *V. Re Cigala*, 47 L. J. Ch. 166 ; 7 Ch. D. 351 : *Colquhoun* v. *Brooks*, 14 App. Ca. 493 ; 61 L. T. 518.

For the present definition of "Property" for the purposes of *Bankruptcy* ; *V.* Bankry. Act, 1883, ss. 44, 168. That will include (and will empower the Trustee to sell), a Bankrupt's claim to have an absolute conveyance set aside and declared to be only a security (*Seear* v. *Lawson*, 49 L. J. Bank. 69 ; 15 Ch. D. 426). So it includes a husband's interest in a wife's *chose in action* which he has not reduced into possession (*Re Biaggi*, 26 S. J. 417); also the Pension of a retired Civil Servant (*Re Huggins*, 51 L. J. Ch. 935; 21 Ch. D. 85). Nor is the power to disclaim, given to Trustees by s. 55, Bankry. Act, 1883, confined to property divisible amongst creditors (*Re Maughan*, 54 L. J. Q. B. 128; 14 Q. B. D. 956).

But not even the wide definitions of the Bankruptcy law will comprise as "Property," the future receipts in a person's business (*Ex p. Nichols*, 52 L. J. Ch. 635; 22 Ch. D. 782: *Sv. Re Toward*, 14 Q. B. D. 310; 54 L. J. Q. B. 126: *Re Davis, Ex p. Rawlings*, 22 Q. B. D. 193).

Alimony is not "Property" within s. 25, 20 & 21 V. c. 85 (*Re Robinson*, 53 L. J. Ch. 986; 27 Ch. D. 160): but a gross or annual sum ordered under s. 32 of that Act (as the order cannot be subsequently withdrawn or modified) is "Property" (*Harrison* v. *Harrison*, 58 L. J. P. D. & A. 28); and an allowance to a wife under a deed of separation, is her "property" within s. 45 of that Act, so that on her adultery the Court may deal with it (*Jump* v. *Jump*, 52 L. J. P. D. & M. 71; 8 P. D. 159).

Unpaid Capital in a Joint Stock Company is not within a power enabling the Directors to mortgage "Property" of the Co. (*Bank of S. Australia* v. *Abrahams*, 44 L. J. P. C. 76; L. R. 6 P. C. 265); *secus*, if the power extends to a Co.'s "Property *and Rights*" (*Howard* v. *Patent Ivory Co.*, 38 Ch. D. 156). *Vf.* Buckl. 151.

"Property," in a Company's Debenture, includes all the Company's property except future calls (*Bower* v. *Foreign & Col. Gas Co.*, W. N. (77) 222).

"Property in the Goods," mentioned in Bill of Lading; *V.* PASS.

"Property held in trust;" *V.* IN TRUST.

"Property vested under" P. H. Act, 1875; *V.* VESTED.

V. SEPARATE PROPERTY: CIVIL RIGHTS: BENEFIT: RECOVERED OR PRESERVED: THE.

PROPERTY AND EFFECTS.—The "Property and Effects" of a business do not include its Goodwill (*Chapman* v. *Hayman*, 1 Times Rep. 397). *V.* EFFECTS: STOCK IN TRADE.

PROPERTY NOT REDUCED INTO MONEY.—*V.* REDUCED INTO MONEY.

PROPERTY OTHER THAN LAND.—"Houses, Buildings and Property *other than land*," s. 33, 3 & 4 W. 4, c. 90;—neither a Railway, a Canal with its towing paths, nor a Dry Dock is within this phrase (*R.* v. *Neath Canal Nav.*, 40 L. J. M. C. 193; nom. *R.* v. *Neath*, L. R. 6 Q. B. 707, discussing *Peto* v. *West Ham*, 28 L. J. M. C. 240; 2 E. & E. 144).

PROPERTY RECOVERED.—*V.* RECOVERED OR PRESERVED.

PROPRIETOR.—In a sale of property for "the Proprietor" (*Sale* v. *Lambert*, 43 L. J. Ch. 470; L. R. 18 Eq. 1; 22 W. R. 478: *Rossiter*

v. *Miller*, 48 L. J. Ch. 10 ; 3 App. Ca. 1124 ; 39 L. T. 173 ; 26 W. R. 865), or for the "Owner," "Mortgagee," or the like (*Jarrett* v. *Hunter*, 56 L. J. Ch. 141 ; 34 Ch. D. 182 ; 55 L. T. 727 ; 35 W. R. 132), or for "the Executor or Personal Representative of A." (*Towle* v. *Topham*, 37 L. T. 308), or for "a Trustee selling under a trust for sale" (*Catling* v. *King*, 46 L. J. Ch. 384 ; 5 Ch. D. 660 ; 36 L. T. 526 ; 25 W. R. 550 : *Va. Bourdillon* v. *Collins*, 19 W. R. 556 ; 24 L. T. 344), or "by direction of the Executors" of a person named (*Hood* v. *Barrington*, L. R. 6 Eq. 218), the description of the vendor is sufficient to satisfy the Statute of Frauds though he be not named ; "but if he is described as 'Vendor,' or as 'Client' or 'Friend' of a named agent, that is not sufficient" (per Kay, J., *Jarrett* v. *Hunter*, sup. : *Vf. Potter* v. *Duffield*, 43 L. J. Ch. 472 ; L. R. 18 Eq. 4 ; 22 W. R. 585 : and jdgmt. of Mellish, L. J., *Catling* v. *King*, sup.). But the description is sufficient if it be for "Vendors" who are described as "a Company in possession of and carrying on mining operations on the property" (*Commins* v. *Scott*, 44 L. J. Ch. 563 ; L. R. 20 Eq. 11 ; 32 L. T. 420 ; 23 W. R. 498).

As to who is the "Proprietor" of a *Design* within s. 61, Patents, Designs and Trade Marks Act, 1883 (46 & 47 V. c. 57) ; *V. Re Guiterman*, 55 L. J. Ch. 309 : "Proprietor" of a *Patent*, s. 87, Ib. ; *V. Van Gelder* v. *Sowerby Bridge Socy.*, 62 L. T. 105.

Proprietor of a *Newspaper ; V.* s. 1, 44 & 45 V. c. 60.

V. OWNER.

PROSECUTE.—To "Prosecute" a Suit or Matter,—that is, begin to prosecute (per Denman, C. J., *Morris* v. *Matthews*, 11 L. J. Q. B. 57 ; 2 Q. B. 293). So to "make and prosecute" an application for a new trial, s. 27, 4 & 5 W. 4, c. 62, was satisfied by obtaining a Rule *nisi*, whatever afterwards became of the Rule (*Haworth* v. *Ormerod*, 13 L. J. Q. B. 265 ; 6 Q. B. 300).

To prosecute an Action for Infringement of a Patent "with Due Diligence," proviso to s. 32, 46 & 47 V. c. 57, does not necessarily require that the action should be carried on to trial (*Colley* v. *Hart*, W. N. (90) 46 ; 34 S. J. 282).

To "prosecute *with Effect*,"—that is, to prosecute to a not unsuccessful termination. *V.* EFFECT.

To "prosecute *with Effect*," an application for extension of time for a Patent, 5 & 6 W. 4, c. 83, s. 4 ; *V. Russell* v. *Ledsam*, 12 L. J. Ex. 439 ; 14 Ib. 353 ; 16 Ib. 145 ; 14 M. & W. 574 ; 16 Ib. 633 ; 1 H. L. Ca. 687.

To "prosecute *without Delay*," is to use due diligence in the business (*Harrison* v. *Wardle*, 5 B. & Ad. 146).

PROSECUTION.—A criminal information for libel, whether *ex officio* or not, is not a "Criminal Prosecution" within s. 3, Newspaper Libel and Registration Act, 1881, 44 & 45 V. c. 60 (*Yates* v. *The Queen*, 54 L. J. Q. B. 258 ; 14 Q. B. D. 648).

"*Such* Prosecution," s. 95, 5 & 6 W. 4, c. 50, means a Prosecution which Justices have power to order, and which is the one which they have actually ordered; and the power given by the section to award costs, cannot be exercised where the Indictment ordered was for non-repair of a general highway, and was amended at the trial so as to charge in respect only of a limited highway (*R.* v. *Lee,* 45 L. J. M. C. 54; 1 Q. B. D. 198).

PROTEST.—*V.* UNDER PROTEST.

PROTESTANT DISSENTERS.—This phrase now includes Unitarians (1 Jarm. 206, n.).

A bequest to "Protestant Dissenters" may be explained by parol (*Drummond* v. *A.-G. of Ireland,* 2 H. L. Ca. 837).

PROVABLE.—"Debt provable in Bankruptcy;" *V.* DEBT.

PROVE.—"To Prove" a thing is to test it, or (when spoken of a legal conclusion) to establish it by litigation; therefore to say of a man's patent that it "has been *proved* to be an infringement" of another patent is actionable, if there has been no litigation under which such infringement has been established (*Crampton* v. *Swete,* 32 S. J. 274; 58 L. T. 516).

"*Admitted or Proved,*" s. 30 (2), Bills of Ex. Act, 1882, "means no more than that some evidence of circumstances in the nature of the fraud, must be given sufficient to be left to the jury" (per Denman, J., *Tatam* v. *Hasler,* 23 Q. B. D. 345; 38 W. R. 110; 58 L. J. Q. B. 432).

PROVIDE.—A bequest to be applied in "*Providing* a proper school" is good, as not necessarily involving the acquisition of land (*Johnston* v. *Swann,* 3 Mad. 457: 1 Jarm. 228, 229). *Cp.* FOUND: ENDOW: ERECT.

"Provide, Furnish or Supply" goods for parochial relief (s. 6, 55 G. 3, c. 137; s. 77, 4 & 5 W. 4, c. 76); *V. Davies* v. *Harvey,* 43 L. J. M. C. 121; L. R. 9 Q. B. 433.

PROVIDE SUITABLY.—"It has been held, in Marriage Articles, that a trust to 'provide suitably' for the settlor's younger children is not too vague to be executed, but the Court will direct an enquiry what the provision should be" (Lewin, 117, citing *Brenan* v. *Brenan,* I. R. 2 Eq. 266).

PROVIDED.—*V.* WHEN: CONDITION.

PROVIDED ALWAYS.—"If a man by Indenture letteth lands for yeeres, Provided alwaies, and it is covenanted and agreed between the said parties that the lessee should not alien; and it was adjudged that this was a condition by force of the *proviso,* and a covenant by force of the other words" (Co. Litt. 203 b: *Vf.* Touch. 122; Elph. 411). But in *Brookes* v.

Drysdale (3 C. P. D. 52 ; 26 W. R. 331), it was held that, in a Lease, the words "Provided always, and these presents are upon this express condition," of themselves, amounted to a Covenant. *V.* PROVISO.

But generally the words "Provided Always" refer to, and qualify what has preceded (*Martelli* v. *Holloway*, L. R. 5 H. L. 532 ; 42 L. J. Ch. 26).

PROVIDED THE FUNDS PERMIT.—These words in the withdrawal clause of a Building Society, do not deprive a member who has given Notice of Withdrawal of his right of priority over other members, in case of a liquidation after the Notice has expired (*Walton* v. *Edge*, 54 L. J. Ch. 362 ; 10 App. Ca. 33,—distinguishing *The Mutual Socy.*, 24 Ch. D. 425 n., and explaining *Blackburn Bg. Socy.* v. *Cunliffe*, 52 L. J. Ch. 92 ; 22 Ch. D. 61).

PROVIDING COVERS.—*V.* COVERS.

PROVISIONAL COMMITTEE.—A Provisional Committee is an association formed for carrying into effect the preliminary arrangements necessary to promote a scheme ; it is not a partnership, for it constitutes no agreement to share in profit or loss (*Reynell* v. *Lewis*, 15 M. & W. 526 ; 16 L. J. Ex. 25).

V. COMMITTEE.

PROVISIONS.—"Provisions," in a Market Act, include Potatoes (*Collier* v. *Worth*, 40 J. P. 342).

"Goods, Materials or Provisions ;" *V.* USE.

PROVISO.—"This word (*proviso*) hath divers operations. Sometime it worketh a Qualification or Limitation; sometime a Condition; and sometime a Covenant" (Co. Litt. 146 b ; *Vf.* Ib. 203 b). "'Proviso' is a condition inserted into any deed, upon the performance whereof the validity of the deed consisteth. Sometimes it is only a covenant, whereof see Coke, l. 2, in the Lord *Cromwel's Case*" (Termes de la Ley).

It is said that "the terms 'Proviso' and 'Condition' are synonymous, and signify some quality annexed to a real estate, by virtue of which it may be defeated, enlarged or created upon an uncertain event" (Woodf. 180). That proposition is probably true when Real Estate is the subject-matter ; but "Proviso" and "Condition" can hardly be regarded as convertible terms for all purposes :—*V.* CONDITION : PROVIDED ALWAYS.

PROVOCATION.—As to what is Provocation that will reduce Murder to Manslaughter; *V.* Steph. Cr. 161, 162 ; Arch. Cr. 721–723 ; Rosc. Cr. 720.

"Provocation" for riot, s. 2 (1), Riot (Damages) Act, 1886, 49 & 50 V. c. 38, may prevent compensation altogether, or reduce its quantum (*Gunter* v. *Metrop. Police*, 5 Times Rep. 58).

PUBLIC ACT OF PARLIAMENT.—*V. Richards* v. *Easto*, 15 L. J. Ex. 163 ; 15 M. & W. 251.

PUBLIC AUCTION.—*V.* AUCTION.

PUBLIC BENEFIT.—What is for the "Public Benefit ;" *V. A.-G.* v. *Terry*, 9 Ch. 423 ; disapproving *R.* v. *Russell*, 6 B. & C. 566.

Bequests for the Public Benefit are good (Tudor, Char. Trusts, 11 *et seq.*).

PUBLIC BRIDGE.—*Vh.* Glen on Highways, 89 *et seq.* and the cases there collected. A bridge of public utility, even though built by an individual if dedicated to and accepted by the community, is a Public Bridge (*R.* v. *Yorkshire*, 2 East, 342: *R.* v. *Bucks*, 12 East, 192). *Vh. R.* v. *Southampton*, 17 Q. B. D. 424 : *Ib.*, 19 Q. B. D. 590.

PUBLIC BUILDING.—A Union Workhouse is a "Public Building" for the purposes of rating under a local Improvement Act (*Bedford Union* v. *Bedford Improvement Commrs.*, 21 L. J. M. C. 229 ; 7 Ex. 777) ; and so is an Infirmary (*Bedford Infirmary* v. *Bedford Improvement Commrs.*, 21 L. J. M. C. 229).

An Ambulance is not a "Public Building" within the Metropolitan Building Acts, 1855 and 1878, so as to require deposit of plans, &c. (*Josolyne* v. *Meeson*, 53 L. T. 319 ; 49 J. P. 805 ; 1 Times Rep. 565).

PUBLIC BUSINESS.—*V.* PUBLIC TRADE OR BUSINESS.

PUBLIC CHARITY.—An institution for the charitable benefit of a large and important body of persons, is a "Public Charity," as well for the purposes of construing that phrase in a Will as for obtaining a statutory exemption from rating (*A.-G.* v. *Pearce*, 2 Atk. 87 : *St. Thomas's Hosp.* v. *Lambeth*, 45 L. J. M. C. 23; L. R. 7 H. L. 477 : *Hall* v. *Derby*, 55 L. J. M. C. 21; 16 Q. B. D. 163 ; 54 L. T. 175 ; 50 J. P. 278 ; 2 Times Rep. 81). *Vf. R.* v. *Stapleton*, 33 L. J. M. C. 17; 4 B. & S. 629.

PUBLIC COMPANY.—*V.* TRADING AND OTHER PUBLIC COMPANIES.

PUBLIC CONVEYANCE.—*V.* RAILWAY.

PUBLIC DANCING-HOUSE.—*V. Marks* v. *Benjamin*, 5 M. & W. 568 ; 9 L. J. M. C. 20.

PUBLIC DRAIN.—The Eau Brink Cut near King's Lynn, is not a "Public or Parish Drain," s. 35, 4 G. 4, c. 55 (*Coulton* v. *Ambler*, 13 M. & W. 403 ; 14 L. J. Ex. 10).

V. DRAIN.

PUBLIC FUNDS.—*V.* Funds : Public Parochial Funds.

PUBLIC HIGHWAY.—Where the access to a road at either end has become impossible by reason of ways leading up to it having been lawfully stopped up, such road ceases to be a "Public Highway" (*Bailey* v. *Jamieson*, 1 C. P. D. 329).

PUBLIC-HOUSE.—Obtaining and using an "off" License for the sale of Beer, is not a breach of a covenant not to use the premises "as a *Public-house* for the sale of beer" (*Pease* v. *Coates*, 36 L. J. Ch. 57 ; L. R. 2 Eq. 688 : *Vf.* on this word, *Fielden*, or *Feilden* v. *Slater*, 38 L. J. Ch. 379 ; L. R. 7 Eq. 523 ; 20 L. T. 112 ; 17 W. R. 485).

A clause, in a lease against the use of the premises "as a Public-house," will prohibit the lessee from using them as a Beer-house (1 W. 4, c. 64, s. 31), and from selling "Wine to be consumed on the premises" under the Wine and Refreshment Houses Acts (*V.* 23 V. c. 27, s. 44).

V. Ale-house : Beer-house.

PUBLIC INTEREST.—*Seymour* v. *Butterworth*, 3 F. & F. 372 : *Cox* v. *Feeney*, 4 Ib. 13 : *Strauss* v. *France*, Ib. 1113 : *Hunter* v. *Sharp*, Ib. 983 : *R.* v. *Labouchere*, 14 Cox C. C. 419.

V. General Interest.

PUBLIC LANDS.—Gold and Silver Mines are not included in the "Public Lands" which, by the 11th Article of the Union of British Columbia to Canada, were to be "conveyed" by British Columbia to the Dominion of Canada (*A.-G. of British Columbia* v. *A.-G. of Canada*, 58 L. J. P. C. 88 ; 14 App. Ca. 295).

PUBLIC PAROCHIAL FUNDS.—By 56 G. 3, c. 139, s. 11, a parish Indenture of Apprenticeship at the expense of "Public Parochial Funds" is invalid unless approved by two justices :—such funds mean those of some one particular parish having an interest in the transaction (*R.* v. *St. Peter's*, 1 B. & Ad. 916) ; and though property given "for the benefit of a parish in general terms might probably be considered as a parochial fund," yet it would not be so if "confined to a particular specified purpose, and not intended to go generally in aid of the parish funds" (*R.* v. *Halesworth*, 1 L. J. M. C. 71 ; 3 B. & Ad. 717 : *Vf. R.* v. *Quainton*, 3 L. J. M. C. 93 ; 1 A. & E. 133 ; 3 N. & M. 289).

PUBLIC PLACE.—A Place is public, within the Criminal law, against Indecency, "if it is so situated that what passes there can be seen by any considerable number of persons if they happen to look" (Steph. Cr. 115). *V.* Place.

V. Street (at end).

PUBLIC POLICY.—" Is a very unruly horse, and when once you get astride of it you never know where it will carry you " (per Burrough, J., *Richardson* v. *Mellish,* 2 Bing. 252). *Vh. Egerton* v. *Brownlow,* 4 H. L. Ca. 1 ; 23 L. J. Ch. 348 : and per Kekewich, J., *Davies* v. *Davies,* 36 Ch. D. 364.

PUBLIC PURPOSES.—A bequest for charitable " or other purposes " is uncertain and bad (*Ellis* v. *Selby,* 4 L. J. Ch. 69 ; 5 Ib. 214 ; 7 Sim. 352 ; 1 My. & C. 286) ; but if given for charities and " other *public* purposes " it is good, the word " public " indicating that the other purposes are to be legally, if not popularly called, charitable (*Dolan* v. *Macdermot,* L. R. 5 Eq. 60 ; 3 Ch. 676. *V.* these cases stated and commented on, 1 Jarm. 215, 216).

A Workhouse is a " House," and the supply of water to it by a Water Co. is for " Domestic " and not " for Public purposes " (*Liskeard Un.* v. *Liskeard W. Works,* 7 Q. B. D. 505).

PUBLIC REFRESHMENT.—Building kept for " Public Refreshment, Resort and Entertainment," s. 6, 23 V. c. 27 ; *V.* ENTERTAINMENT.

PUBLIC RESORT.—*V.* PLACE.

PUBLIC SCHOOL.—The City of London School, though partly supported by the fees payable by the scholars, is a " Public School " within Sch. A., No. VI. (Allowances), to s. 60, Income Tax Act, 1842, 5 & 6 V. c. 35 (*Blake & London Corp.,* 56 L. J. Q. B. 148, 424 ; 19 Q. B. D. 79 ; 35 W. R. 791) ; but some charitable element is implied in the phrase (*Needham* v. *Bowers,* 21 Q. B. D. 442).

In the firstly cited case Denman, J., said that, " a definition of ' Public School ' is nowhere to be found either at common law, or in any law book or Act of Parliament. It is, therefore, a very mixed question of law and fact, though in its nature it is very much a question of fact."

V. HOSPITAL.

PUBLIC SECURITIES.—*Semble,* " Public Securities " is a wider term than GOVERNMENT SECURITIES (per Shadwell, V.-C., *Sampayo* v. *Gould,* 12 Sim. 435).

PUBLIC TRADE OR BUSINESS.—A Girls' School is a breach of a covenant not to suffer " any Public Trade or Business " to be carried on (*Wickenden* v. *Webster,* 25 L. J. Q. B. 264 ; 6 E. & B. 387 ; 27 L. T. O. S. 122 : BUSINESS).

As regards exemption from Distress of goods delivered to a person in the way of his trade, it has been argued that the trade must be " public ; " but Patteson, J., said,—" I do not know what is meant by the phrase ' Public Trade ' " (*Gibson* v. *Ireson,* 3 Q. B. 44).

PUBLIC UNDERTAKING.—*V. Gardner* v. *Lond. C. & Dover Ry.*, 36 L. J. Ch. 323; 2 Ch. 201: *Blaker* v. *Herts & Essex Water Works Co.*, 58 L. J. Ch. 497: UNDERTAKING.

PUBLIC USE.—A "Public Use" of an Invention does not mean a general use, but a use in public as distinguished from one that is secret (*Carpenter* v. *Smith*, 11 L. J. Ex. 213; 9 M. & W. 300; 1 Webster, 530).

PUBLICAN.—The prohibition, in a Lease, of the business "of a Victualler or Publican," will include a Beer-shop (1 W. 4, c. 64, s. 31).

"Victualler;" *V.* Article, 52 J. P. 398, 423.

PUBLICATION: PUBLISH.—"Publication" is accomplished in a variety of ways according to the subject-matter.

A *Book* or other literary matter is published by being surrendered by its author for public use. Thus the sale of an MS. copy of a book is a publication of it (*White* v. *Geroch*, 1 Chitty, 26; 2 B. & Ald. 298; 7 Jarm. Conv. by Sweet, 626). But a gratuitous circulation amongst friends, or pupils, is not (*Queensbury* v. *Shebbeare*, 2 Eden. 329: *Prince Albert* v. *Strange*, 18 L. J. Ch. 120; 2 D. G. & S. 652; 1 Mac. & G. 25; 1 H. & Tw. 1: *Bartlett* v. *Crittenden*, 4 McLean, 300, cited Copinger on Copyright, 2 Ed. 111). Nor is the use of letters as evidence in court, a publication (7 Jarm. Conv. by Sweet, 628, n.).

A *Sculpture*, or *Bust*, is published (54 G. 3, c. 56, s. 1) by being publicly exhibited (*Turner* v. *Robinson*, 10 Ir. Ch. Rep. 516).

Acting a *Play* is not a "publication" of it, according to the primary meaning of that word (Copinger on Copyright, 2 Ed. 295 *et seq.*); but for the purposes of the Copyright Acts the first public representation of a drama or musical composition is equivalent to the first publication of a book (5 & 6 V. c. 45, s. 20).

A *Libel* is published, for the purpose of a civil action, when, its contents being known, or negligently unknown (*Emmens* v. *Pottle*, 55 L. J. Q. B. 51; 16 Q. B. D. 354; 53 L. T. 808; 34 W. R. 116), it is communicated to any one *other than the person libelled;* but the qualification contained in the last five words does not apply in criminal proceedings for libel (Rosc. N. P. 787; Steph. Cr. 199).

An *Award* is published, and "ready to be delivered," as soon as it is completed and executed by the arbitrator (*Brooke* v. *Mitchell*, 6 M. & W. 473; Russell on Arb. 6 Ed. 255).

The "Prior Publication" of an invention which will invalidate a *Patent*, means the prior existence in this country of some document to which the public have access, containing such a description of the invention as will enable a practical man to carry it out from the description given (Terrell on Patents, 41); such access being of such a kind as to raise a reasonable probability that the knowledge on which the invention is based might have been obtained from the document (per Pearson, J., *Otto* v. *Steel*, 55 L. J. Ch. 198; 31 Ch. D. 241; 54 L. T. 157; 34 W. R. 289;—disapproving of the *dicta* in *Lang* v. *Gisborne*, 31 L. J. Ch. 769; 31 Bea. 133, and *Plimpton* v. *Malcolmson*, 45 L. J. Ch. 505; 3 Ch. D. 531). *V.* First Inventor.

As to "publication" of a *Design*; *V. Blank* v. *Footman*, 57 L. J. Ch. 909; 39 Ch. D. 678; 59 L. T. 507; 36 W. R. 921.

As to the publication of *Bye Laws*; *V. Motteram* v. *Eastern Counties Ry.*, 29 L. J. M. C. 57; 7 C. B. N. S. 58.

Publication of a *Will*; *V.* Delivery.

PUBLISHER.—"Publisher," ss. 13, 16, 24, Copyright Act, 1842, 5 & 6 V. c. 45, means the first Publisher (*Weldon* v. *Dicks*, 10 Ch. D. 247; 48 L. J. Ch. 201: *Coote* v. *Judd*, 23 Ch. D. 727; 53 L. J. Ch. 36).

PULL DOWN.—*V.* Demolish: Unnecessary Inconvenience.

PURCHASE.—Speaking technically, a person acquires by "words of Purchase" and is a "Purchaser" when he obtains title in any other mode than by descent or devolution of law (Litt. s. 12; Co. Litt. 18 b.; Termes de la Ley, *Purchase*); a devisee under a Will is accordingly a purchaser in law (Wms. R. P., ch. 4; *Vf.* Watson, Eq. 201, 202). *V.* By Purchase.

But in the Statute of Elizabeth (27 Eliz. c. 4, s. 2) relating to Fraudulent Conveyances as against those "as have *purchased*, or shall afterwards purchase" lands, tenements and hereditaments, "the word 'Purchase,' of course, refers to cases of selling and purchasing in the ordinary and vulgar acceptation of the word, and not in the technical sense of any person who obtains lands otherwise than by descent" (May on Fraudulent Conveyances, 2 Ed. 217). A "purchaser," under this statute, must be "a purchaser for money or other valuable consideration" (*Upton* v. *Bassett*, cited in *Twyne's Case*, 3 Rep. 83 a; *V.* Valuable). This definition includes,—

Mortgages, legal or equitable (*Dolphin* v. *Aylward*, L. R. 4 H. L. 486; 23 L. T. 636: *Lister* v. *Turner*, 5 Hare, 281), even if the mortgage be for a past consideration (*Barton* v. *Vanheythuysen*, 11 Hare, 126: per L. C., *Beavan* v. *Oxford*, 6 D. G. M. & G. 520);

Lessees at rack-rent (*Goodright* v. *Moses*, 2 W. Bl. 1019);

Assignees of Leases (*Price* v. *Jenkins*, 5 Ch. D. 619; 46 L. J. Ch. 805; 37 L. T. 51: *Ex p. Doble*, 26 W. R. 407; 38 L. T. 183: *Harris* v. *Tubb*, 42 Ch. D. 79:—*Price* v. *Jenkins*, dissented from in *Lee* v. *Matthews*, 6 L. R. Ir. 530. But the doctrine of *Price* v. *Jenkins* does not apply to 13 Eliz. c. 5, *Re Ridler*, 22 Ch. D. 74; 52 L. J. Ch. 343; 31 W. R. 93; 48 L. T. 396: *Green* v. *Paterson*, 32 Ch. D. 104); and, *semble*, Sub-Lessees who covenant for performance of the lessee's obligations, *secus*, where there is no such covenant (*Shurmur* v. *Sedgwick*, 53 L. J. Ch. 87; 24 Ch. D. 597);

So of children of a Widow, *quà* Marriage Settlement (*Newstead* v. *Searles*, 1 Atk. 265 ; 9 App. Ca. 320 n.) ; but not those of a Widower (*Re Cameron and Wells*, 57 L. J. Ch. 69 ; 37 Ch. D. 32) ;

Persons becoming partners with the owner under mutual obligations to work the land (*Shaw* v. *Standish*, 2 Vern. 326) ;

"Marriage is a good consideration to make the Feme a Purchaser" (*Douglasse* v. *Waad*, 1 Ch. Ca. 99). As to a post-nuptial Settlement ; *V. Re Foster and Lister*, 6 Ch. D. 87 ; 46 L. J. Ch. 480 ;

Trustees of a Creditors' Deed, when thereby taking a real interest (*Butterfield* v. *Heath*, 15 Bea. 408 ; 22 L. J. Ch. 270), not otherwise (*Cadell* v. *Bewley*, 15 W. R. 703). *Note.—Butterfield* v. *Heath* was disapproved in *Re Foster & Lister* (sup.) ;

Releasors of adverse claims (*Hill* v. *Bishop of Exeter*, 2 Taunt. 69).

But the definition does *not* include,—

Judgment Creditors (*Beavan* v. *Oxford*, 6 D. G. M. & G. 492 ; 25 L. J. Ch. 299 ; 2 Jur. N. S. 121 : *Dolphin* v. *Aylward*, L. R. 4 H. L. 486 ; 23 L. T. 636) ;

Purchaser from Heir or Devisee of grantor (*Lewis* v. *Rees*, 3 K. & J. 132).

V. this subject elaborately discussed, May on Fraudulent Conv., Part 3, ch. 2 : *Va.* Seton, 1376.

In s. 91, Bankry. Act, 1869 (32 & 33 V. c. 71), "Purchaser" means "Buyer" (*Re Pumfrey, Ex p. Hillman*, 10 Ch. D. 622 ; 48 L. J. Bank. 77 ; 27 W. R. 567 ; 40 L. T. 177), or rather, one who gives *quid pro quo* (*Hance* v. *Harding*, 57 L. J. Q. B. 403 ; 20 Q. B. D. 732 ; 59 L. T. 659 ; 36 W. R. 629, explaining *Re Pumfrey*).

For the purposes of the Conv. and L. P. Act, 1881 (s. 2), and the Conv. Act, 1882 (s. 1 (4) ii.), a "purchaser" includes "a lessee or mortgagee or an intending purchaser, lessee or mortgagee, or other person who, for valuable consideration, takes or deals for property." *V.* VALUABLE.

Semble, where a person takes, in the same property, an equitable estate by election, and a legal estate by descent, he is not a "Purchaser" within 3 & 4 W. 4, c. 106, ss. 2, 3 (*Wood* v. *Douglas*, 54 L. J. Ch. 421 ; 28 Ch. D. 327).

V. BONÂ FIDE.

"Purchase" held to mean "Agreement to Purchase" (*Long* v. *Millar*, cited BALANCE).

PURCHASE FOR VALUE.—This phrase does not include a conveyance in consideration of marriage, in the implied covenants for title in a conveyance deed under s. 7 of the Conv. and L. P. Act, 1881 ; *V.* end of sub.-s. A. of s. 7.

PURCHASED.—"Purchased," in a devise of lands, *primâ facie*, means lands acquired in any other way than by descent; and therefore a devise of lands testator has "purchased" will include those he has acquired by exchange (*Doe* d. *Meyrick* v. *Meyrick*, 2 L. J. Ex. 259; 1 Cr. & M. 820; 3 Tyr. 916).

An appointment by a married woman of "all funds and property which have been or shall be *purchased* out of the saving of property to which I have been or shall be entitled to my separate use," does not include separate estate savings, standing to her account at her bankers (*Askew* v. *Rooth*, L. R. 17 Eq. 426; 43 L. J. Ch. 368).

V. PURCHASE.

PURCHASER.—*V.* PURCHASE.

PURE.—"Pure Personalty," "Impure Personalty," in connection with a Charitable Bequest; *V.* Tudor's Char. Trusts, 401 *et seq.*

"Pure and Wholesome *Water*," s. 35, Waterworks Cl. Con. Act, 1847 (10 & 11 V. c. 17); *V. Milnes* v. *Huddersfield*, 56 L. J. Q. B. 1; 11 App. Ca. 511; 55 L. T. 617; 34 W. R. 761; 50 J. P. 676.

V. ADULTERATED.

PURLIEW.—"'Purlue' is all that ground which is neare any Forrest, which being made forrest by Henry the Second, Richard the First, or King John, were by perambulations granted by Henry the Third, severed again from the same" (Termes de la Ley, citing Manwood, Part 2, ch. 20).

"Purliew 'contains such grounds which H. 2, R. 1, or King John added to their ancient forests over other men's grounds, and which were disafforested by force of the Statute of Carta de Foresta, cap. 1, and cap. 3, and the perambulations and grants thereupon;' 4 Inst. 303. As to rights of common in respect of purliew, *V. R.* v. *Rodley*, Hard. 437; *Jenning* v. *Rocke*, Palm. 93." (Elph. 616, 617).

"Purlie Man, is he that hath lands within the purlieu, and being able to dispend forty shillings by the yeare of freehold, is upon these two points licensed to hunt in his owne purlieu" (Termes de la Ley, citing Manwood, Part 1, p. 151, & 177; 1 Jac. c. 27).

PURPORTING.—When validity is given to anything "purporting" to be done in pursuance of a Power, a thing done under it may have validity though done at a time when the power would not be really exerciseable (*Dicker* v. *Angerstein*, 3 Ch. D. 600; 45 L. J. Ch. 754). In that case it was held that the proviso, following conditional powers of Sale in a mortgage, that a "Sale purporting to be made in pursuance" of the powers shall be valid as regards purchasers, enables the mortgagee to confer a good title on a bonâ fide purchaser even though the security be satisfied.

Note.—In the corresponding proviso in the statutory power of sale, the phrase for "purporting" is "professed exercise" (s. 21 (2), Conv. & L. P. Act, 1881).

Vf. Hare v. *Copland*, 13 Ir. C. L. Rep. 426.

V. PURSUANCE.

PURPOSE.—"For any other Purpose;" *V. Re Norris*, W. N. (83) 35, 65.

"For the Purpose of;" *V.* CONSTITUTED.

"Purpose merely Charitable," s. 38, 5 & 6 V. c. 82; *V. A.-G.* v. *Bagot*, 13 Ir. C. L. Rep. 48. *V.* CHARITABLE PURPOSES.

PURPOSES.—"For the Purposes of *the Act;*" *V. Grand Junction Canal Co.* v. *Petty*, 57 L. J. Q. B. 572; 21 Q. B. D. 273; 36 W. R. 795; 52 J. P. 692, and cases therein cited.

Lands "used for the purposes of *the Undertaking*," Lands C. C. Act, 1845; *V. Betts* v. *G. E. Ry.*, 49 L. J. Ex. 197; 28 W. R. 50.

"Purposes of *Trade;*" *V. Bank of India* v. *Wilson*, 3 Ex. D. 113; 47 L. J. Ex. 153.

V. ALL INTENTS AND PURPOSES: DOMESTIC: PUBLIC PURPOSES.

PURPRESTURE.—"By 'Purpresture' is meant, in its present acceptation, an encroachment upon the Crown, either upon part of the demesne lands, or upon the high roads, rivers, forts, or streets; and the difference between purprestures and nuisances consists in this,—that where the jus *privatum* of the Crown is invaded, it is a Purpresture; but where the jus *publicum* is violated, it is a Nuisance" (Dan. Ch. Pr. citing 2 Inst. 38, 272; Harg. Law Tracts, 84, 87; *Vf.* Co. Litt. 277 b; Termes de la Ley; Manwood, *Purpresture;* Elph. 617).

V. NUISANCE.

PURSUANCE.—Notice of Action is in many instances required to be given prior to commencing proceedings for things done "In Pursuance," or "Under or By Virtue," or "In Execution" of a Statute. In strictness anything not authorised by a Statute cannot be "in pursuance" or "under or by virtue" of it, whilst if authorised it would need no other protection. But if effect were given to such a construction it would altogether do away with the protection intended to be given; accordingly it is held that if any public or private body or person, charged with the execution of an Act of Parliament, honestly intends to put the law in motion and really and not unreasonably believes in the existence of facts, which, if existent, would justify his acting and acts accordingly, his conduct will be "in pursuance" or "under or by virtue" of the Statute under which he believes he is acting, although he errs in such belief. The question whether there was in fact reasonable ground for such belief is a subordinate question and one very material to be pressed on the minds of the jury; but the presence or absence of such reasonable ground can only be relied on for the purpose of determining whether the belief was *bonâ fide* or not (*Hermann* v. *Seneschal*, 32 L. J. C. P. 43 ; 13 C. B. N. S. 392, and cases there cited : *Roberts* v. *Orchard*, 2 H. & C. 769 ; 33 L. J. Ex. 65 : *Judge* v. *Selmes*, L. R. 6 Q. B. 724 ; 40 L. J. Q. B. 287 : *Chamberlain* v. *King*, L. R. 6 C. P. 474, nom. *King* v. *Chamberlain*, 40 L. J. C. P. 273 : *Agnew* v. *Jobson*, 47 L. J. M. C. 67 : *Mid. Ry.* v. *Withington*, 52 L. J. Q. B. 689 ; 11 Q. B. D. 788 : *Hughes* v. *Buckland*, 15 M. & W. 346 ; 15 L. J. Ex. 233 : *Lea* v. *Facey*, 56 L. J. Q. B. 536 ; 19 Q. B. D. 352 ; 35 W. R. 721 ; 51 J. P. 756 : *Rochfort* v. *Rynd*, 9 L. R. Ir. 204 : *O'Dea* v. *Hickman*, 18 L. R. Ir. 233. *Vf.* Wilberforce, 87–98 ; Maxwell, 278 ; Rosc. N. P. 1073, 1088, 1095, 1099–1104.

An *omission* to do, in pursuance of a statute, is on the same line as regards notice of action as an actual thing done (*Wilson* v. *Halifax*, L. R. 3 Ex. 114 ; 37 L. J. Ex. 44 : *Joliffe* v. *Wallasey*, L. R. 9 C. P. 62 ; 43 L. J. C. P. 41).

" Persons acting in the execution of this Act," s. 19, *Special Constables Act*, 1 & 2 W. 4, c. 41 ; *V. Bryson* v. *Russell*, 54 L. J. Q. B. 144 ; 14 Q. B. D. 720.

V. Execution of Statutory Powers : Purporting.

PURSUIT.—" Pursuit of Game ; " *V.* Search.

PUT AWAY.—" It shall not be lawful for any Master to *put away* or transfer his Apprentice to any other, or in any way discharge or dismiss him from his service " without consent of magistrates, s. 9, 56 G. 3, c. 139 :—a master not having sufficient employment for a Parish Apprentice agreed with another tradesman that the Apprentice should work for him, he paying to the first master 5*s.* a week ; held, a "putting away " within the section cited, although the apprentice, on one occasion, on demand, returned to his first master and worked for him for 10 days (*R.* v. *Wainfleet*, 9 L. J. M. C. 31 ; 11 A. & E. 656). *Vf. R.* v. *Shipton*, 6 L. J. O. S. M. C. 92 ; 8 B. & C. 88.

V. Assign.

PUT OFF.—To " put off " a bargain for the sale of goods, may mean to postpone its completion, or to procure a resale of the goods to a third person ; the first is the more ordinary meaning, but which is the meaning in a particular case is for the jury (*Thornton* v. *Charles*, 11 L. J. Ex. 302 ; 9 M. & W. 802).

PYKE.—*V.* Gore.

QUA

QUADRANTATA TERRÆ.—$\frac{1}{4}$ of an acre (Elph. 598).

QUALIFICATION.—"The same Qualification," s. 4, 6 V. c. 18, means the same *Property* (*Burton* v. *Gery*, 17 L. J. C. P. 66 ; 5 C. B. 7 ; 10 L. T. O. S. 135).

V. NATURE.

QUALIFIED.—*V.* DULY.

QUALIFIED TO ELECT.—"Qualified to elect," in s. 11, subs. 3, Municipal Corporation Act, 1882 (45 & 46 V. c. 50), is not equivalent to "entitled to vote," in s. 51 of the same Act ; and though, under the latter section, a person on the Register, however he got there, is "entitled to vote," he is not qualified to be elected as a Councillor, as being "qualified to elect to the office" (s. 11, subs. 3) unless, in fact, he really does possess the qualifications to elect that are prescribed by s. 9 (*Flintham* v. *Roxburgh*, 55 L. J. Q. B. 472 ; 17 Q. B. D. 44) ; nor is a woman, "though entitled to vote," capable of being elected a County Councillor (*Beresford-Hope* v. *Sandhurst*, 58 L. J. Q. B. 316).

QUALITY.—*V.* NATURE : DYE : QUANTITY AND QUALITY UNKNOWN.

QUAMDIU.—"*Quamdiu* also is a word of limitation, for if a man grant a rent out of the mannor of D., *quamdiu* the grantor shall bee dwelling upon the mannor, this is good, or *quamdiu se bene gesserit.* And so by these words, *donec, quousque, usque ad, tamdiu, ubicunque*" (Co. Litt. 235 a).

QUANTITY AND QUALITY UNKNOWN.—*Tully* v. *Terry*, 42 L. J. C. P. 240 ; L. R. 8 C. P. 679 : *V. The Ida*, 2 Asp. 551 : CONTENTS UNKNOWN.

QUARENTENA TERRÆ.—"A Furlong ; Co. Litt. 5 b ; Spelm. It is also used in the secondary meaning of a furlong or shot (a division in the common field) ; Seebohm, Eng. Vil. Comm. 4 ; and for that reason, we suppose, 'some hold that by that name land may be demanded ;' Co. Litt. 5 b" (Elph. 617). *V.* STADIUM.

QUARENTINE.—"'Quarentine' is where a man dyeth seized of a manour place, and other Lands, whereof the wife ought to be endowed, then the woman may abide in the manour place, and there live of the store and profits thereof the space of forty dayes, within which time her Dower shall be assigned, as it appeareth in Magna Charta, cap. 6" (Termes de la Ley).

QUARRELS.—"As to this word (*Querelas*), it is to be known that Quarrels extend not only to actions as well real as personal, as it is held in 9 E. 44 a; but also to causes of actions and suits, as it is held in 39 H. 6, 9 b. So that, by release of all 'Quarrels,' not only actions depending in suit, but causes of action and suit also are released . . . . And this word Querela is derived *a querendo, unde etiam querens*, who is the plaintiff; and Quarrels, Controversies and Debates are *synonima*, and of one and the same signification" (*Altham's Case*, 8 Rep. 153 a, 153 b). *Vf.* Termes de la Ley, *Quarels*.

QUARRY.—"The word 'Quarry' is in the *Encyclopædia Metropolitana* stated to be derived from the French word 'quarrière,' and the derivation is followed by this description: 'In the Latin of the lower ages, *quadratarius* was a stone-cutter, *qui marmora quadrat*, and hence 'quarrière,' the place where he quadrates or cuts the stone in squares, the place where the stone is cut in squares, generally a stone-pit,'—clearly, therefore, referring to a place upon or above, and not under the ground" (per Turner, L. J., *Bell* v. *Wilson*, 35 L. J. Ch. 341; 1 Ch. 303; 14 W. R. 493; 14 L. T. 115); and, therefore, distinct from a "Mine" (*Darvill* v. *Roper*, 24 L. J. Ch. 779; 3 Drew. 294; 3 W. R. 467; 25 L. T. O. S. 302). *Vf.* as to the difference between a Quarry and Mine, MacS. 3–5.

For the purposes of the Factory and Workshop Acts, a "Quarry" is defined as "any place, not being a Mine, in which persons work in getting Slate, Stone, Coprolites, or other Minerals" (41 V. c. 16, Sch. 4, Part 2).

V. MINE.

QUARTER OF A YEAR.—"A 'Quarter of a Year' containeth, by legall computation, 91 dayes" (Co. Litt. 135 b).

QUARTER SESSIONS.—*V.* s. 13 (14), Interp. Act, 1889: GENERAL OR QUARTER SESSIONS: NEXT QUARTER SESSIONS: SEPARATE QUARTER SESSIONS.

QUARTERLY.—The power given, by s. 1, 5 V. c. 27, to Incumbents, with consent of Bishop and Patron, to lease glebe lands, is on the condition "that there be reserved on every such Lease, payable to the Incumbent for the time being of such benefice *quarterly* in every year" during the term, the best and most improved yearly rent that can reasonably be gotten; that condition is imperative ; and, therefore, where an Incumbent entered into an agreement to grant a lease at a rent "payable half-yearly," the agreement could not be enforced, nor could the Court modify it so as to make it conform to the provisions of the statute (*Jenkins* v. *Green*, 28 L. J. Ch. 820 ; 27 Bea. 440).

V. YEARLY : HALF YEARLY.

QUEEN ANNE'S BOUNTY.—*V.* s. 12 (16), Interp. Act, 1889.

QUEEN'S ENEMIES.—"The words 'the Queen's Enemies' relate, not to Robbers—for the consequences of whose attacks carriers are liable, unless their liability has been varied by statute or express contract,—but in the case of an English ship, and, in other cases, to the Enemies of the Sovereign of the Shipowner" (1 Maude & P. 351, citing *Russell* v. *Niemann*, 17 C. B. N. S. 163 ; 34 L. J. C. P. 10 : *The Heinrich*, L. R. 3 A. & E. 435 : *The Teutonia*, L. R. 4 P. C. 171 ; 41 L. J. Adm. 57. *Va. The San Roman*, L. R. 3 A. & E. 583 ; 41 L. J. Adm. 72). Pirates are not included herein (1 Maude & P. 351, n. (*h*), 487). *V.* ENEMY.

QUESTION.—"Question in the Action ;" *V. Norris* v. *Beazley*, 2 C. P. D. 80 ; 46 L. J. C. P. 169 : *Horwell* v. *Gen. Omnibus Co.*, 46 L. J. Ex. 700 ; 3 Ex. D. 365 : *Byrne* v. *Brown*, 22 Q. B. D. 657.

By a "Question arising in any Cause or Matter," which may be referred under s. 56, Jud. Act, 1873, is meant a question that must necessarily arise for decision therein (*Weed* v. *Ward*, 58 L. J. Ch. 454).

"Question arising in the Administration of" an Estate or Trust, Ord. 55, R. 3 (g), R. S. C. ; *V. Re Medland, Eland* v. *Medland*, 58 L. J. Ch. 572.

"The Question," in the latter part of s. 41, Regulation of Railways Act, 1868, 31 & 32 V. c. 119, means only, *the* Question of Compensation (*Re East London Ry.*, 38 W. R. 312).

V. BROUGHT INTO QUESTION : FACT : MATTER.

QUIET ENJOYMENT.—The question as to whether or not a Covenant for Quiet Enjoyment has been broken is "in every case a question of fact whether the quiet enjoyment of the land has or has not been interrupted ; and where the ordinary and lawful enjoyment of the land is substantially interfered with by the acts of the lessor (or, other covenantor ?), or those claiming under him, the covenant appears to us to be broken, although neither the title to the land nor the possession of the land may be otherwise affected" (per Willes, J., *Dennett* v. *Atherton*, 41 L. J. Q. B. 165 ; L. R. 7 Q. B. 316). "I take that as an advance upon the older authorities. I accept it and act upon it" (per Lindley, L. J., *Robinson* v. *Kilvert*, 58 L. J. Ch. 396 ; 41 Ch. D. 88).

Vh. Elph. 481–493 ; Woodf. 676–683 ; Touch. 166, 170–172 ; PEACEABLY AND QUIETLY.

QUIET IN HARNESS.—"Quiet in Harness," in a Warranty, refers rather to the behaviour than to the health of the horse (per Pollock, B., *Bush* v. *Freeman*, 3 Times Rep. 449).

QUIT CLAIM.—This is a corruption of "quiet claim" (Litt. s. 445 : *V*. REMISE).

QUOUSQUE.—*V*. QUAMDIU.

RACK-RENT.—"*Rack-rent* is rent of, or approaching to, the full annual value of the property out of which it issues" (Elph. 618).

But this is, perhaps, not quite correct. "Annual value" primarily means *net* annual value (*V.* ANNUAL VALUE); whereas "Rack-rent," or "Annual Rack-rent," means gross rental as distinguished from net annual value (*Stevens* v. *Barnet Water Co.*, 57 L. J. M. C. 82 ; 36 W. R. 924).

Vh. Re Elwes, 28 L. J. Ex. 47 ; 3 H. & N. 719 : 2 Bla. Com. 43.

V. RENT.

RADMANS: RADCHEMISTRES.—*V.* COLEBERTI.

RAIL.—"'Line of Rail,' has, I think, been held to include land covered by an embankment" (per Erle, J., *South Wales Ry.* v. *Swansea* 24 L. J. M. C. 34 ; 4 E. & B. 189).

RAILWAY.—The word "Railway" has no especial technical meaning, but is to be understood in its commonly received sense. Thus in reference to the Railway & Canal Traffic Act, 1854 (17 & 18 V. c. 31), Brett, L. J., made the following observations,—"For instance, if additional points or sidings were requisite for safety at an existing junction, no ordinary person would say that the addition of a set of points or the laying of a siding rail would make a new railway; they would term it an adaptation or improvement of the existing railway: though an order to make a single-line railway from A. to B. into a double-line railway would be considered by all ordinary persons of intelligence to be an order to construct a substantially new line of railway or new railway" (*S. E. Ry.* v. *Ry. Commrs.,* 50 L. J. Q. B. 211 ; 6 Q. B. D. 586).

There is a distinction between "Railway" and "Railway Station." A Station is no part of a railway, nor are offices, warehouses, or other property which are ancillary to its working; but sidings, turntables, and so much of the platform as is to be considered as the side of the railway, do form part of it (*S. Wales Ry.* v. *Swansea,* 24 L. J. M. C. 30 ; 4 E. & B. 189).

Land used only as "a Railway constructed under the powers of an Act of Parliament for Public Conveyance," s. 55, Local Gov. Act, 1858 (21 & 22 V. c. 98), does not exclusively mean a Railway for passengers: any Railway to which the public has a right of access for the conveyance of themselves or their goods is a Railway for Public Conveyance (*R.* v. *Newport Dock Co.,* 31 L. J. M. C. 266). A Railway is, moreover, not less a railway within s. 13 of the Act for Regulating Railways, 1840 (3 & 4 V. c. 97), because it has not yet been opened for passenger traffic (*R.* v. *Bradford*, 29 L. J. M. C. 171 ; Bell, C. C. 268). But a Railway originally constructed by private arrangement is not a " Railway " within s. 55, Loc. Gov. Act, 1858, although subsequently worked under an Act of Parliament (*N. E. Ry.* v. *Leadgate*, 39 L. J. M. C. 65 ; L. R. 5 Q. B. 157).

" Railway," as used in s. 1 (5), Employers' Liability Act, 1880 (43 & 44 V. c. 42), is not restricted to a Railway worked under statutory powers ; but is used in a popular sense, and signifies any way upon which trains pass by means of rails, including a temporary tramway used by a contractor for the passage of engines and trucks during the execution of his contract (*Doughty* v. *Firbank*, 52 L. J. Q. B. 480 ; 10 Q. B. D. 358). *V.* TRAIN.

A Private Railway, however, is not such a " Railway " as to impose on its owner the Rules of the Railway Acts as to Gates and Level Crossings (*Matson* v. *Baird*, 3 App. Ca. 1082).

A short line of railway, part of a dock undertaking, and connecting the dock with other and independent railways, is a " Railway " within s. 3, 30 & 31 V. c. 127 (*G. N. Ry.* v. *Tahourdin*, 53 L. J. Q. B. 69 ; 13 Q. B. D. 320) ; and under the last-named statute a " Railway " is still a railway though closed for traffic and its re-opening doubtful (*Midland Waggon Co.* v. *Potteries, Shrewsbury & North Wales Ry.*, 50 L. J. Q. B. 6 ; 6 Q. B. D. 36) ; but if altogether abandoned as a railway it would probably lose that character (per Stephen, J., Ib.).

A power to make " any Railway," in an Act prior to the invention of steam locomotives, would nevertheless comprise a railway to be worked by such engines (*Bishop* v. *North*, 12 L. J. Ex. 362 ; 11 M. & W. 426).

RAILWAY COMPANY.—A Railway Company which has no rolling stock, and whose line is wholly worked by another Company under a proportional mileage agreement, but maintaining and managing its own line, and collecting and forwarding its own traffic, and wholly employing and paying the staff engaged on its own line, is a " Railway Company " within the Ry. & Canal Traffic Act, 1854, 17 & 18 V. c. 31, and the Regulation of Ry. Act, 1873, 36 & 37 V. c. 48 (*Central Wales Ry.* v. *G. W. Ry.*, 52 L. J. Q. B. 211 ; 10 Q. B. D. 231).

A " Railway Company," to be within the exception in s. 199 of the Companies Act, 1862, and so not liable to be wound up thereunder, must be a Company whose principal object is the construction (or working ?) of a Railway (*Exmouth Docks Co.*, 43 L. J. Ch. 110 ; L. R. 17 Eq. 181) ; and a Tramway Company is not within the exception (*Re Brentford & Isleworth Tramways Co.*, 53 L. J. Ch. 624 ; 26 Ch. D. 527).

But a Dock Company which, under an enabling Act, made and worked on their own land a piece of railway (not a mere siding, but) which was a portion of a larger system, was held a " Railway Company " " constituted by Act of Parliament . . . for the purpose of constructing . . . a Railway" within s. 3, Railway Companies Act, 1867, although the making of a Railway was not one of the purposes for which the Company was originally constituted, nor at any time one of its principal objects (*Re East & West India Dock Co.*, 57 L. J. Ch. 1053 ; 38 Ch. D. 576 ; 59 L. T. 236 ; 36 W. R. 849). *V.* CONSTITUTED.

RAILWAY STATION.—"This term is not in ordinary sense used as a description merely of the actual existing structures at a station ; but as the description of a space actually set apart for, and generally used as, a resting-place for traffic, or a place for dealing with it in a particular way, although every part of the space is not covered with structures or used for passing along or for deposit" (per Brett, L. J., *S. E. Ry.* v. *Ry. Commrs.*, 50 L. J. Q. B. 211).

V. RAILWAY.

RAISE.—"Raise," s. 83 (6), the Metropolitan Building Act, 1855 (18 & 19 V. c. 122), is not confined to raising above-ground, but includes raising a wall by adding to its foundation by under-pinning (*Standard Bank of British South Africa* v. *Stokes*, 47 L. J. Ch. 554 ; 9 Ch. D. 68).

"A covenant to Raise a *Mineral*, means, *primâ facie*, to get or win ; not to bring to the surface" (MacS. 219, citing *Senhouse* v. *Harris*, 5 L. T. 635 : *Kinsman* v. *Jackson*, 42 Ib. 80 ; 28 W. R. 337, 601). *V.* WIN.

"Not to Raise the rent ;" *V.* MOLEST.

A power in a Company's Articles enabling the directors by debentures to "secure the repayment of or *raise* any money authorized to be borrowed," authorises them to issue debentures at a discount (*Re Anglo-Danubian Steam Nav. Co.*, L. R. 20 Eq. 341 ; 44 L. J. Ch. 502),—"Raise" in such a connection being used "to prevent it being contended that the directors could only secure the repayment of the money borrowed" (per Jessel, M. R., Ib.). *V.* REPAYMENT.

RANSOM.—"'*Ransom.*' *Redemptio* is here (Litt. s. 194) taken for grand summe of money for redeeming of a great delinquent from some heinous crime, who is to be captivate in prison untill he payeth it" (Co. Litt. 127 a).

"'Ransome' signifies properly the summe that is payd for the redeeming of one that is taken captive in warre ; but it is used also for a summe of money paid for the pardoning of some great offence, and so it is used in the statute of 1 H. 4, c. 7, and in other statutes. Fine and Ransome going together ; as in 23 Hen. 8, cap. 3, and elsewhere" (Termes de la Ley, *Ransome*).

V. AMERCIAMENT : FINE AND RANSOM.

RAPE.—"'*Rape.*' *Raptus* is, when a man hath carnall knowledge of a woman by force and against her will" (Co. Litt. 123 b).

"Rape is the act of having carnal knowledge of a woman without her conscious permission, such permission not being extorted by force or fear of immediate bodily harm; but if such permission is given, the fact that it was obtained by fraud, or that the woman did not understand the nature of the act, is immaterial. Provided that (1) a husband (it is said) cannot commit rape upon his wife by carnally knowing her himself, but he may do so if he aids another person to have carnal knowledge of her; (2) a boy under 14 years of age is conclusively presumed to be incapable of committing rape" (Steph. Cr. 185, 186). *Vf.* Arch. Cr. 803–805; Rosc. Cr. 897.

V. CARNAL KNOWLEDGE.

RASCAL.—*V.* CHEAT.

RASH AND HAZARDOUS.—Stock Exchange speculations (*Ex p. Salaman*, 54 L. J. Q. B. 238; 14 Q. B. D. 936), or Betting or Gambling (*Ex p. Thornber, Re Barlow,* W. N. (86) 207; 3 Times Rep. 218), or investing in an undeveloped and unproductive Mining Company (*Re Young,* W. N. (85), 12), is a "Rash and Hazardous Speculation" within s. 28, subs. 3 (d), Bankry. Act, 1883. *Vf.* hereon *Ex p. Evans, Re Barnard & Rosenthal,* 31 L. J. Bank. 63: *Ex p. Downman,* 32 L. J. Bank. 49; 11 W. R. 577.

RATE: RATES.—A "Rate" is an impost, usually for current and recurrent expenditure, spread over a district; and is distinct from an amount payable for work done upon or in respect of particular premises (*V.* jdgmt. of Brett, L. J., *Budd* v. *Marshall,* 50 L. J. Q. B. 24; 5 C. P. D. 481).

A lessor's covenant to pay "all Rates and Taxes chargeable in respect of the demised premises," held to include the Water Rate (*Direct Spanish Telegraph Co.* v. *Shepherd,* 53 L. J. Q. B. 420; 13 Q. B. D. 202; 32 W. R. 717). As however the word "Rates" is here associated with "Taxes," it may, perhaps, be doubted whether the meaning of it should not have been confined to parochial or other such like public rates: *V.* TAXES: DEDUCTIONS. And in a subsequent case where a lessor covenanted to pay "all Rates, Taxes and Impositions whatsoever whether parliamentary, parochial, or *imposed* by the Corporation of London or otherwise," it was held by the Court of Appeal (reversing the Divisional Court, acting upon the authority of *Direct Spanish Telegraph Co.* v. *Shepherd*), that that case did not apply, and that the Water Rate was not included (*Badcock* v. *Hunt,* 22 Q. B. D. 145; 58 L. J. Q. B. 134. *Vf.* IMPOSED). In this latter case the Court of Appeal distinguished the words of the covenant from those used in the other case, but the drift of the judgments would seem to justify the conjecture that *Direct Spanish Tel. Co.* v. *Shepherd* was not favourably regarded.

V. DUTIES.

RATED OR ASSESSED.—Under s. 6, Metrop. Man. Act, 1855, a Vestry is to consist of persons "rated or assessed." "An Assessment seems to me to speak of two operations. The Overseers first assess the rate for the whole parish—that is, they consider and determine the amount which is to be raised for the whole parish. That having been done the rate is assessed, but has not been made. The next operation is to calculate the amount for which each person is to be liable. But the mere calculation and fixing of the amount which each person is to pay does not impose any liability, for the rate has not been made; but when the amount has been assessed, the person is rated by putting the amount of the assessment into the rate-book. A person cannot really be assessed, so as in any way to be liable, until he has been rated; nor can he be rated until he has been assessed. The two words 'rated' and 'assessed,' therefore, describe the operation which makes a person liable to the rate. That seems to me to shew that although the words in s. 6, are 'rated *or* assessed,' yet the proper way to read them is 'rated *and* assessed,' as having reference to one operation" (per Esher, M. R., *Mogg* v. *Clark*, 55 L. J. Q. B. 71; 16 Q. B. D. 79). It was held in that case that an owner (not himself the occupier) who has made an agreement to pay poor rates under s. 3, Poor Rate Assessment Act, 1869 (32 & 33 V. c. 41), is not a person "rated or assessed" within the section just referred to. *Va. Goodhew* v. *Williams*, 47 L. J. C. P. 313; 3 C. P. D. 382.

RATE-PAYER.—"By persons *paying* to the Church and Poor must be understood persons *liable to pay*, though they may not have actually paid (*A.-G.* v. *Foster*, 10 Ves. 339, 346); but it seems to be a necessary qualification that they should have been rated (*Edenborough* v. *Canterbury*, 2 Russ. 110), unless, perhaps, the name has been omitted by mistake, or there is the taint of fraud (Ib. 110, 111)." Lewin, 88.

"Ratepayer," *quà* Public Libraries Act, "shall mean every *Inhabitant* who would have to pay the Free Library Assessment in the event of the Act being adopted" (s. 3, 40 & 41 V. c. 54); that definition includes Compound Householders, whose rates are paid for them under the Poor Rate Assessment Act, 1869, 32 & 33 V. c. 41 (*A.-G.* v. *Croydon*, 58 L. J. Ch. 527).

V. Inhabitant.

READY.—"I will be ready to;" held a covenant (*Walker* v. *Walker*, 1 Roll. Ab. 519, pl. 8).

V. Ready and Willing.

READY AND WILLING.—"'Ready and Willing' imply not only the disposition, but the capacity to do the act" (per Abinger, C.B., *De Medina* v. *Norman*, 11 L. J. Ex. 322; 9 M. & W. 827). "I cannot conceive any circumstance more indicative of want of readiness than incapacity" (per Bosanquet, J., *Lawrence* v. *Knowles*, 5 Bing. N. C. 399; 8 L. J. C. P. 210).

V. Ready.

READY MONEY.—A bequest of "Ready Money" includes cash at the bankers, whether balance on current account, or a deposit, or withdrawable after notice (*Parker* v. *Marchant*, 12 L. J. Ch. 385; 1 Phill. 356: *Langdale* v. *Whitfield*, 27 L. J. Ch. 797: *Taylor* v. *Taylor*, 1 Jur. 401: 1 Jarm. 769, n.: *Tallent* v. *Scott*, W. N. (68) 236: *Stein* v. *Ritherdon*, Ib. 65): but not unreceived Dividends on Stock (*May* v. *Grave*, 18 L. J. Ch. 401; 3 D. G. & S. 462). But in *Cooke* v. *Wagster* (23 L. J. Ch. 496; 2 Sm. & G. 296), Stuart, V.-C., said that *May* v. *Grave* was not reconcileable with *Parker* v. *Marchant*, nor with *Fryer* v. *Ranken* (9 L. J. Ch. 337; 11 Sim. 55), and it was held in *Cooke* v. *Wagster*, that a debt would (under the peculiar wording of the Will) pass under a bequest of "Ready Money." (In Wms. Exs. 1194, n. *e*, it is also said that *May* v. *Grave* is difficult to reconcile with *Fryer* v. *Ranken*). In Ireland, it has been held that money in the hands of a Sales-master, is not "Ready Money" (*Smith* v. *Butler*, 9 Ir. Eq. Rep. 398).

A bequest of "whatever remains of the Ready Money already mentioned," held, not to pass a sum of £4,000 Government Stock which was previously mentioned in the Will (*Bevan* v. *Bevan*, 5 L. R. Ir. 57).

Vf. Vaisey v. *Reynolds*, 6 L. J. Ch. O. S. 172; 5 Russ. 12: *Smith* v. *Butler*, 3 J. & La T. 565: and as to admitting extrinsic evidence to widen the meaning of "Ready Money," *V. Knight* v. *Knight*, 30 L. J. Ch. 644; 2 Giff. 616.

V. Money.

READY QUAY BERTH.—Where by a charter-party, a ship, on arriving in port, is to go "to such *ready quay berth* as ordered by charterers," that means that the charterers undertake, for the benefit of the shipowner, that a quay shall be "ready" as soon as the ship is ready to proceed to it (*Harris* v. *Jacobs*, 54 L. J. Q. B. 492; 15 Q. B. D. 247).

READY TO BE DELIVERED.—*V.* Publication, *of Award.*

READY TO LOAD.—A ship to be "Ready to Load" must be completely ready, and discharged in all her holds, so as to give the charterer complete control of every portion of the ship available for cargo (*Groves* v. *Volkart*, 1 Times Rep. 92, 454. *Va. Vaughan* v. *Campbell*, 2 Times Rep. 33).

REAL EFFECTS.—"Do the words 'Real Effects' in law, mean Real Chattels only? No authority has been produced to show that they do. The natural and true meaning of 'Real Effects' in common language and speech is, Real Property" (per Mansfield, C. J., *Hogan* v. *Jackson*, 1 Cowp. 307). "*Hogan* v. *Jackson* decided that 'Real Effects' mean Real

Property" (per Parker, V.-C., *Torrington* v. *Bowman*, 22 L. J. Ch. 236). *Vf.* 1 Jarm. 723, 724 ; 2 Ib. 283.

REAL ESTATE.—"Real Estate" is a term of art to be construed, as a general rule, technically (per Chitty, J., *Butler* v. *Butler*, 54 L. J. Ch. 197; 28 Ch. D. 66). It comprises all a person's freehold and copyhold lands, tenements and heredits, including therein titles of honour and dignity, and also incorporeal hereditaments,—*e.g.* rights of light, air and way : but not including leaseholds for years (Wms. R. P. Introd : *Va.* ESTATE).

For the purposes of the Wills Act (1 V. c. 26) "Real Estate" extends to "Manors, advowsons, messuages, lands, tithes, rents and hereditaments, whether freehold, customary freehold, tenant-right, customary or copyhold, or of any other tenure, and whether corporeal, incorporeal or personal, and to any undivided share thereof and to any estate, right or interest (other than a chattel interest) therein" (s. 1). The phrase "other than a chattel interest" obviously points to leaseholds for years.

V. PERSONAL ESTATE.

Though a devise of "Real Estate" does not *primâ facie* include leaseholds for years, for they are only chattels (Co. Litt. 46 a, and *V. Holmes* v. *Milward*, 47 L. J. Ch. 522 : *Butler* v. *Butler*, sup.), yet leaseholds for years may, by a context, or the circumstances, be included in such a devise (*Swift* v. *Swift*, 29 L. J. Ch. 121 ; 1 D. G. F. & J. 160 : *Gully* v. *Davis*, 39 L. J. Ch. 684 ; L. R. 10 Eq. 562). And so where a testator being possessed of freeholds and long leaseholds at A., and of long leaseholds only at B., devised his "Real Estate" at A. and B., it was held that all the leaseholds passed (*Moase* v. *White*, 3 Ch. D. 763 ; but *V. Moase* v. *White* explained in jdgmt. of Chitty, J., in *Butler* v. *Butler*, sup.). So in *Re Davison* (32 S. J. 273 ; 58 L. T. 304), North, J., followed *Moase* v. *White*, and further held that "Real Estate" was equivalent to "Land" as that latter word is used in s. 26, 1 V. c. 26. *Vf.* Hawk. 33.

A general devise of "Real Estate," or of "Lands," and such like expressions, includes real estate contracted to be purchased by the testator, but not actually conveyed to him (*Atcherley* v. *Vernon*, 10 Mod. 518) ; but unless the testator expresses a contrary intention, any unpaid purchase money is payable by the devisee (17 & 18 V. c. 113 : s. 2, 30 & 31 V. c. 60). Such a devise will not include purchase money of property sold by the testator, but which he has not conveyed (*Knollys* v. *Shepherd*, 1 Jac. & W. 499), *secus*, where the sale is demanded after his death under an option given in his lifetime (*Drant* v. *Vause*, 11 L. J. Ch. 170 ; 1 Y. & C. Ch. 580).

A like devise formerly comprised Trust and Mortgage estates (*Braybroke* v. *Inskip*, 8 Ves. 435 : *Bainbridge* v. *Ashburton*, 6 L. J. Ex. Eq. 73 ; 2 Y. & C. Ex. 347). But all trust and mortgage estates, devolving by death since Dec. 31, 1881, go to the deceased's personal representatives "notwithstanding any testamentary disposition" (s. 30, Conv. & L. P. Act, 1881).

V. LAND.

An action by an heir-at-law against an administratrix for an account of Rents received by her, is not "a Cause or Matter *relating to Real Estate*" within R. 1, Ord. 51, R. S. C. (*Re Staines*, 55 L. J. Ch. 913).

"Interest in the *Nature of Real Estate*," 24 & 25 V. c. 40;—a Gale of mines in the Forest of Dean is within this phrase (*Morgan* v. *Crawshay*, 40 L. J. M. C. 202; L. R. 5 H. L. 304).

REAL AND PERSONAL EFFECTS.—This phrase is "synonymous to SUBSTANCE" (per Mansfield, C. J., *Hogan* v. *Jackson*, 1 Cowp. 307).
V. REAL EFFECTS.

REAL OR PERSONAL PROPERTY.—In the language of conveyancers all kinds of property, and all kinds of proprietary rights, are comprehended in one or other of the two great classes into which such property and rights are divided;—(1) Real, or (2) Personal Property (*V.* Intro. Ch. Wms. Real Pro.). But in the Malicious Injuries to Property Act (24 & 25 V. c. 97), s. 52, the phrase "any real or personal property whatsoever" relates only "to corporeal, tangible and visible property, and not to property which is incorporeal, invisible and not tangible" (per Lopes, J., *Laws* v. *Eltringham*, 51 L. J. M. C. 15), and therefore a right to herbage is not within the section (51 L. J. M. C. 13; 8 Q. B. D. 283): *Vf.* as to this section, WILFUL AND MALICIOUS.

It may probably be stated that "Real Property" and REAL ESTATE are synonymous, and that "Personal Property" is synonymous with PERSONAL ESTATE.

REAL SECURITY.—The obvious meaning of this phrase is a mortgage of Real Estate. But a power to invest on "Real Security" will not authorise trustees to invest on a *Contributory* Mortgage (*Webb* v. *Jonas*, 57 L. J. Ch. 671; 58 L. T. 882), or on an *Equitable* Mortgage (*Swaffield* v. *Nelson*, W. N. (76) 255).

Turnpike-Road Bonds, secured by a mortgage or charge on tolls and toll-houses, are within a power enabling trustees to invest in Real Securities (*Robinson* v. *Robinson*, 21 L. J. Ch. 111; 1 D. G. M. & G. 247); but where a testator bequeathed all his securities for money "except *Mortgages* on real and leasehold security," it was held that mortgages of *Turnpike Tolls*, whether including toll-houses or not, were not within the exception, such mortgages not being within the ordinary meaning of the word "Mortgage" (*Cavendish* v. *Cavendish*, 55 L. J. Ch. 144; 30 Ch. D. 227; 53 L. T. 652).

Though a freehold *Brick-field* is a Real Security in itself, yet so much of its improved value as is derived from the buildings and machinery on it, which are only applicable to the trade of brick-making, should not be estimated for the purpose of the investment of trust funds (*Learoyd* v. *Whiteley*, 57 L. J. Ch. 390; 12 App. Ca. 727; 58 L. T. 93; 36 W. R. 721).

Before the Trustee Act, 1888, *Leaseholds* for years, however long the term, were held not a "Real Security" (*Re Chennell*, 47 L. J. Ch. 583 ; 8 Ch. D. 492 : *Re Boyd*, 49 L. J. Ch. 808 ; 14 Ch. D. 626) ; nor even a long term for raising portions (*Leigh* v. *Leigh*, 56 L. J. Ch. 125 ; 35 W. R. 121 ; 55 L. T. 634 ; 3 Times Rep. 123. *Vh.* Lewin, 327, 328 ; in n. (*a*) at the latter page it is suggested that a long term *at a pepper-corn rent* might be enlarged into the fee simple, Conv. & L. P. Act, 1881, s. 65 ; Conv. Act, 1882, s. 11, and so be available as a Real Security). But by s. 9, Trustee Act, 1888 (51 & 52 V. c. 59), a power to invest trust money in "Real Securities" authorises, and shall be deemed to have always authorised, a Mortgage of Leaseholds held for an unexpired term of not less than 200 years,—and not subject to a greater rent than 1*s.* a year, or to any right of redemption, or to any condition for re-entry except for non-payment of rent.

"Real Securities," *in Ireland*, include Leaseholds for lives renewable for ever (*Macleod* v. *Annesley*, 16 Bea. 600 ; 22 L. J. Ch. 633).

REALIZATION.—As to "Realization" of a bankrupt's property, within s. 24 (3), Bankry. Act, 1883 ; *V.* jdgmt. of Ld. Fitzgerald in *Board of Trade* v. *Block*, 58 L. J. Q. B. 116 ; 13 App. Ca. 570 ; 59 L. T. 734.

REALIZE.—If goods "realize" so much, then commission on excess:— As to what expenses may be deducted from gross proceeds in order to ascertain amount "realized;" *V. Ardree Oyster Co.* v. *Ullmann*, Times, 25th March, 1890.

REALIZED.—Where Articles of Association of a Company provide that "no dividend shall be payable except out of *Realized Profits*," the word "Realized" "must have its ordinary meaning, which, if not equivalent to 'Reduced to actual cash in hand,' must at least be 'Rendered tangible for the purpose of division.' . . . The meaning of the word is the direct converse of 'Estimated'" (per Kay, J., *Re Oxford Bg. Socy.*, 56 L. J. Ch. 102 ; 35 Ch. D. 502 ; 55 L. T. 598 ; 35 W. R. 116).

"Realized *Member*" of a Building Society ; *V. Re Norwich & Norfolk Bg. Socy.*, 45 L. J. Ch. 785.

REALM.—"'*Out of the realme*' (*id est*), *extra regnum ;* as much as to say, as out of the power of the king of England as of his Crowne of England ; for if a man be upon the Sea of England, hee is within the kingdom or realme of England, and within the ligeance of the king of England, as of his Crowne of England. And yet *altum mare* is out of the jurisdiction of the common law, and within the jurisdiction of the lord admirall" (Co. Litt. 260 a, b). A little further on Coke seems to cite Littleton as using "Beyond the Sea" and "Out of the realm" as convertible terms.

The "Realm," in the old Bankry Acts for England, meant England and

Wales, for those parts of the kingdom only were subject to the English bankry law (*Williams* v. *Nunn*, 1 Taunt. 270).

The words "within this Realm," in the Stat. of Monopolies (21 Jac. 1, c. 3), applies to all the United Kingdom (*Robinson's Patent*, 5 Moore. P. C. 65 : *Morgan* v. *Seaward*, 2 M. & W. 544 : *Brown* v. *Annandale*, 8 Cl. & F. 437) ; but not to the Colonies (*Rolls* v. *Isaacs*, 51 L. J. Ch. 170 ; 19 Ch. D. 268).

V. Beyond Seas.

REASON.—When a "Reason" has to be given for an act or for refraining from an act, *semble*, though a discretion be given, such discretion is not absolute (*R.* v. *London Bp.*, 24 Q. B. D. 213).

V. By Reason.

REASONABLE.—It would be unreasonable to expect an exact definition of the word "Reasonable." Reason varies in its conclusions according to the idiosyncrasy of the individual, and the times and circumstances in which he thinks. The reasoning which built up the old scholastic logic, sounds now like the jingling of a child's toy. But mankind must be satisfied with the reasonableness within reach ; and in cases not covered by authority, the verdict of a jury (or the decision of a judge sitting as a jury) usually determines what is "reasonable" in each particular case ; but frequently reasonableness "belongeth to the knowledge of the law, and therefore to be decided by the justices" (Co. Litt. 56 b).

Where a *Contract* has to be performed (*Attwood* v. *Emery*, 26 L. J. C. P. 73 ; 1 C. B. N. S. 110 : *Briddon* v. *G. N. Ry.*, 28 L. J. Ex. 51: *Hales* v. *Lond. & N. W. Ry.*, 32 L. J. Q. B. 292 ; 4 B. & S. 66 ; 11 W. R. 856), or a duty discharged (*Goodwyn* v. *Cheveley*, 28 L. J. Ex. 298 ; 4 H. & N. 631), within a *Reasonable Time*, such time will have to be determined according to the circumstances of the case, and with particular reference to the means and ability of the person by whom the contract is to be performed, or the duty discharged (*Toms* v. *Wilson*, 32 L. J. Q. B. 33 ; Ib. 382 ; 4 B. & S. 455 ; 11 W. R. 117: *Brighty* v. *Norton*, 32 L. J. Q. B. 38 ; 3 B. & S. 305 ; 11 W. R. 167). An obligation to perform a Contract within "a reasonable time" does not require so speedy a fulfilment as one to be done 'directly" or "as soon as possible" (Add. C. 1188). *Vf.* Reasonable Hour.

Six years is a reasonable time within which to present a Cheque for payment, unless loss has been occasioned by unnecessary delay (*Robinson* v. *Hawksford*, 15 L. J. Q. B. 377; 9 Q. B. 52 : *Laws* v. *Rand*, 27 L. J. C. P. 76 ; 30 L. T. O. S. 286 : *Re Bethell*, 34 Ch. D. 566: but *cp. Hare* v. *Henty*, 30 L. J. C. P. 302).

A *Power* to grant *Mining Leases* for such terms as to the donee "shall seem *reasonable and proper*," authorises a Lease for 99 years (*Taylor* v. *Mostyn*, 52 L. J. Ch. 848 ; 23 Ch. D. 583 ; 31 W. R. 3, 686 ; 48 L. T. 715).

"Reasonable Time" for serving a *Magistrate's Summons* prior to hearing; *V. R.* v. *Smith*, L. R. 10 Q. B. 604.

As to reasonable time for service of *Notice to Produce; V.* Rosc. N. P. 12.

As to what is a reasonable *Notice to Quit* in tenancies for less than a year; *V. Huffell* v. *Armistead*, 7 C. & P. 56: *Towne* v. *Campbell*, 16 L. J. C. P. 128; 3 C. B. 921: *Jones* v. *Mills*, 31 L. J. C. P. 66: And as to what is a reasonable *Notice to determine service* in cases other than domestic; *V. Fairman* v. *Oakford*, 29 L. J. Ex. 459; 5 H. & N. 635: *Parker* v. *Ibbetson*, 27 L. J. C. P. 236; 4 C. B. N. S. 346: *Buckingham* v. *Surrey & Hants Canal Co.*, 46 L. T. 885.

"Fair and Reasonable *Compensation*," under 2nd par., s. 5, Agricultural Holdings (England) Act, 1883; *V.* Woodf. 779.

By s. 7, *Railway & Canal Traffic Act*, 1854 (17 & 18 V. c. 31), Railway and Canal Companies are empowered to make such *Conditions* with their customers respecting the receiving, forwarding, or delivering goods, "as shall be adjudged, by the Court or Judge before whom any question relating thereto shall be tried, to be *just and reasonable*." The question of reasonableness under that section is one of law and not of fact (*Simons* v. *G. W. Ry.*, 26 L. J. C. P. 25, 33; 18 C. B. 805, 829); and the onus of showing reasonableness is on the Company (*Peek* v. *N. Staffordsh. Ry.*, 32 L. J. Q. B. 241; 10 H. L. Ca. 473). The solution of this question "will materially depend upon the nature of the articles to be conveyed, the degree of risk attendant upon their conveyance, the rate of charge made, and whether the Company was bound, by the common law or by statute, to carry the articles on being paid the customary hire, or whether it was in its power to reject them altogether and refuse to carry them upon any terms. Whenever, in order to bring a Railway or Canal Company within the protection of a condition or special contract, it is necessary to construe it as excluding responsibility for losses occasioned by the Company's negligence and misconduct, the condition or special contract is unreasonable and unjust, and therefore void, unless an option is given to the customer to have the goods carried on the ordinary terms, at the ordinary rate. Where the terms of the condition are unconditional and would, if valid, protect the Company even in the case of the wilful misconduct of the defendant's own servants, the condition is unreasonable" (Add. C. 556). Applying these principles the following have been held to be

Reasonable Conditions.

Non-liability of Company, for loss of market or other such like delay or detention (*White* v. *G. W. Ry.*, 26 L. J. C. P. 158; 2 C. B. N. S. 7: *Beal* v. *S. Devon Ry.*, 29 L. J. Ex. 441; 5 H. & N. 875: *Lord* v. *Mid. Ry.*, 36 L. J. C. P. 170; L. R. 2 C. P. 339: *Sheridan* v. *Mid. G. W. Ry.*, 24 L. R. Ir. 146); or for goods incorrectly described (*Lewis* v. *G. W. Ry.*, 29 L. J. Ex. 425; 5 H. & N. 867); or for damage in transit to perishable goods, or from restiveness of animals (*Austin* v. *Manchester, S. & L. Ry.*,

21 L. J. C. P. 179 ; 10 C. B. 475 : *Beal* v. *S. Devon Ry.*, sup. : *Sheridan* v. *Mid. G. W. Ry.*, sup.), or from over-crowding (*Sheridan* v. *Mid. G. W. Ry.*, sup.) ; or when a special rate of freight lower than ordinary is taken (*Simons* v. *G. W. Ry.*, 26 L. J. C. P. 25 ; 18 C. B. 805, especially if a *bonâ fide* alternative be given to send the goods at the ordinary rate without condition, *Robinson* v. *G. W. Ry.*, 35 L. J. C. P. 123 : *Brown* v. *Manchester, S. & L. Ry.*, 51 L. J. Q. B. 599 ; 52 Ib. 132 ; 53 Ib. 124 ; 9 Q. B. D. 230 ; 10 Ib. 250 ; 8 App. Ca. 703, or when the exemption does not include wilful misconduct, *Lewis* v. *G. W. Ry.*, 47 L. J. Q. B. 131; 3 Q. B. D. 195) ; or precluding Company's liability unless claim sent in within 7 days after goods delivered (*Lewis* v. *G. W. Ry.*, 29 L. J. Ex. 425 ; 5 H. & N. 867).

But the following (except when warranted by a specially low rate of freight, coupled with the option of sending at ordinary rate without condition) are

Unreasonable Conditions.

Non-liability of Company for loss however occasioned (*Peek* v. *N. Staffordshire Ry.*, 32 L. J. Q. B. 241 ; 10 H. L. Ca. 473 : *Cohen* v. *S. E. Ry.*, 2 Ex. D. 253 ; 46 L. J. Ex. 417 ; and as to horses, &c., *V. M'Manus* v. *Lancashire & Yorkshire Ry.*, 28 L. J. Ex. 353 ; 4 H. & N. 327 : *M'Cance* v. *Lond. & N. W. Ry.*, 31 L. J. Ex. 65 ; 34 Ib. 39 ; 7 H. & N. 477 ; 3 H. & C. 343 : *Ashendon* v. *L. B. & S. Ry.*, 5 Ex. D. 190 : *Gregory* v. *W. Midland Ry.*, 33 L. J. Ex. 155 ; 2 H. & C. 944 : *Rooth* v. *N. E. Ry.*, 36 L. J. Ex. 83 ; L. R. 2 Ex. 173) ; or for loss, detention or damage through insufficient packing (*Simons* v. *G. W. Ry.*, sup : *Garton* v. *Bristol & Exeter Ry.*, 30 L. J. Q. B. 273 ; 1 B. & S. 112) ; or for loss of passenger's luggage "unless fully and properly addressed with the name and destination of the owner" (*Cutler* v. *N. London Ry.*, 56 L. J. Q. B. 648 ; 19 Q. B. D. 64 ; 56 L. T. 639 ; 35 W. R. 575 ; 51 J. P. 774).

As to what is a *bonâ fide* and just *Alternative Rate* ; *V. Dickson* v. *G. N. Ry.*, 56 L. J. Q. B. 111 ; 18 Q. B. D. 176 ; 55 L. T. 868 ; 35 W. R. 202 ; 51 J. P. 388 : and as to what words will give an option, *V. G. W. Ry.* v. *McCarthy*, 56 L. J. P. C. 33 ; 12 App. Ca. 218 ; 56 L. T. 582 ; 35 W. R. 429 ; 51 J. P. 532.

Vf. as to Carriers Act and Ry. & Canal Traffic Act, Add. C. 553–559 ; Rosc. N. P. 566–573.

V. Fair and Reasonable.

REASONABLE ACTS.—*V.* Acts.

REASONABLE AND PROBABLE CAUSE.—"Reasonable and Probable Cause," s. 8, 7 & 8 G. 4, c. 29, relating to Threatening Letters, applies to the money demanded, and not to the accusation threatened (*R.* v. *Hamilton*, 1 C. & K. 212).

"Reasonable and Probable Cause" for detaining a Ship, s. 10, Mer.

Shipping Act, 1876, 39 & 40 V. c. 80, is a question for the jury with the assistance of expert evidence; and the proper question to be left to the jury is, whether the facts in connection with the ship, which would have been apparent to a person of ordinary skill who had had, and had used, all means of examining and enquiring about her, would, in the opinion of the jury, have given such person Reasonable and Probable Cause to suspect the safety of the ship on her outward and homeward voyage, and so to detain her for survey (*Thompson* v. *Farrer*, 51 L. J. Q. B. 534; 9 Q. B. D. 372). *Vf.* *Dixon* v. *Bd. of Trade*, 3 Times Rep. 478. REASONABLY SUSPECTS.

As to evidence of Reasonable and Probable Cause in action for Malicious Prosecution; *V.* Rosc. N. P. 811–813.

"*Lawful* or Reasonable Cause;" *V.* LAWFUL CAUSE.

REASONABLE AND PROPER.—Particulars in an action for infringement of a patent will not be shewn to be "Reasonable and Proper," so as to justify Certificate of Costs for them under s. 29, subs. 6, Patents &c. Act, 1883, 46 & 47 V. c. 57, by merely shewing that they were not unreasonable; the Court will satisfy itself as to whether they were "reasonable and proper" rather by the result, than by considering the position in which the litigant's advisers were placed when settling the Particulars (*Germ Milling Co.* v. *Robinson*, 55 L. T. 282; 2 Times Rep. 785).

REASONABLE CONDITION.—*V.* REASONABLE.

REASONABLE COSTS.—Where an intended mortgagor agreed to pay the "Reasonable Costs" of the mortgagee's solicitor if the matter went off (which happened), held that this did not include the expense of withdrawing the money from a banker and remitting it for payment (*Re Blakesley*, 32 Bea. 379).

REASONABLE DILIGENCE.—*V.* DUE DILIGENCE.

REASONABLE EXCUSE.—The excuses for not causing a child to attend school which may be prescribed by bye-laws under s. 74, 33 & 34 V. c. 75, do not exhaust the instances of "Reasonable Excuse" (*Belper Case*, 51 L. J. M. C. 91; 9 Q. B. D. 259). That case also decides that a parent reasonably and fairly doing his best to send his truant child to school, has a "Reasonable Excuse" against a summons for a penalty for not causing the child to attend. Detaining a child at home to earn money necessary to the support of the family is also a like "Reasonable Excuse" (*London Case*, 53 L. J. M. C. 104; 13 Q. B. D. 176; 32 W. R. 768). But where a child plays truant against the parent's wish, that is not a "Reasonable Excuse" against an application for an order for sending the child to school under s. 11, Elementary Education Act, 1876 (39 & 40 V. c. 79); a "Reasonable Excuse" under that section must be one of the two thereby prescribed (*Hewett* v. *Thompson*, 58 L. J. M. C. 60; 60 L. T. 268).

As to what is a "Reasonable Excuse" (within s. 31, *Divorce* Act, 1857, 20 & 21 V. c. 85) justifying a wife in living separate from her husband; *V. Du Terreaux* v. *Du Terreaux*, 28 L. J. P. & M. 95; and vice versâ, *Haswell* v. *Haswell*, 29 L. J. P. & M. 21.

If rent be only recently due and has not been demanded by the landlord, that is a "Reasonable Excuse," in the mouth of a grantor of a *Bill of Sale*, for the non-production of the receipt for that rent within s. 7, subs. 4, Bills of Sale Act, 1882 (*Ex p. Cotton*, 11 Q. B. D. 301).

REASONABLE EXPECTATION.—A person who begins business without capital and with a mortgage on all his assets and who afterwards becomes bankrupt, has contracted his debts without "reasonable or probable ground of expectation *of being able to pay*" within s. 28 (3), Bankry. Act, 1883. (*Ex p. White*, 54 L. J. Q. B. 384; 14 Q. B. D. 600: *Vf. Ex p. Downman*, 32 L. J. Bank. 49; 11 W. R. 577: *Ex p. Mortimore*, 30 L. J. Bank. 17; 3 D. G. F. & J. 599).

REASONABLE FACILITIES.—*V.* FACILITIES.

REASONABLE HOUR.—In a contract to sell and deliver 10 tons of oil "within the last 14 days of March;" the plaintiff tendered it at half-past eight on the evening of the last day of March. It was found that the tender had been made in time to give the defendant full opportunity to weigh, examine, and receive the oil, but the defendant who was present declined to receive it on the ground that the tender was made at an unreasonable time, but it was held (Denman, C. J., dissenting) that the tender had been made in time (Blackb. 225, citing *Startup* v. *Macdonald*, 6 M. & G. 593; 12 L. J. Ex. 477). In that case Parke, B., said, "Where a thing is to be done *anywhere*, a tender a convenient time before midnight is sufficient; where the thing is to be done at a *particular place*, and where the law implies a duty on the party to whom the thing is to be done to attend, that attendance is to be by daylight, and a convenient time before sunset."

V. REASONABLE.

REASONABLE PORTION.—A power to charge estates "with Reasonable Portions, or Fortunes for younger Children, and for their maintenance and education," is sufficiently certain to be capable of execution; and the word "Reasonable" there, is applicable not only to the amount of the Portion, but also to the time and occasion on which the child would want it (*Edgeworth* v. *Edgeworth*, Beatty, 328).

REASONABLE TIME.—*V.* REASONABLE.

REASONABLY PRACTICABLE.—A direction that a set of affirmative and negative rules shall be observed "so far as is reasonably practicable," will not, unless under very exceptional circumstances indeed, apply to the negative rules. "It is always possible *not* to do that which you are forbidden to do" (per Day, J., *Wales* v. *Thomas*, 55 L. J. M. C. 61 ; 16 Q. B. D. 340 ; 55 L. T. 400 ; 50 J. P. 516 ; 2 Times Rep. 53) ; and it was accordingly held in that case that the rule in s. 51, Coal Mines Regulation Act, 1872 (35 & 36 V. c. 76), prohibiting firing a shot into a mine until the men are out of it, is unqualified by the words at the commencement of the section that the rules thereby laid down "shall be observed so far as is reasonably practicable."

REASONABLY SUSPECTS.—Pawnbrokers' Act, 1872, 35 & 36 V. c. 93, s. 34 ; *V. Howard* v. *Clarke*, 20 Q. B. D. 558.

REBUTTER.—"'*Rebouter*' is a French word, and is in Latine *repellere*, to repell or barre" (Co. Litt. 365 a).

RECEIPT.—A Turnpike Ticket is a "Receipt" (*R.* v. *Fitch*, L. & C. 159), and a Bank Pass Book is an "*Accountable* Receipt" (*R.* v. *Smith*, 31 L. J. M. C. 154 ; L. & C. 168 : *R.* v. *Moody*, 31 L. J. M. C. 156 ; L. & C. 173), within s. 23, 24 & 25 V. c. 98 ; but a "Clearance" certificate from one branch of a Friendly Society to another is not (*R.* v. *French*, 39 L. J. M. C. 58 ; L. R. 1 C. C. R. 217).

Neither a simple Receipt, nor an Inventory of goods and Receipt for their purchase money, is a "Receipt" which, under s. 4, *Bills of Sale Act*, 1878, requires registration, *unless such Receipt, or Inventory and Receipt, make the title of the purchaser* to the goods (*Marsden* v. *Meadows*, 7 Q. B. D. 80 ; 50 L. J. Q. B. 536. *Vf. Thompson* v. *Barrett*, 1 L. T. 268 : *Allsop* v. *Day*, 31 L. J. Ex. 105 ; 7 H. & N. 457 : *Byerley* v. *Prevost*, L. R. 6 C. P. 144 : and *V.* those three cases commented on and distinguished in *Ex p. Odell, Re Walden*, 10 Ch. D. 76 ; 48 L. J. Bank. 1 : and in *Re Baum, Ex p. Cooper*, 10 Ch. D. 313 ; 48 L. J. Bank. 40. But the authority of *Marsden* v. *Meadows* was established by H. L. in *Manchester, S. & L. Ry.* v. *North Central Waggon Co.*, 13 App. Ca. 554. *V.* ASSURANCE).

"Receipt and Acceptance ;" *V.* ACCEPTANCE.

V. RECEIPTS : AUTHORITY OR REQUEST.

RECEIPTS.—This is not a word applicable to corpus (*Troutbeck* v. *Boughey*, 35 L. J. Ch. 840 ; 2 Eq. 53). In that case Kindersley, V.-C., said, "How could a receipt be given for a fee simple ?" *Vf. Johnson* v. *Johnson*, 56 L. J. Ch. 326 ; 35 Ch. D. 345 ; 56 L. T. 163 ; 35 W. R. 329.

V. IN RECEIPT.

RECEIVABLE.—"I myself should have held that the words 'receivable' and 'payable' were the same thing, and that both were equivalent to 'vested ;' but I am happy to find that the judgment of the M. R. in *Hayward* v. *James* (29 L. J. Ch. 822 ; 28 Bea. 523), expresses exactly the same conclusion" (per Malins, V.-C., *West* v. *Miller*, 37 L. J. Ch. 426 ; L. R. 6 Eq. 59). *Vf.* Watson, Eq. 1228.

"Receivable" may be construed "received" (Wms. Exs. 1090, citing *Re Dodgson*, 1 Drew. 440).

V. RECEIVED : PAYABLE.

RECEIVED.—In an executory gift over, "Received" should generally be read "RECEIVABLE," and accordingly as equivalent to PAYABLE (*West* v. *Miller*, 37 L. J. Ch. 423 ; L. R. 6 Eq. 59 : 2 Jarm. 812 *et seq.*). "I take it to be now settled that where there is a gift of property to vest in a person at 21 or marriage, with a gift over in the event of such person dying before the same becomes 'payable,' or the legatee is 'entitled in possession,' these and all similar expressions mean no more than dying before the property becomes '*vested.*' Here the word is 'Received,' that is 'Receivable.' But if one person has to pay, there must be another to receive, and 'receivable' must mean the same as 'payable,' so far as it refers to any period of time . . . In all cases where there is a gift for life, followed by a gift in remainder, which is to vest at the attainment of a particular age, or upon any other event personal to the legatee in remainder, and then a gift over in the event of the latter dying before the legacy is 'payable,' 'receivable,' 'vested in possession,' *or any other form is used which means 'paid' or 'received,'* there all such expressions are to be taken as equivalent to '*vested*'" (per Malins, V.-C., *West* v. *Miller*, sup.).

Where a Charter-party provides that the Bills of Lading shall be "conclusive evidence of the amount of cargo *received*," "received" means "shipped on board" (*Lishman* v. *Christie*, 56 L. J. Q. B. 538 ; 19 Q. B. D. 333 ; 57 L. T. 552 ; 35 W. R. 744, which, as nearly as possible, overrules *Pyman* v. *Burt*, Cab. & El. 207).

Commission "on any Money received ;" *V. Fisher* v. *Drewett*, 48 L. J. Q. B. 32 : *Green* v. *Lucas*, 33 L. T. 584.

V. ACTUALLY RECEIVED : MONEY RECEIVED.

RECEIVING.—As regards the criminal receiving of stolen goods, "a person is said to receive goods improperly obtained as soon as he obtains control over them from the person from whom he receives them.

Where goods are received by a wife or servant, in the husband's or master's absence, with a guilty knowledge on the part of such wife or servant, the husband or master does not become a Receiver only by acquiring a guilty knowledge of the receipt of the goods by such wife or servant, and passively acquiescing therein ; but he does become a Receiver with a guilty knowledge if, having such knowledge, he does any act approving of the receipt of the goods.

Property ceases to be stolen or otherwise improperly obtained, within the meaning of this Article, as soon as it comes into the possession of the general or special owner, and if such general or special owner delivers it to some one who delivers it to a person who receives it knowing of the previous theft or other obtaining, such receiving is not an offence within this article" (Steph. Cr. 282).

Vf. Arch. Cr. 489–499 ; Rosc. Cr. 906–919.

RECEIVING ORDER.—This phrase, in s. 40, subs. (b), Bankry. Act, 1883, means an Order, whether interim or not, "which takes the receipts out of the hands of the debtor, and leaves him no longer the power of satisfying claims for wages and salaries" (per Cave, J., *Re Smith,* 55 L. J. Q. B. 291 ; 17 Q. B. D. 4 ; 54 L. T. 307 ; 34 W. R. 535).

RECITAL OF FACT.—*V.* Fact.

RECLUSE.—"'*Recluse,*' *Reclusus, Heremita, seu Anchorita,* so called by the order of his religion ; he is so mured or shut up, *quòd solus semper sit, et in clausurâ suâ sedet;* and can never come out of his place" (Co. Litt. 258 b ; *V.* s. 434, Litt. for use of "Recluse ;" *Vf.* Termes de la Ley).

RECOGNIZED BRITISH SHIP.—A Vessel registered as a British Ship at the time of action brought, but not so registered when the collision occurred, is not a "Recognized British Ship," *quà* the action, within s. 19, Mer. Shipping Act, 1854, 17 & 18 V. c. 104 (*The Andalusian,* 3 P. D. 182). *V.* British Ship.

RECOMMEND.—*V.* Precatory Trust.

RECORD.—The Record of an Action is a memorial of the pleadings and acts in an action brought in a Court of Record (Co. Litt. 260 a, 117 b), and was formerly written on parchment (Ib. 260 a) ; but see now Ord. 36, R. 30, R. S. C. *V.* Court of Record.

The Issue accompanying a Judge's Order remitting an action to the County Court under 19 & 20 V. c. 108, s. 26, was a sufficient "Record" within s. 5, County Court Act, 1867 (*Taylor* v. *Cass,* L. R. 4 C. P. 614).

V. Debt upon Record.

RECOVER.—The word "Recover" has a technical meaning in law whereby it signifies, to recover by action and by the judgment of the Court (*Vh. Wigens* v. *Cook,* 28 L. J. C. P. 312 ; 6 C. B. N. S. 784 : *Cream* v. *Ray,* 30 L. J. Ex. 110 : *Cooper* v. *Pegg,* 24 L. J. C. P. 167 : *Smith* v. *Edge,* 33 L. J. Ex. 9 ; 2 H. & C. 659 ; 12 W. R. 133 ; *Fergusson* v. *Davison,* 8 Q. B. D. 470 ; 51 L. J. Q. B. 266) : but it is said that there are cases which may be found in which the word has been held to be used in the larger and more popular sense of recover by any legal means, which would include, *e.g.,*—a distress (per Willes, J., *Haines* v. *Welch,* 38 L. J. C. P. 118 ; L. R. 4 C. P. 91 ; 17 W. R. 163). In that case it was held that the word in s. 1, 14 & 15 V. c. 25, includes the right to distrain.

But the amount of a verdict is not "recovered" till judgment can be signed upon it (per Brett, J., *Ings* v. *Lond. & S. W. Ry.,* 38 L. J. C. P. 8 ; L. R. 4 C. P. 17 ; 17 W. R. 120). A Plaintiff does not "recover" a sum paid in under a successful Plea of Tender (*James* v. *Vane*, 29 L. J. Q. B. 169, over-ruling *Cooch* v. *Maltby*, 23 L. J. Q. B. 305).

The proceeds of a sale in a mortgagee's hands are not "*Recovered* by any distress, action or suit," within s. 42, 3 & 4 W. 4, c. 27; and therefore arrears of interest for as far back as 20 years may be retained out of such proceeds (*Edmunds* v. *Waugh*, 35 L. J. Ch. 234; L. R. 1 Eq. 418; 14 W. R. 257: *Re Marshfield*, 34 Ch. D. 721; 56 L. J. Ch. 599; 56 L. T. 694; 35 W. R. 491: *V.* By). So though a loan the interest on which is to vary with trade profits, cannot be "recovered," if the borrower become bankrupt, until the general creditors are satisfied (s. 5, 28 & 29 V. c. 86), yet this word does not extend to deprive the lender of such rights as he may have as mortgagee (*Ex p. Sheil, Re Lonergan*, 4 Ch. D. 789; 46 L. J. Bank. 62; rejecting *Ex p. McArthur*, 40 L. J. Bank. 86). In *Ex p. Sheil* (sup.), James, L. J., said, "I think the word 'Recover' means recover, and does not mean 'Retain.'"

On that principle *Philpott* v. *Jones* (4 L. J. K. B. 65; 2 A. & E. 41; 4 N. & M. 14) decided that a debt for Spirituous Liquors was not "recovered," within the Tippling Act, 24 G. 2, c. 40, s. 12, by crediting an unappropriated payment therefor.

As to "Recover" when used in reference to land.—*e.g.*, s. 2, 3 & 4 W. 4, c. 27,—*V.* jdgmt. of Ex. delivered by Rolfe, B., in *Grant* v. *Ellis*, 11 L. J. Ex. 228; 9 M. & W. 113: *Vth. Irish Land Commission* v. *Grant*, 10 App. Ca. 26.

A power to a body to "Recover," implies the power to sue by its collective designation though not incorporated (*Mills* v. *Scott*, L. R. 8 Q. B. 496; 42 L. J. Q. B. 234).

"Recovered *as Damages*," in a Local Improvement Act incorporating Ry. C. C. Act, 1845, and Towns Imp. Act, 1847, means so recovered before Justices (*Blackburn* v. *Parkinson*, 28 L. J. M. C. 7; 1 E. & E. 71).

"Sum Recovered;" *V. Johnson* v. *Harris*, 24 L. J. C. P. 40; 15 C. B. 357: *Dixon* v. *Walker*, 10 L. J. Ex. 43; 7 M. & W. 214: *James* v. *Vane*, 2 E. & E. 883.

V. Recovered or Preserved: To be recovered.

RECOVERABLE.—In an undertaking by a solicitor to his client that "should the damages or costs not be recoverable in this action, I shall charge you costs out of purse only," the result of the action, and not the solvency of the defendant therein, is referred to (*Re Stretton*, 15 L. J. Ex. 16; 14 M. & W. 806).

RECOVERED OR PRESERVED.—The charge for costs to which the Court is empowered, by s. 28, Solicitors' Act, 1860 (23 & 24 V. c. 127), to declare a solicitor entitled upon the property "Recovered or Preserved" by him, may embrace the whole property saved by his exertions, and is not confined merely to his client's interest therein

(*Greer* v. *Young*, 52 L. J. Ch. 915 ; 24 Ch. D. 545 ; 31 W. R. 930 : *Charlton* v. *Charlton*, 52 L. J. Ch. 971 ; 32 W. R. 91 : over-ruling *Berrie* v. *Howitt*, 39 L. J. Ch. 119 ; L. R. 9 Eq. 1).

As to what is "Property" so "recovered or preserved ;" *V. Emden* v. *D'Oyley Carte*, 51 L. J. Ch. 371; 19 Ch. D. 311; 30 W. R. 17 : *Re Wadsworth*, 54 L. J. Ch. 638 ; 29 Ch. D. 517 : *Pinkerton* v. *Easton*, 42 L. J. Ch. 878 ; L. R. 16 Eq. 490. The Costs recovered in an action, as well as the thing sued for, are such "Property" (*Dallow* v. *Garrold*, 54 L. J. Q. B. 76 ; 14 Q. B. D. 543 ; 33 W. R. 219) ; and so are Costs ordered to be repaid to the Client upon a successful Appeal (*Guy* v. *Churchill*, 35 Ch. D. 489 ; 56 L. J. Ch. 670 ; 57 L. T. 510 ; 35 W. R. 706 ; 3 Times Rep. 600) ; and so is an annual sum which has been secured to a wife under s. 32, 20 & 21 V. c. 85 (*Harrison* v. *Harrison*, 13 P. D. 180) ; and so is property which, by a compromise, has been partially defended from a claim (*Ratcliff* v. *Swift*, 32 S. J. 787), or money received in compromise of an action (*Ross* v. *Buxton*, 58 L. J. Ch. 442). An easement, *e.g.*, a claim of right to light, is *not* such "Property" (*Foxon* v. *Gascoigne*, 43 L. J. Ch. 729 ; 9 Ch. 654). *Vh.* Ann. Pr. notes to Ord. 7, R. 3, R. S. C. : *Ex p. Brown, Re Suffield and Watts*, 20 Q. B. D. 693 ; 58 L. T. 911 ; 36 W. R. 584 : *Keeson* v. *Luxmore*, 61 L. T. 199.

V. Property.

RECOVERY OF LAND.—An action for the "Recovery of Land," as mentioned in the Rules of Court, is equivalent to the old action of ejectment to obtain possession ; and does not include an action for declaration of title (*Gledhill* v. *Hunter*, 49 L. J. Ch. 333 ; 14 Ch. D. 492 ; 28 W. R. 530 : disapproving *Whetstone* v. *Dewis*, 45 L. J. Ch. 49 ; 1 Ch. D. 99).

A Foreclosure or Redemption action is (except as hereafter stated) an action for recovery of land (*Heath* v. *Pugh*, 50 L. J. Q. B. 473 ; 6 Q. B. D. 345 : *Harlock* v. *Ashberry*, 51 L. J. Ch. 394 ; 19 Ch. D. 539) : but not for the recovery of *possession* of land within Ord. 42, R. 5, R. S. C. (*Wood* v. *Wheater*, 52 L. J. Ch. 144 ; 22 Ch. D. 281 ; 31 W. R. 117). And now, for the purposes of R. 2, Ord. 18, R. S. C., neither Foreclosure nor Redemption is to be "deemed an action for the recovery of land" (*V.* provisoes added to the Rule by R. S. C., Dec. 1885 ; *Vf.* Ann. Pr. 278).

RECTOR.—*V.* Clergyman.

RECTORY.—"By the grant of a Rectory, or Parsonage, will pass the house, the glebe, the tithes, and offerings belonging to it. And by the grant of a Vicarage will pass as much as doth belong unto it, as the vicarage house, &c." (Touch. 93).

"The word 'Rectory' comprehends the parish church, with all its rights, glebes, tithes and other profits whatsoever" (5 Cru. Dig., tit. 35, ch. 6, s. 14).

V. Elph. 617 : Advowson.

REDEMPTION.—" Stat. Marlbridge, c. 3. '*Non Ideo puniatur dominus per redemptionem.*' 'Redemption' is fine: and *finis dicitur quia finem litibus imponit*; the party redeems his offence for a sum of money, which makes an end of his transgression and of his imprisonment for it" (Dwar. 690, citing *Griesley's Case*, 8 Rep. 41 a).

REDUCED BY PAYMENT.—This phrase, in s. 7, County Court Act, 1867, meant "Reduced by payment before action brought" (*Osborne* v. *Homburg*, 1 Ex. D. 48; 45 L. J. Ex. 65: *Foster* v. *Usherwood*, 3 Ex. D. 1; 47 L. J. Ex. 30). That section is replaced by s. 65, County Court Act, 1888; but the meaning is the same notwithstanding the introduction into the latter section of the phrase "at any time:" that phrase refers, probably, to the time for making the application to remit (*Hodgson* v. *Bell*, 24 Q. B. D. 302; 38 W. R. 325).

V. Otherwise, p. 549: Payment.

REDUCED INTO MONEY.—The phrase in 36 G. 3, c. 52, s. 22, whereby duty is to be payable on the *valuation* of personalty "which shall not be reduced into money,"—means, which shall not be so reduced *during the administration* of the estate (*A.-G.* v. *Dardier*, 52 L. J. Q. B. 329; 11 Q. B. D. 16).

REDUCTION INTO POSSESSION.—"Reduction into possession, by a husband as regards Choses in Action, means actual payment to the husband in his character of husband, not as trustee or what is equivalent to it. If the property has been paid to his agent, or so dealt with that the property is no longer a chose in action of the wife, but under the exclusive control of the husband; or has been, in the exercise of his exclusive control, placed by him in the hands of, or transferred to, other persons upon some trust inconsistent with the existence of the wife's possible title by survivorship; that will be considered to be a Reduction into Possession" (2 Spence, Eq. Jur. 478, cited by Fry, J., *Nicholson* v. *Drury Building Co.*, 47 L. J. Ch. 194; 7 Ch. D. 48).

RE-EXCHANGE.—"Re-exchange" is the measure of damage sustained by the holder of a dishonoured Bill of Ex. drawn in one country on a person in another country, and is payable in addition to the amount of the Bill (*Willans* v. *Ayers*, 47 L. J. P. C. 1; 3 App. Ca. 133).

REFEREE.—*V.* In case of Need.

REFERENCE.—A power to an arbitrator to give the "Costs of the Reference," includes the Costs of the Award (*Re Walker and Brown*, 51 L. J. Q. B. 424; 9 Q. B. D. 434; 30 W. R. 703). And when the arbitration is by an agreement without action, "Costs of the Reference" include the agreement and those preliminaries which were necessary to bring the parties ad idem; but in a reference at Nisi Prius the "Costs of the

Reference" begin with the reference itself, the prior costs being costs in the cause (*Re Autothreptic Co. and Hook*, 57 L. J. Q. B. 488 ; 21 Q. B. D. 182 ; 59 L. T. 632 ; 37 W. R. 15).

Reference "by Consent ;" *V.* CONSENT.

REFRESHMENT-HOUSE.—*V.* ENTERTAINMENT.

REFUSAL.—"Refusal of an Application ;" *V. International Financial Socy.* v. *Moscow Gas Co.*, 47 L. J. Ch. 258 ; 7 Ch. D. 241.

An angry wife of an Innkeeper who keeps a Constable outside the door whilst she lets him have a piece of her mind, but (that being done) admits him, does not, *semble*, "refuse" to admit the Constable within s. 16, 37 & 38 V. c. 49 ; and at any rate, the Innkeeper being absent, she is not "acting by his *Direction*" within the section (*Caswell* v. *Worcestershire Jus.*, Times, 19th Dec., 1889 ; 53 J. P. 820).

V. WILFUL REFUSAL : OMISSION.

REFUSE.—Ashes from coals burnt in the furnace of a steam-engine which is used only as a force or power for sawing and lifting wood, and other such matters, in a piano manufactory, is "Refuse" of the "*Manufacture or Business*" of piano making, within s. 128, Metrop. Man. Act, 1855 (*Gay* v. *Cadby*, 46 L. J. M. C. 260 ; 2 C. P. D. 391).

Notwithstanding s. 129, a magistrate's decision as to what is "Refuse" is appealable, as the question is one of law (*R.* v. *Bridge*, 59 L. J. M. C. 49).

REFUSING TRUSTEE.—*V.* DECLINING TRUSTEE.

REGARD.—"*Regard being had* to the Scale of Allowances hereinafter contained," s. 1, 29 & 30 V. c. 31 ; *R.* v. *St. George's, Southwark* (56 L. J. Q. B. 652 ; 19 Q. B. D. 533 ; 35 W. R. 841 ; 52 J. P. 6), is overruled ; and this phrase limits the discretion of the Vestry to the amount of allowance prescribed by the Scale, but it has full discretion to act within the Scale (*R.* v. *St. Pancras*, 24 Q. B. D. 371 ; 38 W. R. 311).

V. DUE REGARD.

REGRATOR.—"'Forestaller' is he that buyeth corne, cattell, or other merchandize whatsoever is saleable, by the way as it commeth to Markets, Faires, or such like places to bee sold, to the intent that he may sell the same againe at a more high and deer price, in prejudice and hurt of the common wealth and people" (Termes de la Ley, *Forestaller*).

"'Regrator' is he that hath corn, victuals or other things sufficient for his owne necessary need, occupation or spending, and doth neverthelesse ingrosse and buy up into his hands more corne, victuals, or other such things, to the intent to sell the same againe at a higher and deerer price, in faires, markets or other such like places, whereof see the stat. 5 E. 6, c. 14, for he shall be punished as a forestaller" (Termes de la Ley, *Regrator*).

REGRESS.—*V.* INGRESS.

REGULAR CLERGYMAN.—A "*Regular* Clergyman of the Church of England" does not merely mean one who is duly ordained; he must also be duly inducted, or licensed by the Bishop to perform Divine service or preach, and (if not in his own parish) he must have the consent of the rector or vicar (*Foundling Hospital* v. *Garrett,* 47 L. T. 230; 26 S. J. 631). In that case Brett, L. J., said that "Regular" Clergyman meant not only a Clergyman of the Church of England, "but also a Clergyman who can, without ecclesiastical irregularity, perform duty;" and Cotton, L. J., said, "'Regular Clergyman' at least requires that he shall be regular in performing Divine service, not only with reference to the doctrine he preaches, but as regards performing, in the proper way, the services" in the place of his ministrations.

V. MINISTER.

REGULAR MINISTER.—"Regular Minister of any Dissenting Congregation," s. 28, 5 & 6 W. 4, c. 76; "Regular Minister," "means a Minister who is regularly invited by the congregation to accept the office of their Minister, and who accepts that office,—something quite different from a man who merely temporarily holds the office" (per Mellor, J., *R.* v. *Oldham,* 38 L. J. Q. B. 125; 10 B. & S. 193; L. R. 4 Q. B. 290). In that case it appeared that Mr. Oldham carried on business at Wallingford, and was a deacon in the Baptist chapel there, and had for some years been in the habit of preaching at Pangbourne and its neighbourhood; in Sep., 1867, the congregation at Pangbourne (hearing he was retiring from business, which he did on 1st Sep., 1868) invited him to become their Minister; he declined but subsequently agreed to preach to them every Sunday from 25th March, 1868, to the end of that year, and he did so; on 29th Decr., 1868, the Pangbourne congregation invited Mr. Oldham to continue the services for 1869, to which he agreed, but on the 7th Jan., 1869, the congregation found, by looking at their chapel deed, that they were a Pædo-Baptist congregation and that their Minister must also be of that denomination, which Mr. Oldham was not, and therefore resolved that "we cannot invite Mr. Oldham to become our Regular Permanent Minister:" held, that at the municipal election for Wallingford on the 2nd Nov., 1868, Mr. Oldham was not a "Regular Minister," and was not disqualified under the section cited from being elected a Town Councillor.

REGULAR NOTICE TO QUIT.—*V.* NOTICE TO QUIT.

REGULAR TURNS OF LOADING.—*V.* TURN.

REGULARLY.—*V.* FAIRLY.

REGULATE.—To "regulate" a Supply of Water, does not mean to shut it off altogether. Therefore, where an Act required the consumers of water to provide "proper Ball or Stop-cocks, or other Necessary Apparatus for regulating" the supply, that did not include an out-of-door screw-down valve, whereby the water could be shut off from coming into a consumer's house (*Ward* v. *Folkestone Water Works Co.*, 24 Q. B. D. 334).

REINSTATE.—When a Fire Policy gives the insurers an option to "reinstate or replace" the insured property instead of making payment for damage, "the word 'reinstate' applies to property which is damaged, and the word 'replace' to that which is destroyed" (per Cotton, L. J., *Anderson* v. *Commercial Union Assrce.*, 55 L. J. Q. B. 149); and "when one is dealing with property in the nature of chattels, the term 'reinstate' means to replace (qy. restore) the chattels not *in situ* but *in statu;* and all that the insurers are bound to do is to make the chattels as good as they were before the fire" (per Bowen, L. J., Ib.). Accordingly it was held in that case that the insurer's option, as regards machinery, would not be affected by the mere fact that the building in which it was had been destroyed, or that the term of the assured had been determined.

RELATING.—In *Compagnie Financière* v. *Peruvian Guano Co.* (52 L. J. Q. B. 185; 11 Q. B. D. 55), Brett, L. J., defining words similar to those used in R. S. C. Ord. 31, R. 12, "relating to any matter in question," said:—"It seems to me that any document must be properly held to relate to matters in question in the action which not only would be evidence, but which it is not unreasonable to suppose does contain information which may, either directly or indirectly, enable a party either to advance his own case or to damage the case of his adversary. I used the expression, 'directly or indirectly,' because it seems to me that a document may be properly said to be material if it is one which would naturally lead a party to a chain of enquiry which would lead him to one of those results."

"In relation to;" *V.* GENERALLY.

RELATION.—"'Relation' is a terme in law, where in consideration of law two times or other things are considered so as if they were all one, and by this the thing subsequent is said to take his effect *by relation* at the time preceding" (Termes de la Ley, *Relation, wh. Vf.*).

RELATIONS.—"The strict and accurate meaning of 'Relatives' is 'Legitimate Relatives'" (per Stirling, J., *Jodrell* v. *Seale*, W. N. (89) 230; 34 S. J. 129).

A testamentary gift to a person's "Relations," (or "Relation," *Pyot* v. *Pyot*, 1 Ves. sen. 337), or "Relatives" (*Fielden* v. *Ashworth*, L. R. 20 Eq. 410: *Eagles* v. *Le Breton*, L. R. 15 Eq. 148; 42 L. J. Ch. 362), means to his Next of Kin according to the Statutes of Distribution (2 Jarm. 120,—a rule "not departed from on slight grounds," Ib. 121); but it seems,—(as distinguished from "Heirs" or "Legal Representatives," where either expression is construed statutory next of kin),—*per capita* (Ib. 122, Lewin, 843), and especially so where there are words directing equal distribution

(Ib. 123). But where the words were "to my Relatives, SHARE AND SHARE ALIKE, as the law directs," it was held that the statutory next of kin *per stirpes* were indicated (*Fielden* v. *Ashworth*, sup.). A husband or wife is not included, except that a wife might be included by a context (Ib. 125). *Vf.* Watson, Eq. 1407 : *Lawlor* v. *Henderson*, Ir. Rep. 10 Eq. 150 : *Hibbert* v. *Hibbert*, L. R. 15 Eq. 372 ; 42 L. J. Ch. 383.

Where there is an express reference to the Statute of Distribution, "Relations" take as tenants in common ; otherwise, as joint tenants (*Eagles* v. *Le Breton*, sup.).

Where a gift to Relations is preceded by a life estate, the class is to be determined at the death of the testator (*Eagles* v. *Le Breton*, sup.).

"The objects of a gift to 'Relations' are not varied by its being associated with the word '*near*.' But where the gift is to the '*Nearest* Relations,' the next of kin will take, to the exclusion of those who, under the statute, would have been entitled by representation. Thus surviving brothers and sisters would exclude the children of deceased brothers and sisters, or a living child or grandchild, the issue of a deceased child or grandchild" (2 Jarm. 124 ; *Va.* Watson, Eq. 1408).

Other qualifying adjectives,—*e.g.*, "Poor," "Poorest," "Deserving," "Necessitous,"—are, it is said, generally inoperative because too uncertain (2 Jarm. 126 ; *Vf.* Sug. Pow. 654, 655) ; but the contrary doctrine is strenuously argued for in a note to Lewin, 836, 837 : *Va.* POOREST.

As to the power of making a *selection* amongst "Relations ;" *V.* Lewin, 842, 843 ; Sug. Pow. 655.

"Poor" has been held to have been used as a term of endearment and compassion, and to include a Countess who had not sufficient estate to support her dignity (*Anon.*, 1 P. Wms. 327 : *Svth.* Sug. Pow. 654, 655).

Gifts to "Poor Relations," especially when the intention is to create a perpetual fund, are sometimes regarded as founding a charity (*V.* 2 Jarm. 127 ; 1 Ib. 213, 214 : *Vf.* Wms. Exs. 1121 ; Lewin, 843).

Vh. Chitty, Eq. Ind. 7741–7744.

V. PRECATORY TRUST.

RELEASE.—"'Release' is the giving or discharging of the right or action which any hath or claimeth against another, or his land" (Termes de la Ley, *Release*, *wh. Vf.*).

A "Release" under s. 3, 8 & 9 V. c. 106, must be by Deed (*Gilman* v. *Crowley*, 7 Ir. C. L. Rep. 557).

V. REMISE : DEMAND.

RELIEF.—"Relief," as used in the Poor Law or in Orders thereunder, includes, among other things, the ministrations by ministers of religion (*R.* v. *Haslehurst*, 53 L. J. M. C. 127 ; 13 Q. B. D. 253 : *R.* v. *Braintree Union*, 10 L. J. M. C. 76 ; 1 Q. B. 130).

"A Trust '*for the Relief of the Poor*' has been construed to authorise an application of the funds to the building of a School-house, and the Education of the Poor of the parish" (Lewin, 538, citing *Wilkinson* v. *Malin*, 2 Tyr. 544, 570).

V. PAROCHIAL RELIEF.

As to a feudal "Relief;" *V.* Co. Litt. 76 a; Termes de la Ley.

"*Relief claimed,*" Ord. 40, R. 11, R. S. C. to Jud. Act, 1875 (now Ord. 32, R. 6, R. S. C.); *V. Litton* v. *Litton*, 3 Ch. D. 793; 24 W. R. 962; nom. *Linton* v. *Linton*, 46 L. J. Ch. 64: *Pascoe* v. *Richards*, 50 L. J. Ch. 337.

RELIGION.—"What is Religion? Is it not what a man honestly believes in and approves of and thinks it his duty to inculcate on others, whether with regard to this world or the next? A belief in any system of retribution by an over-ruling power? It must, I think, include the principle of gratitude to an active power who can confer blessings" (per Willes, J., *Baxter* v. *Langley*, 38 L. J. M. C. 5).

V. ENTERED IN RELIGION.

RELIGIOUS.—"Any other Religious Institution or Purpose;" *V. Wilkinson* v. *Lindgren*, 5 Ch. 570.

RELINQUISH.—Property which a Successor "shall be bound to relinquish, or be deprived of," s. 38, Sucn. Dy. Act, 1853;—*V. Le Marchant* v. *Inl. Rev.*, 45 L. J. Ex. 247; 1 Ex. D. 185.

REMAIN.—*V.* LEFT.

"Being out of England, *remains* out of England," s. 4 (d), Bankry. Act, 1883;—This does not include a person whose home is out of England (*Ex p. Crispin*, 42 L. J. Bank. 65; 8 Ch. 374; 21 W. R. 492; 28 L. T. 483: *Ex p. Brandon, Re Trench*, 25 Ch. D. 500; 53 L. J. Ch. 576).

Bequest of Money which might "remain," held to pass Stock (*Rogers* v. *Thomas*, 2 Keen, 8), or a reversionary interest in a sum charged on realty (*Stocks* v. *Barré*, Johns. 54; 5 Jur. N. S. 537).

Bequest to wife, universal in the first instance, but followed by limitations which would cut down her estate to a life interest, is not saved from that cutting down by the limitations being prefaced by "*whatever remains* of my said estate and effects" (*Constable* v. *Bull*, 18 L. J. Ch. 302).

REMAINDER.—*V.* REST: REVERSION.

As used in a residuary clause in a Will this is a technical word, as is also the word "Residue." "Here the words are, 'All the Remainder and Residue of all his estate and effects, both real and personal,'—which includes all the testator's property. All the terms he makes use of, except the word 'effects,' are technical terms: For 'Remainder is applicable to Real Estate, and 'Residue' to Personal Estate" (per Mansfield, C. J., *Hogan* v. *Jackson*, 1 Cowp. 308). *V.* REMAIN: REST.

But "Remainder of my Personal Estate," may mean only a very small surplus, not including a large lapsed legacy (*A.-G.* v. *Johnstone*, 2 Amb. 577: *Page* v. *Leapingwell*, 18 Ves. 466). *Cp.* OVERPLUS : SURPLUS.

Cross-Remainders have been implied from the word "Remainder" (2 Jarm. 552, and cases there cited).

Where a testator directed his debts to be paid out of a specified fund, and "*the* Remainder to be equally divided to my surviving children;" held, a gift of the residue of the specified fund, and not of the general residue (*Jull* v. *Jacobs*, 3 Ch. D. 703). *V.* RESIDUE.

REMAINING.—"Remaining" is an equivocal expression, which may more easily be construed as "other" than the word "surviving" (*Hughes* v. *Whitby*, Ir. Rep. 7 Eq. 99).

V. DISPOSE OF.

REMEDY.—"Require the same to be remedied," s. 46, Coal Mines Regulation Act, 1872, 35 & 36 V. c. 76; *V. R.* v. *Baker*, W. N. (78), 165.

REMISE.—The usual form of words in a Release,—"remise, release, and quit claim,"—are as old as Littleton; but the old, and true, form of "quit" was "quiet" (Litt. s. 445).

"'*Remisisse, relaxâsse, et quietum clamâsse.* Here Littleton sheweth, that there be three proper words of release, and bee much of one effect: besides, there is *renunciare, acquietare*, and there bee many other words of release; as if the lessor grants to the lessee for life, that he shall bee discharged of the rent, this is a good release. *V.* Sect. 532" (Co. Litt. 264 b; *Vf.* Ib. 291 a).

V. DEMAND.

REMITTER.—"Remitter is an antient terme in the law, and is where a man hath two titles to lands or tenements, viz., one a more antient title, and another a more latter title; and if hee come to the land by a latter title, yet the law will adjudge him in by force of the elder title, because the elder title is the more sure and more worthy title. And then when a man is adjudged in by force of his elder title, this is said a Remitter in him" (Litt. s. 659; *Vth.* Co. Litt. 347 b, and Butler's note, 299).

REMOVAL.—"The technical meaning of 'Removal' in 7 & 8 V. c. 101, is not the meaning which the word 'Removal' has in 16 & 17 V. c. 97" (per Cotton, L. J., *R.* v. *Pemberton*, 49 L. J. M. C. 31; 5 Q. B. D. 95).

RENDERING.—"Rendering" rent free of impositions, amounts to a covenant (*Giles* v. *Hooper*, Carth. 135); *Sv.* 2 Platt, 87.

RENEWABLE LEASE.—*V. Hughes* v. *Twisden*, 55 L. J. Ch. 481; 54 L. T. 570; 34 W. R. 498.

RENEWAL.—By Sch. 2, Licensing Act, 1872, the Appeal to Quarter Sessions created by ss. 27, 28 and 29, 9 G. 4, c. 61, is repealed, except in so far as those sections "relate to the Renewal of Licenses, or to the Transfer of Licenses under ss. 4 and 14 of the same Act:"—the tenant of a licensed house gave it up on the 29th Sep., and in the meantime, having received notice of opposition, purposely neglected to apply for a Renewal of his license at the Brewster Sessions held on the 26th Sep.; the in-coming tenant applied for a license at the next Special Sessions held on the 10th Oct.; this was refused and he appealed to Quarter Sessions: held, that such application was not for a new license, but was for a Renewal or Transfer of the old license, and therefore that the right of appeal was not taken away (*Thornton* v. *Clegg*, 24 Q. B. D. 132; 59 L. J. M. C. 6). *V.* New License.

RENT.—"'Rents' be in divers manners, that is Rent service, Rent charge, and Rent secke" (Termes de la Ley, *Rents, wh. Vf.*).

Probably it may be said that the ordinary meaning of "Rent" is the sum certain, in gross, which a tenant pays his landlord for the right of occupying the demised premises (*Vh.* Co. Litt. 141 b, 142 a; Elph. 617–619; Woodf. 375). *V.* Certain Rent.

A covenant to hold clear of all "Rents," includes a Quit Rent (*Hammond* v. *Hill*, 1 Comyn, 180).

"The word *Rent*, in Powers of Leasing, is with great propriety construed to mean not money merely, but any return or equivalent adapted to the nature of the subject demised: therefore, upon a Lease of Mines, a due proportion of the produce may be reserved as a render in lieu of money, although the power requires a 'Rent' generally to be reserved" (Sug. Pow. 791, citing *Campbell* v. *Leach*, 2 Amb. 740: *Bassett's Case*, cited Ib. 748).

"The words 'Rent' and 'Annual Value' are often used indiscriminately;" (per Cleasby, B., *Sheffield Water Works Co.* v. *Bennett*, 41 L. J. Ex. 240). In that case a Water-works Company were empowered to charge each house supplied, according to its "Rent" per annum; which was held to mean the money payment made by the tenant, less tenant's rates payable by the landlord (41 L. J. Ex. 233; 42 Ib. 121; L. R. 7 Ex. 409; 8 Ib. 196: *V.* Annual Rent: Annual Value).

As to such a phrase as "*Gas* Rent;" *V. Re Peake, Ex p. Harrison*, 53 L. J. Ch. 977; 13 Q. B. D. 753: *Ex p. Birmingham and Staffordshire Gas Co.*, 40 L. J. Bank. 52; L. R. 11 Eq. 615: *Ex p. Hill, Re Roberts*, 46 L. J. Bank. 116; 6 Ch. D. 621.

"Rent," s. 1, Stat. Lim., 3 & 4 W. 4, c. 27, includes Tithe Rent-Charge (*Irish Land Commission* v. *Grant*, 10 App. Ca. 14).

"Rent," s. 2, 3 & 4 W. 4, c. 27, "must be confined to rents existing as an inheritance distinct from the land, and for which before the statute the party entitled might have had an assize; such as ancient Rents Service, Fee Farm Rents, or the like" (per Rolfe, B., delivering jdgmt. of the Court in *Grant* v. *Ellis,* 11 L. J. Ex. 232 ; 9 M. & W. 113 : *Va. Ely* v. *Bliss,* 2 D. G. M. & G. 459). *V.* TITHES.

And in the same sense "Rent" is used in the 3rd, 4th, 5th, 7th and 15th sections of the Act just cited ; and whilst in the early part of s. 8 it is used in that sense, yet at the close of that section it means, Rent reserved under a Lease ; and of the *seven* times the word is used in s. 9, in the first, fourth and sixth times it means Rent Charge, whilst in the second, third, fifth and seventh times it means Rent Reserved (per Denman, C. J., in delivering the jdgmt. of the Q. B., *Doe* d. *Angell* v. *Angell,* 15 L. J. Q. B. 193 ; 9 Q. B. 328 : *Va. Baines* v. *Lumley,* 16 W. R. 674).

Vf. as to "Rent" in 3 & 4 W. 4, c. 27 ; Dart, 433, 434, and cases there cited.

Royalties are "Rent" within s. 1, Par. Asst. Act, 6 & 7 W. 4, c. 96 (*R.* v. *Westbrook,* 16 L. J. M. C. 87 ; 10 Q. B. 178 ; 9 L. T. O. S. 21).

"Rent having no Money Value ;" *V.* MONEY VALUE.

V. RACK-RENT : RENTS : ACTUALLY PAID.

RENT PAYABLE.—"Rent payable," in s. 11, 30 & 31 V. c. 142, means the Rent payable between the litigant parties (*Brown* v. *Cocking,* 37 L. J. Q. B. 250 ; L. R. 3 Q. B. 672. *V.*, as to "Value" in this section, *Elston* v. *Rose,* L. R. 4 Q. B. 4 ; 38 L. J. Q. B. 6 : ANNUAL VALUE).

RENTS.—"The use of the word 'Rents' may in some cases shew that the testator intended Leaseholds to be enjoyed in specie" (Watson, Eq. 121, citing *Cafe* v. *Bent,* 5 Hare, 36 : *Cp. Pickup* v. *Atkinson,* 4 Hare, 624 ; 15 L. J. Ch. 213 : *Skirving* v. *Williams,* 24 Bea. 275 : *Blann* v. *Bell,* 2 D. G. M. & G. 775 ; 21 L. J. Ch. 811 ; 5 D. G. & S. 658 : *Vachell* v. *Roberts,* 32 Bea. 140).

"Rents and Profits" in a mortgage of a Wharf ; *V. Anderson* v. *Butler's Co.,* W. N. (79) 163.

V. ANNUAL PROCEEDS : RENT.

RENTS AND PROFITS.—When, under a Contract for the Sale of Realty, the purchaser is to be entitled to all the rents and profits from the day appointed for completion, which time is delayed for a considerable time during which delay the vendor simply remains in possession without arrangement as to rent, the purchaser is nevertheless entitled to a fair occupation rent under the words "all Rents and Profits" (*Metropolitan Ry.* v. *Defries,* 2 Q. B. D. 189, 387).

"A Devise of the 'Rents and Profits,' or of the 'Income,' of lands passes the land itself both at law and in equity ; a rule, it is said, founded on the feudal law, according to which the whole beneficial interest in the land consisted in the right to take the rents and profits. And since 1 V. c. 26, such a devise carries the fee simple ; but before that Act it carried no more than an estate for life unless words of inheritance were added" (1 Jarm. 797). An Advowson will pass under "Rents and Profits" (Ib. 798). *Va.* Co. Litt. 4 b, cited PROFITS.

But in *Johnson* v. *Johnson* (56 L. J. Ch. 326 ; 35 Ch. D. 345 ; 56 L. T. 163 ; 35 W. R. 329), Stirling, J., refused to apply the doctrine just stated to the interpretation of s. 8, M. W. P. Act, 1870 (33 & 34 V. c. 93), and he held that the property of which, under that section, the "Rents and Profits" were to be for the separate use of married women, meant only such property as could be personally enjoyed by a married woman ; and that accordingly no separate use was thereby declared of a fee-simple, and that an unacknowledged conveyance of a fee-simple by a married woman was not saved by the section from being invalid.

In a direction as to the payment or application of property, "the words 'Rents,' 'Issues,' 'Profits,' 'Interest,' 'Dividends' and 'Proceeds,' are all applicable to a life interest, but not to the fee simple" (per Kindersley, V.-C., *Troutbeck* v. *Boughey*, 35 L. J. Ch. 842 ; L. R. 2 Eq. 534).

"Net Rents and Profits ;" *V.* NET.

As to how far a direction to raise money out of "Rents and Profits" will authorize a sale of the property ; *V.* 2 Jarm. 610–612.

As to powers and duties of Trustees to raise Fines on Renewals of Leases out of "Rents, *Issues* and Profits ;" *V.* Lewin, 366–369 ; and as to raising Portions ; *V.* Ib. 419, 420.

"Rents, Issues and Profits" of Real Estate, are, of themselves, sufficient to include the proceeds of sale of a Next Presentation (per Turner, L. J., *Cust* v. *Middleton*, 34 L. J. Ch. 185).

Qy., Does that phrase mean *annual* profits merely, or authorize a sale ? (*Smyth* v. *Foley*, 7 L. J. Ex. Eq. 34 ; 3 Y. & C. Ex. 142).

REPAIR.—The general principle for determining a tenant's liability to "repair," simpliciter, is that, "diminution in value, resulting from the natural operation of time and the elements, falls on the landlord ; but the tenant must take care that the premises do not suffer more damage than the operation of these causes would effect ; and he is bound, by reasonable applications of labour, to keep the house as nearly as possible in the same condition as when it was demised" (per Tindal, C. J., *Gutteridge* v. *Munyard*, 1 Moo. & R. 336).

By an agreement to "repair" and keep in repair, there is no obligation to substitute new buildings for old (*Belcher* v. *McIntosh*, 8 C. & P. 720 ; 2 Moo. & R. 186). But an agreement to "*keep* in repair" a house out of repair, means that the contracting party is first of all to put it in good repair having regard to its age and its class,—*i.e.*, a house in Spitalfields would not be repaired in the same style as one in Grosvenor Square,—but you are not to take into consideration the condition of the premises at the time of the contract (*Payne* v. *Haine*, 16 L. J. Ex. 130 ; 16 M. & W. 541 : *Easton* v. *Pratt*, 33 L. J. Ex. 233 ; 2 H. & C. 683 : *Saner* v. *Bilton*, 47

L. J. Ch. 267 ; 7 Ch. D. 815 ; 38 L. T. 281 ; 26 W. R. 394 : *V.* Keep : *Vf.* Rosc. N. P. 652 *et seq.* ; Woodf. 589).

To put premises in "*Habitable* Repair," means to improve the state of repair, and render the premises reasonably fit for an ordinary occupier of such premises (*Belcher* v. *McIntosh*, sup.).

"The painting of a house is usually provided for by the express terms of a lease, but it would seem that some degree of *painting* is implied in the mere term 'Repair.' It has been ruled for instance, that under a covenant to 'substantially repair, uphold and maintain' a house, the covenantor is bound to keep up the inside painting (*Monk* v. *Noyes*, 1 C. & P. 265) ; but it has been also ruled, on a covenant,—as often as necessary well and sufficiently to repair, uphold, sustain, paint, glaze, cleanse, and scour and keep and leave the premises in such repair, reasonable wear and tear excepted,—that the tenant, if he has repaired within a reasonable time before leaving, is only bound, in addition to the repair of actual dilapidations, to clean the old paint, &c., and not to repaint (*Scales* v. *Lawrence*, 2 F. & F. 289). Questions of this kind will often be more questions of fact than of law ; but if the painting be left to be included in the general term 'Repair,' the only legal obligation would seem to be to paint just as much as is necessary to keep the premises from actual deterioration" (Woodf. 590, 591). To this effect is *Crawford* v. *Newton* (36 W. R. 54).

Vf. as to "*Substantial* Repair," *Brown* v. *Trumper*, 26 Bea. 11.

Under a covenant to repair, the covenantor must *rebuild in case of fire*, unless there be the qualification "Damage by fire excepted" (*Bullock* v. *Dommitt*, 6 T. R. 650 : *Pym* v. *Blackburn*, 3 Ves. 34 : *Vf.* Woodf. 592, and cases there cited).

A covenant by a lessor to repair, "carries with it a license to the lessor to enter upon the premises of the lessee, and to occupy them for a reasonable time to do that which he has contracted to do" (per Fry, J., *Saner* v. *Bilton*, sup.).

"'Improve' and 'Repair' are not equivalent words" (per Brett, L. J., *Truscott* v. *Diamond Rock-Boring Co.*, 51 L. J. Ch. 261).

V. Tenantable Repair : Maintain.

REPAIRS.—"Repairs," in s. 70, 58 G. 3, c. 45, includes not only repairs to the fabric of a church, but also the expenses necessary for the proper and decent performance of divine service, and the other offices to be performed therein and necessarily incident thereto (*R.* v. *Consistory Court*, 31 L. J. Q. B. 106 ; 2 B. & S. 339).

REPARATIONS.—*V.* "Necessary Occasions," sub Necessary.

REPASS.—*V.* Pass and Repass.

REPAYMENT.—"'May secure the Repayment of' (borrowed money)

—a form of expression occurring in Railway Acts, which has been held to preclude the issue of securities at a discount" (per Jessel, M. R., *Anglo-Danubian Steam Nav. Co.*, 44 L. J. Ch. 503). *V.* RAISE.

"Bond given for the Repayment of Money," Stamp Act, 55 G. 3, c. 184,—"Repayment cannot apply to commission or interest" (per Platt, B., *Frith* v. *Rotherham*, 15 L. J. Ex. 136 ; 15 M. & W. 43).

REPLACE.—*V.* REINSTATE.

REPLEVIN.—"'*Replevin*' is derived of *replegiare*, to redeliver to the owner upon pledges or suretie" (Co. Litt. 161 a ; *Vf.* Ib. 145 b).

REPLY.—*V.* WAITING YOUR REPLY.

REPORT.—"The above cargo is accepted on the Report and Samples of Scott & Co.," is a warranty that the bulk is equal to the Report and Samples ; and is not merely a representation that the Report is the genuine report of Scott & Co., and that the Samples were taken by them (*Russell* v. *Nicolopulo*, 8 C. B. N. S. 362).

V. SAMPLE : FAIR REPORT.

REPRESENTATIVE.—A Solicitor is the representative of his client; but Counsel is not, for Counsel "has the whole conduct of the case, and can act even against the instructions of the client" (per Brett, M. R., *R.* v. *Greenwich Co. Co. Registrar*, 54 L. J. Q. B. 392 ; 15 Q. B. D. 54 ; 33 W. R. 671). In that case it was accordingly held that a Solicitor is a "Representative" within subs. 4, s. 17, Bankry. Act, 1883 ; and must be "authorised in writing" to entitle him to question a debtor at a public examination.

REPRESENTATIVES.—"The ordinary legal sense of the term 'Representatives,' without the addition of 'legal,' or 'personal,' is exors or admors" (Wms. Exs. 1134 : *Re Crawford*, 2 Drew. 230 ; 23 L. J. Ch. 625 : *Lindsay* v. *Ellicott*, 46 L. J. Ch. 878) ; but in *Re Horner, Eagleton* v. *Horner* (57 L. J. Ch. 211 ; W. N. (87) 219 ; 4 Times Rep. 100), Stirling, J., contextually construed "Representatives" as "Next of Kin" or as "Descendants." So, in a bequest to A. for life, and, at his death, the principal to be paid "to such children or *Representatives of Children* as he may leave," "Representatives" mean "Descendants" (*Herbert* v. *Forbes*, 1 L. J. Ch. 118).

In *Lindsay* v. *Ellicott* (sup.) Jessel, M. R., said that the rule and observations in *Re Crawford* do not apply where "Representatives" are to take derivatively, and he added,—"Where you have a class who take under the Stat. of Distributions as a primary class, and, by reason of some members being dead, another generation take under the Statute, the second class do take by representation. They represent a dead member of the class. Thus, where an intestate dies leaving brothers and sisters, and leaves children of a dead brother, the children take as representing the dead brother. Therefore, it is the very meaning of the word to describe the persons who take thus as statutory next of kin:" And accordingly in a limitation to persons who would be entitled under the Statute "exclusive of A. and his Representatives," it was held that "Representatives" meant statutory next of kin.

V. LEGAL REPRESENTATIVES.

REPRESENTING OR PERFORMING.—The words, "representing or performing" a dramatic piece or musical composition within the Copyright Act (5 & 6 V. c. 45, s. 20), mean "that there must be publicity in the audience" (per Brett, M. R., *Wall* v. *Taylor*, 52 L. J. Q. B. 562: the judgment at this passage seems to have been incorrectly reported at 11 Q. B. D. 107: *V. Duck* v. *Bates*, 53 L. J. Q. B. 99). *Va. Duck* v. *Bates*, on appeal, 53 L. J. Q. B. 338; 13 Q. B. D. 843; 50 L. T. 778; 32 W. R. 813; 48 J. P. 501, as to what would be publicity: *Vf.* "Place of Dramatic Entertainment," sub PLACE.

REPRISES.—"'Reprises' are deductions, payments, and duties, that goe yearely and are payed out of a mannour: As rent charge, rent secke, pensions, corodies, annuities, fees of stewards or baylifes, and such like" (Termes de la Ley).

REPUTED MANOR.—*V.* MANOR.

REQUEST.—*V.* AUTHORITY OR REQUEST: CONSENT: PRECATORY TRUST: EARNEST.

REQUIRE.—In a contractual obligation whereby one party is to do or permit such things as the other may "require," the word means "reasonably require" (*Braunstein* v. *Accidental Insrce.*, 31 L. J. Q. B. 17; 1 B. & S. 782).

"If Trustees be authorized and *required*, at the instance of the tenant for life, to invest the trust funds in the *purchase of Leaseholds*, they have no option if the tenant for life insist upon his right" (Lewin, 328, citing *Cadogan* v. *Essex*, 2 Drew. 227; 23 L. J. Ch. 487: *Beauclerk* v. *Ashburnham*, 8 Bea. 322); but if they are "required" to lend money to a husband on his personal security at the request of the wife, and the husband become insolvent, they are justified in refusing to lend, because the circumstances and position of the husband have so totally changed (*Boss* v. *Godsall*, 1 Y. & C. Ch. 617: *Va. Luther* v. *Bianconi*, 10 Ir. Ch. Rep. 194: *Costello* v. *O'Rorke*, I. R. 3 Eq. 172: *Vf.* Lewin, 316, 317, 328, 614).

V. CONSENT.

REQUIRED.—The phrase "*is hereby* required" is directory only, as regards a father's consent to the marriage of a minor under s. 16, Marriage Act, 4 G. 4, c. 76 (*R.* v. *Birmingham*, 8 B. & C. 29; 6 L. J. O. S.

M. C. 67; 2 M. & R. 230). In giving judgment in that case Tenterden, C. J., said,—" The language of this section is merely to *require* consent; it does not proceed to make the marriage void if solemnized without consent" (cited by Tindal, C. J., *Cole* v. *Greene*, 13 L. J. C. P. 32). *V.* SHALL.

A difference between Railway Companies is not, by Act of Parliament, "required *or authorised*" to be referred to arbitration within s. 8, Regulation of Railways Act, 1873 (36 & 37 V. c. 48), when a Private Railway Act merely "confirms and makes binding" a provisional agreement, one of the clauses of which provides that all differences between the railway companies parties thereto shall be settled by arbitration (per Smith, J., *G. W. Ry.* v. *Halesowen Ry.*, 52 L. J. Q. B. 473: approved and adopted in *R.* v. *Mid. Ry.*, 56 L. J. Q. B. 585; 19 Q. B. D. 540; 57 L. T. 619; 51 J. P. 550).

When a Railway Company, or other body, is empowered by an Act of Parliament to take such lands "*as may be* required" for their undertaking; that means, such lands as the Company, or other body, may fairly think convenient for its purpose. "I cannot think that 'required' (in this connexion) means, 'absolutely necessary.' 'Required' means, where the Company *bonâ fide* think and are of opinion that the lands are desirable. I think those cases of *Stockton & Darln. Ry.* v. *Brown* (9 H. L. Ca. 246) and *Kemp* v. *S. E. Ry.* (41 L. J. Ch. 404; 7 Ch. 364) . . . really mean this, that the opinion of the railway authorities is to be the governing matter as to whether the things are for the advantage of the railway, if that opinion is an opinion *bonâ fide* expressed and *bonâ fide* laid before the Court" (per Brett, L. J., *Errington* v. *Metrop. Distr. Ry.*, 51 L. J. Ch. 313; 19 Ch. D. 559).

"*If* required;" *V. Wilson* v. *Kynock*, W. N. (77) 164.

"Immediate Possession if required;" *V.* IMMEDIATE POSSESSION.

"Required *to Calculate*," s. 31, Sucn. Dy. Act, 1853; *V. Re Cornwallis*, 25 L. J. Ex. 149; 11 Ex. 580.

"No longer required;" *V.* USELESS.

RESCUE.—"'Rescous,' *Recussus*, is an ancient French word comming from *rescourrer* (*id est*) *recuperare*, that is, to take from, to rescue or recover. *Rescous* is a taking away and setting at liberty against law a distresse taken, or a person arrested by the process or course of law. And all is one, as to the point of the disseisin, to rescue the distresse after it is taken, and before hand to resist and withstand the taking of it; but yet it is no Rescous, untill it be distreyned" (Co. Litt. 160 b: *Vh.* Termes de la Ley, *Rescous;* Woodf. 487).

"Rescue, is the act of forcibly freeing a person from custody against the will of those who have him in custody. If the person rescued is in the custody of a *private* person, the offender must have notice of the fact that the person rescued is in such custody" (Steph. Cr. 99, 100).

RESEMBLING.—"The word 'resembling' means made, or apparently intended, to resemble" (Steph. Cr. 292: *Vh. R.* v. *Robinson*, 34 L. J. M. C. 176; L. & C. 604).

RESERVATION.—"'Reservation' is taken divers wayes, and hath divers natures, as sometimes by way of Exception, to keepe that which a man had before in him . . . . Sometimes a reservation doth get and bring forth another thing which was not before . . . . And note, that in ancient time, their reservations were as well (or for the more part) in victuals, whether flesh, fish, corne, bread, drinke, or what else, as in money, untill at the last, and that chiefly in the raign of King Henry I., by agreement, the reservation of victuals was changed into ready money, as it hath hitherto since continued" (Termes de la Ley).

"Note a diversitie betweene an Exception (which is ever of part of the thing granted and of a thing *in esse*) for which, *exceptis*, *salvo*, *præter*, and the like, be apt words; and a Reservation which is alwayes of a thing not *in esse*, but newly created or reserved out of the land or tenement demised" (Co. Litt. 47 a; *V.* Ib. 143 a: *Va.* Touch. 80, where it is said that a Reservation "doth, most commonly and properly, succeed the *Tenendum*, and is made by one or more of these words, *reddend'*, *reservand'*, *solvend'*, *faciend'*, *inveniend'*, or such like").

"In considering what is required by a power of leasing, we should bear in mind that rent, heriots, suit of mill, and suit of court, are, according to the legal sense and meaning of the word, *Reservations*. A privilege to the lessor to hawk, hunt, fish or fowl, is not either a Reservation or an Exception in point of law" (Sug. Pow. 817).

Therefore a Leasing Power "so as the accustomed yearly *Rents and Reservations* be thereby reserved," would, *semble*, not authorize an Exception of the Mines, Minerals, Quarries, or such like (*Doe* d. *Douglas* v. *Lock*, 2 A. & E. 705; 4 L. J. K. B. 113; 4 N. & M. 807: *Vh.* Sug. Pow. 817, 818).

For an example of words of reservation operating as a grant; *V. Wickham* v. *Hawker*, 10 L. J. Ex. 153; 7 M. & W. 72.

V. RESERVING: CONDITION.

RESERVE.—A direction to "reserve" the pure personalty for a Charitable Bequest, implies marshalling the assets (*Miles* v. *Harrison*, 9 Ch. 316; 43 L. J. Ch. 585: *Re Arnold*, 57 L. J. Ch. 682; 37 Ch. D. 637; 58 L. T. 469; 36 W. R. 424: 1 Jarm. 237, 238). *Cp.* EXCLUSIVELY.

V. WITHOUT RESERVE.

RESERVED BIDDING.—Where Conditions of Sale provide that the auction is made "subject to a Reserved Bidding," that does not give the right *to bid up* to the reserve price; *secus*, if the words were "a right to bid is reserved" (*Gilliat* v. *Gilliat*, 39 L. J. Ch. 142; L. R. 9 Eq. 60, explaining s. 5, Sale of Land by Auction Act, 1867, 30 & 31 V. c. 48).

V. WITHOUT RESERVE.

RESERVING: RESERVED.—" '*Reserving*.' *Reserve* commeth of the Latine word *reservo*, that is, to provide for store; as when a man departeth with his land, he reserveth or provideth for himselfe a rent for his owne livelihood. And sometime it hath the force of *Saving* or *Excepting*. So as sometime it serveth to reserve a new thing, viz., a rent, and sometime to except part of the thing in *esse* that is granted" (Co. Litt. 142 b, 143 a. *Sv.* this passage criticised in the jdgmt. in *Doe* d. *Douglas* v. *Lock*, 4 L. J. K. B. 120; 2 A. & E. 705: *Va.* RESERVATION. But a little further on in the jdgmt. in *Doe* d. *D.* v. *Lock*, occurs this passage:—" It may be said, however, that if the person who creates the Power uses the word 'Reserving' in such a way as to make an Exception a Reservation, it must be so taken; but, we think, not necessarily").

"Reserved," in s. 8, 1 & 2 W. 4, c. 32, "is not used in a technical sense; it points to an arrangement between landlord and tenant; and the game might be reserved by Lease, by Deed, or by Parol contract" (per Lush, J., *Coleman* v. *Bathurst*, L. R. 6 Q. B. 369; 40 L. J. M. C. 134; 24 L. T. 426; 19 W. R. 848: Lush, J., was in a minority only as to whether the agreement there amounted to a Reservation).

V. WITHOUT RESERVE.

RESIDE: RESIDENCE: RESIDENT.—" What is the meaning of the word '*Resides?*' I take it that that word, where there is nothing to show that it is used in a more extensive sense, denotes the place where an individual eats, drinks and sleeps, or where his family or his servants eat, drink and sleep" (per Bayley, J., *R.* v. *North Curry*, 4 B. & C. 959).

"'Residence' has a variety of meanings according to the Statute,—(or document)—in which it is used" (per Erle, C. J., *Naef* v. *Mutter*, 31 L. J. C. P. 359). It is an "ambiguous word" and may receive a different meaning according to the position in which it is found (per Cotton, L. J., *Re Bowie, Ex p. Breull*, 50 L. J. Ch. 384; 16 Ch. D. 484).

A *Condition* to a gift of a house that the donee take actual possession of it "as and for his *Residence* and place of abode," and continue, during his life, to reside therein, does not imply that the donee must continue personally to live in the house;—he will satisfy the condition by keeping up the house as a place of residence in which he, and (qy. or ?) some of the members of his family occasionally dwell (*Warner* v. *Moir*, 53 L. J. Ch. 474; 25 Ch. D. 605: *Vf.* 2 Jarm. 57, 58. It has however been said, "it would seem difficult to reconcile *Warner* v. *Moir* with *Walcot* v. *Botfield*, Kay, 534," Watson, Eq. 1246. *Vf. May* v. *May*, 44 L. T. 412).

A power to "reside in" or "occupy" a building subject to a Condition, —*e.g.*, to repair,—would seem to imply that the privilege once accepted is always accepted *quà* the Condition: thus where there was a power to A. to occupy a Mill so long as he thought proper, "he nevertheless keeping the premises in good and tenantable repair," and A. accepted, but the premises were afterwards totally destroyed by accidental fire; held, that A. was liable to re-instate the premises, and to pay rent therefor in the meanwhile, and could not escape that liability by declining any longer to occupy (*Gregg* v. *Coates*, 23 Bea. 33 ; 4 W. R. 735 ; 2 Jur. N. S. 964).

An Annuity to A., to cease when A. and B. cease to reside together, does not determine by the death of B. (*Sutcliffe* v. *Richardson*, 41 L. J. Ch. 552 ; L. R. 13 Eq. 606). *V.* USUAL PLACE OF ABODE.

The " Residence " of a grantor or an attesting witness, required to be verified on the registration of a *Bill of Sale*, may be where he usually sleeps ; but for this purpose it is sufficient, and perhaps better, to state the place " where he is chiefly to be found " (per Pollock, C. B., *Attenborough* v. *Thompson*, inf.)—*e.g.*, his place of business, or his master's place of business, where he performs his ordinary duties (*Blackwell* v. *England*, 27 L. J. Q. B. 124 ; 8 E. & B. 541 ; 6 W. R. 59 : *Attenborough* v. *Thompson*, 27 L. J. Ex. 23 ; 2 H. & N. 559 ; 6 W. R. 135). If he have more than one, it will be sufficient if one of his Residences be given and verified (*Greenham* v. *Child*, 59 L. J. Q. B. 27 ; herein agreeing with Bacon, V.-C., in *Re Moulson, Ex p. Knightly*, 51 L. J. Ch. 823, and dis-agreeing with him in *Wallis* v. *Smith*, W. N. (82) 77).

So also a person's place of business was his " Residence " under s. 6, *Com. L. Pro. Act*, 1852 (*Ablett* v. *Basham*, 25 L. J. Q. B. 239 ; 5 E. & B. 1019 ; following *Yardley* v. *Jones*, 4 Dowl. 45) ; and was at least, *primâ facie* evidence of his residence within s. 2 of that Act (*Naef* v. *Mutter*, 31 L. J. C. P. 357). But in the Indorsement of a Writ under the R. S. C., where the plaintiff "resides" should be given as at his usual place of residence as distinguished from his place of business (*Re a Solicitor*, 5 Times Rep. 339) ; and so of a person's " Residence " under s. 9, Com. L. Pro. (Ireland) Act, 1853 (*Tom* v. *Nagle*, 13 Ir. C. L. Rep. App. xxxviii).

In *Re Bowie, Ex p. Breull* (50 L. J. Ch. 384 ; 16 Ch. D. 484), James, L. J., held that a man " resides " within the meaning of s. 59, *Bankruptcy Act*, 1869, " where he is to be found daily," *e.g.*,—a Clerk would "reside" at his employer's place of business. But under the Bankruptcy Act, 1883,—*e.g.*, in s. 95,—it would seem that " Residence " means, where the person sleeps, or, at any rate, does not include the place where he carries on business ; for R. 126, and the Forms in the Appendix to the Rules (*V.* Notes to Forms Nos. 3, 4 and 5) employ the word " resides " in a sense opposed to that of " place of business." *Vf.* " Place of Abode," sub PLACE.

A *Company* is only "domiciled or ordinarily *resident*," within Ord. 11, R. 1, R. S. C., where its head office is (*Jones* v. *Scottish Acc. Insrce.*, 55 L. J. Q. B. 415 ; 17 Q. B. D. 421 : *Vh. Newby* v. *Von Oppen Co.*, 41 L. J. Q. B. 148 ; L. R. 7 Q. B. 293 : *Carron Co.* v. *Maclaren*, 5 H. L. Ca. 416 : *Watkins* v. *Scottish Imperial Insrce.*, 58 L. J. Q. B. 495 : *Haggin* v. *Comptoir d'Escompte*, 58 L. J. Q. B. 508 ; 23 Q. B. D. 519). *Vf.* RESIDING.

V. DWELL : CARRY ON.

A place of occasional business is not a Residence within s. 189, *Merchant Shipping* Act, 1854 (*The Blakeney*, Swabey, 428).

For the purpose of a *Bastardy* application a woman may "reside" (s. 3, 35 & 36 V. c. 65) in the Petty Sessional Division to which she, for convenience and without improper motive, goes temporarily to reside for the purpose of making the application (*R.* v. *Hughes*, 26 L. J. M. C. 133 ; Dears. & B. 188) ; but going over night into a Division is not to "reside" there (*Vevers* v. *Mains*, 4 Times Rep. 724) ; and if having made an unsuccessful Application, the woman goes to another Division to make a second Application because she hopes that there she will have a better chance of succeeding, she does not "reside" in the latter Division (*R.* v. *Myott*, 32 L. J. M. C. 138 ; 27 J. P. 119). If she has no settled residence, she "resides" where she happens to be (*Lawrence* v. *Ingmire*, 33 J. P. 339 ; 20 L. T. 391).

The Residence to give a *Pauper* a *Settlement* or a status of Irremovability (s. 34, 39 & 40 V. c. 61) must be his home and fixed place of abode (*Holborn* v. *Chertsey*, 54 L. J. M. C. 53 ; 14 Q. B. D. 289 : *Vf. Merthyr Tydvil* v. *Stepney*, 54 L. J. M. C. 12 : *R.* v. *Abingdon*, 39 L. J. M. C. 153 ; L. R. 5 Q. B. 406 : *R.* v. *Glossop*, 35 L. J. M. C. 148 ; L. R. 1 Q. B. 227 : *R.* v. *St. Leonard's, Shoreditch*, 35 L. J. M. C. 48 ; L. R. 1 Q. B. 21 : *Wolstanton* v. *Northwich*, 46 L. T. 528 : *R.* v. *East Stonehouse*, 23 L. J. M. C. 137 ; 4 E. & B. 901).

Under 3 & 4 W. 4, c. 42, s. 8, "Residence" meant home or domicile (*Lambe* v. *Smythe*, 15 L. J. Ex. 287 ; 15 M. & W. 434).

A Fellow of an Oxford College, having a living where he usually resided 9 miles from Oxford, but having also exclusive occupation of rooms at his College, in which rooms he frequently slept, was held not a "Resident" within s. 48, 17 & 18 V. c. 81, so as to be eligible as a member of the Congregation of the University (*R.* v. *Oxford*, L. R. 7 Q. B. 471).

During imprisonment a man cannot be said to have "resided" at his home, within s. 27, Reform Act, 1832 (*Powell* v. *Guest*, 34 L. J. C. P. 69 ; 18 C. B. N. S. 72 : *Donnelly* v. *Graham*, 24 L. R. Ir. 127).

V. Occupation.

"Resident *Abroad*," for purpose of getting from a plaintiff security for costs ; *V.* Dan. Ch. Pr. 81, 82.

Vh. Article, 88 Law Times, 181.

RESIDING.—A Turkish Corporation, by Turkish law established as a state Bank for the Ottoman Empire with its seat at Constantinople and power to establish branches, established a branch in London under the control of directors resident in England ; held, that the Corporation was not a "person residing in the United Kingdom," *quà* Income Tax, within s. 2, Sch. D., 16 & 17 V. c. 34 (*A.-G.* v. *Alexander*, 44 L. J. Ex. 3 ; L. R. 10 Ex. 20). But a Joint Stock Co. having a registered office in London, from which also its affairs in the United Kingdom were managed by a board of English directors, and to which were sent transcripts of the Co.'s books and also the money for the dividends to English shareholders, was held to be "residing" in the United Kingdom within the section cited, although all the working operations of the Co. were in Italy, where also all its profits were earned under the direction of a Board resident there, and where also its books and general moneys were kept (*Cesena Sulphur Co.* v. *Nicholson*, 45 L. J. Ex. 281; 1 Ex. D. 428 : at same reference *Va. Calcutta Jute Co.* v. *Nicholson*, which was a similar case in India).

V. LIVING : RESIDE.

RESIDUARY BEQUEST OR DEVISE.—*V.* REST..

RESIDUARY EXECUTOR.—*V.* PERSONAL ESTATE, last par.

RESIDUARY LEGATEE.—Like LEGACY, "Residuary Legatee" has, *primâ facie*, reference only to personalty (*Windus* v. *Windus*, 26 L. J. Ch. 185; 6 D. G. M. & G. 549 : *Gethin* v. *Allen*, 23 L. R. Ir. 236) : contextually, however, it may extend to realty (*Hughes* v. *Pritchard*, 46 L. J. Ch. 840; 6 Ch. D. 24); but in that case there was a prior gift of the realty, and where there is no such a gift, *Hughes* v. *Pritchard* is not in point (*Re Methuen and Blore*, 50 L. J. Ch. 464; 16 Ch. D. 696). But the contextual widening of this phrase is supplied in such a case as where a testator directed his exors to sell specified landed property, and then gave legacies and made specific devises of other landed property, and concluded, "I constitute A. my Residuary Legatee," and there it was held that the land not specifically devised (after satisfying the general purposes of the Will) went to A., and not to the heir-at-law (*Singleton* v. *Tomlinson*, 3 App. Ca. 404; 38 L. T. 653; 26 W. R. 722 : *Re Sankey*, W. N. (89) 79). *Vh.* 1 Jarm. 743.

RESIDUARY PERSONAL ESTATE.—*V. Court* v. *Buckland*, 45 L. J. Ch. 214; 1 Ch. D. 605 : 1 Jarm. 761 *et seq.*

RESIDUE.—"A 'Residue' of personal estate means the personal estate which remains after payment of the testator's debts, funeral and testamentary expenses, and the costs of the administration of the estate, including the costs of an administration suit" (Dan. Ch. Pr. 1035, citing *Trethewy* v. *Helyar*, 4 Ch. D. 53; 46 L. J. Ch. 125 : *Fenton* v. *Wills*, 7 Ch. D. 33 : *Blann* v. *Bell*, 7 Ch. D. 382; 47 L. J. Ch. 120 : *Re Jones*, 10 Ch. D. 40). *Vf.* REST : REMAINDER.

"Residue of a Term," sale of; *V.* LEASE.

"Residue of *my Money*," held to include stocks, shares and securities for money (*Re Smith*, W. N. (89) 141). The "Residue of Money," held a gift of the general Residue (*Re White*, 51 L. J. P. D. & A. 40; 7 P. D. 65).

"The Residue of the said sums," in a Settlement; *V. De Lisle* v. *Hodges*, 43 L. J. Ch. 385; L. R. 17 Eq. 440 : *Cp.* OVERPLUS.

RESPECT OF.—*V.* IN RESPECT OF.

RESPECTIVE: RESPECTIVELY. — "Respective," "respectively" are words of severance. Occurring in a testamentary gift to more persons than one, their effect is "to sort out" the devisees or legatees so that they take as tenants in common (*Re Moore,* 31 L. J. Ch. 368; 10 W. R. 315; 6 L. T. 43; wherein Wood, V.-C., explained his own decision in *Re Hodgson,* 1 K. & J. 178: *Va. Sutcliffe* v. *Howard,* 38 L. J. Ch. 472; 17 W. R. 819: *Ive* v. *King,* 16 Bea. 46; 21 L. J. Ch. 560: *Davis* v. *Bennett,* 31 L. J. Ch. 337: *Vf.* 2 Jarm. 257, 259; Wms. Exs. 1469). But a devise to S. M. for life, remainder to the children of her body and the heirs of their "respective" bodies, creates a joint tenancy in the children and several inheritances in tail (*Tiverton Market Act,* 20 Bea. 374; 24 L. J. Ch. 657); in which case it was also held that a tenancy in common in the children would have been created, if the devise had been to the children and the heirs of their bodies "respectively," because in that case the word "respectively" would have had reference to the whole estate. *Vf.* Wms. Exs. 1470: *Vanderplank* v. *King,* 3 Hare, 1; 12 L. J. Ch. 497; 7 Jur. 548: *Gordon* v. *Atkinson,* 1 D. G. & S. 478.

Cross-Remainders may be implied notwithstanding the use of these words (2 Jarm. 545, 551).

In a Power of Sale to Trustees "and their *respective heirs and assigns,*" "respective" was rejected as surplusage, so that surviving Trustees could make a title (*Jones* v. *Price,* 10 L. J. Ch. 195; 11 Sim. 557).

"In Court or in Chambers *respectively,*" s. 39, Jud. Act, 1873, means "*either* in Court or in Chambers" (*Salm-Kyrburg* v. *Pomansky,* 53 L. J. Q. B. 428; 13 Q. B. D. 218: *Amstell* v. *Lesser,* 55 L. J. Q. B. 114; 16 Q. B. D. 189).

S. 10, Jud. Act, 1875, incorporating into the administration of Insolvent Estates and the winding-up of Companies the rules of Bankruptcy as to the "*respective rights* of secured and unsecured creditors," does not affect the rights of either class of creditors *inter se* (*Re Maggi, Winehouse* v. *Winehouse,* 51 L. J. Ch. 560; 20 Ch. D. 545: *Scott v. Murphy,* 13 L. R. Ir. 10: *Re Williams, Jones* v. *Williams,* 36 Ch. D. 573).

RESPONSIBLE.—*V.* INDEMNIFY.

REST.—Phrases in a Will dealing with the residue of a person's property,—*e.g.* "Rest," "Residue" and "Remainder," or either or any of such words,—are not merely most comprehensive in themselves, but will frequently enlarge the scope of other words in association with them.

A Residuary Bequest, always (*Cambridge* v. *Rous,* 8 Ves. 25: *Leake* v. *Robinson,* 2 Mer. 392: *Reynolds* v. *Kortright,* 18 Bea. 427), and a Residuary Devise, since 1 Jany., 1838 (1 V. c. 26, s. 25), carries not only everything not in terms disposed of, but "sweeps in everything (*Sv. Springett* v. *Jenings,* 40 L. J. Ch. 348; 6 Ch. 333) which turns out to be undisposed of" (per Wood, V.-C., *Bernard* v. *Minshull,* 28 L. J. Ch. 657: 1 Jarm. 761,—*wh. V.* to p. 768, as to "Residue;" *Va.* Wms. Exs. 1464, and as to Devises, Jarm. ch. 20; Lewin, 158); except a Share of the Residue itself which, on failing, will go as undisposed of, unless it be the manifest intention of the testator that such lapsed share should belong to the other residuaries (1 Jarm. 764: *Re Rhoades*, 54 L. J. Ch. 573; 29 Ch. D. 142, following *Crawshaw* v. *Crawshaw*, 49 L. J. Ch. 662; 14 Ch. D. 817. *Vf. Re Ballance*, 58 L. J. Ch. 534; 42 Ch. D. 62, in which the somewhat conflicting cases from *Humble* v. *Shore*, 7 Hare, 247, downwards are succinctly stated by Kay, J.).

"All the Rest" (*Attree* v. *Attree*, 40 L. J. Ch. 192; L. R. 11 Eq. 280; 24 L. T. 121; 19 W. R. 464: *Dobson* v. *Bowness*, L. R. 5 Eq. 404), or "the Rest and Residue" (*Smyth* v. *Smyth*, 8 Ch. D. 561; 26 W. R. 736; 38 L. T. 633), may very well include and pass realty, even though found in association with words relating to personalty. In the latter case a gift of "my sheep and all the rest, residue, moneys, chattels, and all other my *effects*" was held (by Malins, V.-C.) to pass realty. *Vh. Marhant* v. *Twisden*, Gilb. Eq. Rep. 30: *Murry* v. *Wise*, 2 Vern. 564: *Meeds* v. *Wood*, 19 Bea. 215: 1 Jarm. 728.

"All the Rest of my Money, however invested;" *V. Re Pringle*, 50 L. J. Ch. 689; 17 Ch. D. 819.

V. Residue: All.

RESTRAINT.—"'Restraint' in a Marine Insurance is the preventing the goods from being got away without laying hands upon them" (per Brett, J., *Rodocanachi* v. *Elliott*, L. R. 8 C. P. 659; 9 Ib. 518; 42 L. J. C. P. 247; 43 Ib. 255). *Vh.* criticism by Cave, J., *Johnston* v. *Hogg*, 52 L. J. Q. B. 343.

RESTRAINT ON ALIENATION.—As to what words will operate as a Restraint on Alienation of property by a married woman, *V.* Elph. 301-303; Watson, Eq. 396: *Vf.* Alienation.

RESTRAINTS OF KINGS.—"The words 'Arrests, Restraints and Detainments of all Kings, Princes and People,' (in a Marine Insurance), are properly applicable only to the ruling power of a country, and not to pirates or any other lawless power (*Nesbitt* v. *Lushington*, 4 T. R. 783). They apply, however, not only to hostile acts, but also to those which are committed by the government of which the assured is a subject; as, for instance, to the seizure of the vessel by the owner's government for the purpose of using her as a fire-ship (*Green* v. *Young*, 2 Ld. Raym. 840), or to the wrongful seizure of an English ship and cargo by a British ship of war (*Lozano* v. *Janson*, 2 E. & E. 160; 28 L. J. Q. B. 337: *Va. Stringer* v. *English and Scottish Mar. Insrce.*, L. R. 5 Q. B. 599; 38 L. J. Q. B. 321; 39 Ib. 214; 10 B. & S. 770), [or to an embargo, for a temporary purpose, by a friendly government: *Aubert* v. *Gray*, 32 L. J. Q. B. 50; 3 B. & S. 163, 169].

"The detention of a neutral vessel within a blockaded port is, it seems, a

'Restraint of Princes' within the meaning of this clause (*Geipel* v. *Smith*, L. R. 7 Q. B. 404 ; 41 L. J. Q. B. 153 : *Rodocanachi* v. *Elliott*, L. R. 8 C. P. 649 ; 9 Ib. 518 ; 43 L. J. C. P. 255)." 1 Maude & P. 488. *Vf. Crew* v. *G. Wn. Steamship Co.*, 4 Times Rep. 148.

In variance of previous decisions (*V.* 1 Maude & P. 352), it seems now the rule, that a reasonable apprehension of Capture will justify delay under the usual exception in Charter-parties of "Restraint of Princes and Rulers" (*The San Roman*, L. R. 5 P. C. 301 ; 42 L. J. Adm. 46 : *The Heinrich*, L. R. 3 A. & E. 435 : *Va. Geipel* v. *Smith* and *Rodocanachi* v. *Elliott*, sup. 1 Maude & P. 352).

V. Enemy.

RESUMPTION.—"'Resumption' is a word used in the statute of 31 H. 6, c. 7, and is there taken for the taking againe into the King's hands such lands or tenements as upon false suggestion or other error he had made livery of to an heire, or granted by patent unto any man" (Termes de la Ley).

RETAIL.—*V.* Wholesale.

For the purposes of the Licensing Acts (*V.* s. 3, 35 & 36 V. c. 94), the sale of Beer, Cider or Perry in any less quantity than 4½ gals. is selling By Retail (4 & 5 W. 4, c. 85, s. 19 ; 35 & 36 V. c. 94, s. 74) ; but as regards Spirits, there seems no definition in these Acts, so that each case must be decided on its own circumstances (Patterson's Licensing Acts, 5 Ed. 5).

Under the Spirits Act, 1880 (43 & 44 V. c. 24, s. 104), "the sale of Spirits in any quantity less than 2 gals., or less than 1 doz. reputed quart bottles, shall be deemed sale By Retail."

By the Sch. to 6 G. 4, c. 81, a Retailer of Beer (other than an Innkeeper) is defined as "Every person, not being a Brewer of Beer, who shall sell Strong Beer only in casks, containing not less than 4½ gallons Imperial Standard Gallon Measure, or in not less than 2 dozen reputed Quart Bottles at one time, to be drank or consumed elsewhere than on his, her or their premises." This provision relating to Quart Bottles no longer obtains : if the quantity sold at one time be 4½ gals. or more, it is not sold "By Retail," though it be delivered in pint or half-pint bottles (*Fairclough* v. *Roberts*, 24 Q. B. D. 350 ; 59 L. J. M. C. 54 ; 34 S. J. 230 ; 6 Times Rep. 180). *Semble*, this principle would also apply to the similar provision in the Spirits Act, 1880, cited above.

Person "licensed to sell Beer by Retail" who, under s. 18, 1 & 2 W. 4, c. 32, is disqualified from having a license to sell Game, means a person who *for the time being* is licensed to sell Beer by Retail ; the disqualification is not confined to Beerhousekeepers (a trade introduced the previous year, 1830, by the 1 W. 4, c. 64), but it also includes persons holding a Grocer's License for selling Beer under s. 1, 26 & 27 V. c. 33 (*Shoolbred* v. *St. Pancras Jus.*, 24 Q. B. D. 346 ; 59 L. J. M. C. 63 ; 38 W. R. 399).

A Covenant, made in 1854, not to carry on the trade of "an hotel or tavern-keeper, publican or beer-shop keeper, or *Seller by Retail* of wine, beer, spirits or spirituous liquors," was held not broken by selling wines and spirits, *in bottles*, by virtue of a license under 24 & 25 V. c. 21, s. 2, because, at the time the covenant was entered into, that would not have been a selling by retail, for at that time the only sellers of Beer, Spirits or Wine *by retail*, were hotel or tavern keepers (per James, V.-C., *Jones* v. *Bone*, L. R. 9 Eq. 674 ; 39 L. J. Ch. 405 ; 23 L. T. 304 ; 18 W. R. 489 ; *Cp. Fielden*, or *Feilden* v. *Slater*, cited SPIRITUOUS LIQUORS). *Jones* v. *Bone* is, accordingly, not of general application ; and a covenant that " no public-house, beer-house, or house for the sale of beer, wine, or spirituous liquors shall be erected, nor shall the trade of an innkeeper, victualler, or *Retailer of Wines, Spirits, or Beer* be carried on," is broken by opening a Bar at a Theatre, at which frequenters to the theatre may obtain wines, spirits, or beer (*Buckle* v. *Fredericks*, 34 S. J. 348 ; affd. Times, 29 March, 1890).

Simons v. *Farren* (4 L. J. C. P. 41 ; 1 Bing. N. C. 126, 272, and cited as to " Retailer of Beer," Woodf. 667), can scarcely be of any use on a question of construction, for it was determined on a point of pleading.

RETAIL LICENSE.—In a contract relating to the sale of a public-house, " Retail License " means the ordinary Retail License, without any condition whatever (*Modlen* v. *Snowball*, 4 D. G. F. & J. 143 ; 29 Bea. 641 ; 31 L. J. Ch. 44 ; 10 W. R. 24 ; 5 L. T. 299).

RETAIN AND EMPLOY.—*V.* EMPLOY.

RETIRE.—" If an Acceptor ' retires ' a Bill at maturity he takes it entirely from circulation, and the Bill is, in effect, paid ; but if an Indorser ' retires ' it, he merely withdraws it from circulation in so far as he himself is concerned, and may hold the Bill with the same remedies as he would have had, had he been called upon in due course, and had paid the amount to his immediate Indorsee " (per Jervis, C. J., delivering jdgmt. of C. P. *Elsam* v. *Denny*, 23 L. J. C. P. 190 ; 15 C. B. 87).

RETIRING TRUSTEE.—" Trustees by paying money into Court *retire* from their trust, and cannot thereafter exercise the powers of the trust " (Lewin, 999, citing *Re Coe*, 4 K. & J. 199 : *Re Williams*, 4 Ib. 87 : *Re Tegg*, 15 L. T. 236 ; 15 W. R. 52 : *Re Nettlefold*, 59 L. T. 315 : *Re Mulqueen*, 7 L. R. Ir. 127). *Va.* DECLINING TRUSTEE.

RETRACT.—" A Condition of Sale that no person shall retract his bidding was originally suggested to me by the case of *Payne* v. *Cave* (3 T. R. 148), and it has now become a common condition. But I always thought it one that could not be enforced. In *Jones* v. *Nanney* (13 Price, 99), Mr. Baron Wood suggested the difficulties. . . . But such a condition in a sale by Order of the Court is binding on the persons who consent to the sale, and upon their agents (*Freer* v. *Rimner*, 14 Sim. 391)." Sug. V. & P. 14.

RETURN.—This word in the Statute of Limitation of 21 Jac. 1, c. 16, does not imply that a plaintiff,—beyond seas when the cause of action arose,—has been in this country before; for, as regards a plaintiff who was never in this country before, it means,—Coming within the jurisdiction having been beyond seas when the cause of action arose (*Strithorst* v. *Græme*, 3 Wils. 145; 2 W. Bl. 723: *Lafond* v. *Raddock*, 22 L. J. C. P. 217; 13 C. B. 813: *Pardo* v. *Bingham*, 39 L. J. Ch. 170; 4 Ch. 735).

A Condition to a legacy, that the legatee "return" to a place, means that he come back to that place; and the condition is not performed if he die, or is lost at sea, whilst returning (*Priestley* v. *Holgate*, 26 L. J. Ch. 448; 3 K. & J. 286: *Sprigg* v. *Sprigg*, 2 Vern. 394). So, if the word is "arrive" (*Burgess* v. *Robinson*, 3 Mer. 7). *Vh.* 2 Jarm. 12, 13.

"Return *to his Work*:"—A person is prevented "from returning to his work" in a Factory, 7 V. c. 15, s. 22, who though he returns to the Factory is unable to work when there (*Lakeman* v. *Stephenson*, 37 L. J. M. C. 57; L. R. 3 Q. B. 192; 9 B. & S. 54).

V. PROCURE: SALE OR RETURN.

RETURN DAY.—In County Court proceedings the "Return Day" means the day *originally* appointed for the hearing (*R.* v. *Leeds Co. Co.*, 55 L. J. Q. B. 365; 16 Q. B. D. 691; 54 L. T. 873; 34 W. R. 487: *Vf.* Co. Co. Act, 1888, s. 186).

V. DAY OF HEARING.

RETURNED NOTE.—"'Returned Note' is an expression which is perfectly understood in the City of London to designate a Note which has been dishonoured" (per Bolland, B., *Hedger* v. *Steavenson*, 2 M. & W. 808; 6 L. J. Ex. 192).

RETURNING FROM.—*V.* GOING TO.

REVELAND.—*V.* TAINLAND.

REVENUE CHARGE.—*V.* *Hutton* v. *West Cork Ry.*, 52 L. J. Ch. 377, 689; 23 Ch. D. 654.

REVEREND.—This is not a title of honour or dignity; but merely a laudatory epithet or mark of respect, which people may inscribe on the tombstone of, *e.g.*, a Wesleyan minister (*Keet* v. *Smith*, 45 L. J. P. C. 10; L. R. 1 P. D. 73).

REVERSION: REMAINDER.—"'*Reversion*,' *Reversio* commeth of the Latine word *revertor*, and signifieth a returning againe" (Co. Litt. 142 b). A "Reversion" is the undisposed of interest in land which reverts to the grantor after the exhaustion of the particular estates,—*e.g.*, for years, for life, or in tail,—which he may have created. "There cannot, in the usual and proper sense of the term, be a Reversion expectant upon an estate in fee-simple" (per Selborne, L. C., *A.-G. of Ontario* v. *Mercer*, 52 L. J. P. C. 86 ; 8 App. Ca. 767) ; and though in the Writ of Escheat the word "revert" is employed, yet an Escheat is not properly a Reversion (Ib.).

A "*Remainder*," on the other hand, is that "residue of an estate in land, depending upon a particular estate and created together with the same ; and in law *Latine* it is called *remanere*" (Co. Litt. 49 a) : *e.g.*, a grant of an estate for life to A. and subject thereto to B. in fee ; the estate of B. is a Remainder.

Vf. Termes de la Ley, *Reversion* ; REMAINDERS.

In brief the meaning of, and difference between, these words are expressed as follows :—The Reversion is what is left ; and the Remainder is that which is created by the grant after the existing possession. Both words are technical phrases. And though it is said in the Touchstone (p. 249) that "a Reversion may be granted by the name of Remainder, or a Remainder by the name of a Reversion ;" yet it needs a very strong context for such a construction. Thus the word "Reversion" as used in s. 8, Prescription Act (2 & 3 W. 4, c. 71) will not be read as including "Remainder" (*Symons* v. *Leaker*, 54 L. J. Q. B. 480 ; 15 Q. B. D. 629 ; 33 W. R. 875 ; 1 Times Rep. 564. *Vf. Laird* v. *Briggs*, 50 L. J. Ch. 260 ; 19 Ch. D. 22).

As to whether the word "Reversion" will raise Cross-Remainders ; *V.* 2 Jarm. 553.

Even before the Wills Act (1 V. c. 26) a devise of a "Remainder" or "Reversion" would carry the fee (2 Jarm. 284 ; *Sv.* 285).

V. PERSON ENTITLED TO ANY REVERSION : REMAINDER.

REVERT.—Property to "Revert to the debtor," s. 35, Bankry. Act, 1883 ; *V. Bailey* v. *Johnson*, 40 L. J. Ex. 189 ; 41 Ib. 211 ; L. R. 6 Ex. 279 ; 7 Ib. 263 : *Vth. Ex p. Morier*, 12 Ch. D. 491.

"Then the same to revert back ;" *Re Norman*, W. N. (79) 175.

Vf. FRIENDS AND RELATIONS.

REVOKE.—As to what is a Revocation of a Will ; *V.* Jarm. ch. 7.

To draw a pen through several parts of a Will, to write on it "*This is revoked*," and then throw it into the waste-paper basket, is not a Revocation (*Cheese* v. *Lovejoy*, 46 L. J. P. D. & A. 66 ; 2 P. D. 251).

REVOLT.—"Make Revolt in a Ship," 11 & 12 W. 3, c. 7, s. 9, would not include force used against the Master to prevent him from committing unlawful homicide (*R.* v. *Rose*, 2 Cox, C. C. 329 : *The Shepherdess*, 5 Rob. C. 266).

REWARD.—"Reward" for a vote,—*e.g.*, 5 & 6 W. 4, c. 76, s. 54,—includes giving an employment (*Harding* v. *Stokes*, 5 L. J. Ex. 178 ; 2 M. & W. 233).

RIDE.—A horse ridden does not include a horse driven ; *e. g.* a Yeomanry Officer was exempt from Turnpike Toll in respect of the horse "*rode* by him in going to or returning from" exercise, &c. (s. 32, 3 G. 4, c. 126); but if, instead of riding his horse, he drove it in a gig the horse was not exempt from Toll (*Humphrey* v. *Bethel*, 35 L. J. M. C. 150; L. R. 1 C. P. 215; 30 J. P. 231). *Cp.* DRIVE.

RIDGE.—*V.* SELION.

RIGHT.—"*Jus, sive rectum* (which Littleton often useth) signifieth properly, and specially in writs and pleadings, when an estate is turned to a right, as by discontinuance, disseisin, &c. where it shall bee said, *quòd jus discendit et non terra.* But (Right) doth also include the estate *in esse* in conveyances; and therefore if tenant in fee simple make a lease for yeares, and release all his right in the land to the lessee and his heires the whole estate in fee simple passeth. And so commonly in fines, the right of the land includeth and passeth the state of the land; as *A. cognovit tenementa prædicta esse jus ipsius, B., &c.* And the statute (West. 2, c. 3) saith, *jus suum defendere,* (which is) *statum suum.* And note that there is *jus recuperandi, jus intrandi, jus habendi, jus retinendi, jus percipiendi, jus possidendi*" (Co. Litt. 345 a, b; *Vh.* Elph. 204–209).

"'Right' is where one hath a thing that was taken from another wrongfully, as by disseisin, discontinuance, or putting out, or such like, and the challenge or claime that he hath who should have the thing, is called Right" (Termes de la Ley, *Droit*).

The saving of every "*Right*, Claim, Privilege, Franchise, Exemption or Immunity" in s. 179, Thames Conservancy Act, 1857 (20 & 21 V. c. cxlvii), means a vested right of property, not a mere general right as one of the public (*Kearns* v. *Cordwainers' Co.*, 28 L. J. C. P. 285: 6 C. B. N. S. 388).

"As *of Right*," s. 5, 2 & 3 W. 4, c. 71; *V. Arkwright* v. *Gell*, 8 L. J. Ex. 201; 5 M. & W. 203: *Mason* v. *Shrewsbury and Hereford Ry.*, L. R. 6 Q. B. 578.

"Rights," &c., "*occupied or enjoyed*;" As to what rights of road, water-course, &c., will pass in a conveyance under the general words "All Rights, &c., to the said heredits belonging, or occupied or enjoyed therewith, or reputed as part, parcel or member thereof;" *V. Watts* v. *Kelson*, 40 L. J. Ch. 126; 6 Ch. 166: *Kay* v. *Oxley*, 44 L. J. Q. B. 210; L. R. 10 Q. B. 360: *Thomas* v. *Owen*, 20 Q. B. D. 231: *Bayley* v. *G. W. Ry.*, 26 Ch. D. 434: *Roe* v. *Siddons*, 22 Q. B. D. 224: APPURTENANCES: RIGHTS.

"Right *of Pasturage* usually enjoyed;" *V. Musgrave* v. *Inclosure Commrs.*, L. R. 9 Q. B. 162: PASTURAGE.

"Right *or Penalty*," s. 230, Bankry. Act, 1861, 24 & 25 V. c. 134; *V. Graham* v. *Robinson*, L. R. 2 Q. B. 387.

"Right, *Power or Privilege*," s. 50, 21 & 22 V. c. 98; *V. Fearon* v. *Mitchell*, L. R. 7 Q. B. 690; 41 L. J. M. C. 170.

V. IN HIS OWN RIGHT: SHARE: RIGHTS AND CREDITS.

RIGHT AND TITLE.—The addition to a devise of lands of all testator's "Right and Title" thereto, would even before the Wills Act pass the fee (*Sharp* v. *Sharp*, 4 Moore & P. 445); so of the word "Interest" therein (*Andrew* v. *Southouse*, 5 T. R. 292 : 2 Jarm. 285).

RIGHT DELIVERY.—Payment of Freight "on Right Delivery of the Cargo," means that the payment and delivery are to be concurrent acts (*Paynter* v. *James*, L. R. 2 C. P. 348).

RIGHT HEIR MALE.—*V. Re Grayson*, 48 L. J. Ch. 354.

RIGHT HEIRS.—"In my judgment the expression 'my own right heir,' or 'right heirs,' means according to the law of England, the heir or heirs of the testator at Common Law" (per Fry, J., *Re Garland*, 47 L. J. Ch. 714; 9 Ch. D. 213); who, if more than one,—*e.g.* females,—take as joint tenants (*Berens* v. *Fellowes*, 56 L. T. 391; 35 W. R. 356; 3 Times Rep. 425).

Vh. Hawes v. *Hawes*, 14 Ch. D. 614.

V. Heirs.

RIGHT OF APPEAL.—"Right of Appeal,"—*e.g.* s. 6, 38 & 39 V. c. 50,—is not limited to a Right of Appeal by statute, but includes a case where a judge has given leave to appeal (*Turner* v. *G. W. Ry.*, 46 L. J. Q. B. 226; 2 Q. B. D. 125).

RIGHT OF COMMON.—This expression as used in s. 1, 2 & 3 W. 4, c. 71, does not include Rights in Gross, "but contemplates only those more usual and ordinary Rights of Common and *profit à prendre* which are in some way appurtenant to land, and are limited to the wants of a dominant tenement" (per Cur., *Shuttleworth* v. *Le Fleming*, 34 L. J. C. P. 311; 19 C. B. N. S. 687).

RIGHT OF SALE.—A contractual "Right of Sale" of an article, or "Right to Sell" it, simply means that the person taking such Right is constituted an Agent for the sale of the article; it does not also mean that the person giving the Right contracts to supply the article (*Fox* v. *Smith*, 6 L. R. Ir. 319): *Semble*, if "the," and not merely "a," Right of Sale be given that imports a sole or exclusive agency (per Ball, C., Ib.). *V.* A : The.

RIGHT TO BID RESERVED.—*V.* Reserved Bidding.

RIGHTS.—The "Rights" which are extinguished by s. 20, Artizans' Dwellings Act, 1875, 38 & 39 V. c. 36, include inchoate or nascent rights; their deprival is "Loss" to be compensated under the same section (*Barlow* v. *Ross*, 24 Q. B. D. 381; 34 S. J. 266; 6 Times Rep. 200). *V.* Right.

RIGHTS AND CREDITS.—A Bequest of "Rights and Credits" will pass the general personal estate (*Hutchinson* v. *Hutchinson*, 13 Ir. Eq. Rep. 322).

S.J.D.

RIOT.—"'Riot' is where three (at the least) or more, do some unlawfull act; as to beat a man, enter upon the possession of another, or such like" (Termes de la Ley, *Riot*).

"A Riot is an unlawful assembly which has actually begun to execute the purpose for which it assembled, by a breach of the peace, and to the terror of the public; or a lawful assembly may become a Riot if the persons assembled form and proceed to execute an unlawful purpose to the terror of the people, although they had not that purpose when they assembled" (Steph. Cr. 49, 50).

Vf. Arch. Cr. 955–961; Rosc. Cr. 923–929: UNLAWFUL ASSEMBLY.

RIOTOUSLY.—Compensation may be given for damage occasioned "by any persons *riotously and tumultuously* assembled together" (s. 2 (1), Riot, Damages, Act, 1886, 49 & 50 V. c. 38), though the assembly be in a private place (*Gunter* v. *Metrop. Police,* 5 Times Rep. 58).

RISK.—"The fallacy in the defendant's argument arises from the double meaning of the word 'Risk.' That means, both the voyage commenced with necessary conditions to make the under-writers liable, and also the chance of loss during its performance" (per Bramwell, L. J., *Bradford* v. *Symondson,* 7 Q. B. D. 464; 50 L. J. Q. B. 586: *Rodocanachi* v. *Elliott,* L. R. 8 C. P. 663, 667, 668). "It is said that the Risk on a vessel, under a policy to a place generally without any provision as to her safety there, terminates on the vessel being safely anchored at her port of destination, in the usual place and manner; and this, I think, is the correct rule" (per Amphlett, B., *Stone* v. *Marine Insrce.,* 1 Ex. D. 86; 45 L. J. Ex. 361).

V. MERCHANT'S RISK: OWN RISK: SHIP'S RISK: WITHOUT RISK.

"Obvious Risk;" *V.* OBVIOUS.

RISK BEGINS TO RUN.—*V.* ATTACHES.

RISK OF COLLISION.—In Art. 14 of Regulations for Preventing Collisions at Sea, 1879, "Risk of Collision," means "a probability or reasonable chance of collision" (1 Maude & P. 599, citing *The Sylph,* 2 Spinks, 75: *The Ericsson,* Swabey, 38: *The Mangerton,* Ib. 120).

RISK OF CRAFT.—*V.* WITHOUT RISK OF CRAFT.

ROAD.—"The word 'Road' used in a Public Act, means in my opinion a public road,—a road over which the public have rights" (per Bramwell, B., *Curtis* v. *Embrey,* 42 L. J. M. C. 40; L. R. 7 Ex. 369; 21 W. R. 143).

V. MAIN ROAD: STREET.

ROAD AUTHORITY.—As to the definition of this phrase in s. 3,

Tramways Act, 1870 (33 & 34 V. c. 78); *V. Wolverhampton Tramways Co.* v. *G. W. Ry.*, 56 L. J. Q. B. 190.

ROADS.—"Dangers of Roads" in the exceptions in a *Bill of Lading*; *V. Rothschild* v. *Royal Mail Steam Packet Co.*, 21 L. J. Ex. 275, 276; 7 Ex. 734: DANGERS.

"Roads" in a *Mining Lease*; *V. Beaufort* v. *Bates*, 31 L. J. Ch. 481; 3 D. G. F. & J. 381; 10 W. R. 200; 6 L. T. 82.

ROBBERS.—"The nature of the transaction" (a Bill of Lading) "shows clearly therefore that the word 'Robbers' means not 'Thieves' but robbers *by force* to whom the term is more usually applied, although in common parlance it is often applied to every description of theft. It is explained also by the word with which it is associated, 'Pirates,'—who certainly take by force and not by stealth. We have no doubt therefore that, in this Bill of Lading, this is the proper meaning of the word 'Robbers;' and this being so, the loss in this case was not by Robbers" (per Pollock, C. B., *Rothschild* v. *Royal Mail Steam Packet Co.*, 21 L. J. Ex. 275, 276; 7 Ex. 743: *Vh.* 1 Maude & P. 353). *V.* THIEVES: DANGERS.

ROBBERY.—"'*Robberie.*' Roberia, properly is when there is a felonious taking away of a man's goods from his person" (Co. Litt. 288 a).

"'Robberie' is when a man taketh anything from the person of another feloniously" (Termes de la Ley).

"If a man take any thing, how little soever it be, from a man's person, feloniously, it is called *Robbery*" (Doctor and Student, Di. 1, ch. 8).

Robbery is Theft, with the additional circumstance that the thing taken "is on the body or in the immediate presence of the person from whom it is taken, and that the taking is by actual violence intentionally used to overcome or prevent his resistance, or by threats of injury to his person, property, or reputation" (Steph. Cr. 224).

Vf. Arch. Cr. 466–478; Rosc. Cr. 931–949.

Cp. THEFT.

ROGUE AND VAGABOND.—*V.* 5 G. 4, c. 83, s. 4; 1 & 2 V. c. 38, s. 2; 36 & 37 V. c. 38, s. 3; 34 & 35 V. c. 108, ss. 7, 10; Steph. Cr. 130.

V. VAGABOND: INCORRIGIBLE ROGUE.

"Thou art a traitorly Rogue" is actionable Slander (*Brunt* v. *Spencer*, 2 Keble, 47).

ROLLS.—*V.* FRENCH BREAD.

RONCARIA.—"*Roncaria* or *Runcaria* signifieth land full of brambles and briers, and is derived of *roncier*, the French word which signifieth the same, and as much as *senticetum*" (Co. Litt. 5 a).

ROOD.—*V.* ACRE.

ROOFED IN.—Houses had been completely roofed in, but they had shop projections with flat roofs, which roofs had only been covered with wood and had not received their intended zinc coverings; held, that the houses were "roofed in" within a Building Agreement (*Lowther* v. *Heaver*, 58 L. J. Ch. 482; 41 Ch. D. 248).

ROOT.—*V.* Product.

ROS.—*V.* Bruera.

ROUGH DRAFT.—A document may be a perfected Agreement though headed "Rough Draft" (*Gray* v. *Smith*, 58 L. J. Ch. 803).

ROUND BALE.—*V.* Bale.

ROUNDING.—*V.* Point.

ROUT.—"'Rout,' is when people do assemble themselves together, and after doe proceed, or ride, or goe forth, or doe move by the instigation of one or more who is their leader: This is called a Rout, because they doe move and proceed in Routs and numbers.

"Also where many assemble themselves together upon their owne quarels and braules: as if the inhabitants of a Towne will gather themselves together to breake hedges, pales and such like, to have common there, or to beat another that hath done to them a common displeasure, or such like, that is a Rout, and against the law, although they have not done or put in execution their mischievous intent. See the statute 1 Ma. c. 5" (Termes de la Ley, *Rout*).

"A Rout is an unlawful assembly which has made a motion towards the execution of the common purpose of the persons assembled" (Steph. Cr. 49).

Vf. Arch. Cr. 956; Rosc. Cr. 955; Unlawful Assembly.

ROYALTIES.—"In its primary and natural sense 'Royalties' is merely the English translation or equivalent of '*Regalitates*,' '*Jura regalia*,' '*Jura regia*.' 'Regalia' and 'regalitates,' according to Ducange, are 'jura regia;' and Spelman (Gloss. Arch.) says, '*Regalia dicuntur jura omnia ad fiscum spectantia*.' The subject was discussed with much fulness of learning in *Dyke* v. *Walford* (5 Moore, P. C. 434), where a Crown grant of *jura regalia*, belonging to the County Palatine of Lancaster, was held to pass the right to *bona vacantia*. 'That it is a *jus* (said Mr. Ellis in his able argument, Ib. p. 480) is indisputable; it must also be *regale*; for the Crown holds it generally through England by royal prerogative and it goes to the successor of the Crown, not to the heir or personal representative of the sovereign. It stands on the same footing as the right to escheats, to the land between high and low water mark, to treasure trove and other analogous rights.' With this statement of the law their Lordships agree" (per Selborne, L. C., *A.-G. of Ontario* v. *Mercer*, 52 L. J. P. C. 89; 8 App. Ca. 767). So "Royalties," in a grant from the Crown, will include gold and silver mines (*A.-G. of British Columbia* v. *A.-G. of Canada*, 58 L. J. P. C. 92; 14 App. Ca. 295). *Vf. Listowel* v. *Gibbings*, 9 Ir. C. L. Rep. 223.

In its secondary senses the word "Royalties" signifies, in mining leases, that part of the *reddendum* which is variable, and depends upon the quantity of minerals gotten (*A.-G. of Ontario* v. *Mercer*, sup.); or the agreed payment to a patentee on every article made according to the patent.

The power to appoint a gamekeeper given, by 22 & 23 Car. 2, c. 25, to lords of "*Manors and other Royalties*," was limited, so far as "Royalties" were concerned, to such Royalties as were inferior to Manors (*Ailesbury* v. *Pattison*, 1 Doug. 28).

RUBBISH.—"Rubbish," 57 G. 3, c. 29, s. 59, are things which have become valueless to the owner and the property in which he has abandoned (*Filbey* v. *Combe*, 2 M. & W. 677; 6 L. J. M. C. 132).

RULES OF COURT.—*V.* s. 14, Interp. Act, 1889.

RULES OR BYE LAWS.—As to what are "Rules or Bye Laws of the Employer," s. 1 (4), Employers' Liability Act, 1880, 43 & 44 V. c. 42; *V. Whatley* v. *Holloway*, 6 Times Rep. 190. In that case Fry, L. J., referring to the compromises manifest in the statute, said,—"Every word represents a conflict or struggle of thought;" and therefore, he said, the Act was to be construed with great care.

RUM.—"Rum," sold simply as such, must not be reduced more than 25 degrees under proof (Sale of Food and Drugs Act Amendment Act, 1879, 42 & 43 V. c. 30, s. 6); *Sv.* GIN and the case there cited.

RUN WITH THE LAND.—"A Covenant is said to 'Run with the Land' when either the liability to perform it, or the right to take advantage of it, passes to the assignee of that land. A covenant is said to 'Run with the Reversion' when either the liability to perform it, or the right to take advantage of it, passes to the assignee of that reversion" (Woodf. 162, citing *Spencer's Case*, 5 Rep. 16 a: *Vth.* 1 Smith's L. C. 65). *Va.* as to what covenants run with the land, Woodf. 162–166; Add. C. 1273–1285: SPIRITUOUS LIQUORS. *Note.*—A purchaser, with notice, is charged with a covenant (*Tulk* v. *Moxhay*, 11 Bea. 571; 18 L. J. Ch. 83), if it be of a *restrictive* character (*Haywood* v. *Brunswick Bg. Socy.*, 51 L. J. Q. B. 73; 8 Q. B. D. 403: *Hall* v. *Ewin*, 37 Ch. D. 74: *Lond. & S. W. Ry.* v. *Gomm*, 51 L. J. Ch. 530; 20 Ch. D. 562: *Mackenzie* v. *Childers*, 43 Ch. D. 265: *Andrew* v. *Aitken*, 52 L. J. Ch. 294; 22 Ch. D. 218: *Warton* v. *Robinson*, 29 S. J. 606, 607).

RUNCARIA.—*V.* RONCARIA.

RUNNING AWAY.—The act of vagrancy by "Running Away" and leaving wife or child chargeable to the parish (s. 4, 5 G. 4, c. 83), may be committed by walking away; but "in order to be within the meaning of the statute, the person must either abscond or so conceal himself that the parish authorities cannot find him, or he must absent himself by going a long distance" (per Erle, C. J., *Cambridge* v. *Parr*, 30 L. J. M. C. 242; 10 C. B. N. S. 99; 25 J. P. 518).

RUNNING DAYS.—"The meaning of 'Running Days' is that the freighter shall not waste time in loading and unloading" (per Abinger, C. B., *Pringle* v. *Mollett*, 6 M. & W. 83).

"Working days vary in different ports and different countries; and merchants and ship-owners, thinking it would be desirable to count Lay-days irrespective of the particular customs of particular ports, introduced the phrase 'Running Days' as distinguished from Working Days. The phrase 'Running Days' is a well-known nautical phrase, and means all the days in which in ordinary course the ship is running, and by that phrase is meant the whole of every day during both day and night. They are the days during which if the ship were at sea she would be running. Therefore 'Running Days' comprehends every day, including Sundays and holidays. In *Brown* v. *Johnson* (11 L. J. Ex. 373; 10 M. & W. 331), Lord Abinger said, 'I think the word *Days* and *Running Days* mean the same thing—namely, consecutive days, *unless there be some particular custom*'" (per Esher, M. R., *Neilsen* v. *Wait*, 55 L. J. Q. B. 89; 16 Q. B. D. 72). In *Neilsen* v. *Wait* a special custom of the Port of Gloucester was affirmed by which "Running Days" does not mean consecutive days.

As to day from which Running Days are to be calculated; *V. Davies* v. *M'Veagh*, 48 L. J. Ex. 686; 4 Ex. D. 265: *Murphy* v. *Coffin*, 12 Q. B. D. 87; *Pyman* v. *Dreyfus*, 24 Q. B. D. 152.

V. DAYS: WORKING DAYS.

RUNNING FREE.—In the Regulations for Preventing Collisions at Sea, 1879, "Running Free" is probably used as opposed to CLOSE-HAULED (1 Maude & P. 599).

RUNNING LANDING NUMBERS.—"These words are in practice treated as referring to the order in which bales are entered in the dock landing book" (Lowndes, 200).

RUSCARIA.—"A man grants *omnes ruscarias suas*, the soile where *rusci*, *i.e.*, kne-holme, or butchers pricks, or broome doe grow shall passe, and so in the verse in the Register it is called; but in F. N. B., fol. 2, in the verse *pischaria* is put instead of *ruscaria*" (Co. Litt. 5 a).

RUST.—As to the frequent exception in a Bill of Lading of "Rust, Leakage and Breakage;" V. LEAKAGE AND BREAKAGE.

SAFE CUSTODY.—As used in s. 76, 24 & 25 V. c. 96; *V. R.* v. *Cooper*, 43 L. J. M. C. 89; L. R. 2 C. C. R. 123; 38 J. P. 341: *R.* v. *Fullagar*, 41 L. T. 448; 44 J. P. 57: *R.* v. *Newman*, 51 L. J. M. C. 87; 8 Q. B. D. 706.

SAFE LOADING PLACE.—A place where a vessel can be rendered safe for loading by reasonable measures of precaution, is a "Safe Loading Place" within the terms of a charter-party (*Smith* v. *Dart*, 14 Q. B. D. 105; 54 L. J. Q. B. 121; 52 L. T. 218; 33 W. R. 455; 1 Times Rep. 99).

SAFE PORT.—"It seems that a port into which a ship cannot enter when fully laden is not a 'Safe Port'" (1 Maude & P. 320, n. (f), citing *General Steam Nav. Co.* v. *Slipper*, 11 C. B. N. S. 493; 31 L. J. C. P. 185. *Vf. Capper* v. *Wallace*, 49 L. J. Q. B. 350; 5 Q. B. D. 163). And, "although the ship can physically get into it (as far as navigation and what may be called the natural incidents are concerned), yet if that would be at the certain risk of confiscation, then the place is not a 'Safe Port'" (per Blackburn, J., *Ogden* v. *Graham*, 31 L. J. Q. B. 29: 1 B. & S. 773).

Va. Duncan v. *Köster; The Teutonia*, 41 L. J. Adm. 57; L. R. 4 P. C. 171: *Smith* v. *Dart*, cited SAFE LOADING PLACE.

V. NEAR THERETO AS SHE MAY SAFELY GET.

SAFELY.—*V.* NEAR THERETO AS SHE MAY SAFELY GET.

"Safely and securely," in a Declaration in Bailment, meant "with due care" (*Ross* v. *Hill*, 15 L. J. C. P. 182; 3 Dowl. & L. 788; 2 C. B. 877).

SAFETY.—As to the usual phrase in a Marine Insurance, "until she hath moored at anchor 24 hours in Good Safety;" *V. Lidgett* v. *Secretan*, L. R. 5 C. P. 190; 39 L. J. C. P. 196, and the authorities there cited and discussed.

SAID.—"The said" has reference to the last antecedent (*Esdaile* v. *Maclean*, 15 M. & W. 277; 16 L. J. Ex. 71: *Va. Wigmore* v. *Wigmore*, W. N. (72) 93).

V. AFORESAID.

SAID ESTATE.—*V. Markham* v. *Hutt*, W. N. (66) 17.

SAID TRUSTEES.—" The power of appointment of new Trustees is sometimes given 'to the *said Trustees*,' and then the question arises whether a sole survivor can appoint. It is conceived that 'the said Trustees' means the persons or person representing the trust for the time being under the Settlement, and that the survivor can therefore exercise the power" (Lewin, 665).

SAIL.—"It is clear that a warranty to 'sail,' without the word *from*, is not complied with by the vessel's raising her anchor, getting under sail, and moving onwards, unless at the time of the performance of these acts she has everything ready for the performance of the voyage, and such acts are done at the commencement of it, nothing remaining to be done afterwards" (per Abbott, C. J., *Lang* v. *Anderdon*, 3 B. & C. 498).

" 'Sail' is a technical word, and means 'Start on Voyage' " (per Byles, J., *Barker* v. *McAndrew*, 34 L. J. C. P. 195 ; 18 C. B. N. S. 759 : *Vh.* 1 Maude & P. 500 : *Thompson* v. *Gillespy*, 24 L. J. Q. B. 340).

Cp. Leave : Depart.

V. Final Sailing.

SAIL WITH CONVOY.—*V.* Convoy.

SAILING.—*V.* Final Sailing.

SAILING VESSEL.—Sailing Vessel "under-way," or "at anchor ;" *V. The Indian Chief*, 14 P. D. 24 ; 58 L. J. P. D. & A. 25 ; 60 L. T. 240, cited Under-Way.

V. Vessel.

ST. LAWRENCE.—" St. Lawrence" is considered to include both the gulf and river of that name (*Birrell* v. *Dryer*, 9 App. Ca. 345).

SAKE.—"The priviledge called 'Sake' is for a man to have the Amerciaments of his tenants in his owne Court" (Termes de la Ley, *Sake*).

SALARY.—" 'Salarie' is a word often used in our bookes, and it signifies a recompense or consideration given unto any man for his paines bestowed upon another man's businesse" (Termes de la Ley, *Salarie*).

The earnings of a Commercial Traveller, whose employment is at so much a year terminable by a week's notice, are a "Salary" within s. 53 (2), Bankry. Act, 1883 (*Ex p. Brindle*, 56 L. T. 498 ; 35 W. R. 596).

V. Wages : Income.

SALE.—" A Sale implies that there shall be one who sells and another who buys" (per Cockburn, C. J., *King* v. *England*, 33 L. J. Q. B. 145 ; 4 B. & S. 782) ; and, accordingly, it was held in that case that a landlord does not "sell" distrained goods, within s. 2, 2 W. & M., sess. 1, c. 5, if he takes them at their appraised value.

Goods are not "sold" within s. 1, Mer. Law Amendment Act, Scotland (19 & 20 V. c. 60), until the purchaser has acquired an enforceable *jus ad rem* in respect of such goods (*Seath* v. *Moore*, 55 L. J. P. C. 54).

The supply at a price by a Club to one of its members of intoxicants to be consumed by him off the premises, is not a "Sale" within s. 3, Licensing Act, 1872, 35 & 36 V. c. 94 (*Graff* v. *Evans*, 51 L. J. M. C. 25 ; 8 Q. B. D. 373 : *Newell* v. *Hemingway*, 58 L. J. M. C. 46).

Covenant against "the Sale," as compared with one against being a "Seller by Retail" of Spirituous Liquors ; *V.* SPIRITUOUS LIQUORS : RETAIL.

A Power enabling a Sale or Exchange of property authorises its PARTITION.

Where goods are "sold" under a *fi. fa.*, the 14 days from time of their "sale," under s. 87, Bankry. Act, 1869 (now s. 46, Bankry. Act, 1883), will begin to run when the sale is completed which the writ authorizes, *i.e.*, the end of the last day of the sale (*Jones* v. *Parsell*, 52 L. J. Q. B. 672 ; 11 Q. B. D. 430 : *Re Cripps, Ross & Co.*, 58 L. J. Q. B. 19).

"Proceeds of Sale," s. 87, Bankry. Act, 1869, meant the amount actually realized by the sale (*Turner* v. *Bridgett*, 51 L. J. Q. B. 374 ; 8 Q. B. D. 392).

As to when a sale is perfected within s. 6, Food & Drugs Act, 1875 (38 & 39 V. c. 63) ; *V. Kirk* v. *Coates*, 55 L. J. M. C. 182.

V. FOR SALE : SELL : SELLER.

SALE ON TRIAL: SALE OR RETURN.—"Other instances of sales, dependent on conditions precedent, are afforded by 'Sales on Trial,' or 'Approval,' and by the bargain known as 'Sale or Return.' In the former class of cases there is no sale till the approval is given, either expressly, or by implication resulting from keeping the goods beyond the time allowed for trial. In the latter case the sale becomes absolute, and the property passes only after a reasonable time has elapsed, without the return of the goods" (Benj. 590, 591, cited with approval *Elphick* v. *Barnes*, 5 C. P. D. 326 ; 49 L. J. C. P. 701).

In sales "*on Trial*," the buyer has the whole of the agreed time in which to exercise his option (Benj. 591).

"Sale *or Return* ;" *Vf. Moss* v. *Sweet*, 16 Q. B. 493 ; 20 L. J. Q. B. 167 : *Ray* v. *Barker*, 4 Ex. D. 279 ; 48 L. J. Ex. 569 : Benj. 591, 592, and other cases there cited.

Where a time is specified in a "Sale or Return" bargain, it will be reckoned from the receipt of the goods by the buyer (*Jacobs* v. *Harbach*, 2 Times Rep. 419).

SALEABLE UNDERWOOD.—What is "Saleable Underwoods"

within 43 Eliz. c. 2, was a question of fact (*R.* v. *Narberth North*, 9 A. & E. 815); and in *Fitzhardinge* v. *Pritchett* (36 L. J. M. C. 49; L. R. 2 Q. B. 135) it was held that Beech trees of 30 years' growth might be cut and managed as "Saleable Underwood" so as to be rateable under that statute.

Note: the provisions of that stat. as to "saleable underwoods" repealed by Rating Act, 1874.

As to what passes under a Grant of "Saleable Underwoods;" *V.* WOOD; Touch. 95.

V. UNDERWOOD.

SALICETUM.—"*Salicetum* doth signifie a wood of willowes. These trees in our bookes are called *sawces*" (Co. Litt. 4 b).

SALIVA.—"By the grant of the boillourie of salt, it is said, that the soile shall passe, for it is the whole profit of the soile. And this is called *saliva*, of the French word *salure* for a salt-pit; and you may read *de saliva* in Domesday, and *selda* signifieth the same thing; and where you shall read in records *de lacertâ in profunditate aquæ salsæ*, there *lacerta* signifieth a fathom" (Co. Litt. 4 b). But a little further on it is said, "*Selda* is a wood of sallowes, willowes, or withies;" *Va.* Touch. 95.

SALT.—In the memorandum of a Policy of Insurance, "Salt" does not include Saltpetre (1 Park, 245; 2 Arn. 791).

To "Salt an Invoice," means the addition of a commission to the price at which goods have been purchased (*Ex p. Johnson*, 30 L. J. Bank. 38).

SALVAGE.—"The taking care of goods left by the tide upon the banks of a navigable river, communicating with the sea, may in a vulgar sense be said to be Salvage; but it has none of the qualities of Salvage, in respect of which the laws of all civilized nations, the laws of *Oleron*, and our own laws in particular, have provided that a recompense is due for the saving, and our law has also provided that this recompense should be a lien upon the goods which have been saved" (per Eyre, C. J., *Nicholson* v. *Chapman*, 2 H. Bl. 257).

"Salvage, in its simple character, is the service which those who recover property from loss or danger at sea, render to the owners, with the responsibility of making restitution, and with a lien for their reward. It is personal in its primary character at least" (per Lord Stowell, *The Thetis*, 3 Hagg. Adm. 48: *Vf. Aitchison* v. *Lohre*, 4 App. Ca. 755; 49 L. J. Q. B. 123).

V. WITHOUT BENEFIT OF SALVAGE.

SAME.—"The same" generally refers to the next preceding antecedent (Co. Litt. 20 b, 385 b).

As to the antecedent to which "the same" refers: *V. Huskisson* v. *Lefevre* (26 Bea. 160); but "the word 'same' may grammatically refer to more than one antecedent" (per Jessel, M. R., *Court* v. *Buckland*, 45

L. J. Ch. 216 ; 1 Ch. D. 605). A devise of "my estate called L." to A. for life "and after his decease I give *the same*" unto B., without words of limitation, was held to give B. only a life interest (*Doe* d. *Lean* v. *Lean*, 10 L. J. Q. B. 60 ; 1 Q. B. 229). But this case was on a Will made previously to 1 V. c. 26, and seems to have turned on the word "Estate" as implying merely local situation, rather than as laying down that because A. was to have a life estate, therefore B. was to have "the same :" *Vf.* 2 Jarm. 282.

"Same Cause ;" *V.* CAUSE.

"Same *Ground* ;" in a commercial traveller's contract for service; *V. Mumford* v. *Gething*, 29 L. J. C. P. 105 ; 7 C. B. N. S. 305.

"Same *Offence* ;" s. 6, Habeas Corpus Act, 31 Car. 2, c. 2 ; *V. A.-G. of Hong Kong* v. *Kwok-a-Sing*, 42 L. J. P. C. 64 ; L. R. 5 P. C. 179.

"Same *Rent and Covenants* ;" "Same *Form* ;"—"On the whole, it is indisputably settled, that the words, 'under the same Rent and Covenants' are not of themselves sufficient to include the covenant for renewal. Nor will a covenant to grant a lease 'in the same Form' include the covenant for renewal" (1 Platt, 724 ; *Vf.* Ib. 713–724).

"Same *State of Investment* ;" *V. Re Morris, Bucknill* v. *Morris*, 54 L. J. Ch. 388 ; 52 L. T. 462 ; 33 W. R. 445 ; W. N. (85) 31.

"The expression 'Passing only over *the same Portion of the Line*' (s. 90, 8 V. c. 20) appears to us to mean passing between the same points of departure and arrival, and passing over no other part of the line. This is the natural interpretation of the words ; it was adopted by Cranworth, L. C., in *Finnie* v. *Glasgow Ry.* (2 Macq. H. L. 77), and by the Court of Session in the recent case of *Murray* v. *Glasgow & S. W. Ry.* (11 Ct. of Sess. Ca. 205) ; and there is no decision in which any other interpretation has been put on the expression" (per Lindley, L. J., in delivering judgmt. of Court of App. in *Manchester, S. & L. Ry.* v. *Denaby Colliery*, 54 L. J. Q. B. 110 ; 14 Q. B. D. 209 ; affd. by H. L., 55 L. J. Q. B. 181 ; 11 App. Ca. 98).

"The expression 'Under the same Circumstances' (s. 90, 8 V. c. 20) must now be taken to mean, under like circumstances *as regards the services performed* by the Railway Company in receiving, carrying and delivering the goods,—*V. G. W. Ry.* v. *Sutton*, 38 L. J. Ex. 177 ; L. R. 4 H. L. 226 : *Lond. & N. W. Ry.* v. *Evershed*, 48 L. J. Q. B. 22 ; 47 Ib. 284 ; 46 Ib. 289 ; 3 App. Ca. 1029 ; 3 Q. B. D. 134, 254" (per Lindley, L. J., *Manchester S. & L. Ry.* v. *Denaby Colliery*, sup.). *Vf. Hull, &c. Ry.* v. *Yorkshire, &c. Coal Co.*, 56 L. J. Q. B. 261.

V. LIKE.

"Same Terms and Conditions," "Same Manner," "Same Time and Manner ;" *V.* AFORESAID.

SAMPLE.—"A sale by Sample, only has reference to the *quality* of the article sold" (per Parke, B., *Nichol* v. *Godts*, 23 L. J. Ex. 315 ; 10 Ex. 191). In that case the contract was for "Foreign Refined Rape Oil, warranted only equal to Samples," and it was held that the buyer was not bound to accept Oil which corresponded with the samples, but was not Foreign Refined Rape Oil. *Va. Azemar* v. *Casella,* 36 L. J. C. P. 263 ; L. R. 2 C. P. 677: and *Cp. Heyworth* v. *Hutchinson,* 36 L. J. Q. B. 270 ; L. R. 2 Q. B. 447.

But a sale "per Sample," simpliciter, is a warranty that the bulk shall be equal to the sample (*Parker* v. *Palmer,* 4 B. & Ald. 387) ; yet a sale by Sample does not exclude implied warranty of merchantable quality respecting such matters as the sample would not disclose to a purchaser using ordinary skill and diligence (*Mody* v. *Gregson,* 38 L. J. Ex. 12 ; L. R. 4 Ex. 49 : *Drummond* v. *Van Ingen,* 56 L. J. Q. B. 563 ; 12 App. Ca. 284 ; 57 L. T. 1 ; 36 W. R. 20).

V. Report.

SATISFACTION.—"*Nota,* 'in satisfaction,' and 'in full satisfaction' is all one" (Co. Litt. 213 a).

"Satisfaction for all Damage," s. 16, Ry. C. C. Act, 1845 ; *V. Re Gower's Walk Schools* v. *London, Tilbury & Southend Ry.,* 59 L. J. Q. B. 162 ; 6 Times Rep. 390.

To "make Satisfaction" to a Creditor, s. 36, 1 & 2 V. c. 110, is to pay his debt (*Hitching,* or *Kitching* v. *Croft,* 10 L. J. Q. B. 18 ; 12 A. & E. 586).

"Making or Tendering Satisfaction" for damage done in the exercise of statutory powers, does not imply a condition precedent to the right of entry ; but means that the act shall not be done without compensation being made (*Lister* v. *Lobley,* or *Hoxley,* 6 L. J. K. B. 200 ; 7 A. & E. 124).

SATISFACTORY.—Where one party has to perform a contractual obligation to the "satisfaction" of the other,—*e.g.,* furnish "proof satisfactory" of death or accident,—this does not give that other the power to act capriciously,—he can only ask for a reasonable fulfilment of the obligation (*Braunstein* v. *Accidental Insrce.,* 31 L. J. Q. B. 17 ; 1 B. & S. 782). So a condition to furnish a Title "satisfactory" to the purchaser, only entitles him to make usual objections (*Lord* v. *Stephens,* 1 Y. & C. Ex. 222).

"Satisfactory *Evidence,*" s. 64, Tithe Commutation Act, 6 & 7 W. 4, c. 71 ;—Though under this section a sealed copy of a Tithe Commutation Map is "Satisfactory Evidence" of its accuracy, that is only so for the purposes of the Act, and not on questions of ownership (*Wilberforce* v. *Hearfield,* 46 L. J. Ch. 584 ; 5 Ch. D. 709).

SATISFACTORILY SOLD.—*V.* Caution.

SATISFIED.—"I desire it to be understood as my clear opinion that a Term does not become 'satisfied,' within 8 & 9 V. c. 112, unless the beneficial interest in the charge secured by the Term, the beneficial interest in the whole charge, and the beneficial interest in the whole estate are united and merged in one person" (per James, L. J., *Anderson* v. *Pignet,* 42

L. J. Ch. 312 ; 8 Ch. 180 ; 27 L. T. 740 ; 21 W. R. 150 : *Va.* cases there cited, and *Shaw* v. *Johnson*, 30 L. J. Ch. 646 ; 1 Dr. & Sm. 412 ; 4 L. T. 461 ; 9 W. R. 629).

"Satisfied *his Contempt*," 53 G. 3, c. 127 ; *V. Dean* v. *Green*, 8 P. D. 79 : *Ex p. Bell Cox*, 20 Q. B. D. 1.

SAVE.—"Can Save ;" *V.* LEFT.

SAWCES.—*V.* SALICETUM.

SAY.—"Say *About* :" "In *M'Connel* v. *Murphy*, L. R. 5 P. C. 203, where the sale was 'of all of the spars manufactured by A., say about 600,' the words 'say about 600' were held to be words of expectation and estimate only, not amounting to an understanding that the quantity should be 600. The effect of the word 'say' when prefixed to the word 'about' was considered as emphatically marking the vendor's purpose to guard himself against being supposed to have made any absolute promise as to quantity" (Benj. 684 ; *Va.* Blackb. 216). But in a Charter-Party a contract to deliver "a full and complete cargo . . . say about" a specified quantity, the words "say about" would bear a different meaning from what they would in an ordinary contract, and would not be mere words of expectation, but are words of limitation and therefore of contract (*Morris* v. *Levison*, 45 L. J. C. P. 409 ; 1 C. P. D. 155 : *V.* Blackb. 216).

"Say *From* :" In a contract for sale "say from 1,000 to 1,200 gallons," these are words of expectation (*Gwillim* v. *Daniel*, 4 L. J. Ex. 174 ; 2 Cr. M. & R. 61). But in *Tanvaco* v. *Lucas* (28 L. J. Q. B. 150, 301 ; nom. *Tamvaco* v. *Lucas*, 1 E. & E. 582), a contract for "about 2,000 quarters, *say from* 1,800 to 2,200 quarters," was, in view of its other stipulations, construed as fixing a minimum and maximum limit.

"Say, *not less than* :" In a contract for sale of wool "Say not less than 100 packs," these are not mere words of expectation ; but amount to a contract to deliver at least that quantity (*Leeming* v. *Snaith*, 16 Q. B. 275 ; 20 L. J. Q. B. 164 : *Va. Bourne* v. *Seymour*, 24 L. J. C. P. 202 ; 16 C. B. 337 : NOT LESS).

Vf. as to the use of the word "Say," *Philips* v. *Astling*, 2 Taunt. 211.

V. MORE OR LESS : THEREABOUTS.

SCANDALOUS.—A pleading is "Scandalous" (Ord. 19, R. 27, R. S. C.) which alleges anything unbecoming the dignity of the Court to hear, or is contrary to good manners, or which charges a crime immaterial to the issue. But the statement of a scandalous fact that is material to the issue is not a scandalous pleading (*Millington* v. *Loring*, 50 L. J. Q. B. 214 ; 6 Q. B. D. 190 ; 29 W. R. 207 : *Christie* v. *Christie*, 42 L. J. Ch. 544 ; 8 Ch. 499).

For examples of Scandalous pleading ; *V. Blake* v. *Albion Assrce.*, 45

L. J. C. P. 663 ; 24 W. R. 677 : *Lee* v. *Ashwin*, 1 Times Rep. 291 : *Coyle* v. *Cuming*, 27 W. R. 529 : *Duncan* v. *Vereker*, W. N. (76) 64 : *Bright* v. *Marner*, W. N. (78) 211.

SCHOOL.—*V.* FREE GRAMMAR SCHOOL.

SCHOOL OF LEARNING.—A school for the education of gentlemen's sons, is a "School of Learning" within 43 Eliz. c. 4 (*A.-G.* v. *Lonsdale*, 1 Sim. 109 : *Va. A.-G.* v. *Nash*, 3 Bro. C. C. 588).

SCHOOLMASTER.—*V.* TUTOR.

SCIENCE.—The 6 & 7 V. c. 36, s. 1, exempts from *Local Rates* premises "belonging to any society instituted for purposes of *Science, Literature or the Fine Arts exclusively*," if supported wholly or in part by annual voluntary contributions, and not making (and the rules of which expressly prohibit, *R.* v. *Jones*, inf.) any dividend to its members; and which has obtained a certificate from the Registrar of Friendly Societies.

The following societies have been held *exempt* :—

Royal Manchester Institution (*R.* v. *Manchester*, 20 L. J. M. C. 113 ; 16 Q. B. 449) : The Linnæan Society of London (*Linnæan Socy.* v. *St. Anne, Westminster*, 23 L. J. M. C. 148 ; 3 E. & B. 793) : The Birmingham New Library (*Ex p. Birmingham*, 18 L. J. M. C. 89 ; nom. *Churchwardens of Birmingham* v. *Shaw*, 10 Q. B. 868) : The Royal Medical and Chirurgical Society of London (*R.* v. *Roy. Med. and Chir. Socy.*, 21 J. P. 789 ; 30 L. T. O. S. 133) : The Bradford Library and Literary Society (*R.* v. *Bradford Library*, 28 L. J. M. C. 73 ; 5 Jur. N. S. 513 ; nom. *Bradford Library Socy.* v. *Churchwardens of Bradford*, 1 E. & E. 88) : The Liverpool Library (*Liverpool Library* v. *Liverpool*, 29 L. J. M. C. 221).

The following societies have been held *not exempt* :—

The Religious Tract Society (*R.* v. *Jones*, 15 L. J. M. C. 129 ; 8 Q. B. 719 : the precise ground of that decision was that the rules of the Society did not expressly prohibit dividends to members ; but Denman, C. J., at the conclusion of his jdgmt., said :—"Upon the words of this statute I greatly doubt whether, under the words 'literary societies,' a religious society can be included :" *V.* this dictum cited with approval in *Scott* v. *St. Martin-in-the-Fields*, 25 L. J. M. C. 42 ; 5 E. & B. 558) : A Society for the purposes of Education (*R.* v. *Pocock*, 15 L. J. M. C. 132 ; 8 Q. B. 729 : *R.* v. *Temple*, 22 L. J. M. C. 129 ; 2 E. & B. 160) : A Society,—*e.g.* The Russell Institution, or the Cambridge Philosophical Society,—one of whose staple objects is to provide a news-room ; for readers of the news of the day are not, whilst so employed, "cultivating science, literature or the fine arts" (*Russell Institution* v. *St. Giles and St. George, Bloomsbury*, 23 L. J. M. C. 65 : 3 E. & B. 416 : *Purchas* v. *Holy Sepulchre*, 24 L. J. M. C.

9; 4 E. & B. 156): A Society whose primary object is the private convenience or amusement of its members (*R.* v. *Brandt*, 20 L. J. M. C. 119; 16 Q. B. 462: *R.* v. *Gaskell*, 21 L. J. M. C. 29; 16 Q. B. 472): The Birmingham News Room (*R.* v. *Phillips*, 17 L. J. M. C. 83; 8 Q. B. 745): The Greenwich Society for the Acquisition and Diffusion of Useful Knowledge (*Purvis* v. *Traill*, 18 L. J. M. C. 57; 3 Ex. 344): The London Library (*Clarendon* v. *St. James, Westminster*, 20 L. J. M. C. 213; 10 C. B. 806): The United Service Institution (*R.* v. *St. Martin's-in-the-Fields*, 21 L. J. M. C. 53; 17 Q. B. 149): The Zoological Society (*R.* v. *Zoological Socy.*, 23 L. J. M. C. 139; nom. *Marylebone Vestry* v. *Zoological Socy.*, 3 E. & B. 807): The Working Men's Educational Union; one of whose objects was the discussion of social and political subjects after the manner of a debating club (*Scott* v. *St Martin's-in-the-Fields*, 25 L. J. M. C. 42; 5 E. & B. 558): The Institution of Civil Engineers; for "Science" ceases to be science, within the meaning of the exemption, when it is acquired, communicated or made use of for the advantage of an individual, or of the members of a particular profession or section of the public (*R.* v. *The Institution of Civil Engineers*, 49 L. J. M. C. 34; 5 Q. B. D. 48; 28 W. R. 253. In that case Field, J., said:—"No doubt it has been thought that the Court of Queen's Bench, in some of the earlier cases, carried the exemption at least to its furthest limits, but all the later cases are in favour of its stricter limitation").

One of the exemptions from *Property Duty* in s. 11, sub-s. 3, Customs and Inland Revenue Act, 1885 (48 & 49 V. c. 51), is for property appropriated "for the promotion of Education, Literature, Science or the Fine Arts." The word "exclusively" does not appear here; "But I apprehend that the meaning of this clause of exemption is that the property or income shall be, if not exclusively, yet certainly in the main and as its chief object, devoted to the promotion of education, literature, science or the fine arts" (per Lord President, *Socy. of Writers to the Signet* v. *Inl. Rev.*, 14 Court Sess. Ca. 4th Series, 34); and accordingly it was there held that the property of the Society of Writers was not exempt. But though that rule of interpretation was adopted in *Re Institution of Civil Engineers* (19 Q. B. D. 610; 20 Ib. 621; 56 L. J. Q. B. 576; 57 Ib. 353; 36 W. R. 523, 598), yet, on the facts, the majority of the Court of Appeal held that that Institution was exempt from the Property Duty. And though in that case Coleridge, C. J., and Field, J. (in the Court below), and Lopes, L. J. (in the Court of Appeal), held that the absence of "exclusively" made no difference, yet as the judgment below was over-ruled and that of Lopes, L. J., was not adopted, it would seem that the absence of that word did make some difference, and explains why the property of the Civil Engineers' Institution is not exempt from Local Rates, but is exempt from Property Duty. Without that explanation it seems difficult to reconcile the two cases.

V. Education.

SCIENTIFIC INVESTIGATION.—*V.* Prolonged Examination.

SCOT.—"A customary contribution laid upon all subjects according to their ability" (Spelm. 505 : *Va.* Cowell's Interpreter). In *Waller* v. *Andrews* (7 L. J. Ex. 67 ; 3 M. & W. 312), "Scots," in a tenant's agreement to pay all outgoings, rates, taxes, scots, &c., was treated as an extensive word, and was held to include an extraordinary assessment by the Commissioners of Sewers for work of permanent benefit (*Vh.* 2 Platt, 170). *V.* Outgoings.

In Termes de la Ley, "Scot" is not spoken of as a contribution or burden; the definition there given is,—"'Scot,' that is to be quit of a certaine custome, as of common tallage made to the use of the Sheriffe or Bayliffe."

SCOT AND LOT.—Those who pay "Scot and Lot," are those who pay to Church and Poor (per Hardwicke, L. C., *A.-G.* v. *Parker*, 3 Atk. 557 ; 1 Ves. 43).

SCOTALE.—"'Scotale' is an extortion prohibited by the statute of Charta de Foresta, c. 7, and it is where any officer of the Forest keepes an ale-house, to the intent that he may have the custome of the inhabitants within the Forrest to come and spend their money with him, and for that he shall winke at their offences committed within the Forrest" (Termes de la Ley).

SCOTCH EDUCATION DEPARTMENT.—*V.* s. 12 (7) Interp. Act, 1889.

SCOUNDREL.—*V.* Cheat.

SCRIVENER.—A "Scrivener" is a person to whom property is entrusted for the purpose of lending it out to others, at a profit payable to his principal, but also at a commission or bonus for himself whereby he seeks, wholly or in part, to gain his livelihood (*Harrison* v. *Harrison*, 1 Esp. 555 : *Lott* v. *Melville*, 3 Sc. N. R. 346 ; 9 Dowl. 882 ; 3 M. & G. 52 : *Ex p. Malkin*, 1 Rose, 406 ; 2 Ib. 27 : *Hutchinson* v. *Gascoigne*, Holt, N. P. 507 : *Ex p. Gem*, 2 Mont. D. & D. 99 ; 5 Jur. 683 : *Ex p. Dufaur* 20 L. J. Bank. 38 ; 2 D. G. M. & G. 246).

SEA.—The Thames at Woolwich is not "the Sea" within s. 1, 48 G. 3, c. 75 (*Woolwich* v. *Robertson*, 50 L. J. M. C. 87 ; 6 Q. B. D. 654). In that case Mathew, J. said, "'Sea' is used, in this Act, in its ordinary and popular sense, and in that sense 'Sea' is always used as distinguished from 'River.'"

"At Sea;" *V.* Mariner.

Ship "proceeding *to Sea* ;" *V.* Proceed to Sea.

V. Perils of the Sea.

SEAL.—" Under the hands and seals ; " an impression made with ink, by means of a wooden block, is a sufficient sealing (*R.* v. *St. Paul's, Covent Garden*, 14 L. J. M. C. 109 ; Sug. Pow. 231, 232 : *Sprange* v. *Barnard*, 2 Bro. C. C. 585). " And if the party seal the deed with any seal besides his own, or with a stick, or any such like thing which makes a print, it is good " (Touch. 57).

SEALED.—The Seal of a Court, with the words " Sealed with the Seal of the Court," proves itself, and will be taken judicial notice of (*Doe* d. *Duncan* v. *Edwards*, 8 L. J. Q. B. 98 ; 9 A. & E. 554 ; 1 P. & D. 408).

SEAM.—*V.* Vein and Seam.

SEAMAN.—*V.* Mariner.

SEAMEN.—In a warranty in the margin of a Marine Policy, " Seamen besides Passengers," mean persons belonging to the ship's company, including cook, surgeon, boys, &c. (*Bean* v. *Stupart*, 1 Doug. 14).

SEARCH.—To "enter or be" on land " in Search or Pursuit of Game," &c., s. 30, 1 & 2 W. 4, c. 32, the Game sought for must be live game (*Kenyon* v. *Hart*, 34 L. J. M. C. 87 ; 6 B. & S. 249 : *Tanton* v. *Jervis*, 43 J. P. 784 ; 68 Law Times, 37) ; but if the Justices find that the shooting from outside the land and the entering to pick up the game, is all one connected act they will, probably, be upheld if they reach the conclusion that there was a " Pursuit " of Game within the section, which pursuit began whilst the Game was alive (*Osbond* v. *Meadows*, 31 L. J. M. C. 238 ; 12 C. B. N. S. 10 : *Sv.* obs. in *Kenyon* v. *Hart*, sup.). *Vh. Dyer* v. *Park*, 38 J. P. 294.

V. Entering or Being.

SEASONABLE TIME.—In the claim of a custom to walk and ride over certain arable land at all Seasonable Times, what is a " Seasonable Time " is a question partly of law and partly of fact ; but when the corn is standing on the land is not a " Seasonable Time " for the exercise of such a custom (*Bell* v. *Wardell*, Willes, 202).

SEAWORTHY.—" By being *seaworthy* ' is meant that the ship shall be in a fit state as to repairs, equipment, and crew, and in all other respects, to encounter the ordinary perils of the voyage insured, at the time of sailing upon it. If the assurance attaches before the voyage commences, it is enough that the state of the ship be commensurate to the then risk ; and, if the voyage be such as to require a different complement of men, or state of equipment in different parts of it, as if it were a voyage down a canal or river and thence across to the open sea, it would be enough if the vessel were, at the commencement of each stage of the navigation, properly manned and equipped for it. But, the assured makes no warranty to the underwriters, that the vessel shall continue seaworthy, or that the master or crew shall do their duty during the voyage, and their negligence or misconduct is no defence to an action on the policy where the loss had been immediately occasioned by the perils insured against ;' per Parke, B., in delivering the jdgmt. of the court in *Dixon* v. *Sadler*, 5 M. & W. 414, confirmed in error 8 Ib. 895 ; 9 L. J. Ex. 48, cited and approved in *Biccard* v. *Shepherd*, 14 Moore P. C. 494 : *Bouillon* v. *Lupton*, 15 C. B. N. S. 113 ; 33 L. J. C. P. 37 : *Davidson* v. *Burnand*, L. R. 4 C. P. 117 : and *Quebec Mar. Insrce.* v. *Commercial Bank of Canada*, L. R. 3 P. C. 234 ; 39 L. J. P. C. 53. An exception of loss from unseaworthiness does not restrict the implied warranty (S. C.). Where the ship is not seaworthy when she sails on her voyage, this is not remedied by her becoming so afterwards and before loss (S. C. ;—following *Forshaw* v. *Chabert*, 3 Brod. & B. 158 ; and over-ruling *Weir* v. *Aberdeen*, 2 B. & Ald. 320, 324, on this point)." Rosc. N. P. 386 : *Vf. Small* v. *Gibson*, 20 L. J. Q. B. 152 ; 16 Q. B. 128 : *Clapham* v. *Langton*, 34 L. J. Q. B. 46 ; 5 B. & S. 729.

SECOND COUSIN.—A testamentary gift to "Second Cousins" of the testator, applies only to persons having the same great-grandfather or great-grandmother as himself, unless the nature of the gift or the wording of the Will, shows that other persons were meant to be included (*Re Parker, Bentham* v. *Wilson*, 50 L. J. Ch. 639 ; 15 Ch. D. 528 ; 17 Ib. 262, and *V.* that case for obs. by Jessel, M. R., on *Mayott* v. *Mayott*, 2 Bro. C. C. 125, and which obs. were afterwards confirmed by James, L. J. : *Vf. Bridgnorth* v. *Collins*, 15 Sim. 538). But where there are no real "Second Cousins," then First Cousins once removed will take ; but not first cousins twice removed (*Slade* v. *Fooks*, 8 L. J. Ch. 41 ; 9 Sim. 386 : *Re Bonner, Tucker* v. *Good*, 51 L. J. Ch. 83 ; 19 Ch. D. 201 : *Wilks* v. *Bannister*, 54 L. J. Ch. 1139 ; 30 Ch. D. 512 : Wms. Exs. 1110).

Vf. Charge v. *Goodyer*, 3 Russ. 140.

V. COUSIN : FIRST COUSIN.

SECOND OFFENCE.—"When a 'Second Offence' is the subject of distinct punishment, it is an offence committed after *conviction* of a first" (Maxwell, 427, citing 2 Inst. 468 ; *Vf.* 1 Hale, P. C. 686) ; and a penalty for a Second Offence can only be inflicted where both convictions are under the same enactment, although each might be supported by the same evidence (*Ex p. Anthers*, or *Authers*, 58 L. J. M. C. 62 ; 22 Q. B. D. 345 ; 60 L. T. 454).

SECOND SON.—*V.* FIRST SON.

SECONDARY.—"'Secondary' is the technical medical word for a disease which is not the primary cause of death. If a man falls through the ice and is drowned, that is death by Accident ; but if he walks home in his wet clothes, and catches a cold which settles on his lungs, and he dies, that is death from a 'Secondary Cause'" (per Mellish, arg. *Smith* v. *Accident Insrce.*, 39 L. J. Ex. 214 ; L. R. 5 Ex. 302 ; *Vh.* jdgmt. Kelly, C. B., therein : the case, however, was decided on another point. *Va. Fitton* v. *Accidental Death Insrce.*, 34 L. J. C. P. 28 ; 17 C. B. N. S. 122). *V.* ACCIDENT.

SECRET DISPOSITION.—"Secret Disposition of the dead body of the said child," s. 60, 24 & 25 V. c. 100 ;—These words "include cases in which the body is placed in a situation where it is not likely to be found, except by accident or upon search ; although the body is in no way concealed from any one who happens to go to that place" (Steph. Cr. 170, citing *R.* v. *Brown*, L. R. 1 C. C. R. 244 ; 39 L. J. M. C. 94 ; 22 L. T. 484 : *Va. R.* v. *Perry*, Dears. 471 ; 24 L. J. M. C. 137 : *R.* v. *Cook*, 22 L. T. 216. In a note to Steph. Cr. 170, the learned author asks,—"If a woman were to leave a child's body by night in the middle of a street, or to drop it by day in a crowd of people, there would be an effectual concealment of the birth, but would there be a 'Secret Disposition' of the body ?")

SECRETARY.—Note signed "for A. B. & Co.,—C. D., Secretary," does not make the Secretary personally liable (*Alexander* v. *Sizer*, 38 L. J. Ex. 59 ; L. R. 4 Ex. 102).

SECRETARY OF STATE.—*V.* s. 12 (3), Interp. Act, 1889.

SECURE.—The direction in s. 32, Divorce Act, 1857 (20 & 21 V. c. 85) to "secure" a gross or annual sum to a wife, does not authorise an order for payment direct to the wife ; but means that the sum is to be secured in such a way as to provide for her (*Medley* v. *Medley*, 51 L. J. P. D. & M. 74 ; 7 P. D. 122).

The words "or otherwise secure," in s. 10, 11 G. 2, c. 19, enlarge the word "impound" with which they are there associated, and give it a wider meaning than if it had been used alone (per Tindal, C. J., *Thomas* v. *Harries*, 1 M. & G. 702 ; 9 L. J. C. P. 308 ; 1 Scott, N. R. 524). *V.* IMPOUND.

SECURED.—*V.* AMOUNT SECURED.

On a sale of a Leasehold Ground-Rent it was described as "*amply secured ;*" it was really secured by an Underlease which was for a longer term than the lessor had, and therefore operated as an Assignment of the original lease, and there was no power of distress ; but the Conditions stated that the purchaser should not object by reason of the term being in excess of the term granted by the original lease, inasmuch as the deeds "may be inspected for 10 days immediately preceding the day of sale by intending purchasers" :—the purchaser was, under those Conditions, held bound to complete, although it was certainly doubtful whether the Ground-Rent was properly secured (*Smith* v. *Watts*, 28 L. J. Ch. 220 ; 4 Drew. 338).

SECURED CREDITOR.—A "Secured Creditor" is one who has security for his debt ; *V.* SECURITY.

In language nearly identical with that in the Bankry. Act of 1869 (s. 16, sub-s. 5), the Bankry. Act, 1883 (s. 168), defines a "Secured Creditor," for bankry purposes, as, "a person holding a Mortgage, Charge or Lien on the property of the debtor, or any part thereof, as a Security for a debt due to him from the debtor." Accordingly it will be seen that a "Secured Creditor," within the Bankry. Act, cannot be defined as a person holding a security as against the whole or some part of the debtor's estate ; that definition would be too wide ; the SECURITY must be of the kind prescribed,—*i.e.* (1) MORTGAGE, (2) CHARGE or (3) LIEN. The appointment of one of the plaintiffs (judgment creditors) as Receiver, without security, of the stock in trade of the defendant, does not make the plaintiffs "Secured Creditors" as against a Bankry Trustee (*Re Dickinson, Ex p. Charrington*, 22 Q. B. D. 187).

But in Administration of a deceased's estate, or of a liquidating Company, the phrase "Secured and Unsecured Creditors" in s. 10, Jud. Act, 1875, does not incorporate the bankry rule which provides for payment of debts *pari passu* except wages and rates and taxes ; and therefore a Judgment Creditor is, in such an administration, entitled to priority (*Re Maggi, Winehouse* v. *Winehouse*, 51 L. J. Ch. 560 ; 20 Ch. D. 545 ; 30 W. R. 729 : *Smith* v. *Morgan*, 49 L. J. C. P. 410 ; 5 C. P. D. 337 : *Scott* v. *Murphy*, 13 L. R. Ir. 10 : *Vf. Re Williams, Jones* v. *Williams*, 36 Ch. D. 573).

SECURELY.—*V.* SAFELY.

SECURITIES.—*V.* SECURITY FOR MONEY : STOCKS.

"Securities," s. 16, Bankry. Act, 1869 ; *V. Re Frith*, 48 L. J. Bank. 122 ; 12 Ch. D. 337.

"*Other* Securities," s. 12, 1 & 2 V. c. 110, "I think, means only Securities *ejusdem generis* with the Securities particularly mentioned in the section ; and I doubt whether the section can be held to apply to goods in pledge" (per North, J., *Re Rollason*, 56 L. J. Ch. 769 ; 34 Ch. D. 495 ; 56 L. T. 303 ; 35 W. R. 607). So a bequest of "Foreign Bonds and other Securities," was held to pass Foreign Securities only, although the testator had large investments in British Funds (*Ferguson* v. *O'Gilby*, 2 Dr. & War. 548).

SECURITY.—A "Security," speaking generally, is anything that makes the money more assured in its payment or more readily recoverable ; as distinguished from (*e.g.*) a mere I. O. U. which is only evidence of a debt.

Thus Bank Notes, Bills of Exchange, Promissory Notes, and Cheques are "Securities" (Byles, *V.* especially Pref. to 1st Ed.).

And writing is not necessary; for a parol deposit of deeds to secure a debt creates an Equitable Mortgage (Fisher, 51 *et seq.*; Coote, ch. 31) and is obviously a "Security."

A *Verdict* before judgment is probably not a "Security" (*Jones* v. *Thompson*, 27 L. J. Q. B. 234; E. B. & E. 63); but "a Judgment is in every sense of the word a Security to a creditor for payment of his claim" (per Kelly, C. B., *West Ham* v. *Ovens*, 42 L. J. M. C. 29; L. R. 8 Ex. 37).

A *Seizure* under a *fi. fa.* (even before sale) gave the execution creditor a "Security" within s. 12, Bankry. Act, 1869 (*Slater* v. *Pinder*, 40 L. J. Ex. 146; 41 Ib. 66; L. R. 6 Ex. 228; 7 Ib. 95; 19 W. R. 778; 20 Ib 441: *Ex p. Rocke, Re Hall*, 40 L. J. Bank. 70; 6 Ch. 795; 19 W. R. 1129; 25 L. T. 287); but no such security was created until seizure (*Ex p. Williams*, 41 L. J. Bank. 38; 7 Ch. 314; 20 W. R. 430); and when the *fi. fa.* was for a sum exceeding £50 and was against a trader, it was defeasible under s. 87. An execution against goods, to be good against bankruptcy must now be "completed by Seizure and Sale" (Bankry. Act, 1883, s. 45: *Vth.* ss. 46, 145).

Seizure under an *elegit* (*Ex p. Abbott, Re Gourlay*, 50 L. J. Ch. 80; 15 Ch. D. 447), or lodging an *elegit* with a sheriff who is remaining in possession under a former elegit (*Ex p. Shaw*, W. N. (84) 60), or the appointment of a Receiver (*Ex p. Evans, Re Watkins*, 49 L. J. Bank. 7; 13 Ch. D. 252; 28 W. R. 127; 41 L. T. 565), gives a Security on land within the Bankry. Act, 1869; and which is not taken away by s. 45, Bankry. Act, 1883. But that latter section is fatal to a Receivership of goods (*Re Dickinson, Ex p. Charrington*, 58 L. J. Q. B. 1; 22 Q. B. D. 187); *V.* SECURED CREDITOR.

A *Garnishee Order*, as soon as served on the garnishee, created a "Security" to the judgment creditor on the debt therein comprised; *V.* CHARGE for cases hereon: but the Order must now be completed "by receipt of the debt" to be good as against bankruptcy (Bankry. Act, 1883, s. 45).

A *Foreign Attachment* out of the Lord Mayor's Court (*Levy* v. *Lovell*, 49 L. J. Ch. 305; 14 Ch. D. 234; 28 W. R. 602), or an attachment in the Tolzey Court of Bristol (*Ex p. Sear*, 51 L. J. Ch. 448; 17 Ch. D. 74), gives no "Security" for the debt sued for, the object of either process being merely to compel the appearance of the defendant.

Money paid into Court to abide the event of an action is a Security to the other litigant (*Ex p. Tate, Re Keyworth*, 43 L. J. Bank. 102; nom. *Ex p. Banner, Re Keyworth*, 9 Ch. 379; 30 L. T. 620: *Ex p. Bouchard, Re Moojen*, 48 L. J. Bank. 105; 12 Ch. D. 26).

As to a Landlord's security for Rent in the liquidation of a Company; *V. Re Oak Pits Co.*, 51 L. J. Ch. 768; 21 Ch. D. 322; 30 W. R. 760.

V. SECURED CREDITOR: VALUABLE: SECURITIES FOR MONEY: MORTGAGE: CHARGE: LIEN.

SECURITY FOR A DEBT.—A Building Agreement which forfeits to the landlord the materials which may be brought on the land on breach by the builder of his obligations, is not a licence to take possession of chattels as "Security for a Debt," and therefore is not a Bill of Sale requiring registration under s. 4, Bills of S. Act, 1878 (*Brown* v. *Bateman*, 36 L. J. C. P. 134 ; L. R. 2 C. P. 272 : *Blake* v. *Izard*, 16 W. R. 108 : *Ex p. Newitt, Re Garrud*, 51 L. J. Ch. 381 ; 16 Ch. D. 522 : *Reeves* v. *Barlow*, 53 L. J. Q. B. 192 ; 11 Q. B. D. 610 ; 12 Ib. 436). *Vh. Ex p. Jay, Re Harrison*, 14 Ch. D. 19 : *Re Yates, Batcheldor* v. *Yates*, 57 L. J. Ch. 697 ; 38 Ch. D. 112 ; 59 L. J. 47 ; 36 W. R. 563 : *Climpson* v. *Coles*, 23 Q. B. D. 465.

A "Security for the *payment of money*," within s. 3, Bills of Sale Act, 1882, is made "whenever the grantor binds himself to pay money to the grantee, whatever may be the reason" (per Esher, M. R., *Hughes* v. *Little*, 56 L. J. Q. B. 98 ; 18 Q. B. D. 32 ; 55 L. T. 476 ; 35 W. R. 36).

SECURITY FOR MONEY.—Mortgages are "Securities for Money" (*Dicks* v. *Lambert*, 4 Ves. 725 : *Ogle* v. *Knipe*, L. R. 8 Eq. 434 ; 38 L. J. Ch. 692). So a bequest of "Securities for Money" will *primâ facie* pass Stock in the Funds (*Bescoby* v. *Pack*, 1 Sim. & St. 500) : but not Bank Stock (Ib. : *Ogle* v. *Knipe*, sup.) ; nor Shares in a Company (*Hudleston* v. *Gouldsbury*, 10 Bea. 547) ; nor an unpaid Legacy (*Re Mason*, 34 Bea. 494 ; 34 L. J. Ch. 603). Such a bequest will pass a Vendor's Lien for unpaid purchase-money (*Callow* v. *Callow*, 58 L. J. Ch. 698 : *Sv. Goold* v. *Teague*, 7 W. R. 84 ; 32 L. T. O. S. 251 ; 5 Jur. N. S. 116, but this latter case disapproved, Sug. V. & P. 684 ; Dart, 827 n.). So it will pass a Life Policy (*Lawrance* v. *Galsworthy*, 3 Jur. N. S. 1049) ; also Bonds (*Dicks* v. *Lambert*, sup.), and Bills of Exchange, Promissory Notes and Cheques (*Barry* v. *Harding*, 1 J. & La T. 475) ; but not Bank Notes, for they are Money (*Southcot* v. *Watson*, 3 Atk. 233). It would not pass money merely evidenced as due by an I. O. U. (*Barry* v. *Harding*, sup.) ; nor a sum shown to be due by a Banker's Deposit Note (*Hopkins* v. *Abbott*, 44 L. J. Ch. 316 ; L. R. 19 Eq. 222) ; still less a mere Debt (*Re Mason*, 34 L. J. Ch. 603 ; 11 Jur. N. S. 835) : but it would seem that money due on a Judgment would pass (*West Ham* v. *Ovens*, 42 L. J. M. C. 29 ; L. R. 8 Ex. 37). *Vh.* Wms. Exs. 1198.

A bequest of "Securities for Money," prior to the Conv. & L. P. Act, 1881, if uncontrolled by context, passed the legal estate in the mortgaged hereditaments (1 Jarm. 699 ; Wms. Exs. 1198 ; Lewin, 228) ; *Sv.* s. 30 of that Act as regards testators dying after 31 Dec. 1881.

"Security for Payment of Money," s. 1, Carriers Act, 11 G. 4 & 1 W. 4, c. 68 ; *V. Stoessiger* v. *S. E. Ry.*, 3 E. & B. 549 ; 23 L. J. Q. B. 293 : *McCall* v. *Taylor*, 19 C. B. N. S. 301 ; 34 L. J. C. P. 365.

"Security for the Payment of Money," s. 3, Bills of S. Act, 1882 ; *V.*

Manchester, S. & L. Ry. v. *North Central Wagon Co.*, 58 L. J. Ch. 219; 13 App. Ca. 554.

V. Money.

SEE BACK.—"See Back" on the face of a (Railway) Cloak Room Ticket, gives to the person taking it notice of the Conditions on the back of it, under which the article is accepted for custody (*Parker* v. *S. E. Ry.*, 46 L. J. C. P. 768; 2 C. P. D. 416). *Vh. Kent* v. *Mid. Ry.*, 44 L. J. Q. B. 18; L. R. 10 Q. B. 1; 23 W. R. 25.

SEED BARLEY.—*V.* Barley.

SEEDS.—"Seeds of another kind;" *V.* Dye.

SEEK A LIVELIHOOD.—*V.* Livelihood.

SEEM MEET.—A power to justices "to make such order thereon as to them shall seem meet" (s. 44, 5 & 6 W. 4, c. 50), does not authorize an order for illegal charges (*Barton* v. *Piggott*, 44 L. J. M. C. 5; L. R. 10 Q. B. 86).

SEIZE.—*V.* Seizure.

SEIZED.—This word, in its relation to real estate, is "one of the most technical words in our law—a word that has no meaning except technical. It has not got into vernacular use that I am aware of" (per James, L. J., *Leach* v. *Jay*, 47 L. J. Ch. 877).

"'Seisin,' or *seison*, is common aswell to the English as to the French, and signifies in the common law, possession; whereof *seisina* a Latin word is made, and *seisire*, a verbe" (Co. Litt. 153 a): actual entry is, generally speaking, necessary to make a seisin (2 Bla. Com. 209; Co. Litt. 29 a; *Sv.* the exceptions there stated and Hargrave's note thereon. *Va.* Wms. R. P. tit. *Feoffment*). Therefore a devise of "all real estate of which I may die seized," will not pass real estate to which the testator is entitled, but of which he has not acquired the actual possession (*Leach* v. *Jay*, 47 L. J. Ch. 876; 9 Ch. D. 42; 39 L. T. 242; 27 W. R. 99).

But though "seized" is a strong technical expression and has its proper relation only to realty, yet if it be the only word relating to realty in a testamentary gift the other expressions of which relate to personalty, it will not be sufficient to pass realty (*Jones* v. *Robinson*, 47 L. J. C. P. 673; 3 C. P. D. 344).

A Recital that a person is "seized of *or otherwise well entitled to*" a property, does not operate as an estoppel that he is seized of the *legal* estate (*Heath* v. *Crealock*, 10 Ch. 22; 44 L. J. Ch. 157).

"Seized *or entitled*," s. 78, District Courts New South Wales Act, 1858; *V. Godfrey* v. *Poole*, 57 L. J. P. C. 78; 13 App. Ca. 497; 58 L. T. 685.

V. ENTITLED.

"Seized in *Fee Simple*," in the exception to 17 G. 3, c. 26, for the Registration of Annuities, included a tenant for life with a general power of appointment (*Halsey* v. *Hales*, 7 T. R. 194).

Meat is not "seized" within ss. 116, 117, P. H. Act, 1875, if, having been purchased, it is, with the consent of the purchaser, taken by an Inspector of Nuisances to a Justice for condemnation (*Vinter* v. *Hind*, 52 L. J. M. C. 93; 10 Q. B. D. 63). *V.* SEIZURE.

SEIZED JOINTLY.—This phrase in s. 10, Trustee Act, 1850 (13 & 14 V. c. 60), is not to be construed as referring only to a strictly legal joint tenancy, but will include coparceners (*Re Greenwood*, 54 L. J. Ch. 623; 27 Ch. D. 359).

SEIZIN.—*V.* SEIZED.

SEIZURE.—The ordinary and natural meaning of "Seizure" is a forcible taking possession (per Cave, J., *Johnston* v. *Hogg*, 52 L. J. Q. B. 343; 10 Q. B. D. 432. *Va. Vinter* v. *Hind*, 52 L. J. M. C. 93; 10 Q. B. D. 63).

Seizure of part of the goods in the house by virtue of a fi. fa. in the name of the whole, is a good seizure of all (per Holt, C. J., *Cole* v. *Davis*, 1 Ld. Raym. 724. *Va. Gladstone* v. *Padwick*, 40 L. J. Ex. 154; L. R. 6 Ex. 203).

An execution against Lands is "completed by Seizure," within s. 45 (2), Bankry. Act, 1883, as soon as the sheriff has delivered the lands to the execution creditor (*Re Hobson*, 55 L. J. Ch. 754; 33 Ch. D. 493; 55 L. T. 255; 34 W. R. 786: *Cp.* DELIVERED IN EXECUTION).

V. ACTUAL: SEIZED.

In a warranty by owners of a ship against "Capture *and Seizure*," in a Marine Insurance, the word "Seizure" has its ordinary and natural meaning and includes the forcible taking possession of a vessel and abandoning her as soon as the cargo has been plundered: "Seizure" is not equivalent to, but is larger than "Capture," as the latter word involves the idea of keeping what has been seized (*Johnston* v. *Hogg*, 52 L. J. Q. B. 343; 10 Q. B. D. 432: and *dicta* there cited). "Seizure" even in this connexion is not confined to a belligerent, hostile or wrongful seizure (*Powell* v. *Hyde*, 25 L. J. Q. B. 65; 5 E. & B. 607: *Kleinwort* v. *Shepard*, 28 L. J. Q. B. 147; 1 E. & E. 447: *Cory* v. *Burr*, 51 L. J. Q. B. 95, 468; 52 Ib. 657; 8 Q. B. D. 313; 9 Ib. 463; 8 App. Ca. 393).

V. CAPTURE.

SELDA.—*V.* SALIVA.

SELECT.—*V.* APPROPRIATE.

SELION.—"By the grant of a selion of land, *selio terræ*, a ridge of land which containeth no certainty, for some be greater and some be lesser; and by the grant *de unâ porcâ*, a ridge doth passe. *Selio* is derived of the French word *sellon*, for a ridge" (Co. Litt. 5 b. *Va.* Termes de la Ley). *V.* PORCA TERRÆ.

SELL.—*V.* SALE; ASSIGN: PARTITION: SELLER.

"Sell, publish, or expose to sale" any Printed Book; *V.* IMPORT FOR SALE.

SELLER.—The person who is the "Seller" of poison within s. 17, Pharmacy Act, 1868 (31 & 32 V. c. 121), is the person who keeps the shop, or actually conducts the business of the place, where the sale is transacted, even though he only sell the article on commission for another person, living elsewhere and having no control over the shop or place (*Templeman* v. *Trafford*, 51 L. J. M. C. 4; 8 Q. B. D. 397).

SEND.—"A threatening letter is 'sent' when it is dropped in the way of the person for whom it is destined, so that he may pick it up (*R.* v. *Jepson*, *R.* v. *Lloyd*, 2 East, P. C. 1115, 1122: *R.* v. *Wagstaff*, Russ. & Ry. 398); or is affixed in some place where he would be likely to see it (*R.* v. *Williams*, 1 Cox, C. C. 16); or is placed on a public road near his house so that it may, however indirectly, reach him, which it eventually does after passing through several hands (*R.* v. *Grimwade*, 1 Den. 30. *Va.* *R.* v. *Jones*, 5 Cox, C. C. 226): although in none of these cases would the paper be popularly said to have been 'sent'" (Maxwell, 336).

Notices of Chargeability or of Appeal were authorized to be sent "*By Post* or otherwise" (s. 79, 4 & 5 W. 4, c. 76; s. 10, 14 & 15 V. c. 105); they were, accordingly, "sent," within s. 9, 11 & 12 V. c. 31, on the day when in the ordinary course of post they ought to have been delivered (*R.* v. *Slawstone*, 21 L. J. M. C. 145; 18 Q. B. 388: *R.* v. *Richmond*, 27 L. J. M. C. 197; E. B. & E. 253; 31 L. T. O. S. 115).

As regards all Acts passed after the 31st Dec. 1889, a document is served "By Post," "by properly addressing, pre-paying, and posting a letter containing the document, and (unless the contrary is proved) to have been effected at the time at which the letter would be delivered in the ordinary course of post" (s. 26, Interp. Act, 1889). *V.* ORDINARY COURSE.

SENTICETUM.—*V.* RONCARIA.

SEPARATE BUILDING.—*V.* DISTINCT.

SEPARATE MAINTENANCE.—A Provision for a married woman for her "Separate Maintenance" may make it for her SEPARATE USE (*Re Tharp*, 3 P. D. 76). *Vf.* COMFORTABLE MAINTENANCE.

SEPARATE PROPERTY.—This phrase, in s. 1, M. W. P. Act, 1882, does not comprise property over which a married woman has a general power of appointment (*Re Armstrong*, 55 L. J. Q. B. 578 ; 21 Q. B. D. 264 ; 34 W. R. 709 ; 2 Times Rep. 745 : *Vh. Re Roper*, 39 Ch. D. 482 : *Mayd* v. *Field*, 3 Ch. D. 587).

Vf. as to this phrase in that section, Greenwood's Real Pro. Statutes, 2 Ed. 354.

SEPARATE QUARTER SESSIONS.—As to this phrase in s. 150, Municipal Corporations Act, 1882, 45 & 46 V. c. 50 ; *V. St. Lawrence, Ramsgate* v. *Kent Jus.*, 51 J. P. 262 ; 3 Times Rep. 519.

SEPARATE USE: SEPARATE ESTATE.—"What words create a trust for Separate Use, has often been a subject of dispute. The principle of construction is stated to be, that the marital right is not to be excluded except by expressions which leave no doubt of the intention" (2 Jarm. 24, n. (*r*) ; *Va.* Elph. 297).

"'Separate' is the proper technical word for excluding the marital right: 'Sole' is not equivalent ; and *primâ facie* a devise or bequest direct to a *single* woman (including the testator's widow) for her 'sole' use will not create a separate estate" (2 Jarm. 25, n. (*r*), citing *Gilbert* v. *Lewis*, 1 D. G. J. & S. 38 ; 32 L. J. Ch. 347 : *Lewis* v. *Mathews*, L. R. 2 Eq. 177 ; 35 L. J. Ch. 638). *Vf.* SOLE.

But "no particular form of words is *necessary* in order to vest property in a married woman to her separate use. That intention though not expressed in terms, may be inferred from the nature of the provisoes annexed to the gift" (per Brougham, L. C., *Stanton* v. *Hall*, 2 Russ. & My. 180).

If, too, the woman were married, or her marriage were in contemplation, at the date of the instrument to be construed, that fact would be of importance, as it would induce the Court the more readily to believe that words pointing to an independent enjoyment were intended to create a separate use (2 Jarm. 25, n. (*r*): *Va.* cases hereon collected, Elph. 298, 299).

For the cases as to what words have been held to create a separate use ; *V.* 2 Jarm. 24, n. (*r*) ; Wms. Exs. 756 ; Theobald, 467 ; Elph. 297–301 ; Lewin, 755–757 ; Watson, Eq. 388–390 ; 2 Story, Eq. 13 Ed. 711–714. *Va.* COMFORTABLE MAINTENANCE : SEPARATE MAINTENANCE.

"Property acquired by a married woman and becoming her separate estate by virtue of the M. W. P. Act, 1882, is not 'property settled to her Separate Use' within the meaning of these words as used in an exception to a covenant for settling a wife's future property in a Settlement before 1883" (Elph. 296, citing *Re Stonor*, 24 Ch. D. 195 ; 52 L. J. Ch. 776 : *Va. Re Whitaker*, 56 L. J. Ch. 251 ; 34 Ch. D. 227 ; 35 W. R. 217). In a discussion of the lastly cited case (31 S. J. 376, 377), it has been said that "the practical effect of the decision is that the words 'for her separate use' should be always added after a gift, limitation, or bequest to a married woman."

Semble,—A gift to a married woman *for her "Separate Use,"* will not take the property out of a *Covenant to settle* (3 Davidson's Prec. 3 Ed. 199, 200 : *Re Alnutt, Pott* v. *Brassey*, 52 L. J. Ch. 299 ; 22 Ch. D. 275 : differing from *Re Mainwaring*, L. R. 2 Eq. 487. *Va. Scholfield* v. *Spooner*, 26 Ch. D. 94.)

SEPARATELY.—A wife may engage in or carry on an employment, trade or occupation "Separately from her husband" (s. 2, M. W. P. Act, 1882), in the house in which they are living together ; "separately," in that connection, does not mean "bodily separate," but means without the husband's interference (*Ashworth* v. *Outram*, 46 L. J. Ch. 687 ; 5 Ch. D. 923 ; 37 L. T. 85 ; 25 W. R. 896 : *Lovell* v. *Newton*, 4 C. P. D. 7 ; 27 W. R. 366 : *Re Dearmer*, 53 L. T. 905).

By Bills of S. Act, 1878, s. 7, "No Fixtures or Growing Crops shall be deemed, under this Act, to be 'separately *assigned or charged*' by reason only that they are assigned by separate words, or that power is given to sever them from the land or building to which they are affixed, or from the land on which they grow, without otherwise taking possession of or dealing with such land or building, or land, if by the same instrument any freehold or leasehold interest in the land or building to which such Fixtures are affixed, or in the land on which such Crops grow, is also conveyed or assigned to the same persons or person. The same rule of construction shall be applied to *all* deeds or instruments including Fixtures or Growing Crops, executed before the commencement of this Act and then subsisting and in force, in all questions arising under any Bankruptcy, Liquidation, Assignment for the Benefit of Creditors, or Execution of any process of any Court, which shall take place or be issued after the commencement of this Act."

SERVANT.—In determining whether a person is entitled to participate in a *Bequest* to "Servants" regard must be had to ;—

1. The Nature of the Service :
2. Its duration :
3. Its conditions.

1. It seems an obvious thing to say that there must be the relationship of master and servant between the testator and the person claiming as "servant :" and therefore a coach-man supplied, with a carriage and horses, by a job-master is not a "servant" of the job-master's customer (*Chilcot* v. *Bromley*, 12 Ves. 114 : *Cp. Howard* v. *Wilson*, 4 Hagg. Ecc. 107 : Wms. Exs. 1152). When, however, there is the relationship of master and servant, the word "Servants," in a bequest and uncontrolled by a context, is very comprehensive. Thus a Land Agent and House Steward, who resided out of the testator's house and had a salary of £300 a year, with permission to use his unemployed time as land agent to several large neighbouring landed proprietors, was held to be included in a bequest to "all my Servants and day labourers" (*Armstrong* v. *Clavering*, 27 Bea. 226 : *Cp.*, however, *Townshend* v. *Windham*, 2 Vern. 546, *wh. Va.* inf.).

So an out-door servant, continuously employed at weekly wages, is within a legacy to "servants;" but a person employed at weekly wages, only a few months in the year, to carry letters to the post is not within the phrase (*Thrupp* v. *Collett*, 26 Bea. 147).

2. When a testator gives to his servants a year's wages, those, and only those, *hired* by the year are included;—the time when the wages have been paid being only useful to determine the nature of the hiring, and being immaterial where the hiring can otherwise be proved to have been a yearly one (*Booth* v. *Dean*, 2 L. J. Ch. 162 ; 1 My. & K. 560 : *Blackwell* v. *Pennant*, 22 L. J. Ch. 155 ; 9 Hare, 551).

3. A bequest to "Servants," *simpliciter*, includes, as a general rule, those, and only those, who pass their whole time in the testator's service; and does not include such servants as Stewards of Courts or persons occasionally employed (*Townshend* v. *Windham*, 2 Vern. 546 : *Thrupp* v. *Collett*, sup. : *Cp. Armstrong* v. *Clavering*, ante) : but a regular servant's temporary absence would not disentitle him (*Herbert* v. *Reid*, 16 Ves. 486). So, service being the cause of such a bequest, only those servants who are in the testator's service at the time of his death (from which date be it observed his Will speaks) are, as a general rule, entitled under a bequest to "servants," *simpliciter* (*Jones* v. *Henley*, 2 Ch. Rep. 162) ; though, of course, if the phrase, controlled and properly construed by its context, is *designatio personarum*, a person so designated would take whether in the service or not at the testator's decease (*Parker* v. *Marchant*, 11 L. J. Ch. 223 ; 1 Y. & C. Ch. 290. This latter case is cited 1 Jarm. 325, for the proposition that a gift to "servants," *simpliciter*, means servants *at the date of the Will; Va.* Theobald, 204 : but with great diffidence I think the rule to be deduced from *Jones* v. *Henley* and *Parker* v. *Marchant* is as I have stated it ; *Va.* Wms. Exs. 1154). When indeed the condition of being in the service "at the time of my decease" is expressly annexed to a gift to "servants" then it is essential to any one taking thereunder that the contract for service should be absolutely unbroken by both of the parties thereto at the time of the decease ; and a wrongful dismissal by the master or a lawful rescission by the servant, or other determination of the service, however reached, in the testator's lifetime, would prevent a person from claiming under such a conditional bequest to "servants" as that just mentioned (*Darlow* v. *Edwards*, 32 L. J. Ex. 51 ; 1 H. & C. 547 ; 6 L. T. 905 ; 10 W. R. 700 : *Venes* v. *Marriott*, 31 L. J. Ch. 519 : *Note.*—The phrase "living *with* me" does not mean "living in my house," but means "living in my service:" per Turner, V.-C., *Blackwell* v. *Pennant*, sup.). The condition of being on testator's "*domestic* establishment," is not fulfilled in the case of a head gardener living in one of the testator's cottages but not dieted by him (*Ogle* v. *Morgan*, 1 D. G. M. & G. 359). *V.* Domestic Servant.

Though the priority *in Bankruptcy* which "Servants" have long had to payment of their wages (*V.* now s. 40 (b), Bankry. Act, 1883) is doubtless intended primarily for, yet it is not the exclusive privilege of, domestic servants. Therefore a Commercial Traveller (*Ex p. Neal*, Mont. & M'A. 194), or a Mate of a Vessel (*Ex p. Homberg*, 2 Mont. D. & D. 642 ; 6 Jur. 898), or a Seaman (*Re Dawson*, 1 Fon. B. C. 229), is within the word "servant" as so used in the Bankry Act. But though a yearly hiring is not necessary to constitute a "servant" within the section just referred to, yet there must be a general and continuous hiring as distinguished from a mere transitory engagement. Therefore a coach-guard and servants at a weekly salary (*Ex p. Skinner*, Mont. & B. 417 ; 3 Dea. & C. 332) ; or weekly labourers or workmen (*Ex p. Crawfoot*, Mont. 270), and still less those paid by the job (*Ex p. Grellier*, Mont. & M'A. 95 ; Mont. 264) ; or a non-resident music-master or a drill-master to a school, who attends the school to give lessons at so much per lesson (*Ex p. Walter*, 42 L. J. Bank. 49 ; L. R. 15 Eq. 412 ; 21 W. R. 523), are not within the section.

The Secretary of a Company in receipt of a salary of £50 a quarter and subject to dismissal at a quarter's notice, is not a "Servant, *Labourer or Workman*" within the Wages Attachment Abolition Act, 1870, 33 & 34 V. c. 30 (*Gordon* v. *Jennings*, 51 L. J. Q. B. 417). In that case Grove, J., said,—"In one sense a Secretary of State is a 'servant,' but it could not have been intended that this Act should apply to such a case."

Every person actually engaged in the performance of a contract of carriage, is a "Servant" of the *Carrier* within s. 8, Carriers Act, 11 G. 4 & 1 W. 4, c. 68 ; and therefore where a Carrier employs a person,—*e.g.*, the proprietor of a receiving house,—and such person employs an assistant, such assistant is a "Servant" in the employ of the Carrier within the section (*Machin*, or *Machu* v. *Lond. & S. W. Ry.*, 17 L. J. Ex. 271 ; 2 Ex. 415). And "where a person is employed by two railways, and receives goods without any instructions as to the railway by which they are to be sent, it may be that the goods are not received for either of the railways ; but when he has determined by which railway they are to be sent, he then holds them for that railway" (per Esher, M. R., *Stephens* v. *Lond. & S. W. Ry.*, 56 L. J. Q. B. 173 ; 18 Q. B. D. 121 ; 56 L. T. 226 : 35 W. R. 161 ; 51 J. P. 324, citing *Syms* v. *Chaplin*, 6 L. J. K. B. 25 ; 5 A. & E. 634).

"Servants," s. 7, Ry. and Canal Traffic Act, 1854, 17 & 18 V. c. 31, include Agents employed by a Ry. Co. to do work which it is under contract to execute (*Doolan* v. *Mid. Ry.*, 2 App. Ca. 792 : approving *Machin* v. *Lond. & S. W. Ry.*, sup.).

As to who is a "Servant *or other Person*" who may dwell in a house for its protection without rendering it liable to the *Inhabited House Duty*, s. 13 (2), 41 V. c. 15, seems to have been very much a question for the Tax Commrs. : therefore, where they found that a Cashier resided (alone) as a caretaker and was such a "Servant or other person," the Court refused to disturb their finding (*Rolfe* v. *Hyde*, 50 L. J. Q. B. 481 ; 6 Q. B. D. 673) ; but in a very similar case (the clerk care-taker, however, having his wife, children and a servant with him), the Court of Appeal reversed the finding of the Commrs., and held that the building was liable to the Duty (*Yewens* v. *Noakes*, 50 L. J. Q. B. 132 ; 6 Q. B. D. 530). Apparently to remedy that uncertainty, s. 24, 44 & 45 V. c. 12, refers to the section just cited, and enacts that " the term ' Servant ' shall be deemed to mean and include only a Menial or Domestic Servant employed by the occupier, and the expression ' Other Person ' shall be deemed to mean any person of a similar grade or description not otherwise employed by the occupier, who shall be engaged by him to dwell in the house or tenement solely for the protection thereof :" *Vth. Weguelin* v. *Wyatt*, 54 L. J. Q. B. 308 ; nom. *Weguelin* v. *Wayall*, 14 Q. B. D. 838 : *London Library* v. *Carter*, 6 Times Rep. 161 ; 34 S. J. 231).

V. Servant in Husbandry : Clerk : Possession.

SERVANT IN HUSBANDRY.—A " Servant in Husbandry " is a person, whether male or female, whose *chief* employment is in works of husbandry ; *i.e.*, the culture or keeping of the ground, or the management or working of horses or cattle, or the gathering in of crops, or any other work strictly pertaining to the manual labour required by farmers. Therefore a Farm Bailiff is not (*Davis* v. *Berwick*, 3 E. & E. 549 ; 30 L. J. M. C. 84), but a Dairy-maid, who also does household work, is a Servant in Husbandry (*Ex p. Hughes*, 23 L. J. M. C. 138).

Cp. Agricultural.

SERVANTS.—" If a man have a licence for himself ' and his Servants ' to hunt in a chase, park, or warren, at his pleasure ; this is a licence of profit ; for by vertue of those words ' for himself and his servants,' the grantee hath a property in the thing hunted, because he may justify hunting by his servants, which is more than a licence of pleasure " (Manwood, *Hunting*, pl. 17. *Vf. Wickham* v. *Hawker*, 10 L. J. Ex. 153 ; 7 M. & W. 72 : Free Liberty). *Vf.* Hunting : Profit à Prendre.

SERVE.—An Industrial Trainer living in a Work-house does not " serve " the Master of the Work-house, within s. 3, Rep. Peo. Act, 1884 (48 V. c. 3) ; nor does a Soldier so " serve " under every one of superior rank to himself in the same regiment (*Adams* v. *Ford*, 55 L. J. Q. B. 13 ; 16 Q. B. D. 239 ; 53 L. T. 666 ; 34 W. R. 64 ; 49 J. P. 711 : *Atkinson* v. *Collard*, 55 L. J. Q. B. 19 ; 16 Q. B. D. 254 ; 53 L. T. 670 ; 34 W. R. 75 ; 50 J. P. 23). A Farm Labourer who by the terms of his hiring is allowed, but not obliged, to occupy a cottage on the farm, does not occupy it *by virtue of Service* (*Marsh* v. *Estcourt*, 59 L. J. Q. B. 100).

A Successive Occupation partly by Service and partly as an Ordinary Tenant, qualifies for the parliamentary franchise (*Nicholson* v. *Yeoman*, 59 L. J. Q. B. 104).

V. Inhabit.

Notice to be " served ;" *V.* Served.

SERVED.—A Notice may generally be either in writing or oral: and if directed to be "given" it may be in either of those modes; but if it is to be "left" or "served," then there is an implication that the notice is to be written (*Wilson* v. *Nightingale*, 15 L. J. Q. B. 309; 8 Q. B. 1034: *R.* v. *Shurmer*, 55 L. J. M. C. 153; 17 Q. B. D. 323; 55 L. T. 126; 34 W. R. 656; 50 J. P. 743; and *V.* especially judgmt. of Coleridge, C. J., in the latter case). But "serve," does not enjoin *personal* service; and, as used in R. 186, Bankry. Rules, 1886, a pre-paid registered letter suffices (*Re McGrath*, 24 Q. B. D. 466).

"Served by Post;" *V.* BY POST: ORDINARY COURSE: SEND.

V. NOTICE.

SERVI.—*V.* VILLANI.

SERVICE.—"In my *service* at the time of my decease;" *V.* SERVANT.

V. MILITARY SERVICE: NAVAL SERVICE: SERVE.

SERVICE OF THE SHIP.—"Hurt or injury in the Service of the Ship," s. 228, Merchant S. Act, 1854; *V.* 1 Maude & P. 208, n. (*i*).

SERVICES.—*V.* CUSTOM.

Annuity for "Services and collecting rents;" *V. Re Muffett*, 56 L. J. Ch. 600; 56 L. T. 685; 51 J. P. 660.

"Services incidental to the duty of a Carrier;" *V.* INCIDENTAL.

SESSIONS.—"'Sessions' in our law is a sitting of Justices in Court upon their commission" (Termes de la Ley).

V. GENERAL OR QUARTER SESSIONS: QUARTER SESSIONS.

SET FIRE.—In Arson, "As to what constitutes 'setting fire,' it is not necessary that flame should be seen (*R.* v. *Stallion*, 1 Moody, 398); but it is not sufficient that wood should be scorched black (*R.* v. *Russell*, C. & M. 541). It is sufficient if the wood has been at a red heat (*R.* v. *Parker*, 9 C. & P. 45). I suppose the question is whether the thing burnt has, or has not, begun to be decomposed by the action of the fire" (Steph. Cr. 318, n. 3). *Vf.* Arch. Cr. 575–594; Rosc. Cr. 284, 289; FIRE.

SET FORTH.—*V.* TRULY SET FORTH.

SET OVER.—*V.* ASSIGN: UNDERLEASE.

SET UP.—Trade, &c., "Set up and commenced," No. 1, 1st set of Rules, Sch. D., s. 100, Income Tax Act, 5 & 6 V. c. 35; *V. Ryhope Co.* v. *Foyer*, 7 Q. B. D. 485; 45 L. T. 404.

"Set up or carry on the business or profession of a Surgeon;" *V. Palmer* v. *Mallett*, 36 Ch. D. 411; 57 L. J. Ch. 226; 58 L. T. 64; 36 W. R. 460: CARRY ON.

Machinery "set up;" *V.* ERECTED.

SETTLE.—As to construction of Covenants to settle property; *V.* AGREED AND DECLARED: DURING: ENTITLED: Elph. ch. 31: "Interest which shall fall into possession," *Sweetapple* v. *Horlock*, 48 L. J. Ch. 660; 11 Ch. D. 745: *Re Jackson*, 13 Ch. D. 189.

As to construction of Marriage Articles, and the Form of Settlement in pursuance of such Articles; *V.* Elph. ch. 32.

As to construction of Testamentary Directions to settle Realty; *V.* 2 Jarm. 344–355; and Personalty, Ib. 567, 578.

"I do hereby settle on my wife," certain property, will create a valid declaration of trust, even though the document may be ineffectual as an assignment (*Baddeley* v. *Baddeley*, 48 L. J. Ch. 36; 9 Ch. D. 113. *Svth. Hayes* v. *Alliance Assrce.*, 8 L. R. Ir. 149).

V. COMING TO SETTLE.

SETTLED.—"The meaning of a 'Settled' Estate, whether in legal or popular language, as contradistinguished from an estate in fee simple, is understood to be one in which the powers of alienation, of devising, and of transmission according to the ordinary rules of descent, are restrained by the limitations of the Settlement: it would be a perversion of language to apply the term 'settled' to an estate taken out of settlement, and brought back to the condition of an estate in fee simple" (per Cockburn, C. J., delivering judgmt. of C. P. in *Micklethwait* v. *Micklethwait*, 28 L. J. C. P. 127; 4 C. B. N. S. 790; affd. 29 L. J. C. P. 75). In that case the phrase to be construed was in a shifting clause in a Will, in the event of a second son succeeding to "the property *settled on the marriage*" of his father.

"Settled Estate" within Settled Estates Act, 1877; *V. Re Morgan*, 49 L. J. Ch. 577.

"Settled *Land*," within Settled Land Act, 1882, is (*V.* s. 2) "Land and any estate or interest therein, which is the subject of a Settlement;" *Vth. Re Wells*, 48 L. T. 859; 31 W. R. 764: *Re Horne*, 39 Ch. D. 84.

V. NOT SETTLED: TO BE SETTLED.

SETTLEMENT.—The Original settlement alone, is "the Settlement" within s. 2 (1), Settled Land Act, 1882 (*Re Knowles*, 54 L. J. Ch. 264; 27 Ch. D. 707; 51 L. T. 655; 33 W. R. 364).

"Settlement," in s. 47, Bankry. Act, 1883 (46 & 47 V. c. 52), "is not confined to a regular Settlement with trusts declared and other usual attributes to a formal settlement, but may include any mere transfer of property, where the object is to preserve the property (whatever its form) for the enjoyment of another person" (per Cave, J., *Re Player*, No. 2, 54 L. J. Q. B. 556). Therefore a gift of money to be invested in a particular manner—*e.g.* in Shares in a Ship—is a "Settlement" within the section (*Re Player*, No. 1, 54 L. J. Q. B. 553); but a gift of money to a child for maintenance, or even to set him up in business, is not (*Re Player*, No. 2, 54 L. J. Q. B. 554; 15 Q. B. D. 682). *Vh. Ex p. Todd*, 19 Q. B. D. 187.

A Settlement, *quà* Stamp Duty, is "Any Instrument, whether voluntary or upon any good or valuable consideration, other than a bonâ fide pecuniary consideration, whereby any *Definite and Certain Principal Sum of Money* (whether charged or chargeable on lands or other hereditaments or heritable subjects or not, or to be laid out in the purchase of lands or other hereditaments or heritable subjects or not), or any *Definite and Certain Amount of Stock*, or any Security, is settled or agreed to be settled in any manner whatsoever" (Sch. Stamp Act, 1870): as to the words italicised, *V. Onslow* v. *Inl. Rev.*, 34 S. J. 231.

SETTLOR.—"Settlor, Disponer," s. 2, Sucn. Dy. Act, 1853; *V. A.-G.* v. *Maule*, 56 L. T. 611; 3 Times Rep. 236.

SEVEN, 14 or 21 YEARS.—*V.* Or.

SEVERAL.—Sometimes read "respectively;" *V. Woodstock* v. *Shillito*, 6 Sim. 416: 1 Jarm. 505.

SEVERAL FISHERY.—*V.* Fishery.

SEVERALLY.—A gift to two or more "severally," or with a limitation to their heirs "as they shall severally die" (*Sheppard* v. *Gibbons*, 2 Atk. 441) creates a tenancy in common.

V. Jointly and Severally: Successively.

SEVERED.—Where the owner of land occupies it himself and demises the right of sporting to another, that right is "severed" from the occupation of the land within s. 6 (2), 37 & 38 V. c. 54 (*Kenrick* v. *Guilsfield*, 49 L. J. M. C. 27; 5 C. P. D. 41, distinguishing *R.* v. *Battle*, 36 L. J. M. C. 1; L. R. 2 Q. B. 8).

SEWAGE PURPOSES.—Where the effluent water from a sewage farm flows into a pool, the cleansing, levelling and concreting the bottom of that pool to prevent the accumulation of Sewage, is a work "for Sewage Purposes" within s. 32, P. H. Act, 1875 (*Wimbledon* v. *Croydon*, 56 L. J. Ch. 159; 32 Ch. D. 421; 55 L. T. 106).

SEWER.—This word as used in the P. H. Act, 1875, should receive "the largest possible interpretation" (per Kay, J., *Acton* v. *Batten*, 54 L. J. Ch. 251; 28 Ch. D. 283; 52 L. T. 17; 49 J. P. 357). A man-hole is part of a "Sewer" (*Swanston* v. *Twickenham*, 48 L. J. Ch. 623; 11 Ch. D. 838). *Vh. Poplar* v. *Knight*, 28 L. J. M. C. 37: *R.* v. *Godmanchester*, 35 L. J. Q. B. 125; L. R. 1 Q. B. 328: *Tottenham* v. *Button*, 2 Times Rep. 828.

"Sewer made by any person for his *own profit*," s. 13 (1), P. H. Act, 1875; *V. Bonella* v. *Twickenham*, 20 Q. B. D. 63.

As to the meaning of "Sewer" in s. 250, Metrop. Man. Act, 1855; *V.*

Bateman v. *Poplar*, 56 L. J. Ch. 149; 33 Ch. D. 360; 55 L. T. 374; 2 Times Rep. 860; 4 Ib. 137.

V. Drain.

Commissioners of Sewers; *V.* Termes de la Ley, *Sewers.*

SHACK.—"'Shack' is a peculiar name of Common, used in the County of Norfolke; and Cattell go to Shack, is as much to say, as to go at liberty, or to goe at large" (Termes de la Ley). *Vf. Corbet's Case,* 7 Rep. 5 a.

SHALL.—Too much care cannot be employed in using or construing this word. Its various meanings range under two general classes according as it is used,—

I. As implying *futurity;* or

II. As implying a *mandate,* or giving *permission* or *direction.*

I. If something is agreed to be done if or when something else "shall" happen, this contemplates futurity; and things that have happened and are existent at the time of the agreement will not accomplish the condition precedent to the fulfilment of the agreement. Thus where by a Marriage Settlement certain specific property belonging to the lady was settled, and in a subsequent part of the settlement there was a covenant to settle all property to which the lady "at any time during the said intended coverture *shall become* seized, possessed of, or entitled unto;" it was held that this covenant did not include property to which the lady was entitled at the date of the settlement and which was not specifically mentioned therein (*Wilton* v. *Colvin*, 3 Drew. 617; 25 L. J. Ch. 850; 27 L. T. O. S. 289; in which case the previous authorities are very fully reviewed: *Va. Archer* v. *Kelly*, 29 L. J. Ch. 911). Where, however, there is one title to a property at the date of the settlement but that title becomes changed into another and a larger title, then the idea of futurity is accomplished, and property so circumstanced would be comprised in a covenant to settle future acquired property; *e.g.* where a tenant in remainder at the date of the settlement becomes a tenant in possession after the settlement (*Maclurcan* v. *Lane*, 7 W. R. 135; 5 Jur. N. S. 56). *Vf.* Entitled.

"Shall *be born*," in the absence of a context, are words of futurity; and, in a Will, mean persons born after its date (*Gibbons* v. *Gibbons*, 50 L. J. P. C. 45; 6 App. Ca. 471).

The phrase, in a divesting clause, if donee of property "shall *become bankrupt*" (as an exception to the rule before stated) seems "to mean, simply being bankrupt" (per Kindersley, V.-C., *Seymour* v. *Lucas*, 29 L. J. Ch. 843); and in such a case it is immaterial whether the bankruptcy has happened before, or shall have happened after, the making of the instrument (*Seymour* v. *Lucas*, sup.: *Manning* v. *Chambers*, 1 D. G. & S. 282; 16 L. J. Ch. 245). So, too, in an independent (as distinguished from a substitutionary) testamentary gift to the issue of a deceased member of a class, the words "shall die" or "shall happen to die" do not necessarily point to a future death, so as inevitably to exclude the issue of a member of the class who may have died before the date of the Will (*Loring* v. *Thomas*, 30 L. J. Ch. 789 ; 1 Dr. & Sm. 497: *Christopherson* v. *Naylor*, 1 Mer. 320 : *Vf.* 2 Jarm. 771). So "a Surrender to such uses as the Testator '*shall*' by Will appoint, applied to a Will antecedently executed, it being considered that the Surrender referred to that Will which should be in existence at Testator's death" (1 Jarm. 58, citing *Spring* v. *Biles*, 1 T. R. 435, n.).

II. Whenever a statute declares that a thing "shall" be done, the natural and proper meaning is that a peremptory mandate is enjoined. But where the thing has reference to :—

a. The time or formality of completing any public act, not being a step in a litigation, or accusation; or,

b. The time or formality of creating an executed contract whereof the benefit has been, or but for their own act might be, received by individuals or private companies or private corporations ;

the enactment will generally be regarded as merely directory, unless there be words making the thing done void if not done in accordance with the prescribed requirements.

The word "Shall" has been held, in the following cases, only

Directory :

As regards the time fixed for the appointment of Overseers under 43 Eliz. c. 2, s. 1 (*R.* v. *Sparrow*, 2 Stra. 1123), or under 54 G. 3, c. 91 (*R.* v. *Staffordshire*, 10 L. J. M. C. 166 ; nom. *R.* v. *Sneyd*, 9 Dowl. 1001); and as regards the time fixed by 8 G. 4, c. xxix., for the Election of Guardians for the Borough of Norwich (*R.* v. *Norwich*, 1 B. & Ad. 310), by 13 G. 3, c. 78, s. 1, for appointment of Surveyors of Highways (*R.* v. *Denbighshire*, 4 East, 142), or by 54 G. 3, c. 84, s. 1, for holding Quarter Sessions (*R.* v. *Leicester*, 5 L. J. O. S. M. C. 95 ; 7 B. & C. 6) ; "and there can be no doubt that the same construction will be put upon" the statutes (11 G. 4 & 1 W. 4, c. 70, s. 35 ; 4 & 5 W. 4, c. 47), which now regulate the time for holding Quarter Sessions (*V.* Chitty's Stat., 3 Ed., Vol. 4, 154, citing Dickinson, Q. S. 65. All the various statutes as to time for holding Quarter Sessions have always been held directory, Dick. Quarter Sess. 6 Ed. 65) :

As regards the transmission of a Conviction by justices to the next Quarter Sessions, under 7 & 8 G. 4, c. 30, s. 40 (*Charter* v. *Greame*, 13 Q. B. 216 ; 18 L. J. M. C. 78):

As regards the time for delivering Burgess Lists and holding Courts for their revision under the Municipal Corporation Act (5 & 6 W. 4, c. 76), s. 18 (*R.* v. *Rochester*, 27 L. J. Q. B. 45 ; 7 E. & B. 910: *Hunt* v. *Hibbs*, 29 L. J. Ex. 222 ; 5 H. & N. 123) :

As regards the time and manner of making out (under ss. 5, 13) the Lists of persons entitled to vote, or (under ss. 47, 48, Registration of

Directory:—

Voters Act, 6 V. c. 18), the time when the Lists of Voters are to be signed and delivered to the sheriff or returning officer (*Morgan* v. *Parry*, 25 L. J. C. P. 141; 17 C. B. 334 : *Brumfitt* v. *Bremner*, 30 L. J. C. P. 33 ; 9 C. B. N. S. 1: *Vf. Wells* v. *Stanforth*, 55 L. J. Q. B. 12 ; 16 Q. B. D. 244 ; 54 L. T. 183 ; 50 J. P. 631) :

As regards stamping the Official Mark on the *back* of a Ballot Paper (*Akers*, or *Ackers* v. *Howard*, 55 L. J. Q. B. 273 ; 16 Q. B. D. 739 ; 54 L. T. 651; 34 W. R. 609 ; 50 J. P. 519) :

As regards the time for depositing the valuation list and transmitting it to the Assessment Committee pursuant to s. 42, Valuation (Metropolis) Act, 1869, 32 & 33 V. c. 67 (*R.* v. *Ingall*, 46 L. J. M. C. 113 ; 2 Q. B. D. 199) ; the time for delivering to the Commissioners of Stamps a return of the names and places of abode of the partners in a Banking Co. pursuant to s. 5, 7 G. 4, c. 46 (*Bosanquet* v. *Woodford*, 13 L. J. Q. B. 93 ; 5 Q. B. 310 ; D. & M. 419 : *Steward* v. *Dunn*, 13 L. J. Ex. 324 ; 12 M. & W. 655 ; 1 Dowl. & L. 642) ; the time for registering at the County Court a married woman's Protection Order pursuant to s. 21, 20 & 21 V. c. 85 (*Re Farraday*, 31 L. J. P. & M. 7; 2 Sw. & Tr. 369):

As regards the 3 cal. months after Avoidance of a Benefice within which the Bishop is to direct the surveyor to report upon dilapidations under s. 29, Ecclesiastical Dilapidations Act, 1871, 34 & 35 V. c. 43 (*Caldow* v. *Pixell*, 46 L. J. C. P. 541; 2 C. P. D. 562) :

As regards the requirement of 33 H. 8, c. 39, that Bonds to the King shall be made payable to him, his heirs or *executors*, a Bond to him, his heirs or *successors* being held to be within the statute (*Yale* v. *The King*, 6 Brown, P. C. 27, 28) :

As regards Consent of father to the marriage of a minor under s. 16, Marriage Act, 4 G. 4, c. 76 (*R.* v. *Birmingham*, 8 B. & C. 29 ; 6 L. J. O. S. M. C. 67; 2 M. & R. 230) :

As regards the Form of making a Poor Rate, under s. 2, 6 & 7 W. 4, c. 96,—except the signature of Justices which is peremptory (*R.* v. *Fordham*, 11 A. & E. 73 ; 9 L. J. M. C. 3) :

As regards the obligation to produce Overseers' Certificate, under s. 2, 3 & 4 V. c. 61, prior to the Excise granting a License to sell beer, &c., under that statute (*Thompson* v. *Harvey*, 28 L. J. M. C. 163 ; 4 H. & N. 254) :

As regards the Questions to be asked a Recruit under s. 55, Mutiny Act, 13 & 14 V. c. 5 (*Wolton* v. *Gavin*, 16 Q. B. 48 ; 20 L. J. Q. B. 73) :

As regards the Particulars to be stated in a doctor's certificate for the detention of a Lunatic under s. 46, 8 & 9 V. c. 100 (*Re Shuttleworth*, 16 L. J. M. C. 18 ; 9 Q. B. 651) :

As regards taking Security on an appointment by Quarter Sessions of a County Treasurer under 12 G. 2, c. 29, s. 6 (*R.* v. *Patteson*, 4 B. & Ad. 9 ; 2 L. J. K. B. 33 ; 1 N. & M. 612) :

Directory :—

As regards the Formalities prior to a Sale by a Bankruptcy Assignee under s. 7, 1 G. 4, c. 119 (*Doe* d. *Phillips* v. *Evans*, 2 L. J. Ex. 179 ; 1 Cr. & M. 450 ; 3 Tyr. 339) :

As regards the things to be done by a Local Board before entering into a Contract under s. 85, P. H. Act, 1848 (*Nowell* v. *Worcester*, 9 Ex. 457; 23 L. J. Ex. 139 : *Sv. Frend* v. *Dennett*, inf.) :

As regards the requirement in a Local Improvement Act that all contracts should be signed by the commissioners, or any three of them, or by their Clerk (*Cole* v. *Greene*, 13 L. J. C. P. 30 ; 6 M. & G. 872) :

As regards Registration of Mortgages and Charges of a Joint-Stock Co., under s. 43, Companies Act, 1862 (*Ex p. Valpy & Chaplin*, 7 Ch. 289 : *Wright* v. *Horton*, 56 L. J. Ch. 873 ; 12 App. Ca. 371 ; 56 L. T. 782 ; 36 W. R. 17 ; 52 J. P. 179) :

As regards the provision of s. 108 of the statute (6 & 7 W. 4, c. cviii), incorporating the Thames Haven Dock & Ry. Co., that the business of the Company should be carried on by *twelve* Directors (*Thames Haven Dock & Ry.* v. *Rose*, 12 L. J. C. P. 90 ; 4 M. & G. 552 ; 5 Sc. N. R. 524) :

As regards the provisions in a private Act as to the mode of keeping the Register of Proprietors in an incorporated Company (*Southampton Dock Co.* v. *Richards*, 1 M. & G. 448 : *London Grand Junc. Ry.* v. *Freeman*, 2 Ib. 606) :

As regards the Countersigning by Secretary, of a bill or note of a Joint-Stock Co., pursuant to s. 45, 7 & 8 V. c. 110 (*Allen* v. *Sea Assurance*, 9 C. B. 574 ; 19 L. J. C. P. 305 : *Aggs* v. *Nicholson*, 1 H. & N. 165 ; 25 L. J. Ex. 348) :

Note.—If a statute directs the time or manner of doing a thing, the penalty (if any) for non-compliance with the direction will be incurred, though such non-compliance may not affect the validity of the act (*Hunt* v. *Hibbs*, 29 L. J. Ex. 222 ; 5 H. & N. 123).

The word "Shall," and words in their ordinary meaning obligatory, have, in the following cases, been held,

Peremptory :

As regards the 3 days, inclusive of Sunday, within which an Appeal Case from Justices "shall" be transmitted to the Court and notice given to the respondent, pursuant to s. 2, 20 & 21 V. c. 43 (*Peacock* v. *The Queen*, 4 C. B. N. S. 264 ; 27 L. J. C. P. 224: *Woodhouse* v. *Woods*, 29 L. J. M. C. 149 : *Morgan* v. *Edwards*, Ib. 108 : *Pennell* v. *Uxbridge*, 31 L. J. M. C. 92), except where the appellant has done all that he can in order to comply with the statute (*V.* jdgmt. *Morgan* v. *Edwards*), and is hindered by the offices of the Court being closed (*Mayer* v. *Harding*, L. R. 2 Q. B. 410 ; 9 B. & S. 27, note *a*), or by respondent not being to be found, and

Peremptory:—

service of notice of appeal in that case being effected on his solicitor within the 3 days (*Syred* v. *Carruthers*, 27 L. J. M. C. 273; E. B. & E. 469):

As regards requirement in R. 18, Summary Jurisdiction Rules, 1886, that application for Special Case "shall be made in writing" (*South Staffordshire W. Works Co.* v. *Stone*, 19 Q. B. D. 168; 56 L. J. M. C. 122; 57 L. T. 368; 36 W. R. 76; 51 J. P. 662: *Lockhart* v. *St. Alban's*, 21 Q. B. D. 188; 57 L. J. M. C. 118; 36 W. R. 800; 52 J. P. 420):

As regards the time for an Appeal from County Court and giving security for its costs under s. 14, 13 & 14 V. c. 61 (*Stone* v. *Dean*, 27 L. J. Q. B. 319; E. B. & E. 504: *Va. Barker* v. *Palmer*, 51 L. J. Q. B. 110):

As regards the 21 days, within which, after its receipt, the Bishop is to send to an accused clergyman a copy of the complaint against him pursuant to s. 9, Public Worship Regulation Act, 1874, 37 & 38 V. c. 85 (*Howard* v. *Bodington*, 2 P. D. 203):

As regards the time for Taxing Parliamentary Costs under s. 3, 28 & 29 V. c. 27 (*Williams* v. *Swansea Canal Navigation*, 37 L. J. Ex. 107; L. R. 3 Ex. 158):

As regards the provision, s. 1, 26 G. 2, c. 14, that table of Justices' Clerks Fees should be made at one Quarter Sessions and should be approved at "the next succeeding Quarter Sessions" (*Bowman* v. *Blyth*, 26 L. J. M. C. 57; 27 Ib. 21; 7 E. & B. 26, 47):

As regards the number of Overseers to be appointed by 43 Eliz. c. 2, s. 1 (*R.* v. *Loxdale*, 1 Burr. 445):

As regards Indorsement on Appeal Case stated by Revising Barrister pursuant to s. 42, 6 V. c. 18 (*Wanklyn* v. *Woollett*, 16 L. J. C. P. 144; 4 C. B. 86: *Sv. Burton* v. *Brooks*, 21 L. J. C. P. 7; 11 C. B. 41; 2 Lutw. 197, and *McKeowne* v. *Bradford*, 7 Ir. Jur. N. S. 169):

As regards the Form of a Municipal Nomination Paper under s. 1, subs. 2, 38 & 39 V. c. 40, repealed (*Henry* v. *Armitage*, 52 L. J. Q. B. 165; reversed, but only on the facts, 32 W. R. 192):

As regards the requirements for creating a Mortgage of a Ship under ss. 55, 56, Merchant Shipping Act, 1854, 17 & 18 V. c. 104 (*Liverpool Boro. Bank* v. *Turner*, 29 L. J. Ch. 827; 30 Ib. 379):

As regards requirement that contracts above £10 by Local Board should be under Seal, &c., pursuant to s. 85, P. H. Act, 1848 (*Frend* v. *Dennett*, 27 L. J. C. P. 314; 4 C. B. N. S. 576: *V. Nowell* v. *Worcester*, sup. and *note* inf.): and now, under s. 174, P. H. Act, 1875, that all contracts by urban authority above £50 shall be under seal (*Young* v. *Royal Leamington Spa*, 51 L. J. Q. B. 292; 52 Ib. 713; 8 App. Ca. 517, following *Hunt* v. *Wimbledon*, 48 L. J. C. P. 207; 4 C. P. D. 48. *Va. Melliss* v. *Shirley*, 16 Q. B. D. 446):

As regards the provisions for Arbitration in s. 180, P. H. Act, 1875

Peremptory :—

(*Re Gifford and Bury*, 57 L. J. Q. B. 181 ; 20 Q. B. D. 368 ; 58 L. T. 522 ; 36 W. R. 468 ; 52 J. P. 119) :

As regards an Arbitration Agreement ; *V. Crump* v. *Adney*, 2 L. J. Ex. 150 ; 1 Cr. & M. 355 ; 3 Tyr. 270 :

As regards the formalities of Sealing and Signature by Directors of contracts by Incorporated Ry. and Dock Companies (*Cope* v. *Thames Haven Dock & Ry.*, 18 L. J. Ex. 345 ; 3 Ex. 841: *Diggle* v. *Lond. & Blackwall Ry.*, 19 L. J. Ex. 308 ; 5 Ex. 442 : *Finlay* v. *Bristol & Ex. Ry.*, 21 L. J. Ex. 117 ; 7 Ex. 409. *V. note,* inf.) :

As regards the ordinary requirement in a Building Contract against Extras without written instructions of the Architect (*Lamprell* v. *Billericay Union,* 18 L. J. Ex. 282 ; 3 Ex. 283) :

Semble, as regards the notice by a tenant of an intended claim under s. 7, Agricultural Holdings (England) Act, 1883 (*Schofield* v. *Hincks,* 37 W. R. 157).

Note.—It was said by counsel in *Young* v. *Royal Leamington Spa,* that *Nowell* v. *Worcester,* sup., might be considered as over-ruled by *Frend* v. *Dennett.* But it is submitted that the two cases are quite in harmony. The first case (*Nowell* v. *Worcester*) decided that the preliminaries which a local board were required to observe under s. 85, P. H. Act, 1848, *before* entering into a contract were directory and, so to speak, a matter between themselves and their constituents : but the latter case (*Frend* v. *Dennett*) decided that the *contract itself* must be vouched in the manner prescribed by the section.

It seems difficult to reconcile *Cope* v. *Thames Haven Dock and Ry.*, and the other two cases cited with it *supra,* with *Cole* v. *Greene, Allen* v. *Sea Assurance,* and *Aggs* v. *Nicholson,* sup., or with sound reasoning. There seems no public policy (like that so forcibly dwelt on in the jdgmt. of Lindley, L. J., in *Young* v. *Royal Leamington Spa*) in letting a Ry. Co. keep an advantage for which they have not paid, simply because the contract under which they have obtained that advantage happens to lack the formality required by the Act establishing the Company. The cases now under criticism seem those referred to by Lindley, L. J. (51 L. J. Q. B. 296), where, referring to executed contracts for corporations, he says,—" The cases on this subject are very numerous and conflicting, and they require review and authoritative exposition by a Court of Appeal."

There is no magic in incorporation as distinguished from any other mode of association for private profit : and it is suggested that *Cope* v. *Thames Haven Dock and Ry.* and other similar cases should be over-ruled, and that the rule of such cases as *Aggs* v. *Nicholson* should be adopted for all kinds of association for private purposes, whether by incorporation or otherwise, so that the canon of construction should run thus :—

In a contract entered into by a *public* body, whether corporate or incorporate, for the public benefit, the formalities which the legislature says "shall" be observed are obligatory and in their absence no rights arise whether the contract be executed or executory: But

In a contract entered into by a *private* association, whether corporate or incorporate, the formalities prescribed (whether by statute, articles of association, or otherwise) for the validation of its contracts are matters chiefly exigent as between the direction and its constituents; and therefore if the contract be *executed* the private association must pay on the assumpsit *quasi ex contractu*, even if not *ex contractu*, though the prescribed contract formalities may be absent: but that no rights would arise out of such a contract the prescribed formalities of which were absent so long as such contract remained merely *executory*. *Vh.* obs. of Brett, L. J., in *Hunt* v. *Wimbledon*, 48 L. J. C. P. 211: *Henderson* v. *Australian Royal Mail Steam Co.*, 5 E. & B. 409: *Sv. Church* v. *Imperial Gas Light and Coke Co.*, 7 L. J. Q. B. 118; 6 A. & E. 858.

For a curious instance of "shall" being used, in the same section, as compulsory and as optional; *V.* per Bowen, L. J., *Cooke* v. *New River Co.*, 57 L. J. Ch. 389; 38 Ch. D. 56; 58 L. T. 830; on app. 14 App. Ca. 698.

V. SHALL AND LAWFULLY MAY; MAY: *Vf.* Maxwell, 286–303; Wilberforce, 193–206.

"Shall" read "should;" *V. Lomax* v. *Holmeden*, 3 P. Wms. 176.

SHALL AND LAWFULLY MAY: SHALL AND MAY: SHALL AND MAY AND THEY ARE HEREBY EMPOWERED.—"The words '*Shall and Lawfully May* are, in their ordinary import, *obligatory*, and ought, according to established rule, to have that construction, unless it would lead to some absurd or inconvenient consequence, or be at variance with the intent of the legislature, to be collected from other parts of the Act" (per Parke, B., delivering the jdgmt. of the Court in *Chapman* v. *Milvain*, 19 L. J. Ex. 230; 1 L. M. & P. 209; 5 Ex. 61). Accordingly, it was held that those words in s. 9, 7 G. 4, c. 46, rendered it necessary for actions by or against a Banking Company to be brought in the name of its Public Officer. *Va. Steward* v. *Greaves*, 10 M. & W. 711; 12 L. J. Ex. 109: *Re London & Eastern Banking Corporation*, 27 L. J. Ch. 457; 2 D. G. & J. 484; 4 K. & J. 273.

So the words "*Shall and May*," in 7 & 8 V. c. 110, s. 66, were held obligatory (*V.* MAY, pp. 464, 465). But though for the offence of allowing an unauthorized person to act in his name, a Solicitor "*shall and may* be struck off the Roll, and for ever after disabled from practising," s. 32, 6 & 7 V. c. 73; yet the infliction of so heavy a penalty is not imperative, and a lesser punishment may be imposed (*Re Grayston*, 4 Times Rep. 749; 58 L. J. Q. B. 451, n. 2: *Re Lamb*, 58 L. J. Q. B. 450; 23 Q. B. D. 477: *Re Sykes*, Times, 19th Feb., 1890).

The words in Sturges Bourne's Act (59 G. 3, c. 12), s. 17, whereby Churchwardens and Overseers "*Shall and May and they are hereby Empowered*" to accept, take and hold real property belonging to a parish, are imperative (*St. Nicholas, Deptford* v. *Sketchley*, 17 L. J. M. C. 17 ; 8 Q. B. 394).

V. SHALL : MAY.

SHALL AND MAY BE LAWFUL.—*V.* IT SHALL BE LAWFUL.

SHALL BECOME ENTITLED.—*V.* ENTITLED.

SHAPE.—"Shape or Configuration," of an article of manufacture, s. 1, 6 & 7 V. c. 65 ; *V. Margetson* v. *Wright*, 2 D. G. & S. 420.

SHARE.—Where there is a testamentary gift to two or more, and the Will speaks of the "Share" of either, a tenancy in common is created (*Gnat* v. *Laurence*, Wight. 395 : *Ive* v. *King*, 21 L. J. Ch. 560 ; 16 Bea. 46 : *Hobgen* v. *Neale*, L. R. 11 Eq. 48). So a bequest in shares to be appointed by a person who is not named, or who fails to appoint, creates a tenancy in common in equal shares (1 Jarm. 361, citing *Robinson* v. *Wheelwright*, 21 Bea. 214 : *Salusbury* v. *Denton*, 26 L. J. Ch. 851 ; 3 K. & J. 529).

A substitutional bequest of a legatee's "Share" will not take effect if the legatee die in the testator's lifetime ; because in that case the legatee could not take a share (*Re Roberts, Tarleton* v. *Bruton*, 53 L. J. Ch. 1023 ; 27 Ch. D. 346 ; affd. 30 Ch. D. 234 ; 53 L. T. 432, following *Stewart* v. *Jones*, 3 D. G. & J. 532 ; *V.* Jarm. 767, and dissenting from *Unsworth* v. *Speakman*, 46 L. J. Ch. 608 ; 4 Ch. D. 620). But would this be so if the legatee were a child of the testator, leaving issue living at testator's death ? *V.* s. 33, 1 V. c. 26.

As to the value of the word "Share," in a substitutionary bequest to the issue of a deceased member of a class, for the purpose of avoiding the rule in *Christopherson* v. *Naylor* (1 Mer. 320 ; 2 Jarm. 771) ; *V. Re Smith* (in note to *Re Sibley*), 5 Ch. D. 494 ; 46 L. J. 387, and *Vth. Re Webster*, 52 L. J. Ch. 769 ; 23 Ch. D. 737 : But *Re Smith* was not followed by Stirling, J., in *Re Chinery* (57 L. J. Ch. 804 ; 39 Ch. D. 614), nor by North, J., in *Re Brown* (58 L. J. Ch. 420).

As to value of "Share" for construing legacy as vested ; *V.* 1 Jarm. 856.

"Share" does not carry an accruing share (2 Jarm. 711 ; Wms. Exs. 1223), unless aided by the context (2 Jarm. 712, 713) ; but "it seems that 'Share *and Interest*' will carry accrued shares proprio vigore" (Ib. 714).

A Devise of "my Share" would, even before the Wills Act, generally carry the fee (Ib. 285) : *Vh. Orange* v. *Martyn*, W. N. (86) 8.

Where a "Power simply authorizes an Appointment of the *shares* to be taken by the objects, the Power necessarily ceases when there is only one object, for he, of course, must take the whole" (Sug. Pow. 416).

Under a bequest of *Shares in a Company*, the Company's Stock will pass if the testator had no Shares (*Trinder* v. *Trinder*, L. R. 1 Eq. 695). *V.* STOCK.

A bequest, by a Shareholder, of all and every his "*Shares and Interest*" in an Insurance Co. does not pass a Policy on his own life effected with the Co. (*Harington* v. *Moffat*, 22 L. J. Ch. 775 ; 4 D. G. M. & G. 1).

A bequest of a person's "*Share, Right and Interest*" in the Goodwill of a Partnership, and in its real and personal estate, does not pass a debt due to the testator from the partnership (*Re Beard, Simpson* v. *Beard*, 57 L. J. Ch. 887 ; 58 L. T. 629 ; 36 W. R. 519).

Vh. Chitty, Eq. Ind. 7826, 7920.

SHARE AND SHARE ALIKE.—The phrase "'Share and Share alike' has the same meaning as 'equally to be divided'" (Sug. Pow. 656, citing *Phillips* v. *Garth*, 3 Bro. C. C. 64 : *Elmsley* v. *Young*, 2 My. & K. 780), and creates a tenancy in common (*Rudge* v. *Barker*, Ca. t. Talb. 124 : *Heathe* v. *Heathe*, 2 Atk. 122 : *Perry* v. *Woods*, 3 Ves. 204 a : *Ashford* v. *Haines*, 21 L. J. Ch. 496 : 2 Jarm. 257 ; Wms. Ex. 1469). *V.* ALIKE.

Accordingly, this phrase, as a context, will control such words as "Legal Representatives" to mean Next of Kin (*King* v. *Cleveland*, cited LEGAL REPRESENTATIVES).

V. RELATIONS.

SHARE-BROKER.—A person who occasionally sold shares for friends was held not a "Share-broker" within the late Bankry definition of "Trader" (*Re Cleland*, 36 L. J. Bank. 33 ; 2 Ch. 466).

SHAREHOLDER.—"Only means the person who holds the shares by having his name on the register" (per Chitty, J., *Re Wala Wynaad Mining Co.*, 52 L. J. Ch. 88 : 21 Ch. D. 849 ; 30 W. R. 915). *Vf. Portal* v. *Emmens*, 46 L. J. C. P. 179 ; 1 C. P. D. 664 : *Kippling* v. *Todd*, 47 L. J. C. P. 617 ; 3 C. P. D. 350 : *Burke* v. *Lechmere*, L. R. 6 Q. B. 297 ; 40 L. J. Q. B. 98.

V. HOLDING.

SHARES.—*V.* STOCK : STOCKS : SHARE.

SHAWE.—*V.* GRAVA.

SHEEPHEAVES.—"Small plots of pasture often in the middle of a waste . . . the soil of which may or may not be in the lord, but the pasture is certainly a private property, and is leased and sold as such" (Cooke, Inclosure Acts, 44).

SHEEPWALK.—*V.* FOLDCOURSE.

SHERIFF.—*Vh.* Co. Litt. 109 b, 168 a.

"Sheriff," in the Bankry. Act, 1883, includes "any officer charged with the execution of a Writ or other process" (s. 168),—*i. e.*, the Officer analogous to the Sheriff : and therefore when the Serjeant-at-Mace, having a levy warrant to execute from the Lord Mayor's Court, finds an officer in possession under a Q. B. D. *fi. fa.*, and (according to custom) intrusts that officer with the warrant to realize the amount leviable thereunder, the Serjeant-at-Mace is the officer to be served with notice under s. 46, sub-s. 2, Bankry. Act, 1883 (*Ex p. Warren, Re Holland,* 54 L. J. Q. B. 320; 15 Q. B. D. 48; 53 L. T. 68; 33 W. R. 572).

V. UNDER-SHERIFF.

"Sheriff," as respects Scotland; *V.* s. 28, Interp. Act, 1889.

SHERIFF CLERK.—In Acts relating to Scotland, "Sheriff Clerk" includes Steward Clerk (s. 7, Interp. Act, 1889).

SHERIFFDOM.—In Acts relating to Scotland, "Sheriffdom" includes a Stewartry (s. 7, Interp. Act, 1889).

SHEW OF BUSINESS.—*V.* OUTWARD MARK.

SHEWN.—"Cause Shown;" *V.* CAUSE.

SHIP.—"Ship," technically taken, designates a particular species of sea-going vessel, square-rigged throughout, which carries three masts with tops and yards to each of them. It has also a generic sense, as designating a vessel of burden, irrespective of rig, and without regard to the particular means of locomotion (1 Arn. 18, 19. *Vf. Hill* v. *Patten,* 8 East, 375: *Forbes* v. *Aspinall,* 13 East, 323).

By s. 2, Merchant Shipping Act, 1854 (17 & 18 V. c. 104; *Va.* 24 V. c. 10, s. 2), "'Ship' shall include every description of vessel used in navigation not propelled by oars." In *Re Ferguson* (40 L. J. Q. B. 105; 19 W. R. 746; L. R. 6 Q. B. 280), Blackburn, J., said:—"Whether a ship is propelled by oars or not, she is still a ship. Most small vessels use something of the kind to propel them. The vessels which came over in the Armada, with perhaps a thousand men on board, were rowed by hundreds of slaves. Yet no one could say they were not ships. I can only suggest that 'Every vessel that substantially goes to sea is a ship.' I do not mean to say that every little boat that goes a mile or two outside a harbour is a ship, but that where it is really and substantially the business of a vessel to go to sea it is a ship. If the absence of oars were the test of a ship, this would take in the case of river steamers which never go to sea. Whenever the vessel is substantially a sea-going vessel, whether it be decked or not decked (or whether propelled with oars or not), it would be a Ship," and within the meaning of the Merchant Shipping Act. Accordingly, in that case it was held that a coble of 10 tons burthen, 24 feet in length, decked forward only, with two moveable masts and a sail for each, and which coble was accustomed to go 20 miles out to sea, and was usually under sail, but was sometimes propelled by oars, was a "Ship." But a vessel to be a "Ship" within the section, need not, necessarily, have been to sea. A launched unfinished vessel intended for navigation is a "ship" (*The Andalusian,* 46 L. J. P. D. & A. 77; 2 P. D. 231; 3 Ib. 182); so is a coble (*Ex p. Hutchinson,* W. N.

(71) 30); so a mud-hopper, used for dredging purposes, not fitted with oars or other means of propulsion, and generally moved by towing, is a "Ship" within the section (*The Mac,* 51 L. J. P. D. & A. 81; 7 P. D. 126). NOTE.—The Merchant Shipping Act, 1854, is only applicable to *British* ships; *Vh. Union Bank of London* v. *Lenanton,* 47 L. J. C. P. 409; 3 C. P. D. 243: SHIPS AND VESSELS.

"Ship," and also "Vessel," in the County Courts Admiralty Jurisdiction Acts, 1868 & 1869 (31 & 32 V. c. 71; 32 & 33 V. c. 51), have the same meaning as "Ship" in the Merchant Shipping Act, 1854, and do not give jurisdiction to try collisions between barges propelled by oars only (*Everard* v. *Kendall,* 39 L. J. C. P. 234; L. R. 5 C. P. 428).

But the Bills of Sale Acts are not coterminous with the Merchant Shipping Act, and the exemption from Registration of an Assignment of a "Ship or Vessel" under the former Acts (s. 4, Bills of S. Act, 1878), is not confined to such ships or vessels as require registration under the Merchant Shipping Act (*Union Bank of London* v. *Lenanton,* 47 L. J. C. P. 409; 3 C. P. D. 243: *Gapp* v. *Bond,* 19 Q. B. D. 200; 56 L. J. Q. B. 438; 57 L. T. 437; 35 W. R. 683; 3 Times Rep. 621).

"Ship lost or not lost;" *V.* LOST OR NOT LOST.

V. SHIPS AND VESSELS: VESSEL: BRITISH SHIP.

SHIP, To.—Dues on Timber "shipped or unshipped within the Harbour or River;" held, that to attach to a log of timber, or a number of logs loosely connected, at one of the ends for the purpose of towing, is not to "ship" the Timber; and that to cast off the tow-rope is not to "unship" it: qy., whether a Raft of Logs so constructed as to be capable of being navigated, can be said to be "unshipped" when, on reaching its destination, it is taken to pieces and landed (*Clyde Nav.* v. *Laird,* 8 App. Ca. 658).

V. SHIPPED: UNSHIPPING.

SHIP DAMAGE.—In a Charter-party between the East India Company and the owners of a ship taken into their service was the following clause,—"But nevertheless the said part owners shall not be charged with any sum of money in respect of goods damaged on board the said ship, either in her outward or homeward-bound voyage, but such as shall, by the condition and appearance of the package thereof, or by some other reasonable proof, appear to be Ship Damage." Part of the homeward-bound cargo was damaged in a storm:—Held, that this was not "Ship Damage," within the meaning of the clause, which is imputable only to such damage as happens by the insufficiency of the ship, or the neglect of those who have charge of her (*East India Co.* v. *Tod,* 1 Brown, P. C. 405).

SHIPMENT.—"Shipment," "For Shipment" is equivalent to "To be shipped;" *V.* SHIPPED.

"Shipment by Steamer or Steamers," "means that if a considerable portion of the goods under the contract in question are shipped by steamer within the time, that is to be a Shipment which will satisfy the contract, and one which the purchaser cannot reject because another portion is not shipped in time" (per Mellish, L. J., *Brandt* v. *Lawrence,* 46 L. J. Q. B. 237 ; 1 Q. B. D. 344). *Vf. Reuter* v. *Sala,* 4 C. P. D. 239.

V. STEAMSHIP.

SHIPPED.—"To be shipped," means to be put on board (*Bowes* v. *Shand,* or *Shand* v. *Bowes,* 46 L. J. Q. B. 561 ; 2 App. Ca. 455, distinguishing *Alexander* v. *Vanderzee,* L. R. 7 C. P. 530 : *Wancke* v. *Wingren,* 58 L. J Q. B. 519. *Vh.* Benj. 569).

"Shipped *for sale* ;" *V. Witham* v. *Vane,* W. N. (81) 79.

V. TO SHIP.

SHIPPING DOCUMENTS.—*V. Tamvaco* v. *Lucas,* 30 L. J. Q. B. 234 ; 31 Ib. 296 ; 1 B. & S. 185 ; 3 Ib. 89 : *North of England Oil Cake Co.* v. *Archangel Insrce.,* L. R. 10 Q. B. 254 ; 44 L. J. Q. B. 121.

"All the Shipping Documents ;" *Cederberg* v. *Borries,* 2 Times Rep. 201.

V. ALL.

SHIPS AND VESSELS.—The Order in Council of Feb. 18, 1854, (which is an addition to 6 G. 4, c. 125, s. 59) exempts from compulsory pilotage "*Ships and Vessels,* trading to ports between Boulogne and the Baltic on their outward passages." *British* ships and vessels are alone comprised in that exemption (*The Vesta,* 51 L. J. P. D. & A. 25 ; 7 P. D. 240).

V. SHIP, p. 732 : VESSEL.

SHIP'S RISK.—A Charter-party provided that the cargo should be taken from the shore to the ship "At the Ship's Risk." In the course of transit of the cargo from the shore to the ship a portion of the cargo was lost, not by the negligence of the shipowner. The charter-party contained the usual clause excepting loss occasioned by "Perils of the Sea." In an action against the shipowner to recover the value of the portion of the cargo lost ; held, that the meaning of "At the Ship's Risk," was to place the goods during their transit from the shore to the ship in the same position as if they were on board ; and that as the cargo was lost by the Perils of the Sea, the loss came within that exception, and the action could not be maintained (*Nottebohm* v. *Richter,* 56 L. J. Q. B. 33 ; 18 Q. B. D. 63 ; 35 W. R. 300 ; 3 Times Rep. 30).

V. RISK.

SHIRE.—*V.* COUNTY.

SHOOTING.—*V.* HUNTING.

SHOP.—The word "Shop" implies a place where a *retail trade* is carried on ; a blacksmith's shop is rather a ware-house than a Shop (*R.* v. *Chapman*, 7 J. P. 132).

"In order to constitute a *Shop*, there must be some structure of a more or less permanent character" (per Mellor, J., *Hooper* v. *Kenshole*, 46 L. J. M. C. 162 ; 2 Q. B. D. 127 : *Vf.* PLACE) : it must be "something more than a mere place for sale ; it imports a place for storing also where the commodities admit of storing" (per Mellor, J., *Pope* v. *Whalley*, 34 L. J. M. C. 80 ; 6 B. & S. 303 : *Va. Llandaff Co.* v. *Lyndon*, 30 L. J. M. C. 105 ; 8 C. B. N. S. 515 : *Fearon* v. *Mitchell*, 41 L. J. M. C. 170 ; L. R. 7 Q. B. 690 : *McHole* v. *Davies*, 45 L. J. M. C. 30 ; 1 Q. B. D. 59). These cases were on the word "Shop" as used in the exception to s. 13, Markets and Fairs Clauses Act, 1847, 10 V. c. 14, and they are referred to thereon ; but they seem of general application. A vessel moored in a canal is not a "Shop" within the exception (*Wiltshire* v. *Baker*, 31 L. J. M. C. 10, n. 1 ; 5 L. T. 355) ; but a wooden shed affixed to a house and supported on wooden posts is within it (*Ashworth* v. *Heyworth*, 10 B. & S. 309 ; L. R. 4 Q. B. 316 ; 38 L. J. M. C. 91 : *Vf. Wiltshire* v. *Willett*, 31 L. J. M. C. 8 ; 11 C. B. N. S. 237; 5 L. T. 355).

If a photographer takes a private house on the ground floor of which he displays and sells photographs, albums or such like things, he converts the house into a shop, even though he make no structural alteration in the building (*Wilkinson* v. *Rogers*, 2 D. G. J. & S. 62 ; 12 W. R. 119, 284 : *V.* CONVERT).

"A Tavern would not come within the definition of 'Shop,'" in an exception from a covenant requiring a property generally to be used for private houses (per Huddleston, B., *Coombs* v. *Cook*, Cab. & El. 75 : Dart, 138).

Cp. BEER-HOUSE and BEER-SHOP.

SHOP FRONT.—A condition in a letting agreement related to a "Shop Front ;" held, that that phrase was not explainable by another document relating to the same premises (*Doe* d. *Nash* v. *Birch*, 1 M. & W. 402 ; 5 L. J. Ex. 185).

"Shop Front," s. 26, sub-s. 2 and 5, 18 & 19 V. c. 122 ; *V. St. Mary, Islington* v. *Goodman*, 58 L. J. M. C. 122.

SHORE.—*V.* KELP-SHORE : ON THE SHORE.

SHOW CAUSE.—Where a party has to "Show Cause," that, by necessary implication, allows the other side to answer (per Brett, L. J., *Davis* v. *Spence*, 1 C. P. D. 721 : *Girvin* v. *Grepe*, 49 L. J. Ch. 63 ; 13 Ch. D. 174 : *Sv.* cases to the contrary cited in the last case).

"Cause Shown ;" *V.* CAUSE.

SHOW OF BUSINESS.—*V.* OUTWARD MARK.

SICK.—A Bequest for "Sick, Aged and Impotent Persons," held to indicate that Hospital, not Educational, purposes were intended (*A.-G.* v. *Northumberland*, 5 Times Rep. 237, 719).

Persons "not under 50 years of age" are "aged" within 43 Eliz. c. 4 (*Re Wall, Pomeroy* v. *Willway*, 42 Ch. D. 510 ; 59 L. J. Ch. 172 ; 61 L. T. 357). *Vf. Thompson* v. *Corby*, 27 Bea. 649 : *Browne* v. *King*, 17 L. R. Ir. 454.

SICKNESS.—"Sickness," means disease (per Campbell, C. J., *R.* v. *Huddersfield*, 26 L. J. M. C. 171) : therefore pregnancy is not, of itself, "Sickness" within s. 4, 9 & 10 V. c. 66 (S. C., 26 L. J. M. C. 169 ; 7 E. & B. 794) : but a woman may be "ill" from pregnancy ; *V.* Ill.

Is Lunacy such a "sickness?" (*R.* v. *Manchester*, 26 L. J. M. C. 1 ; 6 E. & B. 919). Lunacy is "Sickness" within the relief clause of a Friendly Society's Rules (*Burton* v. *Eyden*, 42 L. J. M. C. 115 ; L. R. 8 Q. B. 295 ; 37 J. P. 693, in which case Archibald, J., said, "There can be no doubt that Insanity is a species of Sickness :" *Va. R.* v. *Swindon*, 42 J. P. 407).

Inability to work from mere old age is not "Sickness" (*Dunkley* v. *Harrison*, 51 J. P. 227).

V. Disease.

SIDE.—"No doubt in a certain context the word 'Side' might be so used as to be shewn, by that context, to be contra-distinguished from the top, or bottom, or end of a subject of quadrilateral or any other figure. But for this purpose a determining context is necessary. In the absence of such a context it is accurate, both in scientific and in ordinary language, to say that a quadrilateral table has four sides. In the (Communion) Rubrics not only is there no context to exclude the application of that term to the shorter as well as the longer sides ; but the effect of the context is just the reverse" (per Cairns, L. C., delivering jdgmt. of P. C., *Ridsdale* v. *Clifton*, 2 P. D. 341 ; 46 L. J. P. C. 60, 61 ; 36 L. T. 865).

"The Side or Sides of any *Carriage-way or Cart-way*," s. 51, 27 & 28 V. c. 101, means any land forming part of the Highway, though not part of the metalled road ; but does not include land not part of the highway, though by the side of the road (*Easton* v. *Richmond*, 41 L. J. M. C. 25 ; L. R. 7 Q. B. 69).

To speak of a thing being on the side of some other thing, "contemplates some degree of proximity" (per Fry, L. J., *Ravensthorpe* v. *Hinchcliffe*, 59 L. J. M. C. 22). "It is doubtful, to say no more, whether a building 300 or 400 yards distant from another building can be said to be on one *side* of it," within s. 3, 51 & 52 V. c. 52, which prohibits the bringing forward of a building beyond the front main wall of the house or building "on either side" of it (Ib.).

SIGHT.—*V.* At Sight.

SIGNED: SIGNATURE.—Speaking generally a Signature is the writing, or otherwise affixing, a person's name, or a mark to represent his name, by himself or by his authority (*R.* v. *Kent Jus.*, 42 L. J. M. C. 112; L. R. 8 Q. B. 305), with the intention of authenticating a document as being that of, or as binding on, the person whose name or mark is so written or affixed. But the minute requisite of a Signature will vary according to the nature of the document to which it is affixed; *e.g.*

1. Deeds;
2. Wills;
3. Contracts;
4. Bills of Exchange and Promissory Notes;
5. Solicitors' Bills;
6. Electioneering Papers;
7. Judge's Orders and Legal Proceedings;
8. Office Copies:—

and "in every case where a statute requires a particular document to be signed by a particular person, it must be a pure question on the construction of the statute whether the signature by an Agent is sufficient" (per Bowen, L. J., *Re Whitley*, 55 L. J. Ch. 541; 32 Ch. D. 337; 54 L. T. 912; 34 W. R. 505).

1. *Deeds.*—At common law "a Deed may be good, albeit the party that doth seal it doth never set his name or his mark to it, so as it be duly sealed and delivered" (Touch. 60). Since the Statute of Frauds (29 Car. 2, c. 3), however, it has been a question whether a deed is within its provisions as being an "agreement" and therefore required to be signed. Blackstone thinks it is (2 Com. 306), and herein he is cited and followed by Hilliard in his Edition of the Touchstone (n. 2, p. 56). Mr. Preston, on the contrary, thinks that a Deed is not within the Statute and does not require signing (Touch. n. 24, Preston's Ed.). In *Cooch* v. *Goodman* (11 L. J. Q. B. 225; 2 Q. B. 580), the point was discussed but not decided; and in *Aveline* v. *Whisson* (4 M. & G. 801; 12 L. J. C. P. 58), the point was conceded in the negative without argument. This view was strengthened in *Cherry* v. *Heming* (19 L. J. Ex. 63), where all the judges (Parke, Alderson, Rolfe and Platt) gave it as their opinion (*obiter*) that a Deed is not within the Statute and does not require signing. Thus the weight of authority is against the necessity of signature to a Deed; still, "it would certainly be most unwise to raise the question by leaving any Deed sealed and delivered, but not signed" (Wms. R. P. 127). If it should ultimately be held that a Deed generally must be signed, then, as also in all those particular cases where signature is expressly required, it would seem that the kind of signature may be the same as that required to Wills.

2. *Wills.*—Sec. 9, Wills Act (1 V. c. 26) requires that all Wills "shall be Signed at the foot or end thereof (*V.* 15 & 16 V. c. 24) by the testator or by some other person in his presence and by his direction." Perhaps the most common error as regards the requisites of this signature is the tracing a

former signature with a dry pen. This generally happens where there have been alterations made in a Will since its execution and where accordingly a re-execution of the Will is necessary, but "it cannot be too well understood that tracing with a dry pen is not equivalent to a signature" (per Cresswell, J. O., *Re Cunningham*, 29 L. J. P. M. & A. 71). It will be observed that a dry pen adds nothing to a document, makes no mark or sign upon it; hence its inutility. But when there is a mark or sign (or, it should seem, a seal, per Bayley, B., *Doe* d. *Phillips* v. *Evans*, 2 L. J. Ex. 183) made to a Will, which mark or sign was intended by the testator to be, or to stand for his name, then the Court is not nice as to the kind of mark or sign which is employed. "Whether the mark is made by a pen, or some other instrument cannot make any difference;" and therefore a stamped impression of a testator's signature is sufficient (*Jenkyns* v. *Gaisford*, 32 L. J. P. M. & A. 122; 3 Sw. & Tr. 93; 11 W. R. 854). The mark of the testator (and, it seems, whether he can or cannot write) is a sufficient signature even though his name is not affixed to the mark (*Re Field*, 3 Curt. 752: *Baker* v. *Dening*, 8 A. & E. 94; nom. *Taylor* v. *Dening*, 2 Jur. 775; and particularly, *Re Bryce*, 2 Curt. 325), or even where a wrong name is written against the mark; for in that case "the execution is perfect as soon as the mark is affixed," and therefore, "it matters not what some one else may have written against the mark" (per Cresswell, J. O., *Re Douse*, 31 L. J. P. M. & A. 172: *Va. Re Clarke*, 27 Ib. 18). So if a testator, or witness, writes a name, *not his or her real name*, but intended to represent that real name, the signature will be good. Thus where a woman whose name was "Glover" signed her name as "Reed" (that being the name of her deceased first husband) the signature was held good (*Re Glover*, 5 Notes of Ca. 553; 11 Jur. 1022); and signature in an assumed name is good (*Re Redding*, 2 Rob. Ecc. 339; 14 Jur. 1052). But errors of this kind appear only to be good when done by mistake; and where an attesting witness signed her husband's name instead of her own, it having been desired that the Will should have the appearance of being attested by the husband, the signature was held invalid (*Pryor* v. *Pryor*, 29 L. J. P. M. & A. 114: *Re Leverington*, 55 L. J. P. D. & A. 62; 11 P. D. 80).

Signature by *initials* is good (*Re Wingrove*, 15 Jur. 91: *Re Savory*, Ib. 1042: *Re Hinds*, 16 Ib. 1161). Affixing a seal is not a signing (*Re Byrd*, 3 Curt. 117: *Vf.* 1 Jarm. 78). The hand of a testator may be guided if he is unable from illness to sign (*Wilson* v. *Beddard*, 12 Sim. 28); but the ceremony of execution must be complete whilst the testator is living, for where an intended testator tries to sign his Will, but fails from weakness, the court has no power to decree probate (*Re Wilson*, 2 Curt. 854). *Vf.* 1 Jarm. 82, 78, 79; Wms. Exs. 91; and as to what is an acknowledgment of a testator's signature to a Will, *V.* ACKNOWLEDGMENT.

3. *Contracts.*—At common law a Contract did not require any writing; but by the Statute of Frauds a great many Contracts must be in writing and "signed by the party to be charged therewith, or some other person thereunto

by him lawfully authorized." Observe, first, who is to sign,—" the party to be charged therewith ;" the signature of the person seeking to enforce the contract is not necessary (*Laythoarp* v. *Bryant*, 2 Bing. N. C. 735 : *Vth.* Sug. V. & P. 129) ; and therefore a written signed proposal with the necessary details to support a Contract, accepted by word of mouth, may be enforced by the acceptor against the proposer, though an agreement based on the proposal could not be enforced against such an acceptor (*Warner* v. *Willington*, 3 Drew. 523 ; 25 L. J. Ch. 662 : *Smith* v. *Neale*, 2 C. B. N. S. 67; 26 L. J. C. P. 143 ; 29 L. T. O. S. 93 : *Liverpool Banking Co.* v. *Eccles*, 28 L. J. Ex. 122 : *Peek* v. *North Staffordshire Ry.*, 29 L. J. Q. B. 97). As to the character of the requisite signature to a contract :—In the first place all that has been said as to signature of a Will by a stamped impression, or a mark, or initials, or (it seems) a wrong name, is equally applicable to the signature of a Contract under the Statute of Frauds (*V.* cases collected Add. C. 175, 176. But "whether a signature by initials would suffice, seems not to have been decided expressly," Benj. 220). But in a Contract the latitude as to the manner of signing is carried much farther than in a Will. The signature may appear at the top or bottom of the contract ; and a learned judge has even stated the rule thus widely,—"If the name appears on the contract and be written by the party to be bound, or by his authority, and issued *or accepted* by him, or intended by him as the memorandum of a contract, that is sufficient" (per Blackburn, J., *Durrell* v. *Evans*, 31 L. J. Ex. 345 ; 1 H. & C. 174, in which case *V.* the previous cases hereon collected : *Svth. Murphy* v. *Rose*, L. R. 10 Ex. 126 : *Va.* Rosc. N. P. 289 ; Dart, 269–272). Thus in *Schneider* v. *Norris* (2 M. & S. 286), the name of the seller was printed on a bill of parcels, but he wrote thereon the name of the purchaser, and that was held to be an adoption by the seller of his own printed name, and a signature within the Statute. Assuming that case to be law then, *à fortiori*, tracing a former signature with a dry pen though, as we have seen, not a sufficient signing of a Will would be a sufficient signature to a Contract. *Schneider* v. *Norris* has, however, not passed entirely unquestioned, for in *Jenkyns* v. *Gaisford* (sup.), Cresswell, J. O., said,—" I always had some scruple about that case." Still *Schneider* v. *Norris* was repeatedly cited as an authority in *Durrell* v. *Evans* (sup.). *Vf.* hereon generally Blackb. 66–72 ; Benj. ch. 7.

Generally speaking all contractual documents may be signed by a duly authorised Agent (per Blackburn, J., *R.* v. *Kent Jus.*, 42 L. J. M. C. 112 ; L. R. 8 Q. B. 305 : per Bowen, L. J., *Re Whitley*, 32 Ch. D. 340, 341 : *Browne* v. *Kinsella*, 24 L. R. Ir. 98). But an acknowledgment under Ld. Tenterden's Act (9 G. 4, c. 14) to take a case out of the Statute of Limitations must be signed by the person himself (*Hyde* v. *Johnson*, 5 L. J. C. P. 291 ; 3 Sc. 289 ; 2 Bing. N. C. 776 : *Williams* v. *Mason*, 21 W. R. 386). On the other hand, documents under the Companies Act, 1862, do not need a personal signature, and therefore a Memorandum of Association may be signed by an Agent, who need not be authorised by deed (*Re Whitley*, 55 L. J. Ch. 540). *V.* HIMSELF.

4. *Bills of Ex. and Promissory Notes.*—"No person is liable as Drawer, Indorser or Acceptor of a *Bill* who has not signed it as such: provided that

(1.) Where a person signs a Bill in a Trade or assumed name, he is liable thereon as if he had signed it in his own name:

(2.) The signature of the name of a Firm is equivalent to the signature by the person so signing of the names of all persons liable as partners in that Firm:"

(s. 23, Bills of Ex. Act, 1882): and so of the Maker or Indorser of a Promissory Note (s. 89, Ib.).

"Where, by this Act, any instrument or writing is required to be signed by any person, it is not necessary that he should sign it with his own hand, but it is sufficient if his signature is written thereon by some other person by or under his authority.

(2.) In the case of a Corporation, where, by this Act, any instrument or writing is required to be signed, it is sufficient if the instrument or writing be sealed with the corporate seal" (s. 91, Ib.).

As to signature "per pro.;" *V.* s. 25, Ib.; and by an Agent, s. 26.

5. *Solicitor's Bills.*—By s. 37, 6 & 7 V. c. 73, no action can be brought on a Solicitor's Bill until one month after its delivery, "and which bill shall either be *subscribed* with the *proper hand* of such Solicitor (or in case of a partnership by any of the partners, either with his own name or with the name or style of such partnership), or of the executor, administrator or assignee of such Solicitor, or be enclosed in or accompanied by a letter, subscribed in like manner, referring to such Bill" (*Vh. Re Bush*, 14 L. J. Ch. 6; 8 Bea. 66: *Pilgrim* v. *Hirschfeld*, 12 W. R. 51: *Penley* v. *Anstruther*, 52 L. J. Ch. 367: *Ingle* v. *M'Cutchan*, 53 L. J. Q. B. 311; 12 Q. B. D. 518).

6. *Electioneering Papers.*—Signatures to Electioneering Papers have a few specialities about them distinct from other classes of signatures. In the first place an Objector must sign the Objection himself and not by an agent (*Toms* v. *Cuming*, 7 M. & G. 88; 14 L. J. C. P. 67: *Sv. Davies* v. *Hopkins*, 27 L. J. C. P. 6). This ruling, however, hardly extends to signatures to Voting Papers; for in *R.* v. *Avery* (21 L. J. Q. B. 430), Lord Campbell said, "the burgess is to sign, *or to have another to write his name for him*, in the shape of a signature." This was, however, an obiter dictum: the point decided in that case being that where a party is required merely to sign his name to an electioneering paper his usual mode of signature is sufficient. If however, there were only an initial for the *Surname*, this would seem not enough; for the object of this kind of signature is not merely to authenticate the document but also to give strangers notice who is the party by whom the signature is made. Accordingly a voting paper must be signed by the voter's *correct name*; with this exception, if the Burgess Roll mention him by a wrong name he may vote in the name by which he is therein mentioned (*R.* v. *Thwaites*, 22 L. J. Q. B. 238). And so it may be

further observed that if a mark be used to sign an Electioneering Paper it would seem that there must be the correct name of the person written against the mark ; for a mere mark would not, it should seem, complete such a signature, as it would if the document were a Will or Contract. For the same reason the legibility of the signature, though wholly immaterial in a Will or Contract if it can be in any manner identified, may become an objection to a signature to an Electioneering Paper ; but if such a signature is illegible by itself, but can be made out by reference to the register of voters or other extraneous public document, it will be sufficient (*Trotter* v. *Walker*, 32 L. J. C. P. 60). It appears, however, from that case that if the illegibility were purposely in order to deceive, or if it were an utter illegibility, the signature to an electioneering paper would not be sufficient. The rule laid down in *Jenkyns* v. *Gaisford*, sup. (*i.e.*, that a stamped impression of a signature to a Will is sufficient) has been extended to signatures of electioneering papers (*Bennett* v. *Brumfitt*, 37 L. J. C. P. 25). But that case shows that an Objector must himself, with his own hand, impress his signature. Where the *Christian name* is required to be given, it is not necessary that it should be written at full length ; a well known contraction will be sufficient (*R.* v. *Bradley*, 30 L. J. Q. B. 180). In that case Wightman and Hill, JJ., said (*obiter*) that a mere initial for the christian name would not be sufficient ; but the contrary was held in *Bowden* v. *Besley* (57 L. J. Q. B. 473 ; 21 Q. B. D. 309 ; 59 L. T. 219 ; 36 W. R. 889 ; 52 J. P. 536), if, as in that case, the person signing is sufficiently identified thereby.

7. *Judge's Orders and Legal Proceedings.*—A Judge's Order is well signed by a stamped similitude of the Judge's signature being impressed thereon by his clerk at chambers (*Blades* v. *Lawrence*, 43 L. J. Q. B. 133 ; L. R. 9 Q. B. 374).

But Particulars in a Co. Co. Action are not "signed" by the Plaintiff's Solicitor, so as to entitle him to the costs thereof, if his name is only lithographed thereon ; but, *semble*, his name affixed by his clerk with a stamp would suffice (*R.* v. *Fitzroy Cowper*, 59 L. J. Q. B. 26 ; 38 W. R. 207 : in the Appeal Court, Esher, M. R., was for reversing this decision, but Fry, L. J., agreed with it, and so the appeal fell through ; 34 S. J. 228 ; 6 Times Rep. 179).

8. *Office Copies.*—By s. 45, Insolvent Debtors Act (1 G. 4, c. 119), it was provided that proceedings thereunder should be proved by "a true copy, *signed* by the Officer, certifying the same to be a true copy ; " and it was held, upon a liberal construction, that such a requirement would be satisfied by the office copy being vouched by the seal of the court (per Bayley, B., *Doe* d. *Phillips* v. *Evans*, 2 L. J. Ex. 181, 183).

SIGNED, SEALED AND DELIVERED.—A *Will* signed and sealed by the testator, duly attested, and declared by the testator to be his Will, is a good execution of a Power requiring him to execute it by an

Instrument in Writing, "signed, sealed and *delivered*" by him (*Smith* v. *Adkins*, 41 L. J. Ch. 628 ; L. R. 14 Eq. 402). *V.* DELIVERY.

A *Policy* "signed, sealed and delivered" is complete and binding as against the party executing it, though, in fact, it remains in his possession, unless there is some particular act required to be done by the other party to declare his adoption of it ; and it is not necessary that the assured should formally accept or take away the Policy in order to make the Delivery complete (*Xenos* v. *Wickham*, 36 L. J. C. P. 313 ; L. R. 2 H. L. 296). *Vf. Standing* v. *Bowring*, 31 Ch. D. 282 : *Babington* v. *O'Connor*, 20 L. R. Ir. 254.

SILK.—Silk watch-guards and silk dresses are included in the phrase "Silks in a manufactured or unmanufactured state" as used in s. 1, Carriers Act (*Bernstein* v. *Baxendale*, 28 L. J. C. P. 265 ; 6 C. B. N. S. 259 : overruling *Davey* v. *Mason*, C. & M. 50). So also is silk hose (per Willes, J., citing *Hart* v. *Baxendale*, in *Bernstein* v. *Baxendale*, 28 L. J. C. P. 267). So also is elastic silk webbing composed of ⅓rd silk and ⅔rds india rubber and cotton,—the silk being the most valuable of the materials and the webbing being called in the trade "silk web" as distinguished from cotton web (*Brunt* v. *Mid. Ry.*, 33 L. J. Ex. 187 ; 2 H. & C. 889 ; 12 W. R. 380). The statute speaks of silks "wrought up or not wrought up with other materials." But, of course, that does not mean that any fabric that has silk in it, is necessarily silk within the meaning of the Act. The Court in *Brunt* v. *Mid. Ry.* (sup.) refused to define how much admixture of silk would make a fabric "silk," and held that in cases of doubt it would be a question for the jury. Pollock, C. B., said,—"The line is shifted according to circumstances." But the summary of the facts in that case as given in the jdgmt. of Martin, B., seems to supply as good an indication as could probably be stated as to what the test should be. He said,—"We have here a fabric of which the most valuable portion is silk ; the face of it is silk and the object of the manufacturer is to give it a face of silk ; and an ignorant person would say it was silk."

"*Soft or Organzine* Silk ;" *V. Elliott* v. *Turner*, 15 L. J. C. P. 49 ; 2 C. B. 446.

SILVER.—"Silver" in s. 1, 30 & 31 V. c. 90, does not mean pure silver, but merely what in common parlance is called silver (*Young* v. *Cook*, 47 L. J. M. C. 28 ; 3 Ex. D. 101).

V. METALS : GILD AND SILVER.

SIMILAR.—"Similar Covenants ;" *V. Re Tebb*, W. N. (79) 100.

V. LIKE : SAME.

SINGLE WOMAN.—A "Single Woman," within the Bastardy Act, 35 & 36 V. c. 65, s. 3, includes a Widow (*Antony* v. *Cardenham*, Fort. 309 ; 2 Bott, 6 Ed. 194 : *R.* v. *Wymondham*, 12 L. J. M. C. 74 ; 2 Q. B. 541 ; 2 G. & D. 690), and also a Married Woman living apart from her husband

(*R.* v. *Pilkington*, 2 E. & B. 546 ; nom. *Ex p. Grimes*, 22 L. J. M. C. 153 : *R.* v. *Collingwood*, 17 L. J. M. C. 168 ; 12 Q. B. 681) ; but not a woman single at the time of the birth of her child who has since married and is living with her husband (*Stacey* v. *Lintell*, 48 L. J. M. C. 108 ; 4 Q. B. D. 291 ; 27 W. R. 551 ; 43 J. P. 510), even though she took out the summons before her marriage, and service of it was prevented by the putative father (*Tozer* v. *Lake*, 4 C. P. D. 322 ; 41 L. T. 280 ; 43 J. P. 656).

SINK.—" Warranted free from particular average unless the Ship is stranded, *sunk* or burnt ; " a ship is not " Sunk " within this phrase if she springs a leak and thereby takes in a great deal of water which presses her down very low and much wets the cargo, but notwithstanding she gets into port (*Bryant & May* v. *London Assrce.*, 2 Times Rep. 591). *V.* STRANDING.

" Sink into the Residue ; " *V.* FALL.

SISTER.—*V.* BROTHER.

SITE.—" The term 'Site' in relation to a house, building, or other erection, shall mean the whole space to be occupied by such house, building, or other erection between the level of the bottom of the foundations and the level of the base of the walls " (s. 14, Metrop. Man. Act, 1878). That definition, provided for Part II. of the Act cited, was applied to a Bye-Law made by the Metrop. Bd. of Works (*Blashill* v. *Chambers*, 14 Q. B. D. 479).

SITTING.—" To lose £10 at one 'Time' is to lose it by a single stake or bet ; to lose at one 'Sitting' is to lose it in a course of play where the company never parts, though the person may not be actually gaming the whole time " (per Blackstone, J., *Bones* v. *Booth*, 2 W. Bl. 1226). Therefore money won between one evening and the next in a continuous bout of gaming, except when the party adjourned to dine together, is won at one " Sitting " within s. 2, 9 Anne, c. 14 (*Bones* v. *Booth*, sup.). That was an action in which the losing party sued to recover back his losings ; and it was there suggested that had the action been brought by an Informer (*V.* the section), the Court would have held the Sitting broken into two by the dinner : *Sq. ?*

SITUATE.—*V.* IN : *Crompton* v. *Jarrett*, 54 L. J. Ch. 1109 ; 30 Ch. D. 298.

SITUATION.—" Situation of the Property in respect of which he is enrolled," Form 2, Sch., 38 & 39 V. c. 40 ; *V. Soper* v. *Basingstoke*, 46 L. J. C. P. 422 ; 2 C. P. D. 440.

SIX MONTHS.—A "six months" notice to quit, means a notice served six months prior to the day the tenancy is to be determined, and is

not necessarily equivalent to a "half-year's" notice (*Walker* v. *Constable*, 3 Wils. 25 : *Flower* v. *Darby*, 1 T. R. 159 : *Wilkinson* v. *Calvert*, 47 L. J. C. P. 679 ; 3 C. P. D. 360 : *Barlow* v. *Teal*, 54 L. J. Q. B. 400 ; 15 Q. B. D. 501 ; 1 Times Rep. 491. *Sv. Morgan* v. *Davies*, 3 C. P. D. 260).
V. Half a Year : By Law.

SLAVE-TRADING.—"Each of the following acts and every contract to do any one of them is an act of slave-trading :—(*a*) To deal or trade in, purchase, sell, barter or transfer slaves or persons intended to be dealt with as slaves : (*b*) To carry away or remove slaves or other persons as or in order to their being dealt with as slaves : (*c*) To import or bring into any place whatsoever slaves or other persons as or in order to their being dealt with as slaves : (*d*) To ship, tranship, embark, receive, detain, or confine on board any vessel, slaves or other persons, for the purpose of their being carried away or removed as or in order to their being dealt with as slaves ; or for the purpose of their being imported into any place whatever as or in order to their being dealt with as slaves : (*e*) To fit out, man, navigate, equip, despatch, use, employ, let, or take to freight, or on hire, any vessel, in order to do any act of slave-trading before mentioned : (*f*) To lend or advance, or become security for the loan or advance of money, goods or effects, employed or to be employed in any act of slave-trading before mentioned : (*g*) To become guarantee or security for agents employed, or to be employed, in any act of slave-trading before mentioned : (*h*) To engage in any other manner in any act of slave-trading before mentioned, directly or indirectly as a partner, agent or otherwise : (*i*) To ship, tranship, lade, receive, or put on board of any vessel, money, goods, or effects, to be employed in any act of slave-trading before mentioned : (*j*) To take the charge or command, or to navigate, or enter and embark on board any vessel in any capacity, knowing that such vessel is employed in any act of slave-trading before mentioned, or is intended to be so employed upon the voyage or upon the occasion in which the embarkation takes place : (*k*) To insure slaves or property employed or intended to be employed in slave-trading" (Steph. Cr. 77, 78, epitomising 5 G. 4, c. 113, s. 2). *V.* Ib. Art. 114, as to Piratical Slave Trading. *Vf.* Arch. Cr. 488 ; Rosc. Cr. 868.

SLIP.—"The 'Slip' (in a Marine Policy), is in practice the complete and final contract between the parties, fixing the terms of the insurance and the premium ; and neither party can, without the assent of the other, deviate from the terms thus agreed on without a breach of faith, for which he would suffer severely in his credit and future business" (per Blackburn, J., *Ionides* v. *Pacific Insrce.*, L. R. 6 Q. B. 684. *Vf. Cory* v. *Patton* L. R. 7 Q. B. 308 ; 9 Ib. 577 ; 41 L. J. Q. B. 195 n. ; 43 Ib. 181 : *Morrison* v. *Universal Mar. Insrce.*, L. R. 8 Ex. 199 ; 42 L. J. Ex. 115).

SMALL.—It is laid down in Com. Dig. 'Franchise' (F.), 13, that "a corporation which has a head may give a personal command, and do small *acts* without deed—as it may retain a servant, a cook, butler," &c. As regards the working of the P. H. Act, 1875, the Legislature "intended to get rid of any discussion as to what were Small Matters" (per Brett, L. J., *Hunt* v. *Wimbledon,* 48 L. J. C. P. 212), and therefore by s. 174 has put the limit at £50.

Bequest of "Small Balance;" *V.* BALANCE.

SO.—"So," when used in connection with something to be done,—*e.g.*, "so completed,"—imports the doing of the thing in the manner and so as to satisfy the requirements previously prescribed (*V.* jdgmt. of Smith, J., *G. W. Ry.* v. *Halesowen Ry.*, 52 L. J. Q. B. 479).

"So devised," means "hereinbefore devised" (*Giles* v. *Melsom*, L. R. 6 H. L. 24; 42 L. J. C. P. 122).

SO AS.—"So as, not to violate;" *V.* VIOLATE.

SO FAR AS.—"So far as," "So long as," or "As near as," the rules of law will permit; *V.* jdgmt. of Wood, V.-C., *Scarsdale* v. *Curzon* (29 L. J. Ch. 249; 1 J. & H. 40), which contains an elaborate discussion of the cases: *Va. Christie* v. *Gosling,* 35 L. J. Ch. 667: 2 Jarm. 578, 581.

A Covenant in Restraint of Trade is not rendered vague, and therefore inoperative, by being expressed to be "so far as *the law allows*;" such a covenant means that to the full extent which English law allows a man to contract himself out of the power of carrying on the specified business, the covenantor shall be precluded from carrying it on (*Davies* v. *Davies*, 36 Ch. D. 359; 56 L. J. Ch. 962; 36 W. R. 86; 3 Times Rep. 473).

"So far as applicable;" *V.* APPLICABLE.

"So far as is reasonably practicable;" *V.* REASONABLY PRACTICABLE.

V. POSSIBLE.

SO ILL.—"So ill as not to be able to travel;" *V.* ILL.

SO NEAR THERETO.—*V.* NEAR THERETO AS SHE MAY SAFELY GET.

SO SOON AS.—*V.* WHEN.

SOBER AND TEMPERATE HABITS.—The question as to whether a man is of "Sober and Temperate Habits," within a declaration leading to a Life Policy, is peculiarly one for the jury (*Life Assn. of Scotland* v. *M'Blain*, Ir. Rep. 9 Eq. 176).

V. STRICTLY TEMPERATE.

SOCHEMANS: SOKEMANNI.—*V.* COLEBERTI; Termes de la Ley, *Sockmans.*

SOCIETIES.—" Such Charities, Societies and Institutions . . . . as S. shall nominate ;" *V. Re Douglas*, 56 L. J. Ch. 913 ; 35 Ch. D. 472 ; 56 L. T. 740 ; 35 W. R. 786.

SOCKE.—" Socke" (Termes de la Ley, *Priviledges*), or " Sok" (Ib., *Sok*), " that is suit of men in your Court, according to the custome of the realme" (Ib., *Sok*). *V.* SOKE.

SODOMY.—" Every one commits the felony called Sodomy who (*a*) carnally knows any animal ; or (*b*) being a male, carnally knows any man or any woman (per anum)" (Steph. Cr. 114). *Vf.* Arch. Cr. 824, 825 ; Rosc. Cr. 967.

SOIL.—This word (and notably in Inclosure Acts) frequently means the surface of the land only, and does not include minerals (*Wakefield* v. *Buccleugh*, 36 L. J. Ch. 179 ; L. R. 4 Eq. 613 ; 15 W. R. 247 ; 15 L. T. 462, following *Pretty* v. *Solby*, 26 Bea. 606 ; 33 L. T. O. S. 72. *Wakefield* v. *Buccleugh* was reversed, L. R. 4 H. L. 377 ; 39 L. J. Ch. 441, but on another ground, *V.* especially jdgmt. of Hatherley, L. C.) ; but in the absence of a context it would mean down to the centre of the earth (*Vh. Micklethwait* v. *Winter*, 20 L. J. Ex. 313 ; 6 Ex. 644).

V. WATER AND SOIL : SURFACE.

SOKE.—A manor or lordship (Elph. 620, citing Spelm., *Soca ;* for example *V. Beauchamp* v. *Winn*, L. R. 6 H. L. 243).

V. SOCKE.

SOLD.—*V.* SALE.

SOLDIER.—A militiaman " is a soldier to all intents and purposes" (per Campbell, C. J.), and within the proviso to s. 1, 9 & 10 V. c. 66 (*Horton* v. *Leeds*, 25 L. J. M. C. 38).

A person in the military service of the late East India Company, held a " Soldier" within s. 11, Wills Act, 1 V. c. 26 (*Re Donaldson*, 2 Curt. 386 : *V.* ACTUAL MILITARY SERVICE).

SOLE.—The way in which this word (when used *quà* benefits to be taken by married women) has been judicially interpreted, is not a little curious.

Mr. Hawkins in his Treatise on Construction of Wills (p. 116) lays it down broadly that, " a gift to or for the sole *Use or Benefit* of a woman means, *primâ facie*, Separate Use :"—*i.e.*, that " sole" and " separate," in this connexion are synonymous terms. For this he cites several authorities.

But in *Gilbert* v. *Lewis* (32 L. J. Ch. 347 ; 1 D. G. J. & S. 38 ; 11 W. R. 223), Westbury, L. C., on a review of the same authorities came to an opposite conclusion ; and, in a dictum, intimated that a mere gift to the " sole" use of a woman would not give her a separate estate.

That dictum however was cited by Mr. Hawkins (p. 118) only to discredit it; adding that, "In *Ex p. Killick* (3 Mont. D. & D. 487), Knight-Bruce, V.-C., said, 'I apprehend it is clear that when property is given to a woman whether married or unmarried, for her own *sole* use and benefit, it is vested in her for her separate use, free from the control of the marital right.'"

In *Spirett* v. *Willows* (34 L. J. Ch. 365; 1 Ch. 520; 13 W. R. 329), Ld. Westbury re-asserted the doctrine of *Gilbert* v. *Lewis*; and in *Massy* v. *Rowen* (L. R. 4 H. L. 288) it was again decided that the word "sole," is not equivalent to "separate," use unless such a meaning is plainly deducible from the context (*e.g.*, as in *Re Tarsey*, 35 L. J. Ch. 452; L. R. 1 Eq. 561). But yet in *Re Fox* (28 S. J. 738), Chitty, J., whilst deferring to *Massy* v. *Rowen*, said that some meaning must be attached to the word "sole," and if from the rest of the Will no other meaning could be gathered, then the word was equivalent to "separate." This, if correct, would seem to shift the onus as laid down in *Massy* v. *Rowen*, under which a context was required to give "sole" the meaning of "separate:" *Va.* SEPARATE USE; 1 White & Tudor L. C. 5 Ed. 562; Seton, 690.

"For her sole *Use and Disposal*," excludes the marital right (*Bland* v. *Dawes*, 50 L. J. Ch. 252; 17 Ch. D. 794). *V.* DISPOSAL.

Under a limitation to trustees to the use of a married woman, "for her own sole and separate use," the legal estate will pass to her notwithstanding that phrase (*Williams* v. *Waters*, 14 M. & W. 166).

"For her Sole Use," in a *Life Policy* effected by a Married Woman; *V. Re Suse, Ex p. Dever*, 18 Q. B. D. 660; 56 L. J. Q. B. 552; 3 Times Rep. 400.

"Sole and unmarried;" *V.* UNMARRIED.

SOLE EXECUTOR.—"It seems doubtful whether even the appointment, by subsequent Will, of a 'Sole Executor' amounts, *per se*, to a revocation of the first. *V.*, for revocation, *Re Lowe*, 3 Sw. & Tr. 478; 33 L. J. P. M. & A. 155: *Re Baily*, L. R. 1 P. & M. 628:—Contra, *Geaves* v. *Price*, 3 Sw. & Tr. 71; 32 L. J. P. M. & A. 113: *Re Leese*, 2 Sw. & Tr. 442; 31 L. J. P. M. & A. 169: *Re Morgan*, L. R. 1 P. & D. 323." 1 Jarm. 175.

SOLE HEIR.—"I make my cousin, Giles Bridges, my *Sole Heir* and my Executor;" held to pass testator's lands (*Tayler* v. *Web*, Style, 301, 307, 319: *Marret* v. *Sly*, 2 Sid. 75; cited and commented on in note (*d*), 1 Jarm. 357: *Va. Parker* v. *Nickson*, 32 L. J. Ch. 397; 1 D. G. J. & S. 177: ACKNOWLEDGE).

SOLE NAME OF A DECEASED PERSON.—These words, at commencement of s. 25, Trustee Act, 1850, include the case of stock in the name of two deceased persons as being in the name of the survivor (Seton, 523).

SOLE TRUSTEE.—This phrase in s. 23, Trustee Act, 1850 (13 & 14 V. c. 60), includes two or more Trustees who are solely entitled to any trust property (*Re Hartnall*, 21 L. J. Ch. 384 ; 5 D. G. & S. 111: *Re Hyatt*, 51 L. J. Ch. 742 ; 21 Ch. D. 846 : *Vh.* Lewin, 1022, n. (*d*) ; Watson, Eq. 1020).

SOLELY.—A vehicle sometimes used for the purpose of advertising,—being (as one sometimes sees) painted and placarded as an advertisement, or used for carrying about a band in order to make public announcement,—is not used "solely" in the course of trade so as to give exemption from toll, within subs. 6, s. 19, 32 & 33 V. c. 14 (*Speak* v. *Powell*, 43 L. J. M. C. 19 ; L. R. 9 Ex. 25).

SOLEMNIZATION.—The "Solemnization" of a marriage,—as the word is used in a Marriage Settlement,—means the consummation of a valid and effectual marriage (*Chapman* v. *Bradley*, 33 L. J. Ch. 139 ; 33 Bea. 61; 4 D. G. J. & S. 71; 12 W. R. 140 : *Pawson* v. *Brown*, 49 L. J. Ch. 193 ; 13 Ch. D. 202 : *Addington* v. *Mellor*, 29 S. J. 131).

SOLEMNLY.—Where a thing,—*e.g.* an oath,—has to be done "solemnly,"—that "does not merely mean religiously, but means with all due solemnities" (per Brett, M. R., *A.-G.* v. *Bradlaugh*, 54 L. J. Q. B. 213, 219–221: 14 Q. B. D. 667).

SOLIDATA TERRÆ.—12 acres (Elph. 620).

SOLINUM.—"*Unum solinum* or *solinus terræ* in Domesday booke containeth two plow-lands and somewhat lesse than an halfe ; for there it is said, *septem solini*, or *solina terræ sunt* 17 *carucat*'" (Co. Litt. 5 a). Hargrave's note to this passage is,—"Some think, that *solinus terræ* was frequently synonymous with *carucata terræ*. See Somn. Rom. Ports, 82. Cow. Interpr. ed. 1727, voc. solinus terræ." *Vf.* Elph. 620.

SOLLAR.—The lower part of a house—a room (Elph. 620, citing Spelm. *Solarium*).

SOME.—A bequest of "*some* of my best linen"—is uncertain and void (*Peck* v. *Halsey*, 2 P. Wms. 387; cited 1 Jarm. 358).

"*Some* suit or action," in s. 4, Prescription Act, 2 & 3 W. 4, c. 71, means generally *any* suit or action in which the claim shall have been or shall be brought into question (*Cooper* v. *Hubbuck*, 31 L. J. C. P. 323 ; 12 C. B. N. S. 456, and cases there cited).

SOMETIME.—"'Sometime' is in some places put for the time just past, and 'Late' for the time past long since ; for which reason 'late,' used in the sense of 'sometime,' may be well permitted, and especially in

Counts, which, if they have matter of substance, shall never abate" (*Wrotesley* v. *Adams*, Plowd. 190).

SON.—The word "Son" is quite as flexible as the word "Heir," and can as easily be read "Issue Male" as the word "Heir" can be turned into "Son" (*Jenkins* v. *Clinton*, 26 Bea. 108; nom. *Jenkins* v. *Hughes*, 30 L. J. Ch. 870).

For a collection and discussion of the cases upon the construction of "Son" as a word of limitation; *V.* 2 Jarm. 401 *et seq.: Svth. Beauchant* v. *Usticke*, W. N. (80) 14. Whenever that word is so construed it creates an estate in tail male (2 Jarm. 400: *Va.* Watson, Eq. 1390).

As to a limitation in a *Deed*, as compared with one in a *Will*, to a particular son; *V.* Watson, Eq. 1385.

As to a devise to "*a* Son;" *V. Ashburner* v. *Wilson*, cited ONE.

In an appointment of the remainder of a fund "to be equally divided among my Sons," the sons take as a class (*Fitzroy* v. *Richmond*, 28 L. J. Ch. 750; 27 Bea. 190).

"Either Sons or Daughters," following ISSUE, will control "Issue" to mean "Children" (*Farrant* v. *Nichols*, 15 L. J. Ch. 259; 9 Bea. 327).

"Sons and Daughters," mean legitimate ones; unless those that are illegitimate are indicated (*Vh. Edmunds* v. *Fessey*, 29 Bea. 235; 30 L. J. Ch. 279: DAUGHTER: CHILDREN: NEPHEW).

"*Who being a Son or Sons* shall attain 21," in a limitation which contemplates all the children, will not exclude daughters (*Re Daniel*, 45 L. J. Ch. 105; 1 Ch. D. 375).

Vh. Chitty, Eq. Ind. 7678–7684.

V. ELDEST.

SOON AS POSSIBLE.—*V.* POSSIBLE.

SOONER DETERMINATION.—May be rejected as insensible; *V.* TERM.

SORT.—"Sort," in the expression "kind or sort," is, probably, synonymous with "Quality" or "Nature" (*V.* DYE: NATURE).

SOUND.—"I think the word 'Sound,'"—in a warranty of a horse,—"means that the animal is free from disease at the time he is warranted" (per Parke, B., *Kiddell* v. *Burnard*, 9 M. & W. 669; 11 L. J. Ex. 269; C. & M. 291). In the same case Alderson, B., said, "The word 'Soundness' is explained and qualified by reference to the purposes for which the warranty is given. Any disease, therefore, which tends to impede the use for which the horse is designed, is an unsoundness."

Mere badness of shape, though rendering a horse incapable of work, is not unsoundness (per Alderson, B., *Dickinson* v. *Follett*, 1 Moo. & R. 299).

Bone spavin in the hock is unsoundness, though producing no present apparent lameness (per Tindal, C.J., *Watson* v. *Denton*, 7 C. & P. 85); so is a visible splint on the fore leg, producing subsequent lameness, though the warranty be limited to the condition "at the time of the contract," because the jury found that the seeds of unsoundness were then existing (*Margetson* v. *Wright*, 1 L. J. C. P. 128; 8 Bing. 454; 1 Moore & S. 622).

A receipt "for a grey four-year-old colt, warranted sound in every respect," is a warranty only for the soundness, not for the age (*Budd* v. *Fairmaner*, 1 L. J. C. P. 16; 8 Bing. 48; 1 Moore & S. 74).

Vf. Add. C. 984; Rosc. N. P. 440; Benj. 612.

V. Warranted Sound.

SOVEREIGN.—*V.* Crown.

SOWING.—*V.* Ploughing.

SPECIAL.—"Special *Cause*" for (in Ireland) depriving a successful litigant of costs after a trial by jury, s. 53, 40 & 41 V. c. 57:—In an action of Seduction the woman was 35 years of age and readily consented, the parties were poor, and the jury only gave £10 damages, which the presiding judge thought as much as could have been reasonably expected; held, that there was no "Special Cause" for depriving the plaintiff of costs (*Wilson* v. *M'Mains*, 20 L. R. Ir. 582; *Cp.* Good Cause).

The "Special *Circumstances*" sufficient to enable a client to get taxation of his *Solicitor's Bill after* payment (6 & 7 V. c. 73, s. 41) must, speaking generally but not exhaustively, consist of pressure, or there must be a specified overcharge so gross as to amount to fraud (*Re Harrison*, 16 L. J. Ch. 170; 10 Bea. 57: *Re Lacey*, 53 L. J. Ch. 287; 25 Ch. D. 301: *Re Boycott*, 55 L. J. Ch. 835; 29 Ch. D. 571). The majority of the Court of Appeal in *Re Boycott* adhered to this rule (which culminated in *Re Harrison*), and therefore the disapproval of it in *Re Dearden* (23 L. J. Ex. 14), and in *Re Newman* (36 L. J. Ch. 843; 2 Ch. 707; 15 W. R. 1189), is much lessened. But in *Re Norman* (55 L. J. Q. B. 202; 16 Q. B. D. 673; 54 L. T. 143; 34 W. R. 313) the Court of Appeal declined to be bound by any rigid rule defining these "special circumstances." *Vf. Re Griffith*, 53 L. J. Ch. 303. Charging a Scale Fee where none applicable is a "special circumstance" (*Re Pybus*, 56 L. J. Ch. 921; 35 Ch. D. 568; 57 L. T. 362; 35 W. R. 770).

Protracted litigation is a "Special Circumstance" within Ord. 58, R. 15, R. S. C. (*Va.* R. 113, Bankry. R. 1883), justifying an unusually large deposit as *Security for Costs* on an Appeal (*Re McHenry*, 55 L. J. Q. B. 496; 17 Q. B. D. 351; 35 W. R. 20). Insolvency, or other proved inability to pay costs of appeal if the appellant should be unsuccessful, is generally the "Special Circumstance" acted on under Rule 15 for ordering a deposit as security for costs on an appeal to the Court of Appeal, but the Rule is not confined to such cases (*Weldon* v. *Maples*, 57 L. J. Q. B. 224;

20 Q. B. D. 331 ; 57 L. T. 672 ; 36 W. R. 154 : *Svth. McDougall* v. *Copestake*, 34 S. J. 347). If the appeal is seen to be frivolous (*Usill* v. *Hales*, 47 L. J. C. P. 380 ; 3 C. P. D. 206), or the appellant be a foreigner having no assets in England (*Grant* v. *Banque Franco-Egyptienne*, 47 L. J. C. P. 41), there would be such a "Special Circumstance." *Vf.* Ann. Pr.

As to "Special Circumstances" in s. 73, Court of Probate Act, 1857 (20 & 21 V. c. 77); *V. Re Wensley*, 51 L. J. P. D. & A. 21 ; 7 P. D. 13 : *Re Clayton*, 55 L. J. P. D. & A. 26 ; 11 P. D. 76 ; 34 W. R. 444 ; 50 J. P. 263 : *Re Grundy*, 37 L. J. P. & M. 21 ; L. R. 1 P. & D. 459 : *Re Richardson*, 40 L. J. P. & M. 36 ; L. R. 2 P. & D. 244 : *Re Woodfall*, 42 L. J. P. & M. 64 ; L. R. 3 P. & D. 108 : *Re Turner*, 56 L. J. P. D. & A. 41 ; 12 P. D. 18 ; 57 L. T. 372 ; 35 W. R. 384 : *Re Eccles*, 61 L. T. 652 ; W. N. (89) 198 : *Re Minshull*, 14 P. D. 151.

The "Special Circumstances" justifying a *Change of Venue* of an Election Petition (s. 11, subs. 11, Parl. El. Act, 1868) include local intimidation (*Sligo*, 1 O'M. & H. 300), or a great saving of expense (*Arch* v. *Bentinck*, 18 Q. B. D. 548 ; 56 L. J. Q. B. 458 ; 56 L. T. 360 ; 35 W. R. 476) ; but something more than mere inconvenience must be shown (*Tewkesbury*, 49 L. J. C. P. 685 ; 5 C. P. D. 544).

As to the "Special *Contract*" prescribed in s. 6, *Carriers Act* (11 G. 4 & 1 W. 4, c. 68), and in s. 7, Ry. & Canal Traffic Act, 1854 (17 & 18 V. c. 31); *V. Peek* v. *North Staffordsh. Ry.*, 32 L. J. Q. B. 241 ; 10 H. L. Ca. 473 : *Lewis* v. *G. W. Ry.*, 47 L. J. Q. B. 131 ; 3 Q. B. D. 195 : *Kirby* v. *G. W. Ry.*, 18 L. T. 658.

The "Special Contract" under the *Pawnbrokers Act*, 1872, 35 & 36 V. c. 93, does not prevent the pawnbroker from recovering the balance of his loan remaining due after the sale of the pledge (*Jones* v. *Marshall*, 24 Q. B. D. 269).

"Special *Expenses*," ss. 229, 230, P. H. Act, 1875 ; *V. Darenth Valley* v. *Dartford*, 56 L. J. Q. B. 615 ; 19 Q. B. D. 270 ; 57 L. T. 233 ; 36 W. R. 43 : *Lancashire & Yorkshire Ry.* v. *Bolton*, 5 Times Rep. 610.

The "Special *Grounds*" justifying an Order for Costs on the Higher Scale (R. 9, Ord. 65, R. S. C.) must relate to the importance or difficulty of the cause or matter (*Williamson* v. *North Staffordsh. Ry.*, 55 L. J. Ch. 938 ; 32 Ch. D. 399 ; 55 L. T. 452).

"Special *Grounds*" for admitting further evidence on an Appeal, Ord. 58, R. 4, R. S. C.; *V. Re Chennell*, 47 L. J. Ch. 583 ; 8 Ch. D. 492 : *Arnison* v. *Smith*, 58 L. J. Ch. 645 : Ann. Pr.

A Special "*Indorsement*" of a Writ, under Ord. 3, R. 6, R. S. C., must contain particulars of goods, &c., sued on, giving dates, so as to clearly show what the action is for (*Parpaite* v. *Dickinson*, 38 L. T. 178 ; 26 W. R. 479 : *Walker* v. *Hicks*, 47 L. J. Q. B. 27 ; 3 Q. B. D. 8 : *Godden* v. *Corsten*, W. N. (79) 190) ; or a reference to an account rendered giving such particulars (*Aston* v. *Hurwitz*, 41 L. T. 521). For examples, *V.* Appendix C. s. 4, of the Rules ; *Va. Smith* v. *Wilson*, 49 L. J. C. P. 96 ; 4 C. P. D.

392 ; 5 Ib. 25 : *Bickers* v. *Speight*, 22 Q. B. D. 7 ; 58 L. J. Q. B. 42 ; 37 W. R. 139.

"The 'Special *Licence*' mentioned in the Stat. of Marlebridge (52 H. 3, c. 23, s. 2), is commonly expressed by the well-known phrase 'Without impeachment of Waste'" (*Woodhouse* v. *Walker*, 49 L. J. Q. B. 611 ; 5 Q. B. D. 404).

The "Special *Occasion*" for giving an Innkeeper an extension of hours (s. 29, 35 & 36 V. c. 94), must be determined by the Justices to whom the application is made (*Devine* v. *Keeling*, 34 W. R. 718 ; 50 J. P. 551 ; 2 Times Rep. 692).

Notice specifying "Special *Purpose*" of a Vestry Meeting, s. 1, 58 G. 3, c. 69 ; *V. R.* v. *Powell*, 42 L. J. M. C. 129 ; L. R. 8 Q. B. 403 : *Rand* v. *Green*, 30 L. J. C. P. 80 ; 9 C. B. N. S. 470 : *Smith* v. *Deighton*, 8 Moore P. C. 179.

A Special *Train* is not necessarily one ordered by a passenger or a body of passengers ; but includes a train specially provided by a Railway Company in substitution of, or in addition to, their ordinary service (*Walker* v. *Lond. & S. W. Ry.*, Times, 18th May, 1882): *Va.* ORDINARY TRAIN.

The "Special and Distinctive *Word or Words*," capable of registration under s. 10, Trade-Marks Registration Act, 1875, must have been used before the Act, solely and not in combination with any device, *i.e.*, the word or words must alone have been the trade-mark (*Re Palmer*, 24 Ch. D. 504 : *Re Chorlton*, 53 L. T. 337 ; 34 W. R. 60).

SPECIALLY AUTHORISED.—"Specially authorised Societies," s. 8, subs. 5, Friendly Societies Act, 1875 ; *V. Peat* v. *Fowler*, 55 L. J. Q. B. 271 ; 34 W. R. 366.

SPECIALTY.—A "Specialty" is a contract under seal ; and a "specialty debt" is an obligation secured by such a contract, *e. g.*, a Bond, or Mortgage. So also an obligation arising under a statute is a "Specialty" within the meaning of the Statutes of Limitation : *e.g.*, an action under 2 Ed. 6, for carrying away corn without setting out tithes (*Talory* v. *Jackson*, Cro. Car. 513); an action for an Escape (*Jones* v. *Pope*, 1 Wms. Saund. 36) ; or for Calls on a Shareholder in a Company formed by Act of Parliament (*Cork & Bandon Ry.* v. *Goode*, 22 L. J. C. P. 198 ; 13 C. B. 826), or under the Companies Act, 1862 (s. 17) ; or for Dues authorised by Parliament (*Shepherd* v. *Hills*, 25 L. J. Ex. 6 ; 11 Ex. 55). But a penalty under a Bye-law of a Company founded by Charter under the Great Seal, is not a "Specialty," for such a liability springs out of the member's implied consent to obey the bye-laws, which is in effect a contract without specialty (*Tobacco Pipe Co.* v. *Loder*, 20 L. J. Q. B. 414 ; 16 Q. B. 765) ; so also the mere recital in a deed of a simple contract debt does not make the debt a specialty (*Ivens* v. *Elwes*, 24 L. J. Ch. 249 ; 3 Drew. 25).

SPECIFIC : SPECIFICALLY.—A mortgage or charge "specifically *affecting*" the property of a Joint Stock Co. (s. 43, Companies Act, 1862) means one created by the company itself (*Re General Horticultural Co.*, 29 S. J. 555).

"Specific *Cause*" of Profits falling short, No. 4, 3rd set of Rules, Sch. D, s. 100, Income Tax Act, 5 & 6 V. c. 35 ; *V. Ryhope Co.* v. *Foyer*, 7 Q. B. D. 485 ; 45 L. T. 404.

The statute establishing Poor Rates (43 Eliz. c. 2) imposed no liability on any mines, except coal mines (*Morgan* v. *Crawshay*, 40 L. J. M. C. 202; L. R. 5 H. L. 304). The Rating Act, 1874 (37 & 38 V. c. 54, s. 3) made all mines assessable to the poor rate ; but, by s. 8, a lessee, till then exempt from being rated, became during the continuance of his lease entitled to deduct from his rent one-half of the rate unless he had "specifically *contracted* to pay such rate in the event of the abolition of the said exemption." A lessee of an iron mine who became liable to poor rate under that latter Act, and who before its passing had contracted to pay his rent "free from all deductions whatsoever," and also to pay "all manner of taxes, rates, assessments, charges and impositions whatsoever, parliamentary or parochial, which now are or which shall at any time hereafter" be payable in respect of the mine, was held *not* to have "specifically" contracted himself out of the benefit of s. 8 (*Chaloner* v. *Bolckow*, 47 L. J. C. P. 562 ; 3 App. Ca. 933 : *Devonshire* v. *Barrow Hæmatite Steel Co.*, 46 L. J. Q. B. 435 ; 2 Q. B. D. 286 ; *V.* IMPOSITIONS). "The meaning of the word 'specific' is the reverse of 'general.' You cannot give to a general covenant the force of a specific agreement with regard to a particular tax ; and a covenant in a lease to pay 'all taxes, rates, assessments, charges and impositions whatsoever' cannot be regarded as a 'specific' covenant" (per Ld. Hatherley, *Chaloner* v. *Bolckow*, sup.).

The words "Household furniture and effects, Implements of husbandry," in a Schedule to a Bill of Sale, do not "specifically" *describe* such goods within s. 4, Bills of Sale Act, 1882 ; for the word requires "that amount of separation of one class of articles from another which any business inventory would give" (per Brett, M. R., *Roberts* v. *Roberts*, 53 L. J. Q. B. 313 ; 32 W. R. 605 ; 13 Q. B. D. 794). So a Bill of Sale, by a picture dealer, stating Pictures as being so many,—*e.g.*, 300 Oil Pictures in gilt frames, 20 water-colour pictures,—would be insufficient (*Witt* v. *Banner*, 20 Q. B. D. 114 ; 36 W. R. 115; 57 L. J. Q. B. 141; 58 L. T. 34; 3 Times Rep. 759). But in a Bill of Sale by a private person, "12 Oil Paintings in gilt frames" was held sufficiently specific (*Cooper* v. *Huggins*, 34 S. J. 96). Ordinary cows are specifically described as "21 Milch cows" (*Carpenter* v. *Deen*, 23 Q. B. D. 566 ; 33 S. J. 590 ; 5 Times Rep. 647) ; but in that case Lopes, L. J., said that Sheep should be more definitely described, and that Horses are customarily described by their colour,—*e.g.*, "Bay Mare," "Chestnut Gelding." However, in the case of a small farm in Wales, a description of "All my Farming Stock, comprising 4 Horses, 5 Cows," and mentioning other animals by number only and defining them in no other way, was held sufficient (*Jones* v. *Roberts*, 34 S. J. 254).

To *deny* "specifically" a statement in a Pleading (Ord. 19, R. 13), you "must deal specifically with each allegation of fact" of which you do not admit the truth (Ib. R. 17). *Vth. Thorp* v. *Holdsworth*, 3 Ch. D. 637; 45 L. J. Ch. 406; *Harris* v. *Gamble*, 7 Ch. D. 877; 47 L. J. Ch. 344. *Vf.* Ann. Pr.

"Specifically *devised*;" *V. Giles* v. *Melsom*, L. R. 6 H. L. 24; 42 L. J. C. P. 122.

A "Specific *Sum*," charged by Settlement on realty and exempt from Legacy Duty by the proviso to s. 4, 45 G. 3, c. 28, is not confined to a precise amount fixed by the Settlement, but includes an amount named by the Settlement which may be reduced by the donee of a power thereunder, *e.g.*, a power to appoint a rent-charge *not exceeding* £700 a year (*A.-G.* v. *Hertford*, 14 L. J. Ex. 266; 14 M. & W. 284: *Pickard* v. *A.-G.*, 9 L. J. Ex. 329; 6 M. & W. 348).

V. Specify.

SPECIFY.—A Marine Policy issued by an Association and signed by A. B., manager, "per procuration of the several members of the Association, every member bearing his equal proportion according to the sums mutually insured therein," and which does not by itself afford the means of ascertaining who the insurers were to be, does not "specify" the names of the subscribers or underwriters within the meaning of s. 7, 30 V. c. 23 (*Re Arthur Average Assn.*, 44 L. J. Ch. 569; 10 Ch. 542: *Vth. Smith* v. *Anderson*, 15 Ch. D. 247). But as regards the statute (35 G. 3, c. 63, s. 2), the language of which was employed in s. 7, 30 V. c. 23, it has been held that if the insurers constitute a firm, the name of the firm will be a sufficient specification of the subscribers (*Reid* v. *Allan*, 19 L. J. Ex. 39; 4 Ex. 326: *Dowdall* v. *Allan*, 19 L. J. Q. B. 41: referring to which cases it has been said, "it may easily be held that a partnership name is a sufficient specification;" per James, L. J., *Re Arthur Average Assn.*, 44 L. J. Ch. 576).

V. Specific.

SPEED.—*V.* Convenient Speed.

SPEND.—"Does not spend;" *V.* Left.

SPENT MADDER.—*V. Turner* v. *Mucklow*, 8 Jur. N. S. 870; 6 L. T. 690.

SPINSTERS.—A Bequest for "Spinsters" is Charitable (*Thompson* v. *Corby*, 27 Bea. 649; 8 W. R. 267).

SPIRITS.—"We think that nothing can be taken to be 'Spirits' within the meaning of 6 G. 4, c. 80 (*V.* s. 101), which does not come under the definition of an inflammable liquid produced by distillation, either pure or mixed only with ingredients which do not convert it into some article of commerce not known in common parlance under the generic appellation of 'Spirits'" (per Pollock, C. B., delivering judgment of Court in *A.-G.* v. *Bailey*, 17 L. J. Ex. 12; 1 Ex. 281). It was there also said that 7 W. 4, c. 72, and 5 V. c. 25, were strongly confirmatory of this view; and it was held that Sweet Spirits of Nitre were not "Spirits" within the enactment.

SPIRITUAL.—"Temporal or Spiritual Injury, Damage, Harm, or Loss," s. 2, Corrupt & Illegal Prac. Act, 1883, 46 & 47 V. c. 51;—A Priest may "throw the whole weight of his character into the scale; but he may not appeal to the fears, or terrors, or superstition of those he addresses. He must not hold out hopes of reward here or hereafter, and he must not use threats of temporal injury, or disadvantage, or of punishment hereafter. He must not, *e.g.*, threaten to excommunicate or to withhold the Sacraments or to expose the party to any other religious disability, or denounce the voting for any particular candidate as a sin, or as an offence involving punishment here or hereafter" (per Fitzgerald, J., *Longford*, 2 O'M. & H. 16: *Va. Tipperary*, Ib. 31).

SPIRITUOUS LIQUORS.—A covenant not to use premises "as an Inn, Public-house, or Tap-room, or *for the sale* of Spirituous Liquors or ale or beer," is broken if such Liquors, &c., are sold in any form or manner,—*e.g.*, in bottles (*Fielden*, or *Feilden* v. *Slater*, 38 L. J. Ch. 379; L. R. 7 Eq. 523; 20 L. T. 112; 17 W. R. 485: *Cp. Jones* v. *Bone*, cited RETAIL).

A covenant in the Lease of a tied Public-house that the Lessee shall purchase his beverages from the Lessor, implies, as a condition, that the Lessor shall be willing to supply the same of a good marketable kind (*Luker* v. *Dennis*, 7 Ch. D. 227; 47 L. J. Ch. 174: *Vf. Doe* d. *Calvert* v. *Reid*, 10 B. & C. 849). Such a covenant, if made with the Lessor "and his Assigns," will RUN WITH THE LAND (*Clegg* v. *Hands*, W. N. (90) 59; 34 S. J. 316; 6 Times Rep. 233).

SPOIL.—"Without impeachment of waste, *except Spoil or Destruction*;"—as to the force of this exception, *V.* per Romilly, M. R., *Vincent* v. *Spicer*, 25 L. J. Ch. 591; 22 Bea. 380.

V. WILFUL AND MALICIOUS.

SPONTE.—*V.* WILLINGLY.

SPORTING.—*V.* HUNTING.

SQUARE.—S. 5, 27 G. 3, c. 28, imposed a Duty on all Cast-plate glass which was to be "*squared* into plates of a superficies not less than 1485 inches;" whereon Eyre, C. B. (*A.-G.* v. *Cast-Plate Glass Co.*, 1 Anstr. 44) said,—"I have no doubt in saying, that the legislature used the word 'Square' not in the strict, but in the common acceptation, confining it to rectangular, but not to equilateral figures." *Cp.* SQUARE MILE.

SQUARE BALE.—*V.* Bale.

SQUARE MILE.—The Land Act Amendment Act, 1875, of New South Wales, 39 V. No. 13, s. 31, provides that the holder of Crown lands under lease for pastoral purposes, may, in virtue of intended improvements, apply for the right of pre-emption of such land, "provided that no such application to purchase as aforesaid shall be made for more than one Square Mile within each block of 5 Miles Square out of each lease, or a proportionate quantity out of any holding of less area:" held, that "Square Mile" and "Miles Square" meant areas of those dimensions, and not land geometrically square (*Robertson* v. *Day*, 49 L. J. P. C. 9; 5 App. Ca. 63). *Cp.* Square.

STAB.—*V.* Wound.

STABLESTAND.—"'Stablestand' is a terme of the Forest lawes, and it is when one is found standing in the Forest with his bow bent ready to shoot at any Deere, or with his Greyhounds in a lease ready to slip" (Termes de la Ley, citing Manwood, 133 b).

STACK.—Stack of Hay; *V.* Cock of Hay.

A quantity of Straw packed on a lory, in course of transmission to market, and left for the night in the yard of an Inn, is not a "Stack *of Straw*" within "Stack of corn, grain, pulse, tares, hay, *straw*, haulm, stubble," s. 17, 24 & 25 V. c. 97 (*R.* v. *Satchwell*, 42 L. J. M. C. 63; L. R. 2 C. C. R. 21).

STADIUM.—"By the grant of *Stadium*, *Ferlingus*, or *Quarentena terræ*, doth pass a furlong or furrow long, which anciently was the 8th part of a mile" (Touch. 96; *Va.* Co. Litt. 5 b). "And *de ferlingis et quarentenis* you shall read divers times in the book of Domesday" (Co. Litt. 5 b).

STAGE.—*V.* Entertainment.

STAGE PLAY.—A Duologue is a "Stage Play," within 6 & 7 V. c. 68, s. 23 (*Thorne* v. *Colson*, 25 J. P. 101).

"Entertainment of the Stage:" *V.* Entertainment.

STAGE WAGGON.—By a Local Turnpike Act (4 G. 4, c. xxx), persons who had paid any toll for the passing of any horse and carriage through a toll-gate, were exempt from paying toll again that day, but it was provided that the tolls payable in respect of horses drawing any "Stage-Coach, Diligence, Van, Caravan, *Stage-Waggon* or other Stage-Carriage" should pay on re-passing; held, that "Stage-Waggon" signified a Waggon that went and returned regularly from a fixed place to some other fixed place, at certain definite times (*R.* v. *Ruscoe*, 7 L. J. M. C. 94; 8 A. & E. 386; 3 N. & P. 428).

STAGNUM.—*V.* Pool : Gurges.

STALL.—The continuous occupation of a portion of a Market by an erection placed there for the purpose of selling goods, is a "Stall" for which Stallage is payable although the soil be not interfered with; therefore, a wooden or wicker basket (called in Norfolk, a "Ped"), having a lid which turns back, and which, when supported by a stool or pieces of wood not fixed in the soil, forms a table upon which goods are exposed for sale, is a "Stall" (*Great Yarmouth* v. *Groom*, 32 L. J. Ex. 74 ; 1 H. & C. 102 ; 7 L. T. 161). *Vf. Casswell* v. *Cook*, 31 L. J. M. C. 185 ; 11 C. B. N. S. 637.

STALLAGE AND PICKAGE.—"Stallage is the right of putting up a stall in a fair or market, and also the money paid to the owner of the soil for so doing ; Pickage is the right of picking up the soil for that purpose, and the money paid to the owner of the soil for so doing" (Elph. 620, citing Spelm. *Stallagium* : *R.* v. *Maydenhead*, Palm. 76 ; 2 Rol. Rep. 155. *Vh. Yarmouth* v. *Groom*, 1 H. & C. 102 ; 32 L. J. Ex. 74 ; 8 Jur. N. S. 677 ; 7 L. T. 161).

"'Stallage,' that is to be quit of a certaine custome exacted for the street taken or assigned in Faires and Markets." "'Piccage,' is the payment of money, or the money payd for the breaking of the ground to set up boothes and standings in Faires" (Termes de la Ley).

STANDING.—"Standing in my name," marks a Bequest as specific (*Gordon* v. *Duff*, 3 D. G. F. & J. 662).

Machinery, &c. "standing" on premises ; *V.* Erected.

STANLAWE.—*V.* Law or Lawe.

STATEMENT OF AFFAIRS.—The Statement required to be made and signed by a liquidating or compounding Debtor under the Bankruptcy Act, 1869, meant a full, complete and detailed disclosure, not only of the affairs of his own business, but also and to the same extent of any other (even solvent) business in which he may have been a partner (*Ex p. Amor*, 52 L. J. Ch. 138 ; 21 Ch. D. 594 : 31 W. R. 282 ; 48 L. T. 16).

STATION.—*V.* Railway Station.

STATION TO STATION.—An ordinary contract (and though not as common carriers) to carry from "Station to Station," involves an obligation to unload and deliver at the receiving station, or at least to provide proper appliances for that purpose (per Hawkins, J., *Royal National Life-boat Inst.* v. *Lond. & N. W. Ry.*, 3 Times Rep. 601).

STATIONARY.—To be "stationary," within Article 9 of the Regulations of 1863 for Preventing Collisions at Sea, a Fishing Vessel must not have more way on than is necessary to keep herself under command whilst attached to her nets. If it is necessary, even for the purpose of rendering her fishing more effective, that she should have more way on, she is not "stationary," and must carry the lights of a vessel under way (*The Dunelm*, 53 L. J. P. D. & A. 81 ; 9 P. D. 164).

V. Fixed Engine.

STATUARY.—*V. Sutton* v. *Ciceri*, 16 Sess. Ca., 4th Series, 814; W. N. (90) 67.

STATUTORY DECLARATION.—*V.* Declaration.

STAUNCH.—*V.* Tight.

STAY AND TRADE.—A Policy which covers a Ship during "her Stay and Trade," at a place, means during her stay there for the purposes of trade ; and a stay for a purpose unconnected with trade is a deviation (*African Merchants* v. *British & Foreign Mar. Insrce.*, 42 L. J. Ex. 60 ; L. R. 8 Ex. 154).

STEAMSHIP : STEAMER.—In a Bill of Lading, a Steamship or Steamer means a Ship in which the principal motive-power during the voyage is steam. "I am very far from saying that where it is convenient, as it often is, for a steam vessel to use sailing power instead of steam power when the wind happens to be favourable, it is necessary that the vessel should be at all times and under all circumstances propelled by steam ; but the meaning of a vessel being a steam-ship is that the principal motive-power used shall be the power of steam, and not sails" (per Cockburn, C. J., *Fraser* v. *Telegraph Construction Co.*, L. R. 7 Q. B. 568 ; 41 L. J. Q. B. 250).

"Shipment by Steamer ;" *V.* Shipment.

STEP.—*V.* Fresh Step.

STEP-DAUGHTER.—A bequest of residue to testator's "Step-daughter," held, valid in favour of a daughter by his supposed wife, though such woman had a husband living at the time of the marriage ceremony between her and the testator and which husband was living at testator's death (*Wilkinson* v. *Joughin*, 35 L. J. Ch. 684 ; L. R. 2 Eq. 319).

STETHE OR STEDE.—"*Stethe* or *Stede* betokeneth properly a banke of a river, and many times a place, as *stowe* doth" (Co. Litt. 4 b).

STEWARD.—Steward "is a word of many significations," but in s. 78, Litt., "it signifieth an officer of justice, viz., a Keeper of Courts, &c." (Co. Litt. 61 a, b ; *wh. Vf.*).

STICHE.—A Selion (Elph. 621, citing Spelm. *Selio*).

STIPEND.—A Bequest of "£100 for Masses for the repose of my soul at the Stipend of 5*s*. each ;" held, in Ireland, as meaning "at the Price" of, &c., and as not involving any attempt to create a perpetuity (*Phelan* v. *Slattery*, 19 L. R. Ir. 177).

STIPULATED.—A Bill of Sale payable on demand, provides no "*stipulated* time of payment" within the meaning of the Form prescribed by the schedule to the Bills of Sale Act, 1882 (per Brett, M. R., and Fry, L. J., *Melville* v. *Stringer*, 53 L. J. Q. B. 482 ; 13 Q. B. D. 392 ; 50 L. T. 774 ; 32 W. R. 890).

As to a Condition of Sale that expenses of re-sale, &c., shall be recoverable as "Stipulated Damages,"—"Opinions have differed whether the party should only be allowed to recover what damage he had really sustained (*Randal* v. *Everest*, Moo. & M. 41 : *V. Boys* v. *Ancell*, 5 Bing. N. C. 390), or the stipulated sum (*Crisdee* v. *Bolton*, 3 C. & P. 240). But such a Condition does not preclude the seller from maintaining an action for general damages, where the purchaser breaks off from the contract altogether. It applies in case of a breach of any of the particular Conditions (*Icely* v. *Grew*, 6 N. & M. 467)." Sug. V. & P. 39, 40.

STIRPES.—*V.* Per Stirpes.

STOCK.—"The term 'Stock' or 'Capital Stock' which is used in ss. 61–64, Comp. Cl. Con. Act, 1845 (8 V. c. 16), obviously is derived from the consideration that these were what were called joint stock companies, and that 'stock' was the short name for 'joint stock;' and 'joint stock' in my opinion is only another name for 'shares,' because the owner of part of the capital of a Company is an owner of a part of the joint stock or an owner of a share of the joint stock. The use of the term 'Stock,' appears to me merely to denote that the Company have recognized the fact of the complete payment of the shares, and that the time has come when those shares may be assigned in fragments, which for obvious reasons could not be permitted before ; but that stock shall still be, *e.g.* the qualification of directors, who must possess twenty shares or whatever the number may be, and that the meetings shall be of the persons entitled to this stock, who shall meet as shareholders and vote as shareholders in the proportion of shares which would entitle them to vote before the consolidation into stock. It appears to me that the doubt which has arisen as to the identity of stock and shares has sprung from this circumstance, that it has been supposed, without sufficient attention having been paid to these provisions, that stock in a railway had some sort of analogy to stock in the public funds. It has none whatever. It is possible that *Debenture Stock* in a Railway Company may be said to have some analogy to stock in the public funds ; but the joint stock capital of a Company is a perfectly different thing from stock in the public funds. In my opinion, when, in that state of things, a man has an interest in a railway, and is an owner of stock in a railway, he is said to be a Shareholder in the Company, and would call himself a shareholder in the Company" (per Cairns, L. C., *Morrice* v. *Aylmer*, 44

L. J. Ch. 214 ; 10 Ch. 148 ; affd. 45 L. J. Ch. 614 ; L. R. 7 H. L. 717). It was accordingly held in that case, that a bequest of "Shares" in a Railway carried testator's Stock in that railway.

"Government or other Stock," s. 201, Bankry. Act, 1849, held to include Railway Shares (*Ex p. Copeland*, 22 L. J. Bank. 17 ; 2 D. G. M. & G. 914).

As to effect of converting Shares in a Joint Stock Co. into Stock ; *V.* s. 29, Companies Act, 1862.

V. LIVE AND DEAD STOCK.

A Devise to A. and his "Stock," passed the fee simple (*Counden* v. *Clerke*, Hob. 33).

As to a bequest of "Stock ;" *V. Collison* v. *Curling*, 9 Cl. & F. 88 : *Kirby* v. *Potter*, 4 Ves. 750 : *Measure* v. *Carleton*, 30 Bea. 538 : *Grant* v. *Mussett*, 8 W. R. 330 ; 2 L. T. 133 : STOCKS.

"All my Stock standing in my name *in various Companies*, together with all Bonds, &c. ;" *V. Re Parrott*, 53 L. T. 12 ; W. N. (85) 127.

"Stock," under the Trustee Acts "includes Shares in Ships ; *V.* 18 & 19 V. c. 91, s. 10 ; and Shares in a Joint Stock Bank (*Re Angelo*, 5 D. G. & S. 278)." Seton, 516.

"Stock or Funds of a Foreign Government ;" *V.* FOREIGN GOVERNMENT.

STOCK IN THE FUNDS.—*V.* FUNDS.

STOCK-IN-TRADE.—It is submitted that this phrase comprises all such chattels as are acquired for the purpose of being sold or let to hire in a person's trade. Setting aside a mere dictum in *Elliott* v. *Elliott* (9 M. & W. 23 ; 11 L. J. Ex. 3), the only authority on the interpretation of this phrase, standing alone, seems *Re Richardson* (50 L. J. Ch. 488 ; 44 L. T. 404). In that case the testator was a barge-builder, and, according to the custom of that trade, he would sometimes, on the sale of a new barge, accept an old one in part payment which he would repair and let out on hire ; at the time of his death, he had 5 of such barges :—held, that these barges passed under a bequest of his "Stock-in-Trade as a barge-builder."

On a dissolution of a partnership, "the Stock-in-Trade, Property and Effects of the business" had to be valued and a proportion thereof paid for to the retiring partner ;—held, that Goodwill was not to be included as within the phrase (*Chapman* v. *Hayman*, 1 Times Rep. 397).

STOCK ON FARM.—Is synonymous with FARMING STOCK.

STOCKS.—"According to the Stocks ;" *V.* PER STIRPES.

"Stocks, Shares or Securities of any Company *paying a dividend*,"—as to what investments are authorized under these words ; *V. Consterdine* v. *Consterdine*, 31 Bea. 330 ; 31 L. J. Ch. 807.

STONE.—Blocks cut with wedges from a quarry, and then reduced to certain dimensions and squared to be used as sleepers, are (in an Act imposing Toll) "Stone," as distinguished from "Merchandize" (*Fisher* v. *Lee*, 12 A. & E. 622 ; 10 L. J. Q. B. 1) ; but Coprolites are "Goods, Wares or Merchandize," as distinguished from "Stone" (*Dant* v. *Moore*, 9 L. T. 381).

V. Goods, Wares and Merchandize.

STOP.—To "stop up" a Highway, s. 2, 55 G. 3, c. 68, did not include a power to narrow a road (*R.* v. *Milverton*, 6 L. J. M. C. 73 ; 5 A. & E. 841 ; 1 N. & P. 179) : power to widen was given by s. 16, 13 G. 3, c. 78. *Vf.* s. 84, 5 & 6 W. 4, c. 50, authorising a stopping-up "either entirely or reserving a bridle-way or foot-way along the whole or any part or parts thereof."

STORES.—*V.* Tackle.

STOW.—A valley (Co. Litt. 4 b) ; but a few lines further down "Stowe" is said to signify a place.

STOWAGE.—"Improper Stowage ;" *V.* Improper Navigation.

STRANDING.—In a Marine Insurance, "a touch and go" is not a Stranding; "in order to constitute a Stranding, the Ship must be stationary" (per Ellenborough, C. J., *Macdougle* v. *Royal Exch. Assrce.*, 1 Starkie, 130 ; 4 M. & S. 503). "If the ship merely touches or strikes and gets off again, how much soever she may be injured, she is not stranded ; but if she settles and remains for any time, this is a Stranding, without reference to the degree of damage which she sustains (*Harman* v. *Vaux*, 3 Camp. 429). A resting for 15 or 20 minutes has been held to be a Stranding, whether it be upon a bank or a rock (*Baker* v. *Towry*, 1 Starkie, 436). It is not, however, every stationary taking the ground that constitutes a Stranding. Thus, where a vessel takes the ground in the ordinary and usual course of navigation and management in a tidal river or harbour, upon the ebbing of the tide, or from a natural deficiency of water, so that she may float again upon the flow of the tide or increase of the water, this is not a Stranding within the meaning of the Memorandum (*Magnus* v. *Buttemer*, 11 C. B. 876 ; 21 L. J. C. P. 119 : 2 Kent, Com. 323, n. (*c*) : *Va.* jdgmt. *Corcoran* v. *Gurney*, 1 E. & B. 456 ; 22 L. J. Q. B. 113). So, when a vessel took the ground several times in going up a harbour in the ordinary course of navigation from the shallowness of the water, this was held to be no Stranding (*Hearne* v. *Edmunds*, 1 Brod. & B. 388). Similarly where a vessel took the ground in a tidal harbour, where it was intended she should do so at the time she was moored, and was injured by striking against some hard substance, this was considered not to be a Stranding (*Kingsford* v. *Marshall*, 8 Bing. 458 ; 1 L. J. C. P. 135 ; 1 Moore & S. 657). *Vf. Bryant & May* v. *London Assrce.*, 2 Times Rep. 591.

"But it is otherwise where the ground is taken under circumstances of such an accidental and unforeseen character as not to be in the usual course of navigation (*V.* jdgmt. of Ld. Tenterden, *Wells* v. *Hopwood*, 3 B. & Ad. 20 : *Letchford* v. *Oldham*, 5 Q. B. D. 538 ; 49 L. J. Q. B. 458). And where a ship was improperly fastened to a pier in a basin, so that she took the ground, and, when the tide left her, she fell over and was bilged, this was held to be Stranding (*Carruthers* v. *Sydebotham*, 4 M. & S. 77 : *Va. Bishop* v. *Pentland*, 7 B. & C. 219). So, where the water being drawn off from an inland navigation for the purpose of repairing it, a vessel settled accidentally upon some piles which were not previously known to be there (*Rayner* v. *Godmond*, 5 B. & Ald. 225) ; where a vessel, having struck upon an anchor in a harbour, was injured and in danger of sinking, and was thereupon hauled higher up the harbour and drawn upon the ground, where she remained for some time (*Barrow* v. *Bell*, 4 B. & C. 736) ; where a ship under stress of weather made a tidal harbour, but it being low water she grounded there (*Corcoran* v. *Gurney*, sup.) ; and where a ship was run aground for the purpose of preventing further mischief (*De Mattos* v. *Saunders*, L. R. 7 C. P. 570) ; these were all held to be cases of Stranding." 1 Maude & P. 496.

V. Sink.

STRANGERS IN BLOOD.—Persons who have the legal *status* of "Children" by virtue of a foreign law, applicable to their case, are not "Strangers in Blood," but are "Children" for the purpose of assessment to Legacy Duty (*Skottowe* v. *Young*, 40 L. J. Ch. 366 ; L. R. 11 Eq. 474 : and *V. Re Goodman*, 50 L. J. Ch. 425 ; 17 Ch. D. 266 : *Re Grove*, 40 Ch. D. 216). But where by the foreign law children, illegitimate by the law of England, are not admitted to the full status of lawful children but are merely recognized as entitled to the rights of natural children, such persons are not "Lineal Issue" but are "Strangers in Blood" (*Re Atkinson*, 51 L. J. Ch. 452 ; 21 Ch. D. 100). In that case the point was raised in argument but not referred to in the judgment, as to whether children illegitimate by the law of England, can, under any circumstances, be other than "Strangers in Blood" for the purpose of succession to *Real* estate in England.

STRAY.—*V.* Estray.

STREAM.—"Stream" is used as synonymous with "River" in s. 27, Salmon Fishery Act, 1861, 24 & 25 V. c. 109 (*Rolle* v. *Whyte*, L. R. 3 Q. B. 305 ; 37 L. J. Q. B. 118 ; 8 B. & S. 116).

"Stream," s. 97, 14 G. 3, c. 96, only applies to Artificial Streams (*Smith* v. *Barnham*, 1 Ex. D. 419, cited Watercourse).

"Streams ;" *V. Caldwell* v. *McLaren*, 53 L. J. P. C. 33 ; 9 App. Ca. 392.

"Owners and Occupiers" of a Stream, s. 6, 10 V. c. 17, are the Owners and Occupiers of that portion of it with which a Water Co. may be interfering (*Bush* v. *Trowbridge Water Co.*, cited Take, *wh. Va.* as to "Take or Use" a Stream).

STREET.—The primary meaning of "Street" is a public (or private, *St. Mary, Islington* v. *Barrett,* 43 L. J. M. C. 85 ; L. R. 9 Q. B. 278 : *Midland Ry.* v. *Watton,* 55 L. J. M. C. 99 ; 17 Q. B. D. 30 ; 54 L. T. 482 ; 34 W. R. 524 ; 50 J. P. 405 ; nom. *Midland Ry.* v. *West Ham,* 2 Times Rep. 589) road-way (including its foot-paths, if any) running in front of houses, or buildings, of a sufficient length, and in such a continuous line as to give the road-way the character of a "Street ;" and such a road-way is more emphatically a "Street" if it has a continuous line of houses on *each* side of it. The houses need not be actually contiguous, but must be so near to each other as to form a continuous line. (*Note:*—In *Robinson* v. *Barton,* 53 L. J. Ch. 231 ; 8 App. Ca. 798, Lord Blackburn is reported to have said that the popular and ordinary sense of the word "Street" is,—a highway *with houses on each side.* It is submitted that the legal and ordinary sense of the word "Street," does not require that there should be houses on each side of the roadway ; nor that such roadway should necessarily be a highway. Thus in *Portsmouth* v. *Smith,* 53 L. J. Q. B. 95 ; 13 Q. B. D. 184, Brett, M. R., said,—"The word 'Street,' when popularly used, means *a thoroughfare,* bounded *either on one or both sides* by houses ;" and *V.* obs. of Ld. Blackburn in the same case, on its appeal to House of Lords, 54 L. J. Q. B. 475 ; 10 App. Ca. 364 : *Va. Jowett* v. *Idle,* 36 W. R. 138, 530 ; 4 Times Rep. 101, 442).

Assuming that houses exist in such number and position as to impart the character of "street" to the locality, then the natural and *primâ facie* sense of the word "Street" is the *Roadway* (per Selborne, L. C., *Robinson* v. *Barton,* 53 L. J. Ch. 230). So Jessel, M. R., in *Taylor* v. *Oldham* (46 L. J. Ch. 109 ; 35 L. T. 699 ; 4 Ch. D. 408) said,—

"The definition of a 'Street' is correctly laid down in the Imperial Dictionary :—'The street itself is no doubt, properly, *the paved or prepared road* ; that is the street. It sometimes includes the houses along each side of it. But that is not its proper meaning. It is called a street even without houses. There are some streets with no houses. But the usual common meaning of the word *Street* is,—a road with houses on one or both sides of it.'"

It may be doubted whether, in any sense that would (except under an interpretation clause, or except where a roadway,—*e.g.* a bridge—is a mere connecting link in a street, *Beaver* v. *Manchester,* 26 L. J. Q. B. 311) be recognized by the Courts, a roadway would be held a "Street," without houses or buildings (*V.* in addition to the cases before cited, *R.* v. *Platts,* 49 L. J. Q. B. 848 : *McIntosh* v. *Romford,* 5 Times Rep. 643) ; but the definition from the Imperial Dictionary, having received the approval of so high an authority as that of the late Master of the Rolls, is cited for the purpose of supporting the proposition, that it is the *roadway* which is the "Street," in the primary acceptation of that word (*Va. Lond., Chatham and Dover Ry.* v. *London,* 19 L. T. 250).

But when we have arrived at that conclusion we have, for practical purposes, to acknowledge that "Street" is a most flexible and ambiguous word depending on its context.

"In s. 149, P. H. Act, 1875, and the sections which follow it—(down to and including the 155th ?)—the word 'Street' manifestly has the same sense as when we speak of a man going out of his house into the street;" —*i.e.* its primary meaning of the roadway (per Selborne, L. C., *Robinson* v. *Barton*, 53 L. J. Ch. 229 ; 8 App. Ca. 798. *Va. Mid. Ry.* v. *Watton*, sup.: *Richards* v. *Kessick*, 57 L. J. M. C. 48 ; 59 L. T. 318 ; 52 J. P. 756 : *Coverdale* v. *Charlton*, 48 L. J. Q. B. 128 ; 4 Q. B. D. 104 ; 40 L. T. 88 ; 43 J. P. 268 : *R.* v. *Fullford*, inf. ; *V.* VEST, as to what extent the soil under, and air over, "Streets," vest in local authorities).

But s. 157, P. H. Act, 1875, whilst manifestly comprising the roadways of "streets," also includes the power of making Bye Laws for regulating "the buildings erected or to be erected on each side of them—the whole construction—every part of those buildings external and internal" (per Selborne, L. C., *Robinson* v. *Barton*, sup. : *Baker* v. *Portsmouth*, 47 L. J. Ex. 223 ; 3 Ex. D. 157. *V. Robinson* v. *Barton*, as to what particularity is required in the Bye Laws to justify a Local Authority to compel removal of disapproved buildings ; *V.* NEW STREET). So where the City of London was empowered to take land for the purpose of forming a new "Street" to the Metropolitan Meat Market, it was held that that meant not merely land for the roadway but enough for houses on both its sides (*Galloway* v. *London*, 35 L. J. Ch. 477 ; L. R. 1 H. L. 34 : *Vf. London, Chatham and Dover Ry.* v. *London*, 19 L. T. 250).

The word "Street" may, of course, by an interpretation clause, be made to mean anything, whether in association with houses or not. And for the purposes of the P. H. Act, 1875, it "includes any highway (not being a turnpike road) and any public bridge (not being a county bridge) and any road, lane, footway, square, court, alley, or passage, whether a thoroughfare or not" (s. 4 ; *Vth. Nutter* v. *Accrington*, 48 L. J. Q. B. 487 ; 4 Q. B. D. 375). And a similar definition (though a little larger, as embracing "any mews and a part thereof") is provided for the purposes of the Metropolitan Local Management Acts (18 & 19 V. c. 120, s. 250 ; 25 & 26 V. c. 102, s. 112). "Street" in s. 53 of the latter act includes new, as well as old streets (*St. John, Hampstead* v. *Cotton*, 55 L. J. Q. B. 213 ; 56 Ib. 225 ; 12 App. Ca. 1 ; 56 L. T. 1 ; 35 W. R. 505 ; 51 J. P. 340, following *Sheffield* v. *Fulham*, 1 Ex. D. 395, and dissenting from *Sawyer* v. *Paddington*, 40 L. J. M. C. 8). As to s. 78, 18 & 19 V. c. 120, *V. St. John, Hampstead* v. *Hoopel*, 54 L. J. M. C. 147 ; 15 Q. B. D. 652 ; 1 Times Rep. 584.

Va. definition in s. 3, Waterworks Clauses Act, 1847, 10 V. c. 17.

These statutory definitions do not exclude the ordinary sense of the word "Street" (per Quain, J., *St. Mary, Islington* v. *Barrett*, 43 L. J. M. C. 87 ; L. R. 9 Q. B. 283,—citing *Pound* v. *Plumstead*, 41 L. J. M. C. 51 ;

L. R. 7 Q. B. 183) ; they simply enlarge the meaning of "Street" so as to make that word, *quà* the respective statutes, embrace ways which would not otherwise come within it. A way being ascertained to be a "Street," by means of the interpretation clause, the question then remains as to whether more than the roadway is included ; and *that*, as before explained, will depend on the context to the word in the clause that has to be construed.

It may be added that the object of the interpretation clauses being to *enlarge* the meaning, a Turnpike Road, or any part of it (notwithstanding the exception in the interpretation), will be a "Street," for the purposes of the Acts cited, if in fact it is a street within the ordinary meaning of that word (*R.* v. *Fullford*, sup. : *Thomas* v. *Roberts*, 43 J. P. 574).

Section 3 of the Town Police Clauses Act, 1847 (10 & 11 V. c. 89), (the provisions of which Act, so far as they relate to "obstructions and nuisances in the streets," have been incorporated into the P. H. Act, 1875), declares that "Street" "shall extend to and include any road, square, court, alley and thoroughfare, or public passage within the limits of the Special Act ;" but to be within those words the road, &c. must be of a public, or quasi public character. Therefore an approach to a railway station which is the private property of the Company but only separated from the public highway by a gutter, is not such a "Street" (*Curtis* v. *Embrey*, 42 L. J. M. C. 39 ; L. R. 7 Ex. 369 ; 21 W. R. 143) ; but an open square (in front of, and let with, an hotel), over which for many years the public had freely passed except when the hotel keeper's carriages stood there, was held to be part of the street (*Marks* v. *Ford*, 45 J. P. 157 : *Vf. Foinett* v. *Clark*, 41 J. P. 359).

So where a private Act used the phrase "Street *or Road*," "Street" was held to be deprived of its larger interpretation by being so associated with "Road" (*Bristol W. Works Co.* v. *Bristol*, 5 Times Rep. 203).

Land on the sea-shore between two villages over which the inhabitants of those villages passed at high-tide but by no defined track ; held, not to be a "Street," "Highway" or "Public Place," within s. 3, Gasworks Cl. Act, 1847, 10 V. c. 15 (*Maddock* v. *Wallasey*, 55 L. J. Q. B. 267).

It has been held that whether any given roadway is a "Street" is a question of fact for the jury or the justices (*R.* v. *Fullford*, 33 L. J. M. C. 122 ; 10 L. T. 346 ; 10 Jur. N. S. 522 : *R.* v. *Dayman*, 26 L. J. M. C. 128 : *Maude* v. *Baildon*, 10 Q. B. D. 394). But in *Portsmouth* v. *Smith* (53 L. J. Q. B. 95 ; 13 Q. B. D. 196), Brett, M. R., said, "I am unable to agree with the jdgmt. in *Maude* v. *Baildon*, and think that the Court there was under a misapprehension as to what was decided in *R.* v. *Dayman*" (*V. Portsmouth* v. *Smith*, on app. to H. L., 10 App. Ca. 364 ; 54 L. J. Q. B. 473). The justices, when called on to make an order under s. 150, P. H. Act, 1875, have jurisdiction to enquire whether the place is a "Street" (*Eccles* v. *Wirral*, 55 L. J. M. C. 106 ; 17 Q. B. D. 107 ; 34 W. R. 412 ; 50 J. P. 596).

V. New Street : Highway : Turnpike Road.

For a quaint use of "Street;" *V.* Termes de la Ley, *Stallage*, cited Stallage and Pickage.

STREET OR PLACE.—"Street or Place" in s. 35, Hackney Carriage Act (Metropolitan), 1 & 2 W. 4, c. 22, means a Public Street or Place (*Case* v. *Storey*, L. R. 4 Ex. 319; 38 L. J. M. C. 113). *V.* Ply.

STRICT ENTAIL.—"Where lands are directed to be settled on A. and his heirs 'in Strict Entail,' there seems little doubt that A. ought to be made tenant for life only" (2 Jarm. 354, citing *Graves* v. *Hicks*, 11 Sim. 536; 5 L. J. K. B. 142; 5 A. & E. 38: *Woolmore* v. *Burrows*, 1 Sim. 526); and, as it should seem, "with remainder to his first and other sons successively in tail general, with remainder to his daughters as tenants in common in tail general, &c." (Lewin, 120, citing *Sealey* v. *Stawell*, I. R. 9 Eq. 499).

V. Strict Settlement: Closely entailed.

STRICT SETTLEMENT.—As to what limitations would be inserted in the execution of a direction for a "Strict Settlement;" *V.* 2 Jarm. 344, 345, n. *e*, 354, 355. And *V.* Ib. 577 as to annexing personalty to realty in strict settlement.

In the common form of a Settlement pursuant to a direction for a "Strict Settlement," the tenant for life would be made unimpeachable for Waste (per Wood, V.-C., *Davenport* v. *Davenport*, 33 L. J. Ch. 36; 1 H. & M. 779: *Sv.* Lewin, 507, 508); "but where the executory trust *in terms* gives the first taker a life estate, he is not made dispunishable for Waste" (2 Jarm. 345, n. *e*, citing *Davenport* v. *Davenport*, sup.: *Stanley* v. *Coulthurst*, L. R. 10 Eq. 259; 39 L. J. Ch. 650).

V. Strict Entail.

STRICTLY TEMPERATE.—*V. Thomson* v. *Weems*, 9 App. Ca. 671.

V. Sober and Temperate Habits.

STRIKE.—An excuse for delay in fulfilling a contract on the ground of a "Strike" by workmen, means a Strike against the employer; not a mere refusal to work because an infectious disease is prevalent, or the weather is hot or wet, or such like excuse (*Stephens* v. *Harris*, 57 L. J. Q. B. 203; 3 Times Rep. 720).

STRONG.—*V.* Tight.

STRUCTURE.—*V.* Building.

STUFF.—*V.* Household.

SUBJECT AS AFORESAID.—*V. R.* v. *Local Gov. Bd.*, 54 L. J. Q. B. 104; 15 Q. B. D. 70.

SUBJECT TO.—There is a marked distinction between a testamentary gift "*for*," and one "subject to," a particular purpose. If the particular purpose fail, then, if the gift be "for" that purpose, there will be a resulting Trust for the heir or, *semble* (in case of personalty), a lapse into the residue: *secus*, if the gift be "subject to" the purpose (per Eldon, L. C., *King* v. *Denison*, 1 V. & B. 272: *Vh.* Lewin, 154, 155, and cases there cited. But "for" has been read "charged with," *Abrams* v. *Winshup*, 3 Russ. 350. *Vh.* 1 Jarm. 566, 569).

"Where *lands* are devised to trustees 'subject to,' or 'charged with,' the payment of a yearly sum of money, a legal Rent-Charge is, it seems, created (*Buttery* v. *Robinson*, 3 Bing. 392; 4 L. J. O. S. C. P. 108: *Ramsay* v. *Thorngate*, 16 Sim. 575; 18 L. J. Ch. 238). But where real and personal property together are so given, it is a personal annuity (*Taylor* v. *Martindale*, 12 Sim. 158; 10 L. J. Ch. 339: *Parsons* v. *Parsons*, L. R. 8 Eq. 260), unlike rent reserved on a demise of realty and chattels, which issues out of the land alone (*Farewell* v. *Dickinson*, 6 B. & C. 251; 9 D. & R. 245):" 2 Jarm. 306, n. (*f*).

In an *Assignment of a Lease*, "Subject to" its rent and covenants, no covenant is implied by the assignee to indemnify the assignor against the rent and covenants; the words "subject to," in that connection, being words of qualification and not of contract (*Wolveridge* v. *Steward*, 3 L. J. Ex. 360; 1 Cr. & M. 644; 3 Moore & S. 561; and *V.* that case cited Woodf. 262, 263; Elph. 420; and *Vth. Moule* v. *Garrett*, L. R. 5 Ex. 132).

"Where a *Proposal or Tender* is accepted 'Subject to' the terms of a Contract being arranged and drawn up for signature, there is no concluded bargain until the terms have been arranged and a written contract executed. But an acceptance enclosing a more formal memorandum for signature is sufficient, if the memorandum contains no new terms" (Add. C. 15, and cases there cited; Woodf. 104, 105: *Va. Wilcox* v. *Redhead*, 49 L. J. Ch. 539: *May* v. *Thompson*, 51 L. J. Ch. 917; 20 Ch. D. 705: *Wood* v. *Silcock*, 32 W. R. 845).

So a written memorandum for sale and purchase of land, "Subject to a formal contract being prepared and signed by both parties as approved by their Solicitors," needs the stipulated formal contract to give it effect (*Hawkesworth* v. *Chaffey*, 55 L. J. Ch. 335; 54 L. T. 72, following *Winn* v. *Bull*, 47 L. J. Ch. 139; 7 Ch. D. 29: *Va. Harman* v. *Homer*, 32 S. J. 752: *Harvey* v. *Barnard's Inn*, 50 L. J. Ch. 750.—*Sv. Rossiter* v. *Miller*, 3 App. Ca. 1124; 48 L. J. Ch. 10: *Skinner* v. *McDouall*, 17 L. J. Ch. 347; 2 D. G. & S. 265: *Lewis* v. *Brass*, 3 Q. B. D. 667; 26 W. R. 152: *Bonnewell* v. *Jenkins*, 8 Ch. D. 70; 47 L. J. Ch. 758). And where property is sold, "Subject to approval of Title," the contract (in the absence of *mala fides*) cannot be enforced until that approval is given (*Hussey* v. *Horne-Payne*, 4 App. Ca. 311; 48 L. J. Ch. 846; 41 L. T. 1; 27 W. R. 585: *Vth.*, and as to when a contract is completed by a correspondence, per Jessel, M. R., *Williams* v. *Brisco*, 22 Ch. D. 448: per Kekewich, J., *Wylson* v. *Dunn*,

34 Ch. D. 576 : *Bolton* v. *Lambert*, 41 Ch. D. 295 ; 37 W. R. 434 : *Bristol Aerated Bread Co.* v. *Maggs*, W. N. (90) 60 ; 34 S. J. 318 ; 6 Times Rep. 227 : Woodf. 246 : Add. C. 15 : *Vf. Clack* v. *Wood*, 9 Q. B. D. 276).

"Subject to Insurance;" *V.* FREIGHT IN ADVANCE SUBJECT TO INSURANCE.

"Subject to the Laws and Statutes now in force," 1 Jac. 2, c. 22 ; *V. R.* v. *St. James, Westminster*, 5 A. & E. 391.

"Subject to the Provisions of this Act," s. 19, Jud. Act, 1873 ; *V. Ormerod* v. *Todmorden*, 51 L. J. Q. B. 348 ; 8 Q. B. D. 664 ; 30 W. R. 808.

SUBJECT TO A RESERVED BIDDING. — *V.* RESERVED BIDDING.

SUBMISSION.—"Agreement or Submission to Arbitration *by consent*," s. 17, Com. L. Pro. Act, 1854 ; *Vh. Wadsworth* v. *Smith*, 40 L. J. Q. B. 118 ; L. R. 6 Q. B. 332 : INSTRUMENT IN WRITING. A Submission under s. 25, Lands C. C. Act, 1845, is not within the phrase (*Re Harper and G. E. Ry.*, L. R. 20 Eq. 39, explaining *Ex p. Harper*, L. R. 18 Eq. 539).

SUBMITTED TO.—*V.* ACQUIESCENCE.

SUBORNATION OF PERJURY.—"Subornation of Perjury, is procuring a person to commit a perjury, which he actually commits in consequence of such procurement" (Steph. Cr. 95). *V.* PERJURY.

Vf. Arch. Cr. 940, 942 ; Rosc. Cr. 864.

SUBSCRIBE.—"'Subscribe,' means to write under something," in accordance with prescribed regulations where any such exist (per Brett, M. R., *A.-G.* v. *Bradlaugh*, 54 L. J. Q. B. 213 ; 14 Q. B. D. 667). But though this is the strict primary meaning of the word, it may sometimes be construed as, "to give assent to, or to attest" (*Roberts* v. *Phillips*, 24 L. J. Q. B. 171 ; 4 E. & B. 450).

A statement in a Prospectus of a Company, that share capital has been "subscribed," is not satisfied by the fact that fully paid-up shares have been allotted in payment for property or services (*Arnison* v. *Smith*, 5 Times Rep. 413).

"Subscribe" to an Undertaking, s. 8, Comp. C. C. Act, 1845 ; *V. Burke* v. *Lechmere*, L. R. 6 Q. B. 297 ; 40 L. J. Q. B. 98.

"Subscriber ;" *V. Ex p. Cookney*, 28 L. J. Ch. 12 ; 3 D. G. & J. 170 ; 26 Bea. 6.

V. ATTEST.

SUBSCRIPTION OR CONTRIBUTION.—A "Subscription or Contribution" for any plate, prize, or sum of money to be awarded to the winner "of any lawful game, sport, pastime or exercise," is excepted from the operation of the Gaming Act, and is legal and irrevocable (*V.* proviso to s. 18, 8 & 9 V. c. 109). But to be within that proviso the "Subscription or Contribution" must not itself be a Wager; and therefore if each of two or more persons stake money to form a fund for which they are to compete in a lawful game,—*e.g.*, a foot-race,—that is a Wager, and not a "Subscription or Contribution" within the proviso (*Diggle* v. *Higgs*, 46 L. J. Ex. 721; 2 Ex. D. 422, over-ruling *Batty* v. *Marriott*, 17 L. J. C. P. 215: *Va. Trimble* v. *Hill*, 5 App. Ca. 342).

So if two or more persons play at a lawful game for money, but *do not at the time stake the money*, that is not a "Subscription," but a mere bet upon which no action will lie (*Parsons* v. *Alexander*, 24 L. J. Q. B. 277; 5 E. & B. 263). So the common "Sweep" on a horse-race is not within the above exception, but is a lottery and illegal (*Allport* v. *Nutt*, 14 L. J. C. P. 272; 1 C. B. 989: *Gatty* v. *Field*, 15 L. J. Q. B. 408; 9 Q. B. 431).

SUBSEQUENT.—As to the value of this word in a covenant, in a Marriage Settlement, to settle after-acquired property; *V. Re Garnett*, 55 L. J. Ch. 773; 33 Ch. D. 300; 55 L. T. 562.

SUBSEQUENT ACTION.—A second action commenced after the issue of the Writ but before judgment obtained, in a first action, was held to be a "Subsequent" Action within ss. 2, 5, M. W. P. Act, 1874 (*Fear* v. *Castle*, 51 L. J. Q. B. 279; 8 Q. B. D. 380).

SUBSEQUENT ASSIGNMENT.—"Subsequent" in s. 4, Copyright Act, 1862, 25 & 26 V. c. 68, means subsequent to the first entry; and therefore it is not necessary, under that section, to register the assignment of a copyright to the person who first makes the entry of it (*Troitzsch* v. *Rees*, 3 Times Rep. 773: *Vf. Re Graves*, L. R. 4 Q. B. 715).

SUBSISTING.—Trusts "subsisting and capable of taking effect;" *V. Smyth-Pigott* v. *Smyth-Pigott*, W. N. (84) 149.

SUBSOIL.—"'Subsoil' includes, *primâ facie*, all that is below the actual Surface down to the centre of the earth (*V. Cox* v. *Glue*, 17 L. J. C. P. 162; 5 C. B. 549; 10 L. T. O. S. 374). It is, therefore, a wider term than 'Mines' or 'Quarries,' or even than 'Minerals' (*V. Atkinson* v. *King*, 2 L. R. Ir. 339). And an exception of 'Coals and Coal Mines' will only comprise that portion of the Subsoil which actually consists of Mines of Coal, and will not comprise any intervening or other strata (*V. Ramsay* v. *Blair*, 1 App. Ca. 704)." MacS. 20.

SUBSTANCE.—"What is 'Substance'? It is *every property* a man has. So, in the Stat. 4 & 5 P. & M. c. 8, for the punishment of such as shall take away maidens that be inheritors, the word 'Substance' is made use of, and means *worldly wealth*." "'Substance' includes everything that can be turned into money" (per Mansfield, C. J., *Hogan* v. *Jackson*, 1 Cowp. 307). *V.* WORLDLY ESTATE: WORLDLY GOODS.

A covenant to settle "Fortune or Substance," embraces real estate (*Scully* v. *Scully*, Sugd. Law of Prop. 104). In *Maitland* v. *Adair* (3 Ves. 231 ; cited 1 Jarm. 742), "my Fortune" was, by a context, confined to personalty. *Vf.*, as to "Fortune," *Bacon* v. *Cosby*, 20 L. J. Ch. 213 ; 4 D. G. & S. 261. "Future Fortune ;" *V.* FUTURE.

"Substance" contrasted with "Matter ;" *V.* DESTRUCTIVE.

"Nature, Substance or Quality ;" *V.* NATURE.

V. POINT OF SUBSTANCE.

SUBSTANTIAL.—A *House* was described as "Substantial and Convenient," and having five bed-rooms : held, not a misdescription, although the house was out of repair, and the walls in some places were only half-brick thick, and some of the bed-rooms extremely small inner rooms, and without fireplace. "The description is of a 'Substantial and Convenient Dwelling-house,' a description so relative in its terms as to afford abundant opportunity for a conflict of evidence as to matters which are rather matters of opinion than of fact" (per Stuart, V.-C., *Johnson* v. *Smart*, 2 Giff. 151, 156 ; 2 L. T. 307 ; 6 Jur. N. S. 815).

The Poor Law Statute (43 Eliz. c. 2, s. 1) requires that persons appointed Overseers shall be "Substantial *Householders*." Where, however, a district contained only three houses, two of which were occupied by poor labourers, it was held that the appointment of all the three householders was good (*R.* v. *Stubbs*, 2 T. R. 395). In delivering the jdgmt. of the Court in that case, Ashhurst, J., said: "The word 'Substantial' is a relative term. If there were a great many opulent farmers, there the appointment of a day-labourer might be improper ; but here there were no other persons to serve. They are both householders with some land annexed to their houses, and one of them a proprietor. No better persons can be had than the place affords ; and the want of them is no reason why the poor should not be provided for." *Vh. R.* v. *Spurrell*, L. R. 1 Q. B. 72 ; 35 L. J. M. C. 74.

"Substantial Repair ;" *V.* REPAIR.

SUBSTITUTION.—*V.* ADDITION : LIEU.

SUBSTITUTIONAL GIFTS.—As to construction of ; *V.* 2 Jarm. 771–782.

SUCCEED.—*V. Bagot* v. *Legge*, 34 L. J. Ch. 156.

"If any person shall have *succeeded* to any Trade," &c., No. 4, 3rd set of Rules, Sch. D., s. 100, Income Tax Act, 5 & 6 V. c. 35 ; *V. Ryhope Co.* v. *Foyer*, 7 Q. B. D. 485 ; 45 L. T. 404.

SUCCEEDING.—The phrase "Succeeding *Overseers*," s. 11, 17 G. 2, c. 38, is not confined to Overseers who immediately succeed those who made the Rate ; "succeeding" here, *semble*, means "subsequent" (*East Dean* v. *Everett*, 30 L. J. M. C. 117 ; 3 E. & E. 574).

SUCCESSION.—A devise to A. "and his children *in succession*," gives A. an estate tail (*Tyrone* v. *Waterford*, 29 L. J. Ch. 486; 1 D. G. F. & J. 613).

For the purposes of *Succession Duty*, "Every past or future *Disposition* of property, by reason whereof any person has or shall become beneficially entitled to any property, or the income thereof, upon the death of any person dying after the time appointed for the commencement of this Act (19th May, 1853), either immediately or after any interval, either certainly or contingently, and either originally or by way of substitutive limitation, and every *Devolution by Law* of any beneficial interest in property, or the income thereof, upon the death of any person dying after the time appointed for the commencement of this Act, to any other person in possession or expectancy, shall be deemed to have conferred or to confer on the person entitled by reason of any such Disposition or Devolution a '*Succession*;' and the term '*Successor*' shall denote the person so entitled; and the term '*Predecessor*' shall denote the settlor, disponer, testator, obligor, ancestor, or other person from whom the interest of the Successor is or shall be derived" (s. 2, 16 & 17 V. c. 51). "In framing that Act the word 'Succession' was adopted for the purpose of denoting any property passing upon death from one person to another by virtue of any Gift or Descent; or of any Contract, *not being a bonâ fide contract of purchase or loan*" (per Westbury, L. C., *Floyer* v. *Bankes*, 33 L. J. Ch. 3; 3 D. G. J. & S. 306); and it does not include a conveyance or assignment by way of *bonâ fide* sale (*Fryer* v. *Morland*, 45 L. J. Ch. 817; 3 Ch. D. 675: *Svth. De Rechberg* v. *Beeton*, 38 Ch. D. 192). *Vf. A.-G.* v. *Littledale*, 40 L. J. Ex. 241; L. R. 5 H. L. 290: *A.-G.* v. *Middleton*, 27 L. J. Ex. 229; 3 H. & N. 125: *A.-G.* v. *Sibthorp*, 28 L. J. Ex. 9; 3 H. & N. 424: *A.-G.* v. *Braybrooke*, 9 H. L. Ca. 150; 31 L. J. Ex. 177: Watson, Eq., 1145–1149: Dart, 314–318, 667–669.

V. PREDECESSOR: DERIVE: DISPOSITION.

"*By way of Succession.*" The provision in s. 2 (1), Settled Land Act, 1882, that an instrument limiting or declaring trusts "for any persons By way of Succession" is a Settlement, is adopted from s. 2, Settled Estates Act, 1877, which adopted it from s. 1, 19 & 20 V. c. 120: *Vh. Re Birtle*, 11 W. R. 739; 32 L. J. Ch. 439: *Re Bardin*, 7 W. R. 711; 28 L. J. Ch. 840: *Re Goodwin*, 3 Giff. 620: *Re Horn*, 29 L. T. 830: *Collett* v. *Collett*, L. R. 2 Eq. 203; 35 Bea. 312: *Re Laing*, 35 L. J. Ch. 282; L. R. 1 Eq. 416: *Re Shepheard*, 39 L. J. Ch. 173; L. R. 8 Eq. 571: *Carlyon* v. *Truscott*, L. R. 20 Eq. 348; 44 L. J. Ch. 186: *Re Morgan*, L. R. 9 Eq. 588: *Beioley* v. *Carter*, 38 L. J. Ch. 92, 283; 4 Ch. 230: *Re Morgan*, 49 L. J. Ch. 577: and *V.* most of these cases collected and commented on in Middleton on Settled Estates, 3 ed., 28, 29.

SUCCESSIVELY.—"In many cases devises to several persons *successively*, have been contended to be void on account of the uncertainty respecting the order in which the objects are to take. Where the devise is to several specified individuals in succession, the obvious rule is to hold them to be entitled in the order in which their names occur. If it be to a class of persons, constituted such in virtue of birth,—as to children, sons or brothers,—then priority according to seniority of age may be presumed to be intended. And the circumstance of a condition being imposed on the devisees has been held not to vary the order in which they are successively entitled" (1 Jarm. 374, and *V.* cases there cited).

A devise "to the first son of T. severally and successively in tail male" must be read "to the first, *and every other*, son," as otherwise "severally and successively" would be without meaning (*Parker* v. *Tootal*, 34 L. J. Ex. 198; 11 H. L. Ca. 143: *Vth.* 1 Jarm. 528; 2 Ib. 407).

SUCCESSOR.—*V.* SUCCESSION.

SUCCESSORS.—A Devise to A. "and his Successors," even prior to 1 V. c. 26, passed the fee simple (*Webb* v. *Herring*, 1 Rolle, 399, pl. 25, 8 Vin. Ab. 209, pl. 1; 3 Bulst. 194: *A.-G.* v. *Gilbert*, 10 Bea. 517); so a bequest of personalty to an Earl, "and to his successors, *and to be enjoyed with and go with the title*," is an absolute gift notwithstanding the words italicised (*Re Johnson, Cockerell* v. *Essex*, 53 L. J. Ch. 645; 26 Ch. D. 538; 32 W. R. 634).

But a Grant "to any natural person, to have and to hold to him and his Successors,—by this he hath only an estate for his life" (Touch. 106; *Va.* Co. Litt. 8 b).

In a conveyance of a fee simple to a Corporation the apt words of limitation are "and their Successors;" and in the case of a Corporation Sole, "without these words *Successors*, there passeth no inheritance" (Co. Litt. 8 b; *Vth.* Ib. 94 b; *Va.* FEE SIMPLE).

A Devise to a Minister of Religion "and his successors,"—*e.g.*, "to T. W., Minister of the Roman Catholic Chapel at Kendal, and to his successors for ever,"—is a devise for the benefit of the office held, not of the person named, and is void under the Stat. of Mortmain (*Thornber* v. *Wilson*, 24 L. J. Ch. 667; 3 Drew. 245).

SUCCESSORS IN BUSINESS.—Neither partner of a dissolved firm is the "Successor" in business of such firm, when each partner goes his own way and carries on business for himself (*Eaton* v. *Western*, 52 L. J. Q. B. 41; 9 Q. B. D. 636).

SUCH.—"Such," in Statutes; *V.* Dwar. 601.

"Such," in Testamentary Gifts of a substitutional character; *V. West* v. *Orr*, 47 L. J. Ch. 294; 8 Ch. D. 60: *Heasman* v. *Pearce*, 7 Ch. 285: *Miller* v. *Chapman*, 24 L. J. Ch. 409, discussed 2 Jarm. 779, 780.

As to "Such," wrongly used; *V.* Elph. 82, 403.

"Such *as shall survive*," in a devise to a class, construed as the others or other of them (*Re Tharp*, 33 L. J. Ch. 59; 1 D. G. J. & S. 453). *V.* SURVIVORS.

"Such *Bill*" in s. 38, Solicitors' Act (6 & 7 V. c. 73) refers back to the Bill to be delivered under s. 37, and means a Bill as between Solicitor and Client (*Re Cowdell*, 52 L. J. Ch. 246 : following *Re Grundy*, 50 L. J. Ch. 467 ; 17 Ch. D. 108 ; 29 W. R. 581).

"Such *Craft*" in s. 66, Thames Watermen Act, 1859 (22 & 23 V. c. cxxxiii) means "each" craft (*Elmore* v. *Hunter*, 3 C. P. D. 116 ; 47 L. J. M. C. 8).

"Such *Issue* ;" *V. Re Hutchinson*, 55 L. J. Ch. 574 ; W. N. (86) 63 : and whether prospective or retrospective, *V.* 2 Jarm. 65 : *Strutt* v. *Braithwaite*, 21 L. J. Ch. 609 ; 5 D. G. & S. 369 : *Hope* v. *Potter*, 3 K. & J. 206 : *Harley* v. *Mitford*, 21 Bea. 280. "In default of such Issue ;" *V.* 2 Jarm. 454–457.

"Such *Mines*," in s. 80, Ry. C. C. Act, 1845 ; *V. Midland Ry.* v. *Miles*, 30 Ch. D. 634 ; 53 L. T. 381 ; 34 W. R. 136.

"Such *Order*," in s. 15, 1 & 2 V. c. 110, means a Charging Order *nisi* ; and therefore when the Order has been made absolute it cannot be rescinded under that section (*Jeffryes* v. *Reynolds*, 52 L. J. Q. B. 55).

"Such *other Order* as to the Court shall seem meet," in the prayer of a petition for winding-up a Co. under supervision, enables the Court (petitioner being willing) to make a Compulsory Order (*Re Electric & Magnetic Co.*, 50 L. J. Ch. 491).

A gift of "such *Parts*" of testator's property as the legatee may desire, enables the legatee to take the whole ; and if the gift embraces only a class of testator's property, then the whole of such class may be appropriated by the legatee (*Arthur* v. *Mackinnon*, 48 L. J. Ch. 534 ; 11 Ch. D. 385). *V.* PART.

"Such Prosecution ;" *V.* PROSECUTION.

"Such General or Quarter *Sessions*," s. 14, 5 G. 4, c. 83, refers to the kind of Court, and not the individuals constituting a particular Sessions (*R.* v. *Warwickshire*, 4 L. J. M. C. 62 ; 4 N. & M. 370 ; 2 A. & E. 768).

SUE AND LABOUR.—As to construction of the "Sue and Labour" Clause in a Marine Insurance ; *V. Uzielli* v. *Boston Insrce.*, 54 L. J. Q. B. 142 ; 15 Q. B. D. 11; 52 L. T. 787; 33 W. R. 293 : 1 Maude & P. 490.

SUFFER.—An Annuity, or other life interest, only enjoyable until the beneficiary shall "suffer" anything to deprive him of the right of receiving it, is forfeited by a Garnishee Order served on the trustees (Lewin, 103, citing *Bates* v. *Bates*, W. N. (84) 129) ; or by a Judgment Creditor obtaining a Charging Order (*Roffey* v. *Bent*, L. R. 3 Eq. 759), or registering his judgment as a mortgage against the lands (*Re Moore*, 17 L. R. Ir. 549) ; or the appointment of a Receiver (*Re Detmold*, 58 L. J. Ch. 495) ; or by a Bankry when the act of bankry is such as (under the old practice) neglecting to comply with a debtor's summons (*Ex p. Eyston*, 47 L. J. Bank. 62 ; 7 Ch. D. 145). *Sv. Ex p. Dawes*, cited WOULD.

V. PERMIT : PERMISSION.

There is no real distinction between "permit" and "suffer" in the Licensing Act, 1872, 35 & 36 V. c. 94 (per Stephen, J., *Bond* v. *Evans*, 57 L. J. M. C. 108 ; 21 Q. B. D. 249 ; 59 L. T. 411; 36 W. R. 767; 52 J. P. 613). Some of the sections of that Act (*e.g.* s. 14, and subs. 1, s. 16), deal with offences "knowingly" permitted or suffered, and in those cases knowledge by the licensed person would be an ingredient in the offence. But in other sections (*e.g.* ss. 13, 15, 17), "knowingly" does not occur; and therefore (under s. 13) a licensed person "permits" drunkenness, or sells to one who is drunk, though such person does not know of the drunkenness (*Cundy* v. *Le Cocq*, 53 L. J. M. C. 125 ; 13 Q. B. D. 207) ; and (under s. 17) a licensed person "suffers gaming," if he, *or his servant in charge*, knows or ought to know that gaming is going on (*Bosley* v. *Davies*, 45 L. J. M. C. 27; 1 Q. B. D. 84 ; 39 J. P. 774 : *Redgate* v. *Haynes*, 45 L. J. M. C. 65 ; 1 Q. B. D. 89 ; 40 J. P. 70 : *Crabtree* v. *Hole*, 43 J. P. 799 : *Bond* v. *Evans*, sup.), but not, *semble*, if the knowledge be confined to an irresponsible person not in charge, *e.g.* a potman (*Somerset* v. *Hart*, 53 L. J. M. C. 77; 12 Q. B. D. 360). Note : This prohibition against gaming extends to the licensed person himself and his private friends (*Patten* v. *Rhymer*, 29 L. J. M. C. 189 ; 3 E. & E. 1) ; but the licensed person who is himself drunk, cannot, under s. 13, be convicted of "permitting" drunkenness (*Warden* v. *Tye*, 46 L. J. M. C. 111; 2 C. P. D. 74 : *Cp.* LICENSED PREMISES).

Building "made or *suffered to continue* ;" *V. Pearson* v. *Kingston-upon-Hull*, 35 L. J. M. C. 36 ; 3 H. & C. 921.

SUFFER JUDICIAL PROCEEDING.—A debtor in difficulties owing large sums to his father-in-law consulted his father-in-law's solicitor, who told him he could only act for the father-in-law, and that the debtor must take his own course. The solicitor issued writ for the father-in-law's claim, to which the debtor did not appear ; judgment by default was obtained and debtor's goods were seized under an *elegit* and delivered to the father-in-law. The debtor then filed a liquidation petition, employing therein his father-in-law's solicitor : Held, that the debtor had not "suffered" a judicial proceeding within s. 92, Bankry. Act, 1869 (*Ex p. Lancaster*, 53 L. J. Ch. 1123 ; 25 Ch. D. 311).

SUFFERANCE.—*V.* PERMISSION.

SUFFICE.—*V.* IT SHALL SUFFICE.

SUFFICIENT.—*V.* INSUFFICIENT.

SUFFICIENT CAUSE.—As to what is "other Sufficient Cause," within s. 7 (3), Bankry. Act, 1883, for refusing to make a Receiving Order ; *V. Ex p. Dixon*, 53 L. J. Ch. 769 ; 13 Q. B. D. 118 ; 50 L. T. 414 ; 32 W. R. 837: *Ex p. Oran, Re Watson*, 15 Q. B. D. 399 ; 2 Morr. 199.

As to what is "Sufficient Cause" for non-payment of rate within s. 256, P. H. Act, 1875; *V. Sheffield Waterworks Co.* v. *Sheffield Corp.*, 55 L. J. M. C. 40; 54 L. T. 179; 34 W. R. 153; 50 J. P. 6; 2 Times Rep. 110, distinguishing *Sandgate* v. *Pledge*, 14 Q. B. D. 730.

As to what is an entry in, or omission from, a Register of Shareholders "*Without* Sufficient Cause" within s. 35, Companies Act, 1862; *V.* Buckl. 94.

SUFFICIENT EVIDENCE.—Anything which is duly prescribed as "Sufficient Evidence" of a fact is enough evidence thereon to go to the jury; but the other side is not precluded from controverting it by other evidence (*Barraclough* v. *Greenhough*, 36 L. J. Q. B. 251; 8 B. & S. 623; L. R. 2 Q. B. 612). *Cp.* CONCLUSIVE EVIDENCE.

SUFFICIENT PASTURE.—The measure of what is Sufficient Pasture (*sufficientem pasturam quantum pertinet ad tenementa sua*, Stat. Merton), to be left by a Lord of a Manor when he makes an APPROVEMENT is, that amount which will be sufficient for the full enjoyment by all the Commoners of all their existing rights, whether such rights are likely to be exercised or not (*Robertson* v. *Hartopp*, 34 S. J. 141: in which *Lake* v. *Plaxton*, 10 Ex. 196; 24 L. J. Ex. 52, and *Lascelles* v. *Onslow*, 2 Q. B. D. 433; 46 L. J. Q. B. 333, were questioned, and not followed).

SUFFICIENT PRIVY.—"A Sufficient Watercloset, Earthcloset or Privy," s. 35, P. H. Act, 1875, does not mean a "separate" convenience for each house; if one is, in fact, "sufficient" for two or more houses in common, the statute is satisfied (*R.* v. *Clutton*, 48 L. J. M. C. 135; 4 Q. B. D. 340).

SUFFICIENT REASON.—The "Sufficient Reason" which, under s. 11, Com. L. Pro. Act, 1854 (superseded by s. 4, Arbitration Act, 1889, 52 & 53 V. c. 49), will induce the Court not to stay an action regarding matters which the parties have agreed shall be determined by Arbitration, includes cases where Fraud is charged and the person so charged objects to arbitration (*Russell* v. *Russell*, 14 Ch. D. 471; 49 L. J. Ch. 268), or where defendant's object is delay (*Lury* v. *Pearson*, 1 C. B. N. S. 639), or he has obtained time to plead on terms of accepting short notice of trial (*Smith* v. *British Marine*, W. N. (83) 176), or where submission has been revoked (*Randell* v. *Thompson*, 1 Q. B. D. 748; 45 L. J. Q. B. 713), or the arbitrator chosen is not impartial (*Pickthall* v. *Merthyr*, 2 Times Rep. 805).

The cases in which such "Sufficient Reason" can be shown are few and exceptional (*Russell* v. *Russell*, sup.).

SUFFICIENT WATER.—When a Charter-party provides that the ship shall "discharge in a dock as ordered on arriving, *if sufficient water*, or so near thereunto as she may safely get, always afloat;" the words, "if sufficient water," "are introduced in the interest of the shipowner, and restrict the generality of the power to name a dock. The obligation of the shipowner is to proceed to the dock named if there is sufficient water to enter the dock *when the order is given*; and if there is not then sufficient water, the ship is not bound to discharge in the dock named" (per Cave, J., *Allen* v. *Collart*, 52 L. J. Q. B. 688; 11 Q. B. D. 782).

SUFFICIENT WAYLEAVE.—*V.* Way.

SUICIDE.—"Suicide" does not necessarily involve the idea of a *felonious* self-destruction.—To "commit suicide" is for a person voluntarily to do an act—(or, as it is submitted, to refrain from taking bodily sustenance),—for the purpose of destroying his own life, being conscious of that probable consequence, and having, at the time, sufficient mind to will the destruction of life (*Clift* v. *Schwabe*, 17 L. J. C. P. 2; 3 C. B. 437). In that case the meaning of this word is elaborately discussed, and its history is very learnedly treated by Pollock, C.B., who, however, was in the minority of the Ex. Cham. in upholding the direction of Cresswell, J., at the trial that "Suicide" meant the voluntary self-destruction of a man who at the time was "able to distinguish between right and wrong, and to appreciate the nature and quality of the act that he was doing, so as to be a responsible moral agent." The opposite view, and the one which received the sanction of the majority of the Court, is thus expressed by Patteson, J.:—"Now the words themselves,"—words appearing in a Life Policy, and exonerating the insurers if the insured should "commit suicide,"—"are large enough to embrace all self-destruction as well as self-murder; not, indeed, as was admitted in *Borrodaile* v. *Hunter* (12 L. J. C. P. 225; 5 M. & G. 639), to embrace cases of mere accident, or of insanity extending to unconsciousness of the act done, or of its physical consequences;—because such cases, although comprehended in the very words themselves, cannot be considered to have been in the contemplation of the contracting parties;—but clearly embracing an act of self-destruction committed by a person who was aware of the probable consequence of the act, and intended that consequence to follow."

Vf. Rosc. N. P. 411; Steph. Cr. 165, 166.

V. Die by his own hands: Murder.

SUIT.—"Suit" is a term of wider signification than "Action," and may include proceedings on a Petition (*Re Wallis*, 23 L. R. Ir. 7). *V.* Action.

"And for this word (Sectas) it is to be known that by release of all 'Suits,' executions are barred, for none shall have execution without suit or prayer" (*Altham's Case*, 8 Rep. 153 b). *V.* Actions.

V. Proceeding.

SUITABLE.—Wheels "suitable only to run on the Rail" of a Tramway, s. 62, Tramways Act, 1870, 33 & 34 V. c. 78; *V. Manchester* v. *Andrews*, 5 Times Rep. 470.

"Other Suitable Material;" *V. Ralston* v. *Smith*, 11 H. L. Ca. 223; 35 L. J. C. P. 49.

SUITABLY.—*V.* PROVIDE SUITABLY.

SULLERYE.—"Signifieth a plow-land" (Co. Litt. 5 a). *V.* PLOW-LAND.

SULLINGS.—"Sullings are taken for elders,"—*i. e.*, elder trees (Co. Litt. 4 b).

SUM.—"Provided the Sum or Damages sought to be recovered shall not exceed £50;" "Sum," in such a connection, means "Debt" (*Joule* v. *Taylor*, 21 L. J. Ex. 31; 7 Ex. 58).

V. SUMS: RECOVER.

SUM ADJUDGED.—The "Sum Adjudged" to be paid on a Conviction, "refers to the sum in which the party is convicted, and does not include the costs" (per Crompton, J., delivering jdgmt. of the Court, *R.* v. *Warwickshire*, 25 L. J. M. C. 119; 6 E. & B. 837).

SUM CERTAIN.—An assessment under s. 68, Lands C. C. Act, 1845, does not make the amount of it a "Sum Certain" within 3 & 4 W. 4, c. 42, s. 28, so as to carry interest (per Collier, Co. Co. Judge, *Evans* v. *Lond. & N. W. Ry.*, 31 S. J. 333: *V.* JUDGMENT).

A sum payable by a Bill of Ex. or Promissory Note is a "Sum Certain," within the Bills of Ex. Act, 1882, "although it is required to be paid—

(*a*) With interest.

(*b*) By stated instalments.

(*c*) By stated instalments, with a provision that upon default in payment of any instalment the whole shall become due.

(*d*) According to an indicated rate of exchange, or according to a rate of exchange to be ascertained as directed by the Bill" or Note (ss. 9, 89).

V. CERTAIN TIME.

SUM CLAIMED.—"Sum Claimed," s. 460, Mer. Shipping Act, 1854 (17 & 18 V. c. 104), means "the sum asked before the proceedings commenced" (per Dr. Lushington, *The William and John*, 32 L. J. P. M. & A. 103; Brown & Lush. 49).

"Sum *in Dispute*," s. 464, same Act, does not mean the sum awarded by Justices, and appealed against, but means the sum originally in litigation (*The Andrew Wilson*, 32 L. J. P. M. & A. 104; Brown & Lush. 56). *Vf. The Generous*, L. R. 2 A. & E. 57; 37 L. J. Adm. 37.

SUM IN DISPUTE.—*V.* SUM CLAIMED.

SUM PREVIOUSLY OFFERED.—*V.* PREVIOUSLY OFFERED.

SUM RECOVERED.—*V.* RECOVER: SUM.

SUMMARILY.—Costs of an appeal to Quarter Sessions (enforceable by a Justice's warrant of distress), are "recoverable summarily before a Justice of the Peace" within s. 4 (2) Debtors Act, 1869 (*R.* v. *Pratt,* L. R. 5 Q. B. 176; 39 L. J. M. C. 73).

SUMMARY JURISDICTION.—"Questions of Law which arise in the *Exercise of* Summary Jurisdiction by Justices," 20 & 21 V. c. 43; *V. Sweetman* v. *Guest,* 37 L. J. M. C. 59; L. R. 3 Q. B. 262.

"Summary Jurisdiction Act, 1848;" *V.* s. 13 (6), Interp. Act, 1889.

"Summary Jurisdiction Acts;" *V.* s. 13 (7), (8), (9), (10), Ib.

V. Court of Summary Jurisdiction.

SUMS.—*V.* Money: Money due.

SUNDAY.—"Sunday," s. 1, Sunday Closing (Wales) Act, 1881, has only its ordinary meaning, and does not include Christmas Day (*Forsdike* v. *Colquhoun,* 11 Q. B. D. 71).

V. Days.

SUNK.—*V.* Sink.

SUPERFICIAL YARD.—As used in a building contract; *V. Symonds* v. *Lloyd,* 6 C. B. N. S. 691.

SUPERFLUOUS LAND.—"I think the cases of the *G. W. Ry.* v. *May* (43 L. J. Q. B. 233; L. R. 7 H. L. 283), *Hooper* v. *Bourne* (46 L. J. Q. B. 509; 47 Ib. 437; 49 Ib. 370; 2 Q. B. D. 339; 3 Ib. 258; 5 Ap. Ca. 1; 28 W. R. 493; 42 L. T. 97), and *Betts* v. *G. E. Ry.* (47 L. J. Ex. 461; 49 Ib. 197; 3 Ex. D. 182), have now settled, beyond all controversy, what the meaning of 'Superfluous Land' (in ss. 127, 128, Lands C. C. Act, 1845) is. The test is, whether or not there is *bonâ fide* reason to believe that within no very distant time—it may be years—but that within a reasonable time, having regard to the nature of the undertaking, it will be required for the purposes of the undertaking" (per Manisty, J., *Hobbs* v. *Mid. Ry.,* 51 L. J. Ch. 325; 20 Ch. D. 418).

"Slips of land above and below a tunnel are not superfluous lands" (per Jessel, M. R., *Rosenberg* v. *Cook,* 51 L. J. Q. B. 172; 8 Q. B. D. 162, summarising *Re Metrop. Dist. Ry. & Cosh,* 49 L. J. Ch. 277; 13 Ch. D. 607; 42 L. T. 73; 28 W. R. 685); nor land under arches which carry a railway (*Mulliner* v. *Mid. Ry.,* 48 L. J. Ch. 258: 11 Ch. D. 611); nor Mines under a surface required, or which may be required, for the undertaking (*Hooper* v. *Bourne,* sup.). But the whole of the land beyond the boundary wall of a railway is "superfluous," even though that wall be also a retaining wall thicker at the base than at the surface, and though part of such land would be within a line drawn on the surface vertically above the line of the footings of the wall (*Ware* v. *L. B. & S. Ry.,* 52 L. J. Ch. 198).

When a Company sells, or offers to sell, lands as "Superfluous," that is conclusive as regards the right of pre-emption of the adjoining owner (*Lond. & S. W. Ry.* v. *Blackmore,* 39 L. J. Ch. 713 ; L. R. 4 H. L. 610). But a mere sale to another Company or to an individual, without giving the adjoining owner his chance of pre-emption,—though *primâ facie* evidence that the land is "Superfluous" (and in any view such a sale is *ultra vires*),—does not conclusively show that the land is "Superfluous" (*Hobbs* v. *Mid. Ry.*, 51 L. J. Ch. 320 ; 20 Ch. D. 418. *Vf. Carington* v. *Wycombe Ry.*; 37 L. J. Ch. 213 ; L. R. 2 Eq. 825 ; 3 Ch. 377 : *Beauchamp* v. *G. W. Ry.*, 37 L. J. Ch. 74 ; 38 Ib. 162 ; 3 Ch. 745).

SUPERINTENDENCE.—A gang-way man is not a "person who has *Superintendence* entrusted to him" within sub-s. 2, s. 1 and s. 8, Employers' Liability Act, 1880 (*Shaffers* v. *General Steam Nav. Co.*, 52 L. J. Q. B. 260 ; 10 Q. B. D. 356). *Vh. Kellard* v. *Rooke,* 57 L. J. Q. B. 599 ; 21 Q. B. D. 367 ; 36 W. R. 875 ; 52 J. P. 820.

SUPERIOR COURT.—As to what constitutes a "Superior Court" and as to its difference from an Inferior Court ; *V.* opinion of the judges as delivered by Willes, J., in *Cox* v. *Ld. Mayor of London,* 36 L. J. Ex. 225 ; L. R. 2 H. L. 239 : *Vf. Ex p. Fernandez,* 10 C. B. N. S. 3 ; 30 L. J. C. P. 321 : *Hewitt* v. *Cory,* 39 L. J. Q. B. 279 ; L. R. 5 Q. B. 418 : *Milburn* v. *Lond. & S. W. Ry.*, 40 L. J. Ex. 1 ; L. R. 6 Ex. 4.

SUPERSEDE.—"A Compulsory Order 'supersedes' a Voluntary Winding-up (of a Co.) as from the date of the Order ; but that does not mean that it entirely puts an end to everything that has been previously done in the voluntary winding-up" (per Cotton, L.J., *Thomas* v. *Lionite Co.*, 50 L. J. Ch. 544 ; 17 Ch. D. 250).

SUPPLEMENTAL.—A Deed expressed to be "supplemental" to a previous deed, will, since the Conv. & L. P. Act, 1881, have effect as though it had been endorsed on the previous deed or contained a full recital thereof (s. 53).

SUPPLIED.—"Goods supplied," as used in the consideration for a guarantee ; held, to mean "Goods *to be* supplied," so that the guarantee was not for a past consideration (*Hoad* v. *Grace,* 31 L. J. Ex. 98 ; 7 H. & N. 494). *Vf.* GIVEN.

V. WELL SUPPLIED WITH WATER.

SUPPLY.—The point of "Supply" of gas, s. 6, Metropolis Gas Act, 1860, is the meter from which the gas passes into the customer's pipes (*Gaslight Co.* v. *South Metrop. Gas Co.*, 58 L. T. 899 ; 36 W. R. 455 ; 56 L. J. Ch. 858 : *Imperial Gaslight Co.* v. *West Lond. Gas Co.*, 56 L. J. Ch. 862 n. *V.* those cases, as to "Supply gas *for sale*" in same section).

V. PROVIDE : CONTRACT TO SUPPLY.

SUPPORT.—A bequest "to Support" an institution does not offend the law of Mortmain (*Re Hedgman, Morley* v. *Croxon*, 8 Ch. D. 156: Tudor's Char. Trusts, 410, 413 : 1 Jarm. 230). *V.* FOUND : MAINTENANCE.

V. TOWARDS.

SUPPOSED TO BE.—As to this phrase when prefacing a quantity; *V. Davis* v. *Shepherd*, 35 L. J. Ch. 581 ; 1 Ch. 410 ; 15 L. T. 122.

V. ENTITLED TO VOTE.

SUPPOSITION.—*V.* FAIR AND REASONABLE.

SUPPRESS.—To "Suppress" anything is to put a stop to it when actually existing ; and does not extend to preventing it by suppressing what may lead to it (*Chelsea* v. *King*, 34 L. J. M. C. 9 ; 17 C. B. N. S. 625).

SUPREME COURT.—*V.* s. 13 (1), Interp. Act, 1889.

SURCHARGE.—To "Surcharge" a Common, is to put on to the Common more cattle than the person is entitled to put there. *Vh.* Selwyn's Nisi Prius, tit. *Common.*

"Surcharge and Falsify" a settled account ; *V.* Dan. Ch. Pr. 485.

SURFACE.—"'Surface,' or superficies, *primâ facie*, means, of course, nothing more than the mere *vestimenta terræ*" (MacS. 19). *Vh. Wakefield* v. *Buccleugh*, cited SOIL.

"Surfaces," in a Patent Specification ; *V. Barber* v. *Grace*, 17 L. J. Ex. 122 ; 1 Ex. 339.

SURFACE DAMAGE.—"The expression 'Surface Damage' is a term well known in the North of England in the colliery districts. It is damage to the crops by using the surface, or by the smoke coming from the colliery works or pit-heaps, in respect of which compensation is payable under leases or reservations of coal, or when lords work coal by custom under copyhold lands. It is difficult to say that the injury to the foundations of a house, or the subsidence of the soil, is a Surface Damage ; it may be damage to the house and land, but not Surface Damage" (per Cur. *Allaway* v. *Wagstaff*, 4 H. & N. 681 ; 29 L. J. Ex. 51 : *Vf. Neill's Trustees* v. *Dixon*, 7 Sess. Ca., 4th Series, 741).

SURGEON.—"In strictness, to act as a Surgeon something must be done by the hand" (per Knight-Bruce, L. J., *Ex p. Crabb, Re Palmer*, 25 L. J. Bank. 49).

"A Surgeon, formerly, was a mere operator, who joined his practice to that of a Barber. In latter times all that has been changed, and the profession has risen into great and deserved eminence. But the business of a Surgeon is, properly speaking, with external ailments and injuries of the limbs" (per Best, C. J., *Allison* v. *Haydon*, 4 Bing. 621). But "with a view to the recovery of a patient in a case of that description, he may, perhaps, prescribe and dispense medicine" (Ib.: *Va.* per Cresswell, J., *Apothecaries Co.* v. *Lotinga*, 2 Moo. & R. 499). *V.* APOTHECARY.

Surgeons were formerly a sad lot (*V.* 34 & 35 H. 8, c. 8).

SURGICAL.—*V.* MEDICAL.

SURNAME.—It seems that a bequest to a class of the "Surname" of a particular person, is more readily construed as indicating the "family" or "stock" of that person than if the word NAME were used (2 Jarm. 143, citing *Carpenter* v. *Bott*, 15 Sim. 606; 16 L. J. Ch. 433).

SURPLICE FEES.—"Those fees and dues which go by the name of 'Surplice Fees,' being fees on interments, burials, marriages, and the like. With respect to Surplice Fees it is said that none are due to the Minister as of common right, but depend on special custom only" (2 Steph. Bla. 743;—cited and adopted by Kay, J., *Stewart* v. *West Derby Burial Bd.*, 56 L. J. Ch. 434; 34 Ch. D. 339; 56 L. T. 380; 35 W. R. 268).

SURPLUS.—"Surplus" will not always be construed as "Overplus," in the wide sense of whatever shall turn out to be the Overplus (*Page* v. *Leapingwell*, 18 Ves. 466). *Cp.* OVERPLUS: REMAINDER.

"Surplus" widens the meaning of "Rents, Issues and Profits," in a residuary devise, *e.g.* of "Residuary or Surplus Rents, Issues and Profits" (*Cust* v. *Middleton*, 34 L. J. Ch. 185: *Va.* per Hardwicke, L. C., *Sherrard* v. *Harborough*, Amb. 164).

SURPLUSAGE.—"'Surplusage' comes of the French 'Surplus,' that is, an overplus, and signifies in the law an addition of more then needs, which sometimes is the cause that a writ shall abate, but in pleading many times it is absolutely voyd, and the residue of the plea shall stand good" (Termes de la Ley).

SURRENDER.—"'*Surrender*,' *sursum redditio*, properly is a yeelding up an estate for life or yeares to him that hath an immediate estate in reversion or remainder, wherein the estate for life or yeares may drowne by mutuall agreement between them" (Co. Litt. 337 b; *Vth.* Butler's note, 294, where it is said "a *surrender* differs from a *release* in this respect, that the release operates by the greater estate's descending upon the less:—a surrender is the falling of a less estate into a greater"). *Vh.* Co. Litt. 338 a, *et seq.*

SURVEYOR.—As to meaning of "Surveyor" in P. H. Act, 1875; *V. Lewis* v. *Weston-super-Mare*, 58 L. J. Ch. 39; 40 Ch. D. 55.

SURVIVE.—"Survive" imports that the person who is to survive must be living at the death of the person whom, or at the happening of the event which, he is to survive (*Gee* v. *Liddell*, 35 L. J. Ch. 640; L. R. 2 Eq. 341: *Vth.* 2 Jarm. 691).

In that case Romilly, M. R., said:—"My opinion is, that the meaning of the word 'Survive' or 'Survivor' imports that a person who is to survive must be living at the time of the event which he is to survive. I have consulted several dictionaries on this subject. I have consulted Johnson and Richardson, and the authorities cited by them; and in all instances it appears to me to mean to 'outlive,' that is, to be alive at the time of a particular event, or the death of a particular person which event or person the other is to survive. It is true that Dr. Johnson puts as one of the meanings, 'to live after another' . . . . But all the passages from the English writers cited tend to the conclusion that the person who survives an event, must be living at the time when that event takes place, and that 'to live after,' is somewhat ambiguous."

Bequest, in remainder after life interests, for "*surviving* sister or sisters of my wife, or their heirs;" held, that "surviving" meant surviving the testator (*Stannard* v. *Burt*, 52 L. J. Ch. 355). *Vf. Spurrell* v. *Spurrell*, 22 L. J. Ch. 1076; 11 Hare, 54.

V. SURVIVORS.

SURVIVING SISTERS.—*V. Carver* v. *Burgess*, 24 L. J. Ch. 401; 18 Bea. 541.

SURVIVING TRUSTEE.—*V. Sharp* v. *Sharp*, 2 B. & Ald. 405, stated Lewin, 655: *Vf.* Lewin, 662, 664.

A Power to "Survivor*s*" cannot be executed by last Survivor; but a Power to three or more "and the Surviv*or* of them" may be executed by the Survivor*s* (Lewin, 604: SURVIVOR).

SURVIVOR: SURVIVORS.—"The word 'Survivor' may be either a word of limitation of an estate (denoting the interest certain persons are to take), or it may denote a class of persons" (Theobald, 466).

"If there is a life estate followed by a gift to a number of persons or the Survivors of them, the general rule of construction is that the word 'Survivors' means those who survive the tenant for life; if there is not a life estate, then *primâ facie* as a general rule it refers to those who survive the testator" (per Cotton, L. J., *Ralph* v. *Carrick*, 48 L. J. Ch. 810; 11 Ch. D. 873): or, as it may be otherwise stated, "the word 'Survivors' refers commonly to the time of division" (per Kay, J., *Re Mortimer*, 54 L. J. Ch. 415). *Vf.* as to period of Survivorship, 2 Jarm. 720–751; Theobald, 471–478.

"Survivors," generally speaking, includes "Survivor," and should be read as equivalent to "Survivors or Survivor" (*V.* jdgmt. in *Re Mortimer*, sup.). "But a discretionary power to four Trustees 'and the survivor*s* of them' cannot, it seems, be executed by the last survivor" (Lewin, 604, citing *Hibbard* v. *Lamb*, 1 Amb. 309); though if it be given to "the survivor," it could be executed by the survivors who might be left after the death of one (Lewin, 604).

Read as "Other."

"The question whether the word 'Survivor' (in a Will) is to be read as 'Other' has been the subject of innumerable cases; but there is one never failing guide to all the authorities, viz.,—that it is the duty of the Court to ascertain what the meaning of the testator is, and if it can satisfy itself that the word ought to be read as 'Other,' it is right to substitute the one word for the other" (per Bacon, V.-C., *Re Johnson*, 53 L. J. Ch. 1117); but "when unexplained by other parts of the Will, it is to be interpreted according to its strict and literal meaning" (2 Jarm. 689).

For an elaborate discussion of the cases hereon, *V.* 2 Jarm. 689–710; *Vf.* Wms. Exs. 1472; Theobald, 466–470; Watson, Eq. 1221–1227.

Va. Re Horner, Pomfret v. *Graham*, 51 L. J. Ch. 43; 19 Ch. D. 186: *Re Benn*, 29 Ch. D. 839.

Besides the general rule above enunciated there is, probably, no general rule that can be relied on for construing "Survivor" as "Other" besides the following one, stated by Mr. Hawkins in his work on Construction of Wills (p. 202),—

Where there is a gift to several, or to a class, as tenants in common in tail, with remainder as to the share of each to the "survivors" or "surviving" devisees in tail, with a limitation over on failure of issue of *all* the devisees, the words "survivor" or "surviving" will be construed as "other," so as to create cross-remainders among the devisees by express limitation; either in a Deed or Will (*Doe* v. *Wainewright*, 5 T. R. 427: *Cole* v. *Sewell*, 2 H. L. Ca. 186: *Smith* v. *Osborne*, 6 H. L. Ca. 375).

But in *Re Bowman, Whytehead* v. *Boulton* (41 Ch. D. 531; 37 W. R. 583), Kay, J., said, "It seems to me that the decisions establish the following propositions:—(1) Where the gift is to A., B., and C. equally for their respective lives, and after the death of any to his children, but if any die without children to the survivors for life, with remainder to their children, only children of survivors can take under the gift over; (2) If, to similar words, there is added a limitation over if *all* the tenants for life die without children, then the children of a predeceased tenant for life participate in the share of one who dies without children after their parent; (3) They also participate, *although there is no general gift over,* where the limitations are to A., B., and C. equally for their respective lives, and after the death of any to his children, and, if any die without children, to the surviving tenants for life and their respective children *in the same manner as their original shares.*"

V. this last proposition acutely examined and dissented from, 33 S. J. 572.

Read as "Longest Liver."

In *Re Hill to Chapman* (53 L. J. Ch. 541; 54 Ib. 595), an unsuccessful attempt was made to induce the Court to read "Survivor" as equivalent to "Longest Liver." The rule, in this connection, is thus stated by Turner, L. J., in *White* v. *Baker* (29 L. J. Ch. 577; 2 D. G. F. & J. 55),—"Where there is a bequest to A. for life, and after his death to B. and C., 'or the survivor of them,' some meaning must be attached to the words 'the survivor.' They may refer to any one of three events :—

1. To one of the persons named surviving the other;
2. To one of them only surviving the testator; or
3. To one of them only surviving the tenant for life: and in the absence of any indication to the contrary they are taken to refer to the latter event, as being the more probable one to have been referred to." *V.* jdgmt. of Cotton, L. J., in *Re Hill to Chapman*, sup., for a criticism on *White* v. *Baker*: *Vf. Scurfield* v. *Howes*, 3 Bro. C. C. 90: *Re Hunter*, L. R. 1 Eq. 295.

The word "Survivors," "does not mean 'Longest Livers' in the general sense, but those who are living when the particular event contemplated happens" (per Kay, J., *Re Mortimer*, *Griffiths* v. *Mortimer*, 54 L. J. Ch. 415; 33 W. R. 441). On the words of the Will under consideration in *Re Mortimer*, it was held that on the death of the last survivor of a class of tenants for life who were to take *inter se* by survivorship, the capital fell into the residue and did not belong to the estate of such last survivor. The learned judge followed *Nevill* v. *Boddam* (29 L. J. Ch. 738; 28 Bea. 554), and *Re Corbett* (29 L. J. Ch. 458; Johns. 591; 8 W. R. 257); and commented on *Maden* v. *Taylor* (45 L. J. Ch. 569), and *Davidson* v. *Kimpton* (18 Ch. D. 213; 29 W. R. 912). *Va.* per North, J., *Askew* v. *Askew* (57 L. J. Ch. 629; 36 W. R. 620). But in *Re Roper* (41 Ch. D. 409; 58 L. J. Ch. 439; 33 S. J. 350) Chitty, J., differed from *Re Mortimer*, *Re Corbett*, and *Askew* v. *Askew*, and, following *Maden* v. *Taylor* and *Davidson* v. *Kimpton*, construed "survivors" as "longest livers:" *Va.* per Monroe, J., *Re Hutchins*, 19 L. R. Ir. 223.

V. generally as to limitations to "Survivors," Jarm., ch. 47.

A limitation to A., B. and C. "and the survivors or survivor of them and the heirs of such survivor," makes A., B. and C. joint-tenants for life, with a contingent remainder in fee to the survivor (2 Jarm. 298; *Vf.* Ib. 251).

Vh. Chitty, Eq. Ind. 8012–8038.

SURVIVORSHIP.—*V.* Benefit of Survivorship.

SUSCEPTIBLE OF VALUATION.—Goodwill is "a matter susceptible of valuation" within Partnership Articles (*Steuart* v. *Gladstone*, 47 L. J. Ch. 427; 10 Ch. D. 626).

SUSPEND.—Where there is a clause in a Lease that in case of fire the rent shall be "suspended" until the premises are re-instated, it might be contended that "suspended" means only "postponed;" but more reasonably it means "temporarily extinguished." In this sense the word is obviously used in the following passage from the judgment in *Morrison* v. *Chadwick* (18 L. J. C. P. 192; 7 C. B. 283),—"The eviction by a landlord of his tenant from a part of the premises creates a *Suspension* of the entire rent *during the continuance of the eviction* until the tenant enters and resumes the possession—see the authorities cited in 1 Wms. Saund. 204, n. 2." (*Va.* SUSPENSE). But it would avoid dispute to provide that the rent shall "cease and be suspended" or shall "be suspended and cease to be payable."

"Has suspended, or is about to suspend, payment," Bankry. Act, 1883, s. 4, subs. 1 (h); *V. Ex p. Gibson, Re Lamb*, W. N. (87) 12; 55 L. T. 817; affd. 4 Morr. 25: *Re Crook*, 24 Q. B. D. 320. NOTICE.

SUSPENSE.—"Suspense commeth of *suspendeo*, and in legall understanding is taken when a seigniorie, rent, profit apprender, &c., by reason of unitie of possession of the seigniorie, rent, &c., and of the land out of which they issue, are not *in esse* for a time, *et tunc dormiunt*, but may be revived or awaked. And they are said to be extinguished when they are gone for ever, *et tunc moriuntur*, and can never be revived; that is, when one man hath as high and perdurable an estate in the one as in the other" (Co. Litt. 313 a). *V.* SUSPEND.

SUSTAINED.—"Costs sustained by reason of;" *V.* BY REASON.

SWALLETS. — "Funnel-shaped fissures in the rock forming the Mendip Hills" (Dart, 416).

SWEAR.—*V.* OATH.

SWEEPAGE.—*V.* HERBAGE.

SWEETS.—"In the construction of any enactment relating to the Revenue of Excise, the expression 'Sweets, or Made Wines' shall mean any liquor which is made from fruit and sugar, or from fruit or sugar mixed with any other material, and which has undergone a process of fermentation in the manufacture thereof" (s. 28, Revenue Act, 1889, 52 & 53 V. c. 42).

SWINDLER.—*V.* CHEAT.

SYSTEM.—Death from Causes "arising within the System of the insured;" *V.* ARISING: SECONDARY CAUSE.

TAC—TAK

TACKE.—In the north of England, a Farm (Co. Litt. 5 a).

TACKLE.—"It has been said that by the words 'Tackle, Furniture, Apparel, and all other her Instruments thereunto belonging,' the Boats of a Ship are not transferred (Molloy, De Jure Mar., B. 2, c. 1, s. 8). And it has been held that Ballast is not part of the Furniture of a Merchant Ship (Ib.: *Kynter's Case,* 1 Leon. 46); and that under the words 'Stores, Tackle, Apparel, &c.,' Kintlage does not pass (*Lano* v. *Neale,* 2 Starkie, 105)." 1 Maude & P. 53 n. (*x*).

An insurance upon a ship employed in the Greenland trade on "ship, tackle, apparel, and furniture," does not by the usage of the trade cover the fishing tackle (*Hoskins* v. *Pickersgill,* 3 Doug. 222).

TAIL: ENTAIL.—*V.* HEIRS.

TAINI.—"*Taini,* or *thaini mediocres,*" in Domesday, "were freeholders, and sometimes called *milites regis,* and their land called *tainland.* But *thainus regis* is taken for a baron" (Co. Litt. 5 b). *V.* TAINLAND.

TAINLAND.—"In the book of *Domesday,* land holden by knight's service was called Tainland, and land holden by socage was called Reveland" (Co. Litt. 86 a). But at 5 b, Co. Litt., it is said that land of freeholders generally was called Tainland; *V.* TAINI.

TAKE.—"I think it will be found that in the Lands C. C. Act, 1845, the word 'take' is used in more than one sense. In the first section the word seems to be used in a general sense. In the preamble to sections 6 and 16 a distinction is drawn between 'purchase of lands by agreement,' and 'the purchase *and taking* of lands otherwise than by agreement.' In sec. 68 the word 'taking' occurs, and it is clear, from *Burkinshaw* v. *Birmingham & Oxford Junc. Ry.* (20 L. J. Ex. 246; 5 Ex. 475), that in that section 'take' means actually take, as distinct from serving a notice to treat or any other kind of constructive taking. Looking at the Lands Clauses Act as a whole, and looking at common parlance and at the language of most Acts which give compulsory powers to public bodies, I think we may say that the word 'take' ought not (generally?) to be confined to taking of actual possession. When we turn to the Metropolitan Street Improvements Act, 1877 (40 & 41 V. c. ccxxxv.), and compare the preamble in which the use of the word 'take' is general, with sec. 5, and especially with sec. 31 where the word 'take' is obviously used in a larger sense, I think the safer construction is that 'take' means , either take from the landlord what the landlord has got,—namely, his Title,—or take from the tenant and occupier what the tenant and occupier has got,—namely, Possession" (per Bowen, L. J., *Spencer* v. *Metrop. Bd. of Works*, 52 L. J. Ch. 258 ; *Sv.* as to acquiring the landlord's title obs. of Jessel, M. R., Ib. p. 253). The conditions, therefore, imposed by s. 33 of the Metropolitan Street Improvements Act, 1877, prior to the Board of Works "taking" lands, need not be complied with prior to the Board proceeding with the preliminaries to acquiring title to such lands, such as serving notice to treat and summoning a jury (*Spencer* v. *Metrop. Bd. of Wks.*, 52 L. J. Ch. 249 ; 22 Ch. D. 142 ; 47 L. T. 459 ; 31 W. R. 347).

Lands entered upon and used by a Company, under s. 85, Lands C. C. Act, 1845, are lands "taken" within s. 80 of that Act (*Charlton* v. *Rolleston*, 54 L. J. Ch. 233 ; 28 Ch. D. 237 ; 51 L. T. 612).

As to how far tunnelling under, or arching over, property is a "Taking ;" *V. Sparrow* v. *Oxford, Worc. & Wolv. Ry.*, 2 D. G. M. & G. 94 ; 16 Jur. 703 ; 19 L. T. O. S. 131 : *Pinchin* v. *London & Blackwall Ry.*, 5 D. G. M. & G. 851 ; 24 L. J. Ch. 417 ; 24 L. T. O. S. 125, 196 ; 3 W. R. 52, 125 : *Re Metrop. District Ry. and Cosh*, 13 Ch. D. 607 ; 49 L. J. Ch. 277 ; 42 L. T. 73 ; 28 W. R. 685 : *Tiverton Ry.* v. *Loosemore*, 9 App. Ca. 480 ; 53 L. J. Ch. 812 ; 50 L. T. 637 ; 32 W. R. 929 ; 48 J. P. 372.

To divert part of a *Stream* by a Water Works Co., is not "*to take or use*" the Stream within s. 6, 10 V. c. 17 ; such diversion merely "injuriously affects" the land (*Bush* v. *Trowbridge Water Co.*, 44 L. J. Ch. 235, 645 ; L. R. 19 Eq. 291 ; 10 Ch. 459).

Game is "taken" when it is snared, though it be neither killed nor removed (*R.* v. *Glover*, Russ. & Ry. 269).

"Take" a girl under 16 "out of the possession and against the will of her father or mother," &c., s. 20, 9 G. 4, c. 31, superseded by s. 55, 24 & 25 V. c. 100 ; "Take" in this connection, does not imply force, actual or constructive ; it means being a party to the father, &c., being deprived of the possession of the girl, her willingness being immaterial (*R.* v. *Manktelow*, 22 L. J. M. C. 115 ; Dears. 159 : *R.* v. *Timmins*, 30 L. J. M. C. 45). *V.* Possession.

TAKE AND CARRY AWAY.—For the purposes of the offence of Larceny, "a *thing* is said to be taken and carried away when every part of it is moved from that specific portion of space which it occupied before it was moved (although the whole of it may not be moved from the whole of the space which it occupied), and when it is severed from any person or thing to which it was attached in such a manner that the taker has, for however short a time, complete control of it.

An *animal* is said to be taken and driven or led away when it is caused to move from the place where it was before" (Steph. Cr. 213, 214).

Vf. Arch. Cr. 377–380; Rosc. Cr. 649.

TAKE OR DESTROY.—A penalty for "taking or destroying" the spawn of fish (*Bridger* v. *Richardson*, 2 M. & S. 568), or for "taking or killing" fish (*R.* v. *Mallinson*, 2 Burr. 679), means an improper taking, and not, *e.g.*, removing spawn from one bed to another.

TAKE PLACE.—The mere supply of liquor to a drunken person is not permitting drunkenness "to take place," within s. 13, 35 & 36 V. c. 94 (per Surrey Sessions, *Smith* v. *Eldridge*, 48 J. P. 25).

TALE QUALE.—*V. Wieler* v. *Schilizzi*, 17 C. B. 619; 25 L. J. C. P. 89; cited in the jdgmt. in *Jones* v. *Just*, L. R. 3 Q. B. 204, 205; 37 L. J. Q. B. 94.

TALWOOD.—"'Talwood' is a term used in statutes of 34 & 35 H. 8, c. 3, and 7 E. 6, c. 7, and 43 Eliz. c. 14, and it signifies such wood as is cut into short billets, for the sizing whereof those statutes were made" (Termes de la Ley).

TAMDIU.—*V.* QUAMDIU.

TARRY.—*V.* ELOPE.

TASTE.—*V.* VERTU.

TAVERN.—*V.* ALE-HOUSE.

TAXATION.—*V.* DIRECT TAXATION.

TAXED CART.—*V. Williams* v. *Lear*, 41 L. J. M. C. 76; L. R. 7 Q. B. 285; 25 L. T. 906: dissenting from *Purdy* v. *Smith*, 28 L. J. M. C. 150; 1 E. & E. 511.

TAXES.—"When 'Taxes' are generally spoken of,—if the subject matter will bear it,—they shall be intended Parliamentary Taxes given to the Crown" (per Holt, C. J., *Brewster* v. *Kidgill*, 12 Mod. 167); and the word will include subsequent taxes of the same nature as those in being at the date of the document to be construed, but not those of a different nature (*Brewster* v. *Kidgill*, sup.; sub nom. *Brewster* v. *Kitchin*, 1 Ld. Raym. 317; sub nom. *Brewster* v. *Kitchell*, 1 Salk. 198: *Vf.* Woodf. 555, 556).

The cases relating to Covenants in Leases for payment of *Taxes*, *Rates*, *Assessments*, *Impositions*, *Charges*, *Duties* and other *Outgoings*, seem, at first sight, to run into one another; and it certainly needs a little care to harmonize them. Of course as regards the ordinary public Taxes and the ordinary parochial Rates no difficulty of construction can well arise. Such payments would of course be covered by a covenant to pay Taxes and Rates. But there are a variety of things of a structural kind,—*e.g.*, the cost of abating a nuisance, or of paving the path in front of the tenement, —which though primarily chargeable upon or payable by the landlord may, or may not, be thrown upon the tenant according to the more or less comprehensiveness of his covenant to pay the outgoings in respect of the property demised. It may, perhaps, be safely laid down that where a case is not covered by authority the growing tendency is not to throw exceptional burthens upon the tenant (especially where he holds at a rack-rent; *V.* per Jessel, M. R., *Allum* v. *Dickinson,* 52 L. J. Q. B. 191; 9 Q. B. D. 632), unless he has entered into a clear covenant to bear such burthens. And it is also probably true to say that such burthens are neither Taxes, nor Rates, nor are they "Assessments," or "Impositions," when those words are used in collocation with "Taxes" or "Rates" (*Hartley* v. *Hudson,* 48 L. J. C. P. 751; 4 C. P. D. 367: *Wilkinson* v. *Collyer*, 53 L. J. Q. B. 278: *Tidswell* v. *Whitworth,* 36 L. J. C. P. 103; L. R. 2 C. P. 326).

The practical corollary to the last proposition is, that where a tenant's covenant only embraces "Taxes, Rates, Assessments and Impositions," he will not be liable, thereupon, to pay for exceptional works the costs of which are, by the legislature, imposed on the landlord.

But the tenant's covenant is frequently wider than this, and it is then that difficulty arises. To solve a difficulty of this kind a somewhat close attention to the decided cases is needed. The leading case in favour of the landlord is *Thompson* v. *Lapworth,* whilst that for the tenant is *Tidswell* v. *Whitworth.* Both cases were decided by the same Court of C. P., consisting of Bovill, C. J., and Willes, Keating, and Montague Smith, JJ., —*Thompson* v. *Lapworth* being a few months later than *Tidswell* v. *Whitworth.* Both cases are dealt with *inf.*

Cases in Landlord's Favour.

Where a lessee covenanted to pay rent free from "all parliamentary parochial and other rates, assessments, deductions or abatements," and also to pay "all taxes, rates, *duties*, levies, assessments and payments whatsoever which then were, or during the term might be, rated, levied, assessed or imposed upon or payable in respect of" the demised premises, he was held not entitled to deduct from his rent a payment made by him to a Local Board for paving, which but for the terms of the lease he would have been entitled to deduct (*Payne* v. *Burridge*, 12 M. & W. 727; 13 L. J. Ex. 190: *Va. Sweet* v. *Seager*, 2 C. B. N. S. 119). So where the reservation of rent was "clear of all deductions in respect of land-tax, sewers-rate, and all other taxes, rates, and deductions whatsoever," and the tenant covenanted to "pay and discharge all taxes, rates, *duties* and assessments whatsoever which during the continuance of this present demise shall be taxed, assessed or imposed *on the tenant, or landlord,* of the premises hereby demised in respect thereof, whether parliamentary, parochial or otherwise (except property or income-tax),"—it was held that these words threw the cost of paving, under the 18 & 19 V. c. 120, s. 105, and 25 & 26 V. c. 102, ss. 77 and 96, on the tenant (*Thompson* v. *Lapworth,* L. R. 3 C. P. 149 ; 37 L. J. C. P. 74 ; 16 W. R. 312).

So where the tenant covenanted to "bear, pay and discharge" certain specified taxes and rates, "and all other taxes, rates, *duties* and assessments whatsoever, whether parliamentary, parochial or otherwise, taxed, charged, rated, assessed or imposed upon the said demised premises or any part thereof *or upon the landlords or tenants* in respect thereof,"—it was held that the tenant was liable to pay the expense of abating a nuisance as directed by Justices by an Order obtained by a Sanitary Authority under s. 96, P. H. Act, 1875 (*Budd* v. *Marshall,* 50 L. J. C. P. 24 ; 5 C. P. D. 481).

So where the tenant covenanted to pay "all rates, taxes, *charges* and assessments whatsoever which now are or may be charged or assessed upon the said premises or any part thereof, or *upon any person* or persons in respect thereof (land tax and property tax excepted),"—it was held that the tenant was liable for the expense of sewering, levelling, paving, &c., a street, pursuant to s. 69, P. H. Act, 1848 (*Hartley* v. *Hudson,* 48 L. J. C. P. 751 ; 4 C. P. D. 367 : *Cp. Rawlins* v. *Biggs,* inf.).

So where the tenant covenanted "to bear, pay, and discharge the sewers' rate, tithes, rent-charge in lieu of tithes, and all other taxes, rates, assessments and *outgoings* whatsoever which at any time or times during the said demise should be taxed, rated, charged, assessed or imposed upon the said demised premises, or any part thereof, *or upon the landlord or tenant* in respect thereof, or on the rent thereby reserved,"—it was held that the tenant was liable to pay for the expense of connecting his house-drain with the main sewer, pursuant to s. 10, Sanitary Act, 1866, 29 & 30 V. c. 90 (*Crosse* v. *Raw,* 43 L. J. Ex. 144 ; L. R. 9 Ex. 209 : *Vf.* OUTGOINGS).

Cases in Tenant's Favour.

But where the tenant covenanted "to pay and discharge all taxes, rates, assessments and impositions whatsoever (except property or income tax), payable in respect of the demised premises,"—it was held that he was not liable to pay the expense of paving the street opposite his house, which, under the Manchester General Improvement Act, 1851, had been done by the Corporation, and charged to the landlord (*Tidswell* v. *Whitworth,* 36 L. J. C. P. 103 ; L. R. 2 C. P. 326). So where the tenant covenanted to pay "all and all manner of taxes, rates, *charges,* assessments and impositions whatsoever (except land tax and landlord's property tax), at any time during the said term to be charged, assessed or imposed on the said premises thereby demised, or in respect thereof or of the said rent as aforesaid by authority of Parliament, or otherwise howsoever,"—it was held that he was not liable for the expense of abating a nuisance on the premises under the P. H. Act, 1875 (*Rawlins* v. *Biggs,* 47 L. J. C. P. 487 ; nom. *Rawlins* v. *Briggs,* 3 C. P. D. 368). So where (as in *Thompson* v. *Lapworth,* sup.), a liability for the cost of paving, under the Metropolis Local Management Acts, was sought to be thrown on the tenant, the following words of his covenant were held insufficient for that purpose,—to pay "the sewers and main drainage rates and other district rates and assessments whatsoever, whether parliamentary, parochial or otherwise, which now are or which at any time during the said term shall be taxed, rated, charged, assessed or imposed upon the said demised premises or any part thereof, or upon or payable *by the occupier or tenant* in respect thereof" (*Allum* v. *Dickinson,* 52 L. J. Q. B. 190 ; 9 Q. B. D. 632). And a like ruling in reference to the same statutes, and in respect of a similar cost, was arrived at where the tenant covenanted to pay "all rates, taxes and assessments payable in respect of the premises during the tenancy (except land tax and landlord's property tax)" (*Wilkinson* v. *Collyer,* 53 L. J. Q. B. 278).

How the Cases may be Reconciled.

It will be observed that the covenant in the three first of the above cases in favour of the landlord threw on the tenant the burden of paying all "*Duties* :" and the comprehensiveness of that word is especially pointed out in the jdgmts. of Bramwell and Baggallay, L.JJ., in *Budd* v. *Marshall.* In *Hartley* v. *Hudson* the tenant covenanted to pay all "Charges ;" whilst in *Crosse* v. *Raw* there was the still more comprehensive word "Outgoings."

On the other hand, in the cases (except *Rawlins* v. *Biggs*) where the tenant escaped, the covenant did not go beyond "Rates, Taxes, Assessments and Impositions" (as the controlling words), and exceptional payments of the kind under discussion are not comprised in either term of that phrase.

Besides, in the landlord cases (except the first), the words of the tenant's covenants provided for the payment by him of the obligations, *whether charged on the landlord or tenant* ; whilst in the tenant's cases the covenant was either silent as to this, or only embraced such obligations as were "payable by the occupier or tenant." The importance of this distinction is pointed out by Lindley, J., in *Hartley* v. *Hudson.*

It remains to notice *Rawlins* v. *Biggs* (one of the tenant's cases). *Hartley* v. *Hudson* shows that such an exceptional payment as now under discussion is a "Charge," and it seems a little difficult to see how the learned judge who decided *Hartley* v. *Hudson* was able to say in *Rawlins*

v. *Biggs* that it was not "charged, assessed or imposed on the premises thereby demised, *or in respect thereof.*"

Note : Vf. as to Contracts in Leases as to Taxes, &c. ; *V.* Woodf. 554 *et seq.*

In Wills.

As to when a testamentary direction to pay Income free of Taxes will include Income Tax ; *V.* DEDUCTIONS : 1 Jarm. 187, n.

A direction, in a Will, to make deductions from the income of a tenant for life for "Taxes *or otherwise,*" will include the cost of drainage works under s. 73, 18 & 19 V. c. 120 (*Re Crawley, Acton* v. *Crawley*, 54 L. J. Ch. 652 ; 28 Ch. D. 431 ; 52 L. T. 460 ; 33 W. R. 611 ; 49 J. P. 598).

TAXING OFFICER.—*V. Re Wilson*, 53 L. J. Ch. 989 ; 27 Ch. D. 242.

TEACH AND INSTRUCT.—In the case of an outdoor apprenticeship there is an implication that the master is to perform his covenant "to teach and instruct" at the place where he and his apprentice and the latter's parent resided at the date of the deed (*Eaton* v. *Western*, 52 L. J. Q. B. 41 ; 9 Q. B. D. 636 ; 47 L. T. 593 : over-ruling *Royce* v. *Charlton*, 8 Q. B. D. 1 ; 30 W. R. 274) ; but it would seem there would be no such implication in an indoor apprenticeship (*Eaton* v. *Western*, sup.).

TEAME.—*V.* THEME.

TEAM-WORK.—A lessee's covenant, in an Agricultural Lease, to provide "Team-work," extends to other than agricultural work,—*e.g.*, hauling coals ; but it does not oblige the lessee to find a cart, plough or other machine that may be necessary for the performance of the work (*Marlborough* v. *Osborn*, 33 L. J. Q. B. 148 ; 5 B. & S. 67).

TEAR : TEARING.—A Will may be revoked by "tearing" it (s. 20, 1 V. c. 26),—a word which includes "cutting." The "tearing," or "cutting," need not be of the whole Will ; tearing or cutting off its principal part,—*e.g.*, either of the necessary signatures, or even the seal, when it has been executed under seal (*Price* v. *Powell*, 3 H. & N. 341 ; nom. *Price* v. *Price*, 27 L. J. Ex. 409), is sufficient (1 Jarm. 141 ; *V.* Ib. 131) ; but it is doubtful whether tearing in a fit of anger is a revocation, if the testator afterwards puts the pieces together as well as he can (*Re Colberg*, 2 Curt. 832). "Cutting out a particular clause, or the name of a legatee, is a revocation *pro tanto* only" (1 Jarm. 141). *Vh. Mills* v. *Millward*, 59 L. J. P. D. & A. 23.

Erasing the signature with a knife is a "tearing" that revokes (*Re Morton*, 56 L. J. P. D. & A. 96 ; 12 P. D. 141 ; 57 L. T. 501 ; 35 W. R. 735 ; 51 J. P. 680) ; but would that be so if the erasure were made with a pen ?

V. WEAR AND TEAR.

TEMPERATE.—*V.* Sober and Temperate Habits : Strictly Temperate.

TEMPEST.—" Damage by Tempest ; " *V.* Wear and Tear.

TEMPORAL.—A Testamentary gift of " Temporal *Effects*," held to include realty (*Re Sheridan*, 17 L. R. Ir. 179).

" Temporal *Estate* " is synonymous with Worldly Estate. *Vf. Tanner* v. *Wise*, 3 P. Wms. 295 ; nom. *Tanner* v. *Morse*, Ca. t. Talb. 284 : *Grayson* v. *Atkinson*, 1 Wils. 333 : the latter case is commented on 1 Jarm. 724.

TENANCY IN COMMON.—" A limitation to, or trust for, several either nominatim or as a class, with any words implying a distinctness of interest, makes them tenants in common " (Elph. 284, *wh. V.*; *Vh.* 2 Jarm. ch. 32).

Cp. Joint Tenancy : *V.* Tenant in Common.

TENANT.—" A Tenant is a person who holds of another ; he does not necessarily occupy. In order to occupy, a party must be personally resident by himself or his family " (per Littledale, J., *R.* v. *Ditcheat*, 9 B. & C. 183).

The assignee of a lessee (*Doe* d. *Whitfield* v. *Roe*, 3 Taunt. 402 : *Williams* v. *Bosanquet*, 1 Brod. & B. 238), or a sub-lessee (*Doe* d. *Wyatt* v. *Byron*, 14 L. J. C. P. 207 ; 1 C. B. 623 ; 3 Dowl. & L. 31) is a " Tenant" within s. 210, Com. L. Pro. Act, 1852.

To occupy " As Tenant," within the Acts conferring the parliamentary franchise, involves the idea of some permanent occupation and independent interest, and " excludes some occupations of less independence, such as of servants for their service,—*e.g.*, the porter to a lodge, the gardener at a dwelling in the garden : and also such as that of a surgeon to a hospital of rooms therein (*Dobson* v. *Jones*, 5 M. & G. 112 ; 13 L. J. C. P. 126), also the occupation of premises by objects of a charity, occupying under the permission of the trustees of the charity as in *Heartley* v. *Banks* (28 L. J. C. P. 144), and *Davis* v. *Waddington* (7 M. & G. 37 ; 14 L. J. C. P. 45) " (per Erle, C. J., *Cook* v. *Humber*, 31 L. J. C. P. 77 ; 11 C. B. N. S. 33). *Vf. Smith* v. *Seghill*, L. R. 10 Q. B. 422 ; 44 L. J. M. C. 114 : *Hughes* v. *Chatham*, 1 Lutw. 57 ; 5 M. & G. 54 ; 13 L. J. C. P. 44 : *Bridgewater* v. *Durant*, 11 C. B. N. S. 7 : *Fryer* v. *Bodenham*, 19 L. T. 645 : *Durant* v. *Carter*, 43 L. J. C. P. 17 ; L. R. 9 C. P. 261: *Ford* v. *Pye*, 43 L. J. C. P. 21 ; L. R. 9 C. P. 269.

"*Tenant or Occupier*," entitled to vote for Conservators, s. 15, Wimbledon and Putney Commons Act, 1871 ; *V. Purves* v. *Wimbledon and Putney Com. Conservators*, Times, 29th March, 1890.

In the feudal acceptation, " Tenant " has five significations ;—It signifies (1) the Estate held, (2) the Tenure of the land, (3) Performance of obligation, (4) To be bound, and (5) " To deeme or judge " (Co. Litt. 1 a, b).

" Tenant whose term has expired ; " *V.* Expire.

TENANT AT WILL.—" Tenant at will is, where lands or tenements are let by one man to another, to have and to hold to him at the will of the lessor, by force of which lease the lessee is in possession " (Litt. s. 68 ; *Vth.* Co. Litt. 55 a).

TENANT FOR LIFE.—A Tenant for Life is, as the phrase implies, one who is entitled to the benefit of property for the term of his life.

The large powers now given to the Tenant for Life of settled lands, render the definition of this phrase in connection with such lands a matter of great importance. For the purposes of the Settled Land Act, 1882, a Tenant for Life is, " The person who is for the time being, under a Settlement, beneficially entitled to possession of settled land, for his life " (s. 2, subs. 5 : *V.* also s. 58, for an enumeration of other limited owners who have the same powers as Tenants for Life). Speaking broadly, the result of these sections is that the person intended to have the income of the land is the Tenant for Life for the time being (*Re Jones,* 53 L. J. Ch. 807 ; 26 Ch. D. 736).

As to those who are, or have the powers of, a Tenant for Life under the Settled Land Act; *V. Re Jones,* sup. : *Re Buccleuch,* 54 L. J. Ch. 401 ; 55 Ib. 107 ; 31 Ch. D. 135 ; 53 L. T. 733 ; 34 W. R. 169.

On the contrary ; *V. Re Hazle,* 53 L. J. Ch. 574 ; 54 Ib. 628 ; 29 Ch. D. 78 ; 52 L. T. 947 ; 33 W. R. 759 : *Re Atkinson,* 31 Ch. D. 577 ; 54 L. T. 403 ; 34 W. R. 445 : *Re Strangways,* 34 Ch. D. 423 ; 56 L. J. Ch. 195 ; 55 L. T. 714 ; 35 W. R. 83 : *Re Horne,* 39 Ch. D. 84 ; 57 L. J. Ch. 211 ; 58 L. T. 103 ; 36 W. R. 348. *Re Hazle* was on the phrase "Tenant for years determinable on Life."

As to the phrase " Tenant for life *in possession* ; " *V. Re Wright to Marshall,* 54 L. J. Ch. 60 ; 28 Ch. D. 93 ; 51 L. T. 781 ; 33 W. R. 304.

TENANT IN COMMON.—" Tenants in common are they, which have lands or tenements in fee simple, fee tail, or for term of life, &c., and they have such lands or tenements by several titles, and not by a joint title, and none of them know of this his several, but they ought by the law to occupy these lands or tenements in common, and *pro indiviso* to take the profits in common. And because they come to such lands or tenements by several titles, and not by one joint title, and their occupation and possession shall be by law between them in common, they are called Tenants in Common " (Litt. s. 292).

V. Tenancy in Common.

TENANT-RIGHT.—Away-going future crops fall strictly within the meaning of the words " Tenant-Right yet to come," as contained in a Bill of Sale (*Petch* v. *Tutin,* 15 L. J. Ex. 280).

TENANTABLE REPAIR.—Under an obligation to keep premises in " Tenantable Repair," decorative repair is not included ; papering, always, and painting, unless needed for the protection of the property, are decorative repairs: nor does the obligation extend to repairing, or restoring, what is worn out by age (*Crawford* v. *Newton*, 36 W. R. 54 : *Proudfoot* v. *Hart*, 59 L. J. Q. B. 129) : but Waste, whether voluntary or permissive, is a breach of the obligation (Ib.). For an article discussing the cases on this phrase *V.* 32 S. J. 55.

TENDER.—"'To tender (de tender),' or *tendre*, is a word common both to the *English* and *French*, in *Latine offerre;* and in that sense, and with that *Latine* word it is alwaies used in the common law" (Co. Litt. 211 a).

As to requisites of a Tender *V.* Co. Litt. 207 a, 213 b ; Rosc. N. P. 632–634.

All the precision of a strict legal Tender is not required in "tendering" Rates to Overseers under s. 30, Reform Act, 1832 (per Maule, J.) ; but merely saying "I am prepared to pay them" is not sufficient (*Bishop* v. *Smedley*, 15 L. J. C. P. 73 ; 2 C. B. 90).

"Making or tendering satisfaction ;" *V.* SATISFACTION.

TENEMENT.—"The most comprehensive words of description applicable to Real Estate, are 'Tenements and Hereditaments,' as they include every species of realty, as well corporeal as incorporeal" (1 Jarm. 777 : *Vf.* Co. Litt. 6 a, 19 b, 20 a). And it is said that "by the grant of all Tenements, will pass as much as by the grant of all Hereditaments" (Touch. 91) ; but hereon Preston, in his Ed. of the Touchstone, says "this proposition is too general," and Ld. Coke says that "Tenement" is a large word to grant realty, but "Hereditament" is the largest (1 Inst. 6).

"'Tenement,' though in its vulgar acceptation it is only applied to houses and other buildings, yet in its original proper and legal term signifies everything that may be holden, provided it be of a permanent nature ; whether it be of a substantial and sensible, or of an unsubstantial ideal kind" (2 Bla. Com. 16 ; *Va.* Touch. 91). Thus this word will include an Advowson (*Westfaling* v. *Westfaling*, 3 Atk. 460 : *Gully* v. *Bishop of Exeter*, 4 Bing. 290 : *Sv. Kensey* v. *Langham*, Ca. t. Talb. 145 n. *e*) ; and may include Tithes (*Powell* v. *Bull*, 1 Comyn, 265 : *R.* v. *Skingle*, 1 Stra. 100 : *R.* v. *Barker*, 6 A. & E. 388 : *Sv. R.* v. *Nevill*, 8 Q. B. 452 ; 15 L. J. M. C. 33). So "a Dignity, whether it be granted of a place or not, is a 'Tenement' within the Statute De Donis, and consequently not forfeited on an attainder for felony" (per Chitty, J., in *Re Rivett-Carnac's Will*, 54 L. J. Ch. 1076 ; 30 Ch. D. 136, citing *R.* v. *Knollys*, 2 Salk. 509 ; 1 Ld. Raym. 10 : *Ferrer's Case*, 2 Eden, 373).

A Freehold Rent-Charge, is within the words "Freehold Lands or Tenements" in s. 18, Reform Act, 1832 (*Druitt* v. *Christchurch*, Colt. Reg. Ca. 328).

"An Annuity in fee, not being a rent-charge, is an Hereditament, but not a Tenement; neither is a Condition a Tenement, but it is an Hereditament, 3 Rep. 2; 2 Bla. Com. 17; Salk. 239." Tenement "doth not comprehend a personal Annuity in fee; and an Annuity for life is neither a Tenement or Hereditament; and an office for life is a Tenement, and not an Hereditament" (Preston's Addns. to Touch. 91).

On the other hand "Tenement" sometimes receives its popular meaning of "House" (*Yorkshire Insrce.* v. *Clayton*, 51 L. J. Q. B. 82; 8 Q. B. D. 421). "The common people still use the word, as in the days of Blackstone, to mean a House" (per Cotton, L. J., *Dashwood* v. *Ayles*, 55 L. J. Q. B. 10); or it may, even now, sometimes be the equivalent of "Dwelling-house" (*Minifie* v. *Banger*, 55 L. J. Q. B. 10; W. N. (85) 189).

"With respect to the word 'tenements' or *tenementa*, in Co. Litt. 20 a, it is stated;—'This is the only word which the Stat. of Westm. 2, that created estates taile, useth; and it includeth not only all corporate inheritances which are or may be holden, but also all inheritances issuing out of any of those inheritances, or concerning or annexed to or exerciseable within the same, though they lie not in tenure, therefore all these without question may be entailed.' That is a proper legal definition of 'Tenement.' I think 'Tenement' when used at all in connection with a house or room, must mean something of the same kind, or of the same character, and a thing absolutely immovable from the land" (per Martin, B., *Fredericks* v. *Howie*, 31 L. J. M. C. 249; 1 H. & C. 381; 6 L. T. 544: *Vf. R.* v. *Manchester Water Works Co.*, 1 B. & C. 630: *R.* v. *East London Water Works Co.*, 21 L. J. M. C. 49; 17 Q. B. 512: *Colebrooke* v. *Tickell*, 4 A. & E. 916; 5 L. J. K. B. 180: *Sv. R.* v. *Shrewsbury Gas Co.*, 1 L. J. M. C. 18; 3 B. & Ad. 216). In *Fredericks* v. *Howie*, it was held that a portable booth used by strolling players is not a "Tenement," within s. 46, Metropolitan Police Act (2 & 3 V. c. 47), which prohibits keeping, &c. "any House *or other Tenement*" as an unlicensed theatre. *V.* PLACE.

So "Tenement" in s. 167, Towns Improvement Clauses Act, 1847, 10 & 11 V. c. 34, means property capable of visible and physical occupation, and does not include a Several Fishery (*Redington* v. *Millar*, 24 L. R. Ir. 65).

For a collection of the cases on the word "Tenement" as used in the 13 & 14 Car. 2, c. 12 (which regulated Pauper Settlements); *V.* 3 Chitty's Stat. 3 Ed. 1034.

As to the meaning of "Tenement" in s. 3, Lands C. C. Act, 1845, and as to its being there affected by its context "of any tenure;" *V. G. W. Ry.* v. *Swindon Ry.*, 52 L. J. Ch. 306; 53 Ib. 1075; 22 Ch. D. 677; 9 App. Ca. 787.

V. HEREDITAMENT.

TENOR.—The law attaches a technical meaning to the word "Tenor," as signifying either an exact copy, or a statement of the Libel verbatim. "Tenor" has so strict and technical a meaning as to make it necessary to recite verbatim ; but the expression " Manner and Form " means nothing more than a substantial recital (*Wright* v. *Clements*, 3 B. & Ald. 503).

TENURE.—" The word ' Tenure ' signifies the relation of Tenant to Lord " (per Selborne, L. C., *A.-G. of Ontario* v. *Mercer*, 52 L. J. P. C. 85 ; 8 App. Ca. 767).

Vh. Co. Litt. 1 a, b.

TERM.—" It is said by my Lord Coke, that the word ' Term,' though it is more properly applied to a Term for years, yet may mean an Estate for Life, and it is plainly in this deed used in that sense : the trustees are to permit Robert Dormer to receive the profits during the term of his life ; and the estate to the children is not to commence till the end, or other sooner determination of the said term, which by referring the relative to the last antecedent, must mean the term of his life : as to the words ' *Sooner Determination*,' inserted after the estate for life, these are insensible and may be rejected ; they were probably thrown in, *currente calamo*, or by following a Precedent, and if the Precedent was before the Reformation, when there was a civil death (as well as a natural) by entering into religion, it might then have a meaning " (per Hardwicke, L. C., *Smith* v. *Packhurst*, 3 Atk. 137). *Va. Wrotesley* v. *Adams*, 1 Plowd. 198.

" The word ' Term,' in a covenant in a lease, may signify either the time or the estate granted " (Woodf. 144, and authorities there cited).

Where a " Term " of periods of time is spoken of, successive periods are implied. Therefore residence for " a term of 3 years," to give a Settlement under s. 34, 39 & 40 V. c. 61, must be for three whole consecutive years,—without receiving relief (*Dorchester* v. *Weymouth*, 55 L. J. M. C. 44 ; 16 Q. B. D. 31 ; 54 L. T. 52 ; 50 J. P. 310).

TERM CERTAIN.—" Term or number of years certain," 1 G. 4, c. 87, s. 1 ;—a tenancy for 99 years determinable on lives is not within this phrase (*Doe* d. *Pemberton* v. *Roe*, 7 B. & C. 2 ; 5 L. J. O. S. K. B. 289), nor is a tenancy from quarter to quarter determinable by a 3 months' notice, or on the tenant losing his beer license (*Doe* d. *Carter* v. *Roe*, 12 L. J. Ex. 27 ; 10 M. & W. 670).

TERMINATION.—*V.* DETERMINATION.

TERMS.—" Contract which, *according to the Terms thereof*, ought to be performed within the jurisdiction," Ord. 11, R. 1 (*e*), R. S. C., does not mean that the place of performance is to be stated in terms ; it suffices if such place appears from the contract and its circumstances (*Reynolds* v. *Coleman*, 56 L. J. Ch. 903 ; 36 Ch. D. 453 ; 57 L. T. 588 ; 35 W. R. 813). *Vf.* WITHIN THE JURISDICTION.

TESTAMENT.—" A Testament is the true declaration of our last

Will, of that wee would to be done after our death" (Termes de la Ley, *Testament*).

"Testament" includes a Will, Codicils, &c.; "Instrument" signifies the Will alone (*Fuller* v. *Hooper*, 2 Ves. sen. 242). *V.* INSTRUMENT.

TESTAMENTARY ESTATE.—This phrase in a gift of "personal and testamentary estate" carries the realty; as otherwise it would be inoperative (*Smith* v. *Coffin*, 2 H. Bl. 445: *Roe* d. *Penwarden* v. *Gilbert*, 3 Brod. & B. 85: *Doe* d. *Evans* v. *Walker*, 19 L. J. Q. B. 293; 15 Q. B. 28: cited 1 Jarm. 725). In the last of those cases (*Evans* v. *Walker*), Campbell, C. J., said, "I think the words 'my Testamentary Estate' mean to include all that I can dispose of. They are *primâ facie* sufficiently large to carry both the realty and personalty."

TESTAMENTARY EXPENSES.—"Testamentary Expenses," are those which are incident to the proper performance of the duty of an executor (*Sharp* v. *Lush*, 48 L. J. Ch. 231; 10 Ch. D. 468: *Vh. Brougham* v. *Poulett*, 19 Bea. 134: *Re Young*, 44 L. T. 499).

The costs of all proper parties to proceedings for determining the scope of a devise, are "Testamentary Expenses" (*Morrell* v. *Fisher*, 4 D. G. & S. 422); so are the costs of an administration suit (*Miles* v. *Harrison*, 43 L. J. Ch. 585; 9 Ch. 316: *Harloe* v. *Harloe*, 44 L. J. Ch. 512; L. R. 20 Eq. 471: in which latter case Hall, V.-C. refused to follow *Gilbertson* v. *Gilbertson*, 34 Bea. 354, and *Stringer* v. *Harper*, 26 Ib. 585; 28 L. J. Ch. 643: *Miles* v. *Harrison*, and *Harloe* v. *Harloe*, were followed in *Sharp* v. *Lush*, sup. and in *Penny* v. *Penny*, 48 L. J. Ch. 691; 11 Ch. D. 440: *Vh.* Lewin, 644: *Browne* v. *Groombridge*, 4 Mad. 495); and so are the costs of an unsuccessful opposition to a Will the proof of which has been established under a compromise, one of the terms of which was that such costs should be paid out of the estate (*Brown* v. *Burdett*, 53 L. J. Ch. 56).

By s. 125 (7), Bankry. Act, 1883, "Testamentary Expenses incurred in and about the debtor's estate" by the legal personal representative of a deceased insolvent debtor, are a preferential debt upon the estate: held by Judge Holl, at Newcastle-upon-Tyne County Court, that these words include not merely the cost of obtaining probate, but also the reasonable expenses of investigating the position of the debtor's affairs, and generally of administering his estate prior to the bankruptcy administration Order (*Re Turnbull*, 29 S. J. 557). The phrase also includes costs properly incurred in an Administration Action (*Re York*, 36 Ch. D. 233; 56 L. J. Ch. 552; 56 L. T. 704; 35 W. R. 609).

Funeral expenses, the ascertaining testator's debts and their amounts (including rent current at the decease), and the cost of warehousing specific legacies, are "Testamentary Expenses" (*Sharp* v. *Lush*, sup.).

V. EXECUTORSHIP EXPENSES.

TESTATOR.—"Testator," s. 2, 30 & 31 V. c. 69, applies to any deceased person who has made a Will; even where such Will has not disposed of the testator's beneficial interest in the lands upon which a lien for unpaid purchase money exists (*Dowdall* v. *M'Cartan*, 5 L. R. Ir. 313, 642).

THAINUS.—*V.* TAINI.

THAMES.—In *Leary* v. *Steeves* (Times, 15th Decr., 1881), where the owners of a Bill of Lading had the right to intercept the ship "at the Mouth of the Thames," the jury found that the "Mouth of the Thames" included East Oaze Buoy, off the Mouse Light; the witnesses for the Plaintiffs (in whose favour the verdict was found) stated that, in their opinion, "Mouth of the Thames" was a considerable space of water, the eastern limit of which was between Shoeburyness and Sheerness; one witness gave the western limit as a line between Foulness and Warden Point.

THAT IS TO SAY.—"'That is to say' is the commencement of an ancillary clause which explains the meaning of the principal clause. It has the following properties:—(1) it must not be contrary to the principal clause; (2) it must neither increase nor diminish it; (3) but where the principal clause is general in terms it may restrict it: *V.* this explained with many examples, *Stukeley* v. *Butler*, Hob. 171: *Va. Harrington* v. *Pole*, Dy. 77 b pl. 38" (Elph. 622).

In *Gover* v. *Davis* (30 L. J. Ch. 505; 29 Bea. 225) a bequest of "also the whole of my property and effects, *that is to say*, my box, clothing and bedding, &c. &c.," was held to pass a reversionary interest in a residuary estate; and in like manner Wood, V.-C., held that the wide generality of "my personal property" was not cut down by being immediately followed by "*consisting of* money and clothes" (*Dean* v. *Gibson*, 36 L. J. Ch. 657; L. R. 3 Eq. 713).

V. NAMELY.

THE.—"The *Credit*," in a Guarantee, points to a definite credit,—"Something ascertained and known" (per Bramwell, B., *Broom* v. *Batchelor*, 25 L. J. Ex. 299; 1 H. & N. 255: but the majority of the Court was against him in the conclusion, partly led up to by the dictum just cited).

Where the annual value of "The *House* occupied by" a brewer does not exceed £10 the beer brewed by him is not chargeable with duty (subs. 3, s. 33, Inland Revenue Act, 1880, 43 & 44 V. c. 20). This means the house occupied by him *in which he lives* (*Tippett* v. *Hart*, 52 L. J. M. C. 41; 10 Q. B. D. 483). The words italicised do not actually appear in the judgment in the case cited; but they embody its principle,—Pollock, B. observing, "It was intended to get at the status of the man who brews." It is, however, difficult to see why it was more easy to read into the exception the words "in which he lives," rather than the words "in which he brews" which the Court refused.

"The Minister;" *V.* MINISTER.

"The *Property*" in goods does not pass to an Indorsee in blank of a Bill of Lading (who merely takes as a pledgee), so as to render him liable for freight under s. 1, 18 & 19 V. c. 111: nor (*semble*, per Lord Blackburn) would any pledgee or mortgagee be so liable (*Sewell* v. *Burdick*, 54 L. J. Q. B. 156; 10 App. Ca. 74).

V. A: FISHERY, at end: RIGHT OF SALE.

THEATRE.—"Theatres" in s. 72, subs. 4, Licensing Act, 1872, does not include a Music Hall (*R.* v. *Inl. Rev.*, 57 L. J. M. C. 92; 21 Q. B. D. 569; 59 L. T. 378; 36 W. R. 696; 52 J. P. 390).

THEFT.—"'Theft' is a wrongful taking away of another man's goods, but not from his person, with a mind to steal them against his will whose goods they were" (Termes de la Ley, *Larcenie*).

"Theft is the act of dealing, from any motive whatever, unlawfully and without claim of right, with anything capable of being stolen, in any of the ways in which theft can be committed, with the intention of permanently converting that thing to the use of any person other than the general or special owner thereof" (Steph. Cr. ch. 35, *wh. V.* hereon). *Vf.* Rosc. Cr. 639–694.

Cp. ROBBERY.

THEFT-BOTE.—"'Theft-bote' is when a man taketh any goods of a theefe to favour and maintaine him: And not when a man taketh his owne goods that were stolen from him" (Termes de la Ley).

Vh. Rosc. Cr. 419.

THEIR.—In *Boreham* v. *Bignall* (19 L. J. Ch. 461; 8 Hare, 131), a substitutional gift to "their children" was held by Wigram, V.-C., as conclusively shewing that one wife only of the first beneficiary was in the contemplation of the testator, and that that wife must have been the one living at the date of the Will. *V.* WIFE.

In a covenant by two or more for themselves, "*their* exs. ads. and ass[s]," the word "their" is necessarily read distributively, because the parties do not anticipate that they will have the same exs, &c.; but the word will not convert a covenant otherwise joint into a separate covenant (*Whyte*, or *White* v. *Tyndall*, 13 App. Ca. 263; 57 L. J. P. C. 114; 58 L. T. 741; 52 J. P. 675).

THEME.—"'Theme' (sometimes written *theame* corruptly) is an old Saxon word, and signifieth *potestatem habendi in nativos sive villanos, cum eorum sequelis, terris, bonis et catallis.* But *teame*, sometime corruptly written *theam*, is of another signification; for it is also an old Saxon word, and signifieth where a man cannot produce his warrant of that which he bought according to his voucher" (Co. Litt. 116 a).

THEN.—" If property be given upon certain events to such persons as shall *then* be next of kin or relations of the testator, the persons standing in that relation *at the period in question,*—whether so or not (or not solely so) at the death of the testator,—are, upon the terms of the gift, entitled. But if the gift is, not to those who will then be, but to those who will or would then be entitled as, next of kin by statute, the word ' then ' will be understood as referring to the period when they will be entitled in possession. The persons to take will be, not those who would have been entitled if the testator had then died, but those who would *then* be entitled if the testator, when he died, had died intestate " (2 Jarm. 139, 140).

The cases cited in Jarman for that proposition were thus dealt with by Thesiger, L. J., in *Mortimore* v. *Slater* (47 L. J. Ch. 134 ; 7 Ch. D. 322 ; affd. in H. L. nom. *Mortimore* v. *Mortimore,* 48 L. J. Ch. 470 ; 4 App. Ca. 448) :—" The cases seem to me to divide themselves into three classes. The first of those classes is the one where the word ' then,' as an adverb of time, is attached to the description of the class ; and in that case, as in *Wharton* v. *Barker* (4 K. & J. 483), and *Long* v. *Blackall* (3 Ves. 486), it was decided that the word ' then ' imported the time at which the class so described is to be ascertained. *Wheeler* v. *Addams* (17 Bea. 417), is to a certain extent an exception to that rule ; but I think that may be explained, because we find that in that case there is a reference in the limitation to one of the persons who had been a tenant for life before the limitation came into force.

" The second class of cases consists of those where words of futurity, but without the adverb of time, are attached to the description of the class, and in that class of cases we find no distinction drawn, but in every one of them we find that it was held that the words must speak from the time of the testator's death. The cases cited on that point have been *Holloway* v. *Holloway* (5 Ves. 399), and *Doe* v. *Lawson* (3 East, 292).

" The third class of cases is that where the word ' then,' the adverb of time, is used, but where you find it used not in connection with the description of the class but in connection with the time at which the estate is to come into being. In that class of cases also, without any exception, we find it decided that you are to look at the class at the time of the testator's death. That is to be found in *Cable* v. *Cable* (16 Bea. 507), in *Bullock* v. *Downes* (9 H. L. Ca. 1), and in *Day* v. *Day* (4 Ir. Rep. Eq. 385) ; and it is to be observed that in all these cases we do not find that any distinction is drawn from the use of the additional words, ' as if he had died intestate,' but the point which has been looked at by the learned Judges who decided those cases has been whether the word ' then ' is attached to the description of the class, or to the time when the estate is to come into possession."

" Moreover, ' then ' has more meanings than one, each equally common : it may mean ' at that time ' or ' in that case ; ' and unless the latter meaning be excluded by the context, it will be adopted rather than construe 'next of kin according to the Statute' (the Statute being expressly referred to), as meaning something different from what the Statute says it means" (2 Jarm. 140, and cases there cited).

"Then," used twice in the same sentence, construed in the first instance as pointing to the event, and in the second as an adverb of time (*Gill* v. *Barrett*, 29 Bea. 372).

"Then," construed as an adverb of time, not of contingency (*Baker* v. *Lucas*, 1 Molloy, 481).

Vf. Humfrey v. *Humfrey*, 31 L. J. Ch. 622 ; 2 Dr. & Sm. 49 : *Blight* v. *Hartnoll* (No. 2), 51 L. J. Ch. 162 ; 19 Ch. D. 294 : *Pinder* v. *Pinder*, 28 Bea. 44 ; 29 L. J. Ch. 527 : *Druitt* v. *Seaward*, 31 Ch. D. 234 ; 55 L. J. Ch. 239 ; 34 W. R. 180 : *Re Milne*, 56 L. J. Ch. 543 ; 56 L. T. 852 : Wms. Exs. 1127 : *Boraston's Case*, 3 Rep. 19 : Article, 84 Law Times, 114.

But "then" may be used as equivalent to "further," *e.g.*, where there is a testamentary direction for payment of debts, and "then" a demise of lands (*Willan* v. *Lancaster*, 2 Jarm. 595).

V. Then Living.

THEN IN BEING.—*V. Leader* v. *Duffey*, 17 L. R. Ir. 279 ; 13 App. Ca. 294.

THEN LIVING.—"Where life interests are bequeathed to several persons in succession, terminating with a gift to a class of objects 'then living,' the word 'then' is held to point to the period of the death of the person last named (whether he is or is not the survivor of the several legatees for life), and is not considered as referring to the period of the determination of the several prior interests" (1 Jarm. 851 n., and cases there cited. *Vf.* Wms. Exs. 1472 ; Watson, Eq. 1224–5, 1377 : *Britnell* v. *Walton*, W. N. (69) 238 : *Cooper* v. *Macdonald*, 42 L. J. Ch. 539 ; L. R. 16 Eq. 258 : *Cobden* v. *Bagwell*, 19 L. R. Ir. 168 : Chitty, Eq. Ind. 7385–7388).

V. Then : Living.

THEOLONIO.—Toll : *Vh. Holcroft* v. *Heel*, 1 B. & P. 400, cited arg. *Egremont* v. *Saul*, 6 A. & E. 924 ; 6 L. J. K. B. 205 : Toll : *Cp.* Custom.

THEREABOUTS.—By a charter-party a defendant undertook to load a vessel "of the measurement of 180 to 200 tons *or thereabouts*,"—held, he was not exonerated because the vessel happened to be 257 tons burthen (*Windle* v. *Barker*, 25 L. J. Q. B. 349 ; nom. *Barker* v. *Windle*, 6 E. & B. 675).

"Or thereabouts," when qualifying an estimated quantity of *Mines*, ought to be construed in the same way as if applied to the surface (*Davis* v. *Shepherd*, 35 L. J. Ch. 581 ; 1 Ch. 410 ; 15 L. T. 122).

A bequest of "£3000 *or thereabouts*," to be raised by accumulating income, is not void for uncertainty (*Oddie* v. *Brown*, 28 L. J. Ch. 542 ; 4 D. G. & J. 179, diss. K.-Bruce, L. J. : *Vth.* 1 Jarm. 358).

V. MORE OR LESS : SAY.

THEREAFTER.—*V. Re Manning*, 29 S. J. 683.

THEREAFTER TO BE BORN.—A testamentary gift to a class who may be living at a future event, or "thereafter," or "afterwards," to be born, is an executory gift, and not a contingent remainder, so that all the members of the class, whenever born, are entitled to share (*Miles* v. *Jarvis*, 52 L. J. Ch. 796 ; 24 Ch. D. 633, following *Re Lechmere and Lloyd*, 18 Ch. D. 524, and in opposition to *Brackenbury* v. *Gibbons*, 2 Ch. D. 417). *Vh. Ferguson* v. *Ferguson*, 17 L. R. Ir. 552.

THEREBY.—"Thereupon and thereby ;" *V.* THEREUPON.

THERETO.—"Thereto," in s. 3, 2 & 3 W. 4, c. 71, does not refer to "dwellinghouse, &c.," but to "access and use of light ;" and "the right thereto," in the section, means "the right to the same access and use of light to and for any dwellinghouse, workshop or other building" (per Fry, L. J., *Scott* v. *Pape*, 55 L. J. Ch. 432 ; 31 Ch. D. 554 ; 54 L. T. 399 ; 34 W. R. 465 ; 50 J. P. 645). *Vth. Greenwood* v. *Hornsey*, 33 Ch. D. 471.

"Thereto adjoining ;" *V.* ADJOIN.

"Thereunto belonging ;" *V.* BELONGING.

THERETOFORE.—*V. R.* v. *G. W. Ry.*, 28 L. J. M. C. 246 : *Portsmouth* v. *Smith*, 53 L. J. Q. B. 92 ; 54 Ib. 473 ; 13 Q. B. D. 184 ; 10 App. Ca. 364.

"Theretofore usually demised ;" *V.* USUALLY.

THEREUNTO.—*V.* THERETO.

THEREUPON.—It is as nearly accurate as possible to say that "thereupon" is the equivalent of "IMMEDIATELY" (*Vaughan* v. *Watt*, 9 L. J. Ex. 272 ; 6 M. & W. 492). But "whereupon" confers a right without involving the idea of any time within which it is to be claimed or enforced (*Burslem* v. *Attenborough*, 42 L. J. C. P. 102 ; L. R. 8 C. P. 122).

"Thereupon *and thereby* ;" *V.* these terms distinguished, *Atkinson* v. *Raleigh*, 3 Q. B. 79 ; 11 L. J. Q. B. 165 ; 2 G. & D. 611.

V. UPON.

THEREWITH.—House, &c., with any land "occupied therewith," s. 27, Reform Act, 2 W. 4, c. 45 ; "therewith," in that connection, has reference to time and not to locality ; and therefore, land at a distance from, if occupied at the same time as, a house, &c., can be estimated for the purpose of making up a £10 borough qualification, provided the land and building be so occupied by the claimant during the qualifying year "as owner" or "as tenant under the same landlord" (*Collins* v. *Thomas*, 22 L. J. C. P. 38; 12 C. B. 639; 2 Lutw. 219: *Saunders* v. *Searson*, 50 L. J. C. P. 117).

"Lands held therewith," s. 49, Lands C. C. Act, 1845; *V. Holt* v. *Gas Light and Coke Co.*, 41 L. J. Q. B. 351: L. R. 7 Q. B. 728.

V. TOGETHER WITH.

THESE PRESENTS.—A clause in a mortgage empowered the mortgagee (who was a solicitor) to charge for all business done by him "in or about these presents;" held, that this did not enable him to charge for business relating to the mortgaged property done by him subsequent to the mortgage; "'these presents' mean, not the property, but 'this deed'" (per Kay, J., *Field* v. *Hopkins*, 59 L. J. Ch. 174).

THIEVES.—The exception "Thieves" in a Bill of Lading generally means the same as in a Marine Insurance, and only applies to Thieves external to the ship (*Taylor* v. *Liverpool & G. W. Steam Co.*, 43 L. J. Q. B. 205; L. R. 9 Q. B. 546). In that case Archibald, J., said (43 L. J. Q. B. 208); "No doubt these words, 'Pirates, Robbers, Thieves,' were copied originally from the ordinary Policy of Insurance, and in that Policy the word 'Thieves' refers only to a theft with violence; and as it is capable of that meaning so also it is capable of another meaning, that is, as meaning a *furtum* merely, a furtive theft. Unless it has that ambiguous meaning, we must consider the meaning it has finally acquired in the ordinary Policy of Insurance; and the defts (the ship-owners) not having made it clear that this is an exception for their benefit, we must hold that it has the more restrictive meaning as in the Policy of Insurance." *Vf.* 1 Maude & P. 353.

V. ROBBERS.

THING.—*V.* ARTICLE.

THINGS.—A bequest of "all Things," in a particular house will not pass bonds and other choses in action (*Popham* v. *Aylesbury*, 1 Amb. 68: *Vth.* Wms. Exs. 1184, n. (*k*)).

A residuary bequest of "all Things not before bequeathed," will not pass testator's share in leaseholds (*Cook* v. *Oakley*, 1 P. Wms. 302, cited 1 Jarm. 751; *wh. V.* for further references). *Vf.* VALUABLE.

V. EFFECTS.

"Things duly done;" *V.* DULY.

THINGS IN ACTION.—*V.* CHOSE IN ACTION.

THINK FIT.—*V.* IF THEY SHALL THINK FIT.

In a Lease executed under a Power to Lease "with or without fine, and rendering such rents and services as the donee should think fit," no rent whatever need be reserved (*Talbot* v. *Tipper*, Skinner, 427: *Re Molton*, 2 Ir. C. L. R. 634 : *Muskerry* v. *Chinnery*, L. & G. t. Sug. 185 ; nom. *Sheehy* v. *Muskerry*, 7 Cl. & F. 1 ; 2 Jebb & Sy. 300 ; 1 H. L. Ca. 576 : Sug. Pow. 433–436, 816). If the power were "rendering such *yearly* rents" &c., possibly the rule would be different (*Talbot* v. *Tipper*, sup.).

THIRDS.—By a Settlement a provision out of real and personal estate, was made for the wife "in lieu of Dower or Thirds ;" held, the husband having died intestate, that the provision was in satisfaction of Dower out of realty and of Thirds of personalty, and that the wife could claim nothing under the Stat. of Distributions (*Thompson* v. *Watts*, 31 L. J. Ch. 445 ; 2 J. & H. 291 ; 6 L. T. 817).

THIS.—"This," is a simple word of relation, and its ordinary grammatical meaning will not be extended so as to include something else than that to which it relates (*Bryson* v. *Russell*, 54 L. J. Q. B. 144 ; 14 Q. B. D. 720 ; 52 L. T. 208 ; 33 W. R. 34 ; 49 J. P. 293).

THOUSAND.—Evidence of usage is admissible to show that "Thousand," in a contract, means some other figure than 1000, *e.g.* 1200 (*Smith* v. *Wilson*, 1 L. J. K. B. 194 ; 3 B. & Ad. 728).

THREAT.—A Threat of Legal Proceedings (s. 32, Patents &c. Act, 1883), need not relate only to acts already committed, but may also be contingent warnings directed to future acts ; and are not less Threats because made "without Prejudice" (per Kekewich, J., *Kurtz* v. *Spence*, 57 L. J. Ch. 238 ; 58 L. T. 438, explaining *Challender* v. *Royle*, 56 L. J. Ch. 995 ; 36 Ch. D. 425). *Vh. Combined Weighing Machine Co.* v. *Automatic Weighing Machine Co.*, 58 L. J. Ch. 709 : *Barrett* v. *Day*, 43 Ch. D. 435.

Threat "to limit the number of his Apprentices, or the number or description of his Journeymen, Workmen or Servants," s. 3, 6 G. 4, c. 129 ; *V. Walsby* v. *Anley*, 30 L. J. M. C. 121 ; 9 W. R. 271 : *Shelbourne* v. *Oliver*, 30 L. T. 630 : *O'Neill* v. *Kruger*, 12 W. R. 47 : *Skinner* v. *Kitch*, 36 L. J. M. C. 116 ; L. R. 2 Q. B. 393 : MOLEST.

THREE TIMES GREATER.—Houses and Buildings are to pay Lighting Rate "Three Times Greater" than Land (s. 33, 3 & 4 W. 4, c. 90) ; this does not mean "greater than by three times," but means "three times as great," so that if the whole rate be treated as 6*d.*, Land would pay 1½*d.*, *i.e.* one-fourth (*R.* v. *Somersetshire*, 22 J. P. 431 : *R.* v. *S. E. Ry.*, L. J., Notes of Cases (84), 121).

THROUGH.—Under a grant of way from A. to B. "*in, through, and along*" a particular way, the grantee is not justified in making a transverse road *across* the same (*Senhouse* v. *Christian*, 1 T. R. 560 : *Vh. Wimbledon*

Common Conservators v. *Dixon*, 1 Ch. D. 370 ; 45 L. J. Ch. 353 ; 24 W. R. 466 ; 33 L. T. 679).

The power enabling a Local Authority (s. 16, P. H. Act, 1875) to carry a Sewer "*into, through, or under*" lands, is not confined to carrying it underground (*Roderick* v. *Aston*, 46 L. J. Ch. 802 ; 5 Ch. D. 328.)

"*Through, over, or under*, in a reservation of Wayleave Royalty ; *V. G. W. Ry.* v. *Rous*, L. R. 4 H. L. 650 ; 39 L. J. Ch. 553 ; 19 W. R. 169 ; 23 L. T. 360.

"Through the Intervention ;" *V.* INTERVENTION.

THROUGH TRAFFIC.—"Through Traffic Rate and Route," s. 11, Regulation of Railways Act, 1873, 36 & 37 V. c. 48 ; *V. Central Wales Ry.* v. *G. W. Ry.*, 52 L. J. Q. B. 211 ; 10 Q. B. D. 231, following *Greenock and Wemyss Bay Ry.* v. *Caledonian Ry.*, 3 N. & M. 145.

TIDAL RIVER.—"That is called an arm of the sea where the sea flows and reflows, and so far only as the sea flows and reflows" (Hale, *De Jure Maris*, 12 ; Hargr. Tracts, Pt. 1, Ch. V., p. 17 *et seq.*). Therefore a river is a Tidal River in such parts only as are within the regular ebb and flow of the highest tides (*Reece* v. *Miller*, 51 L. J. M. C. 64 : 8 Q. B. D. 626 : *Vf. Mussett* v. *Burch*, 35 L. T. 486 : *Hudson* v. *McRae*, 33 L. J. M. C. 65 ; 4 B. & S. 585 : *Hargreaves* v. *Diddams*, 44 L. J. M. C. 178 ; L. R. 10 Q. B. 582).

TIDE.—*V.* AT ALL TIMES OF TIDE.

"Tide Permitting ;" *V.* PERMITTING.

TIGHT.—"The representation that the ship is '*Tight, Staunch and Strong*, and every way fitted for the voyage,' seems to be equivalent to the warranty of seaworthiness and fitness, which is implied by law on the part of the shipowner" (Carver, on Carriage by Sea, 145).

TILL.—*V.* UNTIL.

TIMBER.—"By the term 'Timber' is meant properly such trees *only* as are fit to be used in building and repairing houses ; thus Oak, Ash and Elm trees are considered 'timber' in all places, and under whatsoever circumstances they are grown (Co. Litt. 53 a ; Craig on Trees and Woods, 11). But only trees of not less than 6 inches in diameter or two feet girth (allowing for irregularities of shape), appear to be reckoned or considered as 'Timber' (*Whitty* v. *Dillon*, 2 F. & F. 67)," Woodf. 616. And no wood "is timber until of 20 years' growth" (*Dunn* v. *Bryan*, 7 Ir. Eq. 143 : Dart, 149, 150, citing *Foster* v. *Leonard*, Cro. Eliz. 1, and referring further as to what are, and what are not, timber trees to *Honywood* v. *Honywood*, 43 L. J. Ch. 652 ; L. R. 18 Eq. 306).

"Many descriptions of trees, which are not generally considered as timber, are so in some places by the custom of the country, *being there used for the purpose of building;* thus it has been laid down that Horse-chesnuts, Limes, Birch, Beech (*R.* v. *Minchinhampton,* 3 Burr. 1309), Ash, Walnut trees, and the like, may under such circumstances be deemed Timber, and are therefore protected by the law as such (*Chandos* v. *Talbot,* 2 P. Wms. 606 : *Palmer's Case,* Co. Litt. 53 a, Hargrave's note 349). It has been determined that, in the county of York, Birch trees are timber, because they are used in that county for building sheep-houses, cottages, and such mean buildings (*Cumberland's Case,* Moore, 812) : and it would seem that, in Hampshire, Willows have been considered as 'Timber' by the custom of the country (*Layfield* v. *Cowper,* 1 Wood, 330 : *Gruffly* v. *Pindar,* Hob. 219)." Woodf. 616. *Vf. Gordon* v. *Woodford,* 27 Bea. 607 ; 29 L. J. Ch. 222 : Sug. V. & P. 32. To the like effect is the passage in Dart already referred to, where it is laid down that "Timber" includes "by local custom Beech and various other trees ; even trees which are primarily *fruit trees,* as Cherry, Chesnut and Walnut (*Chandos* v. *Talbot,* sup.)." So White-thorn may be Timber (*Palmer's Case,* sup.). But though Dart does not mention the condition italicised in the passage extracted from Woodfall, viz. that to bring trees, not usually regarded as "timber," within that word, they must by the custom be "used for the purpose of building," yet, it would seem, that that at least is an important element in such a construction.

Where Beech trees—or as it should seem any other trees,—are by the custom of the country, and having regard to their nature and age, "Timber," "no evidence can be received to qualify its character of timber by showing that it was not deemed to be such in the county, unless the tree contained 10 feet of solid wood" (Woodf. 617, citing *Aubrey* v. *Fisher,* 10 East, 446 : *Chandos* v. *Talbot,* sup. : Co. Litt. 53).

"Although Pollards have been said not to be timber (Plowd. 470 : Craig on Trees, 12, 13 : *Phillipps* v. *Smith,* 15 L. J. Ex. 201 ; 14 M. & W. 589), yet, Lord King inclined to think them timber, provided their bodies were sound and good : and in an action to recover the value of Pollards under the description of 'timber and timber-like trees,' the plaintiff recovered a verdict (*Rabbett* v. *Raikes,* Suffolk Sum. Ass. 1803, cor. Macdonald, C.B : *Channon* v. *Patch,* 5 B. & C. 897 :" Woodf. 617). Dart says (149, 150), "As a general rule, Pollards would seem not to be timber ; if sound, however, they may be timber by local custom ;" but a little further down the latter page (and citing *Rabbett* v. *Raikes,* sup. ; and 2 P. Wms. 606), it is said that timber and timber-like trees "would seem to include sound Pollards" (*Va.* Sug. V. & P. 32.)

Vh. Craig on Trees and Woods, 11.

Under the words of a grant of "timber and timber-like trees now growing and being or which shall hereafter grow and be upon the said lands," Romilly, M.R., held that "thinnings" were included, and that it was for the grantee to determine what should be cut (*Gordon* v. *Woodford,* sup.).

Ornamental Timber was distinguished from ordinary Timber in *Magennis* v. *Fallon*, 2 Molloy, 590 : *Va. Ford* v. *Tynte*, 2 D. G. J. & S. 127.

Timber "shipped or unshipped ;" *V.* To SHIP.

TIMBERS.—"Main Timbers," in a covenant to repair, will include Iron Beams which are used as substitutes for timbers (*Manchester Bonding Warehouse Co.* v. *Carr*, 49 L. J. C. P. 812 ; 5 C. P. D. 507).

TIME.—"Whenever any expression of Time occurs in any Act of Parliament, Deed, or other legal instrument, the time referred to shall, unless it is otherwise specifically stated, be held, in the case of Great Britain, to be Greenwich Mean Time ; and, in the case of Ireland, Dublin Mean Time" (s. 1, 43 & 44 V. c. 9). *V.* OF THE CLOCK.

There is no general rule, in computing time from an act or event, that the day is to be inclusive or exclusive ; it depends on the reason of the thing according to the circumstances (*Lester* v. *Garland*, 15 Ves. 248).

V. AT ANY TIME : ONE TIME : AT THE PRESENT TIME : AT THE TIME OF : AT ALL TIMES.

TIME BEING.—The phrase "For the time being" may, according to its context, mean the time present, or denote a single period of time ; but its general sense is that of time indefinite, and refers to an indefinite state of facts which will arise in the future, and which may (and probably will) vary from time to time (*Ellison* v. *Thomas*, 31 L. J. Ch. 867 ; 32 L. J. Ch. 32 ; 1 D. G. J. & S. 18 ; 2 Dr. & Sm. 111 : *Coles* v. *Pack*, 39 L. J. C. P. 63 ; L. R. 5 C. P. 65).

A testamentary gift in remainder to testator's "*Next of Kin* for the time being," means the next of kin living at his death (*Moss* v. *Dunlop*, Johns. 490).

"*Owner* for the time being" of Shares in a Co.; held, not to include a holder who had sold his Shares after a Call made, but before it was payable (*Aylesbury Ry.* v. *Thompson*, 2 Ry. Ca. 668 : *Sv. London & Brighton Ry.* v. *Fairclough*, 10 L. J. C. P. 133 ; 2 M. & G. 674 ; 3 Sc. N. S. 68).

A direction to pay Calls on Shares which, at or after his death, might be or become due in respect of Shares "for the time being" constituting part of testator's Residuary Personal Estate ; held, to apply to Calls on Shares held by the testator at his death, but not to Shares afterwards acquired by the Trustees (*Bevan* v. *Waterhouse*, 46 L. J. Ch. 331 ; 3 Ch. D. 752).

Persons who are "for the time being" *Trustees* under s. 2 (8), Settled Land Act, 1882, are those expressly appointed for the purposes of the Act, or else have, at the time of the proposed sale thereunder, a present and immediate power to sell or consent to a sale (*Wheelwright* v. *Walker*, 52 L. J. Ch. 274 ; 23 Ch. D. 752).

"It has been said that if a power to vary the rights of parties be communicated to the '*Trustees* for the time being,' it cannot be exercised by a single trustee" (Lewin, 604, citing *Lancashire* v. *Lancashire*, 2 Phill. 664).

"For the time being," s. 5, Trade Marks Act, 1875 ; *V. Wood* v. *Lambert* (29 S. J. 455).

TIME CERTAIN.—*V.* CERTAIN TIME.

TIME OR SITTING.—S. 2, 9 Anne, c. 14; *V.* SITTING.

TIME OUT OF MIND.—"Some have said that 'Time out of mind' should be said from time of limitation in a writ of right; that is to say, from the time of King Richard the First after the Conquest" (Litt. s. 170), *i.e.*, A.D. 1189. *V.* LONG.

TIME TO TIME.—*V.* FROM TIME TO TIME.

TIMES.—*V.* AT ALL TIMES: AT ALL TIMES OF TIDE.

TITHE FREE.—If property is sold "Tithe Free," that is a material statement, and the purchaser is not bound to complete if it be untrue (*Ker* v. *Clobury*, MS. Sug. V. & P. 321, correcting *Stanhope's Case*, cited *Drewe* v. *Hanson*, 6 Ves. 678).

TITHES.—"Tithes" in 3 & 4 W. 4, c. 27, is confined to Tithes as between adverse claimants to Tithes (*Grant* v. *Ellis*, 11 L. J. Ex. 228; 9 M. & W. 113: *Ely* v. *Cash*, 15 L. J. Ex. 341; 15 M. & W. 617: *Ely* v. *Bliss*, 2 D. G. M. & G. 459: *Bunbury* v. *Fuller*, 23 L. J. Ex. 29; 9 Ex. 128). *Vf. Payne* v. *Esdaile*, 58 L. J. Ch. 299; 13 App. Ca. 613; 37 W. R. 273; 59 L. T. 568.

Tithes in A., will pass under a devise of "Land" in A., if there be no land there belonging to testator (*Ashton* v. *Ashton*, 3 P. Wms. 386; Ca. t. Talb. 152); so they may, or may not, be included in "my real estates" (*Evans* v. *Evans*, 17 Sim. 86; 14 Jur. 383).

V. RENT.

TITHING.—*V.* HUNDRED.

TITLE.—"'Title' properly (as some say) is, when a man hath a lawfull cause of entry into lands whereof another is seized for the which hee can have no action, as title of condition, title of mortmaine, &c. But legally this word (Title) includeth a Right also, as you shall perceive in many places in Littleton: and Title is the more generall word; for every Right is a Title, but every Title is not such a Right for which an action lieth; and therefore *Titulus est justa causa possidendi quod nostrum est,* and signifieth the meanes whereby a man cometh to land, as his title is by Fine or by Feoffment, &c." (Co. Litt. 345 b; *Vh.* Elph. 205).

"The word 'Title' has different meanings. In one sense, it may import whether a party has a right to a thing which is admitted to exist; or it may mean, whether the thing claimed does in fact exist" (per Coleridge, J., *Adey* v. *Trinity House*, 22 L. J. Q. B. 4; nom. *R.* v. *Everett*, 1 E. & B. 273).

A direction that goods bequeathed are "to be enjoyed with and go with the Title" of real or leasehold property, will not create an executed or executory trust, or cut down the legatee's interest in the goods to a life estate (*Re Johnson*, 53 L. J. Ch. 645 ; 26 Ch. D. 538).

Title "accrued ;" *V.* Accrue.

Title "to be approved ;" *V.* Subject to.

TO.—Where a verb of obligation is put in the infinitive mood,—*e.g.*, the tenant "to paint" once every fifth year,—an agreement, or covenant, would obviously be created.

"To" will often mean "*Towards*." The plaintiff effected a Marine Policy, subject to rules one of which was, that ships were not to sail from any port on the east coast of Great Britain *to* any port in the Belts between the 20th Dec. and 15th Feb. The plaintiff's vessel sailed on the 8th Feb. for a port in the Belts, and was lost; held, that the rule in question was a warranty and not an exception; and that the word "*to*" in the rule meant "*towards*" and not "arriving at" (*Colledge* v. *Harty*, 6 Ex. 205 ; 20 L. J. Ex. 146). *V.* Towards.

TO BE.—This phrase is one of futurity, and may (1) create a covenant, (2) impose a qualification of, or condition precedent to, a covenant, or (3) go to define the condition of a gift, or of a state of things.

1 and 2. When a clause in a Deed prescribing something to be done or permitted, is introduced by "To be," or a participle, the effect, speaking generally, is to create either a covenant on the part of the person by whom the thing is to be done or permitted, or to impose a condition precedent on, or a qualification of, some covenant in the deed. The context determines which of these meanings is to prevail. Thus where rent is "*to be paid*" (*Bower* v. *Hodges*, 22 L. J. C. P. 194 ; 13 C. B. 765), or if the ordinary words at the commencement of the reddendum of a Lease,—"Yielding and Paying,"—are used (Elph. 419, 420, 464–466 ; Touch. 162 : *Sear* v. *House Propy. Co.*, 50 L. J. Ch. 77 ; 16 Ch. D. 387), a covenant to pay is created. But where a tenant covenants to repair, he "to be allowed," or the lessor "allowing," necessary timber, such latter clause prescribes a condition precedent, or qualification, of the covenant to repair (*Thomas* v. *Cadwallader*, Willes, 496 : *Vf.* Elph. 420, 421, 464–466 ; Woodf. 159, 160, 167).

3. A condition of a gift is prescribed by "To be" in such a phrase as To be born.

TO BE APPROVED.—Title "to be approved by my solicitor;" *V. Clack* v. *Wood*, 9 Q. B. D. 276, cited Subject to.

TO BE BORN.—The ordinary primary legal meaning of "to be born," or "to be begotten," includes past as well as future children;

though that construction may, by a context, give way to the ordinary meaning of the English language whereby those phrases express futurity (per Fry, L. J., *Locke* v. *Dunlop*, 57 L. J. Ch. 1015 ; 39 Ch. D. 387 ; 59 L. T. 683). That case was an instance in which the latter construction was adopted.

"Gifts to, or trusts for, children '*to be* born,' or '*to be* begotten,' include those already born or begotten ; and *e contra*" (Elph. 328 ; *Va.* Ib. 236).

In class gifts to children "to be born," or "to be begotten," "the established rule is, that if the gift be immediate, so that it would, but for the words in question, have been confined to children (if any) existing at the testator's death, they will have the effect of extending it to *all* the children who shall ever come into existence ; since in order to give to the words in question *some* operation, the gift is necessarily made to comprehend the whole" (2 Jarm. 178).

"This rule of construction, however, does not apply to general pecuniary legacies, where the effect of letting in children born after the death of the testator would be to postpone the distribution of the general estate (out of which the legacies are payable), until the death of the parent of the legatees" (Ib. 179).

"It seems to be established, too, that the expression children '*to be* born,' or '*to be* begotten,' when occurring in a gift under which *some* class of children born after the death of the testator would, independently of this expression of futurity, be entitled, so that the words may be satisfied without departing from the ordinary construction, that construction is unaffected by them" (Ib. 180).

"It has been decided, too, that the words 'which shall be begotten,' or 'to be begotten,' annexed to the description of children or issue, do not *confine* the devise to future children ; but that the description will, notwithstanding these words, include the children or issue in existence before the making of the Will" (Ib. 181) : "and it seems that even the words '*hereafter* to be born' will not exclude previously-born issue" (Ib. 182).

Vh. Chitty, Eq. Ind. 7771–7774.

V. Born.

TO BE CANCELLED.—Charter-party "to be cancelled" in certain events ; *V. Adamson* v. *Newcastle Steamship Insrce.*, 48 L. J. Q. B. 670 ; 4 Q. B. D. 462.

TO BE CONSUMED.—*V.* On the Premises.

TO BE DISPOSED OF.—*V.* Dispose of.

TO BE DIVIDED.—*V.* Divide.

TO BE EXECUTED.—A fi. fa. delivered to a sheriff for execution, but which before seizure is stayed until further orders, and on which subsequently the sheriff is ordered to proceed, is not delivered "to be executed," within s. 16, Stat. of Frauds, 29 Car. 2, c. 3, until the latter order (*Hunt* v. *Hooper*, 13 L. J. Ex. 183 ; 12 M. & W. 664). *V.* EXECUTED.

TO BE PAID.—This phrase in an Agreement inter partes creates a covenant to pay (*Bower* v. *Hodges*, 22 L. J. C. P. 194 ; 13 C. B. 765).

In a Will it is generally synonymous with PAYABLE ; *Vf.* 1 Jarm. 837. In *Martineau* v. *Rogers* (25 L. J. Ch. 398 ; 8 D. G. M. & G. 328), "to be paid" was construed "vested."

V. PAID.

TO BE PERFORMED.—*V.* WITHIN THE JURISDICTION.

TO BE RECOVERED.—"When a statute gives a 'penalty to be recovered before Justices of the Peace,' but prescribes no method of recovering it, the proper method is by Indictment" (Dwar. 673, citing Salk. 606).

V. RECOVER.

TO BE SETTLED.—This phrase held to create an executory trust (*Ballance* v. *Lamphier*, 42 Ch. D. 62 ; 58 L. J. Ch. 534 ; 37 W. R. 600 ; 61 L. T. 158). *Vf.* SETTLED.

TO BE SHIPPED.—*V.* SHIPPED.

TO BEARER.—*V.* BEARER.

TO ORDER.—If a warehouseman gives a Warrant of goods to be held "To Order" of A., and, without getting the Warrant, delivers the goods at A.'s request to some one other than the holder of the Warrant, the warehouseman will be responsible for the goods to the innocent holder for value of the Warrant (*Lond. & County Bank* v. *Fulford*, 2 Times Rep. 703).

TO WIT.—*V.* NAMELY.

TOFT.—"'Toft' is a place wherein a house once stood, but it is now all fallen, or puld downe" (Termes de la Ley).

"Toft is the place where a house has been, but now there is none, and the site of the house can be seen, and by this name it will pass in a grant : 21 Ed. 4, 52, Pl. 15 ; Touch. 95. Spelman says that the house must have been in the country" (Elph. 622).

TOGETHER WITH.—This phrase does not mean "and also," but "at the same time as;" and therefore a Bill of Sale and its affidavit must be registered simultaneously (*Grindell* v. *Brendon*, 28 L. J. C. P. 333 ; 6 C. B. N. S. 698). *V.* THEREWITH.

TOLERATED.—Place of Religious Worship, "tolerated by law on Sundays;" *V.* USUAL PLACE OF RELIGIOUS WORSHIP: Stone's Justices' Manual, 21 Ed. 789.

TOLL.—"Toll," or *Tolnetum* (or THEOLONIO), is a sum of money which is taken in respect of some benefit (per Bramwell & Willes, citing Com. Dig. *Toll,* in *Adey* v. *Trinity House,* 22 L. J. Q. B. 3),—the benefit being, the temporary use of land,—*e.g.*, FAIRS AND MARKET TOLLS, TOLL THOROUGH, TOLL TRAVERSE, ANCHORAGE TOLLS, and Harbour Tolls (*Mayor of Exeter* v. *Warren,* 5 Q. B. 773 : *The London Wharves,* 1 W. Bl. 581). Therefore Harbour Rates (under a Private Act) are "Tolls" (*Adey* v. *Trinity House,* 22 L. J. Q. B. 3 ; nom. *R.* v. *Everett,* 1 E. & B. 273) ; but payments to a Railway Company for the use of locomotive power, as distinguished from the use of their railway, are not (*Hunt* v. *G. N. Ry.*, 20 L. J. Q. B. 349 ; 2 L. M. & P. 268). The proper sense of the word "Toll," as applied to a Ry., is a payment in respect of the use of the railway itself,—the person paying the toll being himself the carrier of the goods or persons along the railway (*Wallis* v. *Lond. & S. W. Ry.*, 39 L. J. Ex. 57 ; L. R. 5 Ex. 62 : *Brown* v. *G. W. Ry.*, 9 Q. B. D. 744 ; 51 L. J. Q. B. 529 : *North Central Wagon Co.* v. *Manchester, S. & L. Ry.*, 55 L. J. Ch. 780 ; 56 Ib. 609 ; 58 Ib. 219 ; 32 Ch. D. 477 ; 35 Ib. 191 ; 13 App. Ca. 554): and those cases show that that is the meaning of the word as used in ss. 95–97, Ry. C. C. Act, 1845. A Railway Co.'s carrier charge is therefore not a Toll : *V.* lastly cited cases and *Gorton* v. *Bristol & Ex. Ry.*, 1 B. & S. 112; 30 L. J. Q. B. 273, for distinction between "Charges" and "Tolls." Yet it would seem that the word "Tolls" in s. 90, 8 V. c. 20, applies to traffic generally, and is not limited to Tolls strictly so called (*Evershed* v. *Lond. & N. W. Ry.*, 46 L. J. Q. B. 289 ; 47 Ib. 284 ; 48 Ib. 22 ; 3 Q. B. D. 134 ; 3 App. Ca. 1029) ; but (per Bramwell, L. J., in that case), the "word does not include a charge for cartage or collection ; it only includes charges for receiving upon transit along, and delivery from, the Railway of the goods entrusted to the Company" (47 L. J. Q. B. 285).

STALLAGE may pass under the word "Toll" (*Bennington* v. *Taylor,* 2 Lutw. E. Ed. 1718, 642 : *Hickman's Case,* 2 Rol. Ab. 123).

Vh. Termes de la Ley, *Tol* or *Tolne.*

V. WITH ALL LIBERTIES : CUSTOM.

TOLL THOROUGH.—Is a toll for passing along a public highway, whether the highway be a road, a river, a ferry, a bridge, or the sea : and it cannot be claimed by prescription, but must be supported (if at all) by a good consideration performed in respect of the precise locality where the toll is claimed, *e. g.* the reparation of *the* highway on which the toll is claimed (Gunning on Tolls, 2–25 : *Hill* v. *Smith,* 4 Taunt. 520 : *V.* ANCHORAGE TOLLS).

TOLL TRAVERSE.—Is a toll payable for passing over the soil of another, or over soil which, though now a public highway, was once private, and which (as a matter of precise proof, or as a legal presumption) was dedicated subject to the toll. It can be claimed by prescription (Gunning on Tolls, 26–42 : *Pelham* v. *Pickersgill*, 1 T. R. 660 : *Lawrence* v. *Hitch*, 37 L. J. Q. B. 209 ; L. R. 3 Q. B. 521).

TO-MORROW.—*V. Duncan* v. *Topham*, 8 C. B. 225 ; 18 L. J. C. P. 310.

TON.—A contract for the sale of goods by "the Ton, long weight," is good, as "the Ton, long weight," though it consists of 240,000 lbs. avoirdupois and is more than 20 cwt. statutory measure, is yet a Multiple of the standard pound, within s. 9, 5 G. 4, c. 74 (*Giles* v. *Jones*, 24 L. J. Ex. 261; 11 Ex. 393). *V.* MULTIPLE.

TOOLS.—*V.* MATERIALS.

TORT.—"A 'Tort' has been defined as a wrong independent of Contract. It may also be defined as the infringement, without lawful excuse, of a right vested in some determinate person, either personally or as a member of the community, and available against the world at large, or against some person or body exercising public functions as such, whereby damage is caused to such determinate person, either intentionally or as a natural consequence of the infringement" (Add. T. 1).

"Action *founded on Tort*," s. 5, County Court Act, 1867;—an action of Detinue is within this phrase (*Bryant* v. *Herbert*, 47 L. J. C. P. 670; 3 C. P. D. 389); so is an action against a Carrier for delivering goods to an insolvent consignee after notice of a stoppage *in transitu* (*Pontifex* v. *Mid. Ry.*, 47 L. J. Q. B. 28 ; 3 Q. B. D. 23). *Cp.* "Action founded on Contract," sub CONTRACT : *Va.* FOUNDED ON.

"Action *of Tort*," s. 10, Co. Co. Act, 1867; Trover is within this phrase (*Clapham* v. *Oliver*, 30 L. T. 365).

TORTURE.—*V.* CRUELTY *to Animals.*

TOTAL LOSS.—"Since the days of *Davy* v. *Milford* (15 East, 559), it seems that the expression, 'Total Loss,' is an ambiguous one; it may mean a total loss of the whole subject-matter of insurance, or a total loss of part" (per Byles, J., *Wilkinson* v. *Hyde*, 3 C. B. N. S. 46 : *Vh. Cossman* v. *West*, 57 L. J. P. C. 17; 13 App. Ca. 160 ; 58 L. T. 122 ; 6 Asp. 233: 2 Arn. 910 *et seq.*, Chs. 6, 7, 8 : Park on Mar. Insrce., Ch. 9, 8 Ed., 332 : Maude & P. 525 *et seq.*).

V. PARTIAL LOSS : LOSS.

TOTIES QUOTIES.—*V.* FROM TIME TO TIME.

TOWARDS.—A bequest of an Annuity to A. "Towards the support of her children until they attain 21," held merely descriptive of the motive of the gift, and that the annuity continued after the children attained 21 (*Farr* v. *Hennis*, W. N. (80) 194). *V.* SUPPORT.

From A. "*towards and unto*" B., in an Indictment for non-repair of a Highway; *V. R.* v. *Downshire*, 5 L. J. K. B. 50; 4 A. & E. 232; 5 N. & M. 662. *V.* To.

TOWN.—"By the name of a towne, *villa*, a mannor may passe" (Co. Litt. 5 a).

"'Towne (ville),'—"*Villa est ex pluribus mansionibus vicinata, et colleta ex pluribus vicinis.* If a towne be decaied so as no houses remaine, yet it is a towne in law. And so if a borough bee decayed, yet shall it send burgesses to the parliament, as Old Salisbury and others doe."—(But the glory of Old Sarum was extinguished by the Reform Act of 1832.)—"It cannot be a towne in law, unlesse it hath, or in time past hath had, a church and celebration of divine service, sacraments and burials" (Co. Litt. 115 b). In *Elliott* v. *S. Devon Ry.* (17 L. J. Ex. 262) Parke, B., said that the legal meaning of the word "Town" was "a place with a constable, or a church."

But generally in modern legislation,—*e.g.* s. 11, Ry. C. C. Act, 1845; ss. 93, 128, Lands C. C. Act, 1845; The Towns Improvement Clauses Act (10 & 11 V. c. 34); and Turnpike Acts,—"Town" is not restricted by its legal meaning, but is expounded popularly and means the space which, for the time being, is covered by, or occupied as accessory to, houses collected together in a mass, and in sufficient number to be ordinarily designated as a Town; and includes unbuilt-on lands that may lie within the ambit of such collected mass of houses (*Elliott* v. *S. Devon Ry.*, 17 L. J. Ex. 262; 2 Ex. 725: *R.* v. *Cottle*, 20 L. J. M. C. 162; 16 Q. B. 412: *Lond. & S. W. Ry.* v. *Blackmore*, 39 L. J. Ch. 713; 23 L. T. 504; 19 W. R. 305; L. R. 4 H. L. 610: *Collier* v. *Worth*, 1 Ex. D. 464; 40 J. P. 808: *Deards* v. *Goldsmith*, 40 L. T. 328; *Vf.* Lloyd on Comp., 5 Ed. 44; Dart, 860, 861); but not lands outside such ambit, though within a borough (*Carington* v. *Wycombe Ry.*, 3 Ch. 377; 37 L. J. Ch. 213; 18 L. T. 96; 16 W. R. 494: *Coventry* v. *L., B. & S. Ry.*, L. R. 5 Eq. 104; 37 L. J. Ch. 90; 16 W. R. 267: *Falkner* v. *Somerset & Dorset Ry.*, L. R. 16 Eq. 458; 42 L. J. Ch. 851).

"Town," in a Turnpike Act; *V. R.* v. *Cottle*, 20 L. J. M. C. 162; 16 Q. B. 412.

"Town," in Towns Improvement (Ireland) Act, 1854; *V. R.* v. *Local Government Bd.*, 2 L. R. Ir. 316.

TOWNSHIP.—*V.* Elph. 624–626.

"Township," s. 1, 3 & 4 V. c. 61; *Preston* v. *Buckley*, 39 L. J. M. C. 105; L. R. 5 Q. B. 391.

TRADE: TRADESMAN.—A "Trade" "has the technical meaning

of buying and selling" (per Willes, J., *Harris* v. *Amery*, 35 L. J. C. P. 92; L. R. 1 C. P. 148): and it is not essential to a "Trade" that the persons carrying it on should make, or desire to make, a profit (per Coleridge, C. J., *Re Law Reporting Council*, 58 L. J. Q. B. 95; 22 Q. B. D. 279).

"The term 'Tradesman' cannot be extended by a reasonable construction to a Farmer" (per Cockburn, C. J., *R.* v. *Silvester*, 33 L. J. M. C. 80; nom. *R.* v. *Cleworth*, 4 B. & S. 927; *Cleworth* v. *Leigh*, 12 W. R. 375).

A Co. "established for any Trade or *Business*," s. 11 (5), Customs & Inl. Rev. Act, 1885, 48 & 49 V. c. 51, may be one not anticipating profit (*Re Law Reporting Council*, sup.); *secus* of the same phrase in s. 13 (2), 41 V. c. 15, because there it is added "by which the occupier seeks a livelihood or profit" (*London Library* v. *Carter*, 6 Times Rep. 161; 34 S. J. 231).

Cp. BUSINESS.

The exemption from Toll for vehicles used "in the course of Trade or *Husbandry*," given by s. 9 (6), 32 & 33 V. c. 14, does not extend to vehicles belonging to the proprietor of a circus, and used by him for carrying his performers and making displays (*Speak* v. *Powell*, 43 L. J. M. C. 19; L. R. 9 Ex. 25).

"Trade, *Manufacture, Adventure, or Concern*," No. 1, 1st set of Rules, Sch. D, s. 100, Income Tax Act, 5 & 6 V. c. 35; *V. Ryhope Co.* v. *Foyer*, 7 Q. B. D. 485; 45 L. T. 404.

V. TRADER: IN HIS TRADE OR BUSINESS: PURPOSES.

TRADE OR COMMERCE.—*V.* CIVIL RIGHTS.

TRADE OR DEALING.—Banking is a "Trade or Dealing for gain or profit;" and, accordingly, a Banking Co., some of whose members were spiritual persons, was held unable to recover on a Bill of Exchange indorsed to it, because its "trade or dealing" was partly carried on by spiritual persons contrary to s. 3, 57 G. 3, c. 39 (*Hall* v. *Franklin*, 3 M. & W. 259; 7 L. J. Ex. 110). *V.* that enactment modified by 4 V. c. 14: *Vth.* Walker on Banking, 2 Ed., 29.

TRADE-MARK.—"A Trade-Mark is—

(a) A mark lawfully used by any person to denote any chattel to be an article or thing of the manufacture, workmanship, production, or merchandise of such person, or to be an article or thing of any peculiar or particular description made or sold by such person;

(b) Any mark or sign which, in pursuance of any statute in force for the time being relating to registered designs, is to be put or placed upon or attached to any chattel or article during the existence or continuance of any copyright or other sole right acquired under the provision of such statutes or any of them" (Steph. Cr. 304, 305, stating 25 & 26 V. c. 88, s. 1).

Vf. Arch. Cr. 998.

TRADE REFUSE—*V.* REFUSE.

TRADER.—For an enumeration of persons who formerly were liable to be adjudicated Bankrupt as "Traders;" *V.* Sch. 1, Bankry. Act, 1869; and for the cases thereon, *V.* Robson on Bankruptcy, 3 Ed. 100–102.

"Trader," s. 5, Bovill's Act, 28 & 29 V. c. 86, includes a trading Joint Stock Co. (*Re House Improvement & Supply Assn.*, Times, 29th Jan., 1890).

"Being a Trader;" *V.* BEING.

V. TRADE: TRADERS.

TRADERS.—In *Tennant* v. *Swansea Harbour Trustees* (3 Times Rep. 129), "Traders" of a person, were held to mean all persons having dealings with him; *i.e.*, his customers.

TRADING.—"Trading," in s. 379 (3), Merchant Shipping Act, 1854 (17 & 18 V. c. 104), means "for the time being Trading," or "when Trading;" and the subsection does not mean that a Ship must be constantly trading to Boulogne, &c., in order to obtain the exemption from compulsory pilotage which the section provides (*Courtney* v. *Cole*, 19 Q. B. D. 447; 56 L. J. M. C. 141; 57 L. T. 409; 36 W. R. 8; 52 J. P. 20; 6 Asp. 169: *Vf. The Wesley*, Lush. 268: *The Sutherland*, 56 L. J. P. D. & A. 95; 12 P. D. 154; 57 L. T. 631; 36 W. R. 13). *Cp.* COASTING TRADE.

"Trading Inwards," "Trading Outwards;" *V. Mersey Docks* v. *Henderson*, 58 L. J. Q. B. 152: *Cross* v. *Pagliano*, L. R. 6 Ex. 9.

TRADING AND OTHER PUBLIC COMPANIES.—This phrase, in s. 5, Apportionment Act, 1870, includes any Public Company, but not a Private Partnership (*Re Griffith, Carr* v. *Griffith*, 12 Ch. D. 655). "What a 'Public Company' is has not been defined, but one test is whether the members have a right to transfer their shares" (Buckl. 3, citing *Re Griffith*, sup.).

TRADING PERSON.—A person who goes from the town in which he resides, and takes a room at another town, and there sells goods which are brought direct from the town of his residence, is a "Trading Person going from town to town" within s. 6, 50 G. 3, c. 41 (*Manson* v. *Hope*, 31 L. J. M. C. 191; 2 B. & S. 498, following *A.-G.* v. *Tongue*, 12 Price, 51: *A.-G.* v. *Woolhouse*, Ib. 65; 1 Y. & J. 463: *Dean* v. *King*, 4 B. & Ald. 517). *V.* HAWKER.

TRAFFIC.—"Traffic," s. 2, Ry. & Canal Traffic Act, 1854 (17 & 18 V. c. 31); *V. East and West India Dock Co.* v. *Shaw*, 39 Ch. D. 524; 57 L. J. Ch. 1038. *V.* FACILITIES.

Receipts from all "Traffic conveyed on the Railway;" "I agree that all things incidental to the Traffic are part of the gross receipts, and I think the receipts of the Cloak Room, and of warehousing, are part of the receipts for carrying the Traffic on the line; but I cannot agree that the receipts from Telegrams are part of those gross receipts" (per Blackburn, J., *R.* v.

Coleridge, 45 L. J. Q. B. 654) ; and Telegram receipts were held not within the phrase, as used in an agreement between two Ry. Companies.

TRAIN.—A series of trucks propelled by hydraulic power into a Goods Station, is a "Train upon a Railway" within s. 1 (5), Employers' Liability Act, 1880 (*Cox* v. *G. W. Ry.*, 9 Q. B. D. 106) : *V.* RAILWAY.

"Special Train ;" *V.* SPECIAL.

TRANSACT BUSINESS.—Going into two shops, and possibly buying tobacco in the one and certainly buying bacon for his own consumption in the other, is not "transacting business" by a member of a Benefit Society, within a Rule forfeiting Sick-pay (*Wallis* v. *Lomas*, Times, 10 Feb., 1890).

TRANSACTION.—*V.* CONTRACT.

"Transaction," in the Canada Civil Code ; *V. King* v. *Pinsoneault*, L. R. 6 P. C. 245 ; 44 L. J. P. C. 42.

TRANSFER.—The operative verb "Transfer,"—"is one of the widest terms that can be used" (per James, L. J., *Gathercole* v. *Smith*, 50 L. J. Ch. 672 ; 17 Ch. D. 1 : *V.* TRANSFERABLE).

"Transfer,"—*e.g.* of a Debt,—"does not necessarily mean Absolute Transfer" (per Cotton, L. J., *Re Combined Weighing Co.*, 43 Ch. D. 104 ; 59 L. J. Ch. 27).

An Agreement accompanying a deposit of a registered Bill of Sale, by way of equitable sub-mortgage, is a "Transfer or Assignment" of the B. of S. within s. 10, Bills of S. Act, 1878, and need not be registered (*Re Parker, Ex p. Turquand*, 54 L. J. Q. B. 242 ; 14 Q. B. D. 636).

A document accompanying an actual pledge of goods is not a "Transfer" requiring registration as a Bill of Sale (*Re Hall, Ex p. Close*, 54 L. J. Q. B. 43 ; 14 Q. B. D. 386 ; 51 L. T. 795 ; 33 W. R. 228 : and *V.* the cases there cited, and *Vth. Ex p. Hubbard, Re Hardwick*, 17 Q. B. D. 695).

A gift of money is a "Transfer of Property" within sub-s. 3, s. 47, Bankry. Act, 1883 (*Re Player, Ex p. Harvey*, No. 1, 54 L. J. Q. B. 553 : *Vf.* SETTLEMENT).

Bankruptcy on a creditor's petition is not an Assignment or Transfer within a clause of forfeiture contemplating a voluntary act by the beneficiary (*Doe* d. *Goodbehere* v. *Bevan*, 3 M. & S. 353 : *Lear* v. *Leggett*, 2 Sim. 479), even though it proceed on a declaration of insolvency (*Graham* v. *Lee*, 23 Bea. 388) : but where there is a *cessio bonorum* in bankruptcy, insolvency, or liquidation based on the *beneficiary's* petition, then there is such a Transfer (*Shee* v. *Hale*, 13 Ves. 409 : *Re Amherst*, 41 L. J. Ch. 222 ; L. R. 13 Eq. 464. *V.* latter case distinguished in *Ex p. Dawes*, cited WOULD).

"Renewal or Transfer" of an Alehouse License ; *V.* RENEWAL.

V. CONVEYANCE : ASSIGN : UNDERLEASE : NEGOTIATE : TRANSMISSION.

TRANSFERABLE.—An interest which by statute or otherwise is made "not transferable" cannot be parted with either by act of parties or by operation of law (*Gathercole* v. *Smith*, 50 L. J. Ch. 671 ; 17 Ch. D. 1 ; 29 W. R. 434). In that case Lush, L. J., said,—"The word 'transferable' is of the widest possible import, and includes *every* means by which the property may be passed from one person to another."

TRANSFEROR.—"(1.) Where the Holder of a Bill, payable to Bearer, negotiates it by Delivery without indorsing it, he is called 'a Transferor by Delivery.'

(2.) A Transferor by Delivery is not liable on the instrument.

(3.) A Transferor by Delivery who negotiates a Bill, thereby warrants to his immediate Transferee being a Holder for Value, that the Bill is what it purports to be, that he has a right to transfer it, and that at the time of the transfer he is not aware of any fact which renders it valueless"

(s. 58, Bills of Ex. Act, 1882) : and so of a Note (s. 89, Ib.).

TRANSHIPMENT.—"PARTIAL LOSS from Transhipment" in a Marine Policy ; *V.* per Mathew, J., *Pink* v. *Fleming*, 6 Times Rep. 213.

TRANSIT.—*V.* DELAY IN TRANSIT.

TRANSMISSIBLE.—A Bequest of Residue to the persons who "shall become entitled to a vested Transmissible Interest," means an Interest "capable of transmission *after death*" (per Stirling, J., *Jodrell* v. *Seale*, W. N. (89) 230 ; 34 S. J. 129 : *Vf. Nannock* v. *Horton*, 7 Ves. 402).

TRANSMISSION.—The phrase "Transmission" of the property in a ship, other than by TRANSFER, occurs in the Merchant Shipping Act, 1854 (17 & 18 V. c. 104), and means "transmission by operation of law, unconnected with any direct act of the party to whom the property is transmitted;" and therefore "a sale by licitation is not such a Transmission" (*Chasteauneuf* v. *Capeyron*, 51 L. J. P. C. 41 ; 7 App. Ca. 127). So "Transmission" of Company Shares is effected by devolution of law as distinguished from a "Transfer" which is accomplished by the act of parties ; and therefore where Table A. applies *simpliciter*, a trustee in bankruptcy is not subject to Art. 10 of that Table (*Re Bentham Mills Co.*, 48 L. J. Ch. 671 ; 11 Ch. D. 900).

A Foreign Executorship created no "Transmission" of interest or liability within Ord. 50, R. 4, Judicature Rules, 1875 : representation must have been obtained in England (per North, J., *Morrice* v. *Smart*, 26 S. J. 752, wherein the learned judge repudiated the reported decision in *Jameson* v. *Marshall*, 46 L. T. 480).

TRANSMIT.—"To Transmit,"—*e.g.* an Appeal Case under s. 3,

20 & 21 V. c. 43,—does that mean to send it off, or does it also include the reception of the thing sent? *Vh.* 37 Law Times, 260, 261.

TRAVELLER.—There are, at least, four classes of "Travellers."

1. A person cannot be a "*bonâ fide* Traveller," within the Licensing Acts, "unless the place where he lodged during the preceding night is, at least, *three miles* distant from the place where he demands to be supplied with liquor, such distance to be calculated by the nearest public thoroughfare" (37 & 38 V. c. 49, s. 10; *Vth. Coulbert* v. *Troke*, 45 L. J. M. C. 7; 1 Q. B. D. 1). For the decisions on this phrase prior to the statutory definition just quoted, *V. Taylor* v. *Humphreys*, 30 L. J. M. C. 242; 10 C. B. N. S. 429; 28 J. P. 793: *Taylor* v. *Humphries*, 34 L. J. M. C. 1; 17 C. B. N. S. 539: *Fisher* v. *Howard*, 34 L. J. M. C. 42: *Peache* v. *Colman*, 35 L. J. M. C. 118; L. R. 1 C. P. 324: *Peplow* v. *Richardson*, L. R. 4 C. P. 168; 33 J. P. 407. Whether business or pleasure be the object of the traveller, was (*Taylor* v. *Humphries*, sup.; *Atkinson* v. *Sellers*, 28 L. J. M. C. 12; 5 C. B. N. S. 442; 23 J. P. 71), and still is wholly immaterial.

2. Persons at a railway station "arriving at, or departing from, such station by railroad," are for the purposes of the Licensing Acts on the same level as *bonâ fide* travellers (37 & 38 V. c. 49, s. 10).

3. Commercial Traveller—*i.e.* "a bonâ fide Traveller" within s. 17, 30 & 31 V. c. 90, on which *V. Stuchbery* v. *Spencer*, 55 L. J. M. C. 141.

4. A traveller entitled at common law to be received as a guest by an Innkeeper, does not include a person resident in the same country town as that in which the Inn is situate and "merely walking about the town for his own recreation and amusement" (*R.* v. *Rymer*, 46 L. J. M. C. 108; 2 Q. B. D. 136). The length of time that a man may remain at an Inn does not affect his character as a traveller; unless he be received for a definite term under a special contract (Add. C. 303, 304, and cases there cited).

V. GUEST.

TRAVERSE.—To traverse;—"'Travers' sometimes signifieth to deny, sometimes to overthrow or undoe a thing done" (Termes de la Ley, *Travers; wh. Vf.* for illustrations).

TREASON.—"'Treason' is in two manners, that is to say, Graund Treason, and Petit Treason" (Termes de la Ley, *Treason*). *V.* HIGH TREASON.

TREASURE TROVE.—"'Treasure trove' is when any money, gold, silver, plate or bullion is found in any place, and no man knoweth to whom the property is, then the property thereof belongeth to the King, and that is called 'Treasure trove,' that is to say, Treasure found. But if any Mine of metell be found in any ground that alway pertaineth to the Lord of the soile, except it be a mine of gold or silver, which shall be alway to the King, in whose ground soever they be found" (Termes de la Ley).

As to the offence of concealing Treasure Trove; *V.* Stephen, Cr. 274.

TREASURY.—*V.* s. 12 (2), Interp. Act, 1889.

TREAT AND VIEW.—An advertisement inviting applications for purchase to be made to A. "to treat and view," gives A. "authority to negotiate and to make and receive proposals, but not to conclude a sale" (per Bovill, C. J., *Godwin* v. *Brind*, 39 L. J. C. P. 122).

TREATING.—For the definition of Treating at Parliamentary Elections, *V.* Corrupt and Illegal Practices Prevention Act, 1883 (46 & 47 V. c. 51), s. 1, adopted also for Municipal Elections (47 & 48 V. c. 70, s. 2); and replacing the definition in s. 4, Corrupt Practices Prevention Act, 1854 (17 & 18 V. c. 102). *Vh.* Leigh and Le Marchant, 4 Ed. 25–29: Mattinson and Macaskie, 2 Ed. 39–53: Rogers, ch. 12.

Vf. Arch. Cr. 1069; Rosc. Cr. 343.

TREES.—"Where the Grant is of all a man's 'Trees,' there shall pass no more of the soil but so much as shall serve for the nutriment of the Trees, and the owner of the soil shall have the grass growing thereupon also" (Touch. 95). *V.* WOOD.

"The word 'Trees,' generally speaking, means wood applicable to buildings, and does not include orchard trees" (per Littledale, J., *Bullen* v. *Denning*, 4 B. & C. 851); and an exception in a Lease of "Trees" will not, as a rule, extend to *fruit* trees, unless specially named; and neither an exception, nor a grant, of "Timber Trees and other Trees" will pass fruit trees (*Bullen* v. *Denning*, sup. *wh. V.* for the old cases hereon). *V.* FRUIT: TIMBER.

Vh. Craig on Trees and Woods, *pass.*

TRENCH.—"Drains, Trenches or Watercourses;" *V.* WATERCOURSE.

TRIAL: TRIED.—A "Trial" is the conclusion, by a competent tribunal, of questions in issue in legal proceedings, whether civil or criminal. Therefore, an assessment of damages by a jury on a judgment by default in an action of tort, is not a Trial within Ord. 65, R. 1, R. S. C. (*Gath* v. *Howarth*, 28 S. J. 427; W. N. (84) 99); nor is the hearing of the reference of an action "and all matters in difference" a Trial within s. 1, 17 & 18 V. c. 34 (*Hall* v. *Brand*, 53 L. J. Q. B. 19; 12 Q. B. D. 39). But an indictment for non-repair of a highway is "tried" within s. 95, Highway Act, 1835 (5 & 6 W. 4, c. 50), if the defendants plead guilty (*R.* v. *Haslemere*, 32 L. J. M. C. 30; 3 B. & S. 313).

V. SALE ON TRIAL.

TRIBUTARY.—A "Tributary" to a river, for the purposes of the Salmon Fishery Act, 1873 (36 & 37 V. c. 71), is another stream which flows into it in an unimpounded course ; and does not include a stream which would have been a tributary but for the fact that its waters are lawfully impounded and used by a Water Company, and only the surplus unused waters of which find their way into the old course of the stream (*Harbottle* v. *Terry*, 52 L. J. M. C. 31 ; 10 Q. B. D. 131).

In that case, Stephen, J., in giving judgment said ;—" Is a pond fed by a stream, and running into a larger stream or river, to be called a 'tributary' of the larger stream? Ordinarily, one would say, no. Ordinarily, by 'tributary,' one means a stream running into another stream. It is not a very exact word, but it has a not very indefinite popular meaning. It is rather by instances that its meaning can be arrived at. I gave as an instance a stream dammed up into a series of pools, and running on through them from one to the other continuously, as being in my opinion a 'tributary.' And again, such a piece of water as Loch Neagh in Ireland, and another lake near Waterville in County Kerry. But take the Serpentine :—it would be a strong thing to call it a 'tributary' of the Thames, and still more so to call the Round Pond one ; yet some of their water finds its way into the Thames."

Where the Secretary of State's Certificate defined the Severn Fishery District as " so much of the River Severn and of the Rivers Vyrynw and Teme, and of all *other* Tributaries of the River Severn as are situate in the counties specified," it was held that "other Tributaries" meant direct Tributaries, as the Vyrynw and Teme are (*Merricks* v. *Cadwallader*, 51 L. J. M. C. 20).

TRINITY HOUSE OUTPORT DISTRICTS. — For the Merchant Shipping Acts, " The Trinity House Outport Districts," comprises " any Pilotage District for the appointment of pilots within which no Particular Provision is made by any Act of Parliament, or Charter" (s. 370, (3) 17 & 18 V. c. 104) ; Ipswich is within that definition (*Hadgraft* v. *Hewitt*, L. R 10 Q. B. 350 ; 44 L. J. M. C. 140). *V.* PARTICULAR PROVISION.

TRINKETS.—" Trinkets" are small articles for personal adornment, or wear, or even use when its object is essentially ornamental. Ivory bracelets, ornamental shirt pins, gilt rings, brooches, tortoise-shell and pearl port-monnaies and scent-bottles, are " Trinkets" within s. 1, Carriers Act (11 G. 4 & 1 W. 4, c. 68) ; but a plain German-silver fusee box is not (*Bernstein* v. *Baxendale*, 28 L. J. C. P. 265 ; 6 C. B. N. S. 259). So ivory fans are included in a bequest of " Trinkets" (*A.-G.* v. *Harley*, 7 L. J. O. S. Ch. 31 ; 5 Russ. 173).

V. PERSONAL ORNAMENTS.

TROUBLE.—The " trouble" of an executorship does not cease by the mere institution of an Administration Action ; nor, accordingly, an Annuity given to an executor for his trouble in superintending testator's affairs (*Baker* v. *Martin*, 8 Sim. 25).

TRUCK-MASTER.—To write of a man that he is a "Truck-Master," is a Libel (*Homer* v. *Taunton*, 29 L. J. Ex. 318 ; 5 H. & N. 661 : Qy. if spoken, would it be slander per se ?). In giving the jdgmt., Pollock, C. B., said the word was not then to be found in any English Dictionary.

TRUE.—When a contract,—*e.g.*, a Life Policy,—proceeds on the basis that statements made by the party to be benefited thereunder are "true," it will be avoided if any material statement is untrue in fact, even though it be made in good faith and be not untrue to the knowledge of the party making it (*Macdonald* v. *Law Union Insrce.*, 43 L. J. Q. B. 131 ; L. R. 9 Q. B. 328).

TRUE AND ANCIENT RENT.—*V. Mountjoy's Case*, 5 Rep. 3 b ; cited Sug. Pow. 730.

TRUE COPY.—A "True Copy" does not mean an absolutely exact copy ; but it means that the copy shall be so true that nobody can by any possibility misunderstand it (per Bacon, C. J., *Re Hewer*, 51 L. J. Ch. 905 ; 21 Ch. D. 871). In that case a Bill of Sale was held well registered though there was a clerical error in the registered copy of it (*Va. Sharp* v. *McHenry*, 38 Ch. D. 428 ; 57 L. J. Ch. 961 ; 57 L. T. 606 ; 3 Times Rep. 847 : *Tuck* v. *Southern Counties Deposit Bank*, 37 W. R. 769 ; 58 L. J. Ch. 699 ; 42 Ch. D. 471). But a served copy of an Order of Court is not a true one, for the purpose of attachment for disobedience, if the title of the cause or matter be omitted (*Re Holt*, 11 Ch. D. 168). As to "True Copy" of a Trader-debtor Summons under Bankry. Act, 1849 ; *V. Re Tindall*, 24 L. J. Bank. 18 ; 6 D. G. M. & G. 741.

TRUE OWNER.—This expression "has a technical meaning in Bankruptcy, and means a person who has acquired (by mortgage, purchase or otherwise) the beneficial interest in personal chattels as distinguished from the vendor, mortgagor or grantor, who is allowed to retain possession of them, and is by means of such possession the reputed or apparent owner" (Robson, 6 Ed. 567, n. *b*). *Vh.* Ib. 498 *et seq.* ; Baldwin, 221 *et seq.* ; Wms. Bank. 182 *et seq.*; Yate Lee, 386 *et seq.*

As to whether the phrase "True Owner" in the Reputed Ownership Clause, includes a Bare Trustee ; *V.* Lewin, 244, 245.

An *un*registered *absolute* Bill of Sale of Chattels, will prevent its giver from being the "True Owner" of the chattels, s. 5, Bills of Sale Act, 1882 ; and a subsequent registered Bill of Sale of the same chattels will thereby be defeated (*Tuck* v. *Southern Counties Deposit Bank*, 37 W. R. 769 ; 58 L. J. Ch. 699 ; 42 Ch. D. 471). But in an unreported case, decided before the lastly cited case, Pollock, B., held, that the grantor of a Bill of Sale, *given by way of mortgage*, remained the "True Owner" of the goods comprised therein, so long as he remained in possession of such goods; and that, therefore, a second Bill of S. registered before a prior one, took precedence of that prior one under s. 10, Bills of S. Act, 1878 (*Price* v. *Russell*, 12 April, 1889).

A Partner in, or other joint owner of, goods is the "True Owner" of *his share* in the goods within s. 5, Bills of Sale Act, 1882 (*Re Tamplin, Ex p. Barrett*, W. N. (90) 48; 38 W. R. 351).

TRULY SET FORTH.—The Bills of Sale Act, 1878, s. 8, requires the consideration of a Bill of Sale to be "set forth" therein, and s. 8 of the Bills of S. Act, 1882, requires the consideration to be "*truly* set forth." The adverb here does not add to the sense (per Smith, J., *Staniforth* v. *Capon*, 2 Times Rep. 493).

Under either Act, the requirement is, that the consideration (but not the sum secured, *Ex p. Challinor, Re Rogers*, 16 Ch. D. 260; 51 L. J. Ch. 476; 29 W. R. 205), shall truly and fairly, according to the ordinary dealings of honest men, appear on the face of the document (*Roberts* v. *Roberts*, 53 L. J. Q. B. 313; 50 L. T. 351; 13 Q. B. D. 794; 32 W. R. 605).

Thus moneys really paid at the request of the grantor to satisfy a debt, due from the grantor, may be stated to have been paid to him (*Ex p. National Mercantile Bank, Re Haynes*, 49 L. J. Bank. 62; 15 Ch. D. 42: *Ex p. Challinor*, sup.: *Hamlyn* v. *Betteley*, 5 C. P. D. 327; 49 L. J. C. P. 465: *Ex p. Bolland, Re Roper*, 21 Ch. D. 543; 52 L. J. Ch. 113: *Va. Carrard* v. *Meek*, 50 L. J. Q. B. 187: *Staniforth* v. *Capon*, sup.); but to bring a case within the doctrine of those decisions the debt so paid must be absolute, prior to the execution of the Bill of S.; and therefore a deduction in respect of a mere inchoate liability as, *e.g.*, for mortgagee's expenses in relation to the security (*Ex p. Firth, Re Cowburn*, 19 Ch. D. 419; 51 L. J. Ch. 473: *Hamilton* v. *Chaine*, 7 Q. B. D. 319; 50 L. J. Q. B. 456: *Ex p. Charing Cross Bank, Re Parker*, 16 Ch. D. 35; 50 L. J. Ch. 157: *Richardson* v. *Harris*, 22 Q. B. D. 268; 37 W. R. 426. *Sv. Re Cann, Ex p. Hunt*, 13 Q. B. D. 36), or for commission on the loan (*Hamilton* v. *Chaine*, sup.), or for prospective interest (*Ex p. Charing Cross Bank, Re Parker*, sup.), or for an agreement to make a future payment (*Ex p. Rolph, Re Spindler*, 19 Ch. D. 98; 51 L. J. Ch. 88; 30 W. R. 52), or a liability on an immature acceptance (*Richardson* v. *Harris*, sup.), cannot be regarded as money paid to the grantor, and if such statement be the only reference to such a deduction the consideration will not be either "truly set forth" or "set forth." But, on the other hand, if the debt be absolute before the execution of the B. of S., then, though it be due to the grantee himself, it will be properly stated as money paid to the grantor, for an allowance to him in account is equivalent to payment (*Credit Co.* v. *Pott*, 6 Q. B. D. 295; 50 L. J. Q. B. 106; 29 W. R. 326: *Ex p. Johnson, Re Chapman*, 26 Ch. D. 338; 53 L. J. Ch. 762; 50 L. T. 214: *Ex p. Nelson*, 55 L. T. 819; 35 W. R. 264).

A Bill of S., given in substitution of a prior defective one, and which contained no reference to that prior document, but stated the pecuniary consideration as "now paid," was held to truly set forth the consideration (*Ex p. Allam, Re Munday*, 14 Q. B. D. 43 : *Sv. Ex p. Berwick*, 29 W. R. 292).

V. PAID : PAYMENT.

Where a Bill of S. was prepared by the grantor's solicitor, and the consideration was a truly stated antecedent debt which the grantor was unable to pay and "in order to induce the grantee not to institute proceedings" the grantor had agreed to make the B. of S.; held, that the consideration was truly set forth, although the grantee had not threatened proceedings (*Ex p. Winter*, 25 S. J. 333).

The consideration must be truly set forth in the B. of S. itself; and an incorrect or imperfect statement of it there, cannot be rectified by reference to a receipt endorsed on it (*Ex p. Charing Cross Bank, Re Parker*, sup.).

Note: Though s. 8, Bills of S. Act, 1878, uses the phrase "set forth" the consideration, s. 10 (3) requires a Defeasance to be "*truly* set forth."

TRUST.—The word "Trust" is not necessary to creat a Trust, nor will its use necessarily create one (1 Jarm. 569 ; Lewin, 148, 149).

"As the doctrines of Trusts are equally applicable to Real and Personal Estate, and the principles which govern the one will be found, *mutatis mutandis*, to govern the other, we cannot better describe the nature of a Trust generally than by adopting Lord Coke's definition of a 'Use,' the term by which, before the Stat. of Uses, a Trust of lands was designated. A Trust, in the words applied to the Use, may be said to be—'a confidence reposed in some other, not issuing out of the land, but as a thing collaterall, annexed in privity to the estate of the land, and to the person touching the land' (Co. Litt. 272 b)." Lewin, 13.

V. Lewin, 1–12, for an Introductory View of the Rise and Progress of Trusts; Ib. ch. 2, s. 1, for a Classification of Trusts, and *V.* Lewin and Watson, Eq. 959–1022, on the subject of Trusts generally.

V. IN TRUST : UPON TRUST.

TRUST: TRUSTING AND CONFIDING.—*V.* PRECATORY TRUST.

TRUSTEE.—As to who may be a Trustee ; *V.* Lewin, ch. 3, s. 2.

As to the Estate taken by Trustees in view of the phrases that may be employed in the instrument creating the Trust ; *V.* Jarm., ch. 34.

As to when a devise is implied in the word "Trustee ;" *V.* Lewin, 215.

"Trustee for Sale" is a sufficient description of a vendor ; *V.* PROPRIETOR.

As regards a hostile *Inspection of Documents*, "the word 'Trustee' is one of wide application, and a party has been considered to hold *as Trustee* where the document is one in which the opposite party has an interest" (per Erle, C. J., *Price* v. *Harrison*, 29 L. J. C. P. 338 ; 8 C. B. N. S. 617 : *Va.* per Wightman, J., *Owen* v. *Nickson*, 30 L. J. Q. B. 125 ; 3 E. & E. 602 : *Brown* v. *Liell*, 16 Q. B. D. 229).

"Trustee," in s. 27, Bankry. Act, 1883, means "Trustee in Bankruptcy" (*V.* s. 168) ; and, therefore, the powers given to a "Trustee" by s. 27 are not applicable to the Trustee of an Arrangement under s. 18 (*Re Grant*, 55 L. J. Q. B. 369 ; 3 Morr. 118).

A "Trustee," in s. 80, Larceny Act, 24 & 25 V. c. 96, means a Trustee who holds property on some express trust created by an instrument in writing (*R.* v. *Fletcher*, 31 L. J. M. C. 206 ; L. & C. 180).

"Trustees" for executing an Act for *Paving, &c.*, s. 2, 20 & 21 V. c. 50 ; *V. Swinford* v. *Keble*, 35 L. J. Q. B. 185 ; L. R. 1 Q. B. 549 ; 7 B. & S. 573.

A vendor who has covenanted to surrender copyholds is a "Trustee" within the Trustee Act, 1850 (*Re Powis*, 29 S. J. 373).

For the purpose of the *Trust Investment* Act, 1889, 52 & 53 V. c. 32, "Trustee" (s. 9) "shall include an exor. or admor., and a trustee whose trust arises by construction or implication of law, as well as an express trustee :"—the Trustees of a Charity are within that definition ; *secus*, the Trustees of a Building Society,—the latter are rather agents for carrying on the business of the Society (*Manchester Infirmary* v. *A.-G.* : *Re National Permanent Bg. Socy.*, 43 Ch. D. 420, 431 ; 34 S. J. 142).

V. TRUST : UPON TRUST.

TRUSTEES FOR THE TIME BEING.—*V.* TIME BEING.

TRUSTEES OF INHERITANCE.—*V.* INHERITANCE.

TUMULTUOUSLY.—*V.* RIOTOUSLY.

TURBARY.—"Common of Turbary is a right to dig turves (*i.e.*, peat, not green turf) in another man's land, or in the lord's waste, for fuel to burn in the house ; and therefore it is appendant or appurtenant to a house only, and not to land ; 5 Assis. 9 : *Tyrringham's Case*, 4 Rep. 36 b ; Tudor's L. C. R. P. : *O'Hare* v. *Fahy*, 10 Ir. C. L. Rep. 318. It cannot be dug for sale ; *Valentine* v. *Penny*, Noy. 145 : *Hayward* v. *Cannington*, 1 Sid. 354 ; 1 Lev. 231 ; 2 Keble, 290, 311. And it does not give a right to take green turf for making grass plots, or repairing the hedges or fences of a garden : *Wilson* v. *Willes*, 7 East, 121 : Wms. on Commons, 187" (Elph. 627).

V. MOSSES.

TURF MOSS.—"I am of opinion that by a grant of 'Bogs and Turf-Mosses' simply, the soil and freehold in both would pass" (per

Brady, C. B., *Boyle* v. *Olpherts*, 4 Ir. Eq. Rep. 249) ; "I believe it cannot be disputed that 'Bog' simply means the soil, and not a mere right of turbary" (per Pennefather, B., Ib.).

TURN.—"In Turn :" These words in a Charter-Party mean (unless explained by the evidence) in the order of readiness (*Robertson* v. *Jackson*, 15 L. J. C. P. 28 ; 2 C. B. 412 : *Lawson* v. *Burness*, 1 H. & C. 396 : *King* v. *Hinde*, 12 L. R. Ir. 113).

"*In Turn to Deliver* :" As to what evidence of usage will enable the Court to construe these words in a Charter-Party in a particular way ; *V. Robertson* v. *Jackson*, sup. *Vh.* 1 Maude & P. 295.

"*In Regular Turns of Loading* :" As to what evidence is admissible to explain this phrase : *Cp. Leidemann* v. *Schultz* (23 L. J. C. P. 17 ; 14 C. B. 38), with *Hudson* v. *Clementson* (25 L. J. C. P. 234 ; 18 C. B. 213) : *Vh. Lawson* v. *Burness*, sup. : 1 Maude & P. 295.

"*Loading in Turn* ;" *V. Taylor* v. *Clay*, 16 L. J. Q. B. 44 ; 9 Q. B. 713.

TURN LOOSE.—*V.* Loose.

TURNE.—The privilege of the Tourne is the power to hold a Court within the precinct of the same authority as the Sheriff's Turne ; and whosoever hath the Leet hath this privilege (Termes de la Ley, *Sheriffes Turne*).

TURNPIKE ROAD.—"A 'Turnpike-road' means a road having toll-gates or bars on it, which were originally called 'turns,' and were first constructed about the middle of the last century. Certain individuals, with the view to the repair of particular roads, subscribed among themselves for that purpose, and erected gates upon the roads, taking tolls from those who passed through them. These were violently opposed at first, and petitions were presented to Parliament against them ; and Acts were in consequence passed for their regulation. This was the origin of turnpike roads. The distinctive mark of a turnpike road is the right of turning back any one who refuses to pay toll" (per Abinger, C. B., *Northam Bridge Co.* v. *Lond. & Southampton Ry.*, 6 M. & W. 438 ; 9 L. J. Ex. 166 ; 4 Jur. 892 ; 1 Ry. Ca. 672 : *Va. R.* v. *East & West India Docks & Birmingham Ry.*, 22 L. J. Q. B. 380 ; 2 E. & B. 466).

Dedication of a road to the public, reserving tolls which are gathered by means of toll-bars, does not make the road a Turnpike Road, unless the scheme have legislative sanction (*Austerberry* v. *Oldham*, 29 Ch. D. 750 ; 55 L. J. Ch. 633 ; 53 L. T. 543 ; 33 W. R. 807 ; 49 J. P. 532 : *Mid. Ry.* v. *Watton*, 55 L. J. M. C. 99 ; 17 Q. B. D. 30 ; 54 L. T. 482 ; 34 W. R. 524 ; 50 J. P. 405).

V. Main Road.

TUTOR.—"Tutor" is not a correct description of a Schoolmaster, *quà* Bills of Sale Acts (*Lee* v. *Turner*, 20 Q. B. D. 773 ; 59 L. T. 320).

TWAITE.—"*Twaite* signifieth a wood grubbed up, and turned to arable" (Co. Litt. 4 b).

TWELVE-MONTH.—"'A Twelve-month' includes all the year according to the Kalendar; but 'Twelve months' shall be reckoned according to twenty-eight days to each month" (*Catesby's Case*, 6 Rep. 62 a: *Va.* 2 Bla. Com. 141; Dwar. 674, 675). *V.* MONTH: YEAR.

A Hiring Agreement "for twelve months *certain*, after which time either party shall be at liberty to determine the agreement by giving the other a three months' notice," means that at the end of the twelve months either party may (without notice) determine the agreement, and that the stipulation as to notice applies only if the engagement be prolonged beyond the twelve months (*Langton* v. *Carleton*, L. R. 9 Ex. 57; 43 L. J. Ex. 54).

UBICUNQUE.—*V.* Quamdiu.

UNABLE.—"Unable to Act;" *V.* Inability.

UNABLE OR UNWILLING.—As to this phrase in Conditions of Sale; *V.* Unwilling.

UNADULTERATED.—*V.* Adulteration: As Unadulterated.

UNADVANCED.—"Unadvanced Member" of a Building Society; *Re Middlesborough Bg. Socy.*, 5 Times Rep. 516. *V.* Withdrawal.

UNAPPRECIABLE.—*V.* Inappreciable.

UNAVOIDABLE OBSTACLE.—"It has been decided that a Condition of Sale for payment of interest, if by reason of any 'Unavoidable Obstacle' the contract could not be completed by a day named, did not apply to a delay occasioned by the state of the title; and therefore interest was not payable under the Condition" (Sug. V. & P. 635, citing *Birch* v. *Podmore,* V.-C., 1828). So of the phrase "Unforeseen or Unavoidable Obstacles" (*Monk* v. *Huskisson*, 4 Russ. 121 n.; *Svth.* Sug. V. & P. 635).

UNBAPTIZED.—A child baptized with water in the name of the Trinity by a Wesleyan minister, not authorized to administer the rite of baptism, is not "unbaptized" within the Burial Service, as incorporated into the Uniformity Act, 13 & 14 Car. 2, c. 4 (*Escott* v. *Martin,* 1 B. & F. 4).

UNBORN.—"Unborn," in s. 30, Trustee Act, 1850, means "non-existent in the character to entitle a person to the property in question" (per Jessel, M. R., *Basnett* v. *Moxon*, 44 L. J. Ch. 559; L. R. 20 Eq. 183). Among other illustrations the learned judge said, "In a sense, the future heir-at-law of a living person, although he may be a living man, is not a living heir. As heir, he comes into existence at a future period." *Vh.* Dan. Ch. Pr. 2110, 2111.

UNCERTAIN RENT.—*V.* Certain Rent.

UNCONDITIONAL.—"Unconditional Order in Writing;" *V.* Bill of Exchange.

UNCONTROLLED.—*V.* Discretion.

UNDER.—*V.* Claiming under : Within and under : Through.
"Under or By Virtue ;" *V.* Pursuance.
Property "Vested under" an Act ; *V.* Vested.
"Under his hand ;" *V.* His hand.

UNDER DECK.—*V. Royal Ex. Co.* v. *Dixon*, 12 App. Ca. 11.

UNDER PAIN.—"Under Pain of forfeiting Body and Goods ;" *V.* Felony.

UNDER PROTEST.—"It is said that the money was received by the petitioner and the receipt given Under Protest. These words are often used on these occasions, but they have no distinct technical meaning, unless accompanied with a statement of circumstances, showing that they were used by way of notice or protest, reserving to the party by reason of such circumstances, a right to a taxation, notwithstanding such payment. The words have no distinct meaning by themselves, and amount to nothing unless explained by the proceedings and circumstances" (per Langdale, M. R., *Re Massey*, 8 Bea. 462 : *Va. Re Dearden*, 23 L. J. Ex. 14 ; 9 Ex. 210 ; 17 Jur. 993 ; 22 L. T. O. S. 90 ; 2 W. R. 18).

UNDERLEASE : UNDERLET.—Though a Covenant against assigning is not broken by an Underlease (*V.* Assign) ; yet a covenant against underletting will restrain an assignment (*Greenaway* v. *Adams*, 12 Ves. 395).

"Letting *Lodgings* has been held not to be a breach of a covenant not 'to grant any Underlease for any term whatsoever, or let, assign, transfer, set over or otherwise part with' without the license of the lessor ; for 'the covenant,' said Lord Ellenborough, 'can only extend to such under-letting as a license might be expected to be applied for ; and whoever heard of a license from a landlord to take in a lodger ?' (*Doe* d. *Pitt* v. *Laming*, 4 Camp. 77). But the same learned judge ruled otherwise where the covenant was not to let the premises, *or any part* thereof (*Roe* v. *Sales*, 1 M. & S. 297), and the ruling itself has been questioned in a later case (per Parke & Alderson, B B., *Greenslade* v. *Tapscott*, 1 Cr. M. & R. 59 ; 3 L. J. Ex. 328 ; 4 Tyr. 566), where land was suffered to be occupied by more persons than one. On principle it would seem that if the covenant be not to sublet the premises *or any part*, the letting Lodgings would be a breach ; otherwise not" (Woodf. 659, 660).

V. Derivative Lease : Lease.

UNDER-SHERIFF.—"Sheriff or Under-Sheriff," s. 46, 6 G. 4, c. 50, does not include a person acting as Under-Sheriff, there being another person holding the formal appointment (*Williams* v. *Thomas*, 19 L. J. Ex. 50 ; 4 Ex. 479).

UNDERTAKE.—The meaning of Rule 6, Solicitors' Remuneration Ord., giving a Solicitor power to elect his mode of remuneration "before undertaking any business," is "that after a Solicitor has accepted the employment and done *any* work in it for his client for which he could charge him if the Scale did not apply, he has *undertaken* the business, and it is too late for him to elect under R. 6" (per Kay, J., *Re Allen*, 56 L. J. Ch. 8 ; affd. Ib. 487 ; 34 Ch. D. 433 ; 56 L. T. 6 ; 35 W. R. 218 : *Re Metcalfe*, 57 L. J. Ch. 82 ; 36 W. R. 137 : *Va. Hester* v. *Hester*, 56 L. J. Ch. 247 ; 34 Ch. D. 607 ; 55 L. T. 862 ; 35 W. R. 233 : *Re Love*, 40 Ch. D. 637 ; 58 L. J. Ch. 272 : *Re Stewart*, 41 Ch. D. 494 : 60 L. T. 737 ; 37 W. R. 484). *V.* BUSINESS.

UNDERTAKING.—This word in a charge contained in a Mortgage Debenture given by a Company would generally be held to cover all its present and future acquired property (*Re Panama Co.*, 5 Ch. 318; 39 L. J. Ch. 482 : *Re Mersey Wood Co.*, 1 Times Rep. 566. *Vh.* Buckl. 152 ; Palmer's Comp. Precedts. 4 Ed. 380) ; but not its uncalled capital (*Re Marine Mansions Co.*, L. R. 4 Eq. 601 ; 37 L. J. Ch. 113).

As to the meaning of the phrase in a Railway Debenture ; *V. Doe* d. *Myatt* v. *St. Helen's Ry.*, 11 L. J. Q. B. 6 ; 2 Q. B. 364 : *Gardner* v. *Lond. C. & Dover Ry.*, 36 L. J. Ch. 323 ; 2 Ch. 201 : and *V.* those cases cited and commented on, 1 Jarm. 224, 225. *Va. Re Southern Ry.*, 17 L. R. Ir. 127 : *Re Bagnalstown & Wexford Ry.*, Ir. Rep. 1 Eq. 275 : *Blaker* v. *Herts & Essex Water W. Co.*, 41 Ch. D. 399 ; 58 L. J. Ch. 497 : and on the last case *V. Re Barton-upon-Humber Water Co.*, 42 Ch. D. 585.

In s. 1, Lands C. C. Act, 1845, "Undertaking" means an undertaking of a public nature ; and does not include such an undertaking as the Westminster Palace Hotel (*Wale* v. *Westminster Palace Hotel Co.*, 8 C. B. N. S. 276), or Sion College (*Re Sion College ; Ex p. London Corp.*, 31 S. J. 378 ; 55 L. T. 589).

"Undertaking *any Business* ;" a Solicitor "undertakes" business, and is deprived of his option under R. 6, General Remuneration Ord. as soon as he does anything, or advises, in relation to it : *V.* UNDERTAKE.

An I. O. U. may be (*R.* v. *Chambers*, 41 L. J. M. C. 15 ; L. R. 1 C. C. R. 341 ; 25 L. T. 507), and a Guarantee by way of suretyship (*R.* v. *Reed*, 2 Moody, 62 : *R.* v. *Stone*, 2 C. & K. 364) or against negligence and dishonesty (*R.* v. *Joyce*, 34 L. J. M. C. 168 ; L. & C. 576), is an "Undertaking *for the payment of money*" within s. 23, 24 & 25 V. c. 98.

UNDER-WAY.—As regards this phrase in Art. 3, Regulations for Preventing Collisions at Sea, 1879,—"A vessel making way through the water is under-way. A sailing vessel hove-to is under-way (*The Rosalie*, 5 P. D. 245 ; 50 L. J. P. D. & A. 3 : *The City of London*, Swabey, 248). A vessel driven from her anchors in a gale of wind, even if wholly unmanageable, is under-way (*The George Arkle*, Lush. 382) ; and a vessel dropping with the tide, although she may have an anchor overboard, is under-way so long as she is not held by her anchor (*The Esk*, L. R. 2 A. & E. 350 ; 38 L. J. Adm. 33)." 1 Maude & P. 589. "The true criterion as to the application of the Regulation must be, whether the vessel be actually holden by, and under the control of, her anchor or not. The moment she ceases to be so, she is in the category of a vessel 'Under-way' and must carry the appointed coloured lights" (per Sir R. Phillimore, *The Esk*, L. R. 2 A. & E. 353 ; 38 L. J. Adm. 34).

A sailing barge having her mast lowered, her anchor on the ground and dredging down Thames, is not a Sailing vessel "Under-way," within Art. 6, Rules for the Navigation of the River Thames, 1880 (*The Indian Chief*, 58 L. J. P. D. & A. 25 ; 14 P. D. 24 ; 60 L. T. 240), nor is she "At Anchor" within Art. 7 (Ib.).

UNDERWOOD.—Generally speaking the term "Underwood" is applied to a species of wood which grows expeditiously and sends up many shoots from one stool, the root remaining perfect from which the shoots are cut, and producing new shoots, and so yielding a succession of profits (per Bayley, J., *R.* v. *Ferrybridge*, 1 B. & C. 384). *V.* SALEABLE UNDERWOOD.

UNDERWRITE.—To "Underwrite" shares, does not mean to "place" them (*V.* PLACE), but means "agreeing to take so many shares as are specified in the underwriting contract, if the public do not subscribe for them" (per Lindley, L. J., *Re Licensed Victuallers' Assn.*, 58 L. J. Ch. 470 ; W. N. (89) 71 ; 5 Times Rep. 369).

V. DISCOUNT : PLACE, *To place.*

UNDISPOSED OF.—"Sum remaining undisposed of ;" *V. M'Cabe* v. *Galsworthy*, W. N. (74) 161.

V. LEFT.

UNDUE INFLUENCE.—Influence to be "undue," so as to vitiate a gift, is of two classes according as the gift is

1. *Inter Vivos* :
2. *Testamentary.*

1. In gifts *inter vivos* a presumption against the gift arises in cases where subsists either of the following relationships ;—Parent and Child : Man and Wife : Doctor and Patient : Confessor and Penitent : or Guardian and Ward. Gifts *inter vivos* brought about by the exercise of either of those influences will be void, unless the donee proves that the donor was placed "in such a position as would enable him to form an entirely free and unfettered judgment independent altogether of any sort of control" (*Archer* v. *Hudson*, 7 Bea. 560 ; 13 L. J. Ch. 380 : *Parfitt* v. *Lawless*, 41 L. J. P. & M. 70 ; L. R. 2 P. & D. 462 : *Vh. Allcard* v. *Skinner*, 56 L. J. Ch. 1052 ; 36 Ch. D. 145 ; 57 L. T. 61).

"Gifts *inter vivos* by a client to a Solicitor are always void" (per Kindersley, V.-C., *Tomson* v. *Judge*, 24 L. J. Ch. 787; 3 Drew. 306: which case see for review of the previous authorities on this point commencing with the leading case of *Welles* v. *Middleton*, 1 Cox Ch. 112): and nothing but a prior severance of the confidential relation will save such gifts (*Morgan* v. *Minett*, 6 Ch. D. 638). N.B. The rule as to *purchases* by a Solicitor from his client is not so strict; *V*. *Tomson* v. *Judge*, sup.

Vf. Watson, Eq. ch. 5; May on Fraudulent Dispositions, Part 5, ch. 5; Dart, 23, 35 *et seq.*

2. But the law regarding testamentary gifts is very different. "The natural influence of the parent or guardian over the child, the husband over the wife, or the attorney over the client, may lawfully be exerted to obtain a Will or Legacy, so long as the testator thoroughly understands what he is doing and is a free agent. There is nothing illegal in the parent or husband pressing his claims on a child or wife, and obtaining a recognition of those claims in a legacy, provided that that persuasion stop short of coercion, and that the volition of the testator, though biassed and impressed by the relation in which he stands to the legatee, is not overborne and subjected to the domination of another. 'The influence which will set aside a Will,' says Mr. Justice Williams (Wms. Exs. 48), 'must amount to force and coercion, destroying free agency; it must not be the influence of affection and attachment; it must not be the mere desire of gratifying the wishes of another, for that would be a very strong ground in support of a testamentary act; further there must be proof that the act was obtained by this coercion, by importunity which could not be resisted, that it was done merely for the sake of peace, so that the motive was tantamount to force and fear'" (per Penzance, J. O., *Parfitt* v. *Lawless*, sup.).

So in directing the jury in *Wingrove* v. *Wingrove* (55 L. J. P. D. & A. 7; 11 P. D. 81; 34 W. R. 260; 50 J. P. 56) Hannen, Pr., said,—

"All men are familiar with the word 'Influence.' They speak of one person having 'unbounded influence' over another, and they speak of good influences and evil influences; but there may be what is commonly called 'unbounded influence,' or there may be good influence or evil influence, and yet such influence may not be 'undue' in the legal sense of the word. There may be the immoral influence of a person of one sex over a person of the other sex which would result in the person subject to such influence yielding to it in a manner which would be very deplorable as regards testamentary disposition: or there may be the case of a person who in the relationship of companion to another of the same sex indulges the inclination of his or her friend for evil courses, and by that means obtains a pernicious influence over him in respect of the disposition of property; and yet it may be that in neither of those cases is there anything which the law would regard as 'undue' influence. To render influence legally 'undue' there must be *coercion*. A testator or testatrix may have been induced to make a Will of which every disinterested person would disapprove, and yet that Will may be in law a perfectly valid one. To establish undue influence, it must be shewn that the testator or testatrix has been coerced to do an act which he or she did not desire to do. Of course this coercion may be of different kinds. To take an extreme case, there may be coercion with actual violence; or it may exist without anything of that sort. From advanced age, or from some other cause, a person may be so weakened that, upon a thing being pressed upon him, he becomes so fatigued in brain as to consent to do it, though it is an act with which his brain does not go. Influence which brings about the execution of a Will by a person in such a condition will be 'undue influence,' because it will amount to coercion; but the fact of a person making a Will being influenced in so doing by mistaken, or even immoral, considerations on his own part or on that of the person influencing him would not be enough to invalidate a Will. The state of things which is sufficient to establish undue influence must shew that the Will was not the expression of the will of the testator, but something which he has been made to represent as his will; and therefore, if it is shewn that the testator's own wishes are expressed in his Will, the fact that the Will is not such as would meet with approbation, or the fact that right-minded persons must condemn the conduct of the person influencing the testator to execute it, will not be enough to establish undue influence.

There is another general proposition which I think it desirable to bring under your notice—namely, that in cases of undue influence it is not enough to shew that the person charged with having exercised such influence had power over the mind of the testator, but it is necessary to prove that such power was exercised in the particular case, and that the testator was thereby induced to make the Will."

Vf. May on Fraudulent Dispositions, 497 *et seq.*

As to *Electoral* "Undue Influence," *V.* Corrupt and Illegal Practices Prevention Act, 1883 (46 & 47 V. c. 51), s. 2; adopted for Municipal Elections (47 & 48 V. c. 70, s. 2). *Vh.* Leigh & Le Marchant, 4 Ed. 29–37; Mattinson & Macaskie, 2 Ed. 53–61; Rogers, ch. 13.

UNDUE MEANS.—*E.g.*,—Arbitrators carrying on examinations separately, instead of jointly (*Re Plews and Middleton*, 6 Q. B. 852; 14 L. J. Q. B. 139).

UNDUE PREFERENCE.—"Undue or unreasonable Preference or Advantage," "Undue or unreasonable Prejudice or Disadvantage," s. 2, Railway and Canal Traffic Act, 1854;—These words "must, it appears to me, be a Preference or Prejudice with reference to competing parties—an inequality, an unfairness with reference to others, or a prejudice to other works—and cannot apply to the suggestion that, because there are excessive charges, a prejudice arises" (per Huddleston, B., *R.* v. *Ry. Commrs.*, 58

L. J. Q. B. 239, 240). *Vh. Ransome* v. *Eastern Counties Ry.*, 26 L. J. C. P. 91 ; 29 Ib. 329 ; 1 C. B. N. S. 437 ; 8 Ib. 709 : *Oxlade* v. *N. E. Ry.*, 26 L. J. C. P. 129 ; 1 C. B. N. S. 454 ; 28 L. T. O. S. 340 : *Baxendale* v. *N. Devon Ry.*, 30 L. T. O. S. 134 : *Harris* v. *Cockermouth Ry.*, 27 L. J. C. P. 162 ; 3 C. B. N. S. 693 ; 30 L. T. O. S. 273 : *Garton* v. *G. W. Ry.*, 28 L. J. C. P. 158 : *Garton* v. *Bristol & Ex. Ry.*, 28 L. J. Ex. 169 ; 30 L. J. Q. B. 273 : *Nicholson* v. *G. W. Ry.*, 28 L. J. C. P. 89 ; 5 C. B. N. S. 366 ; 7 W. R. 49 : *Baxendale* v. *G. W. Ry.*, 28 L. J. C. P. 81 ; 5 C. B. N. S. 336 ; 7 W. R. 64 : *Hungerford Market Co.* v. *City Steam Boat*, 30 L. J. Q. B. 25 ; 3 E. & E. 365 : *Denaby Main Co.* v. *Manchester, S. & L. Ry.*, 11 App. Ca. 97 : *R.* v. *Ry. Commrs.*, 22 Q. B. D. 642.

Vf. Browne & Theobald on Railways, 393–397 ; Hodges on Railways, 6 Ed. 477–480, 503–505 : FACILITIES.

UNEXPIRED.—Lessee or Assignee of "the unexpired Residue, whatever it may be, of any Term originally created for a period of not less than 60 years (whether determinable on a Life or Lives or not)," s. 5, Rep. of the People Act, 1867, 30 & 31 V. c. 102 ; *V. Trotter* v. *Watson*, 38 L. J. C. P. 100 ; L. R. 4 C. P. 434.

V. EXPIRE.

UNFIT.—Bankruptcy renders a Trustee "unfit" (Lewin, 658, citing *Re Roche*, 1 Con. & L. 306 ; 2 Dr. & War. 287). But if the power of appointing new Trustees "be worded 'in case the Trustee shall become *incapable* to act,' without the addition of the words 'or unfit,' a Bankrupt Trustee is not within the description ; for by 'incapable' is meant *personal incapacity*, and not pecuniary embarrassment" (Lewin, 658, citing *Re Watts*, 9 Hare, 106 ; 20 L. J. Ch. 337 : *Turner* v. *Maule*, 15 Jur. 761 : *Re East*, 8 Ch. 735 ; 42 L. J. Ch. 480). Bankruptcy is none the less "unfitness" because occasioned by misfortune (*Re Adams*, 12 Ch. D. 634 ; 48 L. J. Ch. 613 : *Va. Re Barker*, 1 Ch. D. 43 ; 45 L. J. Ch. 52 : *Re Hopkins*, 19 Ch. D. 61) ; but on obtaining his Discharge and ceasing to be impecunious, a Bankrupt Trustee is no longer "unfit" (*Re Bridgman*, 29 L. J. Ch. 844 ; 1 Dr. & Sm. 164).

Temporary Absence abroad is not "unfitness" (*Re Moravian Socy.*, 26 Bea. 101 ; 4 Jur. N. S. 703) ; *secus*, of a settled residence abroad (*Mesnard* v. *Welford*, 22 L. J. Ch. 1053 ; nom. *Mennard* v. *Welford*, 1 Sm. & G. 426 : in this case the word was "incapable").

V. INABILITY : INCAPABLE.

UNFITNESS.—*V.* DUE CAUSE.

UNFORESEEN.—"Unforeseen Cause ;" *V. Hills* v. *Sughrue*, 15 M. & W. 253.

"Unforeseen Obstacle ;" *V.* UNAVOIDABLE OBSTACLE.

UNINTERRUPTEDLY.—*V.* FAIRLY.

UNION.—Poor Law "Union," s. 1, 24 & 25 V. c. 55 ; s. 109, 4 & 5 W. 4, c. 76 ; *V. Machynlleth* v. *Pool,* L. R. 4 Q. B. 592.

"Poor Law Union ;" *V.* s. 16 (2), (4), Interp. Act, 1889.

UNIVERSAL APPLICATION.—British Laws of "universal application ;" *V. Jex* v. *McKinney,* 58 L. J. P. C. 67.

UNJUST.—Scales and Weight are not "Light or Unjust," s. 3, 22 & 23 V. c. 56, if an inaccuracy in them is against the seller (*Booth* v. *Shadgett,* 42 L. J. M. C. 98 ; nom. *Brooke* v. *Shadgate,* L. R. 8 Q. B. 352). *Vh. R.* v. *Baxendale,* 44 J. P. 763 : *Horder* v. *Roberts,* Ib. 256.

UNJUSTIFIABLE EXTRAVAGANCE.—As to what is "Unjustifiable Extravagance in living" (s. 28 (d), Bankry. Act, 1883) ; *V. Ex p. Thornber, Re Barlow,* W. N. (86), 207.

UNKNOWN.—*V.* CONTENTS UNKNOWN.

UNLAWFUL ASSEMBLY.—"Three or more may commit an unlawfull assembly, a riot, or a rout" (Co. Litt. 257 a).

"An Unlawful Assembly is an assembly of three or more persons, (a) with intent to commit a crime by open force ; or (b) with intent to carry out any common purpose, lawful or unlawful, in such a manner as to give firm and courageous persons in the neighbourhood of such assembly reasonable grounds to apprehend a breach of the peace in consequence of it" (Steph. Cr. 48, 49). *Vf.* Arch. Cr. 956 ; Rosc. Cr. 929. *V.* Steph. Cr. 56, as to Unlawful Drilling.

V. RIOT : ROUT.

UNLAWFUL COPIES.—"Unlawful Repetitions, Copies and Imitations," s. 11, Copyright (Works of Art) Act, 1862, 25 & 26 V. c. 68, is a "phrase not well considered, but it means Copies, &c., wrongfully made,—*i.e.*, without the necessary consent" (per Esher, M. R., *Tuck* v. *Priester,* 56 L. J. Q. B. 561 ; 19 Q. B. D. 629 ; 36 W. R. 93 : *Vh. Pollard* v. *Photographic Co.,* 40 Ch. D. 345).

UNLAWFUL GAMING.—"At common law no Game was in itself unlawful" (per Hawkins, J., *Jenks* v. *Turpin,* 53 L. J. M. C. 167). But as common Gaming Houses were prohibited by the common law, all gaming (even at lawful games) in a common Gaming House is "Unlawful Gaming" within s. 4, 17 & 18 V. c. 38 (*Jenks* v. *Turpin,* 53 L. J. M. C. 161 ; 13 Q. B. D. 505).

No "game of mere skill" is now unlawful *per se* (8 & 9 V. c. 109, s. 1). "The Unlawful Games now are,—Ace of Hearts, Pharaoh, Basset, Hazard,

Passage, Roulet, every game of Dice (except Backgammon), and every game of Cards which is not a game of mere skill ; and, I incline to add, any other mere game of chance" of which Baccarat is certainly one (per Hawkins, J., *Jenks* v. *Turpin*, 53 L. J. M. C. 170 : and *V.* same judgment for an elaborate history of the laws relating to Unlawful Gaming).

V. Gaming.

UNLAWFUL PURPOSE.—An "Unlawful Purpose" within s. 4, 5 G. 4, c. 83, means the intention to commit (as distinguished from having been actually guilty of, *R.* v. *Simpson*, 15 J. P. 246, 790) an offence punishable criminally (*Hayes* v. *Stevenson*, 3 L. T. 296 ; 25 J. P. 39); but it is immaterial whether that intention is intended to be carried out in the place where the offender is found (*Re Joy*, 22 L. T. O. S. 80). *Vh. Kirkin* v. *Jenkins*, 32 L. J. M. C. 140.

UNLAWFULLY.—"Unlawfully" is used exceptionally in a wide general sense as regards conspiracy; but its ordinary import is, an act which is "forbidden by some definite law;" and does not embrace that which is merely immoral (per Stephen, J., *R.* v. *Clarence*, 58 L. J. M. C. 18 ; 22 Q. B. D. 23 ; *Va.* jdgmt. of Wills, J.). But an act which would give a right to a Judicial Separation would be done "unlawfully" (Ib.).

The criminal offence of "Unlawfully and Wilfully" Killing a House Dove or Pigeon, s. 23, 24 & 25 V. c. 96, is not committed if it be killed in the honest idea of protecting crops, although to do so may be actionable (*Taylor* v. *Newman*, 32 L. J. M. C. 186 ; 11 W. R. 752 ; 4 B. & S. 89 : *Vf. R.* v. *Stimpson*, 32 L. J. M. C. 208 ; 4 B. & S. 301). But in the very next section of the same Act, relating to taking Fish, "unlawfully and wilfully" means "unlawfully and *intentionally* ;" for that section creates an offence in the nature of poaching (*Hudson* v. *McRae*, 33 L. J. M. C. 65 ; 12 W. R. 80). *V.* Wilfully.

UNLESS.—"Unless," in a clause in a Marine Policy "free from Average unless General," has the same meaning as "except" (*Wilson* v. *Smith*, 3 Burr. 1556).

And "Unless" is, probably, of like value as "Except" in creating a condition precedent (*V. Re Dickinson, Ex p. Rosenthal*, 51 L. J. Ch. 736).

"Unless he shall have paid all such Rates," he shall not be put on the Burgess List, s. 9, 5 & 6 W. 4, c. 76, meant that the payment must have been the person's own act (*R.* v. *Bridgnorth*, 8 L. J. M. C. 86 ; 10 A. & E. 66 ; 2 P. & D. 317).

V. Except.

UNLIQUIDATED DAMAGES.—*V.* Liquidated Damages.

UNLOAD.—*V.* Load.

UNMARRIED.—The primary meaning of "unmarried" is, "never having been married," or "without ever having been married" (*Clarke* v. *Colls*, 9 H. L. Ca. 601: *Dalrymple* v. *Hall*, 50 L. J. Ch. 302; 16 Ch. D. 715: *Re Sergeant*, 54 L. J. Ch. 159; 26 Ch. D. 575): but it is a word of flexible meaning, and "slight circumstances, no doubt, will be sufficient to give the word its other meaning" of, "not having a husband, or wife, at the time in question" (per Pearson, J., *Re Sergeant*, sup.). In *Re Lesingham* (53 L. J. Ch. 333; 24 Ch. D. 703) this secondary meaning was attached to the word as used thus,—"upon trust to pay unto J. H., spinster, if she be then *sole and unmarried*."

The secondary sense was also attached to the word in the following cases:—

Clarke v. *Colls*, sup.:

Pratt v. *Mathew*, 25 L. J. Ch. 409, 686; 22 Bea. 328; 8 D. G. M. & G. 522; 27 L. T. O. S. 74, 267:

Mitchell v. *Colls*, 29 L. J. Ch. 403; Johns. 674:

Day v. *Barnard*, 30 L. J. Ch. 220; 1 Dr. & Sm. 351:

Re Sanders, L. R. 1 Eq. 675.

But the primary meaning was adhered to in—

Blundell v. *De Falbe*, 57 L. J. Ch. 576; 58 L. T. 621:

Heywood v. *Heywood*, 30 L. J. Ch. 155; 29 Bea. 9:

Dalrymple v. *Hall*, sup.:

Re Sergeant, sup.:

Norris v. *Barber*, W. N. (73) 180:

Re Thistlethwayte, 24 L. J. Ch. 712.

Vf. as to both meanings, 1 Jarm. 521–523; Watson, Eq. 657–8; Elph. 333–336.

When a legacy is given to a daughter, who at the date of the Will has never been married, and the gift is conditional upon the legatee being "unmarried" at a given time, the word "unmarried" may properly be construed "a spinster," and not "a widow" (Wms. Exs. 1102, citing *Re Saunders*, 3 K. & J. 156).

A gift to an "unmarried" person does not mean that he is to remain unmarried (*Jubber* v. *Jubber*, 9 Sim. 503: *Hall* v. *Robertson*, 23 L. J. Ch. 241; 4 D. G. M. & G. 781: *Vf.* Wms. Exs. 1282).

"So long as she *continues* unmarried" is not equivalent to "during widowhood," and a divorced woman, if remaining unmarried, continues entitled (*Knox* v. *Wells*, W. N. (83) 58).

V. Without having been married.

UNNECESSARY INCONVENIENCE.—A right to pull down a house in such manner and time as not to cause "Unnecessary Inconvenience," s. 85 (3), 18 & 19 V. c. 122, involves no obligation to protect the privacy of rooms exposed by the pulling down (*Thompson* v. *Hill*, 39 L. J. C. P. 264; L. R. 5 C. P. 564).

UNNECESSARY INTERFERENCE.—Proviso, in a Mining Lease, that the working of the coal should "not be prevented or unnecessarily interfered with ;" *V. Munday* v. *Rutland*, 23 Ch. D. 81.

UNPAID.—A covenant to pay interest at a certain rate so long as the principal secured or any part of it remains "unpaid," does not exclusively mean payment in cash : the word "unpaid" in that connection means, due under the covenant ; and when a judgment has been obtained for the principal, the covenant merges in the judgment and the principal is no longer "unpaid" under the covenant (*Ex p. Fewings, Re Sneyd*, 53 L. J. Ch. 545 ; 25 Ch. D. 338 ; 50 L. T. 109 ; 32 W. R. 352).

V. PAYMENT.

UNREASONABLY.—When a Covenant by a lessee against Underletting without consent is qualified by the Condition that such consent shall not be "unreasonably," or "arbitrarily," or "vexatiously" withheld, a breach of such a Condition gives no right of action to the lessee ; his remedy is to assign without consent (*Sear* v. *House Property Co.*, 16 Ch. D. 387 ; 50 L. J. Ch. 77 ; 29 W. R. 192 ; 43 L. T. 531 : *Treloar* v. *Bigge*, L. R. 9 Ex. 151 ; 43 L. J. Ex. 95 ; 22 W. R. 843 : *Hyde* v. *Warden*, 47 L. J. Ex. 127). In *Treloar* v. *Bigge* (where the phrase was "arbitrarily"), the majority of the Court intimated that a refusal grounded on an expectation that the property would shortly be compulsorily taken by a public body, was not arbitrary.

It has been suggested that a refusal unless a pecuniary consideration were paid for the consent, would be unwarranted (Woodf. 659, n. *t*).

UNSATISFIED.—"Unsatisfied Judgment," s. 98, 9 & 10 V. c. 95 ; *V. Abley* v. *Dale*, 20 L. J. C. P. 233 ; 11 C. B. 378 : *Cookman* v. *Rose*, 3 Jur. N. S. 866.

UNSETTLED ESTATE.—"It cannot be denied that in common parlance the phrase 'Unsettled Estate' means an estate not put into settlement ; and drawing a distinction between its popular meaning and its legal signification, if taken in the former, it would be confined to an estate not put into settlement, while in the latter it is equally open to either interpretation, because it may be either so much of the interest in the settled lands which was not bound by the settlement that was intended to be passed, or the lands which had never been put into settlement. The words in their legal signification will include both." "In all cases the Courts adopt one general rule, whether the words are 'Unsettled,' 'Out of Settlement,' 'Not put into settlement,' or 'Not settled in jointure ;' they say, we will give to the devisee whatever interest the testator had the power to dispose of in the lands bound by the settlement or jointure, giving to the words their full legal signification" (per Sugden, L. C. Ir., *Incorporated Society* v. *Richards*, 4 Ir. Eq. Rep. 192, 194).

V. NOT SETTLED.

UNSHIPPING.—Merely hiring in England a vessel to carry smuggled goods to Ireland where they were unshipped : held, not "assisting or being otherwise concerned in the unshipping" of the goods within s. 45, 6 G. 4, c. 108 (*A.-G.* v. *Kenifeck*, 2 M. & W. 715 ; 6 L. J. Ex. 214). CONCERNED IN.

V. TO SHIP.

UNSOUND MIND.—"'Unsound Mind,' or Insanæ Memoriæ, which all persons must understand to be a Depravity of Reason, or want of it" (per Hardwicke, L. C., *Barnsley's Case*, 2 Eq. Ca. Ab. 580).

For the purposes of the Trustee Act, 1850, 13 & 14 V. c. 60, "the expression 'Person of Unsound Mind' shall mean any person, not an Infant, who, not having been found to be a Lunatic, shall be incapable from infirmity of mind to manage his own affairs" (s. 2) ;—This includes an apoplectic person whose mind is thereby weakened (*Re Critchley*, 83 Law Times, 167) ; or one incapacitated by old age, or by infirmity of mind, *e.g.*, from paralysis (*Re Martin*, 34 Ch. D. 618 ; 56 L. J. Ch. 695, over-ruling *Re Phelps*, 31 Ch. D. 351 ; 55 L. J. Ch. 465) ; but the paralysis must be such as to produce mental infirmity (*Re Barber*, 57 L. J. Ch. 756 ; 39 Ch. D. 187 ; 58 L. T. 756 ; 37 W. R. 182). *V.* LUNATIC : *Cp.* INABILITY : UNFIT.

The power which by R. 196, Divorce Court Rules, is given to the Registrar of assigning a guardian ad litem to a person of "Unsound Mind," should only be exercised in the case of a Lunatic so found by Inquisition (*Fry* v. *Fry*, 34 S. J. 250).

UNSOUNDNESS.—*V.* SOUND.

UNTIL.—This word may be read either as inclusive or exclusive ; it is generally inclusive.

In a memorandum enlarging the time within which an Award may be made it will generally include the whole of the day named (Russ. on Arb., 6 Ed. 146, citing *Kerr* v. *Jeston*, 1 Dowl. N. S. 538 : *Knox* v. *Simmonds*, 3 Bro. C. C. 358. *Vf. Pugh* v. *Leeds*, 2 Cowp. 714). So "it seems that, as a general rule, the word 'Till' is inclusive of the day to which it is prefixed; so that where a defendant was given till a certain day to plead, judgment signed on such day for want of a plea was bad, as the defendant might have delivered a plea during such day (*Dakins* v. *Wagner*, 3 Dowl. 535: *Vá. Kerr* v. *Jeston*, sup.). And the rule is the same in the case of the word 'Until' (*Isaacs* v. *Royal Insrce.*, L. R. 5 Ex. 296 ; 39 L. J. Ex. 189 ; 22 L. T. 681 ; 18 W. R. 982)," Dan. Ch. Pr. 44. So where a Bankrupt was protected from process "until the 29th July," that protection extended during the whole of that day (*Backhouse*, or *Bellhouse* v. *Mellor*, 28 L. J. Ex. 141 ; 4 H. & N. 116 ; 5 Jur. N. S. 175).

But a plaintiff having obtained a judgment, but with a stay of execution "until" a stated day, was held (in Ireland) entitled to issue his execution on that day if the money was not then paid (*Rogers* v. *Davis*, 8 Ir. L. R. 399) :—in that case Burton, J., said, "I think 'until' does not mean 'after.'"

'In Devises and Bequests, "the word '*Until*' is in general coupled with a condition or contingency indicating that some change is intended in the disposition of the property, which, up to that time, is given in a particular way. This, however, will not always be the effect of it. Thus, where there was a gift to A. for life, remainder to her children, *until* they should attain 25, then for such children so attaining 25, with a gift over; it was held that A.'s children took vested interests at birth, and that the gift over was void for remoteness (*Hardcastle* v. *Hardcastle*, 1 H. & M. 405: *V. Bland* v. *Williams*, 3 My. & K. 411; 3 L. J. Ch. 218). Under a devise to A., not to be of age to receive *until* he attain a particular age, A. takes a vested interest subject to being divested on his dying under that age (*Snow* v. *Poulden*, 1 Keen, 186)" Watson, Eq. 1218–9.

UNTIL FURTHER ORDER.—Where an Interim Injunction is granted over a certain day "or Until further Order," the Injunction is not continued after the day named "until further Order," but may be stayed by Order, before the day named (*Bolton* v. *London School Board*, 47 L. J. Ch. 461; 7 Ch. D. 766).

An Order, in an Administration Action, to pay an Annuity "until further Order" is, notwithstanding the latter phrase, *res judicata, quà* appeal (*Peareth* v. *Marriott*, 52 L. J. Ch. 221; 22 Ch. D. 182).

An authority to make periodical payments "until further order" is an ABSOLUTE ASSIGNMENT.

UNTO.—*V.* To: TOWARDS.

UNWILLING.—Referring to the earlier cases on the ordinary clause in *Conditions of Sale* enabling a Vendor to rescind the contract if he should be "unable or unwilling" to answer purchaser's requirements, Turner, L. J., said in *Duddell* v. *Simpson* (2 Ch. 102; 36 L. J. Ch. 72),—"These cases have settled, and I think very wisely settled, that the word 'unwilling' in a Condition of Sale of this description is not to be considered as giving an arbitrary power to the vendor to annul the contract." But though that passage was cited to Bacon, V.-C., in *Dames to Wood* (53 L. J. Ch. 920; 27 Ch. D. 177), he said,—"The word 'unwilling' is as potent as the word 'unable.' Nobody is entitled to ask why he is unwilling; if he refuses to comply with the requisition that is enough" (*Dames* v. *Wood*, affd. 54 L. J. Ch. 771; 29 Ch. D. 626; 53 L. T. 177: *Vf.* jdgmts. of Esher, M. R., and Lindley, L. J., *Terry to White*, 32 Ch. D. 14; 55 L. J. Ch. 345). And the result seems to be that, though "unwilling" means "reasonably unwilling" and does not justify a vendor in capriciously translating it into

"I will not," yet in rescinding the contract he is not bound to give his reason for his unwillingness to complete it, and the onus of proving his caprice or *mala fides* is on the purchaser (*Re Glenton & Saunders*, 53 L. T. 434 : *Re Starr-Bowkett Socy.*, 58 L. J. Ch. 459, 651 ; 42 Ch. D. 375; 60 L. T. 811 : *Woolcott* v. *Peggie*, 15 App. Ca. 42). *Cp.* INSIST.

Vh. Add. C. 895 : Sug. V. & P. 39.

UNWORKABLE.—*V.* WORKABLE.

UPHOLD.—*V.* REPAIR.

UPON.—"'Upon;' This word, in most cases, is used elliptically for 'Upon Condition of:' as, 'upon payment of costs;' 'upon conviction of an offender'" (Dwar. 692).

"The words 'on' or 'upon,' it has been decided, may either mean *before* the act done to which it relates, or *simultaneously with* the act done, or *after* the act done, according as reason and good sense require, with reference to the context and the subject-matter of the enactment" (per Denman, C. J., *R.* v. *Arkwright*, 18 L. J. Q. B. 28 ; 12 Q. B. 970, citing *R.* v. *Humphery*, 7 L. J. Q. B. 202 ; 2 P. & D. 691 ; 10 A. & E. 335 : *Va.* Add. C. 191).

In *R.* v. *Humphery*, sup., "*upon admission*" to public corporate office a person to make a declaration (9 G. 4, c. 17, s. 2), meant that the person could not be called on to declare until *after* admission. So under s. 10, Lord Mayor's Court Act (20 & 21 V. c. clvii), an appeal motion may be made "if *upon the trial*," the judge give leave ; this means at, or within a reasonable time *after*, the trial ; and (in construing that Act) the majority of the Court held that 2 days (whilst Brett, J., thought that 4 days) would be such a reasonable time (*Folkard* v. *Metrop. Ry.*, 42 L. J. C. P. 163 ; L. R. 8 C. P. 470). So the power given (18 & 19 V. c. 43, s. 1) to make a Settlement "upon" *the marriage* of an Infant, means "in the event of" or "on the occasion of" his or her marriage ; and a *post*-nuptial Settlement is thereby authorized (*Re Sampson & Wall*, 53 L. J. Ch. 457 ; 25 Ch. D. 482 : *Re Phillips*, 56 L. J. Ch. 337 ; 34 Ch. D. 467 : *Buckmaster* v. *Buckmaster*, 56 L. J. Ch. 379 ; 35 Ch. D. 21) ; but, *semble*, not if it be long after the marriage (*Re Leigh*, 58 L. J. Ch. 306 ; 40 Ch. D. 290 : *V.* CONTEMPLATION).

But a power to stop up paths "*on notice being* given" in the prescribed manner (59 G. 3, c. 134, s. 39), means that the notice must be given *before* making the order (*R.* v. *Arkwright*, sup.).

"Payment *on* Delivery," means that both acts are to be done simultaneously (*Payntor* v. *James*, L. R. 2 C. P. 348).

V. ON : THEREUPON.

UPON CONDITION.—*V.* CONDITION.

UPON CONVICTION.—*V.* CONVICTION.

UPON SALE.—"Upon Sale or Trial;" *V.* SALE OR TRIAL.

UPON TRUST.—No beneficial interest is taken if property be given or granted "Upon trust," though no trust be declared (Lewin, 147, 148, and cases there cited). But "although the introduction of the words 'Upon trust' may be strong evidence of the intention not to confer a beneficial interest (*Hill* v. *London*, 1 Atk. 620 : *Woollett* v. *Harris*, 5 Mad. 452), yet that construction may be negatived by the context, or the general scope of the instrument (*Dawson* v. *Clarke*, 15 Ves. 409 ; 18 Ib. 247, 257 : *Coningham* v. *Mellish*, Pr. Ch. 31 : *Cook* v. *Hutchinson*, 1 Keen, 42 : *Hughes* v. *Evans*, 13 Sim. 496) ; and in like manner the devisee may be designated as 'Trustee,' but the expression may be explained away (*Batteley* v. *Windle*, 2 Bro. C. C. 31 : *Pratt* v. *Sladden*, 14 Ves. 193 : *Va. Gibbs* v. *Rumsey*, 2 V. & B. 294). On the other hand there may be a total absence of the word 'Trust' or 'Trustee' throughout, and yet the Court may collect the intention that the person taking should be a Trustee (*Saltmarsh* v. *Barrett*, 29 Bea. 474 ; 3 D. G. F. & J. 279 ; 30 L. J. Ch. 853)." Lewin, 148, 149.

V. IN TRUST.

UPON VIEW.—*V.* VIEW.

USAGE OF TRADE.—"The words 'Usage of Trade,' are to be understood as referring to a Particular Usage to be established by evidence; and perfectly distinct from that general custom of merchants, which is the universal established law of the land, to be collected from decisions, legal principles and analogies (not from evidence *in pais*), and the knowledge of which resides in the breasts of the judges" (1 Sm. L. C. 581, 582, and cases there cited).

USE.—"If a man walks with a Gun with intent to kill game, he 'uses' the gun for that purpose without firing, within the statute which makes using a gun, with that intent, penal" (Maxwell, 338, citing 5 Anne, c. 14, s. 4; 1 & 2 W. 4, c. 32, s. 23; *R.* v. *King*, 1 Sess. Ca. 88: *Va. U. S.* v. *Morris*, 14 Peters, 464). So a Net may be "used in taking" Salmon, 24 & 25 V. c. 109, though no salmon be then actually caught (*Rutter* v. *Harris*, 45 L. J. M. C. 103 ; nom. *Ruther* v. *Harris*, 1 Ex. D. 97). And a person "uses" an Engine for killing Game on a Sunday, 1 & 2 W. 4, c. 32, s. 3, who places it on the land prior to, but with the intention for it to remain there during, a Sunday (*Allen* v. *Thompson*, 39 L. J. M. C. 102 ; L. R. 5 Q. B. 336).

An ordinary traveller along a railway in a carriage belonging to the Company, does not "use" the Railway within s. 95, Ry. C. C. Act, 1845, or within enactments of a similar kind (*Brown* v. *G. W. Ry.*, 51 L. J. Q. B. 156, 529 ; 9 Q. B. D. 744, and cases therein cited).

"*Open, keep or use*" a House, Office, Room or other Place, for Betting, ss. 1, 3, 16 & 17 V. c. 119 ; *V. R.* v. *Cook*, 13 Q. B. D. 377 ; 51 L. T. 21 ; 32 W. R. 796 ; 48 J. P. 694 : *Davis* v. *Stephenson*, 6 Times Rep. 242. *Vf.* PLACE, p. 593.

An agreement which, in a passive form, stipulates that the contractor is "*not to use*" premises for other than a specified trade, has not an active operation compelling him *to carry on* that trade (*Doe* d. *Bute* v. *Guest*, 15 M. & W. 160).

V. USING : OCCUPATION : USE AND OCCUPATION.

Bequest for a person's "Use and Disposal ;" *V.* DISPOSAL.

Bequest of Business with "*the use* of the Book Debts, or Capital ;" held, absolute (*Terry* v. *Terry*, 33 Bea. 232 ; 12 W. R. 66 ; 9 L. T. 469).

"Goods, Materials or Provisions *for the use* of any Workhouse," 55 G. 3, c. 137, s. 6, means for use in the Workhouse, and does not comprise repairs to the fabric (*Barber* v. *Waite*, 3 L. J. M. C. 101 ; 1 A. & E. 514 ; 3 N. & M. 611).

An Inclosure Act which authorized the setting apart quarries "for the repair of roads and *for the use* of the Inhabitants" of A., was construed as giving the Inhabitants a right to stone for repairs of roads, but not for private purposes (*Rylatt* v. *Marfleet*, 14 L. J. Ex. 305 ; 14 M. & W. 233).

"Take or Use" a Stream ; *V.* TAKE.

"In Common Use ;" *V.* COMMON TO THE TRADE.

On "Use" as employed in 1 Ric. 3, and on Uses prior to the Stat. of Uses, 27 H. 8, c. 10, *V.* Sanders on Uses, ch. 1 : on Uses since that Stat., *V.* Ib. ch. 2.

USE AND BENEFIT.—*V.* OWN USE AND BENEFIT.

USE AND DISPOSAL.—*V.* DISPOSAL.

USE AND OCCUPATON.—A. devised to his wife the Income of freeholds at B. and leaseholds at P., and bequeathed to her his furniture and effects in his house at E., and desired that she should "have the Free Use and Occupation of the said house ;" held, that she was absolutely entitled to the properties at B. and P., but took only a life interest in the house at E. (*Coward* v. *Larkman*, 60 L. T. 1). *V.* OCCUPATION : RESIDE.

USE OR ENJOYMENT.—*V.* IMMEDIATE USE OR ENJOYMENT.

USE OR PERMIT.—Where a Local Board do no act themselves to create a nuisance, and are endeavouring to put in force their powers to effect a perfect system of drainage, it is no ground of action to an individual that the Board do not take proceedings under their Acts to prevent persons from unlawfully draining into their sewers, in consequence of which draining an additional and serious nuisance is caused to that individual; and they cannot be said "to use or permit to be used" the sewers so as to cause a Nuisance, by abstaining from taking such proceedings (*A.-G.* v. *Dorking*, 51 L. J. Ch. 585; 20 Ch. D. 595).

V. PERMIT.

USED OR ENJOYED.—*V.* APPURTENANCES: HELD.

USELESS.—"Useless, and be no longer required for the purposes of such Road," s. 57, 4 G. 4, c. 95; *V. R.* v. *Greenlaw*, 4 Q. B. D. 447; 48 L. J. Q. B. 409.

V. REQUIRED.

USING.—"The word 'using' at the end of s. 90, 8 & 9 V. c. 20, signifies using in any sense; and is not confined to using by sending engines and other carriages along the line. The section applies to all Tolls without distinction, and, unless 'using' includes using by sending goods, a distinction not warranted by the Act will be drawn between Tolls for Passengers, Engines and Carriages on the one hand, and Tolls for Goods sent in the ordinary way on the other" (per Lindley, L. J., in delivering jdgmt. of Court of Appeal, *Manchester, S. & L. Ry.* v. *Denaby Main Co.*, 54 L. J. Q. B. 110; 14 Q. B. D. 209; 52 L. T. 598; 49 J. P. 181; partly reversed in H. L., 11 App. Ca. 47; 55 L. J. Q. B. 181; 54 L. T. 1: *Va. Evershed's Case*, 48 L. J. Q. B. 22; 3 App. Ca. 1029.)

V. USE.

USQUE AD.—*V.* QUAMDIU.

USUAL.—To determine whether a Clause, Condition, or Thing is "*usual*," the first enquiry is,—Is the subject-matter beyond, or within, recent memory?

I. Where the subject-matter arose *beyond* recent memory, almost any kind of traditive experience may be given in proof. A conspicuous example was furnished when the Ornaments Rubric of the Church came in question, and the Courts, in order to ascertain what is now lawful, had to determine what ornaments were "*in use*" by authority of parliament in the 2nd year of Edward VI. There the literature of the age of the Reformation and the time immediately subsequent, was received in proof (*Hebbert*, or *Elphinstone* v. *Purchas*, L. R. 3 A. & E. 66; 39 L. J. Ecc. 28; L. R. 3 P. C. 245; 40 L. J. Ecc. 33).

II. Where the subject-matter has arisen within recent memory the principles by which what is "usual" is to be determined, are not so easy of statement. What is "usual" is a fact; not a conclusion of law, (*Hampshire* v. *Wickens*, 7 Ch. D. 555; 47 L. J. Ch. 243; 26 W. R. 491). But just as the question of fact of what is reasonable notice to quit as between masters and domestic servants has in process of time crystallized into a set formula of a month's notice or a month's wages, so the courts take judicial notice of some clauses as being "usual" and reject others.

In those cases however where no such judicial conclusion has been arrived at, the question of what is a "usual" clause, condition, or thing is a fact to be established by proof, having regard to (a) the subject-matter, (b) its locality, (c) its time of arising, and (d), sometimes, its circumstances.

a. The *Subject-Matter* must be considered where it is of a special nature, *e.g.* leases of property used for particular trades; "as in the case of leases of public-houses where the brewers have their own forms of leases, and the usual covenants there would mean the covenants *always inserted in the leases of the particular brewer*" (per Jessel, M. R., *Hampshire* v. *Wickens*, 47 L. J. Ch. 245: qy. Should not the words italicised read, "usually inserted in the leases of brewers in the neighbourhood?" In *Hodgkinson* v. *Crowe*, 44 L. J. Ch. 681, James, L. J., said,—"You cannot by the usage between some landlords and some tenants for 10, 20, or even 50 years make a change in the law") So, also referring to a lease of a public-house, Tenterden, C. J., in *Bennett* v. *Wormack* (6 L. J. O. S. K. B. 175; 7 B. & C. 627), said, "That which is usual in leases of one description of property may not be so in leases of another."

b. As to *Locality*. In *Wilbraham* v. *Livesey* (18 Bea. 210) Romilly, M. R., said that in a lease of a house in Grosvenor Square, London, there might be inserted different covenants from those in a lease in a trading locality. So in *Hodgkinson* v. *Crowe* (L. R. 19 Eq. 591; 10 Ch. 622; 44 L. J. Ch. 238, 680; 23 W. R. 406) Bacon, V.-C., admitted evidence of what clauses were usual in mining leases in the district where the property was situate. So also did Fry, J., in *Strelley* v. *Pearson* (15 Ch. D. 113; 49 L. J. Ch. 406; 28 W. R. 752; 43 L. T. 155). *Va. Boardman* v. *Mostyn*, 6 Ves. 467, 471: *Haywood* v. *Silber*, 29 S. J. 649.

c. As to *Time*. "Usual covenants may vary (in their meaning) in different generations. . . . What is well known in one time may in another cease to be usual" (per Jessel, M. R., *Hampshire* v. *Wickens*, 47 L. J. Ch. 245; 7 Ch. D. 555).

d. As to *Circumstances*. "I do *not* think that the word 'usual' is in many cases to be read with reference to the surrounding circumstances; but I agree that the Court has a right to know, and is bound to know, all the material facts which were known to the parties at the time when the agreement, deed, document, will or whatsoever it may be was entered into or made" (per Kay, J., *Hart* v. *Hart*, 50 L. J. Ch. 704, 705. In the report of this passage in the 18 Ch. D. 692, it runs, "I *do* think," and this would seem the correct reading).—But in that case evidence of negotiations preliminary to an agreement for "usual" clauses was rejected. In *Eadie* v. *Addison* (52 L. J. Ch. 80) the circumstances that an intending lessee was a brewer who lived a long distance from the public-house which was the subject of a demise agreement, and that it was not at all likely that the brewer was going to carry on the business at the public-house himself, was strongly relied on by the Court in rejecting a clause against underletting, the agreement there having stipulated for "proper clauses."

In cases not already judicially determined, the proof of what would be "Usual" clauses, having regard to the special subject, its locality or circumstances, would as a rule be furnished by the testimony of such living witnesses, whoever they might be, that might happen to have the information (*Hodgkinson* v. *Crowe*, sup.). But where the question is of a general character the proof of what are "Usual" Clauses may be furnished by,—

1. Considering the provisions of Acts of Parliament, *in pari materia* (*Hodgkinson* v. *Crowe*, 44 L. J. Ch. 682 ; 10 Ch. 622).

2. The evidence of conveyancing counsel (*Hart* v. *Hart*, 50 L. J. Ch. 697 ; 18 Ch. D. 670), and, possibly, of solicitors as being "the most likely to possess extensive and accurate knowledge on this subject" (27 S. J. 130).

3. Books of conveyancers' forms or text books (*Hampshire* v. *Wickens*, sup. : *Hodgkinson* v. *Crowe*, 44 L. J. 682 : *Hart* v. *Hart*, sup. As regards this latter class of evidence it has been thus questioned,—"Books of precedents are not conclusive evidence of the general practice. . . . They provide a precedent in the form in which it may be presented by the party who has to prepare the draft. . . . It is impossible to cross-examine a precedent book" (27 S. J. 130). To which it may be added, "'usual covenants' does not mean universally inserted :" Dwar. 692).

The question as to what are "usual" clauses arises most frequently as regards **Leases.**

The following passage from *Davidson's Precedents*, 3 Ed., "Leases," Vol. 5, Part 1, p. 53, was quoted with approval by Jessel, M. R., in *Hampshire* v. *Wickens*, sup. :—"The result of the authorities appears to be that in a case where the agreement is silent as to the particular covenants to be inserted in the lease, and provides merely for the lease containing usual covenants, or, which is the same thing, is an open agreement without any reference to the covenants ; *and there are no special circumstances* justifying the introduction of other covenants, the following are the only clauses which either party can insist upon, viz. :—Covenants *by the Lessee* ;—

1. To pay rent.
2. To pay taxes, except such as are expressly payable by the landlord.
3. To keep and deliver up the premises in repair. And,
4. To allow the lessor to enter and view the state of repair. A clause for re-entry in default of payment of rent.

The usual qualified clause *by the Lessor* for quiet enjoyment."

In considering what other clauses may be insisted on as "usual" in Leases the jdgmt. in the leading case of *Church* v. *Brown* (15 Ves. 258) should be kept steadily in view. Lord Eldon there (p. 268) expressed himself as follows :—"The safest rule for property is, that a person shall be taken to grant the interest in an estate which he proposes to convey, or the lease he proposes to make, and that *nothing which flows out of that interest as an incident, is to be done away by loose expressions*, to be construed by facts more loose ; that it is upon the party who has forborne to insert a covenant for his own benefit to shew his title to it ; and that it is safer to require the lessor to protect himself by express stipulation, than for Courts of Equity to hold that contracting parties shall insert, not restraints expressed by the contract, or implied by law, but such, more or less in number, as individual conveyancers shall from day to day prescribe, as proper to be imposed upon the lessee" (*V.* this passage cited *Hodgkinson* v. *Crowe*, 44 L. J. Ch. 682).

It would seem that the principles of *Church* v. *Brown* would prevent a lessor of land from insisting on a reservation of Timber, Minerals, or Game unless such a reservation were expressly provided by the contract : and in view of those principles it is perhaps permissible to question the practical value of the suggestions of Bacon, V.-C., towards the conclusion of his jdgmt. in *Hodgkinson* v. *Crowe*, as to what clauses are customary in *Mining Leases* (L. R. 19 Eq. 591 ; 44 L. J. Ch. 238 ; 23 W. R. 406). The reservation in a Mining Lease of liberty to the lessor and his agents and workmen to enter and examine the workings can be insisted on as usual (*Blakesley* v. *Whieldon*, 1 Hare, 176 ; 11 L. J. Ch. 164) ; and in a Mining Lease, granted under a Power, a power enabling the lessee to build conveniently placed cottages for workmen is "necessary or usual" (*Morris* v. *Rhydydefed Co.*, 28 L. J. Ex. 119 ; 3 H. & N. 885).

A clause in a Colliery Lease in Derbyshire (or it should seem anywhere else) to entitle the lessee *to determine the lease* when the mine cannot be worked to a profit, is not usual (*Strelley* v. *Pearson*, 15 Ch. D. 113 ; 49 L. J. Ch. 406 ; 28 W. R. 752 ; 43 L. T. 155).

A proviso *suspending Rent* in case of fire is not "usual" (*Doe* d. *Ellis* v. *Sandham*, 1 T. R. 705). Rent is not even suspended where the landlord has received compensation for injury by fire under a policy effected by him with an Insurance Co. (*Leeds* v. *Cheetham*, 1 Sim. 146 : *Lofft* v. *Dennis*, 1 E. & E. 474 ; 28 L. J. Q. B. 168).

The extract from Davidson above given (*Va.* Woodf. 120) shows that it is usual for a tenant to covenant to pay *Taxes* "except such as are expressly payable by the landlord :"—*e.g.*, as included in such exception, landlord's Property Tax (5 & 6 V. c. 35, ss. 73, 103), the proportionate part of Land Tax (38 G. 3, c. 5, s. 17 ; *Vth.* Woodf. 566), Sewers Rate (Woodf. 569), one half the Cattle Plague Rate (32 & 33 V. c. 70, s. 89), special Paving Rates under Metrop. Man. Acts (*Allum* v. *Dickinson*, 52 L. J. Q. B. 190 ; 9 Q. B. D. 632), and Tithe Rent Charge (6 & 7 W. 4, c. 71, s. 80 : *Parish* v. *Sleeman*, 29 L. J. Ch. 96 ; 1 D. G. F. & J. 326 ; 6 Jur. N. S. 385). Apt words in the agreement may throw all the foregoing landlord's taxes on the tenant, except the landlord's property tax. *V.* Imposed : Net : Outgoings : Taxes.

As regards the covenant to *Repair* the lessee is not (under an agreement for "usual" clauses) entitled to have introduced into the covenant the words, "damage by fire or tempest excepted" (*Sharp* v. *Milligan* (No. 2), 23 Bea. 419 : *Kendall* v. *Hill*, 6 Jur. N. S. 968 ; Woodf. 120) : nor, it should seem, to have inserted the words, "reasonable wear and tear excepted" (27 S. J. 177).

Default in payment of rent (qy. also Bankry of lessee, *Church* v. *Brown*, 15 Ves. 268 : *Haines* v. *Burnett*, 27 Bea. 500 : but certainly not the words "if any execution should issue against him," *Hyde* v. *Warden*, 47 L. J. Ex. 128 ; 3 Ex. D. 72) is the only "Usual" ground of *Forfeiture* (*Hodgkinson* v. *Crowe*, 10 Ch. 622 ; 44 L. J. Ch. 680 ; 23 W. R. 885 : Conv. & L. P. Act, 1881, s. 18, sub-s. 7) : except where the use, or non-use, of the premises for particular purposes is of the essence of the bargain between the parties, *e.g.* a proviso in a lease of a public-house for re-entry in the event of the premises being used for carrying on another business than that of a licensed victualler, which is a "usual" proviso (*Bennett* v. *Wormack*, 6 L. J. O. S. K. B. 175 ; 7 B. & C. 627 : *Vh.* Seton, 1322).

A covenant *against assigning* or underletting is not "Usual," not even when it is stipulated that the landlord's assent shall not be unreasonably withheld (*Church* v. *Brown*, 15 Ves. 258 : *Hodgkinson* v. *Crowe*, sup. : which latter case distinctly over-rules *Haines* v. *Burnett*, 27 Bea. 500 ; 29 L. J. Ch. 289, per Jessel, M. R., *Hampshire* v. *Wickens*, 47 L. J. Ch. 245 ; 7 Ch. D. 555. And of course the *nisi prius* decision of Lord Kenyon in *Morgan* v. *Slaughter*, 1 Esp. 8, is now of no value. *Va. Wilcox* v. *Redhead*, 49 L. J. Ch. 539 : *Buckland* v. *Papillon*, 2 Ch. 67) ; nor is it a "usual" clause which requires a lessee of a public-house to give notice to the lessor or his solicitor of an assignment of the lease (*Brookes* v. *Drysdale*, 3 C. P. D. 52 ; 26 W. R. 331).

Note.—Although the law is thus clear against the usuality of clauses restricting assignment, yet when a clause restricting assignment is in fact inserted in a lease and forfeiture is prescribed to follow on its breach, that is not a forfeiture against which relief is provided by the Conv. & L. P. Act, 1881 (s. 14, sub-s. 6).

A question has been raised (27 S. J. 177) as to whether a covenant obliging the *Lessee to Insure* could be insisted on as "Usual." The opinion there expressed is that it could : Mr. Davidson says that "probably" it could not (Prec. 3 Ed., "Leases," Vol. 5, pt. 1, p. 53) ; and to that effect is *Wilcox* v. *Redhead*, 49 L. J. Ch. 539.

Probably the most difficult question on what "Usual" clauses might be insisted on in leases, would arise as to *Restrictions* prohibiting the absolutely unfettered use and enjoyment of the premises during the term at the free will of the lessee. It is merely common learning to say that, generally speaking, no such restrictions could be insisted on (*Church* v. *Brown* : *Hodgkinson* v. *Crowe*, sup.). But where, as previously suggested, the use, or non-use, of the premises for particular purposes is of the essence of the bargain between the parties, there it would be proper and "usual" to provide for such use, or against such non-use. Such a doctrine would seem to be well within the meaning of "special circumstances" referred to in the extract given above from Davidson and the commentary of the M. R.

thereon in *Hampshire* v. *Wickens*. No doubt the application of the doctrine just enunciated would, in many cases, be difficult. But in *Bennett* v. *Wormack* (sup.) it was held that a lessor of a public-house is entitled, as a "usual" clause, to have a proviso forfeiting the lease in case of the premises being used for a business other than that of a licensed victualler; and *à fortiori* he would be entitled to a *covenant* against such a use: and if so, why should he not be entitled to a similar covenant with an accompanying proviso for re-entry for the purpose of ensuring that the business of a licensed victualler shall be carried on uninterruptedly during the whole of the term and the necessary certificates and licences duly taken out by the lessee? This would be only the completion of the rule of which the other part was established by *Bennett* v. *Wormack*. Without this further provision a lessee might destroy or imperil that part of the property—its character of monopoly as licensed premises,—which is the subject-matter of the lease, and the upholding of which may fairly be regarded as of the essence of the bargain between the parties.

But besides public-houses may not there be other property the peculiar characteristics of which would as much be entitled to protection? Thus in *Hyde* v. *Warden* (47 L. J. 121; 3 Ex. D. 72: *Vth. Reeve* v. *Berridge*, 20 Q. B. D. 523) a covenant not to mow meadow land more than once a year was held not unreasonable or unusual. Of course conditions in restraint of trade are, generally speaking, not "usual" (*Propert* v. *Parker*, 3 My. & K. 280: *Van* v. *Corpe*, Ib. 269; 6 L. J. Ch. 208: *Wilcox* v. *Redhead*, 49 L. J. Ch. 539: *Wilbraham* v. *Livesey*, 18 Bea. 206); but as was suggested in the last-named case, supposing a house be situate in the most fashionable part of London, with circumstances under which to carry on trade in it would be seriously to diminish its value; would not that be *pro tanto* destroying the thing leased, against which the lessor would be entitled to a covenant and clause of forfeiture as a fair and "usual" term of the contract? So, too, of premises where a business of very long standing has been carried on, and the continuance of which business on the premises demised would be fairly collected as of the essence of the bargain. So, too, perhaps, where premises are specially and exclusively adapted for a special kind of occupation, that kind of occupation ought to be preserved by proper "usual" clauses. So again where the continuance of workings goes to the preservation of the thing demised,—*e.g.* pumping water from a mine,—that would seem of the essence of the bargain which the lessor should be able to insist on providing for (*V. Strelley* v. *Pearson*, 15 Ch. D. 113; 49 L. J. Ch. 406; 28 W. R. 752; 43 L. T. 155).

It may be added that an Agreement for a Lease, which stipulates that the lessee is not *to use* the premises for other than a specified trade, and providing for all usual covenants, does not warrant the insertion in the Lease of an affirmative covenant by the lessee that he will *carry on* such trade during the term (*Doe* d. *Bute* v. *Guest*, 15 M. & W. 160).

Vf. as to usual covenants in Leases, Dart. 191, 192; Woodf. 120–123, 664; and in *Mining* Leases, MacS. 196, 197.

Leases under Powers.—Where the power requires that "the Usual and Reasonable covenants" shall be inserted, the lease must contain such covenants as were contained in leases of the same property at the time of the creation of the power; otherwise the power will not be well executed (*Doe* d. *Egremont* v. *Stephens*, 13 L. J. Q. B. 350; 6 Q. B. 208): but, there the court "inclined to think" that such words in a Power as "usually so leased," would not prevent the joining in one lease of tenements that had generally been let separately, provided all the tenements were comprised within the power. *Vf. Doe* d. *Egremont* v. *Williams*, 17 L. J. Q. B. 154; 11 Q. B. 688: Woodf. 205, 206.

As to "Usual" clauses in **Underleases**; *V. Williamson* v. *Williamson*, 43 L. J. Ch. 738; 9 Ch. 729: *Haywood* v. *Silber*, 30 Ch. D. 404; 34 W. R. 114.

As regards **Deeds** in general; what is "Usual" has (when the point is uncovered by authority) to be determined "according to the practice and customs of conveyancers in such cases" (per Kay, J., *Hart* v. *Hart*, 50 L. J. Ch. 702; 18 Ch. D. 670; 30 W. R. 8); in which case it was held that the *dum casta* clause, in a *Deed of Separation* between husband and wife securing an allowance to the latter, is not "usual" (*Va. Gandy* v. *Gandy*, 51 L. J. P. D. & A. 41; 7 P. D. 168: *Harrison* v. *Harrison*, 56 L. J. P. D. & A. 76; 12 P. D. 130; 57 L. T. 119; 35 W. R. 703. *Vf. Lister* v. *Lister*, 24 L. J. Notes of Ca. 104); but a clause that a trustee shall be found for the wife "who will enter into such covenants as in such a deed a trustee usually enters into on behalf of the wife with the husband" (*Hart* v. *Hart*, sup.) is "usual."

A clause providing for a three months' notice prior to sale is usual in a **Mortgage** (*Craddock* v. *Rogers*, 53 L. J. Ch. 968).

As to Usual Clauses in **Partnership Articles**; *V.* Lindl. 830 *et seq.* The cases there digested, though full of valuable suggestion as to what ought to be inserted in Partnership Articles, hardly lay down rules for determining what clauses would be judicially inserted under an agreement stipulating for "usual" clauses. Still they throw much light even on that difficult question.

The following are Usual *Powers* in **Settlements** pursuant to articles:—Leasing for 21 years: Sale and Exchange: Maintenance and Advancement: Varying Securities: Appointment of New Trustees: Partition where Property joint: Leasing Mines: Building Leases where the land is fit for building, unless mere occupation Leases for (say) 21 years have been expressly prescribed and then, on the principle *expressio unius exclusio alterius*, building leases would be excluded (Lewin, 127, 128, and cases there cited). Powers to Jointure or other powers to confer personal privileges would *not*, generally speaking, be "usual" (Ib. 127). *Va.* Settled Land

Act, 1882, ss. 3, 4, 6 *et seq.*; Conv. & L. P. Act, 1881, ss. 42, 66; and *Vth.* Lewin, 129. *Vf.* Macqueen on Husband and Wife, 3 Ed. 240.

In an open Contract to sell a Lease, and even where the liability of the lessee to deliver up in good repair is excluded in the case of "Fire," it is not "usual" to further restrict such liability by adding the words "or other Casualty" (*Crosse* v. *Morgan*, 60 L. T. 703; 37 W. R. 543).

"Usual and Proper" Books of Account; *V.* BUSINESS TRANSACTIONS.

V. PROPER.

USUAL AGENCY TERMS.—"Usual Agency Terms," as between a Country Solicitor and his London Agent, means, that "the London Agent is entitled to be paid by the Country Solicitor all his disbursements out of pocket. But there are a number of other charges which are known as 'Profit Charges,' and the question has been raised whether the London Agent is entitled to half the profit made by the Country Solicitor, or only to half the 'Profit Charges.' We have consulted Mr. Ryland, the Taxing Master, and he has told us that the London Agent is only entitled to half the 'Profit Charges,'—that is, the charges which do not involve any expenditure by him, and that the London Agent has nothing to do with the profit made by the Country Solicitor" (per Cotton, L. J., *Ward* v. *Lawson*, 38 W. R. 300; 43 Ch. D. 353: *Vh.* 34 S. J. 190, 191).

USUAL AND CUSTOMARY MANNER.—"Where by the terms of a Charter-Party the ship is to *Deliver* the Cargo 'in the Usual and Customary Manner,' the obligation which attaches is only that the merchant and shipowner shall each use reasonable despatch in performing his part, and there is no implied contract that the discharge shall *at all events* be performed in the time usually occupied at the particular port. Therefore, where, owing to a threatened bombardment, the authorities at the port of discharge refused for several days to allow the discharge of cargo to proceed, so that during those days neither party to the contract could perform his part of the contract, it was held that the loss from delay must fall on the ship-owner" (1 Maude & P. 409, citing *Ford* v. *Cotesworth*, L. R. 4 Q. B. 127; 5 Ib. 544; 38 L. J. Q. B. 52; 39 Ib. 188; 9 B. & S. 559; 10 Ib. 991: *Cunningham* v. *Dunn*, 3 C. P. D. 443; 48 L. J. C. P. 62).

"*Load* in the usual and customary manner:"—this phrase seems to apply only to the mode of loading when the vessel has arrived at the loading berth, and to have no reference to a detention outside the loading place (1 Maude & P. 408, citing *Tapscott* v. *Balfour*, L. R. 8 C. P. 46; 42 L. J. C. P. 16: per Pollock, C. B., *Lawson* v. *Burness*, 1 H. & C. 400: and per Brett, L. J., *Nelson* v. *Dahl*, 12 Ch. D. 588: *Va. Kay* v. *Field*, 8 Q. B. D. 598; 10 Ib. 241; 52 L. J. Q. B. 17).

USUAL AND MOST APPROVED WAY.—A compliance with a covenant to work *Mines* "in the usual and most approved way" will not exonerate from responsibility on other grounds for letting down the Surface (*Davis* v. *Treharne*, 6 App. Ca. 460 ; 50 L. J. Q. B. 665 ; 29 W. R. 869).

USUAL BUSINESS.—As to what is the "Usual Business of an Hotel and Tavern ;" *V. Simpson* v. *Westminster Palace Hotel Co.*, 29 L. J. Ch. 561 ; 2 D. G. F. & J. 141.

USUAL COVENANTS : CLAUSES.—*V.* USUAL.

USUAL DESPATCH.—"Where Charterers contracted to load a cargo of coals on board 'with Usual Despatch,' it was held that they were bound to load the vessel with the usual despatch of persons who have a cargo ready for loading at the port ; and that they were liable for a delay caused by a severe frost which rendered unnavigable the canal along which coals were to be brought" (1 Maude & P. 317, citing *Kearon* v. *Pearson*, 7 H. & N. 386 ; 31 L. J. Ex. 1).

"To be loaded with the *Usual Despatch of the Port* ;" *V. Ashcroft* v. *Crow Co.*, 43 L. J. Q. B. 194 ; L. R. 9 Q. B. 540.

Vh. Postlethwaite v. *Freeland*, 5 App. Ca. 622 ; 49 L. J. Ex. 630 : *Elliott* v. *Lord*, 52 L. J. P. C. 23 ; 48 L. T. 542 ; 5 Asp. 63.

USUAL PLACE OF ABODE.—A clause of Forfeiture in case of the devisee not making the mansion-house "his Usual and Common Place of Abode and Residence," is not void for uncertainty (*Wynne* v. *Fletcher*, 24 Bea. 430). *V.* RESIDE.

"Last or most Usual Place of Abode," s. 1, 11 & 12 V. c. 43 ; *V. R.* v. *Smith*, L. R. 10 Q. B. 604 : LAST.

"Place of Abode ;" *V.* PLACE.

USUAL PLACE OF RELIGIOUS WORSHIP.—By s. 32, 3 G. 4, c. 126, persons "going to or returning from his, her, or their Usual Place of Religious Worship, tolerated by law on Sundays," were exempted from Turnpike Toll ;—A Primitive Methodist Minister had assigned to him the Sunday and other services of a district comprising the parish of F. The days on which, and the places at which, he was to attend were fixed at regular quarterly meetings of the Methodists and printed on a "Plan." According to this Plan the Minister had to preach at F. on three Sundays each quarter, and elsewhere on other Sundays ; held, that in going to F., on the Sundays indicated in the Plan, to conduct the Services there, the Minister was going to his "Usual Place of Religious Worship," within the exemption (*Smith* v. *Barnett*, L. R. 6 Q. B. 34 ; 40 L. J. M. C. 15 ; 23 L. T. 746 : *Vf. Lewis* v. *Hammond*, 2 B. & Ald. 206). The fact of the carriage being driven by another person than the Minister would not, *semble*, subject the carriage to toll (28 J. P. 735 : *Layard* v. *Ovey*, 37 L. J. M. C. 148 ; L. R. 3 Q. B. 415 ; 18 L. T. 632 ; 32 J. P. 293).

USUAL POWERS.—*V.* Usual.

USUAL PROFESSIONAL CHARGES. — *V.* Professional Charges.

USUAL RENT.—*V.* Ancient Rent.

USUALLY.—A Power to Lease such lands as "theretofore Usually *demised*," or "so as such or more rent shall be reserved as the same lands are *now let at*," will not as a rule apply to lands not previously leased (Watson, Eq. 868). "The words 'Usually or Accustomably Demised' may have two senses; the one signifying the frequent or repeated act of leasing; the other, the common continuance of land in lease, though it has not been more than once demised, as in the case of lands leased for 500 years long since. And this is the more common acceptation of the words 'usually demised;' though, in a literal sense, land once let is not land usually demised. Land twice demised is clearly included in that term" (Platt, 411, 412, citing *Tustian* v. *Roper*, T. Jo. 27; Vaugh. 28); "though lands let by virtue of a contract from year to year for 3 years cannot be said to be usually demised, because it is but one lease, though renewable every year" (1 Platt, 411, 412, citing 2 Rol. Ab. 262, pl. 14: *Vf.* Sug Pow. 730–732).

"Upon the construction of the words 'Usually Demised,' it has been determined that they embrace every species of demise—at will, from year to year, or for years, or lives, and whether granted by parol or by deed, by copy of court-roll, covenant to stand seised, or any other instrument: but whatever the instrument, it must operate as a lease in the sense of the term demise in the given power" (Sug. Pow. 730, and cases there cited).

"Usually *rated*," s. 27, 5 & 6 W. 4, c. 50, means such premises as have been usually actually rated in the parish for which the Rate is made (*R.* v. *Rose*, 13 L. J. M. C. 155; 6 Q. B. 153).

"Usually *sold*," refers to the usage at the date of the statute (*Aerated Bread Co.* v. *Grigg*, cited French Bread).

USURPATION.—"Usurpation hath two significations in the common law: one, when an estranger that no right hath presenteth to a church, and his clerke is admitted and instituted he is said to be an usurper, and the wrongfull act that he hath done is called an usurpation.

"Secondly, when any subject doth use, without lawfull warrant, royall franchises, he is said to usurpe upon the king those franchises" (Co. Litt. 277 b).

UTENSILS.—"By a devise of all Utensils, it is agreed that plate and jewels do not pass" (Touch. 447, citing *Dame Latimer's Case*, 1 Dyer, 59 b, pl. 15; *Va.* Wms. Exs. 1194).

UTILITARIAN PURPOSES.—A bequest to be applied to "utilitarian purposes," is void for uncertainty (*Re Woodgate*, 2 Times Rep. 674).

UTLAND.—Tenemental land (Elph. 627, citing Spelm. *Inland*).

UTMOST.—"Utmost *Efforts*" to obtain payment from Principal Debtor before resort to Surety; *V. Holl* v. *Hadley*, 4 L. J. K. B. 126; 4 N. & M. 515; 2 A. & E. 758.

"Utmost *Endeavours* to improve," in a covenant in a Lease; *V. Croft* v. *Lumley*, 25 L. J. Q. B. 73, 223; 27 Ib. 321; 6 H. L. Ca. 672.

"Utmost endeavours to continue the house open as a Public-House;" *V. Linder* v. *Pryor*, 8 C. & P. 518, stated Woodf. 670.

"Best endeavours to extend the custom and business" of a Public-House; *V. Moore* v. *Robinson*, 48 L. J. Q. B. 156, 158.

"Utmost endeavours" to obtain Renewal of a Lease; *V. Simpson* v. *Clayton*, 8 L. J. C. P. 59; 4 Bing. N. C. 758; 6 Sc. 469; 1 Arnold, 299.

UTTER.—To "utter" a false document is to part with it, or tender it, or use it in some way to get money or other benefit by means of it; and it is immaterial who is to have the money or get the benefit (*R.* v. *Ion*, 21 L. J. M. C. 166; 2 Den. 475). *Vf.* Arch. Cr. 639.

As to uttering Counterfeit, Base, or Foreign Coin; *V.* 24 & 25 V. c. 99, ss. 9–16, 20–23, 30.

Vf. Arch. Cr. 862.

UTTERLY VOID.—*V.* Void.

VACANT.—The site of old buildings recently pulled down, but the rights attaching to which buildings are properly reserved, is not "Vacant *Ground*" within s. 75, Metropolis Management Amendment Act, 1862 (*Auckland* v. *Westminster Bd. of Works*, 41 L. J. Ch. 723; 7 Ch. 597: *Vh. Barlow* v. *St. Mary Abbotts*, 53 L. J. Ch. 899; 55 Ib. 680; 27 Ch. D. 362; 11 App. Ca. 257; 55 L. T. 221; 34 W. R. 521; 50 J. P. 691: *Gilbart* v. *Wandsworth Bd. of Works*, 60 L. T. 149).

V. EMPTY.

As to what is "Vacant *Possession*" within R. 9, Ord. 9, R. S. C.; *V.* Woodf. 799, 800.

VACCARIA.—"By *vaccaria* in law is signified a dairy-house, derived of *vacca*, the cow. In Latine, it is *lactarium*, or *lactitium*, and *vaccarius* is mentioned in Domesday" (Co. Litt. 5 b).

VAGABOND.—"The idea of leading a wandering and vagabond life, is not now at all an ingredient in the description of a Rogue and Vagabond," within the Vagrant Act, 5 G. 4, c. 83 (per Cleasby, B., *Monck* v. *Hilton*, 46 L. J. M. C. 168).

VAGUE.—An Assignment or Contract is not "Vague" merely because it is indefinite or uncertain; "Vague," in this connection, means that which is incapable of being ascertained when the instrument comes to be enforced.

Language has been used with regard to Assignments of, and Contracts relating to, future property "which tends to confuse the idea of Vagueness in the contract itself, with that sort of necessary uncertainty which, at the time when the contract is made, is more or less involved in the idea of futurity. 'Vagueness' is a misleading term. A contract may be too vague *in itself* to be understood; and on that ground it is enforceable neither at law nor in equity. But in the case of a contract to assign future property when the money has been paid, if, when *at the time of the contract coming to be enforced*, the property has fallen into the possession of the assignor, and is of such a character and is sufficiently ascertained to admit of the contract being enforced in equity, there is no necessary Vagueness" (per Bowen, L. J., *Re Clarke, Coombe* v. *Carter*, 56 L. J. Ch. 984; 36 Ch. D. 348: *Vf. Tailby* v. *Official Receiver*, 58 L. J. Q. B. 75; 13 App. Ca. 523, especially jdgmt of Ld. Herschell).

VALUABLE.—A "Valuable *Consideration*" may be money or money's worth; and in this connection, "Valuable" means real, as distinguished from a consideration that is merely illusory or nominal; but it does not mean equivalent. Marriage generally is a Valuable Consideration for a Settlement; but not necessarily so if contracted with the settlor's concubine, nor, indeed, in any case where there is evidence of an intent, of which the wife is cognisant, to make the celebration of marriage part of a scheme to protect property against creditors (*Colombine* v. *Penhall,* 1 Sm. & G. 228 : *Bulmer* v. *Hunter,* 38 L. J. Ch. 543; L. R. 8 Eq. 46 : *Re Pennington,* 5 Morr. 216).

As to what is a "Valuable Consideration" within the statutes of Elizabeth (13 Eliz. c. 5; 27 Eliz. c. 4), *V.* May on Fraudulent Conveyances, Part 4, Ch. 1.

Marriage is not a "Valuable Consideration in *money or money's worth*" within s. 17, Sucn. Dy. Act, 1853 (*Floyer* v. *Bankes,* 3 D. G. J. & S. 306; 33 L. J. Ch. 1).

"(1) Valuable Consideration for a *Bill of Exchange,* may be constituted by,—

(*a*) Any consideration sufficient to support a simple contract;

(*b*) An antecedent debt or liability. Such a debt or liability is deemed Valuable Consideration whether the Bill is payable on demand, or at a future time.

(2) Where value has at any time been given for a Bill, the holder is deemed to be a holder for value as regards the Acceptor and all parties to the Bill who became parties prior to such time.

(3) Where the holder of a Bill has a lien on it, arising either from contract or by implication of law, he is deemed to be a holder for value to the extent of the sum for which he has a lien" (s. 27, Bills of Ex. Act, 1882). So of a Promissory Note (s. 89, Ib.).

V. Good : Further : Full Consideration.

"A '*Valuable Security*' is one on which money is payable irrespective of any contingency" (per Cockburn, C. J., *R.* v. *Tatlock,* 46 L. J. M. C. 711); and accordingly he, and Kelly, C. B., there held that a policy of Insurance was not a "Valuable Security" within ss. 1, 75, 24 & 25 V. c. 96; but the converse was held by Amphlett & Bramwell, B.B. (46 L. J. M. C. 7; 2 Q. B. D. 157). As to describing this "Valuable Security" in an Indictment, *V. R.* v. *Lowrie,* 36 L. J. M. C. 24; L. R. 1 C. C. R. 61.

A Judgment recovered by a pauper, is a "Valuable Security" within 12 & 13 V. c. 103, s. 16 (*West Ham* v. *Ovens,* 42 L. J. M. C. 29; L. R. 8 Ex. 37).

The definition of "Valuable Security" in the Post Office Act, 1837 (s. 47, 1 V. c. 36), is nearly the same as that given in the Larceny Act (s. 1, 24 & 25 V. c. 96).

It has been stated that a Railway Ticket is a "Valuable Security" (Maxwell, 344, citing *R.* v. *Boulton,* 1 Den. 508; 19 L. J. M. C. 67 : *R.* v. *Beecham,* 5 Cox C. C. 181).

"Other Valuable *Things*," in a Bequest, construed *ejusdem generis* (*Cavendish* v. *Cavendish*, 1 Cox, Ch. 77); so of "Things" (*Stuart* v. *Bute*, 1 Dow 73). *Vf.* THINGS.

V. SECURITY.

VALUATION.—"An Arbitration is a proceeding conducted according to judicial rules, and the arbitrator hears the parties and their evidence. A Valuation is a proceeding in which a person specially skilled in the subject-matter decides solely by the use of his eyes and his knowledge" (per Esher, M. R., *Re Dawdy and Hartcup*, 54 L. J. Q. B. 575; 15 Q. B. D. 426).

"Valuation, imperfect or erroneous;" *V.* IMPERFECT.

V. ARBITRATION: FAIR VALUATION.

VALUE.—The "value" of a *Succession* for the purpose of charging duty thereon under s. 10 of the Sucn. Dy. Act, 1853, is to be made by capitalising its "annual value" (s. 21, Ib.). This annual value "must be determined, once for all, when the succession falls, and cannot be left for future ascertainment" (per Ld. Chelmsford, *A.-G.* v. *Sefton*, 34 L. J. Ex. 106), and it means the present actual annual value regardless of a (possible or probable, remote or near) prospective increase or decrease (*A.-G.* v. *Sefton*, 34 L. J. Ex. 98; 11 H. L. Ca. 257; 2 H. & C. 362). But where property,—*e.g.*, unoccupied land,—is not in its existing state yielding or capable of yielding any annual income, but yet is saleable, such property would (probably) be chargeable with Succession Duty; and its annual value would (probably) be a value equal to interest at £3 per cent. on the sum that might be realized if the property were, at once, sold (per Westbury, L. C. and Ld. Chelmsford in the case cited; but Ld. Wensleydale thought it unnecessary for that case to give any opinion on the point).

V. ANNUAL VALUE: CLEAR.

"Value" in *Bills of Ex. Act*, 1882, "means Valuable Consideration" (s. 2): *V.* VALUABLE.

In *Covenants to Settle* after-acquired property "Where the property to be settled is to be of a named minimum value, and the interest accruing is reversionary, the sum named means the value of the property itself when it falls into possession, not the value of the reversion at the time of settlement" (Elph. 526, citing int. al. *Re Mackenzie*, 2 Ch. 345; 36 L. J. Ch. 320: *Cornmell* v. *Keith*, 3 Ch. D. 767; 45 L. J. Ch. 689: *Re Clinton*, L. R. 13 Eq. 295; 41 L. J. Ch. 191: *Re Welstead*, 47 L. T. 331). *Vf.* ONE TIME.

"Value of the *Ship and Freight*;" *V. Gale* v. *Laurie*, 5 B. & C. 156: *Smith* v. *Kirby*, 1 Q. B. D. 131.

Jurisdiction to Co. Co. where "Value of the *Tenements*" did not "exceed £20 *by the year*," s. 11, 30 & 31 V. c. 142, meant the actual marketable value, of which the lettable rent is a fair criterion (*Elstone* v. *Rose*, L. R. 4 Q. B. 4; 38 L. J. Q. B. 6; 9 B. & S. 509).

The "*Actual* Value" of a Railway, taxable under s. 326, Quebec Towns Corporation General Clauses Act, 1876, 44 V. c. 60 (incorporated by s. 98, Quebec Act, 44 V. c. 62), is only that of the land occupied by the road (*St. John* v. *Central Vermont Ry.*, 59 L. J. P. C. 15).

Majority "In Value" of Creditors ; *V.* In Value.

VALUE OF THE SHIP AND FREIGHT.—"Whatever is on board a ship for the object of the voyage and adventure on which she is engaged, belonging to the owners, constitutes a part of the ship and her appurtenances, within the meaning of 53 G. 3, c. 159, s. 1, whether the object be warfare, the conveyance of passengers or goods, or the fishery" (per Abbott, C. J., *Gale* v. *Laurie*, 5 B. & C. 164 : *Vf. Wilson* v. *Dickson*, 2 B. & Ald. 2 : *Cannan* v. *Meaburn*, 1 Bing. 465 ; Maude & P. 79, n. (*h*)).

V. Freight.

VALUE UNKNOWN.—*V.* Contents unknown.

VALUED.—*V.* Hereafter valued and declared.

VAPOUR. — For the conventional chemical distinction between "Vapour" and "Gas ;" *V. Stanley* v. *Western Insrce.*, 37 L. J. Ex. 74.

VARECTUM.—*V.* Warectum.

VARIANCE.—"No objection shall be taken or allowed to any Information, Complaint or Summons . . . . for any *Variance* between such Information, Complaint or Summons and the Evidence" in support of it, s. 1, 11 & 12 V. c. 43 ;—"The word 'Variance' points at some difference between the allegation in the Summons or Information, and the Evidence adduced in support of it" (per Crompton, J., *Martin* v. *Pridgeon*, 28 L. J. M. C. 179 ; 1 E. & E. 778) ; and accordingly it was there held that when the evidence shows a different offence than that alleged in the Summons, the justices cannot convict ; such a difference is not a "Variance" (*Va. Soden* v. *Cray*, 7 L. T. 324 ; nom. *Loadman* v. *Cragg*, 26 J. P. 743). A "Variance" would be, *e.g.*, a misdescription, not misleading, of an employer (*Whittle* v. *Frankland*, 26 J. P. 372), or of an ownership (*Ralph* v. *Hurrell*, 44 L. J. M. C. 145), or of a date (*Exeter* v. *Heaman*, 37 L. T. 535).

"At Variance," s. 25 (9), Jud. Act, 1873; *V. The Bernina*, 55 L. J. P. D. & A. 21; 11 P. D. 33 ; 34 W. R. 595.

VARIED.—*V.* Expressly varied.

VEGETABLE PRODUCTION.—*V. R.* v. *Hodges*, Moo. & M. 341: Product.

VEHICLE.—In the exemption from toll given by subs. 6, s. 19, 32 & 33 V. c. 14, for a trade "Waggon, Cart, or other *Vehicle*," the word "vehicle" means such a cart as that which a tradesman uses for sending his goods from place to place (*Speak* v. *Powell*, 43 L. J. M. C. 19; L. R. 9 Ex. 25).

V. CARRIAGE.

VEIN OR SEAM.—"'Vein' is defined in Webster's Dictionary as 'A Seam or Layer of any substance, more or less wide, intersecting a rock or stratum, and not corresponding with the stratification; often limited in the language of miners to such a layer or course of metal or ore;' and in Richardson's Dictionary as 'Lineal Tubes which convey the blood in animals; Lineal Streaks in mineral or vegetable bodies.' The Encyclopædia Britannica thus describes 'Veins';—'These are Fissures or Cracks in the rocks . . . which are filled . . . with materials of quite a different nature from the rocks in which the fissures occur.' 'Seam' is defined in Webster's Dictionary as 'a thin Layer or Stratum; a narrow vein between two thicker ones, as a Seam of Coal.' 'Vein' and 'Seam' appear, accordingly, to be convertible expressions" (MacS. 1, 2). And a little further on the learned author in contrasting "Mine" and "Vein or Seam" says, "'Mine' appears, in its primary sense, to imply openness; and 'Vein or Seam' appears, in its primary sense, to exclude that notion." *Vf.* Ib. 11.

V. MINE.

VELINDRE.—Welsh for VILL (Elph. 627, citing 4 T. R. 552, n. (*b*)).

VEND.—"I think the proper meaning to be attached to the word 'Vend,' is, the habit of selling" (per Coleridge, J., *Minter* v. *Williams*, 5 L. J. K. B. 60, 62).

VENDOR.—In a contract of sale for "the Vendor," the Vendor is not sufficiently described; *V.* PROPRIETOR.

VENUE.—"'Venew' or 'Visne,' is a term used in the statute of 35 H. 8, c. 6, and often in our bookes, and signifies a place next to that where any thing that comes to be tryed is supposed to be done. And therefore for the better discovery of the truth of the matter in fact upon every tryall, some of the Jury must be of the same Hundred, or sometimes of the same parish in which the thing is supposed to be done, who by intendment may have the best knowledge of the matter. See Coke, 6 Book, 14a, *Arundel's Case*" (Termes de la Ley: *Note.*—The last sentence is curious as throwing light on the original function of the Jury; but the Venue is now often changed to the locality in which the matter has arisen, not because the Jury may have "the best knowledge" of it, but because each locality should bear its own burdens and because the locality of the subject-matter is the place where the witnesses frequently reside).

VERDICT.—"'*Verdict of* 12 *men.*' *Veredictum quasi dictum veritatis,* as *judicium est quasi jurisdictum. Et sicut ad questionem juris, non respondent juratores sed judices: sic ad questionem facti non respondent judices sed juratores.* For jurors are to try the fact, and the judges ought to judge according to the law that riseth upon the fact, for *ex facto jus oritur*" (Co. Litt. 226 a, b).

VERT.—"Whatsoever beareth green leaf, but specially of great and thick coverts" (4 Inst. 317, *wh. V.* for the different kinds of Vert: *Va.* Termes de la Ley; Elph. 627).

VERTU.—A bequest of "Objects of Vertu and Taste" (or "Vertu *or* Taste") will not, *proprio vigore,* comprise Pictures; especially when those words follow an enumeration such as gold and silver plate, china, &c., and where, in the same Will, there is another gift of "Furniture," a word under which Pictures are aptly included (*Re Londesborough,* 50 L. J. Ch. 9).

VESSEL.—"Vessel" does not include everything that floats; *e.g.,* it does not include a Raft or a Wherry (*Gapp* v. *Bond,* 19 Q. B. D. 200; 56 L. J. Q. B. 438; 57 L. T. 437; 35 W. R. 683; 3 Times Rep. 621).

An open Boat 18 feet long; held, within an Act making it penal to set on fire a "Ship or Vessel" (*R.* v. *Bowyer,* 4 C. & P. 559).

For the purposes of the Harbours and Docks Clauses Act, 1847 (10 V. c. 27, s. 3) a "Vessel" includes "Ship, Boat, Lighter and Craft of every kind and whether navigated by steam or otherwise." That definition, by itself, includes a Barge propelled by oars only; but not so when it is qualified as it is in ss. 100, 101, London & St. Katherine's Docks Company Act, 1864, 27 & 28 V. c. clxxviii (*Hedges* v. *London Docks Co.,* 55 L. J. M. C. 46; 16 Q. B. D. 597; 54 L. T. 427; 34 W. R. 503; 50 J. P. 580; 2 Times Rep. 167).

For the purposes of the Swansea Harbour Acts, 1854, 1874, "Vessel" "bound from or to any port or place in the United Kingdom," includes a Barge (*Tennant* v. *Swansea Harbour Trustees,* 3 Times Rep. 128).

A Dumb Barge is a "Vessel" within the exception in s. 4, Bills of Sale Act, 1878, and its assignment does not require registration as a Bill of S. (*Gapp* v. *Bond,* sup.).

V. Ship: Ships and Vessels: Sailing Vessel.

VEST.—"To 'vest,' generally means to give the property in" (per Brett, L. J., *Coverdale* v. *Charlton,* 48 L. J. Q. B. 132). "It may be useful to refer to the history of the word 'vest,' as it is a word which has acquired a definite meaning, carrying with it definite legal consequences. The word 'vest' is found in the Lands C. C. Act, 1845, where it is said, in s. 81, that conveyances 'shall be effectual to *vest* the lands thereby conveyed in the promoters of the Company'; and there is a proviso to the same effect in s. 100. So in the Trustee Act, 1850 (13 & 14 V. c. 60), s. 3 provides that the Chancellor may in certain cases make an order that 'such lands be *vested* in' certain persons. Then again in the Bankry. Act, 1869, it is enacted, by s. 17, that 'on the appointment of a trustee, the property shall forthwith pass to, and *vest* in, the trustee appointed.' So that it is clear that there is an established meaning in which the word 'vest' is employed. I now turn to the P. H. Act, 1875, ss. 12, 13: both contain the word 'vest,' and by the operation of those sections, the sewers become vested in the local board. Then, by s. 149, the streets 'vest in' the same authority; and that means, I think, that the street must, as a matter of property, pass to the local board,—that is, the surface of the street passes and some property in the soil is vested in the local board for the purposes for which the soil of the street is required by those who have to manage the street" (per Cotton, L. J., Ib. 134): that is, the land forming the street does not vest down to the centre of the earth (per Bramwell, L. J., Ib. 130) nor *usque ad cœlum*; but so much *Depth* passes to the local board as is required for the ordinary purposes of the street, including what may be required for water-pipes, gas mains, and the sewer systems (per Brett, L. J., Ib. 133: *Coverdale* v. *Charlton*, also reported 4 Q. B. D. 104; 40 L. T. 88; 43 J. P. 268: *Va. Hinde* v. *Chorlton*, 36 L. J. C. P. 79; L. R. 2 C. P. 104: *Rolls* v. *St. George, Southwark*, 14 Ch. D. 785), and so much *Height* over the street as is required for the preservation of its ordinary user (*Wandsworth* v. *United Telephone Co.*, 53 L. J. Q. B. 449; 13 Q. B. D. 904).

Property of an industrial Society "shall vest" in the Society on registration, s. 6, 25 & 26 V. c. 87; *V. Queensbury Industrial Socy.* v. *Pickles*, 35 L. J. Ex. 1; 3 H. & C. 857; L. R. 1 Ex. 1.

But in the language of Conveyancers, "the word 'to Vest' has several senses which it is important to distinguish :—

I. Originally the word had reference only to real estate. As applied to estates in land, 'to Vest' signifies the acquisition of a portion of the actual ownership or feudal possession of the land: the acquisition, not of an estate *in possession*, but of an actual estate. The fee simple being supposed to be carved out into parts or divisions by the creation of particular estates, a grant to any person of one of these portions of the fee vested him with, or vested in him, an estate in the land. Thus 'Vested' is nearly equivalent to 'Possessed.'

In this, its original sense, 'Vested' has no reference to the absence of *conditional*-ness or contingency. If an estate tail be limited to A., with remainder to B., the estate of B. is a 'vested' remainder, not because the failure of issue of A. is considered an event certain at some time or other to happen, but because such a remainder vests in B. an actual portion of the fee, though the time of its falling into possession is wholly contingent and uncertain. B. is *invested* with a portion of the ownership of the land.

All remainders, not vested, are in fact contingent, not as being necessarily limited on an uncertain event, but because their taking effect depends on the contingency of their happening to vest during the continuance of the particular estate which supports them, and which may determine at any moment. Thus 'Vested' comes to mean the opposite of 'Contingent' or conditional. But the word itself refers, as has been said, not to contingency but to possession.

II. The only definition that can be given of the word 'Vested' in English law, as applied to future interests other than remainders, is, that it means 'not subject to a condition precedent:' what amounts to a condition precedent the cases only can determine. As applied to remainders in land, the word retains its original sense denoting the actual possession of an *estate* in the land" (Hawk. 221–223 : and *V*. Ib. ch. 18) : *Vf.* as to when Devises or Bequests are vested or contingent, *Re Coppard*, 35 Ch. D. 350 ; 56 L. J. Ch. 606 ; 56 L. T. 359 ; 35 W. R. 473 : 1 Jarm. ch. 25 ; Wms. Exs. 1229 *et seq.*; Hawk. ch. 18. As to Vesting of Gifts to Classes, Elph. ch. 25 ; As to the Vesting of Portions, Elph. ch. 26.

Vh. Chitty, Eq. Ind. 7427–7431.

V. VESTED.

VESTED.—In testamentary gifts referring to death contingently, "the proper legal meaning of the word 'vested' is vested in point of interest (*Richardson* v. *Power*, 19 C. B. N. S. 780); but its natural and etymological meaning is said to be, vested in possession (*Young* v. *Robertson*, 4 Macq. H. L. 314 ; 8 Jur. N. S. 825) : and there are many cases of gifts over on the death of the legatee before his legacy has become 'vested,' where, upon the context, the word has been held to bear the latter sense" (2 Jarm. 809, *wh. et seq. V.* for cases in illustration. *Vf. Re Coppard*, cited sup., VEST).

As to when "Vested," in a bequest, may be read as "payable" or "indefeasible;" *V*. 1 Jarm. 849, 850, 859 ; Watson, Eq. 1190.

Inhabitants and Ratepayers having a right under a Founder's Deed to a free education for their children, but having no children whose status is injured by a scheme, have not a "Vested Interest" within s. 39, Endowed Schools Act, 1869 (*Re Shaftoe*, 47 L. J. P. C. 98 ; 3 App. Ca. 872).

"Vested Interest," s. 7, City of London Parochial Charities Act, 1883, 46 & 47 V. c. 36 ; *V. Re St. Alphage, London Wall*, 59 L. T. 614 : *Re St. Edmund*, 60 L. T. 622.

Property "vested under this Act," s. 310, P. H. Act, 1875, in Improvement Commrs. or Local Board, includes property acquired under the powers given by the Act (*Hyde* v. *Bank of Eng.*, 51 L. J. Ch. 747 ; 21 Ch. D. 176).

A landlord's right to Ground Game "is vested" by lease, &c., pursuant to the saving clause (s. 5) of the Ground Game Act, 1880 (43 & 44 V. c. 47), even though it be only reserved by an agreement for a lease executed before, but not coming into operation until after, the Act (*Allhusen* v. *Brooking*, 53 L. J. Ch. 520 ; 26 Ch. D. 559).

V. VEST.

VESTRY.—"In Vestry assembled ;" *V.* PARISHIONER.

VESTURE.—*V.* HERBAGE.

VEXATIOUS.—*V.* FRIVOLOUS.

"Vexatiously ;" *V.* UNREASONABLY.

VI ET ARMIS.—*V.* FORCE.

VICAR.—*V.* CLERGYMAN.

VICARAGE.—*V.* RECTORY.

VICTUALLER.—*V.* PUBLICAN.

VICTUALLING-HOUSE.—A Victualling-house is a house where persons are provided with victuals, but without lodging (1 Burn's Jus. Peace, 30th Ed. 64). It would be, probably, safe to add that a place could scarcely be called a "Victualling-house" unless licensed under the 9 G. 4, c. 61. That technical sense would seem to be impressed on the word by its use in the statute just mentioned in collocation with Inns and Ale-houses. Blackstone (3 Com. 164) speaks of an "Innkeeper or other Victualler ;" but a Victualling-house is differentiated from an Inn, because a Victualling-house does not provide lodging ; but it would seem the exact equivalent of "Ale-house."

V. INN : ALE-HOUSE.

VICTUALS.—"Victuals" comprises everything that is food for man, and everything which, when mixed with something else, constitutes such food (*R.* v. *Hodgkinson*, 10 B. & C. 74).

VIDELICET.—*V.* NAMELY.

VIEW.—*V.* Termes de la Ley, *View.*

"Upon such View," whereby Justices may order Diversion, &c., of a Highway, s. 85, 5 & 6 W. 4, c. 50, means that the Justices making the Order are themselves to have actual and joint inspection of the Highway (*R.* v. *Downshire*, 5 L. J. M. C. 72 ; 4 A. & E. 698 ; 6 N. & M. 92 : *R.* v. *Jones*, 10 L. J. M. C. 5 ; 12 A. & E. 686 : *R.* v. *Cambridgeshire Jus.*, 5 L. J. M. C. 6 ; 4 A. & E. 111 ; 5 N. & M. 440 : *R.* v. *Wallace*, 4 Q. B. D. 641 ; 40 L. T. 518). A compliance with these conditions would be sufficiently stated, by the Order reciting that "having Upon View found" (*R.* v. *Cambridgeshire*, sup.) ; *secus*, if it said "having particularly viewed,"

&c., "and being satisfied," &c. (*R.* v. *Downshire*, sup.), or "having viewed," &c., "and it appearing unto us," &c. (*R.* v. *Jones*, sup.).

V. TREAT AND VIEW.

VILL.—As to distinction between "Vill" and "Parish," as a description of a locality; *V.* Elph. 168, n.

V. VILLAGE: Elph. 624–626.

VILLA.—*V.* DENE: TOWN.

VILLAGE.—In Coke's time "Village" and "Town" seem, in law, to have been synonymous (Co. Litt. 115 b; *Va.* Index to Co. Litt. tit. "Village"). So in the *Touchstone* (p. 92),—"This word (Village or Town) is of large extent. And by the grant of it, a manor, land, meadow and pasture, and divers such like things may pass."

"Village" was discussed in *Waterpark* v. *Fennell*, 7 H. L. Ca. 650. *Va. Anon.*, 12 Mod. pl. 912: *R.* v. *Showler*, 3 Burr. 1391: *R.* v. *Horton*, 1 T. R. 374.

VILLANI.—"*Villani* in Domesday (often named) are not taken there for bondmen, but had their name *de villis*, because they had fermes, and there did worke of husbandry for the lord; and they were ever named before *bordarii, &c.*, and such as are bondmen are called there *servi*" (Co. Litt. 5 b; *Va.* Ib. 116 a). *V.* BORDARII.

To call a man a "Villain" is not actionable, *per se* (per Pollock, C. B., *Barnett* v. *Allen*, 27 L. J. Ex. 412; 3 H. & N. 376; 31 L. T. O. S. 217).

VILLEIN: VILLENAGE.—*V.* Co. Litt. 116 a, *et seq.*: Termes de la Ley, *Villeinage.*

VINTNER.—"Vintner" means one who sells wine, and a covenant prohibiting the trade of a "Vintner" includes a person selling Wine not to be drunk on the premises (*Wells* v. *Attenborough*, 24 L. T. 312; 19 W. R. 465); and, by statute, the prohibition, in a Lease, of the business "of a Vintner," will include the sale of Wines to be consumed on the premises under the Wine & Refreshment Houses Acts (23 V. c. 27, s. 44).

VIOLATE.—A Bequest to found an Institution will, generally, be valid if it be added "so as not to violate the Mortmain Acts" (*Biscoe* v. *Jackson*, 35 Ch. D. 460; 56 L. J. Ch. 540; 35 W. R. 554; 56 L. T. 753; 3 Times Rep. 577). *V.* FOUND, p. 304.

VIRGATA TERRÆ.—*V.* YARDLAND.

VISIBLE MEANS.—This phrase, as used in s. 10, Co. Co. Act, 1867,

(30 & 31 V. c. 142), is not (as was laid down by Whiteside, C. J., in *Counsel* v. *Garvie*, Ir. Rep. 5 C. L. 74, 77) to be narrowed so as to be synonymous with "*tangible* means;" but, at the same time, effect is to be given to the word "visible," and therefore "the words refer to means of paying which are visible to the bodily or mental eye of an attentive observer—means of payment which *the person who makes the affidavit* can fairly ascertain" (per Fry, L.J., *Lea* v. *Parker*, 54 L. J. Q. B. 41; 13 Q. B. D. 835; 33 W. R. 101).

Possession of moveable chattels, the full value of which would merely suffice to cover the probable amount of defendant's costs, does not constitute "Visible Means," within s. 6, Com. L. Pro. (Amendment) Act, Ireland, 1870 (*Watson* v. *M'Cann*, 6 L. R. Ir. 21).

VIVARY.—Vivary, vivarium, is a word of large extent, signifying a place in land or water where living things are kept, *e.g.*, parks, warrens, pischaries or fishings (2 Inst. 100), or a stew (Ib. 162). By the grant of a "Vivarye," "not only the priviledge, but the land itselfe passes" (Co. Litt. 5 b).

VIVER.—"Viver or Vivier:—a Fishpond; 2 Inst. 199" (Elph. 628).

VIZ.—*V.* NAMELY.

VOCATION.—Turf "Book-making" is a "Vocation" within the Income Tax Act (a legal one, per Hawkins, J.), and as such its profits are assessable (*Partridge* v. *Mallandaine*, 56 L. J. Q. B. 251; 18 Q. B. D. 276; 56 L. T. 203; 35 W. R. 276). In that case Denman, J., said that even an illegal Vocation would be taxable on its income; as "if a man were to make a systematic business of receiving stolen goods, and to do nothing else, and were thereby to make a profit of (say) £2,000 a year, the Income Tax Commrs would be quite right in assessing him, if it were, in fact, his Vocation."

VOID.—When a Deed or other transaction is "Void" on default of doing or suffering something by one of the parties thereto, this means,—voidable at the election of the party not in default (*Hughes* v. *Palmer*, 34 L. J. C. P. 279; 19 C. B. N. S. 393: *Molton* v. *Camroux*, 18 L. J. Ex. 68, 356; 2 Ex. 487; 4 Ex. 17). "In a long series of decisions the Courts have construed Clauses of Forfeiture in Leases, declaring in terms however clear and strong that they shall be *void* on breach of conditions by the lessees, to mean that they are voidable only at the option of the lessors. The same rule of construction has been applied to other contracts where a party bound by a condition has sought to take advantage of his own breach of it to annul the contract:—*Doe* d. *Bryan* v. *Bancks*, 4 B. & Ald. 401: *Roberts* v. *Davey*, 4 B. & Ad. 664: notes to *Dumpor's Case*, 1 Smith's L. C. 54" (per Sir M. E. Smith delivering jdgmt. of P. C. in *Davenport* v. *The Queen*,

47 L. J. P. C. 16 ; 3 App. Ca. 128). *Vf. Malins* v. *Freeman*, 4 Bing. N. C. 395 : *Re Tickle*, 3 Morr. 126 : Woodf. 197.

And so of Statutes. "In general, it would seem, that where the enactment has relation only to the benefit of particular persons, the word 'void' would be understood as 'voidable' only, at the election of the persons for whose protection the enactment was made and who are capable of protecting themselves ; but that when it relates to persons not capable of protecting themselves, or when it has some object of public policy in view which requires the strict construction, the word receives its natural full force and effect" (Maxwell, 256, 257, citing per Bayley, J., *R.* v. *Hipswell*, 8 B. & C. 471: *Va. Betham* v. *Gregg*, 10 Bing. 352 ; 3 L. J. C. P. 121; 4 Moore & S. 230 : *Storie* v. *Winchester*, 17 C. B. 653. *V.* cases in illustration, Maxwell, 250–257).

"If it be doubtful whether a statute declaring an act, instrument, or contract void, make it voidable only, another clause in the same statute imposing a penalty on such act, instrument, or contract, is a clear test that it is *ipso facto* void" (Dwar. 640). "The penalty makes it illegal" (Maxwell, 256, citing *Gye* v. *Felton*, 4 Taunt. 876).

When an Act says that anything shall be void "*to all intents and purposes*," the phrase italicised seems little more than an expletive. If a thing is "void," it is empty,—without force. Can a cistern be more than empty, or a body be more than still ? The older authorities seem conformed to this reasoning ; and seem to have established that there was no appreciable difference between declaring a thing "void" and declaring it "void to all intents and purposes." Thus it has been stated, "where Acts of Parliament make a thing void, it shall be void to all intents and have a very violent relation" (Dwar. 653). So that "void" would seem to mean as much without, as with, the added phrase "to all intents and purposes ;" whilst the addition of that phrase has not prevented the judicature, as circumstances have justified, from construing the thing as absolutely void in some, and as only voidable in others, of its aspects. Thus by s. 3, 13 Eliz. c. 10, Leases by Spiritual Persons not made in conformity with that statute "shall be utterly void and of none effect, to all intents, constructions and purposes :" yet it has been frequently held that Leases not in such conformity are good during the life of the lessor ; and are only voidable by the successor, and even he may confirm them (Woodf. 20). The words "*utterly* void" in 13 Eliz. c. 20, s. 1, and the words "utterly void to all intents and purposes" in the Ship Registry Act (26 G. 3, c. 60, s. 17), did not prevent the Courts from giving partial effect to instruments not in conformity with those statutes (*Mouys* v. *Leake*, 8 T. R. 411 : *Kerrison* v. *Cole*, 8 East, 234 : Dwar. 639. *Vf.* cases as to Warrants of Attorney and Judge's Orders, Maxwell, 390).

The decisions on the 5 Eliz. c. 4, whilst they show how little the Courts refused to consider the word "void" as intensified by superadded phrases, show also that on the same words, in the same statute, an informal Indenture of Apprenticeship would be held void for some purposes, and only voidable for others. The language of the statute (s. 41) is that all Indentures of Apprenticeship, not in conformity thereto, shall be "clearly void in law, to all intents and purposes whatsoever." Yet to enable an infant apprentice to gain a parochial settlement, it was held that an apprenticeship, not in conformity, was merely voidable between the parties (*R.* v. *St. Nicholas*, 1 Bott. 525; Burr. S. Ca. 91); but when a master citing that, and other such like cases, sought to recover damages for harbouring an apprentice, who had been bound by an Indenture not in conformity to the statute, it was held he could not recover (*Gye* v. *Felton*, 4 Taunt. 876).

So, in an undeviating course, run the older authorities, which seem to justify the statement that the phrase "to all intents and purposes," in connection with the word "void," is little more than an expletive. But in *Phillpotts* v. *Phillpotts* (20 L. J. C. P. 11; 10 C. B. 85) Maule, J., comments on the absence of the phrase in the provision then under consideration; and in *Re Toomer, Ex p. Blaiberg* (52 L. J. Ch. 461; 23 Ch. D. 254) Jessel, M.R., in some measure, leant on its absence in s. 8 of the Bills of Sale Act, 1878, for the purpose of holding that a Bill of Sale which would have been void against an execution creditor, was not so, under the circumstances, as against a trustee in Bankry; whilst in *Davies* v. *Rees* (55 L. J. Q. B. 364; 17 Q. B. D. 408; 54 L. T. 813; 34 W. R. 573) Esher, M.R., seems to have read the phrase into s. 9, Bills of Sale Act, 1882, for the purpose of giving the word "void" its most absolute effect. (Note: s. 8, Bills of S. Act, 1878, only makes an unregistered B. of S. void as against the persons therein mentioned, *Davies* v. *Goodman*, 5 C. P. D. 128; 49 L. J. C. P. 344: *Cookson* v. *Swire*, 54 L. J. Q. B. 249. Under s. 8 of the Act of 1882, it is void even as between grantor and grantee, *Davies* v. *Rees*, sup.: and per Lindley, L. J., *Re Townsend*, 55 L. J. Q. B. 143; 16 Q. B. D. 532; 53 L. T. 897; 34 W. R. 329).

In s. 2, 27 Eliz. c. 4, vacating Fraudulent Conveyances in favour of purchasers, the phrase is that they shall be "utterly void, frustrate and of none effect": *Vth. Gooch's Case*, 5 Rep. 60 b.

A Deed though declared by statute to be void, may be bad in part and good in part;—*e.g.* a personal covenant to pay is good though contained in a Charge on a Benefice which, under 13 Eliz. c. 20, was "utterly void" (*Mouys* v. *Leake*, 8 T. R. 411; approved by Ellenborough, C. J., *Kerrison* v. *Cole*, 8 East, 234). So of a similar covenant in a Bill of Sale transferring a Ship, which, under 26 G. 3, c. 60, s. 17, was "utterly null and void to all intents and purposes" for not truly reciting certificate of registry (*Anon.*, Dwar. 638, 639: *Va.* other cases cited Maxwell, 492, 493). But though *Kerrison* v. *Cole* (sup.) and several of the cases cited in Maxwell (sup.) were cited in *Davies* v. *Rees* (sup.), yet it was there held that a Bill of Sale, void under s. 9, Bills of S. Act, 1882, because not in the prescribed form, was void altogether even as regards its personal covenant to pay (*Va. Re Townsend*, sup.); but a Bill of Sale void under the Act is good as regards property not within the Act (*Re Burdett*, 20 Q. B. D. 310; 57 L. J. Q. B. 263 : *Va. Re Yates*, 38 Ch. D. 112). It seems a little difficult to reconcile *Davies* v. *Rees* with the Anonymous case in Dwarris (sup.) ; or with *Phillpotts* v. *Phillpotts* (sup.), in which a Conveyance "to multiply voices" and therefore "void and of none effect," under 7 & 8 W. 3, c. 25, s. 7, was nevertheless effective to pass the property as between the parties.

VOIDABLE.—"Voidable" is the concluding word of s. 1, Infants' Relief Act, 1874, 37 & 38 V. c. 62; and in a case in which it somewhat came in question Kekewich, J., said that,—"Voidable" means that a thing is valid until repudiated; not that it is invalid until confirmed (*Duncan* v. *Dixon*, 6 Times Rep. 222).

V. VOID.

VOLUNTARILY.—If a person, without duress of person or goods, does a thing,—*e.g.* appear before a foreign tribunal,—he does that thing "voluntarily" (*Voinet* v. *Barrett*, 55 L. J. Q. B. 39), even though he protests against being called on to do it (*Boissiere* v. *Brockner*, 6 Times Rep. 85). In the latter case Cave, J., said he was unable to supply the reasons for the decisions in *Davies* v. *Price* (34 L. J. Q. B. 8) and *Ringwood* v. *Lowndes* (33 L. J. C. P. 337), and declined to extend the application of those decisions. *V.* VOLUNTARY CONTRIBUTIONS.

VOLUNTARY.—*V.* CONSENT.

VOLUNTARY ANNUITY.—*V.* PECUNIARY CONSIDERATION.

VOLUNTARY CONTRIBUTIONS. — "Voluntary Contributions" and "Voluntary Subscriptions" are synonyms (Tudor, Char. Trusts, 526).

A payment made under a voluntary obligation is a "Voluntary Contribution," within 6 & 7 V. c. 36, s. 1 (*Linnæan Socy.* v. *St. Anne, Westminster*, 23 L. J. M. C. 148 ; 3 E. & B. 793 : *R.* v. *Bradford Library*, 28 L. J. M. C. 73 ; 5 Jur. N. S. 513 ; nom. *Bradford Library* v. *Churchwardens of Bradford*, 1 E. & E. 88) : but it should be "a gift made from disinterested motives for the benefit of others" (per Campbell, C. J., *Russell Institution* v. *St. Giles and St. George, Bloomsbury*, 23 L. J. M. C. 65 ; 3 E. & B. 416).

Exemption from Tax, on "Property acquired by or with funds voluntarily contributed," 48 & 49 V. c. 51, s. 11 (6), does not extend, *e.g.*, to the New University Club (*Re New University Club*, 18 Ch. D. 720 ; 56 L. J. Q. B. 462 ; 56 L. T. 909 ; 35 W. R. 774, following *Socy. of Writers to the Signet* v. *Inl. Rev.*, 14 Sess. Ca., 4th Series, 34).

The phrase "Voluntary Contributions," in s. 62, 16 & 17 V. c. 137, "must not be confined to annual subscriptions ; it must clearly extend to donations" of whatever amount (per Romilly, M. R., *Corporation for Relief of Widows and Children of the Clergy* v. *Sutton*, 27 Bea. 651 ; 29 L. J. Ch. 393). *Vh. Re Wilson*, 19 Bea. 594.

Vf. Tudor, Char. Trusts, 525–528.

VOLUNTARY TRANSFER.—As to what was a "Voluntary Transfer or Delivery" of property within s. 32, 7 G. 4, c. 57 ; *V. Wainwright* v. *Clement*, 4 M. & W. 385 ; 8 L. J. Ex. 25. *V.* FRAUDULENT ASSURANCES.

VOLUNTARY WASTE.—In *Garth* v. *Cotton* (3 Atk. 751 ; 1 Ves. sen. 524, 546 ; 1 Dick. 183), it was considered that the phrase "Without impeachment of waste" was rendered nugatory by adding "except Voluntary Waste." However, in *Vincent* v. *Spicer* (25 L. J. Ch. 589 ; 22 Bea. 380), the words were "Without impeachment of *or for any manner of* Waste, except Spoil or Destruction, or Voluntary or Permissive Waste, or suffering buildings to go out of repair," and under those words Romilly, M. R., held that a tenant for life might cut all timber (except ornamental timber), which an owner in fee, who regarded his own interest and the permanent advantage of the estate, would probably cut.

V. WASTE.

VOTE.—*V.* ENTITLED TO VOTE.

VOUCH TO WARRANTY.—*V.* Co. Litt. 101 b, 102 a.

VOYAGE.—Is a transit at sea from one terminus to another (*Glaholm* v. *Hays*, 2 Sc. N. R. 471 ; 2 M. & G. 257 : *Valente* v. *Gibbs*, 28 L. J. C. P. 229 ; 6 C. B. N. S. 270). "The Word 'Voyage,' standing alone, has an extensive meaning ; it means a passing by water from one place or port to another place or port" (per Byles, J., *Barker* v. *McAndrew*, 34 L. J. C. P. 194 ; 18 C. B. N. S. 759).

As to when a Voyage commences and is completed ; *V. Dahl* v. *Nelson*, 12 Ch. D. 568 ; 6 App. Ca. 38 ; 50 L. J. Ch. 411 : *Re Pyman and Dreyfus*, 24 Q. B. D. 152 ; 59 L. J. Q. B. 13 : 1 Maude & P. 469 *et seq.*

Vh. NEAR THERETO AS SHE MAY SAFELY GET.

"The Outward and Homeward Voyages ;" *V.* Maude & P. 373.

WAGE.—"'Wage,' is the giving security for the performing of any thing; as to wage Law, and to wage Deliverance" (Termes de la Ley, *Wage*).

WAGER.—What is a Wager? *V.* this question discussed 40 J. P. 227.

WAGERING, CONTRACT.—*V.* GAMING OR WAGERING.

WAGES.—"Though this word might be said to include payment for any services,—yet, in general, the word 'Salary' is used for payment of services of a higher class, and 'Wages' is confined to the earnings of labourers and artizans" (per Grove, J., *Gordon* v. *Jennings*, 51 L. J. Q. B. 417. *Vh.* jdgmt. of Parke, B., *Riley* v. *Warden*, 18 L. J. Ex. 120; 2 Ex. 59; and that of Bramwell, B., *Sleeman* v. *Barrett*, 33 L. J. Ex. 153; 2 H. & C. 934, and in *Ingram* v. *Barnes*, 26 L. J. Q. B. 322; 7 E. & B. 132). In the case lastly cited, Bramwell, B., said—"Whatever definition one gives to the term 'Wages,' a portion of what the Plaintiff here gets is 'profits,' made and makeable by the employment of other people under him. If a portion is that,—the whole is not Wages." It would therefore seem that "Wages," are the *personal* earnings of labourers and artizans.

V. SALARY.

Claim for "Wages," s. 3 (2), Co. Co. Admiralty Jur. Act, 1868; *V. The Blessing*, 3 P. D. 35.

Forfeiture of all "Wages *due*;" *V. Walsh* v. *Walley*, 43 L. J. Q. B. 102; L. R. 9 Q. B. 367.

The month's wages payable on dismissing a Domestic Servant without notice, are the money wages; board wages are not included (*Gordon* v. *Potter*, 1 F. & F. 644).

WAGGON.—*V.* CART: STAGE WAGGON.

WAGGON ROAD.—*V.* CART ROAD.

WAIT FOR CONVOY.—*V.* CONVOY.

WAITING YOUR REPLY.—*Semble*, these words at the end of a letter containing a distinct contractual offer, do not make the offer a mere proposal which the writer is at liberty to retract on receiving a reply; therefore, if the receiver of the letter accepts the offer (though only verbally) the writer of it will be bound (*Watts* v. *Ainsworth*, 31 L. J. Ex. 448; 1 H. & C. 83).

WALL.—*V.* PARTY WALL.

WANT.—"Does not want;" *V.* LEFT.

"For want of" objects of preceding limitation; *V.* DIE WITHOUT ISSUE.

WANTING A PILOT.—The words "Wanting a Pilot," 6 G. 4, c. 125, s. 72, are not to be confined to such vessels as are, by the Act, bound to take a pilot, but apply to any vessel, the master or owner of which thinks fit to require one (*Lucey* v. *Ingram*, 6 M. & W. 302; 9 L. J. Ex. 196).

WARECTUM.—"*Warectum* or *wareccum*, or *varectum*, doth signifie fallow" (Co. Litt. 5 b).

WAREHOUSE.—"Warehouse" or "other Building," s. 27, Reform Act, 1832; *V. Watson* v. *Cotton*, 17 L. J. C. P. 68; 5 C. B. 51.

In *R.* v. *Edmundson* (28 L. J. M. C. 213; 2 E. & E. 77) a Warehouse was construed as *ejusdem generis* with "dwelling-house, outhouse, yard, garden, *or other place.*"

WAREHOUSEMAN.—"This is a term well understood in London, and means a person who buys and sells linens, muslins, silks, and woollen goods by wholesale; and does not, it should seem, include in it every person who owns or keeps a Warehouse" (Arch. Bank. 11 Ed. 37: This comment is on "Warehousemen" as contained in the late Bankry definition of "Trader").

WARES.—*V.* GOODS, WARES, AND MERCHANDIZES.

WARRANT.—A Pawnbroker's Ticket is a "Warrant for the delivery of goods" within s. 23, 24 & 25 V. c. 98 (*R.* v. *Morrison*, 28 L. J. M. C. 210; Bell, C. C. 158). *Vf.* Arch. Cr. 407.

"Warrant, Order, Authority or Request;" *V.* AUTHORITY OR REQUEST.

V. JUDICIAL DOCUMENT.

WARRANTED FREE FROM AVERAGE.—"Warranted free," means that the insurers are not to be liable for the things to which the warranty applies. (*Cory* v. *Burr*, 8 App. Ca. 393; 52 L. J. Q. B. 657). *V.* WARRANTY, p. 872.

WARRANTED SOUND.—Horse sold "warranted sound, for one month," means that the warranty is to continue in force for one month only, and that complaint of unsoundness must therefore be made within one month of the sale (*Chapman* v. *Gwyther*, 35 L. J. Q. B. 142; L. R. 1 Q. B. 463; 7 B. & S. 417: *Vf. Bywater* v. *Richardson*, 3 L. J. K. B. 164; 1 A. & E. 508; 3 N. & M. 748).

V. SOUND.

WARRANTY.—"A Warranty is an express, or implied, statement of something which the party undertakes shall be part of a contract, and though part of the contract yet collateral to the express object of it. But in many of the cases, the circumstance of a party selling a particular thing by its proper description has been called a *Warranty* and the breach of such contract a breach of warranty; but it would be better to distinguish such cases as a *Non-compliance* with a contract which a party has engaged to fulfil; as if a man offers to buy *peas* of another and he sends him *beans*, he does not perform his contract; but that is not a Warranty; there is no *warranty* that he should sell him peas; the *contract* is to sell peas and if he sends him anything else in their stead it is non-performance of it" (per Abinger, C. B., *Chanter* v. *Hopkins*, 4 M. & W. 404; 8 L. J. Ex. 16; quoted by Martin, B., *Azemar* v. *Casella*, 36 L. J. C. P. 264).

In Charter-Parties and Marine Insurances, "Warranty" is, and for many years has been, synonymous with "Condition" (per Williams, J., *Behn* v. *Burness*, 32 L. J. Q. B. 205; 3 B. & S. 755).

V. Written Warranty.

In regard to real property "a warrantie is a covenant reall annexed to lands or tenements, whereby a man and his heires are bound to warrant the same" (Co. Litt. 365 a.: *Vf.* Elph. 411).

WARREN.—"'Warren' is a place priviledged by prescription or grant of the King for the preservation of Hares, Conies, Partridges and Phesants, or any of them" (Termes de la Ley).

A Warren, or Free Warren, is a franchise to have and keep game within a manor, or other known place (Wms. on Commons, 238, *wh. V.* for Crown Grant of a Free Warren. *Vf.* Elph. 629).

Although Coke says (Co. Litt. 5 b) that by a grant of a Warren not only the privilege but the land itself passes, yet it has been recently held by the H. L. that the grant of a "Warren"—*e.g.* "Warren of Conies,"—does not, *primâ facie*, pass the soil, though it may do so by a context (*Beauchamp* v. *Winn*, L. R. 6 H. L. 223). *Robinson* v. *Dhuleep Singh* (11 Ch. D. 798; 48 L. J. Ch. 758) is an instance in which, contextually, the word was held (by Fry, J.) to pass the soil.

WASTE.—Waste is an act, or omission, by the tenant in possession, occasioning the destruction of, or injury to, "houses, gardens, woods, trees, or in lands, meadowes, &c., or in exile of men, to the disherison of him in the reversion or remainder. There be two kindes of Waste, viz., Voluntarie or Actuall, and Permissive" (Co. Litt. 53 a. *Va.* Termes de la Ley, *Wast*; 2 Bla. Com. ch. 18, s. 6; Add. T. 381; Woodf. 605).

Voluntary Waste is again divisible into (1) Meliorating Waste,—*i.e.* that which betters, and which, *semble*, is not punishable or restrainable unless substantial damage is proved (*Doherty* v. *Allman*, 3 App. Ca. 709; 26 W. R. 513: *Jones* v. *Chappell*, L. R. 20 Eq. 539; 44 L. J. Ch. 658); and (2) Equitable Waste.

Equitable Waste is the creation of Equity, and arises in cases of destructive or wanton Waste which, at Law, would have been excused by the words "Without impeachment of Waste:"—"'*Without impeachment of waste* (sauns impeachment de wast),' *Absque impetitione vasti* (that is) without any challenge or impeachment of wast, and by force hereof the lessee may cut downe the trees and convert them to his owne use" (Co. Litt. 220 a). But now, the words "Without impeachment of waste" will not confer even "any *legal* right to commit Equitable Waste" (s. 25 (3), Jud. Act, 1873). So that now, both at law and equity, "the term 'Without impeachment of Waste,' contained in a Deed or Will creating a life estate in land, does not enable the life tenant to deal with the property as if he were the absolute owner thereof in fee simple. He may cut down timber and growing trees fit for timber (*Smythe* v. *Smythe*, 2 Swanst. 251: *Gordon* v. *Woodford*, 29 L. J. Ch. 222), and convert them to his own use (*Pyne* v. *Dor*, 1 T. R. 56), and open new mines and work them for his benefit, but he cannot dig and carry off brick-earth, and destroy a field to the prejudice of the inheritance (*London* v. *Web*, 1 P. Wms. 528); and he will be restrained from committing wanton and malicious waste, such as damaging and destroying buildings, pulling down ancient boundary walls and fences (*Aston* v. *Aston*, 1 Ves. sen. 265: *Vane* v. *Barnard*, 2 Vern. 739; 1 T. R. 55: Co. Litt. 220 a: *Leeds* v. *Amherst*, 14 Sim. 357; 15 L. J. Ch. 351; 16 Ib. 5), and cutting down thriving wood unfit for timber, and the felling of which would be destructive to the property (*Chamberlayne* v. *Dummer*, 1 Bro. C. C. 166; 3 Ib. 549); also from cutting down trees which were either planted, or left standing, for the shelter or ornament of a mansion-house (*Micklethwaite* v. *Micklethwaite*, 26 L. J. Ch. 721: *Wellesley* v. *Wellesley*, 6 Sim. 497: *Burges* v. *Lamb*, 16 Ves. 174: *V. Bubb* v. *Yelverton*, L. R. 10 Eq. 465; 40 L. J. Ch. 38). But he is not responsible, although he allows a mansion-house and buildings to go to wreck and ruin for want of timely repairs to the roof and windows (*Powys* v. *Blagrave*, 4 D. G. M. & G. 448; 24 L. J. Ch. 142; Kay, 495: *Lansdowne* v. *Lansdowne*, 1 Jac. & W. 522, over-ruling *Parteriche* v. *Powlett*, 2 Atk. 383); nor if he pulls down a ruinous structure, and uses up the materials in rebuilding it (*Morris* v. *Morris*, 3 D. G. & J. 323; 28 L. J. Ch. 329)" Add. T. 385.

"The words 'Without impeachment of Waste,' *as applied to Trustees of a term for special purposes*, have, however, a very different sense from the same words annexed to a tenancy for life. The Court will not permit Trustees so holding, to execute their trust by cutting down timber (*Downshire* v. *Sandys*, 6 Ves. 115)." Add. T. 385, 386: *Va. Campbell* v. *Allgood*, 17 Bea. 623, there cited. *V.* WITHOUT IMPEACHMENT OF WASTE.

Vf. as to Waste, Co. Litt. 52 b.—54 b. and Tit. "Waste" in Index; Watson, Eq. 1247–1255; Woodf. 605–613; Rosc. N. P. 313–317; Yool on Waste: *Dunn* v. *Bryan*, 7 Ir. R. Eq. 143: *Brooke* v. *Mernagh*, 23 L. R. Ir. 86: *Brooke* v. *Kavanagh*, Ib. 97: and as to when Life Estates limited in pursuance of an Executory Trust are, or are not, to be made impeachable for Waste, Elph. 546.

As to action for Permissive Waste; *V. Re Cartwright, Avis* v. *Newman*, 58 L. J. Ch. 590; 41 Ch. D. 532; 37 W. R. 612. *V.* KEEPING SAME IN REPAIR.

V. VOLUNTARY WASTE.

"Waste" of a Manor; *V.* WASTE GROUND.

WASTE GROUND.—Grant by the Crown, as Lord of the Manor of Englefield, of "all those Coal Mines found, or to be found, within the Commons, *Waste Grounds* or Marshes within the said lordship of E.," with a proviso that the grant should be construed strictly as against the Crown, and most strictly and beneficially for the grantees; held, to pass Coal lying under the fore-shore of the estuary of the Dee, between high and low water marks, and forming part of the Manor (*A.-G.* v. *Hanmer*, 27 L. J. Ch. 837).

WASTE SILK.—*V. Gardiner* v. *Gray*, 4 Camp. 144.

WATCH OR BESET.—*V.* BESET.

WATER AND SOIL.—Reservation in a Lease of "the free running of Water and Soil coming from any other buildings and lands *contiguous* to the premises hereby demised, in and through the sewers and water-courses made, or to be made, within through or under the said premises," extends to Water and Soil coming from contiguous premises, whether arising, in the first instance, on or from such premises, or not; but it does not extend beyond Water, in its natural condition, and such matters as are the product of the ordinary use of land for habitation, and therefore does not give a right of passage for the refuse of tan-pits (*Chadwick* v. *Marsden*, 36 L. J. Ex. 177; L. R. 2 Ex. 285).

WATER CLOSET.—*V.* SUFFICIENT PRIVY.

WATERCOURSE.—"Without saying that a 'Watercourse' may never mean the channel in which water flows, it certainly may mean the stream or flow of the water itself, and whether it means the one or the other in any Instrument, will very materially depend on the context" (per Coleridge, J., in delivering the jdgmt. of the Court in *Doe* d. *Egremont* v. *Williams*, 17 L. J. Q. B. 158; 11 Q. B. 688. *Va.*, as to construction of "Watercourse," *Taylor* v. *St. Helen's*, 46 L. J. Ch. 857; 6 Ch. D. 264: and as to acquisition of Right of Watercourse, *V. Wood* v. *Waud*, 3 Ex. 78; 18 L. J. Ex. 305: *Ramershur Pershad Narain Singh* v. *Koonj Behari Pattuk*, 4 App. Ca. 121).

"A Watercourse means water flowing between banks more or less defined. To constitute a Watercourse in which rights may exist or may be acquired by user or otherwise, the flow of water must possess that unity of character by which the flow on one person's land can be identified with that on his neighbour's land. Water which squanders itself over an indefinite surface is not a Watercourse, nor a proper subject-matter for the acquisition of a right by user (*Briscoe* v. *Drought,* 11 Ir. Com. L. R. 250 : *Rawstron* v. *Taylor,* 11 Ex. 369 ; 25 L. J. Ex. 33 : *Broadbent* v. *Ramsbottom,* 11 Ex. 602, 615 ; 25 L. J. Ex. 115). But the moment the water of a spring runs into a definite channel it constitutes a Watercourse (*Dudden* v. *Clutton Union,* 1 H. & N. 627 ; 26 L. J. Ex. 146). All accessions to such stream, from whatever source, form part of it (*Wood* v. *Waud,* 3 Ex. 748 ; 18 L. J. Ex. 305). Where the question at the trial is whether there is a Watercourse or not, the judge ought, before he leaves that question to the jury, to instruct them as to what constitutes a 'Watercourse' in law (*Briscoe* v. *Drought,* sup. : *Va. Elliott* v. *South Devon Ry.,* 2 Ex. 725 ; 17 L. J. Ex. 262 : *R.* v. *Cottle,* 16 Q. B. 412 ; 20 L. J. M. C. 162 : *Cashill* v. *Wright,* 6 E. & B. 891)." Woodf. 707. *Vh.* Angell on Watercourses.

"*Drains, Trenches, or Watercourses,*" s. 97, 14 G. 3, c. 96, applies only to artificial streams made for improving the navigation of the rivers Aire and Calder, mentioned in the Act, and not to natural streams (*Smith* v. *Barnham,* 1 Ex. D. 419).

V. DRAIN : WATERS.

WATERS.—"If a man grant *aquam suam,* the soile shall not passe, but the pischarie within the water passeth therewith" (Co. Litt. 4 b).

As to the effect of general words in a Conveyance granting "Waters, Watercourses;" *V. Wardle* v. *Brocklehurst,* 29 L. J. Q. B. 145 : *Sanderson* v. *Berwick-upon-Tweed,* 53 L. J. Q. B. 559 ; 13 Q. B. D. 547.

"Waters," in Sch. to 52 G. 3, c. 150, as affected by the repeal in s. 20, 3 & 4 W. 4, c. 97 ; *V. A.-G.* v. *Lamplough,* 47 L. J. Ex. 555 ; 3 Ex. D. 214.

"All other Waters wherein Salmons be taken," 2 Westm. c. 47 ; the Thames is not included herein (2 Inst. 478).

WAY.—"There be three kinde of wayes, whereof you shall read in our ancient bookes. First a foot way which is called *iter, quod est jus eundi vel ambulandi hominis* ; and this was the first way.

"The second is a foot way and horse way, which is called *actus ab agendo* ; and this vulgarly is called packe and prime way, because it is both a foot way, which was the first or prime way, and a packe or drift way also.

"The third is *via* or *aditus,* which containe the other two, and also a cart way, &c., for this is *jus eundi, vehendi, et vehiculum et jumentum ducendi* : and this is twofold, viz., *regia via,* the king's highway for all men, *et communis strata,* belonging to a citie or towne or betweene neighbours and neighbours. This is called in our bookes *chimin,* being a French word for a way, whereof cometh *chiminage, chiminagium,* or *chimmagium,* which signifieth a toll due by custome for having a way thorow a Forest: and in ancient records it is some time also called *pedagium*" (Co. Litt. 56 a).

Besides the Ways enumerated by Ld. Coke there may be a drift way or way for driving cattle, which is not necessarily included in a carriage or horse way (*Ballard* v. *Dyson*, 1 Taunt. 279: *Vth.* per Pearson, J., *Serff* v. *Acton*, 31 Ch. D. 683).

Any right of way may exist for certain purposes only (*Cowling* v. *Higginson*, 7 L. J. Ex. 265; 4 M. & W. 245: *Brunton* v. *Hall*, 10 L. J. Q. B. 258; 1 Q. B. 792: *Wimbledon and Putney Com. Cons.* v. *Dixon*, 45 L. J. Ch. 353; 1 Ch. D. 362: *Bradburn* v. *Morris*, 3 Ch. D. 812).

"A right of way may be created by a covenant by the owner of the servient tenement that the owner of the dominant tenement shall enjoy it" (Elph. 630, citing *Holmes* v. *Seller*, 3 Lev. 305).

When in a deed relating to *Mines* there is a grant of "a *Free and Convenient* Way" (*Senhouse* v. *Christian*, 1 T. R. 560), or of a "*Sufficient* Wayleave" (*Dand* v. *Kingscote*, 9 L. J. Ex. 279; 6 M. & W. 174), or, probably, of a "*Necessary* Wayleave," or the like (S. C.), or to "*Convey Coals*" (*Bishop* v. *North*, 12 L. J. Ex. 362; 11 M. & W. 418), the grantee, *primâ facie*, may for his better accommodation make Waggon-Roads or Tram-Roads on the site over which such a right of way extends. He may even make a Rail-Road if, in the deed, there be a clause requiring him to compensate for damage, and if such a road would not be a nuisance or a source of danger (*Bishop* v. *North*, sup.). *Vf.* MacS. 357–361.

Under the words "Sufficient Way-leave," a party is not confined to such description of way as was in use at the time of the grant (*Dand* v. *Kingscote*, sup.).

The planks placed for walking over a hole in ground where machinery was being erected; held a "Way" within s. 1, subs. 1, *Employers' Liability Act*, 1880, 43 & 44 V. c. 42 (*Bromley* v. *Cavendish Spinning Co.*, 2 Times Rep. 881).

V. WAYS: GATEWAY.

WAYLEAVE.—*V.* WAY.

WAYS.—A grant, by the owner of two closes of land, of one of them, "together with all Ways now used therewith," will pass to the grantee a right of way over a clearly defined path, constructed over the other close, and then actually used as a mode of access to the close granted, even though the path did not exist prior to the unity of possession (*Barkshire* v. *Grubb*, 18 Ch. D. 616: *Vf. Thomson* v. *Waterlow*, L. R. 6 Eq. 36; 37 L. J. Ch. 495: *Langley* v. *Hammond*, L. R. 3 Ex. 161; 37 L. J. Ex. 118: *Kay* v. *Oxley*, L. R. 10 Q. B. 360: *Bayley* v. *G. W. Ry.*, 26 Ch. D. 434: *Brown* v. *Alabaster*, 37 Ch. D. 490).

Ways "now or *heretofore* held or enjoyed"; *V. Roe* v. *Siddons*, 22 Q. B. D. 224.

As to what is included in "Ways" in a Mining Lease ; *V. Beaufort* v. *Bates*, 31 L. J. Ch. 481 ; 3 D. G. F. & J. 381 ; 10 W. R. 200 ; 6 L. T. 82.

WEAR AND TEAR.—"These words ('reasonable Wear and Tear') no doubt, include destruction to some extent,—destruction of surfaces by ordinary friction,—but we do not think they include total destruction by a catastrophe which was never contemplated by either party ;"—even though such catastrophe may have resulted from the reasonable use of the premises demised (per Lindley, J., in delivering the jdgmt. of the Court in *Manchester Bonding Warehouse Co.* v. *Carr*, 49 L. J. C. P. 809 ; 5 C. P. D. 507).

"If those words,—'fair Wear and Tear and Damage by Tempest excepted,'—were not there, any dilapidations found at any time, or at the end of the term, by reason of the wear and tear,—*e.g.*, the wearing out of the walls and floors of a public-house from the constant traffic and so forth,—the lessee would be liable to replace, and if, unfortunately, by a storm his chimney-pot was blown down, or he had his roof broken, he would be bound to put it straight, and restore the place to good and substantial repair" (per Kekewich, J., *Davies* v. *Davies*, 57 L. J. Ch. 1095 ; 38 Ch. D. 499 ; 58 L. T. 514 ; 36 W. R. 399). *V.* Without Impeachment of Waste.

The case of *Bigge* v. *Bigge* (9 Jur. 192) illustrates the distinction between "Wear" and "Tear." In that case a testator had, by handling, *worn* his Will in two,—a very different thing from his having *torn* it in two,—so there was no revocation by "tearing" within s. 20, 1 V. c. 26.

V. Tear.

WEATHER PERMITTING.—*V.* Permitting.

WEEK.—Though "a Week" usually means any consecutive 7 days, it will sometimes be interpreted to mean the ordinary notion of a week reckoning from Sunday to Sunday (*Bazalgette* v. *Lowe*, 24 L. J. Ch. 368, 416).

And, probably, a "week" usually means 7 *clear* days :—thus where a statute provided that Notice of Appeal should be given "within one Week" *before* such appeal was to be heard, and Notice was given on the 22nd for the 29th, it was held that the Notice was insufficient (*R.* v. *Sweeney*, 2 Ir. L. R. 278).

A theatrical engagement to employ at so much "*per week*," may be shewn, by usage, to mean, "per week during every week that the theatre is open" (*Grant* v. *Maddox*, 16 L. J. Ex. 227).

WEEKLY ACCOUNT.—As used in a building contract ; *V. Myers* v. *Sarl*, 3 E. & E. 306 ; 30 L. J. Q. B. 9.

WEIGHT.—*V.* By Weight.

WEIGHT AND MEASUREMENT.—A Cargo of so many tons "of Weight and Measurement;" *V. Pust* v. *Dowie*, 34 L. J. Q. B. 127; 5 B. & S. 33.

WEIGHT UNKNOWN.—*V.* CONTENTS UNKNOWN.

"Not responsible for Weight;" *V. Bradley* v. *Dunipace*, 31 L. J. Ex. 210; 32 Ib. 22; 7 H. & N. 200; 1 H. & C. 521.

WEIR.—*V.* GURGES.

WELL ASSURED.—*V.* PRECATORY TRUST.

WELL KNOW.—*V.* PRECATORY TRUST.

WELL SUPPLIED.—When property is sold under a representation that it is "well supplied with water," that means that the property is "supplied with water by a spring rising in it, or by a running stream passing through or into it, and so supplied as a matter of right, belonging or incident to the property, without rent or payment of any kind for the water or its use" (per Knight-Bruce, L. J., *Leyland* v. *Illingworth*, 29 L. J. Ch. 614).

WERE.—"*Were* is an old Saxon word, sometimes written *wera*, and signifieth the price of the life of a man, *estimatio capitis*, that is, so much as one paid for the killing of a man" (Co. Litt. 287 b; *Va.* Ib. 127 a).

WESTERN BARGE.—A Thames "Western Barge;" *V. Tibble* v. *Beadon*, 24 L. J. M. C. 104: *Doick* v. *Phelps*, 30 L. J. M. C. 2; 3 E. & E. 244.

WET.—"Wet" Oil; *V. Warde* v. *Stuart*, 1 C. B. N. S. 88.

WHARF.—"'Wharfe' is a word used in the statute of 1 Eliz. c. 11, and other statutes, and it is a broad place neare to a creek or hithe of water, upon which goods and wares are laid, which are to bee shipt and transported from place to place" (Termes de la Ley).

WHAT IS LEFT.—Bequest of "What is left, my books and furniture and all other things, I wish to be equally divided amongst the three children," carries the Residue (*Re Cadge*, 37 L. J. P. & M. 15; L. R. 1 P. & M. 543).

V. LEFT.

WHATEVER REMAINS.—*V.* REMAIN.

WHATSOEVER.—"Whatsoever," as a rule, excludes any limitation or qualification, and implies that the genus to which it relates is to be understood in its utmost generality (*V.* per Fry, L. J., *Duck* v. *Bates*, 53 L. J. Q. B. 344; 13 Q. B. D. 843; 50 L. T. 778; 32 W. R. 813; 48 J. P. 501).

"I devise all my goods and chattels, moneys, debts, *and whatsoever else I have in the world not before disposed of*" to A.: held to pass an estate in fee (*Hopewell* v. *Ackland*, 1 Salk. 239 ; 1 Com. 164). So, where the words were "Whatever I may die possessed of" (*Davenport* v. *Coltman*, 9 M. & W. 481 ; 11 L. J. Ex. 114 : *Evans* v. *Jones*, 46 L. J. Ex. 280). *Vh.* 1 Jarm. 738, 739.

WHEEL CARRIAGE.—*V. Radnorshire* v. *Evans*, 32 L. J. M. C. 100 ; 3 B. & S. 400.

WHEN.—"When," usually creates a condition precedent (*Jolly* v. *Hancock*, 22 L. J. Ex. 38 ; 7 Ex. 820).

Where there is a testamentary gift to A., "If," or "When," or "Provided," or "In Case," or "So soon as" (phrases which are synonymous, *Shrimpton* v. *Shrimpton*, 31 Bea. 425), a certain event happens,—*e.g.*, attaining a stated age,—such a gift, standing unaffected by the context, confers only a contingent interest, and requires the happening of the event to give it validity. But with the aid of a context such words may, without difficulty, not defer the vesting of the subject-matter of the gift, but merely refer to the futurity of its possession (1 Jarm. 805, 809, 816, 842, 854, 860 : *Boraston's Case*, 3 Rep. 19 a : *Phipps* v. *Ackers*, 3 Cl. & F. 703 ; nom. *Phipps* v. *Williams*, 5 Sim. 44 : *Scotney* v. *Lomer*, 54 L. J. Ch. 558 ; 55 Ib. 443 ; 29 Ch. D. 535 ; 31 Ib. 380 : *Re Wrey, Stuart* v. *Wrey*, 54 L. J. Ch. 1098 ; 30 Ch. D. 507). It has also been said that "'When' cannot be considered as so strongly indicating contingency as 'Provided' and 'If'" (Watson, Eq. 1217, and cases there cited).

Where the gift is to a class "*who*," or "*as*," shall attain a certain age, the rule (nearly universally applied) is to regard the attainment of the age as part of the description of the beneficiary, and to construe the gift as contingent, "upon the ground that no one could claim who could not predicate of himself that he was of the age required" (per Wigram, V.-C., *Bull* v. *Pritchard*, 16 L. J. Ch. 185 ; 5 Hare, 567 : *Festing* v. *Allen*, 13 L. J. Ex. 74 ; 12 M. & W. 279 ; 5 Hare, 573 : *Vf.* 1 Jarm. 817, 818, 854, 860). But even this construction may yield to a context (*Muskett* v. *Eaton*, 45 L. J. Ch. 22 ; 1 Ch. D. 435 : 1 Jarm. 819, 860, 855–860).

WHEREUPON.—*V.* Thereupon.

WHERRY.—"A 'Wherry' and a 'Lighter' are, in common parlance, boats plying for hire and carrying passengers or goods" (per Erle, J., *Reed* v. *Ingham*, 23 L. J. M. C. 156 ; 3 E. & B. 889).

V. Craft.

WHICH.—*V.* construction of this relative in *Miles* v. *Harrison*, 43 L. J. Ch. 585 ; 9 Ch. 316.

Read "as," in *Whateley* v. *Spooner* (3 K. & J. 542).

WHISKEY.—"Whiskey," sold simply as such, must not be reduced more than 25 degrees under proof (Sale of Food and Drugs Act Amendment Act, 1879, 42 & 43 V. c. 30, s. 6); *Sv.* GIN, and the case there cited.

WHO.—*V.* ATTAIN : HAVE : LIVING : WHEN.

WHOLESALE.—"As a general rule 'Wholesale' merchants deal only with persons who buy to sell again; whilst 'Retail' merchants deal with consumers" (per Bacon, V.-C., *Treacher* v. *Treacher*, W. N. (74) 4).

WHOLESOME.—*V.* PURE.

WHOLLY.—"Wholly Agricultural," "Wholly Pastoral;" *V.* AGRICULTURAL : PASTURE.

"Wholly *disabled*:" A solicitor sprained his ankle, which confined him to his private room, and prevented his going downstairs; some part of his business was stopped, but clerks carried on other parts, and he could write letters, consult law books, and give advice and directions; held, that he was "wholly disabled" "from following his usual business, occupation or pursuits," within an accident policy (*Hooper* v. *Accidental Insrce.*, 29 L. J. Ex. 340, 484; 5 H. & N. 546, 557).

WHOLLY OR IN PART.—*V.* ACCOUNT.

WHOMSOEVER.—A covenant for quiet enjoyment without interruption "by any person or persons whomsoever," extends even to the unlawful acts of all persons therein named or comprised, but not to the unlawful acts of third persons having no title (Woodf. 679, 683, and cases there cited; Touch. 166, 170, 171).

WHOSOEVER WILL GIVE INFORMATION.—A party who had been robbed of bank notes put forth a handbill, wherein it was stated that "Whosoever will give Information" whereby the same might be traced, should, on conviction of the parties, receive a reward. Held, that the only person entitled to the reward was he who first gave information by which the notes were recovered (*Lancaster* v. *Walsh*, 7 L. J. Ex. 209; 4 M. & W. 16 : *Vf. Lockhart* v. *Barnard*, 15 L. J. Ex. 1; 14 M. & W. 674).

WIC.—"A place upon the sea-shore, or upon a river" (Co. Litt. 4 b).

WIDOW.—A woman surviving a man with whom she has gone through the ceremony of marriage, but with regard to whom she had obtained a declaration of nullity of marriage, is not his "Widow" (*Re Boddington*, 52 L. J. Ch. 239; 53 Ib. 475; 22 Ch. D. 597; 25 Ch. D. 685).

V. HUSBAND.

In a gift over on death of testator's "Widow," the use of this word shows that the event was contemplated to happen after testator's death (*Randfield* v. *Randfield*, 2 D. G. & J. 57 ; 4 Drew. 147 : *Cp. Taylor* v. *Stainton*, 2 Jur. N. S. 634, 635).

A charitable gift to the "Widows" of a place is good (*A.-G.* v. *Comber*, 2 Sim. & St. 93 : *Russell* v. *Kellett*, 3 Sm. & G. 264 ; 26 L. T. O. S. 193 ; 2 Jur. N. S. 132 : on *A.-G.* v. *Comber*, *V. Browne* v. *King*, 17 L. R. Ir. 453, 454).

WIDOWED MOTHER.—A widow who has married again, cannot be a "Widowed Mother" within s. 35, Divided Parishes and Poor Law Amendment Act, 1876, 39 & 40 V. c. 61 (*Amersham* v. *London*, 20 Q. B. D. 103 ; 36 W. R. 141 ; 57 L. J. M. C. 6 ; 58 L. T. 83 : *Sv. Highworth* v. *Westbury-on-Severn*, 53 J. P. 580 ; 5 Times Rep. 716). *V.* CHILD, p. 127.

WIDTH.—*V. Stringer* v. *Sykes*, 46 L. J. M. C. 141 ; 2 Ex. D. 240.

WIFE.—"Wife," in s. 35, 39 & 40 V. c. 61, includes a Widow (*Reigate* v. *Croydon* and *Medway* v. *Bedminster*, 53 J. P. 580 ; 5 Times Rep. 716). *V.* CHILD.

"Any Wife," s. 27, Matrimonial Causes Act, 1857, "must certainly include any wife being a natural-born English subject" (per Cresswell, J.O., delivering jdgmt. of the Court, *Deck* v. *Deck*, 29 L. J. P. M. & A. 129 ; 2 Sw. & Tr. 90 : *Va. Bond* v. *Bond*, 29 L. J. P. M. & A. 143 ; 2 Sw. & Tr. 93).

A deserting and adulterous wife, is not a "Wife" within s. 4, 5 G. 4, c. 83, even though the husband has committed adultery since she left him (*R.* v. *Flintan*, 1 B. & Ad. 227). But connivance at a wife's adultery, will preclude a husband from escaping liability for her Necessaries (*Wilson* v. *Glossop*, 20 Q. B. D. 354 ; 57 L. J. Q. B. 161 ; 58 L. T. 707 ; 36 W. R. 296 ; 52 J. P. 246).

A divorced wife, is not a "Wife" within a general bequest or limitation (per Kay, J., *Re Morrieson*, *Hitchins* v. *Morrieson*, 58 L. J. Ch. 80 ; 40 Ch. D. 30 ; 59 L. T. 847, in which the learned judge refused to follow *Re Bullmore*, cited HUSBAND). So a woman who has bigamously become a supposed wife, is not comprised in such a bequest or limitation (*Wilkinson* v. *Joughin*, 35 L. J. Ch. 684 ; L. R. 2 Eq. 319) ; *secus*, in the absence of proof of fraud on her part (*Re Petts*, 29 L. J. Ch. 168 ; 27 Bea. 576).

As to construing *Testamentary Gifts* to a Wife, "the distinctions deducible from general principles, and the authorities, appear to be the following :—

1. That a devise or bequest to the wife of A., who has a wife at the date of the Will, relates to that person, notwithstanding any change of

circumstances which may render the description inapplicable at a subsequent period, and is under *all* circumstances confined to her;

2. If A. have no wife at the date of the Will, the gift embraces the individual sustaining that character at the death of the testator; and

3. If there be no such person, either at the date of the Will or at the death of the testator, it applies to the woman who shall first answer the description of wife at any subsequent period" (1 Jarm. 324). *V.* Beloved Wife: Their: Chitty, Eq. Ind. 7707.

A wife is not included in a gift to a person's "Family" (*Re Hutchinson and Tenant*, 8 Ch. D. 540), or "Relations," or "Next of Kin" (*Nicholls* v. *Savage*, cited 18 Ves. 53).

A bequest to wife "for her own and the children's benefit," she not to diminish principal; *V. Hart* v. *Tribe*, 23 L. J. Ch. 462; 18 Bea. 215.

V. Children of the Wife: Widow.

WIKE.—In Essex, a farm (Co. Litt. 5 a).

WILDFOWL.—By "Wildfowl," "Pheasants and Partridges are not understood, for they are Fowl of Warren (Manwood, cap. 4, s. 3, 4 Ed. p. 363; F. N. B. 86; Rastal, 585). Wildfowl are known in the law, and described by the statute of 25 H. 8, c. 11, which doth take notice of Wildfowl. The title of the statute is 'against destroying of Wildfowl.' It recites that there hath been within this realm great quantities of Wildfowl, as, Ducks, Mallards, Wigeons, Teals, Wildgeese and divers other kind of Wildfowl, which is reasonable to be understood of that sort that do get their prey in that manner. The stat. of 3 & 4 Ed. 6, c. 7, which repeals that of 25 H. 8, takes notice of Wildfowl, and hath the general word 'Wildfowl,' without coming to particulars. Therefore, when the declaration is of 'Wildfowl,' it is not to be understood that sparrows, wrens or robin-red-breasts can be thereby included" (per Holt, C. J., *Keeble* v. *Hickeringill*, 11 East, 577). *V.* Fowl.

WILFUL.—"Wilful is a word of familiar use in every branch of law, and although in some branches of law it may have a special meaning, it generally, as used in Courts of Law, implies nothing blameable, but merely that the person of whose action or default the expression is used is a free agent, and that what has been done arises from the spontaneous action of his will. It amounts to nothing more than this, that he knows what he is doing, and intends to do what he is doing, and is a free agent" (per Bowen, L. J., *Re Young and Harston*, 31 Ch. D. 174; 53 L. T. 837; 34 W. R. 84; 50 J. P. 245).

V. Wilfully.

WILFUL AND MALICIOUS.—In the power which a judge had to give costs to a plaintiff recovering less than 40*s.* damages, if certificate given "that the trespass or grievance in respect of which the action was brought was *wilful and malicious*" (s. 2, 3 & 4 V. c. 24), the words italicised imported personal malice and ill-will to the plaintiff, as distinguished from that legal malice which is essential to sustain an action for libel (*Foster* v. *Pointer*, 10 L. J. Ex. 454 ; 8 M. & W. 395).

"Whoever shall *wilfully or maliciously* commit any *Damage, Injury or Spoil* to, or upon, any Real or Personal Property whatsoever," s. 52, 24 & 25 V. c. 97 ; To constitute this offence there must be some actual damage to the property itself ; and merely gathering mushrooms growing in a wild state in a field, is not such damage to the field (*Gardner* v. *Mansbridge*, 19 Q. B. D. 217 ; 57 L. T. 265 ; 35 W. R. 809 ; 51 J. P. 612). And where a milk-carrier, having accidentally spilt some of the milk that he was taking on his round, added water to conceal the loss, it was held that there was no offence within this section,—for there was an absence of *mens rea* to do damage to anybody, and least of all to the master who was prosecuting (*Hall* v. *Richardson*, 6 Times Rep. 71). A Claim of Right will not take a case of damage out of this section, if the claim be not a reasonable one, of which the Justices are to judge (*White* v. *Feast*, L. R. 7 Q. B. 353 ; 41 L. J. M. C. 81. *Svth. Denny* v. *Thwaites*, 2 Ex. D. 21). *V*. REAL OR PERSONAL PROPERTY.

V. MALICE.

WILFUL DEFAULT.—"Wilful Act, Default or Neglect of the Innkeeper," &c., s. 1, 26 & 27 V. c. 41 ;—In this phrase "Wilful" is only to be read with "Act," and not also with "Default or Neglect" (per Byles, J., *Squire* v. *Wheeler*, 16 L. T. 93). *Cp. Carpenter* v. *Mason*, cited WILFUL WASTE.

"Wilful Default of the person in charge" of a Ship, s. 299, Merchant Shipping Act, 1854, means "by the fault" of such person, whether intentional or negligent, and especially so in view of s. 29, 25 & 26 V. c. 63 (*Grill* v. *General Screw Collier Co.*, 35 L. J. C. P. 321 ; 37 Ib. 205 ; L. R. 1 C. P. 600 ; 3 Ib. 476 ; and especially jdgmt. of Willes, J.). *Cp*. WILFUL NEGLECT.

"Wilful Default of the Vendor ;" *V*. per Bowen, L. J., *Re Young and Harston*, 31 Ch. D. 174 ; 53 L. T. 837 ; 34 W. R. 84 ; 50 J. P. 245 : *Riley to Streatfield*, 34 Ch. D. 386 : Dart, 723 : Sug. V. & P. 638.

V. DEFAULT.

WILFUL DELAY.—Delaying the delivery of a Declaration, in an action for Bribery, for eleven months ; held, that there was "Wilful Delay" in proceeding with the action, within s. 14, 17 & 18 V. c. 102, although delivered within the time then allowed by law, and although plaintiff alleged that he could not sooner acquire the evidence and information necessary to allege the specific charges in the Declaration (*Taylor* v. *Vergette*, 30 L. J. Ex. 400 ; 7 H. & N. 143).

WILFUL MISCONDUCT.—Wrong conduct, wilful in the sense of being intended, but induced by mere honest forgetfulness or genuine mistake, does not amount to "Wilful Misconduct" (*V.* jdgmt. of Grove, J., *Gordon* v. *G. W. Ry.*, 51 L. J. Q. B. 58 ; 8 Q. B. D. 44). "What is meant by 'Wilful Misconduct' is misconduct to which the will is a party : it is something opposed to accidental or negligent ; the *mis* part of it, not the conduct, must be wilful" (per Bramwell, L. J., *Lewis* v. *G. W. Ry.*, 47 L. J. Q. B. 135 ; 3 Q. B. D. 195). *Vf. Stevens* v. *G. W. Ry.*, 52 L. T. 324; 49 J. P. 310 ; 1 Times Rep. 342 : *Spittle* v. *G. W. Ry.*, 2 Times Rep. 618.

Cp. "Wilful *Misbehaviour*," s. 78, Highway Act, 1835, 5 & 6 W. 4, c. 50: WILFUL DEFAULT : WILFUL NEGLECT.

WILFUL NEGLECT.—To "wilfully neglect to do a thing" is intentionally or purposely to omit to do it (per Mellor, J., *R.* v. *Downes*, inf.) ; and therefore to pray, instead of sending for a doctor, is to "wilfully neglect" to provide medical aid within s. 37, 31 & 32 V. c. 122 (*R.* v. *Downes*, 45 L. J. M. C. 8 ; 1 Q. B. D. 25 ; 39 J. P. 760 : *Vf. R.* v. *Morby*, 51 L. J. M. C. 85 ; 8 Q. B. D. 571).

Cp. NEGLECT : WILFUL DEFAULT : OBSTRUCT.

As to what is "Wilful Neglect or Default of the Vendor," in Conditions of Sale ; *V.* WILFUL DEFAULT.

WILFUL REFUSAL.—A "Wilful Refusal" is a refusal without adequate cause ; and therefore a Trustee has not "wilfully refused" to convey trust lands within s. 2, Trustee Act, 1852 (15 & 16 V. c. 55), when his refusal to do so is based on a bonâ fide doubt as to the right of the requesting person (*Re Mills*, 40 Ch. D. 14).

V. REFUSAL.

WILFUL WASTE.—A tenant for life, sans waste "further than Wilful Waste," is entitled to the interest of money produced by sale of decaying timber cut by order of the Court (*Wickham* v. *Wickham*, 19 Ves. 419).

In the phrase "Wilfully Waste or Misapply" property, s. 97, 4 & 5 W. 4, c. 76, "Wilfully" applies to "misapply" as well as to "waste" (*Carpenter* v. *Mason*, 10 L. J. M. C. 1 ; 12 A. & E. 629 ; 4 P. & D. 439). *Cp. Squire* v. *Wheeler*, cited WILFUL DEFAULT.

WILFULLY.—It has been said that the legal meaning of "Wilfully" is purposely, without reference to bona fides or collusion (arg. of counsel in *Hutchinson* v. *Manchester, Bury, & Rossendale Ry.*, 15 L. J. Ex. 295 ; 15 M. & W. 314, citing *R.* v. *Price*, 11 A. & E. 727 ; 9 L. J. M. C. 49). *V.* UNLAWFULLY.

But "'Wilfully' is used in s. 79, 7 & 8 V. c. 84, in a sense denoting *evil intention*, and such is the common use of the word in the English language. Thus Milton :—

'Thou to me
Art all things under heav'n, all places thou,
Who for my *wilful* crime art banish'd hence.'

And Hooker says,—'So full of wilfulness and self-seeking is our nature'" (per Campbell, C. J., *R.* v. *Badger*, 25 L. J. M. C. 90 ; 6 E. & B. 137); and it was held in that case that a Surveyor was not guilty of the offence of "wilfully receiving" a higher fee than he was entitled to, when acting under an honest mistake. *Va. Smith* v. *Barnham*, 1 Ex. D. 419.

V. WILFUL : WILFUL AND MALICIOUS : WILFULLY AND FALSELY : *Cp.* WILFULLY TRESPASS : KNOWINGLY.

WILFULLY AND FALSELY.—"Wilfully and falsely" means Wilful Falsity, not mere incorrectness (*Ellis* v. *Kelly*, 30 L. J. M. C. 35 ; 6 H. & N. 222 ; 25 J. P. 279). That case was on s. 40, 21 & 22 V. c. 90, which imposes a penalty for "wilfully and falsely" pretending to a medical title ; and Pollock, C. B., there said,—"Now 'wilfully' cannot here mean merely 'intentionally,' as opposed to 'accidentally' (which is the meaning it sometimes has), for a man cannot accidentally call himself a Doctor of Medicine ; and, therefore, the section must be read as pointing to Wilful Falsity." *Vh. Andrews* v. *Styrap*, 26 L. T. 704 : *Carpenter* v. *Hamilton*, 41 J. P. 615 ; 37 L. T. 157 : *Pedgrift* v. *Chevallier*, 29 L. J. M. C. 225 : *Steele* v. *Hamilton*, 25 J. P. 643 ; 3 L. T. 322.

V. WILFULLY.

WILFULLY HOLD OVER.—Tenant who "shall wilfully hold over" demised premises, 4 G. 2, c. 28, s. 1 ; "The expression in the statute, 'wilfully hold over,' implies, not only a holding over after the term has expired, but a holding over in the absence of a bonâ fide belief on the part of the tenant that he is justified by the circumstances in so doing" (per Cockburn, C. J., *Swinfen* v. *Bacon*, 30 L. J. Ex. 368 ; 6 H. & N. 846). *Vf. Wright* v. *Smith*, 5 Esp. 203.

WILFULLY OBSTRUCT.—*V.* OBSTRUCT.

WILFULLY OR MALICIOUSLY.—*V.* WILFUL AND MALICIOUS.

WILFULLY TRESPASS.—"Wilfully trespass upon any Railway, and shall refuse to quit upon request," s. 16, 3 & 4 V. c. 96 ;—notwithstanding *Jones* v. *Taylor* (28 L. J. M. C. 204 n. ; 1 E. & E. 20), Blackburn, J., held that a continuing trespass was not, under these words, excused because the offender fancied he had a right to be where he was (*Foulger* v. *Steadman*, 42 L. J. M. C. 3 ; L. R. 8 Q. B. 65). *Cp.* WILFULLY : WILFULLY AND FALSELY : UNLAWFULLY.

WILFULLY WASTE.—*V.* Wilful Waste.

WILL: WILL AND DECLARE: WILL AND DESIRE.—*V.* Precatory Trust.

WILL ONLY.—If a "Power be to appoint by '*Will Only*,' with remainder over in default of appointment, an immediate disposition cannot be made, and it can only take effect under a Will, and after death" (Watson, Eq. 847, citing *Sockett* v. *Wray*, 4 Bro. C. C. 483: *Reid* v. *Shergold*, 10 Ves. 370: *Bradley* v. *Westcott*, 13 Ib. 445: *Anderson* v. *Dawson*, 15 Ib. 532).

WILLING.—*V.* Ready and Willing.

WILLINGLY.—"If a wife willingly (sponte) leave her husband and go away and continue with her avowtrer," she forfeits her dower (13 Edw. 1, St. 1, c. 34); here "Willingly" "is used in contradistinction to a wife being taken away by force by the adulterer" (per Willes, J., *Woodward* v. *Dowse*, 31 L. J. C. P. 72; 10 C. B. N. S. 722), in which case it was held that a wife driven from her home by her husband's cruelty and committing adultery, had "willingly" left her husband within the statute. *Vf.* 2 Inst. 434; Co. Litt. 32 a, b; Elope.

WIMSEY.—A Wimsey is a windlass fixed in the ground, and worked *by a steam engine* for the purpose of drawing materials from the mine (MacS. 246, n. 8, 9; *Cp.* Gin).

WIN.—"It has been doubted whether the money, &c. must be actually obtained, or whether winning a Game by a false pretence would be within the word 'win,' in s. 17, 8 & 9 V. c. 109, if the loser refused to pay the money" (Steph. Cr. 269, n. 5, citing *R.* v. *Moss*, Dears. & B. 104).

"A covenant to 'Win' a *Mineral* means, *primâ facie*, to reach it, and put it in such a condition that it may be continuously worked in the ordinary way" (MacS. 219, citing *Lewis* v. *Fothergill*, 5 Ch. 106). Following which definition the Court of Appeal said in *Rokeby* v. *Elliot* (49 L. J. Ch. 164; 13 Ch. D. 279; 28 W. R. 282; 41 L. T. 537),—"A Coal Field is *won* when full, practicable, available access is given to the coal-hewers so that they may enter on the practical work of getting the coal." *V.* Workable.

WIND AND WATER-TIGHT.—At pp. 597, 598, Woodf., it is stated that the obligation on the part of a tenant to keep his tenement "wind and water tight," "ought to be construed strictly in favour of the tenant. To put an example, it would seem that the broken glass of windows need not be replaced by new glass, but that an exclusion of wet by boards or other unsightly modes would be sufficient." *Sq.?*

WIND AND WEATHER PERMITTING.—*V.* PERMITTING.

WINDING-UP.—"Winding-up the affairs of the Co.;" *V. Re Oriental Bank,* 54 L. J. Ch. 481.

"Winding-up," s. 32 (4), Building Societies Act, 1874, 37 & 38 V. c. 42, means winding-up under the Companies Acts, 1862, 1867 (*Re Sunderland Bg. Socy.,* 21 Q. B. D. 349; 37 W. R. 95).

WINDOW.—A plate-glass shop-front, fixed with wooden wedges, without screws, nails or glue, and removable without injury to the premises (whether or not an "Improvement"), is a "Window" "affixed or belonging" to the premises, within a covenant to deliver up the premises "with all Windows," "Improvements," &c. (*Burt* v. *Haslett,* 18 C. B. 162, 893; 25 L. J. C. P. 201; 27 L. T. O. S. 300). *Semble,* "Improvements," in such a connection, will not include Trade Fixtures (*Cosby* v. *Shaw,* 23 L. R. Ir. 181).

V. FIXED AND FASTENED.

WINE-CELLARS.—A covenant in a Lease of Cellars under a Chapel, that they shall be used "as for Wine-Cellars only, and not for interment or burial," is broken by the user of the Cellars for the storage and sale of Beer and Spirits (*Turner* v. *Marriott,* Dart, 873).

WISH AND DESIRE: WISH AND REQUEST.—*V.* PRECATORY TRUST.

WISTA.—Half a Hide: Great Wista, a Hide (Elph. 630, citing Seebohm, 51; Spelm. *Wista,* where it is said that Wista is sometimes used for VIRGATE).

WIT.—"To wit;" *V.* NAMELY.

WITH.—"'With,' taken to mean 'and as incident thereto'" (Dwar. 692, citing *Durham Ry.* v. *Walker,* 2 Q. B. 966).

"With," in a devise of a House "*with* all the household goods therein," so conjoins the goods with the house that the devisee can have no larger interest in the goods than in the house (*Leeke* v. *Bennett,* 1 Atk. 470).

V. TOGETHER WITH.

WITH A VIEW.—*V.* A.

WITH ALL CONVENIENT SPEED.—*V.* CONVENIENT SPEED.

WITH ALL FAULTS.—*V.* FAULTS.

WITH ALL ITS LIGHTS.—*V.* Dart, 136, and note *f.*

WITH ALL LIBERTIES.—An original grant of a *Fair,* "With all Liberties," merely, does not include Tolls, for Toll is not incident to a Fair; but when Toll, by grant or prescription, is payable in respect of a Fair, and the Fair becomes forfeited to the Crown by whom it is re-granted "cum omnibus libertatibus ad hujusmodi feriam spectantibus," there Toll passes (*Heddy* v. *Wheelhouse*, Cro. Eliz. 591).

So a Grant of a *Market*, "with all Liberties *and Free Customs* to such a market belonging," does not give the right to prevent tradesmen from selling, on market days, marketable articles in shops within the limits of the franchise; though the grantees may acquire such a right by prescription, or, *semble*, it might have been granted by apt words in the charter (*Penryn* v. *Best*, 48 L. J. Ex. 103; 3 Ex. D. 292).

V. Custom: Toll.

WITH ALL MINES.—"Where a man has unopened Mines within his land, and demises for life or years such land 'With all Mines therein,' the lessee may, *primâ facie*, as between himself and his grantor, dig the unopened Mines and will not, by so doing, commit Waste (*Saunders' Case*, 5 Co. 12 a; Co. Litt. 54 b: *Darcy* v. *Askwith*, Hob. 234: *Clegg* v. *Rowland*, L. R. 2 Eq. 160; 35 L. J. Ch. 396; 14 W. R. 530; 14 L. T. 217); for otherwise the words 'With all Mines therein' would have no effect (Co. Litt. 54 b)." MacS. 53.

WITH EFFECT.—*V.* Effect.

WITH FORCE AND ARMS.—*V.* Force.

WITH SERVANTS.—*V.* Servants.

WITHDRAW.—An Agreement by a Partner to "withdraw from the Firm" means to withdraw at once: and it further means (1) "that the withdrawing Partner shall make over to the continuing Partners all his interest in the partnership and in the partnership assets, whether there be real or personal estate, whether there be outstanding contracts, or anything of the kind;" (2) "that the continuing Partners shall indemnify the retiring Partners against all the liabilities of the Firm from that time forth. They take the assets, they take the benefit of the contracts, they take the chances of success for the future, and they must keep him indemnified" (per Kekewich, J., *Gray* v. *Smith*, 58 L. J. Ch. 805).

WITHDRAWAL.—"Withdrawal" Member of a Building Society; *V. Re Norwich & Norfolk Bg. Socy.*, 45 L. J. Ch. 785: *Vth.* per Selborne, L. C., *Walton* v. *Edge*, 10 App. Ca. 39. *Va. Re Sunderland Bg. Socy.*, 24 Q. B. D. 394. *V.* Unadvanced.

WITHHELD.—*V.* Unreasonably.

WITHIN.—Where a statute gave power to assess, for expenses of road-repair, all premises "within" certain streets, it was held that a yard—Kent and Essex Yard, Whitechapel—set back from one of such streets, and having other houses between it and the street, but the only access to which was from the street by means of carriage gates and along a private covered way, was "within" the street (*Baddeley* v. *Gingell*, 17 L. J. Ex. 63 ; 1 Ex. 319). In that case Alderson, B., said,—"You cannot say that any house is literally *within* the street, and we must therefore come to the consideration of what is intended by the expression 'within;'" and the yard was held (*V.* especially jdgmt. of Parke, B.) to be "within" the street because its sole communication was by means of the street, and because it *fronted* and *abutted* on, and derived the benefit of the repairs to, the street.

V. FORMING : FRONTING : IN : NAVIGATING WITHIN.

"Within" a stated time ; *V.* IN : REASONABLE TIME : WEEK : YEAR.

The phrase "within" so many days "after" an event, means clear days (*Williams* v. *Burgess*, 10 L. J. Q. B. 10 ; 12 A. & E. 635 : *Robinson* v. *Waddington*, 18 L. J. Q. B. 250) ; and so of the phrase, within so many days "at least" (*Mitchell* v. *Foster*, 12 A. & E. 472 ; 9 Dowl. 527 : *Freeman* v. *Reed*, 8 L. T. 458 : *R.* v. *Shropshire*, 7 L. J. M. C. 56 ; 3 N. & P. 286 ; 8 A. & E. 173).

"Within" two named times ; *V.* FROM.

"At or Within ;" *V.* AT.

WITHIN HIS PARISH.—*V.* CLERGYMAN.

WITHIN OR UNDER.—It seems difficult to see how a grant of "Minerals" "*within* or under" land is fuller, and less liable to receive a restricted meaning, than if "under" alone were used ; but this suggestion has been made (per Romilly, M. R., *Mid. Ry.* v. *Checkley*, 36 L. J. Ch. 382 ; L. R. 4 Eq. 25 ; observed upon by Wickens, V.-C., *Hext* v. *Gill*, 41 L. J. Ch. 295 ; 7 Ch. 705 n. : *Vf.* MacS. 13).

WITHIN THE JURISDICTION.—Contract which "ought to be performed within the Jurisdiction," Ord. 11, R. 1 (*e*), R. S. C. ; *V.* *Hassall* v. *Lawrence*, 4 Times Rep. 23 : *Robey* v. *Snaefell Co.*, 57 L. J. Q. B. 134 : *Wancke* v. *Wingren*, 58 Ib. 519 : *Reynolds* v. *Coleman*, 56 L. J. Ch. 903 : Ann. Pr. *V.* TERMS.

WITHIN THE REALM.—*V.* REALM.

WITHOUT BENEFIT OF SALVAGE.—A policy on profits is within 19 G. 2, c. 37, s. 1 ; and if made "Without Benefit of Salvage," although "free from average," it is avoided (*De Mattos* v. *North*, L. R. 3 Ex. 185 ; 37 L. J. Ex. 116, following *Smith* v. *Reynolds*, 25 L. J. Ex. 337 ; 1 H. & N. 221 : *V.* FULL INTEREST ADMITTED).

A Policy "Without Benefit of Salvage," omitting the words "to the

Insurers," is within the prohibition of the Act (*Allkins* v. *Jupe*, 46 L. J. C. P. 824 ; 2 C. P. D. 375).

WITHOUT DELAY.—*V.* PROSECUTE.

WITHOUT DISPUTE.—An agreement to accept a title "Without dispute," or "such as the vendor has," will preclude objections (Dart, 169).

WITHOUT HAVING BEEN MARRIED.—*V. Wilson* v. *Atkinson*, 33 Bea. 536 ; 4 D. G. J. & S. 455 ; 33 L. J. Ch. 576 : *Re Ball*, 48 L. J. Ch. 279 ; 11 Ch. D. 270 : *Upton* v. *Brown*, 48 L. J. Ch. 756 ; 12 Ch. D. 872 : *Emmins* v. *Bradford*, 49 L. J. Ch. 222 ; 13 Ch. D. 493 : *Hardman* v. *Maffett*, 13 L. R. Ir. 499 : UNMARRIED.

WITHOUT IMPEACHMENT OF WASTE.—Leases under s. 46, Settled Estates Act, 1877, must "be not made Without Impeachment of Waste" :—a Lease requiring the lessee to deliver up the premises in good repair, "fair Wear and Tear and damage by tempest excepted," offends against that condition and is invalid ; because a tenant for years, in the absence of stipulation, is liable even for Permissive Waste (*Yellowly* v. *Gower*, inf.), from which such an exemption would exempt him (per Kekewich, J., *Davies* v. *Davies*, 57 L. J. Ch. 1093 ; 38 Ch. D. 499 ; 58 L. T. 514 ; 36 W. R. 399, adopting *Yellowly* v. *Gower*, 24 L. J. Ex. 289 ; 11 Ex. 274, notwithstanding that in *Woodhouse* v. *Walker*, 5 Q. B. D. 407 ; 49 L. J. Q. B. 611, the point decided in *Yellowly* v. *Gower* was treated as an open one ; *Va. Barnes* v. *Dowling*, 44 L. T. 809. In Woodf. 610, *Yellowly* v. *Gower* is spoken of "as having been too long accepted to be now overruled").

Vh. Downshire v. *Sandys*, 6 Ves. 107 : Termes de la Ley, *Impeachment of Wast.*

V. WASTE : WEAR AND TEAR.

WITHOUT INJUSTICE.—*V.* INJUSTICE.

WITHOUT INTERRUPTION.—*V.* INTERRUPTION.

WITHOUT ISSUE.—*V.* DIE WITHOUT ISSUE : LEAVING.

WITHOUT PREJUDICE.—A letter "Without Prejudice" cannot be treated "as an admission of right ;" and though Kindersley, V.-C., said, "the party writing it, can use it against the other on the question of costs" (*Williams* v. *Thomas*, 31 L. J. Ch. 676 ; 2 Dr. & Sm. 29 ; 7 L. T. 184 : *Va. Jones* v. *Foxall*, 21 L. J. Ch. 725 ; 15 Bea. 388), yet it has been quite recently held by the Court of Appeal (questioning *Williams* v. *Thomas*), that a letter written "Without Prejudice" cannot be looked at as furnishing Good Cause for depriving a successful litigant of costs (*Walker* v. *Wilsher*, 23 Q. B. D. 335; 58 L. J. Q. B. 501; 37 W. R. 723; 5 Times Rep. 649). This, in effect, seems to establish the principle that a letter "Without Prejudice" cannot be read without the consent of both parties (*Vh.* 34 S. J. 56).

But, even as regards the rights between the parties, a letter "Without Prejudice" is only inadmissible so long as it relates to a negotiation; when the negotiation is closed by an agreement, the privilege ceases (*Holdsworth* v. *Dimsdale*, 19 W. R. 798). *Vf.* *Hoghton* v. *Hoghton*, 15 Bea. 278: *Paddock* v. *Forrester*, 3 M. & G. 903.

The whole of a negotiation is covered if its commencement is "Without Prejudice" (*Ex p. Harris*, 44 L. J. Bank. 33).

As to effect of "Without Prejudice" in a reply to a Requisition on Title; *V.* *Morley* v. *Cook*, 2 Hare, 106.

Threat of Legal Proceedings (s. 32, Patents, &c. Act, 1883), "Without Prejudice;" *V.* *Kurtz* v. *Spence*, 57 L. J. Ch. 238; 58 L. T. 438. *V.* Threat.

WITHOUT RESERVE.—When an auction is advertised as being made "Without Reserve," the vendor cannot bid; and if he bids, or employs any one to bid, the sale is void at the election of the purchaser (*Meadows* v. *Tanner*, 5 Mad. 34: *Thornett* v. *Haines*, 15 L. J. Ex. 230; 15 M. & W. 367: *Robinson* v. *Wall*, 16 L. J. Ch. 401: *Warlow* v. *Harrison*, 29 L. J. Q. B. 14; 1 E. & E. 295; 32 L. T. O. S. 222; 7 W. R. 133: s. 4, 30 & 31 V. c. 48): and when land is the subject of such an auction, it is unlawful for the vendor "to employ any person to bid" (s. 5, 30 & 31 V. c. 48). *Note.*—As to the conflicting rules in Equity and at Law hereon prior to the 30 & 31 V. c. 48; *V.* Dart, 126.

But in *Warlow* v. *Harrison* (sup.) the majority of the Court (Martin and Watson, BB., and Byles, J.) went further, and held that an Auctioneer who puts up property for sale "Without Reserve," "pledges himself that the sale shall be without reserve, or (in other words) contracts that it shall be so; and that this contract is made with the highest *bonâ fide* bidder, and in case of a breach of it that he has a right of action against the Auctioneer." But, though this was a decision of the Ex. Cham., Blackburn, J., in delivering the jdgmt. of the Q. B. in *Mainprice* v. *Westley* (34 L. J. Q. B. 229; 6 B. & S. 420), pointed out that the ultimate decision in *Warlow* v. *Harrison* turned rather on a matter of pleading, and said,—"We do not think, therefore, that we are precluded by it as a judgment of a Court of Error;" and accordingly in *Mainprice* v. *Westley* the Court, without saying whether or not the vendor would be liable *as for a breach of contract* if he authorised biddings in a "peremptory" sale, held, that the auctioneer at such sale would not be liable when acting without deceit and professedly only as an agent.

The authority of *Warlow* v. *Harrison*, on the question whether a

"Peremptory" sale, or a sale "Without Reserve," gives positive contractual rights, was further impaired by *Harris* v. *Nickerson* (42 L. J. Q. B. 171; L. R. 8 Q. B. 286), in which it was held, that an advertisement of an intended auction gives no contractual rights to persons who are put to expense in travelling to attend the auction, and who are disappointed by reason of the sale being at the last moment withdrawn (Add. C. 13). In that case Quain, J., said,—"*Warlow* v. *Harrison* has not been considered a satisfactory decision." And if no contractual rights arise by reason of the withdrawal of an auction, it seems difficult to see how the case is altered, in favour of the highest *bonâ fide* bidder who must be unknown at the commencement of the sale, by the sale being advertised as "Peremptory," or "Without Reserve." A sale "without reserve" might, it seems clear, be withdrawn altogether. If it proceeds, why may it not be withdrawn at any time until an actual contract is made? And if it may be so withdrawn, how can contractual rights arise in favour of one of what may be a large company when all that can be said is that his bidding is prevented from being the highest, and he himself is prevented from being a contracting party, by the intervention of the intending vendor? *Sv.* Add. C. 868.

V. Reserved Bidding.

WITHOUT RISK OF CRAFT.—Where a Lighter was let out, "Without Risk of Craft" and the goods on board were damaged by sea-water, the owner was held not liable for the loss (*Webster* v. *Bond*, Cab. & El. 339). In that case Mathew, J., said,—"I think the words 'without Risk of Craft,' mean without risk or liability to the owner of the craft."

WITNESS.—*V.* Credible Witness.

WOOD: WOODS.—"Wood, *boscus,* contains timber or hautboys and underwood or subboscus. Both the trees and the soil on which they stand pass by the grant of a Wood or Boscus (Co. Litt. 4 b: *Vh. Doe* d. *Kinglake* v. *Beviss*, 18 L. J. C. P. 128; 7 C. B. 456). In like manner by an exception, in a Lease, of the Woods and Underwoods growing or being on the property demised, the soil itself on which they grow is excepted (*Ive's Case*, 5 Rep. 11 a: *Hide* v. *Whilster*, Pop. 146: *Whilster* v. *Paston*, Cro. Jac. 487). On the other hand by an exception of 'Trees' (*Liford's Case*, 11 Rep. 46 b), 'saleable underwoods' now growing on the premises (*Pincombe* v. *Thomas*, Cro. Jac. 524), the soil itself is not excepted. *V. Glover* v. *Andrew*, 1 And. 7" (Elph. 631). *Vf.* Trees: Touch. 94, 95: *Stanley* v. *White*, 14 East, 332.

Lease of "Woods, Groves, Hedgerows, and Springs," by a Chapter, that had no right to fell Timber except for repairs, gave lessee no right to fell timber (*Herring* v. *St. Paul's*, 3 Swanst. 492; 2 Wils. 1).

Vh. Craig on Trees and Woods, *pass.*

"Commissioners of Woods and Forests;" *V.* s. 12 (12), Interp. Act, 1889.

WOODGELD.—"'Woodgeld' seemeth to be the gathering or cutting of wood within the Forrest, or money payd for the same to the Forresters. And the immunity from this by the King's grant is, by Cromp. f. 197, called Woodgeld" (Termes de la Ley).

WORK.—"Work and Maintain" a Railway; *V.* MAINTAIN.

"Work of Necessity;" *V.* NECESSITY.

V. LABOUR: FROM HIS WORK.

WORKABLE.—"An agreement to work a mine as long as it is '*fairly* workable,' does not oblige the tenant to work it at a dead loss (*Jones* v. *Shears*, 7 C. & P. 346); nor does a covenant to 'get the demised clay to the *fullest practicable extent* consistent with the means of sale of bricks and tiles to be derived therefrom,' although a means of sale at an unremunerative rate might be found (per Denman, J., *Newton* v. *Nock*, 43 L. T. 197); but an agreement to work 'in the *most proper and effective manner*' is broken by a cessation from working, although the dead rent be paid (*Kinsman* v. *Jackson*, 42 L. T. 80, 558; 28 W. R. 337. The dictum of Malins, V.-C., *Wheatley* v. *Westminster Brymbo Coal Co.*, L. R. 9 Eq. 538; 39 L. J. Ch. 175; 22 L. T. 7, that it is enough if the dead rent be paid, would seem not to be law; *V.* per Jessel, M. R., 42 L. T. 558). 'Coal Seams *workable as Coal Seams*,' means workable at a profit, including the coal and fire clay, &c., to which the tenant is entitled (*Carr* v. *Benson*, 3 Ch. 524)." Woodf. 669.

As to construction of Covenants to work Mines; *V. R.* v. *Bedworth*, 8 East, 387: *Bute* v. *Thompson*, 14 L. J. Ex. 95; 13 M. & W. 487: *Clifford* v. *Watts*, L. R. 5 C. P. 577: *Jervis* v. *Tomkinson*, 26 L. J. Ex. 41; 1 H. & N. 195: *Foley* v. *Addenbrooke*, 14 L. J. Ex. 169; 13 M. & W. 174: *Quarrington* v. *Arthur*, 11 L. J. Ex. 418; 10 M. & W. 335: *Doe* d. *Bryan* v. *Bancks*, 4 B. & Ald. 401: Woodf. 382, 669, 670: MacS. 219, 229, 230: WORTH THE EXPENSE.

Cp. WROUGHT.

WORKED.—Vessels "*rowed or worked*" may be propelled by steam (per Littledale, J., *Tisdell* v. *Combe*, 7 A. & E. 796).

So a barge, having no motive power of its own, but which is towed by a steamer, is being "*worked and navigated*" within s. 66, Thames Watermen Act, 1859, 22 & 23 V. c. cxxxiii. (*Elmore* v. *Hunter*, 47 L. J. M. C. 8; 3 C. P. D. 116).

WORKING DAYS.—"'Working Days' in a Charter-party will vary in different ports. If by the custom of the port certain days in the year are holidays, so that no work is done in that port on those days, then 'Working Days' do not include those holidays. 'Working Days,' in an English Charter-party, if there is nothing to shew a contrary intention, do not include Christmas-Day and some other days, which are well known to be holidays. Therefore 'Working Days' mean days on which, at the port according to the custom of the port, work is done in loading and unloading ships, and the phrase does not include Sunday" (per Esher, M. R., *Nielsen* v. *Wait*, 16 Q. B. D. 71). *Vh. Straker* v. *Kidd*, 47 L. J. Q. B. 365; 3 Q. B. D. 223.

V. DAYS: RUNNING DAYS.

WORKING MINER.—*V.* PRACTICAL WORKING MINER.

WORKMAN.—For the purposes of the Employers and Workmen Act, 1875 (38 & 39 V. c. 90), a "Workman" "does not include a domestic or menial servant; but, save as aforesaid, means any person, who being a labourer, servant in husbandry, journeyman, artificer, handicraftsman, miner, or otherwise engaged *in manual labour*, whether under the age of 21 years or above that age, has entered into or works under a contract with an employer, whether the contract be express or implied, oral or in writing, and be a contract of service or a contract personally to execute any work or labour" (s. 10); but not including "seamen or apprentices to the sea service" (s. 13),—on which exception, *V. Hanrahan* v. *Limerick Steam Ship Co.*, 18 L. R. Ir. 137: MARINER.

That would seem a good definition of "Workman" for general purposes. With the addition of "a railway servant," it has been adopted as the definition of "Workman" for the purposes of the Employers' Liability Act, 1880 (43 & 44 V. c. 42, s. 8).

Neither an Omnibus Conductor nor a Driver of a Tramcar, is such a "Workman," for the duties of neither involve labour, and those of a Conductor, at least, could not be regarded as manual (*Morgan* v. *Lond. Gen. Omnibus Co.*, 53 L. J. Q. B. 352; 13 Q. B. D. 832; 32 W. R. 759; 48 J. P. 503: *Cook* v. *North Metrop. Trams Co.*, 18 Q. B. D. 683; 56 L. J. Q.B. 309; 56 L. T. 448; 57 Ib. 476; 35 W. R. 577).

Nor is a Designer of Patterns such a "Workman" (*Jackson* v. *Hill*, 13 Q. B. D. 618; 48 J. P. 489).

But one who has to labour manually is not less a "Workman" because he has to employ other manual labour to assist him (*Grainger* v. *Aynsley*, 50 L. J. M. C. 48; 6 Q. B. D. 182; 29 W. R. 242; 45 J. P. 142); and in like manner one, a substantial part of whose time is taken up in manual abour, is a "Workman" within the Acts mentioned, although he is an Overlooker of others (*Leech* v. *Gartside*, 1 Times Rep. 391); and so is a Miner working for a "butty" man (*Brown* v. *Butterley Co.*, 53 L. T. 964; 50 J. P. 230; 2 Times Rep. 159).

V. ARTIFICER: LABOURER: SERVANT: MANUAL LABOUR.

WORKMANLIKE.—*V.* Proper and Workmanlike.

WORKS.—Pit-pans and Levels, held to be "Works," within a Licence to get China-clay (*Martyn* v. *Williams*, 26 L. J. Ex. 117 ; 1 H. & N. 817) ; but Tram-plates fastened to sleepers, not let into but resting on the ground, are not "Works," within a Mining Lease (*Beaufort* v. *Bates*, 31 L. J. Ch. 481 ; 3 D. G. F. & J. 381 ; 10 W. R. 200 ; 6 L. T. 82).

The Completion of "Works" under s. 133, Lands C. C. Act, 1845, includes, —in the case of land speculatively taken by a Local Authority for street improvement,—the disposal, by sale or otherwise, of all the land so acquired ; and, therefore, until the completion of the street and the disposal of all the land, the Local Authority is liable, under the section, to make good any deficiency of Land Tax and Poor Rate in respect of the lands taken (*Bristol Guardians* v. *Bristol Corp.*, 18 Q. B. D. 549 ; 56 L. J. Q. B. 320 ; 56 L. T. 641 ; 35 W. R. 619 ; 51 J. P. 676 ; 3 Times Rep. 271).

V. Accommodation.

"Commissioners of Works ;" *V.* s. 12 (13), Interp. Act, 1889.

WORKSHOP.—A room in which children were taught, and were engaged in, straw-plaiting, by and under the superintendence of a person who had no interest in the work done or the proceeds of it, held a "Workshop" within s. 4, Workshop Regulation Act, 1867, 30 & 31 V. c. 146 (*Beadon* v. *Parrott*, 40 L. J. M. C. 200 ; L. R. 6 Q. B. 718).

WORLD.—To say of a person that he holds himself out "to the world" in any capacity, "is a loose expression" (per Parke, B., *Dickeson* v. *Valpy*, 10 B. & C. 140).

Devise, in remainder, "to the Next Heir of the name of Leach, *as long as the World stands*," is a limitation, and not a devise to the next heir of the name of Leach as a *persona designata* (*Re Catling*, 34 S. J. 364).

WORLDLY ESTATE.—When a man speaks of his "Worldly Estate," that, probably, means all his property, so that the phrase is synonymous with Substance (*Muddle* v. *Fry*, 6 Mad. 270 : *Gall* v. *Esdaile*, 1 L. J. C. P. 95 ; 8 Bing. 323 ; 1 Moore & S. 466 : *Doe* v. *Gwillim*, 2 L. J. K. B. 194 ; 5 B. & Ad. 122 ; 2 N. & M. 247 : *Lloyd* v. *Jackson*, L. R. 1 Q. B. 571 ; 2 Ib. 269). *Cp.* Worldly Goods.

V. Temporal Estate.

WORLDLY GOODS: WORLDLY SUBSTANCE.—"The phrase 'Worldly Goods' is properly applicable only to personal estate" (1 Jarm. 747) : but "'Worldly Substance' includes every property a man has" (per Mansfield, C. J., *Hogan* v. *Jackson*, 1 Cowp. 307). Even "Worldly *Goods*" may be controlled by a context to include realty (*Wright* v. *Shelton*, 18 Jur. 445, cited 1 Jarm. 747). *Cp.* Worldly Estate.

WORLDLY LABOUR.—"Worldly Labour," 29 Car. 2, c. 7; "The expression 'any Worldly Labour' cannot be confined to a man's ordinary calling; but applies to any business he may carry on, whether in his ordinary calling or not" (per Park, J., *Smith* v. *Sparrow*, 4 Bing. 89). *V.* Ordinary Calling.

WORSHIP.—The meaning of the word "Worship" in our Anglican Marriage Service—"with my body I thee worship,"—is "honour." The Puritans always objected to the word; and in 1661 it was agreed that "honour" should be substituted, the alteration being made by Sancroft in Bishop Cosin's revised Prayer Book, instead of the change suggested by Cosin himself. But, either by accident or through a change of mind on the part of the Revision Committee, the old word was allowed to remain. The more exclusive use of this word in connexion with Divine Service is of comparatively modern date. In the *Liber Festivalis,* printed by Caxton in 1483, an Easter homily calls every gentleman's house "a place of worship," and in the same century a prayer begins, "God that commandest to worship fadir and modir." This secular use of it is still continued in the title "your Worship," by which magistrates are addressed, and in the appellation "Worshipful Companies." The expression "with my body I thee worship," or "honour," is equivalent to a bestowal of the man's own self upon the woman, in the same manner in which she is delivered to him by the Church from the hands of her father (*Blunt's Annotated Book of Common Prayer,* 6 Ed. 269: *Va.* for a collection of authorities on this phrase, *Mant's Book of Common Prayer*, 492, 493).

WORSHIP OF GOD.—*V.* Godly Learning.

WORTH.—A testamentary gift of "all I am worth," includes the realty (*Huxstep* v. *Brooman,* 1 Bro. C. C. 437: *Vth.* 1 Jarm. 738, 739: *Va.* All).

V. Ey.

WORTH THE EXPENSE.—"Where a Scotch Lease (of Mines) gave liberty to determine if the Minerals became 'not worth the expense of working,' and they became so through a fall in the market price, the lessees were held entitled to determine" (MacS. 244, n. 4, citing *Shotts Co.* v. *Deas,* 8 Sess. Ca., 4th Series, 530).

V. Workable.

WOULD.—In a clause of Forfeiture of a life interest if the beneficiary shall assign or become bankrupt, "or do or suffer anything whereby the income, if payable to him absolutely, *would* become vested in any other person," "would" does not mean "might," but means "will;" and, therefore, neither the filing of a Bankry Petition, nor the execution of a

Composition Deed by the beneficiary, will work a forfeiture: if the words were "*may* become vested," the case might be different (per Cave, J., *Ex p. Dawes, Re Moon*, 17 Q. B. D. 282). *V.* SUFFER: TRANSFER.

A. had a power of appointment by writing over a Life Policy; in a memorandum he wrote:—"the money from the Equitable Insurance Office I *would have* equally divided between my daughters;" held a good execution of the power (*Proby* v. *Landor*, 30 L. J. Ch. 593). In that case Romilly, M. R., said:—"the word 'would' must be taken to mean 'wish.'"

WOUND.—"'To wound' means to divide the surface of the body, whether it be an internal,—*e.g.*, the inside of the mouth,—or an external surface" (Steph. Cr. 171, citing *R.* v. *Leonard Smith*, 8 C. & P. 173; 1 Russ. Cr. 921). Wounding may be done with the hand (*R.* v. *Bullock*, 37 L. J. M. C. 47; L. R. 1 C. C. R. 115). To break a bone, without breaking the skin, *semble*, is not to wound (*R.* v. *Wood*, 4 C. & P. 381). *Vf. R.* v. *Owens*, 1 Moody, 205: *R.* v. *Hughes*, 2 C. & P. 420: Arch. Cr. 759.

In the collocation "Stab, Cut or Wound," 9 G. 4, c. 31, ss. 11, 12, a Wounding had to be accomplished by an instrument, because "wound" was there associated with "stab, cut," and as a stab or cut must be made by an instrument, so it was held that "wound" meant an injury (other than a "stab" or "cut") made by an instrument (per Alderson, B., *R.* v. *Jennings*, 2 Lewin, C. C. 130, explaining *R.* v. *Stevens*, 1 Moody, 409: *R.* v. *Harris*, 7 C. & P. 446).

WRECK.—"'Wrecke,' or 'Varech' (as the Normans, from whom it came, call it) is where a Ship is perished on the Sea, and no man escapeth alive out of the same, and the Ship, or part of the Ship so perished, or the goods of the Ship come to the Land of any Lord, the Lord shall have that as a Wrecke of the Sea. But if a man, or a dog, or a cat, escape alive, so that the party to whom the goods belong, come within a yeare and a day, and prove the goods to be his, he shall have them againe, by provision of the statute of Westm. 1, c. 4, made in King Ed. I. dayes, who therein followed the decree of H. I., before whose dayes, if a Ship had been cast on shore, torne with tempest, and were not repaired by such as escaped alive within a certaine time, that then this was taken for Wrecke" (Termes de la Ley).

Cp. Doctor and Student, Di. 2, Ch. 51.

"De wreck de mere" (3 Edw. 1, c. 4),—"Wrecke or Shipwrecke, is an English word, in French *Naufrage*, in ancient French, *Varech*, in Latine, *Naufragium*, legally *Wreccum Maris*, Wrecke of the Sea in legall understanding, is applied to such goods as after shipwreck at sea are by the sea cast upon the land; and therefore the jurisdiction thereof pertaineth not to the lord admirall but to the common law. Although this statute speaketh onely of Wrecke, yet this statute extendeth to Flotsam, Jetsam and Lagan" (2 Inst. 167, citing *Constable's Case*, 5 Rep. 106 a).

Section 2, Merchant Shipping Act, 1854, preserves the definition as laid down by *Constable's Case* thus,—"'Wreck,' shall include Jetsam, Flotsam, Lagan, and Derelict found in or on the Shores of the Sea or any Tidal Water" (*Vh. The Zeta*, 44 L. J. Adm. 22; L. R. 4 A. & E. 460). "Timber found floating at sea, without an apparent owner, having drifted from its moorings, is not 'Wreck' within the meaning of the Act" (1 Maude & P. 643, n. (*j*), citing *Palmer* v. *Rouse*, 3 H. & N. 505; 27 L. J. Ex. 437: *Va. Legge* v. *Boyd*, 14 L. J. C. P. 138; 1 C. B. 92: *Barry* v. *Arnaud*, 10 A. & E. 646; 9 L. J. Q. B. 226; 2 P. & D. 633). *Vf.* 1 Maude & P. 643, 675, 677, 679 and authorities there cited.

WRIT OF ERROR.—"Writs of Error upon any Judgment;" held to include Judgments on Writs of Error, as well as original judgments (*Nisbit* v. *Rishton*, 9 A. & E. 426; 9 L. J. Ex. 333; 2 P. & D. 706).

WRIT OF EXECUTION.—"The term 'Writ of Execution' includes writs of *fieri facias*, *capias*, *elegit*, sequestration, and attachment, and all subsequent writs that may issue for giving effect thereto" (Dan. Ch. Pr. 825).

WRIT OF SUMMONS.—Though an Originating Summons is an Action; yet it is not a "Writ of Summons" within Ord. 11, R. 1, R. S. C. and no Order to serve it out of the jurisdiction can be granted (*Re Busfield*, 55 L. J. Ch. 467; 32 Ch. D. 123; 54 L. T. 220; 34 W. R. 372). From the jdgmt. of Cotton, L. J., in that case, it may be stated that a like rule applies to Interpleaders, Petitions and Applications to tax Solicitors' Costs, wherever an Order is sought against the person out of the jurisdiction (*V.* that jdgmt. for review and explanation of *Credits Gerundeuse* v. *Van Weede*, 53 L. J. Q. B. 142; 12 Q. B. D. 171: *Weldon* v. *Gounod*, 15 Q. B. D. 622: *Re Haney*, 44 L. J. Ch. 272; 10 Ch. 275: *Re Bonelli's Co.*, 43 L. J. Ch. 720; L. R. 18 Eq. 655: *Re Naylor*, 28 L. T. 18: *Re Maugham*, 22 W. R. 748: *Re Mewburn*, W. N. (74) 156). *Vf. Re Jellard*, 39 Ch. D. 424: *Re Anglo-African Steamship Co.*, 32 Ch. D. 348: *Re Nathan Newman & Co.*, 35 Ch. D. 1: *Re Liebig, Limd.*, 59 L. T. 315.

WRITING.—In Acts of Parliament, "expressions referring to Writing shall, unless the contrary intention appears, be construed as including references to Printing, Lithography, Photography, and other modes of representing or reproducing words in a visible form" (s. 20, Interp. Act, 1889).

A Will is a "Writing" within the meaning of a Power to appoint "By Writing" (*Lisle* v. *Lisle*, 1 Bro. C. C. 533 : *Orange* v. *Pickford*, 27 L. J. Ch. 808 ; 4 Drew. 363). "If a Power be created to be executed by a Deed, or Instrument in Writing, although the words seem to indicate instruments *inter vivos* only, yet it is settled that it may be well executed by Will" (per Westbury, L. C., *Taylor* v. *Meads*, 34 L. J. Ch. 206 ; 4 D. G. J. & S. 597: *Vh.* Sug. Pow. 214, where it is stated that the leading case on this doctrine is *Kibbet* v. *Lee*, Hob. 312 ; nom. *Hubbard's Case*, Litt. Rep. 218). But if such a Power goes on to prescribe special solemnities for its execution,—*e.g.* that the Writing is to be "under seal,"—such requirements must be followed ; and unless the Power is, *in terms*, a Power to appoint "by Will," a noncompliance with its requirements will not be cured by s. 10, Wills Act, 1 V. c. 26 (*Taylor* v. *Meads*, sup., which distinctly overruled *Buckell* v. *Blenkhorn*, 5 Hare, 131, and established the dicta of the L.JJ. in *Collard* v. *Sampson*, 22 L. J. Ch. 729; 4 D. G. M. & G. 224, and the decision of Wood, V.-C., in *West* v. *Ray*, 23 L. J. Ch. 447; Kay, 385: *Vh.* 1 Jarm. 31, note (*u*) ; Watson, Eq. 888). *V.* SIGNED, SEALED AND DELIVERED.

An Author's MS. is a "Writing" within the Carriers Act, 11 G. 4 & 1 W. 4, c. 68, s. 1 (per Stonor, Co. Co. Judge, *Lawson* v. *Lond. & S. W. Ry.*, 73 Law Times 147).

"Writing under his hand ;" *V.* HIS HAND.

V. NOTE : IN WRITING : INSTRUMENT IN WRITING.

WRITTEN BY.—"Written by," appearing on the title page of a song set to music, refers only to the words of the song and do not mean "written and composed by" (*Barnard* v. *Pillow*, W. N. (68) 94).

WRITTEN CONSENT.—As to what is a sufficient "Written Consent" to an Assignment of a Lease ; *V. West* v. *Dobb*, 39 L. J. Q. B. 190 ; L. R. 5 Q. B. 460).

WRITTEN WARRANTY.—A written description of the quality of goods sold, is not a "Written Warranty" of them within s. 25, Sale of Food and Drugs Act, 1875, 38 & 39 V. c. 63 (*Rook* v. *Hopley*, 47 L. J. M. C. 118 ; 3 Ex. D. 209) ; nor is a written contract for the *future* supply of goods in their pure state such a Warranty, for the Warranty under the statute must accompany each delivery of goods (*Harris* v. *May*, 53 L. J. M. C. 39 ; 12 Q. B. D. 97).

WRONGFUL.—"Wrongful ;" *V.* per Bowen, L. J., *Mogul Co.* v. *McGregor*, cited MALICE.

"Wrongful Act or Default ;" *V.* DEFAULT.

WRONGFULLY CLAIMING.—As to the meaning of this expression in s. 9, 3 & 4 W. 4, c. 27; *V. Williams* v. *Pott*, 40 L. J. Ch. 775; L. R. 12 Eq. 149.

WROUGHT.—A proviso in a Coal Mining Lease, ceasing rent on the Coal being worked out "so far as the same can be Fairly Wrought," relates to the possibility of obtaining coal by fair working" (per Pollock, C. B.), and the question of working at a profit has no bearing (*Griffiths* v. *Rigby*, 25 L. J. Ex. 284; 1 H. & N. 237).

Cp. WORKABLE.

YAR—YEA

YARD.—A yard for bonding foreign timber, in which there were a deal shed and two buildings, with saw-pits ; held, not to be a "Yard" within the Commercial Ry. Act (*Stone* v. *Commercial Ry.*, 9 Sim. 621).

V. Superficial Yard.

YARDLAND.—" *Una virgata terræ,* a yard-land, is in some countries 10, in some 20, in some 24, in some 30, &c." (Co. Litt. 5 a : the "&c." here means "acres," Touch. 93). " By the grant therefore of *virgatam terræ,* or a yard-land, will pass that quantity of land, meadow and pasture, that is called by this name. And so by the grant of half a yard, or a quarter of a yard land" (Touch. 93). *Vf.* Elph. 567, 631.

YARDS.—The parcels in a conveyance were described by reference to coloured parts of a plan. A yard, delineated but not coloured in the plan, was held to pass under the general word "Yards" (*Willis* v. *Watney*, 51 L. J. Ch. 181). *V.* General Words.

YEAR.—" A Year is the time wherein the sun goes around his compass through the twelve signs, viz., 365 days and about 6 hours. But in Leap Year the statute, 24 G. 2, c. 25, enacts that the year shall consist of 366 days ; so that in *R.* v. *Wormingall* (6 M. & S. 350), upon a question of yearly hiring, Ld. Ellenborough said, 'In those years which consist of 366 days, a hiring and service for a year, must be for that same number of days, in like manner as when the year was 365 days, it must have continuance during that number" (Dwar. 693).

An "Agreement not to be performed within the space of one year from the making thereof," s. 4, St. of Frauds, means within 12 calendar months from that date (*V. Bracegirdle* v. *Heald,* 1 B. & Ald. 722 : *Snelling* v. *Huntingfield,* 1 Cr. M. & R. 20). *Vf.* Not to be.

Under the Companies Act, 1862, the Annual List of Members (s. 26), and the General Meetings (s. 49), which are to be sent, or held, "once at least in *every* Year," the word "Year" means the period of time from 1st January to 31st December, not a period of 12 calendar months calculated from the registration of the Co. (*Gibson* v. *Barton,* 44 L. J. M. C. 81 ; L. R. 10 Q. B. 329 : *Edmonds* v. *Foster,* 33 L. T. 690).

In a theatrical engagement, "Year" means "Season" (*Grant* v. *Maddox,* 16 L. J. Ex. 227 ; 15 M. & W. 737). In that case Alderson, B., said,

"The contract is, that the plaintiff is to be paid for 3 years, at a salary of £5, £6, and £7 per week in those years: that means, according to the universal understanding amongst actors, that she is to be paid so much per week, during every week that the theatre is open."

V. TWELVEMONTH.

"By the year;" *V.* VALUE.

Condition of establishing title "Within one year;" *V. Re Hartley*, 34 Ch. D. 742; 56 L. J. Ch. 564; 56 L. T. 565; 35 W. R. 624.

"Space of one whole year," s. 58, 1 & 2 V. c. 106; *V. Bartlett* v. *Kirwood*, 23 L. J. Q. B. 9; 2 E. & B. 771.

YEAR AND A DAY.—In computing a Year and a Day after an event, the day on which the event happens is counted as the first day (Co. Litt. 255 a: Steph. Cr. 155).

YEAR TO YEAR.—"Where parties agree for a tenancy '*from year to year*,' and possession is taken, such a tenancy is thereby created, and may be determined at the end of the first or any subsequent year of the tenancy by a regular notice to quit (*Doe* d. *Clarke* v. *Smaridge*, 7 Q. B. 957; 14 L. J. Q. B. 327: *Doe* d. *Plumer* v. *Mainby*, 10 Q. B. 473; 16 L. J. Q. B. 303). But where a tenancy is created '*for one year certain, and so on from year to year*,' it enures as a tenancy for two years at the least, and cannot be determined at the end of the first year (*Doe* d. *Chadborn* v. *Green*, 9 A. & E. 658; 8 L. J. Q. B. 100; 1 P. & D. 454: *R.* v. *Chawton*, 1 Q. B. 247; 10 L. J. M. C. 55); though it may be determined by notice to quit at the end of the second or any subsequent year of the tenancy. A demise '*for a year*,' or '*for one year certain*,' does not create a tenancy from year to year, nor require any notice to quit at the end of the year (*Cobb* v. *Stokes*, 8 East, 358, 361: *Wilson* v. *Abbott*, 3 B. & C. 88: *Johnstone* v. *Hudlestone*, 4 B. & C. 937)." Woodf. 220, 221.

YEARLING.—"If a breeder of horses should bequeath 'his Yearlings,' and survive into the next year, the Yearlings of the latter year, and not those of the former (now two-year-olds), would probably be held to pass" (1 Jarm. 331, n. (*g*)).

YEARLY.—"The usual 'Yearly' rent means, the yearly rent of so many half-yearly or quarterly payments in the year" (per Abbott, C. J., *Doe* d. *Shrewsbury* v. *Wilson*, 5 B. & Ald. 382). And the better opinion seems to be that in executing a Power of Leasing which requires the reservation of "Yearly" rents, the days of payment, how many and what, are immaterial so long as the rent is a yearly one (*Doe* d. *Douglas* v. *Lock*, 4 L. J. K. B. 117, 119; 2 A. & E. 705: but in that case, after an elaborate review of the somewhat conflicting authorities hereon, the Court refrained from deciding this point and disposed of the case on other grounds). *Vh.* Sug. Pow. 793–795.

In *Doe* d. *Shrewsbury* v. *Wilson* (sup.), the words "made *payable yearly*" were considered the same as if the words had been "payable every year." "In common parlance the word 'yearly' in such Powers, means not a payment of rent once a year, but that the same is to be paid *in or during* every year. In one sense a rent reserved half-yearly is payable yearly, because it is payable during the year" (Sug. Pow. 795).

V. HALF-YEARLY : QUARTERLY.

YEARLY INTEREST.—Interest upon a loan by a banker to a customer for a period less than a year, is not within "any yearly Interest of Money, or any Annuity, or other Annual Payment" (s. 40, 16 & 17 V. c. 34); and therefore the customer is not entitled to deduct Income Tax from such interest (*Goslings* v. *Blake*, 23 Q. B. D. 324 ; 58 L. J. Q. B. 446 ; 5 Times Rep. 605, distinguishing *Bebb and Bunny,* 1 K. & J. 216, and *Dinning* v. *Henderson,* 3 D. G. & S. 702 ; 19 L. J. Ch. 273).

YEARLY RENT.—*V.* CLEAR.

YEARLY VALUE.—*V.* CLEAR : VALUE.

YIELDING AND PAYING.—These words, with which the reddendum clause in a Lease is usually commenced, create, by their own vigour, a covenant by the lessee to pay the rent reserved (*Hellier* v. *Casbard,* 1 Sid. 266 : *Porter* v. *Swetnam,* Style, 406 : *Bower* v. *Hodges,* 22 L. J. C. P. 194 ; 13 C. B. 765, 774. *Vf.* Elph. 419, 420). But they do not create a Condition Precedent (*V.* PAYING).

YOKE.—Used for YARDLAND in Kent (Elph. 631).

YOUNGER : YOUNGEST. — *Primâ facie* "Younger" or "Youngest" has reference to the order of birth (2 Jarm. 213).

An *only* child would take under a bequest to a person's "*youngest* child" (*Emery* v. *England,* 3 Ves. 232).

As to gifts to children "when the *youngest* attains 21 ;" *V.* 2 Jarm. 165–167.

"*Younger Branches*" of a family ; *V. Doe* d. *Smith* v. *Fleming,* 2 Cr. M. & R. 638 ; 5 L. J. Ex. 74 : 2 Jarm. 98.

"*Younger Children,*" are those which were such at the death of the intestate or heir in possession (per Hatherley, L. C., *Catton* v. *Mackenzie,* L. R. 2 H. L. Sc. 203). *Vf. Mason* v. *Westoby,* 42 Ch. D. 590 : *Re Prytherch,* Ib. 591.

"Where an estate is settled on the eldest son, and, subject to that, a Power is given of appointing portions to the younger children, a Younger Child who becomes the Eldest before receiving his portion, is not within the Power (*Chadwick* v. *Doleman,* 2 Vern. 528 : *Teynham* v. *Webb,* 2 Ves. sen. 198 : *Va. Lincoln* v. *Pelham, Bowles* v. *Bowles, Leake* v. *Leake,* 10 Ves. 166,

477 : *Savage* v. *Carroll*, 1 Ball & Beatty, 265 : *Matthews* v. *Paul*, 3 Swanst. 328 : *Peacock* v. *Pares*, 2 Keen, 689) ; but he must become an Eldest or Only Son in the sense of the Settlement, although not fully expressed, to exclude him from a portion ; that is, he must take the estate provided by the Settlement for the Eldest or Only Son (*Spencer* v. *Spencer*, 8 Sim. 87 : *V. Tennison* v. *Moore*, 13 Ir. Eq. Rep. 424), and this even where the Settlement expressly provides that the portion of a Younger Son becoming the Eldest Son in the lifetime of his father shall accrue to the survivors ; therefore if the father and his eldest son bar the estate tail and remainders, and dispose otherwise of the estate, the second son, although he may become, by his brother's death without issue in his father's lifetime, the eldest son entitled according to the Settlement, will still be entitled to his portion as a Younger Son (*Macoubrey* v. *Jones*, 2 K. & J. 684). This is the exception ; but as to the general rule, where a Power was given to appoint a sum amongst Younger Children, provided that the eldest son, or the *son* possessing the estate should have no share of it, and an appointment was made, *nominatim*, to Anthony, the second son, and the other *younger* children, and, after the appointment, Anthony became the eldest son by the death of his elder brother, and the estate descended upon him, Ld. Thurlow held that Anthony could not take any part of the fund, although the appointment was not revoked (*Broadmead* v. *Wood*, 1 Bro. C. C. 77.)" Sug. Pow. 678, 679. *Vf.* Ib. 620, 693 : Elph. ch. 24 : ELDEST.

YOUR.—As to effect of contract for "your" wool, or other specified commodity ; *V. Macdonald* v. *Longbottom*, 28 L. J. Q. B. 293 ; 29 Ib. 256 ; 1 E. & E. 977, 987.

YOUR CLIENT.—*V.* CLIENT.

APPENDIX.

INTERPRETATION ACT, 1889.

(52 & 53 VICT. c. 63).

ARRANGEMENT OF SECTIONS.

Re-enactment of existing Rules.

New General Rules of Construction.

Supplemental.

INDEX TO DEFINITIONS.

An Act for consolidating enactments relating to the Construction of Acts of Parliament and for further shortening the Language used in Acts of Parliament. [*30th August* 1889.]

Be it enacted by the Queen's most Excellent Majesty, by and with the advice and consent of the Lords Spiritual and Temporal, and Commons, in this present Parliament assembled, and by the authority of the same, as follows:

Re-enactment of existing Rules.

1.—(1.) In this Act and in every Act passed *after* the year 1850, whether before or after the commencement of this Act, unless the contrary intention appears,— **Rules as to gender and number.**

(*a.*) words importing the masculine gender shall include females; and

(*b.*) words in the singular shall include the plural, and words in the plural shall include the singular.

(2.) The same rules shall be observed in the construction of every enactment relating to an offence punishable on indictment or on summary conviction, when the enactment is contained in an Act passed *in or before* the year 1850.

2.—(1.) In the construction of every enactment relating to an offence punishable on indictment or on summary conviction, whether contained in an Act passed *before or after the commencement of this Act*, the expression "person" shall, unless the contrary intention appears, include a body corporate. *Cp. s.* 19. **Application of penal Acts to bodies corporate.**

(2.) Where under any Act, whether passed *before or after the commencement of this Act*, any forfeiture or penalty is payable to a party aggrieved, it shall be payable to a body corporate in every case where that body is the party aggrieved.

3. In every Act passed *after* the year 1850, whether before or after the commencement of this Act, the following expressions shall, unless the contrary intention appears, have the meanings hereby respectively assigned to them; namely,— **Meanings of certain words in Acts since 1850.**

The expression "month" shall mean calendar month:

The expression "land" shall include messuages, tenements, and hereditaments, houses, and buildings of any tenure:

The expressions "oath" and "affidavit" shall, in the case of persons for the time being allowed by law to affirm or declare instead of swearing, include affirmation and declaration, and the expression "swear" shall, in the like case, include affirm and declare.

4. In every Act passed *after* the year 1850 *and before the commencement of this Act* the expression "county" shall, unless the contrary intention appears, be construed as including a county of a city and a county of a town. **Meaning of "county" in past Acts.**

5. In every Act passed *after* the year 1866, whether before or after the commencement of this Act, the expression "parish" shall, unless the contrary intention appears, mean, as respects England and Wales, a place for which a separate poor rate is or can be made, or for which a separate overseer is or can be appointed. **Meaning of "parish."**

6. In this Act, and in every Act and Order of Council passed or made *after* the year 1846, whether before or after the commencement of this Act, the expression "county court" shall, unless the contrary intention **Meaning of "county court."**

51 & 52 Vict. c. 43.

appears, mean as respects England and Wales a court under the County Courts Act, 1888. *Cp. s.* 29.

Meaning of "sheriff clerk," &c., in Scotch Acts.

7. In every Act relating to Scotland, whether passed *before or after the commencement of this Act*, unless the contrary intention appears—

The expression "sheriff clerk" shall include steward clerk;

The expression "shire," "sheriffdom," and "county" shall include any stewartry in Scotland.

Sections to be substantive enactments.

8. Every section of an Act shall have effect as a substantive enactment without introductory words.

Acts to be public Acts.

9. Every Act passed *after* the year 1850, whether before or after the commencement of this Act, shall be a public Act and shall be judicially noticed as such, unless the contrary is expressly provided by the Act.

Amendment or repeal of Acts in same session.

10. Any Act may be altered, amended, or repealed in the same session of Parliament.

Effect of repeal in Acts passed since 1850.

11.—(1.) Where an Act passed *after* the year 1850, whether before or after the commencement of this Act, repeals a repealing enactment, it shall not be construed as reviving any enactment previously repealed, unless words are added reviving that enactment.

(2.) Where an Act passed *after* the year 1850, whether before or after the commencement of this Act, repeals wholly or partially any former enactment and substitutes provisions for the enactment repealed, the repealed enactment shall remain in force until the substituted provisions come into operation.

New General Rules of Construction.

Official definitions in past and future Acts.

12. In this Act, and in every other Act whether passed *before or after the commencement of this Act*, the following expressions shall, unless the contrary intention appears, have the meanings hereby respectively assigned to them, namely:—

(1.) The expression "the Lord Chancellor" shall, except when used with reference to Ireland only, mean the Lord High Chancellor of Great Britain for the time being, and when used with reference to Ireland only, shall mean the Lord Chancellor of Ireland for the time being.

(2.) The expression "the Treasury" shall mean the Lord High Treasurer for the time being or the Commissioners for the time being of Her Majesty's Treasury.

(3.) The expression "Secretary of State" shall mean one of Her Majesty's Principal Secretaries of State for the time being.

(4.) The expression "the Admiralty" shall mean the Lord High Admiral of the United Kingdom for the time being, or the Commissioners for the time being for executing the office of Lord High Admiral of the United Kingdom.

(5.) The expression "the Privy Council" shall, except when used with reference to Ireland only, mean the Lords and others for the time being of Her Majesty's Most Honourable Privy Council, and when used with reference to Ireland only, shall mean the Privy Council of Ireland for the time being.

(6.) The expression "the Education Department" shall mean the Lords of the Committee for the time being of the Privy Council appointed for Education.

(7.) The expression "the Scotch Education Department" shall mean the Lords of the Committee for the time being of the Privy Council appointed for Education in Scotland.

(8.) The expression "the Board of Trade" shall mean the Lords of the Committee for the time being of the Privy Council appointed for the consideration of matters relating to trade and foreign plantations.

(9.) The expression "Lord Lieutenant," when used with reference to Ireland, shall mean the Lord Lieutenant of Ireland or other Chief Governors or Governor of Ireland for the time being.

(10.) The expression "Chief Secretary," when used with reference to Ireland, shall mean the Chief Secretary to the Lord Lieutenant for the time being.

(11.) The expression "Postmaster General" shall mean Her Majesty's Postmaster General for the time being.

(12.) The expression "Commissioners of Woods" or "Commissioners of Woods and Forests" shall mean the Commissioners of Her Majesty's Woods, Forests, and Land Revenues for the time being.

(13.) The expression "Commissioners of Works" shall mean the Commissioners of Her Majesty's Works and Public Buildings for the time being.

(14.) The expression "Charity Commissioners" shall mean the Charity Commissioners for England and Wales for the time being.

(15.) The expression "Ecclesiastical Commissioners" shall mean the Ecclesiastical Commissioners for England for the time being.

(16.) The expression "Queen Anne's Bounty" shall mean the Governors of the Bounty of Queen Anne for the augmentation of the maintenance of the poor clergy.

(17.) The expression "National Debt Commissioners" shall mean the Commissioners for the time being for the Reduction of the National Debt.

(18.) The expression "the Bank of England" shall mean, as circumstances require, the Governor and Company of the Bank of England or the bank of the Governor and Company of the Bank of England.

(19.) The expression "the Bank of Ireland" shall mean, as circumstances require, the Governor and Company of the Bank of Ireland or the bank of the Governor and Company of the Bank of Ireland.

(20.) The expression "consular officer" shall include consul-general, consul, vice-consul, consular agent, and any person for the time authorised to discharge the duties of consul-general, consul, or vice-consul.

13. In this Act and in every other Act whether passed *before or after the commencement of this Act*, the following expressions shall, unless the contrary intention appears, have the meanings hereby respectively assigned to them, namely:— Judicial definitions in past and future Acts.

(1). The expression "Supreme Court," when used with reference to England or Ireland, shall mean the Supreme Court of Judicature in England or Ireland, as the case may be, or either branch thereof.

(2). The expression "Court of Appeal," when used with reference to England or Ireland, shall mean Her Majesty's Court of Appeal in England or Ireland, as the case may be.

(3.) The expression "High Court," when used with reference to England or Ireland, shall mean Her Majesty's High Court of Justice in England or Ireland, as the case may be.

(4.) The expression "court of assize" shall, as respects England, Wales, and Ireland, mean a court of assize, a court of oyer and terminer, and a court of gaol delivery, or any of them, and shall, as respects England and Wales, include the Central Criminal Court.

(5.) The expression "assizes," as respects England, Wales, and Ireland, shall mean the courts of assize usually held in every year, and shall include the sessions of the Central Criminal Court, but shall not include any court of assize held by virtue of any special commission, or, as respects Ireland, any court held by virtue of the powers conferred by section sixty-three of the Supreme Court of Judicature Act (Ireland), 1877. 40 & 41 Vict. c. 57.

(6.) The expression "the Summary Jurisdiction Act, 1848," shall mean the Act of the session of the eleventh and twelfth years of the reign of Her present Majesty, chapter forty-three, intituled "An Act to facili-"tate the performance of the duties of justices of the peace out of "sessions within England and Wales with respect to summary convictions "and orders."

(7.) The expression "the Summary Jurisdiction (England) Acts" and the expression "the Summary Jurisdiction (English) Acts" shall respectively mean the Summary Jurisdiction Act, 1848, and the Summary 11 & 12 Vict. c. 43.

42 & 43 Vict. c. 49. Jurisdiction Act, 1879, and any Act, past or future, amending those Acts or either of them.

(8.) The expression "the Summary Jurisdiction (Scotland) Acts" shall mean the Summary Jurisdiction (Scotland) Acts, 1864 and 1881, and any Act, past or future, amending those Acts or either of them.

27 & 28 Vict. c. 53.
44 & 45 Vict. c. 33.

(9.) The expression "the Summary Jurisdiction (Ireland) Acts" shall mean, as respects the Dublin Metropolitan Police District, the Acts regulating the powers and duties of justices of the peace or of the police of that district, and as respects any other part of Ireland, the Petty Sessions (Ireland) Act, 1851, and any Act, past or future, amending the same.

14 & 15 Vict. c. 93.

(10.) The expression "the Summary Jurisdiction Acts" when used in relation to England or Wales shall mean the Summary Jurisdiction (England) Acts, and when used in relation to Scotland the Summary Jurisdiction (Scotland) Acts, and when used in relation to Ireland the Summary Jurisdiction (Ireland) Acts.

(11.) The expression "court of summary jurisdiction" shall mean any justice or justices of the peace, or other magistrate, by whatever name called, to whom jurisdiction is given by, or who is authorised to act under, the Summary Jurisdiction Acts, whether in England, Wales, or Ireland, and whether acting under the Summary Jurisdiction Acts or any of them, or under any other Act, or by virtue of his commission, or under the common law.

(12.) The expression "petty sessional court" shall, as respects England or Wales, mean a court of summary jurisdiction consisting of two or more justices when sitting in a petty sessional court-house, and shall include the Lord Mayor of the city of London, and any alderman of that city, and any metropolitan or borough police magistrate or other stipendiary magistrate when sitting in a court-house or place at which he is authorised by law to do alone any act authorised to be done by more than one justice of the peace.

(13.) The expression "petty sessional court-house" shall, as respects England or Wales, mean a court-house or other place at which justices are accustomed to assemble for holding special or petty sessions, or which is for the time being appointed as a substitute for such a court-house or place, and where the justices are accustomed to assemble for either special or petty sessions at more than one court-house or place in a petty sessional division, shall mean any such court-house or place. The expression shall also include any court-house or place at which the Lord Mayor of the city of London or any alderman of that city, or any metropolitan or borough police magistrate or other stipendiary magistrate is authorised by law to do alone any act authorised to be done by more than one justice of the peace.

(14.) The expression "court of quarter sessions" shall mean the justices of any county, riding, parts, division, or liberty of a county, or of any county of a city, or county of a town, in general or quarter sessions assembled, and shall include the court of the recorder of a municipal borough having a separate court of quarter sessions.

Meaning of "rules of court."

14. In every Act passed *after the commencement of this Act*, unless the contrary intention appears, the expression "rules of court" when used in relation to any court shall mean rules made by the authority having for the time being power to make rules or orders regulating the practice and procedure of such court, and as regards Scotland shall include acts of adjournal and acts of sederunt.

The power of the said authority to make rules of court as above defined shall include a power to make rules of court for the purpose of any Act passed after the commencement of this Act, and directing or authorising anything to be done by rules of court.

Meaning of borough.

15. In this Act and in every Act passed *after* the commencement of this Act the following expressions shall, unless the contrary intention appears, have the meanings hereby respectively assigned to them, namely:—

(1.) The expression "municipal borough" shall mean, as respects England and Wales, any place for the time being subject to the Municipal Corporations Act, 1882, and any reference to the mayor, aldermen, and burgesses of a borough shall include a reference to the mayor, aldermen, and citizens of a city, and any reference to the powers, duties, liabilities or property of the council of a borough shall be construed as a reference to the powers, duties, liabilities, or property of the mayor, aldermen, and burgesses of the borough acting by the council. 45 & 46 Vict. c. 50.

(2.) The expression "municipal borough" shall mean, as respects Ireland, any place for the time being subject to the Act of the session of the third and fourth years of the reign of her present Majesty, chapter one hundred and eight, intituled "An Act for the regulation of municipal corporations in Ireland."

(3.) The expression "parliamentary borough" shall mean any borough, burgh, place or combination of places returning a member or members to serve in Parliament, and not being either a county or division of a county, or a university, or a combination of universities.

(4.) The expression "borough" when used in relation to local government shall mean a municipal borough as above defined, and when used in relation to parliamentary elections or the registration of parliamentary electors shall mean a parliamentary borough as above defined.

16. In this Act and in every Act passed *after* the commencement of this Act the following expressions shall, unless the contrary intention appears, have the meanings hereby respectively assigned to them, namely:— **Meaning of guardians and union.**

(1.) The expression "board of guardians" shall, as respects England and Wales, mean a board of guardians elected under the Poor Law Amendment Act, 1834, and the Acts amending the same, and shall include a board of guardians or other body of persons performing under any local Act the like functions to a board of guardians under the Poor Law Amendment Act, 1834. 4 & 5 Will. 4, c. 76.

(2.) The expression "poor law union" shall, as respects England and Wales, mean any parish or union of parishes for which there is a separate board of guardians.

(3.) The expression "board of guardians" shall, as respects Ireland, mean a board of guardians elected under the Act of the Session of the first and second years of the reign of Her present Majesty, chapter fifty-six, intituled "An Act for the more effectual relief of the destitute poor in Ireland," and the Acts amending the same, and shall include any body of persons appointed by the Local Government Board for Ireland to carry into execution the provisions of those Acts.

(4.) The expression "poor law union" shall, as respects Ireland, mean any townland or place or union, or townlands or places, for which there is a separate board of guardians.

17. In every Act passed *after* the commencement of this Act the following expressions shall, unless the contrary intention appears, have the meanings hereby respectively assigned to them, namely:— **Definitions relating to elections.**

(1.) The expression "parliamentary election" shall mean the election of a member or members to serve in Parliament for a county or division of a county, or parliamentary borough or division of a parliamentary borough, or for a university or combination of universities.

(2.) The expression "parliamentary register of electors" shall mean a register of persons entitled to vote at any parliamentary election.

(3.) The expression "local government register of electors" shall mean as respects an administrative county in England or Wales other than a county borough, the county register, and as respects a county borough or other municipal borough, the burgess roll.

18. In this Act, and in every Act passed *after* the commencement of this Act, the following expressions shall, unless the contrary intention **Geographical and colonial definitions in future Acts.**

appears, have the meanings hereby respectively assigned to them, namely:—

(1.) The expression "British Islands" shall mean the United Kingdom, the Channel Islands, and the Isle of Man.

(2.) The expression "British possession" shall mean any part of Her Majesty's dominions exclusive of the United Kingdom, and where parts of such dominions are under both a central and a local legislature, all parts under the central legislature shall, for the purposes of this definition, be deemed to be one British possession.

(3.) The expression "colony" shall mean any part of Her Majesty's dominions exclusive of the British Islands, and of British India, and where parts of such dominions are under both a central and a local legislature, all parts under the central legislature shall, for the purposes of this definition, be deemed to be one colony.

(4.) The expression "British India" shall mean all territories and places within Her Majesty's dominions which are for the time being governed by Her Majesty through the Governor-General of India or through any governor or other officer subordinate to the Governor-General of India.

(5.) The expression "India" shall mean British India together with any territories of any native prince or chief under the suzerainty of Her Majesty exercised through the Governor-General of India, or through any governor or other officer subordinate to the Governor-General of India.

(6.) The expression "Governor" shall, as respects Canada and India, mean the Governor-General, and include any person who for the time being has the powers of the Governor-General, and as respects any other British possession, shall include the officer for the time being administering the government of that possession.

(7.) The expression "colonial legislature" and the expression "legislature," when used with reference to a British possession, shall respectively mean the authority, other than the Imperial Parliament or Her Majesty the Queen in Council, competent to make laws for a British possession.

Meaning of "person" in future Acts.

19. In this Act and in every Act passed *after* the commencement of this Act the expression "person" shall, unless the contrary intention appears, include any body of persons corporate or unincorporate. *Cp. s.* 2 (1).

Meaning of "writing" in past and future Acts.

20. In this Act and in every other Act whether passed *before or after* the commencement of this Act expressions referring to writing shall, unless the contrary intention appears, be construed as including references to printing, lithography, photography, and other modes of representing or reproducing words in a visible form.

Meaning of "statutory declaration" in past and future Acts. 5 & 6 Will. 4, c. 62.

21. In this Act, and in every other Act, whether passed *before or after* the commencement of this Act, the expression "statutory declaration" shall, unless the contrary intention appears, mean a declaration made by virtue of the Statutory Declarations Act, 1835.

Meaning of "financial year" in future Acts.

22. In this Act and in every Act passed *after* the commencement of this Act the expression "financial year" shall, unless the contrary intention appears, mean as respects any matters relating to the Consolidated Fund or moneys provided by Parliament, or to the Exchequer, or to Imperial taxes or finance, the twelve months ending the thirty-first day of March.

Definition of Lands Clauses Acts. 8 & 9 Vict. c. 18. 23 & 24 Vict. c. 106. 32 & 33 Vict. c. 18.

23. In any Act passed *after* the commencement of this Act, unless the contrary intention appears,—

The expression "Lands Clauses Acts" shall mean—

(*a*) as respects England and Wales, the Lands Clauses Consolidation Act, 1845, the Lands Clauses Consolidation Acts Amendment Act, 1860, the Lands Clauses Consolidation Act, 1869, and the Lands

Clauses (Umpire) Act, 1883, and any Acts for the time being in force amending the same; and 46 & 47 Vict. c. 15.

(*b*) as respects Scotland, the Lands Clauses Consolidation (Scotland) Act, 1845, and the Lands Clauses Consolidation Acts Amendment Act, 1860, and any Acts for the time being in force amending the same; and 8 & 9 Vict. c. 19. 23 & 24 Vict. c. 106.

(*c*) as respects Ireland, the Lands Clauses Consolidation Act, 1845, the Lands Clauses Consolidation Acts Amendment Act, 1860, the Railways Act (Ireland), 1851, the Railways Act (Ireland), 1860, the Railways Act (Ireland), 1864, and the Railways Traverse Act, and any Acts for the time being in force amending the same. 8 & 9 Vict. c. 18. 23 & 24 Vict. c. 97. 14 & 15 Vict. c. 70. 27 & 28 Vict. c. 71. 31 & 32 Vict. c. 70.

Meaning of Irish Valuation Acts.

24. In any Act passed *before or after* the commencement of this Act the expression "Irish Valuation Acts" shall mean the Acts relating to the valuation of rateable property in Ireland.

Meaning of "ordnance map."

25. In this Act and in every other Act, whether passed *before or after* the commencement of this Act, the expression "ordnance map" shall, unless the contrary intention appears, mean a map made under the powers conferred by the Survey (Great Britain) Acts, 1841 to 1870, or by the Survey (Ireland) Acts, 1825 to 1870, and the Acts amending the same respectively.

Meaning of service by post.

26. Where an Act passed *after* the commencement of this Act authorises or requires any document to be served by post, whether the expression "serve," or the expression "give" or "send," or any other expression is used, then, unless the contrary intention appears, the service shall be deemed to be effected by properly addressing, prepaying, and posting a letter containing the document, and unless the contrary is proved to have been effected at the time at which the letter would be delivered in the ordinary course of post.

Meaning of "committed for trial."

27. In every Act passed *after* the commencement of this Act, the expression "committed for trial" used in relation to any person shall, unless the contrary intention appears, mean, as respects England and Wales, committed to prison with the view of being tried before a judge and jury, whether the person is committed in pursuance of section twenty-two or of section twenty-five of the Indictable Offences Act, 1848, or is committed by a court, judge, coroner, or other authority having power to commit a person to any prison with a view to his trial, and shall include a person who is admitted to bail upon a recognizance to appear and take his trial before a judge and jury. 11 & 12 Vict. c. 42.

Meanings of "sheriff," "felony," and "misdemeanour" in future Scotch Acts.

28. In this Act and in every Act passed *after* the commencement of this Act, unless the contrary intention appears—

The expression "sheriff" shall, as respects Scotland, include a sheriff substitute:

The expression "felony" shall, as respects Scotland, mean a high crime and offence:

The expression "misdemeanour" shall, as respects Scotland, mean an offence.

Meaning of "county court" in future Irish Acts.

29. In every Act passed *after* the commencement of this Act, unless the contrary intention appears, the expression "county court" shall, as respects Ireland, mean a civil bill court within the meaning of the County Officers and Courts (Ireland) Act, 1877. *Cp. s.* 6. 40 & 41 Vict. c. 56.

References to the Crown.

30. In this Act and in every other Act, whether passed *before or after* the commencement of this Act, references to the Sovereign reigning at the time of the passing of the Act or to the Crown shall, unless the contrary intention appears, be construed as references to the Sovereign for the time being, and this Act shall be binding on the Crown.

Construction of statutory rules, &c.

31. Where any Act, whether passed *before or after* the commencement of this Act, confers power to make, grant, or issue any instrument, that is to say, any Order in Council, order, warrant, scheme, letters patent, rules, regulations, or byelaws, expressions used in the instrument, *if it is made after the commencement of this Act*, shall, unless the contrary intention appears, have the same respective meanings as in the Act conferring the power.

Construction of provisions as to exercise of powers and duties.

32.—(1.) Where an Act passed *after* the commencement of this Act confers a power or imposes a duty, then, unless the contrary intention appears, the power may be exercised and the duty shall be performed from time to time as occasion requires.

(2.) Where an Act passed *after* the commencement of this Act confers a power or imposes a duty on the holder of an office, as such, then, unless the contrary intention appears, the power may be exercised and the duty shall be performed by the holder for the time being of the office.

(3.) Where an Act passed *after* the commencement of this Act confers a power to make any rules, regulations, or byelaws, the power shall, unless the contrary intention appears, be construed as including a power, exercisable in the like manner and subject to the like consent and conditions, if any, to rescind, revoke, amend, or vary the rules, regulations, or byelaws.

Provisions as to offences under two or more laws.

33. Where an act or omission constitutes an offence under two or more Acts, or both under an Act and at common law, whether any such Act was passed *before or after* the commencement of this Act, the offender shall, unless the contrary intention appears, be liable to be prosecuted and punished under either or any of those Acts or at common law, but shall not be liable to be punished twice for the same offence.

Measurement of distances.

34. In the measurement of any distance for the purposes of any Act passed *after* the commencement of this Act, that distance shall, unless the contrary intention appears, be measured in a straight line on a horizontal plane.

Citation of Acts.

35.—(1.) In any Act, instrument, or document, an Act may be cited by reference to the short title, if any, of the Act, either with or without a reference to the chapter, or by reference to the regnal year in which the Act was passed, and where there are more statutes or sessions than one in the same regnal year, by reference to the statute or the session, as the case may require, and where there are more chapters than one, by reference to the chapter, and any enactment may be cited by reference to the section or sub-section of the Act in which the enactment is contained.

(2.) Where any Act passed *after* the commencement of this Act contains such reference as aforesaid, the reference shall, unless a contrary intention appears, be read as referring, in the case of statutes included in any revised edition of the statutes purporting to be printed by authority, to that edition, and in the case of statutes not so included, and passed before the reign of King George the First, to the edition prepared under the direction of the Record Commission; and in other cases to the copies of the statutes purporting to be printed by the Queen's Printer, or under the superintendence or authority of Her Majesty's Stationery Office.

(3.) In any Act passed *after* the commencement of this Act a description or citation of a portion of another Act shall, unless the contrary intention appears, be construed as including the word, section, or other part mentioned or referred to as forming the beginning and as forming the end of the portion comprised in the description or citation.

"Commencement."

36.—(1.) In this Act, and in every Act passed either *before or after* the commencement of this Act, the expression "commencement," when used with reference to an Act, shall mean the time at which the Act comes into operation.

(2.) Where an Act passed *after* the commencement of this Act, or any Order in Council, order, warrant, scheme, letters patent, rules, regulations, or byelaws made, granted, or issued, under a power conferred by any such Act, is expressed to come into operation on a particular day, the same shall be construed as coming into operation immediately on the expiration of the previous day.

37. Where an Act passed *after* the commencement of this Act is not to come into operation immediately on the passing thereof, and confers power to make any appointment, to make, grant, or issue any instrument, that is to say, any Order in Council, order, warrant, scheme, letters patent, rules, regulations, or byelaws, to give notices, to prescribe forms, or to do any other thing for the purposes of the Act, that power may, unless the contrary intention appears, be exercised at any time after the passing of the Act, so far as may be necessary or expedient for the purpose of bringing the Act into operation at the date of the commencement thereof, subject to this restriction, that any instrument made under the power shall not, unless the contrary intention appears in the Act, or the contrary is necessary for bringing the Act into operation, come into operation until the Act comes into operation. Exercise of statutory powers between passing and commencement of Act.

38.—(1.) Where this Act or any Act passed *after* the commencement of this Act repeals and re-enacts, with or without modification, any provisions of a former Act, references in any other Act to the provisions so repealed, shall, unless the contrary intention appears, be construed as references to the provisions so re-enacted. Effect of repeal in future Acts.

(2.) Where this Act or any Act passed *after* the commencement of this Act repeals any other enactment, then, unless the contrary intention appears, the repeal shall not—

(*a.*) revive anything not in force or existing at the time at which the repeal takes effect; or,

(*b.*) affect the previous operation of any enactment so repealed or anything duly done or suffered under any enactment so repealed; or

(*c.*) affect any right, privilege, obligation, or liability acquired, accrued, or incurred under any enactment so repealed; or

(*d.*) affect any penalty, forfeiture, or punishment incurred in respect of any offence committed against any enactment so repealed; or

(*e.*) affect any investigation, legal proceeding, or remedy in respect of any such right, privilege, obligation, liability, penalty, forfeiture, or punishment as aforesaid;

and any such investigation, legal proceeding, or remedy may be instituted, continued, or enforced, and any such penalty, forfeiture, or punishment may be imposed, as if the repealing Act had not been passed.

Supplemental.

39. In this Act the expression "Act" shall include a local and personal Act and a private Act. Definition of "Act" in this Act.

40. The provisions of this Act respecting the construction of Acts passed *after* the commencement of this Act shall not affect the construction of any Act passed before the commencement of this Act, although it is continued or amended by an Act passed after such commencement. Saving for past Acts.

41. The Acts described in the Schedule to this Act are hereby repealed to the extent appearing in the third column of the Schedule. Repeal.

42. This Act shall come into operation on the first day of January one thousand eight hundred and ninety. Commencement of Act.

43. This Act may be cited as the Interpretation Act, 1889. Short title.

SCHEDULE.

ENACTMENTS REPEALED.

Session and Chapter.	Title or Short Title.	Extent of Repeal.
7 & 8 Geo. 4, c. 28 . .	An Act for further improving the administration of justice in criminal cases in England.	Section fourteen.
9 Geo. 4, c. 54 . . .	An Act for improving the administration of justice in criminal cases in Ireland.	Section thirty-five.
7 Will. 4 & 1 Vict. c. 39	An Act to interpret the word "sheriff," "sheriff clerk," "shire," "sheriffdom," and "county," occurring in Acts of Parliament relating to Scotland.	The whole Act.
13 & 14 Vict. c. 21 . .	An Act for shortening the language used in Acts of Parliament.	The whole Act.
29 & 30 Vict. c. 113 .	The Poor Law Amendment Act of 1866.	Section eighteen, from the beginning to "can be appointed, and."
42 & 43 Vict. c. 49 . .	The Summary Jurisdiction Act, 1879 .	In section twenty the sub-sections numbered (3) and (6). Section fifty.
47 & 48 Vict. c. 43 . .	The Summary Jurisdiction Act, 1884 .	Section seven.
51 & 52 Vict. c. 43 . .	The County Courts Act, 1888 . . .	Section one hundred and eighty-seven, from the beginning to "is meant, and."

NOTE.—The punctuation of this Act is as given in the Queen's Printer's copy.

THE END.

BRADBURY, AGNEW & CO. LIMD., PRINTERS, WHITEFRIARS.

www.ingramcontent.com/pod-product-compliance
Lightning Source LLC
LaVergne TN
LVHW081944200926
848484LV00009B/2506